Course	Financial Accounting: Information for Decisions
Course Number	**Seventh Edition** **John Wild**
	Custom version for Minneapolis Community and Technical College

http://create.mcgraw-hill.com

ISBN-10: 1308175914   ISBN-13: 9781308175911

Contents

Online Supplements

Credits

Online Supplements

Financial Accounting

7th edition

INFORMATION FOR DECISIONS

John J. Wild

University of Wisconsin at Madison

Mc
Graw
Hill
Education

To my students and family, especially **Kimberly**, **Jonathan**, **Stephanie**, and **Trevor.**

FINANCIAL ACCOUNTING: INFORMATION FOR DECISIONS, SEVENTH EDITION

Published by McGraw-Hill Education, 2 Penn Plaza, New York, NY 10121. Copyright © 2015 by McGraw-Hill Education. All rights reserved. Printed in the United States of America. Previous editions © 2013, 2011, and 2008. No part of this publication may be reproduced or distributed in any form or by any means, or stored in a database or retrieval system, without the prior written consent of McGraw-Hill Education, including, but not limited to, in any network or other electronic storage or transmission, or broadcast for distance learning.

Some ancillaries, including electronic and print components, may not be available to customers outside the United States.

This book is printed on acid-free paper.

1 2 3 4 5 6 7 8 9 0 DOW/DOW 1 0 9 8 7 6 5 4

ISBN 978-0-07-802589-1
MHID 0-07-802589-3

Senior Vice President, Products & Markets: *Kurt L. Strand*
Vice President, Content Production
  & Technology Services: *Kimberly Meriwether David*
Managing Director: *Tim Vertovec*
Executive Brand Manager: *Steve Schuetz*
Executive Director of Development: *Ann Torbert*
Managing Development Editor: *Christina A. Sanders*
Director of Digital Content: *Patricia Plumb*
Digital Development Editor: *Julie Hankins*
Digital Product Analyst: *Xin Lin*
Senior Marketing Manager: *Kathleen Klehr*
Director, Content Production: *Terri Schiesl*
Content Project Manager: *Lori Koetters*

Content Project Manager: *Brian Nacik*
Senior Buyer: *Carol A. Bielski*
Design: *Matthew Baldwin*
Cover Images: *Apple store:* © McGraw-Hill Companies/ *Jill Braaten, photographer. Annie's:* © Bloomberg via Getty Images. Groupon: © Bloomberg via Getty Images. Bull statue: © Royalty-Free/CORBIS.
Senior Content Licensing
  Specialist: *Jeremy Cheshareck*
Typeface: *10.5/12 Times Roman*
Compositor: *Aptara®, Inc.*
Printer: *R. R. Donnelley*

All credits appearing on page or at the end of the book are considered to be an extension of the copyright page.

Library of Congress Cataloging-in-Publication Data

Wild, John J.
    Financial accounting : information for decisions / John J. Wild, University of Wisconsin at Madison.
    —7th edition.
      pages cm
    Includes index.
    ISBN 978-0-07-802589-1 (alk. paper) — ISBN 0-07-802589-3 (alk. paper)
    1. Accounting. I. Title.
  HF5635.W695 2015
  657—dc23

                                                            2013042296

The Internet addresses listed in the text were accurate at the time of publication. The inclusion of a website does not indicate an endorsement by the authors or McGraw-Hill Education, and McGraw-Hill Education does not guarantee the accuracy of the information presented at these sites.

Adapting to Today's Students

Financial Accounting, 7e

Enhancements in technology have changed the spectrum of how we live and learn in the world today. Being able to download and work with learning tools on smart phones, tablets, or laptop computers empowers students to drive their own learning by putting increasingly intelligent technology into their hands.

No two students are alike, and whether the goal is to become an accountant or a businessperson or simply to be an informed consumer of accounting information, *Financial Accounting (FA)* has helped generations of students succeed by giving them support in the form of leading-edge accounting content that engages students, paired with state-of-the-art technology that elevates their understanding of key accounting principles.

With *FA* on your side, you'll be provided with **engaging content** in a **motivating style** to help students see the relevance of accounting. Students are motivated when reading materials that are clear and pertinent. *FA* excels at engaging students. Its chapter-opening vignettes showcase dynamic, successful companies guaranteed to **interest and excite students, and highlights the usefulness of accounting to those business owners**. This edition's featured companies—**Apple, Google, and Samsung**—captivate students with their products and annual reports, which are a pathway for learning financial statements. Further, this book's coverage of the accounting cycle fundamentals is widely praised for its clarity and effectiveness.

FA also delivers innovative technology to help student performance. *Connect Accounting* provides students with instant grading and feedback for assignments that are completed online. With our **Intelligent Response Technology**, we have taken our accounting content to the next level, delivering assessment material in a **more intuitive, less restrictive** format that adapts to the needs of today's students.

Our content features:

- **general journal interface** that looks and feels more like that found in practice.
- **auto-calculation** feature that allows students to focus on concepts rather than rote tasks.
- **smart (auto-fill) drop-down design**.
- **NEW General Ledger multi-tab format for select questions.**

The end result is content that better prepares students for the real world. *Connect Accounting* also includes digitally based, interactive adaptive learning tools that provide an opportunity to engage students more effectively by offering varied instructional methods and more personalized learning paths that build on different learning styles, interests, and abilities, allowing students to work at their own pace.

McGraw-Hill LearnSmart™ is an intelligent learning system that uses a series of adaptive questions to pinpoint each student's knowledge gaps. LearnSmart then provides an optimal learning path for each student, so that they spend less time in areas they already know and more time in areas they don't. The result is LearnSmart's adaptive learning path that helps students retain more knowledge, learn faster, and study more efficiently.

Our **Interactive Presentations** teach each chapter's core learning objectives in a rich multimedia format, bringing the content to life. Your students will come to class prepared when you assign Interactive Presentations. Students can also review the Interactive Presentations as they study.

Guided Examples provide students with narrated, animated, step-by-step walkthroughs of exercises similar to those assigned in *Connect*. Students appreciate the Guided Examples because they can help students learn accounting and complete assignments when outside of class.

Connect Plus Accounting integrates a media-rich online version of the textbook with *Connect Accounting*.

About the Author

JOHN J. WILD is a distinguished professor of accounting at the University of Wisconsin at Madison. He previously held appointments at Michigan State University and the University of Manchester in England. He received his BBA, MS, and PhD from the University of Wisconsin.

Professor Wild teaches accounting courses at both the undergraduate and graduate levels. He has received numerous teaching honors, including the Mabel W. Chipman Excellence-in-Teaching Award, the departmental Excellence-in-Teaching Award, and the Teaching Excellence Award from the 2003 and 2005 business graduates at the University of Wisconsin. He also received the Beta Alpha Psi and Roland F. Salmonson Excellence-in-Teaching Award from Michigan State University. Professor Wild has received several research honors and is a past KPMG Peat Marwick National Fellow and is a recipient of fellowships from the American Accounting Association and the Ernst and Young Foundation.

Professor Wild is an active member of the American Accounting Association and its sections. He has served on several committees of these organizations, including the Outstanding Accounting Educator Award, Wildman Award, National Program Advisory, Publications, and Research Committees. Professor Wild is author of *Fundamental Accounting Principles, Financial and Managerial Accounting, Financial Accounting Fundamentals, Managerial Accounting*, and *College Accounting*, each published by McGraw-Hill/Irwin. His research articles on accounting and analysis appear in *The Accounting Review, Journal of Accounting Research, Journal of Accounting and Economics, Contemporary Accounting Research, Journal of Accounting, Auditing and Finance, Journal of Accounting and Public Policy*, and other journals. He is past associate editor of *Contemporary Accounting Research* and has served on several editorial boards including *The Accounting Review*.

In his leisure time, Professor Wild enjoys hiking, sports, travel, people, and spending time with family and friends.

Dear Colleagues/Friends,

As we roll out the new edition of *Financial Accounting*, I thank each of you who provided suggestions to improve the textbook. As teachers, we know how important it is to select the right book for our course. This new edition reflects the advice and wisdom of many dedicated reviewers, symposium and workshop participants, students, and instructors. This book consistently rates number one in customer loyalty because of you. Together, we have created the most readable, concise, current, accurate, and innovative accounting book available today.

Throughout the writing process, I steered this book in the manner you directed. Reviewers, instructors, and students say this book's enhanced presentation, graphics, and technology cater to different learning styles and helps students better understand accounting. *Connect Plus Accounting* offers new features to improve student learning and to assist instructor teaching and grading. You and your students will find all these tools easy to apply.

I owe the success of this book to you and other instructors who graciously took time to help me focus on the changing demands of today's students and their learning needs. I feel fortunate to have witnessed our profession's extraordinary devotion to teaching. Your feedback and suggestions are reflected in everything I write. Please accept my heartfelt thanks for your dedication in helping today's students learn, understand, and appreciate accounting.

With kindest regards,

John J. Wild

Leading Technology Extends Learning

MCGRAW-HILL *CONNECT ACCOUNTING*
Get *Connect Accounting*. Get Results.

McGraw-Hill *Connect Accounting* is a digital teaching and learning environment that gives students the means to better connect with their coursework, with their instructors, and with the important concepts that they will need to know for success now and in the future. With *Connect Accounting*, instructors can deliver assignments, quizzes, and tests easily online. Students can practice important skills at their own pace and on their own schedule.

Online Assignments

Connect Accounting helps students learn more efficiently by providing feedback and practice material when they need it, where they need it. *Connect Accounting* grades homework automatically and gives immediate feedback on any questions students may have missed.

Intelligent Response Technology (IRT)

IRT is a redesigned student interface for our end-of-chapter assessment content. The benefits include improved answer acceptance to reduce students' frustration with formatting issues (such as rounding). Also, select questions have been redesigned to test students' knowledge more fully. They now include tables for students to work through rather than requiring that all calculations be done offline.

General Ledger Simulation

New **general ledger simulation** for select questions provides a much-improved student experience when working with accounting cycle questions. Students' work in the general journal is automatically posted to the ledger, navigation is much simpler, scrolling is no longer an issue, and students can easily link back to their original entries simply by clicking in the ledger if edits are needed. Many questions now have critical thinking components added, to maximize students' foundational knowledge of accounting concepts and principles.

> "I love how the general journal was set up. It felt like what I would be filling out if I had an accounting job."
>
> **—Student, Chabot Community College**

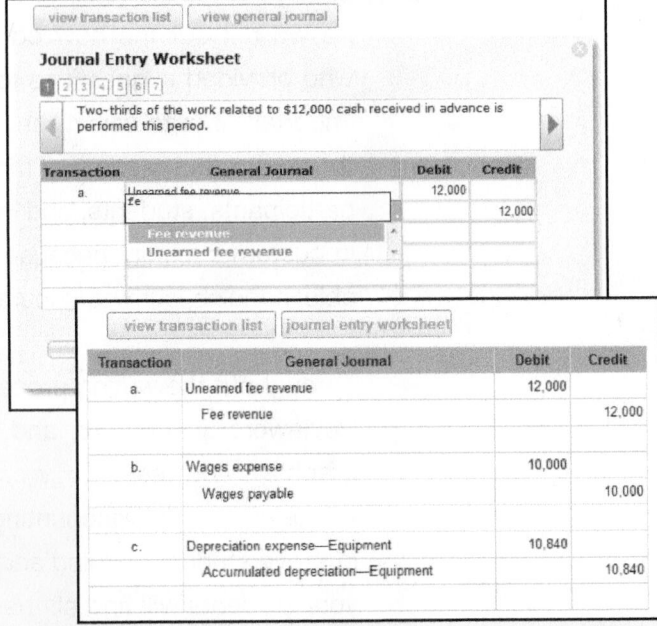

Learn with Adaptive Tools

▣|SMARTBOOK™

Fueled by LearnSmart—the most widely used and intelligent adaptive learning resource—SmartBook is the first and only adaptive reading experience available today.

Distinguishing what a student knows from what they don't, and honing in on concepts they are most likely to forget, SmartBook personalizes content for each student in a continuously adapting reading experience. Reading is no longer a passive and linear experience, but an engaging and dynamic one where students are more likely to master and retain important concepts, coming to class better prepared. Valuable reports provide instructors insight as to how students are progressing through textbook content, and are useful for shaping in-class time or assessment. As a result of the adaptive reading experience found in SmartBook, students are more likely to retain knowledge, stay in class, and get better grades.

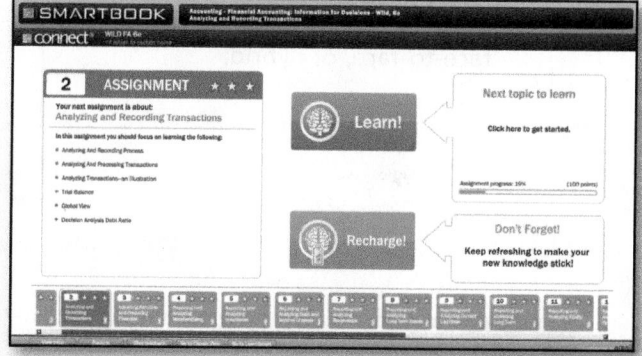

This revolutionary technology is available only from McGraw-Hill Education and for hundreds of course areas as part of the LearnSmart Advantage series.

How Does SmartBook Work?

Each SmartBook contains four components: Preview, Read, Practice, and Recharge. Starting with an initial preview of each chapter and key learning objectives, students read the material and are guided to topics that need the most practice based on their responses to a continuously adapting diagnostic. Read and practice continue until SmartBook directs students to recharge important material they are most likely to forget to ensure concept mastery and retention.

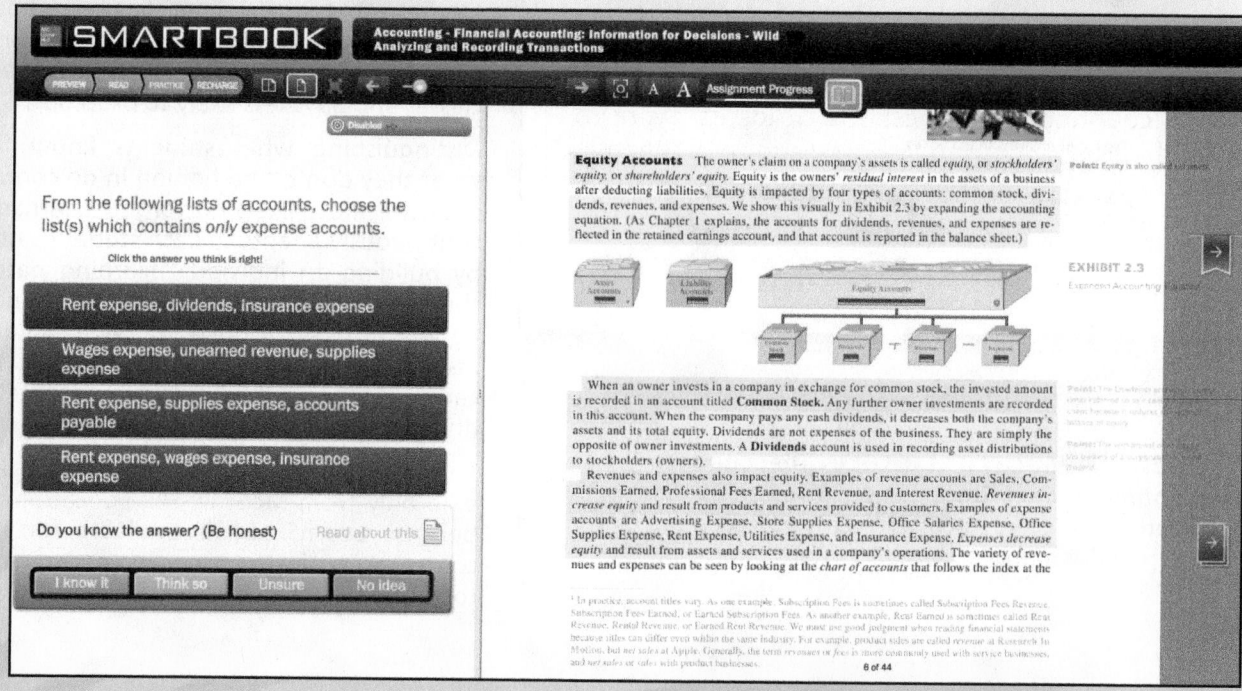

Adapting to the Needs of

Interactive Presentations *Connect Accounting*'s Interactive Presentations teach each chapter's core learning objectives and concepts through an engaging, hands-on presentation, bringing the text content to life. Interactive Presentations harness the full power of technology to truly engage and appeal to all learning styles. Interactive Presentations are ideal in all class formats—online, face-to-face, or hybrid.

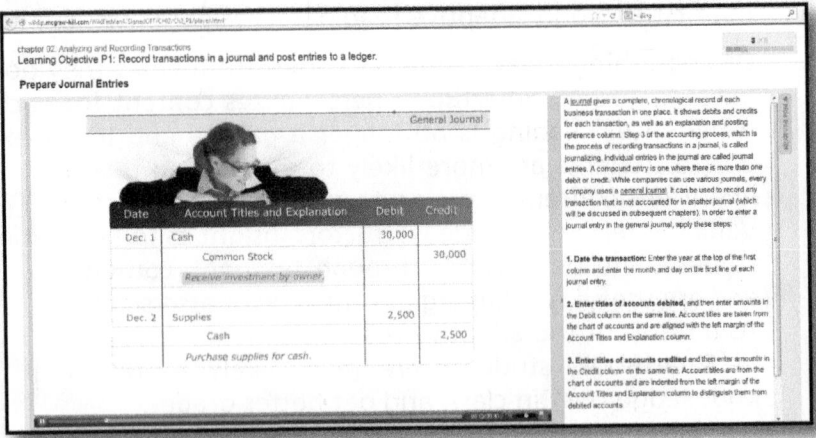

≡LEARNSMART

LearnSmart is one of the most effective and successful adaptive learning resources available on the market today. More than 2 million students have answered more than 1.3 billion questions in LearnSmart since 2009, making it the most widely used and intelligent adaptive study tool that's proven to strengthen memory recall, keep students in class, and boost grades. Students using LearnSmart are 13% more likely to pass their classes and 35% less likely to drop out.

Distinguishing what students know from what they don't, and honing in on concepts they are most likely to forget, LearnSmart continuously adapts to each student's needs by building an individual learning path so they study smarter and retain more knowledge. Turnkey reports provide valuable insight to instructors, so precious class time can be spent on higher-level concepts and discussion.

This revolutionary learning resource is available only from McGraw-Hill Education, and because LearnSmart is available for most course areas, instructors can recommend it to students in almost every class they teach.

Student Resource Library The *Connect Accounting* Student Study Center gives access to additional resources such as recorded lectures, online practice materials, an eBook, and more.

Today's Students!

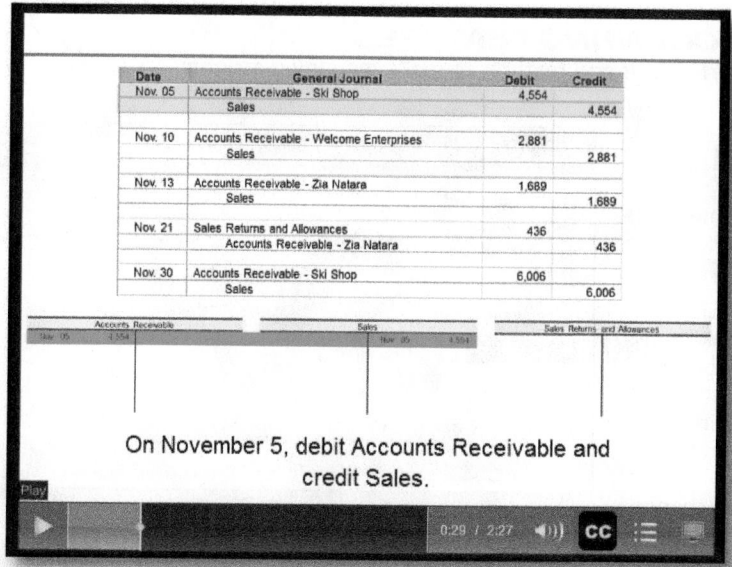

Guided Examples Guided Examples provide narrated, animated, and step-by-step walkthroughs of select exercises similar to those assigned in *Connect Accounting*, allowing the student to identify, review, or reinforce the concepts and activities covered in class. Guided Examples provide immediate feedback and focus on the areas where students need the most help.

Need-to-Know Videos Provide narrated, animated, step-by-step walkthroughs of the Need-to-Know learning activities presented for key concepts in each chapter. These tutorial presentations are directed to maximize student learning and retention of key chapter concepts, procedures, and analyses. Presentations are teacher-structured and student-focused, and are especially beneficial for students outside of the regular classroom.

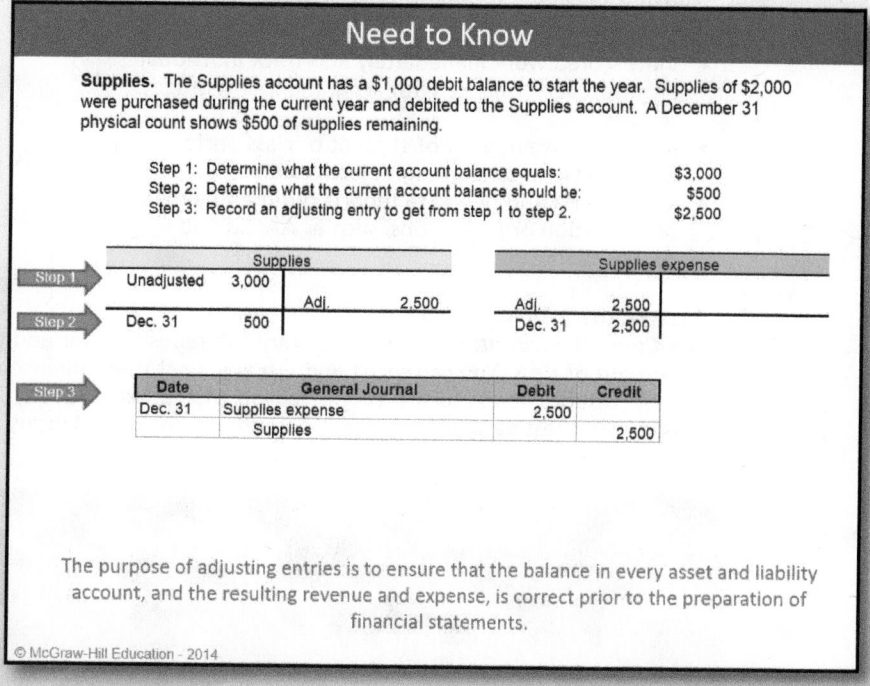

Adapting to the Needs of

MCGRAW-HILL *CONNECT ACCOUNTING* FEATURES

Connect Accounting offers a number of powerful tools and features to make managing assignments easier, so faculty can spend more time teaching.

Simple Assignment Management and Smart Grading

With *Connect Accounting*, creating assignments is easier than ever, so instructors can spend more time teaching and less time managing.

- Create and deliver assignments easily with selectable end-of-chapter questions and Test Bank items.
- Go paperless with the eBook and online submission and grading of student assignments.
- Have assignments scored automatically, giving students immediate feedback on their work and side-by-side comparisons with correct answers.
- Access and review each response; manually change grades or leave comments for students to review.
- Reinforce classroom concepts with practice tests and instant quizzes.

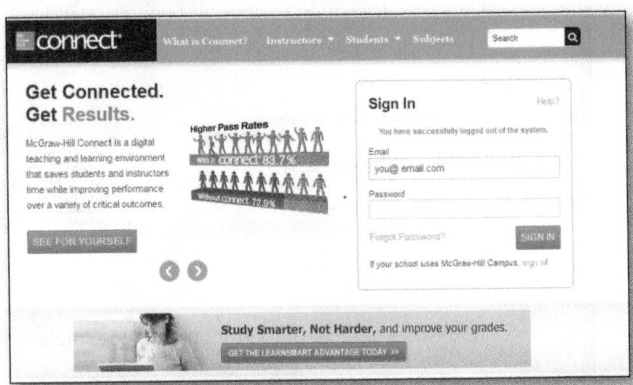

Student Reporting

Connect Accounting keeps instructors informed about how each student, section, and class is performing, allowing for more productive use of lecture and office hours. The progress-tracking function enables you to:

- View scored work immediately and track individual or group performance with assignment and grade reports.
- Access an instant view of student or class performance relative to learning objectives.
- Collect data and generate reports required by many accreditation organizations, such as AACSB and AICPA.

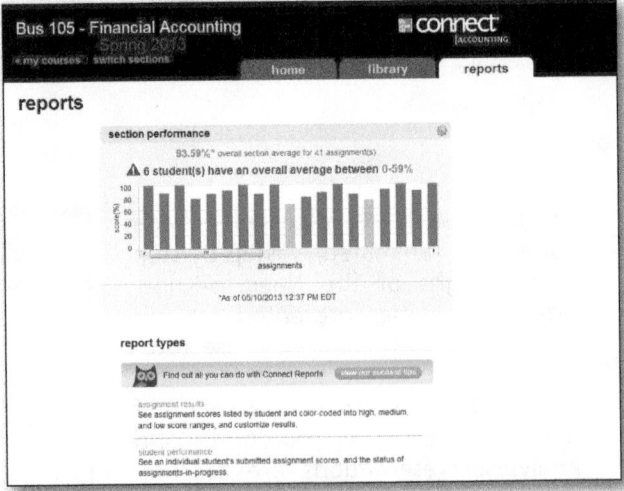

Instructor Library

The *Connect Accounting* Instructor Library is a repository for additional resources to improve student engagement in and out of class. You can select and use any asset that enhances your lecture. The *Connect Accounting* Instructor Library includes access to the eBook version of the text, videos, slide presentations, Solutions Manual, Instructor's Manual, and Test Bank. The *Connect Accounting* Instructor Library also allows you to upload your own files.

> "Connect certainly offers so much for the students and at the same time helps the professors. The professors can offer more learning opportunities to the students without intensive time investment."
>
> —**Constance Hylton, George Mason University**

Today's Instructors

MCGRAW-HILL *CONNECT PLUS ACCOUNTING*

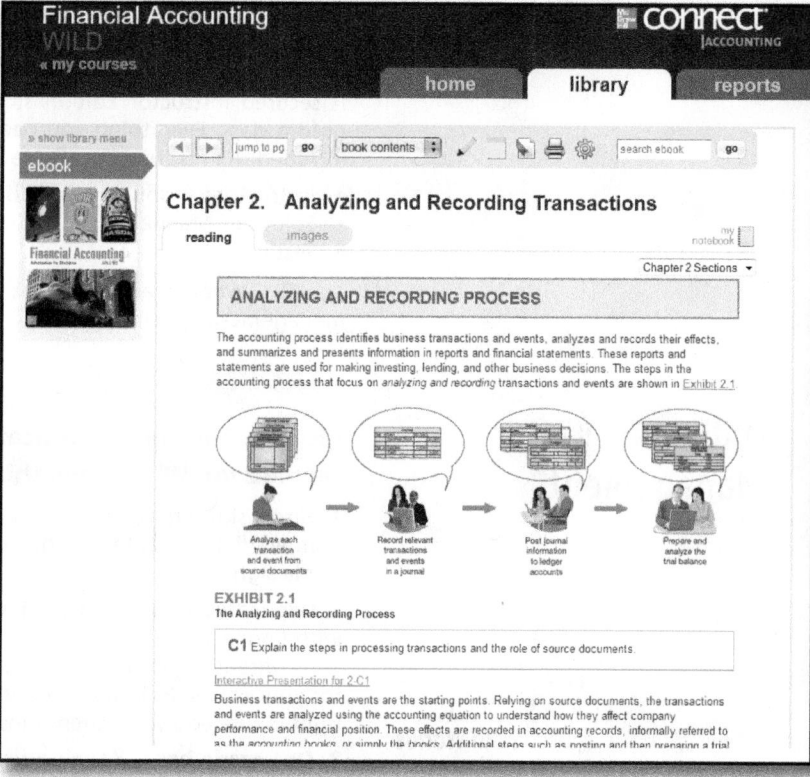

McGraw-Hill reinvents the textbook learning experience for the modern student with *Connect Plus Accounting.* A seamless integration of an eBook and *Connect Accounting, Connect Plus Accounting* provides all of the *Connect Accounting* features plus the following:

- An integrated, media-rich eBook, allowing for anytime, anywhere access to the textbook.
- Media-rich capabilities like embedded audio/visual presentations, highlighting, and sharing notes.
- Dynamic links between the problems or questions you assign to your students and the location in the eBook where that concept is covered.
- A powerful search function to pinpoint key concepts for review.

In short, *Connect Plus Accounting* offers students powerful tools and features that optimize their time and energy, enabling them to focus on learning.

For more information about *Connect Plus Accounting,* go to www.mcgrawhillconnect.com, or contact your local McGraw-Hill sales representative.

Tegrity Campus: Lectures 24/7

Tegrity Campus is a service that makes class time available 24/7 by automatically capturing every lecture. With a simple one-click start-and-stop process, you capture all computer screens and corresponding audio in a format that is easily searchable, frame by frame. Students can replay any part of any class with easy-to-use browser-based viewing on a PC, Mac, iPod, or other mobile device.

To learn more about Tegrity, watch a two-minute Flash demo at http://tegritycampus.mhhe.com.

McGraw-Hill Customer Experience Group Contact Information

At McGraw-Hill, we understand that getting the most from new technology can be challenging. That's why our services don't stop after you purchase our products. You can e-mail our Product Specialists 24 hours a day to get product training online. Or you can search our knowledge bank of Frequently Asked Questions on our support Website. For Customer Support, call 800-331-5094 or visit **www.mhhe.com/support**. One of our Technical Support Analysts will be able to assist you in a timely fashion.

Online Learning Center (OLC)

We offer an Online Learning Center (OLC) that follows *Financial Accounting* chapter by chapter. It doesn't require any building or maintenance on your part. It's ready to go the moment you and your students type in the URL: *www.mhhe.com/wildFA7e*

As students study and learn from *Financial Accounting*, they can visit the Student Edition of the OLC Website to work with a multitude of helpful tools:

- Generic Template Working Papers
- Chapter Learning Objectives
- Interactive Chapter Quizzes
- PowerPoint® Presentations
- Quick Check Exercises

A secured Instructor Edition stores essential course materials to save you prep time before class. Everything you need to run a lively classroom and an efficient course is included. All resources available to students, plus . . .

- Instructor's Resource Manual
- Solutions Manual
- Test Bank

The OLC Website also serves as a doorway to other technology solutions, like course management systems.

Online Course Management

The **Best** of **Both Worlds**

McGraw-Hill Higher Education and Blackboard have teamed up. What does this mean for you?

1. Single sign-on. Now you and your students can access McGraw-Hill's *Connect*™ and Create™ right from within your Blackboard course—all with one single sign-on.

2. Deep integration of content and tools. You get single sign-on with *Connect* and Create, you also get integration of McGraw-Hill content and content engines right in Blackboard. Whether you're choosing a book for your course or building *Connect* assignments, all the tools you need are right where you want them—inside Blackboard.

3. One grade book. Keeping several grade books and manually synchronizing grades in Blackboard is no longer necessary. When a student completes an integrated *Connect* assignment, the grade for that assignment automatically (and instantly) feeds your Blackboard grade center.

4. A solution for everyone. Whether your institution is already using Blackboard or you just want to try Blackboard on your own, we have a solution for you. McGraw-Hill and Blackboard can now offer you easy access to industry-leading technology and content, whether your campus hosts it, or we do. Be sure to ask your local McGraw-Hill representative for details.

 **Campus**

McGraw-Hill Campus™

McGraw-Hill Campus™ is a new one-stop teaching and learning experience available to users of any learning management system. This complimentary integration allows faculty and students to enjoy single sign-on (SSO) access to all McGraw-Hill Higher Education materials and synchronized grade-book with our award-winning McGraw-Hill Connect platform. McGraw-Hill Campus provides faculty with instant access to all McGraw-Hill Higher Education teaching materials (eTextbooks, test banks, PowerPoint slides, animations and learning objects, and so on), allowing them to browse, search, and use any instructor ancillary content in our vast library at no additional cost to instructor or students. Students enjoy SSO access to a variety of free and subscription-based products (McGraw-Hill *Connect*). With this integration enabled, faculty and students will never need to create another account to access McGraw-Hill products and services. For more information on McGraw-Hill Campus please visit our website at **www.mhcampus.com**.

CourseSmart

CourseSmart is a new way to find and buy eTextbooks. CourseSmart has the largest selection of eTextbooks available anywhere, offering thousands of the most commonly adopted textbooks from a wide variety of higher education publishers. CourseSmart eTextbooks are available in one standard online reader with full text search, notes, highlighting, and email tools for sharing between classmates. Visit **www.CourseSmart.com** for more information on ordering.

Instructor Supplements

Online Learning Center Instructor's Library

- **Instructor's Resource Manual**

  Written by April Mohr, Jefferson Community and Technical College, SW.

  This manual contains (for each chapter) a Lecture Outline, a chart linking all assignment materials to Learning Objectives, and additional visuals with transparency masters.

- **Solutions Manual**

  Written by John J. Wild, and Anita Kroll, University of Wisconsin–Madison.

- **Test Bank**

  Revised by Jeannie Folk, College of DuPage.

- **PowerPoint® Presentations**

  Prepared by Anna Boulware, St. Charles Community College.

  Presentations allow for revision of lecture slides, and includes a viewer, allowing screens to be shown with or without the software.

Student Supplements

Working Papers
Available through Create. Contact your publisher representative for details.

Written by John J. Wild.

Connect Accounting with LearnSmart One Semester Access Code Card
ISBN13: 9780077847869
ISBN10: 0077847865

Connect Plus Accounting with LearnSmart One Semester Access Code Card
ISBN13: 9780077844028
ISBN10: 0077844025

Innovative Textbook Features

Topic Flowchart

New! A **Topic Flowchart** is added to provide a handy textual/visual guide at the very start of each chapter to enhance student learning. Students can now begin their reading with a clear understanding of what they will learn and when, allowing them to stay more focused and organized along the way. The new Flowchart also integrates Learning Objectives tied to the CAP Model of learning, which shows the sequencing of learning objectives.

ANALYZING AND RECORDING PROCESS	ANALYZING AND PROCESSING TRANSACTIONS	TRIAL BALANCE AND THE FINANCIAL STATEMENTS
Using financial statements C1 Source documents C2 The account and its analysis Types of accounts Unclassified vs Classified	C3 General ledger C4 Double-entry accounting P1 Journalizing and posting A1 Processing transactions—An illustration	P2 Trial balance preparation & use P3 Financial statement preparation Reading an annual report A2 Analysis of financing sources

CAP Model

The Conceptual/Analytical/Procedural (CAP) Model allows courses to be specially designed to meet your teaching needs or those of a diverse faculty. This model identifies learning objectives, textual materials, assignments, and test items by C, A, or P, allowing different instructors to teach from the same materials, yet easily customize their courses toward a conceptual, analytical, or procedural approach (or a combination thereof) based on personal preferences.

Learning Objectives

C1 Explain the steps in processing transactions and the role of source documents. (p. 56)

C2 Describe an account and its use in recording transactions. (p. 57)

C3 Describe a ledger and a chart of accounts. (p. 60)

C4 Define *debits* and *credits* and explain double-entry accounting. (p. 61)

P1 Record transactions in a journal and post entries to a ledger. (p. 63)

A1 Analyze the impact of transactions on accounts and financial statements. (p. 65)

P2 Prepare and explain the use of a trial balance. (p. 71)

P3 Prepare financial statements from business transactions. (p. 73)

A2 Compute the debt ratio and describe its use in analyzing financial condition. (p. 77)

Using Accounting for Decisions

Whether we prepare, analyze, or apply accounting information, one skill remains essential: decision-making. To help develop good decision-making habits and to illustrate the relevance of accounting, our book uses a unique pedagogical framework we call the Decision Center. This framework is comprised of a variety of approaches and subject areas, giving students insight into every aspect of business decision-making. Answers to Decision Maker and Ethics boxes are at the end of each chapter.

Decision Insight Decision Insight boxes include interesting happenings from the world of business that relate to accounting.

Decision Maker Decision Maker boxes are active learning opportunities for students to take on the persona of a professional who uses accounting information to help resolve practical questions of importance.

Decision Ethics Decision Ethics boxes are active learning opportunities for students to take the perspective of a professional who uses accounting information to help resolve a practical situation that involves issues of ethics.

Decision Analysis Decision Analysis is a separate section at the end of each chapter that introduces important analysis tools/ratios to provide insight into the financial performance or condition of a major corporation.

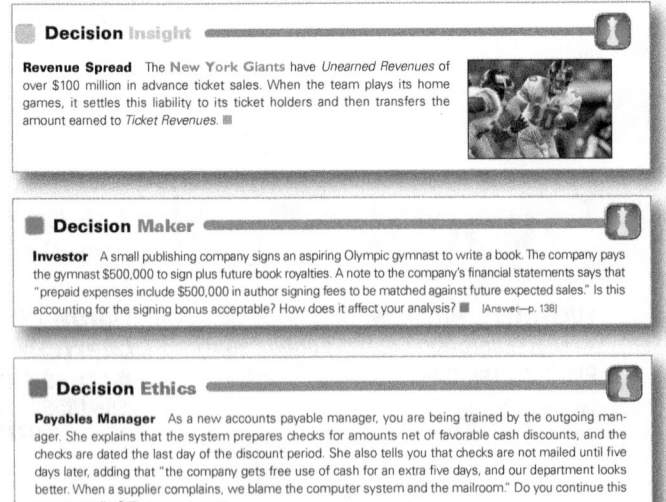

Decision Insight

Revenue Spread The New York Giants have *Unearned Revenues* of over $100 million in advance ticket sales. When the team plays its home games, it settles this liability to its ticket holders and then transfers the amount earned to *Ticket Revenues.*

Decision Maker

Investor A small publishing company signs an aspiring Olympic gymnast to write a book. The company pays the gymnast $500,000 to sign plus future book royalties. A note to the company's financial statements says that "prepaid expenses include $500,000 in author signing fees to be matched against future expected sales." Is this accounting for the signing bonus acceptable? How does it affect your analysis? [Answer—p. 138]

Decision Ethics

Payables Manager As a new accounts payable manager, you are being trained by the outgoing manager. She explains that the system prepares checks for amounts net of favorable cash discounts, and the checks are dated the last day of the discount period. She also tells you that checks are not mailed until five days later, adding that "the company gets free use of cash for an extra five days, and our department looks better. When a supplier complains, we blame the computer system and the mailroom." Do you continue this payment policy? [Answer—p. 171]

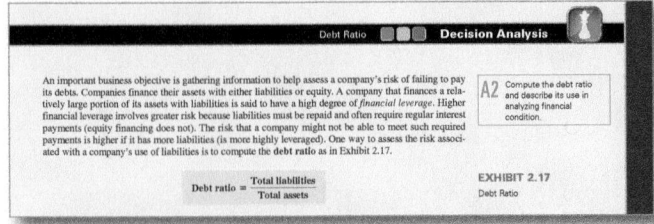

Debt Ratio · **Decision Analysis**

An important business objective is gathering information to help assess a company's risk of failing to pay its debts. Companies finance their assets with either liabilities or equity. A company that finances a relatively large portion of its assets with liabilities is said to have a high degree of *financial leverage*. Higher financial leverage involves greater risk because liabilities must be repaid and often require regular interest payments (equity financing does not). The risk that a company might not be able to meet such required payments is higher if it has more liabilities (is more highly leveraged). One way to assess the risk associated with a company's use of liabilities is to compute the **debt ratio** as in Exhibit 2.17.

A2 Compute the debt ratio and describe its use in analyzing financial condition.

$$\text{Debt ratio} = \frac{\text{Total liabilities}}{\text{Total assets}}$$

EXHIBIT 2.17
Debt Ratio

Bring Accounting To Life

Fraud Boxes

Stewardship is a crucial part of modern business and accounting. Fraud is a gross violation of stewardship. Each chapter introduces one or more new features devoted to accounting's role in fraud detection and prevention. These features describe, or relate to, provocative real-life scenarios of people who pursued fraudulent accounting activities for personal gain.

Fraud

They Fought the Law Our economic and social welfare depends on reliable accounting. Some individuals forgot that and are now paying their dues. They include Raj Rajaratnam (in photo), an investor, convicted of trading stocks using inside information; Bernard Madoff of Madoff Investment Securities, convicted of falsifying securities records; Bernard Ebbers of WorldCom, convicted of an $11 billion accounting scandal; Andrew Fastow of Enron, guilty of hiding debt and inflating income; and Ramalinga Raju of Satyam Computers, accused of overstating assets by $1.5 billion.

NEW Need-to-Know

This new feature asks the key questions that students "need-to-know" to sucessfully navigate the chapter, and provides solutions to allow students to practice.

The Need-to-Know questions are supplemented with a narrated, animated, step-by-step walkthrough video available via Connect Student Resources for additional reinforcement.

NEED-TO-KNOW 1.3

A1

Use the *accounting equation* to compute the missing financial statement amounts.

Company	Assets	Liabilities	Equity
BOSE	$150	$ 30	$__(a)__
VOGUE	$__(b)__	$100	$300

Solution

a. $120 **b.** $400

Use the *expanded accounting equation* to compute the missing financial statement amounts.

Company	Assets	Liabilities	Common Stock	Dividends	Revenues	Expenses
Nikon	$200	$ 80	$100	$0	__(a)__	$40
YouTube	$400	$160	$220	__(b)__	$120	$90

Solution

a. $60 **b.** $10

Do More: QS 1–7, QS 1–8, E 1–8, E 1–9

Marginal Student Annotations

These annotations provide students with additional hints, tips, and examples to help them more fully understand the concepts and retain what they have learned. The annotations also include notes on global implications of accounting and further examples.

Point: The sender (maker) of a *debit memorandum* will debit the account payable of the memo's receiver. The memo's receiver will credit the sender's account receivable.

acquires. Buyers often keep defective but s
acceptable allowance. When a buyer return
issues a **debit memorandum** to inform the s
in the buyer's records.

Purchase Allowances   To illustrate p
Z-Mart (buyer) issues a $300 debit memorar
chandise. Z-Mart's November 15 entry to u
the purchase allowance is

Global View

This section explains international accounting practices relating to the material covered in that chapter. This section is purposefully located at the end of each chapter so that each instructor can decide what emphasis, if at all, is to be assigned to it. The aim of this Global View section is to describe accounting practices and to identify the similarities and differences in international accounting practices versus that in the United States. As we move toward global convergence in accounting practices, and as we witness the evolution of U.S. GAAP and IFRS, the importance of student familiarity with international accounting grows. This innovative section helps us begin down that path of learning and teaching global accounting practices.

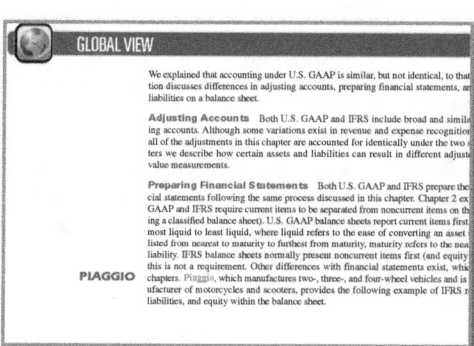

GLOBAL VIEW

We explained that accounting under U.S. GAAP is similar, but not identical, to that tion discusses differences in adjusting accounts, preparing financial statements, an liabilities on a balance sheet.

Adjusting Accounts Both U.S. GAAP and IFRS include broad and simila ing accounts. Although some variations exist in revenue and expense recognition all of the adjustments in this chapter are accounted for identically under the two ters we describe how certain assets and liabilities can result in different adjustm value measurements.

Preparing Financial Statements Both U.S. GAAP and IFRS prepare the cial statements following the same process discussed in this chapter. Chapter 2 ex GAAP and IFRS require current items to be separated from noncurrent items on th ing a classified balance sheet). U.S. GAAP balance sheets report current items first most liquid to least liquid, where liquid refers to the ease of converting an asset listed from nearest to maturity to furthest from maturity, maturity refers to the nea liability. IFRS balance sheets normally present noncurrent items first (and equity this is not a requirement. Other differences with financial statements exist, whic chapters. Piaggio, which manufactures two-, three-, and four-wheel vehicles and is ufacturer of motorcycles and scooters, provides the following example of IFRS liabilities, and equity within the balance sheet.

PIAGGIO

xv

Outstanding Assignment Material

Once a student has finished reading the chapter, how well he or she retains the material can depend greatly on the questions, exercises, and problems that reinforce it. This book leads the way in comprehensive, accurate assignments.

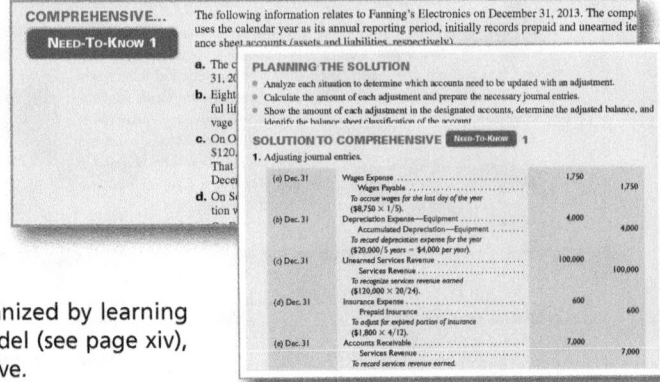

Comprehensive Need-to-Know Problems
are located at the end of each chapter and present both a problem and a complete solution, allowing students to review the entire problem-solving process.

Chapter Summaries provide students with a review organized by learning objectives. Chapter Summaries are a component of the CAP model (see page xiv), which recaps each conceptual, analytical, and procedural objective.

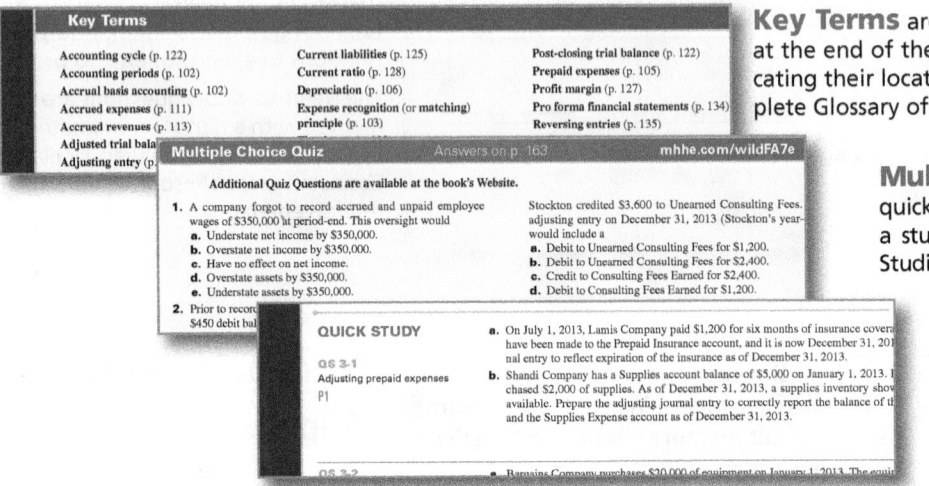

Key Terms are bolded in the text and repeated at the end of the chapter with page numbers indicating their location. The book also includes a complete Glossary of Key Terms.

Multiple Choice Quiz questions quickly test chapter knowledge before a student moves on to complete Quick Studies, Exercises, and Problems.

Quick Study assignments are short exercises that often focus on one learning objective. Most are included in *Connect Accounting*. There are usually 8-10 Quick Study assignments per chapter.

Exercises are one of this book's many strengths and a competitive advantage. There are about 10-15 per chapter and are included in *Connect Accounting*. The Exercises cover all learning objectives and all key topics in each chapter.

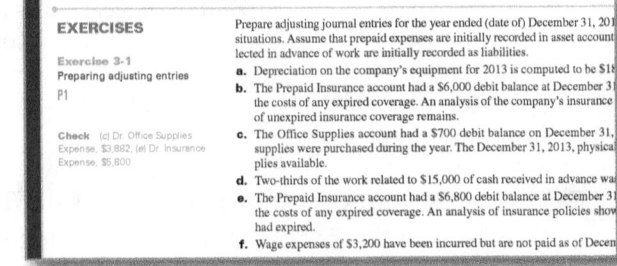

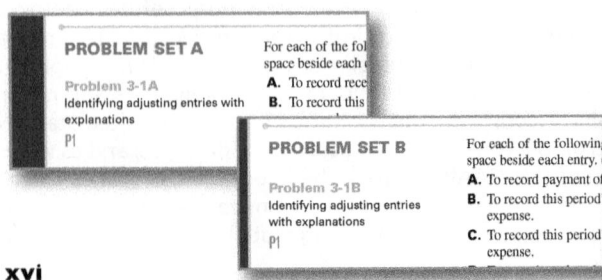

Problem Sets A & B are proven problems that can be assigned as homework or for in-class projects. All problems are coded according to the CAP model (see page xiv), and Set A is included in *Connect Accounting*.

Helps Students Master Key Concepts

Beyond the Numbers exercises ask students to use accounting figures and understand their meaning. Students also learn how accounting applies to a variety of business situations. These creative and fun exercises are all new or updated, and are divided into sections:

- Reporting in Action
- Comparative Analysis
- Ethics Challenge
- Communicating in Practice
- Taking It To The Net
- Teamwork in Action
- Hitting the Road
- Entrepreneurial Decision
- Global Decision

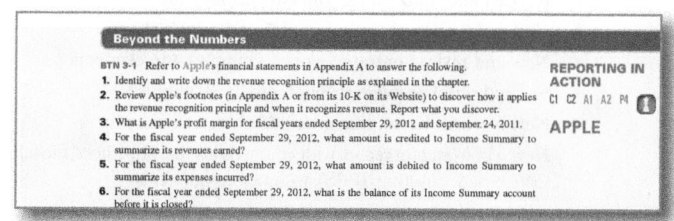

Serial Problem uses a continuous running case study to illustrate chapter concepts in a familiar context. The Serial Problem can be followed continuously from the first chapter or picked up at any later point in the book; enough information is provided to ensure students can get right to work.

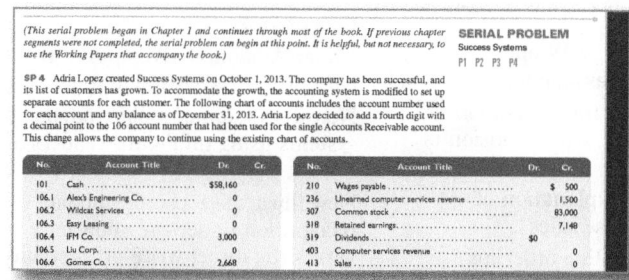

New General Ledger Problems—Only Available in Connect. Every transaction affects one or more financial statements. This General Ledger simulation automates many of the steps in the accounting cycle, which allows students to see the impact each transaction has on the financial statements in real-time. Students can easily link back to their original entries simply by clicking in the ledger if edits are needed. Many questions now have critical thinking components added to maximize the student's foundational knowledge of accounting concepts and principles.

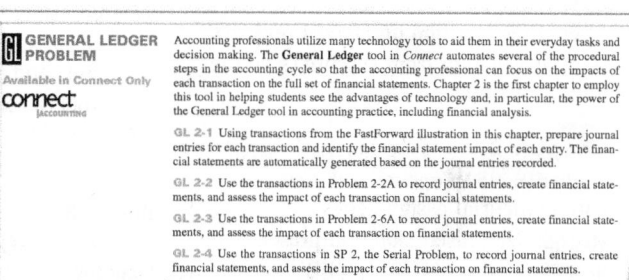

The End of the Chapter Is Only the Beginning. Our valuable and proven assignments aren't just confined to the book. From problems that require technological solutions to materials found exclusively online, this book's end-of-chapter material is fully integrated with its technology package.

QC1

- Quick Studies, Exercises, and Problems available in *Connect* are marked with an icon.
- Assignments that focus on global accounting practices and companies are often identified with an icon.
- The QC icon in the margin indicates that Quick Check questions with solutions are available via the text Website for additional practice.

Enhancements in This Edition

This edition's revisions are driven by instructors and students. General revisions to the entire book follow (including chapter-by-chapter revisions):

- Revised and updated assignments throughout
- Updated ratio/tool analysis and data for each chapter
- New and revised entrepreneurial examples and elements
- Revised serial problem through nearly all chapters
- New Need-to-Know examples added to each chapter
- New Apple annual report with comparisons to competitors, including Google and Samsung (IFRS), with new assignments

- Updated graphics added to each chapter's analysis section
- New technology content integrated and referenced in the book
- Updated Global View section in each chapter
- New innovative assignments sprinkled throughout the book
- New General Ledger questions added to most chapters

Chapter 1

Apple NEW opener with new entrepreneurial assignment

Streamlined and reorganized discussion of the users of accounting information

New discussion on the joint role of the FASB and IASB in standard setting

Revised layout for accounting principles and assumptions

Updated accounting salary information

Added titles to revenue and expense entries in columnar layout of transaction analysis

Streamlined section on Dodd-Frank act

New survey data from executives on the impact of fraud

Chapter 2

LinkedIn NEW opener with new entrepreneurial assignment

Reorganized discussion and presentation of assets, liabilities, and equity accounts

Enhanced 4-step process of journalizing and posting transactions

New Section on Using Financial Statements, including ratio analysis

New coverage of classified and unclassifed balance sheets

Revised global view and new Samsung's (abbreviated) balance sheet

Updated debt ratio discussion using recent Skechers's information

Chapter 3

Facebook NEW opener with new entrepreneurial assignment

Updated innovative 3-step process for adjusting accounts

New example of unearned revenues using USA Today

Updated IFRS and FASB revenue recognition convergence

Added new Quick Studies to directly apply the three-step adjustment process

Chapter 4

Buffalo Wild Wings NEW opener with new entrepreneurial assignment

Enhanced exhibit on transportation costs and FOB terms, with inclusion of entries

Highlight two-step explanation of recording merchandise sales

New discussion of online ordering, tracking numbers, RFID, and FOB

Revised visual display of a sales invoice

Revised discussion of merchandising purchases and sales

New Volkswagen example of IFRS income statement

Chapter 5

Boston Beer Company NEW opener with new entrepreneurial assignment

New focus on periodic valuation (perpetual in appendix)

New exhibits visually show cost flows for each method

New explanatory boxes added to selected exhibits as learning aids

Expanded assignments covering periodic and perpetual inventory measurement

Chapter 6

Google NEW opener with new entrepreneurial assignment

Expanded presentation of 'Hacker's Guide'

New discussion of the lock box and its purpose

New data on sources of fraud complaints

New evidence on methods to override controls

New visual on document to bond (insure) an employee

New example of MLB controls, and lack thereof

Chapter 7

Under Armour NEW opener with new entrepreneurial assignment

New discussion of mobile payment systems using mini-card-readers and iPads

New illustration comparing bad debts recognition under the allowance method versus the direct write-off method

Revised exhibit on aging of accounts receivable, including all detailed accounts

New illustration on why the banker's rule is commonly applied

Chapter 8

Nathan's Famous NEW opener with new entrepreneurial assignment

New learning boxes added to selected exhibits identifying salvage value

New explanation on how asset purchases occurring on different days of the month are commonly processed

New example of extraordinary repairs applied to the stealth bomber

New notes added to emphasize that depreciation is cost allocation, and not valuation

New explanation on how drugmakers fight patent expirations

New information on the Mickey Mouse Protection Act for intangibles

New goodwill example using Google's purchase of YouTube

Chapter 9

Annie's, Inc. NEW opener with new entrepreneurial assignment

Revised unearned revenues example based on Rihanna ticket sales

For Better Learning and Retention

Added explanation on the role of sellers as tax collection 'agents' for the government

New information on franchise costs and how they are accounted for

Added select formulas to enhance the exhibit on payroll deductions

Updated payroll rates to 2013 with discussion on likely adjustments for 2014

Added discussion on maximum withholding allowances claimed

New discussion on IRS actions against companies that fail to pay employment taxes

New evidence on payroll fraud, its median loss, and time taken to uncover such frauds

Chapter 10

Zynga NEW opener with new entrepreneurial assignment

New explanation on why debt (credit) financing is less costly than equity financing

New margin graphics (four) illustrating how a debt's carrying value is periodically adjusted until it equals maturity value at the end of its life

New margin boxes on calculator functions to compute the price of bonds

New explanation of what is investment grade debt

New discussion on the role of unreported liabilities and the financial crisis

Reference to changes in lease accounting

New discussion of collateral and its role in debt financing

New separate appendix learning objectives on amortizing a discount or a premium using effective interest

Chapter 11

Groupon NEW opener with new entrepreneurial assignment

Revised presentation of corporate form

New discussion of Facebook's IPO and the role of accounting information

New reference to corporate governance

New reference to state laws and where companies incorporate

New examples using Target for stock quotes and Google for stock splits

New discussion of fraudulent information dissemination and stock prices

Updated the global view on equity accounting

Chapter 12

Salesforce.com NEW opener with new entrepreneurial assignment

Revised graphics to better illustrate cash inflows and outflows for operating, investing, and financing activities

Revised graphic to better reflect cash and cash equivalents

Added discussion on the use of T-accounts for reconstructing transactions impacting cash

New margin clarification for computing free cash flow

New discussion on the potential for IASB and FASB to issue guidance for the statement of cash flow that would require the direct method... stay tuned

Chapter 13

Morgan Stanley NEW opener with new entrepreneurial assignment

New companies—Apple, Google, and Samsung—data throughout the chapter, exhibits, and illustrations

New boxed discussion on the role of financial statement analysis to fight and prevent fraud

Enhanced horizontal, vertical, ratio analysis using new companies and industry data

New analysis of segment data

Streamlined global view section

Appendix C

New discussion of the two optional presentations for comprehensive income

Revised discussion of accounting for securities

New reference to Greek debt in the context of international operations

New Google example of comprehensive income

Appendix D

New examples of LLPs and their prevalence among professional services

New discussion of the potential for multiple drawing accounts in practice

Revised and streamlined three-step process to liquidate a partnership

Appendix E

Expanded discussion and examples of hackers and internal controls

New pneumonic tool for system principles

Enhanced exhibit on system components

New discussion on voice recognition controls

New discussion on cloud computing, its implications to accounting, and its risks

New references to XBRL, Dynamics GP, and QuickBooks in accounting

Updated discussion and examples for ERP

New! Corporate / Entrepreneurial Flavor

This edition marries three motivating factors. First, we know that student learning increases when students are engaged. Second, students tell us that entrepreneurial stories of success motivate them. Third, students say that reports of how accounting helps those entrepreneurs motivate them to study accounting. In response, we made several key decisions:

• Each chapter launches with an entrepreneur who uses accounting and has achieved success

• Each entrepreneurial company is publicly traded, meaning that students can access its accounting data

• "Decision" features (see page xiv) introduce business decisions, ethics, ratios, and real world events in accounting

• Real world assignments give students hands-on experience with data from practice

• Other elements, such as excerpts from Apple and Google, combine to create our new corporate/entrepreneurial flavor!

Assurance of Learning Ready

Many educational institutions today are focused on the notion of assurance of learning, an important element of some accreditation standards. *Financial Accounting* is designed specifically to support your assurance of learning initiatives with a simple, yet powerful solution. Each test bank question for *Financial Accounting* maps to a specific chapter learning objective listed in the text. You can use, EZ Test Online or *Connect Accounting* to easily query for learning objectives that directly relate to the learning objectives for your course. You can then use the reporting features of EZ Test to aggregate student results in similar fashion, making the collection and presentation of assurance of learning data simple and easy.

> "This textbook does address many learning styles and at the same time allows for many teaching styles ... our faculty have been very pleased with the continued revisions and supplements. From working papers ... to continually improved homework sites and e-books. I'm a 'Wild' fan!"
>
> **—Rita Hays, Southwestern Oklahoma State University**

AACSB Statement

The McGraw-Hill Companies is a proud corporate member of AACSB International. Understanding the importance and value of AACSB accreditation, *Financial Accounting* recognizes the curricula guidelines detailed in the AACSB standards for business accreditation by connecting selected questions in the test bank to the six general knowledge and skill guidelines in the AACSB standards. The statements contained in *Financial Accounting* are provided only as a guide for the users of this textbook. The AACSB leaves content coverage and assessment within the purview of individual schools, the mission of the school, and the faculty. While *Financial Accounting* and the teaching package make no claim of any specific AACSB qualification or evaluation, we have within *Financial Accounting* labeled select questions according to the six general knowledge and skills areas.

Acknowledgments

John J. Wild and McGraw-Hill/Irwin would like to recognize the following instructors for their valuable feedback and involvement in the development of *Financial Accounting, 7e*. We are thankful for their suggestions, counsel, and encouragement.

Thomas Arcuri, Florida State University

Sidney Askew, Borough of Manhattan Community College

Richard Barnhart, Grand Rapids Community College

Jaswinder Bhangal, Chabot College

Patrick Borja, Citrus College

Anna Boulware, St. Charles Community College

Billy Brewster, University of Texas at Arlington

Marci Butterfield, University of Utah

Colleen Chung, Miami Dade College-Kendall

Kwang-Hyun Chung, Pace University

Robert Churchman, Harding University

Marilyn Ciolino, Delgado Community College

Robin Clement, University of Oregon

Ken Couvillion, Delta College

Karen Crisonino, County College of Morris

Stan Davis, University of Tennessee at Chattanooga

Walter DeAguero, Saddleback College

Stephanie and Mike Derr, Derr Properties

Mike Deschamps, MiraCosta College

Ron Dustin, Fresno City College

Magdy Farag, California State Polytechnic University-Pomona

Albert Fisher, College of Southern Nevada

Linda Flowers, Houston Community College

Jeannie Folk, College of DuPage

Ernesto Gonzalez, Florida National College

Ann Gregory, South Plains College

Rebecca Hancock, El Paso Community College-Valley Verde

Laurie Hays, Western Michigan University

Rita Hays, Southwestern Oklahoma State University

Bambi Hora, University of Central Oklahoma

Constance Hylton, George Mason University

Todd Jensen, Sierra College

Gina M. Jones, Aims Community College

Jeff Jones, College of Southern Nevada

Sandra Jordan, Florida State College at Jacksonville

Dmitriy Kalyagin, Chabot College

Thomas Kam, Hawaii Pacific University

Ann Kelley, Providence College

Shirly A. Kleiner, Johnson County Community College

Jo Koehn, University of Central Missouri

Sudha Krishnan, California State University-Long Beach

Anita Kroll, University of Wisconsin-Madison

David Krug, Johnson County Community College

Christopher Kwak, DeAnza College

David Laurel, South Texas College

Charles Lewis, Houston Community College

Jeannie Liu, Chaffey College

Thomas S. Marsh, Northern Virginia Community College-Annandale

Stacie Mayes, Rose State College

Donald McWilliams, Jackson State University

Jeanine Metzler, Northampton Community College

Edna C. Mitchell, Polk State College

Kathleen O'Donnell, Onondaga Community College

Yvonne Phang, Borough of Manhattan Community College

James Racic, Lakeland Community College

Ruthie Reynolds, Howard University

Helen Roybark, Radford University

Richard Sarkisian, Camden County College

Linda Schain, Hofstra University

Tracy Schmeltzer, Wayne Community College

Debbie Schmidt, Cerritos College

Raymond Shaffer, Youngstown State University

Geeta Shankhar, University of Dayton

Regina Shea, Community College of Baltimore County—Essex

Jaye Simpson, Tarrant County College

Erik Slayter, California Polytechnic State University San Luis Obispo

Gerald Smith, University of Northern Iowa

Dominique Svarc, William Rainey Harper College

Ulysses Taylor, Fayetteville State University

Anthony Teng, Saddleback College

Teresa Thompson, Chaffey Community College

Tom Thompson, Madison College

Jerri Tittle, Rose State College

Bob Urell, Irvine Valley College

Patricia Walczak, Lansing Community College

Dave Welch, Franklin University

Jean Wells-Jessup, Howard University

Christopher Widmer, Tidewater Community College

Gayle Williams, Sacramento City College

Kenneth L. Wild, University of London

Jonathan M. Wild, University of Wisconsin

John Woodward, Polk State College

Wanda Wong, Chabot College

Qiang Wu, Rensselaer Polytechnic Institute

Judy Zander, Grossmont College

The author extends a special thank you to our contributing and technology supplement authors:

Contributing Authors: Anita Kroll, University of Wisconsin; Jo Lynne Koehn, University of Central Missouri; Kathleen O'Donnell, Onondaga Community College

Accuracy Checkers: Dave Krug, Johnson County Community College; Albert Fisher, College of Southern Nevada; Judy Zander, Grossmont College; Ann McCarthy, Eastern Carolina University; Mark McCarthy, East Carolina University; Helen Roybark, Radford University; Beth Woods; and Barbara Schnathorst

LearnSmart Author: April Mohr, Jefferson Community and Technical College, SW

Online Quizzes: Constance Hylton, George Mason University

Interactive Presentations: Jeannie Folk, College of DuPage

PowerPoint: Anna Boulware, St. Charles Community College

Instructor Resource Manual: April Mohr, Jefferson Community and Technical College, SW

Test Bank: Jeannie Folk, College of DuPage

In addition to the helpful and generous colleagues listed above, I thank the entire McGraw-Hill/Irwin *Financial Accounting*, 7e team, including Tim Vertovec, Steve Schuetz, Christina Sanders, Lori Koetters, Matthew Baldwin, Carol Bielski, Patricia Plumb, Jeremy Cheshareck, Ron Nelms, Xin Lin, Julie Hankins, and Brian Nacik. I also thank the great marketing and sales support staff, including Michelle Nolte and Kathleen Klehr. Many talented educators and professionals worked hard to create the supplements for this book, and for their efforts I'm grateful. Finally, many more people I either did not meet or whose efforts I did not personally witness nevertheless helped to make this book everything that it is, and I thank them all.

John J. Wild

Brief Contents

* Appendixes D & E are available on the book's Website, **mhhe.com/wildFA7e**, and as print copy from a McGraw-Hill representative.

Contents

4 Reporting and Analyzing Merchandising Operations 164

5 Reporting and Analyzing Inventories 212

6 Reporting and Analyzing Cash and Internal Controls 262

7 Reporting and Analyzing Receivables 308

8 Reporting and Analyzing Long-Term Assets 344

9 Reporting and Analyzing Current Liabilities 388

* Appendixes D & E are available on the book's Website, **mhhe.com/wildFA7e**, and as print copy from a McGraw-Hill representative.

1 Introducing Financial Accounting

Chapter Flowchart is organized by key topics and includes key learning objectives

IMPORTANCE OF ACCOUNTING	FUNDAMENTALS OF ACCOUNTING	TRANSACTION ANALYSIS	FINANCIAL STATEMENTS
C1 Purpose of accounting	C3 Ethics—key concept	A1 Accounting equation and its components	P2 Income statement
C2 Accounting information users	C4 Generally accepted accounting principles	P1 Transaction analysis—illustrated	Statement of retained earnings
Opportunities in accounting	International standards		Balance sheet
	Conceptual framework		Statement of cash flows
			A2 Financial analysis

Learning Objectives are classified as conceptual, analytical, or procedural (and are listed in the order covered as shown in the Flowchart above)

Learning Objectives

C1 Explain the purpose and importance of accounting. (p. 4)

C2 Identify users and uses of, and opportunities in, accounting. (p. 4)

C3 Explain why ethics are crucial to accounting. (p. 7)

C4 Explain generally accepted accounting principles and define and apply several accounting principles. (p. 9)

A1 Define and interpret the accounting equation and each of its components. (p. 15)

P1 Analyze business transactions using the accounting equation. (p. 16)

P2 Identify and prepare basic financial statements and explain how they interrelate. (p. 21)

A2 Compute and interpret return on assets. (p. 25)

A3 *Appendix 1A*—Explain the relation between return and risk. (p. 29)

C5 *Appendix 1B*—Identify and describe the three major activities of organizations. (p. 29)

*A **Decision Feature** launches each chapter showing the relevance of accounting for a real entrepreneur. An **Entrepreneurial Decision** problem at the end of the assignments returns to this feature with a mini-case.*

Wizard of Woz

"Wherever smart people work, doors are unlocked . . ."

—STEVE WOZNIAK

CUPERTINO, CA—"When I designed the Apple stuff," says Steve Wozniak (a.k.a. Woz, also known as the *Wizard of Woz*), "I never thought in my life I would have enough money to fly to Hawaii or make a down-payment on a house." Today, **Apple** (**Apple.com**) boasts a value of over $400 billion and revenues of over $156 billion (recent years' revenues follow).

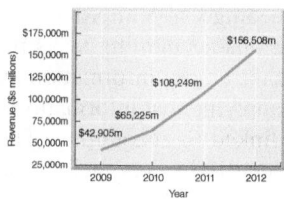

Woz, along with Steve Jobs, founded Apple on April 1, 1976. Immediately, Woz and Jobs confronted many accounting issues, including how to finance their new company. Their decision was to sell some of their prized possessions, such as Woz's HP scientific calculator and Jobs's Volkswagen van, thereby raising $1,300 to launch Apple. They quickly spent the funds on electronic equipment for Woz to build the first Apple computer.

Apple Inc.
NASDAQ: AAPL

$176,064 mil. assets
73,000 employees

Revenue Sources

In setting up their company, the two young entrepreneurs had to make a decision on what type of entity to form: partnership or corporation. They decided on a partnership and had Ron Wayne type it. "He sat down at a typewriter and typed our partnership contract right out of his head," recalls Woz. "He did an etching of Newton under the apple tree for the cover of our Apple I manual [and] he wrote the manual." Interestingly, the original partnership agreement included Wayne as a third partner with 10% ownership. However, 10 days later, Wayne had a change of heart when he considered the unlimited liability of a partnership and he pulled out, leaving Woz and Jobs holding 50% each. Within nine months, Woz and Jobs saw advantages to the corporate form of business organization, and they converted Apple to a corporation on January 3, 1977.

As the new company grew, Woz and Steve had to learn some accounting along with details of preparing and interpreting financial statements. Important questions involving transaction analysis and financial reporting arose, and the owners took care to do things right. "Everything we did," asserts Woz, "we were setting the tone for the world." Still, there were some doubters, including Woz's father. "A person like him shouldn't have that much money," said his father after finding $250,000 of uncashed checks lying around in Woz's Porsche.

Information for business decisions is the focus of Apple's accounting records. Woz believes that Apple is integral to the language of technology, just as accounting is the language of business. In retrospect, Woz says, "every dream I have ever had in life has come true ten times over." He adds: "in the end, I hope there's a little note somewhere that says I designed a good computer."

Sources: *Woz Website,* Woz.org, January 2014; *iWoz: From Computer Geek to Cult Icon,* W.W.Norton & Co., 2006; Founders at Work, Apress, 2007; *Apple Website,* January 2014

IMPORTANCE OF ACCOUNTING

C1 Explain the purpose and importance of accounting.

Why is accounting so popular on campus? Why are there so many openings for accounting jobs? Why is accounting so important to companies? Why do politicians and business leaders focus on accounting regulations? The answer is that we live in an information age, where that information, and its reliability, impacts us all.

Accounting is an information and measurement system that identifies, records, and communicates relevant, reliable, and comparable information about an organization's business activities. *Identifying* business activities requires that we select relevant transactions and events. Examples are the sale of iPads by Apple and the receipt of ticket money by TicketMaster. *Recording* business activities requires that we keep a chronological log of transactions and events measured in dollars. *Communicating* business activities requires that we prepare accounting reports such as financial statements, which we analyze and interpret. (The financial statements and notes of Apple are shown in Appendix A near the end of this book. This appendix also shows the financial statements of Google and Samsung.) Exhibit 1.1 summarizes accounting activities.

Real company names are printed in bold magenta.

EXHIBIT 1.1

Accounting Activities

Identifying	Recording	Communicating
Select transactions and events	Input, measure, and log	Prepare, analyze, and interpret

Accounting is part of our everyday lives. Our most common contact with accounting is through credit approvals, checking accounts, tax forms, and payroll. These experiences tend to focus on the recordkeeping parts of accounting. **Recordkeeping,** or **bookkeeping,** is the recording of transactions and events, either manually or electronically. This is just one part of accounting. Accounting also identifies and communicates information on transactions and events, and it includes the crucial processes of analysis and interpretation.

Technology is a key part of modern business and plays a major role in accounting. Technology reduces the time, effort, and cost of recordkeeping while improving clerical accuracy. Some small organizations continue to perform various accounting tasks manually, but even they are impacted by technology. As technology makes more information available, the demand for accounting increases and so too the skills for applying that information. Consulting, planning, and other financial services are now closely linked to accounting. These services require sorting through data, interpreting their meaning, identifying key factors, and analyzing their implications.

Point: Technology is only as useful as the accounting data available, and users' decisions are only as good as their understanding of accounting. The best software and recordkeeping cannot make up for lack of accounting knowledge.

Users of Accounting Information

C2 Identify users and uses of, and opportunities in, accounting.

Accounting is called the *language of business* because all organizations set up an accounting information system to communicate data to help people make better decisions. Exhibit 1.2 shows that accounting serves many users (this is a partial listing) who can be divided into two groups: external users and internal users.

External Information Users   **External users** of accounting information are *not* directly involved in running the organization. They include shareholders (investors), lenders, directors, customers, suppliers, regulators, lawyers, brokers, and the press. External users have limited access to an organization's information. Yet their business decisions depend on information that is reliable, relevant, and comparable. **Financial accounting** is the area of accounting aimed at

External users

• Lenders   • Consumer groups
• Shareholders   • External auditors
• Governments   • Customers

Internal users

• Officers   • Sales staff
• Managers   • Budget officers
• Internal auditors • Controllers

EXHIBIT 1.2

Users of Accounting Information

Infographics reinforce key concepts through visual learning.

serving external users by providing them with *general-purpose financial statements*. The term *general-purpose* refers to the broad range of purposes for which external users rely on these statements. Following is a partial list of external users and some decisions they make with accounting information.

- *Lenders* (creditors) loan money or other resources to an organization. Banks, savings and loans, co-ops, and mortgage and finance companies are lenders. Lenders look for information to help them assess whether an organization is likely to repay its loans with interest.

- *Shareholders* (*investors*) are the owners of a corporation. They use accounting reports in deciding whether to buy, hold, or sell stock.

- *Directors* are typically elected to a *board of directors* to oversee their interests in an organization. Since directors are responsible to shareholders, their information needs are similar.

- *External* (independent) *auditors* examine financial statements to verify that they are prepared according to generally accepted accounting principles.

- *Nonexecutive employees* and *labor unions* use financial statements to judge the fairness of wages, assess job prospects, and bargain for better wages.

- *Regulators* often have legal authority over certain activities of organizations. For example, the Internal Revenue Service (IRS) and other tax authorities require organizations to file accounting reports in computing taxes. Other regulators include utility boards that use accounting information to set utility rates and securities regulators that require reports for companies that sell their stock to the public.

- *Voters, legislators,* and *government officials* use accounting information to monitor and evaluate government receipts and expenses.

- *Contributors* to nonprofit organizations use accounting information to evaluate the use and impact of their donations.

- *Suppliers* use accounting information to judge the soundness of a customer before making sales on credit.

- *Customers* use financial reports to assess the staying power of potential suppliers.

Internal Information Users   **Internal users** of accounting information are those directly involved in managing and operating an organization such as the chief executive officer (CEO), chief financial officer (CFO), chief audit executive (CAE), treasurer, and other executive and managerial-level employees. They use the information to help improve the efficiency and effectiveness of an organization. **Managerial accounting** is the area of accounting that serves the decision-making needs of internal users. Internal reports are not subject to the same rules as external reports and instead are designed with the special needs of internal users in mind. Following is a partial list of internal users and some decisions they make with accounting information.

- *Research and development managers* need information about projected costs and revenues of any proposed changes in products and services.

- *Purchasing managers* need to know what, when, and how much to purchase.

- *Human resource managers* need information about employees' payroll, benefits, performance, and compensation.
- *Production managers* depend on information to monitor costs and ensure quality.
- *Distribution managers* need reports for timely, accurate, and efficient delivery of products and services.
- *Marketing managers* use reports about sales and costs to target consumers, set prices, and monitor consumer needs, tastes, and price concerns.
- *Service managers* require information on the costs and benefits of looking after products and services.

Opportunities in Accounting

Accounting information is in all aspects of our lives. When we earn money, pay taxes, invest savings, budget earnings, and plan for the future, we use accounting. Accounting has four broad areas of opportunities: financial, managerial, taxation, and accounting-related. Exhibit 1.3 lists selected opportunities in each area.

EXHIBIT 1.3

Accounting Opportunities

EXHIBIT 1.4

Accounting Jobs by Area

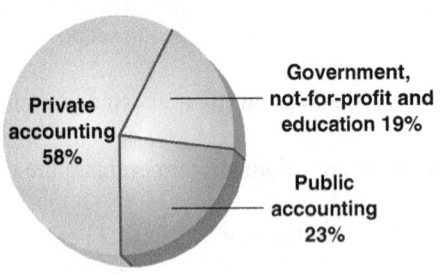

Point: The largest accounting firms are Deloitte, Ernst & Young, KPMG, and PricewaterhouseCoopers.

Margin notes further enhance the textual material.

Point: Census Bureau (2011) reports that for workers 25 and over, higher education yields higher average pay:

Advanced degree	$81,568
Bachelor's degree.	57,326
High school degree	36,876
No high school degree.	26,124

Point: U.S. Bureau of Labor (June 2011) reports higher education is associated with a lower unemployment rate:

Bachelor's degree or more	4.4%
High school degree	10.0%
No high school degree.	14.3%

Exhibit 1.4 shows that the majority of opportunities are in *private accounting,* which are employees working for businesses. *Public accounting* offers the next largest number of opportunities, which involve services such as auditing and tax advice. Still other opportunities exist in government and not-for-profit agencies, including business regulation and investigation of law violations.

Accounting specialists are highly regarded and their professional standing is often denoted by a certificate. Certified public accountants (CPAs) must meet education and experience requirements, pass an examination, and exhibit ethical character. Many accounting specialists hold certificates in addition to or instead of the CPA. Two of the most common are the certificate in management accounting (CMA) and the certified internal auditor (CIA). Employers also look for specialists with designations such as certified bookkeeper (CB), certified payroll professional (CPP), personal financial specialist (PFS), certified fraud examiner (CFE), and certified forensic accountant (CrFA).

Demand for accounting specialists is strong. Exhibit 1.5 reports average annual salaries for several accounting positions. Salary variation depends on location, company size, professional designation, experience, and other factors. For example, salaries for chief financial officers (CFO) range from under $100,000 to more than $1 million per year. Likewise, salaries for bookkeepers range from under $30,000 to more than $80,000.

Field	Title (experience)	2011 Salary	2016 Estimate*
Public Accounting	Partner	$202,000	$223,000
	Manager (6–8 years)	97,500	107,500
	Senior (3–5 years)	75,000	83,000
	Junior (0–2 years)	57,500	63,500
Private Accounting	CFO	242,000	267,000
	Controller/Treasurer	157,500	174,000
	Manager (6–8 years)	91,500	101,000
	Senior (3–5 years)	74,500	82,000
	Junior (0–2 years)	53,000	58,500
Recordkeeping	Full-charge bookkeeper	59,500	65,500
	Accounts manager	52,000	57,500
	Payroll manager	55,500	61,000
	Accounting clerk (0–2 years)	38,500	42,500

EXHIBIT 1.5

Accounting Salaries for Selected Fields

* Estimates assume a 2% compounded annual increase over current levels (rounded to nearest $500).

Point: For updated salary information:
Abbott-Langer.com
www.AICPA.org
Kforce.com

NEED-TO-KNOWs highlight key procedures and concepts in learning accounting.

Identify the following users of accounting information as either an (a) external, or (b) internal user.

NEED-TO-KNOW 1.1

C1   C2

1. ___ Regulator	**4.** ___ Controller	**7.** ___ Production Manager
2. ___ CEO	**5.** ___ Executive Employee	**8.** ___ Nonexecutive
3. ___ Shareholder	**6.** ___ External Auditor	Employee

Do More: QS 1-1, QS 1-2, E 1-1, E 1-2, E 1-3

Solution

1. a **2.** b **3.** a **4.** b **5.** b **6.** a **7.** b **8.** a

QC1

QC icon indicates Quick Check self-review questions available on text Website

FUNDAMENTALS OF ACCOUNTING

Accounting is guided by principles, standards, concepts, and assumptions. This section describes several of these key fundamentals of accounting.

Ethics—A Key Concept

The goal of accounting is to provide useful information for decisions. For information to be useful, it must be trusted. This demands ethics in accounting. **Ethics** are beliefs that distinguish right from wrong. They are accepted standards of good and bad behavior.

Identifying the ethical path is sometimes difficult. The preferred path is a course of action that avoids casting doubt on one's decisions. For example, accounting users are less likely to trust an auditor's report if the auditor's pay depends on the client's success . To avoid such concerns, ethics rules are often set. For example, auditors are banned from direct investment in their client and cannot accept pay that depends on figures in the client's reports. Exhibit 1.6 gives a three-step process for making ethical decisions.

C3 Explain why ethics are crucial to accounting.

Point: Sarbanes-Oxley Act requires each issuer of securities to disclose whether it has adopted a code of ethics for its senior officers and the contents of that code.

1. Identify ethical concerns

Use personal ethics to recognize an ethical concern.

2. Analyze options

Consider all good and bad consequences.

3. Make ethical decision

Choose best option after weighing all consequences.

EXHIBIT 1.6

Guidelines for Ethical Decision Making

Accountants face many ethical choices as they prepare financial reports. These choices can affect the price a buyer pays and the wages paid to workers. They can even affect the success of products and services. Misleading information can lead to a wrongful closing of a division that harms workers, customers, and suppliers. There is an old saying: *Good ethics are good business.*

Some people extend ethics to *social responsibility,* which refers to a concern for the impact of actions on society. An organization's social responsibility can include donations to hospitals, colleges, community programs, and law enforcement. It also can include programs to reduce pollution, increase product safety, improve worker conditions, and support continuing education. These programs are not limited to large companies. For example, many small businesses offer discounts to students and senior citizens. Still others help sponsor events such as the Special Olympics and summer reading programs.

Point: The American Institute of Certified Public Accountants' *Code of Professional Conduct* is available at **www.AICPA.org**.

Decision Insight boxes highlight relevant items from practice.

Decision Insight

Virtuous Returns Virtue is not always its own reward. Compare the S&P 500 with the Domini Social Index (DSI), which covers 400 companies that have especially good records of social responsibility. We see that returns for companies with socially responsible behavior are roughly on par with those of the S&P 500 for the past 10-year period (Domini.com, 2011 Annual Report). Copyright © 2005 by KLD Research & Analytics, Inc. The "Domini 400 Social Index" is a service mark of KLD Research & Analytics. ■

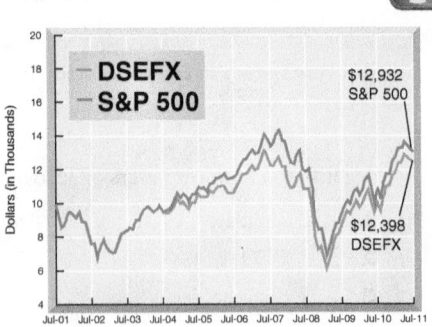

Fraud Triangle

The fraud triangle is a model created by a criminologist that asserts the following *three* factors must exist for a person to commit fraud: opportunity, pressure, and rationalization.

- *Opportunity.* A person must envision a way to commit fraud with a low perceived risk of getting caught. Employers can directly reduce this risk. An example of some control on opportunity is a pre-employment background check.
- *Pressure,* or incentive. A person must have some pressure to commit fraud. Examples are unpaid bills and addictions.
- *Rationalization,* or attitude. A person who rationalizes fails to see the criminal nature of the fraud or justifies the action.

It is important to recognize that all three factors of the fraud triangle must usually exist for fraud to occur. The absence of one or more factors suggests fraud is unlikely. The key to dealing with fraud is to focus on prevention. It is less expensive and more effective to prevent fraud from happening than it is to try to detect the crime. By the time the fraud is discovered, the money is gone and chances are slim that it will be recovered. Additionally, it is costly and time-consuming to investigate a fraud.

Both internal and external users rely on internal controls to reduce the likelihood of fraud. *Internal controls* are procedures set up to protect company property and equipment, ensure reliable accounting reports, promote efficiency, and encourage adherence to company policies. Examples are good records, physical controls (locks, passwords, guards), and independent reviews.

Fraud

They Fought the Law Our economic and social welfare depends on reliable accounting. Some individuals forgot that and are now paying their dues. They include Raj Rajaratnam (in photo), an investor, convicted of trading stocks using inside information; Bernard Madoff of Madoff Investment Securities, convicted of falsifying securities records; Bernard Ebbers of WorldCom, convicted of an $11 billion accounting scandal; Andrew Fastow of Enron, guilty of hiding debt and inflating income; and Ramalinga Raju of Satyam Computers, accused of overstating assets by $1.5 billion.

Generally Accepted Accounting Principles

Financial accounting is governed by concepts and rules known as **generally accepted accounting principles (GAAP).** We must understand these principles to best use accounting data. GAAP aims to make information *relevant, reliable,* and *comparable.* Relevant information affects decisions of users. Reliable information is trusted by users. Comparable information is helpful in contrasting organizations.

In the United States, the **Securities and Exchange Commission (SEC),** a government agency, has the legal authority to set GAAP. The SEC also oversees proper use of GAAP by companies that raise money from the public through issuances of their stock and debt. Those companies that issue their stock on U.S. exchanges include both *U.S. SEC registrants* (companies incorporated in the United States) and *non-U.S. SEC registrants* (companies incorporated under non-U.S. laws). The SEC has largely delegated the task of setting U.S. GAAP to the **Financial Accounting Standards Board (FASB),** which is a private-sector group that sets both broad and specific principles.

International Standards

In today's global economy, there is increased demand by external users for comparability in accounting reports. This demand often arises when companies wish to raise money from lenders and investors in different countries. To that end, the **International Accounting Standards Board (IASB),** an independent group (consisting of individuals from many countries), issues **International Financial Reporting Standards (IFRS)** that identify preferred accounting practices.

If standards are harmonized, one company can potentially use a single set of financial statements in all financial markets. Differences between U.S. GAAP and IFRS are decreasing as the FASB and IASB pursue a *convergence* process aimed to achieve a single set of accounting standards for global use. More than 115 countries now require or permit companies to prepare financial reports following IFRS. Further, non-U.S. SEC registrants can use IFRS in financial reports filed with the SEC (with no reconciliation to U.S. GAAP). This means there are *two* sets of accepted accounting principles in the United States: (1) U.S. GAAP for U.S. SEC registrants and (2) either IFRS or U.S. GAAP for non-U.S. SEC registrants.

The SEC is encouraging the FASB to change U.S. GAAP over a period of several years by endorsing, and thereby incorporating, individual IFRS standards into U.S. GAAP. This endorsement process would still allow the FASB to modify IFRS when necessary. The SEC would:

- Maintain its statutory oversight of the FASB, including authority to prescribe accounting principles and standards for U.S. issuers.
- Contribute to oversight and governance of the IASB through its involvement on the IFRS Foundation Monitoring Board.

The FASB would continue, but its role would be to provide input and support to the IASB in crafting high-quality, global standards. The FASB is to develop a transition plan to effect these changes over the next five years or so. For updates on this roadmap, we can check with the AICPA (IFRS.com), FASB (FASB.org), and IASB (ifrs.org).

 IFRS

Like the FASB, the IASB uses a conceptual framework to aid in revising or drafting new standards. However, unlike the FASB, the IASB's conceptual framework is used as a reference when specific guidance is lacking. The IASB also requires that transactions be accounted for according to their substance (not only their legal form), and that financial statements give a fair presentation, whereas the FASB narrows that scope to fair presentation *in accordance with U.S. GAAP.* ∎

Conceptual Framework and Convergence

The FASB and IASB are attempting to converge and enhance the **conceptual framework** that guides standard setting. The FASB framework consists broadly of the following:

- **Objectives**—to provide information useful to investors, creditors, and others.
- **Qualitative Characteristics**—to require information that is *relevant, reliable,* and *comparable.*

C4 Explain generally accepted accounting principles and define and apply several accounting principles.

Point: State ethics codes require CPAs who audit financial statements to disclose areas where those statements fail to comply with GAAP. If CPAs fail to report noncompliance, they can lose their licenses and be subject to criminal and civil actions and fines.

- **Elements**—to define items that financial statements can contain.
- **Recognition and Measurement**—to set criteria that an item must meet for it to be recognized as an element; and how to measure that element.

For updates on this joint FASB and IASB conceptual framework convergence we can check with FASB.org or ifrs.org Websites. We must remember that U.S. GAAP and IFRS are two similar, but not identical, systems. However, their similarities greatly outweigh any differences. The remainder of this section describes key principles and assumptions of accounting.

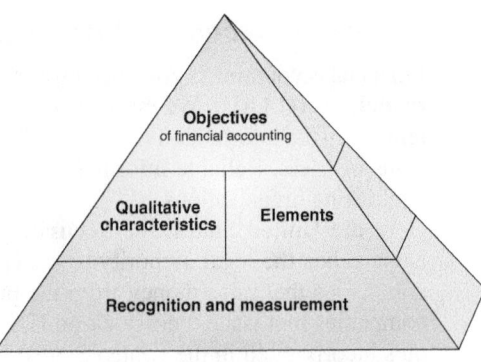

Decision Insight

Principles and Scruples   Auditors, directors, and lawyers are using principles to improve accounting reports. Examples include accounting restatements at **Navistar**, financial restatements at **Nortel**, accounting reviews at **Echostar**, and expense adjustments at **Electronic Data Systems**. Principles-based accounting has led accounting firms to drop clients deemed too risky. Examples include **Grant Thornton**'s resignation as auditor of **Fremont General** due to alleged failures in providing information when promised, and **Ernst and Young**'s resignation as auditor of **Catalina Marketing** due to alleged accounting errors. ■

Principles and Assumptions of Accounting   Accounting principles (and assumptions) are of two types. *General principles* are the basic assumptions, concepts, and guidelines for preparing financial statements. *Specific principles* are detailed rules used in reporting business transactions and events. General principles stem from long-used accounting practices. Specific principles arise more often from the rulings of authoritative groups.

We need to understand both general and specific principles to effectively use accounting information. Several general principles are described in this section that are relied on in later chapters. General principles (in purple font with white shading) and assumptions (in red font with white shading) are portrayed as building blocks of GAAP in Exhibit 1.7. The specific principles are described as we encounter them in the book.

EXHIBIT 1.7

Building Blocks for GAAP

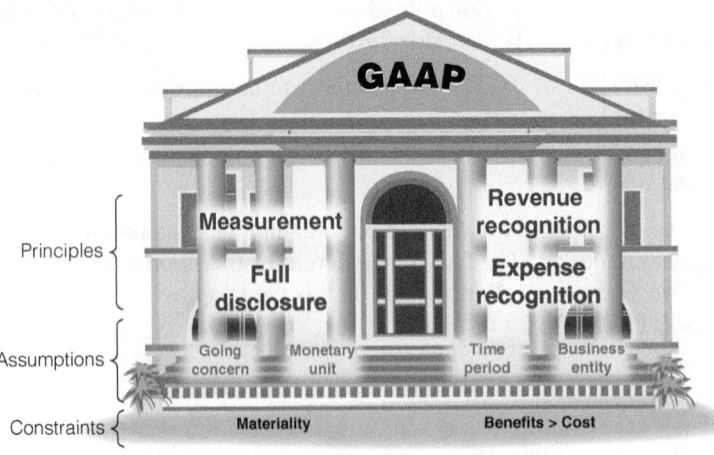

Accounting Principles   General principles consist of at least four basic principles, four assumptions, and two constraints.

- *Measurement* The **measurement principle,** also called the **cost principle,** usually prescribes that accounting information is based on actual cost (with a potential for subsequent adjustments to market). Cost is measured on a cash or equal-to-cash basis. This means if cash

Point: The cost principle is also called the *historical cost principle.*

is given for a service, its cost is measured as the amount of cash paid. If something besides cash is exchanged (such as a car traded for a truck), cost is measured as the cash value of what is given up or received. The cost principle emphasizes reliability and verifiability, and information based on cost is considered objective. *Objectivity* means that information is supported by independent, unbiased evidence; it demands more than a person's opinion. To illustrate, suppose a company pays $5,000 for equipment. The cost principle requires that this purchase be recorded at $5,000. It makes no difference if the owner thinks this equipment is worth $7,000. Later in the book we introduce *fair value* measures.

- *Revenue recognition* Revenue (sales) is the amount received from selling products and services. The **revenue recognition principle** provides guidance on when a company must recognize revenue. To *recognize* means to record it. If revenue is recognized too early, a company would look more profitable than it is. If revenue is recognized too late, a company would look less profitable than it is. Three concepts are important to revenue recognition. (1) *Revenue is recognized when earned.* The earnings process is normally complete when services are performed or a seller transfers ownership of products to the buyer. (2) *Proceeds from selling products and services need not be in cash.* A common noncash proceed received by a seller is a customer's promise to pay at a future date, called *credit sales.* (3) *Revenue is measured by the cash received plus the cash value of any other items received.*

  Example: When a bookstore sells a textbook on credit is its earnings process complete? *Answer:* A bookstore can record sales for these books minus an amount expected for returns.

- *Expense recognition* The **expense recognition principle,** also called the **matching principle,** prescribes that a company record the expenses it incurred to generate the revenue reported. The principles of matching and revenue recognition are key to modern accounting.

- *Full disclosure* The **full disclosure principle** prescribes that a company report the details behind financial statements that would impact users' decisions. Those disclosures are often in footnotes to the statements.

Decision Insight

Revenues for the **Green Bay Packers, New England Patriots, New York Giants,** and other professional football teams include ticket sales, television and cable broadcasts, radio rights, concessions, and advertising. Revenues from ticket sales are earned when the NFL team plays each game. Advance ticket sales are not revenues; instead, they represent a liability until the NFL team plays the game for which the ticket was sold. At that point, the liability is removed and revenues are reported. ▪

Accounting Assumptions   There are four accounting assumptions: the going-concern assumption, the monetary unit assumption, the time period assumption, and the business entity assumption.

- *Going concern* The **going-concern assumption** means that accounting information reflects a presumption that the business will continue operating instead of being closed or sold. This implies, for example, that property is reported at cost instead of, say, liquidation values that assume closure.

- *Monetary unit* The **monetary unit assumption** means that we can express transactions and events in monetary, or money, units. Money is the common denominator in business. Examples of monetary units are the dollar in the United States, Canada, Australia, and Singapore; and the peso in Mexico, the Philippines, and Chile. The monetary unit a company uses in its accounting reports usually depends on the country where it operates, but many companies today are expressing reports in more than one monetary unit.

  Point: For currency conversion: xe.com

- *Time period* The **time period assumption** presumes that the life of a company can be divided into time periods, such as months and years, and that useful reports can be prepared for those periods.

Point: Abuse of the entity assumption was a main culprit in **Enron**'s collapse.

● *Business entity* The **business entity assumption** means that a business is accounted for separately from other business entities, including its owner. The reason for this assumption is that separate information about each business is necessary for good decisions. A business entity can take one of three legal forms: *proprietorship, partnership,* or *corporation.*

1. A **sole proprietorship,** or simply **proprietorship,** is a business owned by one person in which that person and the company are viewed as one entity for tax and liability purposes. No special legal requirements must be met to start a proprietorship. It is a separate entity for accounting purposes, but it is *not* a separate legal entity from its owner. This means, for example, that a court can order an owner to sell personal belongings to pay a proprietorship's debt. This *unlimited liability* of a proprietorship is a disadvantage. However, an advantage is that a proprietorship's income is not subject to a business income tax but is instead reported and taxed on the owner's personal income tax return. Proprietorship attributes are summarized in Exhibit 1.8, including those for partnerships and corporations.

EXHIBIT 1.8

Attributes of Businesses

Attribute Present	Proprietorship	Partnership	Corporation
One owner allowed............	yes	no	yes
Business taxed	no	no	yes
Limited liability...............	no*	no*	yes
Business entity	yes	yes	yes
Legal entity....................	no	no	yes
Unlimited life	no	no	yes

* Proprietorships and partnerships that are set up as LLCs provide limited liability.

Point: Search for "Apple Computer Company Partnership Agreement" to see the original document.

2. A **partnership** is a business owned by two or more people, called *partners,* which are jointly liable for tax and other obligations. Like a proprietorship, no special legal requirements must be met in starting a partnership. The only requirement is an agreement between partners to run a business together. The agreement can be either oral or written and usually indicates how income and losses are to be shared. A partnership, like a proprietorship, is *not* legally separate from its owners. This means that each partner's share of profits is reported and taxed on that partner's tax return. It also means *unlimited liability* for its partners. However, at least three types of partnerships limit liability. A *limited partnership (LP)* includes a general partner(s) with unlimited liability and a limited partner(s) with liability restricted to the amount invested. A *limited liability partnership (LLP)* restricts partners' liabilities to their own acts and the acts of individuals under their control. This protects an innocent partner from the negligence of another partner, yet all partners remain responsible for partnership debts. A *limited liability company (LLC)* offers the limited liability of a corporation and the tax treatment of a partnership (and proprietorship). Most proprietorships and partnerships are now organized as LLCs.

Point: Proprietorships and partnerships are usually managed by their owners. In a corporation, the owners (shareholders) elect a board of directors who appoint managers to run the business.

3. A **corporation,** also called *C corporation,* is a business legally separate from its owner or owners, meaning it is responsible for its own acts and its own debts. Separate legal status means that a corporation can conduct business with the rights, duties, and responsibilities of a person. A corporation acts through its managers, who are its legal agents. Separate legal status also means that its owners, who are called **shareholders** (or **stockholders**), are not personally liable for corporate acts and debts. This limited liability is its main advantage. A main disadvantage is what's called *double taxation*—meaning that (1) the corporation income is taxed and (2) any distribution of income to its owners through dividends is taxed as part of the owners' personal income, usually at the individual's income tax rate. (For "qualified" dividends, the tax rate is 0%, 15%, or 20%, depending on the individual's tax bracket.) An *S corporation,* a corporation with special attributes, does not owe corporate income tax. Owners of S corporations report their share of corporate income with their personal income. Ownership of all corporations is

divided into units called **shares** or **stock.** When a corporation issues only one class of stock, we call it **common stock** (or *capital stock*).

▣ Decision **Ethics**

Decision Ethics *boxes are role-playing exercises that stress ethics in accounting and business.*

Entrepreneur   You and a friend develop a new design for in-line skates that improves speed by 25% to 30%. You plan to form a business to manufacture and market those skates. You and your friend want to minimize taxes, but your prime concern is potential lawsuits from individuals who might be injured on these skates. What form of organization do you set up? ■   [Answer—p. 30]

Accounting Constraints   There are two basic constraints on financial reporting.

- *Materiality* The **materiality constraint** prescribes that only information that would influence the decisions of a reasonable person need be disclosed. This constraint looks at both the importance and relative size of an amount.
- *Benefit exceeds cost* The **cost-benefit constraint** prescribes that only information with benefits of disclosure greater than the costs of providing it need be disclosed.

Conservatism and *industry practices* are also sometimes referred to as accounting constraints.

Sarbanes–Oxley (SOX)

Congress passed the **Sarbanes–Oxley Act,** also called *SOX,* to help curb financial abuses at companies that issue their stock to the public. SOX requires that these public companies apply both accounting oversight and stringent internal controls. The desired results include more transparency, accountability, and truthfulness in reporting transactions.

Point: An audit examines whether financial statements are prepared using GAAP. It does *not* attest to absolute accuracy of the statements.

Compliance with SOX requires documentation and verification of internal controls and increased emphasis on internal control effectiveness. Failure to comply can yield financial penalties, stock market delisting, and criminal prosecution of executives. Management must issue a report stating that internal controls are effective. CEOs and CFOs who knowingly sign off on bogus accounting reports risk millions of dollars in fines and years in prison. **Auditors** also must verify the effectiveness of internal controls.

Point: *Business Week* reports that external audit costs run about $35,000 for start-ups, up from $15,000 pre-SOX.

A listing of some of the more publicized accounting scandals in recent years follows.

Company	Alleged Accounting Abuses
Enron	Inflated income, hid debt, and bribed officials
WorldCom	Understated expenses to inflate income and hid debt
Fannie Mae	Inflated income
Adelphia Communications	Understated expenses to inflate income and hid debt
AOL Time Warner	Inflated revenues and income
Xerox	Inflated income
Bristol-Myers Squibb	Inflated revenues and income
Nortel Networks	Understated expenses to inflate income
Global Crossing	Inflated revenues and income
Tyco	Hid debt, and CEO evaded taxes
Halliburton	Inflated revenues and income
Qwest Communications	Inflated revenues and income

To reduce the risk of accounting fraud, companies set up *governance systems.* A company's governance system includes its owners, managers, employees, board of directors, and other important stakeholders, who work together to reduce the risk of accounting fraud and increase confidence in accounting reports.

The impact of SOX regulations for accounting and business is discussed throughout this book. Ethics and investor confidence are key to company success. Lack of confidence in accounting numbers impacts company value as evidenced by huge stock price declines for Enron, WorldCom, Tyco, and ImClone after accounting misconduct was uncovered.

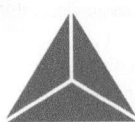

Fraud

Economic Downturn, Fraud Upturn? Executives polled show that 80% believe that the economic downturn has or will have a significant impact on fraud control in their companies (Deloitte 2010). The top three responses to the question "What activity would best counter this increased fraud risk?" are tallied in the graphic to the right.

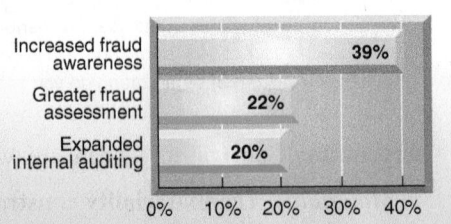

Dodd-Frank

Congress passed the **Dodd-Frank Wall Street Reform and Consumer Protection Act**, or *Dodd-Frank*, to (1) promote accountability and transparency in the financial system, (2) put an end to the notion of "too big to fail," (3) protect the taxpayer by ending bailouts, and (4) protect consumers from abusive financial services. It includes provisions whose impacts are unknown until regulators set detailed rules. However, a few proposals are notable, such as the following:

- *Exemption* Exemption from Section 404(b) of SOX for smaller public entities from the requirement to obtain an external audit on effectiveness of internal control over financial reporting.
- *Independence* Independence for all members of the compensation committee (including additional disclosures); in the event of an accounting restatement, an entity must set policies mandating recovery ("clawback") of excess incentive compensation.
- *Whistleblower* Requires the SEC, when sanctions exceed $1 million, to pay whistleblowers between 10% and 30% of the sanction.

NEED-TO-KNOW 1.2

C3   C4

Identify the following terms/phrases as either an accounting (a) principle, (b) assumption, or (c) constraint.

1. ____ Materiality   **4.** ____ Going concern   **7.** ____ Full disclosure

2. ____ Measurement   **5.** ____ Expense recognition   **8.** ____ Revenue recognition

3. ____ Business entity   **6.** ____ Time period

Solution

1. c   **2.** a   **3.** b   **4.** b   **5.** a   **6.** b   **7.** a   **8.** a

Complete the following table with either a yes or a no regarding the attributes of a partnership and a corporation.

Attribute Present	Partnership	Corporation
Business taxed..........	a. ____	e. ____
Limited liability	b. ____	f. ____
Legal entity	c. ____	g. ____
Unlimited life..........	d. ____	h. ____

Do More: QS 1-3, QS 1-4, QS 1-5, QS 1-6, E 1-4, E 1-5, E 1-7

QC2

Solution

a. no   **b.** no   **c.** no   **d.** no   **e.** yes   **f.** yes   **g.** yes   **h.** yes

TRANSACTION ANALYSIS AND THE ACCOUNTING EQUATION

To understand accounting information, we need to know how an accounting system captures relevant data about transactions, and then classifies, records, and reports data.

Accounting Equation

The accounting system reflects two basic aspects of a company: what it owns and what it owes. *Assets* are resources a company owns or controls. Examples are cash, supplies, equipment, and land, where each carries expected benefits. The claims on a company's assets—what it owes—are separated into owner and nonowner claims. *Liabilities* are what a company owes its non-owners (creditors) in future payments, products, or services. *Equity* (also called owner's equity or capital) refers to the claims of its owner(s). Together, liabilities and equity are the source of funds to acquire assets. The relation of assets, liabilities, and equity is reflected in the following **accounting equation:**

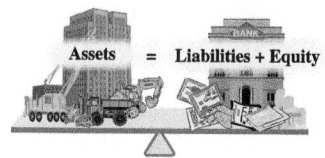

A1 Define and interpret the accounting equation and each of its components.

$$\text{Assets} = \text{Liabilities} + \text{Equity}$$

Liabilities are usually shown before equity in this equation because creditors' claims must be paid before the claims of owners. (The terms in this equation can be rearranged; for example, Assets − Liabilities = Equity.) The accounting equation applies to all transactions and events, to all companies and forms of organization, and to all points in time. For example, Apple's assets equal \$176,064, its liabilities equal \$57,854, and its equity equals \$118,210 (\$ in millions). Let's now look at the accounting equation in more detail.

Assets   Assets are resources a company owns or controls. These resources are expected to yield future benefits. Examples are Web servers for an online services company, musical instruments for a rock band, and land for a vegetable grower. The term *receivable* is used to refer to an asset that promises a future inflow of resources. A company that provides a service or product on credit is said to have an account receivable from that customer.

Point: The phrases "on credit" and "on account" imply that cash payment will occur at a future date.

Liabilities   Liabilities are creditors' claims on assets. These claims reflect company obligations to provide assets, products or services to others. The term *payable* refers to a liability that promises a future outflow of resources. Examples are wages payable to workers, accounts payable to suppliers, notes payable to banks, and taxes payable to the government.

Equity   Equity is the owner's claim on assets, and is equal to assets minus liabilities. This is the reason equity is also called *net assets* or *residual equity*.

Equity is the owner's claim on assets and is *equal to assets minus liabilities;* which is why equity is also called net assets or residual equity. A corporation's equity—also called stockholders' or shareholders' equity—has two parts: contributed capital and retained earnings. **Contributed capital** is the amount stockholders invest in the company. **Retained earnings** is the accumulated revenues *less* the accumulated expenses and dividends since the company began. To better illustrate, these two parts are separated into four categories.

*Key **terms** are printed in bold and defined again in the end-of-book glossary.*

- *Common Stock* **Common stock,** which is part of contributed capital, is the amount that stockholders invest in the company (later chapters identify other parts of contributed capital).
- *Dividends* The distribution of assets to stockholders is called **dividends,** which reduce retained earnings.
- *Revenues* **Revenues** increase retained earnings and are resources from a company's earnings activities. Examples are consulting services provided, sales of products, facilities rented to others, and commissions from services.
- *Expenses* **Expenses** decrease retained earnings and are the cost of assets or services used to earn revenues. Examples are costs of employee time, use of supplies, advertising, utilities, and insurance fees.

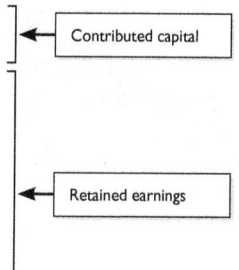

Contributed capital

Retained earnings

This breakdown of equity yields the following **expanded accounting equation:**

$$\underset{\text{Assets = Liabilities + Contributed Capital + Retained Earnings}}{\overset{\text{Equity}}{}}$$

$$\text{= Liabilities + Common Stock − Dividends + Revenues − Expenses}$$

Net income occurs when revenues exceed expenses. Net income increases equity. A **net loss** occurs when expenses exceed revenues, which decreases equity.

■ **Decision** Insight

Web Info   Most organizations maintain Websites that include accounting data— see Apple (Apple.com) as an example. The SEC keeps an online database called EDGAR (www.SEC.gov/edgar.shtml), which has accounting information for thousands of companies that issue stock to the public. The annual report filing for most publicly traded U.S. companies is known as Form 10-K, and the quarterly filing is Form 10-Q. Information services such as Finance.Google.com and Finance.Yahoo.com offer online data and analysis. ■

NEED-TO-KNOW 1.3

A1

Use the *accounting equation* to compute the missing financial statement amounts.

Company	Assets	Liabilities	Equity
BOSE	$150	$ 30	$__(a)__
VOGUE	$__(b)__	$100	$300

Solution

a. $120   **b.** $400

Use the *expanded accounting equation* to compute the missing financial statement amounts.

Company	Assets	Liabilities	Common Stock	Dividends	Revenues	Expenses
Nikon	$200	$ 80	$100	$0	__(a)__	$40
YouTube	$400	$160	$220	__(b)__	$120	$90

Solution

Do More: QS 1-7, QS 1-8, E 1-8, E 1-9

a. $60   **b.** $10

Transaction Analysis

P1   Analyze business transactions using the accounting equation.

Business activities can be described in terms of transactions and events. **External transactions** are exchanges of value between two entities, which yield changes in the accounting equation. An example is the sale of *AppleCare+ Protection Plan* by Apple. **Internal transactions** are exchanges within an entity, which may or may not affect the accounting equation. An example is Twitter's use of its supplies, which are reported as expenses when used. **Events** refer to happenings that affect the accounting equation *and* are reliably measured. They include business events such as changes in the market value of certain assets and liabilities and natural events such as floods and fires that destroy assets and create losses. They do not include, for example, the signing of service or product contracts, which by themselves do not impact the accounting equation.

This section uses the accounting equation to analyze 11 selected transactions and events of FastForward, a start-up consulting (service) business, in its first month of operations. Remember that each transaction and event leaves the equation in balance and that assets *always* equal the sum of liabilities and equity.

Transaction 1: Investment by Owner   On December 1, Chas Taylor forms a consulting business, named FastForward and set up as a corporation, that focuses on assessing the performance of footwear and accessories. Taylor owns and manages the business. The marketing plan for the business is to focus primarily on publishing online reviews and consulting with clubs, athletes, and others who place orders for footwear and accessories with manufacturers. Taylor personally invests $30,000 cash in the new company and deposits the cash in a bank account opened under the name of FastForward. After this transaction, the cash (an asset) and the stockholders' equity each equal $30,000. The source of increase in equity is the owner's investment (stock issuance), which is included in the column titled Common Stock. The effect of this transaction on FastForward is reflected in the accounting equation as follows (we label the equity entries):

Point: There are 3 basic types of company operations: (1) **Services**—providing customer services for profit, (2) **Merchandisers**—buying products and re-selling them for profit, and (3) **Manufacturers**—creating products and selling them for profit.

	Assets	=	Liabilities	+	Equity
	Cash	=			**Common Stock**
(1)	+$30,000	=			+$30,000 owner investment

Transaction 2: Purchase Supplies for Cash   FastForward uses $2,500 of its cash to buy supplies of brand name footwear for performance testing over the next few months. This transaction is an exchange of cash, an asset, for another kind of asset, supplies. It merely changes the form of assets from cash to supplies. The decrease in cash is exactly equal to the increase in supplies. The supplies of footwear are assets because of the expected future benefits from the test results of their performance. This transaction is reflected in the accounting equation as follows:

		Assets			=	Liabilities	+	Equity
	Cash	+	**Supplies**	=				**Common Stock**
Old Bal.	$30,000			=				$30,000
(2)	−2,500	+	$2,500					
New Bal.	$27,500	+	$ 2,500	=				$30,000
		$30,000					$30,000	

Transaction 3: Purchase Equipment for Cash   FastForward spends $26,000 to acquire equipment for testing footwear. Like transaction 2, transaction 3 is an exchange of one asset, cash, for another asset, equipment. The equipment is an asset because of its expected future benefits from testing footwear. This purchase changes the makeup of assets but does not change the asset total. The accounting equation remains in balance.

			Assets			=	Liabilities	+	Equity
	Cash	+	**Supplies**	+	**Equipment**	=			**Common Stock**
Old Bal.	$27,500	+	$2,500			=			$30,000
(3)	−26,000			+	$26,000				
New Bal.	$ 1,500	+	$2,500	+	$ 26,000	=			$30,000
			$30,000					$30,000	

Transaction 4: Purchase Supplies on Credit   Taylor decides more supplies of footwear and accessories are needed. These additional supplies total $7,100, but as we see from the accounting equation in transaction 3, FastForward has only $1,500 in cash. Taylor arranges to purchase them on credit from CalTech Supply Company. Thus, FastForward acquires supplies in exchange for a promise to pay for them later. This purchase increases assets by $7,100 in supplies, and liabilities (called *accounts payable* to CalTech Supply) increase by the same amount. The effects of this purchase follow:

	Assets					=	Liabilities	+	Equity
	Cash	+	**Supplies**	+	**Equipment**	=	**Accounts Payable**	+	**Common Stock**
Old Bal.	$1,500	+	$2,500	+	$26,000	=			$30,000
(4)		+	7,100				+$7,100		
New Bal.	$1,500	+	$9,600	+	$26,000	=	$ 7,100	+	$30,000
			$37,100				$37,100		

Transaction 5: Provide Services for Cash   FastForward earns revenues by selling online ad space to manufacturers and by consulting with clients about test results on footwear and accessories. It earns net income only if its revenues are greater than its expenses incurred in earning them. In one of its first jobs, FastForward provides consulting services to a power-walking club and immediately collects $4,200 cash. The accounting equation reflects this increase in cash of $4,200 and in equity of $4,200. This increase in equity is identified in the far right column under Revenues because the cash received is earned by providing consulting services.

	Assets					=	Liabilities	+	Equity		
	Cash	+	**Supplies**	+	**Equipment**	=	**Accounts Payable**	+	**Common Stock**	+	**Revenues**
Old Bal.	$1,500	+	$9,600	+	$26,000	=	$7,100	+	$30,000		
(5)	+4,200									+	$4,200 Consulting
New Bal.	$5,700	+	$9,600	+	$26,000	=	$7,100	+	$30,000	+	$ 4,200
			$41,300						$41,300		

Transactions 6 and 7: Payment of Expenses in Cash   FastForward pays $1,000 rent to the landlord of the building where its facilities are located. Paying this amount allows FastForward to occupy the space for the month of December. The rental payment is reflected in the following accounting equation as transaction 6. FastForward also pays the biweekly $700 salary of the company's only employee. This is reflected in the accounting equation as transaction 7. Both transactions 6 and 7 are December expenses for FastForward. The costs of both rent and salary are expenses, as opposed to assets, because their benefits are used in December (they have no future benefits after December). These transactions also use up an asset (cash) in carrying out FastForward's operations. The accounting equation shows that both transactions reduce cash and equity. The far right column identifies these decreases as Expenses.

By definition, increases in expenses yield decreases in equity.

	Assets					=	Liabilities	+	Equity				
	Cash	+	**Supplies**	+	**Equipment**	=	**Accounts Payable**	+	**Common Stock**	+	**Revenues**	−	**Expenses**
Old Bal.	$5,700	+	$9,600	+	$26,000	=	$7,100	+	$30,000	+	$4,200		
(6)	−1,000											−	$1,000 Rent
Bal.	4,700	+	9,600	+	26,000	=	7,100	+	30,000	+	4,200	−	1,000
(7)	− 700											−	700 Salaries
New Bal.	$4,000	+	$9,600	+	$26,000	=	$7,100	+	$30,000	+	$4,200	−	$ 1,700
			$39,600						$39,600				

Transaction 8: Provide Services and Facilities for Credit   FastForward provides consulting services of $1,600 and rents its test facilities for $300 to a podiatric services center. The rental involves allowing members to try recommended footwear and accessories at FastForward's testing area. The center is billed for the $1,900 total. This transaction results in a new asset, called *accounts receivable,* from this client. It also yields an increase in equity from the two revenue components reflected in the Revenues column of the accounting equation:

	Assets						=	Liabilities	+			Equity		
	Cash	+	**Accounts Receivable**	+	**Supplies**	+	**Equipment**	=	**Accounts Payable**	+	**Common Stock**	+	**Revenues**	−	**Expenses**
Old Bal.	$4,000	+		+	$9,600	+	$26,000	=	$7,100	+	$30,000	+	$4,200	−	$1,700
(8)		+	$1,900									+	1,600 Consulting		
												+	300 Rental		
New Bal.	$4,000	+	$1,900	+	$9,600	+	$26,000	=	$7,100	+	$30,000	+	$6,100	−	$1,700

$41,500 = $41,500

Transaction 9: Receipt of Cash from Accounts Receivable   The client in transaction 8 (the podiatric center) pays $1,900 to FastForward 10 days after it is billed for consulting services. This transaction 9 does not change the total amount of assets and does not affect liabilities or equity. It converts the receivable (an asset) to cash (another asset). It does not create new revenue. Revenue was recognized when FastForward rendered the services in transaction 8, not when the cash is now collected. This emphasis on the earnings process instead of cash flows is a goal of the revenue recognition principle and yields useful information to users. The new balances follow:

Point: Receipt of cash is not always a revenue.

	Assets						=	Liabilities	+			Equity		
	Cash	+	**Accounts Receivable**	+	**Supplies**	+	**Equipment**	=	**Accounts Payable**	+	**Common Stock**	+	**Revenues**	−	**Expenses**
Old Bal.	$4,000	+	$1,900	+	$9,600	+	$26,000	=	$7,100	+	$30,000	+	$6,100	−	$1,700
(9)	+1,900	−	1,900												
New Bal.	$5,900	+	$ 0	+	$9,600	+	$26,000	=	$7,100	+	$30,000	+	$6,100	−	$1,700

$41,500 = $41,500

Transaction 10: Payment of Accounts Payable   FastForward pays CalTech Supply $900 cash as partial payment for its earlier $7,100 purchase of supplies (transaction 4), leaving $6,200 unpaid. The accounting equation shows that this transaction decreases FastForward's cash by $900 and decreases its liability to CalTech Supply by $900. Equity does not change. This event does not create an expense even though cash flows out of FastForward (instead the expense is recorded when FastForward derives the benefits from these supplies).

	Assets						=	Liabilities	+			Equity		
	Cash	+	**Accounts Receivable**	+	**Supplies**	+	**Equipment**	=	**Accounts Payable**	+	**Common Stock**	+	**Revenues**	−	**Expenses**
Old Bal.	$5,900	+	$ 0	+	$9,600	+	$26,000	=	$7,100	+	$30,000	+	$6,100	−	$1,700
(10)	− 900								− 900						
New Bal.	$5,000	+	$ 0	+	$9,600	+	$26,000	=	$6,200	+	$30,000	+	$6,100	−	$1,700

$40,600 = $40,600

Transaction 11: Payment of Cash Dividend FastForward declares and pays a $200 cash dividend to its owner (the sole shareholder). Dividends (decreases in equity) are not reported as expenses because they are not part of the company's earnings process. Since dividends are not company expenses, they are not used in computing net income.

By definition, increases in dividends yield decreases in equity.

	Assets				=	Liabilities	+			Equity		
	Cash	+ Accounts Receivable	+ Supplies	+ Equipment	=	Accounts Payable	+ Common Stock	− Dividends		+ Revenues	− Expenses
Old Bal.	$5,000	+ $ 0	+ $9,600	+ $26,000	=	$6,200	+ $30,000			+ $6,100	− $1,700
(11)	− 200							− $200 Dividend			
New Bal.	$4,800	+ $ 0	+ $9,600	+ $26,000	=	$6,200	+ $30,000	− $200		+ $6,100	− $1,700

$40,400 $40,400

Point: Knowing how financial statements are prepared improves our analysis of them. We develop the skills for analysis of financial statements throughout the book. Chapter 13 focuses on financial statement analysis.

EXHIBIT 1.9

Summary of Transactions Using the Accounting Equation

Summary of Transactions

We summarize in Exhibit 1.9 the effects of these 11 transactions of FastForward using the accounting equation. First, we see that the accounting equation remains in balance after each transaction. Second, transactions can be analyzed by their effects on components of the accounting equation. For example, in transactions 2, 3, and 9, one asset increased while another asset decreased by equal amounts.

	Assets				=	Liabilities	+		Equity		
	Cash	+ Accounts Receivable	+ Supplies	+ Equipment	=	Accounts Payable	+ Common Stock	− Dividends	+ Revenues	− Expenses
(1)	$30,000				=		$30,000			
(2)	− 2,500		+ $2,500							
Bal.	27,500		+ 2,500		=		30,000			
(3)	−26,000			+ $26,000						
Bal.	1,500		+ 2,500	+ 26,000	=		30,000			
(4)			+ 7,100			+$7,100				
Bal.	1,500		+ 9,600	+ 26,000	=	7,100	+ 30,000			
(5)	+ 4,200								+ $4,200	
Bal.	5,700		+ 9,600	+ 26,000	=	7,100	+ 30,000		+ 4,200	
(6)	− 1,000									− $1,000
Bal.	4,700		+ 9,600	+ 26,000	=	7,100	+ 30,000		+ 4,200	− 1,000
(7)	− 700									− 700
Bal.	4,000		+ 9,600	+ 26,000	=	7,100	+ 30,000		+ 4,200	1,700
(8)		+ $1,900							+ 1,600	
									+ 300	
Bal.	4,000	+ 1,900	+ 9,600	+ 26,000	=	7,100	+ 30,000		+ 6,100	− 1,700
(9)	+ 1,900	− 1,900								
Bal.	5,900	+ 0	+ 9,600	+ 26,000	=	7,100	+ 30,000		+ 6,100	− 1,700
(10)	− 900					− 900				
Bal.	5,000	+ 0	+ 9,600	+ 26,000	=	6,200	+ 30,000		+ 6,100	− 1,700
(11)	− 200							− $200		
Bal.	$ 4,800	+ $ 0	+ $ 9,600	+ $ 26,000	=	$ 6,200	+ $ 30,000	− $ 200	+ $6,100	− $ 1,700

NEED-TO-KNOW 1.4

P1

Assume Tata began operations on January 1 and completed the following transactions during its first month of operations. Arrange the following asset, liability, and equity titles in a table like Exhibit 1.9: Cash; Accounts Receivable; Equipment; Accounts Payable; Common Stock; Dividends; Revenues; and Expenses.

Jan.   1   Ms Jamsetji invested $4,000 cash in the Tata company in exchange for its common stock.
    5   The company purchased $2,000 of equipment on credit.
  14   The company provided $540 of services for a client on credit.
  21   The company paid $250 cash for an employee's salary.

Do More: QS 1-10, QS 1-11, E 1-11, E 1-13

Solution

	Assets			=	Liabilities	+		Equity			
	Cash	+	Accounts Receivable	+ Equipment =	Accounts Payable	+	Common Stock	− Dividends +	Revenues	−	Expenses
Jan. 1	$4,000			=			$4,000				
Jan. 5				+$2,000 =	+$2,000						
Bal.	4,000			2,000 =	2,000		4,000				
Jan. 14			+$540						+$540		
Bal.	4,000		540	2,000 =	2,000		4,000		540		
Jan. 21	−250									−	$250
Bal.	3,750		540	2,000 =	2,000		4,000		540	−	250

QC3

FINANCIAL STATEMENTS

This section introduces us to how financial statements are prepared from the analysis of business transactions. The four financial statements and their purposes are:

P2 Identify and prepare basic financial statements and explain how they interrelate.

1. **Income statement**—describes a company's revenues and expenses along with the resulting net income or loss over a period of time due to earnings activities.
2. **Statement of retained earnings**—explains changes in equity from net income (or loss) and from any dividends over a period of time.
3. **Balance sheet**—describes a company's financial position (types and amounts of assets, liabilities, and equity) at a point in time.
4. **Statement of cash flows**—identifies cash inflows (receipts) and cash outflows (payments) over a period of time.

We prepare these financial statements, in this order, using the 11 selected transactions of Fast-Forward. (These statements are technically called *unadjusted*—we explain this in Chapters 2 and 3.)

Income Statement

FastForward's income statement for December is shown at the top of Exhibit 1.10. Information about revenues and expenses is conveniently taken from the Equity columns of Exhibit 1.9. Revenues are reported first on the income statement. They include consulting revenues of $5,800 from transactions 5 and 8 and rental revenue of $300 from transaction 8. Expenses are reported after revenues. (For convenience in this chapter, we list larger amounts first, but we can sort expenses in different ways.) Rent and salary expenses are from transactions 6 and 7. Expenses reflect the costs to generate the revenues reported. Net income (or loss) is reported at the bottom of the statement and is the amount earned in December. Stockholders' investments and dividends are *not* part of income.

Point: Net income is sometimes called *earnings* or *profit.*

Statement of Retained Earnings

The statement of retained earnings reports information about how retained earnings changes over the reporting period. This statement shows beginning retained earnings, events that increase it (net income), and events that decrease it (dividends and net loss). Ending retained earnings is computed in this statement and is carried over and reported on the balance sheet. FastForward's statement of retained earnings is the second report in Exhibit 1.10. The beginning balance is measured as of the start of business on December 1. It is zero because FastForward did not exist before then. An existing business reports the beginning balance equal to that as of the end of the prior reporting period (such as from November 30). FastForward's statement shows the $4,400 of net income earned during the period. This links the income statement to the

Point: The statement of retained earnings is also called the *statement of changes in retained earnings.* Note: Beg. Retained Earnings + Net Income − Dividends = End. Retained Earnings

EXHIBIT 1.10

Financial Statements and
Their Links

Point: A statement's heading identifies
the company, the statement title, and
the date or time period.

Point: Arrow lines show how the
statements are linked. ① Net income
is used to compute equity. ② Retained
earnings is used to prepare the balance
sheet. ③ Cash from the balance sheet
is used to reconcile the statement of
cash flows.

Point: The income statement, the
statement of retained earnings, and the
statement of cash flows are prepared
for a *period* of time. The balance sheet is
prepared as of a *point* in time.

FASTFORWARD
Income Statement
For Month Ended December 31, 2013

Revenues		
Consulting revenue ($4,200 + $1,600)................	$ 5,800	
Rental revenue	300	
Total revenues		$ 6,100
Expenses		
Rent expense	1,000	
Salaries expense	700	
Total expenses		1,700
Net income		$ 4,400

FASTFORWARD
Statement of Retained Earnings
For Month Ended December 31, 2013

Retained earnings, December 1, 2013.............................	$ 0	①
Plus: Net income..	4,400	
	4,400	
Less: Dividends	200	
Retained earnings, December 31, 2013.............................	$ 4,200	

FASTFORWARD
Balance Sheet
December 31, 2013

Assets		Liabilities		
Cash	$ 4,800	Accounts payable.............	$ 6,200	②
Supplies	9,600	Total liabilities	6,200	
Equipment........	26,000	**Equity**		
		Common stock	30,000	
		Retained earnings	4,200	
		Total equity	34,200	
Total assets	$ 40,400	Total liabilities and equity	$ 40,400	

FASTFORWARD
Statement of Cash Flows
For Month Ended December 31, 2013

Cash flows from operating activities		
Cash received from clients ($4,200 + $1,900).........	$ 6,100	
Cash paid for supplies ($2,500 + $900)..............	(3,400)	
Cash paid for rent	(1,000)	
Cash paid to employee	(700)	
Net cash provided by operating activities		$ 1,000
Cash flows from investing activities		
Purchase of equipment	(26,000)	
Net cash used by investing activities		(26,000)
Cash flows from financing activities		
Investments by stockholder.......................	30,000	
Dividends to stockholder	(200)	
Net cash provided by financing activities		29,800
Net increase in cash		$ 4,800
Cash balance, December 1, 2013		0
Cash balance, December 31, 2013		$ 4,800

③

Point: A single ruled line denotes an
addition or subtraction. Final totals are
double underlined. Negative amounts are
often in parentheses.

statement of retained earnings (see line ①). The statement also reports the $200 cash dividend and FastForward's end-of-period retained earnings balance.

Balance Sheet

FastForward's balance sheet is the third report in Exhibit 1.10. This statement refers to FastForward's financial condition at the close of business on December 31. The left side of the balance sheet lists FastForward's assets: cash, supplies, and equipment. The upper right side of the balance sheet shows that FastForward owes $6,200 to creditors. Any other liabilities (such as a bank loan) would be listed here. The equity balance is $34,200. Line ② shows the link between the ending balance of the statement of retained earnings and the retained earnings balance on the balance sheet. (This presentation of the balance sheet is called the *account form:* assets on the left and liabilities and equity on the right. Another presentation is the *report form:* assets on top, followed by liabilities and then equity at the bottom. Either presentation is acceptable.) As always, we see the accounting equation applies: Assets of $40,400 = Liabilities of $6,200 + Equity of $34,200.

Statement of Cash Flows

FastForward's statement of cash flows is the final report in Exhibit 1.10. The first section reports cash flows from *operating activities*. It shows the $6,100 cash received from clients and the $5,100 cash paid for supplies, rent, and employee salaries. Outflows are in parentheses to denote subtraction. Net cash provided by operating activities for December is $1,000. If cash paid exceeded the $5,100 cash received, we would call it "cash used by operating activities." The second section reports *investing activities*, which involve buying and selling assets such as land and equipment that are held for *long-term use* (typically more than one year). The only investing activity is the $26,000 purchase of equipment. The third section shows cash flows from *financing activities*, which include the *long-term* borrowing and repaying of cash from lenders and the cash investments from, and dividends to, stockholders. FastForward reports $30,000 from the owner's initial investment and the $200 cash dividend. The net cash effect of all financing transactions is a $29,800 cash inflow. The final part of the statement shows FastForward increased its cash balance by $4,800 in December. Since it started with no cash, the ending balance is also $4,800—see line ③. We see that cash flow numbers are different from income statement (*accrual*) numbers, which is common.

Point: Statement of cash flows has three main sections: operating, investing, and financing.

Point: Payment for supplies is an operating activity because supplies are expected to be used up in short-term operations (typically less than one year).

Point: Investing activities refer to long-term asset investments by the company, *not* to owner investments.

Prepare the (a) income statement, (b) statement of retained earnings, and (c) balance sheet, for Apple using the following condensed data from its fiscal year ended September 29, 2012.

NEED-TO-KNOW 1.5

P2

Common stock	$ 16,422	Tax expense	$ 14,030
Accounts payable	21,175	Investments and other assets	138,936
Other liabilities	37,178	Land and equipment	15,452
Cost of sales (expense)	87,846	Selling and other expense	12,899
Cash	10,746	Accounts receivable	10,930
Retained earnings, Sep. 29, 2012	101,289	Net income	41,733
Dividends in fiscal year 2012	3,285	Retained earnings, Sep. 24, 2011	62,841
Revenues	156,508		

Solution

APPLE
Income Statement
For Fiscal Year Ended September 29, 2012

Revenues		$156,508
Expenses		
Cost of sales (expense)	$87,846	
Selling and other expenses	12,899	
Tax expense	14,030	
Total expenses		114,775
Net income		$ 41,733

APPLE Statement of Retained Earnings For Fiscal Year Ended September 29, 2012	
Retained earnings, Sep. 24, 2011	$ 62,841
Plus: Net income...	41,733
	104,574
Less: Dividends	3,285
Retained earnings, Sep. 29, 2012	$101,289

APPLE Balance Sheet September 29, 2012			
Assets		**Liabilities**	
Cash............................	$ 10,746	Accounts payable	$ 21,175
Accounts receivable	10,930	Other liabilities.................	37,178
Land and equipment.................	15,452	Total liabilities	58,353
Investments and other assets	138,936	**Equity**	
		Common stock.................	16,422
		Retained earnings	101,289
		Total equity	117,711
Total assets	$176,064	Total liabilities and equity	$176,064

Do More: QS 1-12, QS 1-13, QS 1-14, E 1-14,
E 1-15, E 1-16, E 1-17

QC4

GLOBAL VIEW

Accounting according to U.S. GAAP is similar, but not identical, to IFRS. Throughout the book we use this last section to identify major similarities and differences between IFRS and U.S. GAAP for the materials in each chapter.

Basic Principles Both U.S. GAAP and IFRS include broad and similar guidance for accounting. However, neither system specifies particular account names nor the detail required. (A typical *chart of accounts* is shown near the end of this book.) IFRS does require certain minimum line items be reported in the balance sheet along with other minimum disclosures that U.S. GAAP does not. On the other hand, U.S. GAAP requires disclosures for the current and prior two years for the income statement, statement of cash flows, and statement of retained earnings (equity), while IFRS requires disclosures for the current and prior year. Still, the basic principles behind these two systems are similar.

Transaction Analysis Both U.S. GAAP and IFRS apply transaction analysis identically as shown in this chapter. Although some variations exist in revenue and expense recognition and other principles, all of the transactions in this chapter are accounted for identically under these two systems. It is often said that U.S. GAAP is more *rules-based* whereas IFRS is more *principles-based*. The main difference on the rules versus principles focus is with the approach in deciding how to account for certain transactions. Under U.S. GAAP, the approach is more focused on strictly following the accounting rules; under IFRS, the approach is more focused on a review of the situation and how accounting can best reflect it. This difference typically impacts advanced topics beyond the introductory course.

Samsung

Financial Statements Both U.S. GAAP and IFRS prepare the same four basic financial statements. To illustrate, a condensed version of Samsung's income statement follows (numbers are in thousands of U.S. dollars). Similar condensed versions can be prepared for the other three statements (see Appendix A).

SAMSUNG Income Statement (in $ thousands) For Year Ended December 31, 2012	
Revenues	187,754,283
Cost of sales	118,244,730
Cost of selling, wages, depreciation, and other expenses, net	41,580,305
Tax expense	5,666,822
Net income (profit)	22,262,426

Status of IFRS Accounting impacts companies across the world, which requires us to take a global view. IFRS is now adopted or accepted in over 115 countries, including over 30 member-states of the EU (see gold and light tan shading in the map below). Teal shading in the map reflects a system other than IFRS. The FASB and IASB continue to work on the convergence of IFRS and U.S. GAAP. Further, the SEC has a "roadmap" for ultimate use of IFRS by U.S. companies. Currently, the roadmap extends out over the next several years.

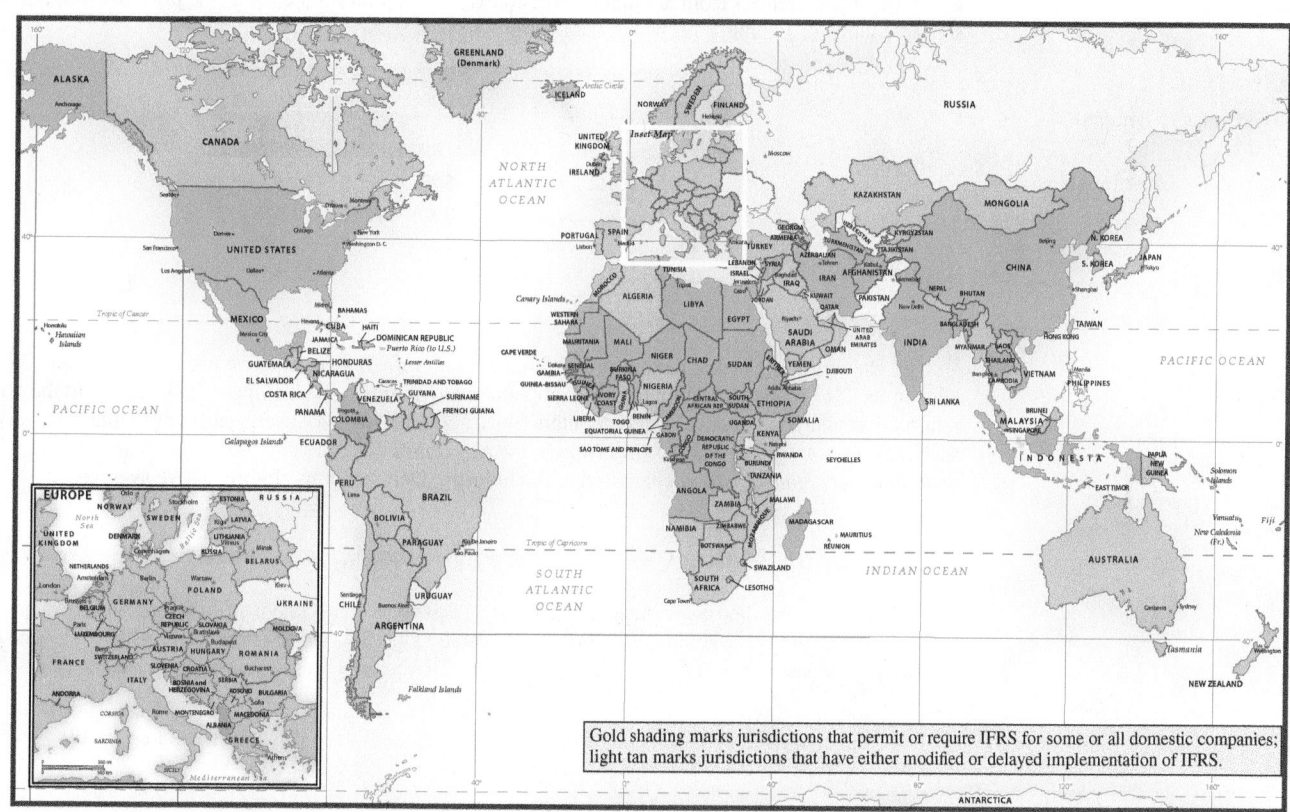

Gold shading marks jurisdictions that permit or require IFRS for some or all domestic companies; light tan marks jurisdictions that have either modified or delayed implementation of IFRS.

Decision Analysis (a section at the end of each chapter) introduces and explains ratios helpful in decision making using real company data. Instructors can skip this section and cover all ratios in Chapter 13.

Return on Assets  **Decision Analysis**

A *Decision Analysis* section at the end of each chapter is devoted to financial statement analysis. We organize financial statement analysis into four areas: (1) liquidity and efficiency, (2) solvency, (3) profitability, and (4) market prospects—Chapter 13 has a ratio listing with definitions and groupings by area. When analyzing ratios, we need benchmarks to identify good, bad, or average levels. Common benchmarks include the company's prior levels and those of its competitors.

A2 Compute and interpret return on assets.

This chapter presents a profitability measure: return on assets. Return on assets is useful in evaluating management, analyzing and forecasting profits, and planning activities. Dell has its marketing department compute return on assets for *every* order. **Return on assets (ROA),** also called *return on investment* (*ROI*), is defined in Exhibit 1.11.

EXHIBIT 1.11

Return on Assets

$$\text{Return on assets} = \frac{\text{Net income}}{\text{Average total assets}}$$

Net income is from the annual income statement, and average total assets is computed by adding the beginning and ending amounts for that same period and dividing by 2. To illustrate, Dell reports net income of $2,372 million for fiscal year 2013. At the beginning of fiscal 2013, its total assets are $44,533 million and at the end of fiscal 2013, they total $47,540 million. Dell's return on assets for fiscal 2013 is:

$$\text{Return on assets} = \frac{\$2,372 \text{ million}}{(\$47,540 \text{ million} + \$44,533 \text{ million})/2} = 5.2\%$$

Is an 5.2% return on assets good or bad for Dell? To help answer this question, we compare (benchmark) Dell's return with its prior performance, the returns of competitors (such as Hewlett-Packard, IBM, and Lenovo), and the returns from alternative investments. Dell's return for each of the prior five years is in the second column of Exhibit 1.12, which ranges from 4.8% to 9.2%.

EXHIBIT 1.12

Dell and Industry Returns

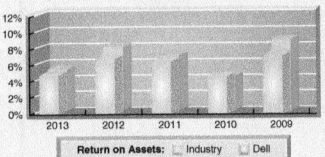

Fiscal Year	Return on Assets	
	Dell	Industry
2013	5.2%	4.9%
2012	8.4	6.9
2011	7.3	6.5
2010	4.8	4.7
2009	9.2	7.2

Dell shows a fairly stable pattern of good returns that reflect its productive use of assets. There is a decline in its 2013 return reflecting a more competitive environment. We compare Dell's return to the normal return for similar manufacturers of computers (third column). Industry averages are available from services such as Dun & Bradstreet's *Industry Norms and Key Ratios* and The Risk Management Association *Annual Statement Studies*. When compared to the industry, Dell performs slightly above average.

*Each **Decision Analysis** section ends with a role-playing scenario to show the usefulness of ratios.*

■ **Decision** Maker ═══════════════════════════════

Business Owner   You own a small winter ski resort that earns a 21% return on its assets. An opportunity to purchase a winter ski equipment manufacturer is offered to you. This manufacturer earns a 19% return on its assets. The industry return for this manufacturer is 14%. Do you purchase this manufacturer? ■ [Answer—p. 31]

*The **Comprehensive Need-to-Know** is a review of key chapter content. The Planning the Solution offers strategies in solving the problem.*

COMPREHENSIVE...

NEED-TO-KNOW

After several months of planning, Jasmine Worthy started a haircutting business called Expressions. The following events occurred during its first month of business.

a. On August 1, Worthy invested $3,000 cash and $15,000 of equipment in Expressions in exchange for its common stock.

b. On August 2, Expressions paid $600 cash for furniture for the shop.

c. On August 3, Expressions paid $500 cash to rent space in a strip mall for August.

d. On August 4, it purchased $1,200 of equipment on credit for the shop (using a long-term note payable).

e. On August 5, Expressions opened for business. Cash received from haircutting services in the first week and a half of business (ended August 15) was $825.

f. On August 15, it provided $100 of haircutting services on account.

g. On August 17, it received a $100 check for services previously rendered on account.

h. On August 17, it paid $125 cash to an assistant for hours worked during the grand opening.

i. Cash received from services provided during the second half of August was $930.

j. On August 31, it paid a $400 installment toward principal on the note payable entered into on August 4.

k. On August 31, it paid $900 cash in dividends to Worthy (sole shareholder).

Required

1. Arrange the following asset, liability, and equity titles in a table similar to the one in Exhibit 1.9: Cash; Accounts Receivable; Furniture; Store Equipment; Note Payable; Common Stock; Dividends; Revenues; and Expenses. Show the effects of each transaction using the accounting equation.

2. Prepare an income statement for August.

3. Prepare a statement of retained earnings for August.

4. Prepare a balance sheet as of August 31.

5. Prepare a statement of cash flows for August.

6. Determine the return on assets ratio for August.

PLANNING THE SOLUTION

- Set up a table like Exhibit 1.9 with the appropriate columns for accounts.
- Analyze each transaction and show its effects as increases or decreases in the appropriate columns. Be sure the accounting equation remains in balance after each transaction.
- Prepare the income statement, and identify revenues and expenses. List those items on the statement, compute the difference, and label the result as *net income* or *net loss*.
- Use information in the Equity columns to prepare the statement of retained earnings.
- Use information in the last row of the transactions table to prepare the balance sheet.
- Prepare the statement of cash flows; include all events listed in the Cash column of the transactions table. Classify each cash flow as operating, investing, or financing.
- Calculate return on assets by dividing net income by average assets.

SOLUTION TO COMPREHENSIVE NEED-TO-KNOW

1.

	Cash	+	Accounts Receivable	+	Furniture	+	Store Equipment	=	Note Payable	+	Common Stock	−	Dividends	+	Revenues	−	Expenses
a.	$3,000						$15,000				$18,000						
b.	− 600			+	$600												
Bal.	2,400	+		+	600	+	15,000	=			18,000						
c.	− 500															−	$500
Bal.	1,900	+		+	600	+	15,000	=			18,000					−	500
d.						+	1,200		+$1,200								
Bal.	1,900	+		+	600	+	16,200	=	1,200	+	18,000					−	500
e.	+ 825													+	$ 825		
Bal.	2,725	+		+	600	+	16,200	=	1,200	+	18,000			+	825	−	500
f.		+	$100											+	100		
Bal.	2,725	+	100	+	600	+	16,200	=	1,200	+	18,000			+	925	−	500
g.	+ 100	−	100														
Bal.	2,825	+	0	+	600	+	16,200	=	1,200	+	18,000			+	925	−	500
h.	− 125															−	125
Bal.	2,700	+	0	+	600	+	16,200	=	1,200	+	18,000			+	925	−	625
i.	+ 930													+	930		
Bal.	3,630	+	0	+	600	+	16,200	=	1,200	+	18,000			+	1,855	−	625
j.	− 400								− 400								
Bal.	3,230	+	0	+	600	+	16,200	=	800	+	18,000			+	1,855	−	625
k.	− 900											−	$900				
Bal.	$ 2,330	+	0	+	$600	+	$ 16,200	=	$ 800	+	$ 18,000	−	$900	+	$1,855	−	$625

2.

EXPRESSIONS
Income Statement
For Month Ended August 31

Revenues		
Haircutting services revenue		$1,855
Expenses		
Rent expense	$500	
Wages expense	125	
Total expenses		625
Net Income		$1,230

3.

EXPRESSIONS
Statement of Retained Earnings
For Month Ended August 31

Retained earnings, August 1*	$ 0
Plus: Net income	1,230
	1,230
Less: Dividend to owner	900
Retained earnings, August 31.........	$ 330

* If Expressions had been an existing business from a prior period, the beginning retained earnings balance would equal the retained earnings balance from the end of the prior period.

4.

EXPRESSIONS
Balance Sheet
August 31

Assets		Liabilities	
Cash	$ 2,330	Note payable	$ 800
Furniture	600	**Equity**	
Store equipment	16,200	Common stock	18,000
		Retained earnings................	330
		Total equity	18,330
Total assets	$19,130	Total liabilities and equity	$19,130

5.

EXPRESSIONS
Statement of Cash Flows
For Month Ended August 31

Cash flows from operating activities		
Cash received from customers	$1,855	
Cash paid for rent	(500)	
Cash paid for wages	(125)	
Net cash provided by operating activities		$1,230
Cash flows from investing activities		
Cash paid for furniture		(600)
Cash flows from financing activities		
Cash investments from stockholders	3,000	
Cash dividends to stockholders	(900)	
Partial repayment of (long-term) note payable	(400)	
Net cash provided by financing activities		1,700
Net increase in cash................................		$2,330
Cash balance, August 1		0
Cash balance, August 31.............................		$2,330

6. Return on assets $= \dfrac{\text{Net income}}{\text{Average assets}} = \dfrac{\$1,230}{(\$18,000^* + \$19,130)/2} = \dfrac{\$1,230}{\$18,565} = \underline{\underline{\mathbf{6.63\%}}}$

* Uses the initial \$18,000 investment as the beginning balance for the *start-up period only*.

Return and Risk Analysis

This appendix explains return and risk analysis and its role in business and accounting.

Net income is often linked to **return.** Return on assets (ROA) is stated in ratio form as income divided by assets invested. For example, banks report return from a savings account in the form of an interest return such as 4%. If we invest in a savings account or in U.S. Treasury bills, we expect a return of around 2% to 7%. We could also invest in a company's stock, or even start our own business. How do we decide among these investment options? The answer depends on our trade-off between return and risk.

A3 Explain the relation between return and risk.

Risk is the uncertainty about the return we will earn. All business investments involve risk, but some investments involve more risk than others. The lower the risk of an investment, the lower is our expected return. The reason that savings accounts pay such a low return is the low risk of not being repaid with interest (the government guarantees most savings accounts from default). If we buy a share of eBay or any other company, we might obtain a large return. However, we have no guarantee of any return; there is even the risk of loss.

The bar graph in Exhibit 1A.1 shows recent returns for 10-year bonds with different risks. *Bonds* are written promises by organizations to repay amounts loaned with interest. U.S. Treasury bonds provide a low expected return, but they also offer low risk since they are backed by the U.S. government. High-risk corporate bonds offer a much larger potential return but with much higher risk.

The trade-off between return and risk is a normal part of business. Higher risk implies higher, but riskier, expected returns. To help us make better decisions, we use accounting information to assess both return and risk.

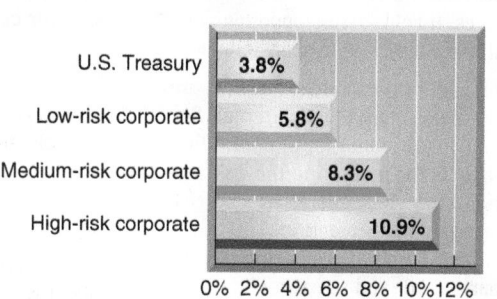

EXHIBIT 1A.1

Average Returns for Bonds with Different Risks

Business Activities and the Accounting Equation

This appendix explains how the accounting equation is derived from business activities.

There are three major types of business activities: financing, investing, and operating. Each of these requires planning. *Planning* involves defining an organization's ideas, goals, and actions. Most public corporations use the *Management Discussion and Analysis* section in their annual reports to communicate plans. However, planning is not cast in stone. This adds *risk* to both setting plans and analyzing them.

C5 Identify and describe the three major activities of organizations.

Financing   *Financing activities* provide the means organizations use to pay for resources such as land, buildings, and equipment to carry out plans. Organizations are careful in acquiring and managing financing activities because they can determine success or failure. The two sources of financing are owner and nonowner. *Owner financing* refers to resources contributed by the owner along with any income the owner leaves in the organization. *Nonowner* (or *creditor*) *financing* refers to resources contributed by creditors (lenders). *Financial management* is the task of planning how to obtain these resources and to set the right mix between owner and creditor financing.

Point: Management must understand accounting data to set financial goals, make financing and investing decisions, and evaluate operating performance.

Investing   *Investing activities* are the acquiring and disposing of resources (assets) that an organization uses to acquire and sell its products or services. Assets are funded by an organization's financing. Organizations differ on the amount and makeup of assets. Some require land and factories to operate. Others need only an office. Determining the amount and type of assets for operations is called *asset management*. Invested

Point: Investing (assets) and financing (liabilities plus equity) totals are *always* equal.

amounts are referred to as *assets*. Financing is made up of creditor and owner financing, which hold claims on assets. Creditors' claims are called *liabilities*, and the owner's claim is called *equity*. This basic equality is called the *accounting equation* and can be written as: Assets = Liabilities + Equity.

EXHIBIT 1B.1

Activities of Organizations

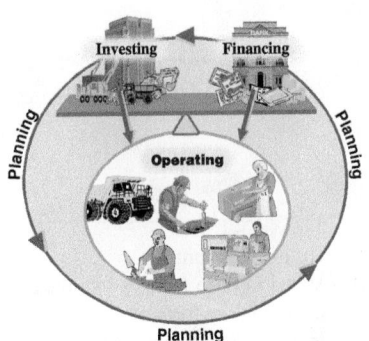

Operating   *Operating activities* involve using resources to research, develop, purchase, produce, distribute, and market products and services. Sales and revenues are the inflow of assets from selling products and services. Costs and expenses are the outflow of assets to support operating activities. *Strategic management* is the process of determining the right mix of operating activities for the type of organization, its plans, and its market.

Exhibit 1B.1 summarizes business activities. Planning is part of each activity and gives them meaning and focus. Investing (assets) and financing (liabilities and equity) are set opposite each other to stress their balance. Operating activities are below investing and financing activities to show that operating activities are the result of investing and financing.

Summary

← A Summary organized by learning objectives concludes each chapter.

C1 **Explain the purpose and importance of accounting.** Accounting is an information and measurement system that aims to identify, record, and communicate relevant, reliable, and comparable information about business activities. It helps assess opportunities, products, investments, and social and community responsibilities.

C2 **Identify users and uses of, and opportunities in, accounting.** Users of accounting are both internal and external. Some users and uses of accounting include (a) managers in controlling, monitoring, and planning; (b) lenders for measuring the risk and return of loans; (c) shareholders for assessing the return and risk of stock; (d) directors for overseeing management; and (e) employees for judging employment opportunities. Opportunities in accounting include financial, managerial, and tax accounting. They also include accounting-related fields such as lending, consulting, managing, and planning.

C3 **Explain why ethics are crucial to accounting.** The goal of accounting is to provide useful information for decision making. For information to be useful, it must be trusted. This demands ethical behavior in accounting.

C4 **Explain generally accepted accounting principles and define and apply several accounting principles.** Generally accepted accounting principles are a common set of standards applied by accountants. Accounting principles aid in producing relevant, reliable, and comparable information. Four principles underlying financial statements were introduced: cost, revenue recognition, matching, and full disclosure. Financial statements also reflect four assumptions: going-concern, monetary unit, time period, and business entity.

C5[B] **Identify and describe the three major activities of organizations.** Organizations carry out three major activities: financing, investing, and operating. Financing is the means used to

pay for resources such as land, buildings, and machines. Investing refers to the buying and selling of resources used in acquiring and selling products and services. Operating activities are those necessary for carrying out the organization's plans.

A1 **Define and interpret the accounting equation and each of its components.** The accounting equation is: Assets = Liabilities + Equity. Assets are resources owned by a company. Liabilities are creditors' claims on assets. Equity is the owner's claim on assets (*the residual*). The expanded accounting equation is: Assets = Liabilities + [Common Stock − Dividends + Revenues − Expenses].

A2 **Compute and interpret return on assets.** Return on assets is computed as net income divided by average assets. For example, if we have an average balance of $100 in a savings account and it earns $5 interest for the year, the return on assets is $5/$100, or 5%.

A3[A] **Explain the relation between return and risk.** *Return* refers to income, and *risk* is the uncertainty about the return we hope to make. All investments involve risk. The lower the risk of an investment, the lower is its expected return. Higher risk implies higher, but riskier, expected return.

P1 **Analyze business transactions using the accounting equation.** A *transaction* is an exchange of economic consideration between two parties. Examples include exchanges of products, services, money, and rights to collect money. Transactions always have at least two effects on one or more components of the accounting equation. This equation is always in balance.

P2 **Identify and prepare basic financial statements and explain how they interrelate.** Four financial statements report on an organization's activities: balance sheet, income statement, statement of retained earnings, and statement of cash flows.

Guidance Answers to Decision Maker and Decision Ethics

Entrepreneur   (p. 13) You should probably form the business as a corporation if potential lawsuits are of prime concern. The corporate form of organization protects your personal property from lawsuits

directed at the business and places only the corporation's resources at risk. A downside of the corporate form is double taxation: The corporation must pay taxes on its income, and you normally must pay taxes on any money distributed to you from the business (even though the corporation already paid taxes on this money). You should also examine the ethical and socially responsible aspects of starting a business in which you anticipate injuries to others. Formation as an LLC or S corp. should also be explored.

Business Owner   (p. 26) The 19% return on assets for the manufacturer exceeds the 14% industry return (and many others). This is a

positive factor for a potential purchase. Also, the purchase of this manufacturer is an opportunity to spread your risk over two businesses as opposed to one. Still, you should hesitate to purchase a business whose return of 19% is lower than your current resort's return of 21%. You are probably better off directing efforts to increase investment in your resort, assuming you can continue to earn a 21% return.

A list of key terms with page references concludes each chapter (a complete glossary is at the end of the book)

Key Terms

Accounting (p. 4)
Accounting equation (p. 15)
Assets (p. 15)
Audit (p. 13)
Auditors (p. 13)
Balance sheet (p. 21)
Bookkeeping (p. 4)
Business entity assumption (p. 12)
Common stock (p. 13, 15)
Conceptual framework (p. 9)
Contributed capital (p. 15)
Corporation (p. 12)
Cost-benefit constraint (p. 13)
Cost principle (p. 10)
Dividends (p. 15)
Dodd-Frank Wall Street Reform and Consumer Protection Act (p. 14)
Equity (p. 15)
Ethics (p. 7)
Events (p. 16)
Expanded accounting equation (p. 16)
Expense recognition principle (p. 11)
Expenses (p. 15)

External transactions (p. 16)
External users (p. 4)
Financial accounting (p. 4)
Financial Accounting Standards Board (FASB) (p. 9)
Full disclosure principle (p. 11)
Generally accepted accounting principles (GAAP) (p. 9)
Going-concern assumption (p. 11)
Income (p. 16)
Income statement (p. 21)
Internal transactions (p. 16)
Internal users (p. 5)
International Accounting Standards Board (IASB) (p. 9)
International Financial Reporting Standards (IFRS) (p. 9)
Liabilities (p. 15)
Managerial accounting (p. 5)
Matching principle (p. 11)
Materiality constraint (p. 13)
Measurement principle (p. 10)
Monetary unit assumption (p. 11)

Net income (p. 16)
Net loss (p. 16)
Partnership (p. 12)
Proprietorship (p. 12)
Recordkeeping (p. 4)
Retained earnings (p. 15)
Return (p. 29)
Return on assets (p. 26)
Revenue recognition principle (p. 11)
Revenues (p. 15)
Risk (p. 29)
Sarbanes–Oxley Act (p. 13)
Securities and Exchange Commission (SEC) (p. 9)
Shareholders (p. 12)
Shares (p. 13)
Sole proprietorship (p. 12)
Statement of cash flows (p. 21)
Statement of retained earnings (p. 21)
Stock (p. 13)
Stockholders (p. 12)
Time period assumption (p. 11)

Multiple Choice Quiz   Answers on p. 51   mhhe.com/wildFA7e

Additional Quiz Questions are available at the book's Website.

1. A building is offered for sale at $500,000 but is currently assessed at $400,000. The purchaser of the building believes the building is worth $475,000, but ultimately purchases the building for $450,000. The purchaser records the building at:
   a. $50,000
   b. $400,000
   c. $450,000
   d. $475,000
   e. $500,000
2. On December 30, 2012, KPMG signs a $150,000 contract to provide accounting services to one of its clients in 2013. KPMG

has a December 31 year-end. Which accounting principle or assumption requires KPMG to record the accounting services revenue from this client in 2013 and not 2012?
   a. Business entity assumption
   b. Revenue recognition principle
   c. Monetary unit assumption
   d. Cost principle
   e. Going-concern assumption
3. If the assets of a company increase by $100,000 during the year and its liabilities increase by $35,000 during the same

year, then the change in equity of the company during the year must have been:
   a. An increase of $135,000.
   b. A decrease of $135,000.
   c. A decrease of $65,000.
   d. An increase of $65,000.
   e. An increase of $100,000.

4. Brunswick borrows $50,000 cash from Third National Bank. How does this transaction affect the accounting equation for Brunswick?
   a. Assets increase by $50,000; liabilities increase by $50,000; no effect on equity.
   b. Assets increase by $50,000; no effect on liabilities; equity increases by $50,000.
   c. Assets increase by $50,000; liabilities decrease by $50,000; no effect on equity.
   d. No effect on assets; liabilities increase by $50,000; equity increases by $50,000.
   e. No effect on assets; liabilities increase by $50,000; equity decreases by $50,000.

5. Geek Squad performs services for a customer and bills the customer for $500. How would Geek Squad record this transaction?
   a. Accounts receivable increase by $500; revenues increase by $500.
   b. Cash increases by $500; revenues increase by $500.
   c. Accounts receivable increase by $500; revenues decrease by $500.
   d. Accounts receivable increase by $500; accounts payable increase by $500.
   e. Accounts payable increase by $500; revenues increase by $500.

A(B) *Superscript letter A (B) denotes assignments based on Appendix 1A (1B).*

🔘 Icon denotes assignments that involve decision making.

Discussion Questions

1. What is the purpose of accounting in society?

2. Technology is increasingly used to process accounting data. Why then must we study and understand accounting?

3. 🔘 Identify four kinds of external users and describe how they use accounting information.

4. 🔘 What are at least three questions business owners and managers might be able to answer by looking at accounting information?

5. Identify three actual businesses that offer services and three actual businesses that offer products.

6. 🔘 Describe the internal role of accounting for organizations.

7. Identify three types of services typically offered by accounting professionals.

8. 🔘 What type of accounting information might be useful to the marketing managers of a business?

9. Why is accounting described as a service activity?

10. What are some accounting-related professions?

11. How do ethics rules affect auditors' choice of clients?

12. What work do tax accounting professionals perform in addition to preparing tax returns?

13. What does the concept of *objectivity* imply for information reported in financial statements? Why?

14. A business reports its own office stationery on the balance sheet at its $400 cost, although it cannot be sold for more than $10 as scrap paper. Which accounting principle and/or assumption justifies this treatment?

15. Why is the revenue recognition principle needed? What does it demand?

16. Describe the three basic forms of business organization and their key attributes.

17. Define (*a*) *assets,* (*b*) *liabilities,* (*c*) *equity,* and (*d*) *net assets.*

18. What events or transactions change equity?

19. Identify the two main categories of accounting principles.

20. What do accountants mean by the term *revenue?*

21. Define *net income* and explain its computation.

22. Identify the four basic financial statements of a business.

23. 🔘 What information is reported in an income statement?

24. Give two examples of expenses a business might incur.

25. What is the purpose of the statement of retained earnings?

26. 🔘 What information is reported in a balance sheet?

27. The statement of cash flows reports on what major activities?

28. 🔘 Define and explain return on assets.

29.ᴬ 🔘 Define return and risk. Discuss the trade-off between them.

30.ᴮ Describe the three major business activities in organizations.

31.ᴮ Explain why investing (assets) and financing (liabilities and equity) totals are always equal.

32. Refer to the financial statements of Apple in Appendix A near the end of the book. To what **APPLE** level of significance are dollar amounts rounded? What time period does its income statement cover?

33. Identify the dollar amounts of Google's 2012 assets, liabilities, and equity as reported in **GOOGLE** its statements in Appendix A near the end of the book.

34. Refer to Samsung's 2012 balance sheet in Appendix A near the end of the book. Con- **Samsung** firm that its total assets equal its total liabilities plus total equity.

35. 🔘 Access the SEC EDGAR database (www.sec. gov) and retrieve Apple's 2012 10-K (filed **APPLE** October 31, 2012). Identify its auditor. What responsibility does its independent auditor claim regarding Apple's financial statements?

Connect *reproduces assignments online, in static or algorithmic mode, which allows instructors to monitor, promote, and assess student learning. It can be used for practice, homework, or exams.*

Quick Study exercises give readers a brief test of key elements.

QUICK STUDY

Choose from the following list of terms/phrases to best complete the following statements.

a. Accounting   **c.** Recording   **e.** Recordkeeping (bookkeeping)   **g.** Language of business

b. Identifying   **d.** Communicating   **f.** Technology   **h.** Governmental

1. _____ reduces the time, effort, and cost of recordkeeping while improving clerical accuracy.

2. _____ business activities requires that we keep a chronological log of transactions and events measured in dollars.

3. _____ is the recording of transactions and events, either manually or electronically.

QS 1-1
Understanding accounting   C1

Identify the following users as either external users (E) or internal users (I).

_____ **a.** Customers   _____ **e.** Managers   _____ **i.** Controllers

_____ **b.** Suppliers   _____ **f.** District attorney   _____ **j.** FBI and IRS

_____ **c.** Brokers   _____ **g.** Shareholders   _____ **k.** Consumer group

_____ **d.** Business press   _____ **h.** Lenders   _____ **l.** Sales clerks

QS 1-2
Identifying accounting users
C2

a. Accounting professionals must sometimes choose between two or more acceptable methods of accounting for business transactions and events. Explain why these situations can involve difficult matters of ethical concern.

b. An important responsibility of many accounting professionals is to design and implement internal control procedures for organizations. Explain the purpose of internal control procedures. Provide two examples of internal controls applied by companies.

QS 1-3
Identifying ethical concerns   C3
This icon highlights assignments that enhance decision-making skills.

Identify the following terms/phrases as either an accounting (a) principle, (b) assumption, or (c) constraint.

_____ **1.** Materiality   _____ **3.** Benefit exceeds cost

_____ **2.** Time period   _____ **4.** Revenue recognition

QS 1-4
Identifying principles, assumptions and constraints   C4

Complete the following table with either a yes or no regarding the attributes of a proprietorship, partnership and corporation.

Attribute Present	Proprietorship	Partnership	Corporation
1. Business taxed.............	_____	_____	_____
2. Business entity.............	_____	_____	_____
3. Legal entity	_____	_____	_____

QS 1-5
Identifying attributes of businesses
C4

Identify which accounting principle or assumption best describes each of the following practices:

a. In December 2012, Chavez Landscaping received a customer's order and cash prepayment to install sod at a new house that would not be ready for installation until March 2013. Chavez should record the revenue from the customer order in March 2013, not in December 2012.

b. If $51,000 cash is paid to buy land, the land is reported on the buyer's balance sheet at $51,000.

c. Jo Keene owns both Sailing Passions and Dockside Supplies. In preparing financial statements for Dockside Supplies, Keene makes sure that the expense transactions of Sailing Passions are kept separate from Dockside's transactions and financial statements.

QS 1-6
Identifying accounting principles
C4

a. Total assets of Charter Company equal $700,000 and its equity is $420,000. What is the amount of its liabilities?

b. Total assets of Martin Marine equal $500,000 and its liabilities and equity amounts are equal to each other. What is the amount of its liabilities? What is the amount of its equity?

QS 1-7
Applying the accounting equation   A1

QS 1-8
Applying the accounting equation
A1

1. Use the accounting equation to compute the missing financial statement amounts (*a*), (*b*), and (*c*).

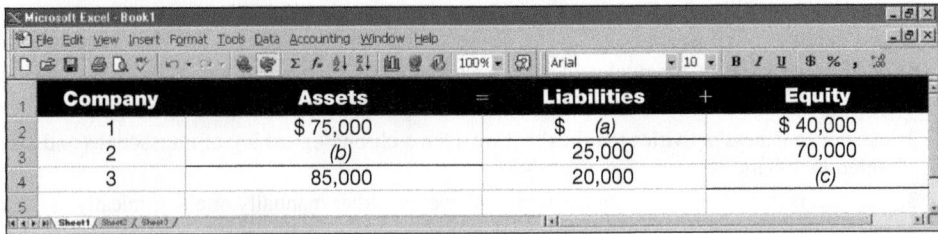

Company	Assets	=	Liabilities	+	Equity
1	$ 75,000		$ (a)		$ 40,000
2	(b)		25,000		70,000
3	85,000		20,000		(c)

2. Use the accounting equation to compute the missing financial statement amounts (*a*) and (*b*).

Company	Assets	Liabilities	Common Stock	Dividends	Revenues	Expenses
1	$ 40,000	$ 16,000	$ 20,000	$ 0	(a)	$ 8,000
2	$ 80,000	$ 32,000	$ 44,000	(b)	$ 24,000	$ 18,000

QS 1-9
Identifying and computing assets, liabilities, and equity   A1

Samsung

Use Samsung's December 31, 2012, financial statements, in Appendix A near the end of the book, to answer the following:

a. Identify the dollar amounts of its 2012 (1) assets, (2) liabilities, and (3) equity.

b. Using amounts from part *a*, verify that Assets = Liabilities + Equity.

QS 1-10
Identifying effects of transactions using accounting equation— Revenues and Expenses

P1

Create a table like the one in Exhibit 1.9, using the following headings for columns: Cash; Accounts Receivable; Accounts Payable; Common Stock; Dividends; Revenues; and Expenses. Then use additions and subtractions to show the effects of each transaction on individual items of the accounting equation (identify each revenue and expense type, such as commissions revenue or rent expense).

a. The company completed consulting work for a client and immediately collected $5,500 cash earned.

b. The company completed commission work for a client and sent a bill for $4,000 to be received within 30 days.

c. The company paid an assistant $1,400 cash as wages for the period.

d. The company collected $2,000 cash as a partial payment for the amount owed by the client in transaction b.

e. The company paid $700 cash for this period's cleaning services.

QS 1-11
Identifying effects of transactions using accounting equation— Assets and Liabilities

P1

Create a table like the one in Exhibit 1.9, using the following headings for columns: Cash; Supplies; Equipment; Land; Accounts Payable; Notes Payable; Common Stock; Dividends; Revenues; and Expenses. Then use additions and subtractions to show the effects of each transaction on individual items of the accounting equation.

a. The owner invested $15,000 cash in the company in exchange for its common stock.

b. The company purchased supplies for $500 cash.

c. The company purchased $10,000 in equipment on credit (record liability as Note Payable).

d. The company purchased $200 of additional supplies on credit.

e. The company purchased land for $9,000 cash.

QS 1-12
Identifying items with financial statements

P2

Indicate in which financial statement each item would most likely appear: income statement (I), balance sheet (B), statement of retained earnings (E), or statement of cash flows (CF).

_____ **a.** Assets

_____ **b.** Cash from operating activities

_____ **c.** Dividends

_____ **d.** Equipment

_____ **e.** Expenses

_____ **f.** Liabilities

_____ **g.** Net decrease (or increase) in cash

_____ **h.** Revenues

_____ **i.** Total liabilities and equity

Classify each of the following items as revenues (R), expenses (EX), or dividends (D).

_____ **1.** Cost of sales (expense)   _____ **3.** Wages expense

_____ **2.** Service revenue   _____ **4.** Dividend

QS 1-13

Identifying revenues, expenses and dividends P2

Classify each of the following items as assets (A), liabilities (L), or equity (EQ).

_____ **1.** Land   _____ **3.** Retained earnings   _____ **5.** Accounts receivable

_____ **2.** Common stock   _____ **4.** Accounts payable

QS 1-14

Identifying assets, liabilities and equity P2

In a recent year's financial statements, Home Depot reported the following results. Compute and interpret Home Depot's return on assets (assume competitors average a 8.0% return on assets).

Sales	$67,997 million
Net income	3,338 million
Average total assets	40,501 million

QS 1-15

Computing and interpreting return on assets

A2

Answer each of the following questions related to international accounting standards.

a. The International Accounting Standards Board (IASB) issues preferred accounting practices that are referred to as what?

b. The FASB and IASB are working on a convergence process for what purpose?

c. The SEC has proposed a roadmap for use of IFRS by U.S. companies. What is the proposed time period (as suggested by the SEC) for the FASB to endorse IFRS (with necessary exceptions) as U.S. GAAP?

QS 1-16

International accounting standards C4

This icon highlights assignments that focus on IFRS-related content.

---

connect

Many accounting professionals work in one of the following three areas:

A. Managerial accounting   **B.** Financial accounting   **C.** Tax accounting

Identify the area of accounting that is most involved in each of the following responsibilities:

_____ **1.** Internal auditing.   _____ **5.** Investigating violations of tax laws.

_____ **2.** External auditing.   _____ **6.** Planning transactions to minimize taxes.

_____ **3.** Cost accounting.   _____ **7.** Preparing external financial statements.

_____ **4.** Budgeting.   _____ **8.** Reviewing reports for SEC compliance.

EXERCISES

Exercise 1-1

Describing accounting responsibilities

C2

Accounting is an information and measurement system that identifies, records, and communicates relevant, reliable, and comparable information about an organization's business activities. Classify the following activities as part of the identifying (I), recording (R), or communicating (C) aspects of accounting.

_____ **1.** Analyzing and interpreting reports.   _____ **6.** Establishing revenues generated from a product.

_____ **2.** Presenting financial information.   _____ **7.** Determining employee tasks behind a service.

_____ **3.** Maintaining a log of service costs.

_____ **4.** Measuring the costs of a product.

_____ **5.** Preparing financial statements.

Exercise 1-2

Classifying activities reflected in the accounting system

C1

Part A. Identify the following users of accounting information as either an internal (I) or an external (E) user.

_____ **1.** Research and development director   _____ **5.** Distribution managers

_____ **2.** Human resources director   _____ **6.** Creditors

_____ **3.** Nonexecutive employee   _____ **7.** Production supervisors

_____ **4.** Shareholders   _____ **8.** Purchasing manager

Part B. Identify the following questions as most likely to be asked by an internal (I) or an external (E) user of accounting information.

_____ **1.** What are reasonable payroll benefits and wages?   _____ **5.** Should we spend further research on our product?

_____ **2.** Should we make a five-year loan to that business?   _____ **6.** Which firm reports the highest sales and income?

_____ **3.** What are the costs of our product's ingredients?   _____ **7.** What are the costs of our service to customers?

_____ **4.** Do income levels justify the current stock price?

Exercise 1-3

Identifying accounting users and uses

C2

Exercise 1-4

Identifying ethical concerns

C3

Assume the following role and describe a situation in which ethical considerations play an important part in guiding your decisions and actions:

   a. You are a student in an introductory accounting course.

   b. You are a manager with responsibility for several employees.

   c. You are an accounting professional preparing tax returns for clients.

   d. You are an accounting professional with audit clients that are competitors in business.

Exercise 1-5

Identifying accounting principles and assumptions

C4

Match each of the numbered descriptions with the principle or assumption it best reflects. Enter the letter for the appropriate principle or assumption in the blank space next to each description.

A. General accounting principle   **E.** Specific accounting principle

B. Cost principle   **F.** Matching (expense recognition) principle

C. Business entity assumption   **G.** Going-concern assumption

D. Revenue recognition principle   **H.** Full disclosure principle

   _____ **1.** Usually created by a pronouncement from an authoritative body.

   _____ **2.** Financial statements reflect the assumption that the business continues operating.

   _____ **3.** Derived from long-used and generally accepted accounting practices.

   _____ **4.** Every business is accounted for separately from its owner or owners.

   _____ **5.** Revenue is recorded only when the earnings process is complete.

   _____ **6.** Information is based on actual costs incurred in transactions.

   _____ **7.** A company records the expenses incurred to generate the revenues reported.

   _____ **8.** A company reports details behind financial statements that would impact users' decisions.

Exercise 1-6

Learning the language of business

C1–C3

Match each of the numbered descriptions with the term or phrase it best reflects. Indicate your answer by writing the letter for the term or phrase in the blank provided.

A. Audit   **C.** Ethics   **E.** SEC   **G.** Net income

B. GAAP   **D.** Tax accounting   **F.** Public accountants   **H.** IASB

   _____ **1.** Principles that determine whether an action is right or wrong.

   _____ **2.** Accounting professionals who provide services to many clients.

   _____ **3.** An accounting area that includes planning future transactions to minimize taxes paid.

   _____ **4.** An examination of an organization's accounting system and records that adds credibility to financial statements.

   _____ **5.** Amount a business earns after paying all expenses and costs associated with its sales and revenues.

Exercise 1-7

Distinguishing business organizations

C4

The following describe several different business organizations. Determine whether the description refers to a sole proprietorship, partnership, or corporation.

   a. Ownership of Zander Company is divided into 1,000 shares of stock.

   b. Wallingford is owned by Trent Malone, who is personally liable for the company's debts.

   c. Micah Douglas and Nathan Logan own Financial Services, a financial services provider. Neither Douglas nor Logan has personal responsibility for the debts of Financial Services.

   d. Riley and Kay own Speedy Packages, a courier service. Both are personally liable for the debts of the business.

   e. IBC Services does not have separate legal existence apart from the one person who owns it.

   f. Physio Products does not pay income taxes and has one owner.

   g. AJ pays its own income taxes and has two owners.

Exercise 1-8

Using the accounting equation

A1 P1

Check (c) Beg. equity, $60,000

Answer the following questions. (*Hint:* Use the accounting equation.)

   a. Office Store has assets equal to $123,000 and liabilities equal to $47,000 at year-end. What is the total equity for Office Store at year-end?

   b. At the beginning of the year, Addison Company's assets are $300,000 and its equity is $100,000. During the year, assets increase $80,000 and liabilities increase $50,000. What is the equity at the end of the year?

   c. At the beginning of the year, Quaker Company's liabilities equal $70,000. During the year, assets increase by $60,000, and at year-end assets equal $190,000. Liabilities decrease $5,000 during the year. What are the beginning and ending amounts of equity?

Determine the missing amount from each of the separate situations *a*, *b*, and *c* below.

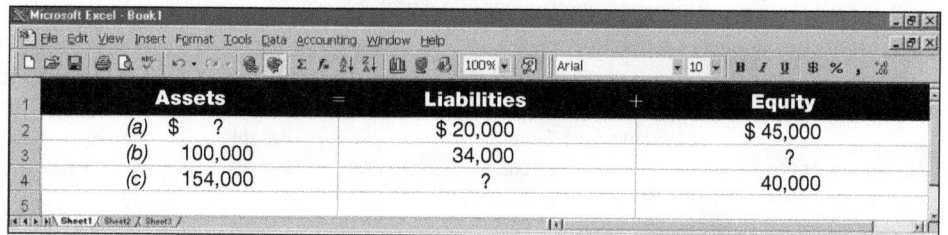

	Assets	=	Liabilities	+	Equity
(a)	$?		$ 20,000		$ 45,000
(b)	100,000		34,000		?
(c)	154,000		?		40,000

Exercise 1-9
Using the accounting equation
A1

Provide an example of a transaction that creates the described effects for the separate cases *a* through *g*.

a. Decreases an asset and decreases equity.

b. Increases an asset and increases a liability.

c. Decreases a liability and increases a liability.

d. Decreases an asset and decreases a liability.

e. Increases an asset and decreases an asset.

f. Increases a liability and decreases equity.

g. Increases an asset and increases equity.

Exercise 1-10
Identifying effects of transactions on the accounting equation
P1

Lena Holden began a professional practice on June 1 and plans to prepare financial statements at the end of each month. During June, Holden (the owner) completed these transactions:

a. Owner invested $60,000 cash in the company along with equipment that had a $15,000 market value in exchange for its common stock.

b. The company paid $1,500 cash for rent of office space for the month.

c. The company purchased $10,000 of additional equipment on credit (payment due within 30 days).

d. The company completed work for a client and immediately collected the $2,500 cash earned.

e. The company completed work for a client and sent a bill for $8,000 to be received within 30 days.

f. The company purchased additional equipment for $6,000 cash.

g. The company paid an assistant $3,000 cash as wages for the month.

h. The company collected $5,000 cash as a partial payment for the amount owed by the client in transaction *e*.

i. The company paid $10,000 cash to settle the liability created in transaction *c*.

j. The company paid $1,000 cash in dividends to the owner (sole shareholder).

Exercise 1-11
Identifying effects of transactions using the accounting equation
P1

Required

Create a table like the one in Exhibit 1.9, using the following headings for columns: Cash; Accounts Receivable; Equipment; Accounts Payable; Common Stock; Dividends; Revenues; and Expenses. Then use additions and subtractions to show the effects of the transactions on individual items of the accounting equation. Show new balances after each transaction.

Check   Net income, $6,000

Zen began a new consulting firm on January 5. The accounting equation showed the following balances after each of the company's first five transactions. Analyze the accounting equation for each transaction and describe each of the five transactions with their amounts.

Exercise 1-12
Analysis using the accounting equation
P1

	Assets								=	Liabilities	+	Equity		
Trans-action	Cash	+	Accounts Receiv-able	+	Office Sup-plies	+	Office Furni-ture	=	Payable	+	Common Stock	+	Revenues
a.	$40,000	+	$ 0	+	$ 0	+	$ 0	=	$ 0	+	$40,000	+	$ 0
b.	38,000	+	0	+	3,000	+	0	=	1,000	+	40,000	+	0
c.	30,000	+	0	+	3,000	+	8,000	=	1,000	+	40,000	+	0
d.	30,000	+	6,000	+	3,000	+	8,000	=	1,000	+	40,000	+	6,000
e.	31,000	+	6,000	+	3,000	+	8,000	=	1,000	+	40,000	+	7,000

Exercise 1-13

Identifying effects of transactions on accounting equation

P1

The following table shows the effects of five transactions (*a* through *e*) on the assets, liabilities, and equity of Trista's Boutique. Write short descriptions of the probable nature of each transaction.

	Assets				=	Liabilities	+	Equity		
	Cash	+ Accounts Receivable	+ Office Supplies	+ Land	=	Accounts Payable	+ Common Stock	+ Revenues		
	$ 21,000	+ $ 0	+ $3,000	+ $19,000	=	$ 0	+ $43,000	+ $ 0		
a.	− 4,000			+ 4,000						
b.			+ 1,000			+1,000				
c.		+ 1,900						+ 1,900		
d.	− 1,000					−1,000				
e.	+ 1,900	− 1,900								
	$ 17,900	+ $ 0	+ $4,000	+ $23,000	=	$ 0	+ $43,000	+ $1,900		

Exercise 1-14

Preparing an income statement

P2

Check Net income, $2,110

On October 1, Keisha King organized Real Answers, a new consulting firm; on October 3, the owner contributed $84,000 cash. On October 31, the company's records show the following items and amounts. Use this information to prepare an October income statement for the business.

Cash	$11,360		Cash dividends	$ 2,000
Accounts receivable	14,000		Consulting fees earned.	14,000
Office supplies	3,250		Rent expense	3,550
Land	46,000		Salaries expense	7,000
Office equipment	18,000		Telephone expense.	760
Accounts payable.	8,500		Miscellaneous expenses	580
Common stock	84,000			

Exercise 1-15

Preparing a statement of retained earnings   P2

Use the information in Exercise 1-14 to prepare an October statement of retained earnings for Real Answers.

Exercise 1-16

Preparing a balance sheet   P2

Use the information in Exercise 1-14 (if completed, you can also use your solution to Exercise 1-15) to prepare an October 31 balance sheet for Real Answers.

Exercise 1-17

Preparing a statement of cash flows

P2

Check Net increase in cash, $11,360

Use the information in Exercise 1-14 to prepare an October 31 statement of cash flows for Real Answers. Also assume the following:

a. The owner's initial investment consists of $38,000 cash and $46,000 in land in exchange for its common stock.

b. The company's $18,000 equipment purchase is paid in cash.

c. The accounts payable balance of $8,500 consists of the $3,250 office supplies purchase and $5,250 in employee salaries yet to be paid.

d. The company's rent, telephone, and miscellaneous expenses are paid in cash.

e. No cash has been collected on the $14,000 consulting fees earned.

Exercise 1-18

Analysis of return on assets

A2

Swiss Group reports net income of $40,000 for 2013. At the beginning of 2013, Swiss Group had $200,000 in assets. By the end of 2013, assets had grown to $300,000. What is Swiss Group's 2013 return on assets? How would you assess its performance if competitors average a 10% return on assets?

Exercise 1-19

Identifying sections of the statement of cash flows

P2

Indicate the section where each of the following would appear on the statement of cash flows.

O. Cash flows from operating activity

I. Cash flows from investing activity

F. Cash flows from financing activity

_____ **1.** Cash paid for advertising   _____ **5.** Cash paid for rent

_____ **2.** Cash paid for wages   _____ **6.** Cash paid on an account payable

_____ **3.** Cash paid for dividends   _____ **7.** Cash received from stock issued

_____ **4.** Cash purchase of equipment   _____ **8.** Cash received from clients

Match each transaction or event to one of the following activities of an organization: financing activities (F), investing activities (I), or operating activities (O).

a. _____ An owner contributes resources to the business in exchange for its common stock.

b. _____ An organization sells some of its land.

c. _____ An organization purchases equipment.

d. _____ An organization advertises a new product.

e. _____ The organization borrows money from a bank.

Exercise 1-20[B]
Identifying business activities
C5

Nintendo Company reports the following income statement accounts for the year ended March 31, 2011. (Japanese yen in millions.)

Exercise 1-21
Preparing an income statement for a global company
P2

Net sales	¥1,014,345
Cost of sales	626,379
Selling, general and administrative expenses	216,889
Other expenses	93,456

Use this information to prepare Nintendo's income statement for the year ended March 31, 2011.

*Problem Set B located at the end of **Problem Set A** is provided for each problem to reinforce the learning process.*

≡ connect

The following financial statement information is from five separate companies:

PROBLEM SET A

Problem 1-1A
Computing missing information using accounting knowledge
A1   P1

	Company A	Company B	Company C	Company D	Company E
December 31, 2012					
Assets.........................	$55,000	$34,000	$24,000	$60,000	$119,000
Liabilities	24,500	21,500	9,000	40,000	?
December 31, 2013					
Assets.........................	58,000	40,000	?	85,000	113,000
Liabilities	?	26,500	29,000	24,000	70,000
During year 2013					
Stock issuances	6,000	1,400	9,750	?	6,500
Net income (loss)	8,500	?	8,000	14,000	20,000
Cash dividends	3,500	2,000	5,875	0	11,000

Required

1. Answer the following questions about Company A:

   a. What is the amount of equity on December 31, 2012?

   b. What is the amount of equity on December 31, 2013?

   c. What is the amount of liabilities on December 31, 2013?

2. Answer the following questions about Company B:

   a. What is the amount of equity on December 31, 2012?

   b. What is the amount of equity on December 31, 2013?

   c. What is net income for year 2013?

3. Calculate the amount of assets for Company C on December 31, 2013.

4. Calculate the amount of stock issuances for Company D during year 2013.

5. Calculate the amount of liabilities for Company E on December 31, 2012.

Check   (1*b*) $41,500

(2*c*) $1,600

(3) $55,875

Problem 1-2A
Identifying effects of
transactions on financial
statements

A1 P1

Identify how each of the following separate transactions affects financial statements. For the balance sheet, identify how each transaction affects total assets, total liabilities, and total equity. For the income statement, identify how each transaction affects net income. For the statement of cash flows, identify how each transaction affects cash flows from operating activities, cash flows from financing activities, and cash flows from investing activities. For increases, place a "+" in the column or columns. For decreases, place a "−" in the column or columns. If both an increase and a decrease occur, place a "+/−" in the column or columns. The first transaction is completed as an example.

	Transaction	Balance Sheet Total Assets	Total Liab.	Total Equity	Income Statement Net Income	Statement of Cash Flows Operating Activities	Financing Activities	Investing Activities
1	Owner invests cash for its stock	+		+			+	
2	Receives cash for services provided							
3	Pays cash for employee wages							
4	Incurs legal costs on credit							
5	Borrows cash by signing long-term note payable							
6	Pays cash dividend							
7	Buys land by signing note payable							
8	Provides services on credit							
9	Buys office equipment for cash							
10	Collects cash on receivable from (8)							

Problem 1-3A
Preparing an income
statement

P2

The following is selected financial information for Elko Energy Company for the year ended December 31, 2013: revenues, $55,000; expenses, $40,000; net income, $15,000.

Required

Prepare the 2013 calendar-year income statement for Elko Energy Company.

Problem 1-4A
Preparing a balance sheet

P2

The following is selected financial information for Amity Company as of December 31, 2013: liabilities, $44,000; equity, $46,000; assets, $90,000.

Required

Prepare the balance sheet for Amity Company as of December 31, 2013.

Problem 1-5A
Preparing a statement of
cash flows

P2

Following is selected financial information of ABM Company for the year ended December 31, 2013.

Cash used by investing activities	$(2,000)
Net increase in cash	1,200
Cash used by financing activities	(2,800)
Cash from operating activities	6,000
Cash, December 31, 2012	2,300

Check   Cash balance, Dec. 31,
2013, $3,500

Required

Prepare the 2013 statement of cash flows for ABM Company.

Problem 1-6A
Preparing a statement of
retained earnings

P2

Following is selected financial information for Kasio Co. for the year ended December 31, 2013.

Retained Earnings, Dec. 31, 2013	$14,000	Cash dividends	$1,000
Net income	8,000	Retained Earnings, Dec. 31, 2012	7,000

Required

Prepare the 2013 statement of retained earnings for Kasio.

Holden Graham started The Graham Co., a new business that began operations on May 1. The Graham Co. completed the following transactions during its first month of operations.

May 1   H. Graham invested $40,000 cash in the company in exchange for its common stock.
     1   The company rented a furnished office and paid $2,200 cash for May's rent.
     3   The company purchased $1,890 of office equipment on credit.
     5   The company paid $750 cash for this month's cleaning services.
     8   The company provided consulting services for a client and immediately collected $5,400 cash.
    12   The company provided $2,500 of consulting services for a client on credit.
    15   The company paid $750 cash for an assistant's salary for the first half of this month.
    20   The company received $2,500 cash payment for the services provided on May 12.
    22   The company provided $3,200 of consulting services on credit.
    25   The company received $3,200 cash payment for the services provided on May 22.
    26   The company paid $1,890 cash for the office equipment purchased on May 3.
    27   The company purchased $80 of advertising in this month's (May) local paper on credit; cash payment is due June 1.
    28   The company paid $750 cash for an assistant's salary for the second half of this month.
    30   The company paid $300 cash for this month's telephone bill.
    30   The company paid $280 cash for this month's utilities.
    31   The company paid $1,400 cash in dividends to the owner (sole shareholder).

Required

1. Arrange the following asset, liability, and equity titles in a table like Exhibit 1.9: Cash; Accounts Receivable; Office Equipment; Accounts Payable; Common Stock; Dividends; Revenues; and Expenses.
2. Show effects of the transactions on the accounts of the accounting equation by recording increases and decreases in the appropriate columns. Do not determine new account balances after each transaction. Determine the final total for each account and verify that the equation is in balance.
3. Prepare an income statement for May, a statement of retained earnings for May, a May 31 balance sheet, and a statement of cash flows for May.

Helga Ander started a new business and completed these transactions during December.

Dec. 1   Helga Ander transferred $65,000 cash from a personal savings account to a checking account in the name of Ander Electric in exchange for its common stock.
      2   The company rented office space and paid $1,000 cash for the December rent.
      3   The company purchased $13,000 of electrical equipment by paying $4,800 cash and agreeing to pay the $8,200 balance in 30 days.
      5   The company purchased office supplies by paying $800 cash.
      6   The company completed electrical work and immediately collected $1,200 cash for these services.
      8   The company purchased $2,530 of office equipment on credit.
     15   The company completed electrical work on credit in the amount of $5,000.
     18   The company purchased $350 of office supplies on credit.
     20   The company paid $2,530 cash for the office equipment purchased on December 8.
     24   The company billed a client $900 for electrical work completed; the balance is due in 30 days.
     28   The company received $5,000 cash for the work completed on December 15.
     29   The company paid the assistant's salary of $1,400 cash for this month.
     30   The company paid $540 cash for this month's utility bill.
     31   The company paid $950 cash in dividends to the owner (sole shareholder).

Required

1. Arrange the following asset, liability, and equity titles in a table like Exhibit 1.9: Cash; Accounts Receivable; Office Supplies; Office Equipment; Electrical Equipment; Accounts Payable; Common Stock; Dividends; Revenues; and Expenses.
2. Use additions and subtractions to show the effects of each transaction on the accounts in the accounting equation. Show new balances after each transaction.
3. Use the increases and decreases in the columns of the table from part 2 to prepare an income statement, a statement of retained earnings, and a statement of cash flows—each of these for the current month. Also prepare a balance sheet as of the end of the month.

Analysis Component

4. Assume that the owner investment transaction on December 1 was $49,000 cash instead of $65,000 and that Ander Electric obtained another $16,000 in cash by borrowing it from a bank. Explain the effect of this change on total assets, total liabilities, and total equity.

Problem 1-9A
Analyzing effects of transactions
C4 P1 P2 A1

Isabel Lopez started Biz Consulting, a new business, and completed the following transactions during its first year of operations.

a. I. Lopez invests $70,000 cash and office equipment valued at $10,000 in the company in exchange for its common stock.

b. The company purchased a $150,000 building to use as an office. Biz paid $20,000 in cash and signed a note payable promising to pay the $130,000 balance over the next ten years.

c. The company purchased office equipment for $15,000 cash.

d. The company purchased $1,200 of office supplies and $1,700 of office equipment on credit.

e. The company paid a local newspaper $500 cash for printing an announcement of the office's opening.

f. The company completed a financial plan for a client and billed that client $2,800 for the service.

g. The company designed a financial plan for another client and immediately collected an $4,000 cash fee.

h. The company paid $3,275 cash in dividends to the owner (sole shareholder).

i. The company received $1,800 cash as partial payment from the client described in transaction *f*.

j. The company made a partial payment of $700 cash on the equipment purchased in transaction *d*.

k. The company paid $1,800 cash for the office secretary's wages for this period.

Required

1. Create a table like the one in Exhibit 1.9, using the following headings for the columns: Cash; Accounts Receivable; Office Supplies; Office Equipment; Building; Accounts Payable; Notes Payable; Common Stock; Dividends; Revenues; and Expenses.

Check (2) Ending balances: Cash, $34,525; Expenses, $2,300; Notes Payable, $130,000

(3) Net income, $4,500

2. Use additions and subtractions within the table created in part *1* to show the dollar effects of each transaction on individual items of the accounting equation. Show new balances after each transaction.

3. Once you have completed the table, determine the company's net income.

Problem 1-10A
Computing and interpreting return on assets
A2

Coca-Cola and PepsiCo both produce and market beverages that are direct competitors. Key financial figures (in $ millions) for these businesses over the past year follow.

Key Figures ($ millions)	Coca-Cola	PepsiCo
Sales	$46,542	$66,504
Net income	8,634	6,462
Average assets	76,448	70,518

Required

Check (1*a*) 11.3%; (1*b*) 9.2%

1. Compute return on assets for (*a*) Coca-Cola and (*b*) PepsiCo.

2. Which company is more successful in its total amount of sales to consumers?

3. Which company is more successful in returning net income from its assets invested?

Analysis Component

4. Write a one-paragraph memorandum explaining which company you would invest your money in and why. (Limit your explanation to the information provided.)

Problem 1-11A
Determining expenses, liabilities, equity, and return on assets
A1 A2

Kyzera manufactures, markets, and sells cellular telephones. The average total assets for Kyzera is $250,000. In its most recent year, Kyzera reported net income of $65,000 on revenues of $475,000.

Required

1. What is Kyzera's return on assets?

2. Does return on assets seem satisfactory for Kyzera given that its competitors average a 12% return on assets?

Check (3) $410,000

(4) $250,000

3. What are total expenses for Kyzera in its most recent year?

4. What is the average total amount of liabilities plus equity for Kyzera?

All business decisions involve aspects of risk and return.

Required

Identify both the risk and the return in each of the following activities:
1. Investing $2,000 in a 5% savings account.
2. Placing a $2,500 bet on your favorite sports team.
3. Investing $10,000 in Yahoo! stock.
4. Taking out a $15,000 college loan toward earning an accounting degree.

Problem 1-12A^A

Identifying risk and return

A3

A start-up company often engages in the following transactions in its first year of operations. Classify those transactions in one of the three major categories of an organization's business activities.

F. Financing   **I.** Investing   **O.** Operating

_____ **1.** Owner investing land in business.   _____ **5.** Purchasing equipment.
_____ **2.** Purchasing a building.   _____ **6.** Selling and distributing products.
_____ **3.** Purchasing land.   _____ **7.** Paying for advertising.
_____ **4.** Borrowing cash from a bank.   _____ **8.** Paying employee wages.

Problem 1-13A^B

Describing organizational activities

C5

An organization undertakes various activities in pursuit of business success. Identify an organization's three major business activities, and describe each activity.

Problem 1-14A^B

Describing organizational activities   C5

The following financial statement information is from five separate companies.

PROBLEM SET B

Problem 1-1B
Computing missing information using accounting knowledge

A1 P1

	Company V	Company W	Company X	Company Y	Company Z
December 31, 2012					
Assets.........................	$54,000	$80,000	$141,500	$92,500	$144,000
Liabilities	25,000	60,000	68,500	51,500	?
December 31, 2013					
Assets.........................	59,000	100,000	186,500	?	170,000
Liabilities	36,000	?	65,800	42,000	42,000
During year 2013					
Stock issuances	5,000	20,000	?	48,100	60,000
Net income or (loss)...........	?	40,000	18,500	24,000	32,000
Cash dividends	5,500	2,000	0	20,000	8,000

Required

1. Answer the following questions about Company V:
   a. What is the amount of equity on December 31, 2012?
   b. What is the amount of equity on December 31, 2013?
   c. What is the net income or loss for the year 2013?
2. Answer the following questions about Company W:
   a. What is the amount of equity on December 31, 2012?
   b. What is the amount of equity on December 31, 2013?
   c. What is the amount of liabilities on December 31, 2013?
3. Calculate the amount of stock issuances for Company X during 2013.
4. Calculate the amount of assets for Company Y on December 31, 2013.
5. Calculate the amount of liabilities for Company Z on December 31, 2012.

Check   (1*b*) $23,000

(2*c*) $22,000

(4) $135,100

Problem 1-2B
Identifying effects of transactions on financial statements   A1   P1

Identify how each of the following separate transactions affects financial statements. For the balance sheet, identify how each transaction affects total assets, total liabilities, and total equity. For the income statement, identify how each transaction affects net income. For the statement of cash flows, identify how each transaction affects cash flows from operating activities, cash flows from financing activities, and cash flows from investing activities. For increases, place a "+" in the column or columns. For decreases, place a "−" in the column or columns. If both an increase and a decrease occur, place "+/−" in the column or columns. The first transaction is completed as an example.

	Transaction	Balance Sheet			Income Statement	Statement of Cash Flows		
		Total Assets	Total Liab.	Total Equity	Net Income	Operating Activities	Financing Activities	Investing Activities
1	Owner invests cash for its stock	+		+			+	
2	Buys building by signing note payable							
3	Pays cash for salaries incurred							
4	Provides services for cash							
5	Pays cash for rent incurred							
6	Incurs utilities costs on credit							
7	Buys store equipment for cash							
8	Pays cash dividend							
9	Provides services on credit							
10	Collects cash on receivable from (9)							

Problem 1-3B
Preparing an income statement
P2

Selected financial information for Offshore Co. for the year ended December 31, 2013, follows.

Revenues	$68,000	Expenses	$40,000	Net income	$28,000

Required
Prepare the 2013 income statement for Offshore Company.

Problem 1-4B
Preparing a balance sheet
P2

The following is selected financial information for TLC Company as of December 31, 2013.

Liabilities	$64,000	Equity	$50,000	Assets	$114,000

Required
Prepare the balance sheet for TLC Company as of December 31, 2013.

Problem 1-5B
Preparing a statement of cash flows
P2

Selected financial information of HalfLife Company for the year ended December 31, 2013, follows.

Cash from investing activities	$1,600
Net increase in cash	400
Cash from financing activities	1,800
Cash used by operating activities	(3,000)
Cash, December 31, 2012	1,300

Required
Prepare the 2013 statement of cash flows for HalfLife Company.

Problem 1-6B
Preparing a statement of retained earnings
P2

Following is selected financial information of ATV Company for the year ended December 31, 2013.

Retained Earnings, Dec. 31, 2013	$47,000	Cash dividends	$ 7,000
Net income	5,000	Retained Earnings, Dec. 31, 2012	49,000

Required
Prepare the 2013 statement of retained earnings for ATV Company.

Holly Nikolas launched a new business, Holly's Maintenance Co., that began operations on June 1. The following transactions were completed by the company during that first month.

Problem 1-7B

Analyzing transactions and preparing financial statements

C4 P1 P2

June 1   H. Nikolas invested $130,000 cash in the company in exchange for its common stock.
2   The company rented a furnished office and paid $6,000 cash for June's rent.
4   The company purchased $2,400 of equipment on credit.
6   The company paid $1,150 cash for this month's advertising of the opening of the business.
8   The company completed maintenance services for a customer and immediately collected $850 cash.
14   The company completed $7,500 of maintenance services for City Center on credit.
16   The company paid $800 cash for an assistant's salary for the first half of the month.
20   The company received $7,500 cash payment for services completed for City Center on June 14.
21   The company completed $7,900 of maintenance services for Paula's Beauty Shop on credit.
24   The company completed $675 of maintenance services for Build-It Coop on credit.
25   The company received $7,900 cash payment from Paula's Beauty Shop for the work completed on June 21.
26   The company made payment of $2,400 cash for equipment purchased on June 4.
28   The company paid $800 cash for an assistant's salary for the second half of this month.
29   The company paid $4,000 cash in dividends to the owner (sole shareholder).
30   The company paid $150 cash for this month's telephone bill.
30   The company paid $890 cash for this month's utilities.

Required

1. Arrange the following asset, liability, and equity titles in a table like Exhibit 1.9: Cash; Accounts Receivable; Equipment; Accounts Payable; Common Stock; Dividends; Revenues; and Expenses.
2. Show the effects of the transactions on the accounts of the accounting equation by recording increases and decreases in the appropriate columns. Do not determine new account balances after each transaction. Determine the final total for each account and verify that the equation is in balance.
3. Prepare a June income statement, a June statement of retained earnings, a June 30 balance sheet, and a June statement of cash flows.

Check   (2) Ending balances: Cash, $130,060; Expenses, $9,790

(3) Net income, $7,135; Total assets, $133,135

Truro Excavating Co., owned by Raul Truro, began operations in July and completed these transactions during that first month of operations.

Problem 1-8B

Analyzing transactions and preparing financial statements

C4 P1 P2

July 1   R. Truro invested $80,000 cash in the company in exchange for its common stock.
2   The company rented office space and paid $700 cash for the July rent.
3   The company purchased excavating equipment for $5,000 by paying $1,000 cash and agreeing to pay the $4,000 balance in 30 days.
6   The company purchased office supplies for $600 cash.
8   The company completed work for a customer and immediately collected $7,600 cash for the work.
10   The company purchased $2,300 of office equipment on credit.
15   The company completed work for a customer on credit in the amount of $8,200.
17   The company purchased $3,100 of office supplies on credit.
23   The company paid $2,300 cash for the office equipment purchased on July 10.
25   The company billed a customer $5,000 for work completed; the balance is due in 30 days.
28   The company received $8,200 cash for the work completed on July 15.
30   The company paid an assistant's salary of $1,560 cash for this month.
31   The company paid $295 cash for this month's utility bill.
31   The company paid $1,800 cash in dividends to the owner (sole shareholder).

Required

1. Arrange the following asset, liability, and equity titles in a table like Exhibit 1.9: Cash; Accounts Receivable; Office Supplies; Office Equipment; Excavating Equipment; Accounts Payable; Common Stock; Dividends; Revenues; and Expenses.
2. Use additions and subtractions to show the effects of each transaction on the accounts in the accounting equation. Show new balances after each transaction.
3. Use the increases and decreases in the columns of the table from part 2 to prepare an income statement, a statement of retained earnings, and a statement of cash flows—each of these for the current month. Also prepare a balance sheet as of the end of the month.

Check   (2) Ending balances: Cash, $87,545; Accounts Payable, $7,100

(3) Net income, $18,245; Total assets, $103,545

Analysis Component

4. Assume that the $5,000 purchase of excavating equipment on July 3 was financed from an owner investment of another $5,000 cash in the business in exchange for more common stock (instead of the purchase conditions described in the transaction). Explain the effect of this change on total assets, total liabilities, and total equity.

Problem 1-9B
Analyzing effects of transactions
C4 P1 P2 A1

Nico Mitchell started a new business, Nico's Solutions, and completed the following transactions during its first year of operations.

a. N. Mitchell invests $90,000 cash and office equipment valued at $20,000 in the company in exchange for its common stock.

b. The company purchased a $150,000 building to use as an office. It paid $40,000 in cash and signed a note payable promising to pay the $110,000 balance over the next ten years.

c. The company purchased office equipment for $25,000 cash.

d. The company purchased $1,200 of office supplies and $1,700 of office equipment on credit.

e. The company paid a local newspaper $750 cash for printing an announcement of the office's opening.

f. The company completed a financial plan for a client and billed that client $2,800 for the service.

g. The company designed a financial plan for another client and immediately collected a $4,000 cash fee.

h. The company paid $11,500 cash in dividends to the owner (sole shareholder).

i. The company received $1,800 cash from the client described in transaction *f*.

j. The company made a payment of $700 cash on the equipment purchased in transaction *d*.

k. The company paid $2,500 cash for the office secretary's wages.

Required

Check (2) Ending balances: Cash, $15,350; Expenses, $3,250; Notes Payable, $110,000

(3) Net income, $3,550

1. Create a table like the one in Exhibit 1.9, using the following headings for the columns: Cash; Accounts Receivable; Office Supplies; Office Equipment; Building; Accounts Payable; Notes Payable; Common Stock; Dividends; Revenues; and Expenses.

2. Use additions and subtractions within the table created in part *1* to show the dollar effects of each transaction on individual items of the accounting equation. Show new balances after each transaction.

3. Once you have completed the table, determine the company's net income.

Problem 1-10B
Computing and interpreting
return on assets
A2

AT&T and Verizon produce and market telecommunications products and are competitors. Key financial figures (in $ millions) for these businesses over the past year follow.

Key Figures ($ millions)	AT&T	Verizon
Sales	$126,723	$110,875
Net income	4,184	10,198
Average assets	269,868	225,233

Required

Check (1a) 1.6%; (1b) 4.5%

1. Compute return on assets for (*a*) AT&T and (*b*) Verizon.

2. Which company is more successful in the total amount of sales to consumers?

3. Which company is more successful in returning net income from its assets invested?

Analysis Component

4. Write a one-paragraph memorandum explaining which company you would invest your money in and why. (Limit your explanation to the information provided.)

Problem 1-11B
Determining expenses, liabilities,
equity, and return on assets

A1 A2

Carbondale Company manufactures, markets, and sells snowmobile and snowmobile equipment and accessories. The average total assets for Carbondale is $3,000,000. In its most recent year, Carbondale reported net income of $201,000 on revenues of $1,400,000.

Required

1. What is Carbondale Company's return on assets?
2. Does return on assets seem satisfactory for Carbondale given that its competitors average a 9.5% return on assets?
3. What are the total expenses for Carbondale Company in its most recent year?
4. What is the average total amount of liabilities plus equity for Carbondale Company?

Check (3) $1,199,000

(4) $3,000,000

All business decisions involve aspects of risk and return.

Problem 1-12B[A]

Identifying risk and return

A3

Required

Identify both the risk and the return in each of the following activities:

1. Stashing $500 cash under your mattress.
2. Placing a $250 bet on a horse running in the Kentucky Derby.
3. Investing $20,000 in Nike stock.
4. Investing $35,000 in U.S. Savings Bonds.

A start-up company often engages in the following activities during its first year of operations. Classify each of the following activities into one of the three major activities of an organization.

Problem 1-13B[B]

Describing organizational activities

C5

F. Financing   **I.** Investing   **O.** Operating

_____ **1.** Providing client services.
_____ **2.** Obtaining a bank loan.
_____ **3.** Purchasing machinery.
_____ **4.** Research for its products.

_____ **5.** Supervising workers.
_____ **6.** Owner investing money in business.
_____ **7.** Renting office space.
_____ **8.** Paying utilities expenses.

Identify in outline format the three major business activities of an organization. For each of these activities, identify at least two specific transactions or events normally undertaken by the business's owners or its managers.

Problem 1-14B[B]

Describing organizational activities C5

This serial problem starts in this chapter and continues throughout most chapters of the book. It is most readily solved if you use the Working Papers that accompany this book (but working papers are not required).

SP 1 On October 1, 2013, Adria Lopez launched a computer services company, **Success Systems,** that is organized as a corporation and provides consulting services, computer system installations, and custom program development. Lopez adopts the calendar year for reporting purposes and expects to prepare the company's first set of financial statements on December 31, 2013.

SERIAL PROBLEM
Success Systems

C4   P1

Required

Create a table like the one in Exhibit 1.9 using the following headings for columns: Cash; Accounts Receivable; Computer Supplies; Computer System; Office Equipment; Accounts Payable; Common Stock; Dividends; Revenues; and Expenses. Then use additions and subtractions within the table created to show the dollar effects for each of the following October transactions for Success Systems on the individual items of the accounting equation. Show new balances after each transaction.

Oct. 1   A. Lopez invested $55,000 cash, a $20,000 computer system, and $8,000 of office equipment in the company in exchange for its common stock.
3   The company purchased $1,420 of computer supplies on credit from Harris Office Products.
6   The company billed Easy Leasing $4,800 for services performed in installing a new Web server.
8   The company paid $1,420 cash for the computer supplies purchased from Harris Office Products on October 3.
10   The company hired Lyn Addie as a part-time assistant for $125 per day, as needed.
12   The company billed Easy Leasing another $1,400 for services performed.

15   The company received $4,800 cash from Easy Leasing as partial payment toward its account.
17   The company paid $805 cash to repair computer equipment damaged when moving it.
20   The company paid $1,940 cash for advertisements published in the local newspaper.
22   The company received $1,400 cash from Easy Leasing toward its account.
28   The company billed IFM Company $5,208 for services performed.
31   The company paid $875 cash for Lyn Addie's wages for seven days of work this month.
31   The company paid $3,600 cash in dividends to the owner (sole shareholder).

Check   Ending balances: Cash, $52,560; Revenues, $11,408; Expenses, $3,620

 **GENERAL LEDGER PROBLEM**

Available in Connect Only

connect
|ACCOUNTING

Accounting professionals apply many technology tools to aid them in their everyday tasks and decision making. The **General Ledger** tool in *Connect* automates several of the procedural steps in the accounting cycle so that the accounting professional can focus on the impacts of each transaction on the full set of financial statements. Chapter 2 is the first chapter to exploit this tool in helping students see the advantages of technology and, in particular, the power of the General Ledger tool in accounting practice, including financial analysis and "what if" scenarios.

Beyond the Numbers (BTN) is a special problem section aimed to refine communication, conceptual, analysis, and research skills. It includes many activities helpful in developing an active learning environment.

Beyond the Numbers

REPORTING IN ACTION

A1 A2 A3

APPLE

Check   (2) 28.5%

BTN 1-1   Key financial figures for Apple's fiscal year ended September 29, 2012, follow.

Key Figure	In Millions
Liabilities + Equity.........	$176,064
Net income	41,733
Revenues	156,508

Required

1. What is the total amount of assets invested in Apple?
2. What is Apple's return on assets for 2012? Its assets at September 24, 2011, equal $116,371 (in millions).
3. How much are total expenses for Apple for the year ended September 29, 2012?
4. Does Apple's return on assets for 2012 seem satisfactory if competitors average a 10% return?

Fast Forward

5. Access Apple's financial statements (Form 10-K) for years ending after September 29, 2012, from its Website (Apple.com) or from the SEC Website (www.SEC.gov) and compute its return on assets for those years. Compare the September 29, 2012, year-end return on assets to any subsequent years' returns you are able to compute, and interpret the results.

COMPARATIVE ANALYSIS

A1 A2 A3

APPLE

GOOGLE

BTN 1-2   Key comparative figures ($ millions) for both Apple and Google follow.

Key Figure	Apple	Google
Liabilities + Equity.........	$176,064	$93,798
Net income	41,733	10,737
Revenues and sales	156,508	50,175

Required

1. What is the total amount of assets invested in (*a*) Apple and (*b*) Google?
2. What is the return on assets for (*a*) Apple and (*b*) Google? Apple's beginning-year assets equal $116,371 (in millions) and Google's beginning-year assets equal $72,574 (in millions).
3. How much are expenses for (*a*) Apple and (*b*) Google?
4. Is return on assets satisfactory for (*a*) Apple and (*b*) Google? (Assume competitors average a 10% return.)
5. What can you conclude about Apple and Google from these computations?

Check (2b) 12.9%

BTN 1-3 Craig Thorne works in a public accounting firm and hopes to eventually be a partner. The management of Allnet Company invites Thorne to prepare a bid to audit Allnet's financial statements. In discussing the audit fee, Allnet's management suggests a fee range in which the amount depends on the reported profit of Allnet. The higher its profit, the higher will be the audit fee paid to Thorne's firm.

ETHICS CHALLENGE

C3 C4

Required

1. Identify the parties potentially affected by this audit and the fee plan proposed.
2. What are the ethical factors in this situation? Explain.
3. Would you recommend that Thorne accept this audit fee arrangement? Why or why not?
4. Describe some ethical considerations guiding your recommendation.

BTN 1-4 Refer to this chapter's opening feature about Apple. Assume that the owners, sometime during their first five years of business, desire to expand their computer product services to meet people's demands regarding technical support. They eventually decide to meet with their banker to discuss a loan to allow Apple to expand.

COMMUNICATING IN PRACTICE

A1 C2

Required

1. Prepare a half-page report outlining the information you would request from the owners if you were the loan officer.
2. Indicate whether the information you request and your loan decision are affected by the form of business organization for Apple.

BTN 1-5 Visit the EDGAR database at (www.sec.gov). Access the Form 10-K report of Rocky Mountain Chocolate Factory (ticker RMCF) filed on May 24, 2011, covering its 2011 fiscal year.

TAKING IT TO THE NET

A2

Required

1. Item 6 of the 10-K report provides comparative financial highlights of RMCF for the years 2007–2011. How would you describe the revenue trend for RMCF over this five-year period?
2. Has RMCF been profitable (see net income) over this five-year period? Support your answer.

BTN 1-6 Teamwork is important in today's business world. Successful teams schedule convenient meetings, maintain regular communications, and cooperate with and support their members. This assignment aims to establish support/learning teams, initiate discussions, and set meeting times.

TEAMWORK IN ACTION

C1

Required

1. Form teams and open a team discussion to determine a regular time and place for your team to meet between each scheduled class meeting. Notify your instructor via a memorandum or e-mail message as to when and where your team will hold regularly scheduled meetings.
2. Develop a list of telephone numbers and/or e-mail addresses of your teammates.

ENTREPRENEURIAL DECISION

A1 P1

BTN 1-7 Refer to this chapter's opening feature about Apple. Assume that the owners decide to open a new Website and an innovative mobile App devoted to micro-blogging for accountants and those learning accounting. This new company will be called AccountApp.

Required

1. AccountApp obtains a $500,000 loan and the two owners contribute $250,000 in total from their own savings in exchange for common stock in the new company.
   a. What is the new company's total amount of liabilities plus equity?
   b. What is the new company's total amount of assets?

2. If the new company earns $80,250 in net income in the first year of operation, compute its return on assets (assume average assets equal $750,000). Assess its performance if competitors average a 10% return.

Check (2) 10.7%

HITTING THE ROAD

C2

BTN 1-8 You are to interview a local business owner. (This can be a friend or relative.) Opening lines of communication with members of the business community can provide personal benefits of business networking. If you do not know the owner, you should call ahead to introduce yourself and explain your position as a student and your assignment requirements. You should request a 30-minute appointment for a face-to-face or phone interview to discuss the form of organization and operations of the business. Be prepared to make a good impression.

Required

1. Identify and describe the main operating activities and the form of organization for this business.
2. Determine and explain why the owner(s) chose this particular form of organization.
3. Identify any special advantages and/or disadvantages the owner(s) experiences in operating with this form of business organization.

GLOBAL DECISION

A1 A2 A3

Samsung
APPLE
GOOGLE

BTN 1-9 Samsung (Samsung.com) is a leading global manufacturer, and it competes with both Apple and Google. Key financial figures for Samsung follow.

Key Figure*	Korean Won in Millions
Average assets..........	₩168,435,917
Net income.............	₩ 23,845,285
Revenue...............	₩201,103,613
Return on assets........	14.2%

* Figures prepared in accordance with International Financial Reporting Standards as adopted by the Republic of Korea.

Required

1. Identify any concerns you have in comparing Samsung's income and revenue figures to those of Apple and Google (in BTN 1-2) for purposes of making business decisions.
2. Identify any concerns you have in comparing Samsung's return on assets ratio to those of Apple and Google (computed for BTN 1-2) for purposes of making business decisions.

ANSWERS TO MULTIPLE CHOICE QUIZ

1. c; $450,000 is the actual cost incurred.

2. b; revenue is recorded when earned.

3. d;

Assets	=	Liabilities	+	Equity
+$100,000	=	+35,000	+	?

Change in equity = $100,000 − $35,000 = $65,000

4. a

5. a

2

Accounting System and Financial Statements

ANALYZING AND RECORDING PROCESS	ANALYZING AND PROCESSING TRANSACTIONS	TRIAL BALANCE AND THE FINANCIAL STATEMENTS
Using financial statements C1 Source documents C2 The account and its analysis Types of accounts Unclassified vs Classified	C3 General ledger C4 Double-entry accounting P1 Journalizing and posting A1 Processing transactions—An illustration	P2 Trial balance preparation & use P3 Financial statement preparation Reading an annual report A2 Analysis of financing sources

Learning Objectives

C1 Explain the steps in processing transactions and the role of source documents. (p. 56)

C2 Describe an account and its use in recording transactions. (p. 57)

C3 Describe a ledger and a chart of accounts. (p. 60)

C4 Define *debits* and *credits* and explain double-entry accounting. (p. 61)

P1 Record transactions in a journal and post entries to a ledger. (p. 63)

A1 Analyze the impact of transactions on accounts and financial statements. (p. 65)

P2 Prepare and explain the use of a trial balance. (p. 71)

P3 Prepare financial statements from business transactions. (p. 73)

A2 Compute the debt ratio and describe its use in analyzing financial condition. (p. 77)

King of Connections

"Starting a company is like throwing yourself off the cliff and assembling an airplane on the way down"
—REID HOFFMAN

MOUNTAIN VIEW, CA—Reid Hoffman grew up like so many other kids, enjoying video games and getting Bs and Cs in middle school. He also loved to study the link between computing and human intelligence, and eventually earned a college degree in philosophy. Reid was aiming for a teaching career when he had an epiphany. "When you write a scholarly work, it tends to be understood by very few," explains Reid. "When you build a service, you can touch millions, to hundreds of millions." With that philosophy, Reid set out on an entrepreneurial path, eventually leading to the launch of **LinkedIn (LinkedIn.com),** which is the world's largest professional network on the Internet.

To pursue his business ambitions, Reid studied entrepreneurial activities and learned the value of accounting information. He established recordkeeping processes, transaction analysis, control procedures, and financial statement reporting. I had to get a handle on my financial situation, explains Reid, as I wanted to be successful. To this day, Reid has had many entrepreneurial successes and has a reliable accounting system to help him make good business decisions. "Be persistent," advises Reid, "and hang on to your vision."

LinkedIn Corporation
(NYSE:LNKD)

4,000 employees
240 mil. members
2002 founded

Revenue Sources
Premium Subscriptions 20%
Marketing Solutions 27%
Talent Solutions 54%

Reid recalls how his team had to account and control for numerous expenses and then obtain sufficient revenues to survive. At the same time, he maintained his vision and strategy. "The thing I'm working on with LinkedIn is to create something massive," insists Reid. "If you don't shoot for something really big, you're never going to get there." He explains that LinkedIn generates revenue from three sources: Talent Solutions, Marketing Solutions, and Premium Subscriptions. Reid reports that LinkedIn generated nearly $1 billion in net revenue this past year, with a very positive trend in revenue, income, and assets as shown here:

($ millions)	2010	2011	2012
Net revenues	$243	$522	$ 972
Net income	3	12	22
Total assets	238	874	1,382

Reid continues to track and account for all revenues and expenses. He maintains that success requires proper accounting for and analysis of the financial side of business. That discipline carries over to his personal philosophy. "You have to decide early on what you're going to hold yourself accountable for," explains Reid. So far, the investment community likes LinkedIn's accountability as reflected in its stock price over the past three years.

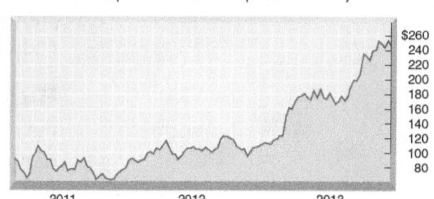

The bigger message of LinkedIn, insists Reid, is promoting careers. "LinkedIn is a tool to solve their [users'] problems," says Reid. "Think of it as a place to get business intelligence, to research problems, to establish an online presence." He adds, "If [we] really learned how to use LinkedIn, it would raise the country's GDP!"

Sources: *LinkedIn Website,* January 2014; *Wired,* March 2012; *KISSmetrics,* April 2013; *New York Times,* November 2011; *Bottom Line,* May 2013; *LinkedIn 10-K,* December 2012

USING FINANCIAL STATEMENTS

We introduced the four financial statements in Chapter 1. This chapter extends that discussion to include financial statement analysis and transaction analysis. Our approach is to gradually develop both skills. Specifically, the basics of transaction analysis are slowly introduced over Chapters 1, 2 and 3. The basics of financial statement analysis are introduced throughout Chapters 1 through 13. We begin this chapter with a discussion of *financial statement analysis,* which refers to applying analytical tools to financial statements for making business decisions.

Analyzing Financial Statements   Financial statement analysis is used by both internal and external users of accounting. Internal users use this analysis to improve company efficiency and effectiveness in providing products and services. External users use financial analysis for investing, lending, and monitoring management. For example, analysts such as Dun & Bradstreet, Moody's, and Standard & Poor's use financial statements in making buy/sell recommendations and in setting credit ratings. The common goal of all users is to evaluate company performance and its financial condition.

Assessing Company Results   When interpreting measures of analysis, we must decide whether the measures indicate good, bad, or average performance. To make such judgments, we need standards (benchmarks) for comparisons that include the following:

- *Intracompany*—comparing company results across two or more periods; an example is comparing Apple's current income to its prior-year income.
- *Intercompany*—comparing results across competitors; an example is comparing Nike's profit margin to Adidas.
- *Industry*—comparing results to industry norms; an example is comparing Google's debt level to the industry average.
- *Guidelines (rules of thumb)*—comparing results to standards based on experience; an example is the 2:1 level for the current ratio.

Using Ratios to Analyze Financial Statements

Ratio analysis is the most widely used tool of financial analysis. A ratio, which expresses a mathematical relation between two quantities, can help uncover a condition or trend. It can be expressed as a percent, rate, or proportion. For instance, a change in an account balance from $100 to $250 can be expressed as (1) 150% increase, (2) 2.5 times, or (3) 2.5 to 1 (or 2.5:1). To be meaningful, a ratio must refer to an economically important relation. For example, an important relation exists between a product's sales price and its cost. Accordingly, the ratio of cost of goods sold to sales is meaningful. However, no useful relation exists between delivery expense and cleaning costs.

Building Blocks of Analysis

Financial statement analysis focuses on one or more of four basic *building blocks* of analysis:

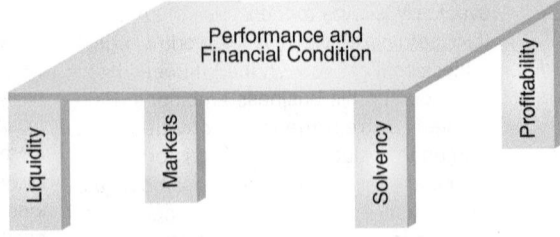

- **Liquidity**—ability to meet short-term obligations and generate revenues.
- **Solvency**—ability to generate future revenues and meet long-term obligations.
- **Profitability**—ability to provide financial rewards sufficient to attract and retain financing.
- **Market prospects**—ability to generate positive market expectations.

The four building blocks focus on different, but interrelated, aspects of a company's financial condition or performance. We can view these blocks as making up the four legs of a table, where the four must work for the table to perform properly.

Liquidity (and Efficiency)

Liquidity refers to the availability of resources to meet short-term cash requirements. (*Efficiency* refers to how productive a company is in using its assets.) Liquidity and efficiency are important and complementary. If a company fails to meet its current obligations, its continued existence is doubtful. Moreover, inefficient use of assets can cause liquidity problems. Liquidity is often assessed by the current ratio, defined as current assets divided by current liabilities (where "current" is defined in the next section). For Apple's statements in Appendix A, its current ratio follows:

Current Ratio = Current Assets/Current Liabilities
1.50   = $57,653/$38,542

For comparison, Google's current ratio is 4.22, which is higher (implying greater liquidity, which is better).

Solvency

Solvency refers to a company's long-run financial viability and its ability to cover long-term obligations. Solvency analysis focuses on a company's ability to both meet its obligations and provide security to its creditors *over the long run.* Solvency is often assessed by the debt ratio, defined as total liabilities divided by total assets. For Apple's statements in Appendix A, its debt ratio follows:

Debt Ratio = Total Liabilities/Total Assets
0.33   = $57,854/$176,064

For comparison, Google's debt ratio is 0.24, which is lower (implying greater solvency, which is better). To better understand, the larger the debt, the larger the contractual obligations to outsiders.

Profitability

Profitability refers to a company's ability to use its assets to produce profits (and positive cash flows). It is commonly assessed by comparing income to sales or to the amount invested. One such measure is the profit margin ratio, defined as net income divided by net sales. For Apple's statements in Appendix A, its profit margin follows:

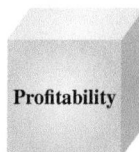

Profit Margin = Net Income/Net Sales
0.27   = $41,733/$156,508

For comparison, Google's profit margin ratio is 0.21, which is lower (implying less profitability, which is worse for Google's future performance).

Market Prospects

Market measures are useful for analyzing companies with publicly traded stock. Market measures use stock price, which reflects the market's (public's) expectations for the company. This includes expectations of both company return and risk. One measure of market performance is the price-to-earnings ratio, defined as price per share divided by earnings per share. For Apple's statements in Appendix A, its price-to-earnings follows:

Price-to-Earnings = Price per Share/Earnings per Share
14.69   = $655.88/$44.64

For comparison, Google's price-to-earnings ratio is 21.46, which is higher (implying greater market expectations for Google's future performance).

Summarizing Ratios

Exhibit 13.16 in Chapter 13 lists additional measures of liquidity, solvency, profitability, and market prospects. This summary includes each ratio's title, its formula, and the purpose for which it is commonly used. The final section of each chapter includes one or more of these ratios relevant to that specific chapter.

ANALYZING AND REPORTING ACCOUNTS

 C1 Explain the steps in processing transactions and the role of source documents.

The accounting process identifies business transactions and events, analyzes and records their effects, and summarizes and presents information in reports and financial statements. These reports and statements are used for making investing, lending, and other business decisions. The steps in the accounting process that focus on *analyzing and recording* transactions and events are shown in Exhibit 2.1.

EXHIBIT 2.1

The Analyzing and Recording Process

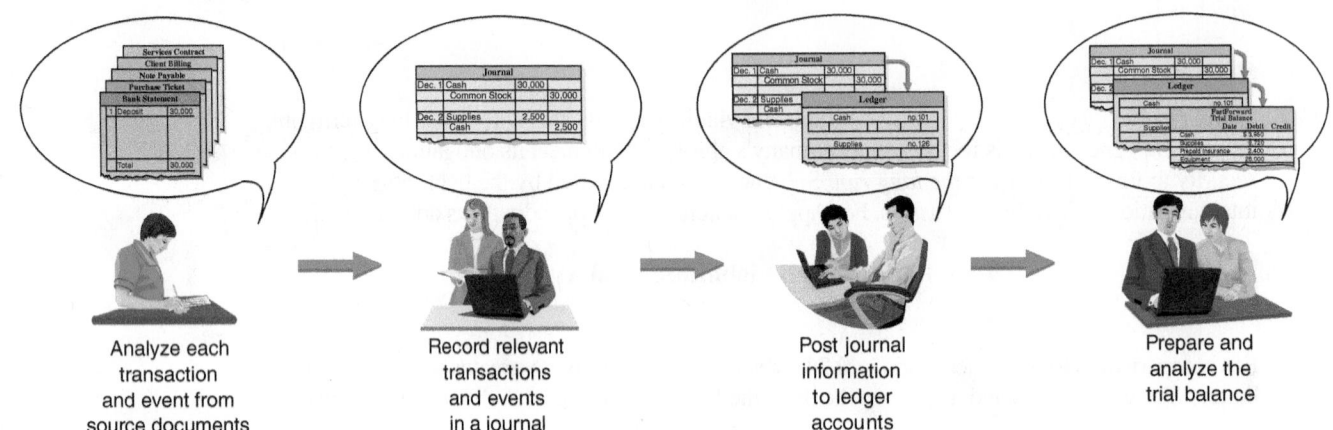

Analyze each transaction and event from source documents

Record relevant transactions and events in a journal

Post journal information to ledger accounts

Prepare and analyze the trial balance

Business transactions and events are the starting points. Relying on source documents, the transactions and events are analyzed using the accounting equation to understand how they affect company performance and financial position. These effects are recorded in accounting records, informally referred to as the *accounting books,* or simply the *books.* Additional steps such as posting and then preparing a trial balance help summarize and classify the effects of transactions and events. Ultimately, the accounting process provides information in useful reports or financial statements to decision makers.

Source Documents

Source documents identify and describe transactions and events entering the accounting process. They are the sources of accounting information and can be in either hard copy or electronic form. Examples are sales tickets, checks, purchase orders, bills from suppliers, employee earnings records, and bank statements. To illustrate, when an item is purchased on credit, the seller usually prepares at least two copies of a sales invoice. One copy is given to the buyer. Another copy, often sent electronically, results in an entry in the seller's information system to record the sale. Sellers use invoices for recording sales and for control; buyers use them for recording purchases and for monitoring purchasing activity. Many cash registers record information for each sale on a tape or electronic file locked inside the register. This record can be used as a source document for recording sales in the accounting records. Source documents, especially if obtained from outside the organization, provide objective and reliable evidence about transactions and events and their amounts.

Point: To ensure that all sales are rung up on the register, most sellers require customers to have their receipts to exchange or return purchased items.

 **Decision Ethics**

Cashier Your manager requires that you, as cashier, immediately enter each sale. Recently, lunch hour traffic has increased and the assistant manager asks you to avoid delays by taking customers' cash and making change without entering sales. The assistant manager says she will add up cash and enter sales after lunch. She says that, in this way, the register will always match the cash amount when the manager arrives at three o'clock. What do you do? ■ [Answer—p. 81]

The Account and Its Analysis

An **account** is a record of increases and decreases in a specific asset, liability, equity, revenue, or expense item. Information from an account is analyzed, summarized, and presented in reports and financial statements. The **general ledger,** or simply **ledger,** is a record containing all accounts used by a company. The ledger is often in electronic form. While most companies' ledgers contain similar accounts, a company often uses one or more unique accounts because of its type of operations.

C2 Describe an account and its use in recording transactions.

Unclassified Balance Sheet Asset, liability, and equity accounts are reported in a balance sheet. An *unclassified balance sheet* broadly groups accounts into assets, liabilities, and equity as shown in Exhibit 2.2a following the accounting equation.

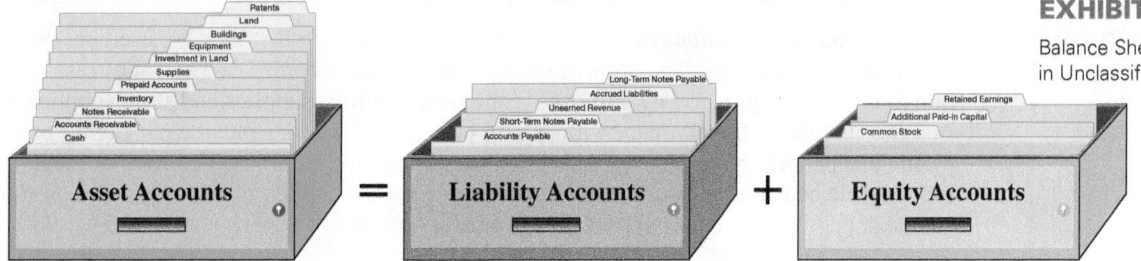

EXHIBIT 2.2a

Balance Sheet Accounts Reported in Unclassified Manner

Classified Balance Sheet A *classified balance sheet* organizes assets and liabilities into subgroups that have similar attributes as shown in Exhibit 2.2b. A key classification is the separation between current and noncurrent items for both assets and liabilities. Current items are those expected to come due (either collected or owed) within one year or the company's operating cycle, whichever is longer. The next chapter explains this in detail. For now, a classified balance sheet reports current assets before noncurrent assets and current liabilities before noncurrent liabilities.

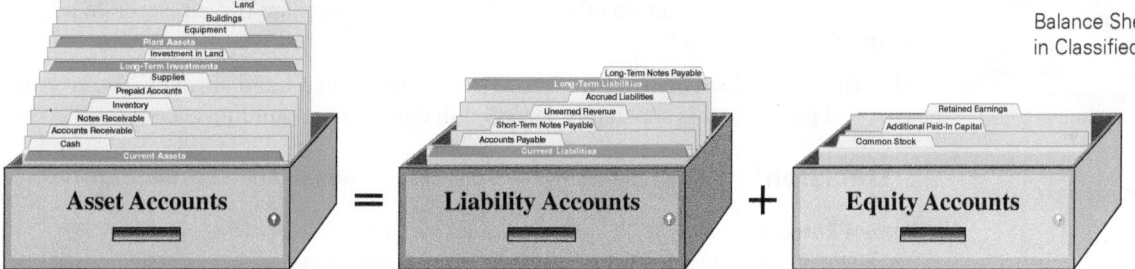

EXHIBIT 2.2b

Balance Sheet Accounts Reported in Classified Manner

Asset Accounts Assets are resources owned or controlled by a company, and those resources have expected future benefits. Most accounting systems include (at a minimum) separate accounts for the assets described here.

Cash A *Cash* account reflects a company's cash balance. All increases and decreases in cash are recorded in the Cash account. It includes money and any medium of exchange that a bank accepts for deposit (coins, checks, money orders, and checking account balances).

Accounts Receivable *Accounts receivable* are held by a seller and refer to promises of payment from customers to sellers. These transactions are often called *credit sales* or *sales on account* (or *on credit*). Accounts receivable are increased by credit sales and are decreased by customer payments. A company needs a separate record for each customer, but for now, we use the simpler practice of recording all increases and decreases in receivables in a single account called Accounts Receivable.

Point: Customers and others who owe a company are called its **debtors.**

Note Receivable A *note receivable,* or promissory note, is a written promise of another entity to pay a definite sum of money on a specified future date to the holder of the note. A company holding a promissory note signed by another entity has an asset that is recorded in a Note (or Notes) Receivable account.

Prepaid Accounts *Prepaid accounts* (also called *prepaid expenses*) are assets that represent prepayments of future expenses (*not* current expenses). When the expenses are later incurred, the amounts in prepaid accounts are transferred to expense accounts. Common examples of prepaid

Point: A college parking fee is a prepaid account from the student's standpoint. At the beginning of the term, it represents an asset that entitles a student to park on or near campus. The benefits of the parking fee expire as the term progresses. At term-end, prepaid parking (asset) equals zero as it has been entirely recorded as parking expense.

Point: Prepaid accounts that apply to current and future periods are assets. These assets are adjusted at the end of each period to reflect only those amounts that have not yet expired, and to record as expenses those amounts that have expired.

accounts include prepaid insurance, prepaid rent, and prepaid services (such as club memberships). Prepaid accounts expire with the passage of time (such as with rent) or through use (such as with prepaid meal tickets). When financial statements are prepared, prepaid accounts are adjusted so that (1) all expired and used prepaid accounts are recorded as regular expenses and (2) all unexpired and unused prepaid accounts are recorded as assets (reflecting future use in future periods). To illustrate, when an insurance fee, called a *premium,* is paid in advance, the cost is typically recorded in the asset account Prepaid Insurance. Over time, the expiring portion of the insurance cost is removed from this asset account and reported in expenses on the income statement. Any unexpired portion remains in Prepaid Insurance and is reported on the balance sheet as an asset. (An exception exists for prepaid accounts that will expire or be used before the end of the current accounting period when financial statements are prepared. In this case, the prepayments *can* be recorded immediately as expenses.)

Supplies Accounts   *Supplies* are assets until they are used. When they are used up, their costs are reported as expenses. The costs of unused supplies are recorded in a Supplies asset account. Supplies are often grouped by purpose—for example, office supplies and store supplies. *Office supplies* include stationery, paper, toner, and pens. *Store supplies* include packaging materials, plastic and paper bags, gift boxes and cartons, and cleaning materials. The costs of these unused supplies can be recorded in an Office Supplies or a Store Supplies asset account. When supplies are used, their costs are transferred from the asset accounts to expense accounts.

Equipment Accounts   *Equipment* is an asset. When equipment is used and gets worn down, its cost is gradually reported as an expense (called depreciation). Equipment is often grouped by its purpose—for example, office equipment and store equipment. *Office equipment* includes computers, printers, desks, chairs, and shelves. Costs incurred for these items are recorded in an Office Equipment asset account. The *Store Equipment* account includes the costs of assets used in a store, such as counters, showcases, ladders, hoists, and cash registers.

Buildings Accounts   *Buildings* such as stores, offices, warehouses, and factories are assets because they provide expected future benefits to those who control or own them. Their costs are recorded in a Buildings asset account. When several buildings are owned, separate accounts are sometimes kept for each of them.

Land   The cost of *land* owned by a business is recorded in a Land account. The cost of buildings located on the land is separately recorded in one or more building accounts.

Point: Some assets are described as *intangible* because they do not have physical existence or their benefits are highly uncertain. A recent balance sheet for **Coca-Cola Company** shows nearly $1 billion in intangible assets.

Decision Insight

Women Entrepreneurs   SPANX has given more than $20 million to charity. The Center for Women's Business Research reports that women-owned businesses, such as SPANX (owner Sara Blakely in photo), are growing and that they:

- Total approximately 11 million and employ nearly 20 million workers.
- Generate $2.5 trillion in annual sales and tend to embrace technology.
- Are philanthropic—70% of owners volunteer at least once per month.
- Are more likely funded by individual investors (73%) than venture firms (15%). ■

Liability Accounts   Liabilities are claims (by creditors) against assets, which means they are obligations to transfer assets or provide products or services to others. **Creditors** are individuals and organizations that have rights to receive payments from a company. If a company fails to pay its obligations, the law gives creditors a right to force the sale of that company's assets to obtain the money to meet creditors' claims. When assets are sold under these conditions, creditors are paid first, but only up to the amount of their claims. Any remaining money, the residual, goes to the owners of the company. Creditors often use a balance sheet to help decide whether to loan money to a company. A loan is less risky if the borrower's liabilities are small in comparison to assets because this means there are more resources than claims on resources. Common liability accounts are described here.

Point: Accounts payable are also called *trade payables.*

Accounts Payable   *Accounts payable* refer to oral or implied promises to pay later, which usually arise from purchases of merchandise. Payables can also arise from purchases of supplies, equipment, and services. Accounting systems keep separate records about each creditor. We describe these individual records in Chapter 4.

Note Payable A *note payable* refers to a formal promise, usually denoted by the signing of a promissory note, to pay a future amount. It is recorded in either a short-term Note Payable account or a long-term Note Payable account, depending on when it must be repaid. We explain details of short- and long-term classification in Chapter 3.

Unearned Revenue Accounts **Unearned revenue** refers to a liability that is settled in the future when a company delivers its products or services. When customers pay in advance for products or services (before revenue is earned), the revenue recognition principle requires that the seller consider this payment as unearned revenue. Examples of unearned revenue include magazine subscriptions collected in advance by a publisher, sales of gift certificates by stores, and season ticket sales by sports teams. The seller would record these in liability accounts such as Unearned Subscriptions, Unearned Store Sales, and Unearned Ticket Revenue. When products and services are later delivered, the earned portion of the unearned revenue is transferred to revenue accounts such as Subscription Fees, Store Sales, and Ticket Sales.[1]

Point: If a subscription is canceled, the publisher is expected to refund the unused portion to the subscriber.

Accrued Liabilities *Accrued liabilities* are amounts owed that are not yet paid. Examples are wages payable, taxes payable, and interest payable. These are often recorded in separate liability accounts by the same title. If they are not large in amount, one or more ledger accounts can be added and reported as a single amount on the balance sheet. (Financial statements often have amounts reported that are a summation of several ledger accounts.)

🔲 **Decision** Insight

Revenue Spread The New York Giants have *Unearned Revenues* of over $100 million in advance ticket sales. When the team plays its home games, it settles this liability to its ticket holders and then transfers the amount earned to *Ticket Revenues*. ▨

Equity Accounts The owner's claim on a company's assets is called *equity,* or *stockholders' equity,* or *shareholders' equity.* Equity is the owners' *residual interest* in the assets of a business after deducting liabilities. Equity is impacted by four types of accounts: common stock, dividends, revenues, and expenses. We show this visually in Exhibit 2.3 by expanding the accounting equation. (As Chapter 1 explains, the accounts for dividends, revenues, and expenses are reflected in the retained earnings account, and that account is reported in the balance sheet.)

Point: Equity is also called *net assets.*

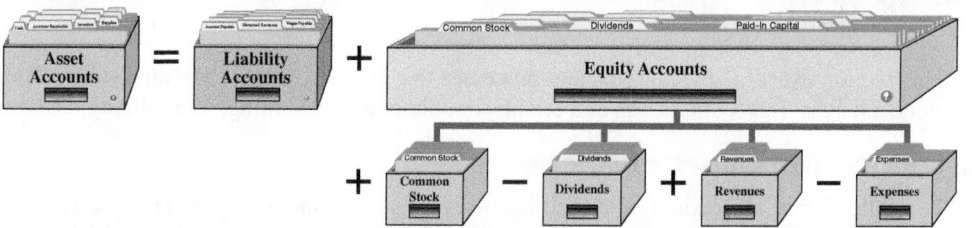

EXHIBIT 2.3

Expanded Accounting Equation

Common Stock When an owner invests in a company in exchange for common stock, the invested amount is recorded in an account titled **Common Stock.** Any further owner investments are recorded in this account.

Point: The Dividends account is sometimes referred to as a *contra equity* account because it reduces the normal balance of equity.

Dividends When the company pays any cash dividends, it decreases both the company's assets and its total equity. Dividends are not expenses of the business. They are simply the opposite of owner investments. A **Dividends** account is used in recording asset distributions to stockholders (owners).

Point: The withdrawal of assets by the owners of a corporation is called a *dividend.*

Revenue Accounts Revenues and expenses also impact equity. Examples of revenue accounts are Sales, Commissions Earned, Professional Fees Earned, Rent Revenue, and Interest Revenue. *Revenues increase equity* and result from products and services provided to customers.

---

[1] In practice, account titles vary. As one example, Subscription Fees is sometimes called Subscription Fees Revenue, Subscription Fees Earned, or Earned Subscription Fees. As another example, Rent Earned is sometimes called Rent Revenue, Rental Revenue, or Earned Rent Revenue. We must use good judgment when reading financial statements because titles can differ even within the same industry. For example, product sales are called *net sales* at Apple, *revenues* at Google, and *revenue* at Samsung. Generally, the term *revenues* or *fees* is more commonly used with service businesses, and *net sales* or *sales* with product businesses.

Expense Accounts   Examples of expense accounts are Advertising Expense, Store Supplies Expense, Office Salaries Expense, Office Supplies Expense, Rent Expense, Utilities Expense, and Insurance Expense. *Expenses decrease equity* and result from assets and services used in a company's operations. The variety of revenues and expenses can be seen by looking at the *chart of accounts* that follows the index at the back of this book. (Different companies sometimes use different account titles than those in this book's chart of accounts. For example, some might use Interest Revenue instead of Interest Earned, or Rental Expense instead of Rent Expense. It is important only that an account title describe the item it represents.)

■ **Decision** Insight ═══════════════════════════════

Sporting Accounts   The Miami Heat, Los Angeles Lakers, Chicago Bulls, and the other NBA teams have the following major revenue and expense accounts:

Revenues	Expenses
Basketball ticket sales	Team salaries
TV & radio broadcast fees	Game costs
Advertising revenues	NBA franchise costs
Basketball playoff receipts	Promotional costs ■

NEED-TO-KNOW 2.1

C1   C2

Classify each of the following accounts as assets (A), liabilities (L), or equity (EQ).

1. ____ Prepaid Rent   **5.** ____ Accounts Receivable   **9.** ____ Land

2. ____ Common Stock   **6.** ____ Equipment   **10.** ____ Prepaid Insurance

3. ____ Note Receivable   **7.** ____ Interest Payable

4. ____ Accounts Payable   **8.** ____ Unearned Revenue

Solution

1. A **2.** EQ **3.** A **4.** L **5.** A **6.** A **7.** L **8.** L **9.** A **10.** A

Do More: QS 2-2, QS 2-3

ANALYZING AND PROCESSING TRANSACTIONS

This section explains several tools and processes that comprise an accounting system. These include a ledger, T-account, debits and credits, double-entry accounting, journalizing, and posting.

Ledger and Chart of Accounts

C3   Describe a ledger and a chart of accounts.

The collection of all accounts and their balances for an information system is called a *ledger* (or *general ledger*). If accounts are in files on a hard drive, the sum of those files is the ledger. If the accounts are pages in a file, that file is the ledger. A company's size and diversity of operations affect the number of accounts needed. A small company can get by with as few as 20 or 30 accounts; a large company can require several thousand. The **chart of accounts** is a list of all ledger accounts and includes an identification number assigned to each account. A small business might use the following numbering system for its accounts:

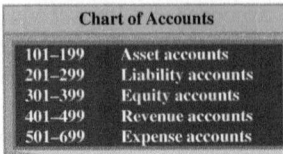

Chart of Accounts	
101–199	Asset accounts
201–299	Liability accounts
301–399	Equity accounts
401–499	Revenue accounts
501–699	Expense accounts

These numbers provide a three-digit code that is useful in recordkeeping. In this case, the first digit assigned to asset accounts is a 1, the first digit assigned to liability accounts is a 2, and so on. The second and third digits relate to the accounts' subcategories. Exhibit 2.4 shows a partial chart of accounts for FastForward, the focus company of Chapter 1. (Please review the more complete chart of accounts that follows the index at the back of this book.)

Chart of Accounts								
Acct. No.	**Account Name**		**Acct. No.**	**Account Name**		**Acct. No.**	**Account Name**	
101	Cash		236	Unearned consulting		406	Rental revenue	
106	Accounts receivable			revenue		622	Salaries expense	
126	Supplies		307	Common stock		637	Insurance expense	
128	Prepaid insurance		318	Retained earnings		640	Rent expense	
167	Equipment		319	Dividends		652	Supplies expense	
201	Accounts payable		403	Consulting revenue		690	Utilities expense	

EXHIBIT 2.4

Partial Chart of Accounts for FastForward

Debits and Credits

A **T-account** represents a ledger account and is a tool used to understand the effects of one or more transactions. Its name comes from its shape like the letter T. The layout of a T-account, shown in Exhibit 2.5, is (1) the account title on top, (2) a left, or debit side, and (3) a right, or credit, side.

The left side of an account is called the **debit** side, often abbreviated *Dr.* The right side is called the **credit** side, abbreviated *Cr.*[2] To enter amounts on the left side of an account is to *debit* the account. To enter amounts on the right side is to *credit* the account. Do not make the error of thinking that the terms *debit* and *credit* mean increase or decrease. Whether a

Account Title	
(Left side)	(Right side)
Debit	*Credit*

debit or a credit is an increase or decrease depends on the account. For an account where a debit is an increase, the credit is a decrease; for an account where a debit is a decrease, the credit is an increase. The difference between total debits and total credits for an account, including any beginning balance, is the **account balance.** When the sum of debits exceeds the sum of credits, the account has a *debit balance.* It has a *credit balance* when the sum of credits exceeds the sum of debits. When the sum of debits equals the sum of credits, the account has a *zero balance.*

C4 Define *debits* and *credits* and explain double-entry accounting.

EXHIBIT 2.5

The T-Account

Point: Think of *debit* and *credit* as accounting directions for left and right.

Double-Entry Accounting

Double-entry accounting requires that for each transaction:

- At least two accounts are involved, with at least one debit and one credit.
- The total amount debited must equal the total amount credited.
- The accounting equation must not be violated.

This means the sum of the debits for all entries must equal the sum of the credits for all entries, and the sum of debit account balances in the ledger must equal the sum of credit account balances.

The system for recording debits and credits follows from the usual accounting equation—see Exhibit 2.6. Two points are important here. First, like any simple mathematical relation, net

"Total debits equal total credits for each entry."

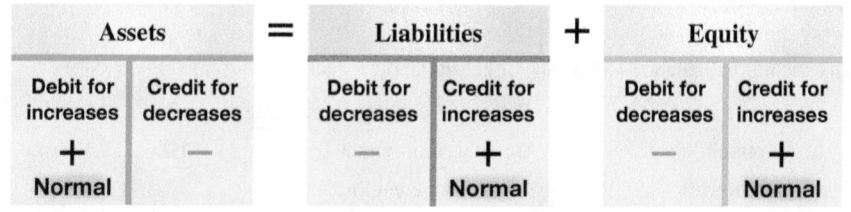

EXHIBIT 2.6

Debits and Credits in the Accounting Equation

---

[2] These abbreviations are remnants of 18th-century English recordkeeping practices where the terms *debitor* and *creditor* were used instead of *debit* and *credit.* The abbreviations use the first and last letters of these terms, just as we still do for Saint (St.) and Doctor (Dr.).

increases or decreases on one side have equal net effects on the other side. For example, a net increase in assets must be accompanied by an identical net increase on the liabilities and equity side. Recall that some transactions affect only one side of the equation, meaning that two or more accounts on one side are affected, but their net effect on this one side is zero. Second, the left side is the *normal balance* side for assets, and the right side is the *normal balance* side for liabilities and equity. This matches their layout in the accounting equation where assets are on the left side of this equation, and liabilities and equity are on the right.

Point: Debits and credits do not mean favorable or unfavorable. A debit to an asset increases it, as does a debit to an expense. A credit to a liability increases it, as does a credit to a revenue.

Recall that equity increases from revenues and stock issuances, and it decreases from expenses and dividends. These important equity relations are conveyed by expanding the accounting equation to include debits and credits in double-entry form as shown in Exhibit 2.7.

EXHIBIT 2.7

Debit and Credit Effects for Component Accounts

Assets		=	Liabilities		+	Common Stock		−	Dividends		+	Revenues		−	Expenses	
						Equity										
Dr. for increases	Cr. for decreases		Dr. for decreases	Cr. for increases		Dr. for decreases	Cr. for increases		Dr. for increases	Cr. for decreases		Dr. for decreases	Cr. for increases		Dr. for increases	Cr. for decreases
+	−		−	+		−	+		+	−		−	+		+	−
Normal				Normal			Normal		Normal				Normal		Normal	

Increases (credits) to common stock and revenues *increase* equity; increases (debits) to dividends and expenses *decrease* equity. The normal balance of each account (asset, liability, common stock, dividends, revenue, or expense) refers to the left or right (debit or credit) side where *increases* are recorded. Understanding these diagrams and rules is required to prepare, analyze, and interpret financial statements.

The T-account for FastForward's Cash account, reflecting its first 11 transactions (from Exhibit 1.9), is shown in Exhibit 2.8. The total increases in its Cash account are $36,100, the total decreases are $31,300, and the account's debit balance is $4,800. (We illustrate use of T-accounts later in this chapter.)

EXHIBIT 2.8

Computing the Balance for a T-Account

Cash			
Receive investment by owner for stock	30,000	Purchase of supplies	2,500
Consulting services revenue earned	4,200	Purchase of equipment	26,000
Collection of account receivable	1,900	Payment of rent	1,000
		Payment of salary	700
		Payment of account payable	900
		Payment of cash dividend	200
Balance	4,800		

Point: The ending balance is on the side with the larger dollar amount. Also, a plus (+) and minus (−) are not used in a T-account.

NEED-TO-KNOW 2.2

C3 C4

Identify the normal balance (debit [Dr] or credit [Cr]) for each of the following accounts.

1. ____ Prepaid Rent
2. ____ Common Stock
3. ____ Note Receivable
4. ____ Accounts Payable
5. ____ Accounts Receivable
6. ____ Equipment
7. ____ Interest Payable
8. ____ Unearned Revenue
9. ____ Land
10. ____ Prepaid Insurance

Do More: QS 2-4, QS 2-5, QS 2-6, E 2-4

QC1

Solution

1. Dr. **2.** Cr. **3.** Dr. **4.** Cr. **5.** Dr. **6.** Dr. **7.** Cr. **8.** Cr. **9.** Dr. **10.** Dr.

Journalizing and Posting Transactions

Processing transactions is a crucial part of accounting. The four usual steps of this process are depicted in Exhibit 2.9. Steps 1 and 2—involving transaction analysis and the accounting equation—were introduced in prior sections. This section extends that discussion and focuses on steps 3 and 4 of the accounting process. Step 3 is to record each transaction chronologically in a journal. A **journal** gives a complete record of each transaction in one place. It also shows debits and credits for each transaction. The process of recording transactions in a journal is called **journalizing.** Step 4 is to transfer (or *post*) entries from the journal to the ledger. The process of transferring journal entry information to the ledger is called **posting.**

P1 Record transactions in a journal and post entries to a ledger.

Step 1: Identify transactions and source documents.

	Services Contract	
	Client Billing	
	Note Payable	
	Purchase Ticket	
	Bank Statement	
1	Deposit	30,000
	TOTAL	

Step 2: Analyze transactions using the accounting equation.

Cash — Assets = Liabilities + Equity

Step 3: Record journal entry.

General Journal

Dec. 1	Cash	30,000	
	Common Stock		30,000
Dec. 2	Supplies	2,500	
	Cash		2,500

Step 4: Post entry to ledger.

General Journal
Ledger

EXHIBIT 2.9

Steps in Processing Transactions

Journalizing Transactions   The process of journalizing transactions requires an understanding of a journal. While companies can use various journals, every company uses a **general journal.** It can be used to record any transaction and includes the following information about each transaction: ⓐ date of transaction, ⓑ titles of affected accounts, ⓒ dollar amount of each debit and credit, and ⓓ explanation of the transaction. Exhibit 2.10 shows how the first two transactions of FastForward are recorded in a general journal. This process is similar for manual and computerized systems. Computerized journals are often designed to look like a manual journal page, and also include error-checking routines that ensure debits equal credits for each entry. Shortcuts allow recordkeepers to select account names and numbers from pull-down menus.

EXHIBIT 2.10

Partial General Journal for FastForward

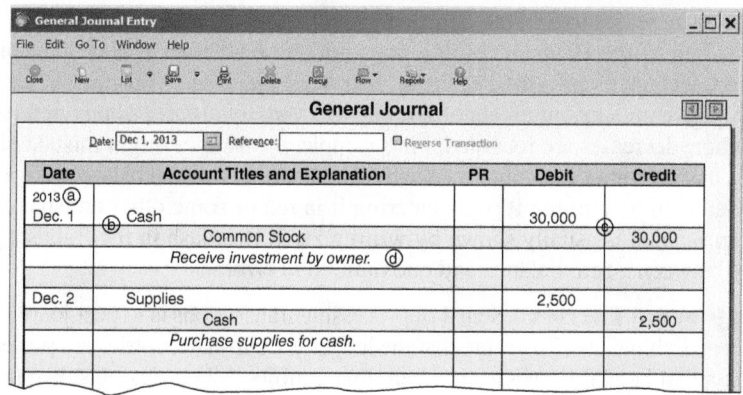

To record entries in a general journal, apply these steps; refer to the entries in Exhibit 2.10 when reviewing these steps.

a. Date the transaction: Enter the year at the top of the first column and the month and day on the first line of each journal entry.

b. Enter titles of accounts debited and then enter amounts in the Debit column on the same line. Account titles are taken from the chart of accounts and are aligned with the left margin of the Account Titles and Explanation column.

c. Enter titles of accounts credited and then enter amounts in the Credit column on the same line. Account titles are from the chart of accounts and are indented from the left margin of the Account Titles and Explanation column to distinguish them from debited accounts.

d. Enter a brief explanation of the transaction on the line below the entry (it often references a source document). This explanation is indented about half as far as the credited account titles to avoid confusing it with accounts, and it is italicized.

A blank line is left between each journal entry for clarity. When a transaction is first recorded, the **posting reference (PR) column** is left blank (in a manual system). Later, when posting entries to the ledger, the identification numbers of the individual ledger accounts are entered in the PR column.

 IFRS _____

IFRS requires that companies report the following four basic financial statements with explanatory notes:

- Balance sheet
- Income statement
- Statement of changes in equity (or statement of recognized revenue and expense)
- Statement of cash flows

IFRS does not prescribe specific formats; and comparative information is required for the preceding period only. ■

Balance Column Account   T-accounts are simple and direct means to show how the accounting process works. However, actual accounting systems need more structure and therefore use **balance column accounts,** such as that in Exhibit 2.11.

EXHIBIT 2.11

Cash Account in Balance
Column Format

General Ledger						
		Cash			Account No. 101	
Date	Explanation	PR	Debit	Credit	Balance	
2013 Dec. 1		G1	30,000		30,000	
Dec. 2		G1		2,500	27,500	
Dec. 3		G1		26,000	1,500	
Dec. 10		G1	4,200		5,700	

The balance column account format is similar to a T-account in having columns for debits and credits. It is different in including transaction date and explanation columns. It also has a column with the balance of the account after each entry is recorded. To illustrate, FastForward's Cash account in Exhibit 2.11 is debited on December 1 for the $30,000 owner investment, yielding a $30,000 debit balance. The account is credited on December 2 for $2,500, yielding a $27,500 debit balance. On December 3, it is credited again, this time for $26,000, and its debit balance is reduced to $1,500. The Cash account is debited for $4,200 on December 10, and its debit balance increases to $5,700; and so on.

The heading of the Balance column does not show whether it is a debit or credit balance. Instead, an account is assumed to have a *normal balance*. Unusual events can sometimes temporarily give an account an abnormal balance. An *abnormal balance* refers to a balance on the side where decreases are recorded. For example, a customer might mistakenly overpay a bill. This gives that customer's account receivable an abnormal (credit) balance. An abnormal balance is often identified by circling it or by entering it in red or some other unusual color. A zero balance for an account is usually shown by writing zeros or a dash in the Balance column to avoid confusion between a zero balance and one omitted in error.

Posting Journal Entries   Step 4 of processing transactions is to post journal entries to ledger accounts (see Exhibit 2.9). To ensure that the ledger is up-to-date, entries are posted as soon as possible. This might be daily, weekly, or when time permits. All entries must be posted to the ledger before financial statements are prepared to ensure that account balances are up-to-date. When entries are posted to the ledger, the debits in journal entries are transferred into ledger accounts as debits, and credits are transferred into ledger accounts as credits. Exhibit 2.12 shows the *four steps to post a journal entry*. First, identify the ledger account that is debited in the entry; then, in the ledger, enter the entry date, the journal and page in its PR column, the debit amount, and the new

Point: There are no exact rules for writing journal entry explanations. An explanation should be short yet describe why an entry is made.

Point: Explanations are typically included in ledger accounts only for unusual transactions or events.

Point: Computerized systems often provide a code beside a balance such as *dr.* or *cr.* to identify its balance. Posting is automatic and immediate with accounting software.

Point: A journal is often referred to as the *book of original entry.* The ledger is referred to as the *book of final entry* because financial statements are prepared from it.

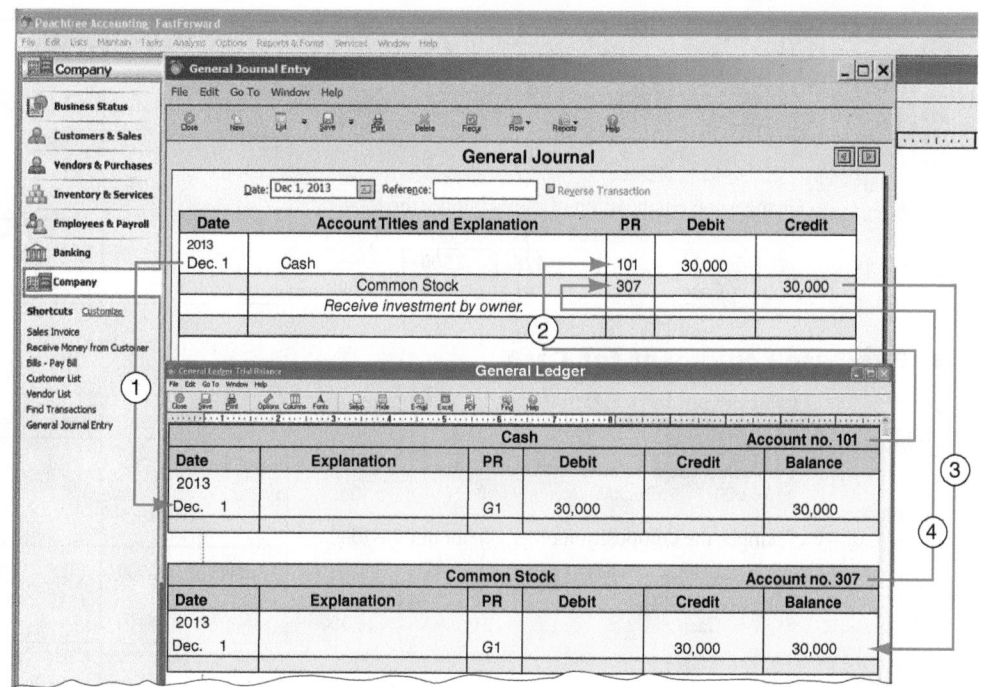

EXHIBIT 2.12

Posting an Entry to the Ledger

Key:
1. Identify debit account in Ledger: enter date, journal page, amount, and balance.
2. Enter the debit account number from the Ledger in the PR column of the journal.
3. Identify credit account in Ledger: enter date, journal page, amount, and balance.
4. Enter the credit account number from the Ledger in the PR column of the journal.

Point: The fundamental concepts of a manual (pencil-and-paper) system are identical to those of a computerized information system.

balance of the ledger account. (The letter *G* shows it came from the General Journal.) Second, enter the ledger account number in the PR column of the journal. Steps 3 and 4 repeat the first two steps for credit entries and amounts. The posting process creates a link between the ledger and the journal entry. This link is a useful cross-reference for tracing an amount from one record to another.

Analyzing Transactions — An Illustration

We return to the activities of FastForward to show how double-entry accounting is useful in analyzing and processing transactions. Analysis of each transaction follows the four steps of Exhibit 2.9.

A1 Analyze the impact of transactions on accounts and financial statements.

Step 1 Identify the transaction and any source documents.
Step 2 Analyze the transaction using the accounting equation.
Step 3 Record the transaction in journal entry form applying double-entry accounting.
Step 4 Post the entry (for simplicity, we use T-accounts to represent ledger accounts).

Study each transaction thoroughly before proceeding to the next. The first 11 transactions are from Chapter 1, and we analyze five additional December transactions of FastForward (numbered 12 through 16) that were omitted earlier.

Point: In the Need-To-Know at the chapter end we show how to use "balance column accounts" for the ledger.

1. Receive investment by Owner

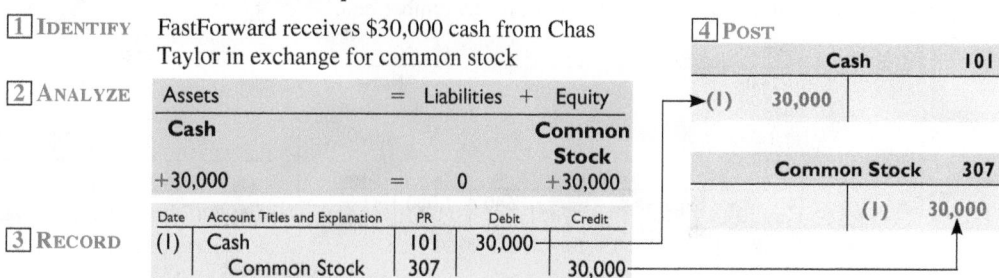

2. Purchase Supplies for Cash

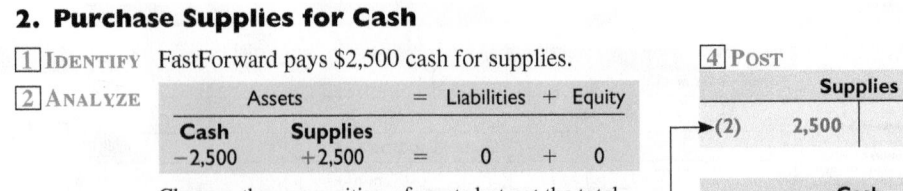

① **IDENTIFY** FastForward pays $2,500 cash for supplies.

② **ANALYZE**

Assets		= Liabilities	+ Equity
Cash	**Supplies**		
−2,500	+2,500	= 0	+ 0

Changes the composition of assets but not the total.

③ **RECORD**

Date	Account Titles and Explanation	PR	Debit	Credit
(2)	Supplies	126	2,500	
	Cash	101		2,500

④ **POST**

Supplies		126
(2)	2,500	

Cash		101	
(1)	30,000	(2)	2,500

3. Purchase Equipment for Cash

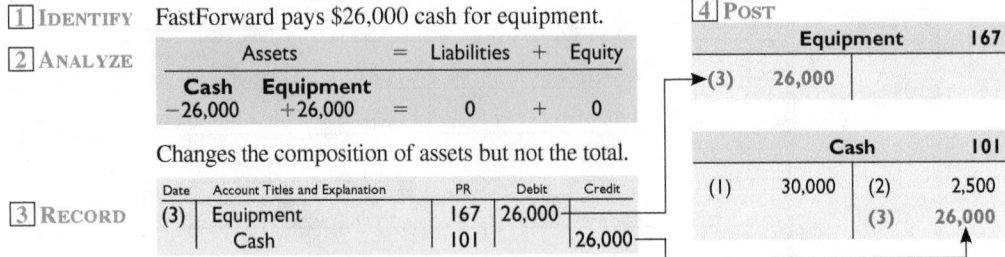

① **IDENTIFY** FastForward pays $26,000 cash for equipment.

② **ANALYZE**

Assets		= Liabilities	+ Equity
Cash	**Equipment**		
−26,000	+26,000	= 0	+ 0

Changes the composition of assets but not the total.

③ **RECORD**

Date	Account Titles and Explanation	PR	Debit	Credit
(3)	Equipment	167	26,000	
	Cash	101		26,000

④ **POST**

Equipment		167
(3)	26,000	

Cash		101	
(1)	30,000	(2)	2,500
		(3)	26,000

4. Purchase Supplies on Credit

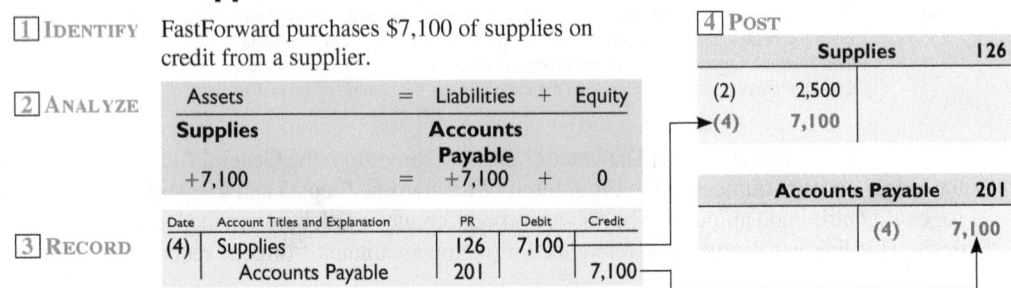

① **IDENTIFY** FastForward purchases $7,100 of supplies on credit from a supplier.

② **ANALYZE**

Assets	= Liabilities	+ Equity
Supplies	**Accounts Payable**	
+7,100	= +7,100	+ 0

③ **RECORD**

Date	Account Titles and Explanation	PR	Debit	Credit
(4)	Supplies	126	7,100	
	Accounts Payable	201		7,100

④ **POST**

Supplies		126
(2)	2,500	
(4)	7,100	

Accounts Payable		201
	(4)	7,100

5. Provide Services for Cash

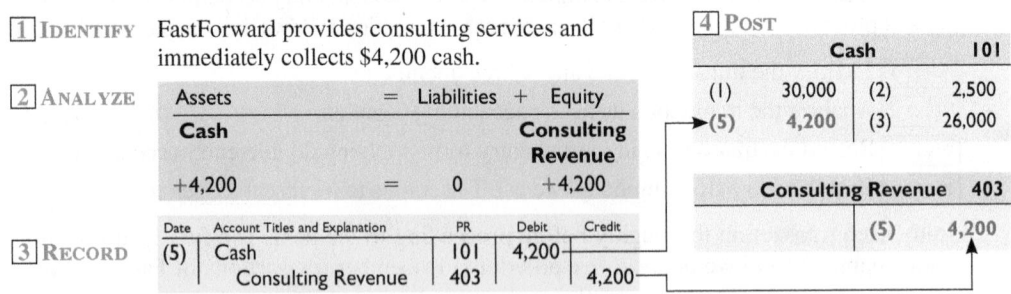

① **IDENTIFY** FastForward provides consulting services and immediately collects $4,200 cash.

② **ANALYZE**

Assets	= Liabilities	+ Equity
Cash		**Consulting Revenue**
+4,200	= 0	+4,200

③ **RECORD**

Date	Account Titles and Explanation	PR	Debit	Credit
(5)	Cash	101	4,200	
	Consulting Revenue	403		4,200

④ **POST**

Cash		101	
(1)	30,000	(2)	2,500
(5)	4,200	(3)	26,000

Consulting Revenue		403
	(5)	4,200

6. Payment of Expense in Cash

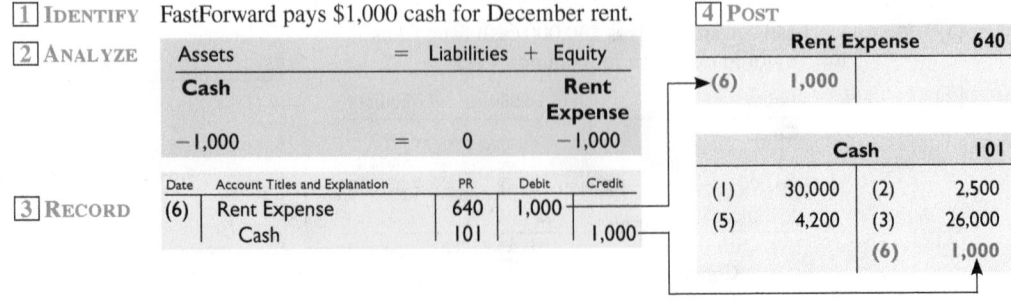

① **IDENTIFY** FastForward pays $1,000 cash for December rent.

② **ANALYZE**

Assets	= Liabilities	+ Equity
Cash		**Rent Expense**
−1,000	= 0	−1,000

③ **RECORD**

Date	Account Titles and Explanation	PR	Debit	Credit
(6)	Rent Expense	640	1,000	
	Cash	101		1,000

④ **POST**

Rent Expense		640
(6)	1,000	

Cash		101	
(1)	30,000	(2)	2,500
(5)	4,200	(3)	26,000
		(6)	1,000

7. Payment of Expense in Cash

1 IDENTIFY   FastForward pays $700 cash for employee salary.

2 ANALYZE

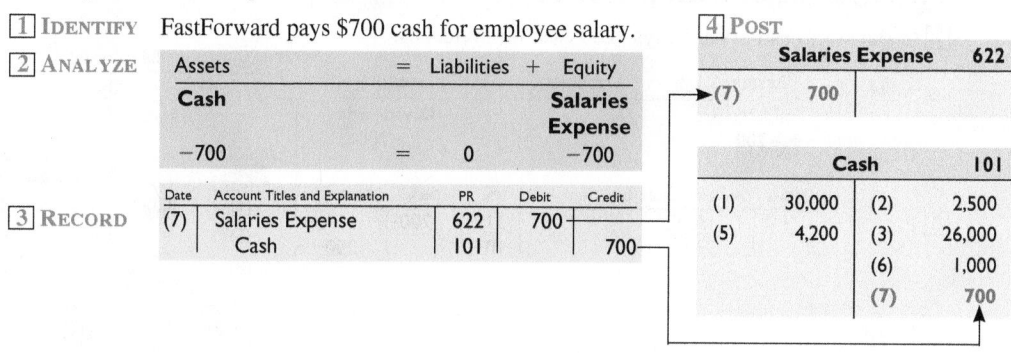

Assets		=	Liabilities	+	Equity
Cash					**Salaries Expense**
−700		=	0		−700

3 RECORD

Date	Account Titles and Explanation	PR	Debit	Credit
(7)	Salaries Expense	622	700	
	Cash	101		700

4 POST

Salaries Expense		622
(7)	700	

Cash			101
(1)	30,000	(2)	2,500
(5)	4,200	(3)	26,000
		(6)	1,000
		(7)	700

Point: *Salary* usually refers to compensation for an employee who receives a fixed amount for a given time period, whereas *wages* usually refers to compensation based on time worked.

8. Provide Consulting and Rental Services on Credit

1 IDENTIFY   FastForward provides consulting services of $1,600 and rents its test facilities for $300. The customer is billed $1,900 for these services.

2 ANALYZE

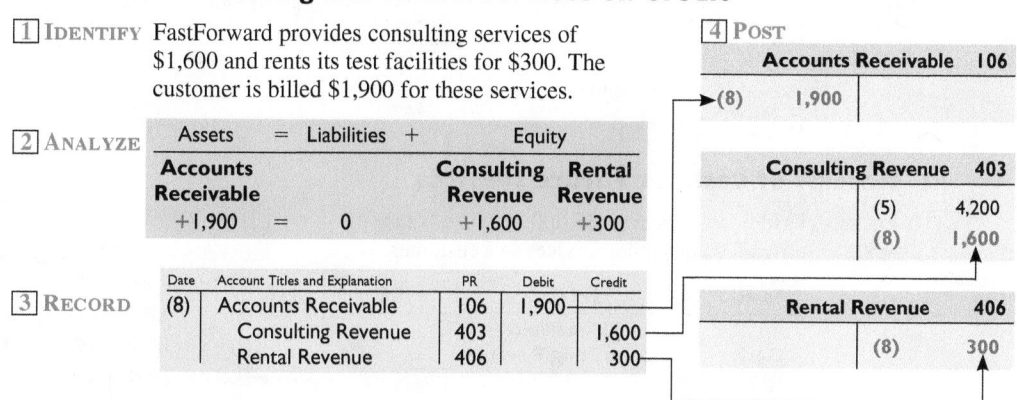

Assets	=	Liabilities	+	Equity	
Accounts Receivable				**Consulting Revenue**	**Rental Revenue**
+1,900	=	0		+1,600	+300

3 RECORD

Date	Account Titles and Explanation	PR	Debit	Credit
(8)	Accounts Receivable	106	1,900	
	Consulting Revenue	403		1,600
	Rental Revenue	406		300

4 POST

Accounts Receivable		106
(8)	1,900	

Consulting Revenue		403
	(5)	4,200
	(8)	1,600

Rental Revenue		406
	(8)	300

Point: Transaction 8 is a **compound journal entry,** which affects three or more accounts.

9. Receipt of Cash on Account

1 IDENTIFY   FastForward receives $1,900 cash from the client billed in transaction 8.

2 ANALYZE

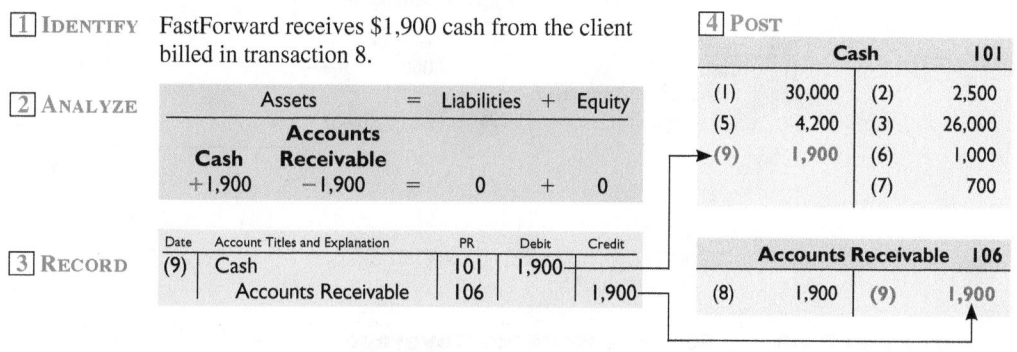

Assets		=	Liabilities	+	Equity
Cash	**Accounts Receivable**				
+1,900	−1,900	=	0	+	0

3 RECORD

Date	Account Titles and Explanation	PR	Debit	Credit
(9)	Cash	101	1,900	
	Accounts Receivable	106		1,900

4 POST

Cash			101
(1)	30,000	(2)	2,500
(5)	4,200	(3)	26,000
(9)	1,900	(6)	1,000
		(7)	700

Accounts Receivable			106
(8)	1,900	(9)	1,900

Point: The *revenue recognition principle* requires revenue to be recognized when earned, which is when the company provides products and services to a customer. This is not necessarily the same time that the customer pays. A customer can pay before or after products or services are provided.

10. Partial Payment of Accounts Payable

1 IDENTIFY   FastForward pays CalTech Supply $900 cash toward the payable of transaction 4.

2 ANALYZE

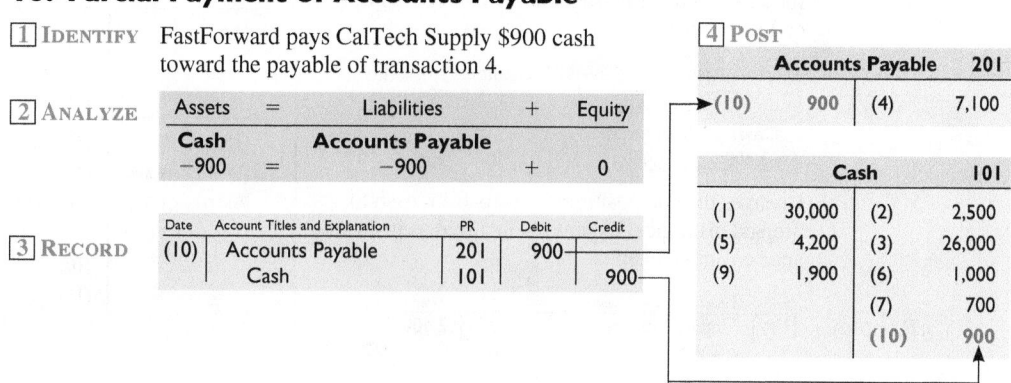

Assets	=	Liabilities	+	Equity
Cash		**Accounts Payable**		
−900	=	−900	+	0

3 RECORD

Date	Account Titles and Explanation	PR	Debit	Credit
(10)	Accounts Payable	201	900	
	Cash	101		900

4 POST

Accounts Payable			201
(10)	900	(4)	7,100

Cash			101
(1)	30,000	(2)	2,500
(5)	4,200	(3)	26,000
(9)	1,900	(6)	1,000
		(7)	700
		(10)	900

11. Payment of Cash Dividend

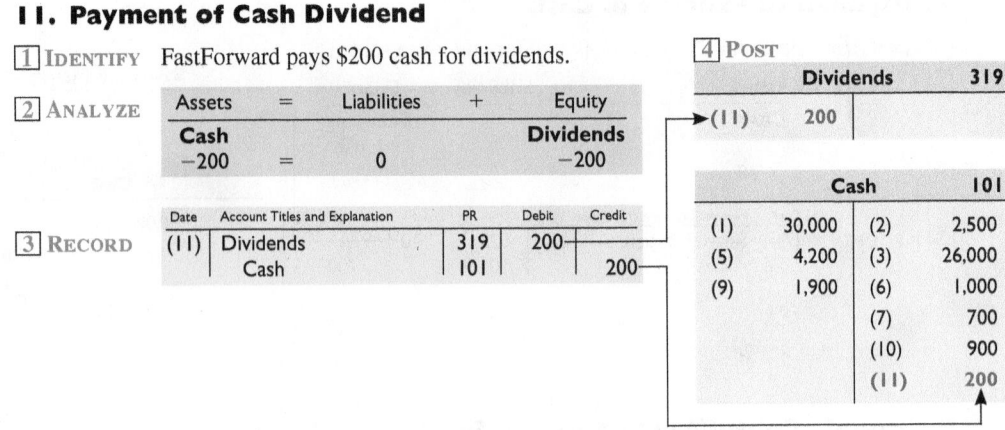

1 IDENTIFY   FastForward pays $200 cash for dividends.

2 ANALYZE

Assets	=	Liabilities	+	Equity
Cash				**Dividends**
−200	=	0		−200

3 RECORD

Date	Account Titles and Explanation	PR	Debit	Credit
(11)	Dividends	319	200	
	Cash	101		200

4 POST

Dividends		319
►(11)	200	

	Cash		101
(1)	30,000	(2)	2,500
(5)	4,200	(3)	26,000
(9)	1,900	(6)	1,000
		(7)	700
		(10)	900
		(11)	200

12. Receipt of Cash for Future Services

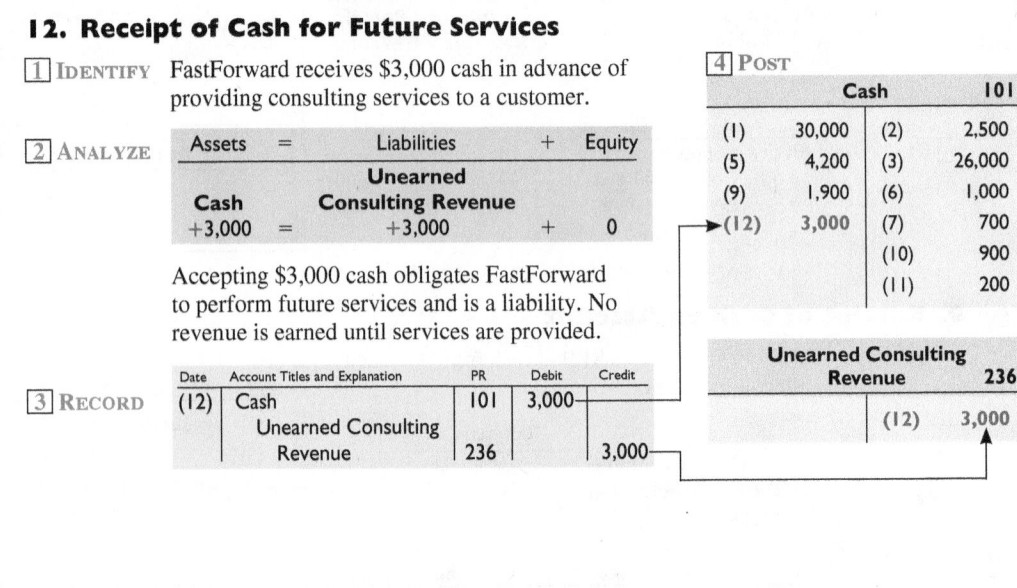

1 IDENTIFY   FastForward receives $3,000 cash in advance of providing consulting services to a customer.

2 ANALYZE

Assets	=	Liabilities	+	Equity
		Unearned		
Cash		**Consulting Revenue**		
+3,000	=	+3,000	+	0

Accepting $3,000 cash obligates FastForward to perform future services and is a liability. No revenue is earned until services are provided.

3 RECORD

Date	Account Titles and Explanation	PR	Debit	Credit
(12)	Cash	101	3,000	
	Unearned Consulting			
	Revenue	236		3,000

4 POST

	Cash		101
(1)	30,000	(2)	2,500
(5)	4,200	(3)	26,000
(9)	1,900	(6)	1,000
►(12)	3,000	(7)	700
		(10)	900
		(11)	200

Unearned Consulting Revenue		236
	(12)	3,000

13. Pay Cash for Future Insurance Coverage

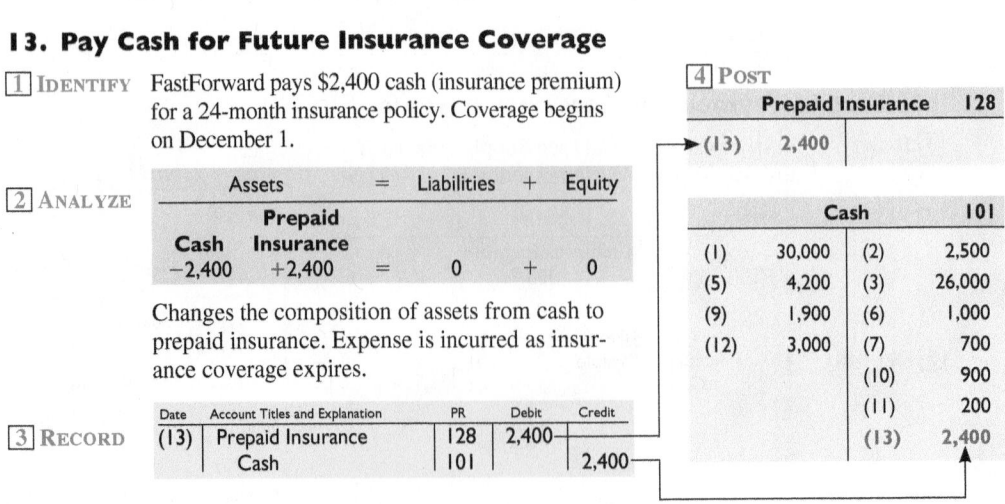

1 IDENTIFY   FastForward pays $2,400 cash (insurance premium) for a 24-month insurance policy. Coverage begins on December 1.

2 ANALYZE

Assets		=	Liabilities	+	Equity
	Prepaid				
Cash	**Insurance**				
−2,400	+2,400	=	0	+	0

Changes the composition of assets from cash to prepaid insurance. Expense is incurred as insurance coverage expires.

3 RECORD

Date	Account Titles and Explanation	PR	Debit	Credit
(13)	Prepaid Insurance	128	2,400	
	Cash	101		2,400

4 POST

Prepaid Insurance		128
►(13)	2,400	

	Cash		101
(1)	30,000	(2)	2,500
(5)	4,200	(3)	26,000
(9)	1,900	(6)	1,000
(12)	3,000	(7)	700
		(10)	900
		(11)	200
		(13)	2,400

14. Purchase Supplies for Cash

☐ IDENTIFY   FastForward pays $120 cash for supplies.

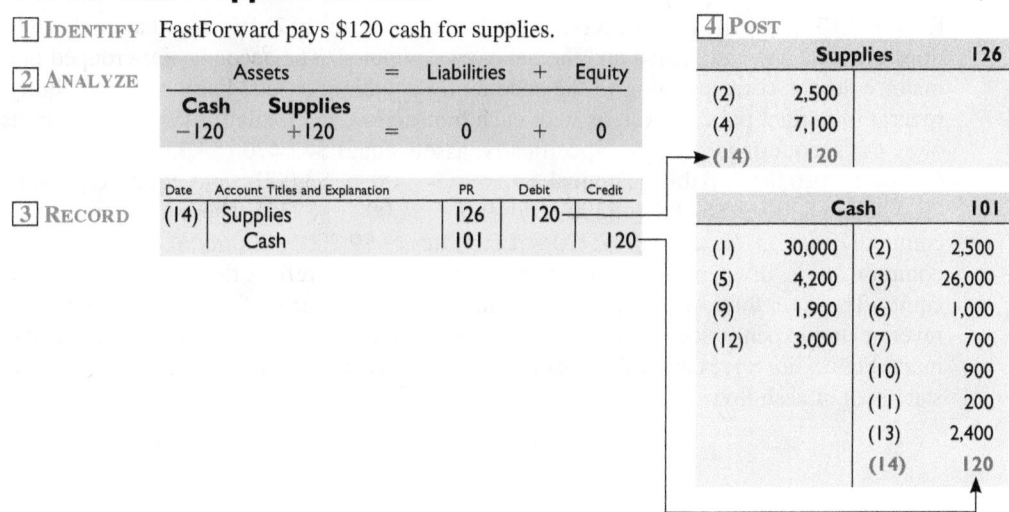

15. Payment of Expense in Cash

☐ IDENTIFY   FastForward pays $230 cash for December utilities expense.

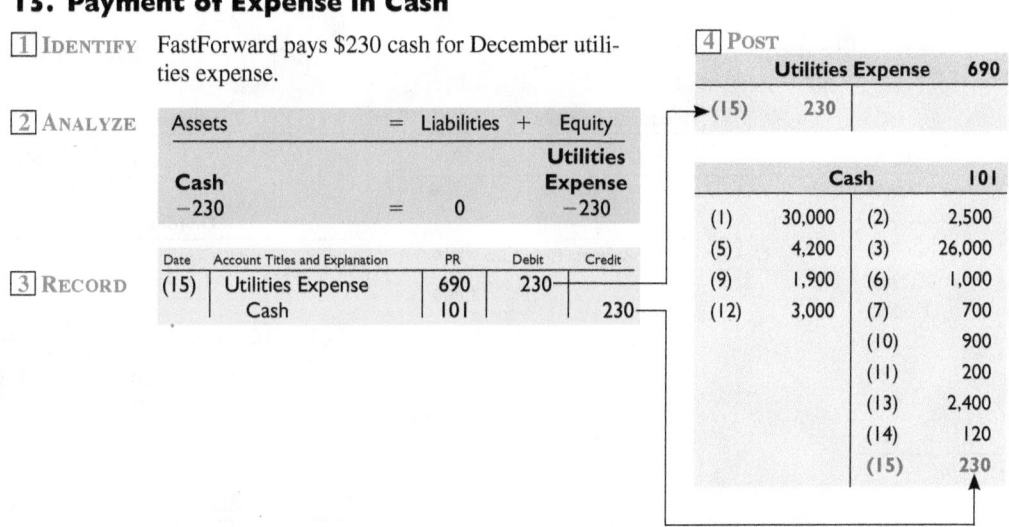

16. Payment of Expense in Cash

☐ IDENTIFY   FastForward pays $700 cash in employee salary for work performed in the latter part of December.

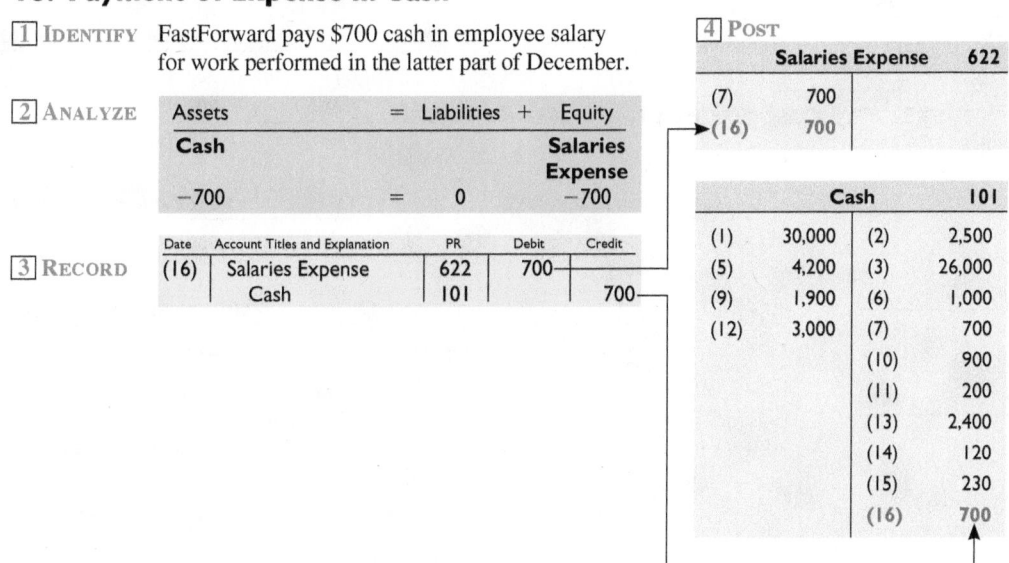

Point: We could merge transactions 15 and 16 into one *compound entry*.

Accounting Equation Analysis

Point: Technology does not provide the judgment required to analyze most business transactions. Analysis requires the expertise of skilled and ethical professionals.

Exhibit 2.13 shows the ledger accounts (in T-account form) of FastForward after all 16 transactions are recorded and posted and the balances computed. The accounts are grouped into three major columns corresponding to the accounting equation: assets, liabilities, and equity. Note several important points. First, as with each transaction, the totals for the three columns must obey the accounting equation. Specifically, assets equal $42,470 ($4,350 + $0 + $9,720 + $2,400 + $26,000); liabilities equal $9,200 ($6,200 + $3,000); and equity equals $33,270 ($30,000 − $200 + $5,800 + $300 − $1,400 − $1,000 − $230). These numbers prove the accounting equation: Assets of $42,470 = Liabilities of $9,200 + Equity of $33,270. Second, the common stock, dividends, revenue, and expense accounts reflect the transactions that change equity. The latter three account categories underlie the statement of retained earnings. Third, the revenue and expense account balances will be summarized and reported in the income statement. Fourth, increases and decreases in the cash account make up the elements reported in the statement of cash flows.

EXHIBIT 2.13

Ledger for FastForward (in T-Account Form)

General Ledger

Assets = **Liabilities** + **Equity**

Cash   101

(1)	30,000	(2)	2,500
(5)	4,200	(3)	26,000
(9)	1,900	(6)	1,000
(12)	3,000	(7)	700
		(10)	900
		(11)	200
		(13)	2,400
		(14)	120
		(15)	230
		(16)	700
Balance	4,350		

Accounts Receivable   106

(8)	1,900	(9)	1,900
Balance	0		

Supplies   126

(2)	2,500
(4)	7,100
(14)	120
Balance	9,720

Prepaid Insurance   128

(13)	2,400

Equipment   167

(3)	26,000

Accounts Payable   201

(10)	900	(4)	7,100
		Balance	6,200

Unearned Consulting Revenue   236

	(12)	3,000

Common Stock   307

	(1)	30,000

Dividends   319

(11)	200

Consulting Revenue   403

	(5)	4,200
	(8)	1,600
	Balance	5,800

Rental Revenue   406

	(8)	300

Salaries Expense   622

(7)	700
(16)	700
Balance	1,400

Rent Expense   640

(6)	1,000

Utilities Expense   690

(15)	230

Accounts in this white area reflect those reported on the income statement.

$42,470	=	$9,200	+	$33,270

Assume Tata began operations on January 1 and completed the following transactions during its first month of operations. For each transaction, (a) analyze the transaction using the accounting equation, (b) record the transaction in journal entry form, and (c) post the entry using T-accounts to represent ledger accounts. Tata has the following (partial) chart of accounts—account numbers in parenthesis: Cash (101); Accounts Receivable (106); Equipment (167); Accounts Payable (201); Common Stock (307); Dividends (319); Services Revenue (403); and Wages Expense (601).

NEED-TO-KNOW 2.3

P1   A1

Jan. 1 Ms Jamsetji invested $4,000 cash in the Tata company in exchange for its common stock.
    5 Tata Company purchased $2,000 of equipment on credit.
    14 Tata Company provided $540 of services for a client on credit.

Solution

Jan. 1 Receive investment by Owner

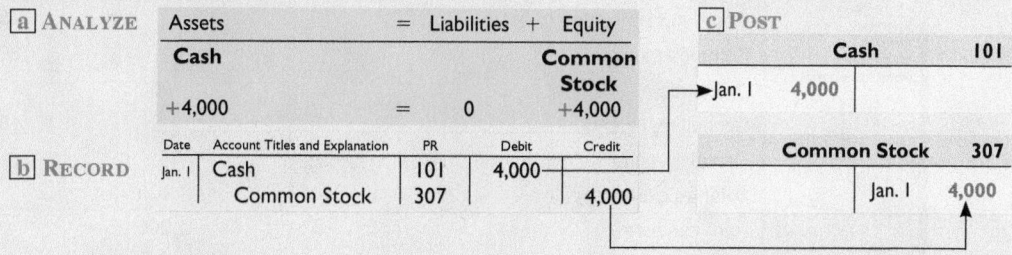

Jan. 5 Purchase Equipment on Credit

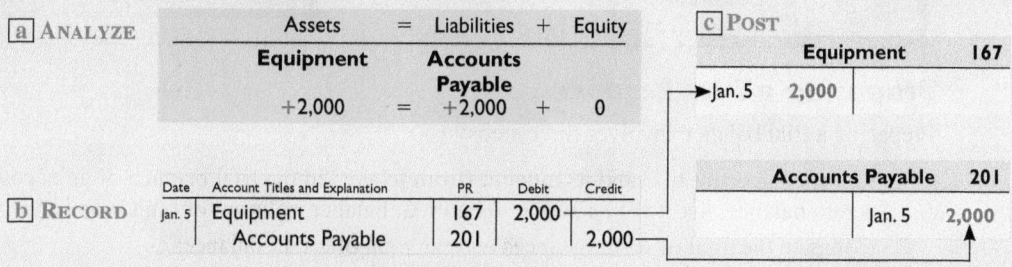

Jan. 14 Provide Services on Credit

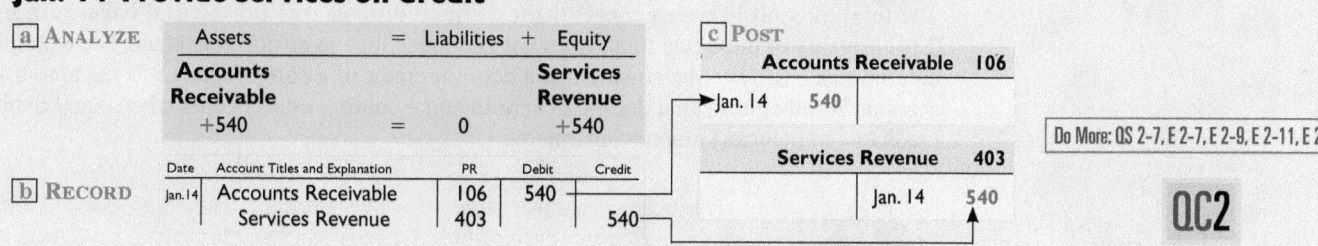

Do More: QS 2-7, E 2-7, E 2-9, E 2-11, E 2-12

QC2

TRIAL BALANCE

Double-entry accounting requires the sum of debit account balances to equal the sum of credit account balances. A trial balance is used to confirm this. A **trial balance** is a list of accounts and their balances at a point in time. Account balances are reported in their appropriate debit or credit columns of a trial balance. A trial balance can be used to confirm this and to follow up on any abnormal or unusual balances. Exhibit 2.14 shows the trial balance for FastForward after its 16 entries have been posted to the ledger. (This is an *unadjusted* trial balance—Chapter 3 explains the necessary adjustments.)

P2 Prepare and explain the use of a trial balance.

EXHIBIT 2.14

Trial Balance (Unadjusted)

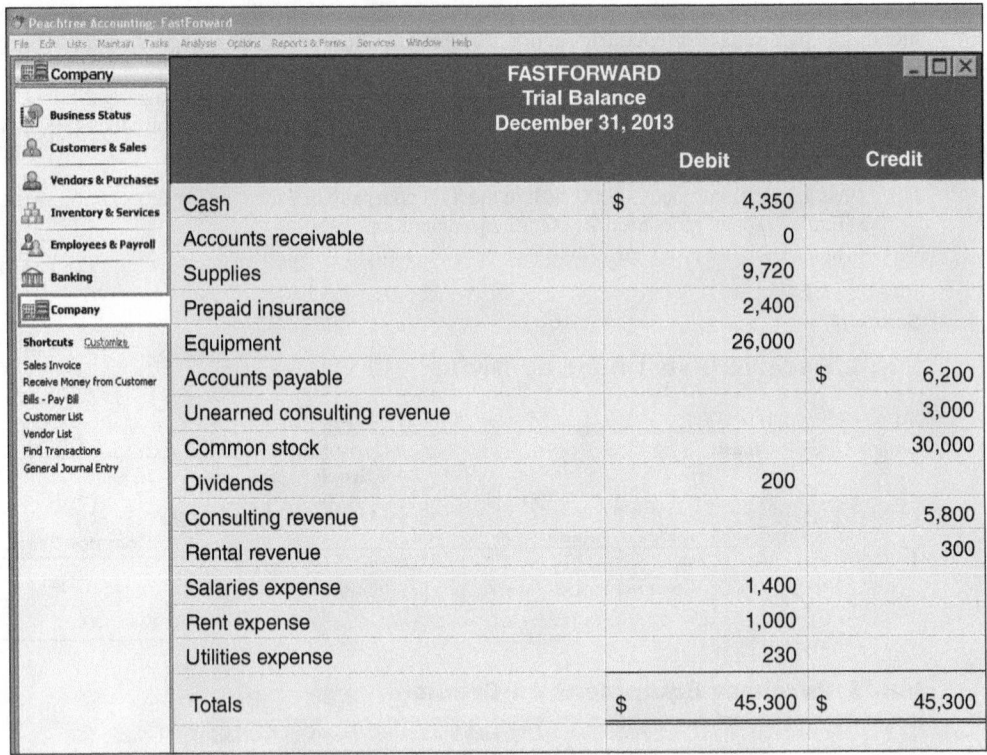

Point: The ordering of accounts in a trial balance follows their identification number from the chart of accounts, which is in the following order: asset, liability, equity, revenue, and expense accounts.

Preparing a Trial Balance

Preparing a trial balance involves three steps:

1. List each account title and its amount (from ledger) in the trial balance. If an account has a zero balance, list it with a zero in its normal balance column (or omit it entirely).
2. Compute the total of debit balances and the total of credit balances.
3. Verify (*prove*) total debit balances equal total credit balances.

The total of debit balances equals the total of credit balances for the trial balance in Exhibit 2.14. Equality of these two totals does not guarantee that no errors were made. For example, the column totals still will be equal when a debit or credit of a correct amount is made to a wrong account. Another error that does not cause unequal column totals occurs when equal debits and credits of an incorrect amount are entered.

> **Fraud**
>
> **Heavenly accounting.** Religious organizations are especially vulnerable to fraud. Due to "trust" among religious cohorts, the opportunity factor in the fraud triangle looms large for such entities. In many cases, the recording of transactions has few or no controls. For example, a mother and son team from Morristown, Tennessee, pleaded guilty to defrauding a local church. They had recorded nearly 2,000 checks to "cash," amounting to more than $1.5 million, which they cashed and pocketed. An independent review of transactions or a requirement for documentation would have reduced the opportunity factor.

Searching for and Correcting Errors   If the trial balance does not balance (when its columns are not equal), the error (or errors) must be found and corrected. An efficient way to search for an error is to check the journalizing, posting, and trial balance preparation in *reverse order.* Step 1 is to verify that the trial balance columns are correctly added. If step 1 fails to find the error, step 2 is to verify that account balances are accurately entered from the ledger. Step 3 is to see whether a debit (or credit) balance is mistakenly listed in the trial balance as a credit (or debit). A clue to this error is when the difference between total debits

Point: A trial balance is *not* a financial statement but a mechanism for checking equality of debits and credits in the ledger. Financial statements do not have debit and credit columns.

and total credits equals twice the amount of the incorrect account balance. If the error is still undiscovered, Step 4 is to recompute each account balance in the ledger. Step 5 is to verify that each journal entry is properly posted. Step 6 is to verify that the original journal entry has equal debits and credits. At this point, the errors should be uncovered.[3]

If an error in a journal entry is discovered before the error is posted, it can be corrected in a manual system by drawing a line through the incorrect information. The correct information is written above it to create a record of change for the auditor. Many computerized systems allow the operator to replace the incorrect information directly.

If an error in a journal entry is not discovered until after it is posted, we do not strike through both erroneous entries in the journal and ledger. Instead, we correct this error by creating a *correcting entry* that removes the amount from the wrong account and records it to the correct account. As an example, suppose a $100 purchase of supplies is journalized with an incorrect debit to Equipment, and then this incorrect entry is posted to the ledger. The Supplies ledger account balance is understated by $100, and the Equipment ledger account balance is overstated by $100. The correcting entry is: debit Supplies and credit Equipment (both for $100).

Using a Trial Balance to Prepare Financial Statements

This section shows how to prepare *financial statements* from the trial balance in Exhibit 2.14 and from information on the December transactions of FastForward. These statements differ from those in Chapter 1 because of several additional transactions. These statements are also more precisely called *unadjusted statements* because we need to make some further accounting adjustments (described in Chapter 3).

How financial statements are linked in time is illustrated in Exhibit 2.15. A balance sheet reports on an organization's financial position at a *point in time*. The income statement, statement of retained earnings, and statement of cash flows report on financial performance over a *period of time*. The three statements in the middle column of Exhibit 2.15 link balance sheets from the beginning to the end of a reporting period. They explain how financial position changes from one point to another.

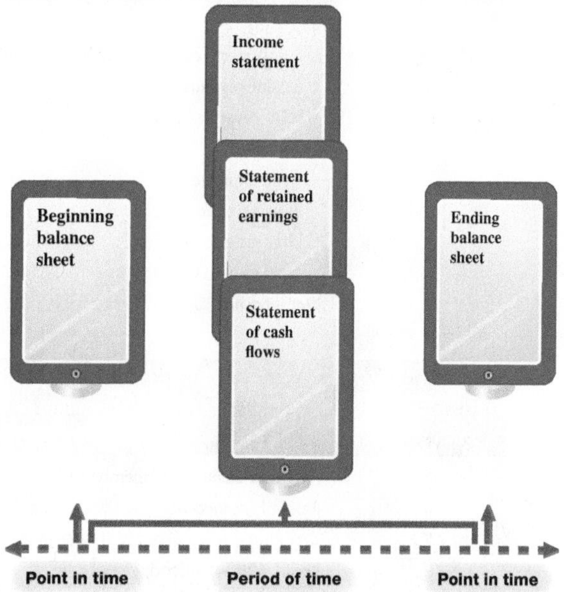

Preparers and users (including regulatory agencies) determine the length of the reporting period. A one-year, or annual, reporting period is common, as are semi-annual, quarterly, and monthly periods. The one-year reporting period is known as the *accounting,* or *fiscal, year.*

EXHIBIT 2.15

Links between Financial Statements across Time

| P3 | Prepare financial statements from business transactions. |

Businesses whose accounting year begins on January 1 and ends on December 31 are known as *calendar-year* companies. Google is a calendar-year company. Many companies choose a fiscal year ending on a date other than December 31. Apple is a *noncalendar-year* company as reflected in the headings of its September 29 year-end financial statements in Appendix A near the end of the book.

[3] *Transposition* occurs when two digits are switched, or transposed, within a number. If transposition is the only error, it yields a difference between the two trial balance totals that is evenly divisible by 9. For example, assume that a $691 debit in an entry is incorrectly posted to the ledger as $619. Total credits in the trial balance are then larger than total debits by $72 ($691 − $619). The $72 error is *evenly* divisible by 9 (72/9 = 8). The first digit of the quotient (in our example it is 8) equals the difference between the digits of the two transposed numbers (the 9 and the 1). The number of digits in the quotient also tells the location of the transposition, starting from the right. The quotient in our example had only one digit (8), so it tells us the transposition is in the first digit. Consider another example where a transposition error involves posting $961 instead of the correct $691. The difference in these numbers is $270, and its quotient is 30 (270/9). The quotient has two digits, so it tells us to check the second digit from the right for a transposition of two numbers that have a difference of 3.

Sidebar:

Example: If a credit to Unearned Revenue was incorrectly posted from the journal as a credit to the Revenue ledger account, would the ledger still balance? Would the financial statements be correct? *Answers:* The ledger would balance, but liabilities would be understated, equity would be overstated, and income would be overstated (all because of overstated revenues).

Point: The IRS requires companies to keep records that can be audited.

Point: A statement's heading lists the 3 W's: **W**ho—name of organization, **W**hat—name of statement, **W**hen—statement's point in time or period of time.

Income Statement   An income statement reports the revenues earned less the expenses incurred by a business over a period of time. FastForward's income statement for December is shown at the top of Exhibit 2.16. Information about revenues and expenses is conveniently taken from the trial balance in Exhibit 2.14. Net income of $3,470 is reported at the bottom of the statement. Owner investments and dividends are *not* part of income.

Statement of Retained Earnings   The statement of retained earnings reports informa-tion about how retained earnings change over the reporting period. FastForward's statement of retained earnings is the second report in Exhibit 2.16. It shows the $3,470 of net income, the $200 dividend, and the $3,270 end-of-period balance. (The beginning balance in the statement of retained earnings is rarely zero; an exception is for the first period of operations. The begin-ning balance in January 2014 is $3,270, which is December's ending balance.)

Balance Sheet   The balance sheet reports the financial position of a company at a point in time, usually at the end of a month, quarter, or year. FastForward's balance sheet is the third report in Exhibit 2.16. This statement refers to financial condition at the close of business on December 31. The left side of the balance sheet lists its assets: cash, supplies, prepaid insurance, and equipment. The upper right side of the balance sheet shows that it owes $6,200 to creditors and $3,000 in ser-vices to customers who paid in advance. The equity section shows an ending balance of $33,270. Note the link between the ending balance of the statement of retained earnings and the retained

Point: An income statement is also called an *earnings statement, a statement of operations,* or a *P&L* (profit and loss) *statement.* A balance sheet is also called a *statement of financial position.*

EXHIBIT 2.16

Financial Statements and Their Links

Point: Arrow lines show how the statements are linked.

FASTFORWARD
Income Statement
For Month Ended December 31, 2013

Revenues		
Consulting revenue ($4,200 + $1,600)	$ 5,800	
Rental revenue	300	
Total revenues		$ 6,100
Expenses		
Rent expense	1,000	
Salaries expense	1,400	
Utilities expense	230	
Total expenses		2,630
Net income		$ 3,470

FASTFORWARD
Statement of Retained Earnings
For Month Ended December 31, 2013

Retained earnings, December 1, 2013		$ 0
Plus: Net income		3,470
		3,470
Less: Cash dividends........................		200
Retained earnings, December 31, 2013		$ 3,270

FASTFORWARD
Balance Sheet
December 31, 2013

Assets		Liabilities	
Cash	$ 4,350	Accounts payable	$ 6,200
Supplies	9,720	Unearned revenue	3,000
Prepaid insurance ..	2,400	Total liabilities	9,200
Equipment	26,000	**Equity**	
		Common stock	30,000
		Retained earnings	3,270
		Total equity	33,270
Total assets	$42,470	Total liabilities and equity ..	$42,470

Point: To *foot* a column of numbers is to add them.

earnings balance. (Recall that this presentation of the balance sheet is called the *account form:* assets on the left and liabilities and equity on the right. Another presentation is the *report form:* assets on top, followed by liabilities and then equity. Either presentation is acceptable.)

■ Decision Maker

Entrepreneur   You open a wholesale business selling entertainment equipment to retail outlets. You find that most of your customers demand to buy on credit. How can you use the balance sheets of these customers to decide which ones to extend credit to? ■   [Answer—p. 81]

Presentation Issues   Dollar signs are not used in journals and ledgers. They do appear in financial statements and other reports such as trial balances. The usual practice is to put dollar signs beside only the first and last numbers in a column. Apple's financial statements in Appendix A show this. When amounts are entered in a journal, ledger, or trial balance, commas are optional to indicate thousands, millions, and so forth. However, commas are always used in financial statements. Companies also commonly round amounts in reports to the nearest dollar, or even to a higher level. Apple is typical of many companies in that it rounds its financial statement amounts to the nearest million. This decision is based on the perceived impact of rounding for users' business decisions.

Reading and Using an Annual Report   An *annual report* is required of more than 10,000 corporations in the United States that trade their stock *publicly*. This requirement is imposed by the SEC. Another nearly 5 million corporations in the United States do not trade their shares publicly and are called *private* or *closely held* corporations, which are not subject to SEC oversight. Appendix A, near the end of this book, shows key excerpts from the annual report of Apple. This appendix also reproduces financial statements from the annual reports of Google and Samsung. The key excerpts are identified and explained on Page A-1. We review and use the annual report for many business decisions, especially for valuing corporate stock.

Point: While revenues increase equity, and expenses decrease equity, the amounts are not reported in detail in the statement of retained earnings. Instead, their effects are reflected through net income.

Point: Knowing how financial statements are prepared improves our analysis of them.

off the mark.com   by Mark Parisi
offthemark.com

HE CONTINUED ACCOUNTING RIGHT THROUGH HIS COFFEE BREAK...THEN HIS LUNCH BREAK. CLEARLY, MYRON WAS "IN THE ZONE."

Prepare a trial balance for Apple using the following condensed data from its fiscal year ended September 29, 2012.

NEED-TO-KNOW 2.4

P2

Common stock	$ 16,422	Tax expense	$ 14,030
Accounts payable	21,175	Investments and other assets	138,936
Other liabilities	37,178	Land and equipment	15,452
Cost of sales (expense)	87,846	Selling and other expense	12,899
Cash	10,746	Accounts receivable	10,930
Revenues	156,508	Retained earnings	62,841
Dividends	3,285		

Solution

APPLE Trial Balance September 29, 2012		
	Debit	**Credit**
Cash	$ 10,746	
Accounts receivable	10,930	
Land and equipment	15,452	
Investments and other assets	138,936	
Accounts payable		$ 21,175
Other liabilities		37,178
Common stock		16,422
Retained earnings		62,841
Dividends	3,285	
Revenues		156,508
Cost of sales	87,846	
Selling and other expense	12,899	
Tax expense	14,030	
Totals	$294,124	$294,124

Do More: E 2-8, E 2-10

QC3

GLOBAL VIEW

Financial accounting according to U.S. GAAP is similar, but not identical, to IFRS. This section discusses differences in analyzing and recording transactions, and with the preparation of financial statements.

Analyzing and Recording Transactions   Both U.S. GAAP and IFRS include broad and similar guidance for financial accounting. As the FASB and IASB work toward a common conceptual framework over the next few years, even those differences will fade. Further, both U.S. GAAP and IFRS apply transaction analysis and recording as shown in this chapter—using the same debit and credit system and accrual accounting. Although some variations exist in revenue and expense recognition and other accounting principles, all of the transactions in this chapter are accounted for identically under these two systems.

Financial Statements   Both U.S. GAAP and IFRS prepare the same four basic financial statements. A few differences within each statement do exist and we will discuss those throughout the book. For example, both U.S. GAAP and IFRS require balance sheets to separate current items from noncurrent items. However, while U.S. GAAP balance sheets report current items first, IFRS balance sheets normally (but are not required to) present noncurrent items first, and equity before liabilities. To illustrate, a condensed version of Samsung's balance sheet follows (numbers using Korean won in millions).

Samsung

SAMSUNG Balance Sheet (in millions of Korean won) December 31, 2012			
Assets		**Equity and Liabilities**	
Current assets	₩ 87,269,017	Current liabilities	₩ 46,933,052
Noncurrent assets	93,802,553	Noncurrent liabilities	12,658,312
		Total equity	121,480,206
Total assets	₩181,071,570	Total equity and liabilities	₩181,071,570

Accounting Controls and Assurance   Accounting systems depend on control procedures that assure the proper principles were applied in processing accounting information. The passage of SOX legislation strengthened U.S. control procedures in recent years. However, global standards for control are diverse and so are enforcement activities. Consequently, while global accounting standards are converging, their application in different countries can yield different outcomes depending on the quality of their auditing standards and enforcement.

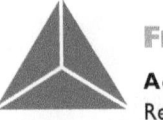

Fraud

Accounting Control   Recording valid transactions, and not recording fraudulent transactions, enhances the quality of financial statements. The graph here shows the percentage of employees in information technology that report observing specific types of misconduct within the past year [Source: KPMG 2009].

An important business objective is gathering information to help assess a company's risk of failing to pay its debts. Companies finance their assets with either liabilities or equity. A company that finances a relatively large portion of its assets with liabilities is said to have a high degree of *financial leverage*. Higher financial leverage involves greater risk because liabilities must be repaid and often require regular interest payments (equity financing does not). The risk that a company might not be able to meet such required payments is higher if it has more liabilities (is more highly leveraged). One way to assess the risk associated with a company's use of liabilities is to compute the **debt ratio** as in Exhibit 2.17.

A2 Compute the debt ratio and describe its use in analyzing financial condition.

$$\text{Debt ratio} = \frac{\text{Total liabilities}}{\text{Total assets}}$$

To see how to apply the debt ratio, let's look at Skechers's liabilities and assets. The company designs, markets, and sells footwear for men, women, and children under the Skechers brand. Exhibit 2.18 computes and reports its debt ratio at the end of each year from 2006 to 2011.

EXHIBIT 2.17

Debt Ratio

Point: Compare the equity amount to the liability amount to assess the extent of owner versus nonowner financing.

EXHIBIT 2.18

Computation and Analysis of Debt Ratio

$ in millions	2011	2010	2009	2008	2007	2006
Total liabilities	$ 389	$ 359	$246	$204	$201	$288
Total assets	$1,282	$1,305	$996	$876	$828	$737
Debt ratio	0.30	0.28	0.25	0.23	0.24	0.39
Industry debt ratio	0.47	0.49	0.51	0.50	0.46	0.48

Skechers's debt ratio ranges from a low of 0.23 to a high of 0.39—also, see graph in margin. Its ratio is lower, compared with the industry ratio. This analysis implies a low risk from its financial leverage. Is financial leverage good or bad for Skechers? To answer that question we need to compare the company's return on the borrowed money to the rate it is paying creditors. If the company's return is higher, it is successfully borrowing money to make more money. A company's success with making money from borrowed money can quickly turn unprofitable if its own return drops below the rate it is paying creditors.

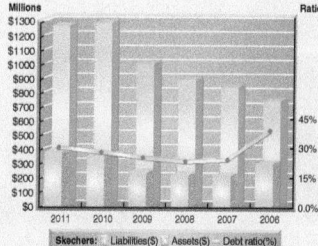

◼ **Decision Maker** ━━━━━━━━━━━━━━━━━━━━━━━◗

Investor You consider buying stock in Converse. As part of your analysis, you compute its debt ratio for 2011, 2012, and 2013 as: 0.35, 0.74, and 0.94, respectively. Based on the debt ratio, is Converse a low-risk investment? Has the risk of buying Converse stock changed over this period? (The industry debt ratio averages 0.40.) ◼ [Answer—p. 81]

(This problem extends the **COMPREHENSIVE NEED-TO-KNOW** problem of Chapter 1.) After several months of planning, Jasmine Worthy started a haircutting business called Expressions. The following events occurred during its first month.

COMPREHENSIVE...

NEED-TO-KNOW

a. On August 1, Worthy invested $3,000 cash and $15,000 of equipment in Expressions in exchange for common stock.

b. On August 2, Expressions paid $600 cash for furniture for the shop.

c. On August 3, Expressions paid $500 cash to rent space in a strip mall for August.

d. On August 4, it purchased $1,200 of equipment on credit for the shop (using a long-term note payable).

e. On August 5, Expressions opened for business. Cash received from haircutting services in the first week and a half of business (ended August 15) was $825.

f. On August 15, it provided $100 of haircutting services on account.

g. On August 17, it received a $100 check for services previously rendered on account.

h. On August 17, it paid $125 to an assistant for hours worked during the grand opening.

i. Cash received from services provided during the second half of August was $930.

j. On August 31, it paid a $400 installment toward principal on the note payable entered into on August 4.

k. On August 31, it paid $900 cash in dividends to Worthy (sole shareholder).

Required

1. Open the following ledger accounts in balance column format (account numbers are in parentheses): Cash (101); Accounts Receivable (102); Furniture (161); Store Equipment (165); Note Payable (240); Common Stock (307); Dividends (319); Haircutting Services Revenue (403); Wages Expense (623); and Rent Expense (640). Prepare general journal entries for the transactions.

2. Post the journal entries from (1) to the ledger accounts.

3. Prepare a trial balance as of August 31.

4. Prepare an income statement for August.

5. Prepare a statement of retained earnings for August.

6. Prepare a balance sheet as of August 31.

7. Determine the debt ratio as of August 31.

Extended Analysis

8. In the coming months, Expressions will experience a greater variety of business transactions. Identify which accounts are debited and which are credited for the following transactions. (*Hint:* We must use some accounts not opened in part 1.)

    a. Purchase supplies with cash.

    b. Pay cash for future insurance coverage.

    c. Receive cash for services to be provided in the future.

    d. Purchase supplies on account.

PLANNING THE SOLUTION

- Analyze each transaction and use the debit and credit rules to prepare a journal entry for each.
- Post each debit and each credit from journal entries to their ledger accounts and cross-reference each amount in the posting reference (PR) columns of the journal and ledger.
- Calculate each account balance and list the accounts with their balances on a trial balance.
- Verify that total debits in the trial balance equal total credits.
- To prepare the income statement, identify revenues and expenses. List those items on the statement, compute the difference, and label the result as *net income* or *net loss*.
- Use information in the ledger to prepare the statement of retained earnings.
- Use information in the ledger to prepare the balance sheet.
- Calculate the debt ratio by dividing total liabilities by total assets.
- Analyze the future transactions to identify the accounts affected and apply debit and credit rules.

SOLUTION TO COMPREHENSIVE NEED-TO-KNOW

1. General journal entries:

					Page 1
Date	Account Titles and Explanation	PR	Debit	Credit
Aug. 1	Cash	101	3,000	
	Store Equipment	165	15,000	
	Common Stock	307		18,000
	Owner's investment for stock.			
2	Furniture	161	600	
	Cash	101		600
	Purchased furniture for cash.			
3	Rent Expense	640	500	
	Cash	101		500
	Paid rent for August.			
4	Store Equipment	165	1,200	
	Note Payable	240		1,200
	Purchased additional equipment on credit.			

[continued on next page]

[continued from previous page]

15	Cash	101	825	
	Haircutting Services Revenue	403		825
	Cash receipts from first half of August.			
15	Accounts Receivable	102	100	
	Haircutting Services Revenue	403		100
	To record revenue for services provided on account.			
17	Cash	101	100	
	Accounts Receivable	102		100
	To record cash received as payment on account.			
17	Wages Expense	623	125	
	Cash	101		125
	Paid wages to assistant.			
31	Cash	101	930	
	Haircutting Services Revenue	403		930
	Cash receipts from second half of August.			
31	Note Payable	240	400	
	Cash	101		400
	Paid an installment on the note payable.			
31	Dividends	319	900	
	Cash	101		900
	Paid cash dividend.			

2. Post journal entries from part 1 to the ledger accounts:

General Ledger

Cash   **Account No. 101**

Date	PR	Debit	Credit	Balance
Aug. 1	G1	3,000		3,000
2	G1		600	2,400
3	G1		500	1,900
15	G1	825		2,725
17	G1	100		2,825
17	G1		125	2,700
31	G1	930		3,630
31	G1		400	3,230
31	G1		900	2,330

Accounts Receivable   **Account No. 102**

Date	PR	Debit	Credit	Balance
Aug. 15	G1	100		100
17	G1		100	0

Furniture   **Account No. 161**

Date	PR	Debit	Credit	Balance
Aug. 2	G1	600		600

Store Equipment   **Account No. 165**

Date	PR	Debit	Credit	Balance
Aug. 1	G1	15,000		15,000
4	G1	1,200		16,200

Note Payable   **Account No. 240**

Date	PR	Debit	Credit	Balance
Aug. 4	G1		1,200	1,200
31	G1	400		800

Common Stock   **Account No. 307**

Date	PR	Debit	Credit	Balance
Aug. 1	G1		18,000	18,000

Dividends   **Account No. 319**

Date	PR	Debit	Credit	Balance
Aug. 31	G1	900		900

Haircutting Services Revenue   **Account No. 403**

Date	PR	Debit	Credit	Balance
Aug. 15	G1		825	825
15	G1		100	925
31	G1		930	1,855

Wages Expense   **Account No. 623**

Date	PR	Debit	Credit	Balance
Aug. 17	G1	125		125

Rent Expense   **Account No. 640**

Date	PR	Debit	Credit	Balance
Aug. 3	G1	500		500

3. Prepare a trial balance from the ledger:

EXPRESSIONS Trial Balance August 31		
	Debit	**Credit**
Cash	$ 2,330	
Accounts receivable	0	
Furniture	600	
Store equipment	16,200	
Note payable		$ 800
Common stock....................		18,000
Dividends	900	
Haircutting services revenue		1,855
Wages expense	125	
Rent expense	500	
Totals	$20,655	$20,655

4.

EXPRESSIONS Income Statement For Month Ended August 31		
Revenues		
Haircutting services revenue		$1,855
Operating expenses		
Rent expense	$500	
Wages expense	125	
Total operating expenses		625
Net income		$1,230

5.

EXPRESSIONS Statement of Retained Earnings For Month Ended August 31	
Retained earnings, August 1	$ 0
Plus: Net income	1,230
	1,230
Less: Cash dividends	900
Retained earnings, August 31	$ 330

6.

EXPRESSIONS Balance Sheet August 31			
Assets		**Liabilities**	
Cash	$ 2,330	Note payable	$ 800
Furniture	600	**Equity**	
Store equipment	16,200	Common stock.................	18,000
		Retained earnings	330
		Total equity	18,330
Total assets	$19,130	Total liabilities and equity	$19,130

7. Debt ratio $= \dfrac{\text{Total liabilities}}{\text{Total assets}} = \dfrac{\$800}{\$19{,}130} = \underline{\underline{4.18\%}}$

8a. Supplies *debited*
    Cash *credited*

8b. Prepaid Insurance *debited*
    Cash *credited*

8c. Cash *debited*
    Unearned Services Revenue *credited*

8d. Supplies *debited*
    Accounts Payable *credited*

Summary

C1 Explain the steps in processing transactions and the role of source documents. The accounting process identifies business transactions and events, analyzes and records their effects, and summarizes and prepares information useful in making decisions. Transactions and events are the starting points in the accounting process. Source documents identify and describe transactions and events. Examples are sales tickets, checks, purchase orders, bills, and bank statements. Source documents provide objective and reliable evidence, making information more useful. The effects of transactions and events are recorded in journals. Posting along with a trial balance helps summarize and classify these effects.

C2 Describe an account and its use in recording transactions. An account is a detailed record of increases and decreases in a specific asset, liability, equity, revenue, or expense. Information from accounts is analyzed, summarized, and presented in reports and financial statements for decision makers.

C3 Describe a ledger and a chart of accounts. The ledger (or general ledger) is a record containing all accounts used by a company and their balances. It is referred to as the *books*. The chart of accounts is a list of all accounts and usually includes an identification number assigned to each account.

C4 Define *debits* and *credits* and explain double-entry accounting. *Debit* refers to left, and *credit* refers to right. Debits increase assets, expenses, and dividends while credits decrease them. Credits increase liabilities, common stock, and revenues; debits decrease them. Double-entry accounting means each transaction affects at least two accounts and has at least one debit and one credit. The system for recording debits and credits follows from the accounting equation. The left side of an account is the normal balance for assets, dividends, and expenses, and the right side is the normal balance for liabilities, common stock, and revenues.

A1 Analyze the impact of transactions on accounts and financial statements. We analyze transactions using concepts of double-entry accounting. This analysis is performed by determining a transaction's effects on accounts. These effects are recorded in journals and posted to ledgers.

A2 Compute the debt ratio and describe its use in analyzing financial condition. A company's debt ratio is computed as total liabilities divided by total assets. It reveals how much of the assets are financed by creditor (nonowner) financing. The higher this ratio, the more risk a company faces because liabilities must be repaid at specific dates.

P1 Record transactions in a journal and post entries to a ledger. Transactions are recorded in a journal. Each entry in a journal is posted to the accounts in the ledger. This provides information that is used to produce financial statements. Balance column accounts are widely used and include columns for debits, credits, and the account balance.

P2 Prepare and explain the use of a trial balance. A trial balance is a list of accounts from the ledger showing their debit or credit balances in separate columns. The trial balance is a summary of the ledger's contents and is useful in preparing financial statements and in revealing recordkeeping errors.

P3 Prepare financial statements from business transactions. The balance sheet, the statement of retained earnings, the income statement, and the statement of cash flows use data from the trial balance (and other financial statements) for their preparation.

Guidance Answers to Decision Maker **and** Decision Ethics

Cashier The advantages to the process proposed by the assistant manager include improved customer service, fewer delays, and less work for you. However, you should have serious concerns about internal control and the potential for fraud. In particular, the assistant manager could steal cash and simply enter fewer sales to match the remaining cash. You should reject her suggestion without the manager's approval. Moreover, you should have an ethical concern about the assistant manager's suggestion to ignore store policy.

Entrepreneur We can use the accounting equation (Assets = Liabilities + Equity) to help us identify risky customers to whom we would likely not want to extend credit. A balance sheet provides amounts for each of these key components. The lower a customer's equity is relative to liabilities, the less likely you would extend credit. A low equity means the business has little value that does not already have creditor claims to it.

Investor The debt ratio suggests the stock of Converse is of higher risk than normal and that this risk is rising. The average industry ratio of 0.40 further supports this conclusion. The 2013 debt ratio for Converse is twice the industry norm. Also, a debt ratio approaching 1.0 indicates little to no equity.

Key Terms

Account (p. 57)
Account balance, or Balance (p. 61)
Balance column account (p. 64)
Chart of accounts (p. 60)
Common stock (p. 59)
Compound journal entry (p. 67)
Credit (p. 61)
Creditors (p. 58)

Debit (p. 61)
Debt ratio (p. 77)
Dividends (p. 59)
Double-entry accounting (p. 61)
General journal (p. 63)
General ledger (p. 57)
Journal (p. 63)
Journalizing (p. 63)

Posting (p. 63)
Posting reference (PR) column (p. 74)
Source documents (p. 56)
T-accounts (p. 61)
Trial balance (p. 71)
Unearned revenue (p. 59)

Multiple Choice Quiz   Answers on p. 99   mhhe.com/wildFA7e

Additional Quiz Questions are available at the book's Website.

1. Amalia Company received its utility bill for the current period of $700 and immediately paid it. Its journal entry to record this transaction includes a
   a. Credit to Utility Expense for $700.
   b. Debit to Utility Expense for $700.
   c. Debit to Accounts Payable for $700.
   d. Debit to Cash for $700.
   e. Credit to Common Stock for $700.

2. On May 1, Mattingly Lawn Service collected $2,500 cash from a customer in advance of five months of lawn service. Mattingly's journal entry to record this transaction includes a
   a. Credit to Unearned Lawn Service Fees for $2,500.
   b. Debit to Lawn Service Fees Earned for $2,500.
   c. Credit to Cash for $2,500.
   d. Debit to Unearned Lawn Service Fees for $2,500.
   e. Credit to Common Stock for $2,500.

3. Liang Shue contributed $250,000 cash and land worth $500,000 to open his new business, Shue Consulting Corporation. Which of the following journal entries does Shue Consulting make to record this transaction?
   a. Cash Assets 750,000
       Common Stock   750,000
   b. Common Stock 750,000
       Assets   750,000
   c. Cash 250,000
       Land 500,000
         Common Stock   750,000

   d. Common Stock 750,000
       Cash   250,000
       Land   500,000

4. A trial balance prepared at year-end shows total credits exceed total debits by $765. This discrepancy could have been caused by
   a. An error in the general journal where a $765 increase in Accounts Payable was recorded as a $765 decrease in Accounts Payable.
   b. The ledger balance for Accounts Payable of $7,650 being entered in the trial balance as $765.
   c. A general journal error where a $765 increase in Accounts Receivable was recorded as a $765 increase in Cash.
   d. The ledger balance of $850 in Accounts Receivable was entered in the trial balance as $85.
   e. An error in recording a $765 increase in Cash as a credit.

5. Bonaventure Company has total assets of $1,000,000, liabilities of $400,000, and equity of $600,000. What is its debt ratio (rounded to a whole percent)?
   a. 250%
   b. 167%
   c. 67%
   d. 150%
   e. 40%

🔃 Icon denotes assignments that involve decision making.

Discussion Questions

1. Provide the names of two (*a*) asset accounts, (*b*) liability accounts, and (*c*) equity accounts.

2. What is the difference between a note payable and an account payable?

3. 🔃 Discuss the steps in processing business transactions.

4. What kinds of transactions can be recorded in a general journal?

5. Are debits or credits typically listed first in general journal entries? Are the debits or the credits indented?

6. Should a transaction be recorded first in a journal or the ledger? Why?

7. If assets are valuable resources and asset accounts have debit balances, why do expense accounts also have debit balances?

8. Why does the recordkeeper prepare a trial balance?

9. If an incorrect amount is journalized and posted to the accounts, how should the error be corrected?

10. Identify the four financial statements of a business.

11. What information is reported in a balance sheet?

12. What information is reported in an income statement?

13. Why does the user of an income statement need to know the time period that it covers?

14. Define (*a*) *assets,* (*b*) *liabilities,* (*c*) *equity,* and (*d*) *net assets.*

15. Which financial statement is sometimes called the *statement of financial position?*

16. Review the Apple balance sheet in Appendix A. Identify three accounts on its balance sheet **APPLE** that carry debit balances and three accounts on its balance sheet that carry credit balances.

17. Review the Google balance sheet in Appendix A. Identify an asset with the word *receivable* in its account title and a liability with the word *payable* in its account title. **GOOGLE**

18. Review the Samsung balance sheet in Appendix A. Identify three current liabilities and three noncurrent liabilities in its balance sheet. **Samsung**

19. Review the Google balance sheet in Appendix A. Compute its current ratio, debt ratio, profit margin, and price-to-earnings. **GOOGLE**

⊞ connect

Identify the items from the following list that are likely to serve as source documents.

a. Sales ticket   **d.** Telephone bill   **g.** Balance sheet
b. Income statement   **e.** Invoice from supplier **h.** Prepaid insurance
c. Trial balance   **f.** Company revenue account **i.** Bank statement

QUICK STUDY

QS 2-1
Identifying source documents
C1

Classify each of the following accounts as an asset (A), liability (L), or equity (EQ) account.

a. Office equipment   **d.** Prepaid insurance   **g.** Cash
b. Dividends   **e.** Office supplies   **h.** Unearned rent revenue
c. Retained earnings   **f.** Prepaid rent   **i.** Accounts payable

QS 2-2
Identifying financial statement accounts
C2

A chart of accounts is a list of all ledger accounts and an identification number for each. One example of a chart of accounts is near the end of the book on pages CA-1 and CA-2. Using that chart, identify the following accounts as either an asset (A), liability (L), equity (EQ), revenue (R) or expense (E) account, along with its identification number.

a. Advertising expense   **d.** Patents   **g.** Notes payable
b. Rent revenue   **e.** Rent payable   **h.** Retained earnings
c. Rent receivable   **f.** Furniture   **i.** Utilities expense

QS 2-3
Reading a chart of accounts
C3

Identify the normal balance (debit or credit) for each of the following accounts.

a. Office Supplies   **d.** Wages Expense   **g.** Wages Payable
b. Dividends   **e.** Accounts Receivable **h.** Building
c. Fees Earned   **f.** Prepaid Rent   **i.** Common Stock

QS 2-4
Identifying normal balance
C4

Indicate whether a debit or credit *decreases* the normal balance of each of the following accounts.

a. Service Revenue   **e.** Common Stock   **i.** Dividends
b. Interest Payable   **f.** Prepaid Insurance **j.** Unearned Revenue
c. Accounts Receivable   **g.** Buildings   **k.** Accounts Payable
d. Salaries Expense   **h.** Interest Revenue   **l.** Land

QS 2-5
Linking debit or credit with normal balance
C4

Identify whether a debit or credit yields the indicated change for each of the following accounts.

a. To increase Land   **f.** To decrease Prepaid Rent
b. To decrease Cash   **g.** To increase Notes Payable
c. To increase Office Expense **h.** To decrease Accounts Receivable
d. To increase Fees Earned   **i.** To increase Common Stock
e. To decrease Unearned Revenue **j.** To increase Store Equipment

QS 2-6
Analyzing debit or credit by account
A1

QS 2-7

Analyzing transactions and preparing journal entries

P1

For each transaction, (1) analyze the transaction using the accounting equation, (2) record the transaction in journal entry form, and (3) post the entry using T-accounts to represent ledger accounts. Use the following (partial) chart of accounts—account numbers in parenthesis: Cash (101); Accounts Receivable (106); Office Supplies (124); Trucks (153); Equipment (167); Accounts Payable (201); Unearned Landscaping Revenue (236); Common Stock (307); Retained Earnings (318); Landscaping Revenue (403); Wages Expense (601), and Landscaping Expense (696).

a. On May 15, DeShawn Tyler opens a landscaping company called Elegant Lawns by investing $70,000 in Cash along with equipment having a $30,000 value in exchange for common stock.

b. On May 21, Elegant Lawns purchases office supplies on credit for $280.

c. On May 25, Elegant Lawns receives $7,800 cash for performing landscaping services.

d. On May 30, Elegant Lawns receives $1,000 cash in advance of providing landscaping services to a customer.

QS 2-8

Identifying a posting error

P2

A trial balance has total debits of $20,000 and total credits of $24,500. Which one of the following errors would create this imbalance? Explain.

a. A $2,250 debit to Utilities Expense in a journal entry is incorrectly posted to the ledger as a $2,250 credit, leaving the Utilities Expense account with a $3,000 debit balance.

b. A $4,500 debit to Salaries Expense in a journal entry is incorrectly posted to the ledger as a $4,500 credit, leaving the Salaries Expense account with a $750 debit balance.

c. A $2,250 credit to Consulting Fees Earned in a journal entry is incorrectly posted to the ledger as a $2,250 debit, leaving the Consulting Fees Earned account with a $6,300 credit balance.

d. A $2,250 debit posting to Accounts Receivable was posted mistakenly to Land.

e. A $4,500 debit posting to Equipment was posted mistakenly to Cash.

f. An entry debiting Cash and crediting Accounts Payable for $4,500 was mistakenly not posted.

QS 2-9

Classifying accounts in financial statements

P3

Indicate the financial statement on which each of the following items appears. Use I for income statement, E for statement of retained earnings, and B for balance sheet.

a. Services Revenue

b. Interest Payable

c. Accounts Receivable

d. Salaries Expense

e. Equipment

f. Prepaid Insurance

g. Buildings

h. Rental Revenue

i. Dividends

j. Office Supplies

k. Interest Expense

l. Insurance Expense

QS 2-10

International accounting standards

C4

Answer each of the following questions related to international accounting standards.

a. What type of entry system is applied when accounting follows IFRS?

b. Identify the number and usual titles of the financial statements prepared under IFRS.

c. How do differences in accounting controls and enforcement impact accounting reports prepared across different countries?

≡ connect

EXERCISES

Exercise 2-1

Steps in analyzing and recording transactions   C1

Order the following steps in the accounting process that focus on analyzing and recording transactions.

_____ **a.** Analyze each transaction from source documents.

_____ **b.** Prepare and analyze the trial balance.

_____ **c.** Record relevant transactions in a journal.

_____ **d.** Post journal information to ledger accounts.

Exercise 2-2

Identifying and classifying accounts

C2

Enter the number for the item that best completes each of the descriptions below.

1. Asset   **3.** Account   **5.** Three

2. Equity   **4.** Liability

a. An _____ is a record of increases and decreases in a specific asset, liability, equity, revenue, or expense item.

b. Accounts payable, unearned revenue, and note payable are examples of _____ accounts.

c. Accounts receivable, prepaid accounts, supplies, and land are examples of _____ accounts.

d. Accounts are arranged into _____ general categories.

e. Common stock and dividends are examples of _____ accounts.

Enter the number for the item that best completes each of the descriptions below.

1. Chart   **2.** General ledger

a. The _____ is a record containing all accounts used by a company.

b. A _____ of accounts is a list of all accounts a company uses.

For each of the following (1) identify the type of account as an asset, liability, equity, revenue, or expense, (2) identify the normal balance of the account, and (3) enter *debit* (*Dr.*) or *credit* (*Cr.*) to identify the kind of entry that would increase the account balance.

a. Cash   **e.** Accounts Receivable   **i.** Fees Earned
b. Legal Expense   **f.** Dividends   **j.** Equipment
c. Prepaid Insurance   **g.** License Fee Revenue   **k.** Notes Payable
d. Land   **h.** Unearned Revenue   **l.** Common Stock

Use the information in each of the following separate cases to calculate the unknown amount.

a. Corentine Co. had $152,000 of accounts payable on September 30 and $132,500 on October 31. Total purchases on account during October were $281,000. Determine how much cash was paid on accounts payable during October.

b. On September 30, Valerian Co. had a $102,500 balance in Accounts Receivable. During October, the company collected $102,890 from its credit customers. The October 31 balance in Accounts Receivable was $89,000. Determine the amount of sales on account that occurred in October.

c. During October, Alameda Company had $102,500 of cash receipts and $103,150 of cash disbursements. The October 31 Cash balance was $18,600. Determine how much cash the company had at the close of business on September 30.

Groro Co. bills a client $62,000 for services provided and agrees to accept the following three items in full payment: (1) $10,000 cash, (2) computer equipment worth $80,000, and (3) to assume responsibility for a $28,000 note payable related to the computer equipment. The entry Groro makes to record this transaction includes which one or more of the following?

a. $28,000 increase in a liability account   **d.** $62,000 increase in an asset account
b. $10,000 increase in the Cash account   **e.** $62,000 increase in a revenue account
c. $10,000 increase in a revenue account   **f.** $62,000 increase in an equity account

---

Prepare general journal entries for the following transactions of a new company called Pose-for-Pics.

Aug. 1 Madison Harris, the owner, invested $6,500 cash and $33,500 of photography equipment in the company in exchange for common stock.
       2 The company paid $2,100 cash for an insurance policy covering the next 24 months.
       5 The company purchased office supplies for $880 cash.
      20 The company received $3,331 cash in photography fees earned.
      31 The company paid $675 cash for August utilities.

Use the information in Exercise 2-7 to prepare an August 31 trial balance for Pose-for-Pics. Begin by opening these T-accounts: Cash; Office Supplies; Prepaid Insurance; Photography Equipment; Common Stock; Photography Fees Earned; and Utilities Expense. Then, post the general journal entries to these T-accounts (which will serve as the ledger), and prepare the trial balance.

Prepare general journal entries to record the transactions below for Spade Company by using the following accounts: Cash; Accounts Receivable; Office Supplies; Office Equipment; Accounts Payable; Common Stock; Dividends; Fees Earned; and Rent Expense. Use the letters beside each transaction to identify entries. After recording the transactions, post them to T-accounts, which serves as the general ledger for this assignment. Determine the ending balance of each T-account.

a. Kacy Spade, owner, invested $100,750 cash in the company in exchange for common stock.

b. The company purchased office supplies for $1,250 cash.

c. The company purchased $10,050 of office equipment on credit.

d. The company received $15,500 cash as fees for services provided to a customer.

e. The company paid $10,050 cash to settle the payable for the office equipment purchased in transaction *c*.

f. The company billed a customer $2,700 as fees for services provided.

g. The company paid $1,225 cash for the monthly rent.

h. The company collected $1,125 cash as partial payment for the account receivable created in transaction *f*.

i. The company paid $10,000 cash in dividends to Spade (sole shareholder).

Check Cash ending balance, $94,850

Exercise 2-10
Preparing a trial balance P2

After recording the transactions of Exercise 2-9 in T-accounts and calculating the balance of each account, prepare a trial balance. Use May 31, 2013, as its report date.

Exercise 2-11
Analyzing and journalizing revenue transactions

A1 P1

Examine the following transactions and identify those that create revenues for Valdez Services, a company owned by Brina Valdez. Prepare general journal entries to record those revenue transactions and explain why the other transactions did not create revenues.

a. Brina Valdez invests $39,350 cash in the company in exchange for common stock.

b. The company provided $2,300 of services on credit.

c. The company provided services to a client and immediately received $875 cash.

d. The company received $10,200 cash from a client in payment for services to be provided next year.

e. The company received $3,500 cash from a client in partial payment of an account receivable.

f. The company borrowed $120,000 cash from the bank by signing a promissory note.

Exercise 2-12
Analyzing and journalizing expense transactions

A1 P1

Examine the following transactions and identify those that create expenses for Valdez Services. Prepare general journal entries to record those expense transactions and explain why the other transactions did not create expenses.

a. The company paid $12,200 cash for payment on a 16-month old liability for office supplies.

b. The company paid $1,233 cash for the just completed two-week salary of the receptionist.

c. The company paid $39,200 cash for equipment purchased.

d. The company paid $870 cash for this month's utilities.

e. The company paid $4,500 cash in dividends.

Exercise 2-13
Preparing an income statement

C3 P3

Carmen Camry operates a consulting firm called Help Today, which began operations on August 1. On August 31, the company's records show the following accounts and amounts for the month of August. Use this information to prepare an August income statement for the business.

Cash	$ 25,360		Dividends	$ 6,000
Accounts receivable	22,360		Consulting fees earned	27,000
Office supplies	5,250		Rent expense	9,550
Land	44,000		Salaries expense.........................	5,600
Office equipment	20,000		Telephone expense	860
Accounts payable	10,500		Miscellaneous expenses....................	520
Common stock	102,000			

Check Net income, $10,470

Exercise 2-14
Preparing a statement of retained earnings P3

Use the information in Exercise 2-13 to prepare an August statement of retained earnings for Help Today. (The owner invested a total of $102,000 in the company in exchange for common stock on August 1.)

Exercise 2-15
Preparing a balance sheet P3

Use the information in Exercise 2-13 (if completed, you can also use your solution to Exercise 2-14) to prepare an August 31 balance sheet for Help Today.

Exercise 2-16
Computing net income

A1

A corporation had the following assets and liabilities at the beginning and end of this year.

	Assets	Liabilities
Beginning of the year	$ 60,000	$20,000
End of the year	105,000	36,000

Determine the net income earned or net loss incurred by the business during the year for each of the following *separate* cases:

a. Owner made no investments in the business and no dividends were paid during the year.

b. Owner made no investments in the business but dividends were $1,250 cash per month.

c. No dividends were paid during the year but the owner did invest an additional $55,000 cash in exchange for common stock.

d. Dividends were $1,250 cash per month and the owner invested an additional $35,000 cash in exchange for common stock.

Compute the missing amount for each of the following separate companies *a* through *d*.

Exercise 2-17
Analyzing changes in a company's equity

P3

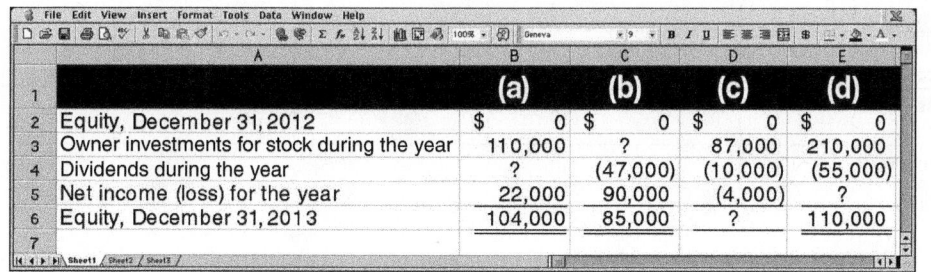

	(a)	(b)	(c)	(d)
Equity, December 31, 2012	$ 0	$ 0	$ 0	$ 0
Owner investments for stock during the year	110,000	?	87,000	210,000
Dividends during the year	?	(47,000)	(10,000)	(55,000)
Net income (loss) for the year	22,000	90,000	(4,000)	?
Equity, December 31, 2013	104,000	85,000	?	110,000

Assume the following T-accounts reflect Belle Co.'s general ledger and that seven transactions *a* through *g* are posted to them. Provide a short description of each transaction. Include the amounts in your descriptions.

Exercise 2-18
Interpreting and describing transactions from T-accounts

A1

Cash			
(a)	6,000	(b)	4,800
(e)	4,500	(c)	900
		(f)	1,600
		(g)	820

Office Supplies	
(c)	900
(d)	300

Prepaid Insurance	
(b)	4,800

Equipment	
(a)	7,600
(d)	9,700

Automobiles	
(a)	12,000

Accounts Payable			
(f)	1,600	(d)	10,000

Common Stock			
		(a)	25,600

Delivery Services Revenue			
		(e)	4,500

Gas and Oil Expense	
(g)	820

Use information from the T-accounts in Exercise 2-18 to prepare general journal entries for each of the seven transactions *a* through *g*.

Exercise 2-19
Preparing general journal entries

P1

Posting errors are identified in the following table. In column (1), enter the amount of the difference between the two trial balance columns (debit and credit) due to the error. In column (2), identify the trial balance column (debit or credit) with the larger amount if they are not equal. In column (3), identify the account(s) affected by the error. In column (4), indicate the amount by which the account(s) in column (3) is under- or overstated. Item (a) is completed as an example.

Exercise 2-20
Identifying effects of posting errors on the trial balance

A1 P2

		(1)	(2)	(3)	(4)
	Description of Posting Error	Difference between Debit and Credit Columns	Column with the Larger Total	Identify Account(s) Incorrectly Stated	Amount that Account(s) Is Over- or Understated
a.	$3,600 debit to Rent Expense is posted as a $1,340 debit.	$2,260	Credit	Rent Expense	Rent Expense understated $2,260
b.	$6,500 credit to Cash is posted twice as two credits to Cash.				
c.	$10,900 debit to the Dividends account is debited to Common Stock.				
d.	$2,050 debit to Prepaid Insurance is posted as a debit to Insurance Expense.				
e.	$38,000 debit to Machinery is posted as a debit to Accounts Payable.				
f.	$5,850 credit to Services Revenue is posted as a $585 credit.				
g.	$1,390 debit to Store Supplies is not posted.				

Exercise 2-21

Analyzing a trial balance error

A1 P2

You are told the column totals in a trial balance are not equal. After careful analysis, you discover only one error. Specifically, a correctly journalized credit purchase of an automobile for $18,950 is posted from the journal to the ledger with a $18,950 debit to Automobiles and another $18,950 debit to Accounts Payable. The Automobiles account has a debit balance of $37,100 on the trial balance. Answer each of the following questions and compute the dollar amount of any misstatement.

a. Is the debit column total of the trial balance overstated, understated, or correctly stated?

b. Is the credit column total of the trial balance overstated, understated, or correctly stated?

c. Is the Automobiles account balance overstated, understated, or correctly stated in the trial balance?

d. Is the Accounts Payable account balance overstated, understated, or correctly stated in the trial balance?

e. If the debit column total of the trial balance is $200,000 before correcting the error, what is the total of the credit column before correction?

Exercise 2-22

Interpreting the debt ratio and return on assets

A2

a. Calculate the debt ratio and the return on assets using the year-end information for each of the following six separate companies ($ thousands).

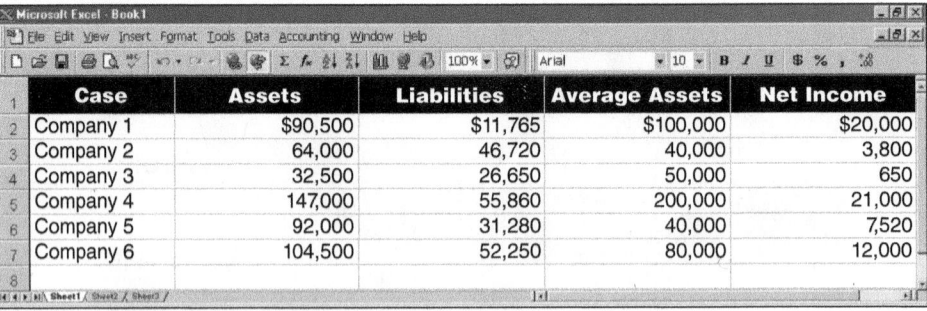

Case	Assets	Liabilities	Average Assets	Net Income
Company 1	$90,500	$11,765	$100,000	$20,000
Company 2	64,000	46,720	40,000	3,800
Company 3	32,500	26,650	50,000	650
Company 4	147,000	55,860	200,000	21,000
Company 5	92,000	31,280	40,000	7,520
Company 6	104,500	52,250	80,000	12,000

b. Of the six companies, which business relies most heavily on creditor financing?

c. Of the six companies, which business relies most heavily on equity financing?

d. Which two companies indicate the greatest risk?

e. Which two companies earn the highest return on assets?

f. Which one company would investors likely prefer based on the risk–return relation?

Exercise 2-23

Preparing a balance sheet following IFRS

P3

BMW reports the following balance sheet accounts for the year ended December 31, 2011 (euro in millions). Prepare the balance sheet for this company as of December 31, 2011, following the usual IFRS formats.

Current liabilities	€11,519	Noncurrent liabilities	€7,767
Current assets	17,682	Noncurrent assets	9,826
Total equity	8,222		

connect

Aracel Engineering completed the following transactions in the month of June.

a. To launch the company, Jenna Aracel, the owner, invested $100,000 cash, office equipment with a value of $5,000, and $60,000 of drafting equipment in exchange for common stock.

b. The company purchased land worth $49,000 for an office by paying $6,300 cash and signing a long-term note payable for $42,700.

c. The company purchased a portable building with $55,000 cash and moved it onto the land acquired in b.

d. The company paid $3,000 cash for the premium on an 18-month insurance policy.

e. The company completed and delivered a set of plans for a client and collected $6,200 cash.

f. The company purchased $20,000 of additional drafting equipment by paying $9,500 cash and signing a long-term note payable for $10,500.

g. The company completed $14,000 of engineering services for a client. This amount is to be received in 30 days.

h. The company purchased $1,150 of additional office equipment on credit.

i. The company completed engineering services for $22,000 on credit.

j. The company received a bill for rent of equipment that was used on a recently completed job. The $1,333 rent cost must be paid within 30 days.

k. The company collected $7,000 cash in partial payment from the client described in transaction g.

l. The company paid $1,200 cash for wages to a drafting assistant.

m. The company paid $1,150 cash to settle the account payable created in transaction h.

n. The company paid $925 cash for minor maintenance of its drafting equipment.

o. The company paid $9,480 cash in dividends.

p. The company paid $1,200 cash for wages to a drafting assistant.

q. The company paid $2,500 cash for advertisements on the Web during June.

Required

1. Prepare general journal entries to record these transactions (use the account titles listed in part 2).

2. Open the following ledger accounts—their account numbers are in parentheses (use the balance column format): Cash (101); Accounts Receivable (106); Prepaid Insurance (108); Office Equipment (163); Drafting Equipment (164); Building (170); Land (172); Accounts Payable (201); Notes Payable (250); Common Stock (307); Dividends (319); Engineering Fees Earned (402); Wages Expense (601); Equipment Rental Expense (602); Advertising Expense (603); and Repairs Expense (604). Post the journal entries from part 1 to the accounts and enter the balance after each posting.

3. Prepare a trial balance as of the end of June.

PROBLEM SET A

Problem 2-1A
Preparing and posting journal entries; preparing a trial balance
C3 C4 A1 P1 P2

Check (2) Ending balances: Cash, $22,945; Accounts Receivable, $29,000; Accounts Payable, $1,333

(3) Trial balance totals, $261,733

Denzel Brooks opens a Web consulting business called Venture Consultants and completes the following transactions in March.

March 1 Brooks invested $150,000 cash along with $22,000 in office equipment in the company in exchange for common stock.
      2 The company prepaid $6,000 cash for six months' rent for an office. (*Hint:* Debit Prepaid Rent for $6,000.)
      3 The company made credit purchases of office equipment for $3,000 and office supplies for $1,200. Payment is due within 10 days.
      6 The company completed services for a client and immediately received $4,000 cash.
      9 The company completed a $7,500 project for a client, who must pay within 30 days.
     12 The company paid $4,200 cash to settle the account payable created on March 3.
     19 The company paid $5,000 cash for the premium on a 12-month insurance policy. (*Hint:* Debit Prepaid Insurance for $5,000.)
     22 The company received $3,500 cash as partial payment for the work completed on March 9.
     25 The company completed work for another client for $3,820 on credit.
     29 The company paid $5,100 cash in dividends.
     30 The company purchased $600 of additional office supplies on credit.
     31 The company paid $500 cash for this month's utility bill.

Problem 2-2A
Preparing and posting journal entries; preparing a trial balance
C3 C4 A1 P1 P2

Required

1. Prepare general journal entries to record these transactions (use the account titles listed in part 2).
2. Open the following ledger accounts—their account numbers are in parentheses (use the balance column format): Cash (101); Accounts Receivable (106); Office Supplies (124); Prepaid Insurance (128); Prepaid Rent (131); Office Equipment (163); Accounts Payable (201); Common Stock (307); Dividends (319); Services Revenue (403); and Utilities Expense (690). Post the journal entries from part 1 to the ledger accounts and enter the balance after each posting.
3. Prepare a trial balance as of the end of March.

Problem 2-3A
Preparing and posting journal entries; preparing a trial balance
C3 C4 A1 P1 P2

Karla Tanner opens a Web consulting business called Linkworks and completes the following transactions in its first month of operations.

April 1 Tanner invests $80,000 cash along with office equipment valued at $26,000 in the company in exchange for common stock.
       2 The company prepaid $9,000 cash for 12 months' rent for office space. (*Hint:* Debit Prepaid Rent for $9,000.)
       3 The company made credit purchases for $8,000 in office equipment and $3,600 in office supplies. Payment is due within 10 days.
       6 The company completed services for a client and immediately received $4,000 cash.
       9 The company completed a $6,000 project for a client, who must pay within 30 days.
      13 The company paid $11,600 cash to settle the account payable created on April 3.
      19 The company paid $2,400 cash for the premium on a 12-month insurance policy. (*Hint:* Debit Prepaid Insurance for $2,400.)
      22 The company received $4,400 cash as partial payment for the work completed on April 9.
      25 The company completed work for another client for $2,890 on credit.
      28 The company paid $5,500 cash in dividends.
      29 The company purchased $600 of additional office supplies on credit.
      30 The company paid $435 cash for this month's utility bill.

Required

1. Prepare general journal entries to record these transactions (use account titles listed in part 2).
2. Open the following ledger accounts—their account numbers are in parentheses (use the balance column format): Cash (101); Accounts Receivable (106); Office Supplies (124); Prepaid Insurance (128); Prepaid Rent (131); Office Equipment (163); Accounts Payable (201); Common Stock (307); Dividends (319); Services Revenue (403); and Utilities Expense (690). Post journal entries from part 1 to the ledger accounts and enter the balance after each posting.
3. Prepare a trial balance as of April 30.

Problem 2-4A
Computing net income from equity analysis, preparing a balance sheet, and computing the debt ratio
C2 A1 A2 P3

The accounting records of Nettle Distribution show the following assets and liabilities as of December 31, 2012 and 2013.

December 31	2012	2013
Cash	$ 64,300	$ 15,640
Accounts receivable	26,240	19,390
Office supplies	3,160	1,960
Office equipment	44,000	44,000
Trucks	148,000	157,000
Building	0	80,000
Land	0	60,000
Accounts payable	3,500	33,500
Note payable	0	40,000

Late in December 2013, the business purchased a small office building and land for $140,000. It paid $100,000 cash toward the purchase and a $40,000 note payable was signed for the balance. Mr. Nettle had to invest $35,000 cash in the business (in exchange for common stock) to enable it to pay the $100,000 cash. The business also pays $3,000 cash per month for dividends.

Required

1. Prepare balance sheets for the business as of December 31, 2012 and 2013. (*Hint:* Report only total equity on the balance sheet and remember that total equity equals the difference between assets and liabilities.)

2. By comparing equity amounts from the balance sheets and using the additional information presented in this problem, prepare a calculation to show how much net income was earned by the business during 2013.

3. Compute the 2013 year-end debt ratio (in percent and rounded to one decimal).

Check (2) Net income, $23,290

(3) Debt ratio, 19.4%

Yi Min started an engineering firm called Min Engineering. He began operations and completed seven transactions in May, which included his initial investment of $18,000 cash. After those seven transactions, the ledger included the following accounts with normal balances.

Cash	$37,641
Office supplies	890
Prepaid insurance	4,600
Office equipment	12,900
Accounts payable	12,900
Common stock	18,000
Dividends	3,329
Engineering fees earned	36,000
Rent expense	7,540

Problem 2-5A
Analyzing account balances and reconstructing transactions

C1 C3 A1 P2

Required

1. Prepare a trial balance for this business as of the end of May.

Analysis Components

2. Analyze the accounts and their balances and prepare a list that describes each of the seven most likely transactions and their amounts.

3. Prepare a report of cash received and cash paid showing how the seven transactions in part 2 yield the $37,641 ending Cash balance.

Check (1) Trial balance totals, $66,900

(3) Cash paid, $16,359

Business transactions completed by Hannah Venedict during the month of September are as follows.

a. Venedict invested $60,000 cash along with office equipment valued at $25,000 in exchange for common stock of a new company named HV Consulting.

b. The company purchased land valued at $40,000 and a building valued at $160,000. The purchase is paid with $30,000 cash and a long-term note payable for $170,000.

c. The company purchased $2,000 of office supplies on credit.

d. Venedict invested her personal automobile in the company in exchange for more common stock. The automobile has a value of $16,500 and is to be used exclusively in the business.

e. The company purchased $5,600 of additional office equipment on credit.

f. The company paid $1,800 cash salary to an assistant.

g. The company provided services to a client and collected $8,000 cash.

h. The company paid $635 cash for this month's utilities.

i. The company paid $2,000 cash to settle the account payable created in transaction *c*.

j. The company purchased $20,300 of new office equipment by paying $20,300 cash.

k. The company completed $6,250 of services for a client, who must pay within 30 days.

l. The company paid $1,800 cash salary to an assistant.

m. The company received $4,000 cash in partial payment on the receivable created in transaction *k*.

n. The company paid $2,800 cash in dividends.

Problem 2-6A
Recording transactions; posting to ledger; preparing a trial balance

C3 A1 P1 P2

Required

1. Prepare general journal entries to record these transactions (use account titles listed in part 2).

2. Open the following ledger accounts—their account numbers are in parentheses (use the balance column format): Cash (101); Accounts Receivable (106); Office Supplies (108); Office Equipment (163); Automobiles (164); Building (170); Land (172); Accounts Payable (201); Notes Payable (250); Common Stock

Check (2) Ending balances: Cash, $12,665; Office Equipment, $50,900

(3) Trial balance totals,

$291,350

(307); Dividends (319); Fees Earned (402); Salaries Expense (601); and Utilities Expense (602). Post the journal entries from part 1 to the ledger accounts and enter the balance after each posting.

3. Prepare a trial balance as of the end of September.

PROBLEM SET B

Problem 2-1B

Preparing and posting journal entries; preparing a trial balance

C3 C4 A1 P1 P2

At the beginning of April, Bernadette Grechus launched a custom computer solutions company called Softworks. The company had the following transactions during April.

a. Bernadette Grechus invested $65,000 cash, office equipment with a value of $5,750, and $30,000 of computer equipment in the company in exchange for common stock.

b. The company purchased land worth $22,000 for an office by paying $5,000 cash and signing a long-term note payable for $17,000.

c. The company purchased a portable building with $34,500 cash and moved it onto the land acquired in b.

d. The company paid $5,000 cash for the premium on a two-year insurance policy.

e. The company provided services to a client and immediately collected $4,600 cash.

f. The company purchased $4,500 of additional computer equipment by paying $800 cash and signing a long-term note payable for $3,700.

g. The company completed $4,250 of services for a client. This amount is to be received within 30 days.

h. The company purchased $950 of additional office equipment on credit.

i. The company completed client services for $10,200 on credit.

j. The company received a bill for rent of a computer testing device that was used on a recently completed job. The $580 rent cost must be paid within 30 days.

k. The company collected $5,100 cash in partial payment from the client described in transaction i.

l. The company paid $1,800 cash for wages to an assistant.

m. The company paid $950 cash to settle the payable created in transaction h.

n. The company paid $608 cash for minor maintenance of the company's computer equipment.

o. The company paid $6,230 cash in dividends.

p. The company paid $1,800 cash for wages to an assistant.

q. The company paid $750 cash for advertisements on the Web during April.

Required

1. Prepare general journal entries to record these transactions (use account titles listed in part 2).

Check (2) Ending balances: Cash, $17,262; Accounts Receivable, $9,350; Accounts Payable, $580

2. Open the following ledger accounts—their account numbers are in parentheses (use the balance column format): Cash (101); Accounts Receivable (106); Prepaid Insurance (108); Office Equipment (163); Computer Equipment (164); Building (170); Land (172); Accounts Payable (201); Notes Payable (250); Common Stock (307); Dividends (319); Fees Earned (402); Wages Expense (601); Computer Rental Expense (602); Advertising Expense (603); and Repairs Expense (604). Post the journal entries from part 1 to the accounts and enter the balance after each posting.

(3) Trial balance totals,

$141,080

3. Prepare a trial balance as of the end of April.

Problem 2-2B

Preparing and posting journal entries; preparing a trial balance

C3 C4 A1 P1 P2

Zucker Management Services opens for business and completes these transactions in November.

Nov. 1 Matt Zucker, the owner, invested $30,000 cash along with $15,000 of office equipment in the company in exchange for common stock.

2 The company prepaid $4,500 cash for six months' rent for an office. (*Hint:* Debit Prepaid Rent for $4,500.)

4 The company made credit purchases of office equipment for $2,500 and of office supplies for $600. Payment is due within 10 days.

8 The company completed work for a client and immediately received $3,400 cash.

12 The company completed a $10,200 project for a client, who must pay within 30 days.

13 The company paid $3,100 cash to settle the payable created on November 4.

19 The company paid $1,800 cash for the premium on a 24-month insurance policy.

22 The company received $5,200 cash as partial payment for the work completed on November 12.

24 The company completed work for another client for $1,750 on credit.

28 The company paid $5,300 cash in dividends.

29 The company purchased $249 of additional office supplies on credit.

30 The company paid $831 cash for this month's utility bill.

Required

1. Prepare general journal entries to record these transactions (use account titles listed in part 2).

2. Open the following ledger accounts—their account numbers are in parentheses (use the balance column format): Cash (101); Accounts Receivable (106); Office Supplies (124); Prepaid Insurance (128); Prepaid Rent (131); Office Equipment (163); Accounts Payable (201); Common Stock (307); Dividends (319); Services Revenue (403); and Utilities Expense (690). Post the journal entries from part 1 to the ledger accounts and enter the balance after each posting.

3. Prepare a trial balance as of the end of November.

Check   (2) Ending balances: Cash, $23,069; Accounts Receivable, $6,750; Accounts Payable, $249

(3) Total debits, $60,599

Humble Management Services opens for business and completes these transactions in September.

Problem 2-3B
Preparing and posting journal entries; preparing a trial balance
C3 C4 A1 P1 P2

Sept. 1 Henry Humble, the owner, invests $38,000 cash along with office equipment valued at $15,000 in the company in exchange for common stock.
    2 The company prepaid $9,000 cash for 12 months' rent for office space. (*Hint:* Debit Prepaid Rent for $9,000.)
    4 The company made credit purchases for $8,000 in office equipment and $2,400 in office supplies. Payment is due within 10 days.
    8 The company completed work for a client and immediately received $3,280 cash.
   12 The company completed a $15,400 project for a client, who must pay within 30 days.
   13 The company paid $10,400 cash to settle the payable created on September 4.
   19 The company paid $1,900 cash for the premium on an 18-month insurance policy. (*Hint:* Debit Prepaid Insurance for $1,900.)
   22 The company received $7,700 cash as partial payment for the work completed on September 12.
   24 The company completed work for another client for $2,100 on credit.
   28 The company paid $5,300 cash in dividends.
   29 The company purchased $550 of additional office supplies on credit.
   30 The company paid $860 cash for this month's utility bill.

Required

1. Prepare general journal entries to record these transactions (use account titles listed in part 2).

2. Open the following ledger accounts—their account numbers are in parentheses (use the balance column format): Cash (101); Accounts Receivable (106); Office Supplies (124); Prepaid Insurance (128); Prepaid Rent (131); Office Equipment (163); Accounts Payable (201); Common Stock (307); Dividends (319); Service Fees Earned (401); and Utilities Expense (690). Post journal entries from part 1 to the ledger accounts and enter the balance after each posting.

3. Prepare a trial balance as of the end of September.

Check   (2) Ending balances: Cash, $21,520; Accounts Receivable, $9,800; Accounts Payable, $550

(3) Total debits, $74,330

The accounting records of Tama Co. show the following assets and liabilities as of December 31, 2012 and 2013.

Problem 2-4B
Computing net income from equity analysis, preparing a balance sheet, and computing the debt ratio
C2 A1 A2 P3

December 31	2012	2013
Cash	$20,000	$ 5,000
Accounts receivable	35,000	25,000
Office supplies	8,000	13,500
Office equipment	40,000	40,000
Machinery	28,500	28,500
Building	0	250,000
Land	0	50,000
Accounts payable	4,000	12,000
Note payable	0	250,000

Late in December 2013, the business purchased a small office building and land for $300,000. It paid $50,000 cash toward the purchase and a $250,000 note payable was signed for the balance. Joe Tama, the owner, had to invest an additional $15,000 cash (in exchange for common stock) to enable it to pay the $50,000 cash toward the purchase. The business also pays $250 cash per month for dividends.

Required

1. Prepare balance sheets for the business as of December 31, 2012 and 2013. (*Hint:* Report only total equity on the balance sheet and remember that total equity equals the difference between assets and liabilities.)

2. By comparing equity amounts from the balance sheets and using the additional information presented in the problem, prepare a calculation to show how much net income was earned by the business during 2013.

3. Calculate the December 31, 2013, debt ratio (in percent and rounded to one decimal).

Problem 2-5B

Analyzing account balances and reconstructing transactions

C1   C3   A1   P2

Roshaun Gould started a Web consulting firm called Gould Solutions. He began operations and completed seven transactions in April that resulted in the following accounts, which all have normal balances.

Cash	$19,982
Office supplies	760
Prepaid rent	1,800
Office equipment	12,250
Accounts payable	12,250
Common stock	15,000
Dividends	5,200
Consulting fees earned	20,400
Operating expenses	7,658

Required

1. Prepare a trial balance for this business as of the end of April.

Analysis Component

2. Analyze the accounts and their balances and prepare a list that describes each of the seven most likely transactions and their amounts.

3. Prepare a report of cash received and cash paid showing how the seven transactions in part 2 yield the $19,982 ending Cash balance.

Problem 2-6B

Recording transactions; posting to ledger; preparing a trial balance

C3   A1   P1   P2

Nuncio Consulting completed the following transactions during June.

a. Armand Nuncio, the owner, invested $35,000 cash along with office equipment valued at $11,000 in the new company in exchange for common stock.

b. The company purchased land valued at $7,500 and a building valued at $40,000. The purchase is paid with $15,000 cash and a long-term note payable for $32,500.

c. The company purchased $500 of office supplies on credit.

d. A. Nuncio invested his personal automobile in the company in exchange for more common stock. The automobile has a value of $8,000 and is to be used exclusively in the business.

e. The company purchased $1,200 of additional office equipment on credit.

f. The company paid $1,000 cash salary to an assistant.

g. The company provided services to a client and collected $3,200 cash.

h. The company paid $540 cash for this month's utilities.

i. The company paid $500 cash to settle the payable created in transaction *c*.

j. The company purchased $3,400 of new office equipment by paying $3,400 cash.

k. The company completed $4,200 of services for a client, who must pay within 30 days.

l. The company paid $1,000 cash salary to an assistant.

m. The company received $2,200 cash in partial payment on the receivable created in transaction *k*.

n. The company paid $1,100 cash in dividends.

Required

1. Prepare general journal entries to record these transactions (use account titles listed in part 2).

2. Open the following ledger accounts—their account numbers are in parentheses (use the balance column format): Cash (101); Accounts Receivable (106); Office Supplies (108); Office Equipment (163); Automobiles (164); Building (170); Land (172); Accounts Payable (201); Notes Payable (250); Common Stock (307); Dividends (319); Fees Earned (402); Salaries Expense (601); and Utilities Expense (602). Post the journal entries from part 1 to the ledger accounts and enter the balance after each posting.

3. Prepare a trial balance as of the end of June.

(This serial problem started in Chapter 1 and continues through most of the chapters. If the Chapter 1 segment was not completed, the problem can begin at this point. It is helpful, but not necessary, to use the Working Papers that accompany this book.)

SERIAL PROBLEM
Success Systems

A1   P1   P2

SP 2   On October 1, 2013, Adria Lopez launched a computer services company called **Success Systems,** which provides consulting services, computer system installations, and custom program development. Adria adopts the calendar year for reporting purposes and expects to prepare the company's first set of financial statements on December 31, 2013. The company's initial chart of accounts follows.

Account	No.	Account	No.
Cash......................	101	Common Stock....................	307
Accounts Receivable	106	Dividends........................	319
Computer Supplies	126	Computer Services Revenue	403
Prepaid Insurance	128	Wages Expense....................	623
Prepaid Rent	131	Advertising Expense	655
Office Equipment	163	Mileage Expense	676
Computer Equipment	167	Miscellaneous Expenses	677
Accounts Payable	201	Repairs Expense—Computer........	684

Required

1. Prepare journal entries to record each of the following transactions for Success Systems.

Oct. 1   Adria Lopez invested $55,000 cash, a $20,000 computer system, and $8,000 of office equipment in the company in exchange for its common stock.

    2   The company paid $3,300 cash for four months' rent. (*Hint:* Debit Prepaid Rent for $3,300.)

    3   The company purchased $1,420 of computer supplies on credit from Harris Office Products.

    5   The company paid $2,220 cash for one year's premium on a property and liability insurance policy. (*Hint:* Debit Prepaid Insurance for $2,220.)

    6   The company billed Easy Leasing $4,800 for services performed in installing a new Web server.

    8   The company paid $1,420 cash for the computer supplies purchased from Harris Office Products on October 3.

    10   The company hired Lyn Addie as a part-time assistant for $125 per day, as needed.

    12   The company billed Easy Leasing another $1,400 for services performed.

    15   The company received $4,800 cash from Easy Leasing as partial payment on its account.

    17   The company paid $805 cash to repair computer equipment that was damaged when moving it.

    20   The company paid $1,940 cash for advertisements published in the local newspaper.

    22   The company received $1,400 cash from Easy Leasing on its account.

    28   The company billed IFM Company $5,208 for services performed.

    31   The company paid $875 cash for Lyn Addie's wages for seven days' work.

    31   The company paid $3,600 cash in dividends.

Nov. 1   The company reimbursed Adria Lopez in cash for business automobile mileage allowance (Lopez logged 1,000 miles at $0.32 per mile).

    2   The company received $4,633 cash from Liu Corporation for computer services performed.

    5   The company purchased computer supplies for $1,125 cash from Harris Office Products.

    8   The company billed Gomez Co. $5,668 for services performed.

    13   The company received notification from Alex's Engineering Co. that Success Systems' bid of $3,950 for an upcoming project is accepted.

    18   The company received $2,208 cash from IFM Company as partial payment of the October 28 bill.

    22   The company donated $250 cash to the United Way in the company's name.

    24   The company completed work for Alex's Engineering Co. and sent it a bill for $3,950.

    25   The company sent another bill to IFM Company for the past-due amount of $3,000.

    28   The company reimbursed Adria Lopez in cash for business automobile mileage (1,200 miles at $0.32 per mile).

    30   The company paid $1,750 cash for Lyn Addie's wages for 14 days' work.

    30   The company paid $2,000 cash in dividends.

2. Open ledger accounts (in balance column format) and post the journal entries from part 1 to them.

3. Prepare a trial balance as of the end of November.

Check   (2) Cash, Nov. 30 bal., $48,052

           (3) Trial bal. totals, $108,659

 **GENERAL LEDGER PROBLEM**

Available in Connect Only

|ACCOUNTING

Accounting professionals utilize many technology tools to aid them in their everyday tasks and decision making. The **General Ledger** tool in *Connect* automates several of the procedural steps in the accounting cycle so that the accounting professional can focus on the impacts of each transaction on the full set of financial statements. Chapter 2 is the first chapter to employ this tool in helping students see the advantages of technology and, in particular, the power of the General Ledger tool in accounting practice, including financial analysis.

GL 2-1 Using transactions from the FastForward illustration in this chapter, prepare journal entries for each transaction and identify the financial statement impact of each entry. The financial statements are automatically generated based on the journal entries recorded.

GL 2-2 Use the transactions in Problem 2-2A to record journal entries, create financial statements, and assess the impact of each transaction on financial statements.

GL 2-3 Use the transactions in Problem 2-6A to record journal entries, create financial statements, and assess the impact of each transaction on financial statements.

GL 2-4 Use the transactions in SP 2, the Serial Problem, to record journal entries, create financial statements, and assess the impact of each transaction on financial statements.

Beyond the Numbers

REPORTING IN ACTION

A1 A2

APPLE

BTN 2-1   Refer to Apple's financial statements in Appendix A for the following questions.

Required

1. What amount of total liabilities does it report for each of the fiscal years ended September 29, 2012, and September 24, 2011?

2. What amount of total assets does it report for each of the fiscal years ended September 29, 2012, and September 24, 2011?

3. Compute its debt ratio for each of the fiscal years ended September 29, 2012, and September 24, 2011. (Report ratio in percent and round it to one decimal.)

4. In which fiscal year did it employ more financial leverage (September 29, 2012, or September 24, 2011)? Explain.

Fast Forward

5. Access its financial statements (10-K report) for a fiscal year ending after September 29, 2012, from its Website (Apple.com) or the SEC's EDGAR database (www.sec.gov). Recompute its debt ratio for any subsequent year's data and compare it with the debt ratio for 2012 and 2011.

COMPARATIVE ANALYSIS

A1 A2

APPLE

GOOGLE

BTN 2-2   Key comparative figures for Apple and Google follow.

(in millions)	Apple Current Year	Apple Prior Year	Google Current Year	Google Prior Year
Total liabilities	$ 57,854	39,756	22,083	14,429
Total assets	176,064	116,371	93,798	72,574

1. What is the debt ratio for Apple in the current year and for the prior year?

2. What is the debt ratio for Google in the current year and for the prior year?

3. Which of the two companies has the higher degree of financial leverage? What does this imply?

BTN 2-3   Review the *Decision Ethics* case from the first part of this chapter involving the cashier. The guidance answer suggests that you should not comply with the assistant manager's request.

ETHICS CHALLENGE

C1

Required

Propose and evaluate two other courses of action you might consider, and explain why.

BTN 2-4   Lila Corentine is an aspiring entrepreneur and your friend. She is having difficulty understanding the purposes of financial statements and how they fit together across time.

COMMUNICATING IN PRACTICE

C1 C2 A1 P3

Required

Write a one-page memorandum to Corentine explaining the purposes of the four financial statements and how they are linked across time.

BTN 2-5   Access EDGAR online (www.sec.gov) and locate the 2011 year 10-K report of Amazon.com (ticker AMZN) filed on February 1, 2012. Review its financial statements reported for years ended 2011, 2010, and 2009 to answer the following questions.

TAKING IT TO THE NET

A1

Required

1. What are the amounts of its net income or net loss reported for each of these three years?
2. Does Amazon's operating activities provide cash or use cash for each of these three years?
3. If Amazon has a 2011 net income of more than $600 million and 2011 operating cash flows of nearly $4,000 million, how is it possible that its cash balance at December 31, 2011, increases by less than $1,500 million relative to its balance at December 31, 2010?

BTN 2-6   The expanded accounting equation consists of assets, liabilities, common stock, dividends, revenues, and expenses. It can be used to reveal insights into changes in a company's financial position.

TEAMWORK IN ACTION

C1 C2 C4 A1

Required

1. Form *learning teams* of six (or more) members. Each team member must select one of the six components and each team must have at least one expert on each component: (*a*) assets, (*b*) liabilities, (*c*) common stock, (*d*) dividends, (*e*) revenues, and (*f*) expenses.
2. Form *expert teams* of individuals who selected the same component in part 1. Expert teams are to draft a report that each expert will present to his or her learning team addressing the following:
   a. Identify for its component the (i) increase and decrease side of the account and (ii) normal balance side of the account.
   b. Describe a transaction, with amounts, that increases its component.
   c. Using the transaction and amounts in (*b*), verify the equality of the accounting equation and then explain any effects on the income statement and statement of cash flows.
   d. Describe a transaction, with amounts, that decreases its component.
   e. Using the transaction and amounts in (*d*), verify the equality of the accounting equation and then explain any effects on the income statement and statement of cash flows.
3. Each expert should return to his/her learning team. In rotation, each member presents his/her expert team's report to the learning team. Team discussion is encouraged.

**ENTREPRENEURIAL
DECISION**

A1 A2 P3

BTN 2-7 Assume Reid Hoffman of **LinkedIn** plans on expanding his business to accommodate more specialized lines of professional listings. He is considering financing the expansion in one of two ways: (1) contributing more of his own funds to the business or (2) borrowing the funds from a bank.

Required

Identify at least two issues that Reid should consider when trying to decide on the method for financing his expansion.

**ENTREPRENEURIAL
DECISION**

A1 A2 P3

BTN 2-8 Angel Martin is a young entrepreneur who operates Martin Music Services, offering singing lessons and instruction on musical instruments. Martin wishes to expand but needs a $30,000 loan. The bank requests Martin to prepare a balance sheet and key financial ratios. Martin has not kept formal records but is able to provide the following accounts and their amounts as of December 31, 2013.

Cash	$ 3,600	Accounts Receivable	$ 9,600	Prepaid Insurance	$ 1,500
Prepaid Rent	9,400	Store Supplies	6,600	Equipment	50,000
Accounts Payable	2,200	Unearned Lesson Fees . . .	15,600	Total Equity*	62,900
Annual net income . . .	40,000				

* The total equity amount reflects all owner investments, dividends, revenues, and expenses as of December 31, 2013.

Required

1. Prepare a balance sheet as of December 31, 2013, for Martin Music Services. (Report only the total equity amount on the balance sheet.)
2. Compute Martin's debt ratio and its return on assets (the latter ratio is defined in Chapter 1). Assume average assets equal its ending balance.
3. Do you believe the prospects of a $30,000 bank loan are good? Why or why not?

HITTING THE ROAD

C1

BTN 2-9 Obtain a recent copy of the most prominent newspaper distributed in your area. Research the classified section and prepare a report answering the following questions (attach relevant classified clippings to your report). Alternatively, you may want to search the Web for the required information. One suitable Website is CareerOneStop (www.CareerOneStop.org). For documentation, you should print copies of Websites accessed.

1. Identify the number of listings for accounting positions and the various accounting job titles.
2. Identify the number of listings for other job titles, with examples, that require or prefer accounting knowledge/experience but are not specifically accounting positions.
3. Specify the salary range for the accounting and accounting-related positions if provided.
4. Indicate the job that appeals to you, the reason for its appeal, and its requirements.

GLOBAL DECISION

A2

Samsung
APPLE
GOOGLE

BTN 2-10 **Samsung** (www.Samsung.com) is a market leader in high-tech electronics manufacturing and digital media, and it competes to some extent with both **Apple** and **Google**. Key financial ratios for the current fiscal year follow.

Key Figure	Samsung	Apple	Google
Return on assets	14.2%	28.5%	12.9%
Debt ratio	32.9%	32.9%	23.5%

Required

1. Which company is most profitable according to its return on assets?
2. Which company is most risky according to the debt ratio?
3. Which company deserves increased investment based on a joint analysis of return on assets and the debt ratio? Explain.

ANSWERS TO MULTIPLE CHOICE QUIZ

1. b; debit Utility Expense for $700, and credit Cash for $700.

2. a; debit Cash for $2,500, and credit Unearned Lawn Service Fees for $2,500.

3. c; debit Cash for $250,000, debit Land for $500,000, and credit Common Stock for $750,000.

4. d

5. e; Debt ratio = $400,000/$1,000,000 = <u>40%</u>

3 Adjusting Accounts for Financial Statements

TIME PERIODS AND ADJUSTING ACCOUNTS	PREPARING FINANCIAL STATEMENTS AND CLOSING	CLASSIFIED BALANCE SHEET AND ANALYSIS
C1 Accounting period	P2 Adjusted trial balance	C4 Classified balance sheet— Structure and categories
C2 Accrual vs cash	P3 Financial statement preparation illustrated	A2 Profit margin analysis
P1 Adjustments—Illustrated	P4 Closing entries	A3 Current ratio analysis
A1 Adjustments—Summarized	P5 Post-closing trial balance	
	C3 Accounting cycle summary	

Learning Objectives

C1 Explain the importance of periodic reporting and the time period assumption. (p. 102)

C2 Explain accrual accounting and how it improves financial statements. (p. 102)

P1 Prepare and explain adjusting entries. (p. 104)

A1 Explain how accounting adjustments link to financial statements. (p. 115)

P2 Explain and prepare an adjusted trial balance. (p. 116)

P3 Prepare financial statements from an adjusted trial balance. (p. 116)

P4 Describe and prepare closing entries. (p. 118)

P5 Explain and prepare a post-closing trial balance. (p. 120)

C3 Identify steps in the accounting cycle. (p. 122)

C4 Explain and prepare a classified balance sheet. (p. 123)

A2 Compute profit margin and describe its use in analyzing company performance. (p. 127)

A3 Compute the current ratio and describe what it reveals about a company's financial condition. (p. 128)

P6 *Appendix 3A*—Explain the alternatives in accounting for prepaids. (p. 131)

P7 *Appendix 3B*—Prepare a work sheet and explain its usefulness. (p. 133)

P8 *Appendix 3C*—Prepare reversing entries and explain their purpose. (p. 137)

Facebook Opens Its Books

"We are focused on . . . helping people share information"
—MARK ZUCKERBERG

PALO ALTO, CA—"Open Society" conjures up philosophical thoughts and political ideologies. However, for Mark Zuckerberg, his vision of an open society "is to give people the power to share and make the world more open and connected." That vision led Mark to create **Facebook** (**Facebook.com**) from his college dorm. Today, Facebook is the highest-profile social networking site. Along the way, Mark had to learn accounting and the details of preparing and interpreting financial statements.

"It's all been very interesting," says Mark. Important questions involving business formation, transaction analysis, and financial reporting arose. Mark answered them and in the process has set his company apart. "I'm here to build something for the long term," declares Mark. "Anything else is a distraction."

Information is the focus—both within Facebook and within its accounting records. Mark recalls that when he launched his business, there were, "all these reasons why they could not aggregate this [personal] information." He took a similar tactic in addressing accounting information. "There's an intense focus on . . . information, as both

Facebook, Inc.

NASDAQ:FB

$63 billion valuation
Founded 2004
$5 bil. annual sales

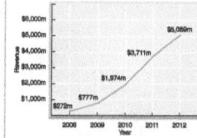

an ideal and a practical strategy to get things done," insists Mark. This includes using accounting information to make key business decisions.

While Facebook is the language of social networking, accounting is the language of business networking. "As a company we are very focused on what we are building," says Mark. "We are adding a certain amount of value to people's lives if we build a very good product." That value is reflected in its financial statements, which are based on transaction analysis and accounting adjustments. For example, Facebook's prepaid assets are $471 million, and its accrued expenses are $423 million. Mark signs off on the proper adjustments for those accounts and others.

Facebook's success is reflected in its revenues, which continue to grow and

exhibit what people call the monetizing of social networking (see graphic). "Social Ads are doing pretty well," asserts Mark. "We are happy with how we are doing in terms of numbers of advertisers and revenue." Facebook also tracks its expenses and asset purchases. "We expect to achieve . . . profitability," states Mark. "It means we will be able to fund all of our operations and server purchases from the cash we generate." This is saying a lot as Facebook's operating expenditures must support more than 900 million monthly active users.

Mark emphasizes that his financial house must be in order for Facebook to realize its full potential—and that potential is in his sights. "We believe really deeply that if people are sharing more, then the world will be a more open place where people can understand what is going on with the people around them."

Sources: *Facebook Website,* January 2014; *CNN,* October 2008; *Mercury News,* April 2009; *VentureBeat,* March 2008; *FastCompany.com,* May 2007; *Wired,* June 2009; *Facebook 10-K Report,* February 2013

TIMING AND REPORTING

This section describes the importance of reporting accounting information at regular intervals and its impact for recording revenues and expenses.

The Accounting Period

C1 Explain the importance of periodic reporting and the time period assumption.

The value of information is often linked to its timeliness. Useful information must reach decision makers frequently and promptly. To provide timely information, accounting systems prepare reports at regular intervals. This results in an accounting process impacted by the time period (or periodicity) assumption. The **time period assumption** presumes that an organization's activities can be divided into specific time periods such as a month, a three-month quarter, a six-month interval, or a year. Exhibit 3.1 shows various **accounting**, or *report-ing*, **periods.** Most organizations use a year as their primary accounting period. Reports covering a one-year period are known as **annual financial statements.** Many organizations also prepare **interim financial statements** covering one, three, or six months of activity.

"Apple announces annual income of . . ."

EXHIBIT 3.1

Accounting Periods

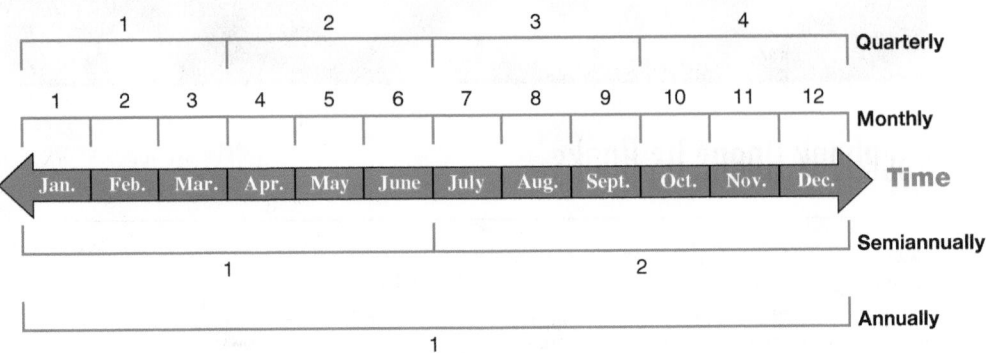

The annual reporting period is not always a calendar year ending on December 31. An organization can adopt a **fiscal year** consisting of any 12 consecutive months. It is also acceptable to adopt an annual reporting period of 52 weeks. For example, Gap's fiscal year consistently ends the final week of January or the first week of February each year.

Companies with little seasonal variation in sales often choose the calendar year as their fiscal year. Facebook, Inc., uses calendar year reporting. However, the financial statements of The Kellogg Company (the company that controls characters such as Tony the Tiger, Snap! Crackle! Pop!, and Keebler Elf) reflect a fiscal year that ends on the Saturday nearest December 31. Companies experiencing seasonal variations in sales often choose a **natural business year** end, which is when sales activities are at their lowest level for the year. The natural business year for retailers such as Walmart, Target, and Macy's usually ends around January 31, after the holiday season.

Accrual Basis versus Cash Basis

C2 Explain accrual accounting and how it improves financial statements.

After external transactions and events are recorded, several accounts still need adjustments before their balances appear in financial statements. This need arises because internal transactions and events remain unrecorded. **Accrual basis accounting** uses the adjusting process to recognize revenues when earned and expenses when incurred (matched with revenues).

Cash basis accounting recognizes revenues when cash is received and records expenses when cash is paid. This means that cash basis net income for a period is the difference between cash receipts and cash payments. Cash basis accounting is not consistent with generally accepted accounting principles (neither U.S. GAAP nor IFRS).

It is commonly held that accrual accounting better reflects business performance than information about cash receipts and payments. Accrual accounting also increases the *comparability* of financial statements from one period to another. Yet cash basis accounting is useful for several business decisions—which is the reason companies must report a statement of cash flows.

To see the difference between these two accounting systems, let's consider FastForward's Prepaid Insurance account. FastForward paid $2,400 for 24 months of insurance coverage that began on December 1, 2013. Accrual accounting requires that $100 of insurance expense be reported on December 2013's income statement. Another $1,200 of expense is reported in year 2014, and the remaining $1,100 is reported as expense in the first 11 months of 2015. Exhibit 3.2 illustrates this allocation of insurance cost across these three years. Any unexpired premium is reported as a Prepaid Insurance asset on the accrual basis balance sheet.

EXHIBIT 3.2

Accrual Accounting for Allocating Prepaid Insurance to Expense

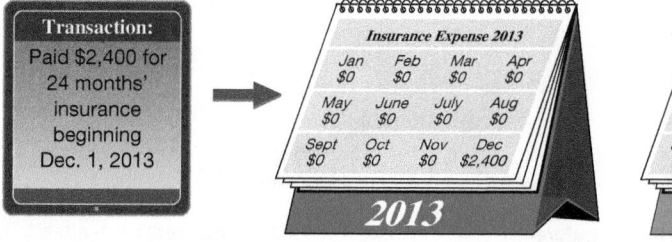

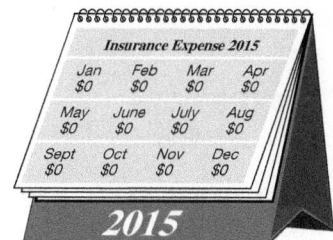

Alternatively, a cash basis income statement for December 2013 reports insurance expense of $2,400, as shown in Exhibit 3.3. The cash basis income statements for years 2014 and 2015 report no insurance expense. The cash basis balance sheet never reports an insurance asset because it is immediately expensed. This shows that cash basis income for 2013–2015 fails to match the cost of insurance with the insurance benefits received for those years and months.

EXHIBIT 3.3

Cash Accounting for Allocating Prepaid Insurance to Expense

Recognizing Revenues and Expenses

We use the time period assumption to divide a company's activities into specific time periods, but not all activities are complete when financial statements are prepared. Thus, adjustments often are required to get correct account balances.

We rely on two principles in the adjusting process: revenue recognition and expense recognition (the latter is often referred to as matching). Chapter 1 explained that the *revenue recognition principle* requires that revenue be recorded when earned, not before and not after. Most companies earn revenue when they provide services and products to customers. A major goal of the adjusting process is to have revenue recognized (reported) in the time period when it is earned. The **expense recognition** (or **matching**) **principle** aims to record expenses in the same accounting period as the revenues that are earned as a result of those expenses. This matching of expenses with the revenue benefits is a major part of the adjusting process.

Matching expenses with revenues often requires us to predict certain events. When we use financial statements, we must understand that they require estimates and therefore include measures that are not precise. Walt Disney's annual report explains that its production costs from

Point: Recording revenue early overstates current-period revenue and income; recording it late understates current-period revenue and income.

Point: Recording expense early overstates current-period expense and understates current-period income; recording it late understates current-period expense and overstates current-period income.

movies, such as its *Pirates of the Caribbean* series, are matched to revenues based on a ratio of current revenues from the movie divided by its predicted total revenues.

 **Decision** Insight

Diamond Foods, Inc., a popular snack maker, was recently investigated for postponing expenses related to payments to its walnut growers. This alleged late expense recognition caused income to be overstated in 2011. Further, this misstatement threatened completion of its recent acquisition of **Pringles** (for more details, see *BusinessWeek*, January 17, 2012). ▦

QC1

ADJUSTING ACCOUNTS

Adjusting accounts is a three-step process:

> **Step 1:** Determine what the current account balance *equals*.
>
> **Step 2:** Determine what the current account balance *should equal*.
>
> **Step 3:** Record an adjusting entry to get from step *1* to step *2*.

Framework for Adjustments

P1 Prepare and explain adjusting entries.

Adjustments are necessary for transactions and events that extend over more than one period. It is helpful to group adjustments by the timing of cash receipt or cash payment in relation to the recognition of the related revenues or expenses. Exhibit 3.4 identifies four types of adjustments.

EXHIBIT 3.4

Types of Adjustments

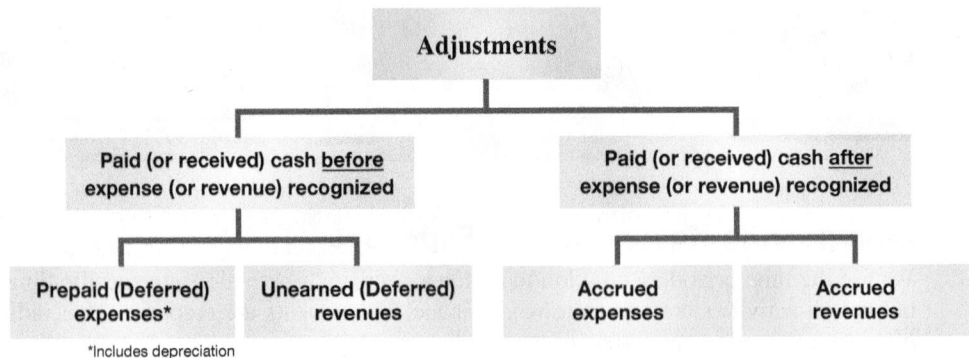

Point: Source documents provide information for most daily transactions, and in many businesses the recordkeepers record them. Adjustments require more knowledge and are usually handled by senior accounting professionals.

   The left half of this exhibit shows prepaid expenses (including depreciation) and unearned revenues, which reflect transactions when cash is paid or received *before* a related expense or revenue is recognized. They are also called *deferrals* because the recognition of an expense (or revenue) is *deferred* until after the related cash is paid (or received). The right half of this exhibit shows accrued expenses and accrued revenues, which reflect transactions when cash is paid or received *after* a related expense or revenue is recognized. Adjusting entries are necessary for each of these so that revenues, expenses, assets, and liabilities are correctly reported. Specifically, an **adjusting entry** is made at the end of an accounting period to reflect a transaction or event that is not yet recorded. Each adjusting entry affects one or more income statement accounts *and* one or more balance sheet accounts (but never the Cash account).

Prepaid (Deferred) Expenses

Prepaid expenses refer to items *paid for* in advance of receiving their benefits. Prepaid expenses are assets. When these assets are used, their costs become expenses. Adjusting entries for prepaids increase expenses and decrease assets as shown in the T-accounts of Exhibit 3.5. Such adjustments reflect transactions and events that use up prepaid expenses (including passage of time). To illustrate the accounting for prepaid expenses, we look at prepaid insurance, supplies, and depreciation.

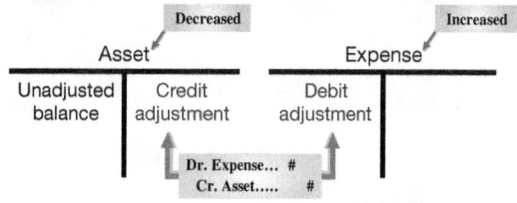

EXHIBIT 3.5

Adjusting for Prepaid Expenses

Prepaid Insurance   We use our 3-step process for this and all accounting adjustments.

Step 1:   We determine that the current balance of FastForward's prepaid insurance is equal to its $2,400 payment for 24 months of insurance benefits that began on December 1, 2013.

Step 2:   With the passage of time, the benefits of the insurance gradually expire and a portion of the Prepaid Insurance asset becomes expense. For instance, one month's insurance coverage expires by December 31, 2013. This expense is $100, or 1/24 of $2,400, which leaves $2,300.

Step 3:   The adjusting entry to record this expense and reduce the asset, along with T-account postings, follows:

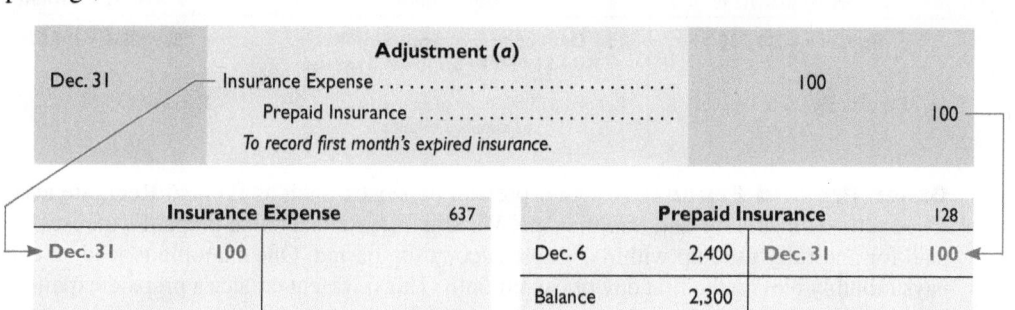

Assets = Liabilities + Equity
−100   −100

Explanation   After adjusting and posting, the $100 balance in Insurance Expense and the $2,300 balance in Prepaid Insurance are ready for reporting in financial statements. *Not* making the adjustment on or before December 31 would (1) understate expenses by $100 and overstate net income by $100 for the December income statement and (2) overstate both prepaid insurance (assets) and equity (because of net income) by $100 in the December 31 balance sheet. (Exhibit 3.2 showed that 2014's adjustments must transfer a total of $1,200 from Prepaid Insurance to Insurance Expense, and 2015's adjustments must transfer the remaining $1,100 to Insurance Expense.) The following table highlights the December 31, 2013, adjustment for prepaid insurance.

Point: Many companies record adjusting entries only at the end of each year because of the time and cost necessary.

Before Adjustment	Adjustment	After Adjustment
Prepaid Insurance = $2,400	**Deduct $100 from Prepaid Insurance Add $100 to Insurance Expense**	**Prepaid Insurance = $2,300**
Reports $2,400 policy for 24-months' coverage.	Record current month's $100 insurance expense and $100 reduction in prepaid amount.	Reports $2,300 in coverage for remaining 23 months.

Supplies   Supplies are a prepaid expense requiring adjustment.

Step 1:   FastForward purchased $9,720 of supplies in December and some of them were used during this month. When financial statements are prepared at December 31, the cost of supplies used during December must be recognized.

Step 2:   When FastForward computes (takes physical count of) its remaining unused supplies at December 31, it finds $8,670 of supplies remaining of the $9,720 total supplies. The $1,050 difference between these two amounts is December's supplies expense.

Step 3:   The adjusting entry to record this expense and reduce the Supplies asset account, along with T-account postings, follows:

Assets = Liabilities + Equity
−1,050   −1,050

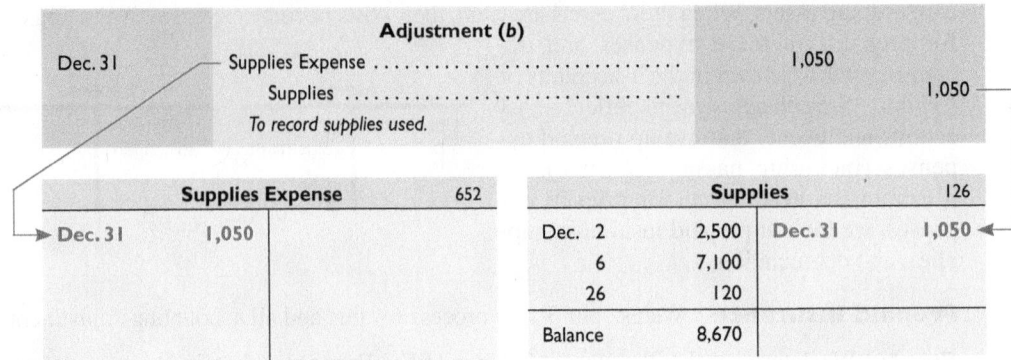

Adjustment (b)		
Dec. 31 Supplies Expense	1,050	
Supplies		1,050
To record supplies used.		

Supplies Expense		652
Dec. 31	1,050	

Supplies				126
Dec. 2	2,500	Dec. 31	1,050	
6	7,100			
26	120			
Balance	8,670			

Explanation   The balance of the Supplies account is $8,670 after posting—equaling the cost of the remaining supplies. *Not* making the adjustment on or before December 31 would (1) understate expenses by $1,050 and overstate net income by $1,050 for the December income statement and (2) overstate both supplies and equity (because of net income) by $1,050 in the December 31 balance sheet. The following table highlights the adjustment for supplies.

Before Adjustment	**Adjustment**	**After Adjustment**
Supplies = $9,720	**Deduct $1,050 from Supplies Add $1,050 to Supplies Expense**	**Supplies = $8,670**
Reports $9,720 in supplies.	Record $1,050 in supplies used and $1,050 as supplies expense.	Reports $8,670 in supplies.

Other Prepaid Expenses   Other prepaid expenses, such as Prepaid Rent, are accounted for exactly as Insurance and Supplies are. We should note that some prepaid expenses are both paid for and fully used up within a single accounting period. One example is when a company pays monthly rent on the first day of each month. This payment creates a prepaid expense on the first day of each month that fully expires by the end of the month. In these special cases, we can record the cash paid with a debit to an expense account instead of an asset account. This practice is described more completely later in the chapter.

Point: We assume that prepaid and unearned items are recorded in balance sheet accounts. An alternative is to record them in income statement accounts; Appendix 3A discusses this alternative. The adjusted financial statements are identical.

▌ **Decision** Maker ════════════════════════════════════

Investor   A small publishing company signs an aspiring Olympic gymnast to write a book. The company pays the gymnast $500,000 to sign plus future book royalties. A note to the company's financial statements says that "prepaid expenses include $500,000 in author signing fees to be matched against future expected sales." Is this accounting for the signing bonus acceptable? How does it affect your analysis? ■   [Answer—p. 138]

Point: Plant assets are also called *Plant & Equipment,* or *Property, Plant & Equipment.*

Point: Depreciation does not necessarily measure decline in market value.

Point: An asset's expected value at the end of its useful life is called *salvage value.*

Depreciation   A special category of prepaid expenses is **plant assets,** which refers to long-term tangible assets used to produce and sell products and services. Plant assets are expected to provide benefits for more than one period. Examples of plant assets are buildings, machines, vehicles, and fixtures. All plant assets, with a general exception for land, eventually wear out or decline in usefulness. The costs of these assets are deferred but are gradually reported as expenses in the income statement over the assets' useful lives (benefit periods). **Depreciation** is the process of allocating the costs of these assets over their expected useful lives. Depreciation expense is recorded with an adjusting entry similar to that for other prepaid expenses.

Step 1:   Recall that FastForward purchased equipment for $26,000 in early December to use in earning revenue. This equipment's cost must be depreciated.

Step 2:   The equipment is expected to have a useful life (benefit period) of four years and to be worth about $8,000 at the end of four years. This means the *net* cost of this equipment over its useful life is $18,000 ($26,000 − $8,000). We can use any of several methods to allocate this $18,000 net cost to expense. FastForward uses a method called **straight-line depreciation,** which allocates equal amounts of the asset's net cost to depreciation during its useful life. Dividing the $18,000 net cost by the 48 months in the asset's useful life gives a monthly cost of $375 ($18,000/48).

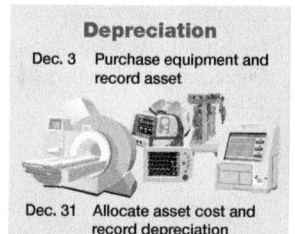

Depreciation

Dec. 3 Purchase equipment and record asset

Dec. 31 Allocate asset cost and record depreciation

Step 3: The adjusting entry to record monthly depreciation expense, along with T-account postings, follows:

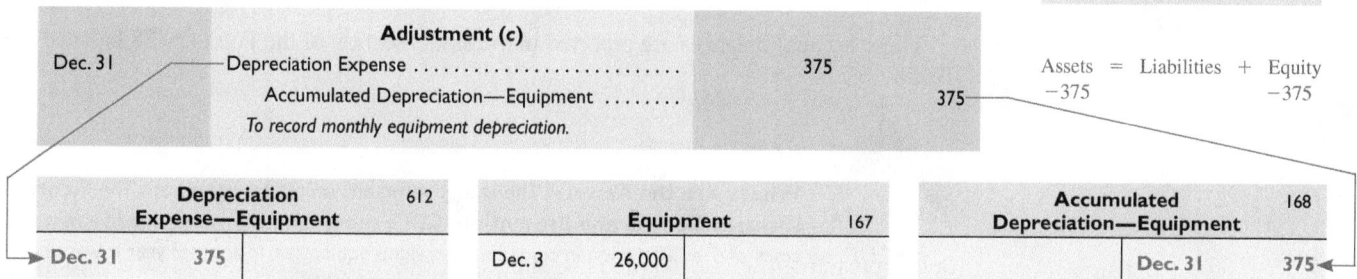

Explanation After posting the adjustment, the Equipment account ($26,000) less its Accumulated Depreciation ($375) account equals the $25,625 net cost (made up of $17,625 for the 47 remaining months in the benefit period plus the $8,000 value at the end of that time). The $375 balance in the Depreciation Expense account is reported in the December income statement. *Not* making the adjustment at December 31 would (1) understate expenses by $375 and overstate net income by $375 for the December income statement and (2) overstate both assets and equity (because of income) by $375 in the December 31 balance sheet. The following table highlights the adjustment for depreciation.

Before Adjustment	Adjustment	After Adjustment
Equipment, net = $26,000	**Deduct $375 from Equipment, net Add $375 to Depreciation Expense**	**Equipment, net = $25,625**
Reports $26,000 in equipment.	Record $375 in depreciation and $375 as accumulated depreciation, which is deducted from equipment.	Reports $25,625 in equipment, net of accumulated depreciation.

Accumulated depreciation is kept in a separate contra account. A **contra account** is an account linked with another account, it has an opposite normal balance, and it is reported as a subtraction from that other account's balance. For instance, FastForward's contra account of Accumulated Depreciation—Equipment is subtracted from the Equipment account in the balance sheet (see Exhibit 3.7). This contra account allows balance sheet readers to know both the full costs of assets and the total depreciation.

Equipment		167
Dec. 3	26,000	

Accumulated Depreciation—Equipment		168
	Dec. 31	375
	Jan. 31	375
	Feb. 28	375
	Balance	1,125

EXHIBIT 3.6

Accounts after Three Months of Depreciation Adjustments

The title of the contra account, *Accumulated Depreciation,* reveals that this account includes total depreciation expense for all prior periods for which the asset was used. To illustrate, the Equipment and the Accumulated Depreciation accounts appear as in Exhibit 3.6 on February 28, 2014, after three months of adjusting entries. The $1,125 balance in the accumulated depreciation account can be subtracted from its related $26,000 asset cost. The difference ($24,875) between these two balances is the cost of the asset that has not yet been depreciated. This difference is called the **book value,** or the *net amount,* which equals the asset's costs less its accumulated depreciation.

Point: The cost principle requires an asset to be initially recorded at acquisition cost. Depreciation causes the asset's book value (cost less accumulated depreciation) to decline over time.

Point: The net cost of equipment is also called the *depreciable basis.*

EXHIBIT 3.7

Equipment and Accumulated
Depreciation on February 28
Balance Sheet

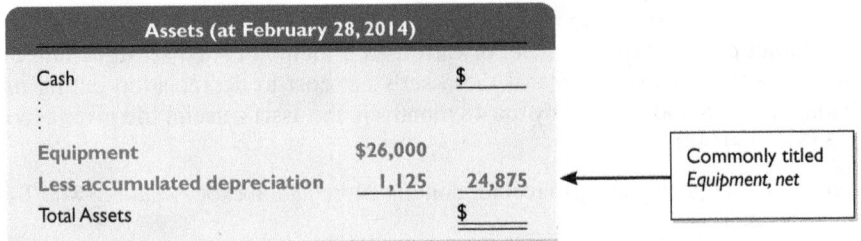

Assets (at February 28, 2014)		
Cash		$
⋮		
Equipment	$26,000	
Less accumulated depreciation	1,125	24,875
Total Assets		$

Commonly titled
Equipment, net

These account balances are reported in the assets section of the February 28 balance sheet in Exhibit 3.7.

Fraud

Where Are the Assests? The U.S. government seems to lose assets. The **Center for Diseases Control and Prevention** (CDC) seems especially vulnerable. In a recent year, the CDC lost track of over $8 million in computer and video equipment, In another year it was unable to account for nearly $6 million in computers, microscopes, and vehicles. The president of *Citizens Against Government Waste* said "It's just a good thing they haven't lost any diseases!"

NEED-TO-KNOW 3.1

P1

For each separate case below, follow the three-step process for adjusting the prepaid asset account. Step 1: Determine what the current account balance equals. Step 2: Determine what the current account balance should equal. Step 3: Record an adjusting entry to get from step 1 to step 2. *Assume no other adjusting entries are made during the year.*

1. **Prepaid Insurance.** The Prepaid Insurance account has a $5,000 debit balance to start the year and no insurance payments were made during the year. A review of insurance policies and payments shows that $1,000 of unexpired insurance remains at year-end.

2. **Prepaid Rent.** On October 1 of the current year, the company prepaid $12,000 for one year of rent for facilities being occupied from that day forward. The company debited Prepaid Rent and credited Cash for $12,000. December 31 year-end statements must be prepared.

3. **Supplies.** The Supplies account has a $1,000 debit balance to start the year. Supplies of $2,000 were purchased during the current year and debited to the Supplies account. A December 31 physical count shows $500 of supplies remaining.

4. **Accumulated Depreciation.** The company has only one fixed asset (equipment) that it purchased at the start of this year. That asset had cost $38,000, had an estimated life of 10 years, and is expected to be valued at $8,000 at the end of the 10-year life.

Solution

1. Step 1: Prepaid Insurance equals $5,000
   Step 2: Prepaid Insurance should equal $1,000 (the unexpired part)
   Step 3: Adjusting entry to get from Step 1 to Step 2

Insurance Expense	4,000	
Prepaid Insurance		4,000
To record insurance coverage that expired ($5,000 − $1,000).		

2. Step 1: Prepaid Rent equals $12,000
   Step 2: Prepaid Rent should equal $9,000 (the unexpired part)*
   Step 3: Adjusting entry to get from Step 1 to Step 2

Rent Expense	3,000	
Prepaid Rent		3,000
*To record prepaid rent that expired *($12,000 − $3,000 = $9,000)*		
where $3,000 is from: ($12,000/12 months) × 3 months		

3. Step 1: Supplies equal $3,000 (from $1,000 + $2,000)
Step 2: Supplies should equal $500 (what's left)
Step 3: Adjusting entry to get from Step 1 to Step 2*

Supplies Expense	2,500	
Supplies		2,500
*To record supplies used. *$1,000 + $2,000 purchased − Supplies used = $500 remaining*		

4. Step 1: Accumulated Depreciation equals $0
Step 2: Accumulated Depreciation should equal $3,000 (after current period depreciation of $3,000)*
Step 3: Adjusting entry to get from Step 1 to Step 2

Depreciation Expense—Equipment..................................	3,000	
Accumulated Depreciation—Equipment		3,000
*To record depreciation expense for the period. *($38,000 − $8,000)/10 years*		

Do More: QS 3-1, QS 3-2, QS 3-14, QS 3-15, QS 3-16, E 3-5

Unearned (Deferred) Revenues

The term **unearned revenues** refers to cash received in advance of providing products and services. Unearned revenues, also called *deferred revenues,* are liabilities. When cash is accepted, an obligation to provide products or services is accepted. As products or services are provided, the unearned revenues become *earned* revenues. Adjusting entries for unearned revenues involve increasing revenues and decreasing unearned revenues, as shown in Exhibit 3.8.

Point: To *defer* is to postpone. We postpone reporting amounts received as revenues until they are earned.

EXHIBIT 3.8

Adjusting for Unearned Revenues

An example of unearned revenues is from Gannett Co., Inc., publisher of USA TODAY, which reports unexpired (unearned subscriptions) of $224 million: "Revenue is recognized in the period in which it is earned (as newspapers are delivered)." Unearned revenues are nearly 25% of the current liabilities for Gannett. Another example comes from the Boston Celtics. When the Celtics receive cash from advance ticket sales and broadcast fees, they record it in an unearned revenue account called *Deferred Game Revenues.* The Celtics recognize this unearned revenue with adjusting entries on a game-by-game basis. Since the NBA regular season begins in October and ends in April, revenue recognition is mainly limited to this period. For a recent season, the Celtics' quarterly revenues were $0 million for July–September; $34 million for October–December; $48 million for January–March; and $17 million for April–June.

Returning to FastForward, it also has unearned revenues. It agreed on December 26 to provide consulting services to a client for a fixed fee of $3,000 for 60 days.

Step 1: On December 26, the client paid the 60-day fee in advance, covering the period December 27 to February 24. The entry to record the cash received in advance is

Dec. 26	Cash	3,000	
	Unearned Consulting Revenue		3,000
	Received advance payment for services over the next 60 days.		

Assets = Liabilities + Equity
+3,000   +3,000

This advance payment increases cash and creates an obligation to do consulting work over the next 60 days.

Step 2: As time passes, FastForward earns this payment through consulting. By December 31, it has provided five days' service and earned 5/60 of the $3,000 unearned revenue. This amounts to $250 ($3,000 × 5/60). The *revenue recognition principle* implies that $250 of unearned revenue must be reported as revenue on the December income statement.

Step 3:   The adjusting entry to reduce the liability account and recognize earned revenue, along with T-account postings, follows:

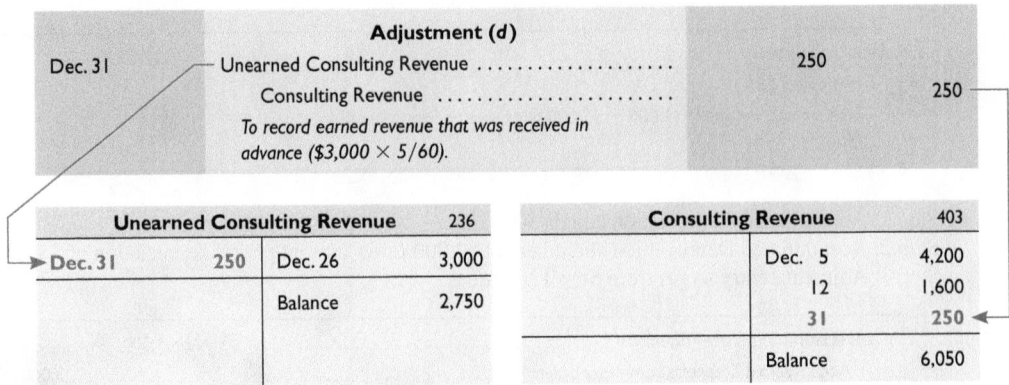

Assets = Liabilities + Equity
           −250   +250

Adjustment (d)		
Dec. 31 Unearned Consulting Revenue	250	
Consulting Revenue		250
To record earned revenue that was received in advance ($3,000 × 5/60).		

Unearned Consulting Revenue			236
Dec. 31	250	Dec. 26	3,000
		Balance	2,750

Consulting Revenue		403
	Dec. 5	4,200
	12	1,600
	31	250
	Balance	6,050

Explanation   The adjusting entry transfers $250 from unearned revenue (a liability account) to a revenue account. *Not* making the adjustment (1) understates revenue and net income by $250 in the December income statement and (2) overstates unearned revenue and understates equity by $250 on the December 31 balance sheet. The following highlights the adjustment for unearned revenue.

Before Adjustment	Adjustment	After Adjustment
Unearned Consulting Revenue = $3,000	**Deduct $250 from Unearned Consulting Revenue Add $250 to Consulting Revenue**	**Unearned Consulting Revenue = $2,750**
Reports $3,000 in unearned revenue for consulting services promised for 60 days.	Record 5 days of earned consulting revenue, which is 5/60 of unearned amount.	Reports $2,750 in unearned revenue for consulting services owed over next 55 days.

Accounting for unearned revenues is crucial to many companies. For example, the National Retail Federation reports that gift card sales, which are unearned revenues for sellers, exceed $20 billion annually. Gift cards are now the top selling holiday gift; 57.3% of all gift givers planned to give at least one gift card in 2011 (source: NRF Website).

NEED-TO-KNOW 3.2

P1

For each separate case below, follow the three-step process for adjusting the unearned revenue liability account. Step 1: Determine what the current account balance equals. Step 2: Determine what the current account balance should equal. Step 3: Record an adjusting entry to get from step 1 to step 2. *Assume no other adjusting entries are made during the year.*

a. Unearned Rent Revenue. The company collected $24,000 rent in advance on September 1, debiting Cash and crediting Unearned Rent Revenue. The tenant was paying 12 months rent in advance and occupancy began September 1.

b. Unearned Services Revenue. The company charges $100 per month to spray a house for insects. A customer paid $600 on November 1 in advance for six treatments, which was recorded with a debit to Cash and a credit to Unearned Services Revenue. At year-end, the company has applied two treatments for the customer.

Solution

a. Step 1: Unearned Rent Revenue equals $24,000
   Step 2: Unearned Rent Revenue should equal $16,000 (current period earned revenue is $8,000*)
   Step 3: Adjusting entry to get from Step 1 to Step 2

Unearned Rent Revenue...	8,000	
Rent Revenue		8,000
To record earned portion of rent received in advance.		
*($24,000/12 months) × 4 months rental usage		

b. Step 1: Unearned Services Revenue equals $600
Step 2: Unearned Services Revenue should equal $400 (current period earned revenue is $200*)
Step 3: Adjusting entry to get from Step 1 to Step 2

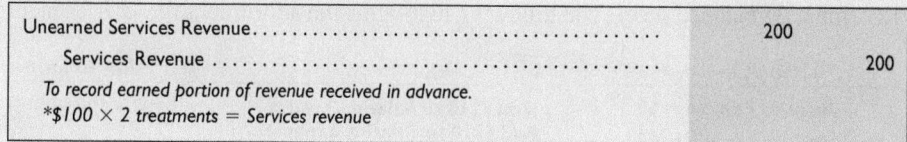

Unearned Services Revenue...	200	
Services Revenue		200
To record earned portion of revenue received in advance.		
*$100 × 2 treatments = Services revenue		

Do More: QS 3-5, QS 3-17

Accrued Expenses

Accrued expenses refer to costs that are incurred in a period but are both unpaid and unrecorded. Accrued expenses must be reported on the income statement for the period when incurred. Adjusting entries for recording accrued expenses involve increasing expenses and increasing liabilities as shown in Exhibit 3.9. This adjustment recognizes expenses incurred in a period but not yet paid. Common examples of accrued expenses are salaries, interest, rent, and taxes. We use salaries and interest to show how to adjust accounts for accrued expenses.

Point: Accrued expenses are also called accrued liabilities.

EXHIBIT 3.9

Adjusting for Accrued Expenses

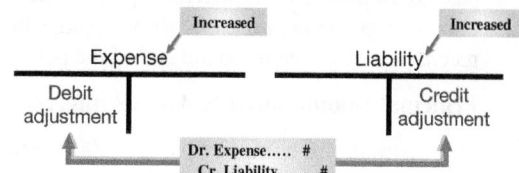

Accrued Salaries Expense   FastForward's employee earns $70 per day, or $350 for a five-day workweek beginning on Monday and ending on Friday.

Step 1:   Its employee is paid every two weeks on Friday. On December 12 and 26, the wages are paid, recorded in the journal, and posted to the ledger.

Step 2:   The calendar in Exhibit 3.10 shows three working days after the December 26 payday (29, 30, and 31). This means the employee has earned three days' salary by the close of business

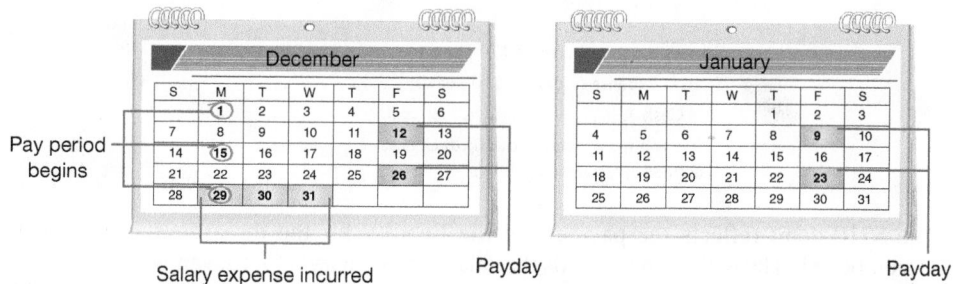

Salary expense incurred   Payday   Payday

EXHIBIT 3.10

Salary Accrual and Paydays

on Wednesday, December 31, yet this salary cost has not been paid or recorded. The financial statements would be incomplete if FastForward failed to report the added expense and liability to the employee for unpaid salary from December 29, 30, and 31.

Point: An employer records salaries expense and a vacation pay liability when employees earn vacation pay.

Step 3:   The adjusting entry to account for accrued salaries, along with T-account postings, follows:

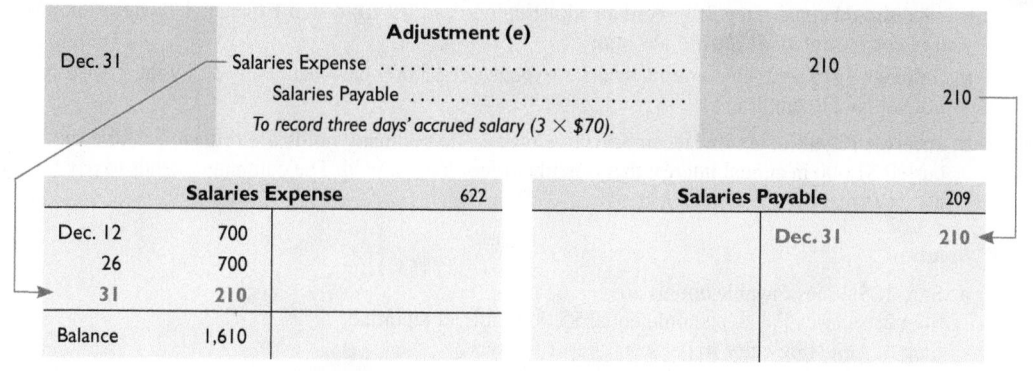

	Adjustment (e)		
Dec. 31	Salaries Expense	210	
	Salaries Payable		210
	To record three days' accrued salary (3 × $70).		

Assets = Liabilities + Equity
+210   −210

Salaries Expense		622
Dec. 12	700	
26	700	
31	210	
Balance	1,610	

| **Salaries Payable** | | 209 |
| | Dec. 31 | 210 |

Explanation   Salaries expense of $1,610 is reported on the December income statement and $210 of salaries payable (liability) is reported in the balance sheet. *Not* making the adjustment (1) understates salaries expense and overstates net income by $210 in the December income statement and (2) understates salaries payable (liabilities) and overstates equity by $210 on the December 31 balance sheet. The following highlights the adjustment for salaries incurred.

Before Adjustment	Adjustment	After Adjustment
Salaries Payable = $0	**Add $210 to Salaries Payable** **Add $210 to Salaries Expense**	**Salaries Payable = $210**
Reports $0 from employee salaries incurred but not yet paid in cash.	Record 3 days' salaries owed to employee, but not yet paid, at $70 per day.	Reports $210 salaries payable to employee but not yet paid.

Accrued Interest Expense   Companies commonly have accrued interest expense on notes payable and other long-term liabilities at the end of a period. Interest expense is incurred with the passage of time. Unless interest is paid on the last day of an accounting period, we need to adjust for interest expense incurred but not yet paid. This means we must accrue interest cost from the most recent payment date up to the end of the period. The formula for computing accrued interest is:

Principal amount owed × Annual interest rate × Fraction of year since last payment date.

Point: Interest computations assume a 360-day year; known as the *bankers' rule.*

To illustrate, if a company has a $6,000 loan from a bank at 6% annual interest, then 30 days' accrued interest expense is $30—computed as $6,000 × 0.06 × 30/360. The adjusting entry would be to debit Interest Expense for $30 and credit Interest Payable for $30.

Future Payment of Accrued Expenses   Adjusting entries for accrued expenses foretell cash transactions in future periods. Specifically, accrued expenses at the end of one accounting period result in *cash payment* in a *future period*(s). To illustrate, recall that FastForward recorded accrued salaries of $210. On January 9, the first payday of the next period, the following entry settles the accrued liability (salaries payable) and records salaries expense for seven days of work in January:

Assets = Liabilities + Equity
−700   −210   −490

Jan. 9	Salaries Payable (3 days at $70 per day)	210	
	Salaries Expense (7 days at $70 per day)	490	
	Cash		700
	Paid two weeks' salary including three days accrued in December.		

The $210 debit reflects the payment of the liability for the three days' salary accrued on December 31. The $490 debit records the salary for January's first seven working days (including the New Year's Day holiday) as an expense of the new accounting period. The $700 credit records the total amount of cash paid to the employee.

NEED-TO-KNOW 3.3

P1

For each separate case below, follow the three-step process for adjusting the accrued expense account. Step 1: Determine what the current account balance equals. Step 2: Determine what the current account balance should equal. Step 3: Record an adjusting entry to get from step 1 to step 2. *Assume no other adjusting entries are made during the year.*

a. Salaries Payable. At year-end, salaries expense of $5,000 has been incurred by the company, but is not yet paid to employees.

b. Interest Payable. At its December 31 year-end, the company holds a mortgage payable that has incurred $1,000 in annual interest that is neither recorded nor paid. The company intends to pay the interest on January 3 of the next year.

Solution

a. Step 1: Salaries Payable equals $0
Step 2: Salaries Payable should equal $5,000 (not yet recorded)
Step 3: Adjusting entry to get from Step 1 to Step 2

Salaries Expense	5,000	
Salaries Payable		5,000
To record employee salaries earned but not yet paid.		

b. Step 1: Interest Payable equals $0
Step 2: Interest Payable should equal $1,000 (not yet recorded)
Step 3: Adjusting entry to get from Step 1 to Step 2

Interest Expense	1,000	
Interest Payable		1,000
To record interest incurred but not yet paid.		

Do More: QS 3-4, QS 3-18, E 3-3, E 3-4

Accrued Revenues

The term **accrued revenues** refers to revenues earned in a period that are both unrecorded and not yet received in cash (or other assets). An example is a technician who bills customers only when the job is done. If one-third of a job is complete by the end of a period, then the technician must record one-third of the expected billing as revenue in that period—even though there is no billing or collection. The adjusting entries for accrued revenues increase assets and increase revenues as shown in Exhibit 3.11. Accrued revenues commonly arise from services, products, interest, and rent. We use service fees and interest to show how to adjust for accrued revenues.

Point: Accrued revenues are also called *accrued assets.*

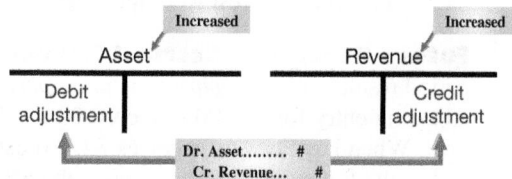

EXHIBIT 3.11
Adjusting for Accrued Revenues

Accrued Services Revenue Accrued revenues are not recorded until adjusting entries are made at the end of the accounting period. These accrued revenues are earned but unrecorded because either the buyer has not yet paid for them or the seller has not yet billed the buyer. FastForward provides an example.

Step 1: In the second week of December, it agreed to provide 30 days of consulting services to a local fitness club for a fixed fee of $2,700. The terms of the initial agreement call for FastForward to provide services from December 12, 2013, through January 10, 2014, or 30 days of service. The club agrees to pay FastForward $2,700 on January 10, 2014, when the service period is complete.

Step 2: At December 31, 2013, 20 days of services have already been provided. Since the contracted services have not yet been entirely provided, FastForward has neither billed the club nor recorded the services already provided. Still, FastForward has earned two-thirds of the 30-day fee, or $1,800 ($2,700 × 20/30). The *revenue recognition principle* implies that it must report the $1,800 on the December income statement. The balance sheet also must report that the club owes FastForward $1,800.

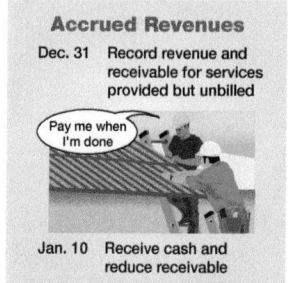

Accrued Revenues
Dec. 31 Record revenue and receivable for services provided but unbilled

Jan. 10 Receive cash and reduce receivable

Step 3: The year-end adjusting entry to account for accrued services revenue is

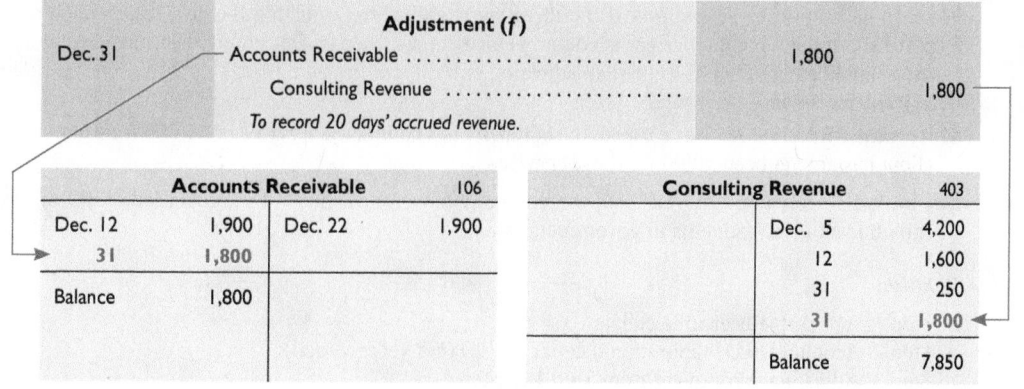

Dec. 31	Adjustment (f)		
	Accounts Receivable	1,800	
	Consulting Revenue		1,800
	To record 20 days' accrued revenue.		

Assets = Liabilities + Equity
+1,800   +1,800

Accounts Receivable			106
Dec. 12	1,900	Dec. 22	1,900
31	1,800		
Balance	1,800		

Consulting Revenue		403
	Dec. 5	4,200
	12	1,600
	31	250
	31	1,800
	Balance	7,850

Example: What is the adjusting entry if the 30-day consulting period began on December 22? *Answer:* One-third of the fee is earned:

Accounts Receivable   900
    Consulting Revenue. . . .   900

Explanation   Accounts receivable are reported on the balance sheet at $1,800, and the $7,850 total of consulting revenue is reported on the income statement. *Not* making the adjustment would understate (1) both consulting revenue and net income by $1,800 in the December income statement and (2) both accounts receivable (assets) and equity by $1,800 on the December 31 balance sheet. The following table highlights the adjustment for accrued revenue.

Before Adjustment	Adjustment	After Adjustment
Accounts Receivable = $0	**Add $1,800 to Accounts Receivable** **Add $1,800 to Consulting Revenue**	**Accounts Receivable = $1,800**
Reports $0 from revenue earned but not yet received in cash.	Record 20 days of earned consulting revenue, which is 20/30 of total contract amount.	Reports $1,800 in accounts receivable from consulting services provided.

Accrued Interest Revenue   In addition to the accrued interest expense we described earlier, interest can yield an accrued revenue when a debtor owes money (or other assets) to a company. If a company is holding notes or accounts receivable that produce interest revenue, we must adjust the accounts to record any earned and yet uncollected interest revenue. The adjusting entry is similar to the one for accruing services revenue. Specifically, we debit Interest Receivable (asset) and credit Interest Revenue.

Future Receipt of Accrued Revenues   Accrued revenues at the end of one accounting period result in *cash receipts* in a *future period*(s). To illustrate, recall that FastForward made an adjusting entry for $1,800 to record 20 days' accrued revenue earned from its consulting contract. When FastForward receives $2,700 cash on January 10 for the entire contract amount, it makes the following entry to remove the accrued asset (accounts receivable) and recognize the revenue earned in January. The $2,700 debit reflects the cash received. The $1,800 credit reflects the removal of the receivable, and the $900 credit records the revenue earned in January.

Assets = Liabilities + Equity
+2,700   +900
−1,800

Jan. 10	Cash	2,700	
	Accounts Receivable (20 days at $90 per day)		1,800
	Consulting Revenue (10 days at $90 per day)		900
	Received cash for the accrued asset and recorded earned consulting revenue for January.		

Decision Maker

Loan Officer   The owner of a custom audio, video, and home theater store applies for a business loan. The store's financial statements reveal large increases in current-year revenues and income. Analysis shows that these increases are due to a promotion that let consumers buy now and pay nothing until January 1 of next year. The store recorded these sales as accrued revenue. Does your analysis raise any concerns? ■   [Answer—p. 138]

NEED-TO-KNOW 3.4

P1

For each separate case below, follow the three-step process for adjusting the accrued revenue account. Step 1: Determine what the current account balance equals. Step 2: Determine what the current account balance should equal. Step 3: Record an adjusting entry to get from step 1 to step 2. *Assume no other adjusting entries are made during the year.*

a. Accounts Receivable. At year-end, the company has completed services of $1,000 for a client, but the client has not yet been billed for those services.

b. Interest Receivable. At year-end, the company has earned, but not yet recorded, $500 of interest earned from its investments in government bonds.

Solution

a. Step 1: Accounts Receivable equals $0
   Step 2: Accounts Receivable should equal $1,000 (not yet recorded)
   Step 3: Adjusting entry to get from Step 1 to Step 2

Accounts Receivable..	1,000	
Services Revenue		1,000
To record services revenue earned but not yet received.		

b. Step 1: Interest Receivable equals $0
Step 2: Interest Receivable should equal $500 (not yet recorded)
Step 3: Adjusting entry to get from Step 1 to Step 2

Interest Receivable...	500	
Interest Revenue		500
To record interest earned but not yet received.		

> Do More: QS 3-3, QS 3-19

Links to Financial Statements

The process of adjusting accounts is intended to bring an asset or liability account balance to its correct amount. It also updates a related expense or revenue account. These adjustments are necessary for transactions and events that extend over more than one period. (Adjusting entries are posted like any other entry.)

> **A1** Explain how accounting adjustments link to financial statements.

Exhibit 3.12 summarizes the four types of transactions requiring adjustment. Understanding this exhibit is important to understanding the adjusting process and its importance to financial statements. Remember that each adjusting entry affects one or more income statement accounts *and* one or more balance sheet accounts (but never cash).

| | **BEFORE** Adjusting | | |
Category	**Balance Sheet**	**Income Statement**	**Adjusting Entry**
Prepaid expenses†	Asset overstated	Expense understated	Dr. Expense
	Equity overstated		Cr. Asset*
Unearned revenues†	Liability overstated	Revenue understated	Dr. Liability
	Equity understated		Cr. Revenue
Accrued expenses	Liability understated	Expense understated	Dr. Expense
	Equity overstated		Cr. Liability
Accrued revenues	Asset understated	Revenue understated	Dr. Asset
	Equity understated		Cr. Revenue

EXHIBIT 3.12

Summary of Adjustments and Financial Statement Links

* For depreciation, the credit is to Accumulated Depreciation (contra asset).

† Exhibit assumes that prepaid expenses are initially recorded as assets and that unearned revenues are initially recorded as liabilities.

Information about some adjustments is not always available until several days or even weeks after the period-end. This means that some adjusting and closing entries are recorded later than, but dated as of, the last day of the period. One example is a company that receives a utility bill on January 10 for costs incurred for the month of December. When it receives the bill, the company records the expense and the payable as of December 31. Other examples include long-distance phone usage and costs of many Web billings. The December income statement reflects these additional expenses incurred, and the December 31 balance sheet includes these payables, although the amounts were not actually known on December 31.

> **Point:** CFOs often feel pressure to pursue fraudulent accounting due to pressure applied by their superiors, such as overbearing CEOs or aggressive boards.

■ **Decision Ethics**

Financial Officer   At year-end, the president instructs you, the financial officer, not to record accrued expenses until next year because they will not be paid until then. The president also directs you to record in current-year sales a recent purchase order from a customer that requires merchandise to be delivered two weeks after the year-end. Your company would report a net income instead of a net loss if you carry out these instructions. What do you do? ■   [Answer—p. 138]

> **QC2**

Adjusted Trial Balance

P2   Explain and prepare an adjusted trial balance.

An **unadjusted trial balance** is a list of accounts and balances prepared *before* adjustments are recorded. An **adjusted trial balance** is a list of accounts and balances prepared *after* adjusting entries have been recorded and posted to the ledger.

Exhibit 3.13 shows both the unadjusted and the adjusted trial balances for FastForward at December 31, 2013. The order of accounts in the trial balance is usually set up to match the order in the chart of accounts. Several new accounts arise from the adjusting entries.

EXHIBIT 3.13

Unadjusted and Adjusted Trial Balances

FASTFORWARD
Trial Balances
December 31, 2013

Acct. No.	Account Title	Unadjusted Trial Balance Dr.	Unadjusted Trial Balance Cr.	Adjustments Dr.	Adjustments Cr.	Adjusted Trial Balance Dr.	Adjusted Trial Balance Cr.
101	Cash	$ 4,350				$ 4,350	
106	Accounts receivable	0		(f) $1,800		1,800	
126	Supplies	9,720			(b) $1,050	8,670	
128	Prepaid insurance	2,400			(a) 100	2,300	
167	Equipment	26,000				26,000	
168	Accumulated depreciation—Equip.		$ 0		(c) 375		$ 375
201	Accounts payable		6,200				6,200
209	Salaries payable		0		(e) 210		210
236	Unearned consulting revenue		3,000	(d) 250			2,750
307	Common stock		30,000				30,000
318	Retained earnings		0				0
319	Dividends	200				200	
403	Consulting revenue		5,800		(d) 250		7,850
					(f) 1,800		
406	Rental revenue		300				300
612	Depreciation expense—Equip.	0		(c) 375		375	
622	Salaries expense	1,400		(e) 210		1,610	
637	Insurance expense	0		(a) 100		100	
640	Rent expense	1,000				1,000	
652	Supplies expense	0		(b) 1,050		1,050	
690	Utilities expense	230				230	
	Totals	$45,300	$45,300	$3,785	$3,785	$47,685	$47,685

Each adjustment (see middle columns) is identified by a letter in parentheses that links it to an adjusting entry explained earlier. Each amount in the Adjusted Trial Balance columns is computed by taking that account's amount from the Unadjusted Trial Balance columns and adding or subtracting any adjustment(s). To illustrate, Supplies has a $9,720 Dr. balance in the unadjusted columns. Subtracting the $1,050 Cr. amount shown in the adjustments columns yields an adjusted $8,670 Dr. balance for Supplies. An account can have more than one adjustment, such as for Consulting Revenue. Also, some accounts might not require adjustment for this period, such as Accounts Payable.

PREPARING FINANCIAL STATEMENTS

P3   Prepare financial statements from an adjusted trial balance.

Point: Sarbanes-Oxley Act requires that financial statements filed with the SEC be certified by the CEO and CFO, including a declaration that the statements fairly present the issuer's operations and financial condition. Violators can receive fines and/or prison terms.

We can prepare financial statements directly from information in the *adjusted* trial balance. An adjusted trial balance (see the right-most columns in Exhibit 3.13) includes all accounts and balances appearing in financial statements, and is easier to work from than the entire ledger when preparing financial statements.

Exhibit 3.14 shows how revenue and expense balances are transferred from the adjusted trial balance to the income statement (red lines). The net income and the dividends amount are then used to prepare the statement of retained earnings (black lines). Asset and liability balances on the adjusted trial balance are then transferred to the balance sheet (blue lines). The ending retained

EXHIBIT 3.14

Preparing Financial Statements (Adjusted Trial Balance from Exhibit 3.13)

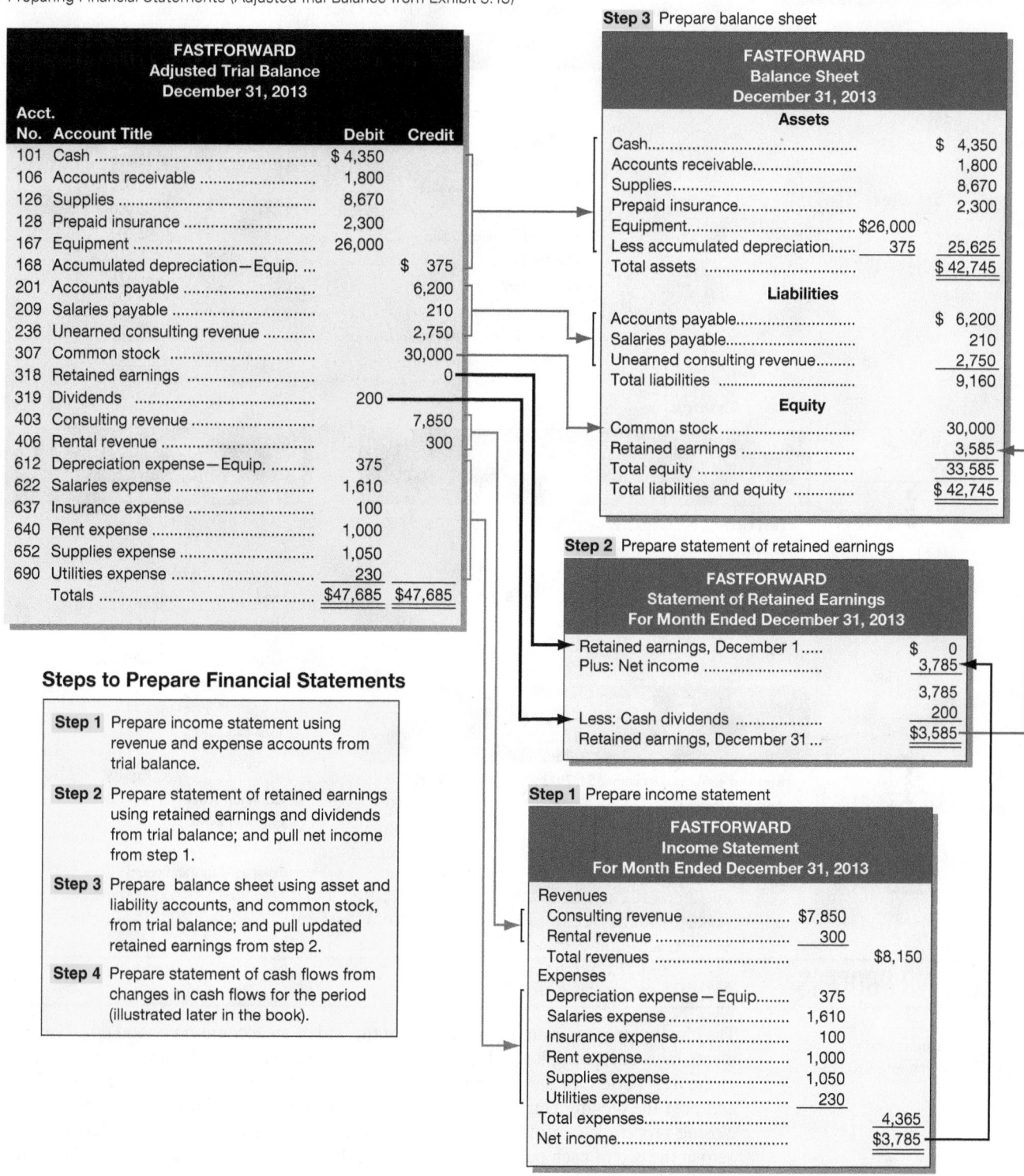

Step 3 Prepare balance sheet

FASTFORWARD
Adjusted Trial Balance
December 31, 2013

Acct. No.	Account Title	Debit	Credit
101	Cash	$ 4,350	
106	Accounts receivable	1,800	
126	Supplies	8,670	
128	Prepaid insurance	2,300	
167	Equipment	26,000	
168	Accumulated depreciation—Equip.		$ 375
201	Accounts payable		6,200
209	Salaries payable		210
236	Unearned consulting revenue		2,750
307	Common stock		30,000
318	Retained earnings		0
319	Dividends	200	
403	Consulting revenue		7,850
406	Rental revenue		300
612	Depreciation expense—Equip.	375	
622	Salaries expense	1,610	
637	Insurance expense	100	
640	Rent expense	1,000	
652	Supplies expense	1,050	
690	Utilities expense	230	
	Totals	$47,685	$47,685

Steps to Prepare Financial Statements

Step 1 Prepare income statement using revenue and expense accounts from trial balance.

Step 2 Prepare statement of retained earnings using retained earnings and dividends from trial balance; and pull net income from step 1.

Step 3 Prepare balance sheet using asset and liability accounts, and common stock, from trial balance; and pull updated retained earnings from step 2.

Step 4 Prepare statement of cash flows from changes in cash flows for the period (illustrated later in the book).

FASTFORWARD
Balance Sheet
December 31, 2013

Assets

Cash		$ 4,350
Accounts receivable		1,800
Supplies		8,670
Prepaid insurance		2,300
Equipment	$26,000	
Less accumulated depreciation	375	25,625
Total assets		$ 42,745

Liabilities

Accounts payable	$ 6,200
Salaries payable	210
Unearned consulting revenue	2,750
Total liabilities	9,160

Equity

Common stock	30,000
Retained earnings	3,585
Total equity	33,585
Total liabilities and equity	$ 42,745

Step 2 Prepare statement of retained earnings

FASTFORWARD
Statement of Retained Earnings
For Month Ended December 31, 2013

Retained earnings, December 1	$ 0
Plus: Net income	3,785
	3,785
Less: Cash dividends	200
Retained earnings, December 31	$3,585

Step 1 Prepare income statement

FASTFORWARD
Income Statement
For Month Ended December 31, 2013

Revenues		
Consulting revenue	$7,850	
Rental revenue	300	
Total revenues		$8,150
Expenses		
Depreciation expense—Equip.	375	
Salaries expense	1,610	
Insurance expense	100	
Rent expense	1,000	
Supplies expense	1,050	
Utilities expense	230	
Total expenses		4,365
Net income		$3,785

earnings is determined on the statement of retained earnings and transferred to the balance sheet (green lines).

We prepare financial statements in the following order: income statement, statement of retained earnings, and balance sheet. This order makes sense because the balance sheet uses information from the statement of retained earnings, which in turn uses information from the income statement. The statement of cash flows is usually the final statement prepared.

Point: Each trial balance amount is used in only *one* financial statement and, when financial statements are completed, each account will have been used once.

NEED-TO-KNOW 3.5

P3

Use the following adjusted trial balance of Magic Company to prepare its (1) income statement, (2) statement of retained earnings, and (3) balance sheet (unclassified), for the year ended, or date of, December 31, 2014. The retained earnings account balance is $45,000 at December 31, 2013.

Account Title	Debit	Credit
Cash	$ 13,000	
Accounts receivable	17,000	
Land	85,000	
Accounts payable		$ 12,000
Long-term notes payable		33,000
Common stock		30,000
Retained earnings......................		45,000
Dividends	20,000	
Fees earned		79,000
Salaries expense	56,000	
Office supplies expense	8,000	
Totals	$199,000	$199,000

Solution

MAGIC COMPANY
Income Statement
For Year Ended December 31, 2014

Fees earned		$79,000
Expenses		
Salaries expense	$56,000	
Office supplies expense	8,000	
Total expenses		64,000
Net income		$15,000

MAGIC COMPANY
Statement of Retained Earnings
For Year Ended December 31, 2014

Retained earnings, December 31, 2013.........	$ 45,000
Add: Net income	15,000
	60,000
Less: Dividends............................	(20,000)
Retained earnings, December 31, 2014.........	$ 40,000

Do More: E 3-11, P 3-5

QC3

MAGIC COMPANY
Balance Sheet
December 31, 2014

Assets	
Cash	$ 13,000
Accounts receivable.............	17,000
Land	85,000
Total assets	$115,000

Liabilities	
Accounts payable	$ 12,000
Long-term notes payable.........	33,000
Total liabilities	45,000

Equity	
Common stock	30,000
Retained earnings	40,000
Total equity.....................	70,000
Total liabilities and equity	$115,000

CLOSING PROCESS

P4 Describe and prepare closing entries.

The **closing process** is an important step at the end of an accounting period *after* financial statements have been completed. It prepares accounts for recording the transactions and the events of the *next* period. In the closing process we must (1) identify accounts for closing, (2) record and post the closing entries, and (3) prepare a post-closing trial balance. The purpose of the closing process is twofold. First, it resets revenue, expense, and dividends account balances to zero at the end of each period. This is done so that these accounts can properly measure income and dividends for the next period. Second, it helps in summarizing a period's revenues and expenses. This section explains the closing process.

Temporary and Permanent Accounts

Temporary (or *nominal*) **accounts** accumulate data related to one accounting period. They include all income statement accounts, the dividends account, and the Income Summary account. They are temporary because the accounts are opened at the beginning of a period, used to record transactions and events for that period, and then closed at the end of the period. *The closing process applies only to temporary accounts.* **Permanent** (or *real*) **accounts** report on activities related to one or more future accounting periods. They carry their ending balances into the next period and generally consist of all balance sheet accounts. These asset, liability, and equity accounts are not closed.

Recording Closing Entries

To record and post **closing entries** is to transfer the end-of-period balances in revenue, expense, and dividends accounts to the permanent retained earnings account. Closing entries are necessary at the end of each period after financial statements are prepared because

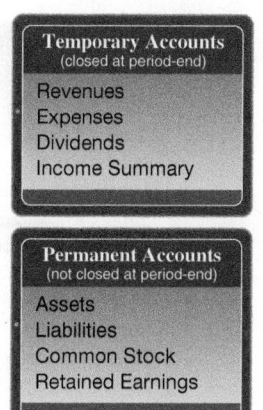

- Revenue, expense, and dividends accounts must begin each period with zero balances.
- Retained earnings must reflect prior periods' revenues, expenses, and dividends.

An income statement aims to report revenues and expenses for a *specific accounting period.* The statement of retained earnings reports similar information, including dividends. Since revenue, expense, and dividends accounts must accumulate information separately for each period, they must start each period with zero balances. To close these accounts, we transfer their balances first to an account called *Income Summary.* **Income Summary** is a temporary account (only used for the closing process) that contains a credit for the sum of all revenues (and gains) and a debit for the sum of all expenses (and losses). Its balance equals net income or net loss and it is transferred to retained earnings. Next the dividends account balance is transferred to retained earnings. After these closing entries are posted, the revenue, expense, dividends, and Income Summary accounts have zero balances. These accounts are then said to be *closed* or *cleared.*

Exhibit 3.15 uses the adjusted account balances of FastForward (from the left side of Exhibit 3.14) to show the four steps necessary to close its temporary accounts. We explain each step.

Point: To understand the closing process, focus on its *outcomes—updating* the retained earnings account balance to its proper ending balance, and getting *temporary accounts* to show *zero balances* for purposes of accumulating data for the next period.

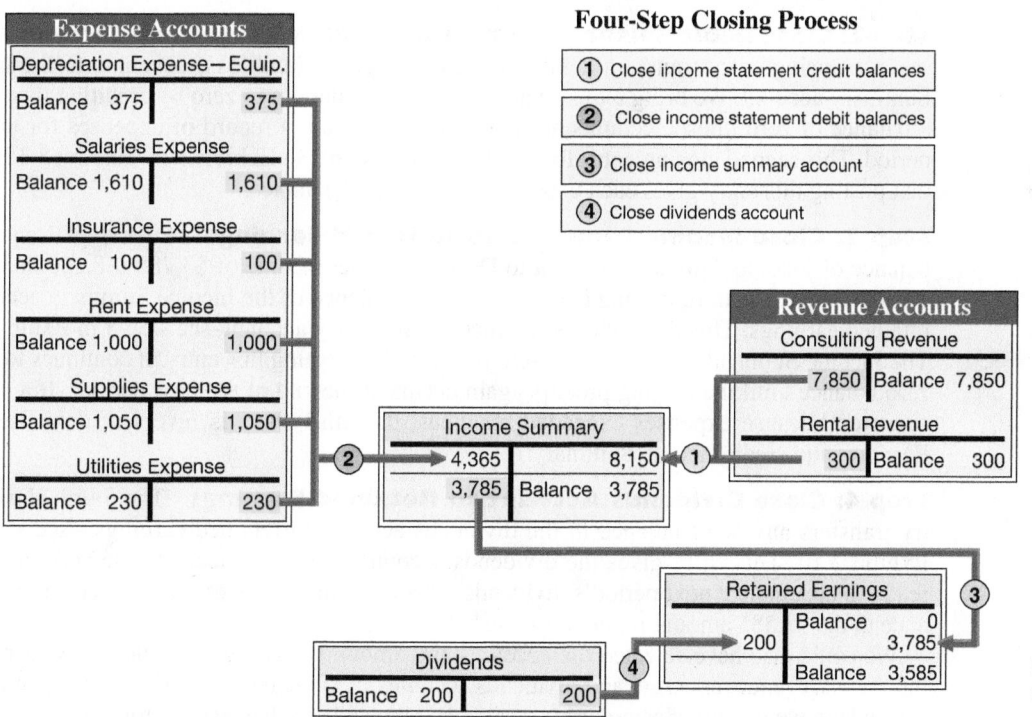

EXHIBIT 3.15
Four-Step Closing Process

Point: Retained Earnings is the only *permanent account* in Exhibit 3.15.

Step 1: Close Credit Balances in Revenue Accounts to Income Summary

The first closing entry transfers credit balances in revenue (and gain) accounts to the Income Summary account. We bring accounts with credit balances to zero by debiting them. For FastForward, this journal entry is step 1 in Exhibit 3.16. This entry closes revenue accounts and leaves them with zero balances. The accounts are now ready to record revenues when they occur in the next period. The $8,150 credit entry to Income Summary equals total revenues for the period.

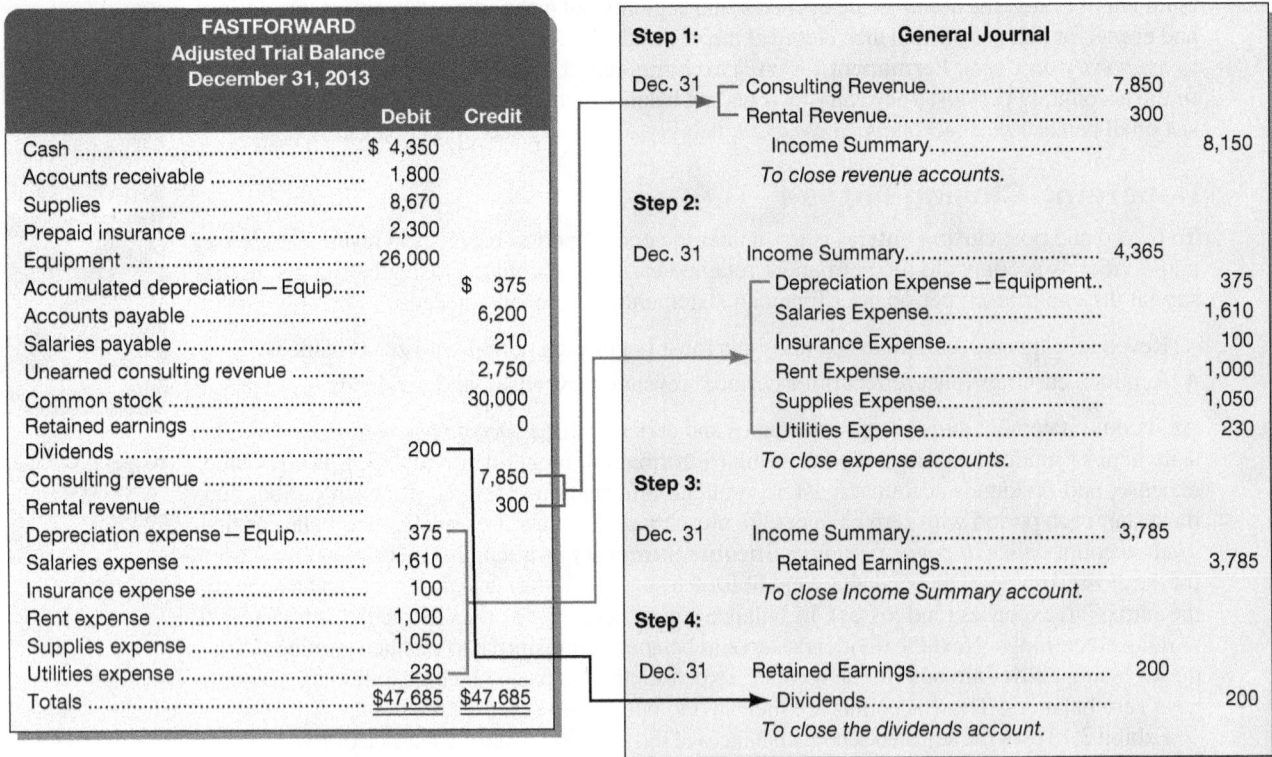

EXHIBIT 3.16

Preparing Closing Entries

Point: It is possible to close revenue and expense accounts directly to retained earnings. Computerized accounting systems do this.

Step 2: Close Debit Balances in Expense Accounts to Income Summary   The second closing entry transfers debit balances in expense (and loss) accounts to the Income Summary account. We bring expense accounts' debit balances to zero by crediting them. With a balance of zero, these accounts are ready to accumulate a record of expenses for the next period. This second closing entry for FastForward is step 2 in Exhibit 3.16. Exhibit 3.15 shows that posting this entry gives each expense account a zero balance.

Step 3: Close Income Summary to Retained Earnings   After steps 1 and 2, the balance of Income Summary is equal to December's net income of $3,785 ($8,150 credit less $4,365 debit). The third closing entry transfers the balance of the Income Summary account to retained earnings. This entry closes the Income Summary account–see step 3 in Exhibit 3.16. The Income Summary account has a zero balance after posting this entry. It continues to have a zero balance until the closing process again occurs at the end of the next period. (If a net loss occurred because expenses exceeded revenues, the third entry is reversed: debit Retained Earnings and credit Income Summary.)

Step 4: Close Dividends Account to Retained Earnings   The fourth closing entry transfers any debit balance in the dividends account to retained earnings—see step 4 in Exhibit 3.16. This entry gives the dividends account a zero balance, and the account is now ready to accumulate next period's dividends. This entry also reduces the retained earnings balance to the $3,585 amount reported on the balance sheet.

We could also have selected the accounts and amounts needing to be closed by identifying individual revenue, expense, and dividends accounts in the ledger. This is illustrated in Exhibit 3.16 where we prepare closing entries using the adjusted trial balance. (Information for closing entries is also in the financial statement columns of a work sheet—see Appendix 3B.)

Post-Closing Trial Balance

P5 Explain and prepare a post-closing trial balance.

Exhibit 3.17 shows the entire ledger of FastForward as of December 31 after adjusting and closing entries are posted. (The transaction entries are in Chapter 2.) The temporary accounts (revenues, expenses, and dividends) have ending balances equal to zero.

EXHIBIT 3.17

General Ledger after the Closing Process for FastForward

Asset Accounts

Cash   Acct. No. 101

Date	Explan.	PR	Debit	Credit	Balance
2013					
Dec. 1	(1)	G1	30,000		30,000
2	(2)	G1		2,500	27,500
3	(3)	G1		26,000	1,500
5	(5)	G1	4,200		5,700
6	(13)	G1		2,400	3,300
12	(6)	G1		1,000	2,300
12	(7)	G1		700	1,600
22	(9)	G1	1,900		3,500
24	(10)	G1		900	2,600
24	(11)	G1		200	2,400
26	(12)	G1	3,000		5,400
26	(14)	G1		120	5,280
26	(15)	G1		230	5,050
26	(16)	G1		700	**4,350**

Accounts Receivable   Acct. No. 106

Date	Explan.	PR	Debit	Credit	Balance
2013					
Dec. 12	(8)	G1	1,900		1,900
22	(9)	G1		1,900	0
31	Adj.(f)	G1	1,800		**1,800**

Supplies   Acct. No. 126

Date	Explan.	PR	Debit	Credit	Balance
2013					
Dec. 2	(2)	G1	2,500		2,500
6	(4)	G1	7,100		9,600
26	(14)	G1	120		9,720
31	Adj.(b)	G1		1,050	**8,670**

Prepaid Insurance   Acct. No. 128

Date	Explan.	PR	Debit	Credit	Balance
2013					
Dec. 6	(13)	G1	2,400		2,400
31	Adj.(a)	G1		100	**2,300**

Equipment   Acct. No. 167

Date	Explan.	PR	Debit	Credit	Balance
2013					
Dec. 3	(3)	G1	26,000		**26,000**

Accumulated Depreciation— Equipment   Acct. No. 168

Date	Explan.	PR	Debit	Credit	Balance
2013					
Dec. 31	Adj.(c)	G1		375	**375**

Liability and Equity Accounts

Accounts Payable   Acct. No. 201

Date	Explan.	PR	Debit	Credit	Balance
2013					
Dec. 6	(4)	G1		7,100	7,100
24	(10)	G1	900		**6,200**

Salaries Payable   Acct. No. 209

Date	Explan.	PR	Debit	Credit	Balance
2013					
Dec. 31	Adj.(e)	G1		210	**210**

Unearned Consulting Revenue   Acct. No. 236

Date	Explan.	PR	Debit	Credit	Balance
2013					
Dec. 26	(12)	G1		3,000	3,000
31	Adj.(d)	G1	250		**2,750**

Common Stock   Acct. No. 307

Date	Explan.	PR	Debit	Credit	Balance
2013					
Dec. 1	(1)	G1		30,000	30,000

Retained Earnings   Acct. No. 318

Date	Explan.	PR	Debit	Credit	Balance
2013					
Dec. 31	Clos.(3)	G1		3,785	3,785
31	Clos.(4)	G1	200		3,585

Dividends   Acct. No. 319

Date	Explan.	PR	Debit	Credit	Balance
2013					
Dec. 24	(11)	G1	200		200
31	Clos.(4)	G1		200	0

Revenue and Expense Accounts (Including Income Summary)

Consulting Revenue   Acct. No. 403

Date	Explan.	PR	Debit	Credit	Balance
2013					
Dec. 5	(5)	G1		4,200	4,200
12	(8)	G1		1,600	5,800
31	Adj.(d)	G1		250	6,050
31	Adj.(f)	G1		1,800	**7,850**
31	Clos.(1)	G1	7,850		0

Rental Revenue   Acct. No. 406

Date	Explan.	PR	Debit	Credit	Balance
2013					
Dec. 12	(8)	G1		300	300
31	Clos.(1)	G1	300		0

Depreciation Expense— Equipment   Acct. No. 612

Date	Explan.	PR	Debit	Credit	Balance
2013					
Dec. 31	Adj.(c)	G1	375		375
31	Clos.(2)	G1		375	0

Salaries Expense   Acct. No. 622

Date	Explan.	PR	Debit	Credit	Balance
2013					
Dec. 12	(7)	G1	700		700
26	(16)	G1	700		1,400
31	Adj.(e)	G1	210		**1,610**
31	Clos.(2)	G1		1,610	0

Insurance Expense   Acct. No. 637

Date	Explan.	PR	Debit	Credit	Balance
2013					
Dec. 31	Adj.(a)	G1	100		100
31	Clos.(2)	G1		100	0

Rent Expense   Acct. No. 640

Date	Explan.	PR	Debit	Credit	Balance
2013					
Dec. 12	(6)	G1	1,000		**1,000**
31	Clos.(2)	G1		1,000	0

Supplies Expense   Acct. No. 652

Date	Explan.	PR	Debit	Credit	Balance
2013					
Dec. 31	Adj.(b)	G1	1,050		**1,050**
31	Clos.(2)	G1		1,050	0

Utilities Expense   Acct. No. 690

Date	Explan.	PR	Debit	Credit	Balance
2013					
Dec. 26	(15)	G1	230		**230**
31	Clos.(2)	G1		230	0

Income Summary   Acct. No. 901

Date	Explan.	PR	Debit	Credit	Balance
2013					
Dec. 31	Clos.(1)	G1		8,150	8,150
31	Clos.(2)	G1	4,365		3,785
31	Clos.(3)	G1	3,785		0

A **post-closing trial balance** is a list of permanent accounts and their balances from the ledger after all closing entries have been journalized and posted. It lists the balances for all accounts not closed. These accounts comprise a company's assets, liabilities, and equity, which are identical to those in the balance sheet. The aim of a post-closing trial balance is to verify that (1) total debits equal total credits for permanent accounts and (2) all temporary accounts have zero balances. FastForward's post-closing trial balance is shown in Exhibit 3.18. The post-closing trial balance usually is the last step in the accounting process.

EXHIBIT 3.18

Post-Closing Trial Balance

FASTFORWARD **Post-Closing Trial Balance** **December 31, 2013**	Debit	Credit
Cash	$ 4,350	
Accounts receivable	1,800	
Supplies	8,670	
Prepaid insurance	2,300	
Equipment	26,000	
Accumulated depreciation—Equipment		$ 375
Accounts payable		6,200
Salaries payable		210
Unearned consulting revenue		2,750
Common stock		30,000
Retained earnings...........................		3,585
Totals	$43,120	$43,120

Accounting Cycle

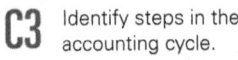

C3   Identify steps in the accounting cycle.

The term **accounting cycle** refers to the steps in preparing financial statements. It is called a *cycle* because the steps are repeated each reporting period. Exhibit 3.19 shows the 10 steps in the cycle, beginning with analyzing transactions and ending with a post-closing trial balance or

EXHIBIT 3.19

Steps in the Accounting Cycle*

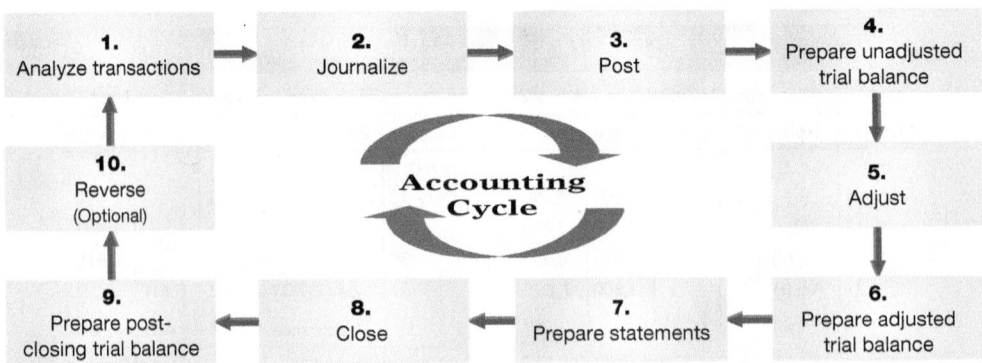

Explanations

1. Analyze transactions	Analyze transactions to prepare for journalizing.
2. Journalize	Record accounts, including debits and credits, in a journal.
3. Post	Transfer debits and credits from the journal to the ledger.
4. Prepare unadjusted trial balance	Summarize unadjusted ledger accounts and amounts.
5. Adjust	Record adjustments to bring account balances up to date; journalize and post adjustments.
6. Prepare adjusted trial balance	Summarize adjusted ledger accounts and amounts.
7. Prepare statements	Use adjusted trial balance to prepare financial statements.
8. Close	Journalize and post entries to close temporary accounts.
9. Prepare post-closing trial balance	Test clerical accuracy of the closing procedures.
10. Reverse (optional)	Reverse certain adjustments in the next period—optional step; see Appendix 3C.

* Steps 4, 6, and 9 can be done on a work sheet. A work sheet is useful in planning adjustments, but adjustments (step 5) must always be journalized and posted. Steps 3, 4, 6, and 9 are automatic with a computerized system.

reversing entries. Steps 1 through 3 usually occur regularly as a company enters into transactions. Steps 4 through 9 are done at the end of a period. *Reversing entries* in step 10 are optional and are explained in Appendix 3C.

Use the adjusted trial balance of Magic Company from Need-To-Know 3.5 to prepare its closing entries.

NEED-TO-KNOW 3.6

P4

Dec. 31	Fees Earned....................................	79,000	
	Income Summary		79,000
	To close the revenue account.		
31	Income Summary	64,000	
	Salaries Expense		56,000
	Office Supplies Expense		8,000
	To close the expense accounts.		
31	Income Summary	15,000	
	Retained Earnings		15,000
	To close Income Summary.		
31	Retained Earnings	20,000	
	Dividends		20,000
	To close the Dividends account.		

Do More: QS 3-23, E 3-16

QC4

CLASSIFIED BALANCE SHEET

Our discussion to this point has been limited to unclassified financial statements. This section describes a classified balance sheet. The next chapter describes a classified income statement. An **unclassified balance sheet** is one whose items are broadly grouped into assets, liabilities, and equity. One example is FastForward's balance sheet in Exhibit 3.14. A **classified balance sheet** organizes assets and liabilities into important subgroups that provide more information to decision makers.

C4 Explain and prepare a classified balance sheet.

Classification Structure

A classified balance sheet has no required layout, but it usually contains the categories in Exhibit 3.20. One of the more important classifications is the separation between current and noncurrent items for both assets and liabilities. Current items are those expected to come due (either collected or owed) within one year or the company's operating cycle, whichever is longer. The **operating cycle** is the time span from when *cash is used* to acquire goods and services until *cash is received* from the sale of goods and services. "Operating" refers to company operations and "cycle" refers to the circular flow of cash used for company inputs and then cash received from its outputs. The length of a company's operating cycle depends on its activities. For a service company, the operating cycle is the time span between (1) paying employees who perform the services and (2) receiving cash from customers. For a merchandiser selling products, the operating cycle is the time span between (1) paying suppliers for merchandise and (2) receiving cash from customers.

Point: Current and Noncurrent are also referred to as Short-Term and Long-Term, respectively.

Assets	Liabilities and Equity
Current assets	Current liabilities
Noncurrent assets	Noncurrent liabilities
Long-term investments	Equity
Plant assets	
Intangible assets	

EXHIBIT 3.20

Typical Categories in a Classified Balance Sheet

Most operating cycles are less than one year. This means most companies use a one-year period in deciding which assets and liabilities are current. A few companies have an operating cycle longer than one year. For instance, producers of certain beverages (wine) and products (ginseng) that require aging for several years have operating cycles longer than one year. A balance sheet lists current assets before noncurrent assets and current liabilities before noncurrent liabilities. This consistency in presentation allows users to quickly identify current assets that are most easily converted to cash and current liabilities that are shortly coming due. Items in current assets and current liabilities are listed in the order of how quickly they will be converted to, or paid in, cash.

Classification Categories

This section describes the most common categories in a classified balance sheet. The balance sheet for Snowboarding Components in Exhibit 3.21 shows the typical categories. Its

EXHIBIT 3.21

Example of a Classified Balance Sheet

SNOWBOARDING COMPONENTS
Balance Sheet
January 31, 2013

Assets

Current assets		
Cash	$ 6,500	
Short-term investments	2,100	
Accounts receivable, net	4,400	
Merchandise inventory	27,500	
Prepaid expenses	2,400	
Total current assets		$ 42,900
Long-term investments		
Notes receivable	1,500	
Investments in stocks and bonds	18,000	
Land held for future expansion	48,000	
Total long-term investments		67,500
Plant assets		
Equipment and buildings	203,200	
Less accumulated depreciation	53,000	
Equipment and buildings, net		150,200
Land		73,200
Total plant assets		223,400
Intangible assets		10,000
Total assets		$343,800

Liabilities

Current liabilities		
Accounts payable	$ 15,300	
Wages payable	3,200	
Notes payable	3,000	
Current portion of long-term liabilities	7,500	
Total current liabilities		$ 29,000
Long-term liabilities (net of current portion)		150,000
Total liabilities		179,000

Equity

Common stock		50,000
Retained earnings		114,800
Total equity		164,800
Total liabilities and equity		$343,800

assets are classified as either current or noncurrent. Its noncurrent assets include three main categories: long-term investments, plant assets, and intangible assets. Its liabilities are classified as either current or long-term. Not all companies use the same categories of assets and liabilities for their balance sheets. **K2 Sports**, a manufacturer of snowboards, reported a balance sheet with only three asset classes: current assets; property, plant and equipment; and other assets.

Current Assets Current assets are cash and other resources that are expected to be sold, collected, or used within one year or the company's operating cycle, whichever is longer. Examples are cash, short-term investments, accounts receivable, short-term notes receivable, goods for sale (called *merchandise* or *inventory*), and prepaid expenses. The individual prepaid expenses of a company are usually small in amount compared to many other assets and are often combined and shown as a single item. The prepaid expenses likely include items such as prepaid insurance, prepaid rent, office supplies, and store supplies. Prepaid expenses are usually listed last because they will not be converted to cash (instead, they are used).

Long-Term Investments A second major balance sheet classification is **long-term** (or *noncurrent*) **investments.** Notes receivable and investments in stocks and bonds are long-term assets when they are expected to be held for more than the longer of one year or the operating cycle. Land held for future expansion is a long-term investment because it is *not* used in operations.

Plant Assets Plant assets are tangible assets that are both *long-lived* and *used to produce* or *sell products and services*. Examples are equipment, machinery, buildings, and land that are used to produce or sell products and services. The order listing for plant assets is usually from most liquid to least liquid such as equipment and machinery to buildings and land.

Point: Plant assets are also called *fixed assets; property, plant and equipment;* or *long-lived assets.*

Intangible Assets Intangible assets are long-term resources that benefit business operations, usually lack physical form, and have uncertain benefits. Examples are patents, trademarks, copyrights, franchises, and goodwill. Their value comes from the privileges or rights granted to or held by the owner. **K2 Sports**, reported intangible assets of $228 million, which is nearly 20 percent of its total assets. Its intangibles included trademarks, patents, and licensing agreements.

Point: Furniture and fixtures are referred to as F&F, which are classified as noncurrent assets.

Current Liabilities Current liabilities are obligations due to be paid or settled within one year or the operating cycle, whichever is longer. They are usually settled by paying out current assets such as cash. Current liabilities often include accounts payable, notes payable, wages payable, taxes payable, interest payable, and unearned revenues. Also, any portion of a long-term liability due to be paid within one year or the operating cycle, whichever is longer, is a current liability. Unearned revenues are current liabilities when they will be settled by delivering products or services within one year or the operating cycle, whichever is longer. Current liabilities are reported in the order of those to be settled first.

Point: Many financial ratios are distorted if accounts are not classified correctly.

Long-Term Liabilities Long-term liabilities are obligations *not* due within one year or the operating cycle, whichever is longer. Notes payable, mortgages payable, bonds payable, and lease obligations are common long-term liabilities. If a company has both short- and long-term items in each of these categories, they are commonly separated into two accounts in the ledger.

Point: Only assets and liabilities are classified as current or noncurrent.

Equity Equity is the owner's claim on assets. The equity section for a corporation is divided into two main subsections, common stock and retained earnings.

NEED-TO-KNOW 3.7

C4

Use the adjusted trial balance of Magic Company from Need-To-Know 3.5 to prepare its classified balance sheet as of December 31, 2014. (*Hint:* The retained earnings account balance is $40,000 at December 31, 2014.)

MAGIC COMPANY Balance Sheet December 31, 2014		
Assets		
Current assets		
Cash	$ 13,000	
Accounts receivable	17,000	
Total current assets	30,000	
Plant assets		
Land	85,000	
Total plant assets	85,000	
Total assets	$115,000	
Liabilities		
Current liabilities		
Accounts payable	$ 12,000	
Total current liabilities	12,000	
Long-term notes payable	33,000	
Total liabilities	45,000	
Equity		
Common stock	30,000	
Retained earnings	40,000	
Total equity	70,000	
Total liabilities and equity	$115,000	

Do More: QS 3-21, E 3-12, P 3-6

QC5

GLOBAL VIEW

We explained that accounting under U.S. GAAP is similar, but not identical, to that under IFRS. This section discusses differences in adjusting accounts, preparing financial statements, and reporting assets and liabilities on a balance sheet.

Adjusting Accounts   Both U.S. GAAP and IFRS include broad and similar guidance for adjusting accounts. Although some variations exist in revenue and expense recognition and other principles, all of the adjustments in this chapter are accounted for identically under the two systems. In later chapters we describe how certain assets and liabilities can result in different adjusted amounts using fair value measurements.

Preparing Financial Statements   Both U.S. GAAP and IFRS prepare the same four basic financial statements following the same process discussed in this chapter. Chapter 2 explained how both U.S. GAAP and IFRS require current items to be separated from noncurrent items on the balance sheet (yielding a classified balance sheet). U.S. GAAP balance sheets report current items first. Assets are listed from most liquid to least liquid, where liquid refers to the ease of converting an asset to cash. Liabilities are listed from nearest to maturity to furthest from maturity, maturity refers to the nearness of paying off the liability. IFRS balance sheets normally present noncurrent items first (and equity before liabilities), but this is not a requirement. Other differences with financial statements exist, which we identify in later

PIAGGIO   chapters. Piaggio, which manufactures two-, three-, and four-wheel vehicles and is Europe's leading manufacturer of motorcycles and scooters, provides the following example of IFRS reporting for its assets, liabilities, and equity within the balance sheet.

PIAGGIO Balance Sheet (in thousands of Euro) December 31, 2011			
Assets		**Equity and Liabilities**	
Noncurrent assets		Total equity	€ 446,218
Intangible assets	€ 649,420	Noncurrent liabilities	
Property, plant and equipment. . . .	274,871	Financial liabilities falling due after one year	329,200
Other noncurrent assets	86,185	Other long-term liabilities	100,489
Total noncurrent assets	1,010,476	Total noncurrent liabilities	429,689
Current assets		Current liabilities	
Trade receivables	65,560	Financial liabilities falling due within one year	170,261
Other receivables	28,028	Trade payables	375,263
Short-term tax receivables	27,245	Tax payables	20,920
Inventories	236,988	Other short-term payables	64,718
Cash and cash equivalents	151,887	Current portion of other long-term provisions . . .	13,115
Total current assets	509,708	Total current liabilities	644,277
Total assets	€1,520,184	Total equity and liabilities.	€1,520,184

Point: IASB and FASB are working to improve financial statements. One proposal would reorganize the balance sheet to show assets and liabilities classified as operating, investing, or financing.

Closing Process   The closing process is identical under U.S. GAAP and IFRS. Although unique accounts can arise under either system, the closing process remains the same.

IFRS: New revenue recognition rules proposed by the FASB and the IASB reduce variation between U.S. GAAP and IFRS when accounting for revenue.

 IFRS

Revenue and expense recognition are key to recording accounting adjustments. IFRS tends to be more *principles-based* relative to U.S. GAAP, which is viewed as more *rules-based*. A principles-based system depends heavily on control procedures to reduce the potential for fraud or misconduct. Failure in judgment led to improper accounting adjustments at Fannie Mae, Xerox, WorldCom, and others. A KPMG survey of accounting and finance employees found that more than 10% of them had witnessed falsification or manipulation of accounting data within the past year. Internal controls and governance processes are directed at curtailing such behavior. Yet, a 2011 KPMG fraud survey found that one in seven frauds was uncovered by chance, which emphasizes our need to improve internal controls and governance. ∎

Financial Pressure

Profit Margin and Current Ratio  **Decision Analysis**

Profit Margin

A useful measure of a company's operating results is the ratio of its net income to net sales. This ratio is called **profit margin,** or *return on sales,* and is computed as in Exhibit 3.22.

A2 Compute profit margin and describe its use in analyzing company performance.

$$\text{Profit margin} = \frac{\text{Net income}}{\text{Net sales}}$$

EXHIBIT 3.22

Profit Margin

This ratio is interpreted as reflecting the percent of profit in each dollar of sales. To illustrate how we compute and use profit margin, let's look at the results of Limited Brands, Inc., in Exhibit 3.23 for its fiscal years 2007 through 2011.

EXHIBIT 3.23

Limited Brands' Profit Margin

$ in millions	2011	2010	2009	2008	2007
Net income	$ 805	$ 448	$ 220	$ 718	$ 676
Net sales	$9,613	$8,632	$9,043	$10,134	$10,671
Profit margin	8.4%	5.2%	2.4%	7.1%	6.3%
Industry profit margin	2.1%	0.9%	0.3%	1.1%	1.6%

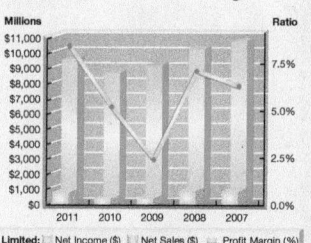

The Limited's average profit margin is 5.9% during this 5-year period. This favorably compares to the average industry profit margin of 1.2%. However, Limited's profit margin has rebounded in the most recent two years—from 2.4% in 2009 to 5.2% and 8.4% for the recent recovery periods (see margin graph). Future success depends on Limited maintaining its market share and increasing its profit margin.

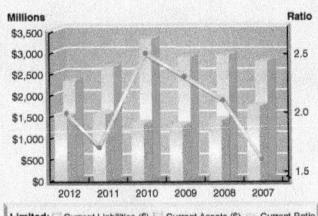

A3 Compute the current ratio and describe what it reveals about a company's financial condition.

Current Ratio

An important use of financial statements is to help assess a company's ability to pay its debts in the near future. Such analysis affects decisions by suppliers when allowing a company to buy on credit. It also affects decisions by creditors when lending money to a company, including loan terms such as interest rate, due date, and collateral requirements. It can also affect a manager's decisions about using cash to pay debts when they come due. The **current ratio** is one measure of a company's ability to pay its short-term obligations. It is defined in Exhibit 3.24 as current assets divided by current liabilities.

EXHIBIT 3.24

Current Ratio

$$\text{Current ratio} = \frac{\text{Current assets}}{\text{Current liabilities}}$$

Using financial information from Limited Brands, Inc., we compute its current ratio for the recent five-year period. The results are in Exhibit 3.25.

EXHIBIT 3.25

Limited Brands' Current Ratio

$ in millions	2012	2011	2010	2009	2008	2007
Current assets	$2,368	$2,592	$3,250	$2,867	$2,919	$2,771
Current liabilities	$1,526	$1,504	$1,322	$1,255	$1,374	$1,709
Current ratio	1.6	1.7	2.5	2.3	2.1	1.6
Industry current ratio	1.6	1.7	1.9	2.0	2.1	2.3

Limited Brands' current ratio averaged 2.0 for its fiscal years 2007 through 2012. The current ratio for each of these years suggests that the company's short-term obligations can be covered with its short-term assets. However, if its ratio would approach 1.0, Limited would expect to face challenges in covering liabilities. If the ratio were *less* than 1.0, current liabilities would exceed current assets, and the company's ability to pay short-term obligations could be in doubt. Limited Brand's liquidity, as evidenced by its current ratio, declines in 2011 and 2012, after growing steadily from 2008–2010.

■ Decision Maker ━━━━━━━━━━━━━━━━━━━━━━━━━━━━━━━

Analyst   You are analyzing the financial condition of a company to assess its ability to meet upcoming loan payments. You compute its current ratio as 1.2. You also find that a major portion of accounts receivable is due from one client who has not made any payments in the past 12 months. Removing this receivable from current assets lowers the current ratio to 0.7. What do you conclude? ■ [Answer—p. 138]

COMPREHENSIVE...

NEED-TO-KNOW 1

The following information relates to Fanning's Electronics on December 31, 2013. The company, which uses the calendar year as its annual reporting period, initially records prepaid and unearned items in balance sheet accounts (assets and liabilities, respectively).

a. The company's weekly payroll is $8,750, paid each Friday for a five-day workweek. Assume December 31, 2013, falls on a Monday, but the employees will not be paid their wages until Friday, January 4, 2014.

b. Eighteen months earlier, on July 1, 2012, the company purchased equipment that cost $20,000. Its useful life is predicted to be five years, at which time the equipment is expected to be worthless (zero salvage value).

c. On October 1, 2013, the company agreed to work on a new housing development. The company is paid $120,000 on October 1 in advance of future installation of similar alarm systems in 24 new homes. That amount was credited to the Unearned Services Revenue account. Between October 1 and December 31, work on 20 homes was completed.

d. On September 1, 2013, the company purchased a 12-month insurance policy for $1,800. The transaction was recorded with an $1,800 debit to Prepaid Insurance.

e. On December 29, 2013, the company completed a $7,000 service that has not been billed and not recorded as of December 31, 2013.

Required

1. Prepare any necessary adjusting entries on December 31, 2013, in relation to transactions and events *a* through *e*.

2. Prepare T-accounts for the accounts affected by adjusting entries, and post the adjusting entries. Determine the adjusted balances for the Unearned Revenue and the Prepaid Insurance accounts.

3. Complete the following table and determine the amounts and effects of your adjusting entries on the year 2013 income statement and the December 31, 2013, balance sheet. Use up (down) arrows to indicate an increase (decrease) in the Effect columns.

Entry	Amount in the Entry	Effect on Net Income	Effect on Total Assets	Effect on Total Liabilities	Effect on Total Equity

PLANNING THE SOLUTION

- Analyze each situation to determine which accounts need to be updated with an adjustment.
- Calculate the amount of each adjustment and prepare the necessary journal entries.
- Show the amount of each adjustment in the designated accounts, determine the adjusted balance, and identify the balance sheet classification of the account.
- Determine each entry's effect on net income for the year and on total assets, total liabilities, and total equity at the end of the year.

SOLUTION TO COMPREHENSIVE NEED-TO-KNOW 1

1. Adjusting journal entries.

(a) Dec. 31	Wages Expense	1,750	
	Wages Payable		1,750
	To accrue wages for the last day of the year		
	($8,750 × 1/5).		
(b) Dec. 31	Depreciation Expense—Equipment	4,000	
	Accumulated Depreciation—Equipment		4,000
	To record depreciation expense for the year		
	($20,000/5 years = $4,000 per year).		
(c) Dec. 31	Unearned Services Revenue	100,000	
	Services Revenue		100,000
	To recognize services revenue earned		
	($120,000 × 20/24).		
(d) Dec. 31	Insurance Expense	600	
	Prepaid Insurance		600
	To adjust for expired portion of insurance		
	($1,800 × 4/12).		
(e) Dec. 31	Accounts Receivable	7,000	
	Services Revenue		7,000
	To record services revenue earned.		

2. T-accounts for adjusting journal entries *a* through *e*.

Wages Expense		
(a)	1,750	

Wages Payable		
	(a)	1,750

Depreciation Expense—Equipment		
(b)	4,000	

Accumulated Depreciation— Equipment		
	(b)	4,000

Unearned Services Revenue		
	Unadj. Bal.	120,000
(c)	100,000	
	Adj. Bal.	20,000

Services Revenue		
	(c)	100,000
	(e)	7,000
	Adj. Bal.	107,000

Insurance Expense		
(d)	600	

Prepaid Insurance		
Unadj. Bal.	1,800	
	(d)	600
Adj. Bal.	1,200	

Accounts Receivable		
(e)	7,000	

3. Financial statement effects of adjusting journal entries.

Entry	Amount in the Entry	Effect on Net Income	Effect on Total Assets	Effect on Total Liabilities	Effect on Total Equity
a	$ 1,750	$ 1,750 ↓	No effect	$ 1,750 ↑	$ 1,750 ↓
b	4,000	4,000 ↓	$4,000 ↓	No effect	4,000 ↓
c	100,000	100,000 ↑	No effect	$100,000 ↓	100,000 ↑
d	600	600 ↓	$ 600 ↓	No effect	600 ↓
e	7,000	7,000 ↑	$7,000 ↑	No effect	7,000 ↑

COMPREHENSIVE...

NEED-TO-KNOW 2

Use the following adjusted trial balance to answer questions 1–3.

CHOI COMPANY Adjusted Trial Balance December 31		
	Debit	Credit
Cash	$ 3,050	
Accounts receivable	400	
Prepaid insurance	830	
Supplies	80	
Equipment	217,200	
Accumulated depreciation—Equipment		$ 29,100
Wages payable		880
Interest payable		3,600
Unearned rent		460
Long-term notes payable		150,000
Common stock		10,000
Retained earnings		30,340
Dividends	21,000	
Rent earned		57,500
Wages expense	25,000	
Utilities expense	1,900	
Insurance expense	3,200	
Supplies expense	250	
Depreciation expense—Equipment	5,970	
Interest expense	3,000	
Totals	$281,880	$281,880

1. Prepare the annual income statement from the adjusted trial balance of Choi Company.

Answer:

CHOI COMPANY Income Statement For Year Ended December 31		
Revenues		
Rent earned		$57,500
Expenses		
Wages expense	$25,000	
Utilities expense	1,900	
Insurance expense	3,200	
Supplies expense	250	
Depreciation expense—Equipment	5,970	
Interest expense	3,000	
Total expenses		39,320
Net income		$18,180

2. Prepare a statement of retained earnings from the adjusted trial balance of Choi Company.

Answer:

CHOI COMPANY
Statement of Retained Earnings
For Year Ended December 31

Retained earnings, December 31 prior year-end	$30,340
Plus: Net income	18,180
	48,520
Less: Dividends	21,000
Retained earnings, December 31 current year-end	$27,520

3. Prepare a balance sheet (unclassified) from the adjusted trial balance of Choi Company.

Answer:

CHOI COMPANY
Balance Sheet
December 31

Assets		
Cash		$ 3,050
Accounts receivable		400
Prepaid insurance		830
Supplies		80
Equipment	$217,200	
Less accumulated depreciation	29,100	188,100
Total assets		$192,460
Liabilities		
Wages payable		$ 880
Interest payable		3,600
Unearned rent		460
Long-term notes payable		150,000
Total liabilities		154,940
Equity		
Common stock		10,000
Retained earnings		27,520
Total equity		37,520
Total liabilities and equity		$192,460

APPENDIX

Alternative Accounting for Prepayments

3A

This appendix explains an alternative in accounting for prepaid expenses and unearned revenues.

RECORDING PREPAYMENT OF EXPENSES <u>IN EXPENSE ACCOUNTS</u>

An alternative method is to record *all* prepaid expenses with debits to expense accounts. If any prepaids remain unused or unexpired at the end of an accounting period, then adjusting entries must transfer the cost of the unused portions from expense accounts to prepaid expense (asset) accounts. This alternative method is acceptable. The financial statements are identical under either method, but the adjusting entries

P6 Explain the alternatives in accounting for prepaids.

are different. To illustrate the differences between these two methods, let's look at FastForward's cash payment of December 6 for 24 months of insurance coverage beginning on December 1. FastForward recorded that payment with a debit to an asset account, but it could have recorded a debit to an expense account. These alternatives are shown in Exhibit 3A.1.

EXHIBIT 3A.1

Alternative Initial Entries for Prepaid Expenses

			Payment Recorded as Asset	Payment Recorded as Expense
Dec. 6	Prepaid Insurance		2,400	
	Cash			2,400
Dec. 6	Insurance Expense			2,400
	Cash			2,400

At the end of its accounting period on December 31, insurance protection for one month has expired. This means $100 ($2,400/24) of insurance coverage expired and is an expense for December. The adjusting entry depends on how the original payment was recorded. This is shown in Exhibit 3A.2.

EXHIBIT 3A.2

Adjusting Entry for Prepaid Expenses for the Two Alternatives

			Payment Recorded as Asset	Payment Recorded as Expense
Dec. 31	Insurance Expense		100	
	Prepaid Insurance		100	
Dec. 31	Prepaid Insurance			2,300
	Insurance Expense			2,300

When these entries are posted to the accounts in the ledger, we can see that these two methods give identical results. The December 31 adjusted account balances in Exhibit 3A.3 show Prepaid Insurance of $2,300 and Insurance Expense of $100 for both methods.

EXHIBIT 3A.3

Account Balances under Two Alternatives for Recording Prepaid Expenses

Payment Recorded as Asset			
Prepaid Insurance			128
Dec. 6	2,400	Dec. 31	100
Balance	2,300		

Payment Recorded as Expense			
Prepaid Insurance			128
Dec. 31	2,300		

Insurance Expense			637
Dec. 31	100		

Insurance Expense			637
Dec. 6	2,400	Dec. 31	2,300
Balance	100		

RECORDING PREPAYMENT OF REVENUES IN REVENUE ACCOUNTS

As with prepaid expenses, an alternative method is to record *all* unearned revenues with credits to revenue accounts. If any revenues are unearned at the end of an accounting period, then adjusting entries must transfer the unearned portions from revenue accounts to unearned revenue (liability) accounts. This alternative method is acceptable. The adjusting entries are different for these two alternatives, but the financial statements are identical. To illustrate the accounting differences between these two methods, let's look at FastForward's December 26 receipt of $3,000 for consulting services covering the period December 27 to February 24. FastForward recorded this transaction with a credit to a liability account. The alternative is to record it with a credit to a revenue account, as shown in Exhibit 3A.4.

EXHIBIT 3A.4

Alternative Initial Entries for Unearned Revenues

			Receipt Recorded as Liability	Receipt Recorded as Revenue
Dec. 26	Cash		3,000	
	Unearned Consulting Revenue			3,000
Dec. 26	Cash			3,000
	Consulting Revenue			3,000

By the end of its accounting period on December 31, FastForward has earned $250 of this revenue. This means $250 of the liability has been satisfied. Depending on how the initial receipt is recorded, the adjusting entry is as shown in Exhibit 3A.5.

		Receipt Recorded as Liability	Receipt Recorded as Revenue
Dec. 31	Unearned Consulting Revenue	250	
	Consulting Revenue	250	
Dec. 31	Consulting Revenue		2,750
	Unearned Consulting Revenue		2,750

EXHIBIT 3A.5

Adjusting Entry for Unearned Revenues for the Two Alternatives

After adjusting entries are posted, the two alternatives give identical results. The December 31 adjusted account balances in Exhibit 3A.6 show unearned consulting revenue of $2,750 and consulting revenue of $250 for both methods.

Receipt Recorded as Liability

Unearned Consulting Revenue			236
Dec. 31	250	Dec. 26	3,000
		Balance	2,750

Consulting Revenue			403
		Dec. 31	250

Receipt Recorded as Revenue

Unearned Consulting Revenue			236
		Dec. 31	2,750

Consulting Revenue			403
Dec. 31	2,750	Dec. 26	3,000
		Balance	250

EXHIBIT 3A.6

Account Balances under Two Alternatives for Recording Unearned Revenues

---

APPENDIX

Work Sheet as a Tool

3B

Information preparers use various analyses and internal documents when organizing information for internal and external decision makers. Internal documents are often called **working papers.** One widely used working paper is the **work sheet,** which is a useful tool for preparers in working with accounting information. It is usually not available to external decision makers.

Benefits of a Work Sheet (Spreadsheet)   A work sheet is *not* a required report, yet using a manual or electronic work sheet has several potential benefits. Specifically, a work sheet:

P7 Prepare a work sheet and explain its usefulness.

- Aids the preparation of financial statements.
- Reduces the possibility of errors when working with many accounts and adjustments.
- Links accounts and adjustments to their impacts in financial statements.
- Assists in planning and organizing an audit of financial statements—as it can be used to reflect any adjustments necessary.
- Helps in preparing interim (monthly and quarterly) financial statements when the journalizing and posting of adjusting entries are postponed until the year-end.
- Shows the effects of proposed or "what if" transactions.

Use of a Work Sheet (Spreadsheet)   When a work sheet is used to prepare financial statements, it is constructed at the end of a period before the adjusting process. The complete work sheet includes a list of the accounts, their balances and adjustments, and their sorting into financial statement columns. It provides two columns each for the unadjusted trial balance, the adjustments, the adjusted trial balance, the income statement, and the balance sheet. To describe and interpret the work sheet, we

Point: Since a work sheet is *not* a required report or an accounting record, its format is flexible and can be modified by its user to fit his/her preferences.

use the information from FastForward. Preparing the work sheet has five important steps. Each step, 1 through 5, is color-coded and explained with reference to Exhibit 3B.1.

① Step 1. Enter Unadjusted Trial Balance

The first step in preparing a work sheet is to list the title of every account and its account number that is expected to appear on its financial statements. This includes all accounts in the ledger plus any new ones from adjusting entries. Most adjusting entries—including expenses from salaries, supplies, depreciation, and insurance—are predictable and recurring. The unadjusted balance for each account is then entered in the appropriate Debit or Credit column of the unadjusted trial balance columns. The totals of these two columns must be equal. Exhibit 3B.1 shows FastForward's work sheet after completing this first step. Sometimes blank lines are left on the work sheet based on past experience to indicate where lines will be needed for adjustments to certain accounts. Exhibit 3B.1 shows Consulting Revenue as one example. An alternative is to squeeze adjustments on one line or to combine the effects of two or more adjustments in one amount. In the unusual case when an account is not predicted, we can add a new line for such an account following the *Totals* line.

② Step 2. Enter Adjustments

The second step in preparing a work sheet is to enter adjustments in the Adjustments columns. The adjustments shown are the same ones shown in Exhibit 3.13. An identifying letter links the debit and credit of each adjusting entry. This is called *keying* the adjustments. After preparing a work sheet, adjusting entries must still be entered in the journal and posted to the ledger. The Adjustments columns provide the information for those entries.

③ Step 3. Prepare Adjusted Trial Balance

Point: To avoid omitting the transfer of an account balance, start with the first line (cash) and continue in account order.

The adjusted trial balance is prepared by combining the adjustments with the unadjusted balances for each account. As an example, the Prepaid Insurance account has a $2,400 debit balance in the Unadjusted Trial Balance columns. This $2,400 debit is combined with the $100 credit in the Adjustments columns to give Prepaid Insurance a $2,300 debit in the Adjusted Trial Balance columns. The totals of the Adjusted Trial Balance columns confirm the equality of debits and credits.

④ Step 4. Sort Adjusted Trial Balance Amounts to Financial Statements

This step involves sorting account balances from the adjusted trial balance to their proper financial statement columns. Expenses go to the Income Statement Debit column and revenues to the Income Statement Credit column. Assets and Dividends go to the Balance Sheet Debit column. Liabilities, Retained Earnings, and Common Stock go to the Balance Sheet Credit column.

⑤ Step 5. Total Statement Columns, Compute Income or Loss, and Balance Columns

Each financial statement column (from Step 4) is totaled. The difference between the totals of the Income Statement columns is net income or net loss. This occurs because revenues are entered in the Credit column and expenses in the Debit column. If the Credit total exceeds the Debit total, there is net income. If the Debit total exceeds the Credit total, there is a net loss. For FastForward, the Credit total exceeds the Debit total, giving a $3,785 net income.

The net income from the Income Statement columns is then entered in the Balance Sheet Credit column. Adding net income to the last Credit column implies that it is to be added to retained earnings. If a loss occurs, it is added to the Debit column. This implies that it is to be subtracted from retained earnings. The ending balance of retained earnings does not appear in the last two columns as a single amount, but it is computed in the statement of retained earnings using these account balances. When net income or net loss is added to the proper Balance Sheet column, the totals of the last two columns must balance. If they do not, one or more errors have been made. The error can either be mathematical or involve sorting one or more amounts to incorrect columns.

Work Sheet Applications and Analysis   A work sheet does not substitute for financial statements. It is a tool we can use at the end of an accounting period to help organize data and prepare financial statements. FastForward's financial statements are shown in Exhibit 3.14. Its income statement amounts are taken from the Income Statement columns of the work sheet. Similarly, amounts for its balance sheet and its statement of retained earnings are taken from the Balance Sheet columns of the work sheet.

Work sheets are also useful in analyzing the effects of proposed, or what-if, transactions. This is done by entering financial statement amounts in the Unadjusted (what-if) columns. Proposed transactions are then entered in the Adjustments columns. We then compute "adjusted" amounts from these proposed transactions. The extended amounts in the financial statement columns show the effects of these proposed transactions. These financial statement columns yield **pro forma financial statements** because they show the statements *as if* the proposed transactions occurred.

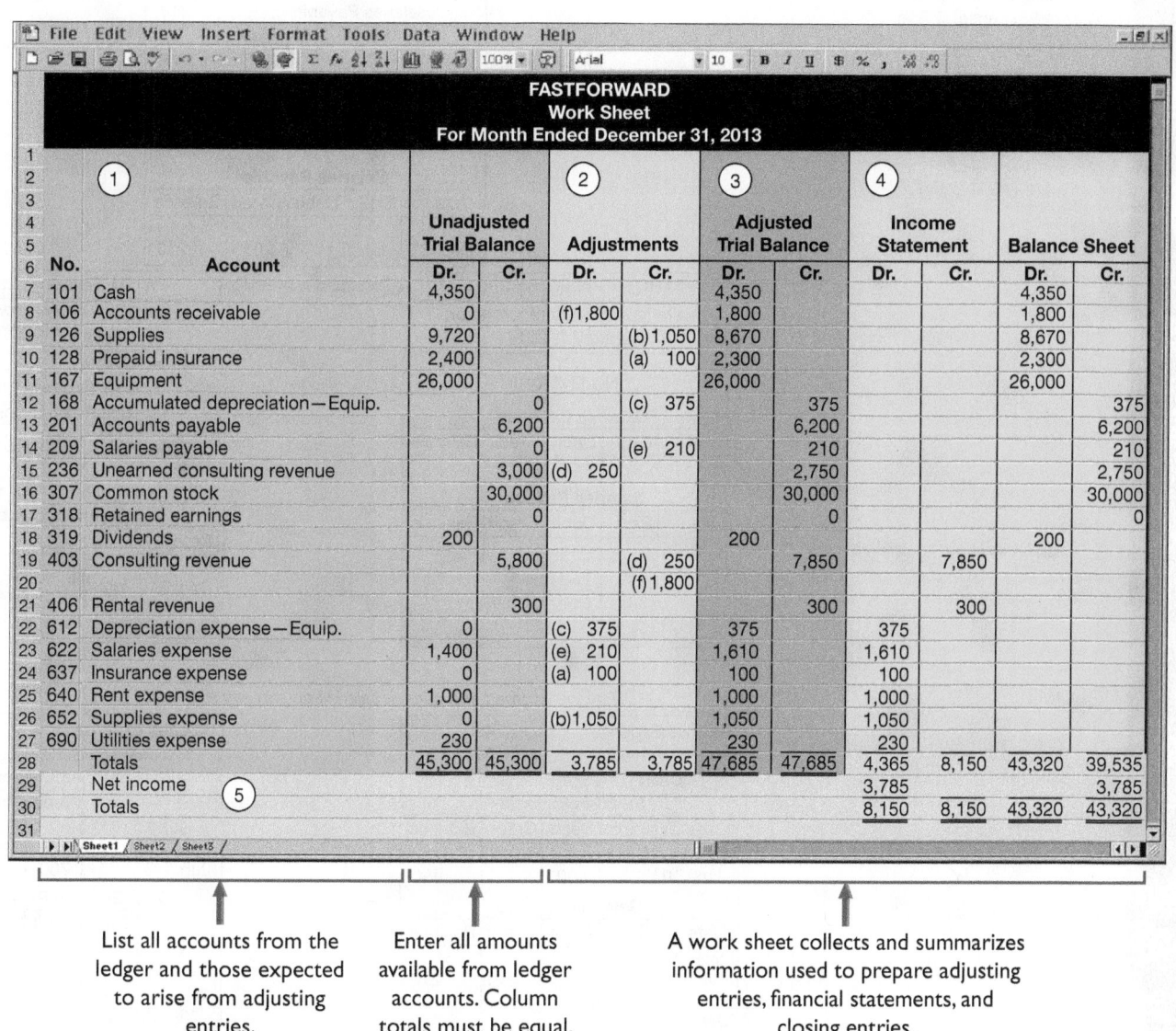

List all accounts from the ledger and those expected to arise from adjusting entries.

Enter all amounts available from ledger accounts. Column totals must be equal.

A work sheet collects and summarizes information used to prepare adjusting entries, financial statements, and closing entries.

APPENDIX

Reversing Entries

3C

Reversing entries are optional. They are recorded in response to accrued assets and accrued liabilities that were created by adjusting entries at the end of a reporting period. The purpose of reversing entries is to simplify a company's recordkeeping. Exhibit 3C.1 shows an example of FastForward's reversing entries. The top of the exhibit shows the adjusting entry FastForward recorded on December 31 for its employee's earned but unpaid salary. The entry recorded three days' salary of $210, which increased December's total salary expense to $1,610. The entry also recognized a liability of $210. The expense is reported on December's income statement. The expense account is then closed. The ledger on January 1, 2014, shows a $210 liability and a zero balance in the Salaries Expense account. At this point, the choice is made between using or not using reversing entries.

Point: As a general rule, adjusting entries that create new asset or liability accounts are likely candidates for reversing.

EXHIBIT 3C.1

Reversing Entries for an
Accrued Expense

Accrue salaries expense on December 31, 2013

Salaries Expense 210
    Salaries Payable 210

Salaries Expense

Date	Expl.	Debit	Credit	Balance
2013				
Dec. 12	(7)	700		700
26	(16)	700		1,400
31	(e)	210		1,610

Salaries Payable

Date	Expl.	Debit	Credit	Balance
2013				
Dec. 31	(e)		210	210

WITHOUT Reversing Entries	**WITH Reversing Entries**

No reversing entry recorded on — OR — *Reversing entry recorded on*
January 1, 2014   *January 1, 2014*

WITHOUT side:

NO ENTRY

Salaries Expense

Date	Expl.	Debit	Credit	Balance
2014				

Salaries Payable

Date	Expl.	Debit	Credit	Balance
2013				
Dec. 31	(e)		210	210
2014				

WITH side:

Salaries Payable 210
    Salaries Expense 210

Salaries Expense*

Date	Expl.	Debit	Credit	Balance
2014				
Jan. 1			210	(210)

Salaries Payable

Date	Expl.	Debit	Credit	Balance
2013				
Dec. 31	(e)		210	210
2014				
Jan. 1		210		0

Pay the accrued and current salaries on January 9, the first payday in 2014

WITHOUT side:

Salaries Expense 490
Salaries Payable 210
    Cash 700

Salaries Expense

Date	Expl.	Debit	Credit	Balance
2014				
Jan. 9		490		490

Salaries Payable

Date	Expl.	Debit	Credit	Balance
2013				
Dec. 31	(e)		210	210
2014				
Jan. 9		210		0

WITH side:

Salaries Expense 700
    Cash 700

Salaries Expense*

Date	Expl.	Debit	Credit	Balance
2014				
Jan. 1			210	(210)
Jan. 9		700		490

Salaries Payable

Date	Expl.	Debit	Credit	Balance
2013				
Dec. 31	(e)		210	210
2014				
Jan. 1		210		0

Under both approaches, the expense and liability accounts have
identical balances after the cash payment on January 9.

Salaries Expense $490
Salaries Payable .... $ 0

Circled numbers in the Balance *column indicate abnormal balances.*

Accounting *without* Reversing Entries   The path down the left side of Exhibit 3C.1 is described in the chapter. To summarize here, when the next payday occurs on January 9, we record payment with a compound entry that debits both the expense and liability accounts and credits Cash. Posting that entry creates a $490 balance in the expense account and reduces the liability account balance to zero because the debt has been settled. The disadvantage of this approach is the slightly more complex entry required on January 9. Paying the accrued liability means that this entry differs from the routine entries made on all other paydays. To construct the proper entry on January 9, we must recall the effect of the December 31 adjusting entry. Reversing entries overcome this disadvantage.

Point: Firms that use reversing entries hope that this simplification will reduce errors.

Accounting *with* Reversing Entries   The right side of Exhibit 3C.1 shows how a reversing entry on January 1 overcomes the disadvantage of the January 9 entry when not using reversing entries. A reversing entry is the exact opposite of an adjusting entry. For FastForward, the Salaries Payable liability account is debited for $210, meaning that this account now has a zero balance after the entry is posted. The Salaries Payable account temporarily understates the liability, but this is not a problem since financial statements are not prepared before the liability is settled on January 9. The credit to the Salaries Expense account is unusual because it gives the account an *abnormal credit balance.* We highlight an abnormal balance by circling it. Because of the reversing entry, the January 9 entry to record payment is straightforward. This entry debits the Salaries Expense account and credits Cash for the full $700 paid. It is the same as all other entries made to record 10 days' salary for the employee. Notice that after the payment entry is posted, the Salaries Expense account has a $490 balance that reflects seven days' salary of $70 per day (see the lower right side of Exhibit 3C.1). The zero balance in the Salaries Payable account is now correct. The lower section of Exhibit 3C.1 shows that the expense and liability accounts have exactly the same balances whether reversing entries are used or not. This means that both approaches yield identical results.

P8	Prepare reversing entries and explain their purpose.

Summary

C1 **Explain the importance of periodic reporting and the time period assumption.** The value of information is often linked to its timeliness. To provide timely information, accounting systems prepare periodic reports at regular intervals. The time period assumption presumes that an organization's activities can be divided into specific time periods for periodic reporting.

C2 **Explain accrual accounting and how it improves financial statements.** Accrual accounting recognizes revenue when earned and expenses when incurred—not necessarily when cash inflows and outflows occur. This information is valuable in assessing a company's financial position and performance.

C3 **Identify steps in the accounting cycle.** The accounting cycle consists of 10 steps: (1) analyze transactions, (2) journalize, (3) post, (4) prepare an unadjusted trial balance, (5) adjust accounts, (6) prepare an adjusted trial balance, (7) prepare statements, (8) close, (9) prepare a post-closing trial balance, and (10) prepare (optional) reversing entries.

C4 **Explain and prepare a classified balance sheet.** Classified balance sheets report assets and liabilities in two categories: current and noncurrent. Noncurrent assets often include long-term investments, plant assets, and intangible assets. A corporation separates equity into common stock and retained earnings.

A1 **Explain how accounting adjustments link to financial statements.** Accounting adjustments bring an asset or liability account balance to its correct amount. They also update related expense or revenue accounts. Every adjusting entry affects one or more income statement accounts *and* one or more balance sheet accounts. An adjusting entry never affects cash.

A2 **Compute profit margin and describe its use in analyzing company performance.** *Profit margin* is defined as the reporting period's net income divided by its net sales. Profit margin reflects on a company's earnings activities by showing how much income is in each dollar of sales.

A3 **Compute the current ratio and describe what it reveals about a company's financial condition.** A company's current ratio is defined as current assets divided by current liabilities. We use it to evaluate a company's ability to pay its current liabilities out of current assets.

P1 **Prepare and explain adjusting entries.** *Prepaid expenses* refer to items paid for in advance of receiving their benefits. Prepaid expenses are assets. Adjusting entries for prepaids involve increasing (debiting) expenses and decreasing (crediting) assets. *Unearned* (or *prepaid*) *revenues* refer to cash received in advance of providing products and services. Unearned revenues are liabilities. Adjusting entries for unearned revenues involve increasing (crediting) revenues and decreasing (debiting) unearned revenues. *Accrued expenses* refer to costs incurred in a period that are both unpaid and unrecorded. Adjusting entries for recording accrued expenses involve increasing (debiting) expenses and increasing (crediting) liabilities. *Accrued revenues* refer to revenues earned in a period that are both unrecorded and not yet received in cash. Adjusting entries for recording accrued revenues involve increasing (debiting) assets and increasing (crediting) revenues.

P2 **Explain and prepare an adjusted trial balance.** An adjusted trial balance is a list of accounts and balances prepared after recording and posting adjusting entries. Financial statements are often prepared from the adjusted trial balance.

P3 **Prepare financial statements from an adjusted trial balance.** Revenue and expense balances are reported on the income statement. Asset, liability, and equity balances are reported on the balance sheet. We usually prepare statements in the following order: income statement, statement of retained earnings, balance sheet, and statement of cash flows.

P4 **Describe and prepare closing entries.** Closing entries involve four steps: (1) close credit balances in revenue (and gain) accounts to Income Summary, (2) close debit balances in expense (and loss) accounts to Income Summary, (3) close Income Summary to the retained earnings, and (4) close dividends account to retained earnings.

P5 **Explain and prepare a post-closing trial balance.** A post-closing trial balance is a list of permanent accounts and their balances after all closing entries have been journalized and posted. Its purpose is to verify that (1) total debits equal total credits for permanent accounts and (2) all temporary accounts have zero balances.

P6^A **Explain the alternatives in accounting for prepaids.** Charging all prepaid expenses to expense accounts when they are purchased is acceptable. When this is done, adjusting entries must transfer any unexpired amounts from expense accounts to asset accounts. Crediting all unearned revenues to revenue accounts when cash is received is also acceptable. In this case, the adjusting entries must transfer any unearned amounts from revenue accounts to unearned revenue accounts.

P7^B **Prepare a work sheet and explain its usefulness.** A work sheet can be a useful tool in preparing and analyzing financial statements. It is helpful at the end of a period in

preparing adjusting entries, an adjusted trial balance, and financial statements. A work sheet usually contains five pairs of columns: Unadjusted Trial Balance, Adjustments, Adjusted Trial Balance, Income Statement, and Balance Sheet & Statement of Equity.

P8^C **Prepare reversing entries and explain their purpose.** Reversing entries are an optional step. They are applied to accrued expenses and revenues. The purpose of reversing entries is to simplify subsequent journal entries. Financial statements are unaffected by the choice to use or not use reversing entries.

Guidance Answers to Decision Maker and Decision Ethics

Investor   Prepaid expenses are items paid for in advance of receiving their benefits. They are assets and are expensed as they are used up. The publishing company's treatment of the signing bonus is acceptable provided future book sales can at least match the $500,000 expense. As an investor, you are concerned about the risk of future book sales. The riskier the likelihood of future book sales is, the more likely your analysis is to treat the $500,000, or a portion of it, as an expense, not a prepaid expense (asset).

Loan Officer   Your concern in lending to this store arises from analysis of current-year sales. While increased revenues and income are fine, your concern is with collectibility of these promotional sales. If the owner sold products to customers with poor records of paying bills, then collectibility of these sales is low. Your analysis must assess this possibility and recognize any expected losses.

Financial Officer   Omitting accrued expenses and recognizing revenue early can mislead financial statement users. One action is to request a second meeting with the president so you can explain that accruing expenses when incurred and recognizing revenue when earned are required practices. If the president persists, you might discuss the situation with legal counsel and any auditors involved. Your ethical action might cost you this job, but the potential pitfalls for falsification of statements, reputation and personal integrity loss, and other costs are too great.

Analyst   A current ratio of 1.2 suggests that current assets are sufficient to cover current liabilities, but it implies a minimal buffer in case of errors in measuring current assets or current liabilities. Removing the past due receivable reduces the current ratio to 0.7. Your assessment is that the company will have some difficulty meeting its loan payments.

Key Terms

Additional Quiz Questions are available at the book's Website.

1. A company forgot to record accrued and unpaid employee wages of $350,000 at period-end. This oversight would
   a. Understate net income by $350,000.
   b. Overstate net income by $350,000.
   c. Have no effect on net income.
   d. Overstate assets by $350,000.
   e. Understate assets by $350,000.

2. Prior to recording adjusting entries, the Supplies account has a $450 debit balance. A physical count of supplies shows $125 of unused supplies still available. The required adjusting entry is:
   a. Debit Supplies $125; Credit Supplies Expense $125.
   b. Debit Supplies $325; Credit Supplies Expense $325.
   c. Debit Supplies Expense $325; Credit Supplies $325.
   d. Debit Supplies Expense $325; Credit Supplies $125.
   e. Debit Supplies Expense $125; Credit Supplies $125.

3. On May 1, 2013, a two-year insurance policy was purchased for $24,000 with coverage to begin immediately. What is the amount of insurance expense that appears on the company's income statement for the year ended December 31, 2013?
   a. $4,000
   b. $8,000
   c. $12,000
   d. $20,000
   e. $24,000

4. On November 1, 2013, Stockton Co. receives $3,600 cash from Hans Co. for consulting services to be provided evenly over the period November 1, 2013, to April 30, 2014—at which time

Stockton credited $3,600 to Unearned Consulting Fees. The adjusting entry on December 31, 2013 (Stockton's year-end) would include a
   a. Debit to Unearned Consulting Fees for $1,200.
   b. Debit to Unearned Consulting Fees for $2,400.
   c. Credit to Consulting Fees Earned for $2,400.
   d. Debit to Consulting Fees Earned for $1,200.
   e. Credit to Cash for $3,600.

5. If a company had $15,000 in net income for the year, and its sales were $300,000 for the same year, what is its profit margin?
   a. 20%
   b. 2,000%
   c. $285,000
   d. $315,000
   e. 5%

6. Based on the following information from Repicor Company's balance sheet, what is Repicor Company's current ratio?

Current assets	$ 75,000	Current liabilities	50,000
Investments	30,000	Long-term liabilities ...	60,000
Plant assets	300,000	Common stock	295,000

   a. 2.10
   b. 1.50
   c. 1.00
   d. 0.95
   e. 0.67

A(B,C) *Superscript letter A(B,C) denotes assignments based on Appendix 3A(3B,3C).*
🔲 Icon denotes assignments that involve decision making.

1. What is the difference between the cash basis and the accrual basis of accounting?

2. 🔲 Why is the accrual basis of accounting generally preferred over the cash basis?

3. What type of business is most likely to select a fiscal year that corresponds to its natural business year instead of the calendar year?

4. What is a prepaid expense and where is it reported in the financial statements?

5. 🔲 What type of assets requires adjusting entries to record depreciation?

6. 🔲 What contra account is used when recording and reporting the effects of depreciation? Why is it used?

7. 🌐 Assume Samsung has unearned revenue. What is unearned revenue and where is it reported in financial statements?   **Samsung**

8. What is an accrued revenue? Give an example.

9.ᴬ If a company initially records prepaid expenses with debits to expense accounts, what type of account is debited in the adjusting entries for those prepaid expenses?

10. 🔲 Review the balance sheet of Apple in Appendix A. Identify one asset account that requires adjustment before annual financial statements can be prepared. What would be the effect on the income statement if this asset account were not adjusted? (Number not required, but comment on over- or understating of net income.)   **APPLE**

11. 🔲 Review the balance sheet of Google in Appendix A. Identify the amount for property and equipment. What adjusting entry is necessary (no numbers required) for this account when preparing financial statements?   **GOOGLE**

12. 🌐 Refer to Samsung's balance sheet in Appendix A. If it made an adjustment for unpaid wages at year-end, where would the accrued wages be reported on its balance sheet?   **Samsung**

13. What are the steps in recording closing entries?

14. What accounts are affected by closing entries? What accounts are not affected?

15. 🔲 What two purposes are accomplished by recording closing entries?

16. What is the purpose of the Income Summary account?

17. 🔲 Explain whether an error has occurred if a post-closing trial balance includes a Depreciation Expense account.

18.[B] What tasks are aided by a work sheet?

19.[B] Why are the debit and credit entries in the Adjustments columns of the work sheet identified with letters?

20. What is a company's operating cycle?

21. What classes of assets and liabilities are shown on a typical classified balance sheet?

22. How is unearned revenue classified on the balance sheet?

23. What are the characteristics of plant assets?

24.[C] How do reversing entries simplify recordkeeping?

25.[C] If a company recorded accrued salaries expense of $500 at the end of its fiscal year, what reversing entry could be made? When would it be made?

26. 🔲 Refer to the most recent balance sheet for Apple in Appendix A. What five main noncurrent asset categories are used on its classified balance sheet? **APPLE**

27. Refer to Samsung's most recent balance sheet in Appendix A. Identify and list its 8 current assets. **Samsung**

28. 🔲 Refer to Google's most recent balance sheet in Appendix A. Identify the 8 accounts listed as current liabilities. **GOOGLE**

29. 🔲 Refer to Samsung's financial statements in Appendix A. What journal entry was likely recorded as of December 31, 2012, to close its Income Summary account? **Samsung**

≣**connect**

QUICK STUDY

QS 3-1

Adjusting prepaid expenses

P1

a. On July 1, 2013, Lamis Company paid $1,200 for six months of insurance coverage. No adjustments have been made to the Prepaid Insurance account, and it is now December 31, 2013. Prepare the journal entry to reflect expiration of the insurance as of December 31, 2013.

b. Shandi Company has a Supplies account balance of $5,000 on January 1, 2013. During 2013, it purchased $2,000 of supplies. As of December 31, 2013, a supplies inventory shows $800 of supplies available. Prepare the adjusting journal entry to correctly report the balance of the Supplies account and the Supplies Expense account as of December 31, 2013.

QS 3-2

Adjusting for depreciation

P1

a. Bargains Company purchases $20,000 of equipment on January 1, 2013. The equipment is expected to last five years and be worth $2,000 at the end of that time. Prepare the entry to record one year's depreciation expense of $3,600 for the equipment as of December 31, 2013.

b. Welch Company purchases $10,000 of land on January 1, 2013. The land is expected to last indefinitely. What depreciation adjustment, if any, should be made with respect to the Land account as of December 31, 2013?

QS 3-3

Identifying accounting adjustments

P1

Classify the following adjusting entries as involving prepaid expenses (PE), unearned revenues (UR), accrued expenses (AE), or accrued revenues (AR).

a. _____ To record expiration of prepaid insurance.

b. _____ To record revenue earned but not yet billed (nor recorded).

c. _____ To record wages expense incurred but not yet paid (nor recorded).

d. _____ To record annual depreciation expense.

e. _____ To record revenue earned that was previously received as cash in advance.

QS 3-4

Accruing salaries

A1 P1

Jasmine Culpepper employs one college student every summer in her coffee shop. The student works the five weekdays and is paid on the following Monday. (For example, a student who works Monday through Friday, June 1 through June 5, is paid for that work on Monday, June 8.) Culpepper adjusts her books monthly, if needed, to show salaries earned but unpaid at month-end. The student works the last week of July—Friday is August 1. If the student earns $100 per day, what adjusting entry must Culpepper make on July 31 to correctly record accrued salaries expense for July?

a. Tao Co. receives $10,000 cash in advance for 4 months of legal services on October 1, 2013, and records it by debiting Cash and crediting Unearned Revenue both for $10,000. It is now December 31, 2013, and Tao has provided legal services as planned. What adjusting entry should Tao make to account for the work performed from October 1 through December 31, 2013?

b. A. Caden started a new publication called *Contest News*. Its subscribers pay $24 to receive 12 monthly issues. With every new subscriber, Caden debits Cash and credits Unearned Subscription Revenue for the amounts received. The company has 100 new subscribers as of July 1, 2013. It sends *Contest News* to each of these subscribers every month from July through December. Assuming no changes in subscribers, prepare the journal entry that Caden must make as of December 31, 2013, to adjust the Subscription Revenue account and the Unearned Subscription Revenue account.

QS 3-5
Adjusting for unearned revenues
A1 P1

In its first year of operations, Roma Co. earned $45,000 in revenues and received $37,000 cash from these customers. The company incurred expenses of $25,500 but had not paid $5,250 of them at year-end. The company also prepaid $6,750 cash for expenses that would be incurred the next year. Calculate the first year's net income under both the cash basis and the accrual basis of accounting.

QS 3-6
Computing accrual and cash income C2 A1

Adjusting entries affect at least one balance sheet account and at least one income statement account. For the following entries, identify the account to be debited and the account to be credited. Indicate which of the accounts is the income statement account and which is the balance sheet account.

a. Entry to record revenue earned that was previously received as cash in advance.

b. Entry to record wage expenses incurred but not yet paid (nor recorded).

c. Entry to record revenue earned but not yet billed (nor recorded).

d. Entry to record expiration of prepaid insurance.

e. Entry to record annual depreciation expense.

QS 3-7
Recording and analyzing adjusting entries
A1

During the year, Sereno Co. recorded prepayments of expenses in asset accounts, and cash receipts of unearned revenues in liability accounts. At the end of its annual accounting period, the company must make three adjusting entries: (1) accrue salaries expense, (2) adjust the Unearned Services Revenue account to recognize earned revenue, and (3) record services revenue earned for which cash will be received the following period. For each of these adjusting entries (1), (2), and (3), indicate the account from *a* through *i* to be debited and the account to be credited.

a. Prepaid Salaries

b. Cash

c. Salaries Payable

d. Unearned Services Revenue

e. Salaries Expense

f. Services Revenue

g. Accounts Receivable

h. Accounts Payable

i. Equipment

QS 3-8
Preparing adjusting entries
P1

The following information is taken from Brooke Company's unadjusted and adjusted trial balances.

QS 3-9
Interpreting adjusting entries
C2 P2

	Unadjusted		Adjusted	
	Debit	Credit	Debit	Credit
Prepaid insurance.........	$4,100		$3,700	
Interest payable		$ 0		$800

Given this information, which of the following is likely included among its adjusting entries?

a. A $400 debit to Insurance Expense and an $800 debit to Interest Payable.

b. A $400 debit to Insurance Expense and an $800 debit to Interest Expense.

c. A $400 credit to Prepaid Insurance and an $800 debit to Interest Payable.

In making adjusting entries at the end of its accounting period, Chao Consulting failed to record $3,200 of insurance coverage that had expired. This $3,200 cost had been initially debited to the Prepaid Insurance account. The company also failed to record accrued salaries expense of $2,000. As a result of these two oversights, the financial statements for the reporting period will [choose one] (1) understate assets by $3,200; (2) understate expenses by $5,200; (3) understate net income by $2,000; or (4) overstate liabilities by $2,000.

QS 3-10
Determining effects of adjusting entries
A1

QS 3-11
Analyzing profit margin   A2

Deklin Company reported net income of $48,025 and net sales of $425,000 for the current year. Calculate the company's profit margin and interpret the result. Assume that its competitors earn an average profit margin of 15%.

QS 3-12ᴬ
Preparing adjusting entries
P6

Calvin Consulting initially records prepaid and unearned items in income statement accounts. Given this company's accounting practices, which of the following applies to the preparation of adjusting entries at the end of its first accounting period?

  a. Unearned fees (on which cash was received in advance earlier in the period) are recorded with a debit to Consulting Fees Earned of $500 and a credit to Unearned Consulting Fees of $500.

  b. Unpaid salaries of $400 are recorded with a debit to Prepaid Salaries of $400 and a credit to Salaries Expense of $400.

  c. Office supplies purchased for the period were $1,000. The cost of unused office supplies of $650 is recorded with a debit to Supplies Expense of $650 and a credit to Office Supplies of $650.

  d. Earned but unbilled (and unrecorded) consulting fees for the period were $1,200, which are recorded with a debit to Unearned Consulting Fees of $1,200 and a credit to Consulting Fees Earned of $1,200.

QS 3-13
International accounting
standards   P3

Answer each of the following questions related to international accounting standards.

  a. Do financial statements prepared under IFRS normally present assets from least liquid to most liquid or vice-versa?

  b. Do financial statements prepared under IFRS normally present liabilities from furthest from maturity to nearest to maturity or vice-versa?

QS 3-14
Prepaid (deferred) expenses
adjustments
P1

For each separate case below, follow the 3-step process for adjusting the prepaid asset account: Step 1: Determine what the current account balance equals. Step 2: Determine what the current account balance should equal. Step 3: Record an adjusting entry to get from step 1 to step 2. *Assume no other adjusting entries are made during the year.*

  a. Prepaid Insurance. The Prepaid Insurance account has a $4,700 debit balance to start the year. A review of insurance policies and payments shows that $900 of unexpired insurance remains at year-end.

  b. Prepaid Insurance. The Prepaid Insurance account has a $5,890 debit balance at the start of the year. A review of insurance policies and payments shows $1,040 of insurance has expired by year-end.

  c. Prepaid Rent. On September 1 of the current year, the company prepaid $24,000 for 2 years of rent for facilities being occupied that day. The company debited Prepaid Rent and credited Cash for $24,000.

QS 3-15
Prepaid (deferred) expenses
adjustments
P1

For each separate case below, follow the 3-step process for adjusting the supplies asset account: Step 1: Determine what the current account balance equals. Step 2: Determine what the current account balance should equal. Step 3: Record an adjusting entry to get from step 1 to step 2. *Assume no other adjusting entries are made during the year.*

  a. Supplies. The Supplies account has a $300 debit balance to start the year. No supplies were purchased during the current year. A December 31 physical count shows $110 of supplies remaining.

  b. Supplies. The Supplies account has an $800 debit balance to start the year. Supplies of $2,100 were purchased during the current year and debited to the Supplies account. A December 31 physical count shows $650 of supplies remaining.

  c. Supplies. The Supplies account has a $4,000 debit balance to start the year. During the current year, supplies of $9,400 were purchased and debited to the Supplies account. The inventory of supplies available at December 31 totaled $2,660.

QS 3-16
Accumulated depreciation
adjustments
P1

For each separate case below, follow the 3-step process for adjusting the accumulated depreciation account: Step 1: Determine what the current account balance equals. Step 2: Determine what the current account balance should equal. Step 3: Record an adjusting entry to get from step 1 to step 2. *Assume no other adjusting entries are made during the year.*

  a. Accumulated Depreciation. The Krug Company's Accumulated Depreciation account has a $13,500 balance to start the year. A review of depreciation schedules reveals that $14,600 of depreciation expense must be recorded for the year.

  b. Accumulated Depreciation. The company has only one fixed asset (truck) that it purchased at the start of this year. That asset had cost $44,000, had an estimated life of 5 years, and is expected to have zero value at the end of the 5 years.

  c. Accumulated Depreciation. The company has only one fixed asset (equipment) that it purchased at the start of this year. That asset had cost $32,000, had an estimated life of 7 years, and is expected to be valued at $4,000 at the end of the 7 years.

For each separate case below, follow the 3-step process for adjusting the unearned revenue liability account: Step 1: Determine what the current account balance equals. Step 2: Determine what the current account balance should equal. Step 3: Record an adjusting entry to get from step 1 to step 2. *Assume no other adjusting entries are made during the year.*

a. Unearned Rent Revenue. The Krug Company collected $6,000 rent in advance on November 1, debiting Cash and crediting Unearned Rent Revenue. The tenant was paying twelve months rent in advance and occupancy began November 1.

b. Unearned Services Revenue. The company charges $75 per month to spray a house for insects. A customer paid $300 on October 1 in advance for four treatments, which was recorded with a debit to Cash and a credit to Unearned Services Revenue. At year-end, the company has applied three treatments for the customer.

c. Unearned Rent Revenue. On September 1, a client paid the company $24,000 cash for six months of rent in advance (the client leased a building and took occupancy immediately). The company recorded the cash as Unearned Rent Revenue.

QS 3-17
Unearned (deferred) revenues adjustments
P1

For each separate case below, follow the 3-step process for adjusting the accrued expense account: Step 1: Determine what the current account balance equals. Step 2: Determine what the current account balance should equal. Step 3: Record an adjusting entry to get from step 1 to step 2. *Assume no other adjusting entries are made during the year.*

a. Salaries Payable. At year-end, salaries expense of $15,500 has been incurred by the company, but is not yet paid to employees.

b. Interest Payable. At its December 31 year-end, the company owes $250 of interest on a line-of-credit loan. That interest will not be paid until sometime in January of the next year.

c. Interest Payable. At its December 31 year-end, the company holds a mortgage payable that has incurred $875 in annual interest that is neither recorded nor paid. The company intends to pay the interest on January 7 of the next year.

QS 3-18
Accrued expenses adjustments
P1

For each separate case below, follow the 3-step process for adjusting the accrued revenue account: Step 1: Determine what the current account balance equals. Step 2: Determine what the current account balance should equal. Step 3: Record an adjusting entry to get from step 1 to step 2. *Assume no other adjusting entries are made during the year.*

a. Accounts Receivable. At year-end, the Krug Company has completed services of $19,000 for a client, but the client has not yet been billed for those services.

b. Interest Receivable. At year-end, the company has earned, but not yet recorded, $390 of interest earned from its investments in government bonds.

c. Accounts Receivable. A painting company collects fees when jobs are complete. The work for one customer, whose job was bid at $1,300, has been completed, but the customer has not yet been billed.

QS 3-19
Accrued revenues adjustments
P1

List the following steps of the accounting cycle in their proper order.

a. Posting the journal entries.
b. Journalizing and posting adjusting entries.
c. Preparing the adjusted trial balance.
d. Journalizing and posting closing entries.
e. Analyzing transactions and events.
f. Preparing the financial statements.
g. Preparing the unadjusted trial balance.
h. Journalizing transactions and events.
i. Preparing the post-closing trial balance.

QS 3-20
Identifying the accounting cycle
C3

The following are common categories on a classified balance sheet.

A. Current assets
B. Long-term investments
C. Plant assets
D. Intangible assets
E. Current liabilities
F. Long-term liabilities

For each of the following items, select the letter that identifies the balance sheet category where the item typically would appear.

_____ **1.** Land not currently used in operations
_____ **2.** Notes payable (due in five years)
_____ **3.** Accounts receivable
_____ **4.** Trademarks
_____ **5.** Accounts payable
_____ **6.** Store equipment
_____ **7.** Wages payable
_____ **8.** Cash

QS 3-21
Classifying balance sheet items
C4

QS 3-22

Identifying current accounts and computing the current ratio

A3

Compute Chavez Company's current ratio using the following information.

Accounts receivable	$18,000	Long-term notes payable	$21,000
Accounts payable	11,000	Office supplies	2,800
Buildings	45,000	Prepaid insurance	3,560
Cash	7,000	Unearned services revenue	3,000

QS 3-23

Prepare closing entries from the ledger   P4

The ledger of Mai Company includes the following accounts with normal balances: Common Stock $9,000; Dividends $800; Services Revenue $13,000; Wages Expense $8,400; and Rent Expense $1,600. Prepare the necessary closing entries from the available information at December 31.

QS 3-24

Identify post-closing accounts   P5

Identify which of the following accounts would be included in a post-closing trial balance.

a. Accounts receivable   **c.** Goodwill   **e.** Income tax expense

b. Salaries expense   **d.** Land

QS 3-25ᴮ

Preparing a partial work sheet

P7

The ledger of Claudell Company includes the following unadjusted normal balances: Prepaid Rent $1,000, Services Revenue $55,600, and Wages Expense $5,000. Adjusting entries are required for (a) prepaid rent expired, $200; (b) accrued services revenue $900; and (c) accrued wages expense $700. Enter these unadjusted balances and the necessary adjustments on a work sheet and complete the work sheet for these accounts. *Note:* Also include the following accounts: Accounts Receivable, Wages Payable, and Rent Expense.

QS 3-26ᶜ

Reversing entries

P8

On December 31, 2012, Yates Co. prepared an adjusting entry for $12,000 of earned but unrecorded management fees. On January 16, 2013, Yates received $26,700 cash in management fees, which included the accrued fees earned in 2012. Assuming the company uses reversing entries, prepare the January 1, 2013, reversing entry and the January 16, 2013, cash receipt entry.

connect

EXERCISES

Exercise 3-1

Preparing adjusting entries

P1

Prepare adjusting journal entries for the year ended (date of) December 31, 2013, for each of these separate situations. Assume that prepaid expenses are initially recorded in asset accounts. Also assume that fees collected in advance of work are initially recorded as liabilities.

a. Depreciation on the company's equipment for 2013 is computed to be $18,000.

b. The Prepaid Insurance account had a $6,000 debit balance at December 31, 2013, before adjusting for the costs of any expired coverage. An analysis of the company's insurance policies showed that $1,100 of unexpired insurance coverage remains.

Check (c) Dr. Office Supplies Expense, $3,882; (e) Dr. Insurance Expense, $5,800

c. The Office Supplies account had a $700 debit balance on December 31, 2012; and $3,480 of office supplies were purchased during the year. The December 31, 2013, physical count showed $298 of supplies available.

d. Two-thirds of the work related to $15,000 of cash received in advance was performed this period.

e. The Prepaid Insurance account had a $6,800 debit balance at December 31, 2013, before adjusting for the costs of any expired coverage. An analysis of insurance policies showed that $5,800 of coverage had expired.

f. Wage expenses of $3,200 have been incurred but are not paid as of December 31, 2013.

Exercise 3-2

Preparing adjusting entries

P1

For each of the following separate cases, prepare adjusting entries required of financial statements for the year ended (date of) December 31, 2013. (Assume that prepaid expenses are initially recorded in asset accounts and that fees collected in advance of work are initially recorded as liabilities.)

a. One-third of the work related to $15,000 cash received in advance is performed this period.

b. Wages of $8,000 are earned by workers but not paid as of December 31, 2013.

c. Depreciation on the company's equipment for 2013 is $18,531.

d. The Office Supplies account had a $240 debit balance on December 31, 2012. During 2013, $5,239 of office supplies are purchased. A physical count of supplies at December 31, 2013, shows $487 of supplies available.

Check (e) Dr. Insurance Expense, $2,800; (f) Cr. Interest Revenue, $1,050

e. The Prepaid Insurance account had a $4,000 balance on December 31, 2012. An analysis of insurance policies shows that $1,200 of unexpired insurance benefits remain at December 31, 2013.

f. The company has earned (but not recorded) $1,050 of interest from investments in CDs for the year ended December 31, 2013. The interest revenue will be received on January 10, 2014.

g. The company has a bank loan and has incurred (but not recorded) interest expense of $2,500 for the year ended December 31, 2013. The company must pay the interest on January 2, 2014.

Pablo Management has five part-time employees, each of whom earns $250 per day. They are normally paid on Fridays for work completed Monday through Friday of the same week. Assume that December 28, 2013, was a Friday, and that they were paid in full on that day. The next week, the five employees worked only four days because New Year's Day was an unpaid holiday. (*a*) Assuming that December 31, 2013, was a Monday, prepare the adjusting entry that would be recorded at the close of that day. (*b*) Assuming that January 4, 2014, was a Friday, prepare the journal entry that would be made to record payment of the employees' wages.

Exercise 3-3
Adjusting and paying accrued wages
C1 P1

The following three separate situations require adjusting journal entries to prepare financial statements as of April 30. For each situation, present both the April 30 adjusting entry and the subsequent entry during May to record the payment of the accrued expenses.

a. On April 1, the company retained an attorney for a flat monthly fee of $3,500. Payment for April legal services was made by the company on May 12.

b. A $900,000 note payable requires 10% annual interest, or $9,000 to be paid at the 20th day of each month. The interest was last paid on April 20 and the next payment is due on May 20. As of April 30, $3,000 of interest expense has accrued.

c. Total weekly salaries expense for all employees is $10,000. This amount is paid at the end of the day on Friday of each five-day workweek. April 30 falls on Tuesday of this year, which means that the employees had worked two days since the last payday. The next payday is May 3.

Exercise 3-4
Adjusting and paying accrued expenses
A1

Check (*b*) May 20 Dr. Interest Expense, $6,000

Determine the missing amounts in each of these four separate situations *a* through *d*.

Exercise 3-5
Determining cost flows through accounts
C1 A1

	a	b	c	d
Supplies available—prior year-end	$ 400	$1,200	$1,260	?
Supplies purchased during the current year	2,800	6,500	?	$3,000
Supplies available—current year-end	650	?	1,350	700
Supplies expense for the current year	?	1,200	8,400	4,588

Following are two income statements for Alexis Co. for the year ended December 31. The left column is prepared before any adjusting entries are recorded, and the right column includes the effects of adjusting entries. The company records cash receipts and payments related to unearned and prepaid items in balance sheet accounts. Analyze the statements and prepare the eight adjusting entries that likely were recorded. (*Note:* 30% of the $7,000 adjustment for Fees Earned has been earned but not billed, and the other 70% has been earned by performing services that were paid for in advance.)

Exercise 3-6
Analyzing and preparing adjusting entries
A1 P3

ALEXIS CO. Income Statements For Year Ended December 31		
	Unadjusted	Adjusted
Revenues		
Fees earned	$18,000	$25,000
Commissions earned	36,500	36,500
Total revenues	54,500	61,500
Expenses		
Depreciation expense—Computers	0	1,600
Depreciation expense—Office furniture	0	1,850
Salaries expense	13,500	15,750
Insurance expense	0	1,400
Rent expense	3,800	3,800
Office supplies expense	0	580
Advertising expense	2,500	2,500
Utilities expense	1,245	1,335
Total expenses	21,045	28,815
Net income	$33,455	$32,685

Exercise 3-7

Computing and interpreting
profit margin

A2

Use the following information to compute profit margin for each separate company *a* through *e*.

	Net Income	Net Sales		Net Income	Net Sales
a.	$ 4,361	$ 44,500	**d.**	$65,646	$1,458,800
b.	97,706	398,800	**e.**	80,142	435,500
c.	111,281	257,000			

Which of the five companies is the most profitable according to the profit margin ratio? Interpret that company's profit margin ratio.

Exercise 3-8ᴬ

Adjusting for prepaids recorded
as expenses and unearned
revenues recorded as revenues

P6

Check (*f*) Cr. Insurance Expense,
$1,200; (*g*) Dr. Remodeling Fees
Earned, $11,130

Ricardo Construction began operations on December 1. In setting up its accounting procedures, the company decided to debit expense accounts when it prepays its expenses and to credit revenue accounts when customers pay for services in advance. Prepare journal entries for items *a* through *d* and the adjusting entries as of its December 31 period-end for items *e* through *g*.

a. Supplies are purchased on December 1 for $2,000 cash.

b. The company prepaid its insurance premiums for $1,540 cash on December 2.

c. On December 15, the company receives an advance payment of $13,000 cash from a customer for remodeling work.

d. On December 28, the company receives $3,700 cash from another customer for remodeling work to be performed in January.

e. A physical count on December 31 indicates that the Company has $1,840 of supplies available.

f. An analysis of the insurance policies in effect on December 31 shows that $340 of insurance coverage had expired.

g. As of December 31, only one remodeling project has been worked on and completed. The $5,570 fee for this project had been received in advance and recorded as remodeling fees earned.

Exercise 3-9ᴬ

Recording and reporting
revenues received in advance

P6

Check (*c*) Fees Earned—using
entries from part *b*, $10,500

Costanza Company experienced the following events and transactions during July.

July	1	Received $3,000 cash in advance of performing work for Vivian Solana.
	6	Received $7,500 cash in advance of performing work for Iris Haru.
	12	Completed the job for Solana.
	18	Received $8,500 cash in advance of performing work for Amina Jordan.
	27	Completed the job for Haru.
	31	None of the work for Jordan has been performed.

a. Prepare journal entries (including any adjusting entries as of the end of the month) to record these events using the procedure of initially crediting the Unearned Fees account when payment is received from a customer in advance of performing services.

b. Prepare journal entries (including any adjusting entries as of the end of the month) to record these events using the procedure of initially crediting the Fees Earned account when payment is received from a customer in advance of performing services.

c. Under each method, determine the amount of earned fees reported on the income statement for July and the amount of unearned fees reported on the balance sheet as of July 31.

Exercise 3-10

Preparing a balance sheet
following IFRS

P3

adidas AG reports the following balance sheet accounts for the year ended December 31, 2011 (euros in millions). Prepare the balance sheet for this company as of December 31, 2011, following usual IFRS practices.

Tangible and other assets	€ 255		Intangible assets	€ 154
Total equity	2,322		Total current liabilities	345
Receivables and other assets	1,767		Inventories	30
Total noncurrent liabilities	3,379		Total liabilities	3,724
Cash and cash equivalents	383		Other current assets	28
Total current assets	2,208		Total noncurrent assets	3,838
Other noncurrent assets	3,429			

Exercise 3-11

Preparing financial statements

C3 P3

Use the following adjusted trial balance of Wilson Trucking Company to prepare the (1) income statement and (2) statement of retained earnings, for the year ended December 31, 2013. The retained earnings account balance is $145,000 at December 31, 2012.

Account Title	Debit	Credit
Cash	$ 8,000	
Accounts receivable	17,500	
Office supplies	3,000	
Trucks	172,000	
Accumulated depreciation—Trucks		$ 36,000
Land	85,000	
Accounts payable		12,000
Interest payable		4,000
Long-term notes payable		53,000
Common stock		30,000
Retained earnings		145,000
Dividends	20,000	
Trucking fees earned		130,000
Depreciation expense—Trucks	23,500	
Salaries expense	61,000	
Office supplies expense	8,000	
Repairs expense—Trucks	12,000	
Totals	$410,000	$410,000

Use the information in the adjusted trial balance reported in Exercise 3-11 to prepare Wilson Trucking Company's classified balance sheet as of December 31, 2013.

Exercise 3-12
Preparing a classified balance sheet **C4**

Check Total assets, $249,500

Use the information in the adjusted trial balance reported in Exercise 3-11 to compute the current ratio as of the balance sheet date (round the ratio to two decimals). Interpret the current ratio for the Wilson Trucking Company. (Assume that the industry average for the current ratio is 1.5.)

Exercise 3-13
Computing the current ratio

A3

Calculate the current ratio in each of the following separate cases (round the ratio to two decimals). Identify the company case with the strongest liquidity position. (These cases represent competing companies in the same industry.)

Exercise 3-14
Computing and analyzing the current ratio

A3

	Current Assets	Current Liabilities
Case 1	$ 79,040	$ 32,000
Case 2	104,880	76,000
Case 3	45,080	49,000
Case 4	85,680	81,600
Case 5	61,000	100,000

The following two events occurred for Trey Co. on October 31, 2013, the end of its fiscal year.

a. Trey rents a building from its owner for $2,800 per month. By a prearrangement, the company delayed paying October's rent until November 5. On this date, the company paid the rent for both October and November.

b. Trey rents space in a building it owns to a tenant for $850 per month. By prearrangement, the tenant delayed paying the October rent until November 8. On this date, the tenant paid the rent for both October and November.

Exercise 3-15ᴬ
Preparing reversing entries

P8

Required

1. Prepare adjusting entries that the company must record for these events as of October 31.

2. Assuming Trey does *not* use reversing entries, prepare journal entries to record Trey's payment of rent on November 5 and the collection of the tenant's rent on November 8.

3. Assuming that the company uses reversing entries, prepare reversing entries on November 1 and the journal entries to record Trey's payment of rent on November 5 and the collection of the tenant's rent on November 8.

Exercise 3-16
Preparing closing entries
P4

Following are Nintendo's revenue and expense accounts for a recent calendar year (yen in millions). Prepare the company's closing entries for its revenues and its expenses.

Net sales	¥1,014,345
Cost of sales	626,379
Advertising expense	96,359
Other expense, net	213,986

Exercise 3-17
Completing a work sheet
P7

The following data are taken from the unadjusted trial balance of the Westcott Company at December 31, 2013. Each account carries a normal balance and the accounts are shown here in alphabetical order.

Accounts Payable	$ 6	Prepaid Insurance	$18	Retained earnings	$32
Accounts Receivable...............	12	Revenue	75	Dividends	6
Accumulated Depreciation—Equip.	15	Salaries Expense.......	18	Unearned Revenue	12
Cash...........................	21	Supplies	24	Utilities Expense	12
Equipment......................	39	Common stock	10		

1. Use the data above to prepare a work sheet. Enter the accounts in proper order and enter their balances in the correct debit or credit column.

2. Use the following adjustment information to complete the work sheet.

    a. Depreciation on equipment, $3

    b. Accrued salaries, $6

    c. The $12 of unearned revenue has been earned

    d. Supplies available at December 31, 2013, $15

    e. Expired insurance, $15

PROBLEM SET A

Problem 3-1A
Identifying adjusting entries with explanations
P1

For each of the following entries, enter the letter of the explanation that most closely describes it in the space beside each entry. (You can use letters more than once.)

A. To record receipt of unearned revenue.

B. To record this period's earning of prior unearned revenue.

C. To record payment of an accrued expense.

D. To record receipt of an accrued revenue.

E. To record an accrued expense.

F. To record an accrued revenue.

G. To record this period's use of a prepaid expense.

H. To record payment of a prepaid expense.

I. To record this period's depreciation expense.

_____	1.	Interest Expense	1,000
		Interest Payable	1,000
_____	2.	Depreciation Expense	4,000
		Accumulated Depreciation	4,000
_____	3.	Unearned Professional Fees	3,000
		Professional Fees Earned	3,000
_____	4.	Insurance Expense	4,200
		Prepaid Insurance	4,200
_____	5.	Salaries Payable	1,400
		Cash	1,400
_____	6.	Prepaid Rent	4,500
		Cash	4,500
_____	7.	Salaries Expense	6,000
		Salaries Payable	6,000
_____	8.	Interest Receivable	5,000
		Interest Revenue	5,000
_____	9.	Cash..	9,000
		Accounts Receivable (from consulting)	9,000
_____	10.	Cash..	7,500
		Unearned Professional Fees	7,500
_____	11.	Cash..	2,000
		Interest Receivable	2,000
_____	12.	Rent Expense	2,000
		Prepaid Rent	2,000

Arnez Co. follows the practice of recording prepaid expenses and unearned revenues in balance sheet accounts. The company's annual accounting period ends on December 31, 2013. The following information concerns the adjusting entries to be recorded as of that date.

Problem 3-2A
Preparing adjusting and subsequent journal entries

C1 A1 P1

a. The Office Supplies account started the year with a $4,000 balance. During 2013, the company purchased supplies for $13,400, which was added to the Office Supplies account. The inventory of supplies available at December 31, 2013, totaled $2,554.

b. An analysis of the company's insurance policies provided the following facts.

Policy	Date of Purchase	Months of Coverage	Cost
A	April 1, 2011	24	$14,400
B	April 1, 2012	36	12,960
C	August 1, 2013	12	2,400

The total premium for each policy was paid in full (for all months) at the purchase date, and the Prepaid Insurance account was debited for the full cost. (Year-end adjusting entries for Prepaid Insurance were properly recorded in all prior years.)

c. The company has 15 employees, who earn a total of $1,960 in salaries each working day. They are paid each Monday for their work in the five-day workweek ending on the previous Friday. Assume that December 31, 2013, is a Tuesday, and all 15 employees worked the first two days of that week. Because New Year's Day is a paid holiday, they will be paid salaries for five full days on Monday, January 6, 2014.

d. The company purchased a building on January 1, 2013. It cost $960,000 and is expected to have a $45,000 salvage value at the end of its predicted 30-year life. Annual depreciation is $30,500.

e. Since the company is not large enough to occupy the entire building it owns, it rented space to a tenant at $3,000 per month, starting on November 1, 2013. The rent was paid on time on November 1, and the amount received was credited to the Rent Earned account. However, the tenant has not paid the December rent. The company has worked out an agreement with the tenant, who has promised to pay both December and January rent in full on January 15. The tenant has agreed not to fall behind again.

f. On November 1, the company rented space to another tenant for $2,800 per month. The tenant paid five months' rent in advance on that date. The payment was recorded with a credit to the Unearned Rent account.

Required

1. Use the information to prepare adjusting entries as of December 31, 2013.
2. Prepare journal entries to record the first subsequent cash transaction in 2014 for parts *c* and *e*.

Check   (1*b*) Dr. Insurance Expense, $7,120 (1*d*) Dr. Depreciation Expense, $30,500

Wells Technical Institute (WTI), a school owned by Tristana Wells, provides training to individuals who pay tuition directly to the school. WTI also offers training to groups in off-site locations. Its unadjusted trial balance as of December 31, 2013, follows. WTI initially records prepaid expenses and unearned revenues in balance sheet accounts. Descriptions of items *a* through *h* that require adjusting entries on December 31, 2013, follow.

Problem 3-3A
Preparing adjusting entries, adjusted trial balance, and financial statements

A1 P1 P2 P3

Additional Information Items

a. An analysis of WTI's insurance policies shows that $2,400 of coverage has expired.

b. An inventory count shows that teaching supplies costing $2,800 are available at year-end 2013.

c. Annual depreciation on the equipment is $13,200.

d. Annual depreciation on the professional library is $7,200.

e. On November 1, WTI agreed to do a special six-month course (starting immediately) for a client. The contract calls for a monthly fee of $2,500, and the client paid the first five months' fees in advance. When the cash was received, the Unearned Training Fees account was credited. The fee for the sixth month will be recorded when it is collected in 2014.

f. On October 15, WTI agreed to teach a four-month class (beginning immediately) for an individual for $3,000 tuition per month payable at the end of the class. The class started on October 15, but no payment has yet been received. (WTI's accruals are applied to the nearest half-month; for example, October recognizes one-half month accrual.)

g. WTI's two employees are paid weekly. As of the end of the year, two days' salaries have accrued at the rate of $100 per day for each employee.

h. The balance in the Prepaid Rent account represents rent for December.

		Debit	Credit
	WELLS TECHNICAL INSTITUTE		
	Unadjusted Trial Balance		
	December 31, 2013		
3	Cash	$ 34,000	
4	Accounts receivable	0	
5	Teaching supplies	8,000	
6	Prepaid insurance	12,000	
7	Prepaid rent	3,000	
8	Professional library	35,000	
9	Accumulated depreciation—Professional library		$ 10,000
10	Equipment	80,000	
11	Accumulated depreciation—Equipment		15,000
12	Accounts payable		26,000
13	Salaries payable		0
14	Unearned training fees		12,500
15	Common stock		10,000
16	Retained earnings		80,000
17	Dividends	50,000	
18	Tuition fees earned		123,900
19	Training fees earned		40,000
20	Depreciation expense—Professional library	0	
21	Depreciation expense—Equipment	0	
22	Salaries expense	50,000	
23	Insurance expense	0	
24	Rent expense	33,000	
25	Teaching supplies expense	0	
26	Advertising expense	6,000	
27	Utilities expense	6,400	
28	Totals	$ 317,400	$ 317,400

Required

1. Prepare T-accounts (representing the ledger) with balances from the unadjusted trial balance.

2. Prepare the necessary adjusting journal entries for items *a* through *h* and post them to the T-accounts. Assume that adjusting entries are made only at year-end.

3. Update balances in the T-accounts for the adjusting entries and prepare an adjusted trial balance.

4. Prepare Wells Technical Institute's income statement and statement of retained earnings for the year 2013 and prepare its balance sheet as of December 31, 2013.

Problem 3-4A

Interpreting unadjusted and adjusted trial balances, and preparing financial statements

A1 P1 P2 P3

A six-column table for JKL Company follows. The first two columns contain the unadjusted trial balance for the company as of July 31, 2013. The last two columns contain the adjusted trial balance as of the same date.

Required

Analysis Component

1. Analyze the differences between the unadjusted and adjusted trial balances to determine the eight adjustments that likely were made. Show the results of your analysis by inserting these adjustment amounts in the table's two middle columns. Label each adjustment with a letter *a* through *h* and provide a short description of it at the bottom of the table.

Preparation Component

2. Use the information in the adjusted trial balance to prepare the company's (*a*) income statement and its statement of retained earnings for the year ended July 31, 2013 (*Note:* retained earnings at July 31, 2012, was $25,000, and the current-year dividends were $5,000), and (*b*) the balance sheet as of July 31, 2013.

	Unadjusted Trial Balance		Adjustments		Adjusted Trial Balance	
Cash	$ 34,000				$ 34,000	
Accounts receivable	14,000				22,000	
Office supplies	16,000				2,000	
Prepaid insurance	8,540				2,960	
Office equipment	84,000				84,000	
Accum. depreciation—						
Office equip.		$ 14,000				$ 20,000
Accounts payable		9,100				10,000
Interest payable		0				1,000
Salaries payable		0				7,000
Unearned consulting fees		18,000				15,000
Long-term notes payable		52,000				52,000
Common stock..............		15,000				15,000
Retained earnings		25,000				25,000
Dividends	5,000				5,000	
Consulting fees earned		123,240				134,240
Depreciation expense—						
Office equip.	0				6,000	
Salaries expense	67,000				74,000	
Interest expense	1,200				2,200	
Insurance expense	0				5,580	
Rent expense	14,500				14,500	
Office supplies expense	0				14,000	
Advertising expense	12,100				13,000	
Totals	$256,340	$256,340			$279,240	$279,240

The adjusted trial balance for Chiara Company as of December 31, 2013, follows.

Problem 3-5A
Preparing financial statements from the adjusted trial balance and calculating profit margin

P3   A1   A2

	Debit	Credit
Cash	$ 30,000	
Accounts receivable	52,000	
Interest receivable	18,000	
Notes receivable (due in 90 days)	168,000	
Office supplies	16,000	
Automobiles	168,000	
Accumulated depreciation—Automobiles		$ 50,000
Equipment................................	138,000	
Accumulated depreciation—Equipment		18,000
Land	78,000	
Accounts payable		96,000
Interest payable		20,000
Salaries payable		19,000
Unearned fees		30,000
Long-term notes payable		138,000
Common stock............................		20,000
Retained earnings		235,800
Dividends	46,000	
Fees earned		484,000
Interest earned		24,000
Depreciation expense—Automobiles	26,000	
Depreciation expense—Equipment	18,000	
Salaries expense	188,000	
Wages expense	40,000	
Interest expense	32,000	
Office supplies expense	34,000	
Advertising expense	58,000	
Repairs expense—Automobiles	24,800	
Totals	$1,134,800	$1,134,800

Required

1. Use the information in the adjusted trial balance to prepare (*a*) the income statement for the year ended December 31, 2013; (*b*) the statement of retained earnings for the year ended December 31, 2013; and (*c*) the balance sheet as of December 31, 2013.

2. Calculate the profit margin for year 2013.

Problem 3-6A

Determining balance sheet classifications

C4

In the blank space beside each numbered balance sheet item, enter the letter of its balance sheet classification. If the item should not appear on the balance sheet, enter a *Z* in the blank.

A. Current assets   **D.** Intangible assets   **F.** Long-term liabilities
B. Long-term investments   **E.** Current liabilities   **G.** Equity
C. Plant assets

_____ **1.** Long-term investment in stock   _____ **11.** Unearned services revenue
_____ **2.** Depreciation expense—Building   _____ **12.** Accumulated depreciation—Trucks
_____ **3.** Prepaid rent   _____ **13.** Cash
_____ **4.** Interest receivable   _____ **14.** Buildings
_____ **5.** Taxes payable   _____ **15.** Store supplies
_____ **6.** Automobiles   _____ **16.** Office equipment
_____ **7.** Notes payable (due in 3 years)   _____ **17.** Land (used in operations)
_____ **8.** Accounts payable   _____ **18.** Repairs expense
_____ **9.** Prepaid insurance   _____ **19.** Office supplies
_____ **10.** Common stock   _____ **20.** Current portion of long-term note payable

---

Problem 3-7A

Applying the accounting cycle

P1 P2 P3 P4 P5

On April 1, 2013, Jiro Nozomi created a new travel agency, Adventure Travel. The following transactions occurred during the company's first month.

April 1	Nozomi invested $30,000 cash and computer equipment worth $20,000 in the company in exchange for common stock.
2	The company rented furnished office space by paying $1,800 cash for the first month's (April) rent.
3	The company purchased $1,000 of office supplies for cash.
10	The company paid $2,400 cash for the premium on a 12-month insurance policy. Coverage begins on April 11.
14	The company paid $1,600 cash for two weeks' salaries earned by employees.
24	The company collected $8,000 cash on commissions from airlines on tickets obtained for customers.
28	The company paid $1,600 cash for two weeks' salaries earned by employees.
29	The company paid $350 cash for minor repairs to the company's computer.
30	The company paid $750 cash for this month's telephone bill.
30	The company paid $1,500 cash for dividends.

The company's chart of accounts follows:

101	Cash	209	Salaries Payable	622	Salaries Expense
106	Accounts Receivable	307	Common Stock	637	Insurance Expense
124	Office Supplies	318	Retained Earnings	640	Rent Expense
128	Prepaid Insurance	319	Dividends	650	Office Supplies Expense
167	Computer Equipment	405	Commissions Earned	684	Repairs Expense
168	Accumulated	612	Depreciation	688	Telephone Expense
	Depreciation—Computer Equip.		Expense—Computer Equip.	901	Income Summary

Required

1. Use the balance column format to set up each ledger account listed in its chart of accounts.

2. Prepare journal entries to record the transactions for April and post them to the ledger accounts. The company records prepaid and unearned items in balance sheet accounts.

3. Prepare an unadjusted trial balance as of April 30.

4. Use the following information to journalize and post adjusting entries for the month:

a. Two-thirds (or $133) of one month's insurance coverage has expired.

b. At the end of the month, $600 of office supplies are still available.

c. This month's depreciation on the computer equipment is $500.

d. Employees earned $420 of unpaid and unrecorded salaries as of month-end.

e. The company earned $1,750 of commissions that are not yet billed at month-end.

5. Prepare the adjusted trial balance as of April 30. Prepare the income statement and the statement of retained earnings for the month of April and the balance sheet at April 30, 2013.

6. Prepare journal entries to close the temporary accounts and post these entries to the ledger.

7. Prepare a post-closing trial balance.

(5) Net income, $2,197; Total assets, $51,117

(7) P-C trial balance totals, $51,617

The adjusted trial balance for Tybalt Construction as of December 31, 2013, follows.

Problem 3-8A
Preparing closing entries, financial statements, and ratios
C4 A2 A3 P3 P4

	TYBALT CONSTRUCTION Adjusted Trial Balance December 31, 2013		
No.	**Account Title**	**Debit**	**Credit**
101	Cash	$ 5,000	
104	Short-term investments	23,000	
126	Supplies	8,100	
128	Prepaid insurance	7,000	
167	Equipment	40,000	
168	Accumulated depreciation—Equipment		$ 20,000
173	Building	150,000	
174	Accumulated depreciation—Building		50,000
183	Land	55,000	
201	Accounts payable		16,500
203	Interest payable		2,500
208	Rent payable		3,500
210	Wages payable		2,500
213	Property taxes payable		900
233	Unearned professional fees		7,500
251	Long-term notes payable		67,000
307	Common stock............................		5,000
318	Retained earnings		121,400
319	Dividends	13,000	
401	Professional fees earned		97,000
406	Rent earned		14,000
407	Dividends earned		2,000
409	Interest earned		2,100
606	Depreciation expense—Building	11,000	
612	Depreciation expense—Equipment	6,000	
623	Wages expense	32,000	
633	Interest expense..........................	5,100	
637	Insurance expense	10,000	
640	Rent expense	13,400	
652	Supplies expense	7,400	
682	Postage expense	4,200	
683	Property taxes expense	5,000	
684	Repairs expense	8,900	
688	Telephone expense	3,200	
690	Utilities expense..........................	4,600	
	Totals	$411,900	$411,900

O. Tybalt invested $1,000 cash in the business in exchange for more common stock during year 2013; the December 31, 2012, credit balance of retained earnings was $121,400. Tybalt Construction is required to make a $7,000 payment on its long-term notes payable during 2014.

Required

1. Prepare the income statement and the statement of retained earnings for the calendar year 2013 and the classified balance sheet at December 31, 2013.

2. Prepare the necessary closing entries at December 31, 2013.

3. Use the information in the financial statements to compute these ratios: (*a*) return on assets (total assets at December 31, 2012, was $200,000), (*b*) debt ratio, (*c*) profit margin ratio (use total revenues as the denominator), and (*d*) current ratio. Round ratios to three decimals for parts *a* and *c*, and to two decimals for parts *b* and *d*.

Check (1) Total assets (12/31/2013), $218,100; Net income, $4,300

PROBLEM SET B

Problem 3-1B
Identifying adjusting entries
with explanations
P1

For each of the following entries, enter the letter of the explanation that most closely describes it in the space beside each entry. (You can use letters more than once.)

A. To record payment of a prepaid expense.

B. To record this period's use of a prepaid expense.

C. To record this period's depreciation expense.

D. To record receipt of unearned revenue.

E. To record this period's earning of prior unearned revenue.

F. To record an accrued expense.

G. To record payment of an accrued expense.

H. To record an accrued revenue.

I. To record receipt of accrued revenue.

_____	1.	Interest Receivable	3,500
		Interest Revenue	3,500
_____	2.	Salaries Payable	9,000
		Cash	9,000
_____	3.	Depreciation Expense	8,000
		Accumulated Depreciation	8,000
_____	4.	Cash	9,000
		Unearned Professional Fees	9,000
_____	5.	Insurance Expense	4,000
		Prepaid Insurance	4,000
_____	6.	Interest Expense	5,000
		Interest Payable	5,000
_____	7.	Cash	1,500
		Accounts Receivable (from services)	1,500
_____	8.	Salaries Expense	7,000
		Salaries Payable	7,000
_____	9.	Cash	1,000
		Interest Receivable	1,000
_____	10.	Prepaid Rent	3,000
		Cash	3,000
_____	11.	Rent Expense	7,500
		Prepaid Rent	7,500
_____	12.	Unearned Professional Fees	6,000
		Professional Fees Earned	6,000

Problem 3-2B
Preparing adjusting and
subsequent journal entries
C1 A1 P1

Natsu Co. follows the practice of recording prepaid expenses and unearned revenues in balance sheet accounts. The company's annual accounting period ends on October 31, 2013. The following information concerns the adjusting entries that need to be recorded as of that date.

a. The Office Supplies account started the fiscal year with a $600 balance. During the fiscal year, the company purchased supplies for $4,570, which was added to the Office Supplies account. The supplies available at October 31, 2013, totaled $800.

b. An analysis of the company's insurance policies provided the following facts.

Policy	Date of Purchase	Months of Coverage	Cost
A	April 1, 2012	24	$6,000
B	April 1, 2013	36	7,200
C	August 1, 2013	12	1,320

The total premium for each policy was paid in full (for all months) at the purchase date, and the Prepaid Insurance account was debited for the full cost. (Year-end adjusting entries for Prepaid Insurance were properly recorded in all prior fiscal years.)

c. The company has four employees, who earn a total of $1,000 for each workday. They are paid each Monday for their work in the five-day workweek ending on the previous Friday. Assume that October 31, 2013, is a Monday, and all four employees worked the first day of that week. They will be paid salaries for five full days on Monday, November 7, 2013.

d. The company purchased a building on November 1, 2010, that cost $175,000 and is expected to have a $40,000 salvage value at the end of its predicted 25-year life. Annual depreciation is $5,400.

e. Since the company does not occupy the entire building it owns, it rented space to a tenant at $1,000 per month, starting on September 1, 2013. The rent was paid on time on September 1, and the amount received was credited to the Rent Earned account. However, the October rent has not been paid. The company has worked out an agreement with the tenant, who has promised to pay both October and November rent in full on November 15. The tenant has agreed not to fall behind again.

f. On September 1, the company rented space to another tenant for $725 per month. The tenant paid five months' rent in advance on that date. The payment was recorded with a credit to the Unearned Rent account.

Required

1. Use the information to prepare adjusting entries as of October 31, 2013.

2. Prepare journal entries to record the first subsequent cash transaction in November 2013 for parts *c* and *e*.

Check (1*b*) Dr. Insurance Expense, $4,730; (1*d*) Dr. Depreciation Expense, $5,400.

Following is the unadjusted trial balance for Augustus Institute as of December 31, 2013, which initially records prepaid expenses and unearned revenues in balance sheet accounts. The Institute provides one-on-one training to individuals who pay tuition directly to the business and offers extension training to groups in off-site locations. Shown after the trial balance are items *a* through *h* that require adjusting entries as of December 31, 2013.

Problem 3-3B
Preparing adjusting entries, adjusted trial balance, and financial statements

A1 P1 P2 P3

AUGUSTUS INSTITUTE Unadjusted Trial Balance December 31, 2013	Debit	Credit
Cash	$ 60,000	
Accounts receivable	0	
Teaching supplies	70,000	
Prepaid insurance	19,000	
Prepaid rent	3,800	
Professional library	12,000	
Accumulated depreciation—Professional library		$ 2,500
Equipment	40,000	
Accumulated depreciation—Equipment		20,000
Accounts payable		11,200
Salaries payable		0
Unearned training fees		28,600
Common stock		11,000
Retained earnings		60,500
Dividends	20,000	
Tuition fees earned		129,200
Training fees earned		68,000
Depreciation expense—Professional library	0	
Depreciation expense—Equipment	0	
Salaries expense	44,200	
Insurance expense	0	
Rent expense	29,600	
Teaching supplies expense	0	
Advertising expense	19,000	
Utilities expense	13,400	
Totals	$ 331,000	$331,000

Additional Information Items

a. An analysis of the Institute's insurance policies shows that $9,500 of coverage has expired.

b. An inventory count shows that teaching supplies costing $20,000 are available at year-end 2013.

c. Annual depreciation on the equipment is $5,000.

d. Annual depreciation on the professional library is $2,400.

e. On November 1, the Institute agreed to do a special five-month course (starting immediately) for a client. The contract calls for a $14,300 monthly fee, and the client paid the first two months' fees in advance. When the cash was received, the Unearned Training Fees account was credited. The last two month's fees will be recorded when collected in 2014.

f. On October 15, the Institute agreed to teach a four-month class (beginning immediately) to an individual for $2,300 tuition per month payable at the end of the class. The class started on October 15, but no payment has yet been received. (The Institute's accruals are applied to the nearest half-month; for example, October recognizes one-half month accrual.)

g. The Institute's only employee is paid weekly. As of the end of the year, three days' salaries have accrued at the rate of $150 per day.

h. The balance in the Prepaid Rent account represents rent for December.

Required

1. Prepare T-accounts (representing the ledger) with balances from the unadjusted trial balance.

2. Prepare the necessary adjusting journal entries for items *a* through *h*, and post them to the T-accounts. Assume that adjusting entries are made only at year-end.

3. Update balances in the T-accounts for the adjusting entries and prepare an adjusted trial balance.

4. Prepare the company's income statement and statement of retained earnings for the year 2013, and prepare its balance sheet as of December 31, 2013.

Problem 3-4B

Interpreting unadjusted and adjusted trial balances, and preparing financial statements

A1 P1 P2 P3

A six-column table for Yan Consulting Company follows. The first two columns contain the unadjusted trial balance for the company as of December 31, 2013, and the last two columns contain the adjusted trial balance as of the same date.

	Unadjusted Trial Balance		Adjustments		Adjusted Trial Balance	
Cash	$ 45,000				$ 45,000	
Accounts receivable	60,000				66,660	
Office supplies	40,000				17,000	
Prepaid insurance	8,200				3,600	
Office equipment	120,000				120,000	
Accumulated depreciation—						
Office equip.		$ 20,000				$ 30,000
Accounts payable		26,000				32,000
Interest payable		0				2,150
Salaries payable		0				16,000
Unearned consulting fees		40,000				27,800
Long-term notes payable		75,000				75,000
Common stock...............		4,000				4,000
Retained earnings		76,200				76,200
Dividends....................	20,000				20,000	
Consulting fees earned		234,600				253,460
Depreciation expense—						
Office equip.	0				10,000	
Salaries expense	112,000				128,000	
Interest expense	8,600				10,750	
Insurance expense	0				4,600	
Rent expense	20,000				20,000	
Office supplies expense	0				23,000	
Advertising expense	42,000				48,000	
Totals....................	$475,800	$475,800			$516,610	$516,610

Required

Analysis Component

1. Analyze the differences between the unadjusted and adjusted trial balances to determine the eight adjustments that likely were made. Show the results of your analysis by inserting these adjustment amounts in the table's two middle columns. Label each adjustment with a letter *a* through *h* and provide a short description of it at the bottom of the table.

Preparation Component

2. Use the information in the adjusted trial balance to prepare this company's (*a*) income statement and its statement of retained earnings for the year ended December 31, 2013 (*Note:* retained earnings at December 31, 2012, was $76,200, and the current-year dividends were $20,000), and (*b*) the balance sheet as of December 31, 2013.

The adjusted trial balance for Speedy Courier as of December 31, 2013, follows.

Problem 3-5B
Preparing financial statements
from the adjusted trial balance
and calculating profit margin

P3 A1 A2

	Debit	Credit
Cash	$ 58,000	
Accounts receivable	120,000	
Interest receivable	7,000	
Notes receivable (due in 90 days)	210,000	
Office supplies	22,000	
Trucks	134,000	
Accumulated depreciation—Trucks		$ 58,000
Equipment	270,000	
Accumulated depreciation—Equipment		200,000
Land	100,000	
Accounts payable		134,000
Interest payable		20,000
Salaries payable		28,000
Unearned delivery fees		120,000
Long-term notes payable		200,000
Common stock		15,000
Retained earnings		110,000
Dividends	50,000	
Delivery fees earned		611,800
Interest earned		34,000
Depreciation expense—Trucks	29,000	
Depreciation expense—Equipment	48,000	
Salaries expense	74,000	
Wages expense	300,000	
Interest expense	15,000	
Office supplies expense	31,000	
Advertising expense	27,200	
Repairs expense—Trucks	35,600	
Totals	$1,530,800	$1,530,800

Required

1. Use the information in the adjusted trial balance to prepare (*a*) the income statement for the year ended December 31, 2013, (*b*) the statement of retained earnings for the year ended December 31, 2013, and (*c*) the balance sheet as of December 31, 2013.

2. Calculate the profit margin for year 2013.

Check   (1) Total assets, $663,000

In the blank space beside each numbered balance sheet item, enter the letter of its balance sheet classification. If the item should not appear on the balance sheet, enter a *Z* in the blank.

Problem 3-6B
Determining balance sheet
classifications

C4

A. Current assets
B. Long-term investments
C. Plant assets
D. Intangible assets

E. Current liabilities
F. Long-term liabilities
G. Equity

_____ **1.** Commissions earned
_____ **2.** Interest receivable
_____ **3.** Long-term investment in stock
_____ **4.** Prepaid insurance
_____ **5.** Machinery
_____ **6.** Notes payable (due in 15 years)
_____ **7.** Copyrights
_____ **8.** Current portion of long-term note payable
_____ **9.** Accumulated depreciation—Trucks
_____ **10.** Office equipment

_____ **11.** Rent receivable
_____ **12.** Salaries payable
_____ **13.** Income taxes payable
_____ **14.** Common stock
_____ **15.** Office supplies
_____ **16.** Interest payable
_____ **17.** Rent revenue
_____ **18.** Notes receivable (due in 120 days)
_____ **19.** Land (used in operations)
_____ **20.** Depreciation expense—Trucks

Problem 3-7B
Applying the accounting cycle

P1 P2 P3 P4 P5

On July 1, 2013, Lula Plume created a new self-storage business, Safe Storage Co. The following transactions occurred during the company's first month.

July 1   Plume invested $30,000 cash and buildings worth $150,000 in the company in exchange for common stock.
      2   The company rented equipment by paying $2,000 cash for the first month's (July) rent.
      5   The company purchased $2,400 of office supplies for cash.
     10   The company paid $7,200 cash for the premium on a 12-month insurance policy. Coverage begins on July 11.
     14   The company paid an employee $1,000 cash for two weeks' salary earned.
     24   The company collected $9,800 cash for storage fees from customers.
     28   The company paid $1,000 cash for two weeks' salary earned by an employee.
     29   The company paid $950 cash for minor repairs to a leaking roof.
     30   The company paid $400 cash for this month's telephone bill.
     31   The company paid $2,000 cash for dividends.

The company's chart of accounts follows:

No.	Account	No.	Account
101	Cash	401	Storage Fees Earned
106	Accounts Receivable	606	Depreciation Expense—Buildings
124	Office Supplies	622	Salaries Expense
128	Prepaid Insurance	637	Insurance Expense
173	Buildings	640	Rent Expense
174	Accumulated Depreciation—Buildings	650	Office Supplies Expense
209	Salaries Payable	684	Repairs Expense
307	Common Stock	688	Telephone Expense
318	Retained Earnings	901	Income Summary
319	Dividends		

Required

1. Use the balance column format to set up each ledger account listed in its chart of accounts.

2. Prepare journal entries to record the transactions for July and post them to the ledger accounts. Record prepaid and unearned items in balance sheet accounts.

Check (3) Unadj. trial balance totals, $189,800

3. Prepare an unadjusted trial balance as of July 31.

4. Use the following information to journalize and post adjusting entries for the month:

   (4a) Dr. Insurance Expense, $400

   a. Two-thirds of one month's insurance coverage has expired.
   b. At the end of the month, $1,525 of office supplies are still available.
   c. This month's depreciation on the buildings is $1,500.
   d. An employee earned $100 of unpaid and unrecorded salary as of month-end.
   e. The company earned $1,150 of storage fees that are not yet billed at month-end.

   (5) Net income, $2,725; Total assets, $180,825

5. Prepare the adjusted trial balance as of July 31. Prepare the income statement and the statement of retained earnings for the month of July and the balance sheet at July 31, 2013.

6. Prepare journal entries to close the temporary accounts and post these entries to the ledger.

   (7) P-C trial balance totals, $182,325

7. Prepare a post-closing trial balance.

Problem 3-8B
Preparing closing entries, financial statements, and ratios

C4 A2 A3 P3 P4

The adjusted trial balance for Anara Co. as of December 31, 2013, follows.

No.	Account Title	Debit	Credit
	ANARA COMPANY		
	Adjusted Trial Balance		
	December 31, 2013		
101	Cash	$ 7,400	
104	Short-term investments	11,200	
126	Supplies	4,600	
128	Prepaid insurance	1,000	

[continued on next page]

[continued from previous page]

167	Equipment	24,000	
168	Accumulated depreciation—Equipment		$ 4,000
173	Building	100,000	
174	Accumulated depreciation—Building		10,000
183	Land	30,500	
201	Accounts payable		3,500
203	Interest payable		1,750
208	Rent payable		400
210	Wages payable		1,280
213	Property taxes payable		3,330
233	Unearned professional fees		750
251	Long-term notes payable		40,000
307	Common stock............................		40,000
318	Retained earnings		52,800
319	Dividends	8,000	
401	Professional fees earned		59,600
406	Rent earned		4,500
407	Dividends earned		1,000
409	Interest earned		1,320
606	Depreciation expense—Building	2,000	
612	Depreciation expense—Equipment	1,000	
623	Wages expense	18,500	
633	Interest expense..........................	1,550	
637	Insurance expense	1,525	
640	Rent expense	3,600	
652	Supplies expense	1,000	
682	Postage expense	410	
683	Property taxes expense	4,825	
684	Repairs expense	679	
688	Telephone expense	521	
690	Utilities expense..........................	1,920	
	Totals	$224,230	$224,230

P. Anara invested $4,000 cash in the business in exchange for more common stock during year 2013; the December 31, 2012, credit balance of retained earnings was $52,800. Anara Company is required to make a $8,400 payment on its long-term notes payable during 2014.

Required

1. Prepare the income statement and the statement of retained earnings for the calendar year 2013 and the classified balance sheet at December 31, 2013.

2. Prepare the necessary closing entries at December 31, 2013.

3. Use the information in the financial statements to calculate these ratios: (*a*) return on assets (total assets at December 31, 2012, were $160,000), (*b*) debt ratio, (*c*) profit margin ratio (use total revenues as the denominator), and (*d*) current ratio. Round ratios to three decimals for parts *a* and *c*, and to two decimals for parts *b* and *d*.

Check (1) Total assets (12/31/2013), $164,700; Net income, $28,890

This serial problem began in Chapter 1 and continues through most of the book. If previous chapter segments were not completed, the serial problem can still begin at this point. It is helpful, but not necessary, to use the Working Papers that accompany the book.

SERIAL PROBLEM
Success Systems

P1 P2 P3 P4 P5

SP 3 After the success of the company's first two months, Adria Lopez continues to operate Success Systems. (Transactions for the first two months are described in the serial problem of Chapter 2.) The November 30, 2013, unadjusted trial balance of Success Systems (reflecting its transactions for October and November of 2013) follows.

No.	Account Title	Debit	Credit
101	Cash	$ 48,052	
106	Accounts receivable	12,618	
126	Computer supplies	2,545	
128	Prepaid insurance	2,220	
131	Prepaid rent	3,300	
163	Office equipment	8,000	
164	Accumulated depreciation—Office equipment		$ 0
167	Computer equipment............................	20,000	
168	Accumulated depreciation—Computer equipment		0
201	Accounts payable		0
210	Wages payable		0
236	Unearned computer services revenue		0
307	Common stock................................		83,000
318	Retained earnings		0
319	Dividends	5,600	
403	Computer services revenue		25,659
612	Depreciation expense—Office equipment	0	
613	Depreciation expense—Computer equipment	0	
623	Wages expense	2,625	
637	Insurance expense	0	
640	Rent expense	0	
652	Computer supplies expense	0	
655	Advertising expense	1,940	
676	Mileage expense	704	
677	Miscellaneous expenses	250	
684	Repairs expense—Computer	805	
	Totals	$108,659	$108,659

Success Systems had the following transactions and events in December 2013.

Dec.	2	Paid $1,025 cash to Hillside Mall for Success Systems' share of mall advertising costs.
	3	Paid $500 cash for minor repairs to the company's computer.
	4	Received $3,950 cash from Alex's Engineering Co. for the receivable from November.
	10	Paid cash to Lyn Addie for six days of work at the rate of $125 per day.
	14	Notified by Alex's Engineering Co. that Success Systems' bid of $7,000 on a proposed project has been accepted. Alex's paid a $1,500 cash advance to Success Systems.
	15	Purchased $1,100 of computer supplies on credit from Harris Office Products.
	16	Sent a reminder to Gomez Co. to pay the fee for services recorded on November 8.
	20	Completed a project for Liu Corporation and received $5,625 cash.
22–26		Took the week off for the holidays.
	28	Received $3,000 cash from Gomez Co. on its receivable.
	29	Reimbursed A. Lopez for business automobile mileage (600 miles at $0.32 per mile).
	31	The business paid $1,500 cash for dividends.

The following additional facts are collected for use in making adjusting entries prior to preparing financial statements for the company's first three months:

a. The December 31 inventory count of computer supplies shows $580 still available.

b. Three months have expired since the 12-month insurance premium was paid in advance.

c. As of December 31, Lyn Addie has not been paid for four days of work at $125 per day.

d. The computer system, acquired on October 1, is expected to have a four-year life with no salvage value.

e. The office equipment, acquired on October 1, is expected to have a five-year life with no salvage value.

f. Three of the four months' prepaid rent has expired.

Required

1. Prepare journal entries to record each of the December transactions and events for Success Systems. Post those entries to the accounts in the ledger.

2. Prepare adjusting entries to reflect *a* through *f*. Post those entries to the accounts in the ledger.

3. Prepare an adjusted trial balance as of December 31, 2013.

4. Prepare an income statement for the three months ended December 31, 2013.

5. Prepare a statement of retained earnings for the three months ended December 31, 2013.

6. Prepare a balance sheet as of December 31, 2013.

7. Record and post the necessary closing entries for Success Systems.

8. Prepare a post-closing trial balance as of December 31, 2013.

Check   (3) Adjusted trial balance totals, $119,034

(6) Total assets, $93,248

Check   Post-closing trial balance totals, $94,898

Accounting professionals utilize many technology tools to aid them in their everyday tasks and decision making. The **General Ledger** tool in *Connect* automates several of the procedural steps in the accounting cycle so that the accounting professional can focus on the impacts of each transaction on the full set of financial statements. The assignments below utilize this tool in helping students see the advantages of technology and, in particular, the power of the General Ledger tool in accounting practice, including financial analysis.

GENERAL LEDGER PROBLEM

Available in Connect Only

connect
|ACCOUNTING

GL 3-1   This assignment is a continuation of the FastForward Company from Chapter 2. Beginning with the unadjusted trial balance, prepare the necessary adjusting entry for each of the transactions illustrated in this chapter. The financial statements are automatically generated, which will allow us to identify the impact of each adjustment on the financial statements. Finally, the closing entries must be prepared.

GL 3-2   Use the unadjusted trial balance in Problem 3-3A to record adjusting entries, create financial statements, and prepare closing entries. Identify the income statement impact of each entry.

GL 3-3   Use the transactions in Problem 3-7A to record adjusting entries, create financial statements, and prepare closing entries. Identify the income statement impact of each entry.

GL 3-4   Use the unadjusted trial balance in SP 3, the Serial Problem, to record adjusting entries, create financial statements, and prepare closing entries. Identify the income statement impact of each entry.

Beyond the Numbers

BTN 3-1   Refer to Apple's financial statements in Appendix A to answer the following.

1. Identify and write down the revenue recognition principle as explained in the chapter.

2. Review Apple's footnotes (in Appendix A or from its 10-K on its Website) to discover how it applies the revenue recognition principle and when it recognizes revenue. Report what you discover.

3. What is Apple's profit margin for fiscal years ended September 29, 2012 and September 24, 2011.

4. For the fiscal year ended September 29, 2012, what amount is credited to Income Summary to summarize its revenues earned?

5. For the fiscal year ended September 29, 2012, what amount is debited to Income Summary to summarize its expenses incurred?

6. For the fiscal year ended September 29, 2012, what is the balance of its Income Summary account before it is closed?

Fast Forward

7. Access Apple's annual report (10-K) for fiscal years ending after September 29, 2012, at its Website (Apple.com) or the SEC's EDGAR database (www.sec.gov). Assess and compare the September 29, 2012, fiscal year profit margin to any subsequent year's profit margin that you compute.

REPORTING IN ACTION

C1 C2 A1 A2 P4

APPLE

BTN 3-2   Key figures for the recent two years of both Apple and Google follow.

($ millions)	Apple		Google	
	Current Year	Prior Year	Current Year	Prior Year
Net income............	$ 41,733	$ 25,922	$10,737	$ 9,737
Net sales..............	156,508	108,249	50,175	37,905
Current assets	57,653	44,988	60,454	52,758
Current liabilities	38,542	27,970	14,337	8,913

COMPARATIVE ANALYSIS

A2 A3

APPLE
GOOGLE

Required

1. Compute profit margins for (*a*) Apple and (*b*) Google for the two years of data shown.
2. Which company is more successful on the basis of profit margin? Explain.
3. Compute the current ratio for both years for both companies.
4. Which company has the better ability to pay short-term obligations according to the current ratio?
5. Analyze and comment on each company's current ratios for the past two years.
6. How do Apple's and Google's current ratios compare to their industry (assumed) average ratio of 2.0?

ETHICS CHALLENGE

C1 C2 A1

BTN 3-3 Jessica Boland works for Sea Biscuit Co. She and Farah Smith, her manager, are preparing adjusting entries for annual financial statements. Boland computes depreciation and records it as

Depreciation Expense—Equipment	123,000	
Accumulated Depreciation—Equipment		123,000

Smith agrees with her computation but says the credit entry should be directly to the Equipment account. Smith argues that while accumulated depreciation is technically correct, "it is less hassle not to use a contra account and just credit the Equipment account directly. And besides, the balance sheet shows the same amount for total assets under either method."

Required

1. How should depreciation be recorded? Do you support Boland or Smith?
2. Evaluate the strengths and weaknesses of Smith's reasons for preferring her method.
3. Indicate whether the situation Boland faces is an ethical problem. Explain.

COMMUNICATING IN PRACTICE

P4

BTN 3-4 Assume that one of your classmates states that a company's books should be ongoing and therefore not closed until that business is terminated. Write a half-page memo to this classmate explaining the concept of the closing process by drawing analogies between (1) a scoreboard for an athletic event and the revenue and expense accounts of a business or (2) a sports team's record book and retained earnings. (*Hint:* Think about what would happen if the scoreboard is not cleared before the start of a new game.)

TAKING IT TO THE NET

C1 A2

BTN 3-5 Access EDGAR online (www.sec.gov) and locate the 10-K report of The Gap, Inc., (ticker GPS) filed on March 26, 2012. Review its financial statements reported for the year ended January 28, 2012, to answer the following questions.

Required

1. What are Gap's main brands?
2. What is Gap's fiscal year-end?
3. What is Gap's net sales for the period ended January 28, 2012?
4. What is Gap's net income for the period ended January 28, 2012?
5. Compute Gap's profit margin for the year ended January 28, 2012.
6. Do you believe Gap's decision to use a year-end of late January or early February relates to its natural business year? Explain.

TEAMWORK IN ACTION

A1 P1

BTN 3-6 Four types of adjustments are described in the chapter: (1) prepaid expenses, (2) unearned revenues, (3) accrued expenses, and (4) accrued revenues.

Required

1. Form *learning teams* of four (or more) members. Each team member must select one of the four adjustments as an area of expertise (each team must have at least one expert in each area).
2. Form *expert teams* from the individuals who have selected the same area of expertise. Expert teams are to discuss and write a report that each expert will present to his or her learning team addressing the following:
   a. Description of the adjustment and why it's necessary.
   b. Example of a transaction or event, with dates and amounts, that requires adjustment.
   c. Adjusting entry(ies) for the example in requirement *b*.

d. Status of the affected account(s) before and after the adjustment in requirement *c*.

e. Effects on financial statements of not making the adjustment.

3. Each expert should return to his or her learning team. In rotation, each member should present his or her expert team's report to the learning team. Team discussion is encouraged.

BTN 3-7 Review the opening feature of this chapter dealing with Facebook and the entrepreneurial owner Mark Zuckerberg.

ENTREPRENEURIAL DECISION

A2

Required

1. Assume that Facebook receives $300 cash in advance of providing advertising space for a new client. Prepare the journal entry for the (*a*) collection of the cash in return for future advertising for the client and (*b*) revenue from the subsequent publishing of advertising for the client.

2. Assume that Mark Zuckerberg is considering expanding Facebook's operation into actual merchandising of products (much like Amazon). Under one scenario, this would involve Facebook carrying inventory of merchandise for sale. Mark desires your advice on the pros and cons of carrying such inventory. Provide at least one reason for and one reason against carrying inventory.

BTN 3-8 Select a company that you can visit in person or interview on the telephone. Call ahead to the company to arrange a time when you can interview an employee (preferably an accountant) who helps prepare the annual financial statements. Inquire about the following aspects of its *accounting cycle*:

HITTING THE ROAD

C1

1. Does the company prepare interim financial statements? What time period(s) is used for interim statements?

2. Does the company use the cash or accrual basis of accounting?

3. Does the company use a work sheet in preparing financial statements? Why or why not?

4. Does the company use a spreadsheet program? If so, which software program is used?

5. How long does it take after the end of its reporting period to complete annual statements?

BTN 3-9 Samsung (Samsung.com) is a leading manufacturer of consumer electronic products. The following selected information is available from Samsung's financial statements.

GLOBAL DECISION

A2 A3 C1 C2

Samsung

(millions of Korean won)	Current Year	Prior Year
Current assets	₩87,269,017	₩71,502,063
Current liabilities	46,933,052	44,319,014

Required

1. Locate the notes to its December 31, 2012, financial statements at the company's Website, and read note *2.24 Summary of Significant Accounting Policies—Revenue Recognition,* first paragraph only. When is revenue recognized by Samsung?

2. Refer to Samsung's financials in Appendix A. What is Samsung's profit margin for the year ended December 31, 2012?

3. Compute Samsung's current ratio for both the current year and the prior year.

4. Comment on any change from the prior year to the current year for the current ratio.

ANSWERS TO MULTIPLE CHOICE QUIZ

1. b; the forgotten adjusting entry is: *dr.* Wages Expense, *cr.* Wages Payable.

2. c; Supplies used = $450 − $125 = $325

3. b; Insurance expense = $24,000 × (8/24) = $8,000; adjusting entry is: *dr.* Insurance Expense for $8,000, *cr.* Prepaid Insurance for $8,000.

4. a; Consulting fees earned = $3,600 × (2/6) = $1,200; adjusting entry is: *dr.* Unearned Consulting Fee for $1,200, *cr.* Consulting Fees Earned for $1,200.

5. e; Profit margin = $15,000/$300,000 = 5%

6. b

4

Reporting and Analyzing Merchandising Operations

MERCHANDISING ACTIVITIES	MERCHANDISING PURCHASES	MERCHANDISING SALES	MERCHANDISE REPORTING AND ANALYSIS
C1 Reporting income and inventory C2 Operating cycles and inventory systems	P1 Accounting for: Purchase discounts Purchase returns and allowances Transportation costs	P2 Accounting for: Sales of merchandise Sales discounts Sales returns and allowances	P3 Adjusting and closing for merchandisers P4 Multiple-step and single-step income statements A1 Acid-test analysis A2 Gross margin analysis

Learning Objectives

C1 Describe merchandising activities and identify income components for a merchandising company. (p. 166)

C2 Identify and explain the inventory asset and cost flows of a merchandising company. (p. 166)

P1 Analyze and record transactions for merchandise purchases using a perpetual system. (p. 168)

P2 Analyze and record transactions for merchandise sales using a perpetual system. (p. 173)

P3 Prepare adjustments and close accounts for a merchandising company. (p. 176)

P4 Define and prepare multiple-step and single-step income statements. (p. 179)

A1 Compute the acid-test ratio and explain its use to assess liquidity. (p. 183)

A2 Compute the gross margin ratio and explain its use to assess profitability. (p. 183)

P5 *Appendix 4A*—Record and compare merchandising transactions using both periodic and perpetual inventory systems. (p. 188)

Tracking Buffalo Wild Wings

"Our vision is to provide the ultimate social experience"
—**SALLY SMITH**

MINNEAPOLIS—Twenty years ago, **Buffalo Wild Wings, Inc. (BuffaloWildWings.com)**, was a small chain with about 50 restaurants. The founders, Jim Disbrow and Scott Lowery, pursued their business as a labor of love. But they knew help was needed if they were going to take the business to another level. They hired a new CEO to do just that. However, the new CEO never showed up for work!

Jim and Scott huddled, and they decided that Sally Smith, the accountant for Buffalo Wild Wings, would make a good CEO. Recalls Sally, "I really didn't have a chance to say no!" Thank goodness she didn't. "Jim and Scott were great at understanding franchises and guests," explains Sally. "I always looked at myself as a caretaker for their vision."

The one-time accountant with KPMG quickly focused on getting the accounting house in order. "Bankers would ask for our balance sheet," recalls Sally, "and [Scott] would open his wallet and say, 'We have $27.'" In response, Sally set up an accounting system to measure, track, summarize, and report on all operations, and especially purchases. She also computerized the accounting system, prepared monthly financial statements by restaurant, developed annual budgets, produced audited financial statements, and managed all bank accounts

Buffalo Wild Wings
(NASDAQ: BWLD)

20,000 employees
1,000 restaurants
1.3 bil. wings sold/year

and payables. "What we did was apply some business discipline," explains Sally.

That discipline fundamentally altered Buffalo Wild Wings' accounting system and renewed its focus on quality products including the tracking of purchases, purchase returns, and purchase allowances. Developing an accounting system to capture all aspects of the operations is worth the effort, according to Sally. "We will be at 1,000 [restaurants] by the end of 2013!" proclaims Sally. Buffalo Wild Wings' revenues, net income, and asset growth for the past four years reflect her optimism:

($ millions)	2009	2010	2011	2012
Revenues........	$489	$555	$717	$964
Net income......	31	38	50	57
Total assets......	309	380	495	591

"We are very fortunate . . . because we have a strong balance sheet," says Sally. The financial markets are equally enthused about

the accounting discipline and vision introduced by Sally into Buffalo Wild Wings as reflected in its stock price over this same period.

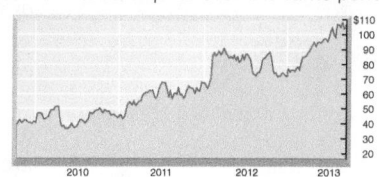

The company is flying high with the right accounting for long-run success. "We would like to have 3,000 restaurants worldwide in the next decade," insists Sally. "We are also seeing different kinds of opportunities to work with vendors." Moreover, much of Sally's executive team consists of women when, interestingly, Buffalo Wild Wings has a reputation as a guy-centric sports bar. "Our goal," explains Sally, "is to make all the restaurants very comfortable for women and families. I think the balance we have on our team has helped."

Today, Sally jokes that she isn't sure she could pass the CPA exam. Fortunately, she doesn't need to. Explains Sally, "I love what I do. I am really excited about our next steps."

Sources: *Buffalo Wild Wings Website,* January 2014; *Buffalo Wild Wings 10-K,* 2012; *Tulsa World,* January 2012; *Twin Cities Business,* June 2012; *FSR Magazine,* October 2012; *USA Today,* July 2011

MERCHANDISING ACTIVITIES

C1 | Describe merchandising activities and identify income components for a merchandising company.

Previous chapters emphasized the accounting and reporting activities of service companies. A merchandising company's activities differ from those of a service company. **Merchandise** consists of products, also called *goods,* that a company acquires to resell to customers. A **merchandiser** earns net income by buying and selling merchandise. Merchandisers are often identified as either wholesalers or retailers. A **wholesaler** is an *intermediary* that buys products from manufacturers or other wholesalers and sells them to retailers or other wholesalers. A **retailer** is an intermediary that buys products from manufacturers or wholesalers and sells them to consumers. Many retailers sell both products and services.

Reporting Income for a Merchandiser

Net income for a merchandiser equals revenues from selling merchandise minus both the cost of merchandise sold to customers and the cost of other expenses for the period, see Exhibit 4.1.

EXHIBIT 4.1

Computing Income for a Merchandising Company versus a Service Company

Service Company

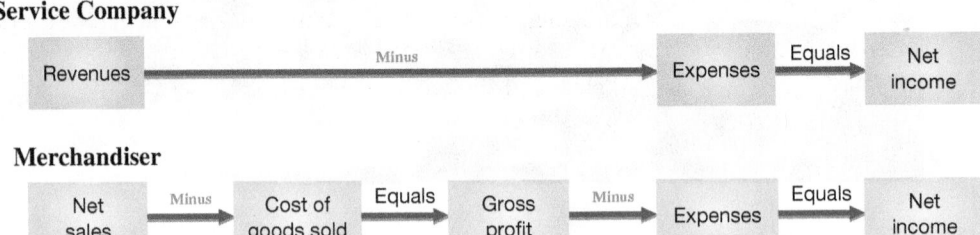

Merchandiser

Point: Fleming, SuperValu, and SYSCO are wholesalers. Aeropostale, Coach, Target, and Walmart are retailers.

The usual accounting term for revenues from selling merchandise is *sales,* and the term used for the expense of buying and preparing the merchandise is **cost of goods sold.** (Some service companies use the term *sales* instead of revenues; and cost of goods sold is also called *cost of sales.*)

The income statement for Z-Mart in Exhibit 4.2 illustrates these key components of a merchandiser's net income. The first two lines show that products are acquired at a cost of $230,400 and sold for $314,700. The third line shows an $84,300 **gross profit,** also called **gross margin,** which equals net sales less cost of goods sold. Additional expenses of $71,400 are reported, which leaves $12,900 in net income.

EXHIBIT 4.2

Merchandiser's Income Statement

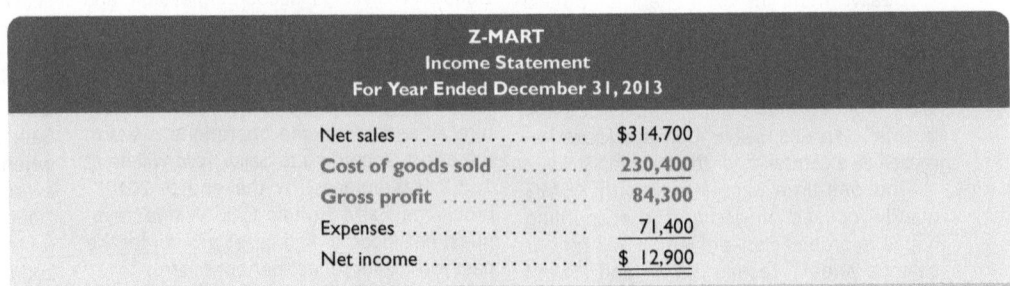

Z-MART	
Income Statement	
For Year Ended December 31, 2013	
Net sales	$314,700
Cost of goods sold	230,400
Gross profit	84,300
Expenses	71,400
Net income	$ 12,900

Reporting Inventory for a Merchandiser

C2 | Identify and explain the inventory asset and cost flows of a merchandising company.

A merchandiser's balance sheet includes a current asset called *merchandise inventory,* an item not on a service company's balance sheet. **Merchandise inventory,** or simply *inventory,* refers to products that a company owns and intends to sell. The cost of this asset includes the cost incurred to buy the goods, ship them to the store, and make them ready for sale.

Operating Cycle for a Merchandiser

A merchandising company's operating cycle begins by purchasing merchandise and ends by collecting cash from selling the merchandise. The length of an operating cycle differs across the types of businesses. Department stores often have operating cycles of two to five months. Operating cycles for grocery merchants usually range from two to eight weeks. A grocer has more operating cycles in a year than, say, clothing or electronics retailers.

Exhibit 4.3 illustrates an operating cycle for a merchandiser with credit sales. The cycle moves from (*a*) cash purchases of merchandise to (*b*) inventory for sale to (*c*) credit sales to (*d*) accounts receivable to (*e*) cash. Companies try to keep their operating cycles short because assets tied up in inventory and receivables are not productive. Cash sales shorten operating cycles.

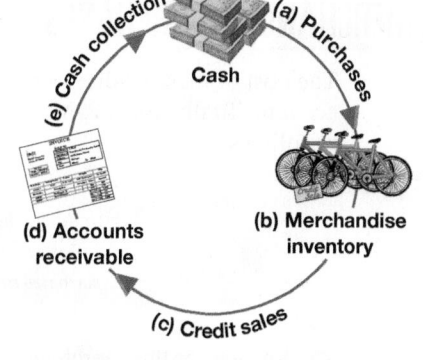

EXHIBIT 4.3

Merchandiser's Operating Cycle

Inventory Systems

Cost of goods sold is the cost of merchandise sold to customers during a period. It is often the largest single expense on a merchandiser's income statement. **Inventory** refers to products a company owns and expects to sell in its normal operations. Exhibit 4.4 shows that a company's merchandise available for sale consists of what it begins with (beginning inventory) and what it purchases (net purchases). The merchandise available is either sold (cost of goods sold) or kept for future sales (ending inventory).

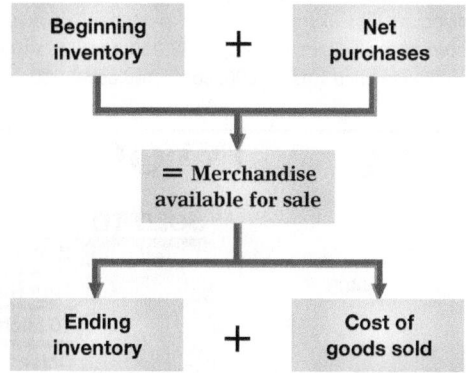

EXHIBIT 4.4

Merchandiser's Cost Flow for a Single Time Period

Point: Mathematically, Exhibit 4.4 says
$$BI + NP = MAS,$$
where BI is beginning inventory, NP is net purchases, and MAS is merchandise available for sale. Exhibit 4.4 also says
$$MAS = EI + COGS,$$
which can be rewritten as MAS − EI = COGS or MAS − COGS = EI, where EI is ending inventory and COGS is cost of goods sold. In both equations above, if we know two of the three values, we can solve for the third.

Two alternative inventory accounting systems can be used to collect information about cost of goods sold and cost of inventory: *perpetual system* or *periodic system*. The **perpetual inventory system** continually updates accounting records for merchandising transactions—specifically, for those records of inventory available for sale and inventory sold. The **periodic inventory system** updates the accounting records for merchandise transactions only at the *end of a period.* Technological advances and competitive pressures have dramatically increased the use of the perpetual system. It gives managers immediate access to detailed information on sales and inventory levels, where they can strategically react to sales trends, cost changes, consumer tastes, and so forth, to increase gross profit. (Some companies use a *hybrid* system where the perpetual system is used for tracking units available and the periodic system is used to compute cost of sales.)

Point: Growth of superstores such as Costco and Sam's is fueled by efficient use of perpetual inventory. Such large stores evolved only after scannable UPC codes to help control inventory were invented.

The following sections, consisting of the next 10 pages on purchasing, selling, and adjusting merchandise, use the perpetual system. Appendix 4A uses the periodic system (with the perpetual results on the side). An instructor can choose to cover either one or both inventory systems.

ACCOUNTING FOR MERCHANDISE PURCHASES

P1 Analyze and record transactions for merchandise purchases using a perpetual system.

The cost of merchandise purchased for resale is recorded in the Merchandise Inventory asset account. To illustrate, Z-Mart records a $1,200 cash purchase of merchandise on November 2 as follows:

Assets = Liabilities + Equity
+1,200
−1,200

Nov. 2	Merchandise Inventory	1,200	
	Cash		1,200
	Purchased merchandise for cash.		

Point: The Merchandise Inventory account reflects the cost of goods available for resale. Costs recorded in Merchandise Inventory are sometimes called *inventoriable costs.*

The invoice for this merchandise is shown in Exhibit 4.5. The buyer usually receives the original invoice, and the seller keeps a copy. This *source document* serves as the purchase invoice of Z-Mart (buyer) and the sales invoice for Trex (seller). The amount recorded for merchandise inventory includes its purchase cost, shipping fees, taxes, and any other costs necessary to make it ready for sale. This section explains how we compute the recorded cost of merchandise purchases.

Decision Insight

Trade Discounts   When a manufacturer or wholesaler prepares a catalog of items it has for sale, it usually gives each item a **list price**, also called a *catalog price*. However, an item's intended *selling price* equals list price minus a given percent called a **trade discount.** The amount of trade discount usually depends on whether a buyer is a wholesaler, retailer, or final consumer. A wholesaler buying in large quantities is often granted a larger discount than a retailer buying in smaller quantities. A buyer records the net amount of list price minus trade discount. For example, in the November 2 purchase of merchandise by Z-Mart, the merchandise was listed in the seller's catalog at $2,000 and Z-Mart received a 40% trade discount. This meant that Z-Mart's purchase price was $1,200, computed as $2,000 − (40% × $2,000). ∎

Point: **Lowes** and **Home Depot** offer trade discounts to construction companies and contractors. Trade discounts help create loyalty among customers.

EXHIBIT 4.5

Invoice

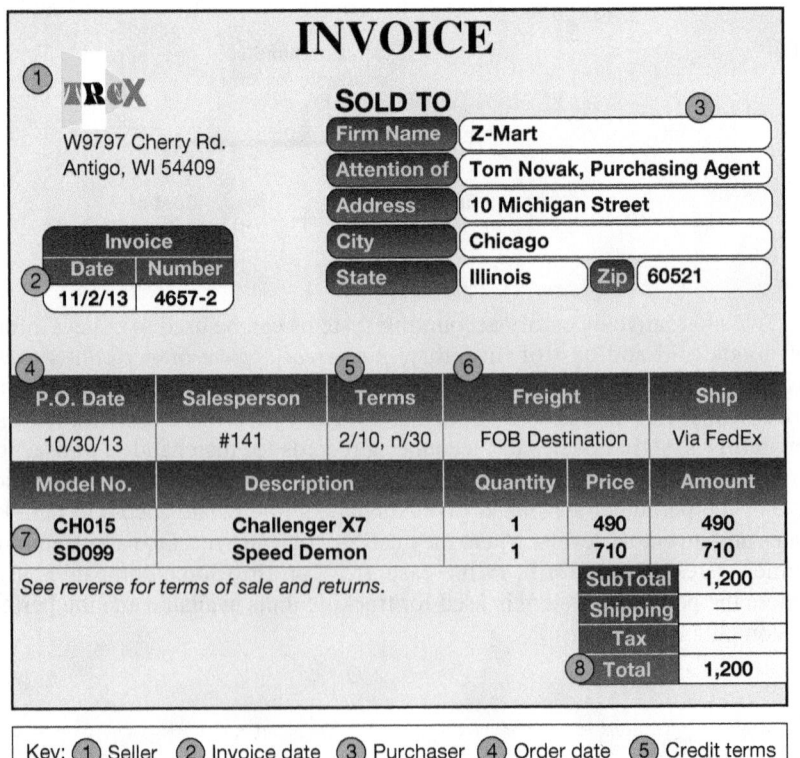

Purchase Discounts

The purchase of goods on credit requires a clear statement of expected future payments and dates to avoid misunderstandings. **Credit terms** for a purchase include the amounts and timing of payments from a buyer to a seller. Credit terms usually reflect an industry's practices. To illustrate, when sellers require payment within 10 days after the end of the month of the invoice date, the invoice will show credit terms as "n/10 EOM," which stands for net 10 days after end of month (**EOM**). When sellers require payment within 30 days after the invoice date, the invoice shows credit terms of "n/30," which stands for *net 30 days*.

Exhibit 4.6 portrays credit terms. The amount of time allowed before full payment is due is called the **credit period.** Sellers can grant a **cash discount** to encourage buyers to pay earlier. A buyer views a cash discount as a **purchase discount.** A seller views a cash discount as a **sales discount.** Any cash discounts are described in the credit terms on the invoice. For example, credit terms of "2/10, n/60" mean that full payment is due within a 60-day credit period, but the buyer can deduct 2% of the invoice amount if payment is made within 10 days of the invoice date. This reduced payment applies only for the **discount period.**

Point: Since both the buyer and seller know the invoice date, this date is used in setting the discount and credit periods.

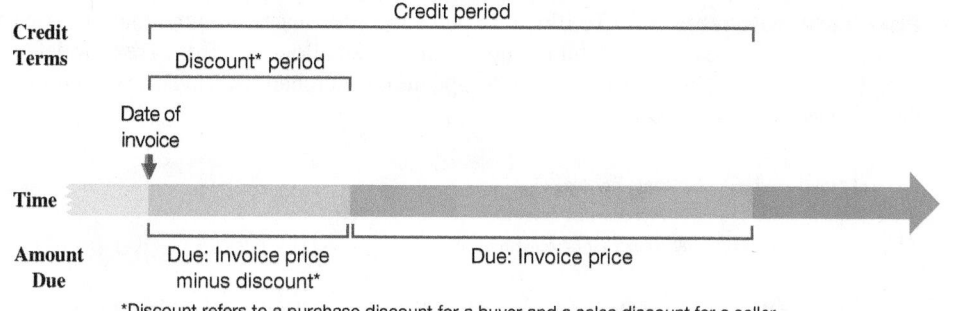

EXHIBIT 4.6

Credit Terms

*Discount refers to a purchase discount for a buyer and a sales discount for a seller.

To illustrate how a buyer accounts for a purchase discount, assume that Z-Mart's $1,200 purchase of merchandise is on credit with terms of 2/10, n/30. Its entry is

Point: Appendix 4A repeats journal entries *a* through *f* using a periodic inventory system.

(*a*) Nov. 2	Merchandise Inventory	1,200	
	Accounts Payable		1,200
	Purchased merchandise on credit, invoice		
	dated Nov. 2, terms 2/10, n/30.		

Assets = Liabilities + Equity
+1,200   +1,200

If Z-Mart pays the amount due on (or before) November 12, the entry is

(*b*) Nov. 12	Accounts Payable	1,200	
	Merchandise Inventory		24
	Cash		1,176
	Paid for the $1,200 purchase of Nov. 2 less the		
	discount of $24 (2% × $1,200).		

Assets = Liabilities + Equity
−24   −1,200
−1,176

The Merchandise Inventory account after these entries reflects the net cost of merchandise purchased, and the Accounts Payable account shows a zero balance. Both ledger accounts, in T-account form, follow:

Point: These entries illustrate what is called the *gross method* of accounting for purchases with discount terms.

Merchandise Inventory					Accounts Payable				
Nov. 2	1,200	Nov. 12	24		Nov. 12	1,200	Nov. 2	1,200	
Balance	1,176						Balance	0	

A buyer's failure to pay within a discount period can be expensive. To illustrate, if Z-Mart does not pay within the 10-day 2% discount period, it can delay payment by 20 more days. This delay costs Z-Mart $24, computed as 2% × $1,200. Most buyers take advantage of a purchase

Point: Buyers sometimes make partial payments toward amounts owed. Assume that credit terms apply to both partial and full payments.

discount because of the usually high interest rate implied from not taking it.[1] Also, good cash management means that no invoice is paid until the last day of the discount or credit period.

■ Decision Maker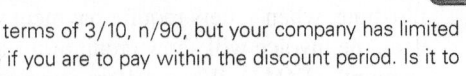

Entrepreneur You purchase a batch of products on terms of 3/10, n/90, but your company has limited cash and you must borrow funds at an 11% annual rate if you are to pay within the discount period. Is it to your advantage to take the purchase discount? Explain. ■   [Answer—p. 193]

Purchase Returns and Allowances

Purchase returns refer to merchandise a buyer acquires but then returns to the seller. A *purchase allowance* is a reduction in the cost of defective or unacceptable merchandise that a buyer acquires. Buyers often keep defective but still marketable merchandise if the seller grants an acceptable allowance. When a buyer returns or takes an allowance on merchandise, the buyer issues a **debit memorandum** to inform the seller of a debit made to the seller's account payable in the buyer's records.

> **Point:** The sender (maker) of a *debit memorandum* will debit the account payable of the memo's receiver. The memo's receiver will credit the sender's account receivable.

Purchase Allowances   To illustrate purchase allowances, assume that on November 15, Z-Mart (buyer) issues a $300 debit memorandum for an allowance from Trex for defective merchandise. Z-Mart's November 15 entry to update its Merchandise Inventory account to reflect the purchase allowance is

> Assets = Liabilities + Equity
> −300   −300

(c) Nov. 15	Accounts Payable.............................	300	
	Merchandise Inventory......................		300
	Allowance for defective merchandise.		

The buyer's allowance for defective merchandise is usually offset against the buyer's current account payable balance to the seller. When cash is refunded, the Cash account is debited instead of Accounts Payable.

Purchase Returns   Returns are recorded at the net costs charged to buyers. To illustrate the accounting for returns, suppose Z-Mart purchases $1,000 of merchandise on June 1 with terms 2/10, n/60. Two days later, Z-Mart returns $100 of goods before paying the invoice. When Z-Mart later pays on June 11, it takes the 2% discount only on the $900 remaining balance. When goods are returned, a buyer can take a purchase discount on only the remaining balance of the invoice. The resulting discount is $18 (2% × $900) and the cash payment is $882 ($900 − $18). The following entries reflect this illustration.

> **Point:** In the perpetual system, all purchases, purchase discounts, purchase returns, and cost of sales are recorded in the Merchandise Inventory account. This is different from the periodic system as explained in Appendix 4A.

June 1	Merchandise Inventory.........................	1,000	
	Accounts Payable...........................		1,000
	Purchased merchandise, invoice dated June 1,		
	terms 2/10, n/60.		
June 3	Accounts Payable..............................	100	
	Merchandise Inventory......................		100
	Returned merchandise to seller.		
June 11	Accounts Payable..............................	900	
	Merchandise Inventory......................		18
	Cash.......................................		882
	Paid for $900 merchandise ($1,000 − $100)		
	less $18 discount (2% × $900).		

> **Example:** Assume Z-Mart pays $980 cash for $1,000 of merchandise purchased within its 2% discount period. Later, it returns $100 of the original $1,000 merchandise. The return entry is
> Cash.................... 98
>   Merchandise Inventory 98

---

[1] The *implied annual interest rate* formula is:

$$[365 \text{ days} \div (\text{Credit period} - \text{Discount period})] \times \text{Cash discount rate}.$$

For terms of 2/10, n/30, missing the 2% discount for an additional 20 days is equal to an annual interest rate of 36.5%, computed as [365 days/(30 days − 10 days)] × 2% discount rate. *Favorable purchase discounts* are those with implied annual interest rates that exceed the purchaser's annual rate for borrowing money.

Decision Ethics

Payables Manager   As a new accounts payable manager, you are being trained by the outgoing manager. She explains that the system prepares checks for amounts net of favorable cash discounts, and the checks are dated the last day of the discount period. She also tells you that checks are not mailed until five days later, adding that "the company gets free use of cash for an extra five days, and our department looks better. When a supplier complains, we blame the computer system and the mailroom." Do you continue this payment policy? ■ [Answer—p. 171]

Transportation Costs and Ownership Transfer

The buyer and seller must agree on who is responsible for paying any freight costs and who bears the risk of loss during transit for merchandising transactions. This is essentially the same as asking at what point ownership transfers from the seller to the buyer. The point of transfer is called the **FOB** (*free on board*) point, which determines who pays transportation costs (and often other incidental costs of transit such as insurance).

Exhibit 4.7 identifies two alternative points of transfer. (1) *FOB shipping point,* also called *FOB factory,* means the buyer accepts ownership when the goods depart the seller's place of business. The buyer is then responsible for paying shipping costs and bearing the risk of damage or loss when goods are in transit. The goods are part of the buyer's inventory when they are in

Seller   **Buyer**

Shipping point   Carrier   Destination

EXHIBIT 4.7

Ownership Transfer and Transportation Costs

Shipping Terms	Ownership Transfers When Goods Passed to	Transportation Costs Paid by	
FOB shipping point	Carrier	Buyer	Merchandise Inventory... # Cash .... #
FOB destination	Buyer	Seller	Delivery Expense .... # Cash .... #

Point: If we place an order online and receive free shipping, we have terms FOB destination.

transit since ownership has transferred to the buyer. 1-800-FLOWERS.COM, a floral and gift merchandiser, and Bare Escentuals, a cosmetic manufacturer, both use FOB shipping point. (2) *FOB destination* means ownership of goods transfers to the buyer when the goods arrive at the buyer's place of business. The seller is responsible for paying shipping charges and bears the risk of damage or loss in transit. The seller does not record revenue from this sale until the goods arrive at the destination because this transaction is not complete before that point. Kyocera, a manufacturer, uses FOB destination.

Z-Mart's $1,200 purchase on November 2 is on terms of FOB destination. This means Z-Mart is not responsible for paying transportation costs. When a buyer is responsible for paying transportation costs, the payment is made to a carrier or directly to the seller depending on the agreement. The cost principle requires that any necessary transportation costs of a buyer (often called *transportation-in* or *freight-in*) be included as part of the cost of purchased merchandise. To illustrate, Z-Mart's entry to record a $75 freight charge from an independent carrier for merchandise purchased FOB shipping point is

Point: The party not responsible for shipping costs sometimes pays the carrier. In these cases, the party paying these costs either bills the party responsible or, more commonly, adjusts its account payable or account receivable with the other party. For example, a buyer paying a carrier when terms are FOB destination can decrease its account payable to the seller by the amount of shipping cost. Assume that any freight payments to carriers are *not* applied in computing merchandise discounts.

(d) Nov. 24	Merchandise Inventory	75	
	Cash		75
	Paid freight costs on purchased merchandise.		

Assets = Liabilities + Equity
+75
−75

A seller records the costs of shipping goods to customers in a Delivery Expense account when the seller is responsible for these costs. Delivery Expense, also called *transportation-out* or *freight-out*, is reported as a selling expense in the seller's income statement.

In summary, purchases are recorded as debits to Merchandise Inventory. Any later purchase discounts, returns, and allowances are credited (decreases) to Merchandise Inventory. Transportation-in is debited (added) to Merchandise Inventory. Z-Mart's itemized costs of merchandise purchases for year 2013 are in Exhibit 4.8.

Point: With *tracking numbers* it is possible to know the exact time shipped goods arrive at their destination.

EXHIBIT 4.8

Itemized Costs of Merchandise Purchases

Z-MART Itemized Costs of Merchandise Purchases For Year Ended December 31, 2013	
Invoice cost of merchandise purchases	$ 235,800
Less: Purchase discounts received	(4,200)
Purchase returns and allowances	(1,500)
Add: Costs of transportation-in	2,300
Total cost of merchandise purchases	$232,400

Point: Some companies have separate accounts for purchase discounts, returns and allowances, and transportation-in. These accounts are then transferred to Merchandise Inventory at period-end. This is a *hybrid system* of perpetual and periodic. That is, Merchandise Inventory is updated on a perpetual basis but only for purchases and cost of goods sold.

The accounting system described here does not provide separate records (accounts) for total purchases, total purchase discounts, total purchase returns and allowances, and total transportation-in. Yet nearly all companies collect this information in supplementary records because managers need this information to evaluate and control each of these cost elements. **Supplementary records,** also called *supplemental records,* refer to information outside the usual general ledger accounts.

NEED-TO-KNOW 4.1

P1

Prepare journal entries to record each of the following purchases transactions of a merchandising company. Show supporting calculations and assume a perpetual inventory system.

Oct. 1   Purchased 125 units of a product at a cost of $4 per unit. Terms of the sale are 2/10, n/30, and FOB shipping point; the invoice is dated October 1.
Oct. 3   Paid $30 cash for freight charges from UPS for the October 1 purchase.
Oct. 7   Returned 50 defective units from the October 1 purchase and received full credit.
Oct. 11   Paid the amount due from the October 1 purchase, less the return on October 7.
Oct. 31   *Assume the October 11 payment was never made* and, instead, payment of the amount due on the October 1 purchase, less the return on October 7, occurred on October 31.

Solution

Oct. 1	Merchandise Inventory	500	
	Accounts Payable		500
	To record credit purchase (125 units × $4).		
Oct. 1	Merchandise Inventory.	30	
	Cash		30
	Paid freight costs on good purchased FOB shipping point.		
Oct. 7	Accounts Payable	200	
	Merchandise Inventory		200
	Returned defective units (50 units × $4).		
Oct. 11	Accounts Payable	300	
	Cash		294
	Merchandise Inventory*		6
	*Paid for purchases less cash discount *[($500 − $200) × 2%].*		
Oct. 31	Accounts Payable	300	
	Cash		300
	Paid for purchases (no cash discount received).		

Do More: QS 4-3, QS 4-16, E 4-2, E 4-5

QC2

ACCOUNTING FOR MERCHANDISE SALES

Merchandising companies also must account for sales, sales discounts, sales returns and allowances, and cost of goods sold. A merchandising company such as Z-Mart reflects these items in its gross profit computation, as shown in Exhibit 4.9. This section explains how this information is derived from transactions.

P2 Analyze and record transactions for merchandise sales using a perpetual system.

EXHIBIT 4.9

Gross Profit Computation

Z-MART Computation of Gross Profit For Year Ended December 31, 2013		
Sales.		$321,000
Less: Sales discounts	$4,300	
Sales returns and allowances	2,000	6,300
Net sales		314,700
Cost of goods sold		230,400
Gross profit		$ 84,300

Sales of Merchandise

Each sales transaction for a seller of merchandise involves two parts.

1. **Revenue received in the form of an asset from the customer.**
2. **Cost recognized for the merchandise sold to the customer.**

Accounting for a sales transaction under the perpetual system requires recording information about both parts. This means that each sales transaction for merchandisers, whether for cash or on credit, requires *two entries:* one for revenue and one for cost. To illustrate, Z-Mart sold $2,400 of merchandise on credit on November 3. The revenue part of this transaction is recorded as

(e) Nov. 3	Accounts Receivable	2,400	
	Sales		2,400
	Sold merchandise on credit.		

Assets = Liabilities + Equity
+2,400   +2,400

This entry reflects an increase in Z-Mart's assets in the form of accounts receivable. It also shows the increase in revenue (Sales). If the sale is for cash, the debit is to Cash instead of Accounts Receivable.

The cost part of each sales transaction ensures that the Merchandise Inventory account under a perpetual inventory system reflects the updated cost of the merchandise available for sale. For example, the cost of the merchandise Z-Mart sold on November 3 is $1,600, and the entry to record the cost part of this sales transaction is

(e) Nov. 3	Cost of Goods Sold	1,600	
	Merchandise Inventory		1,600
	To record the cost of Nov. 3 sale.		

Assets = Liabilities + Equity
−1,600   −1,600

Decision Insight

Suppliers and Demands Large merchandising companies often bombard suppliers with demands. These include discounts for bar coding and technology support systems, and fines for shipping errors. Merchandisers' goals are to reduce inventories, shorten lead times, and eliminate errors. Many colleges now offer programs in supply chain management and logistics to train future employees that can help merchandisers meet such goals. ■

Sales Discounts

Sales discounts on credit sales can benefit a seller by decreasing the delay in receiving cash and reducing future collection efforts. At the time of a credit sale, a seller does not know whether a

Point: Radio-frequency identification (RFID) tags attach to objects for tracking purposes. Such tags help find items in a store, monitor shipments, and help check on production progress.

customer will pay within the discount period and take advantage of a discount. This means the seller usually does not record a sales discount until a customer actually pays within the discount period. To illustrate, Z-Mart completes a credit sale for $1,000 on November 12 with terms of 2/10, n/60. The entry to record the revenue part of this sale is

Assets = Liabilities + Equity
+1,000   +1,000

Nov. 12	Accounts Receivable	1,000	
	Sales		1,000
	Sold merchandise under terms of 2/10, n/60.		

This entry records the receivable and the revenue as if the customer will pay the full amount. The customer has two options, however. One option is to wait 60 days until January 11 and pay the full $1,000. In this case, Z-Mart records that payment as

Assets = Liabilities + Equity
+1,000
−1,000

Jan. 11	Cash	1,000	
	Accounts Receivable		1,000
	Received payment for Nov. 12 sale.		

The customer's second option is to pay $980 within a 10-day period ending November 22. If the customer pays on (or before) November 22, Z-Mart records the payment as

Assets = Liabilities + Equity
+980   −20
−1,000

Nov. 22	Cash	980	
	Sales Discounts	20	
	Accounts Receivable		1,000
	Received payment for Nov. 12 sale less discount.		

Sales Discounts is a contra revenue account, meaning the Sales Discounts account is deducted from the Sales account when computing a company's net sales (see Exhibit 4.9). Management monitors Sales Discounts to assess the effectiveness and cost of its discount policy.

Sales Returns and Allowances

Point: Published income statements rarely disclose sales discounts, returns and allowances.

Sales returns refer to merchandise that customers return to the seller after a sale. Many companies allow customers to return merchandise for a full refund. *Sales allowances* refer to reductions in the selling price of merchandise sold to customers. This can occur with damaged or defective merchandise that a customer is willing to purchase with a decrease in selling price. Sales returns and allowances usually involve dissatisfied customers and the possibility of lost future sales, and managers monitor information about returns and allowances.

Sales Returns   To illustrate, recall Z-Mart's sale of merchandise on November 3 for $2,400 that had cost $1,600. Assume that the customer returns part of the merchandise on November 6, and the returned items sell for $800 and cost $600. The revenue part of this transaction must reflect the decrease in sales from the customer's return of merchandise as follows:

Assets = Liabilities + Equity
−800   −800

(f) Nov. 6	Sales Returns and Allowances	800	
	Accounts Receivable		800
	Customer returns merchandise of Nov. 3 sale.		

If the merchandise returned to Z-Mart is not defective and can be resold to another customer, Z-Mart returns these goods to its inventory. The entry to restore the cost of such goods to the Merchandise Inventory account is

Assets = Liabilities + Equity
+600   +600

Nov. 6	Merchandise Inventory	600	
	Cost of Goods Sold		600
	Returned goods added to inventory.		

This entry changes if the goods returned are defective. In this case the returned inventory is recorded at its estimated value, not its cost. To illustrate, if the goods (costing $600) returned to Z-Mart are defective and estimated to be worth $150, the following entry is made: Dr. Merchandise Inventory for $150, Dr. Loss from Defective Merchandise for $450, and Cr. Cost of Goods Sold for $600.

Point: Some sellers charge buyers a re-stocking fee for returns.

Fraud

Reversing Returns. On May 3, 2011, Green Mountain Coffee Roasters beat analysts' earnings estimates by $0.10 per share for the 13-week period ended March 26, 2011. The next day the stock price rose $11.91 per share to close at $75.98 per share, an 18.5% increase over the prior day's closing price. In the weeks that followed, some analysts raised questions about the quality of Green Mountain's earnings because of its accounting for sales returns. They allege that a large part of that earnings increase was due to an accounting adjustment that reversed much of a reserve that was set up for sales returns in prior periods.

Sales Allowances   To illustrate sales allowances, assume that $800 of the merchandise Z-Mart sold on November 3 is defective but the buyer decides to keep it because Z-Mart offers a $100 price reduction. Z-Mart records this allowance as follows:

Nov. 6	Sales Returns and Allowances	100	
	Accounts Receivable		100
	To record sales allowance on Nov. 3 sale.		

Assets = Liabilities + Equity
−100   −100

The seller usually prepares a credit memorandum to confirm a buyer's return or allowance. A seller's **credit memorandum** informs a buyer of the seller's credit to the buyer's Account Receivable (on the seller's books).

Point: The sender (maker) of a credit memorandum will *credit* the account of the receiver. The receiver of a credit memorandum will *debit* the sender's account.

Prepare journal entries to record each of the following sales transactions of a merchandising company. Show supporting calculations and assume a perpetual inventory system.

NEED-TO-KNOW 4.2

P2

June 1   Sold 500 units of merchandise to a customer for $14 per unit under credit terms of 2/10, n/30, FOB shipping point, and the invoice is dated June 1. The merchandise had cost $10 per unit.

June 7   The customer returns 20 units because those units did not fit the customer's needs. The seller restores those units to its inventory.

June 8   The customer discovers that 30 units are damaged but are still of some use and, therefore, keeps the units because the seller sends the buyer a credit memorandum for $90 to compensate for the damage.

June 11   The customer discovers that 10 units are the wrong color, but keeps 8 of these units because the seller sends a $12 credit memorandum to compensate. The customer returns the remaining 2 units to the seller. The seller restores the 2 returned units to its inventory.

Solution

June 1	Accounts Receivable	7,000	
	Sales		7,000
	Sold merchandise on credit (500 × $14).		
June 1	Cost of Goods Sold	5,000	
	Merchandise Inventory		5,000
	To record cost of sale (500 × $10).		
June 7	Sales Returns and Allowances	280	
	Accounts Receivable		280
	Accepted a return from a customer (20 × $14).		
June 7	Merchandise Inventory	200	
	Cost of Goods Sold		200
	Returned merchandise to inventory (20 × $10).		
June 8	Sales Returns and Allowances	90	
	Accounts Receivable		90
	Granted allowance for damaged merchandise.		
June 11	Sales Returns and Allowances	40	
	Accounts Receivable		40
	Granted allowance for mis-colored merchandise and accepted a return from a customer for the mis-colored merchandise [$12 + (2 × $14)].		
June 11	Merchandise Inventory	20	
	Cost of Goods Sold		20
	Returned merchandise to inventory (2 × $10).		

Do More: QS 4-4, E 4-4

QC3

COMPLETING THE ACCOUNTING CYCLE

Exhibit 4.10 shows the flow of merchandising costs during a period and where these costs are reported at period-end. Specifically, beginning inventory plus the net cost of purchases is the merchandise available for sale. As inventory is sold, its cost is recorded in cost of goods sold on the income statement; what remains is ending inventory on the balance sheet. A period's ending inventory is the next period's beginning inventory.

EXHIBIT 4.10

Merchandising Cost Flow in the Accounting Cycle

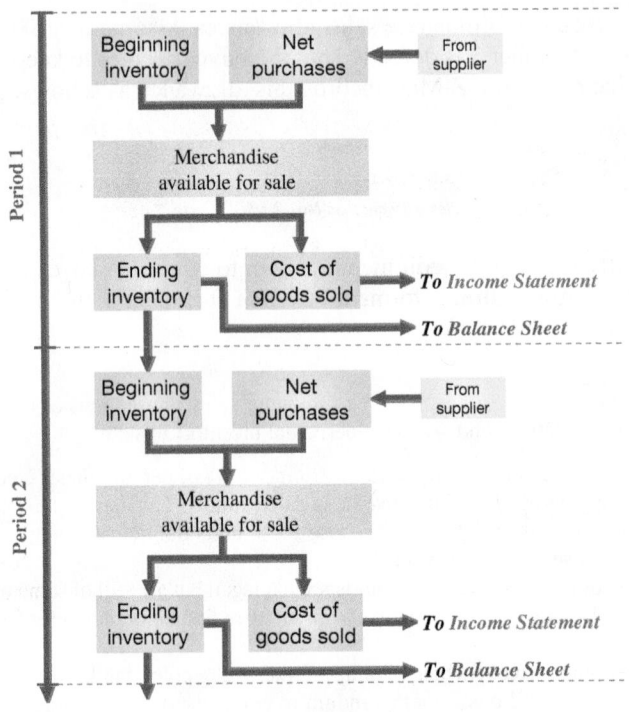

Adjusting Entries for Merchandisers

Each of the steps in the accounting cycle described in the prior chapter for a service company applies to a merchandiser. This section and the next two further explain three steps of the accounting cycle for a merchandiser—adjustments, statement preparation, and closing.

Adjusting entries are generally the same for merchandising companies and service companies, including those for prepaid expenses (including depreciation), accrued expenses, unearned revenues, and accrued revenues. However, a merchandiser using a perpetual inventory system is usually required to make another adjustment to update the Merchandise Inventory account to reflect any loss of merchandise, including theft and deterioration. **Shrinkage** is the term used to refer to the loss of inventory and it is computed by comparing a physical count of inventory with recorded amounts. A physical count is usually performed at least once annually.

To illustrate, Z-Mart's Merchandise Inventory account at the end of year 2013 has a balance of $21,250, but a physical count reveals that only $21,000 of inventory exists. The adjusting entry to record this $250 shrinkage is

Point: About two-thirds of shoplifting losses are thefts by employees.

Assets = Liabilities + Equity
−250   −250

Dec. 31	Cost of Goods Sold	250	
	Merchandise Inventory		250
	To adjust for $250 shrinkage revealed by a physical count of inventory.		

Preparing Financial Statements

The financial statements of a merchandiser, and their preparation, are similar to those for a service company described in Chapters 2 and 3. The income statement mainly differs by the inclusion of *cost of goods sold* and *gross profit*. Also, net sales is affected by discounts, returns, and allowances, and some additional expenses are possible such as delivery expense and loss from defective merchandise. The balance sheet mainly differs by the inclusion of *merchandise inventory* as part of current assets. The statement of retained earnings is unchanged. A work sheet can be used to help prepare these statements, and one is illustrated in Appendix 4B for Z-Mart.

Point: Staples's costs of shipping merchandise to its stores is included in its costs of inventories as required by the cost principle.

Closing Entries for Merchandisers

Closing entries are similar for service companies and merchandising companies using a perpetual system. The difference is that we must close some new temporary accounts that arise from merchandising activities. Z-Mart has several temporary accounts unique to merchandisers: Sales (of goods), Sales Discounts, Sales Returns and Allowances, and Cost of Goods Sold. Their existence in the ledger means that the first two closing entries for a merchandiser are slightly different from the ones described in the prior chapter for a service company. These differences are set in **red boldface** in the closing entries of Exhibit 4.11.

Point: The Inventory account is not affected by the closing process under a perpetual system.

Step 1: Close Credit Balances in Temporary Accounts to Income Summary.

Dec. 31	Sales	321,000	
	Income Summary		321,000
	To close credit balances in temporary accounts.		

Step 2: Close Debit Balances in Temporary Accounts to Income Summary.

Dec. 31	Income Summary	308,100	
	Sales Discounts		4,300
	Sales Returns and Allowances		2,000
	Cost of Goods Sold		230,400
	Depreciation Expense		3,700
	Salaries Expense		43,800
	Insurance Expense		600
	Rent Expense..............................		9,000
	Supplies Expense		3,000
	Advertising Expense		11,300
	To close debit balances in temporary accounts.		

Step 3: Close Income Summary to Retained Earnings.

The third closing entry is identical for a merchandising company and a service company. The $12,900 amount is net income reported on the income statement.

Dec. 31	Income Summary	12,900	
	Retained Earnings		12,900
	To close the Income Summary account.		

Step 4: Close Dividends Account to Retained Earnings.

The fourth closing entry is identical for a merchandising company and a service company. It closes the Dividends account and adjusts the Retained Earnings account to the amount shown on the balance sheet.

Dec. 31	Retained Earnings	4,000	
	Dividends.................................		4,000
	To close the Dividends account.		

EXHIBIT 4.11

Closing Entries for a Merchandiser

Summary of Merchandising Entries

Exhibit 4.12 summarizes the key adjusting and closing entries of a merchandiser (using a perpetual inventory system) that are different from those of a service company described in prior chapters (the Comprehensive Need-To-Know 2 illustrates these merchandising entries).

EXHIBIT 4.12

Summary of Merchandising Entries

Merchandising Transactions		Merchandising Entries	Dr.	Cr.
Purchases	Purchasing merchandise for resale.	Merchandise Inventory .... Cash or Accounts Payable..........	#	#
	Paying freight costs on purchases; FOB shipping point.	Merchandise Inventory .... Cash..............................	#	#

	Paying within discount period.	Accounts Payable ....
		    Merchandise Inventory ....
		    Cash..............................
			#	#
				 #

	Recording purchase returns or allowances.	Cash or Accounts Payable............. Merchandise Inventory	#	#

Sales	Selling merchandise.	Cash or Accounts Receivable ....
		    Sales.............................
		
		 Cost of Goods Sold ....
		    Merchandise Inventory ....
			#
			
			 #
				#
				
				 #

	Receiving payment within discount period.	Cash................................ Sales Discounts .... Accounts Receivable	# #	#

	Granting sales returns or allowances.	Sales Returns and Allowances ....
		    Cash or Accounts Receivable ....
		
		 Merchandise Inventory ....
		    Cost of Goods Sold ....
			#
			
			 #
				#
				
				 #

	Paying freight costs on sales; FOB destination.	Delivery Expense .... Cash	#	#

Merchandising Events		Adjusting and Closing Entries		
Adjusting	Adjusting due to shrinkage (occurs when recorded amount larger than physical inventory).	Cost of Goods Sold .... Merchandise Inventory	#	#
Closing	Closing temporary accounts with credit balances.	Sales................................ Income Summary	#	#

	Closing temporary accounts with debit balances.	Income Summary ....
		    Sales Returns and Allowances ....
		    Sales Discounts ....
		    Cost of Goods Sold ....
		    Delivery Expense ....
		    "Other Expenses" ....
			#	#
				 #
				 #
				 #
				 #

NEED-TO-KNOW 4.3

P3

A merchandising company's ledger on May 31, its fiscal year-end, includes the following selected accounts that have normal balances (it uses the perpetual inventory system). A physical count of its May 31 year-end inventory reveals that the cost of the merchandise inventory still available is $718. (a) Prepare the entry to record any inventory shrinkage. (b) Prepare journal entries to close the balances in temporary revenue and expense accounts.

Merchandise inventory..........	$ 756	Sales returns and allowances	$ 130
Retained earnings..............	2,306	Cost of goods sold	2,100
Dividends	140	Depreciation expense...............	206
Sales........................	3,204	Salaries expense...................	650
Sales discounts...............	94	Other operating expenses	100

Solution

May 31	Cost of Goods Sold .... Merchandise Inventory .... *To adjust for shrinkage based on physical count* *[$756 − $718].*	38	38
May 31	Sales .... Income Summary .... *To close temporary accounts with credit balances.*	3,204	3,204

[continued on next page]

[continued from previous page]

May 31	Income Summary		3,318	
	Sales Discounts			94
	Sales Returns and Allowances			130
	Cost of Goods Sold*			2,138
	Depreciation Expense			206
	Salaries Expense			650
	Other Operating Expenses			100
	To close temporary accounts with debit balances.			
	(*$2,100 + $38[from shrinkage])			

Do More: QS 4-6, QS 4-7, E 4-9, P 4-5

QC4

FINANCIAL STATEMENT FORMATS

Generally accepted accounting principles do not require companies to use any one presentation format for financial statements so we see many different formats in practice. This section describes two common income statement formats: multiple-step and single-step. The classified balance sheet of a merchandiser is also explained.

P4 Define and prepare multiple-step and single-step income statements.

Multiple-Step Income Statement

A **multiple-step income statement** format shows detailed computations of net sales and other costs and expenses, and reports subtotals for various classes of items. Exhibit 4.13 shows a multiple-step income statement for Z-Mart. The statement has three main parts: (1) *gross profit,* determined by net sales less cost of goods sold, (2) *income from operations,* determined by

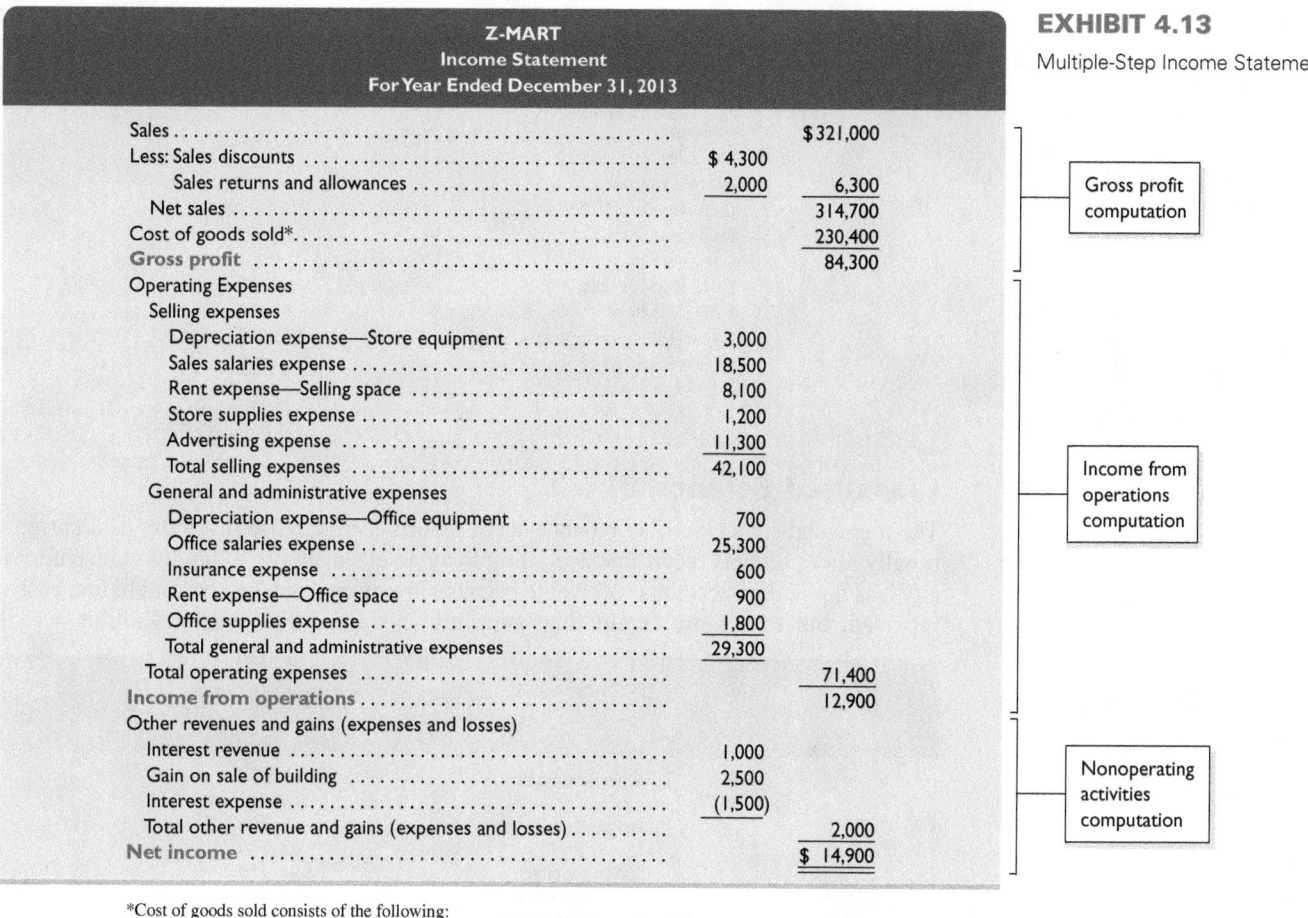

EXHIBIT 4.13

Multiple-Step Income Statement

Z-MART
Income Statement
For Year Ended December 31, 2013

Sales		$321,000	
Less: Sales discounts	$ 4,300		Gross profit computation
Sales returns and allowances	2,000	6,300	
Net sales		314,700	
Cost of goods sold*		230,400	
Gross profit		84,300	
Operating Expenses			
Selling expenses			
Depreciation expense—Store equipment	3,000		
Sales salaries expense	18,500		
Rent expense—Selling space	8,100		
Store supplies expense	1,200		
Advertising expense	11,300		
Total selling expenses	42,100		Income from operations computation
General and administrative expenses			
Depreciation expense—Office equipment	700		
Office salaries expense	25,300		
Insurance expense	600		
Rent expense—Office space	900		
Office supplies expense	1,800		
Total general and administrative expenses	29,300		
Total operating expenses		71,400	
Income from operations		12,900	
Other revenues and gains (expenses and losses)			
Interest revenue	1,000		
Gain on sale of building	2,500		Nonoperating activities computation
Interest expense	(1,500)		
Total other revenue and gains (expenses and losses)		2,000	
Net income		$ 14,900	

*Cost of goods sold consists of the following:

Beginning inventory...............	$ 19,000		Less ending inventory	21,000
Cost of goods purchased	232,400		Cost of goods sold	$230,400
Goods available for sale..........	251,400			

gross profit less operating expenses, and (3) *net income,* determined by income from operations adjusted for nonoperating items.

Operating expenses are classified into two sections. **Selling expenses** include the expenses of promoting sales by displaying and advertising merchandise, making sales, and delivering goods to customers. **General and administrative expenses** support a company's overall operations and include expenses related to accounting, human resource management, and financial management. Expenses are allocated between sections when they contribute to more than one. Z-Mart allocates rent expense of $9,000 from its store building between two sections: $8,100 to selling expense and $900 to general and administrative expense.

Nonoperating activities consist of other expenses, revenues, losses, and gains that are unrelated to a company's operations. *Other revenues and gains* commonly include interest revenue, dividend revenue, rent revenue, and gains from asset disposals. *Other expenses and losses* commonly include interest expense, losses from asset disposals, and casualty losses. When a company has no reportable nonoperating activities, its income from operations is simply labeled net income.

Single-Step Income Statement

A **single-step income statement** is another widely used format and is shown in Exhibit 4.14 for Z-Mart. It lists cost of goods sold as another expense and shows only one subtotal for total expenses. Expenses are grouped into very few, if any, categories. Many companies use formats that combine features of both the single- and multiple-step statements. Provided that income statement items are shown sensibly, management can choose the format. (In later chapters, we describe some items, such as extraordinary gains and losses, that must be reported in certain locations on the income statement.) Similar presentation options are available for the statement of retained earnings and statement of cash flows.

Point: Z-Mart did not have any non-operating activities; however, Exhibit 4.13 includes some for illustrative purposes.

Point: Many companies report interest expense and interest revenue in separate categories after operating income and before subtracting income tax expense. As one example, see **Samsung's** income statements and footnote 28 in Appendix A.

Example: Sometimes interest revenue and interest expense are reported on the income statement as *interest, net.* To illustrate, if a company has $1,000 of interest expense and $600 of interest revenue, it might report $400 as *interest, net.*

EXHIBIT 4.14

Single-Step Income Statement

Z-MART Income Statement For Year Ended December 31, 2013		
Revenues		
Net sales		$314,700
Interest revenue		1,000
Gain on sale of building		2,500
Total revenues		318,200
Expenses		
Cost of goods sold	$230,400	
Selling expenses	42,100	
General and administrative expenses	29,300	
Interest expense	1,500	
Total expenses		303,300
Net income		$ 14,900

Classified Balance Sheet

The merchandiser's classified balance sheet reports merchandise inventory as a current asset, usually after accounts receivable according to an asset's nearness to liquidity. Inventory is usually less liquid than accounts receivable because inventory must first be sold before cash can be received; but it is more liquid than supplies and prepaid expenses. Exhibit 4.15 shows

EXHIBIT 4.15

Classified Balance Sheet (partial) of a Merchandiser

Z-MART Balance Sheet (partial) December 31, 2013	
Current assets	
Cash	$ 8,200
Accounts receivable	11,200
Merchandise inventory	21,000
Office supplies	550
Store supplies	250
Prepaid insurance	300
Total current assets	$41,500

the current asset section of Z-Mart's classified balance sheet (other sections are as shown in Chapter 3).

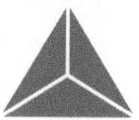

Fraud

Merchandising Shenanigans Accurate invoices are important to both sellers and buyers. Merchandisers rely on invoices to make certain they receive all monies for products provided—no more, no less. To achieve this, controls are set up. Still, failures arise. A survey reports that 9% of employees in sales and marketing witnessed false or misleading invoices sent to customers. Another 14% observed employees violating contract terms with customers (KPMG 2009).

Assume Target's adjusted trial balance on April 31, 2014, its fiscal year-end, follows. (a) Prepare a multiple-step income statement that includes separate categories for selling expenses and for general and administrative expenses. (b) Prepare a single-step income statement that includes these expense categories: cost of goods sold, selling expenses, and general and administrative expenses.

NEED-TO-KNOW 4.4

P4

Merchandise inventory................	$ 820	
Other (noninventory) assets...........	2,608	
Total liabilities......................		$ 500
Common stock		200
Retained earnings...................		1,891
Dividends	160	
Sales		4,512
Sales discounts.....................	45	
Sales returns and allowances...........	240	
Cost of goods sold..................	1,490	
Sales salaries expense	640	
Rent expense — Selling space..........	160	
Store supplies expense	30	
Advertising expense	260	
Office salaries expense	570	
Rent expense — Office space	72	
Office supplies expense	8	
Totals	$7,103	$7,103

Solution

a. Multiple-step income statement

TARGET Income Statement For Year Ended April 31, 2014		
Sales		$4,512
Less: Sales discounts.....................	$ 45	
Sales returns and allowances................	240	285
Net sales......................................		4,227
Cost of goods sold*...........................		1,490
Gross profit		2,737
Expenses		
Selling expenses		
Sales salaries expense	640	
Rent expense—Selling space................	160	
Store supplies expense	30	
Advertising expense......................	260	
Total selling expenses		1,090
General and administrative expenses		
Office salaries expense	570	
Rent expense—Office space	72	
Office supplies expense	8	
Total general and administrative expenses		650
Total expenses		1,740
Net income		$ 997

b. Single-step income statement

TARGET Income Statement For Year Ended April 31, 2014		
Net sales......................................		$4,227
Expenses		
Cost of goods sold	$1,490	
Selling expenses.........................	1,090	
General and administrative expenses	650	
Total expenses		3,230
Net income		$ 997

Do More: QS 4-10, E 4-15, P 4-4

GLOBAL VIEW

This section discusses similarities and differences between U.S. GAAP and IFRS in accounting and reporting for merchandise purchases and sales, and for the income statement.

Accounting for Merchandise Purchases and Sales   Both U.S. GAAP and IFRS include broad and similar guidance for the accounting of merchandise purchases and sales. Specifically, all of the transactions presented and illustrated in this chapter are accounted for identically under the two systems. The closing process for merchandisers also is identical for U.S. GAAP and IFRS. In the next chapter we describe how inventory valuation can, in some cases, be different for the two systems.

Income Statement Presentation   We explained that net income, profit, and earnings refer to the same (*bottom line*) item. However, IFRS tends to use the term *profit* more than any other term, whereas U.S. statements tend to use *net income* more than any other term. Both U.S. GAAP and IFRS income statements begin with the net sales or net revenues (*top line*) item. For merchandisers and manufacturers, this is followed by cost of goods sold. The presentation is similar for the remaining items with the following differences.

- U.S. GAAP offers little guidance about the presentation or order of expenses. IFRS requires separate disclosures for financing costs (interest expense), income tax expense, and some other special items.
- Both systems require separate disclosure of items when their size, nature, or frequency are important.
- IFRS permits expenses to be presented by their function or their nature. U.S. GAAP provides no direction but the SEC requires presentation by function.
- Neither U.S. GAAP nor IFRS define *operating* income, which results in latitude in reporting.
- IFRS permits alternative income measures on the income statement; U.S. GAAP does not.

VOLKSWAGEN   Volkswagen Group provides the following example of income statement reporting. We see the separate disclosure of finance costs, taxes, and other items. We also see the unusual practice of using the minus symbol in an income statement.

VOLKSWAGEN GROUP Income Statement (in Euros million) For Year Ended December 31, 2011	
Sales revenue	€ 159,337
Cost of sales	−131,371
Gross profit	27,966
Distribution expenses	−14,582
Administrative expenses	−4,384
Other operating income (net of other expenses)	2,271
Operating profit	11,271
Finance costs	−2,047
Other financial results (including equity investments)	9,702
Profit before tax	18,926
Income tax	−3,127
Profit	€ 15,799

Balance Sheet Presentation   Chapters 2 and 3 explained how both U.S. GAAP and IFRS require current items to be separated from noncurrent items on the balance sheet (yielding a *classified balance sheet*). As discussed, U.S. GAAP balance sheets report current items first. Assets are listed from most liquid to least liquid, whereas liabilities are listed from nearest to maturity to furthest from maturity. IFRS balance sheets normally present noncurrent items first (and equity before liabilities), but this is *not* a requirement as evidenced by Samsung's balance in Appendix A.

Samsung

Acid-Test and Gross Margin Ratios ▢▢▢ **Decision Analysis**

Acid-Test Ratio

For many merchandisers, inventory makes up a large portion of current assets. Inventory must be sold and any resulting accounts receivable must be collected before cash is available. Chapter 3 explained that the current ratio, defined as current assets divided by current liabilities, is useful in assessing a company's ability to pay current liabilities. Because it is sometimes unreasonable to assume that inventories are a source of payment for current liabilities, we look to other measures.

A1 Compute the acid-test ratio and explain its use to assess liquidity.

One measure of a merchandiser's ability to pay its current liabilities (referred to as its *liquidity*) is the acid-test ratio. It differs from the current ratio by excluding less liquid current assets such as inventory and prepaid expenses that take longer to be converted to cash. The **acid-test ratio,** also called *quick ratio,* is defined as *quick assets* (cash, short-term investments, and current receivables) divided by current liabilities—see Exhibit 4.16.

$$\text{Acid-test ratio} = \frac{\text{Cash and cash equivalents} + \text{Short-term investments} + \text{Current receivables}}{\text{Current liabilities}}$$

EXHIBIT 4.16

Acid-Test (Quick) Ratio

Exhibit 4.17 shows both the acid-test and current ratios of retailer JCPenney for fiscal years 2008 through 2012—also see margin graph. JCPenney's acid-test ratio reveals a general increase from 2008 through 2011 that exceeds the industry average, and then a marked decline in 2012. Further, JCPenney's current ratio shows a marked decline in 2012 to 1.84, which suggests that its short-term obligations are less confidently covered with short-term assets compared with prior years.

EXHIBIT 4.17

JCPenney's Acid-Test and Current Ratios

($ millions)	2012	2011	2010	2009	2008
Total quick assets	$1,920	$2,956	$3,406	$2,704	$2,845
Total current assets	5,081	$6,370	$6,652	$6,220	$6,751
Total current liabilities	2,756	$2,647	$3,249	$2,794	$3,338
Acid-test ratio	0.70	1.12	1.05	0.97	0.85
Current ratio	1.84	2.41	2.05	2.23	2.02
Industry acid-test ratio	0.54	0.61	0.59	0.63	0.62
Industry current ratio	2.01	2.27	2.15	2.31	2.39

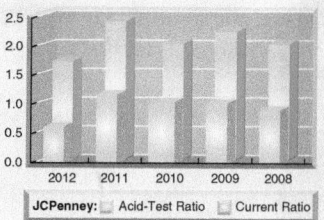

An acid-test ratio less than 1.0 means that current liabilities exceed quick assets. A rule of thumb is that the acid-test ratio should have a value near, or higher than, 1.0 to conclude that a company is unlikely to face near-term liquidity problems. A value much less than 1.0 raises liquidity concerns unless a company can generate enough cash from inventory sales or if much of its liabilities are not due until late in the next period. Similarly, a value slightly larger than 1.0 can hide a liquidity problem if payables are due shortly and receivables are not collected until late in the next period. Analysis of JCPenney shows some need for concern regarding its liquidity as its acid-test ratio is less than one. However, retailers such as JCPenney pay many current liabilities from inventory sales and in all years, JCPenney's acid-test ratios exceed the industry norm (and its inventory is fairly liquid).

Point: Successful use of a just-in-time inventory system can narrow the gap between the acid-test ratio and the current ratio.

▮ **Decision** Maker ━━━━━━━━━━━━━━━━━━

Supplier A retailer requests to purchase supplies on credit from your company. You have no prior experience with this retailer. The retailer's current ratio is 2.1, its acid-test ratio is 0.5, and inventory makes up most of its current assets. Do you extend credit? ■ [Answer—p. 193]

Gross Margin Ratio

The cost of goods sold makes up much of a merchandiser's expenses. Without sufficient gross profit, a merchandiser will likely fail. Users often compute the gross margin ratio to help understand this relation. It differs from the profit margin ratio in that it excludes all costs except cost of goods sold. The **gross margin ratio** (also called *gross profit ratio*) is defined as *gross margin* (net sales minus cost of goods sold) divided by net sales—see Exhibit 4.18.

A2 Compute the gross margin ratio and explain its use to assess profitability.

$$\text{Gross margin ratio} = \frac{\text{Net sales} - \text{Cost of goods sold}}{\text{Net sales}}$$

EXHIBIT 4.18

Gross Margin Ratio

Point: The power of a ratio is often its ability to identify areas for more detailed analysis.

Exhibit 4.19 shows the gross margin ratio of JCPenney for fiscal years 2008 through 2012. For JCPenney, each $1 of sales in 2012 yielded about 36.0¢ in gross margin to cover all other expenses and still produce a net income. This 36.0¢ margin is down from 38.6¢ in 2008. This decrease is not a favorable development. Success for merchandisers such as JCPenney depends on adequate gross margin. For example, the 2.60¢ decrease in the gross margin ratio, computed as 36.0¢ − 38.6¢, means that JCPenney has $448.76 million less in gross margin! (This is computed as net sales of $17,260 million multiplied by the 2.6% decrease in gross margin.) Management's discussion in its annual report attributes this decline to "softer than expected selling environment and the resulting increased promotional activity and the costs associated with implementing our new pricing strategy."

EXHIBIT 4.19

JCPenney's Gross Margin Ratio

($ millions)	2012	2011	2010	2009	2008
Gross margin	$ 6,218	$ 6,960	$ 6,910	$ 6,915	$ 7,671
Net sales	$17,260	$17,759	$17,556	$18,486	$19,860
Gross margin ratio	36.0%	39.2%	39.4%	37.4%	38.6%

■ **Decision** Maker

Financial Officer Your company has a 36% gross margin ratio and a 17% net profit margin ratio. Industry averages are 44% for gross margin and 16% for net profit margin. Do these comparative results concern you? ■ [Answer—p. 193]

COMPREHENSIVE...

NEED-TO-KNOW 1

Use the following adjusted trial balance and additional information to complete the requirements.

KC ANTIQUES
Adjusted Trial Balance
December 31, 2013

	Debit	Credit
Cash	$ 7,000	
Accounts receivable	13,000	
Merchandise inventory	60,000	
Store supplies	1,500	
Equipment	45,600	
Accumulated depreciation—Equipment		$ 16,600
Accounts payable		9,000
Salaries payable		2,000
Common stock		20,000
Retained earnings		59,000
Dividends	10,000	
Sales		343,250
Sales discounts	5,000	
Sales returns and allowances	6,000	
Cost of goods sold	159,900	
Depreciation expense—Store equipment	4,100	
Depreciation expense—Office equipment	1,600	
Sales salaries expense	30,000	
Office salaries expense	34,000	
Insurance expense	11,000	
Rent expense (70% is store, 30% is office)	24,000	
Store supplies expense	5,750	
Advertising expense	31,400	
Totals	$449,850	$449,850

KC Antiques' *supplementary records* for 2013 reveal the following itemized costs for merchandising activities:

Invoice cost of merchandise purchases	$150,000
Purchase discounts received	2,500
Purchase returns and allowances	2,700
Cost of transportation-in	5,000

Required

1. Use the supplementary records to compute the total cost of merchandise purchases for 2013.

2. Prepare a 2013 multiple-step income statement. (Inventory at December 31, 2012, is $70,100.)

3. Prepare a single-step income statement for 2013.

4. Prepare closing entries for KC Antiques at December 31, 2013.

5. Compute the acid-test ratio and the gross margin ratio. Explain the meaning of each ratio and interpret them for KC Antiques.

PLANNING THE SOLUTION

- Compute the total cost of merchandise purchases for 2013.

- To prepare the multiple-step statement, first compute net sales. Then, to compute cost of goods sold, add the net cost of merchandise purchases for the year to beginning inventory and subtract the cost of ending inventory. Subtract cost of goods sold from net sales to get gross profit. Then classify expenses as selling expenses or general and administrative expenses.

- To prepare the single-step income statement, begin with net sales. Then list and subtract the expenses.

- The first closing entry debits all temporary accounts with credit balances and opens the Income Summary account. The second closing entry credits all temporary accounts with debit balances. The third entry closes the Income Summary account to the retained earnings account, and the fourth entry closes the dividends account to the retained earnings account.

- Identify the quick assets on the adjusted trial balance. Compute the acid-test ratio by dividing quick assets by current liabilities. Compute the gross margin ratio by dividing gross profit by net sales.

SOLUTION TO COMPREHENSIVE NEED-TO-KNOW 1

1.

Invoice cost of merchandise purchases	$150,000
Less: Purchases discounts received	2,500
Purchase returns and allowances	2,700
Add: Cost of transportation-in	5,000
Total cost of merchandise purchases	$149,800

2. Multiple-step income statement

KC ANTIQUES Income Statement For Year Ended December 31, 2013		
Sales		$343,250
Less: Sales discounts	$ 5,000	
Sales returns and allowances	6,000	11,000
Net sales.....................................		332,250
Cost of goods sold*		159,900
Gross profit		172,350
Expenses		
Selling expenses		
Depreciation expense—Store equipment	4,100	
Sales salaries expense	30,000	
Rent expense—Selling space	16,800	
Store supplies expense	5,750	
Advertising expense	31,400	
Total selling expenses	88,050	

[continued on next page]

[continued from previous page]

General and administrative expenses		
Depreciation expense—Office equipment	1,600	
Office salaries expense	34,000	
Insurance expense	11,000	
Rent expense—Office space	7,200	
Total general and administrative expenses	53,800	
Total operating expenses		141,850
Net income		$ 30,500

* Cost of goods sold can also be directly computed (applying concepts from Exhibit 4.4):

Merchandise inventory, December 31, 2012	$ 70,100
Total cost of merchandise purchases (from part 1)	149,800
Goods available for sale	219,900
Merchandise inventory, December 31, 2013	60,000
Cost of goods sold	$159,900

3. Single-step income statement

KC ANTIQUES
Income Statement
For Year Ended December 31, 2013

Net sales		$332,250
Expenses		
Cost of goods sold	$159,900	
Selling expenses	88,050	
General and administrative expenses	53,800	
Total expenses		301,750
Net income		$ 30,500

4.

Dec. 31	Sales	343,250	
	Income Summary		343,250
	To close credit balances in temporary accounts.		
Dec. 31	Income Summary	312,750	
	Sales Discounts		5,000
	Sales Returns and Allowances		6,000
	Cost of Goods Sold		159,900
	Depreciation Expense—Store Equipment		4,100
	Depreciation Expense—Office Equipment		1,600
	Sales Salaries Expense		30,000
	Office Salaries Expense		34,000
	Insurance Expense		11,000
	Rent Expense		24,000
	Store Supplies Expense		5,750
	Advertising Expense		31,400
	To close debit balances in temporary accounts.		
Dec. 31	Income Summary	30,500	
	Retained Earnings		30,500
	To close the Income Summary account.		
Dec. 31	Retained Earnings	10,000	
	Dividends		10,000
	To close the Dividends account.		

5. Acid-test ratio = (Cash and equivalents + Short-term investments + Current receivables)/
Current liabilities

= (Cash + Accounts receivable/(Accounts payable + Salaries payable)

= ($7,000 + $13,000)/($9,000 + $2,000) = $20,000/$11,000 = 1.82

Gross margin ratio = Gross profit/Net sales = $172,350/$332,250 = 0.52 (or 52%)

KC Antiques has a healthy acid-test ratio of 1.82. This means it has more than $1.80 in liquid assets to satisfy each $1.00 in current liabilities. The gross margin of 0.52 shows that KC Antiques spends 48¢ ($1.00 − $0.52) of every dollar of net sales on the costs of acquiring the merchandise it sells. This leaves 52¢ of every dollar of net sales to cover other expenses incurred in the business and to provide a net profit.

Prepare journal entries to record the following merchandising transactions for both the seller (BMX) and buyer (Sanuk).

COMPREHENSIVE...

NEED-TO-KNOW 2

May 4	BMX sold $1,500 of merchandise on account to Sanuk, terms FOB shipping point, n/45, invoice dated May 4. The cost of the merchandise was $900.
May 6	Sanuk paid transportation charges of $30 on the May 4 purchase from BMX.
May 8	BMX sold $1,000 of merchandise on account to Sanuk, terms FOB destination, n/30, invoice dated May 8. The cost of the merchandise was $700.
May 10	BMX paid transportation costs of $50 for delivery of merchandise sold to Sanuk on May 8.
May 16	BMX issued Sanuk a $200 credit memorandum for merchandise returned. The merchandise was purchased by Sanuk on account on May 8. The cost of the merchandise returned was $140.
May 18	BMX received payment from Sanuk for purchase of May 8.
May 21	BMX sold $2,400 of merchandise on account to Sanuk, terms FOB shipping point, 2/10, n/EOM. BMX prepaid transportation costs of $100, which were added to the invoice. The cost of the merchandise was $1,440.
May 31	BMX received payment from Sanuk for purchase of May 21, less discount (2% × $2,400).

SOLUTION TO COMPREHENSIVE NEED-TO-KNOW 2

BMX (Seller)

		Debit	Credit
May 4	Accounts Receivable—Sanuk	1,500	
	Sales		1,500
	Cost of Goods Sold	900	
	Merchandise Inventory		900
6	No entry.		
8	Accounts Receivable—Sanuk	1,000	
	Sales		1,000
	Cost of Goods Sold	700	
	Merchandise Inventory		700
10	Delivery Expense	50	
	Cash		50
16	Sales Returns & Allowances	200	
	Accounts Receivable—Sanuk		200
	Merchandise Inventory	140	
	Cost of Goods Sold		140
18	Cash	800	
	Accounts Receivable—Sanuk		800
21	Accounts Receivable—Sanuk	2,400	
	Sales		2,400
	Accounts Receivable—Sanuk	100	
	Cash		100
	Cost of Goods Sold	1,440	
	Merchandise Inventory		1,440
31	Cash	2,452	
	Sales Discounts	48	
	Accounts Receivable—Sanuk		2,500

Sanuk (Buyer)

		Debit	Credit
May 4	Merchandise Inventory	1,500	
	Accounts Payable—BMX		1,500
6	Merchandise Inventory	30	
	Cash		30
8	Merchandise Inventory	1,000	
	Accounts Payable—BMX		1,000
10	No entry.		
16	Accounts Payable—BMX	200	
	Merchandise Inventory		200
18	Accounts Payable—BMX	800	
	Cash		800
21	Merchandise Inventory	2,500	
	Accounts Payable—BMX		2,500
31	Accounts Payable—BMX	2,500	
	Merchandise Inventory		48
	Cash		2,452

4A Periodic Inventory System

A periodic inventory system requires updating the inventory account only at the *end of a period* to reflect the quantity and cost of both the goods available and the goods sold. Thus, during the period, the Merchandise Inventory balance remains unchanged. It reflects the beginning inventory balance until it is updated at the end of the period. During the period the cost of merchandise is recorded in a temporary *Purchases* account. When a company sells merchandise, it records revenue **but not the cost of the goods sold.** At the end of the period when a company prepares financial statements, it takes a *physical count of inventory* by counting the quantities and costs of merchandise available. The cost of goods sold is then computed by subtracting the ending inventory amount from the cost of merchandise available for sale.

> **P5** Record and compare merchandising transactions using both periodic and perpetual inventory systems.

Recording Merchandise Transactions   Under a periodic system, purchases, purchase returns and allowances, purchase discounts, and transportation-in transactions are recorded in separate temporary accounts. At period-end, each of these temporary accounts is closed and the Merchandise Inventory account is updated. To illustrate, journal entries under the periodic inventory system are shown for the most common transactions (codes *a* through *f* link these transactions to those in the chapter, and we drop explanations for simplicity). For comparison, perpetual system journal entries are shown to the right of each periodic entry, where differences are in green font.

Purchases   The periodic system uses a temporary *Purchases* account that accumulates the cost of all purchase transactions during each period. Z-Mart's November 2 entry to record the purchase of merchandise for $1,200 on credit with terms of 2/10, n/30 is

(a)

Periodic				Perpetual		
Purchases	1,200			Merchandise Inventory	1,200	
Accounts Payable		1,200		Accounts Payable		1,200

Purchase Discounts   The periodic system uses a temporary *Purchase Discounts* account that accumulates discounts taken on purchase transactions during the period. If payment in (*a*) is delayed until after the discount period expires, the entry is to debit Accounts Payable and credit Cash for $1,200 each. However, if Z-Mart pays the supplier for the previous purchase in (*a*) within the discount period, the required payment is $1,176 ($1,200 × 98%) and is recorded as

(b)

Periodic				Perpetual		
Accounts Payable	1,200			Accounts Payable	1,200	
Purchase Discounts		24		Merchandise Inventory		24
Cash		1,176		Cash		1,176

> **Point:** Purchase Discounts and Purchase Returns and Allowances are both classified as contra-purchases accounts *and* have normal credit balances.

Purchase Returns and Allowances   Z-Mart returned merchandise purchased on November 2 because of defects. In the periodic system, the temporary *Purchase Returns and Allowances* account accumulates the cost of all returns and allowances during a period. The recorded cost (including discounts) of the defective merchandise is $300, and Z-Mart records the November 15 return with this entry:

(c)

Periodic				Perpetual		
Accounts Payable	300			Accounts Payable	300	
Purchase Returns and Allowances		300		Merchandise Inventory		300

Transportation-In   Z-Mart paid a $75 freight charge to transport merchandise to its store. In the periodic system, this cost is charged to a temporary *Transportation-In* account.

(d)

Periodic			Perpetual		
Transportation-In	75		Merchandise Inventory	75	
Cash		75	Cash		75

Sales   Under the periodic system, the cost of goods sold is *not* recorded at the time of each sale. (We later show how to compute total cost of goods sold at the end of a period.) Z-Mart's November 3 entry to record sales of $2,400 in merchandise on credit (when its cost is $1,600) is:

(e)

Periodic			Perpetual		
Accounts Receivable	2,400		Accounts Receivable	2,400	
Sales		2,400	Sales		2,400
			Cost of Goods Sold	1,600	
			Merchandise Inventory		1,600

Sales Returns   A customer returned part of the merchandise from the transaction in (e), where the returned items sell for $800 and cost $600. (*Recall:* The periodic system records only the revenue effect, not the cost effect, for sales transactions.) Z-Mart restores the merchandise to inventory and records the November 6 return as

(f)

Periodic			Perpetual		
Sales Returns and Allowances	800		Sales Returns and Allowances	800	
Accounts Receivable ...		800	Accounts Receivable		800
			Merchandise Inventory	600	
			Cost of Goods Sold		600

Sales Discounts   To illustrate sales discounts, assume that the remaining $1,600 of receivables (computed as $2,400 from *e* less $800 for *f*) has credit terms of 3/10, n/90 and that customers all pay within the discount period. Z-Mart records this payment as

Periodic			Perpetual		
Cash	1,552		Cash	1,552	
Sales Discounts ($1,600 × .03)	48		Sales Discounts ($1,600 × .03) ...	48	
Accounts Receivable ...		1,600	Accounts Receivable		1,600

Adjusting and Closing Entries   The periodic and perpetual inventory systems have slight differences in adjusting and closing entries. The period-end Merchandise Inventory balance (unadjusted) is $19,000 under the periodic system and $21,250 under the perpetual system. Since the periodic system does not update the Merchandise Inventory balance during the period, the $19,000 amount is the beginning inventory. However, the $21,250 balance under the perpetual system is the recorded ending inventory before adjusting for any inventory shrinkage.

A physical count of inventory taken at the end of the period reveals $21,000 of merchandise available. The adjusting and closing entries for the two systems are shown in Exhibit 4A.1. The periodic system records the ending inventory of $21,000 in the Merchandise Inventory account (which includes

EXHIBIT 4A.1

Comparison of Adjusting and Closing Entries—Periodic and Perpetual

PERIODIC			PERPETUAL		
Adjusting Entry—Shrinkage			Adjusting Entry—Shrinkage		
None			Cost of Goods Sold	250	
			Merchandise Inventory		250

[continued on next page]

[continued from previous page]

PERIODIC		
Closing Entries		
(1) Sales	321,000	
Merchandise Inventory	21,000	
Purchase Discounts	4,200	
Purchase Returns and Allowances	1,500	
Income Summary		347,700
(2) Income Summary	334,800	
Sales Discounts		4,300
Sales Returns and Allowances		2,000
Merchandise Inventory		19,000
Purchases		235,800
Transportation-In		2,300
Depreciation Expense		3,700
Salaries Expense		43,800
Insurance Expense		600
Rent Expense		9,000
Supplies Expense		3,000
Advertising Expense		11,300
(3) Income Summary	12,900	
Retained Earnings		12,900
(4) Retained Earnings	4,000	
Dividends		4,000

PERPETUAL		
Closing Entries		
(1) Sales	321,000	
Income Summary		321,000
(2) Income Summary	308,100	
Sales Discounts		4,300
Sales Returns and Allowances		2,000
Cost of Goods Sold		230,400
Depreciation Expense		3,700
Salaries Expense		43,800
Insurance Expense		600
Rent Expense		9,000
Supplies Expense		3,000
Advertising Expense		11,300
(3) Income Summary	12,900	
Retained Earnings		12,900
(4) Retained Earnings	4,000	
Dividends		4,000

shrinkage) in the first closing entry and removes the $19,000 beginning inventory balance from the account in the second closing entry.[2]

By updating Merchandise Inventory and closing Purchases, Purchase Discounts, Purchase Returns and Allowances, and Transportation-In, the periodic system transfers the cost of goods sold amount to Income Summary. Review the periodic side of Exhibit 4A.1 and notice that the **boldface** items affect Income Summary as follows.

Credit to Income Summary in the first closing entry includes amounts from:	
Merchandise inventory (ending)	$ 21,000
Purchase discounts	4,200
Purchase returns and allowances	1,500
Debit to Income Summary in the second closing entry includes amounts from:	
Merchandise inventory (beginning)	(19,000)
Purchases	(235,800)
Transportation-in	(2,300)
Net effect on Income Summary	$(230,400)

This $230,400 effect on Income Summary is the cost of goods sold amount. The periodic system transfers cost of goods sold to the Income Summary account but without using a Cost of Goods Sold account. Also, the periodic system does not separately measure shrinkage. Instead, it computes cost of goods available

---

[2] This approach is called the *closing entry method*. An alternative approach, referred to as the *adjusting entry method*, would not make any entries to Merchandise Inventory in the closing entries of Exhibit 4A.1, but instead would make two adjusting entries. Using Z-Mart data, the two adjusting entries would be: (1) Dr. Income Summary and Cr. Merchandise Inventory for $19,000 each, and (2) Dr. Merchandise Inventory and Cr. Income Summary for $21,000 each. The first entry removes the beginning balance of Merchandise Inventory, and the second entry records the actual ending balance.

for sale, subtracts the cost of ending inventory, and defines the difference as cost of goods sold, which includes shrinkage.

Preparing Financial Statements   The financial statements of a merchandiser using the periodic system are similar to those for a service company described in prior chapters. The income statement mainly differs by the inclusion of *cost of goods sold* and *gross profit*—of course, net sales is affected by discounts, returns, and allowances. The cost of goods sold section under the periodic system follows

Calculation of Cost of Goods Sold For Year Ended December 31, 2013	
Beginning inventory....................	$ 19,000
Cost of goods purchased	232,400
Cost of goods available for sale	251,400
Less ending inventory	21,000
Cost of goods sold..................	$230,400

The balance sheet mainly differs by the inclusion of *merchandise inventory* in current assets—see Exhibit 4.15. The statement of retained earnings is unchanged. A work sheet can be used to help prepare these statements. The only differences under the periodic system from the work sheet illustrated in Appendix 4B using the perpetual system are highlighted as follows in blue boldface font.

File Edit View Insert Format Tools Data Accounting Window Help

		Unadjusted Trial Balance		Adjustments		Adjusted Trial Balance		Income Statement		Balance Sheet	
No.	Account	Dr.	Cr.	Dr.	Cr.	Dr.	Cr.	Dr.	Cr.	Dr.	Cr.
101	Cash	8,200				8,200				8,200	
106	Accounts receivable	11,200				11,200				11,200	
119	**Merchandise Inventory**	19,000				19,000		19,000	21,000	21,000	
126	Supplies	3,800			(b) 3,000	800				800	
128	Prepaid insurance	900			(a) 600	300				300	
167	Equipment	34,200				34,200				34,200	
168	Accumulated depr.—Equip.		3,700		(c) 3,700		7,400				7,400
201	Accounts payable		16,000				16,000				16,000
209	Salaries payable				(d) 800		800				800
307	Common stock		10,000				10,000				10,000
318	Retained earnings		32,600				32,600				32,600
319	Dividends	4,000				4,000				4,000	
413	Sales		321,000				321,000		321,000		
414	Sales returns and allowances	2,000				2,000		2,000			
415	Sales discounts	4,300				4,300		4,300			
505	**Purchases**	**235,800**				235,800		235,800			
506	**Purchases returns & allowance**		**1,500**				1,500		1,500		
507	**Purchases discounts**		**4,200**				4,200		4,200		
508	**Transportation-in**	**2,300**				2,300		2,300			
612	Depreciation expense—Equip.			(c) 3,700		3,700		3,700			
622	Salaries expense	43,000		(d) 800		43,800		43,800			
637	Insurance expense			(a)` 600		600		600			
640	Rent expense	9,000				9,000		9,000			
652	Supplies expense			(b) 3,000		3,000		3,000			
655	Advertising expense	11,300				11,300		11,300			
	Totals	389,000	389,000	8,100	8,100	393,500	393,500	334,800	347,700	79,700	66,800
	Net income							12,900			12,900
	Totals							347,700	347,700	79,700	79,700

Sheet1 Sheet2 Sheet3

4B   Work Sheet—Perpetual System

Exhibit 4B.1 shows the work sheet for preparing financial statements of a merchandiser. It differs slightly from the work sheet layout in Chapter 3—the differences are in **red boldface**. Also, the adjustments in the work sheet reflect the following: (*a*) Expiration of $600 of prepaid insurance. (*b*) Use of $3,000 of supplies. (*c*) Depreciation of $3,700 for equipment. (*d*) Accrual of $800 of unpaid salaries. (*e*) Inventory shrinkage of $250. Once the adjusted amounts are extended into the financial statement columns, the information is used to develop financial statements.

EXHIBIT 4B.1

Work Sheet for Merchandiser (using a perpetual system)

No.	Account	Unadjusted Trial Balance Dr.	Cr.	Adjustments Dr.	Cr.	Adjusted Trial Balance Dr.	Cr.	Income Statement Dr.	Cr.	Balance Sheet Dr.	Cr.
101	Cash	8,200				8,200				8,200	
106	Accounts receivable	11,200				11,200				11,200	
119	Merchandise Inventory	21,250			(e) 250	21,000				21,000	
126	Supplies	3,800			(b) 3,000	800				800	
128	Prepaid insurance	900			(a) 600	300				300	
167	Equipment	34,200				34,200				34,200	
168	Accumulated depr.—Equip.		3,700		(c) 3,700		7,400				7,400
201	Accounts payable		16,000				16,000				16,000
209	Salaries payable				(d) 800		800				800
307	Common stock		10,000				10,000				10,000
318	Retained earnings		32,600				32,600				32,600
319	Dividends	4,000				4,000				4,000	
413	Sales		321,000				321,000		321,000		
414	Sales returns and allowances	2,000				2,000		2,000			
415	Sales discounts	4,300				4,300		4,300			
502	Cost of goods sold	230,150		(e) 250		230,400		230,400			
612	Depreciation expense—Equip.			(c) 3,700		3,700		3,700			
622	Salaries expense	43,000		(d) 800		43,800		43,800			
637	Insurance expense			(a) 600		600		600			
640	Rent expense	9,000				9,000		9,000			
652	Supplies expense			(b) 3,000		3,000		3,000			
655	Advertising expense	11,300				11,300		11,300			
	Totals	383,300	383,300	8,350	8,350	387,800	387,800	308,100	321,000	79,700	66,800
	Net income							12,900			12,900
	Totals							321,000	321,000	79,700	79,700

Summary

C1 Describe merchandising activities and identify income components for a merchandising company. Merchandisers buy products and resell them. Examples of merchandisers include Walmart, Home Depot, The Limited, and Barnes & Noble. A merchandiser's costs on the income statement include an amount for cost of goods sold. Gross profit, or gross margin, equals sales minus cost of goods sold.

C2 Identify and explain the inventory asset and cost flows of a merchandising company. The current asset section of a merchandising company's balance sheet includes *merchandise inventory,* which refers to the products a merchandiser sells and are available for sale at the balance sheet date. Cost of merchandise purchases flows into Merchandise Inventory and from there to Cost of Goods Sold on the income statement. Any remaining inventory is reported as a current asset on the balance sheet.

A1 **Compute the acid-test ratio and explain its use to assess liquidity.** The acid-test ratio is computed as quick assets (cash, short-term investments, and current receivables) divided by current liabilities. It indicates a company's ability to pay its current liabilities with its existing quick assets. An acid-test ratio equal to or greater than 1.0 is often adequate.

A2 **Compute the gross margin ratio and explain its use to assess profitability.** The gross margin ratio is computed as gross margin (net sales minus cost of goods sold) divided by net sales. It indicates a company's profitability before considering other expenses.

P1 **Analyze and record transactions for merchandise purchases using a perpetual system.** For a perpetual inventory system, purchases of inventory (net of trade discounts) are added to the Merchandise Inventory account. Purchase discounts and purchase returns and allowances are subtracted from Merchandise Inventory, and transportation-in costs are added to Merchandise Inventory.

P2 **Analyze and record transactions for merchandise sales using a perpetual system.** A merchandiser records sales at list price less any trade discounts. The cost of items sold is transferred from Merchandise Inventory to Cost of Goods Sold. Refunds or credits given to customers for unsatisfactory merchandise are recorded in Sales Returns and Allowances, a contra account to Sales. If merchandise is returned and restored to inventory, the cost of this merchandise is removed from Cost of Goods

Sold and transferred back to Merchandise Inventory. When cash discounts from the sales price are offered and customers pay within the discount period, the seller records Sales Discounts, a contra account to Sales.

P3 **Prepare adjustments and close accounts for a merchandising company.** With a perpetual system, it is often necessary to make an adjustment for inventory shrinkage. This is computed by comparing a physical count of inventory with the Merchandise Inventory balance. Shrinkage is normally charged to Cost of Goods Sold. Temporary accounts closed to Income Summary for a merchandiser include Sales, Sales Discounts, Sales Returns and Allowances, and Cost of Goods Sold.

P4 **Define and prepare multiple-step and single-step income statements.** Multiple-step income statements include greater detail for sales and expenses than do single-step income statements. They also show details of net sales and report expenses in categories reflecting different activities.

P5[A] **Record and compare merchandising transactions using both periodic and perpetual inventory systems.** A perpetual inventory system continuously tracks the cost of goods available for sale and the cost of goods sold. A periodic system accumulates the cost of goods purchased during the period and does not compute the amount of inventory or the cost of goods sold until the end of a period. Transactions involving the sale and purchase of merchandise are recorded and analyzed under both the periodic and perpetual inventory systems. Adjusting and closing entries for both inventory systems are illustrated and explained.

Guidance Answers to Decision Maker and Decision Ethics

Entrepreneur   For terms of 3/10, n/90, missing the 3% discount for an additional 80 days equals an implied annual interest rate of 13.69%, computed as (365 days ÷ 80 days) × 3%. Since you can borrow funds at 11% (assuming no other processing costs), it is better to borrow and pay within the discount period. You save 2.69% (13.69% − 11%) in interest costs by paying early.

Payables Manager   Your decision is whether to comply with prior policy or to create a new policy and not abuse discounts offered by suppliers. Your first step should be to meet with your superior to find out if the late payment policy is the actual policy and, if so, its rationale. If it is the policy to pay late, you must apply your own sense of ethics. One point of view is that the late payment policy is unethical. A deliberate plan to make late payments means the company lies when it pretends to make payment within the discount period. Another view is that the late payment policy is acceptable. In some markets, attempts to take discounts through late payments are accepted as a continued phase of "price negotiation." Also, your company's suppliers can respond by billing your company for the discounts not accepted because of late payments. However, this is a dubious viewpoint, especially since the prior manager proposes that you dishonestly explain late payments as computer or mail problems and since some suppliers have complained.

Supplier   A current ratio of 2.1 suggests sufficient current assets to cover current liabilities. An acid-test ratio of 0.5 suggests, however, that quick assets can cover only about one-half of current liabilities. This implies that the retailer depends on money from sales of inventory to pay current liabilities. If sales of inventory decline or profit margins decrease, the likelihood that this retailer will default on its payments increases. Your decision is probably not to extend credit. If you do extend credit, you are likely to closely monitor the retailer's financial condition. (It is better to hold unsold inventory than uncollectible receivables.)

Financial Officer   Your company's net profit margin is about equal to the industry average and suggests typical industry performance. However, gross margin reveals that your company is paying far more in cost of goods sold or receiving far less in sales price than competitors. Your attention must be directed to finding the problem with cost of goods sold, sales, or both. One positive note is that your company's expenses make up 19% of sales (36% − 17%). This favorably compares with competitors' expenses that make up 28% of sales (44% − 16%).

Key Terms

Acid-test ratio (p. 183)
Cash discount (p. 169)
Cost of goods sold (p. 166)
Credit memorandum (p. 175)
Credit period (p. 169)
Credit terms (p. 169)
Debit memorandum (p. 170)
Discount period (p. 169)
EOM (p. 169)
FOB (p. 171)
General and administrative expenses (p. 180)

Gross margin (p. 166)
Gross margin ratio (p. 183)
Gross profit (p. 166)
Inventory (p. 167)
List price (p. 168)
Merchandise (p. 166)
Merchandise inventory (p. 166)
Merchandiser (p. 166)
Multiple-step income statement (p. 179)
Periodic inventory system (p. 167)
Perpetual inventory system (p. 167)

Purchase discount (p. 169)
Retailer (p. 166)
Sales discount (p. 169)
Selling expenses (p. 180)
Shrinkage (p. 176)
Single-step income statement (p. 180)
Supplementary records (p. 172)
Trade discount (p. 168)
Wholesaler (p. 166)

Multiple Choice Quiz   Answers on p. 211   mhhe.com/wildFA7e

Additional Quiz Questions are available at the book's Website.

1. A company has $550,000 in net sales and $193,000 in gross profit. This means its cost of goods sold equals
   a. $743,000
   b. $550,000
   c. $357,000
   d. $193,000
   e. $(193,000)

2. A company purchased $4,500 of merchandise on May 1 with terms of 2/10, n/30. On May 6, it returned $250 of that merchandise. On May 8, it paid the balance owed for merchandise, taking any discount it is entitled to. The cash paid on May 8 is
   a. $4,500
   b. $4,250
   c. $4,160
   d. $4,165
   e. $4,410

3. A company has cash sales of $75,000, credit sales of $320,000, sales returns and allowances of $13,700, and sales discounts of $6,000. Its net sales equal
   a. $395,000
   b. $375,300

   c. $300,300
   d. $339,700
   e. $414,700

4. A company's quick assets are $37,500, its current assets are $80,000, and its current liabilities are $50,000. Its acid-test ratio equals
   a. 1.600
   b. 0.750
   c. 0.625
   d. 1.333
   e. 0.469

5. A company's net sales are $675,000, its costs of goods sold are $459,000, and its net income is $74,250. Its gross margin ratio equals
   a. 32%
   b. 68%
   c. 47%
   d. 11%
   e. 34%

A(B) *Superscript letter A (B) denotes assignments based on Appendix 4A (4B).*

🚹 Icon denotes assignments that involve decision making.

Discussion Questions

1. What items appear in financial statements of merchandising companies but not in the statements of service companies?

2. In comparing the accounts of a merchandising company with those of a service company, what additional accounts would the merchandising company likely use, assuming it employs a perpetual inventory system?

3. 🚹 Explain how a business can earn a positive gross profit on its sales and still have a net loss.

4. 🚹 Why do companies offer a cash discount?

5. How does a company that uses a perpetual inventory system determine the amount of inventory shrinkage?

6. Distinguish between cash discounts and trade discounts. Is the amount of a trade discount on purchased merchandise recorded in the accounts?

7. What is the difference between a sales discount and a purchase discount?

8. 🔲 Why would a company's manager be concerned about the quantity of its purchase returns if its suppliers allow unlimited returns?

9. Does the sender (maker) of a debit memorandum record a debit or a credit in the recipient's account? What entry (debit or credit) does the recipient record?

10. What is the difference between the single-step and multiple-step income statement formats?

11. 🔲 Refer to the balance sheet and income statement for Apple in Appendix A. What does the company title its inventory account? Does the company present a detailed calculation of its cost of goods sold? **APPLE**

12. Refer to Google's income statement in Appendix A. What title does it use for cost of goods sold? **GOOGLE**

13. Refer to the income statement for Samsung in Appendix A. What does Samsung title its cost of goods sold account? **Samsung**

14. Refer to the income statement of Samsung in Appendix A. Does its income statement report a gross profit figure? If yes, what is the amount? **Samsung**

15. 🔲 Buyers negotiate purchase contracts with suppliers. What type of shipping terms should a buyer attempt to negotiate to minimize freight-in costs?

⬛connect

Enter the letter for each term in the blank space beside the definition that it most closely matches.

A. Sales discount	**E.** FOB shipping point	**H.** Purchase discount
B. Credit period	**F.** Gross profit	**I.** Cash discount
C. Discount period	**G.** Merchandise inventory	**J.** Trade discount
D. FOB destination		

QUICK STUDY

QS 4-1
Applying merchandising terms
C1

_____ **1.** Goods a company owns and expects to sell to its customers.
_____ **2.** Time period that can pass before a customer's payment is due.
_____ **3.** Seller's description of a cash discount granted to buyers in return for early payment.
_____ **4.** Reduction below list or catalog price that is negotiated in setting the price of goods.
_____ **5.** Ownership of goods is transferred when the seller delivers goods to the carrier.
_____ **6.** Purchaser's description of a cash discount received from a supplier of goods.
_____ **7.** Reduction in a receivable or payable if it is paid within the discount period.
_____ **8.** Difference between net sales and the cost of goods sold.
_____ **9.** Time period in which a cash discount is available.
_____ **10.** Ownership of goods is transferred when delivered to the buyer's place of business.

Costs of $5,000 were incurred to make goods ready for sale. The goods were shipped to the store (FOB shipping point) for a cost of $200. Costs of $400 were incurred to buy the goods. What is the total cost of merchandise inventory?

a. $5,000
b. $5,200
c. $5,400
d. $5,600

QS 4-2
Identifying inventory costs
C2

Prepare journal entries to record each of the following purchases transactions of a merchandising company. Show supporting calculations and assume a perpetual inventory system.

Nov. 5   Purchased 600 units of product at a cost of $10 per unit. Terms of the sale are 2/10, n/60; the invoice is dated November 5.
Nov. 7   Returned 25 defective units from the November 5 purchase and received full credit.
Nov. 15   Paid the amount due from the November 5 purchase, less the return on November 7.

QS 4-3
Recording purchases—
perpetual system
P1

Prepare journal entries to record each of the following sales transactions of a merchandising company. Show supporting calculations and assume a perpetual inventory system.

Apr. 1   Sold merchandise for $3,000, granting the customer terms of 2/10, EOM; invoice dated April 1. The cost of the merchandise is $1,800.
Apr. 4   The customer in the April 1 sale returned merchandise and received credit for $600. The merchandise, which had cost $360, is returned to inventory.
Apr. 11   Received payment for the amount due from the April 1 sale less the return on April 4.

QS 4-4
Recording sales—
perpetual system
P2

QS 4-5

Computing and analyzing gross margin

A2

Compute net sales, gross profit, and the gross margin ratio for each separate case *a* through *d*. Interpret the gross margin ratio for case *a*.

	a	b	c	d
Sales	$150,000	$550,000	$38,700	$255,700
Sales discounts	5,000	17,500	600	4,800
Sales returns and allowances	20,000	6,000	5,100	900
Cost of goods sold	79,750	329,589	24,453	126,500

QS 4-6

Accounting for shrinkage— perpetual system

P3

Nix'It Company's ledger on July 31, its fiscal year-end, includes the following selected accounts that have normal balances (Nix'It uses the perpetual inventory system).

Merchandise inventory	$ 37,800	Sales returns and allowances	$ 6,500
Retained earnings	115,300	Cost of goods sold	105,000
Dividends	7,000	Depreciation expense	10,300
Sales	160,200	Salaries expense	32,500
Sales discounts	4,700	Miscellaneous expenses	5,000

A physical count of its July 31 year-end inventory discloses that the cost of the merchandise inventory still available is $35,900. Prepare the entry to record any inventory shrinkage.

QS 4-7

Closing entries   P3

Refer to QS 4-6 and prepare journal entries to close the balances in temporary revenue and expense accounts. Remember to consider the entry for shrinkage that is made to solve QS 4-6.

QS 4-8

Computing and interpreting acid-test ratio

A1

Use the following information on current assets and current liabilities to compute and interpret the acid-test ratio. Explain what the acid-test ratio of a company measures.

Cash	$1,490	Prepaid expenses	$ 700
Accounts receivable	2,800	Accounts payable	5,750
Inventory	6,000	Other current liabilities	850

QS 4-9

Contrasting liquidity ratios   A1

Identify similarities and differences between the acid-test ratio and the current ratio. Compare and describe how the two ratios reflect a company's ability to meet its current obligations.

QS 4-10

Multiple-step income statement

P4

For each item below indicate whether the statement describes a multiple-step income statement or a single-step income statement.

a. Multiple-step income statement   **b.** Single-step income statement

_____ **1.** Shows detailed computations of net sales and other costs and expenses.

_____ **2.** Statement limited to two main categories (revenues and expenses).

_____ **3.** Reports gross profit as a separate line item.

_____ **4.** Reports net income equal to income from operations adjusted for any nonoperating items.

QS 4-11[A]

Contrasting periodic and perpetual systems

P5

Identify whether each description best applies to a periodic or a perpetual inventory system.

a. Updates the inventory account only at period-end.

b. Requires an adjusting entry to record inventory shrinkage.

c. Markedly increased in frequency and popularity in business within the past decade.

d. Records cost of goods sold each time a sales transaction occurs.

e. Provides more timely information to managers.

QS 4-12[A]

Recording purchases— periodic system   P5

Refer to QS 4-3 and prepare journal entries to record each of the merchandising transactions assuming that the periodic inventory system is used.

Refer to QS 4-4 and prepare journal entries to record each of the merchandising transactions assuming that the periodic inventory system is used.

QS 4-13[A]

Recording purchases—
periodic system   P5

Income statement information for adidas Group, a German footwear, apparel, and accessories manufacturer, for the year ended December 31, 2011, follows. The company applies IFRS, as adopted by the European Union, and reports its results in millions of Euros. Prepare its calendar year 2011 (1) multiple-step income statement and (2) single-step income statement.

QS 4-14

IFRS income statement
presentation

P4

Net income	€ 670
Financial income	31
Financial expenses	115
Operating profit	1,011
Cost of sales	7,000
Income taxes	257
Income before taxes	927
Gross profit	6,344
Royalty and commission income	93
Other operating income	98
Other operating expenses	5,524
Net sales	13,344

Answer each of the following questions related to international accounting standards.

a. Explain how the accounting for merchandise purchases and sales is different between accounting under IFRS versus U.S. GAAP.

b. Income statements prepared under IFRS usually report an item titled *finance costs*. What do finance costs refer to?

c. U.S. GAAP prohibits alternative measures of income reported on the income statement. Does IFRS permit such alternative measures on the income statement?

QS 4-15

International accounting
standards

C1

On August 1, Gilmore Company purchased merchandise from Hendren with an invoice price of $60,000 and credit terms of 2/10, n/30. Gilmore Company paid Hendren on August 11. Prepare any required journal entry(ies) for Gilmore Company (the purchaser) on: (*a*) August 1, and (*b*) August 11. Assume Gilmore uses the perpetual inventory method.

QS 4-16

Recording discounts
taken—perpetual   P1

On September 15, Krug Company purchased merchandise inventory from Makarov with an invoice price of $35,000 and credit terms of 2/10, n/30. Krug Company paid Makarov on September 28. Prepare any required journal entry(ies) for Krug Company (the purchaser) on: (*a*) September 15, and (*b*) September 28. Assume Krug uses the perpetual inventory method.

QS 4-17

Recording discounts
missed—perpetual   P1

Use the following information (in random order) from a service company and from a merchandiser to compute net income. For the merchandiser, also compute gross profit, the goods available for sale, and the cost of goods sold. *Hint:* Not all information may be necessary.

QS 4-18

Merchandise equations
and flows

C2

Krug Service Company		Kleiner Merchandising Company	
Expenses	$ 8,500	Accumulated depreciation	$ 700
Revenues	14,000	Beginning inventory	5,000
Dividends	1,600	Common stock	50
Cash	700	Retained earnings	900
Prepaid rent	800	Ending inventory	1,700
Accounts payable	200	Operating expenses	1,450
Common stock	500	Purchases	3,900
Retained earnings	2,500	Sales	9,500
Equipment	1,300	Dividends	1,600

EXERCISES

Exercise 4-1

Operating cycle for merchandiser

C2

The operating cycle of a merchandiser with credit sales includes the following five activities. Starting with merchandise acquisition, identify the chronological order of these five activities.

a. _____ inventory made available for sale.

b. _____ cash collections from customers.

c. _____ credit sales to customers.

d. _____ purchases of merchandise.

e. _____ accounts receivable accounted for.

Exercise 4-2

Recording entries for merchandise purchases

P1

Prepare journal entries to record the following transactions for a retail store. Assume a perpetual inventory system.

Apr. 2 Purchased merchandise from Lyon Company under the following terms: $4,600 price, invoice dated April 2, credit terms of 2/15, n/60, and FOB shipping point.

       3 Paid $300 for shipping charges on the April 2 purchase.

       4 Returned to Lyon Company unacceptable merchandise that had an invoice price of $600.

      17 Sent a check to Lyon Company for the April 2 purchase, net of the discount and the returned merchandise.

      18 Purchased merchandise from Frist Corp. under the following terms: $8,500 price, invoice dated April 18, credit terms of 2/10, n/30, and FOB destination.

      21 After negotiations, received from Frist a $1,100 allowance on the April 18 purchase.

      28 Sent check to Frist paying for the April 18 purchase, net of the discount and allowance.

Check   April 28, Cr. Cash $7,252

Exercise 4-3

Analyzing and recording merchandise transactions— both buyer and seller

P1 P2

Santa Fe Company purchased merchandise for resale from Mesa Company with an invoice price of $24,000 and credit terms of 3/10, n/60. The merchandise had cost Mesa $16,000. Santa Fe paid within the discount period. Assume that both buyer and seller use a perpetual inventory system.

1. Prepare entries that the buyer should record for (*a*) the purchase and (*b*) the cash payment.

2. Prepare entries that the seller should record for (*a*) the sale and (*b*) the cash collection.

3. Assume that the buyer borrowed enough cash to pay the balance on the last day of the discount period at an annual interest rate of 8% and paid it back on the last day of the credit period. Compute how much the buyer saved by following this strategy. (Assume a 365-day year and round dollar amounts to the nearest cent, including computation of interest per day.)

Check   (3) $465 savings

Exercise 4-4

Recording sales returns and allowances   P2

Allied Parts was organized on May 1, 2013, and made its first purchase of merchandise on May 3. The purchase was for 2,000 units at a price of $10 per unit. On May 5, Allied Parts sold 1,500 of the units for $14 per unit to Baker Co. Terms of the sale were 2/10, n/60. Prepare entries for Allied Parts to record the May 5 sale and each of the following separate transactions *a* through *c* using a perpetual inventory system.

a. On May 7, Baker returns 200 units because they did not fit the customer's needs. Allied Parts restores the units to its inventory.

b. On May 8, Baker discovers that 300 units are damaged but are still of some use and, therefore, keeps the units. Allied Parts sends Baker a credit memorandum for $600 to compensate for the damage.

Check   (c) Dr. Merchandise Inventory $400

c. On May 15, Baker discovers that 100 units are the wrong color. Baker keeps 60 of these units because Allied Parts sends a $120 credit memorandum to compensate. Baker returns the remaining 40 units to Allied Parts. Allied Parts restores the 40 returned units to its inventory.

Exercise 4-5

Recording purchase returns and allowances   P1

Refer to Exercise 4-4 and prepare the appropriate journal entries for Baker Co. to record the May 5 purchase and each of the three separate transactions *a* through *c*. Baker is a retailer that uses a perpetual inventory system and purchases these units for resale.

Exercise 4-6

Sales returns and allowances

C1

Business decision makers desire information on sales returns and allowances. (1) Explain why a company's manager wants the accounting system to record customers' returns of unsatisfactory goods in the Sales Returns and Allowances account instead of the Sales account. (2) Explain whether this information would be useful for external decision makers.

Exercise 4-7

Analyzing and recording merchandise transactions— both buyer and seller   P1 P2

On May 11, Sydney Co. accepts delivery of $40,000 of merchandise it purchases for resale from Troy Corporation. With the merchandise is an invoice dated May 11, with terms of 3/10, n/90, FOB shipping point. The goods cost Troy $30,000. When the goods are delivered, Sydney pays $345 to Express Shipping for delivery charges on the merchandise. On May 12, Sydney returns $1,400 of goods to Troy, who receives them one day later and restores them to inventory. The returned goods had cost Troy $800. On May 20, Sydney mails a check to Troy Corporation for the amount owed. Troy receives it the following day. (Both Sydney and Troy use a perpetual inventory system.)

1. Prepare journal entries that Sydney Co. records for these transactions.

2. Prepare journal entries that Troy Corporation records for these transactions.

Check (1) May 20, Cr. Cash $37,442

The following supplementary records summarize Tosca Company's merchandising activities for year 2013. Set up T-accounts for Merchandise Inventory and Cost of Goods Sold. Then record the summarized activities in those T-accounts and compute account balances.

Exercise 4-8
Recording effects of merchandising activities
P1 P2

Cost of merchandise sold to customers in sales transactions	$196,000
Merchandise inventory, December 31, 2012	25,000
Invoice cost of merchandise purchases	192,500
Shrinkage determined on December 31, 2013	800
Cost of transportation-in	2,900
Cost of merchandise returned by customers and restored to inventory	2,100
Purchase discounts received	1,700
Purchase returns and allowances	4,000

Check Year-End Merchandise Inventory Dec. 31, $20,000

The following list includes selected permanent accounts and all of the temporary accounts from the December 31, 2013, unadjusted trial balance of Emiko Co., a business owned by Kumi Emiko. Use these account balances along with the additional information to journalize (*a*) adjusting entries and (*b*) closing entries. Emiko Co. uses a perpetual inventory system.

Exercise 4-9
Preparing adjusting and closing entries for a merchandiser
P3

	Debit	Credit
Merchandise inventory	$ 30,000	
Prepaid selling expenses	5,600	
Dividends	33,000	
Sales		$529,000
Sales returns and allowances	17,500	
Sales discounts	5,000	
Cost of goods sold	212,000	
Sales salaries expense	48,000	
Utilities expense	15,000	
Selling expenses	36,000	
Administrative expenses	105,000	

Additional Information

Accrued sales salaries amount to $1,700. Prepaid selling expenses of $3,000 have expired. A physical count of year-end merchandise inventory shows $28,450 of goods still available.

Check Entry to close Income Summary: Cr. Retained Earnings $84,250

Using your accounting knowledge, fill in the blanks in the following separate income statements *a* through *e*. Identify any negative amount by putting it in parentheses.

Exercise 4-10
Computing revenues, expenses, and income
C1 C2

	a	b	c	d	e
Sales	$62,000	$43,500	$46,000	$?	$25,600
Cost of goods sold					
Merchandise inventory (beginning)	8,000	17,050	7,500	8,000	4,560
Total cost of merchandise purchases	38,000	?	?	32,000	6,600
Merchandise inventory (ending)	?	(3,000)	(9,000)	(6,600)	?
Cost of goods sold	34,050	16,000	?	?	7,000
Gross profit	?	?	3,750	45,600	?
Expenses	10,000	10,650	12,150	3,600	6,000
Net income (loss)	$?	$16,850	$ (8,400)	$42,000	$?

Exercise 4-11

Interpreting a physical count
error as inventory shrinkage

A1

A retail company recently completed a physical count of ending merchandise inventory to use in preparing adjusting entries. In determining the cost of the counted inventory, company employees failed to consider that $3,000 of incoming goods had been shipped by a supplier on December 31 under an FOB shipping point agreement. These goods had been recorded in Merchandise Inventory as a purchase, but they were not included in the physical count because they were in transit. Explain how this overlooked fact affects the company's financial statements and the following ratios: return on assets, debt ratio, current ratio, and acid-test ratio.

Exercise 4-12

Physical count error and profits

A2

Refer to the information in Exercise 4-11 and explain how the error in the physical count affects the company's gross margin ratio and its profit margin ratio.

Exercise 4-13

Computing and analyzing
acid-test and current ratios

A1

Compute the current ratio and acid-test ratio for each of the following separate cases. (Round ratios to two decimals.) Which company case is in the best position to meet short-term obligations? Explain.

	Case X	Case Y	Case Z
Cash......................	$2,000	$ 110	$1,000
Short-term investments	0	0	600
Current receivables	350	590	700
Inventory	2,650	2,300	4,100
Prepaid expenses	200	500	900
Total current assets	$5,200	$3,500	$7,300
Current liabilities	$2,200	$1,200	$3,750

Exercise 4-14

Preparing journal entries—
perpetual system

P1 P2

Journalize the following merchandising transactions for Chilton Systems assuming it uses a perpetual inventory system.

1. On November 1, Chilton Systems purchases merchandise for $1,500 on credit with terms of 2/5, n/30, FOB shipping point; invoice dated November 1.
2. On November 5, Chilton Systems pays cash for the November 1 purchase.
3. On November 7, Chilton Systems discovers and returns $200 of defective merchandise purchased on November 1 for a cash refund.
4. On November 10, Chilton Systems pays $90 cash for transportation costs with the November 1 purchase.
5. On November 13, Chilton Systems sells merchandise for $1,600 on credit. The cost of the merchandise is $800.
6. On November 16, the customer returns merchandise from the November 13 transaction. The returned items are priced at $300 and cost $130; the items were not damaged and were returned to inventory.

Exercise 4-15

Multiple-step income statement

P4

A company reports the following sales related information: Sales (gross) of $200,000; Sales discounts of $4,000; Sales returns and allowances of $16,000; Sales salaries expense of $10,000. Prepare the net sales portion only of this company's multiple-step income statement.

Exercise 4-16[A]

Recording purchases—
periodic system   P5

Refer to Exercise 4-2 and prepare journal entries to record each of the merchandising transactions assuming that the periodic inventory system is used.

Exercise 4-17[A]

Recording purchases and sales—
periodic system   P5

Refer to Exercise 4-3 and prepare journal entries to record each of the merchandising transactions assuming that the periodic inventory system is used by both the buyer and the seller. (Skip the part 3 requirement.)

Exercise 4-18[A]

Buyer and seller transactions—
periodic system   P5

Refer to Exercise 4-7 and prepare journal entries to record each of the merchandising transactions assuming that the periodic inventory system is used by both the buyer and the seller.

Exercise 4-19[A]

Recording purchases—
periodic system   P5

Refer to Exercise 4-14 and prepare journal entries to record each of the merchandising transactions assuming that the periodic inventory system is used.

L'Oréal reports the following income statement accounts for the year ended December 31, 2011 (euros in millions). Prepare the income statement for this company for the year ended December 31, 2011, following usual IFRS practices.

Exercise 4-20
Preparing an income statement following IFRS

P4

Net profit	€ 2,440.9	Income tax expense	€1,025.8
Finance costs	19.6	Profit before tax expense	3,466.7
Net sales	20,343.1	Research and development expense	720.5
Gross profit	14,491.6	Selling, general and administrative expense	4,186.9
Other income	193.7	Advertising and promotion expense	6,291.6
Cost of sales	5,851.5		

connect

Prepare journal entries to record the following merchandising transactions of Blink Company, which applies the perpetual inventory system. (*Hint:* It will help to identify each receivable and payable; for example, record the purchase on July 1 in Accounts Payable—Boden.)

July 1 Purchased merchandise from Boden Company for $6,000 under credit terms of 1/15, n/30, FOB shipping point, invoice dated July 1.

2 Sold merchandise to Creek Co. for $900 under credit terms of 2/10, n/60, FOB shipping point, invoice dated July 2. The merchandise had cost $500.

3 Paid $125 cash for freight charges on the purchase of July 1.

8 Sold merchandise that had cost $1,300 for $1,700 cash.

9 Purchased merchandise from Leight Co. for $2,200 under credit terms of 2/15, n/60, FOB destination, invoice dated July 9.

11 Received a $200 credit memorandum from Leight Co. for the return of part of the merchandise purchased on July 9.

12 Received the balance due from Creek Co. for the invoice dated July 2, net of the discount.

16 Paid the balance due to Boden Company within the discount period.

19 Sold merchandise that cost $800 to Art Co. for $1,200 under credit terms of 2/15, n/60, FOB shipping point, invoice dated July 19.

21 Issued a $200 credit memorandum to Art Co. for an allowance on goods sold on July 19.

24 Paid Leight Co. the balance due after deducting the discount.

30 Received the balance due from Art Co. for the invoice dated July 19, net of discount.

31 Sold merchandise that cost $4,800 to Creek Co. for $7,000 under credit terms of 2/10, n/60, FOB shipping point, invoice dated July 31.

PROBLEM SET A

Problem 4-1A
Preparing journal entries for merchandising activities—perpetual system

P1 P2

Check July 12, Dr. Cash $882
July 16, Cr. Cash $5,940

July 24, Cr. Cash $1,960
July 30, Dr. Cash $980

Prepare journal entries to record the following merchandising transactions of Sheng Company, which applies the perpetual inventory system. (*Hint:* It will help to identify each receivable and payable; for example, record the purchase on August 1 in Accounts Payable—Arotek.)

Aug. 1 Purchased merchandise from Arotek Company for $7,500 under credit terms of 1/10, n/30, FOB destination, invoice dated August 1.

5 Sold merchandise to Laird Corp. for $5,200 under credit terms of 2/10, n/60, FOB destination, invoice dated August 5. The merchandise had cost $4,000.

8 Purchased merchandise from Waters Corporation for $5,400 under credit terms of 1/10, n/45, FOB shipping point, invoice dated August 8. The invoice showed that at Sheng's request, Waters paid the $140 shipping charges and added that amount to the bill. (*Hint:* Discounts are not applied to freight and shipping charges.)

9 Paid $125 cash for shipping charges related to the August 5 sale to Laird Corp.

10 Laird returned merchandise from the August 5 sale that had cost Sheng $400 and been sold for $600. The merchandise was restored to inventory.

12 After negotiations with Waters Corporation concerning problems with the merchandise purchased on August 8, Sheng received a credit memorandum from Waters granting a price reduction of $700.

14 At Arotek's request, Sheng paid $200 cash for freight charges on the August 1 purchase, reducing the amount owed to Arotek.

Problem 4-2A
Preparing journal entries for merchandising activities—perpetual system

P1 P2

Check Aug. 9, Dr. Delivery Expense, $125

Aug. 18, Cr. Cash $4,793

15   Received balance due from Laird Corp. for the August 5 sale less the return on August 10.
18   Paid the amount due Waters Corporation for the August 8 purchase less the price reduction granted.
19   Sold merchandise to Tux Co. for $4,800 under credit terms of 1/10, n/30, FOB shipping point, invoice dated August 19. The merchandise had cost $2,400.
22   Tux requested a price reduction on the August 19 sale because the merchandise did not meet specifications. Sheng sent Tux a $500 credit memorandum to resolve the issue.

Aug. 29, Dr. Cash $4,257

29   Received Tux's cash payment for the amount due from the August 19 sale.
30   Paid Arotek Company the amount due from the August 1 purchase.

Problem 4-3A
Preparing adjusting entries and income statements; and computing gross margin, acid-test, and current ratios

A1   A2   P3   P4

The following unadjusted trial balance is prepared at fiscal year-end for Nelson Company.

NELSON COMPANY
Unadjusted Trial Balance
January 31, 2013

	Debit	Credit
Cash	$ 1,000	
Merchandise inventory	12,500	
Store supplies	5,800	
Prepaid insurance	2,400	
Store equipment	42,900	
Accumulated depreciation—Store equipment		$ 15,250
Accounts payable		10,000
Common stock		5,000
Retained earnings		27,000
Dividends	2,200	
Sales		111,950
Sales discounts	2,000	
Sales returns and allowances	2,200	
Cost of goods sold	38,400	
Depreciation expense—Store equipment	0	
Salaries expense	35,000	
Insurance expense	0	
Rent expense	15,000	
Store supplies expense	0	
Advertising expense	9,800	
Totals	$169,200	$169,200

Rent expense and salaries expense are equally divided between selling activities and the general and administrative activities. Nelson Company uses a perpetual inventory system.

Required

1. Prepare adjusting journal entries to reflect each of the following:
   a. Store supplies still available at fiscal year-end amount to $1,750.
   b. Expired insurance, an administrative expense, for the fiscal year is $1,400.
   c. Depreciation expense on store equipment, a selling expense, is $1,525 for the fiscal year.
   d. To estimate shrinkage, a physical count of ending merchandise inventory is taken. It shows $10,900 of inventory is still available at fiscal year-end.

Check (2) Gross profit, $67,750; (3) Total expenses, $106,775; Net income, $975

2. Prepare a multiple-step income statement for fiscal year 2013.
3. Prepare a single-step income statement for fiscal year 2013.
4. Compute the current ratio, acid-test ratio, and gross margin ratio as of January 31, 2013. (Round ratios to two decimals.)

Valley Company's adjusted trial balance on August 31, 2013, its fiscal year-end, follows.

	Debit	Credit
Merchandise inventory	$ 41,000	
Other (noninventory) assets	130,400	
Total liabilities		$ 25,000
Common stock		10,000
Retained earnings.		94,550
Dividends	8,000	
Sales		225,600
Sales discounts	2,250	
Sales returns and allowances	12,000	
Cost of goods sold	74,500	
Sales salaries expense	32,000	
Rent expense—Selling space	8,000	
Store supplies expense	1,500	
Advertising expense	13,000	
Office salaries expense	28,500	
Rent expense—Office space	3,600	
Office supplies expense	400	
Totals	$355,150	$355,150

On August 31, 2012, merchandise inventory was $25,400. Supplementary records of merchandising activities for the year ended August 31, 2013, reveal the following itemized costs.

Invoice cost of merchandise purchases	$92,000
Purchase discounts received	2,000
Purchase returns and allowances	4,500
Costs of transportation-in	4,600

Required

1. Compute the company's net sales for the year.
2. Compute the company's total cost of merchandise purchased for the year.
3. Prepare a multiple-step income statement that includes separate categories for selling expenses and for general and administrative expenses.
4. Prepare a single-step income statement that includes these expense categories: cost of goods sold, selling expenses, and general and administrative expenses.

Use the data for Valley Company in Problem 4-4A to complete the following requirements.

Problem 4-5A
Preparing closing entries and
interpreting information about
discounts and returns

C2 P3

Required

1. Prepare closing entries as of August 31, 2013 (the perpetual inventory system is used).

Analysis Component

2. The company makes all purchases on credit, and its suppliers uniformly offer a 3% sales discount. Does it appear that the company's cash management system is accomplishing the goal of taking all available discounts? Explain.

3. In prior years, the company experienced a 4% returns and allowance rate on its sales, which means approximately 4% of its gross sales were eventually returned outright or caused the company to grant allowances to customers. How do this year's results compare to prior years' results?

Problem 4-6A[B]
Preparing a work sheet for
a merchandiser
P3

Refer to the data and information in Problem 4-3A.

Required

Prepare and complete the entire 10-column work sheet for Nelson Company. Follow the structure of Exhibit 4B.1 in Appendix 4B.

PROBLEM SET B

Problem 4-1B
Preparing journal entries for
merchandising activities—
perpetual system
P1 P2

Prepare journal entries to record the following merchandising transactions of Yarvelle Company, which applies the perpetual inventory system. (*Hint:* It will help to identify each receivable and payable; for example, record the purchase on May 2 in Accounts Payable—Havel.)

May 2 Purchased merchandise from Havel Co. for $10,000 under credit terms of 1/15, n/30, FOB shipping point, invoice dated May 2.
4 Sold merchandise to Heather Co. for $11,000 under credit terms of 2/10, n/60, FOB shipping point, invoice dated May 4. The merchandise had cost $5,600.
5 Paid $250 cash for freight charges on the purchase of May 2.
9 Sold merchandise that had cost $2,000 for $2,500 cash.
10 Purchased merchandise from Duke Co. for $3,650 under credit terms of 2/15, n/60, FOB destination, invoice dated May 10.
12 Received a $400 credit memorandum from Duke Co. for the return of part of the merchandise purchased on May 10.
14 Received the balance due from Heather Co. for the invoice dated May 4, net of the discount.
17 Paid the balance due to Havel Co. within the discount period.
20 Sold merchandise that cost $1,450 to Tameron Co. for $2,800 under credit terms of 2/15, n/60, FOB shipping point, invoice dated May 20.
22 Issued a $400 credit memorandum to Tameron Co. for an allowance on goods sold from May 20.
25 Paid Duke Co. the balance due after deducting the discount.
30 Received the balance due from Tameron Co. for the invoice dated May 20, net of discount and allowance.
31 Sold merchandise that cost $3,600 to Heather Co. for $7,200 under credit terms of 2/10, n/60, FOB shipping point, invoice dated May 31.

Check May 14, Dr. Cash $10,780
May 17, Cr. Cash $9,900

May 30, Dr. Cash $2,352

Problem 4-2B
Preparing journal entries for
merchandising activities—
perpetual system
P1 P2

Prepare journal entries to record the following merchandising transactions of Mason Company, which applies the perpetual inventory system. (*Hint:* It will help to identify each receivable and payable; for example, record the purchase on July 3 in Accounts Payable—OLB.)

July 3 Purchased merchandise from OLB Corp. for $15,000 under credit terms of 1/10, n/30, FOB destination, invoice dated July 3.
7 Sold merchandise to Brill Co. for $11,500 under credit terms of 2/10, n/60, FOB destination, invoice dated July 7. The merchandise had cost $7,750.
10 Purchased merchandise from Rupert Corporation for $14,200 under credit terms of 1/10, n/45, FOB shipping point, invoice dated July 10. The invoice showed that at Mason's request, Rupert paid the $500 shipping charges and added that amount to the bill. (*Hint:* Discounts are not applied to freight and shipping charges.)
11 Paid $300 cash for shipping charges related to the July 7 sale to Brill Co.
12 Brill returned merchandise from the July 7 sale that had cost Mason $1,450 and been sold for $1,850. The merchandise was restored to inventory.
14 After negotiations with Rupert Corporation concerning problems with the merchandise purchased on July 10, Mason received a credit memorandum from Rupert granting a price reduction of $2,000.
15 At OLB's request, Mason paid $150 cash for freight charges on the July 3 purchase, reducing the amount owed to OLB.
17 Received balance due from Brill Co. for the July 7 sale less the return on July 12.
20 Paid the amount due Rupert Corporation for the July 10 purchase less the price reduction granted.
21 Sold merchandise to Brown for $11,000 under credit terms of 1/10, n/30, FOB shipping point, invoice dated July 21. The merchandise had cost $7,000.
24 Brown requested a price reduction on the July 21 sale because the merchandise did not meet specifications. Mason sent Brown a credit memorandum for $1,300 to resolve the issue.
30 Received Brown's cash payment for the amount due from the July 21 sale.
31 Paid OLB Corp. the amount due from the July 3 purchase.

Check July 17, Dr. Cash $9,457
July 20, Cr. Cash $12,578

July 30, Dr. Cash $9,603

The following unadjusted trial balance is prepared at fiscal year-end for Foster Products Company.

Problem 4-3B
Preparing adjusting entries
and income statements; and
computing gross margin,
acid-test, and current ratios

A1 A2 P3 P4

	File Edit View Insert Format Tools Data Accounting Window Help	_ |_| x|
	□ ☞ ■ ⬛ ⬛ ❤ ⟋ ⟋ ⬛ ⬛ Σ ʄ ₂↓ ₂↓ ⬛ ⬛ ⬛ 100% ▾ ⬛ ‖ Arial ▾ 10 ▾ B I U $ % , ⁺⁸ ⁺⁹	

	FOSTER PRODUCTS COMPANY Unadjusted Trial Balance October 31, 2013		
1		**Debit**	**Credit**
2	Cash	$ 7,400	
3	Merchandise inventory	24,000	
4	Store supplies	9,700	
5	Prepaid insurance	6,600	
6	Store equipment	81,800	
7	Accumulated depreciation—Store equipment		$ 32,000
8	Accounts payable		18,000
9	Common stock		3,000
10	Retained earnings		40,000
11	Dividends	2,000	
12	Sales		227,100
13	Sales discounts	1,000	
14	Sales returns and allowances	5,000	
15	Cost of goods sold	75,800	
16	Depreciation expense—Store equipment	0	
17	Salaries expense	63,000	
18	Insurance expense	0	
19	Rent expense	26,000	
20	Store supplies expense	0	
21	Advertising expense	17,800	
22	Totals	$320,100	$320,100
23			
	Sheet1 ⟋ Sheet2 ⟋ Sheet3 ⟋	‖◄‖ ►‖	

Rent expense and salaries expense are equally divided between selling activities and the general and administrative activities. Foster Products Company uses a perpetual inventory system.

Required

1. Prepare adjusting journal entries to reflect each of the following.
  a. Store supplies still available at fiscal year-end amount to $3,700.
  b. Expired insurance, an administrative expense, for the fiscal year is $2,800.
  c. Depreciation expense on store equipment, a selling expense, is $3,000 for the fiscal year.
  d. To estimate shrinkage, a physical count of ending merchandise inventory is taken. It shows $21,300 of inventory is still available at fiscal year-end.
2. Prepare a multiple-step income statement for fiscal year 2013.
3. Prepare a single-step income statement for fiscal year 2013.
4. Compute the current ratio, acid-test ratio, and gross margin ratio as of October 31, 2013. (Round ratios to two decimals.)

Check (2) Gross profit, $142,600;
(3) Total expenses, $197,100;
Net income, $24,000

Barkley Company's adjusted trial balance on March 31, 2013, its fiscal year-end, follows.

Problem 4-4B
Computing merchandising
amounts and formatting
income statements

C1 C2 P4

	Debit	Credit
Merchandise inventory	$ 56,500	
Other (noninventory) assets	202,600	
Total liabilities		$ 42,500
Common stock		10,000
Retained earnings.		154,425

[continued on next page]

[continued from previous page]

Dividends	3,000	
Sales		332,650
Sales discounts	5,875	
Sales returns and allowances	20,000	
Cost of goods sold	115,600	
Sales salaries expense	44,500	
Rent expense—Selling space	16,000	
Store supplies expense	3,850	
Advertising expense	26,000	
Office salaries expense	40,750	
Rent expense—Office space	3,800	
Office supplies expense	1,100	
Totals	$539,575	$539,575

On March 31, 2012, merchandise inventory was $37,500. Supplementary records of merchandising activities for the year ended March 31, 2013, reveal the following itemized costs.

Invoice cost of merchandise purchases	$138,500
Purchase discounts received	2,950
Purchase returns and allowances	6,700
Costs of transportation-in	5,750

Required

1. Calculate the company's net sales for the year.

Check   (2) $134,600;

2. Calculate the company's total cost of merchandise purchased for the year.

(3) Gross profit, $191,175;
Net income, $55,175;

(4) Total expenses, $251,600

3. Prepare a multiple-step income statement that includes separate categories for selling expenses and for general and administrative expenses.

4. Prepare a single-step income statement that includes these expense categories: cost of goods sold, selling expenses, and general and administrative expenses.

Problem 4-5B

Preparing closing entries and interpreting information about discounts and returns

C2 P3

Check   (1) $55,175 Dr. to close
Income Summary

(3) Current-year rate, 6.0%

Use the data for Barkley Company in Problem 4-4B to complete the following requirements.

Required

1. Prepare closing entries as of March 31, 2013 (the perpetual inventory system is used).

Analysis Component

2. The company makes all purchases on credit, and its suppliers uniformly offer a 3% sales discount. Does it appear that the company's cash management system is accomplishing the goal of taking all available discounts? Explain.

3. In prior years, the company experienced a 5% returns and allowance rate on its sales, which means approximately 5% of its gross sales were eventually returned outright or caused the company to grant allowances to customers. How do this year's results compare to prior years' results?

Problem 4-6B[B]

Preparing a work sheet for a merchandiser

P3

Refer to the data and information in Problem 4-3B.

Required

Prepare and complete the entire 10-column work sheet for Foster Products Company. Follow the structure of Exhibit 4B.1 in Appendix 4B.

(This serial problem began in Chapter 1 and continues through most of the book. If previous chapter segments were not completed, the serial problem can begin at this point. It is helpful, but not necessary, to use the Working Papers that accompany the book.)

SP 4 Adria Lopez created Success Systems on October 1, 2013. The company has been successful, and its list of customers has grown. To accommodate the growth, the accounting system is modified to set up separate accounts for each customer. The following chart of accounts includes the account number used for each account and any balance as of December 31, 2013. Adria Lopez decided to add a fourth digit with a decimal point to the 106 account number that had been used for the single Accounts Receivable account. This change allows the company to continue using the existing chart of accounts.

No.	Account Title	Dr.	Cr.
101	Cash	$58,160	
106.1	Alex's Engineering Co.	0	
106.2	Wildcat Services	0	
106.3	Easy Leasing	0	
106.4	IFM Co.	3,000	
106.5	Liu Corp.	0	
106.6	Gomez Co.	2,668	
106.7	Delta Co.	0	
106.8	KC, Inc.	0	
106.9	Dream, Inc.	0	
119	Merchandise inventory	0	
126	Computer supplies	580	
128	Prepaid insurance	1,665	
131	Prepaid rent	825	
163	Office equipment	8,000	
164	Accumulated depreciation—Office equipment		$ 400
167	Computer equipment	20,000	
168	Accumulated depreciation—Computer equipment		1,250
201	Accounts payable		1,100

No.	Account Title	Dr.	Cr.
210	Wages payable		$ 500
236	Unearned computer services revenue		1,500
307	Common stock		83,000
318	Retained earnings		7,148
319	Dividends	$0	
403	Computer services revenue		0
413	Sales		0
414	Sales returns and allowances	0	
415	Sales discounts	0	
502	Cost of goods sold	0	
612	Depreciation expense—Office equipment	0	
613	Depreciation expense—Computer equipment	0	
623	Wages expense	0	
637	Insurance expense	0	
640	Rent expense	0	
652	Computer supplies expense	0	
655	Advertising expense	0	
676	Mileage expense	0	
677	Miscellaneous expenses	0	
684	Repairs expense—Computer	0	

In response to requests from customers, A. Lopez will begin selling computer software. The company will extend credit terms of 1/10, n/30, FOB shipping point, to all customers who purchase this merchandise. However, no cash discount is available on consulting fees. Additional accounts (Nos. 119, 413, 414, 415, and 502) are added to its general ledger to accommodate the company's new merchandising activities. Also, Success Systems does not use reversing entries and, therefore, all revenue and expense accounts have zero beginning balances as of January 1, 2014. Its transactions for January through March follow:

Jan. 4 The company paid cash to Lyn Addie for five days' work at the rate of $125 per day. Four of the five days relate to wages payable that were accrued in the prior year.
 5 Adria Lopez invested an additional $25,000 cash in the company in exchange for more common stock.
 7 The company purchased $5,800 of merchandise from Kansas Corp. with terms of 1/10, n/30, FOB shipping point, invoice dated January 7.
 9 The company received $2,668 cash from Gomez Co. as full payment on its account.
 11 The company completed a five-day project for Alex's Engineering Co. and billed it $5,500, which is the total price of $7,000 less the advance payment of $1,500.
 13 The company sold merchandise with a retail value of $5,200 and a cost of $3,560 to Liu Corp., invoice dated January 13.
 15 The company paid $600 cash for freight charges on the merchandise purchased on January 7.
 16 The company received $4,000 cash from Delta Co. for computer services provided.
 17 The company paid Kansas Corp. for the invoice dated January 7, net of the discount.
 20 Liu Corp. returned $500 of defective merchandise from its invoice dated January 13. The returned merchandise, which had a $320 cost, is discarded. (The policy of Success Systems is to leave the cost of defective products in cost of goods sold.)

Check Jan. 11, Dr. Unearned Computer Services Revenue $1,500

Check Jan. 20, No entry to Cost of Goods Sold

	22	The company received the balance due from Liu Corp., net of both the discount and the credit for the returned merchandise.

22   The company received the balance due from Liu Corp., net of both the discount and the credit for the returned merchandise.

24   The company returned defective merchandise to Kansas Corp. and accepted a credit against future purchases. The defective merchandise invoice cost, net of the discount, was $496.

26   The company purchased $9,000 of merchandise from Kansas Corp. with terms of 1/10, n/30, FOB destination, invoice dated January 26.

26   The company sold merchandise with a $4,640 cost for $5,800 on credit to KC, Inc., invoice dated January 26.

31   The company paid cash to Lyn Addie for 10 days' work at $125 per day.

Feb. 1   The company paid $2,475 cash to Hillside Mall for another three months' rent in advance.

3   The company paid Kansas Corp. for the balance due, net of the cash discount, less the $496 amount in the credit memorandum.

5   The company paid $600 cash to the local newspaper for an advertising insert in today's paper.

11   The company received the balance due from Alex's Engineering Co. for fees billed on January 11.

15   The company paid $4,800 cash for dividends.

23   The company sold merchandise with a $2,660 cost for $3,220 on credit to Delta Co., invoice dated February 23.

26   The company paid cash to Lyn Addie for eight days' work at $125 per day.

27   The company reimbursed Adria Lopez for business automobile mileage (600 miles at $0.32 per mile).

Mar. 8   The company purchased $2,730 of computer supplies from Harris Office Products on credit, invoice dated March 8.

9   The company received the balance due from Delta Co. for merchandise sold on February 23.

11   The company paid $960 cash for minor repairs to the company's computer.

16   The company received $5,260 cash from Dream, Inc., for computing services provided.

19   The company paid the full amount due to Harris Office Products, consisting of amounts created on December 15 (of $1,100) and March 8.

24   The company billed Easy Leasing for $8,900 of computing services provided.

25   The company sold merchandise with a $2,002 cost for $2,800 on credit to Wildcat Services, invoice dated March 25.

30   The company sold merchandise with a $1,100 cost for $2,220 on credit to IFM Company, invoice dated March 30.

31   The company reimbursed Adria Lopez for business automobile mileage (400 miles at $0.32 per mile).

The following additional facts are available for preparing adjustments on March 31 prior to financial statement preparation:

a. The March 31 amount of computer supplies still available totals $2,005.

b. Three more months have expired since the company purchased its annual insurance policy at a $2,220 cost for 12 months of coverage.

c. Lyn Addie has not been paid for seven days of work at the rate of $125 per day.

d. Three months have passed since any prepaid rent has been transferred to expense. The monthly rent expense is $825.

e. Depreciation on the computer equipment for January 1 through March 31 is $1,250.

f. Depreciation on the office equipment for January 1 through March 31 is $400.

g. The March 31 amount of merchandise inventory still available totals $704.

Required

1. Prepare journal entries to record each of the January through March transactions.

2. Post the journal entries in part 1 to the accounts in the company's general ledger. (*Note:* Begin with the ledger's post-closing adjusted balances as of December 31, 2013.)

3. Prepare a partial work sheet consisting of the first six columns (similar to the one shown in Exhibit 4B.1) that includes the unadjusted trial balance, the March 31 adjustments (*a*) through (*g*), and the adjusted trial balance. Do not prepare closing entries and do not journalize the adjustments or post them to the ledger.

4. Prepare an income statement (from the adjusted trial balance in part 3) for the three months ended March 31, 2014. Use a single-step format. List all expenses without differentiating between selling expenses and general and administrative expenses.

5. Prepare a statement of retained earnings (from the adjusted trial balance in part 3) for the three months ended March 31, 2014.

6. Prepare a classified balance sheet (from the adjusted trial balance) as of March 31, 2014.

Check (2) Ending balances at March 31: Cash, $77,845; Sales, $19,240;

(3) Unadj. totals, $161,198; Adj. totals, $163,723;

(4) Net income, $18,686;

(6) Total assets, $129,909

The following General Ledger questions highlight the operating cycle of a merchandising company. In each case, the trial balance is automatically updated from the journal entries recorded. Three options exist for displaying the trial balance: unadjusted, adjusted, or post-closing.

GL 4-1 Refer to the merchandising transactions in Problem 4-1A to record the transactions, prepare a partial income statement, and determine the impact of each merchandising transaction on net income.

GL 4-2 Refer to the unadjusted trial balance in Problem 4-3A to prepare the necessary adjusting entries, a single-step and a multiple-step income statement, a classified balance sheet, and the closing entries for the merchandiser. Some key financial ratios are also computed.

Beyond the Numbers

BTN 4-1 Refer to Apple's financial statements in Appendix A to answer the following.

REPORTING IN ACTION

A1

APPLE

Required

1. Assume that the amounts reported for inventories and cost of sales reflect items purchased in a form ready for resale. Compute the net cost of goods purchased for the year ended September 29, 2012.
2. Compute the current ratio and acid-test ratio as of September 29, 2012 and September 24, 2011. Interpret and comment on the ratio results. How does Apple compare to the industry average of 1.5 for the current ratio and 1.25 for the acid-test ratio?

Fast Forward

3. Access Apple's financial statements (form 10-K) for fiscal years ending after September 29, 2012, from its Website (Apple.com) or the SEC's EDGAR database (www.SEC.gov). Recompute and interpret the current ratio and acid-test ratio for these current fiscal years.

BTN 4-2 Key comparative figures for both Apple and Google follow.

COMPARATIVE ANALYSIS

A2

APPLE
GOOGLE

($ millions)	Apple		Google	
	Current Year	Prior Year	Current Year	Prior Year
Net sales	$156,508	$108,249	$50,175	$37,905
Cost of sales	87,846	64,431	20,634	13,188

Required

1. Compute the dollar amount of gross margin and the gross margin ratio for the two years shown for each of these companies.
2. Which company earns more in gross margin for each dollar of net sales? How do they compare to the industry average of 45.0%?
3. Did the gross margin ratio improve or decline for these companies?

BTN 4-3 Amy Martin is a student who plans to attend approximately four professional events a year at her college. Each event necessitates a financial outlay of $100 to $200 for a new suit and accessories. After incurring a major hit to her savings for the first event, Amy developed a different approach. She buys the suit on credit the week before the event, wears it to the event, and returns it the next week to the store for a full refund on her charge card.

ETHICS CHALLENGE

C1 P2

Required

1. Comment on the ethics exhibited by Amy and possible consequences of her actions.
2. How does the merchandising company account for the suits that Amy returns?

COMMUNICATING IN PRACTICE

C2 P3 P5

BTN 4-4 You are the financial officer for Music Plus, a retailer that sells goods for home entertainment needs. The business owner, Vic Velakturi, recently reviewed the annual financial statements you prepared and sent you an e-mail stating that he thinks you overstated net income. He explains that although he has invested a great deal in security, he is sure shoplifting and other forms of inventory shrinkage have occurred, but he does not see any deduction for shrinkage on the income statement. The store uses a perpetual inventory system.

Required

Prepare a brief memorandum that responds to the owner's concerns.

TAKING IT TO THE NET

A2 C1

BTN 4-5 Access the SEC's EDGAR database (www.SEC.gov) and obtain the March 19, 2012, filing of its fiscal 2012 10-K report (for year ended January 28, 2012) for J. Crew Group, Inc. (ticker: JCG).

Required

Prepare a table that reports the gross margin ratios for J. Crew using the revenues and cost of goods sold data from J. Crew's income statement for each of its most recent three years. Analyze and comment on the trend in its gross margin ratio.

TEAMWORK IN ACTION

C1 C2

BTN 4-6 Official Brands' general ledger and supplementary records at the end of its current period reveal the following.

Sales	$600,000	Merchandise inventory (beginning of period)	$ 98,000
Sales returns and allowances	20,000	Invoice cost of merchandise purchases	360,000
Sales discounts	13,000	Purchase discounts received	9,000
Cost of transportation-in	22,000	Purchase returns and allowances	11,000
Operating expenses	50,000	Merchandise inventory (end of period)	84,000

Required

1. *Each* member of the team is to assume responsibility for computing *one* of the following items. You are not to duplicate your teammates' work. Get any necessary amounts to compute your item from the appropriate teammate. Each member is to explain his or her computation to the team in preparation for reporting to the class.

    a. Net sales
    b. Total cost of merchandise purchases
    c. Cost of goods sold
    d. Gross profit
    e. Net income

2. Check your net income with the instructor. If correct, proceed to step 3.
3. Assume that a physical inventory count finds that actual ending inventory is $76,000. Discuss how this affects previously computed amounts in step 1.

Point: In teams of four, assign the same student *a* and *e*. Rotate teams for reporting on a different computation and the analysis in step 3.

ENTREPRENEURIAL DECISION

C1 C2 P4

BTN 4-7 Refer to the opening feature about Buffalo Wild Wings. Buffalo Wild Wings has a small segment of its business devoted to merchandising shirts, mugs, hats, and other related items tied to its branding strategy. That merchandising segment has current annual sales of approximately $10 million and prepares the following income statement.

BUFFALO WILD WINGS	
Income Statement—Merchandising Segment	
For Year Ended January 31, 2013	
Net sales	$10,000,000
Cost of sales	6,100,000
Expenses (other than cost of sales)	2,000,000
Net income	$ 1,900,000

This segment sells to individuals and retailers, ranging from small shops to large chains. Assume that it currently offers credit terms of 1/15, n/60, and ships FOB destination. To improve cash flow, it is considering changing credit terms to 3/10, n/30. In addition, it proposes to change shipping terms to FOB shipping point. The segment's manager expects that the increase in discount rate will increase net sales by 9%, but the gross margin ratio (and ratio of cost of sales divided by net sales) is expected to remain unchanged. The segment's manager also expects that delivery expenses will be zero under this proposal; thus, expenses other than cost of sales are expected to increase only 6%.

Required

1. Prepare a forecasted income statement (for this segment) for the year ended January 31, 2014, based on the proposal.

2. Based on the forecasted income statement alone (from your part 1 solution), do you recommend that Buffalo Wild Wings implement the new sales policies? Explain.

3. What else should Buffalo Wild Wings consider before deciding whether or not to implement the new policies? Explain.

BTN 4-8   Arrange an interview (in person or by phone) with the manager of a retail shop in a mall or in the downtown area of your community. Explain to the manager that you are a student studying merchandising activities and the accounting for sales returns and sales allowances. Ask the manager what the store policy is regarding returns. Also find out if sales allowances are ever negotiated with customers. Inquire whether management perceives that customers are abusing return policies and what actions management takes to counter potential abuses. Be prepared to discuss your findings in class.

HITTING THE ROAD

C1

Point: This activity complements the Ethics Challenge assignment.

BTN 4-9   Samsung (www.Samsung.com), Apple, and Google are competitors in the global marketplace. Key comparative figures for each company follow.

GLOBAL DECISION

A2 P4

Samsung
APPLE
GOOGLE

	Net Sales	Cost of Sales
Samsung*	₩201,103,613	₩126,651,931
Apple[†]	$ 156,508	$ 87,846
Google[†]	$ 50,175	$ 20,634

* Millions of Korean won for Samsung.

[†] $ millions for Apple and Google.

Required

1. Rank the three companies (highest to lowest) based on the gross margin ratio.

2. Which of the companies uses a multiple-step income statement format? (These companies' income statements are in Appendix A.)

ANSWERS TO MULTIPLE CHOICE QUIZ

1. c; Gross profit = $550,000 − $193,000 = $357,000
2. d; ($4,500 − $250) × (100% − 2%) = $4,165
3. b; Net sales = $75,000 + $320,000 − $13,700 − $6,000 = $375,300

4. b; Acid-test ratio = $37,500/$50,000 = 0.750
5. a; Gross margin ratio = ($675,000 − $459,000)/$675,000 = 32%

5 Reporting and Analyzing Inventories

INVENTORY BASICS	INVENTORY COSTING	INVENTORY VALUATION, ERRORS, AND ANALYSIS
C1 Determining inventory items **C2** Determining inventory costs Internal control of inventory and taking a physical count	**P1** Cost flow assumptions using: Specific identification First-in, first-out Last-in, first-out Weighted average **A1** Effects on financial statements	**P2** Inventory valuation at lower of cost or market **A2** Financial statement effects of inventory errors **A3** Inventory management **P4** Inventory estimation

Learning Objectives

C1 Identify the items making up merchandise inventory. (p. 214)

C2 Identify the costs of merchandise inventory. (p. 214)

P1 Compute inventory in a periodic system using the methods of specific identification, FIFO, LIFO, and weighted average. (p. 217)

A1 Analyze the effects of inventory methods for both financial and tax reporting. (p. 221)

P2 Compute the lower of cost or market amount of inventory. (p. 223)

A2 Analyze the effects of inventory errors on current and future financial statements. (p. 225)

A3 Assess inventory management using both inventory turnover and days' sales in inventory. (p. 227)

P3 *Appendix 5A*—Compute inventory in a perpetual system using the methods of specific identification, FIFO, LIFO, and weighted average. (p. 234)

P4 *Appendix 5B*—Apply both the retail inventory and gross profit methods to estimate inventory. (p. 240)

Crafting the Dream

"Know when to pull the plug and move on"
—JIM KOCH

BOSTON—"My dad was a brewmaster and my mother was a teacher," recounts Jim Koch. "I thought, I can start my own brewery." Such is the unlikely story behind the Boston Beer Company (**BostonBeer.com**). "When I told my dad I wanted to start a brewery, his reaction was, 'Jim, you've done some stupid things before. This is about the dumbest.'"

But Jim persevered. He rekindled an old family recipe for a lager and started brewing. "I wanted an assertively American name [for the lager]," explains Jim, "and Samuel Adams was a brewer, a patriot, and a revolutionary, so we named the beer after him. I wanted to create a beer revolution." With his family recipe, success quickly followed. "Six weeks after it came out, we got picked at the Great American Beer Festival as the best beer in America."

Jim insists that inventory management is key to his company's success. The company proudly proclaims that its "flagship style was, and is still, created using only the world's finest, all natural ingredients." Its Website adds, "the hops farmers always comment on how Jim doesn't just sniff the hops, he 'dives' into them." This attention to the details of inventory quality and management separates Boston Beer from its competitors and is

Boston Beer Company

(NYSE: SAM)

80 employees
31 distinct beers
2.7 mil. barrels sold/year

reflected in its sales, income, inventory, and asset growth over the past few years:

($ millions)	2009	2010	2011	2012
Revenues........	$453	$506	$558	$629
Cost of sales.....	201	207	228	265
Inventories	26	27	34	44
Total assets	263	259	272	359

"We have a roll-up-your-sleeves, no bureaucracy, get-it-done company culture," explains Jim. Just getting his inventory to market was a challenge when he started. "We'd distribute it with a truck that I rented, and we did all the sales ourselves." He set up an inventory system, learned to prepare and read inventory reports, and applied inventory management tools. The inventory system tracks all transactions, and he regularly analyzes inventory reports when making decisions. The company further claims that it "is the only brewer with a cooperative

program . . . to buy back its beer when it's past its peak freshness date."

The financial markets seem equally enthused about the inventory of Boston Beer, as reflected in its stock price over this same four-year period.

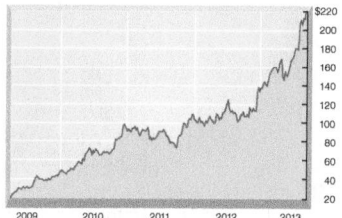

Boston Beer cautions, however, that its 'Freshest Beer Program' could substantially increase inventory cost and it will reassess the long run viability of this inventory buyback program. "Moving forward, I'm just focused on making great beer and working hard to sell it," explains Jim. "If we can get great beer into the mouths of our consumers, we'll do just fine." Somewhere we believe his dad is proud!

Sources: *Boston Beer Website,* January 2014; *Boston Beer 10-K,* 2012; *Fortune,* March 2013; *AmericanCraftBeer.com,* April 2013

INVENTORY BASICS

This section identifies the items and costs making up merchandise inventory. It also describes the importance of internal controls in taking a physical count of inventory.

Determining Inventory Items

C1 Identify the items making up merchandise inventory.

Merchandise inventory includes all goods that a company owns and holds for sale. This rule holds regardless of where the goods are located when inventory is counted. Certain inventory items require special attention, including goods in transit, goods on consignment, and goods that are damaged or obsolete.

Goods in Transit   Does a purchaser's inventory include goods in transit from a supplier? The answer is that if ownership has passed to the purchaser, the goods are included in the purchaser's inventory. We determine this by reviewing the shipping terms: *FOB destination* or *FOB shipping point*. If the purchaser is responsible for paying freight, ownership passes when goods are loaded on the transport vehicle. If the seller is responsible for paying freight, ownership passes when goods arrive at their destination.

Point: FOB shipping point is also called *FOB origin* or *FOB supplier's warehouse*.

Goods on Consignment   Goods on consignment are goods shipped by the owner, called the **consignor,** to another party, the **consignee.** A consignee sells goods for the owner. The consignor continues to own the consigned goods and reports them in its inventory. Upper Deck, for instance, pays sports celebrities such as Aaron Rodgers of the Green Bay Packers to sign memorabilia, which are offered to shopping networks on consignment. Upper Deck, the consignor, must report these items in its inventory until sold.

Goods Damaged or Obsolete   Damaged and obsolete (and deteriorated) goods are not counted in inventory if they cannot be sold. If these goods can be sold at a reduced price, they are included in inventory at a conservative estimate of their **net realizable value.** Net realizable value is sales price minus the cost of making the sale. The period when damage or obsolescence (or deterioration) occurs is the period when the loss in value is reported.

■ Decision Insight

A wireless portable device with a two-way radio allows clerks to quickly record inventory by scanning bar codes and to instantly send and receive inventory data. It gives managers access to up-to-date information on inventory and its location. ▨

Determining Inventory Costs

C2 Identify the costs of merchandise inventory.

Merchandise inventory includes costs of expenditures necessary, directly or indirectly, to bring an item to a salable condition and location. This means that the cost of an inventory item includes its invoice cost minus any discount, and plus any incidental costs necessary to put it in a place and condition for sale. Incidental costs can include import tariffs, freight, storage, insurance, and costs incurred in an aging process (for example, aging wine or cheese).

Accounting principles prescribe that incidental costs be added to inventory. Also, the *matching (expense recognition) principle* states that inventory costs should be recorded against revenue in the period when inventory is sold. However, some companies use the *materiality constraint (cost-to-benefit constraint)* to avoid assigning some incidental costs of acquiring merchandise to inventory. Instead, they expense them to cost of goods sold when incurred. These companies argue either that those incidental costs are immaterial or that the effort in assigning them outweighs the benefit.

Internal Controls and Taking a Physical Count

Events can cause the Inventory account balance to differ from the actual inventory available. Such events include theft, loss, damage, and errors. Thus, nearly all companies take a *physical count of inventory* at least once each year—informally called *taking an inventory*. This often occurs at the end of a fiscal year or when inventory amounts are low. This physical count is used to adjust the Inventory account balance to the actual inventory available.

Fraud: Auditors commonly observe employees as they take a physical inventory. Auditors take their own test counts to monitor the accuracy of a company's count.

Fraud

A company applies internal controls when taking a physical count of inventory that usually include the following procedures to minimize fraud and to increase reliability:

- *Prenumbered inventory tickets* are distributed to *counters*—each ticket must be accounted for.
- Counters of inventory are assigned and do not include those responsible for inventory.
- Counters confirm the validity of inventory, including its existence, amount, and quality.
- A second count is taken by a different counter.
- A manager confirms that all inventories are ticketed once, and only once.

Point: The Inventory account is a controlling account for the inventory subsidiary ledger. This *subsidiary ledger* contains a separate record (units and costs) for each separate product, and it can be in electronic or paper form. Subsidiary records assist managers in planning and monitoring inventory.

1. A master carver of wooden birds operates her business out of a garage. At the end of the current period, the carver has 17 units (carvings) in her garage, three of which were damaged by water and cannot be sold. The distributor also has another five units in her truck, ready to deliver per a customer order, terms FOB destination, and another 11 units out on consignment at several small retail stores. How many units does the carver include in business's period-end inventory?

2. A distributor of artistic iron-based fixtures acquires a piece for $1,000, terms FOB shipping point. Additional costs in obtaining it and offering it for sale include $150 for transportation-in, $300 for import duties, $100 for insurance during shipment, $200 for advertising, a $50 voluntary gratuity to the delivery person, $75 for enhanced store lighting, and $250 for sales staff salaries. For computing inventory, what cost is assigned to this artistic piece?

NEED-TO-KNOW 5.1

C1, C2

Solutions

Part 1

Units in ending inventory	
Units in storage	17 units
Less damaged (unsalable) units	(3)
Plus units in transit.	5
Plus units on consignment	11
Total units in ending inventory	30 units

Part 2

Merchandise cost.	$1,000
Plus	
Transportation-in	150
Import duties	300
Insurance	100
Total inventory cost.	$1,550

Do More: QS 5-17, QS 5-18, E 5-1, E 5-2

QC1

INVENTORY COSTING UNDER A PERIODIC SYSTEM

Accounting for inventory affects both the balance sheet and the income statement. A major goal in accounting for inventory is to properly match costs with sales. We use the *expense recognition* (or *matching*) *principle* to decide how much of the cost of the goods available for sale is deducted from sales and how much is carried forward as inventory and matched against future sales.

Management decisions in accounting for inventory involve the following:

- Items included in inventory and their costs.
- Costing method (specific identification, FIFO, LIFO, or weighted average).
- Inventory system (perpetual or periodic).
- Use of market values or other estimates.

The first point was explained on the prior two pages. The second and third points will be addressed now. The fourth point is the focus at the end of this chapter. Decisions on these points affect the reported amounts for inventory, cost of goods sold, gross profit, income, current assets, and other accounts.

One of the most important issues in accounting for inventory is determining the per unit costs assigned to inventory items. When all units are purchased at the same unit cost, this process is simple. When identical items are purchased at different costs, however, a question arises as to which amounts to record in cost of goods sold and which amounts remain in inventory.

EXHIBIT 5.1

Frequency in Use of
Inventory Methods

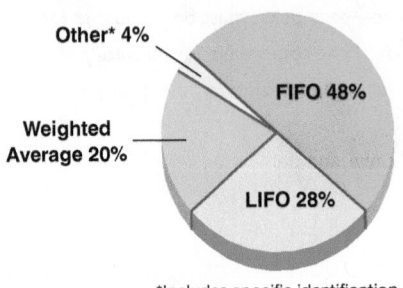

*Includes specific identification.

Four methods are commonly used to assign costs to inventory and to cost of goods sold: (1) specific identification; (2) first-in, first-out; (3) last-in, first-out; and (4) weighted average. Exhibit 5.1 shows the frequency in the use of these methods.

Each method assumes a particular pattern for how costs flow through inventory. Each of these four methods is acceptable whether or not the actual physical flow of goods follows the cost flow assumption. Physical flow of goods depends on the type of product and the way it is stored. (Perishable goods such as fresh fruit demand that a business attempt to sell them in a first-in, first-out physical flow. Other products such as crude oil and minerals such as coal, gold, and decorative stone can be sold in a last-in, first-out physical flow.) Physical flow and cost flow need not be the same.

Inventory Cost Flow Assumptions

Point: Cost of goods sold is abbreviated COGS.

This section introduces inventory cost flow assumptions. For this purpose, assume that three identical units are purchased separately at the following three dates and costs: May 1 at $45, May 3 at $65, and May 6 at $70. One unit is then sold on May 7 for $100. Exhibit 5.2 gives a visual layout of the flow of costs to either the gross profit section of the income statement or the inventory reported on the balance sheet for FIFO, LIFO, and weighted average.

EXHIBIT 5.2

Cost Flow Assumptions

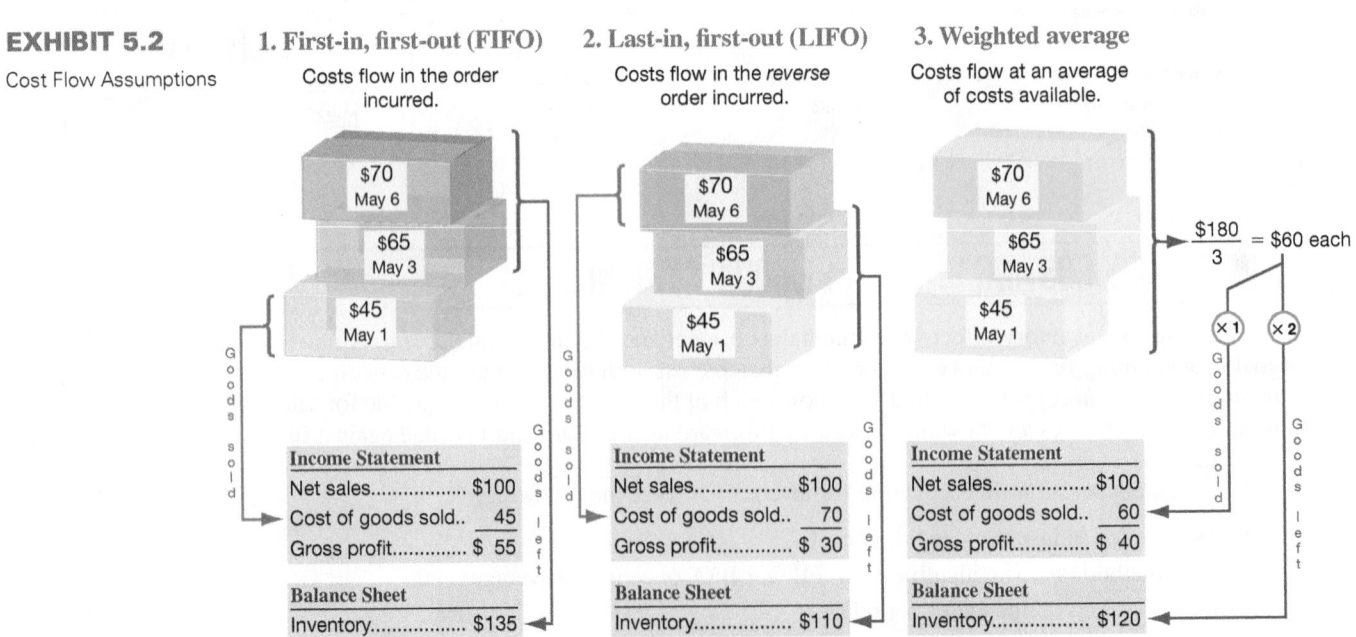

(1) *FIFO assumes costs flow in the order incurred.* The unit purchased on May 1 for $45 is the earliest cost incurred—it is sent to cost of goods sold on the income statement first. The remaining two units ($65 and $70) are reported in inventory on the balance sheet.

(2) *LIFO assumes costs flow in the reverse order incurred.* The unit purchased on May 6 for $70 is the most recent cost incurred—it is sent to cost of goods sold on the income statement. The remaining two units ($45 and $65) are reported in inventory on the balance sheet.

(3) *Weighted average assumes costs flow at an average of the costs available.* The units available at the May 7 sale average $60 in cost, computed as ($45 + $65 + $70)/3. One unit's $60 average cost is sent to cost of goods sold on the income statement. The remaining two units' average costs are reported in inventory at $120 on the balance sheet.

Cost flow assumptions can markedly impact gross profit and inventory numbers. Exhibit 5.2 shows that gross profit as a percent of net sales ranges from 30% to 55% due to nothing else but the cost flow assumption.

Point: It is helpful to recall the cost flow of inventory from Exhibit 4.4.

The following sections on inventory costing use the periodic system. Appendix 5A uses the perpetual system. An instructor can choose to cover either one or both systems. If the periodic system is skipped, then read Appendix 5A and return to the Decision Maker box (on page 221) titled "Cost Analyst."

Inventory Costing Illustration

This section provides a comprehensive illustration of inventory costing methods. We use information from Trekking, a sporting goods store. Among its many products, Trekking carries one type of mountain bike whose sales are directed at resorts that provide inexpensive mountain bikes for complimentary guest use. Its customers usually purchase in amounts of 10 or more bikes. We use Trekking's data from August. Its mountain bike (unit) inventory at the beginning of August and its purchases and sales during August are shown in Exhibit 5.3. It ends August with 12 bikes remaining in inventory.

P1 Compute inventory in a periodic system using the methods of specific identification, FIFO, LIFO, and weighted average.

Date	Activity	Units Acquired at Cost	Units Sold at Retail	Unit Inventory
Aug. 1	Beginning inventory	10 units @ $ 91 = $ 910		10 units
Aug. 3	Purchases	15 units @ $106 = $ 1,590		25 units
Aug. 14	Sales		20 units @ $130	5 units
Aug. 17	Purchases	20 units @ $115 = $ 2,300		25 units
Aug. 28	Purchases	10 units @ $119 = $ 1,190		35 units
Aug. 31	Sales		23 units @ $150	12 units
	Totals	55 units $5,990	43 units	
		Units available for sale Goods available for sale	Units sold	Units left

EXHIBIT 5.3

Purchases and Sales of Goods

Trekking uses the periodic inventory system, which means that its merchandise inventory account is updated at the end of each period (monthly for Trekking) to reflect purchases and sales. **(Appendix 5A describes the assignment of costs to inventory using a perpetual system.)** Regardless of what inventory method or system is used, cost of goods available for sale must be allocated between cost of goods sold and ending inventory.

Point: Beginning inventory units plus purchased units equals units available for sale (UAFS).

Specific Identification

When each item in inventory can be identified with a specific purchase and invoice, we can use **specific identification** or **SI** (also called *specific invoice inventory pricing*) to assign costs. We

Point: Three key variables determine the value assigned to ending inventory: (1) inventory quantity, (2) unit costs of inventory, and (3) cost flow assumption.

also need sales records that identify exactly which items were sold and when. Trekking's internal documents reveal the following specific unit sales:

August 14   Sold 8 bikes costing $91 each and 12 bikes costing $106 each

August 31   Sold 2 bikes costing $91 each, 3 bikes costing $106 each, 15 bikes costing $115 each, and 3 bikes costing $119 each

Applying specific identification, and using the information above and from Exhibit 5.3, we prepare Exhibit 5.4. This exhibit begins with the $5,990 in total units available for sale—this is from Exhibit 5.3. Applying specific identification, we know that for the 20 units sold on August 14, the company specifically identified that 8 of them had cost $91 each and 12 had cost $106 each, resulting in an August 14 cost of sales of $2,000. Next, for the 23 units sold on August 31, the company specifically identified that 2 of them had cost $91 each, that 3 had cost $106 each, that 15 had cost $115 each, and 3 had cost $119 each, resulting in an August 31 cost of sales of $2,582. This yields a total cost of sales for the period of $4,582. We then subtract this $4,582 in cost of goods sold from the $5,990 in cost of goods available to get $1,408 in ending inventory. Carefully study this exhibit and the explanations to see the flow of costs. Each unit, whether sold or remaining in inventory, has its own specific cost attached to it.

EXHIBIT 5.4

Specific Identification Computations

Total cost of 55 units available for sale (from Exhibit 5.3)		$5,990
Cost of goods sold*		
Aug. 14 (8 @ $91) + (12 @ $106)	$2,000	
Aug. 31 (2 @ $91) + (3 @ $106) + (15 @ $115) + (3 @ $119)	2,582	4,582
Ending inventory		$1,408

* Identification of items sold (and their costs) is obtained from internal documents that track each unit from its purchase to its sale.

Point: Specific identification is usually practical for companies with expensive or custom-made inventory. Examples include car dealerships, implement dealers, jewelers, and fashion designers.

When using specific identification, Trekking's cost of goods sold reported on the income statement totals $4,582, the sum of $2,000 and $2,582 from the cost of goods sold section of Exhibit 5.4. Trekking's ending inventory reported on the balance sheet is $1,408, which is the final inventory balance from Exhibit 5.4. The following graphic visually reflects the computations under specific identification.

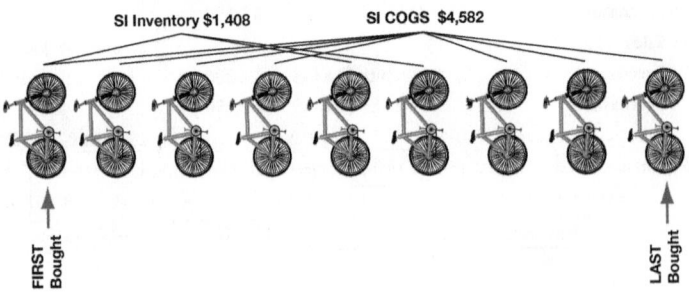

SI Inventory $1,408   SI COGS $4,582

FIRST Bought   LAST Bought

First-In, First-Out

The **first-in, first-out (FIFO)** method of assigning costs to both inventory and cost of goods sold assumes that inventory items are sold in the order acquired. When sales occur, the costs of the earliest units acquired are charged to cost of goods sold. This leaves the costs from the most recent purchases in ending inventory. Use of FIFO for computing the cost of inventory and cost of goods sold is shown in Exhibit 5.5.

This exhibit starts with computing $5,990 in total units available for sale—this is from Exhibit 5.3. Applying FIFO, we know that the 12 units in ending inventory will be reported at the cost of the most recent 12 purchases. Reviewing purchases in reverse order, we assign costs to the 12 bikes in ending inventory as follows: $119 cost to 10 bikes and $115 cost to 2 bikes. This yields 12 bikes costing $1,420 in ending inventory. We then subtract this $1,420 in ending inventory from $5,990 in cost of goods available to get $4,570 in cost of goods sold.

Point: Under FIFO, a unit sold is assigned the earliest (oldest) cost from inventory. This leaves the most recent costs in ending inventory.

EXHIBIT 5.5

FIFO Computations—Periodic System

Total cost of 55 units available for sale (from Exhibit 5.3)	$5,990
Less ending inventory priced using FIFO	
10 units from August 28 purchase at $119 each $1,190	
2 units from August 17 purchase at $115 each 230	
Ending inventory	1,420
Cost of goods sold	$4,570

Exhibit 5.3 shows that the 12 units in ending inventory consist of 10 units from the latest purchase on Aug. 28 and 2 units from the next latest purchase on Aug. 17.

Trekking's ending inventory reported on the balance sheet is $1,420, and its cost of goods sold reported on the income statement is $4,570. The following graphic visually reflects the computations under FIFO.

Point: The assignment of costs to the goods sold and to inventory using FIFO is the same for both the periodic and perpetual systems.

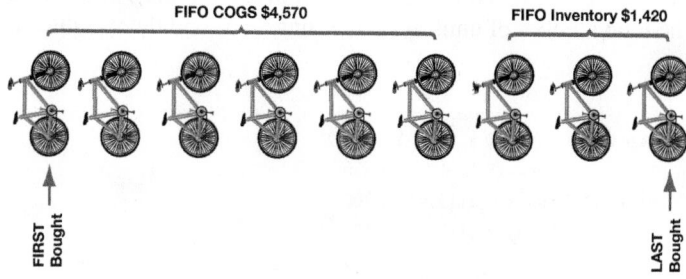

FIFO COGS $4,570   FIFO Inventory $1,420

FIRST Bought   LAST Bought

Last-In, First-Out

The **last-in, first-out (LIFO)** method of assigning costs assumes that the most recent purchases are sold first. These more recent costs are charged to the goods sold, and the costs of the earliest purchases are assigned to inventory. LIFO results in costs of the most recent purchases being assigned to cost of goods sold, which means that LIFO comes close to matching current costs of goods sold with revenues. Use of LIFO for computing cost of inventory and cost of goods sold is shown in Exhibit 5.6.

This exhibit starts with computing $5,990 in total units available for sale—this is from Exhibit 5.3. Applying LIFO, we know that the 12 units in ending inventory will be reported at the cost of the earliest 12 purchases. Reviewing the earliest purchases in order, we assign costs to the 12 bikes in ending inventory as follows: $91 cost to 10 bikes and $106 cost to 2 bikes. This yields 12 bikes costing $1,122 in ending inventory. We then subtract this $1,122 in ending inventory from $5,990 in cost of goods available to get $4,868 in cost of goods sold.

EXHIBIT 5.6

LIFO Computations—Periodic System

Total cost of 55 units available for sale (from Exhibit 5.3)	$5,990
Less ending inventory priced using LIFO	
10 units in beginning inventory at $91 each $910	
2 units from August 3 purchase at $106 each. 212	
Ending inventory	1,122
Cost of goods sold	$4,868

Exhibit 5.3 shows that the 12 units in ending inventory consist of 10 units from the earliest purchase (beg. inv.) and 2 units from the next earliest purchase on Aug. 3.

Trekking's ending inventory reported on the balance sheet is $1,122, and its cost of goods sold reported on the income statement is $4,868. The following graphic visually reflects the computations under LIFO.

Point: Under LIFO, a unit sold is assigned the most recent (latest) cost from inventory. This leaves the oldest costs in inventory.

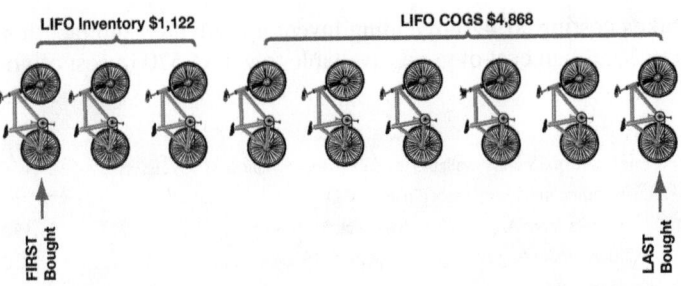

Weighted Average

The **weighted average** or **WA** (also called **average cost**) method of assigning cost requires that we use the average cost per unit of inventory at the end of the period. Weighted average cost per unit equals the cost of goods available for sale divided by the units available. The weighted average method of assigning cost involves three important steps. The first two steps are shown in Exhibit 5.7a. First, multiply the per unit cost for beginning inventory and each particular purchase by the corresponding number of units (from Exhibit 5.3). Second, add these amounts and divide by the total number of units available for sale to find the weighted average cost per unit.

EXHIBIT 5.7a

Weighted Average Cost per Unit

Example: In Exhibit 5.7a, if 5 more units had been purchased at $120 each, what would be the weighted average cost per unit?

Answer: $109.83 ($6,590/60)

Step 1:	10 units @ $ 91 =	$ 910	
	15 units @ $106 =	1,590	
	20 units @ $115 =	2,300	
	10 units @ $119 =	1,190	
	55	$5,990	
Step 2:	$5,990/55 units =	**$108.91** weighted average cost per unit	

The third step is to use the weighted average cost per unit to assign costs to inventory and to the units sold as shown in Exhibit 5.7b.

EXHIBIT 5.7b

Weighted Average Computations—Periodic

Step 3:	Total cost of 55 units available for sale (from Exhibit 5.3)	$ 5,990
	Less **ending inventory** priced on a weighted average cost basis: 12 units at $108.91 each (from Exhibit 5.7a)	1,307
	Cost of goods sold	$4,683

Trekking's ending inventory reported on the balance sheet is $1,307, and its cost of goods sold reported on the income statement is $4,683 when using the weighted average (periodic) method. The following graphic visually reflects the computations under weighted average.

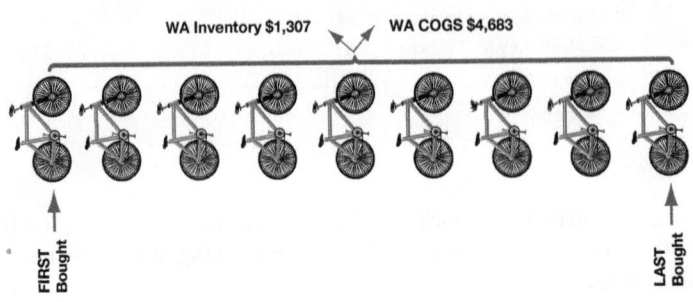

Fraud

Inventory Control Inventory safeguards include restricted access, use of authorized requisitions, security measures, and controlled environments to prevent damage. Proper accounting includes matching inventory received with purchase order terms and quality requirements, preventing misstatements, and controlling access to inventory records. A study reports that 23% of employees in purchasing and procurement observed inappropriate kickbacks or gifts from suppliers. Another study reports that submission of fraudulent supplier invoices is now common, and perpetrators are often employees (KPMG 2011).

Financial Statement Effects of Costing Methods

When purchase prices do not change, each inventory costing method assigns the same cost amounts to inventory and to cost of goods sold. When purchase prices are different, however, the methods nearly always assign different cost amounts. We show these differences in Exhibit 5.8 using Trekking's data.

A1 Analyze the effects of inventory methods for both financial and tax reporting.

TREKKING COMPANY For Month Ended August 31				
	Specific Identification	FIFO	LIFO	Weighted Average
Income Statement				
Sales	$ 6,050	$ 6,050	$ 6,050	$ 6,050
Cost of goods sold	4,582	4,570	4,868	4,683
Gross profit	1,468	1,480	1,182	1,367
Expenses	450	450	450	450
Income before taxes	1,018	1,030	732	917
Income tax expense (30%)	305	309	220	275
Net income	$ 713	$ 721	$ 512	$ 642
Balance Sheet				
Inventory	$1,408	$1,420	$1,122	$1,307

EXHIBIT 5.8

Financial Statement Effects of Inventory Costing Methods

This exhibit reveals two important results. First, when purchase costs *regularly rise,* as in Trekking's case, observe the following:

- FIFO assigns the lowest amount to cost of goods sold—yielding the highest gross profit and net income.
- LIFO assigns the highest amount to cost of goods sold—yielding the lowest gross profit and net income, which also yields a temporary tax advantage by postponing payment of some income tax.
- Weighted average yields results between FIFO and LIFO.
- Specific identification always yields results that depend on which units are sold.

Point: Managers prefer FIFO when costs are rising *and* incentives exist to report higher income for reasons such as bonus plans, job security, and reputation.

Second, when costs *regularly decline,* the reverse occurs for FIFO and LIFO. FIFO gives the highest cost of goods sold—yielding the lowest gross profit and income. And LIFO gives the lowest cost of goods sold—yielding the highest gross profit and income.

All four inventory costing methods are acceptable in practice. A company must disclose the inventory method it uses. Each method offers certain advantages as follows:

- FIFO assigns an amount to inventory on the balance sheet that approximates its current cost; it also mimics the actual flow of goods for most businesses.
- LIFO assigns an amount to cost of goods sold on the income statement that approximates its current cost; it also better matches current costs with revenues in computing gross profit.
- Weighted average tends to smooth out erratic changes in costs.
- Specific identification exactly matches the costs of items with the revenues they generate.

Point: LIFO inventory is often less than the inventory's replacement cost because LIFO inventory is valued using the oldest inventory purchase costs.

■ Decision Maker ━━━━━━━━━━━━━━━━━━

Cost Analyst Your supervisor says she finds managing product costs easier if the balance sheet reflects inventory values that closely reflect replacement cost. Which inventory costing method do you advise adopting? ■ [Answer—p. 243]

Tax Effects of Costing Methods   Trekking's segment income statement in Exhibit 5.8 includes income tax expense (at a rate of 30%) because it was formed as a corporation. Since inventory costs affect net income, they have potential tax effects. Trekking gains a temporary tax advantage by using LIFO. Many companies use LIFO for this reason.

Point: *LIFO conformity rule* may be revised if IFRS is adopted for U.S. companies as IFRS currently does not permit LIFO (see Global View).

Companies can and often do use different costing methods for financial reporting and tax reporting. *The only exception is when LIFO is used for tax reporting; in this case, the IRS requires that it also be used in financial statements*—called the LIFO conformity rule.

Consistency in Using Costing Methods

The **consistency concept** prescribes that a company use the same accounting methods period after period so that financial statements are comparable across periods—the only exception is when a change from one method to another will improve its financial reporting. The *full-disclosure principle* prescribes that the notes to the statements report this type of change, its justification, and its effect on income.

The consistency concept does *not* require a company to use one method exclusively. For example, it can use different methods to value different categories of inventory.

■ **Decision Ethics**

Inventory Manager   Your compensation as inventory manager includes a bonus plan based on gross profit. Your superior asks your opinion on changing the inventory costing method from FIFO to LIFO. Since costs are expected to continue to rise, your superior predicts that LIFO would match higher current costs against sales, thereby lowering taxable income (and gross profit). What do you recommend? ■   [Answer—p. 243]

NEED-TO-KNOW 5.2

P1

A company reported the following December purchases and sales data for its only product.

Date	Activities	Units Acquired at Cost	Units Sold at Retail
Dec. 1	Beginning inventory.........	5 units @ $3.00 = $ 15.00	
Dec. 8	Purchase	10 units @ $4.50 = 45.00	
Dec. 9	Sales......................		8 units @ $7.00
Dec. 19	Purchase	13 units @ $5.00 = 65.00	
Dec. 24	Sales......................		18 units @ $8.00
Dec. 30	Purchase	8 units @ $5.30 = 42.40	
Totals	....	36 units $167.40	26 units

The company uses a *periodic inventory system*. Determine the cost assigned to ending inventory and to cost of goods sold using (*a*) specific identification, (*b*) FIFO, (*c*) LIFO, and (*d*) weighted average. (Round per unit costs and inventory amounts to cents.) For specific identification, ending inventory consists of 10 units, where eight are from the December 30 purchase and two are from the December 8 purchase.

Solutions

a. Specific identification: Ending inventory—eight units from December 30 purchase and two units from December 8 purchase

Specific Identification	Ending Inventory	Cost of Goods Sold
(8 × $5.30) + (2 × $4.50)...	$51.40	
(5 × $3.00) + (8 × $4.50) + (13 × $5.00) + (0 × $5.30)...............		$116.00
or $167.40 [Total Goods Available] − $51.40 [Ending Inventory].........		$116.00

b. FIFO

FIFO	Ending Inventory	Cost of Goods Sold
(8 × $5.30) + (2 × $5.00)	$52.40	
(5 × $3.00) + (10 × $4.50) + (11 × $5.00)		$115.00
or $167.40 [Total Goods Available] − $52.40 [Ending Inventory]		$115.00

c. LIFO

LIFO	Ending Inventory	Cost of Goods Sold
(5 × $3.00) + (5 × $4.50)	$37.50	
(8 × $5.30) + (13 × $5.00) + (5 × $4.50)		$129.90
or $167.40 [Total Goods Available] − $37.50 [Ending Inventory]		$129.90

d. WA

WA	Ending Inventory	Cost of Goods Sold
10 × $4.65 (computed from $167.40/36)	$46.50	
26 × $4.65 (computed from $167.40/36)		$120.90
or $167.40 [Total Goods Available] − $46.50 [Ending Inventory]		$120.90

> Do More: QS 5-4, QS 5-5, QS 5-6, QS 5-12, QS 5-13, QS 5-14, QS 5-15

QC2

VALUING INVENTORY AT LCM AND THE EFFECTS OF INVENTORY ERRORS

This section examines the role of market costs in determining inventory on the balance sheet and also the financial statement effects of inventory errors.

Lower of Cost or Market

We explained how to assign costs to ending inventory and cost of goods sold using one of four costing methods (FIFO, LIFO, weighted average, or specific identification). However, *accounting principles require that inventory be reported at the market value (cost) of replacing inventory when market value is lower than cost.* Merchandise inventory is then said to be reported on the balance sheet at the **lower of cost or market (LCM).**

> **P2** Compute the lower of cost or market amount of inventory.

Computing the Lower of Cost or Market Market in the term LCM is defined as the current replacement cost of purchasing the same inventory items in the usual manner. A decline in replacement cost reflects a loss of value in inventory. When the recorded cost of inventory is higher than the replacement cost, a loss is recognized. When the recorded cost is lower, no adjustment is made.

LCM is applied in one of three ways: (1) to each individual item separately, (2) to major categories of items, or (3) to the whole of inventory. The less similar the items that make up inventory, the more likely companies are to apply LCM to individual items or categories. With the increasing application of technology and inventory tracking, companies increasingly apply LCM to each individual item separately. Accordingly, we show that method only; however, advanced courses cover the other two methods. To illustrate LCM, we apply it to the ending inventory of a motorsports retailer in Exhibit 5.9.

LCM Applied to Individual Items When LCM is applied to individual *items* of inventory, the number of comparisons equals the number of items. For Roadster, $140,000 is the lower of the $160,000 cost and the $140,000 market. For Sprint, $50,000 is the lower of the $50,000 cost

EXHIBIT 5.9

Lower of Cost or Market
Computations

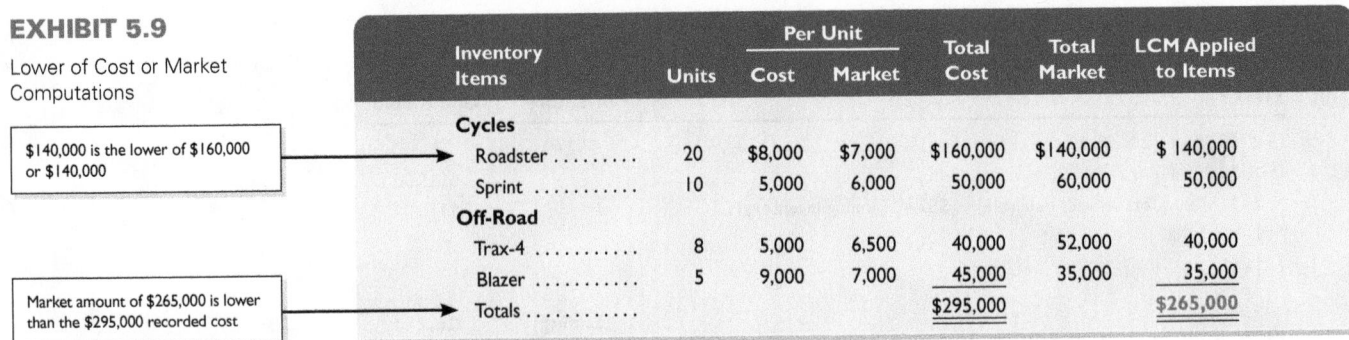

Inventory Items	Units	Per Unit		Total Cost	Total Market	LCM Applied to Items
		Cost	Market			
Cycles						
Roadster	20	$8,000	$7,000	$160,000	$140,000	$ 140,000
Sprint	10	5,000	6,000	50,000	60,000	50,000
Off-Road						
Trax-4	8	5,000	6,500	40,000	52,000	40,000
Blazer	5	9,000	7,000	45,000	35,000	35,000
Totals				$295,000		$265,000

$140,000 is the lower of $160,000 or $140,000

Market amount of $265,000 is lower than the $295,000 recorded cost

Point: Advances in technology encourage the individual-item approach for LCM.

Global: IFRS requires LCM applied to individual items; this results in the most conservative inventory amount.

and the $60,000 market. For Trax-4, $40,000 is the lower of the $40,000 cost and the $52,000 market. For Blazer, $35,000 is the lower of the $45,000 cost and the $35,000 market. This yields a $265,000 reported inventory, computed from $140,000 for Roadster plus $50,000 for Sprint plus $40,000 for Trax-4 plus $35,000 for Blazer.

The retailer The Buckle applies LCM and reports that its "inventory is stated at the lower of cost or market. Cost is determined using the average cost method."

Recording the Lower of Cost or Market   Inventory must be adjusted downward when market is less than cost. To illustrate, if LCM is applied to the individual items of inventory in Exhibit 5.9, the Merchandise Inventory account must be adjusted from the $295,000 recorded cost down to the $265,000 market amount as follows.

Cost of Goods Sold	30,000	
Merchandise Inventory		30,000
To adjust inventory cost to market.		

Accounting rules require that inventory be adjusted to market when market is less than cost, but inventory normally cannot be written up to market when market exceeds cost. If recording inventory down to market is acceptable, why are companies not allowed to record inventory up to market? One view is that a gain from a market increase should not be realized until a sales transaction verifies the gain. However, this view also applies when market is less than cost. A second and primary reason is the **conservatism constraint,** which prescribes the use of the less optimistic amount when more than one estimate of the amount to be received or paid exists and these estimates are about equally likely.

NEED-TO-KNOW 5.3

P2

A company has the following products in its ending inventory. (a) Compute the lower of cost or market for its inventory when applied separately to each product. (b) If the market amount is less than the recorded cost of the inventory, then record the December 31 LCM adjustment to the Merchandise Inventory account.

Road bikes	5	$1,000	$800
Mountain bikes.........	4	500	600
Town bikes	10	400	450

Solution

Inventory Items	Units	Per Unit		Total Cost	Total Market	LCM-Items
		Cost	Market			
Road bikes	5	$1,000	$800	$ 5,000	$4,000	$ 4,000
Mountain bikes.....................	4	500	600	2,000	2,400	2,000
Town bikes	10	400	450	4,000	4,500	4,000
				$11,000		$ 10,000
LCM applied to each product						$10,000

Dec. 31	Cost of Goods Sold	1,000	
	Merchandise Inventory		1,000
	To adjust inventory cost to market ($11,000 − $10,000).		

Do More: QS 5-19, E 5-10

Financial Statement Effects of Inventory Errors

Companies must take care in both taking a physical count of inventory and in assigning a cost to it. An inventory error causes misstatements in cost of goods sold, gross profit, net income, current assets, and equity. It also causes misstatements in the next period's statements because ending inventory of one period is the beginning inventory of the next. As we consider the financial statement effects in this section, it is helpful if we recall the following *inventory relation.*

A2 Analyze the effects of inventory errors on current and future financial statements.

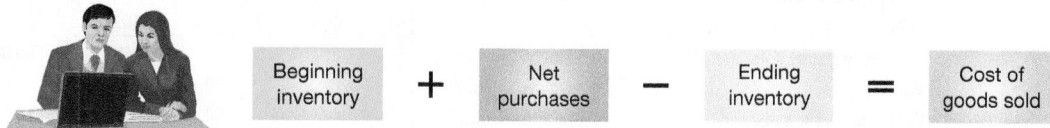

$$\text{Beginning inventory} + \text{Net purchases} - \text{Ending inventory} = \text{Cost of goods sold}$$

Income Statement Effects Exhibit 5.10 shows the effects of inventory errors on key amounts in the current and next periods' income statements. Let's look at row 1 and year 1. We see that understating ending inventory overstates cost of goods sold. This can be seen from the above inventory relation where we subtract a smaller ending inventory amount in computing cost of goods sold. Then a higher cost of goods sold yields a lower income.

To understand year 2 of row 1, remember that an understated ending inventory for year 1 becomes an understated beginning inventory for year 2. Using the above inventory relation, we see that if beginning inventory is understated, then cost of goods sold is understated (because we are starting with a smaller amount). A lower cost of goods sold yields a higher income.

Turning to overstatements, let's look at row 2 and year 1. If ending inventory is overstated, we use the inventory relation to see that cost of goods sold is understated. A lower cost of goods sold yields a higher income.

For year 2 of row 2, we again recall that an overstated ending inventory for year 1 becomes an overstated beginning inventory for year 2. If beginning inventory is overstated, we use the inventory relation to see that cost of goods sold is overstated. A higher cost of goods sold yields a lower income.

	Year 1		Year 2	
Ending Inventory	**Cost of Goods Sold**	**Net Income**	**Cost of Goods Sold**	**Net Income**
Understated ↓	Overstated ↑	Understated ↓	Understated ↓	Overstated ↑
Overstated* ↑	Understated ↓	Overstated ↑	Overstated ↑	Understated ↓

EXHIBIT 5.10

Effects of Inventory Errors on the Income Statement

* This error is less likely under a perpetual system versus a periodic because it implies more inventory than is recorded (or less shrinkage than expected). Management will normally follow up and discover and correct this error before it impacts any accounts.

To illustrate, consider an inventory error for a company with $100,000 in sales for each of the years 2012, 2013, and 2014. If this company maintains a steady $20,000 inventory level during this period and makes $60,000 in purchases in each of these years, its cost of goods sold is $60,000 and its gross profit is $40,000 each year.

Ending Inventory Understated—Year 1 Assume that this company errs in computing its 2012 ending inventory and reports $16,000 instead of the correct amount of $20,000. The effects of this error are shown in Exhibit 5.11. The $4,000 understatement of 2012 ending inventory causes a $4,000 overstatement in 2012 cost of goods sold and a $4,000 understatement in both gross profit and net income for 2012. We see that these effects match the effects predicted in Exhibit 5.10.

Ending Inventory Understated—Year 2 The 2012 understated ending inventory becomes the 2013 understated *beginning* inventory. We see in Exhibit 5.11 that this error causes an understatement in 2013 cost of goods sold and a $4,000 overstatement in both gross profit and net income for 2013.

Ending Inventory Understated—Year 3 Exhibit 5.11 shows that the 2012 ending inventory error affects only that period and the next. It does not affect 2014 results or any period thereafter. An inventory error is said to be *self-correcting* because it always yields an offsetting error in

Example: If 2012 ending inventory in Exhibit 5.11 is overstated by $3,000 (not understated by $4,000), what is the effect on cost of goods sold, gross profit, assets, and equity? *Answer:* Cost of goods sold is understated by $3,000 in 2012 and overstated by $3,000 in 2013. Gross profit and net income are overstated in 2012 and understated in 2013. Assets and equity are overstated in 2012.

EXHIBIT 5.11

Effects of Inventory Errors on Three Periods' Income Statements

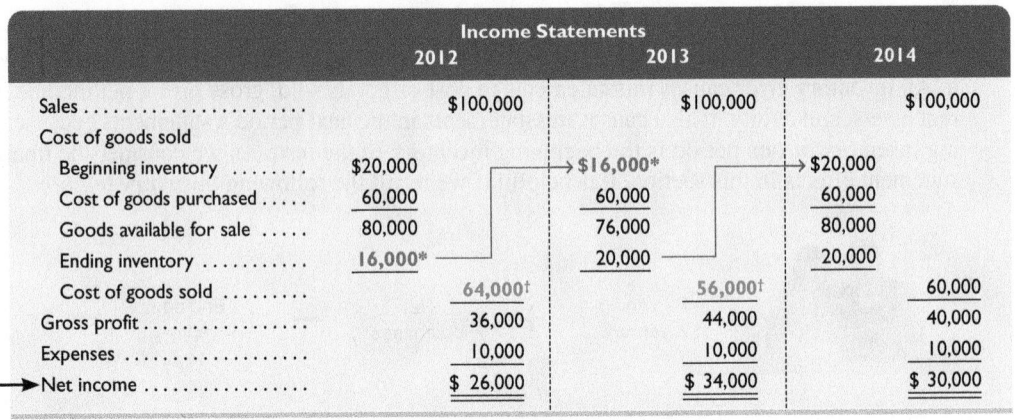

	Income Statements		
	2012	2013	2014
Sales	$100,000	$100,000	$100,000
Cost of goods sold			
Beginning inventory	$20,000	→$16,000*	→$20,000
Cost of goods purchased	60,000	60,000	60,000
Goods available for sale	80,000	76,000	80,000
Ending inventory	16,000*	20,000	20,000
Cost of goods sold	64,000†	56,000†	60,000
Gross profit	36,000	44,000	40,000
Expenses	10,000	10,000	10,000
Net income	$ 26,000	$ 34,000	$ 30,000

Correct income is $30,000 for each year

* Correct amount is $20,000.   † Correct amount is $60,000.

the next period. This does not reduce the severity of inventory errors. Managers, lenders, owners, and others make important decisions from analysis of income and costs.

We can also do an analysis of beginning inventory errors. The income statement effects are the opposite of those for ending inventory.

Balance Sheet Effects   Balance sheet effects of an inventory error can be seen by considering the accounting equation: Assets = Liabilities + Equity. For example, understating ending inventory understates both current and total assets. An understatement in ending inventory also yields an understatement in equity because of the understatement in net income. Exhibit 5.12 shows the effects of inventory errors on the current period's balance sheet amounts. Errors in *beginning* inventory do not yield misstatements in the end-of-period balance sheet, but they do affect that current period's income statement.

Point: A former internal auditor at Coca-Cola alleges that just before midnight at a prior calendar year-end, fully loaded Coke trucks were ordered to drive about 2 feet away from the loading dock so that Coke could record millions of dollars in extra sales.

EXHIBIT 5.12

Effects of Inventory Errors on Current Period's Balance Sheet

Ending Inventory	Assets	Equity
Understated ↓	Understated ↓	Understated ↓
Overstated ↑	Overstated ↑	Overstated ↑

NEED-TO-KNOW 5.4

A2

A company had $10,000 of sales in each of three consecutive years, 2012–2014, and it purchased merchandise costing $7,000 in each of those years. It also maintained a $2,000 physical inventory from the beginning to the end of that three-year period. In accounting for inventory, it made an error at the end of year 2012 that caused its year-end 2012 inventory to appear on its statements as $1,600 rather than the correct $2,000. (a) Determine the correct amount of the company's gross profit in each of the years 2012–2014. (b) Prepare comparative income statements as in Exhibit 5.11 to show the effect of this error on the company's cost of goods sold and gross profit for each of the years 2012–2014.

Solution

a. Correct gross profit = $10,000 − $7,000 = $3,000 (for each year)

b. Cost of goods sold and gross profit figures

	Year 2012	Year 2013	Year 2014
Sales	$10,000	$10,000	$10,000
Cost of goods sold			
Beginning inventory	$2,000	$1,600	$2,000
Cost of purchases	7,000	7,000	7,000
Good available for sale	9,000	8,600	9,000
Ending inventory	1,600	2,000	2,000
Cost of goods sold..........	7,400	6,600	7,000
Gross profit	$ 2,600	$ 3,400	$ 3,000

Do More: QS 5-20, E 5-12

QC3

 **GLOBAL VIEW**

This section discusses differences between U.S. GAAP and IFRS in the items and costs making up merchandise inventory, in the methods to assign costs to inventory, and in the methods to estimate inventory values.

Items and Costs Making Up Inventory   Both U.S. GAAP and IFRS include broad and similar guidance for the items and costs making up merchandise inventory. Specifically, under both accounting systems, merchandise inventory includes all items that a company owns and holds for sale. Further, merchandise inventory includes costs of expenditures necessary, directly or indirectly, to bring those items to a salable condition and location.

Assigning Costs to Inventory   Both U.S. GAAP and IFRS allow companies to use specific identification in assigning costs to inventory. Further, both systems allow companies to apply a *cost flow assumption.* The usual cost flow assumptions are: FIFO, Weighted Average, and LIFO. However, IFRS does not (currently) allow use of LIFO. As the convergence project progresses, this prohibition may or may not persist.

Estimating Inventory Costs   The value of inventory can change while it awaits sale to customers. That value can decrease or increase.

Decreases in Inventory Value   Both U.S. GAAP and IFRS require companies to write down (reduce the cost recorded for) inventory when its value falls below the cost recorded. This is referred to as the *lower of cost or market* method explained in this chapter. U.S. GAAP prohibits any later increase in the recorded value of that inventory even if that decline in value is reversed through value increases in later periods. However, IFRS allows reversals of those write-downs up to the original acquisition cost. For example, if Apple wrote down its 2012 inventory from $791 million to $750 million, it could not reverse this in future periods even if its value increased to more than $791 million. However, if Apple applied IFRS, it could reverse that previous loss. (Another difference is that value refers to *replacement cost* under U.S. GAAP, but *net realizable value* under IFRS.)

APPLE

Increases in Inventory Value   Neither U.S. GAAP nor IFRS allow inventory to be adjusted upward beyond the original cost. (One exception is that IFRS requires agricultural assets such as animals, forests, and plants to be measured at fair value less point-of-sale costs.)

Nokia provides the following description of its inventory valuation procedures:

NOKIA

> Inventories are stated at the lower of cost or net realizable value. Cost ... approximates actual cost on a FIFO (First-in First-out) basis. Net realizable value is the amount that can be realized from the sale of the inventory in the normal course of business after allowing for the costs of realization.

Inventory Turnover and Days' Sales in Inventory **Decision Analysis**

Inventory Turnover

Earlier chapters described two important ratios useful in evaluating a company's short-term liquidity: current ratio and acid-test ratio. A merchandiser's ability to pay its short-term obligations also depends on how quickly it sells its merchandise inventory. **Inventory turnover,** also called *merchandise inventory turnover* or, simply, *turns,* is one ratio used to assess this and is defined in Exhibit 5.13.

A3 Assess inventory management using both inventory turnover and days' sales in inventory.

$$\text{Inventory turnover} = \frac{\text{Cost of goods sold}}{\text{Average inventory}}$$

EXHIBIT 5.13

Inventory Turnover

This ratio reveals how many *times* a company turns over (sells) its inventory during a period. If a company's inventory greatly varies within a year, average inventory amounts can be computed from interim periods such as quarters or months.

Users apply inventory turnover to help analyze short-term liquidity and to assess whether management is doing a good job controlling the amount of inventory available. A low ratio compared to that of competitors suggests inefficient use of assets. The company may be holding more inventory than it needs to support its sales volume. Similarly, a very high ratio compared to that of competitors suggests inventory might be too low. This can cause lost sales if customers must back-order merchandise. Inventory turnover has no simple rule except to say *a high ratio is preferable provided inventory is adequate to meet demand.*

Point: We must take care when comparing turnover ratios across companies that use different costing methods (such as FIFO and LIFO).

Days' Sales in Inventory

To better interpret inventory turnover, many users measure the adequacy of inventory to meet sales demand. **Days' sales in inventory,** also called *days' stock on hand,* is a ratio that reveals how much inventory is available in terms of the number of days' sales. It can be interpreted as the number of days one can sell from inventory if no new items are purchased. This ratio is often viewed as a measure of the buffer against out-of-stock inventory and is useful in evaluating liquidity of inventory. It is defined in Exhibit 5.14.

EXHIBIT 5.14

Days' Sales in Inventory

Point: Days' sales in inventory for many Ford models has risen: Freestyle, 122 days; Montego, 109 days; Five Hundred, 118 days. The industry average is 73 days. (*BusinessWeek*)

$$\text{Days' sales in inventory} = \frac{\text{Ending inventory}}{\text{Cost of goods sold}} \times 365$$

Days' sales in inventory focuses on ending inventory and it estimates how many days it will take to convert inventory at the end of a period into accounts receivable or cash. Days' sales in inventory focuses on *ending* inventory whereas inventory turnover focuses on *average* inventory.

■ Decision Insight

Short Shelf Life   Whole Foods Market, Inc., is committed to foods that are fresh, wholesome, and safe to eat. To fulfill those values, Whole Foods Market focuses on inventory management. It turns its inventory 20 times a year with days' sales in inventory of 19 days. ■

Analysis of Inventory Management

Inventory management is a major emphasis for merchandisers. They must both plan and control inventory purchases and sales. Toys "R" Us is one of those merchandisers. Its inventory in fiscal year 2011 was $2,104 million. This inventory constituted 58% of its current assets and 24% of its total assets. We apply the analysis tools in this section to Toys "R" Us, as shown in Exhibit 5.15—also see margin graph.

EXHIBIT 5.15

Inventory Turnover and Days' Sales in Inventory for Toys "R" Us

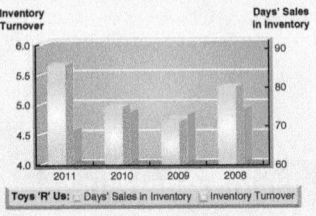

($ millions)	2011	2010	2009	2008
Cost of goods sold	$8,939	$8,790	$8,976	$8,987
Ending inventory	$2,104	$1,810	$1,781	$1,998
Inventory turnover	4.6 times	4.9 times	4.8 times	4.9 times
Industry inventory turnover	3.3 times	3.5 times	3.2 times	3.4 times
Days' sales in inventory	86 days	75 days	72 days	81 days
Industry days' sales in inventory	132 days	129 days	124 days	135 days

Its 2011 inventory turnover of 4.6 times means that Toys "R" Us turns over its inventory 4.6 times per year, or once every 79 days (365 days ÷ 4.6). We prefer inventory turnover to be high provided inventory is not out of stock and the company is not losing customers. The second metric, the 2011 days' sales in inventory of 86 days, reveals that it is carrying 86 days of sales in inventory. This inventory buffer seems more than adequate. The increased days' sales in inventory suggests that Toys "R" Us would benefit from further management efforts to increase inventory turnover and reduce inventory levels.

■ Decision Maker

Entrepreneur   Analysis of your retail store yields an inventory turnover of 5.0 and a days' sales in inventory of 73 days. The industry norm for inventory turnover is 4.4 and for days' sales in inventory is 74 days. What is your assessment of inventory management? ■   [Answer—p. 243]

Information: Craig Company buys and sells one product. Its beginning inventory, purchases, and sales during calendar year 2013 follow:

Date		Activity	Units Acquired at Cost	Units Sold at Retail	Unit Inventory
Jan.	1	Beg. Inventory	400 units @ $14 = $ 5,600		400 units
Jan.	15	Sale		200 units @ $30	200 units
March	10	Purchase........	200 units @ $15 = $ 3,000		400 units
April	1	Sale		200 units @ $30	200 units
May	9	Purchase........	300 units @ $16 = $ 4,800		500 units
Sept.	22	Purchase........	250 units @ $20 = $ 5,000		750 units
Nov.	1	Sale		300 units @ $35	450 units
Nov.	28	Purchase........	100 units @ $21 = $ 2,100		550 units
		Totals	1,250 units $20,500	700 units	

Additional tracking data for specific identification: (1) January 15 sale—200 units @ $14, (2) April 1 sale—200 units @ $15, and (3) November 1 sale—200 units @ $14 and 100 units @ $20.

Required

1. Calculate the cost of goods available for sale.

2. Apply the four different methods of inventory costing (FIFO, LIFO, weighted average, and specific identification) to calculate ending inventory and cost of goods sold under each method using the periodic system.

3. Compute gross profit earned by the company for each of the four costing methods in part 2. Also, report the inventory amount reported on the balance sheet for each of the four methods.

4. In preparing financial statements for year 2013, the financial officer was instructed to use FIFO but failed to do so and instead computed cost of goods sold according to LIFO. Determine the impact on year 2013's income from the error. Also determine the effect of this error on year 2014's income. Assume no income taxes.

PLANNING THE SOLUTION

- Compute cost of goods available for sale by multiplying the units of beginning inventory and each purchase by their unit costs to determine the total cost of goods available for sale.

- Prepare a periodic FIFO computation starting with cost of units available and subtracting FIFO ending inventory amounts to obtain FIFO cost of goods sold (see Exhibit 5.5).

- Prepare a periodic LIFO computation starting with cost of units available and subtracting LIFO ending inventory amounts to obtain LIFO cost of goods sold (see Exhibit 5.6).

- Apply the three-step process illustrated in Exhibits 5.7a and 5.7b.

- Prepare a table showing the computation of cost of goods sold and ending inventory using the specific identification method (see Exhibit 5.4).

- Compare the year-end 2013 inventory amounts under FIFO and LIFO to determine the misstatement of year 2013 income that results from using LIFO. The errors for year 2013 and 2014 are equal in amount but opposite in effect.

SOLUTION TO COMPREHENSIVE NEED-TO-KNOW

1. Cost of goods available for sale (this amount is the same for all methods).

Date			Units	Unit Cost	Cost
Jan.	1	Beg. Inventory	400	$14	$ 5,600
March	10	Purchase..............	200	15	3,000
May	9	Purchase..............	300	16	4,800
Sept.	22	Purchase..............	250	20	5,000
Nov.	28	Purchase..............	100	21	2,100
		Total goods available for sale........	1,250		$20,500

2a. FIFO periodic method (FIFO under periodic and perpetual yields identical results).

Cost of goods available for sale (from part 1)		$ 20,500
Ending inventory*		
Nov. 28 Purchase (100 @ $21)	$2,100	
Sept. 22 Purchase (250 @ $20)	5,000	
May 9 Purchase (200 @ $16)	3,200	
Ending inventory		10,300
Cost of goods sold...........................		$10,200

* Since FIFO assumes that the earlier costs are the first to flow out, we determine ending inventory by assigning the most recent costs to the remaining items.

2b. LIFO periodic method.

Cost of goods available for sale (from part 1)		$ 20,500
Ending inventory*		
January 1 Beg. Inventory (400 @ $14)...........	$5,600	
March 10 Purchase (150 @ $15)	2,250	
Ending inventory		7,850
Cost of goods sold...........................		$12,650

* Since LIFO assumes that the most recent (newest) costs are the first to flow out, we determine ending inventory by assigning the earliest (oldest) costs to the remaining items.

2c. Weighted average periodic method.

Step 1:	400 units @ $14 = $ 5,600	
	200 units @ $15 = 3,000	
	300 units @ $16 = 4,800	
	250 units @ $20 = 5,000	
	100 units @ $21 = 2,100	
	1,250 $20,500	

Step 2:	$20,500/1,250 units = **$16.40** weighted average cost per unit	
Step 3:	Total cost of 1,250 units available for sale	$20,500
	Less **ending inventory** priced on a weighted average cost basis: 550 units at $16.40 each	9,020
	Cost of goods sold	$11,480

2d. Specific identification method.

Total cost of 1,250 units available for sale..........		$20,500
Cost of goods sold		
Jan. 15 (200 @ $14)	$2,800	
Apr. 1 (200 @ $15).......................	3,000	
Nov. 1 (200 @ $14) + (100 @ $20)..........	4,800	10,600
Ending inventory		$ 9,900

3.

	FIFO	LIFO	Weighted Average	Specific Identification
Income Statement				
Sales*	$ 22,500	$22,500	$ 22,500	$22,500
Cost of goods sold............	10,200	12,650	11,480	10,600
Gross profit	$ 12,300	$ 9,850	$ 11,020	$11,900
Balance Sheet				
Inventory....................	$10,300	$ 7,850	$ 9,020	$ 9,900

* Sales = (200 units × $30) + (200 units × $30) + (300 units × $35) = $22,500

4. Mistakenly using LIFO, when FIFO should have been used, overstates cost of goods sold in year 2013 by $2,450, which is the difference between the FIFO and LIFO amounts of ending inventory. It understates income in 2013 by $2,450. In year 2014, income is overstated by $2,450 because of the understatement in beginning inventory.

Refer to the information in Comprehensive Need-To-Know 1 to answer the following requirements.

Required

1. Calculate the cost of goods available for sale.

2. Apply the four different methods of inventory costing (FIFO, LIFO, weighted average, and specific identification) to calculate ending inventory and cost of goods sold under each method using the perpetual system.

3. Compute gross profit earned by the company for each of the four costing methods in part 2. Also, report the inventory amount reported on the balance sheet for each of the four methods.

4. In preparing financial statements for year 2013, the financial officer was instructed to use FIFO but failed to do so and instead computed cost of goods sold according to LIFO. Determine the impact of the error on year 2013's income. Also determine the effect of this error on year 2014's income. Assume no income taxes.

5. Management wants a report that shows how changing from FIFO to another method would change net income. Prepare a table showing (1) the cost of goods sold amount under each of the four methods, (2) the amount by which each cost of goods sold total is different from the FIFO cost of goods sold, and (3) the effect on net income if another method is used instead of FIFO.

PLANNING THE SOLUTION

- Compute cost of goods available for sale by multiplying the units of beginning inventory and each purchase by their unit costs to determine the total cost of goods available for sale.
- Prepare a perpetual FIFO table starting with beginning inventory and showing how inventory changes after each purchase and after each sale (see Exhibit 5A.3).
- Prepare a perpetual LIFO table starting with beginning inventory and showing how inventory changes after each purchase and after each sale (see Exhibit 5A.4).
- Make a table of purchases and sales recalculating the average cost of inventory prior to each sale to arrive at the weighted average cost of ending inventory. Total the average costs associated with each sale to determine cost of goods sold (see Exhibit 5A.5).
- Prepare a table showing the computation of cost of goods sold and ending inventory using the specific identification method (see Exhibit 5.4).
- Compare the year-end 2013 inventory amounts under FIFO and LIFO to determine the misstatement of year 2013 income that results from using LIFO. The errors for year 2013 and 2014 are equal in amount but opposite in effect.
- Create a table showing cost of goods sold under each method and how net income would differ from FIFO net income if an alternate method is adopted.

SOLUTION TO COMPREHENSIVE NEED-TO-KNOW

1. The solution is identical to the solution for part 1 of Comprehensive Need-To-Know 1.

2a. FIFO perpetual method (FIFO yields identical results under periodic and perpetual).

Date	Goods Purchased	Cost of Goods Sold	Inventory Balance	
Jan. 1	Beginning balance		400 @ $14	= $ 5,600
Jan. 15		200 @ $14 = $2,800	200 @ $14	= $ 2,800
Mar. 10	200 @ $15 = $3,000		200 @ $14 200 @ $15 }	= $ 5,800
April 1		200 @ $14 = $2,800	200 @ $15	= $ 3,000
May 9	300 @ $16 = $4,800		200 @ $15 300 @ $16 }	= $ 7,800
Sept. 22	250 @ $20 = $5,000		200 @ $15 300 @ $16 250 @ $20 }	= $12,800
Nov. 1		200 @ $15 = $3,000 100 @ $16 = $1,600	200 @ $16 250 @ $20 }	= $ 8,200
Nov. 28	100 @ $21 = $2,100		200 @ $16 250 @ $20 100 @ $21 }	= $10,300
	Total cost of goods sold	$10,200		

Note to students: **In a classroom situation,** once we compute cost of goods available for sale, we can compute the amount for either cost of goods sold or ending inventory—it is a matter of preference. **In practice,** the costs of items sold are identified as sales are made and immediately transferred from the inventory account to the cost of goods sold account. The previous solution showing the line-by-line approach illustrates actual application in practice. The following alternate solutions illustrate that, once the concepts are understood, other solution approaches are available. Although this is only shown for FIFO, it could be shown for all methods.

Alternate Methods to Compute FIFO Perpetual Numbers

[FIFO Alternate No. 1: Computing cost of goods sold first]

Cost of goods available for sale (from part 1)			$ 20,500
Cost of goods sold			
Jan. 15	Sold (200 @ $14)	$2,800	
April 1	Sold (200 @ $14)	2,800	
Nov. 1	Sold (200 @ $15 and 100 @ $16)	4,600	10,200
Ending inventory			$10,300

[FIFO Alternate No. 2: Computing ending inventory first]

Cost of goods available for sale (from part 1)			$ 20,500
Ending inventory*			
Nov. 28	Purchase (100 @ $21)	$2,100	
Sept. 22	Purchase (250 @ $20)	5,000	
May 9	Purchase (200 @ $16)	3,200	
Ending inventory			10,300
Cost of goods sold			$10,200

* Since FIFO assumes that the earlier costs are the first to flow out, we determine ending inventory by assigning the most recent costs to the remaining items.

2b. LIFO perpetual method.

Date	Goods Purchased	Cost of Goods Sold	Inventory Balance
Jan. 1	Beginning balance		400 @ $14 = $ 5,600
Jan. 15		200 @ $14 = $2,800	200 @ $14 = $ 2,800
Mar. 10	200 @ $15 = $3,000		200 @ $14 200 @ $15 } = $ 5,800
April 1		200 @ $15 = $3,000	200 @ $14 = $ 2,800
May 9	300 @ $16 = $4,800		200 @ $14 300 @ $16 } = $ 7,600
Sept. 22	250 @ $20 = $5,000		200 @ $14 300 @ $16 250 @ $20 } = $12,600
Nov. 1		250 @ $20 = $5,000 50 @ $16 = $ 800	200 @ $14 250 @ $16 } = $ 6,800
Nov. 28	100 @ $21 = $2,100		200 @ $14 250 @ $16 100 @ $21 } = $ 8,900
Total cost of goods sold		$11,600	

2c. Weighted average perpetual method.

Date	Goods Purchased	Cost of Goods Sold	Inventory Balance	
Jan. 1	Beginning balance		400 @ $14	= $ 5,600
Jan. 15		200 @ $14 = $2,800	200 @ $14	= $ 2,800
Mar. 10	200 @ $15 = $3,000		200 @ $14 ⎫ 200 @ $15 ⎬ (avg. cost is $14.5)	= $ 5,800
April 1		200 @ $14.5 = $2,900	200 @ $14.5	= $ 2,900
May 9	300 @ $16 = $4,800		200 @ $14.5 ⎫ 300 @ $16 ⎬ (avg. cost is $15.4)	= $ 7,700
Sept. 22	250 @ $20 = $5,000		200 @ $14.5 ⎫ 300 @ $16 ⎬ 250 @ $20 ⎭ (avg. cost is $16.93)	= $ 12,700
Nov. 1		300 @ $16.93 = $5,079	450 @ $16.93	= $ 7,618.5
Nov. 28	100 @ $21 = $2,100		450 @ $16.93 ⎫ 100 @ $21 ⎬	= $9,718.5
Total cost of goods sold*		$10,779		

* The cost of goods sold ($10,779) plus ending inventory ($9,718.5) is $2.5 less than the cost of goods available for sale ($20,500) due to rounding.

2d. Specific identification method.

The solution is identical to the solution shown in part 2d of Comprehensive Need-To-Know 1. This is because specific identification is *not* a cost flow assumption; instead, this method specifically identifies each item in inventory and each item that is sold.

3.

	FIFO	LIFO	Weighted Average	Specific Identification
Income Statement				
Sales*	$ 22,500	$22,500	$ 22,500	$22,500
Cost of goods sold...........	10,200	11,600	10,779	10,600
Gross profit................	$ 12,300	$10,900	$ 11,721	$11,900
Balance Sheet				
Inventory....................	$10,300	$ 8,900	$9,718.5	$ 9,900

* Sales = (200 units × $30) + (200 units × $30) + (300 units × $35) = $22,500

4. Mistakenly using LIFO, when FIFO should have been used, overstates cost of goods sold in year 2013 by $1,400, which is the difference between the FIFO and LIFO amounts of ending inventory. It understates income in 2013 by $1,400. In year 2014, income is overstated by $1,400 because of the understatement in beginning inventory.

5. Analysis of the effects of alternative inventory methods.

	Cost of Goods Sold	Difference from FIFO Cost of Goods Sold	Effect on Net Income If Adopted Instead of FIFO
FIFO	$10,200	—	—
LIFO	11,600	+$1,400	$1,400 lower
Weighted average	10,779	+ 579	579 lower
Specific identification	10,600	+ 400	400 lower

5A   Inventory Costing under a Perpetual System

P3A *Appendix 5A—Compute inventory in a perpetual system using the methods of specific identification, FIFO, LIFO, and weighted average.*

This section illustrates inventory costing methods. We use information from Trekking, a sporting goods store. Among its products, Trekking carries one type of mountain bike whose sales are directed at resorts that provide inexpensive mountain bikes for complimentary guest use. These resorts usually purchase in amounts of 10 or more bikes. We use Trekking's data from August. Its mountain bike (unit) inventory at the beginning of August and its purchases and sales during August are in Exhibit 5A.1. It ends August with 12 bikes in inventory. Trekking uses the perpetual inventory system, which means that its merchandise inventory account is continually updated to reflect purchases and sales. Regardless of what inventory method or system is used, cost of goods available for sale must be allocated between cost of goods sold and ending inventory.

EXHIBIT 5A.1

Purchases and Sales of Goods

Date	Activity	Units Acquired at Cost	Units Sold at Retail	Unit Inventory
Aug. 1	Beginning inventory	10 units @ $ 91 = $ 910		10 units
Aug. 3	Purchases	15 units @ $106 = $ 1,590		25 units
Aug. 14	Sales		20 units @ $130	5 units
Aug. 17	Purchases	20 units @ $115 = $ 2,300		25 units
Aug. 28	Purchases	10 units @ $119 = $ 1,190		35 units
Aug. 31	Sales		23 units @ $150	12 units
	Totals	55 units $5,990	43 units	

Units available for sale   Goods available for sale   Units sold   Units left

Specific Identification   When each item in inventory can be identified with a specific purchase and invoice, we can use **specific identification** (also called *specific invoice inventory pricing*) to assign costs. We also need sales records that identify exactly which items were sold and when. Trekking's internal data reveal the following specific unit sales:

August 14   Sold 8 bikes costing $91 each and 12 bikes costing $106 each
August 31   Sold 2 bikes costing $91 each, 3 bikes costing $106 each, 15 bikes costing $115 each, and 3 bikes costing $119 each

Point: Three key variables determine the value assigned to ending inventory: (1) inventory quantity, (2) unit costs of inventory, and (3) cost flow assumption.

Applying specific identification and using the information above, we prepare Exhibit 5A.2. This exhibit begins with the $5,990 in total units available for sale—this is from Exhibit 5.3. Applying specific identification, we know that for the 20 units sold on August 14, the company specifically identified that 8 of them had cost $91 each and 12 had cost $106 each, resulting in an August 14 cost of sales of $2,000. Next, for the 23 units sold on August 31, the company specifically identified that 2 of them had cost $91 each, that 3 had cost $106 each, that 15 had cost $115 each, and 3 had cost $119 each, resulting in an August 31 cost of sales of $2,582. This yields a total cost of sales for the period of $4,582. We then subtract this $4,582 in cost of goods sold from the $5,990 in cost of goods available to get $1,408 in ending inventory. Carefully study Exhibit 5A.2 to see the flow of costs. Each unit, whether sold or remaining in inventory, has its own specific cost attached to it.

Point: The assignment of costs to the goods sold and to inventory using specific identification is the same for both the perpetual and periodic systems.

EXHIBIT 5A.2

Specific Identification Computations

Total cost of 55 units available for sale (from Exhibit 5.3)		$5,990
Cost of goods sold*		
Aug. 14 (8 @ $91) + (12 @ $106)	$2,000	
Aug. 31 (2 @ $91) + (3 @ $106) + (15 @ $115) + (3 @ $119)	2,582	4,582
Ending inventory		$1,408

* Identification of items sold (and their costs) is obtained from internal documents that track each unit from its purchase to its sale.

When using specific identification, Trekking's cost of goods sold reported on the income statement totals $4,582, the sum of $2,000 and $2,582 from the cost of goods sold section of Exhibit 5A.2. Trekking's ending inventory reported on the balance sheet is $1,408, which is the final inventory balance. The purchases and sales entries for Exhibit 5A.2 follow (the colored boldface numbers are those impacted by the cost flow assumption):

Point: Specific identification is usually practical only for companies with expensive, custom-made inventory. Examples include car dealerships, implement dealers, jewelers, and fashion designers.

Purchases			
Aug. 3	Merchandise Inventory	1,590	
	Accounts Payable		1,590
17	Merchandise Inventory	2,300	
	Accounts Payable		2,300
28	Merchandise Inventory	1,190	
	Accounts Payable		1,190

Sales			
Aug. 14	Accounts Receivable	2,600	
	Sales		2,600
14	Cost of Goods Sold	2,000	
	Merchandise Inventory		2,000
31	Accounts Receivable	3,450	
	Sales		3,450
31	Cost of Goods Sold	2,582	
	Merchandise Inventory		2,582

First-In, First-Out   The **first-in, first-out (FIFO)** method of assigning costs to both inventory and cost of goods sold assumes that inventory items are sold in the order acquired. When sales occur, the costs of the earliest units acquired are charged to cost of goods sold. This leaves the costs from the most recent purchases in ending inventory. Use of FIFO for computing the cost of inventory and cost of goods sold is shown in Exhibit 5A.3.

Point: The "Goods Purchased" column is identical for all methods. Data are taken from Exhibit 5A.1.

This exhibit starts with beginning inventory of 10 bikes at $91 each. On August 3, 15 more bikes costing $106 each are bought for $1,590. Inventory now consists of 10 bikes at $91 each and 15 bikes at $106 each, for a total of $2,500. On August 14, 20 bikes are sold—applying FIFO, the first 10 sold cost $91 each and the next 10 sold cost $106 each, for a total cost of $1,970. This leaves 5 bikes costing $106 each, or $530, in inventory. On August 17, 20 bikes costing $2,300 are purchased, and on August 28, another 10 bikes costing $1,190 are purchased, for a total of 35 bikes costing $4,020 in inventory. On August 31, 23 bikes are sold—applying FIFO, the first 5 bikes sold cost $530 and the next 18 sold cost $2,070, which leaves 12 bikes costing $1,420 in ending inventory.

Date	Goods Purchased	Cost of Goods Sold	Inventory Balance
Aug. 1	Beginning balance		10 @ $ 91 = $ 910
Aug. 3	15 @ $106 = $1,590		10 @ $ 91 } 15 @ $106 } = $2,500
Aug. 14		10 @ $ 91 = $ 910 } 10 @ $106 = $1,060 } = $1,970	5 @ $106 = $ 530
Aug. 17	20 @ $115 = $2,300		5 @ $106 } 20 @ $115 } = $2,830
Aug. 28	10 @ $119 = $1,190		5 @ $106 } 20 @ $115 } = $4,020 10 @ $119 }
Aug. 31		5 @ $106 = $ 530 } 18 @ $115 = $2,070 } = $2,600 $4,570	2 @ $115 } = $1,420 10 @ $119 }

EXHIBIT 5A.3

FIFO Computations—Perpetual System

For the 20 units sold on Aug. 14, the first 10 sold are assigned the earliest cost of $91 (from beg. bal.). The next 10 sold are assigned the next earliest cost of $106.

For the 23 units sold on Aug. 31, the first 5 sold are assigned the earliest available cost of $106 (from Aug. 3 purchase). The next 18 sold are assigned the next earliest cost of $115 (from Aug. 17 purchase).

Trekking's FIFO cost of goods sold reported on its income statement (reflecting the 43 units sold) is $4,570 ($1,970 + $2,600), and its ending inventory reported on the balance sheet (reflecting the 12 units unsold) is $1,420. These amounts are the same as those computed using the periodic system. This always occurs because the most recent purchases are in ending inventory under both systems.

Point: Under FIFO, a unit sold is assigned the earliest (oldest) cost from inventory. This leaves the most recent costs in ending inventory.

Point: *LOSH (last ones still here)* can help remember what costs are in FIFO ending inventory.

The purchases and sales entries for Exhibit 5A.3 follow (the colored boldface numbers are those affected by the cost flow assumption).

Purchases				Sales		
Aug. 3	Merchandise Inventory 1,590		Aug. 14	Accounts Receivable 2,600	
	Accounts Payable	1,590		Sales	2,600
17	Merchandise Inventory 2,300		14	Cost of Goods Sold 1,970	
	Accounts Payable	2,300		Merchandise Inventory	1,970
28	Merchandise Inventory 1,190		31	Accounts Receivable 3,450	
	Accounts Payable	1,190		Sales	3,450
			31	Cost of Goods Sold 2,600	
				Merchandise Inventory	2,600

Last-In, First-Out The **last-in, first-out (LIFO)** method of assigning costs assumes that the most recent purchases are sold first. These more recent costs are charged to the goods sold, and the costs of the earliest purchases are assigned to inventory. As with other methods, LIFO is acceptable even when the physical flow of goods does not follow a last-in, first-out pattern. One appeal of LIFO is that by assigning costs from the most recent purchases to cost of goods sold, LIFO comes closest to matching current costs of goods sold with revenues (compared to FIFO or weighted average).

Point: Under LIFO, a unit sold is assigned the most recent (latest) cost from inventory. This leaves the oldest costs in inventory.

Point: *FOSH (first ones still here)* can help remember what costs are in LIFO ending inventory.

Exhibit 5A.4 shows the LIFO computations. It starts with beginning inventory of 10 bikes at $91 each. On August 3, 15 more bikes costing $106 each are bought for $1,590. Inventory now consists of 10 bikes at $91 each and 15 bikes at $106 each, for a total of $2,500. On August 14, 20 bikes are sold—applying LIFO, the first 15 sold are from the most recent purchase costing $106 each, and the next 5 sold are from the next most recent purchase costing $91 each, for a total cost of $2,045. This leaves 5 bikes costing $91 each, or $455, in inventory. On August 17, 20 bikes costing $2,300 are purchased, and on August 28, another 10 bikes costing $1,190 are purchased, for a total of 35 bikes costing $3,945 in inventory. On August 31, 23 bikes are sold—applying LIFO, the first 10 bikes sold are from the most recent purchase costing $1,190, and the next 13 sold are from the next most recent purchase costing $1,495, which leaves 12 bikes costing $1,260 in ending inventory.

EXHIBIT 5A.4

LIFO Computations— Perpetual System

Date	Goods Purchased	Cost of Goods Sold	Inventory Balance
Aug. 1	Beginning balance		10 @ $ 91 = $ 910
Aug. 3	15 @ $106 = $1,590		10 @ $ 91 } = $ 2,500 15 @ $106 }
Aug. 14		15 @ $106 = $1,590 } 5 @ $ 91 = $ 455 } = $2,045	5 @ $ 91 = $ 455
Aug. 17	20 @ $115 = $2,300		5 @ $ 91 } = $ 2,755 20 @ $115 }
Aug. 28	10 @ $119 = $1,190		5 @ $ 91 } 20 @ $115 } = $ 3,945 10 @ $119 }
Aug. 31		10 @ $119 = $1,190 } 13 @ $115 = $1,495 } = $2,685 $4,730	5 @ $ 91 } = $1,260 7 @ $115 }

For the 20 units sold on Aug. 14, the first 15 sold are assigned the most recent cost of $106. The next 5 sold are assigned the next most recent cost of $91.

For the 23 units sold on Aug. 31, the first 10 sold are assigned the most recent cost of $119. The next 13 sold are assigned the next most recent cost of $115.

Trekking's LIFO cost of goods sold reported on the income statement is $4,730 ($2,045 + $2,685), and its ending inventory reported on the balance sheet is $1,260. When LIFO is used with the perpetual system, cost of goods sold is assigned costs from the most recent purchases at the point of each sale. With the periodic system, cost of goods sold is assigned costs from the most recent purchases for the period.

The purchases and sales entries for Exhibit 5A.4 follow (the colored boldface numbers are those affected by the cost flow assumption).

Purchases		
Aug. 3	Merchandise Inventory 1,590	
	Accounts Payable	1,590
17	Merchandise Inventory 2,300	
	Accounts Payable	2,300
28	Merchandise Inventory 1,190	
	Accounts Payable	1,190

Sales		
Aug. 14	Accounts Receivable 2,600	
	Sales	2,600
14	Cost of Goods Sold 2,045	
	Merchandise Inventory	2,045
31	Accounts Receivable 3,450	
	Sales	3,450
31	Cost of Goods Sold 2,685	
	Merchandise Inventory	2,685

Point: Grocers prefer a FIFO physical flow of milk cartons. Consumers prefer a LIFO flow as they desire a long refrigerator life and reach for recently stocked milk. However, the cost flow in accounting need not match the physical flow in the store.

Weighted Average   The **weighted average** (also called **average cost**) method of assigning cost requires that we use the weighted average cost per unit of inventory at the time of each sale. Weighted average cost per unit at the time of each sale equals the cost of goods available for sale divided by the units available. The results using weighted average (WA) for Trekking are shown in Exhibit 5A.5.

Date	Goods Purchased	Cost of Goods Sold	Inventory Balance
Aug. 1	Beginning balance		10 @ $ 91 = $ 910
Aug. 3	15 @ $106 = $1,590		10 @ $ 91 } 15 @ $106 } = $2,500 (or $100 per unit)[a]
Aug. 14		20 @ $100 = **$2,000**	5 @ $100 = $ 500 (or $100 per unit)[b]
Aug. 17	20 @ $115 = $2,300		5 @ $100 } 20 @ $115 } = $2,800 (or $112 per unit)[c]
Aug. 28	10 @ $119 = $1,190		5 @ $100 } 20 @ $115 } = $3,990 (or $114 per unit)[d] 10 @ $119 }
Aug. 31		23 @ $114 = **$2,622**	12 @ $114 = $1,368 (or $114 per unit)[e]
		$4,622	

EXHIBIT 5A.5

Weighted Average
Computations—Perpetual System

For the 20 units sold on Aug. 14, the cost assigned is the $100 *average cost* per unit from the inventory balance column at the time of sale.

For the 23 units sold on Aug. 31, the cost assigned is the $114 *average cost* per unit from the inventory balance column at the time of sale.

[a] $100 per unit = ($2,500 inventory balance ÷ 25 units in inventory).
[b] $100 per unit = ($500 inventory balance ÷ 5 units in inventory).
[c] $112 per unit = ($2,800 inventory balance ÷ 25 units in inventory).
[d] $114 per unit = ($3,990 inventory balance ÷ 35 units in inventory).
[e] $114 per unit = ($1,368 inventory balance ÷ 12 units in inventory).

This exhibit starts with beginning inventory of 10 bikes at $91 each. On August 3, 15 more bikes costing $106 each are bought for $1,590. Inventory now consists of 10 bikes at $91 each and 15 bikes at $106 each, for a total of $2,500. The average cost per bike for that inventory is $100, computed as $2,500/(10 bikes + 15 bikes). On August 14, 20 bikes are sold—applying WA, the 20 sold are assigned the $100 average cost, for a total cost of $2,000. This leaves 5 bikes with an average cost of $100 each, or $500, in inventory. On August 17, 20 bikes costing $2,300 are purchased, and on August 28, another 10 bikes costing $1,190 are purchased, for a total of 35 bikes costing $3,990 in inventory at August 28. The average cost per bike for the August 28 inventory is $114, computed as $3,990/(5 bikes + 20 bikes + 10 bikes). On August 31, 23 bikes are sold—applying WA, the 23 sold are assigned the $114 average cost, for a total cost of $2,622. This leaves 12 bikes costing $1,368 in ending inventory.

Point: Weighted average usually yields different results for the perpetual and the periodic systems because under a perpetual system it recomputes the per unit cost prior to each sale, whereas under a periodic system, the per unit cost is computed only at the end of a period.

Trekking's cost of goods sold reported on the income statement (reflecting the 43 units sold) is $4,622 ($2,000 + $2,622), and its ending inventory reported on the balance sheet (reflecting the 12 units unsold) is $1,368.

The purchases and sales entries for Exhibit 5A.5 follow (the colored boldface numbers are those affected by the cost flow assumption).

Purchases			Sales		
Aug. 3 Merchandise Inventory 1,590			Aug. 14 Accounts Receivable 2,600		
Accounts Payable		1,590	Sales		2,600
17 Merchandise Inventory 2,300			14 Cost of Goods Sold 2,000		
Accounts Payable		2,300	Merchandise Inventory		2,000
28 Merchandise Inventory 1,190			31 Accounts Receivable 3,450		
Accounts Payable		1,190	Sales		3,450
			31 Cost of Goods Sold 2,622		
			Merchandise Inventory		2,622

This completes computations under the four most common perpetual inventory costing methods. Advances in technology have greatly reduced the cost of a perpetual inventory system. Many companies now ask whether they can afford *not* to have a perpetual inventory system because timely access to inventory information is a competitive advantage and it can help reduce the amount of inventory, which reduces costs.

Financial Statement Effects of Costing Methods   When purchase prices do not change, each inventory costing method assigns the same cost amounts to inventory and to cost of goods sold. When purchase prices are different, however, the methods nearly always assign different cost amounts. We show these differences in Exhibit 5A.6 using Trekking's data.

EXHIBIT 5A.6

Financial Statement Effects of Inventory Costing Methods

TREKKING COMPANY For Month Ended August 31				
	Specific Identification	FIFO	LIFO	Weighted Average
Income Statement				
Sales	$ 6,050	$ 6,050	$ 6,050	$ 6,050
Cost of goods sold	4,582	4,570	4,730	4,622
Gross profit	1,468	1,480	1,320	1,428
Expenses	450	450	450	450
Income before taxes	1,018	1,030	870	978
Income tax expense (30%)	305	309	261	293
Net income	$ 713	$ 721	$ 609	$ 685
Balance Sheet				
Inventory	$1,408	$1,420	$1,260	$1,368

This exhibit reveals two important results. First, when purchase costs *regularly rise,* as in Trekking's case, the following occurs:

● FIFO assigns the lowest amount to cost of goods sold—yielding the highest gross profit and net income.

● LIFO assigns the highest amount to cost of goods sold—yielding the lowest gross profit and net income, which also yields a temporary tax advantage by postponing payment of some income tax.

● Weighted average yields results between FIFO and LIFO.

● Specific identification always yields results that depend on which units are sold.

Second, when costs *regularly decline,* the reverse occurs for FIFO and LIFO. Namely, FIFO gives the highest cost of goods sold—yielding the lowest gross profit and income. However, LIFO then gives the lowest cost of goods sold—yielding the highest gross profit and income.

All four inventory costing methods are acceptable. However, a company must disclose the inventory method it uses in its financial statements or notes. Each method offers certain advantages as follows:

- FIFO assigns an amount to inventory on the balance sheet that approximates its current cost; it also mimics the actual flow of goods for most businesses.
- LIFO assigns an amount to cost of goods sold on the income statement that approximates its current cost; it also better matches current costs with revenues in computing gross profit.
- Weighted average tends to smooth out erratic changes in costs.
- Specific identification exactly matches the costs of items with the revenues they generate.

A company reported the following December purchases and sales data for its only product.

Date	Activities	Units Acquired at Cost	Units Sold at Retail
Dec. 1	Beginning inventory........	5 units @ $3.00 = $ 15.00	
Dec. 8	Purchase	10 units @ $4.50 = 45.00	
Dec. 9	Sales.....................		8 units @ $7.00
Dec. 19	Purchase	13 units @ $5.00 = 65.00	
Dec. 24	Sales....................		18 units @ $8.00
Dec. 30	Purchase	8 units @ $5.30 = 42.40	
Totals	....	36 units $167.40	26 units

The company uses a *perpetual inventory system.* Determine the cost assigned to ending inventory and to cost of goods sold using (a) specific identification, (b) FIFO, (c) LIFO, and (d) weighted average. (Round per unit costs and inventory amounts to cents.) For specific identification, ending inventory consists of 10 units, where eight are from the December 30 purchase and two are from the December 8 purchase.

Solutions

a. Specific identification: Ending inventory—eight units from December 30 purchase and two units from December 8 purchase

Specific Identification	Ending Inventory	Cost of Goods Sold
(8 × $5.30) + (2 × $4.50)...	$51.40	
(5 × $3.00) + (2 × $4.50) + (13 × $5.00) + (0 × $5.30)		$116.00
or $167.40 [Total Goods Available] − $51.40 [Ending Inventory].........		$116.00

b. FIFO—Perpetual

Date	Goods Purchased	Cost of Goods Sold	Inventory Balance
12/1			5 @ $3.00 = $15.00
12/8	10 @ $4.50		5 @ $3.00 } = $60.00 10 @ $4.50 }
12/9		5 @ $3.00 } = $ 28.50 3 @ $4.50 }	7 @ $4.50 = $31.50
12/19	13 @ $5.00		7 @ $4.50 } = $96.50 13 @ $5.00 }
12/24		7 @ $4.50 } = $ 86.50 11 @ $5.00 }	2 @ $5.00 = $10.00
12/30	8 @ $5.30		2 @ $5.00 } = $52.40 8 @ $5.30 }
		$115.00	

OR "short-cut" FIFO—Perpetual

FIFO	Ending Inventory	Cost of Goods Sold
$(8 \times \$5.30) + (2 \times \$5.00)$	$52.40	
$(5 \times \$3.00) + (10 \times \$4.50) + (11 \times \$5.00)$		$115.00
or $167.40 [Total Goods Available] − $52.40 [Ending Inventory].........		$115.00

c. LIFO—Perpetual

Date	Goods Purchased	Cost of Goods Sold	Inventory Balance	
12/1			5 @ $3.00	= $15.00
12/8	10 @ $4.50		5 @ $3.00 10 @ $4.50 }	= $60.00
12/9		8 @ $4.50 = $ 36.00	5 @ $3.00 2 @ $4.50 }	= $24.00
12/19	13 @ $5.00		5 @ $3.00 2 @ $4.50 13 @ $5.00 }	= $89.00
12/24		13 @ $5.00 2 @ $4.50 } = $ 83.00 3 @ $3.00	2 @ $3.00	= $ 6.00
12/30	8 @ $5.30	 $119.00	2 @ $3.00 8 @ $5.30 }	= $48.40

d. Weighted Average—Perpetual

Date	Goods Purchased	Cost of Goods Sold	Inventory Balance	
12/1			5 @ $3.00	= $15.00
12/8	10 @ $4.50		5 @ $3.00 10 @ $4.50 } (avg. cost is $4.00)	= $60.00
12/9		8 @ $4.00 = $ 32.00	7 @ $4.00	= $28.00
12/19	13 @ $5.00		7 @ $4.00 13 @ $5.00 } (avg. cost is $4.65)	= $93.00
12/24		18 @ $4.65 = $ 83.70	2 @ $4.65	= $ 9.30
12/30	8 @ $5.30	 $115.70	2 @ $4.65 8 @ $5.30 } (avg. cost is $5.17)	= $51.70

Do More: QS 5-1, QS 5-2, QS 5-3, QS 5-8, QS 5-9, QS 5-10, QS 5-11

APPENDIX

5B

Inventory Estimation Methods

P4 Apply both the retail inventory and gross profit methods to estimate inventory.

Inventory sometimes requires estimation for two reasons. First, companies often require **interim statements** (financial statements prepared for periods of less than one year), but they only annually take a physical count of inventory. Second, companies may require an inventory estimate if some casualty such as fire or flood makes taking a physical count impossible. Estimates are usually only required for companies that use the periodic system. Companies using a perpetual system would presumably have updated inventory data.

This appendix describes two methods to estimate inventory.

Retail Inventory Method   To avoid the time-consuming and expensive process of taking a physical inventory each month or quarter, some companies use the **retail inventory method** to estimate cost of goods sold and ending inventory. Some companies even use the retail inventory method to prepare the annual statements. Home Depot, for instance, says in its annual report: "Inventories are stated at the lower of cost (first-in, first-out) or market, as determined by the retail inventory method." A company may also estimate inventory for audit purposes or when inventory is damaged or destroyed.

The retail inventory method uses a three-step process to estimate ending inventory. We need to know the amount of inventory a company had at the beginning of the period in both *cost* and *retail* amounts. We already explained how to compute the cost of inventory. The *retail amount of inventory* refers to its dollar amount measured using selling prices of inventory items. We also need to know the net amount of goods purchased (minus returns, allowances, and discounts) in the period, both at cost and at retail. The amount of net sales at retail is also needed. The process is shown in Exhibit 5B.1.

The reasoning behind the retail inventory method is that if we can get a good estimate of the cost-to-retail ratio, we can multiply ending inventory at retail by this ratio to estimate ending inventory at cost. We show in Exhibit 5B.2 how these steps are applied to estimate ending inventory for a typical company. First, we find that $100,000 of goods (at retail selling prices) were available for sale. We see that $70,000 of these goods were sold, leaving $30,000 (retail value) of merchandise in ending inventory. Second, the cost of these goods is 60% of the $100,000 retail value. Third, since cost for these goods is 60% of retail, the estimated cost of ending inventory is $18,000.

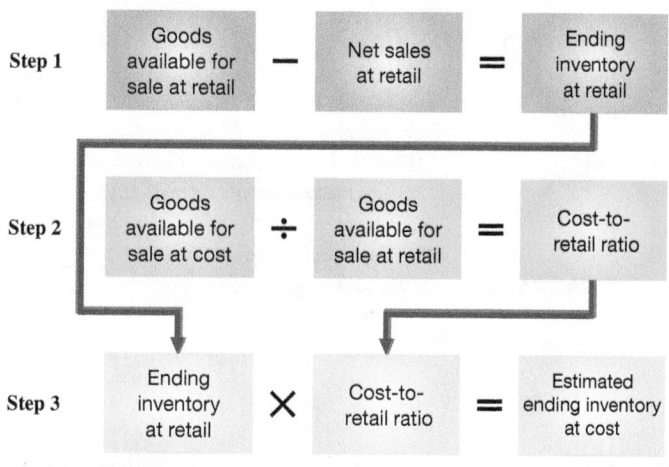

EXHIBIT 5B.1

Retail Inventory Method of Inventory Estimation

Point: When a retailer takes a physical inventory, it can restate the retail value of inventory to a cost basis by applying the cost-to-retail ratio. It can also estimate the amount of shrinkage by comparing the inventory computed with the amount from a physical inventory.

Example: What is the cost of ending inventory in Exhibit 5B.2 if the cost of beginning inventory is $22,500 and its retail value is $34,500? *Answer:* $30,000 × 62% = $18,600

		At Cost	At Retail
Goods available for sale			
Beginning inventory		$ 20,500	$ 34,500
Cost of goods purchased.......................		39,500	65,500
Step 1: { Goods available for sale		60,000	100,000
Deduct net sales at retail			70,000
Ending inventory at retail			$ 30,000
Step 2:	Cost-to-retail ratio: ($60,000 ÷ $100,000) = 60%		
Step 3:	Estimated ending inventory at cost ($30,000 × 60%)	$18,000	

EXHIBIT 5B.2

Estimated Inventory Using the Retail Inventory Method

Point: A retailer such as Target can speed up its year-end physical count by using the retail inventory method. Inventory counters can record the item's retail price without having to look up the cost of each item.

Gross Profit Method   The **gross profit method** estimates the cost of ending inventory by applying the gross profit ratio to net sales (at retail). This type of estimate often is needed when inventory is destroyed, lost, or stolen. These cases require an inventory estimate so that a company can file a claim with its insurer. Users also apply this method to see whether inventory amounts from a physical count are reasonable. This method uses the historical relation between cost of goods sold and net sales to estimate the proportion of cost of goods sold making up current sales. This cost of goods sold estimate is then subtracted from cost of goods available for sale to estimate the ending inventory at cost. These two steps are shown in Exhibit 5B.3.

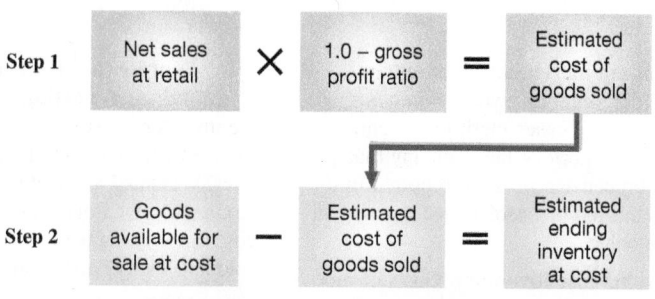

EXHIBIT 5B.3

Gross Profit Method of Inventory Estimation

Point: A fire or other catastrophe can result in an insurance claim for lost inventory or income. Backup and off-site storage of data help ensure coverage for such losses.

Point: Reliability of the gross profit method depends on an accurate and stable estimate of the gross profit ratio.

To illustrate, assume that a company's inventory is destroyed by fire in March 2013. When the fire occurs, the company's accounts show the following balances for January through March: sales, $31,500; sales returns, $1,500; inventory (January 1, 2013), $12,000; and cost of goods purchased, $20,500. If this company's gross profit ratio is 30%, then 30% of each net sales dollar is gross profit and 70% is cost of goods sold. We show in Exhibit 5B.4 how this 70% is used to estimate lost inventory of $11,500. To understand this exhibit, think of subtracting the cost of goods sold from the goods available for sale to get the ending inventory.

EXHIBIT 5B.4

Estimated Inventory Using the Gross Profit Method

Goods available for sale		
Inventory, January 1, 2013	$12,000	
Cost of goods purchased	20,500	
Goods available for sale (at cost)	32,500	
Net sales at retail ($31,500 − $1,500)		$30,000
Step 1: Estimated cost of goods sold ($30,000 × 70%)	(21,000) ← × 0.70	
Step 2: Estimated March inventory at cost	$11,500	

NEED-TO-KNOW 5.6

P4

Using the retail method and the following data, estimate the cost of ending inventory.

	Cost	Retail
Beginning inventory	$324,000	$530,000
Cost of goods purchased	195,000	335,000
Net sales		320,000

Solution

Estimated ending inventory (at cost) is $327,000. It is computed as follows:

Step 1: ($530,000 + $335,000) − $320,000 = $545,000

Step 2: $\dfrac{\$324,000 + \$195,000}{\$530,000 + \$335,000} = 60\%$

Do More: QS 5-22, E 5-16, E 5-17

Step 3: $545,000 × 60% = \underline{\$327,000}$

Summary

C1 Identify the items making up merchandise inventory.
Merchandise inventory refers to goods owned by a company and held for resale. Three special cases merit our attention. Goods in transit are reported in inventory of the company that holds ownership rights. Goods on consignment are reported in the consignor's inventory. Goods damaged or obsolete are reported in inventory at their net realizable value.

C2 Identify the costs of merchandise inventory. Costs of merchandise inventory include expenditures necessary to bring an item to a salable condition and location. This includes its invoice cost minus any discount plus any added or incidental costs necessary to put it in a place and condition for sale.

A1 Analyze the effects of inventory methods for both financial and tax reporting. When purchase costs are rising or falling, the inventory costing methods are likely to assign different costs to inventory. Specific identification exactly matches costs and revenues. Weighted average smooths out cost changes. FIFO assigns an amount to inventory closely approximating current replacement cost. LIFO assigns the most recent costs incurred to cost of goods sold and likely better matches current costs with revenues.

A2 Analyze the effects of inventory errors on current and future financial statements. An error in the amount of ending inventory affects assets (inventory), net income (cost of goods sold), and equity for that period. Since ending inventory is next period's beginning inventory, an error in ending inventory affects next period's cost of goods sold and net income. Inventory errors in one period are offset in the next period.

A3 **Assess inventory management using both inventory turnover and days' sales in inventory.** We prefer a high inventory turnover, provided that goods are not out of stock and customers are not turned away. We use days' sales in inventory to assess the likelihood of goods being out of stock. We prefer a small number of days' sales in inventory if we can serve customer needs and provide a buffer for uncertainties.

P1 **Compute inventory in a periodic system using the methods of specific identification, FIFO, LIFO, and weighted average.** Periodic inventory systems allocate the cost of goods available for sale between cost of goods sold and ending inventory *at the end of a period*. Specific identification and FIFO give identical results whether the periodic or perpetual system is used. LIFO assigns costs to cost of goods sold assuming the last units purchased for the period are the first units sold. The weighted average cost per unit is computed by dividing the total cost of beginning inventory and net purchases for the period by the total number of units available. Then, it multiplies cost per unit by the number of units sold to give cost of goods sold.

P2 **Compute the lower of cost or market amount of inventory.** Inventory is reported at market cost when market is *lower* than recorded cost, called the *lower of cost or market (LCM) inventory*. Market is typically measured as replacement cost. Lower of cost or market can be applied separately to each item, to major categories of items, or to the entire inventory.

P3A **Compute inventory in a perpetual system using the methods of specific identification, FIFO, LIFO, and weighted average.** Costs are assigned to the cost of goods sold account *each time* a sale occurs in a perpetual system. Specific identification assigns a cost to each item sold by referring to its actual cost (for example, its net invoice cost). Weighted average assigns a cost to items sold by dividing the current balance in the inventory account by the total items available for sale to determine cost per unit. We then multiply the number of units sold by this cost per unit to get the cost of each sale. FIFO assigns cost to items sold assuming that the earliest units purchased are the first units sold. LIFO assigns cost to items sold assuming that the most recent units purchased are the first units sold.

P4B **Apply both the retail inventory and gross profit methods to estimate inventory.** The retail inventory method involves three steps: (1) goods available at retail minus net sales at retail equals ending inventory at retail, (2) goods available at cost divided by goods available at retail equals the cost-to-retail ratio, and (3) ending inventory at retail multiplied by the cost-to-retail ratio equals estimated ending inventory at cost. The gross profit method involves two steps: (1) net sales at retail multiplied by 1 minus the gross profit ratio equals estimated cost of goods sold, and (2) goods available at cost minus estimated cost of goods sold equals estimated ending inventory at cost.

Guidance Answers to Decision Maker and Decision Ethics

Cost Analyst   Explain to your supervisor that when inventory costs are increasing, FIFO results in an inventory valuation that approximates replacement cost. The most recently purchased goods are assigned to ending inventory under FIFO and are likely closer to replacement values than earlier costs that would be assigned to inventory if LIFO were used.

Inventory Manager   It seems your company can save (or at least postpone) taxes by switching to LIFO, but the switch is likely to reduce bonus money that you think you have earned and deserve. Since the U.S. tax code requires companies that use LIFO for tax reporting also to use it for financial reporting, your options are further constrained. Your best decision is to tell your superior about the tax savings with LIFO. You also should discuss your bonus plan and how this is likely to hurt you unfairly. You might propose to compute inventory under the LIFO method for reporting purposes but use the FIFO method for your bonus calculations. Another solution is to revise the bonus plan to reflect the company's use of the LIFO method.

Entrepreneur   Your inventory turnover is markedly higher than the norm, whereas days' sales in inventory approximates the norm. Since your turnover is already 14% better than average, you are probably best served by directing attention to days' sales in inventory. You should see whether you can reduce the level of inventory while maintaining service to customers. Given your higher turnover, you should be able to hold less inventory.

Key Terms

Average cost (pp. 220, 237)
Conservatism constraint (p. 224)
Consignee (p. 214)
Consignor (p. 214)
Consistency concept (p. 222)
Days' sales in inventory (p. 228)

First-in, first-out (FIFO) (pp. 218, 235)
Gross profit method (p. 241)
Interim statements (p. 240)
Inventory turnover (p. 227)
Last-in, first-out (LIFO) (pp. 219, 236)
Lower of cost or market (LCM) (p. 223)

Net realizable value (p. 214)
Retail inventory method (p. 241)
Specific identification (p. 217, 234)
Weighted average (p. 220, 237)

Multiple Choice Quiz Answers on p. 260 mhhe.com/wildFA7e

Additional Quiz Questions are available at the book's Website.

Use the following information from Marvel Company for the month of July to answer questions 1 through 4.

July 1	Beginning inventory	75 units @ $25 each
July 3	Purchase	348 units @ $27 each
July 8	Sale	300 units
July 15	Purchase	257 units @ $28 each
July 23	Sale	275 units

1. **Periodic:** Assume that Marvel uses a *periodic* FIFO inventory system. What is the dollar value of its ending inventory?
   a. $2,940   d. $2,852
   b. $2,685   e. $2,705
   c. $2,625

2. **Periodic:** Assume that Marvel uses a *periodic* specific identification inventory system. Its ending inventory consists of 20 units from beginning inventory, 40 units from the July 3 purchase, and 45 units from the July 15 purchase. What is the dollar value of its ending inventory?
   a. $2,940   d. $2,852
   b. $2,685   e. $2,840
   c. $2,625

3. **Perpetual:** Assume that Marvel uses a *perpetual* LIFO inventory system. What is the dollar value of its ending inventory?
   a. $2,940   d. $2,852
   b. $2,685   e. $2,705
   c. $2,625

4. **Perpetual:** Assume that Marvel uses a *perpetual* FIFO inventory system. What is the dollar value of its ending inventory?
   a. $2,940   d. $2,852
   b. $2,685   e. $2,705
   c. $2,625

5. **Periodic:** A company reports the following beginning inventory and purchases, and it ends the period with 30 units in inventory.

Beginning inventory	100 units at $10 cost per unit
Purchase 1	40 units at $12 cost per unit
Purchase 2	20 units at $14 cost per unit

   a. Compute ending inventory using the FIFO *periodic* system.
   b. Compute cost of goods sold using the LIFO *periodic* system.

6. A company has cost of goods sold of $85,000 and ending inventory of $18,000. Its days' sales in inventory equals:
   a. 49.32 days   d. 77.29 days
   b. 0.21 days   e. 1,723.61 days
   c. 4.72 days

B Superscript letter A (B) denotes assignments based on Appendix 5A (5B).

Icon denotes assignments that involve decision making.

Discussion Questions

1. Describe how costs flow from inventory to cost of goods sold for the following methods: (*a*) FIFO and (*b*) LIFO.
2. Where is the amount of merchandise inventory disclosed in the financial statements?
3. Why are incidental costs sometimes ignored in inventory costing? Under what accounting constraint is this permitted?
4. If costs are declining, will the LIFO or FIFO method of inventory valuation yield the lower cost of goods sold? Why?
5. What does the full-disclosure principle prescribe if a company changes from one acceptable accounting method to another?
6. Can a company change its inventory method each accounting period? Explain.
7. Does the accounting concept of consistency preclude any changes from one accounting method to another?
8. If inventory errors are said to correct themselves, why are accounting users concerned when such errors are made?
9. Explain the following statement: "Inventory errors correct themselves."
10. What is the meaning of *market* as it is used in determining the lower of cost or market for inventory?

11. What guidance does the accounting constraint of conservatism offer?
12. What factors contribute to (or cause) inventory shrinkage?
13.B When preparing interim financial statements, what two methods can companies utilize to estimate cost of goods sold and ending inventory?
14. Refer to Google's financial statements in Appendix A. On December 31, 2012, what **GOOGLE** percent of current assets are represented by inventory?
15. Refer to Apple's financial statements in Appendix A and compute its cost of goods avail- **APPLE** able for sale for the year ended September 29, 2012.
16. Refer to Samsung's financial statements in Appendix A. Compute its cost of goods **Samsung** available for sale for the year ended December 31, 2012.
17. Refer to Samsung's financial statements in Appendix A. What percent of its current **Samsung** assets are inventory as of December 31, 2012 and 2011?

connect

Information: A company reports the following beginning inventory and purchases for the month of January. On January 26, the company sells 350 units. 150 units remain in ending inventory at January 31.

	Units	Unit Cost
Beginning inventory on January 1	320	$3.00
Purchase on January 9	80	3.20
Purchase on January 25	100	3.34

Required

Assume the perpetual inventory system is used and then determine the costs assigned to ending inventory when costs are assigned based on the FIFO method. (Round per unit costs and inventory amounts to cents.)

QS 5-1[A]
Perpetual: Inventory costing with FIFO

P3

Refer to the **information** in QS 5-1 and assume the perpetual inventory system is used. Determine the costs assigned to ending inventory when costs are assigned based on LIFO. (Round per unit costs and inventory amounts to cents.)

QS 5-2[A]
Perpetual: Inventory costing with LIFO P3

Refer to the **information** in QS 5-1 and assume the perpetual inventory system is used. Determine the costs assigned to ending inventory when costs are assigned based on the weighted average method. (Round per unit costs and inventory amounts to cents.)

QS 5-3[A]
Perpetual: Inventory costing with weighted average P3
Check $465

Refer to the **information** in QS 5-1 and assume the periodic inventory system is used. Determine the costs assigned to ending inventory when costs are assigned based on the FIFO method. (Round per unit costs and inventory amounts to cents.)

QS 5-4
Periodic: Inventory costing with FIFO P1

Refer to the **information** in QS 5-1 and assume the periodic inventory system is used. Determine the costs assigned to ending inventory when costs are assigned based on the LIFO method. (Round per unit costs and inventory amounts to cents.)

QS 5-5
Periodic: Inventory costing with LIFO P1

Refer to the **information** in QS 5-1 and assume the periodic inventory system is used. Determine the costs assigned to ending inventory when costs are assigned based on the weighted average method. (Round per unit costs and inventory amounts to cents.)

QS 5-6
Periodic: Inventory costing with weighted average P1

Wattan Company reports beginning inventory of 10 units at $60 each. Every week for four weeks it purchases an additional 10 units at respective costs of $61, $62, $65 and $70 per unit for weeks 1 through 4. Calculate the cost of goods available for sale and the units available for sale for this four-week period. Assume that no sales occur during those four weeks.

QS 5-7
Computing goods available for sale P3

Information: Trey Monson starts a merchandising business on December 1 and enters into the following three inventory purchases. During December, Monson sells 15 units for $20 each on December 15.

QS 5-8[A]
Perpetual: Assigning costs with FIFO

P3

Purchases on December 7	10 units @ $ 6.00 cost
Purchases on December 14	20 units @ $12.00 cost
Purchases on December 21	15 units @ $14.00 cost

Required

Monson uses a perpetual inventory system. Determine the costs assigned to the December 31 ending inventory based on the FIFO method. (Round per unit costs and inventory amounts to cents.)

Refer to the **information** in QS 5-8 and assume the perpetual inventory system is used. Determine the costs assigned to ending inventory when costs are assigned based on the LIFO method. (Round per unit costs and inventory amounts to cents.)

QS 5-9[A]
Perpetual: Inventory costing with LIFO P3

Refer to the **information** in QS 5-8 and assume the perpetual inventory system is used. Determine the costs assigned to ending inventory when costs are assigned based on the weighted average method. (Round per unit costs and inventory amounts to cents.)

QS 5-10[A]
Perpetual: Inventory costing with weighted average P3
Check End. Inv. = $360

QS 5-11[A] **Perpetual:** Inventory costing with specific identification P3	Refer to the **information** in QS 5-8 and assume the perpetual inventory system is used. Determine the costs assigned to ending inventory when costs are assigned based on specific identification. Of the units sold, eight are from the December 7 purchase and seven are from the December 14 purchase. (Round per unit costs and inventory amounts to cents.)
QS 5-12 **Periodic:** Inventory costing with FIFO P1	Refer to the **information** in QS 5-8 and assume the periodic inventory system is used. Determine the costs assigned to ending inventory when costs are assigned based on the FIFO method. (Round per unit costs and inventory amounts to cents.)
QS 5-13 **Periodic:** Inventory costing with LIFO P1	Refer to the **information** in QS 5-8 and assume the periodic inventory system is used. Determine the costs assigned to ending inventory when costs are assigned based on the LIFO method. (Round per unit costs and inventory amounts to cents.)
QS 5-14 **Periodic:** Inventory costing with weighted average P1 **Check** End. Inv. = $339.90	Refer to the **information** in QS 5-8 and assume the periodic inventory system is used. Determine the costs assigned to ending inventory when costs are assigned based on the weighted average method. (Round per unit costs and inventory amounts to cents.)
QS 5-15 **Periodic:** Inventory costing with specific identification P1	Refer to the **information** in QS 5-8 and assume the periodic inventory system is used. Determine the costs assigned to ending inventory when costs are assigned based on specific identification. Of the units sold, eight are from the December 7 purchase and seven are from the December 14 purchase. (Round per unit costs and inventory amounts to cents.)

QS 5-16 Contrasting inventory costing methods A1	Identify the inventory costing method best described by each of the following separate statements. Assume a period of increasing costs. **1.** Yields a balance sheet inventory amount often markedly less than its replacement cost. **2.** Results in a balance sheet inventory amount approximating replacement cost. **3.** Provides a tax advantage (deferral) to a corporation when costs are rising. **4.** Recognizes (matches) recent costs against net sales. **5.** The preferred method when each unit of product has unique features that markedly affect cost.
QS 5-17 Inventory ownership C1	Homestead Crafts, a distributor of handmade gifts, operates out of owner Emma Finn's house. At the end of the current period, Emma reports she has 1,300 units (products) in her basement, 20 of which were damaged by water and cannot be sold. She also has another 350 units in her van, ready to deliver per a customer order, terms FOB destination, and another 80 units out on consignment to a friend who owns a retail store. How many units should Emma include in her company's period-end inventory?
QS 5-18 Inventory costs C2	A car dealer acquires a used car for $14,000, terms FOB shipping point. Additional costs in obtaining and offering the car for sale include $250 for transportation-in, $900 for import duties, $300 for insurance during shipment, $150 for advertising, and $1,250 for sales staff salaries. For computing inventory, what cost is assigned to the used car?
QS 5-19 Applying LCM to inventories P2	Ames Trading Co. has the following products in its ending inventory. Compute lower of cost or market for inventory applied separately to each product.

Product	Quantity	Cost per Unit	Market per Unit
Mountain bikes	11	$600	$550
Skateboards	13	350	425
Gliders	26	800	700

QS 5-20 Inventory errors A2	In taking a physical inventory at the end of year 2013, Grant Company forgot to count certain units. Explain how this error affects the following: (*a*) 2013 cost of goods sold, (*b*) 2013 gross profit, (*c*) 2013 net income, (*d*) 2014 net income, (*e*) the combined two-year income, and (*f*) income for years after 2014.
QS 5-21 Analyzing inventory A3	Endor Company begins the year with $150,000 of goods in inventory. At year-end, the amount in inventory has increased to $180,000. Cost of goods sold for the year is $1,200,000. Compute Endor's inventory turnover and days' sales in inventory. Assume that there are 365 days in the year.

Kauai Store's inventory is destroyed by a fire on September 5, 2013. The following data for year 2013 are available from the accounting records. Estimate the cost of the inventory destroyed.

QS 5-22ᴮ
Estimating inventories—gross profit method
P4

Jan. 1 inventory	$190,000
Jan. 1 through Sept. 5 purchases (net)	$352,000
Jan. 1 through Sept. 5 sales (net)	$685,000
Year 2013 estimated gross profit rate	44%

Answer each of the following questions related to international accounting standards.

a. Explain how the accounting for items and costs making up merchandise inventory is different between IFRS and U.S. GAAP.

b. Can companies reporting under IFRS apply a cost flow assumption in assigning costs to inventory? If yes, identify at least two acceptable cost flow assumptions.

c. Both IFRS and U.S. GAAP apply the lower of cost or market method for reporting inventory values. If inventory is written down from applying the lower of cost or market method, explain in general terms how IFRS and U.S. GAAP differ in accounting for any subsequent period reversal of that reported decline in inventory value.

QS 5-23
International accounting standards
C1 C2 P2

connect

1. Harris Company has shipped $20,000 of goods to Harlow Co., and Harlow Co. has arranged to sell the goods for Harris. Identify the consignor and the consignee. Which company should include any unsold goods as part of its inventory?

2. At year-end, Harris Co. had shipped $12,500 of merchandise FOB destination to Harlow Co. Which company should include the $12,500 of merchandise in transit as part of its year-end inventory?

EXERCISES

Exercise 5-1
Inventory ownership C1

Walberg Associates, antique dealers, purchased the contents of an estate for $75,000. Terms of the purchase were FOB shipping point, and the cost of transporting the goods to Walberg Associates' warehouse was $2,400. Walberg Associates insured the shipment at a cost of $300. Prior to putting the goods up for sale, they cleaned and refurbished them at a cost of $980. Determine the cost of the inventory acquired from the estate.

Exercise 5-2
Inventory costs
C2

Information: Laker Company reported the following January purchases and sales data for its only product.

Exercise 5-3ᴬ
Perpetual: Inventory costing methods
P3

Date	Activities	Units Acquired at Cost	Units Sold at Retail
Jan. 1	Beginning inventory	140 units @ $6.00 = $ 840	
Jan. 10	Sales		100 units @ $15
Jan. 20	Purchase	60 units @ $5.00 = 300	
Jan. 25	Sales		80 units @ $15
Jan. 30	Purchase	180 units @ $4.50 = 810	
	Totals	380 units $1,950	180 units

Required

The Company uses a perpetual inventory system. Determine the cost assigned to ending inventory and to cost of goods sold using (a) specific identification, (b) weighted average, (c) FIFO, and (d) LIFO. (Round per unit costs and inventory amounts to cents.) For specific identification, ending inventory consists of 200 units, where 180 are from the January 30 purchase, 5 are from the January 20 purchase, and 15 are from beginning inventory.

Check Ending inventory: LIFO, $930; WA, $918

Use the data in Exercise 5-3 to prepare comparative income statements for the month of January for Laker Company similar to those shown in Exhibit 5.8 for the four inventory methods. Assume expenses are $1,250, and that the applicable income tax rate is 40%. (Round amounts to cents.)

1. Which method yields the highest net income?

2. Does net income using weighted average fall between that using FIFO and LIFO?

3. If costs were rising instead of falling, which method would yield the highest net income?

Exercise 5-4ᴬ
Perpetual: Income effects of inventory methods
A1

Exercise 5-5
Periodic: Inventory costing P1

Check Ending inventory: LIFO, $1,140; WA, $1,026

Refer to the **information** in Exercise 5-3 and assume the periodic inventory system is used. Determine the costs assigned to ending inventory and to cost of goods sold using (*a*) specific identification, (*b*) weighted average, (*c*) FIFO, and (*d*) LIFO. (Round per unit costs and inventory amounts to cents.)

Exercise 5-6
Periodic: Income effects of inventory methods

A1

Use the data in Exercise 5-5 to prepare comparative income statements for the month of January for the company similar to those shown in Exhibit 5.8 for the four inventory methods. Assume expenses are $1,250, and that the applicable income tax rate is 40%. (Round amounts to cents.)

Required

1. Which method yields the highest net income?
2. Does net income using weighted average fall between that using FIFO and LIFO?
3. If costs were rising instead of falling, which method would yield the highest net income?

Exercise 5-7[A]
Perpetual: Inventory costing methods—FIFO and LIFO

P3

Information: Hemming Co. reported the following current-year purchases and sales for its only product.

Date	Activities	Units Acquired at Cost	Units Sold at Retail
Jan. 1	Beginning inventory	200 units @ $10 = $ 2,000	
Jan. 10	Sales		150 units @ $40
Mar. 14	Purchase	350 units @ $15 = 5,250	
Mar. 15	Sales		300 units @ $40
July 30	Purchase	450 units @ $20 = 9,000	
Oct. 5	Sales		430 units @ $40
Oct. 26	Purchase	100 units @ $25 = 2,500	
	Totals	1,100 units $18,750	880 units

Required

Check Ending inventory: LIFO, $4,150

Hemming uses a perpetual inventory system. Determine the costs assigned to ending inventory and to cost of goods sold using (*a*) FIFO and (*b*) LIFO. Compute the gross margin for each method. (Round amounts to cents.)

Exercise 5-8
Specific identification P3

Refer to the **information** in Exercise 5-7. Ending inventory consists of 45 units from the March 14 purchase, 75 units from the July 30 purchase, and all 100 units from the October 26 purchase. Using the specific identification method, calculate (*a*) the cost of goods sold and (*b*) the gross profit. (Round amounts to cents.)

Exercise 5-9
Periodic: Inventory costing P1
Check Ending inventory: LIFO, $2,300

Refer to the **information** in Exercise 5-7 and assume the periodic inventory system is used. Determine the costs assigned to ending inventory and to cost of goods sold using (*a*) FIFO and (*b*) LIFO. Then (*c*) compute the gross margin for each method.

Exercise 5-10
Lower of cost or market

P2

Martinez Company's ending inventory includes the following items. Compute the lower of cost or market for ending inventory applied separately to each product.

		Per Unit	
Product	Units	Cost	Market
Helmets	24	$50	$54
Bats	17	78	72
Shoes	38	95	91
Uniforms	42	36	36

Check LCM = $7,394

Cruz Company uses LIFO for inventory costing and reports the following financial data. It also recomputed inventory and cost of goods sold using FIFO for comparison purposes.

Exercise 5-11

Comparing LIFO numbers to FIFO numbers; ratio analysis

A1 A3

	2013	2012
LIFO inventory	$160	$110
LIFO cost of goods sold	740	680
FIFO inventory	240	110
FIFO cost of goods sold	660	645
Current assets (using LIFO)	220	180
Current liabilities	200	170

1. Compute its current ratio, inventory turnover, and days' sales in inventory for 2013 using (*a*) LIFO numbers and (*b*) FIFO numbers. (Round answers to one decimal.)

2. Comment on and interpret the results of part 1.

Check   (1) FIFO: Current ratio, 1.5; Inventory turnover, 3.8 times

---

Vibrant Company had $850,000 of sales in each of three consecutive years 2012–2014, and it purchased merchandise costing $500,000 in each of those years. It also maintained a $250,000 physical inventory from the beginning to the end of that three-year period. In accounting for inventory, it made an error at the end of year 2012 that caused its year-end 2012 inventory to appear on its statements as $230,000 rather than the correct $250,000.

Exercise 5-12

Analysis of inventory errors

A2

1. Determine the correct amount of the company's gross profit in each of the years 2012–2014.

2. Prepare comparative income statements as in Exhibit 5.11 to show the effect of this error on the company's cost of goods sold and gross profit for each of the years 2012–2014.

Check   2012 reported gross profit, $330,000

Use the following information for Palmer Co. to compute inventory turnover for 2013 and 2012, and its days' sales in inventory at December 31, 2013 and 2012. (Round answers to one decimal.) Comment on Palmer's efficiency in using its assets to increase sales from 2012 to 2013.

Exercise 5-13

Inventory turnover and days' sales in inventory

A3

	2013	2012	2011
Cost of goods sold	$643,825	$426,650	$391,300
Ending inventory	97,400	87,750	92,500

Martinez Co. reported the following current-year data for its only product. The company uses a periodic inventory system, and its ending inventory consists of 150 units—50 from each of the last three purchases. Determine the cost assigned to ending inventory and to cost of goods sold using (*a*) specific identification, (*b*) weighted average, (*c*) FIFO, and (*d*) LIFO. (Round per unit costs and inventory amounts to cents.) Which method yields the highest net income?

Exercise 5-14

Periodic: Cost flow assumptions

P1

Jan.	1	Beginning inventory	96 units @ $2.00 = $	192
Mar.	7	Purchase	220 units @ $2.25 =	495
July	28	Purchase	544 units @ $2.50 =	1,360
Oct.	3	Purchase	480 units @ $2.80 =	1,344
Dec.	19	Purchase	160 units @ $2.90 =	464
		Totals	1,500 units	$3,855

Check   Inventory; LIFO, $313.50; FIFO, $435.00

Flora's Gifts reported the following current-monthly data for its only product. The company uses a periodic inventory system, and its ending inventory consists of 60 units—50 units from the January 6 purchase, and 10 units from the January 25 purchase. Determine the cost assigned to ending inventory and to cost of goods sold using (*a*) specific identification, (*b*) weighted average, (*c*) FIFO, and (*d*) LIFO. (Round per unit costs and inventory amounts to cents.) Which method yields the lowest net income?

Exercise 5-15

Periodic: Cost flow assumptions

P1

Jan.	1	Beginning inventory	138 units @ $3.00 = $	414
Jan.	6	Purchase	300 units @ $2.80 =	840
Jan.	17	Purchase	540 units @ $2.30 =	1,242
Jan.	25	Purchase	22 units @ $2.00 =	44
		Totals	1,000 units	$2,540

Check   Inventory: LIFO, $180.00; FIFO, $131.40

Exercise 5-16ᴮ
Estimating ending inventory—retail method

P4

Check End. Inventory, $35,860

In 2013, Dakota Company had net sales (at retail) of $260,000. The following additional information is available from its records at the end of 2013. Use the retail inventory method to estimate Dakota's 2013 ending inventory at cost.

	At Cost	At Retail
Beginning inventory	$ 63,800	$128,400
Cost of goods purchased	115,060	196,800

Exercise 5-17ᴮ
Estimating ending inventory—gross profit method

P4

On January 1, JKR Shop had $225,000 of inventory at cost. In the first quarter of the year, it purchased $795,000 of merchandise, returned $11,550, and paid freight charges of $18,800 on purchased merchandise, terms FOB shipping point. The company's gross profit averages 30%, and the store had $1,000,000 of net sales (at retail) in the first quarter of the year. Use the gross profit method to estimate its cost of inventory at the end of the first quarter.

Exercise 5-18
Accounting for inventory following IFRS

P2

Samsung Electronics reports the following regarding its accounting for inventories.

> Inventories are stated at the lower of cost or net realizable value. Cost is determined using the average cost method, except for materials-in-transit. Inventories are reduced for the estimated losses arising from excess, obsolescence, and the decline in value. This reduction is determined by estimating market value based on future customer demand. The losses on inventory obsolescence are recorded as a part of cost of sales.

1. What cost flow assumption(s) does Samsung apply in assigning costs to its inventories?
2. If at year-end 2011 there was an increase in the value of its inventories such that there was a reversal of ₩550 (₩ is Korean won) million for the 2010 write-down, how would Samsung account for this under IFRS? Would Samsung's accounting be different for this reversal if it reported under U.S. GAAP? Explain.

≢ connect

PROBLEM SET A

Problem 5-1Aᴬ
Perpetual: Alternative cost flows

P3

Information: Warnerwoods Company uses a perpetual inventory system. It entered into the following purchases and sales transactions for March. (For specific identification, the March 9 sale consisted of 80 units from beginning inventory and 340 units from the March 5 purchase; the March 29 sale consisted of 40 units from the March 18 purchase and 120 units from the March 25 purchase.)

Date	Activities	Units Acquired at Cost	Units Sold at Retail
Mar. 1	Beginning inventory	100 units @ $50.00 per unit	
Mar. 5	Purchase.	400 units @ $55.00 per unit	
Mar. 9	Sales		420 units @ $85.00 per unit
Mar. 18	Purchase.	120 units @ $60.00 per unit	
Mar. 25	Purchase.	200 units @ $62.00 per unit	
Mar. 29	Sales		160 units @ $95.00 per unit
	Totals	820 units	580 units

Required

1. Compute cost of goods available for sale and the number of units available for sale.
2. Compute the number of units in ending inventory.
3. Compute the cost assigned to ending inventory using (*a*) FIFO, (*b*) LIFO, (*c*) weighted average, and (*d*) specific identification. (Round all amounts to cents.)
4. Compute gross profit earned by the company for each of the four costing methods in part 3.

Check (3) Ending Inventory: FIFO, $14,800; LIFO, $13,680, WA, $14,352
(4) LIFO gross profit, $17,980

Problem 5-2A
Periodic: Alternative cost flows

P3

Check (3) Ending Inventory: FIFO, $14,800.00; LIFO, $12,700.00; WA, $13,639.20
(4) LIFO gross profit, $17,000.00

Refer to the **information** in Problem 5-1A and assume the periodic inventory system is used.

Required

1. Compute cost of goods available for sale and the number of units available for sale.
2. Compute the number of units in ending inventory.
3. Compute the cost assigned to ending inventory using (*a*) FIFO, (*b*) LIFO, (*c*) weighted average, and (*d*) specific identification. (Round all amounts to cents.)
4. Compute gross profit earned by the company for each of the four costing methods in part 3.

Information: Montoure Company uses a perpetual inventory system. It entered into the following calendar-year 2013 purchases and sales transactions. (For specific identification, units sold consist of 600 units from beginning inventory, 300 from the February 10 purchase, 200 from the March 13 purchase, 50 from the August 21 purchase, and 250 from the September 5 purchase.)

Problem 5-3A[A]

Perpetual: Alternative cost flows

P3

Date	Activities	Units Acquired at Cost	Units Sold at Retail
Jan. I	Beginning inventory	600 units @ $45.00 per unit	
Feb. 10	Purchase	400 units @ $42.00 per unit	
Mar. 13	Purchase	200 units @ $27.00 per unit	
Mar. 15	Sales		800 units @ $75.00 per unit
Aug. 21	Purchase	100 units @ $50.00 per unit	
Sept. 5	Purchase	500 units @ $46.00 per unit	
Sept. 10	Sales		600 units @ $75.00 per unit
	Totals	1,800 units	1,400 units

Required

1. Compute cost of goods available for sale and the number of units available for sale.
2. Compute the number of units in ending inventory.
3. Compute the cost assigned to ending inventory using (*a*) FIFO, (*b*) LIFO, (*c*) weighted average, and (*d*) specific identification. (Round all amounts to cents.)
4. Compute gross profit earned by the company for each of the four costing methods in part 3.

Analysis Component

5. If the company's manager earns a bonus based on a percent of gross profit, which method of inventory costing will the manager likely prefer?

Check   (3) Ending inventory: FIFO, $18,400; LIFO, $18,000; WA, $17,760; (4) LIFO gross profit, $45,800

Refer to the **information** in Problem 5-3A and assume the periodic inventory system is used.

Problem 5-4A

Periodic: Alternative cost flows

P3

Required

1. Compute cost of goods available for sale and the number of units available for sale.
2. Compute the number of units in ending inventory.
3. Compute the cost assigned to ending inventory using (*a*) FIFO, (*b*) LIFO, (*c*) weighted average, and (*d*) specific identification. (Round all amounts to cents.)
4. Compute gross profit earned by the company for each of the four costing methods in part 3.

Check   (3) Ending inventory: FIFO, $18,400; LIFO, $18,000; WA, $17,156; (4) LIFO gross profit, $45,800

Analysis Component

5. If the company's manager earns a bonus based on a percentage of gross profit, which method of inventory costing will the manager likely prefer?

A physical inventory of Liverpool Company taken at December 31 reveals the following.

Problem 5-5A

Lower of cost or market

P2

File Edit View Insert Format Tools Data Accounting Window Help

			Per Unit	
	Item	**Units**	**Cost**	**Market**
3	Audio equipment			
4	Receivers	345	$ 90	$ 98
5	CD players	260	111	100
6	MP3 players	326	86	95
7	Speakers	204	52	41
8	Video equipment			
9	Handheld LCDs	480	150	125
10	VCRs	291	93	84
11	Camcorders	212	310	322
12	Car audio equipment			
13	Satellite radios	185	70	84
14	CD/MP3 radios	170	97	105

Sheet1 / Sheet2 / Sheet3 /

Required

1. Calculate the lower of cost or market for the inventory applied separately to each item.
2. If the market amount is less than the recorded cost of the inventory, then record the LCM adjustment to the Merchandise Inventory account.

Problem 5-6A
Analysis of inventory errors

A2

Navajo Company's financial statements show the following. The company recently discovered that in making physical counts of inventory, it had made the following errors: Inventory on December 31, 2012, is understated by $56,000, and inventory on December 31, 2013, is overstated by $20,000.

For Year Ended December 31		2012	2013	2014
(a)	Cost of goods sold	$ 615,000	$ 957,000	$ 780,000
(b)	Net income.....................	230,000	285,000	241,000
(c)	Total current assets	1,255,000	1,365,000	1,200,000
(d)	Total equity.....................	1,387,000	1,530,000	1,242,000

Required

1. For each key financial statement figure—(a), (b), (c), and (d) above—prepare a table similar to the following to show the adjustments necessary to correct the reported amounts.

Figure: _____	2012	2013	2014
Reported amount			
Adjustments for: 12/31/2012 error			
12/31/2013 error			
Corrected amount			

Analysis Component

2. What is the error in total net income for the combined three-year period resulting from the inventory errors? Explain.
3. Explain why the understatement of inventory by $56,000 at the end of 2012 results in an understatement of equity by the same amount in that year.

Problem 5-7A
Periodic: Alternative cost flows

P1

Information: Seminole Company began year 2013 with 23,000 units of product in its January 1 inventory costing $15 each. It made successive purchases of its product in year 2013 as follows. The company uses a periodic inventory system. On December 31, 2013, a physical count reveals that 40,000 units of its product remain in inventory.

Mar. 7	30,000 units @ $18.00 each
May 25	39,000 units @ $20.00 each
Aug. 1	23,000 units @ $25.00 each
Nov. 10	35,000 units @ $26.00 each

Required

1. Compute the number and total cost of the units available for sale in year 2013.
2. Compute the amounts assigned to the 2013 ending inventory and the cost of goods sold using (a) FIFO, (b) LIFO, and (c) weighted average. (Round all amounts to cents.)

Problem 5-8A
Periodic: Income comparisons and cost flows

A1 P1

Information: QP Corp. sold 4,000 units of its product at $50 per unit in year 2013 and incurred operating expenses of $5 per unit in selling the units. It began the year with 700 units in inventory and made successive purchases of its product as follows.

Jan. 1	Beginning inventory	700 units @ $18.00 per unit
Feb. 20	Purchase	1,700 units @ $19.00 per unit
May 16	Purchase	800 units @ $20.00 per unit
Oct. 3	Purchase	500 units @ $21.00 per unit
Dec. 11	Purchase	2,300 units @ $22.00 per unit
	Total	6,000 units

Required

1. Prepare comparative income statements similar to Exhibit 5.8 for the three inventory costing methods of FIFO, LIFO, and weighted average. (Round all amounts to cents.) Include a detailed cost of goods sold section as part of each statement. The company uses a periodic inventory system, and its income tax rate is 40%.

2. How would the financial results from using the three alternative inventory costing methods change if the Company had been experiencing declining costs in its purchases of inventory?

3. What advantages and disadvantages are offered by using (*a*) LIFO and (*b*) FIFO? Assume the continuing trend of increasing costs.

Check (1) Net income: FIFO, $61,200; LIFO, $57,180; WA, $59,196

The records of Alaska Company provide the following information for the year ended December 31.

Problem 5-9Aᴮ
Retail inventory method
P4

	At Cost	At Retail
January 1 beginning inventory	$ 469,010	$ 928,950
Cost of goods purchased	3,376,050	6,381,050
Sales		5,595,800
Sales returns		42,800

Required

1. Use the retail inventory method to estimate the company's year-end inventory at cost.

2. A year-end physical inventory at retail prices yields a total inventory of $1,686,900. Prepare a calculation showing the company's loss from shrinkage at cost and at retail.

Check (1) Inventory, $924,182 cost; (2) Inventory shortage at cost, $36,873

Wayward Company wants to prepare interim financial statements for the first quarter. The company wishes to avoid making a physical count of inventory. Wayward's gross profit rate averages 34%. The following information for the first quarter is available from its records.

Problem 5-10Aᴮ
Gross profit method
P4

January 1 beginning inventory	$ 302,580
Cost of goods purchased	941,040
Sales	1,211,160
Sales returns	8,410

Required

Use the gross profit method to estimate the company's first quarter ending inventory.

Check Estimated ending inventory, $449,805

Information: TDS Company uses a perpetual inventory system. It entered into the following purchases and sales transactions for April. (For specific identification, the April 9 sale consisted of 8 units from beginning inventory and 27 units from the April 6 purchase; the April 30 sale consisted of 12 units from beginning inventory 3 units from the April 6 purchase and 10 units from the April 25 purchase.)

PROBLEM SET B

Problem 5-1Bᴬ
Perpetual: Alternative cost flows
P3

Date	Activities	Units Acquired at Cost	Units Sold at Retail
Apr. 1	Beginning inventory	20 units @ $3,000.00 per unit	
Apr. 6	Purchase	30 units @ $3,500.00 per unit	
Apr. 9	Sales		35 units @ $12,000.00 per unit
Apr. 17	Purchase	5 units @ $4,500.00 per unit	
Apr. 25	Purchase	10 units @ $4,800.00 per unit	
Apr. 30	Sales		25 units @ $14,000.00 per unit
	Total	65 units	60 units

Required

1. Compute cost of goods available for sale and the number of units available for sale.
2. Compute the number of units in ending inventory.

3. Compute the cost assigned to ending inventory using (*a*) FIFO, (*b*) LIFO, (*c*) weighted average, and (*d*) specific identification. (Round all amounts to cents.)
4. Compute gross profit earned by the company for each of the four costing methods in part 3.

Problem 5-2B
Periodic: Alternative cost flows
P3

Refer to the **information** in Problem 5-1B and assume the periodic inventory system is used.

Required

1. Compute cost of goods available for sale and the number of units available for sale.
2. Compute the number of units in ending inventory.
3. Compute the cost assigned to ending inventory using (*a*) FIFO, (*b*) LIFO, (*c*) weighted average, and (*d*) specific identification. (Round all amounts to cents.)
4. Compute gross profit earned by the company for each of the four costing methods in part 3.

Problem 5-3B[A]
Perpetual: Alternative cost flows
P3

Information: Aloha Company uses a perpetual inventory system. It entered into the following calendar-year 2013 purchases and sales transactions. (For specific identification, the May 9 sale consisted of 80 units from beginning inventory and 100 units from the May 6 purchase; the May 30 sale consisted of 200 units from the May 6 purchase and 100 units from the May 25 purchase.)

Date	Activities	Units Acquired at Cost	Units Sold at Retail
May 1	Beginning inventory	150 units @ $300.00 per unit	
May 6	Purchase	350 units @ $350.00 per unit	
May 9	Sales		180 units @ $1,200.00 per unit
May 17	Purchase	80 units @ $450.00 per unit	
May 25	Purchase	100 units @ $458.00 per unit	
May 30	Sales	_____	300 units @ $1,400.00 per unit
	Total	680 units	480 units

Required

1. Compute cost of goods available for sale and the number of units available for sale.
2. Compute the number of units in ending inventory.

3. Compute the cost assigned to ending inventory using (*a*) FIFO, (*b*) LIFO, (*c*) weighted average, and (*d*) specific identification. (Round all amounts to cents.)
4. Compute gross profit earned by the company for each of the four costing methods in part 3.

Analysis Component

5. If the company's manager earns a bonus based on a percent of gross profit, which method of inventory costing will the manager likely prefer?

Problem 5-4B
Periodic: Alternative cost flows
P3

Refer to the **information** in Problem 5-3B and assume the periodic inventory system is used.

Required

1. Compute cost of goods available for sale and the number of units available for sale.
2. Compute the number of units in ending inventory.
3. Compute the cost assigned to ending inventory using (*a*) FIFO, (*b*) LIFO, (*c*) weighted average, and (*d*) specific identification. (Round all amounts to cents.)
4. Compute gross profit earned by the company for each of the four costing methods in part 3.

Analysis Component

5. If the company's manager earns a bonus based on a percentage of gross profit, which method of inventory costing will the manager likely prefer?

A physical inventory of Office Necessities taken at December 31 reveals the following.

Problem 5-5B
Lower of cost or market
P2

| | | Per Unit | |
Item	Units	Cost	Market
Office furniture			
Desks	536	$261	$305
Credenzas	395	227	256
Chairs	687	49	43
Bookshelves	421	93	82
Filing cabinets			
Two-drawer	114	81	70
Four-drawer	298	135	122
Lateral	75	104	118
Office equipment			
Fax machines	370	168	200
Copiers	475	317	288
Telephones	302	125	117

Required

1. Compute the lower of cost or market for the inventory applied separately to each item.
2. If the market amount is less than the recorded cost of the inventory, then record the LCM adjustment to the Merchandise Inventory account.

Check (1) $580,054

Hallam Company's financial statements show the following. The company recently discovered that in making physical counts of inventory, it had made the following errors: Inventory on December 31, 2012, is overstated by $18,000, and inventory on December 31, 2013, is understated by $26,000.

Problem 5-6B
Analysis of inventory errors
A2

For Year Ended December 31	2012	2013	2014
(a) Cost of goods sold	$207,200	$213,800	$197,030
(b) Net income	175,800	212,270	184,910
(c) Total current assets	276,000	277,500	272,950
(d) Total equity	314,000	315,000	346,000

Required

1. For each key financial statement figure—(a), (b), (c), and (d) above—prepare a table similar to the following to show the adjustments necessary to correct the reported amounts.

Figure: _____	2012	2013	2014
Reported amount			
Adjustments for: 12/31/2012 error			
12/31/2013 error			
Corrected amount			

Check (1) Corrected net income: 2012, $157,800; 2013, $256,270; 2014, $158,910

Analysis Component

2. What is the error in total net income for the combined three-year period resulting from the inventory errors? Explain.
3. Explain why the overstatement of inventory by $18,000 at the end of 2012 results in an overstatement of equity by the same amount in that year.

Problem 5-7B

Periodic: Alternative cost flows

P1

Information: Seneca Co. began year 2013 with 6,500 units of product in its January 1 inventory costing $35 each. It made successive purchases of its product in year 2013 as follows. The company uses a periodic inventory system. On December 31, 2013, a physical count reveals that 8,500 units of its product remain in inventory.

Jan. 4	11,500 units @ $33 each
May 18	13,400 units @ $32 each
July 9	11,000 units @ $29 each
Nov. 21	7,600 units @ $27 each

Required

Check (2) Cost of goods sold: FIFO, $1,328,700; LIFO, $1,266,500; WA, $1,294,800

1. Compute the number and total cost of the units available for sale in year 2013.
2. Compute the amounts assigned to the 2013 ending inventory and the cost of goods sold using (*a*) FIFO, (*b*) LIFO, and (*c*) weighted average. (Round all amounts to cents.)

Problem 5-8B

Periodic: Income comparisons and cost flows

A1 P1

Information: Shepard Company sold 4,000 units of its product at $100 per unit in year 2013 and incurred operating expenses of $15 per unit in selling the units. It began the year with 840 units in inventory and made successive purchases of its product as follows.

Jan. 1	Beginning inventory	840 units @ $58 per unit
April 2	Purchase	600 units @ $59 per unit
June 14	Purchase	1,205 units @ $61 per unit
Aug. 29	Purchase	700 units @ $64 per unit
Nov. 18	Purchase	1,655 units @ $65 per unit
	Total	5,000 units

Required

Check (1) Net income: LIFO, $52,896; FIFO, $57,000; WA, $55,200

1. Prepare comparative income statements similar to Exhibit 5.8 for the three inventory costing methods of FIFO, LIFO, and weighted average. (Round all amounts to cents.) Include a detailed cost of goods sold section as part of each statement. The company uses a periodic inventory system, and its income tax rate is 40%.
2. How would the financial results from using the three alternative inventory costing methods change if the company had been experiencing decreasing prices in its purchases of inventory?
3. What advantages and disadvantages are offered by using (*a*) LIFO and (*b*) FIFO? Assume the continuing trend of increasing costs.

Problem 5-9B[B]

Retail inventory method

P4

The records of Macklin Co. provide the following information for the year ended December 31.

	At Cost	At Retail
January 1 beginning inventory	$ 90,022	$115,610
Cost of goods purchased	502,250	761,830
Sales		782,300
Sales returns		3,460

Required

Check (1) Inventory, $66,555 cost; (2) Inventory shortage at cost, $12,251.25

1. Use the retail inventory method to estimate the company's year-end inventory.
2. A year-end physical inventory at retail prices yields a total inventory of $80,450. Prepare a calculation showing the company's loss from shrinkage at cost and at retail.

Problem 5-10B[B]

Gross profit method

P4

Otingo Equipment Co. wants to prepare interim financial statements for the first quarter. The company wishes to avoid making a physical count of inventory. Otingo's gross profit rate averages 35%. The following information for the first quarter is available from its records.

January 1 beginning inventory	$ 802,880
Cost of goods purchased	2,209,636
Sales	3,760,260
Sales returns	79,300

Required

Use the gross profit method to estimate the company's first quarter ending inventory.

Check Estim. ending inventory, $619,892

(This serial problem began in Chapter 1 and continues through most of the book. If previous chapter segments were not completed, the serial problem can begin at this point.)

SERIAL PROBLEM
Success Systems

P2 A3

SP 5

Part A

Adria Lopez of Success Systems is evaluating her inventory to determine whether it must be adjusted based on lower of cost or market rules. Her company has three different types of software in its inventory and the following information is available for each.

Inventory Items	Units	Per Unit	
		Cost	Market
Office productivity	3	$ 76	$ 74
Desktop publishing	2	103	100
Accounting	3	90	96

Required

1. Compute the lower of cost or market for ending inventory assuming Lopez applies the lower of cost or market rule to inventory as a whole. Must Lopez adjust the reported inventory value? Explain.

2. Assume that Lopez had instead applied the lower of cost or market rule to each product in inventory. Under this assumption, must Lopez adjust the reported inventory value? Explain.

Part B

Selected accounts and balances for the three months ended March 31, 2014, for Success Systems follow.

January I beginning inventory	$ 0
Cost of goods sold	14,052
March 31 ending inventory	704

Required

1. Compute inventory turnover and days' sales in inventory for the three months ended March 31, 2014.

2. Assess the company's performance if competitors average 15 times for inventory turnover and 29 days for days' sales in inventory.

Beyond the Numbers

BTN 5-1   Refer to Apple's financial statements in Appendix A to answer the following.

REPORTING IN ACTION

C2 A3

APPLE

Required

1. What amount of inventories did Apple report as a current asset on September 29, 2012? On September 24, 2011?

2. Inventories represent what percent of total assets on September 29, 2012? On September 24, 2011?

3. Comment on the relative size of Apple's inventories compared to its other types of assets.

4. What accounting method did Apple use to compute inventory amounts on its balance sheet?

5. Compute inventory turnover for fiscal year ended September 29, 2012, and days' sales in inventory as of September 29, 2012.

Fast Forward

6. Access Apple's financial statements for fiscal years ended after September 29, 2012, from its Website (Apple.com) or the SEC's EDGAR database (www.sec.gov). Answer questions 1 through 5 using the current Apple information and compare results to those prior years.

**COMPARATIVE
ANALYSIS**

A3

APPLE

GOOGLE

BTN 5-2   Comparative figures for Apple and Google follow.

($ millions)	Apple			Google		
	Current Year	One Year Prior	Two Years Prior	Current Year	One Year Prior	Two Years Prior
Inventory	$ 791	$ 776	$ 1,051	$ 505	$ 35	$ 0
Cost of sales	87,846	64,431	39,541	20,634	13,188	10,417

Required

1. Compute inventory turnover for each company for the most recent two years shown.
2. Compute days' sales in inventory for each company for the three years shown.
3. Comment on and interpret your findings from parts 1 and 2. Assume an industry average for inventory turnover of 5.

**ETHICS
CHALLENGE**

A1

BTN 5-3   Golf Challenge Corp. is a retail sports store carrying golf apparel and equipment. The store is at the end of its second year of operation and is struggling. A major problem is that its cost of inventory has continually increased in the past two years. In the first year of operations, the store assigned inventory costs using LIFO. A loan agreement the store has with its bank, its prime source of financing, requires the store to maintain a certain profit margin and current ratio. The store's owner is currently looking over Golf Challenge's preliminary financial statements for its second year. The numbers are not favorable. The only way the store can meet the required financial ratios agreed on with the bank is to change from LIFO to FIFO. The store originally decided on LIFO because of its tax advantages. The owner recalculates ending inventory using FIFO and submits those numbers and statements to the loan officer at the bank for the required bank review. The owner thankfully reflects on the available latitude in choosing the inventory costing method.

Required

1. How does Golf Challenge's use of FIFO improve its net profit margin and current ratio?
2. Is the action by Golf Challenge's owner ethical? Explain.

**COMMUNICATING
IN PRACTICE**

A1

BTN 5-4   You are a financial adviser with a client in the wholesale produce business that just completed its first year of operations. Due to weather conditions, the cost of acquiring produce to resell has escalated during the later part of this period. Your client, Javonte Gish, mentions that because her business sells perishable goods, she has striven to maintain a FIFO flow of goods. Although sales are good, the increasing cost of inventory has put the business in a tight cash position. Gish has expressed concern regarding the ability of the business to meet income tax obligations.

Required

Prepare a memorandum that identifies, explains, and justifies the inventory method you recommend your client, Ms. Gish, adopt.

**TAKING IT TO
THE NET**

A3

BTN 5-5   Access the September 24, 2011, 10-K report for Apple, Inc. (Ticker AAPL), filed on October 26, 2011, from the EDGAR filings at www.sec.gov.

Required

1. What products are manufactured by Apple?
2. What inventory method does Apple use? (*Hint:* See the Note 1 to its financial statements.)
3. Compute its gross margin and gross margin ratio for the 2011 fiscal year. Comment on your computations—assume an industry average of 40% for the gross margin ratio.
4. Compute its inventory turnover and days' sales in inventory for the year ended September 24, 2011. Comment on your computations—assume an industry average of 40 for inventory turnover and 9 for days' sales in inventory.

BTN 5-6ᴬ   Each team member has the responsibility to become an expert on an inventory method. This expertise will be used to facilitate teammates' understanding of the concepts relevant to that method.

1. Each learning team member should select an area for expertise by choosing one of the following inventory methods: specific identification, LIFO, FIFO, or weighted average.

2. Form expert teams made up of students who have selected the same area of expertise. The instructor will identify where each expert team will meet.

3. Using the following data, each expert team must collaborate to develop a presentation that illustrates the relevant concepts and procedures for its inventory method. Each team member must write the presentation in a format that can be shown to the learning team.

TEAMWORK IN ACTION

A1 P3

Point: Step 1 allows four choices or areas for expertise. Larger teams will have some duplication of choice, but the specific identification method should not be duplicated.

Data

The company uses a *perpetual* inventory system. It had the following beginning inventory and current year purchases of its product.

Jan.	1	Beginning inventory	50 units @ $100 = $ 5,000
Jan.	14	Purchase	150 units @ $120 = 18,000
Apr.	30	Purchase	200 units @ $150 = 30,000
Sept.	26	Purchase	300 units @ $200 = 60,000

The company transacted sales on the following dates at a $350 per unit sales price.

Jan.	10	30 units	(specific cost: 30 @ $100)
Feb.	15	100 units	(specific cost: 100 @ $120)
Oct.	5	350 units	(specific cost: 100 @ $150 and 250 @ $200)

Concepts and Procedures to Illustrate in Expert Presentation

a. Identify and compute the costs to assign to the units sold. (Round per unit costs to three decimals.)

b. Identify and compute the costs to assign to the units in ending inventory. (Round inventory balances to the dollar.)

c. How likely is it that this inventory costing method will reflect the actual physical flow of goods? How relevant is that factor in determining whether this is an acceptable method to use?

d. What is the impact of this method versus others in determining net income and income taxes?

e. How closely does the ending inventory amount reflect replacement cost?

4. Re-form learning teams. In rotation, each expert is to present to the team the presentation developed in part 3. Experts are to encourage and respond to questions.

BTN 5-7   Review the chapter's opening feature highlighting Jim Koch and his company, Boston Beer Company. Assume that the company consistently maintains an inventory level of $3,000,000, meaning that its average and ending inventory levels are the same. Also assume its annual cost of sales is $12,000,000. To cut costs, the company proposes to slash inventory to a constant level of $1,500,000 with no impact on cost of sales. It plans to work with suppliers to get quicker deliveries and to order smaller quantities more often.

ENTREPRENEURIAL DECISION

A3

Required

1. Compute the company's inventory turnover and its days' sales in inventory under (*a*) current conditions and (*b*) proposed conditions.

2. Evaluate and comment on the merits of their proposal given your analysis for part 1. Identify any concerns you might have about the proposal.

HITTING THE ROAD

C1 C2

BTN 5-8 Visit four retail stores with another classmate. In each store, identify whether the store uses a bar-coding system to help manage its inventory. Try to find at least one store that does not use bar-coding. If a store does not use bar-coding, ask the store's manager or clerk whether he or she knows which type of inventory method the store employs. Create a table that shows columns for the name of store visited, type of merchandise sold, use or nonuse of bar-coding, and the inventory method used if bar-coding is not employed. You might also inquire as to what the store's inventory turnover is and how often physical inventory is taken.

GLOBAL DECISION

A3

Samsung
APPLE
GOOGLE

BTN 5-9 Following are key figures (in millions of Korean won) for Samsung (www.Samsung.com), which is a leading manufacturer of consumer electronics products.

₩ in millions	Current Year	One Year Prior	Two Years Prior
Inventory............	₩ 17,747,413	₩ 15,716,715	₩ 13,364,524
Cost of sales.........	126,651,931	112,145,120	118,244,730

Required

1. Use these data and those from BTN 5-2 to compute (*a*) inventory turnover and (*b*) days' sales in inventory for the most recent two years shown for Samsung, Apple, and Google.
2. Comment on and interpret your findings from part 1.

ANSWERS TO MULTIPLE CHOICE QUIZ

1. a; FIFO periodic

Date	Goods Purchased	Cost of Goods Sold	Inventory Balance
July 1			75 units @ $25 = $ 1,875
July 3	348 units @ $27 = $9,396		75 units @ $25 348 units @ $27 } = $ 11,271
July 8		75 units @ $25 225 units @ $27 } = $ 7,950	123 units @ $27 = $ 3,321
July 15	257 units @ $28 = $7,196		123 units @ $27 257 units @ $28 } = $ 10,517
July 23		123 units @ $27 152 units @ $28 } = $ 7,577	105 units @ $28 = $ 2,940
		$15,527	

2. e; Specific identification (perpetual and periodic are identical for specific identification)—Ending inventory computation.

20 units @ $25	$ 500
40 units @ $27	1,080
45 units @ $28	1,260
105 units	$2,840

3. b; LIFO perpetual

Date	Goods Purchased	Cost of Goods Sold	Inventory Balance
July 1			75 units @ $25 = $ 1,875
July 3	348 units @ $27 = $9,396		75 units @ $25 ⎫ 348 units @ $27 ⎬ = $11,271
July 8		300 units @ $27 = $ 8,100	75 units @ $25 ⎫ 48 units @ $27 ⎬ = $ 3,171
July 15	257 units @ $28 = $7,196		75 units @ $25 ⎫ 48 units @ $27 ⎬ = $10,367 257 units @ $28 ⎭
July 23		257 units @ $28 ⎫ 18 units @ $27 ⎬ = $ 7,682	75 units @ $25 ⎫ 30 units @ $27 ⎬ = $ 2,685
		$15,782	

4. a; FIFO perpetual. Ending inventory computation:
105 units @ $28 each = $2,940; The FIFO periodic inventory computation is identical to the FIFO perpetual inventory computation (see question 1).

5. a; FIFO periodic inventory = $(20 \times \$14) + (10 \times \$12)$
$= \$400$

a; LIFO periodic cost of goods sold = $(20 \times \$14) + (40 \times \$12) + (70 \times \$10)$
$= \$1,460$

6. d; Days' sales in inventory = (Ending inventory/Cost of goods sold $\times$ 365)
$= (\$18,000/\$85,000) \times 365 = 77.29$ days

6

Reporting and Analyzing Cash and Internal Controls

INTERNAL CONTROL	CONTROL OF CASH	TOOLS OF CONTROL AND ANALYSIS
C1 Purpose and principles of controls Technology and controls Limitations of controls	C2 Definition and reporting of cash P1 Control of cash receipts and cash disbursements	P2 Control of petty cash P3 Bank reconciliation as a control tool A1 Assessing liquidity

Learning Objectives

C1 Define internal control and identify its purpose and principles. (p. 264)

C2 Define cash and cash equivalents and explain how to report them. (p. 270)

P1 Apply internal control to cash receipts and disbursements. (p. 270)

P2 Explain and record petty cash fund transactions. (p. 274)

P3 Prepare a bank reconciliation. (p. 279)

A1 Compute the days' sales uncollected ratio and use it to assess liquidity. (p. 285)

P4 *Appendix 6A—Describe the use of documentation and verification to control cash disbursements.* (p. 287)

P5 *Appendix 6B—Apply the net method to control purchase discounts.* (p. 290)

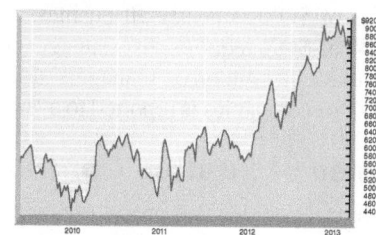

Genesis, Geniuses and Google

"Our goal is to organize the world's information"

——LARRY PAGE

MOUNTAIN VIEW, CA—You know you've hit it big when you are profiled in a comic book series! Enter Larry Page and Sergey Brin, founders of **Google, Inc. (Google.com)**, who are the focus of Bluewater Productions' new business leaders comic book series. Yet, their real life story is just as amazing.

Larry and Sergey met in college, where it is said they disagreed "about most everything." However, a college project on measuring the importance of a Website led the two to develop an algorithm for an improved search engine. The duo ran their project out of their dorm rooms but soon were getting 10,000 searches per day. With some trepidation, they borrowed $15,000, wrote a business plan, and launched Google (Google is based on the word "googol," a mathematical term for the number 1 followed by 100 zeros). Larry recalls the night, at 23 years old, when he woke from a dream, "grabbed a pen and started writing . . . scribbling out the details and convincing myself it would work."

Google is now the dominant search engine and has expanded into several markets to now compete head-to-head with Apple on many fronts. Google's revenues and net income for the past four years follow:

($ billions)	2009	2010	2011	2012
Revenues	$24	$29	$38	$50
Net income	4	7	9	11

Google, Inc.

(NASDAQ: GOOG)   Founded 1998

55,000 employees (20,000 in R&D)
$37 billion in costs ($7 billion in R&D)

The financial markets similarly see Google in a positive light, viewing it as an innovative company with dynamic leaders. Its stock prices over the past four years reflect that enthusiasm.

An important part of Google's success is setting up systems of internal controls, including controls over cash, to enable future success. Larry explains that proper internal controls are important to Google's future and to the integrity of its systems. This includes establishing control procedures to monitor business activities and safeguard its assets. Both Larry and Sergey claim that such controls and management practices raise productivity, cut expenses, and enhance the user experience.

That focus on internal controls extends to its cash. Google's cash balances have continued to grow and currently make up nearly 16% of total assets as shown here:

($ billions)	2009	2010	2011	2012
Cash	$10	$14	$10	$15
Total assets	40	58	73	94

If we add in its current marketable securities of $33 billion, its liquid assets make up more than one-half of its total assets. This "excess liquidity" concerns investors as the return on such assets is low. Also, with such large cash balances, Google invests substantial resources into cash management, including controls over cash receipts, disbursements, and petty cash. The effective use of bank reconciliations is one of many tools that it uses. The owners also take advantage of readily available banking services to enhance controls over its cash.

Larry and Sergey, however, insist that much of that cash be devoted to R&D. They call it the 70-20-10 rule. "About 70% . . . [spent] on the core efforts of the company," explains Sergey, and "about 20% to adjacent areas and expansion." And, "for the final 10%," admits Sergey, "to anything goes!"

Sources: *Google Website*, January 2014; *Google 10-K*, 2012; *Entrepreneur*, October 2008; *Fortune, April* 2012

INTERNAL CONTROL

This section describes internal control and its fundamental principles. We also discuss the impact of technology on internal control and the limitations of control procedures.

Purpose of Internal Control

C1 Define internal control and identify its purpose and principles.

Managers (or owners) of small businesses often control the entire operation. These managers usually purchase all assets, hire and manage employees, negotiate all contracts, and sign all checks. They know from personal contact and observation whether the business is actually receiving the assets and services paid for. Most companies, however, cannot maintain this close personal supervision. They must delegate responsibilities and rely on formal procedures rather than personal contact in controlling business activities.

Internal Control System   Managers use an internal control system to monitor and control business activities. An **internal control system** consists of the policies and procedures managers use to

- Protect assets.
- Ensure reliable accounting.
- Promote efficient operations.
- Urge adherence to company policies.

A properly designed internal control system is a key part of systems design, analysis, and performance. Managers place a high priority on internal control systems because they can prevent avoidable losses, help managers plan operations, and monitor company and employee performance. For example, internal controls for health care must protect patient records and privacy. Internal controls do not provide guarantees, but they lower the company's risk of loss.

Sarbanes-Oxley Act (SOX)   The **Sarbanes-Oxley Act (SOX)** requires the managers and auditors of companies whose stock is traded on an exchange (called *public companies*) to document and certify the system of internal controls. Following are some of the specific requirements:

- Auditors must evaluate internal controls and issue an internal control report.
- Auditors of a client are restricted as to what consulting services they can provide that client.
- The person leading an audit can serve no more than seven years without a two-year break.
- Auditors' work is overseen by the *Public Company Accounting Oversight Board* (PCAOB).
- Harsh penalties exist for violators—sentences up to 25 years in prison with severe fines.

SOX has markedly impacted companies, and the costs of its implementation are high. Importantly, **Section 404** of SOX requires that managers document and assess the effectiveness of all internal control processes that can impact financial reporting. The benefits include greater confidence in accounting systems and their related reports. However, the public continues to debate the costs versus the benefits of SOX as nearly all business activities of these companies are impacted by SOX. Section 404 of SOX requires that managers document and assess their internal controls *and* that auditors provide an opinion on managers' documentation and assessment. Costs of complying with Section 404 for companies is reported to average $4 million (source: Financial Executives Institute).

Principles of Internal Control

Internal control policies and procedures vary from company to company according to such factors as the nature of the business and its size. Certain fundamental internal control principles apply to all companies. The **principles of internal control** are to

1. Establish responsibilities.
2. Maintain adequate records.
3. Insure assets and bond key employees.
4. Separate recordkeeping from custody of assets.
5. Divide responsibility for related transactions.
6. Apply technological controls.
7. Perform regular and independent reviews.

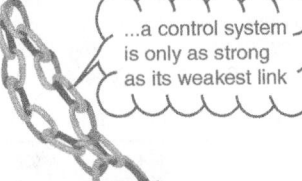

...a control system is only as strong as its weakest link

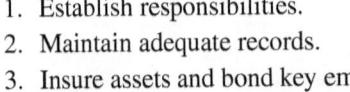

This section explains these seven principles and describes how internal control procedures minimize the risk of fraud and theft. These procedures also increase the reliability and accuracy of accounting records. A framework for how these seven principles improve the quality of financial reporting is provided by the **Committee of Sponsoring Organizations (COSO)** (www.COSO.org). Specifically, these principles link to five aspects of internal control: control activities, control environment, risk assessment, monitoring, and communication.

Point: Sarbanes-Oxley Act (SOX) requires that each annual report contain an *internal control report,* which must: (1) state managers' responsibility for establishing and maintaining adequate internal controls for financial reporting; and (2) assess the effectiveness of those controls.

Establish Responsibilities   Proper internal control means that responsibility for a task is clearly established and assigned to one person. When a problem occurs in a company where responsibility is not identified, determining who is at fault is difficult. For instance, if two salesclerks share the same cash register and there is a cash shortage, neither clerk can be held accountable. To prevent this problem, one clerk might be given responsibility for handling all cash sales. Alternately, a company can use a register with separate cash drawers for each clerk. Most of us have waited at a retail counter during a shift change while employees swap cash drawers.

Maintain Adequate Records   Good recordkeeping is part of an internal control system. It helps protect assets and ensures that employees use prescribed procedures. Reliable records are also a source of information that managers use to monitor company activities. When detailed records of equipment are kept, for instance, items are unlikely to be lost or stolen without detection. Similarly, transactions are less likely to be entered in wrong accounts if a chart of accounts is set up and carefully used. Many preprinted forms and internal documents are also designed for use in a good internal control system. When sales slips are properly designed, for instance, sales personnel can record needed information efficiently with less chance of errors or delays to customers. When sales slips are prenumbered and controlled, each one issued is the responsibility of one salesperson, preventing the salesperson from pocketing cash by making a sale and destroying the sales slip. Computerized point-of-sale systems achieve the same control results.

Point: Many companies have a mandatory vacation policy for employees who handle cash. When another employee must cover for the one on vacation, it is more difficult to hide cash frauds.

Insure Assets and Bond Key Employees   Good internal control means that assets are adequately insured against casualty and that employees handling large amounts of cash and easily transferable assets are bonded. An employee is *bonded* when a company purchases an insurance policy, or a bond, against losses from theft by that employee. Bonding reduces the risk of loss. It also discourages theft because bonded employees know an independent bonding company will be involved when theft is uncovered and is unlikely to be sympathetic with an employee involved in theft. (A common question on job applications is whether you are bonded or bondable.)

Fraud

Tagging Assets A novel technique exists for marking physical assets. It involves embedding a less than one-inch-square tag of fibers that creates a unique optical signature recordable by scanners. Manufacturers hope to embed tags in everything from compact discs and credit cards to designer clothes for purposes of internal control and efficiency.

Separate Recordkeeping from Custody of Assets   A person who controls or has access to an asset must not keep that asset's accounting records. This principle reduces the risk of theft or waste of an asset because the person with control over it knows that another person keeps its records. Also, a recordkeeper who does not have access to the asset has no reason to falsify records. This means that to steal an asset and hide the theft from the records, two or more people must *collude*—or agree in secret to commit the fraud. Some payroll cash checking services require fingerprint ID before the payroll check is cashed.

Point: The Association of Certified Fraud Examiners (acfe.com) estimates that employee fraud costs small companies more than $100,000 per incident.

Divide Responsibility for Related Transactions   Good internal control divides responsibility for a transaction or a series of related transactions between two or more individuals or departments. This is to ensure that the work of one individual acts as a check on the other. This principle, often called *separation of duties,* is not a call for duplication of work. Each employee or department should perform unduplicated effort. Examples of transactions with divided responsibility are placing purchase orders, receiving merchandise, and paying vendors. These tasks should not be given to one individual or department. Assigning responsibility for two or more of these tasks to one party increases mistakes and perhaps fraud. Having an independent person, for example, check incoming goods for quality and quantity encourages more care and attention to detail than having the person who placed the order do the checking. Added protection can result from identifying a third person to approve payment of the invoice. A company can even designate a fourth person with authority to write checks as another protective measure.

Point: There's a new security device—a person's ECG (electrocardiogram) reading—that is as unique as a fingerprint and a lot harder to lose or steal than a PIN. ECGs can be read through fingertip touches. An ECG also shows that a living person is actually there, whereas fingerprint and facial recognition software can be fooled.

Apply Technological Controls   Cash registers, check protectors, time clocks, and personal identification scanners are examples of devices that can improve internal control. Technology often improves the effectiveness of controls. A cash register with a locked-in tape or electronic file makes a record of each cash sale. A check protector perforates the amount of a check into its face and makes it difficult to alter the amount. A time clock registers the exact time an employee both arrives at and departs from the job. Mechanical change and currency counters quickly and accurately count amounts, and personal scanners limit access to only authorized individuals. Each of these and other technological controls are an effective part of many internal control systems. Some companies video record workers as they clock in and out, which discourages them from clocking in or out for others.

Decision Insight

Face Reading   Face-recognition software snaps a digital picture of the face and converts key facial features—say, the distance between the eyes—into a series of numerical values. These can be stored on an ID or ATM card as a simple bar code to prohibit unauthorized access. ■

Point: COSO organizes control components into five types:
- Control environment
- Control activities
- Risk assessment
- Monitoring
- Information and communication

Perform Regular and Independent Reviews   Changes in personnel, stress of time pressures, and technological advances present opportunities for shortcuts and lapses. To counter these factors, regular reviews of internal control systems are needed to ensure that procedures are followed. These reviews are preferably done by internal auditors not directly involved in the activities. Their impartial perspective encourages an evaluation of the efficiency as well as the effectiveness of the internal control system. Many companies also pay for audits by independent, external auditors. These external auditors test the company's financial records to give an opinion as to whether its financial statements are presented fairly. Before external auditors decide on how much testing is needed, they evaluate the effectiveness of the internal control system. This evaluation is often helpful to a client. Independent, external audits are usually performed by auditors who work for public accounting firms.

Decision Maker

Entrepreneur   As owner of a start-up information services company, you hire a systems analyst. The analyst sees that your company only employs two workers. She recommends you improve controls and says that as owner you must serve as a compensating control. What does the analyst mean? ■   [Answer—p. 292]

Technology and Internal Control

The fundamental principles of internal control are relevant no matter what the technological state of the accounting system, from purely manual to fully automated systems. Technology impacts an internal control system in several important ways. Perhaps the most obvious is that technology allows us quicker access to databases and information. Used effectively, technology greatly improves managers' abilities to monitor and control business activities. This section describes some technological impacts we must be alert to.

Point: Information on Internet fraud can be found at these Websites:
sec.gov/investor/pubs/cyberfraud.htm
ftc.gov/bcp/consumer.shtm
www.fraud.org

Reduced Processing Errors   Technologically advanced systems reduce the number of errors in processing information. Provided the software and data entry are correct, the risk of mechanical and mathematical errors is nearly eliminated. However, we must remember that erroneous software or data entry does exist. Also, less human involvement in data processing can cause data entry errors to go undiscovered. Moreover, errors in software can produce consistent

Point: Evidence of any internal control failure for a company reduces user confidence in its financial statements.

but erroneous processing of transactions. Continually checking and monitoring all types of systems are important.

More Extensive Testing of Records A company's review and audit of electronic records can include more extensive testing when information is easily and rapidly accessed. When accounting records are kept manually, auditors and others likely select only small samples of data to test. When data are accessible with computer technology, however, auditors can quickly analyze large samples or even the entire database.

Limited Evidence of Processing Many data processing steps are increasingly done by computer. Accordingly, fewer hard-copy items of documentary evidence are available for review. Yet technologically advanced systems can provide new evidence. They can, for instance, record who made the entries, the date and time, the source of the entry, and so on. Technology can also be designed to require the use of passwords or other identification before access to the system is granted. This means that internal control depends more on the design and operation of the information system and less on the analysis of its resulting documents.

Crucial Separation of Duties Technological advances in accounting information systems often yield some job eliminations or consolidations. While those who remain have the special skills necessary to operate advanced programs and equipment, a company with a reduced workforce risks losing its crucial separation of duties. The company must establish ways to control and monitor employees to minimize risk of error and fraud. For instance, the person who designs and programs the information system must not be the one who operates it. The company must also separate control over programs and files from the activities related to cash receipts and disbursements. For instance, a computer operator should not control check-writing activities. Achieving acceptable separation of duties can be especially difficult and costly in small companies with few employees.

Point: We look to several sources when assessing a company's internal controls. Sources include the auditor's report, management report on controls (if available), management discussion and analysis, and financial press.

Increased E-Commerce Technology has encouraged the growth of e-commerce. Amazon.com and eBay are examples of companies that have successfully exploited e-commerce. Most companies have some e-commerce transactions. All such transactions involve at least three risks. (1) *Credit card number theft* is a risk of using, transmitting, and storing such data online. This increases the cost of e-commerce. (2) *Computer viruses* are malicious programs that attach themselves to innocent files for purposes of infecting and harming other files and programs. (3) *Impersonation* online can result in charges of sales to bogus accounts, purchases of inappropriate materials, and the unknowing giving up of confidential information to hackers. Companies use both firewalls and encryption to combat some of these risks—firewalls are points of entry to a system that require passwords to continue, and encryption is a mathematical process to rearrange contents that cannot be read without the process code. Nearly 5% of Americans already report being victims of identity theft, and roughly 10 million say their privacy has been compromised.

"Worst case of identity theft I've ever seen!"

Copyright 2004 by Randy Glasbergen. www.glasbergen.com

 Decision Insight

Winnings and Controls Certified Fraud Examiners Website reports the following: Andrew Cameron stole Jacqueline Boanson's credit card. Cameron headed to the racetrack and promptly charged two bets for $150 on the credit card—winning $400. Unfortunately for Cameron the racetrack refused to pay him cash as its internal control policy is to credit winnings from bets made on a credit card to that same card. Cameron was later nabbed; and the racetrack let Ms. Boanson keep the winnings. ■

Limitations of Internal Control

All internal control policies and procedures have limitations that usually arise from either (1) the human element or (2) the cost–benefit principle.

Internal control policies and procedures are applied by people. This human element creates several potential limitations that we can categorize as either (1) human error or (2) human fraud.

Human error can occur from negligence, fatigue, misjudgment, or confusion. *Human fraud* involves intent by people to defeat internal controls, such as *management override,* for personal gain. Fraud also includes collusion to thwart the separation of duties. The human element highlights the importance of establishing an *internal control environment* to convey management's commitment to internal control policies and procedures. Human fraud is driven by the *triple-threat* of fraud:

● **Opportunity**—refers to internal control deficiencies in the workplace.
● **Pressure**—refers to financial, family, society, and other stresses to succeed.
● **Rationalization**—refers to employees justifying fraudulent behavior.

The second major limitation on internal control is the *cost–benefit principle,* which dictates that the costs of internal controls must not exceed their benefits. Analysis of costs and benefits must consider all factors, including the impact on morale. Most companies, for instance, have a legal right to read employees' e-mails, yet companies seldom exercise that right unless they are confronted with evidence of potential harm to the company. The same holds for drug testing, phone tapping, and hidden cameras. The bottom line is that managers must establish internal control policies and procedures with a net benefit to the company.

Point: Cybercrime.gov pursues computer and intellectual property crimes, including that of e-commerce.

Hacker's Guide to Cyberspace

Pharming Viruses attached to e-mails and Websites load software onto your PC that monitors keystrokes; when you sign on to financial Websites, it steals your passwords.

Phishing Hackers send e-mails to you posing as banks; you are asked for information using fake Websites where they reel in your passwords and personal data.

WI-Phishing Cybercrooks set up wireless networks hoping you use them to connect to the Web; your passwords and data are stolen as you use their network.

Bot-Networking Hackers send remote-control programs to your PC that take control to send out spam and viruses; they even rent your bot to other cybercrooks.

Typo-Squatting Hackers set up Websites with addresses similar to legit outfits; when you make a typo and hit their sites, they infect your PC with viruses or take them over as bots.

Hackers also have their own self-identification system...
• *Hackers,* or *external attackers,* crack systems and take data for illicit gains (as unauthorized users).
• *Rogue insiders,* or *internal attackers,* crack systems and take data for illicit gains or revenge (as authorized users).
• *Ethical hackers,* or *good-guys* or *white-hat hackers,* crack systems and reveal vulnerabilities to enhance controls.
• *Crackers,* or *criminal hackers,* crack systems illegally for illicit gains, fame, or revenge.

■ **Decision** Insight

Ball Control Ryan Braun of the Milwaukee Brewers won an appeal of a 50-game Major League Baseball (MLB) suspension for a positive drug test. Braun claimed that MLB did not maintain control over his sample through the testing process and raised the risk that his sample was tainted. This control failure led to dismissal of that particular test result and him winning the appeal. Controls are crucial when people's livelihoods and reputations are on the line. (A caveat: Two years later, Braun was suspended for 65 games, costing him $3.25 million, resulting from the Biogenesis probe.) ■

Identify the following phrases/terms as best linked with the (a) purposes of an internal control system, (b) principles of internal control, or (c) limitations of internal control.

1. ____ Protect assets
2. ____ Establish responsibilities
3. ____ Human error
4. ____ Maintain adequate records
5. ____ Apply technological controls
6. ____ Ensure reliable accounting
7. ____ Insure assets and bond key employees
8. ____ Human fraud
9. ____ Separate recordkeeping from custody of assets
10. ____ Divide responsibility for related transactions
11. ____ Cost-benefit principle
12. ____ Promote efficient operations
13. ____ Perform regular and independent reviews
14. ____ Urge adherence to company policies

Do More: QS 6-1, E 6-1, E 6-3, P 6-1

Solution

1. a **2.** b **3.** c **4.** b **5.** b **6.** a **7.** b **8.** c **9.** b **10.** b **11.** c **12.** a **13.** b **14.** a

QC1

CONTROL OF CASH

Cash is a necessary asset of every company. Most companies also own *cash equivalents* (defined below), which are assets similar to cash. Cash and cash equivalents are the most liquid of all assets and are easily hidden and moved. Cash is also the most desired asset as other assets must be *fenced* (sold in a secondary market). An effective system of internal controls protects cash assets and it should meet three basic guidelines:

1. Handling cash is separate from recordkeeping of cash.
2. Cash receipts are promptly deposited in a bank.
3. Cash disbursements are made by check.

The first guideline applies separation of duties to minimize errors and fraud. When duties are separated, two or more people must collude to steal cash and conceal this action in the accounting records. The second guideline uses immediate (say, daily) deposits of all cash receipts to produce a timely independent record of the cash received. It also reduces the likelihood of cash theft (or loss) and the risk that an employee could personally use the money before depositing it. The third guideline uses payments by check to develop an independent bank record of cash disbursements. This guideline also reduces the risk of cash theft (or loss).

This section begins with definitions of cash and cash equivalents. Discussion then focuses on controls and accounting for both cash receipts and disbursements. The exact procedures used to achieve control over cash vary across companies. They depend on factors such as company size, number of employees, volume of cash transactions, and sources of cash.

Cash, Cash Equivalents, and Liquidity

Good accounting systems help in managing the amount of cash and controlling who has access to it. Cash is the usual means of payment when paying for assets, services, or liabilities. **Liquidity** refers to a company's ability to pay for its near-term obligations. Cash and similar assets are called **liquid assets** because they can be readily used to settle such obligations. A company needs liquid assets to effectively operate.

Cash includes currency and coins along with the amounts on deposit in bank accounts, checking accounts (called *demand deposits*), and many savings accounts (called *time deposits*). Cash also includes items that are acceptable for deposit in these accounts such as customer checks, cashier's checks, certified checks, and money orders. **Cash equivalents** are short-term, highly liquid investment assets meeting two criteria: (1) readily convertible to a known cash amount and (2) sufficiently close to their due date so that their market value is not sensitive to interest rate changes. Only investments purchased within three months of their due date usually

C2 Define cash and cash equivalents and explain how to report them.

Point: The most liquid assets are usually reported first on a balance sheet; the least liquid assets are reported last.

satisfy these criteria. Examples of cash equivalents are short-term investments in assets such as U.S. Treasury bills and money market funds. To increase their return, many companies invest idle cash in cash equivalents. Most companies combine cash equivalents with cash as a single item on the balance sheet.

Cash Management

When companies fail, one of the most common causes is their inability to manage cash. Companies must plan both cash receipts and cash payments. The goals of cash management are twofold:

1. Plan cash receipts to meet cash payments when due.
2. Keep a minimum level of cash necessary to operate.

The *treasurer* of the company is responsible for cash management. Effective cash management involves applying the following cash management principles.

- **Encourage collection of receivables.** The more quickly customers and others pay the company, the more quickly that company can use the money. Some companies have cash-only sales policies. Others might offer discounts for payments received early.

- **Delay payment of liabilities.** The more delayed a company is in paying others, the more time it has to use the money. Some companies regularly wait to pay their bills until the last possible day allowed—although, a company must take care not to hurt its credit standing.

- **Keep only necessary levels of assets.** The less money tied up in idle assets, the more money to invest in productive assets. Some companies maintain *just-in-time* inventory; meaning they plan inventory to be available at the same time orders are filled. Others might lease out excess warehouse space or rent equipment instead of buying it.

- **Plan expenditures.** Money should be spent only when it is available. Companies must look at seasonal and business cycles to plan expenditures.

- **Invest excess cash.** Excess cash earns no return and should be invested. Excess cash from seasonal cycles can be placed in a bank account or other short-term investment for income. Excess cash beyond what's needed for regular business should be invested in productive assets like factories and inventories.

Decision Insight

Days' Cash Expense Coverage   The ratio of *cash (and cash equivalents) to average daily cash expenses* indicates the number of days a company can operate without additional cash inflows. It reflects on company liquidity and on the potential of excess cash. ∎

Control of Cash Receipts

P1 Apply internal control to cash receipts and disbursements.

Internal control of cash receipts ensures that cash received is properly recorded and deposited. Cash receipts can arise from transactions such as cash sales, collections of customer accounts, receipts of interest earned, bank loans, sales of assets, and owner investments. This section explains internal control over two important types of cash receipts: over-the-counter and by mail.

Over-the-Counter Cash Receipts   For purposes of internal control, over-the-counter cash receipts from sales should be recorded on a cash register at the time of each sale. To help ensure that correct amounts are entered, each register should be located so customers can read the amounts entered. Clerks also should be required to enter each sale before wrapping merchandise and to give the customer a receipt for each sale. The design of each cash register should provide a permanent, locked-in record of each transaction. In many systems, the register is directly linked with computing and accounting services. Less advanced registers simply print a record of each transaction on a paper tape or electronic file locked inside the register.

   Proper internal control prescribes that custody over cash should be separate from its record-keeping. For over-the-counter cash receipts, this separation begins with the cash sale. The clerk who has access to cash in the register should not have access to its locked-in record. At the end of the clerk's work period, the clerk should count the cash in the register, record the amount, and turn over the cash and a record of its amount to the company cashier. The cashier, like the clerk, has access to the cash but should not have access to accounting records (or the register tape or file). A third employee, often a supervisor, compares the record of total register transactions (or the register tape or file) with the cash receipts reported by the cashier. This record is the basis for a journal entry recording over-the-counter cash receipts. The third employee has access to the records for cash but not to the actual cash. The clerk and the cashier have access to cash but not to the accounting records. None of them can make a mistake or divert cash without the difference being revealed—see the following diagram.

Point: Convenience stores sometimes display a sign: *Cashier has no access to cash in locked floor (or wall) safe.* Such signs help thwart theft and holdups because of lack of access to the floor (or wall) safe.

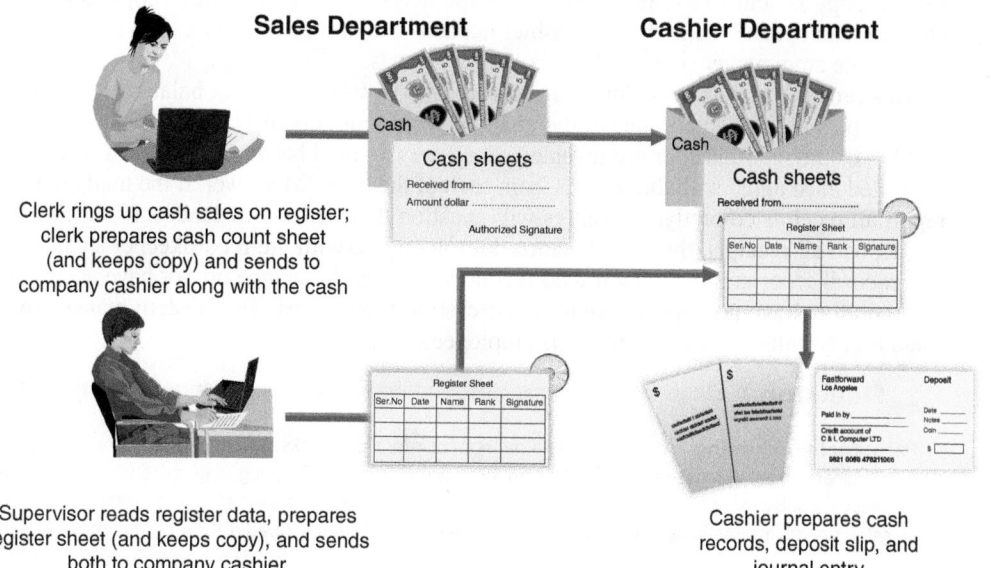

Sales Department

Clerk rings up cash sales on register; clerk prepares cash count sheet (and keeps copy) and sends to company cashier along with the cash

Supervisor reads register data, prepares register sheet (and keeps copy), and sends both to company cashier

Cashier Department

Cashier prepares cash records, deposit slip, and journal entry

Cash over and short.   Sometimes errors in making change are discovered from differences between the cash in a cash register and the record of the amount of cash receipts. Although a clerk is careful, one or more customers can be given too much or too little change. This means that at the end of a work period, the cash in a cash register might not equal the record of cash receipts. This difference is reported in the **Cash Over and Short** account, also called *Cash Short and Over*, which is an income statement account recording the income effects of cash overages and cash shortages. To illustrate, if a cash register's record shows $550 but the count of cash in the register is $555, the entry to record cash sales and its overage is

Point: Retailers often require cashiers to restrictively endorse checks immediately on receipt by stamping them "For deposit only."

Cash	555	
Cash Over and Short		5
Sales		550
To record cash sales and a cash overage.		

Assets = Liabilities + Equity
+555   +   5
                   +550

On the other hand, if a cash register's record shows $625 but the count of cash in the register is $621, the entry to record cash sales and its shortage is

Cash	621	
Cash Over and Short	4	
Sales		625
To record cash sales and a cash shortage.		

Assets = Liabilities + Equity
+621   −   4
                   +625

Since customers are more likely to dispute being shortchanged than being given too much change, the Cash Over and Short account usually has a debit balance at the end of an accounting period. A debit balance reflects an expense. It is reported on the income statement as part of general and administrative expenses. (Since the amount is usually small, it is often combined

Point: Merchants begin a business day with a *change fund* in their cash register. The accounting for a change fund is similar to that for petty cash, including that for cash shortages or overages.

with other small expenses and reported as part of *miscellaneous expenses*—or as part of *miscellaneous revenues* if it has a credit balance.)

Cash Receipts by Mail   Control of cash receipts that arrive through the mail starts with the person who opens the mail. Preferably, two people are assigned the task of, and are present for, opening the mail. In this case, theft of cash receipts by mail requires collusion between these two employees. Specifically, the person(s) opening the mail enters a list (in triplicate) of money received. This list should contain a record of each sender's name, the amount, and an explanation of why the money is sent. The first copy is sent with the money to the cashier. A second copy is sent to the recordkeeper in the accounting area. A third copy is kept by the clerk(s) who opened the mail. The cashier deposits the money in a bank, and the recordkeeper records the amounts received in the accounting records.

Point: Collusion implies that two or more individuals are knowledgeable or involved with the activities of the other(s).

This process reflects good internal control. That is, when the bank balance is reconciled by another person (explained later in the chapter), errors or acts of fraud by the mail clerks, the cashier, or the recordkeeper are revealed. They are revealed because the bank's record of cash deposited must agree with the records from each of the three. Moreover, if the mail clerks do not report all receipts correctly, customers will question their account balances. If the cashier does not deposit all receipts, the bank balance does not agree with the recordkeeper's cash balance. The recordkeeper and the person who reconciles the bank balance do not have access to cash and therefore have no opportunity to divert cash to themselves. This system makes errors and fraud highly unlikely. The exception is employee collusion.

 Decision Insight

Perpetual Accounting   Walmart uses a network of information links with its point-of-sale cash registers to coordinate sales, purchases, and distribution. Its supercenters, for instance, ring up 15,000 separate sales on heavy days. By using cash register information, the company can fix pricing mistakes quickly and capitalize on sales trends. Interestingly, Sam Walton, the founder, was a self-described distruster of computers. ■

Control of Cash Disbursements

Control of cash disbursements is especially important as most large thefts occur from payment of fictitious invoices. One key to controlling cash disbursements is to require all expenditures to be made by check. The only exception is small payments made from petty cash. Another key is to deny access to the accounting records to anyone other than the owner who has the authority to sign checks. A small business owner often signs checks and knows from personal contact that the items being paid for are actually received. This arrangement is impossible in large businesses. Instead, internal control procedures must be substituted for personal contact. Such procedures are designed to assure the check signer that the obligations recorded are properly incurred and should be paid. This section describes these and other internal control procedures, including the voucher system and petty cash system. A method for management of cash disbursements for purchases is described in Appendix 6B.

Cash Budget   Projected cash receipts and cash disbursements are often summarized in a *cash budget*. Provided that sufficient cash exists for effective operations, companies wish to minimize the cash they hold because of its risk of theft and its low return versus other investment opportunities.

 Decision Insight

Lock Box   Some companies do not receive cash in the mail but, instead, elect to have customers send deposits directly to the bank using a *lock box* system. Bank employees are charged with receipting the cash and depositing it in the correct business bank account. ■

Voucher System of Control   A **voucher system** is a set of procedures and approvals designed to control cash disbursements and the acceptance of obligations. The voucher system of control establishes procedures for

- Verifying, approving, and recording obligations for eventual cash disbursement.
- Issuing checks for payment of verified, approved, and recorded obligations.

A reliable voucher system follows standard procedures for every transaction. This applies even when multiple purchases are made from the same supplier.

A voucher system's control over cash disbursements begins when a company incurs an obligation that will result in payment of cash. A key factor in this system is that only approved departments and individuals are authorized to incur such obligations. The system often limits the type of obligations that a department or individual can incur. In a large retail store, for instance, only a purchasing department should be authorized to incur obligations for merchandise inventory. Another key factor is that procedures for purchasing, receiving, and paying for merchandise are divided among several departments (or individuals). These departments include the one requesting the purchase, the purchasing department, the receiving department, and the accounting department. To coordinate and control responsibilities of these departments, a company uses several different business documents. Exhibit 6.1 shows how documents are accumulated in a **voucher,** which is an internal document (or file) used to accumulate information to control cash disbursements and to ensure that a transaction is properly recorded. This specific example begins with a *purchase requisition* and concludes with a *check* drawn against cash. Appendix 6A describes the documentation and verification necessary for a voucher system of control. It also describes the internal control objective served by each document.

Point: MCI, formerly WorldCom, paid a whopping $500 million in SEC fines for accounting fraud. Among the charges were that it inflated earnings by as much as $10 billion. Its CEO, Bernard Ebbers, was sentenced to 25 years.

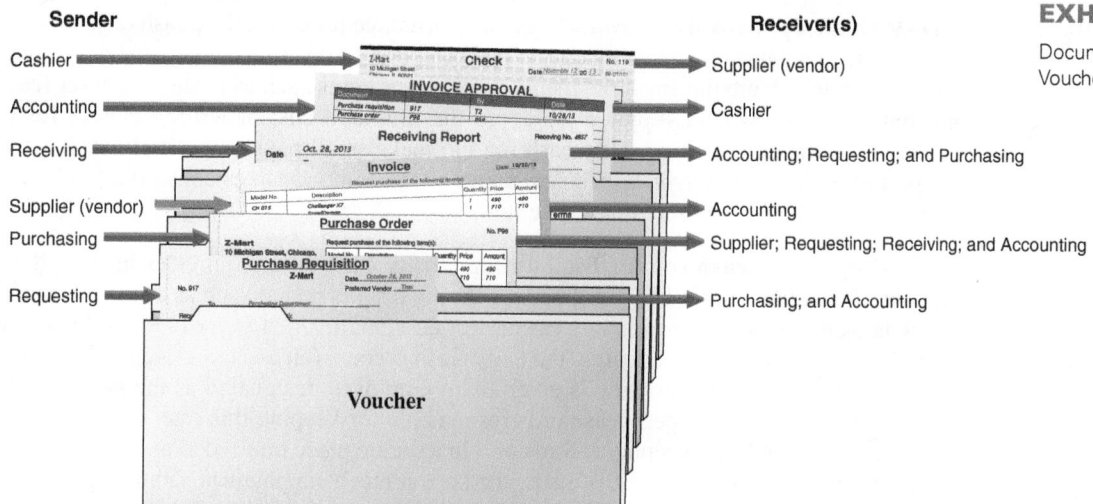

EXHIBIT 6.1

Document Flow in a Voucher System

A voucher system should be applied not only to purchases of inventory but to all expenditures. To illustrate, when a company receives a monthly telephone bill, it should review and verify the charges, prepare a voucher (file), and insert the bill. This transaction is then recorded with a journal entry. If the amount is currently due, a check is issued. If not, the voucher is filed for payment on its due date. If no voucher is prepared, verifying the invoice and its amount after several days or weeks can be difficult. Also, without records, a dishonest employee could collude with a dishonest supplier to get more than one payment for an obligation, payment for excessive amounts, or payment for goods and services not received. An effective voucher system helps prevent such frauds.

Point: A *voucher* is an internal document (or file).

Point: The basic purposes of paper and electronic documents are similar. However, the internal control system must change to reflect different risks, including confidential and competitive-sensitive information that is at greater risk in electronic systems.

Fraud

Cyber Setup The FTC is on the cutting edge of cybersleuthing. Opportunists in search of easy money are lured to www.wemarket4u.net/sundaestation/ and www.wemarket4u.net/fatfoe/. Take the bait and you get warned. The top 5 fraud complaints as compiled by the Federal Trade Commission are shown to the right.

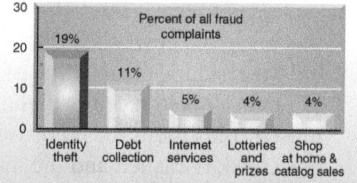

NEED-TO-KNOW 6.2

P1, C2

Do More: QS 6-3, E 6-2, E 6-4

QC2

A good system of internal control for cash provides adequate procedures for protecting both cash receipts and cash disbursements. Which of the following statements is true regarding the control of cash receipts and cash disbursements?

1. ____ Over-the-counter cash receipts from sales should be recorded on a cash register at the time of each sale.

2. ____ Custody over cash should be separate from the recordkeeping of cash.

3. ____ For control of cash receipts that arrive through the mail, two people should be assigned the task of, and be present for, opening that mail.

4. ____ One key to controlling cash disbursements is to require that no expenditures be made by check; instead, all expenditures should be made from petty cash.

5. ____ A voucher system of control should be applied only to purchases of inventory and never to other expenditures.

Solution

1. True   **2.** True   **3.** True   **4.** False   **5.** False

---

P2 Explain and record petty cash fund transactions.

Petty Cash System of Control   A basic principle for controlling cash disbursements is that all payments must be made by check. An exception to this rule is made for *petty cash disbursements,* which are the small payments required for items such as postage, courier fees, minor repairs, and low-cost supplies. To avoid the time and cost of writing checks for small amounts, a company sets up a petty cash fund to make small payments. (**Petty cash** activities are part of an *imprest system,* which designates advance money to establish the fund, to withdraw from the fund, and to reimburse the fund.)

Operating a petty cash fund.   Establishing a petty cash fund requires estimating the total amount of small payments likely to be made during a short period such as a week or month. A check is then drawn by the company cashier for an amount slightly in excess of this estimate. This check is recorded with a debit to the Petty Cash account (an asset) and a credit to Cash. The check is cashed, and the currency is given to an employee designated as the *petty cashier* or *petty cash custodian.* The petty cashier is responsible for keeping this cash safe, making payments from the fund, and keeping records of it in a secure place referred to as the *petty cashbox.*

When each cash disbursement is made, the person receiving payment should sign a prenumbered *petty cash receipt,* also called *petty cash ticket*—see Exhibit 6.2. The petty cash receipt is then placed in the petty cashbox with the remaining money. Under this system, the sum of all receipts plus the remaining cash equals the total fund amount. A $100 petty cash fund, for instance, contains any combination of cash and petty cash receipts that totals $100 (examples are $80 cash plus $20 in receipts, or $10 cash plus $90 in receipts). Each disbursement reduces cash and increases the amount of receipts in the petty cashbox.

Point: A petty cash fund is used only for business expenses.

EXHIBIT 6.2

Petty Cash Receipt

Z-Mart   No. 9

PETTY CASH RECEIPT

For *Freight charges*
Date *November 5, 2013*   Approved by *RL Grill*
Charge to *Merchandise Inventory*
Amount *$6.75*   Received by *DL Fibb*

Point: Petty cash receipts with either no signature or a forged signature usually indicate misuse of petty cash. Companies respond with surprise petty cash counts for verification.

The petty cash fund should be reimbursed when it is nearing zero and at the end of an accounting period when financial statements are prepared. For this purpose, the petty cashier sorts the paid receipts by the type of expense or account and then totals the receipts. The petty cashier presents all paid receipts to the company cashier, who stamps all receipts *paid* so they cannot be reused, files them for recordkeeping, and gives the petty cashier a check for their sum. When this check is cashed and the money placed in the cashbox, the total money in the cashbox is restored to its original amount. The fund is now ready for a new cycle of petty cash payments.

Illustrating a petty cash fund.   To illustrate, assume Z-Mart establishes a petty cash fund on November 1 and designates one of its office employees as the petty cashier. A $75 check is drawn, cashed, and the proceeds given to the petty cashier. The entry to record the setup of this petty cash fund is

Nov. 1	Petty Cash	75	
	Cash		75
	To establish a petty cash fund.		

Assets = Liabilities + Equity
+75
−75

After the petty cash fund is established, the Petty Cash account is not debited or credited again unless the amount of the fund is changed. (A fund should be increased if it requires reimbursement too frequently. On the other hand, if the fund is too large, some of its money should be redeposited in the Cash account.)

Next, assume that Z-Mart's petty cashier makes several November payments from petty cash. Each person who received payment is required to sign a receipt. On November 27, after making a $26.50 cash payment for tile cleaning, only $3.70 cash remains in the fund. The petty cashier then summarizes and totals the petty cash receipts as shown in Exhibit 6.3.

Point: Reducing or eliminating a petty cash fund requires a credit to Petty Cash.

Point: Although *individual* petty cash disbursements are not evidenced by a check, the initial petty cash fund is evidenced by a check, and later petty cash expenditures are evidenced by a check to replenish them *in total.*

Z-MART		
Petty Cash Payments Report		
Miscellaneous Expenses		
Nov. 2 Cleaning of LCD panels	$20.00	
Nov. 27 Tile cleaning	26.50	$ 46.50
Merchandise Inventory (transportation-in)		
Nov. 5 Transport of merchandise purchased	6.75	
Nov. 20 Transport of merchandise purchased	8.30	15.05
Delivery Expense		
Nov. 18 Customer's package delivered		5.00
Office Supplies Expense		
Nov. 15 Purchase of office supplies immediately used		4.75
Total		$71.30

EXHIBIT 6.3

Petty Cash Payments Report

Point: This report can also include receipt number and names of those who approved and received cash payment (see Need-To-Know 6.3).

The petty cash payments report and all receipts are given to the company cashier in exchange for a $71.30 check to reimburse the fund. The petty cashier cashes the check and puts the $71.30 cash in the petty cashbox. The company records this reimbursement as follows.

Nov. 27	Miscellaneous Expenses	46.50	
	Merchandise Inventory	15.05	
	Delivery Expense	5.00	
	Office Supplies Expense	4.75	
	Cash		71.30
	To reimburse petty cash.		

Assets = Liabilities + Equity
−71.30   −46.50
                          −15.05
                          − 5.00
                          − 4.75

A petty cash fund is usually reimbursed at the end of an accounting period so that expenses are recorded in the proper period, even if the fund is not low on money. If the fund is not reimbursed at the end of a period, the financial statements would show both an overstated cash asset and understated expenses (or assets) that were paid out of petty cash. Some companies do not reimburse the petty cash fund at the end of each period under the notion that this amount is immaterial to users of financial statements.

Point: To avoid errors in recording petty cash reimbursement, follow these steps: (1) prepare payments report, (2) compute cash needed by subtracting cash remaining from total fund amount, (3) record entry, and (4) check "Dr. = Cr." in entry. Any difference is Cash Over and Short.

Increasing or decreasing a petty cash fund.   A decision to increase or decrease a petty cash fund is often made when reimbursing it. To illustrate, assume Z-Mart decides to *increase* its petty cash fund from $75 to $100 on November 27 when it reimburses the fund. The entries required are to (1) reimburse the fund as usual (see the preceding November 27 entry) and (2) increase the fund amount as follows.

Nov. 27	Petty Cash	25	
	Cash		25
	To increase the petty cash fund amount.		

Alternatively, if Z-Mart *decreases* the petty cash fund from $75 to $55 on November 27, the entry is to (1) credit Petty Cash for $20 (decreasing the fund from $75 to $55) and (2) debit Cash for $20 (reflecting the $20 transfer from Petty Cash to Cash).

Summary of Petty Cash Accounting

Event	Petty Cash	Cash	Expenses
Set up fund	Dr.	Cr.	—
Reimburse fund ..	—	Cr.	Dr.
Increase fund....	Dr.	Cr.	—
Decrease fund ...	Cr.	Dr.	—

Cash over and short. Sometimes a petty cashier fails to get a receipt for payment or overpays for the amount due. When this occurs and the fund is later reimbursed, the petty cash payments report plus the cash remaining will not total to the fund balance. This mistake causes the fund to be *short.* This shortage is recorded as an expense in the reimbursing entry with a debit to the Cash Over and Short account. (An overage in the petty cash fund is recorded with a credit to Cash Over and Short in the reimbursing entry.) To illustrate, prepare the June 1 entry to reimburse a $200 petty cash fund when its payments report shows $178 in miscellaneous expenses and $15 cash remains.

$200 Petty Cash Fund

$15 Cash $7 Short $178 Receipts

June 1	Miscellaneous Expenses	178	
	Cash Over and Short	7	
	Cash		185
	To reimburse petty cash.		

Fraud

Warning Signs There are clues to internal control violations. Warning signs from accounting include (1) an increase in customer refunds—could be fake, (2) missing documents—could be used for fraud, (3) differences between bank deposits and cash receipts—could be cash embezzled, and (4) delayed recording—could reflect fraudulent records. Warning signs from employees include (1) lifestyle change—could be embezzlement, (2) too close with suppliers—could signal fraudulent transactions, and (3) failure to leave job, even for vacations—could conceal fraudulent activities.

NEED-TO-KNOW 6.3

P2

Bacardi Company established a $150 petty cash fund with Eminem as the petty cashier. When the fund balance reached $19 cash, Eminem prepared a petty cash payments report, which follows.

Petty Cash Payments Report

Receipt No.	Account Charged		Approved by	Received by
12	Delivery Expense	$ 29	Eminem	A. Smirnoff
13	Merchandise Inventory	18	Eminem	J. Daniels
15	(Omitted)	32	Eminem	C. Carlsberg
16	Miscellaneous Expense	41	(Omitted)	J. Walker
	Total	$120		

Required

1. Identify four internal control weaknesses from the petty cash payments report.
2. Prepare general journal entries to record:
   a. Establishment of the petty cash fund.
   b. Reimbursement of the fund. (Assume for this part only that petty cash receipt no. 15 was issued for miscellaneous expenses.)
3. What is the Petty Cash account balance immediately before reimbursement? Immediately after reimbursement?

Solution

1. Four internal control weaknesses that are apparent from the payments report include:

   a. Petty cash ticket no. 14 is missing. Its omission raises questions about the petty cashier's management of the fund.

   b. The $19 cash balance means that $131 has been withdrawn ($150 − $19 = $131). However, the total amount of the petty cash receipts is only $120 ($29 + $18 + $32 + $41). The fund is $11 short of cash ($131 − $120 = $11). Was petty cash receipt no. 14 issued for $11? Management should investigate.

   c. The petty cashier (Eminem) did not sign petty cash receipt no. 16. This omission could have been an oversight on his part or he might not have authorized the payment. Management should investigate.

   d. Petty cash receipt no. 15 does not indicate which account to charge. This omission could have been an oversight on the petty cashier's part. Management could check with C. Carlsberg and the petty cashier (Eminem) about the transaction. Without further information, debit Miscellaneous Expense.

2. Petty cash general journal entries.

   a. Entry to establish the petty cash fund.

Petty Cash	150	
Cash		150

   b. Entry to reimburse the fund.

Delivery Expense	29	
Merchandise Inventory.................	18	
Miscellaneous Expense ($41 + $32)	73	
Cash Over and Short.................	11	
Cash		131

Do More: QS 6-5, E 6-5, E 6-6, E 6-8

3. The Petty Cash account balance *always* equals its fund balance, in this case $150. This account balance does not change unless the fund is increased or decreased.

QC3

BANKING ACTIVITIES AS CONTROLS

Banks (and other financial institutions) provide many services, including helping companies control cash. Banks safeguard cash, provide detailed and independent records of cash transactions, and are a source of cash financing. This section describes these services and the documents provided by banking activities that increase managers' control over cash.

Basic Bank Services

This section explains basic bank services—such as the bank account, the bank deposit, and checking—that contribute to the control of cash.

Bank Account, Deposit, and Check   A *bank account* is a record set up by a bank for a customer. It permits a customer to deposit money for safekeeping and helps control withdrawals. To limit access to a bank account, all persons authorized to write checks on the account must sign a **signature card,** which bank employees use to verify signatures on checks. Many companies have more than one bank account to serve different needs and to handle special transactions such as payroll.

   Each bank deposit is supported by a **deposit ticket,** which lists items such as currency, coins, and checks deposited along with their corresponding dollar amounts. The bank gives the customer a copy of the deposit ticket or a deposit receipt as proof of the deposit. Exhibit 6.4 shows one type of deposit ticket.

   To withdraw money from an account, the depositor can use a **check,** which is a document signed by the depositor instructing the bank to pay a specified amount of money to a designated recipient. A check involves three parties: a *maker* who signs the check, a *payee* who is the recipient, and a *bank* (or *payer*) on which the check is drawn. The bank provides a depositor the checks that are serially numbered and imprinted with the name and address of both the depositor and bank. Both checks and deposit tickets are imprinted with identification codes in magnetic ink

Point: Online banking services include the ability to stop payment on a check, move money between accounts, get up-to-date balances, and identify cleared checks and deposits.

EXHIBIT 6.4

Deposit Ticket

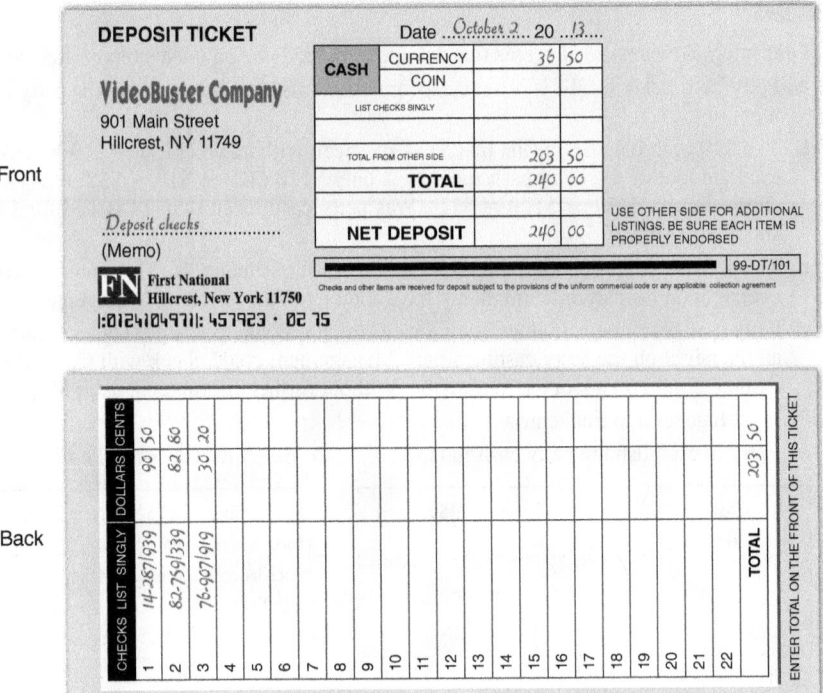

for computer processing. Exhibit 6.5 shows one type of check. It is accompanied with an optional *remittance advice* explaining the payment. When a remittance advice is unavailable, the *memo* line is often used for a brief explanation.

Electronic Funds Transfer   **Electronic funds transfer (EFT)** is the electronic transfer of cash from one party to another. No paper documents are necessary. Banks simply transfer

EXHIBIT 6.5

Check with Remittance Advice

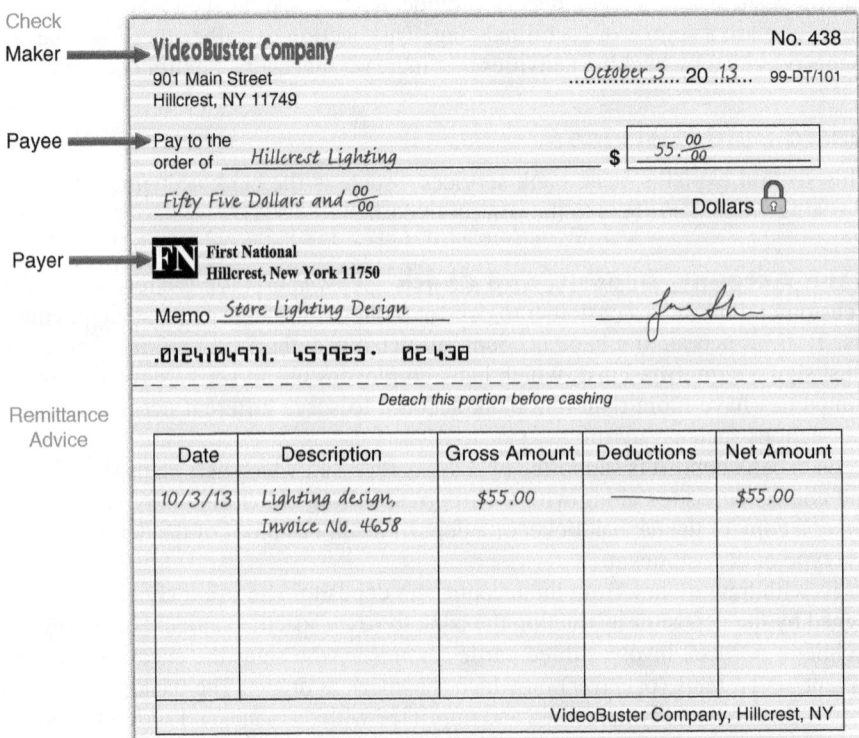

cash from one account to another with a journal entry. Companies are increasingly using EFT because of its convenience and low cost. For instance, it can cost up to 50 cents to process a check through the banking system, whereas EFT cost is near zero. We now commonly see items such as payroll, rent, utilities, insurance, and interest payments being handled by EFT. The bank statement lists cash withdrawals by EFT with the checks and other deductions. Cash receipts by EFT are listed with deposits and other additions. A bank statement is sometimes a depositor's only notice of an EFT. *Automated teller machines (ATMs)* are one form of EFT, which allows bank customers to deposit, withdraw, and transfer cash.

Bank Statement

Usually once a month, the bank sends each depositor a **bank statement** showing the activity in the account. Although a monthly statement is common, companies often regularly access information on their banking transactions. (Companies can choose to record any accounting adjustments required from the bank statement immediately or later, say, at the end of each day, week, month, or when reconciling a bank statement.) Different banks use different formats for their bank statements, but all of them include the following items of information:

1. Beginning-of-period balance of the depositor's account.
2. Checks and other debits decreasing the account during the period.
3. Deposits and other credits increasing the account during the period.
4. End-of-period balance of the depositor's account.

This information reflects the bank's records. Exhibit 6.6 shows one type of bank statement. Identify each of these four items in that statement. Part Ⓐ of Exhibit 6.6 summarizes changes in the account. Part Ⓑ lists paid checks along with other debits. Part Ⓒ lists deposits and credits to the account, and part Ⓓ shows the daily account balances.

In reading a bank statement note that a depositor's account is a liability on the bank's records. This is so because the money belongs to the depositor, not the bank. When a depositor increases the account balance, the bank records it with a *credit* to that liability account. This means that debit memos from the bank produce *credits* on the depositor's books, and credit memos from the bank produce *debits* on the depositor's books.

Enclosed with a bank statement is a list of the depositor's canceled checks (or the actual canceled checks) along with any debit or credit memoranda affecting the account. Increasingly, banks are showing canceled checks electronically via online access to accounts. **Canceled checks** are checks the bank has paid and deducted from the customer's account during the period. Other deductions that can appear on a bank statement include (1) service charges and fees assessed by the bank, (2) checks deposited that are uncollectible, (3) corrections of previous errors, (4) withdrawals through automated teller machines (ATMs), and (5) periodic payments arranged in advance by a depositor. (Most company checking accounts do not allow ATM withdrawals because of the company's desire to make all disbursements by check.) Except for service charges, the bank notifies the depositor of each deduction with a debit memorandum when the bank reduces the balance. A copy of each debit memorandum is usually sent with the statement (again, this information is often available earlier via online access and notifications).

Transactions that increase the depositor's account include amounts the bank collects on behalf of the depositor and the corrections of previous errors. Credit memoranda notify the depositor of all increases when they are recorded. A copy of each credit memorandum is often sent with the bank statement. Banks that pay interest on checking accounts often compute the amount of interest earned on the average cash balance and credit it to the depositor's account each period. In Exhibit 6.6, the bank credits $8.42 of interest to the account.

Bank Reconciliation

When a company deposits all cash receipts and makes all cash payments (except petty cash) by check, it can use the bank statement for proving the accuracy of its cash records. This is done using

Point: Good internal control is to deposit all cash receipts daily and make all payments for goods and services by check. This controls access to cash and creates an independent record of all cash activities.

Global: If cash is in more than one currency, a company usually translates these amounts into U.S. dollars using the exchange rate as of the balance sheet date. Also, a company must disclose any restrictions on cash accounts located outside the U.S.

P3   Prepare a bank reconciliation.

EXHIBIT 6.6

Bank Statement

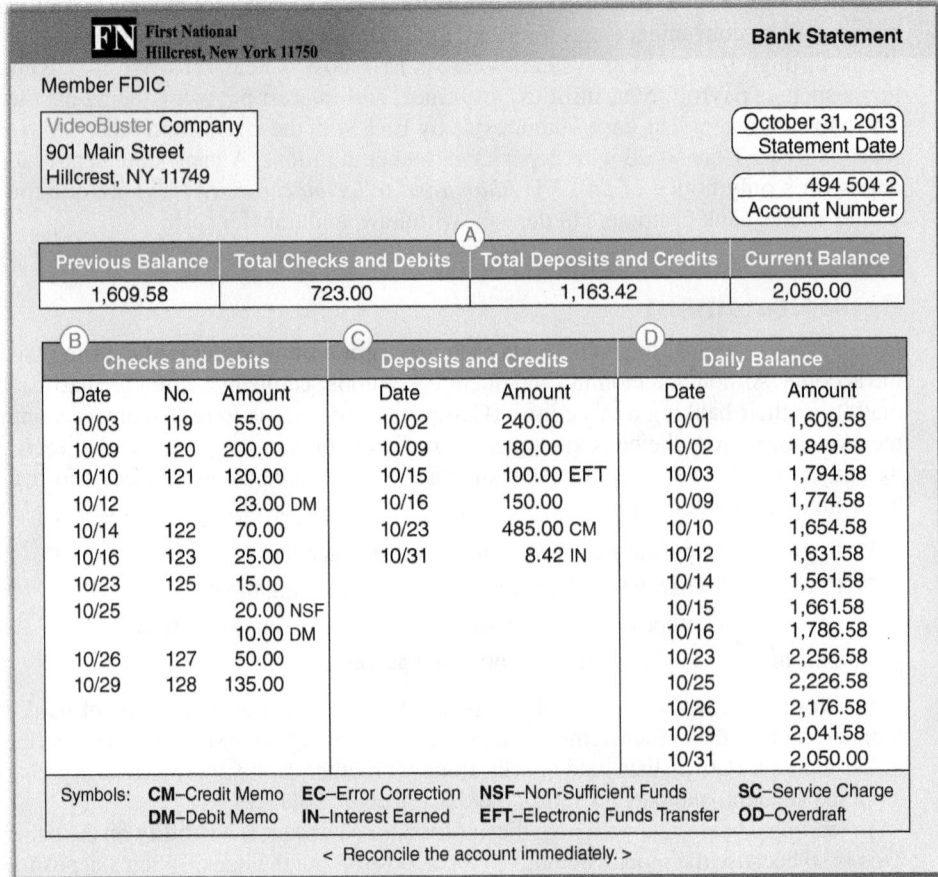

		First National Hillcrest, New York 11750				Bank Statement

Member FDIC

VideoBuster Company
901 Main Street
Hillcrest, NY 11749

October 31, 2013
Statement Date

494 504 2
Account Number

Ⓐ

Previous Balance	Total Checks and Debits	Total Deposits and Credits	Current Balance
1,609.58	723.00	1,163.42	2,050.00

Ⓑ Checks and Debits　　Ⓒ Deposits and Credits　　Ⓓ Daily Balance

Date	No.	Amount	Date	Amount	Date	Amount
10/03	119	55.00	10/02	240.00	10/01	1,609.58
10/09	120	200.00	10/09	180.00	10/02	1,849.58
10/10	121	120.00	10/15	100.00 EFT	10/03	1,794.58
10/12		23.00 DM	10/16	150.00	10/09	1,774.58
10/14	122	70.00	10/23	485.00 CM	10/10	1,654.58
10/16	123	25.00	10/31	8.42 IN	10/12	1,631.58
10/23	125	15.00			10/14	1,561.58
10/25		20.00 NSF			10/15	1,661.58
		10.00 DM			10/16	1,786.58
10/26	127	50.00			10/23	2,256.58
10/29	128	135.00			10/25	2,226.58
					10/26	2,176.58
					10/29	2,041.58
					10/31	2,050.00

Symbols:	**CM**–Credit Memo	**EC**–Error Correction	**NSF**–Non-Sufficient Funds	**SC**–Service Charge
	DM–Debit Memo	**IN**–Interest Earned	**EFT**–Electronic Funds Transfer	**OD**–Overdraft

< Reconcile the account immediately. >

Point: Many banks separately report other debits and credits apart from checks and deposits.

a **bank reconciliation,** which is a report explaining any differences between the checking account balance according to the depositor's records and the balance reported on the bank statement. The figure below reflects this process, which we describe in the following sections.

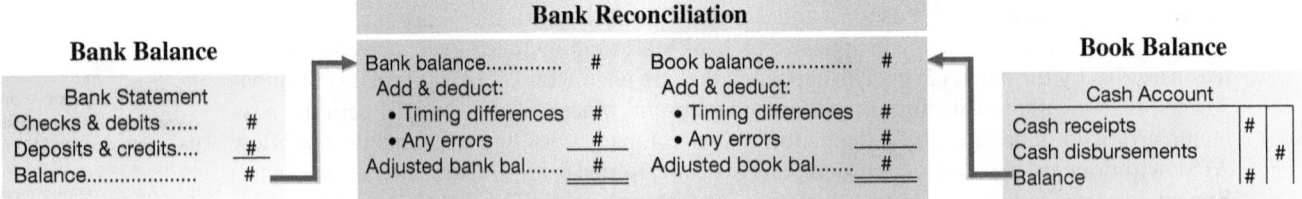

Bank Balance

Bank Statement
Checks & debits ...... #
Deposits & credits.... #
Balance.................... #

Bank Reconciliation

Bank balance.............. #	Book balance.............. #
Add & deduct:	Add & deduct:
• Timing differences #	• Timing differences #
• Any errors #	• Any errors #
Adjusted bank bal....... #	Adjusted book bal....... #

Book Balance

Cash Account
Cash receipts | #
Cash disbursements | #
Balance | #

Purpose of Bank Reconciliation　The balance of a checking account reported on the bank statement rarely equals the balance in the depositor's accounting records. This is usually due to information that one party has that the other does not. We must therefore prove the accuracy of both the depositor's records and those of the bank. This means we must *reconcile* the two balances and explain or account for any differences in them. Among the factors causing the bank statement balance to differ from the depositor's book balance are these:

● **Outstanding checks. Outstanding checks** are checks written (or drawn) by the depositor, deducted on the depositor's records, and sent to the payees but not yet received by the bank for payment at the bank statement date.

● **Deposits in transit** (also called **outstanding deposits**). **Deposits in transit** are deposits made and recorded by the depositor but not yet recorded on the bank statement. For example, companies can make deposits (in the night depository) at the end of a business day after the bank is closed. If such a deposit occurred on a bank statement date, it would not appear on this period's statement. The bank would record such a deposit on the next business day, and it would appear on the next period's bank statement. Deposits mailed to the bank near the end of a period also can be in transit and unrecorded when the statement is prepared.

- **Deductions for uncollectible items and for services.** A company sometimes deposits another party's check that is uncollectible (usually meaning the balance in that party's account is not large enough to cover the check). This check is called a *nonsufficient funds (NSF)* check. The bank would have initially credited the depositor's account for the amount of the check. When the bank learns the check is uncollectible, it debits (reduces) the depositor's account for the amount of that check. The bank may also charge the depositor a fee for processing an uncollectible check and notify the depositor of the deduction by sending a debit memorandum. The depositor should record each deduction when a debit memorandum is received, but an entry is sometimes not made until the bank reconciliation is prepared. Other possible bank charges to a depositor's account that are first reported on a bank statement include printing new checks and service fees.

- **Additions for collections and for interest.** Banks sometimes act as collection agents for their depositors by collecting notes and other items. Banks can also receive electronic funds transfers to the depositor's account. When a bank collects an item, it is added to the depositor's account, less any service fee. The bank also sends a credit memorandum to notify the depositor of the transaction. When the memorandum is received, the depositor should record it; yet it sometimes remains unrecorded until the bank reconciliation is prepared. The bank statement also includes a credit for any interest earned.

- **Errors.** Both banks and depositors can make errors. Bank errors might not be discovered until the depositor prepares the bank reconciliation. Also, depositor errors are sometimes discovered when the bank balance is reconciled. Error testing includes: (a) comparing deposits on the bank statement with deposits in the accounting records and (b) comparing canceled checks on the bank statement with checks recorded in the accounting records.

Illustration of a Bank Reconciliation   We follow nine steps in preparing the bank reconciliation. It is helpful to refer to the bank reconciliation in Exhibit 6.7 when studying steps ① through ⑨.

Forms of Check Fraud (CkFraud.org)
- Forged signatures—legitimate blank checks with fake payer signature
- Forged endorsements—stolen check that is endorsed and cashed by someone other than the payee
- Counterfeit checks—fraudulent checks with fake payer signature
- Altered checks—legitimate check altered (such as changed payee or amount) to benefit perpetrator
- Check kiting—deposit check from one bank account (without sufficient funds) into a second bank account

Point: Small businesses with few employees often allow recordkeepers to both write checks and keep the general ledger. If this is done, it is essential that the owner do the bank reconciliation.

Point: The person preparing the bank reconciliation should not be responsible for processing cash receipts, managing checks, or maintaining cash records.

EXHIBIT 6.7
Bank Reconciliation

VIDEOBUSTER Bank Reconciliation October 31, 2013						
① Bank statement balance		$ 2,050.00	⑤ Book balance			$ 1,404.58
② Add			⑥ Add			
Deposit of Oct. 31 in transit		145.00	Collect $500 note less $15 fee	$485.00		
		2,195.00	Interest earned	8.42		493.42
③ Deduct						1,898.00
Outstanding checks			⑦ Deduct			
No. 124	$150.00		Check printing charge	23.00		
No. 126	200.00	350.00	NSF check plus service fee	30.00		53.00
④ **Adjusted bank balance**		**$1,845.00**	⑧ **Adjusted book balance**			**$1,845.00**
		⑨ Balances are equal (reconciled)				

¹ Identify the bank statement balance of the cash account (*balance per bank*). VideoBuster's bank balance is $2,050.

² Identify and list any unrecorded deposits and any bank errors understating the bank balance. Add them to the bank balance. VideoBuster's $145 deposit placed in the bank's night depository on October 31 is not recorded on its bank statement.

³ Identify and list any outstanding checks and any bank errors overstating the bank balance. Deduct them from the bank balance. VideoBuster's comparison of canceled checks with its books shows two checks outstanding: No. 124 for $150 and No. 126 for $200.

Point: Outstanding checks are identified by comparing canceled checks on the bank statement with checks recorded. This includes identifying any outstanding checks listed on the *previous* period's bank reconciliation that are not included in the canceled checks on this period's bank statement.

4 Compute the *adjusted bank balance*, also called the *corrected* or *reconciled balance*.

5 Identify the company's book balance of the cash account (*balance per book*). VideoBuster's book balance is $1,404.58.

6 Identify and list any unrecorded credit memoranda from the bank, any interest earned, and errors understating the book balance. Add them to the book balance. VideoBuster's bank statement includes a credit memorandum showing the bank collected a note receivable for the company on October 23. The note's proceeds of $500 (minus a $15 collection fee) are credited to the company's account. VideoBuster's bank statement also shows a credit of $8.42 for interest earned on the average cash balance. There was no prior notification of this item, and it is not yet recorded.

7 Identify and list any unrecorded debit memoranda from the bank, any service charges, and errors overstating the book balance. Deduct them from the book balance. Debits on Video-Buster's bank statement that are not yet recorded include (a) a $23 charge for check printing and (b) an NSF check for $20 plus a related $10 processing fee. (The NSF check is dated October 16 and was included in the book balance.)

8 Compute the *adjusted book balance*, also called *corrected* or *reconciled balance*.

9 Verify that the two adjusted balances from steps 4 and 8 are equal. If so, they are reconciled. If not, check for accuracy and missing data to achieve reconciliation.

Point: Adjusting entries can be combined into one compound entry.

Adjusting Entries from a Bank Reconciliation

A bank reconciliation often identifies unrecorded items that need recording by the company. In VideoBuster's reconciliation, the adjusted balance of $1,845 is the correct balance as of October 31. But the company's accounting records show a $1,404.58 balance. We must prepare journal entries to adjust the book balance to the correct balance. It is important to remember that only the items reconciling the *book balance* require adjustment. A review of Exhibit 6.7 indicates that four entries are required for VideoBuster.

Collection of note.   The first entry is to record the proceeds of its note receivable collected by the bank less the expense of having the bank perform that service.

Assets = Liabilities + Equity
+485   −15
−500

Oct. 31	Cash	485	
	Collection Expense	15	
	Notes Receivable		500
	To record the collection fee and proceeds		
	for a note collected by the bank.		

Interest earned.   The second entry records interest credited to its account by the bank.

Assets = Liabilities + Equity
+8.42   +8.42

Oct. 31	Cash	8.42	
	Interest Revenue		8.42
	To record interest earned on the cash		
	balance in the checking account.		

Check printing.   The third entry records expenses for the check printing charge.

Assets = Liabilities + Equity
−23   −23

Oct. 31	Miscellaneous Expenses	23	
	Cash		23
	Check printing charge.		

NSF check.   The fourth entry records the NSF check that is returned as uncollectible. The $20 check was originally received from T. Woods in payment of his account and then deposited. The bank charged $10 for handling the NSF check and deducted $30 total from VideoBuster's account. This means the entry must reverse the effects of the original entry made when the check was received and must record (add) the $10 bank fee.

Point: The company will try to collect the entire NSF amount of $30 from customer.

Oct. 31	Accounts Receivable—T. Woods	30	
	Cash		30
	To charge Woods' account for $20 NSF check and $10 bank fee.		

Assets = Liabilities + Equity
+30
−30

After these four entries are recorded, the book balance of cash is adjusted to the correct amount of $1,845 (computed as $1,404.58 + $485 + $8.42 − $23 − $30). The Cash T-account to the side shows the same computation, where entries are keyed to the numerical codes in Exhibit 6.7.

		Cash		
Unadj. bal.	1,404.58			
⑥	485.00	⑦		23.00
⑥	8.42	⑦		30.00
Adj. bal.	1,845.00			

Point: The Need-To-Know 6.4 shows an adjusting entry for an error correction.

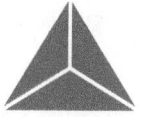 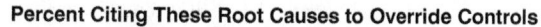

Fraud

Fraud A survey reports that 74% of employees had 'personally seen' or had 'firsthand knowledge of' fraud or misconduct within the past year. Another survey found that fraudsters exploited weak internal controls in 74% of the frauds—up from 47% four years earlier—see graphic (KPMG 2011).

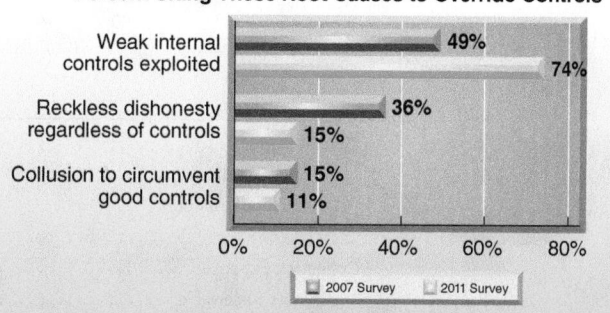

Percent Citing These Root Causes to Override Controls

Weak internal controls exploited: 49% / 74%
Reckless dishonesty regardless of controls: 36% / 15%
Collusion to circumvent good controls: 15% / 11%

☐ 2007 Survey   ☐ 2011 Survey

The following information is available to reconcile Gucci's book balance of cash with its bank statement cash balance as of December 31, 2014.

a. The December 31 cash balance according to the accounting records is $1,610, and the bank statement cash balance for that date is $1,900.

b. Gucci's December 31 daily cash receipts of $800 were placed in the bank's night depository on December 31, but do not appear on the December 31 bank statement.

c. Check No. 6273 for $400 and Check No. 6282 for $100, both written and entered in the accounting records in December, are not among the canceled checks. Two checks, No. 6231 for $2,000 and No. 6242 for $200, were outstanding on the most recent November 30 reconciliation. Check No. 6231 is listed with the December canceled checks, but Check No. 6242 is not.

d. When the December checks are compared with entries in the accounting records, it is found that Check No. 6267 had been correctly drawn for $340 to pay for office supplies but was erroneously entered in the accounting records as $430.

e. A credit memorandum indicates that the bank collected $500 cash on a note receivable for the company, deducted a $30 collection fee, and credited the balance to the company's Cash account. Gucci had not recorded this transaction before receiving the statement.

f. Two debit memoranda are enclosed with the statement and are unrecorded at the time of the reconciliation. One debit memorandum is for $150 and dealt with an NSF check for $140 received from a customer, Prada Inc., in payment of its account. The bank assessed a $10 fee for processing it. The second debit memorandum is a $20 charge for check printing. Gucci had not recorded these transactions before receiving the statement.

Required

1. Prepare the bank reconciliation for this company as of December 31, 2014.

2. Prepare the journal entries necessary to bring Gucci's book balance of cash into conformity with the reconciled cash balance as of December 31, 2014.

Solutions

Part 1

GUCCI					
Bank Reconciliation					
December 31, 2014					
Bank statement balance.........		$1,900	Book balance.................		$1,610
Add			Add		
Deposit of Dec. 31..........		800	Error (Ck 6267)	$ 90	
		2,700	Proceeds of note		
			less $30 fee	470	560
					2,170
Deduct			Deduct		
Checks No. 6242	$200		NSF check	$150	
6273	400		Printing fee.................	20	
6282	100	700			170
Adjusted bank balance..........		$2,000	Adjusted book balance		$2,000

Part 2

Dec. 31	Cash	90	
	Office Supplies		90
	To correct an entry error.		
Dec. 31	Cash	470	
	Collection Expense	30	
	Notes Receivable		500
	To record note collection less fees.		
Dec. 31	Accounts Receivable—Prada Inc.	150	
	Cash		150
	To charge account for NSF check plus fees.		
Dec. 31	Miscellaneous Expenses	20	
	Cash		20
	To record check printing charge.		

Do More: QS 6-4, QS 6-6, QS 6-7, E 6-7, E 6-10, E 6-11

GLOBAL VIEW

This section discusses similarities and differences between U.S. GAAP and IFRS regarding internal controls and in the accounting and reporting of cash.

Internal Control Purposes, Principles, and Procedures   Both U.S. GAAP and IFRS aim for high-quality financial reporting. That aim translates into enhanced internal controls worldwide. Specifically, the purposes and principles of internal control systems are fundamentally the same across the globe. However, culture and other realities suggest different emphases on the mix of control procedures, and some sensitivity to different customs and environments when establishing that mix. Nevertheless, the discussion in this chapter applies internationally. Nokia provides the following description of its control activities.

NOKIA

> Nokia has an internal audit function that acts as an independent appraisal function by examining and evaluating the adequacy and effectiveness of the company's system of internal control.

Control of Cash   Accounting definitions for cash are similar for U.S. GAAP and IFRS. The need for control of cash is universal and applies globally. This means that companies worldwide desire to apply cash management procedures as explained in this chapter and aim to control both cash receipts and disbursements. Accordingly, systems that employ tools such as cash monitoring mechanisms, verification of documents, and petty cash processes are applied worldwide. The basic techniques explained in this chapter are part of those control procedures.

Banking Activities as Controls   There is a global demand for banking services, bank statements, and bank reconciliations. To the extent feasible, companies utilize banking services as part of their effective control procedures. Further, bank statements are similarly used along with bank reconciliations to control and monitor cash.

 **IFRS** _____

Internal controls are crucial to companies that convert from U.S. GAAP to IFRS. Major risks include misstatement of financial information and fraud. Other risks are ineffective communication of the impact of this change for investors, creditors and others, and management's inability to certify the effectiveness of controls over financial reporting. ▪

Days' Sales Uncollected ▢▢▢   **Decision Analysis**

An important part of cash management is monitoring the receipt of cash from receivables. If customers and others who owe money to a company are delayed in payment, then that company can find it difficult to pay its obligations when they are due. A company's customers are crucial partners in its cash management. Many companies attract customers by selling to them on credit. This means that cash receipts from customers are delayed until accounts receivable are collected.

A1 Compute the days' sales uncollected ratio and use it to assess liquidity.

One measure of how quickly a company can convert its accounts receivable into cash is the **days' sales uncollected,** also called _days' sales in receivables_. This measure is computed by dividing the current balance of receivables by net credit sales over the year just completed and then multiplying by 365 (number of days in a year). Since net credit sales usually are not reported to external users, the net sales (or revenues) figure is commonly used in the computation as in Exhibit 6.8.

$$\text{Days' sales uncollected} = \frac{\text{Accounts receivable}}{\text{Net sales}} \times 365$$

EXHIBIT 6.8

Days' Sales Uncollected

We use days' sales uncollected to estimate how much time is likely to pass before the current amount of accounts receivable is received in cash. For evaluation purposes, we need to compare this estimate to that for other companies in the same industry. We also make comparisons between current and prior periods.

To illustrate, we select data from the annual reports of two toy manufacturers, Hasbro and Mattel. Their days' sales uncollected figures are shown in Exhibit 6.9.

Company	Figure ($ millions)	2011	2010	2009	2008	2007
Hasbro	Accounts receivable	$1,035	$961	$1,039	$612	$655
	Net sales	$4,286	$4,002	$4,068	$4,022	$3,838
	Days' sales uncollected	88 days	88 days	93 days	56 days	62 days
Mattel	Accounts receivable	$1,247	$1,146	$749	$874	$991
	Net sales	$6,266	$5,856	$5,431	$5,918	$5,970
	Days' sales uncollected	73 days	71 days	50 days	54 days	61 days

EXHIBIT 6.9

Analysis Using Days' Sales Uncollected

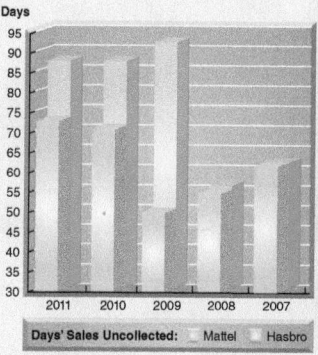

Days' sales uncollected for Hasbro in 2011 is computed as ($1,035/$4,286) × 365 days = 88 days. This means that it will take about 88 days to collect cash from ending accounts receivable. This number reflects one or more of the following factors: a company's ability to collect receivables, customer financial health, customer payment strategies, and discount terms. To further assess days' sales uncollected for Hasbro, we compare it to four prior years and to those of Mattel. We see that Hasbro's days' sales uncollected has worsened since 2008 as it takes much longer to collect its receivables relative to 2007 and 2008. In comparison, Mattel has also worsened from 50 days in 2009 up to 73 days in 2011. For all years, Mattel is superior to Hasbro on this measure of cash management. The less time that money is tied up in receivables often translates into increased profitability.

 **Decision** Maker

Sales Representative   The sales staff is told to take action to help reduce days' sales uncollected for cash management purposes. What can you, a salesperson, do to reduce days' sales uncollected? ■   [Answer—p. 292]

COMPREHENSIVE...

NEED-TO-KNOW

Prepare a bank reconciliation for Jamboree Enterprises for the month ended November 30, 2013. The following information is available to reconcile Jamboree Enterprises' book balance of cash with its bank statement balance as of November 30, 2013:

a. After all posting is complete on November 30, the company's book balance of Cash has a $16,380 debit balance, but its bank statement shows a $38,520 balance.

b. Checks No. 2024 for $4,810 and No. 2026 for $5,000 are outstanding.

c. In comparing the canceled checks on the bank statement with the entries in the accounting records, it is found that Check No. 2025 in payment of rent is correctly drawn for $1,000 but is erroneously entered in the accounting records as $880.

Point: Generally, the party that is not the initial recorder of an item, but is later informed, includes that item on its "book" of the bank reconciliation. For example, the bank records an NSF check and then informs the company. The company, as not the initial recorder of the item, reports it on the book side of its reconciliation.

d. The November 30 deposit of $17,150 was placed in the night depository after banking hours on that date, and this amount does not appear on the bank statement.

e. In reviewing the bank statement, a check written by Jumbo Enterprises in the amount of $160 was erroneously drawn against Jamboree's account.

f. A credit memorandum enclosed with the bank statement indicates that the bank collected a $30,000 note and $900 of related interest on Jamboree's behalf. This transaction was not recorded by Jamboree prior to receiving the statement.

g. A debit memorandum for $1,100 lists a $1,100 NSF check received from a customer, Marilyn Welch. Jamboree had not recorded the return of this check before receiving the statement.

h. Bank service charges for November total $40. These charges were not recorded by Jamboree before receiving the statement.

PLANNING THE SOLUTION

● Set up a bank reconciliation with a bank side and a book side (as in Exhibit 6.7). Leave room to both add and deduct items. Each column will result in a reconciled, equal balance.

● Examine each item *a* through *h* to determine whether it affects the book or the bank balance and whether it should be added or deducted from the bank or book balance.

● After all items are analyzed, complete the reconciliation and arrive at a reconciled balance between the bank side and the book side.

● For each reconciling item on the book side, prepare an adjusting entry. Additions to the book side require an adjusting entry that debits Cash. Deductions on the book side require an adjusting entry that credits Cash.

SOLUTION TO COMPREHENSIVE NEED-TO-KNOW

JAMBOREE ENTERPRISES
Bank Reconciliation
November 30, 2013

Bank statement balance			$ 38,520	Book balance		$ 16,380
Add				Add		
Deposit of Nov. 30	$17,150			Collection of note	$30,000	
Bank error (Jumbo)	160		17,310	Interest earned	900	30,900
			55,830			47,280
Deduct				Deduct		
Outstanding checks				NSF check (M. Welch)	1,100	
No. 2024	4,810			Recording error (# 2025) ...	120	
No. 2026	5,000		9,810	Service charge	40	1,260
Adjusted bank balance ...			**$46,020**	**Adjusted book balance**		**$46,020**

Required Adjusting Entries for Jamboree

Nov. 30	Cash	30,900	
	Notes Receivable		30,000
	Interest Earned		900
	To record collection of note with interest.		
Nov. 30	Accounts Receivable—M. Welch	1,100	
	Cash		1,100
	To reinstate account due from an NSF check.		
Nov. 30	Rent Expense	120	
	Cash		120
	To correct recording error on check no. 2025.		
Nov. 30	Bank Service Charges	40	
	Cash		40
	To record bank service charges.		

Point: Error correction can alternatively involve (1) reversing the error entry, and (2) recording the correct entry.

Documentation and Verification

This appendix describes the important business documents of a voucher system of control.

Purchase Requisition   Department managers are usually not allowed to place orders directly with suppliers for control purposes. Instead, a department manager must inform the purchasing department of its needs by preparing and signing a **purchase requisition,** which lists the merchandise needed and requests that it be purchased—see Exhibit 6A.1. Two copies of the purchase requisition are sent to the purchasing department, which then sends one copy to the accounting department. When the accounting department receives a purchase requisition, it creates and maintains a voucher for this transaction. The requesting department keeps the third copy.

P4 Describe the use of documentation and verification to control cash disbursements.

EXHIBIT 6A.1

Purchase Requisition

Purchase Order   A **purchase order** is a document the purchasing department uses to place an order with a **vendor** (seller or supplier). A purchase order authorizes a vendor to ship ordered merchandise at the stated price and terms—see Exhibit 6A.2. When the purchasing department receives a purchase requisition, it prepares at least five copies of a purchase order. The copies are distributed as follows: *copy 1* to the vendor as a purchase request and as authority to ship merchandise; *copy 2,* along with a copy of the purchase

Point: A voucher system is designed to uniquely meet the needs of a specific business. Thus, we should read this appendix as one example of a common voucher system design, but *not* the only design.

EXHIBIT 6A.2

Purchase Order

Point: Shipping terms and credit terms are shown on the purchase order.

Z-Mart	PURCHASE ORDER
10 Michigan Street	
Chicago, Illinois 60521	No. P98

		Date	10/30/13
To:	Trex	FOB	Destination
	W9797 Cherry Road	Ship by	As soon as possible
	Antigo, Wisconsin 54409	Terms	2/15, n/30

Request shipment of the following item(s):

Model No.	Description	Quantity	Price	Amount
CH 015	Challenger X7	1	490	490
SD 099	SpeedDemon	1	710	710

All shipments and invoices must include purchase order number

_J.W._

ORDERED BY

requisition, to the accounting department, where it is entered in the voucher and used in approving payment of the invoice; *copy 3* to the requesting department to inform its manager that action is being taken; *copy 4* to the receiving department without order quantity so it can compare with goods received and provide independent count of goods received; and *copy 5* retained on file by the purchasing department.

Invoice   An **invoice** is an itemized statement of goods prepared by the vendor listing the customer's name, items sold, sales prices, and terms of sale. An invoice is also a bill sent to the buyer from the supplier. From the vendor's point of view, it is a *sales invoice*. The buyer, or **vendee,** treats it as a *purchase invoice*. When receiving a purchase order, the vendor ships the ordered merchandise to the buyer and includes or mails a copy of the invoice covering the shipment to the buyer. The invoice is sent to the buyer's accounting department where it is placed in the voucher. (Refer back to Exhibit 4.5, which shows Z-Mart's purchase invoice.)

Receiving Report   Many companies maintain a separate department to receive all merchandise and purchased assets. When each shipment arrives, this receiving department counts the goods and checks them for damage and agreement with the purchase order. It then prepares four or more copies of a **receiving report,** which is used within the company to notify the appropriate persons that ordered goods have been received and to describe the quantities and condition of the goods. One copy is sent to accounting and placed in the voucher. Copies are also sent to the requesting department and the purchasing department to notify them that the goods have arrived. The receiving department retains a copy in its files.

Invoice Approval   When a receiving report arrives, the accounting department should have copies of the following documents in the voucher: purchase requisition, purchase order, and invoice. With the information in these documents, the accounting department can record the purchase and approve its payment. In approving an invoice for payment, it checks and compares information across all documents. To facilitate this checking and to ensure that no step is omitted, it often uses an **invoice approval,** also called *check authorization*—see Exhibit 6A.3. An invoice approval is a checklist of steps necessary for approving

EXHIBIT 6A.3

Invoice Approval

INVOICE APPROVAL			
DOCUMENT		BY	DATE
Purchase requisition	917	TZ	10/28/13
Purchase order	P98	JW	10/30/13
Receiving report	R85	SK	11/03/13
Invoice:	4657		11/12/13
Price		JK	11/12/13
Calculations		JK	11/12/13
Terms		JK	11/12/13
Approved for payment		BC	

an invoice for recording and payment. It is a separate document either filed in the voucher or preprinted (or stamped) on the voucher.

As each step in the checklist is approved, the person initials the invoice approval and records the current date. Final approval implies the following steps have occurred:

1. **Requisition check:** Items on invoice are requested per purchase requisition.
2. **Purchase order check:** Items on invoice are ordered per purchase order.
3. **Receiving report check:** Items on invoice are received per receiving report.
4. **Invoice check: Price:** Invoice prices are as agreed with the vendor.
   Calculations: Invoice has no mathematical errors.
   Terms: Terms are as agreed with the vendor.

Voucher   Once an invoice has been checked and approved, the voucher is complete. A complete voucher is a record summarizing a transaction. Once the voucher certifies a transaction, it authorizes recording an obligation. A voucher also contains approval for paying the obligation on an appropriate date. The physical form of a voucher varies across companies. Many are designed so that the invoice and other related source documents are placed inside the voucher, which can be a folder.

Completion of a voucher usually requires a person to enter certain information on both the inside and outside of the voucher. Typical information required on the inside of a voucher is shown in Exhibit 6A.4, and that for the outside is shown in Exhibit 6A.5. This information is taken from the invoice and the supporting documents filed in the voucher. A complete voucher is sent to an authorized individual (often called an *auditor*). This person performs a final review, approves the accounts and amounts for debiting (called the *accounting distribution*), and authorizes recording of the voucher.

Point: Recording a purchase is initiated by an invoice approval, not an invoice. An invoice approval verifies that the amount is consistent with that requested, ordered, and received. This controls and verifies purchases and related liabilities.

Point: Auditors, when auditing inventory, check a sampling of purchases by reviewing the purchase order, receiving report, and invoice.

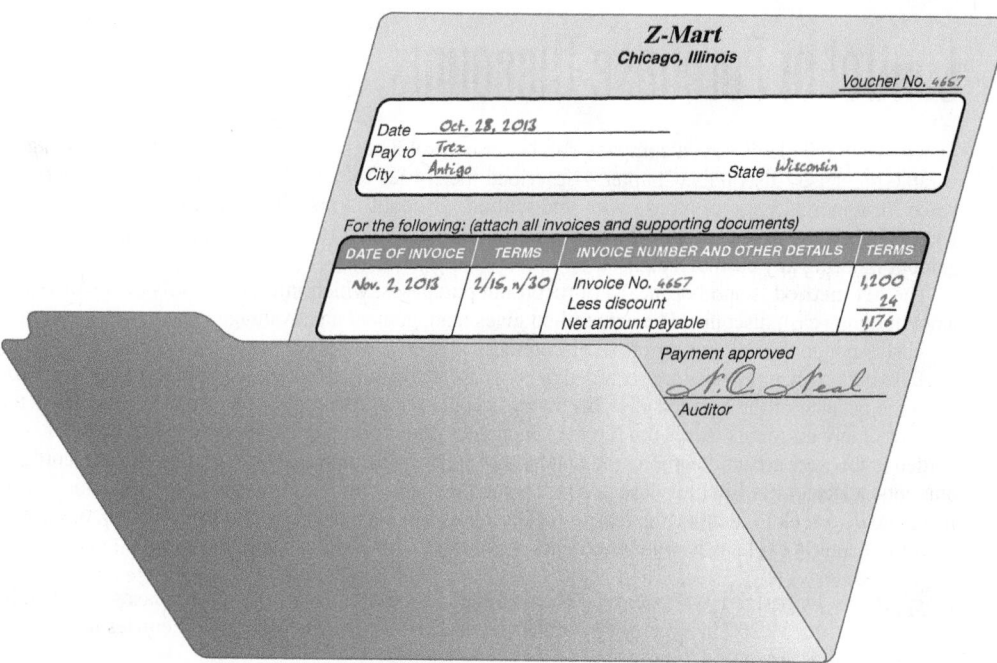

EXHIBIT 6A.4

Inside of a Voucher

After a voucher is approved and recorded (in a journal called a **voucher register**), it is filed by its due date. A check is then sent on the payment date from the cashier, the voucher is marked "paid," and the voucher is sent to the accounting department and recorded (in a journal called the **check register**). The person issuing checks relies on the approved voucher and its signed supporting documents as proof that an obligation has been incurred and must be paid. The purchase requisition and purchase order confirm the purchase was authorized. The receiving report shows that items have been received, and the invoice approval form verifies that the invoice has been checked for errors. There is little chance for error and even less chance for fraud without collusion unless all the documents and signatures are forged.

EXHIBIT 6A.5

Outside of a Voucher

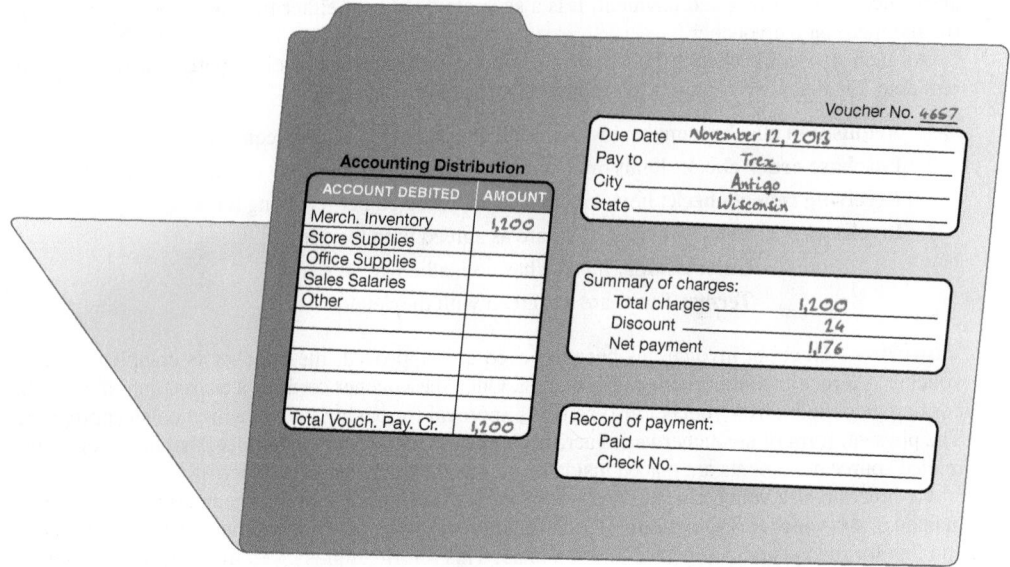

APPENDIX

6B   Control of Purchase Discounts

P5 Apply the net method to control purchase discounts.

This appendix explains how a company can better control its cash *disbursements* to take advantage of favorable purchases discounts. Chapter 4 described the entries to record the receipt and payment of an invoice for a merchandise purchase with and without discount terms. Those entries were prepared under what is called the **gross method** of recording purchases, which initially records the invoice at its *gross* amount ignoring any cash discount.

The **net method** is another means of recording purchases, which initially records the invoice at its *net* amount of any cash discount. The net method gives management an advantage in controlling and monitoring cash payments involving purchase discounts.

To explain, when invoices are recorded at *gross* amounts, the amount of any discounts taken is deducted from the balance of the Merchandise Inventory account when cash payment is made. This means that the amount of any discounts lost is not reported in any account or on the income statement. Lost discounts recorded in this way are unlikely to come to the attention of management. When purchases are recorded at *net* amounts, a **Discounts Lost** expense account is recorded and brought to management's attention. Management can then seek to identify the reason for discounts lost such as oversight, carelessness, or unfavorable terms. (Chapter 4 explains how managers assess whether a discount is favorable or not.)

Perpetual Inventory System   To illustrate, assume that a company purchases merchandise on November 2 at a $1,200 invoice price with terms of 2/10, n/30. Its November 2 entries under the gross and net methods are

Gross Method—Perpetual				**Net Method—Perpetual**		
Merchandise Inventory	1,200			Merchandise Inventory	1,176	
Accounts Payable		1,200		Accounts Payable		1,176

If the invoice is paid on November 12 within the discount period, it records the following:

Gross Method—Perpetual				**Net Method—Perpetual**		
Accounts Payable	1,200			Accounts Payable	1,176	
Merchandise Inventory		24		Cash		1,176
Cash		1,176				

If the invoice is *not* paid within the discount period, it records the following November 12 entry (which is the date corresponding to the end of the discount period):

Gross Method—Perpetual		Net Method—Perpetual	
No entry		Discounts Lost 24	
		Accounts Payable	24

Then, when the invoice is later paid on December 2, outside the discount period, it records the following:

Gross Method—Perpetual		Net Method—Perpetual	
Accounts Payable 1,200		Accounts Payable 1,200	
Cash......................	1,200	Cash	1,200

(The discount lost can be recorded when the cash payment is made with a single entry. However, in this case, when financial statements are prepared after a discount is lost and before the cash payment is made, an adjusting entry is required to recognize any unrecorded discount lost in the period when incurred.)

Periodic Inventory System   The preceding entries assume a perpetual inventory system. If a company is using a periodic system, its November 2 entries under the gross and net methods are

Gross Method—Periodic		Net Method—Periodic	
Purchases 1,200		Purchases 1,176	
Accounts Payable	1,200	Accounts Payable	1,176

If the invoice is paid on November 12 within the discount period, it records the following:

Gross Method—Periodic		Net Method—Periodic	
Accounts Payable 1,200		Accounts Payable 1,176	
Purchases Discounts	24	Cash	1,176
Cash......................	1,176		

If the invoice is *not* paid within the discount period, it records the following November 12 entry:

Gross Method—Periodic		Net Method—Periodic	
No entry		Discounts Lost 24	
		Accounts Payable	24

Then, when the invoice is later paid on December 2, outside the discount period, it records the following:

Gross Method—Periodic		Net Method—Periodic	
Accounts Payable 1,200		Accounts Payable 1,200	
Cash	1,200	Cash	1,200

Summary

C1   **Define internal control and identify its purpose and principles.** An internal control system consists of the policies and procedures managers use to protect assets, ensure reliable accounting, promote efficient operations, and urge adherence to company policies. It can prevent avoidable losses and help managers both plan operations and monitor company and human performance. Principles of good internal control include establishing responsibilities, maintaining adequate records, insuring assets and bonding employees, separating recordkeeping from custody of assets, dividing responsibilities for related transactions, applying technological controls, and performing regular independent reviews.

C2   **Define cash and cash equivalents and explain how to report them.** Cash includes currency, coins, and amounts on (or acceptable for) deposit in checking and savings accounts. Cash equivalents are short-term, highly liquid investment assets readily convertible to a known cash amount and sufficiently close to their maturity date so that market value is not sensitive to interest rate changes. Cash and cash equivalents are liquid assets because they are readily converted into other assets or can be used to pay for goods, services, or liabilities.

A1   **Compute the days' sales uncollected ratio and use it to assess liquidity.** Many companies attract customers by selling to them on credit. This means that cash receipts from customers are delayed until accounts receivable are collected. Users want to know how quickly a company can convert its accounts receivable into cash. The days' sales uncollected ratio, one measure reflecting company liquidity, is computed by dividing the ending balance of receivables by annual net sales, and then multiplying by 365.

P1 **Apply internal control to cash receipts and disbursements.** Internal control of cash receipts ensures that all cash received is properly recorded and deposited. Attention focuses on two important types of cash receipts: over-the-counter and by mail. Good internal control for over-the-counter cash receipts includes use of a cash register, customer review, use of receipts, a permanent transaction record, and separation of the custody of cash from its recordkeeping. Good internal control for cash receipts by mail includes at least two people assigned to open mail and a listing of each sender's name, amount, and explanation. (Banks offer several services that promote the control and safeguarding of cash.)

P2 **Explain and record petty cash fund transactions.** Petty cash disbursements are payments of small amounts for items such as postage, courier fees, minor repairs, and supplies. A company usually sets up one or more petty cash funds. A petty cash fund cashier is responsible for safekeeping the cash, making payments from this fund, and keeping receipts and records. A Petty Cash account is debited only when the fund is established or increased in amount. When the fund is replenished, petty cash disbursements are recorded with debits to expense (or asset) accounts and a credit to cash.

P3 **Prepare a bank reconciliation.** A bank reconciliation proves the accuracy of the depositor's and the bank's records. The bank statement balance is adjusted for items such as outstanding checks and unrecorded deposits made on or before the bank statement date but not reflected on the statement. The book balance is adjusted for items such as service charges, bank collections for the depositor, and interest earned on the account.

P4ᴬ **Describe the use of documentation and verification to control cash disbursements.** A voucher system is a set of procedures and approvals designed to control cash disbursements and acceptance of obligations. The voucher system of control relies on several important documents, including the voucher and its supporting files. A key factor in this system is that only approved departments and individuals are authorized to incur certain obligations.

P5ᴮ **Apply the net method to control purchase discounts.** The net method aids management in monitoring and controlling purchase discounts. When invoices are recorded at gross amounts, the amount of discounts taken is deducted from the balance of the Inventory account. This means that the amount of any discounts lost is not reported in any account and is unlikely to come to the attention of management. When purchases are recorded at net amounts, a Discounts Lost account is brought to management's attention as an operating expense. Management can then seek to identify the reason for discounts lost, such as oversight, carelessness, or unfavorable terms.

Guidance Answers to Decision Maker and Decision Ethics

Entrepreneur   To achieve proper separation of duties, a minimum of three employees are required. Transaction authorization, recording, and asset custody are ideally handled by three employees. Many small businesses do not employ three workers. In such cases, an owner must exercise more oversight to make sure that the lack of separation of duties does not result in fraudulent transactions.

Sales Representative   A salesperson can take several steps to reduce days' sales uncollected. These include (1) decreasing the ratio of sales on account to total sales by encouraging more cash sales, (2) identifying customers most delayed in their payments and encouraging earlier payments or cash sales, and (3) applying stricter credit policies to eliminate credit sales to customers that never pay.

Key Terms

Bank reconciliation (p. 280)

Bank statement (p. 279)

Canceled checks (p. 279)

Cash (p. 269)

Cash equivalents (p. 269)

Cash Over and Short (p. 271)

Check (p. 277)

Check register (p. 290)

Committee of Sponsoring Organizations (COSO) (p. 265)

Days' sales uncollected (p. 285)

Deposit ticket (p. 277)

Deposits in transit (p. 280)

Discounts lost (p. 290)

Electronic funds transfer (EFT) (p. 278)

Gross method (p. 290)

Internal control system (p. 264)

Invoice (p. 288)

Invoice approval (p. 288)

Liquid assets (p. 269)

Liquidity (p. 269)

Net method (p. 290)

Outstanding checks (p. 280)

Petty cash (p. 274)

Principles of internal control (p. 264)

Purchase order (p. 287)

Purchase requisition (p. 287)

Receiving report (p. 288)

Sarbanes-Oxley Act (p. 264)

Section 404 (of SOX) (p. 264)

Signature card (p. 277)

Vendee (p. 288)

Vendor (p. 287)

Voucher (p. 289)

Voucher register (p. 289)

Voucher system (p. 272)

Additional Quiz Questions are available at the book's Website.

1. A company needs to replenish its $500 petty cash fund. Its petty cash box has $75 cash and petty cash receipts of $420. The journal entry to replenish the fund includes
   a. A debit to Cash for $75.
   b. A credit to Cash for $75.
   c. A credit to Petty Cash for $420.
   d. A credit to Cash Over and Short for $5.
   e. A debit to Cash Over and Short for $5.

2. The following information is available for Hapley Company:
   - The November 30 bank statement shows a $1,895 balance.
   - The general ledger shows a $1,742 balance at November 30.
   - A $795 deposit placed in the bank's night depository on November 30 does not appear on the November 30 bank statement.
   - Outstanding checks amount to $638 at November 30.
   - A customer's $335 note was collected by the bank in November. A collection fee of $15 was deducted by the bank and the difference deposited in Hapley's account.
   - A bank service charge of $10 is deducted by the bank and appears on the November 30 bank statement.

   How will the customer's note appear on Hapley's November 30 bank reconciliation?
   a. $320 appears as an addition to the book balance of cash.
   b. $320 appears as a deduction from the book balance of cash.
   c. $320 appears as an addition to the bank balance of cash.
   d. $320 appears as a deduction from the bank balance of cash.
   e. $335 appears as an addition to the bank balance of cash.

3. Using the information from question 2, what is the reconciled balance on Hapley's November 30 bank reconciliation?
   a. $2,052
   b. $1,895
   c. $1,742
   d. $2,201
   e. $1,184

4. A company had net sales of $84,000 and accounts receivable of $6,720. Its days' sales uncollected is
   a. 3.2 days
   b. 18.4 days
   c. 230.0 days
   d. 29.2 days
   e. 12.5 days

5.[B] A company records its purchases using the net method. On August 1, it purchases merchandise on account for $6,000 with terms of 2/10, n/30. The August 1 journal entry to record this transaction includes a
   a. Debit to Merchandise Inventory for $6,000.
   b. Debit to Merchandise Inventory for $5,880.
   c. Debit to Merchandise Inventory for $120.
   d. Debit to Accounts Payable for $5,880.
   e. Credit to Accounts Payable for $6,000.

A(B) *Superscript letter A(B) denotes assignments based on Appendix 6A (6B).*

[i] Icon denotes assignments that involve decision making.

Discussion Questions

1. List the seven broad principles of internal control.
2. [i] Internal control procedures are important in every business, but at what stage in the development of a business do they become especially critical?
3. [i] Why should responsibility for related transactions be divided among different departments or individuals?
4. [i] Why should the person who keeps the records of an asset not be the person responsible for its custody?
5. [i] When a store purchases merchandise, why are individual departments not allowed to directly deal with suppliers?
6. What are the limitations of internal controls?
7. Which of the following assets is most liquid? Which is least liquid? Inventory, building, accounts receivable, or cash.
8. What is a petty cash receipt? Who should sign it?
9. Why should cash receipts be deposited on the day of receipt?
10. Apple's statement of cash flows in Appendix A **APPLE** describes changes in cash and cash equivalents for the year ended September 29, 2012. What total amount is provided (used) by investing activities? What amount is provided (used) by financing activities?
11. Refer to Google's financial statements in Appendix A. Identify Google's net earnings **GOOGLE** (income) for the year ended December 31, 2012. Is its net earnings equal to the increase in cash and cash equivalents for the year? Explain the difference between net earnings and the increase in cash and cash equivalents.
12. [i] Refer to Samsung's balance sheet in Appendix A. How does its cash (titled **Samsung** "Cash and cash equivalents") compare with its other current assets (both in amount and percent) as of December 31, 2012? Compare and assess its cash at December 31, 2012, with its cash at December 31, 2011.
13. [i] Samsung's balance sheet in Appendix A reports that cash and equivalents in- **Samsung** creased during the year ended December 31, 2012. Identify the cash generated (or used) by operating activities, by investing activities, and by financing (funding) activities.

QUICK STUDY

QS 6-1

Internal control objectives

C1

An internal control system consists of all policies and procedures used to protect assets, ensure reliable accounting, promote efficient operations, and urge adherence to company policies. Evaluate each of the following statements and indicate which are true and which are false regarding the objectives of an internal control system.

_____ **1.** Separation of recordkeeping for assets from the custody over assets is intended to reduce theft and fraud.

_____ **2.** The primary objective of internal control procedures is to safeguard the revenues of the business.

_____ **3.** The main objective of internal control procedures is best accomplished by designing an operational system with managerial policies that protect the assets from waste, fraud and theft.

_____ **4.** Separating the responsibility for a transaction between two or more individuals or departments will not help prevent someone from creating a fictitious invoice and paying the money to herself or himself.

QS 6-2

Cash and equivalents

C2

Choose from the following list of terms/phrases to best complete the following statements.

    a. Cash   **c.** Outstanding check   **e.** Bank reconciliation

    b. Cash equivalents   **d.** Liquidity   **f.** Current assets

_____ **1.** The _____ category includes currency and coins along with amounts on deposit in bank accounts, checking accounts, and savings accounts.

_____ **2.** The term _____ refers to a company's ability to pay for its near-term obligations.

_____ **3.** The _____ category includes short-term, highly liquid investment assets that are readily convertible to a known cash amount and sufficiently close to their due dates so that their market value is not sensitive to interest rate changes.

QS 6-3

Internal control for cash

P1

A good system of internal control for cash provides adequate procedures for protecting both cash receipts and cash disbursements. Which of the following statements is true regarding this protection?

    a. A basic guideline for safeguarding cash is that all cash receipts be deposited weekly or monthly.

    b. A voucher system of control is a control system exclusively for cash receipts.

    c. A basic guideline for safeguarding cash is to separate the duties of those who have custody of cash from those who keep cash records.

    d. A petty cash system is not a control procedure for safeguarding cash.

QS 6-4

Bank reconciliation

P3

1. For each of the following items, indicate whether its amount (i) affects the bank or book side of a bank reconciliation and (ii) represents an addition or a subtraction in a bank reconciliation.

    a. Interest on cash balance   **d.** Outstanding checks   **g.** Outstanding deposits

    b. Bank service charges   **e.** Credit memos

    c. Debit memos   **f.** NSF checks

2. Which of the items in part 1 require an adjusting journal entry?

QS 6-5

Petty cash accounting

P2

1. The petty cash fund of the Brooks Agency is established at $150. At the end of the current period, the fund contained $28 and had the following receipts: film rentals, $24, refreshments for meetings, $46 (both expenditures to be classified as Entertainment Expense); postage, $30; and printing, $22. Prepare journal entries to record (a) establishment of the fund and (b) reimbursement of the fund at the end of the current period.

2. Identify the two events that cause a Petty Cash account to be credited in a journal entry.

QS 6-6

Bank reconciliation

P3

Nolan Company deposits all cash receipts on the day when they are received and it makes all cash payments by check. At the close of business on June 30, 2013, its Cash account shows an $22,352 debit balance. Nolan's June 30 bank statement shows $21,332 on deposit in the bank. Prepare a bank reconciliation for the company using the following information.

    a. Outstanding checks as of June 30 total $3,713.

    b. The June 30 bank statement included a $41 debit memorandum for bank services; the company has not yet recorded the cost of these services.

    c. In reviewing the bank statement, a $90 check written by the company was mistakenly recorded in the company's books at $99.

d. June 30 cash receipts of $4,724 were placed in the bank's night depository after banking hours and were not recorded on the June 30 bank statement.

e. The bank statement included a $23 credit for interest earned on the cash in the bank.

An entrepreneur commented that a bank reconciliation may not be necessary as she regularly reviews her online bank statement for any unusual items and errors.

a. Describe how a bank reconciliation and an online review (or reading) of the bank statement are not equivalent.

b. Identify and explain at least two frauds or errors that would be uncovered through a bank reconciliation and that would *not* be uncovered through an online review of the bank statement.

The following annual account balances are taken from Armour Sports at December 31.

	2013	2012
Accounts receivable	$ 85,692	$ 80,485
Net sales	2,691,855	2,396,858

What is the change in the number of days' sales uncollected between years 2012 and 2013? (Round the number of days to one decimal.) According to this analysis, is the company's collection of receivables improving? Explain.

Management uses a voucher system to help control and monitor cash disbursements. Which of the four documents listed below are prepared as part of a voucher system of control?

_____ **a.** Purchase Order   _____ **b.** Outstanding Check   _____ **c.** Invoice   _____ **d.** Voucher

---

An important part of cash management is knowing when, and if, to take purchase discounts.

a. Which accounting method uses a Discounts Lost account?

b. What is the advantage of this method for management?

Answer each of the following related to international accounting standards.

a. Explain how the purposes and principles of internal controls are different between accounting systems reporting under IFRS versus U.S. GAAP.

b. Cash presents special internal control challenges. How do internal controls for cash differ for accounting systems reporting under IFRS versus U.S. GAAP? How do the procedures applied differ across those two accounting systems?

■ **connect**

Franco Company is a rapidly growing start-up business. Its recordkeeper, who was hired six months ago, left town after the company's manager discovered that a large sum of money had disappeared over the past three months. An audit disclosed that the recordkeeper had written and signed several checks made payable to her fiancé and then recorded the checks as salaries expense. The fiancé, who cashed the checks but never worked for the company, left town with the recordkeeper. As a result, the company incurred an uninsured loss of $184,000. Evaluate Franco's internal control system and indicate which principles of internal control appear to have been ignored.

Some of Crown Company's cash receipts from customers are received by the company with the regular mail. The company's recordkeeper opens these letters and deposits the cash received each day. (*a*) Identify any internal control problem(s) in this arrangement. (*b*) What changes to its internal control system do you recommend?

What internal control procedures would you recommend in each of the following situations?

1. A concession company has one employee who sells towels, coolers, and sunglasses at the beach. Each day, the employee is given enough towels, coolers, and sunglasses to last through the day and enough cash to make change. The money is kept in a box at the stand.

2. An antique store has one employee who is given cash and sent to garage sales each weekend. The employee pays cash for any merchandise acquired that the antique store resells.

Exercise 6-4

Cash, liquidity, and return

C2

Good accounting systems help with the management and control of cash and cash equivalents.

1. Define and contrast the terms *liquid asset* and *cash equivalent.*
2. Why would companies invest their idle cash in cash equivalents?
3. Identify five principles of effective cash management.

Exercise 6-5

Petty cash fund accounting

P2

Check   (3) Cr. Cash $162 & $250

Palmona Co. establishes a $200 petty cash fund on January 1. On January 8, the fund shows $38 in cash along with receipts for the following expenditures: postage, $74; transportation-in, $29; delivery expenses, $16; and miscellaneous expenses, $43. Palmona uses the perpetual system in accounting for merchandise inventory. Prepare journal entries to (1) establish the fund on January 1, (2) reimburse it on January 8, and (3) both reimburse the fund and increase it to $450 on January 8, assuming no entry in part 2. (*Hint*: Make two separate entries for part 3.)

Exercise 6-6

Petty cash fund with a shortage

P2

Check   (2) Cr. Cash $246 and (3) Cr. Cash $50

Waupaca Company establishes a $350 petty cash fund on September 9. On September 30, the fund shows $104 in cash along with receipts for the following expenditures: transportation-in, $40; postage expenses, $123; and miscellaneous expenses, $80. The petty cashier could not account for a $3 shortage in the fund. The company uses the perpetual system in accounting for merchandise inventory. Prepare (1) the September 9 entry to establish the fund, (2) the September 30 entry to reimburse the fund, and (3) an October 1 entry to increase the fund to $400.

Exercise 6-7

Bank reconciliation and adjusting entries

P3

Prepare a table with the following headings for a monthly bank reconciliation dated September 30.

Bank Balance		Book Balance			Not Shown on the Reconciliation
Add	Deduct	Add	Deduct	Adjust	

For each item 1 through 12, place an *x* in the appropriate column to indicate whether the item should be added to or deducted from the book or bank balance, or whether it should not appear on the reconciliation. If the book balance is to be adjusted, place a *Dr.* or *Cr.* in the Adjust column to indicate whether the Cash balance should be debited or credited. At the left side of your table, number the items to correspond to the following list.

1. NSF check from customer is returned on September 25 but not yet recorded by this company.
2. Interest earned on the September cash balance in the bank.
3. Deposit made on September 5 and processed by the bank on September 6.
4. Checks written by another depositor but charged against this company's account.
5. Bank service charge for September.
6. Checks outstanding on August 31 that cleared the bank in September.
7. Check written against the company's account and cleared by the bank; erroneously not recorded by the company's recordkeeper.
8. Principal and interest on a note receivable to this company is collected by the bank but not yet recorded by the company.
9. Checks written and mailed to payees on October 2.
10. Checks written by the company and mailed to payees on September 30.
11. Night deposit made on September 30 after the bank closed.
12. Special bank charge for collection of note in part 8 on this company's behalf.

Exercise 6-8

Voucher system

P1

The voucher system of control is designed to control cash disbursements and the acceptance of obligations.

1. The voucher system of control establishes procedures for what two processes?
2. What types of expenditures should be overseen by a voucher system of control?
3. When is the voucher initially prepared? Explain.

Exercise 6-9

Bank reconciliation

P3

Wright Company deposits all cash receipts on the day when they are received and it makes all cash payments by check. At the close of business on May 31, 2013, its Cash account shows a $27,500 debit balance. The company's May 31 bank statement shows $25,800 on deposit in the bank. Prepare a bank reconciliation for the company using the following information.

a. The May 31 bank statement included a $100 debit memorandum for bank services; the company has not yet recorded the cost of these services.

b. Outstanding checks as of May 31 total $5,600.

c. May 31 cash receipts of $6,200 were placed in the bank's night depository after banking hours and were not recorded on the May 31 bank statement.

d. In reviewing the bank statement, a $400 check written by Smith Company was mistakenly drawn against Wright's account.

e. A debit memorandum for $600 refers to a $600 NSF check from a customer; the company has not yet recorded this NSF check.

Check Reconciled bal., $26,800

Del Gato Clinic deposits all cash receipts on the day when they are received and it makes all cash payments by check. At the close of business on June 30, 2013, its Cash account shows a $11,589 debit balance. Del Gato Clinic's June 30 bank statement shows $10,555 on deposit in the bank. Prepare a bank reconciliation for Del Gato Clinic using the following information:

a. Outstanding checks as of June 30 total $1,829.

b. The June 30 bank statement included a $16 debit memorandum for bank services.

c. Check No. 919, listed with the canceled checks, was correctly drawn for $467 in payment of a utility bill on June 15. Del Gato Clinic mistakenly recorded it with a debit to Utilities Expense and a credit to Cash in the amount of $476.

d. The June 30 cash receipts of $2,856 were placed in the bank's night depository after banking hours and were not recorded on the June 30 bank statement.

Exercise 6-10
Bank reconciliation
P3

Check Reconciled bal., $11,582

Prepare the adjusting journal entries that Del Gato Clinic must record as a result of preparing the bank reconciliation in Exercise 6-10.

Exercise 6-11
Adjusting entries from bank reconciliation P3

Bargains Co. reported annual net sales for 2012 and 2013 of $665,000 and $747,000, respectively. Its year-end balances of accounts receivable follow: December 31, 2012, $61,000; and December 31, 2013, $93,000. (*a*) Calculate its days' sales uncollected at the end of each year. Round the number of days to one decimal. (*b*) Evaluate and comment on any changes in the amount of liquid assets tied up in receivables.

Exercise 6-12
Liquid assets and accounts receivable

A1

Match each document in a voucher system in column one with its description in column two.

Exercise 6-13ᴬ
Documents in a voucher system
P4

Document

1. Purchase requisition
2. Purchase order
3. Invoice
4. Receiving report
5. Invoice approval
6. Voucher

Description

A. An itemized statement of goods prepared by the vendor listing the customer's name, items sold, sales prices, and terms of sale.

B. An internal file used to store documents and information to control cash disbursements and to ensure that a transaction is properly authorized and recorded.

C. A document used to place an order with a vendor that authorizes the vendor to ship ordered merchandise at the stated price and terms.

D. A checklist of steps necessary for the approval of an invoice for recording and payment; also known as a check authorization.

E. A document used by department managers to inform the purchasing department to place an order with a vendor.

F. A document used to notify the appropriate persons that ordered goods have arrived, including a description of the quantities and condition of goods.

Piere Imports uses the perpetual system in accounting for merchandise inventory and had the following transactions during the month of October. Prepare entries to record these transactions assuming that Piere Imports records invoices (*a*) at gross amounts and (*b*) at net amounts.

Exercise 6-14ᴮ
Record invoices at gross or net amounts
P5

Oct. 2 Purchased merchandise at a $3,000 price, invoice dated October 2, terms 2/10, n/30.
    10 Received a $500 credit memorandum (at full invoice price) for the return of merchandise that it purchased on October 2.
    17 Purchased merchandise at a $5,400 price, invoice dated October 17, terms 2/10, n/30.
    27 Paid for the merchandise purchased on October 17, less the discount.
    31 Paid for the merchandise purchased on October 2. Payment was delayed because the invoice was mistakenly filed for payment today. This error caused the discount to be lost.

■ connect

PROBLEM SET A

Problem 6-1A

Analyzing internal control

C1

For each of these five separate cases, identify the principle(s) of internal control that is violated. Recommend what the business should do to ensure adherence to principles of internal control.

1. Chi Han records all incoming customer cash receipts for her employer and posts the customer payments to their respective accounts.

2. At Tico Company, Julia and Justine alternate lunch hours. Julia is the petty cash custodian, but if someone needs petty cash when he is at lunch, Jose fills in as custodian.

3. Nori Nozumi posts all patient charges and payments at the Hopeville Medical Clinic. Each night Nori backs up the computerized accounting system to a tape and stores the tape in a locked file at her desk.

4. Benedict Shales prides himself on hiring quality workers who require little supervision. As office manager, Benedict gives his employees full discretion over their tasks and for years has seen no reason to perform independent reviews of their work.

5. Carla Farah's manager has told her to reduce costs. Cala decides to raise the deductible on the plant's property insurance from $5,000 to $10,000. This cuts the property insurance premium in half. In a related move, she decides that bonding the plant's employees is a waste of money since the company has not experienced any losses due to employee theft. Cala saves the entire amount of the bonding insurance premium by dropping the bonding insurance.

Problem 6-2A

Establish, reimburse, and increase petty cash

P2

Nakashima Gallery had the following petty cash transactions in February of the current year.

Feb. 2   Wrote a $400 check, cashed it, and gave the proceeds and the petty cashbox to Chloe Addison, the petty cashier.
       5   Purchased bond paper for the copier for $14.15 that is immediately used.
       9   Paid $32.50 COD shipping charges on merchandise purchased for resale, terms FOB shipping point. Nakashima uses the perpetual system to account for merchandise inventory.
      12   Paid $7.95 postage to express mail a contract to a client.
      14   Reimbursed Adina Sharon, the manager, $68 for business mileage on her car.
      20   Purchased stationery for $67.77 that is immediately used.
      23   Paid a courier $20 to deliver merchandise sold to a customer, terms FOB destination.
      25   Paid $13.10 COD shipping charges on merchandise purchased for resale, terms FOB shipping point.
      27   Paid $54 for postage expenses.
      28   The fund had $120.42 remaining in the petty cash box. Sorted the petty cash receipts by accounts affected and exchanged them for a check to reimburse the fund for expenditures.
      28   The petty cash fund amount is increased by $100 to a total of $500.

Required

1. Prepare the journal entry to establish the petty cash fund.

2. Prepare a petty cash payments report for February with these categories: delivery expense, mileage expense, postage expense, merchandise inventory (for transportation-in), and office supplies expense. Sort the payments into the appropriate categories and total the expenditures in each category.

Check   (3a & 3b) Total Cr. to Cash $379.58

3. Prepare the journal entries (in dollars and cents) for part 2 to both (*a*) reimburse and (*b*) increase the fund amount.

Problem 6-3A

Establish, reimburse, and adjust petty cash

P2

Kiona Co. set up a petty cash fund for payments of small amounts. The following transactions involving the petty cash fund occurred in May (the last month of the company's fiscal year).

May 1   Prepared a company check for $300 to establish the petty cash fund.
     15   Prepared a company check to replenish the fund for the following expenditures made since May 1.
         a.   Paid $88 for janitorial services.
         b.   Paid $53.68 for miscellaneous expenses.
         c.   Paid postage expenses of $53.50.
         d.   Paid $47.15 to *The County Gazette* (the local newspaper) for an advertisement.
         e.   Counted $62.15 remaining in the petty cash box.

16   Prepared a company check for $200 to increase the fund to $500.

31   The petty cashier reports that $288.20 cash remains in the fund. A company check is drawn to replenish the fund for the following expenditures made since May 15.

    f.   Paid postage expenses of $147.36.

    g.   Reimbursed the office manager for business mileage, $23.50.

    h.   Paid $34.75 to deliver merchandise to a customer, terms FOB destination.

31   The company decides that the May 16 increase in the fund was too large. It reduces the fund by $100, leaving a total of $400.

Required

1. Prepare journal entries (in dollars and cents) to establish the fund on May 1, to replenish it on May 15 and on May 31, and to reflect any increase or decrease in the fund balance on May 16 and May 31.

Check   (1) Cr. to Cash: May 15, $237.85; May 16, $200.00

Analysis Component

2. Explain how the company's financial statements are affected if the petty cash fund is not replenished and no entry is made on May 31.

The following information is available to reconcile Branch Company's book balance of cash with its bank statement cash balance as of July 31, 2013.

Problem 6-4A

Prepare a bank reconciliation and record adjustments

P3

a. On July 31, the company's Cash account has a $27,497 debit balance, but its July bank statement shows a $27,233 cash balance.

b. Check No. 3031 for $1,482 and Check No. 3040 for $558 were outstanding on the June 30 bank reconciliation. Check No. 3040 is listed with the July canceled checks, but Check No. 3031 is not. Also, Check No. 3065 for $382 and Check No. 3069 for $2,281, both written in July, are not among the canceled checks on the July 31 statement.

c. In comparing the canceled checks on the bank statement with the entries in the accounting records, it is found that Check No. 3056 for July rent was correctly written and drawn for $1,270 but was erroneously entered in the accounting records as $1,250.

d. A credit memorandum enclosed with the July bank statement indicates the bank collected $8,000 cash on a non-interest-bearing note for Branch, deducted a $45 collection fee, and credited the remainder to its account. Branch had not recorded this event before receiving the statement.

e. A debit memorandum for $805 lists a $795 NSF check plus a $10 NSF charge. The check had been received from a customer, Evan Shaw. Branch has not yet recorded this check as NSF.

f. Enclosed with the July statement is a $25 debit memorandum for bank services. It has not yet been recorded because no previous notification had been received.

g. Branch's July 31 daily cash receipts of $11,514 were placed in the bank's night depository on that date, but do not appear on the July 31 bank statement.

Required

1. Prepare the bank reconciliation for this company as of July 31, 2013.

2. Prepare the journal entries necessary to bring the company's book balance of cash into conformity with the reconciled cash balance as of July 31, 2013.

Check   (1) Reconciled balance, $34,602; (2) Cr. Notes Receivable $8,000

Analysis Component

3. Assume that the July 31, 2013, bank reconciliation for this company is prepared and some items are treated incorrectly. For each of the following errors, explain the effect of the error on (i) the adjusted bank statement cash balance and (ii) the adjusted cash account book balance.

    a. The company's unadjusted cash account balance of $27,497 is listed on the reconciliation as $27,947.

    b. The bank's collection of the $8,000 note less the $45 collection fee is added to the bank statement cash balance on the reconciliation.

Chavez Company most recently reconciled its bank statement and book balances of cash on August 31
and it reported two checks outstanding, No. 5888 for $1,028.05 and No. 5893 for $494.25. The following
information is available for its September 30, 2013, reconciliation.

From the September 30 Bank Statement

PREVIOUS BALANCE	TOTAL CHECKS AND DEBITS	TOTAL DEPOSITS AND CREDITS	CURRENT BALANCE
16,800.45	9,620.05	11,272.85	18,453.25

CHECKS AND DEBITS			DEPOSITS AND CREDITS		DAILY BALANCE	
Date	No.	Amount	Date	Amount	Date	Amount
09/03	5888	1,028.05	09/05	1,103.75	08/31	16,800.45
09/04	5902	719.90	09/12	2,226.90	09/03	15,772.40
09/07	5901	1,824.25	09/21	4,093.00	09/04	15,052.50
09/17		600.25 NSF	09/25	2,351.70	09/05	16,156.25
09/20	5905	937.00	09/30	12.50 IN	09/07	14,332.00
09/22	5903	399.10	09/30	1,485.00 CM	09/12	16,558.90
09/22	5904	2,090.00			09/17	15,958.65
09/28	5907	213.85			09/20	15,021.65
09/29	5909	1,807.65			09/21	19,114.65
					09/22	16,625.55
					09/25	18,977.25
					09/28	18,763.40
					09/29	16,955.75
					09/30	18,453.25

From Chavez Company's Accounting Records

Cash Receipts Deposited		
Date		Cash Debit
Sept. 5		1,103.75
12		2,226.90
21		4,093.00
25		2,351.70
30		1,682.75
		11,458.10

Cash Disbursements		
Check No.		Cash Credit
5901		1,824.25
5902		719.90
5903		399.10
5904		2,060.00
5905		937.00
5906		982.30
5907		213.85
5908		388.00
5909		1,807.65
		9,332.05

Cash						Acct. No. 101
Date		Explanation	PR	Debit	Credit	Balance
Aug.	31	Balance				15,278.15
Sept.	30	Total receipts	R12	11,458.10		26,736.25
	30	Total disbursements	D23		9,332.05	17,404.20

Additional Information

Check No. 5904 is correctly drawn for $2,090 to pay for computer equipment; however, the recordkeeper
misread the amount and entered it in the accounting records with a debit to Computer Equipment and a
credit to Cash of $2,060. The NSF check shown in the statement was originally received from a customer,
S. Nilson, in payment of her account. Its return has not yet been recorded by the company. The credit

memorandum is from the collection of a $1,500 note for Chavez Company by the bank. The bank deducted a $15 collection fee. The collection and fee are not yet recorded.

Required

1. Prepare the September 30, 2013, bank reconciliation for this company.
2. Prepare the journal entries (in dollars and cents) to adjust the book balance of cash to the reconciled balance.

Analysis Component

3. The bank statement reveals that some of the prenumbered checks in the sequence are missing. Describe three situations that could explain this.

Check   (1) Reconciled balance, $18,271.45 (2) Cr. Notes Receivable $1,500.00

For each of these five separate cases, identify the principle(s) of internal control that is violated. Recommend what the business should do to ensure adherence to principles of internal control.

1. Latisha Tally is the company's computer specialist and oversees its computerized payroll system. Her boss recently asked her to put password protection on all office computers. Latisha has put a password in place that allows only the boss access to the file where pay rates are changed and personnel are added or deleted from the payroll.
2. Marker Theater has a computerized order-taking system for its tickets. The system is active all week and backed up every Friday night.
3. Sutton Company has two employees handling acquisitions of inventory. One employee places purchase orders and pays vendors. The second employee receives the merchandise.
4. The owner of Super Pharmacy uses a check protector to perforate checks, making it difficult for anyone to alter the amount of the check. The check protector is on the owner's desk in an office that contains company checks and is normally unlocked.
5. Lavina Company is a small business that has separated the duties of cash receipts and cash disbursements. The employee responsible for cash disbursements reconciles the bank account monthly.

PROBLEM SET B

Problem 6-1B
Analyzing internal control

C1

Blues Music Center had the following petty cash transactions in March of the current year.

March	5	Wrote a $250 check, cashed it, and gave the proceeds and the petty cashbox to Jen Rouse, the petty cashier.
	6	Paid $12.50 COD shipping charges on merchandise purchased for resale, terms FOB shipping point. Blues uses the perpetual system to account for merchandise inventory.
	11	Paid $10.75 delivery charges on merchandise sold to a customer, terms FOB destination.
	12	Purchased file folders for $14.13 that are immediately used.
	14	Reimbursed Bob Geldof, the manager, $11.65 for office supplies purchased and used.
	18	Purchased printer paper for $20.54 that is immediately used.
	27	Paid $45.10 COD shipping charges on merchandise purchased for resale, terms FOB shipping point.
	28	Paid postage expenses of $18.
	30	Reimbursed Geldof $56.80 for business car mileage.
	31	Cash of $61.53 remained in the fund. Sorted the petty cash receipts by accounts affected and exchanged them for a check to reimburse the fund for expenditures.
	31	The petty cash fund amount is increased by $50 to a total of $300.

Problem 6-2B
Establish, reimburse, and increase petty cash

P2

Required

1. Prepare the journal entry to establish the petty cash fund.
2. Prepare a petty cash payments report for March with these categories: delivery expense, mileage expense, postage expense, merchandise inventory (for transportation-in), and office supplies expense. Sort the payments into the appropriate categories and total the expenses in each category.
3. Prepare the journal entries (in dollars and cents) for part 2 to both (*a*) reimburse and (*b*) increase the fund amount.

Check   (2) Total expenses $189.47

(3a & 3b) Total Cr. to Cash $238.47

Moya Co. establishes a petty cash fund for payments of small amounts. The following transactions involving the petty cash fund occurred in January (the last month of the company's fiscal year).

Jan. 3   A company check for $150 is written and made payable to the petty cashier to establish the petty cash fund.

Problem 6-3B
Establishing, reimbursing, and adjusting petty cash

P2

14   A company check is written to replenish the fund for the following expenditures made since
      January 3.
      a.   Purchased office supplies for $14.29 that are immediately used up.
      b.   Paid $19.60 COD shipping charges on merchandise purchased for resale, terms FOB ship-
             ping point. Moya uses the perpetual system to account for inventory.
      c.   Paid $38.57 to All-Tech for minor repairs to a computer.
      d.   Paid $12.82 for items classified as miscellaneous expenses.
      e.   Counted $62.28 remaining in the petty cash box.
15   Prepared a company check for $50 to increase the fund to $200.
31   The petty cashier reports that $17.35 remains in the fund. A company check is written to replen-
      ish the fund for the following expenditures made since January 14.
      f.   Paid $50 to *The Smart Shopper* for an advertisement in January's newsletter.
      g.   Paid $48.19 for postage expenses.
      h.   Paid $78 to Smooth Delivery for delivery of merchandise, terms FOB destination.
31   The company decides that the January 15 increase in the fund was too little. It increases the fund
      by another $50, leaving a total of $250.

Required

Check (1) Cr. to Cash: Jan. 14,
$87.72; Jan. 31 (total), $232.65

1. Prepare journal entries (in dollars and cents) to establish the fund on January 3, to replenish it on
   January 14 and January 31, and to reflect any increase or decrease in the fund balance on January 15
   and 31.

Analysis Component

2. Explain how the company's financial statements are affected if the petty cash fund is not replenished
   and no entry is made on January 31.

Problem 6-4B

Prepare a bank reconciliation
and record adjustments

P3

The following information is available to reconcile Severino Co.'s book balance of cash with its bank
statement cash balance as of December 31, 2013.

a. The December 31 cash balance according to the accounting records is $32,878.30, and the bank state-
ment cash balance for that date is $46,822.40.

b. Check No. 1273 for $4,589.30 and Check No. 1282 for $400, both written and entered in the accounting records in December, are not among the canceled checks. Two checks, No. 1231 for $2,289 and
No. 1242 for $410.40, were outstanding on the most recent November 30 reconciliation. Check No. 1231
is listed with the December canceled checks, but Check No. 1242 is not.

c. When the December checks are compared with entries in the accounting records, it is found that
Check No. 1267 had been correctly drawn for $3,456 to pay for office supplies but was erroneously
entered in the accounting records as $3,465.

d. Two debit memoranda are enclosed with the statement and are unrecorded at the time of the reconciliation. One debit memorandum is for $762.50 and dealt with an NSF check for $745 received from a
customer, Titus Industries, in payment of its account. The bank assessed a $17.50 fee for processing
it. The second debit memorandum is a $99 charge for check printing. Severino did not record these
transactions before receiving the statement.

e. A credit memorandum indicates that the bank collected $19,000 cash on a note receivable for the
company, deducted a $20 collection fee, and credited the balance to the company's Cash account.
Severino did not record this transaction before receiving the statement.

f. Severino's December 31 daily cash receipts of $9,583.10 were placed in the bank's night depository
on that date, but do not appear on the December 31 bank statement.

Required

Check (1) Reconciled balance,
$51,005.80; (2) Cr. Notes Receivable
$19,000.00

1. Prepare the bank reconciliation for this company as of December 31, 2013.
2. Prepare the journal entries (in dollars and cents) necessary to bring the company's book balance of
   cash into conformity with the reconciled cash balance as of December 31, 2013.

Analysis Component

3. Explain the nature of the communications conveyed by a bank when the bank sends the depositor
   (*a*) a debit memorandum and (*b*) a credit memorandum.

Shamara Systems most recently reconciled its bank balance on April 30 and reported two checks outstanding at that time, No. 1771 for $781 and No. 1780 for $1,425.90. The following information is available for its May 31, 2013, reconciliation.

Problem 6-5B

Prepare a bank reconciliation
and record adjustments

P3

From the May 31 Bank Statement

PREVIOUS BALANCE	TOTAL CHECKS AND DEBITS	TOTAL DEPOSITS AND CREDITS	CURRENT BALANCE
18,290.70	13,094.80	16,566.80	21,762.70

CHECKS AND DEBITS			DEPOSITS AND CREDITS		DAILY BALANCE	
Date	No.	Amount	Date	Amount	Date	Amount
05/01	1771	781.00	05/04	2,438.00	04/30	18,290.70
05/02	1783	382.50	05/14	2,898.00	05/01	17,509.70
05/04	1782	1,285.50	05/22	1,801.80	05/02	17,127.20
05/11	1784	1,449.60	05/25	7,350.00 CM	05/04	18,279.70
05/18		431.80 NSF	05/26	2,079.00	05/11	16,830.10
05/25	1787	8,032.50			05/14	19,728.10
05/26	1785	63.90			05/18	19,296.30
05/29	1788	654.00			05/22	21,098.10
05/31		14.00 SC			05/25	20,415.60
					05/26	22,430.70
					05/29	21,776.70
					05/31	21,762.70

From Shamara Systems' Accounting Records

Cash Receipts Deposited					Cash Disbursements		
Date			Cash Debit		Check No.		Cash Credit
May	4		2,438.00		1782		1,285.50
	14		2,898.00		1783		382.50
	22		1,801.80		1784		1,449.60
	26		2,079.00		1785		63.90
	31		2,727.30		1786		353.10
			11,944.10		1787		8,032.50
					1788		644.00
					1789		639.50
							12,850.60

Cash						Acct. No. 101
Date		Explanation	PR	Debit	Credit	Balance
Apr.	30	Balance				16,083.80
May	31	Total receipts	R7	11,944.10		28,027.90
	31	Total disbursements	D8		12,850.60	15,177.30

Additional Information

Check No. 1788 is correctly drawn for $654 to pay for May utilities; however, the recordkeeper misread the amount and entered it in the accounting records with a debit to Utilities Expense and a credit to Cash for $644. The bank paid and deducted the correct amount. The NSF check shown in the statement was originally received from a customer, W. Sox, in payment of her account. The company has not yet recorded its return. The credit memorandum is from a $7,400 note that the bank collected for the company.

The bank deducted a $50 collection fee and deposited the remainder in the company's account. The collection and fee have not yet been recorded.

Required

1. Prepare the May 31, 2013, bank reconciliation for Shamara Systems.
2. Prepare the journal entries (in dollars and cents) to adjust the book balance of cash to the reconciled balance.

Analysis Component

3. The bank statement reveals that some of the prenumbered checks in the sequence are missing. Describe three possible situations to explain this.

SERIAL PROBLEM
Success Systems

P3

(This serial problem began in Chapter 1 and continues through most of the book. If previous chapter segments were not completed, the serial problem can begin at this point. It is helpful, but not necessary, to use the Working Papers that accompany the book.)

SP 6 Adria Lopez receives the March bank statement for Success Systems on April 11, 2014. The March 31 bank statement shows an ending cash balance of $77,354. A comparison of the bank statement with the general ledger Cash account, No. 101, reveals the following.

a. A. Lopez notices that the bank erroneously cleared a $500 check against her account in March that she did not issue. The check documentation included with the bank statement shows that this check was actually issued by a company named Sierra Systems.

b. On March 25, the bank issued a $50 debit memorandum for the safety deposit box that Success Systems agreed to rent from the bank beginning March 25.

c. On March 26, the bank issued a $102 debit memorandum for printed checks that Success Systems ordered from the bank.

d. On March 31, the bank issued a credit memorandum for $33 interest earned on Success Systems' checking account for the month of March.

e. A. Lopez notices that the check she issued for $128 on March 31, 2014, has not yet cleared the bank.

f. A. Lopez verifies that all deposits made in March do appear on the March bank statement.

g. The general ledger Cash account, No. 101, shows an ending cash balance per books of $77,845 as of March 31 (prior to any reconciliation).

Required

1. Prepare a bank reconciliation for Success Systems for the month ended March 31, 2014.
2. Prepare any necessary adjusting entries. Use Miscellaneous Expenses, No. 677, for any bank charges. Use Interest Revenue, No. 404, for any interest earned on the checking account for the month of March.

GL GENERAL LEDGER PROBLEM

Available in Connect Only

connect
|ACCOUNTING

The following General Ledger assignment focuses on transactions related to the petty cash fund and highlights the impact each transaction has on net income, if any.

GL 6-1 (This assignment is adapted from Problem 6-3A.) Prepare the journal entries related to the petty cash fund. Then, assess the impact of each transaction on the company's net income, if any, using the **General Ledger** tool.

Beyond the Numbers

REPORTING IN ACTION

C2 A1 **APPLE**

BTN 6-1 Refer to Apple's financial statements in Appendix A to answer the following.

1. For both fiscal years ended September 29, 2012 and September 24, 2011, identify the total amount of cash and cash equivalents. Determine the percent (rounded to one decimal) that this amount represents of total current assets, total current liabilities, total shareholders' equity, and total assets for both years. Comment on any trends.

2. For fiscal years ended September 29, 2012, and September 24, 2011, use the information in the statement of cash flows to determine the percent change (rounded to one decimal) between the beginning and ending year amounts of cash and cash equivalents.

3. Compute the days' sales uncollected (rounded to two decimals) as of September 29, 2012, and September 24, 2011. Has the collection of receivables improved? Are accounts receivable an important asset for Apple? Explain.

Fast Forward

4. Access Apple's financial statements for fiscal years ending after September 29, 2012, from its Website (Apple.com) or the SEC's EDGAR database (www.sec.gov). Recompute its days' sales uncollected for years ending after September 29, 2012. Compare this to the days' sales uncollected for fiscal years ended September 29, 2012, and September 24, 2011.

BTN 6-2   Key comparative figures for Apple and Google follow.

($ millions)	Apple		Google	
	Current Year	Prior Year	Current Year	Prior Year
Accounts receivable	$ 10,930	$ 5,369	$ 7,885	$ 5,427
Net sales	156,508	108,249	50,175	37,905

COMPARATIVE ANALYSIS

A1

APPLE
GOOGLE

Required

Compute days' sales uncollected (rounded to two decimals) for these companies for each of the two years shown. Comment on any trends for the companies. Which company has the largest percent change (rounded to two decimals) in days' sales uncollected?

BTN 6-3   Harriet Knox, Ralph Patton, and Marcia Diamond work for a family physician, Dr. Gwen Conrad, who is in private practice. Dr. Conrad is knowledgeable about office management practices and has segregated the cash receipt duties as follows. Knox opens the mail and prepares a triplicate list of money received. She sends one copy of the list to Patton, the cashier, who deposits the receipts daily in the bank. Diamond, the recordkeeper, receives a copy of the list and posts payments to patients' accounts. About once a month the office clerks have an expensive lunch they pay for as follows. First, Patton endorses a patient's check in Dr. Conrad's name and cashes it at the bank. Knox then destroys the remittance advice accompanying the check. Finally, Diamond posts payment to the customer's account as a miscellaneous credit. The three justify their actions by their relatively low pay and knowledge that Dr. Conrad will likely never miss the money.

ETHICS CHALLENGE

C1

Required

1. Who is the best person in Dr. Conrad's office to reconcile the bank statement?
2. Would a bank reconciliation uncover this office fraud?
3. What are some procedures to detect this type of fraud?
4. Suggest additional internal controls that Dr. Conrad could implement.

BTN 6-4ᴮ   Assume you are a business consultant. The owner of a company sends you an e-mail expressing concern that the company is not taking advantage of its discounts offered by vendors. The company currently uses the gross method of recording purchases. The owner is considering a review of all invoices and payments from the previous period. Due to the volume of purchases, however, the owner recognizes that this is time-consuming and costly. The owner seeks your advice about monitoring purchase discounts in the future. Provide a response in memorandum form.

COMMUNICATING IN PRACTICE

P5

TAKING IT TO THE NET

C1　P1

BTN 6-5　Visit the Association of Certified Fraud Examiners Website at acfe.com. Find and open the file "2010 Report to the Nation." Read the two-page Executive Summary and fill in the following blanks. (The report is under its *Fraud Resources* tab or under its *About the ACFE* tab [under Press Room]; we can also use the *Search* tab.)

1. The median loss caused by occupational frauds was $_____.
2. Nearly _____ of fraud cases involved losses of at least $1 million in losses.
3. Companies lose ___% of their annual revenues to fraud; this figure translates to a potential total fraud loss of more than $_____ trillion.
4. The typical length of fraud schemes was _____ months from the time the fraud began until it was detected.
5. Less than ___% of victim organizations conducted surprise audits, however these organizations have lower fraud losses and detect fraud more quickly than those without surprise audits.
6. Asset misappropriation schemes were most common at ___% of cases with a median loss of $_____.
7. Financial statement fraud schemes made up less than ___% of cases with a median loss of more than $_____ million.
8. Corruption schemes comprised ___% of cases with a median loss of $_____.
9. Less than ___% of the perpetrators had convictions prior to committing their frauds.

TEAMWORK IN ACTION

C1

BTN 6-6　Organize the class into teams. Each team must prepare a list of 10 internal controls a consumer could observe in a typical retail department store. When called upon, the team's spokesperson must be prepared to share controls identified by the team that have not been shared by another team's spokesperson.

ENTREPRENEURIAL DECISION

C1　P1

BTN 6-7　Review the opening feature of this chapter that highlights Larry Page and Sergey Brin and their company Google, Inc. Assume that Google is considering opening up retail outlets to sell its portable mobile, gaming, and communication products to consumers.

Required

1. List the seven principles of internal control and explain how a retail outlet might implement each of the principles in its store.
2. Do you believe that a retail outlet will need to add controls to the business as it expands? Explain.

HITTING THE ROAD

C1

BTN 6-8　Visit an area of your college that serves the student community with either products or services. Some examples are food services, libraries, and bookstores. Identify and describe between four and eight internal controls being implemented.

GLOBAL DECISION

C2　A1

 Samsung

BTN 6-9　The following information is from Samsung (www.Samsung.com), which is a leading manufacturer of consumer electronic products.

₩ in millions	Current Year	Prior Year
Cash	₩ 18,791,460	₩ 14,691,761
Accounts receivable	26,674,596	24,153,028
Current assets	87,269,017	71,502,063
Total assets	181,071,570	155,800,263
Current liabilities	46,933,052	44,319,014
Shareholders' equity	121,480,206	101,313,630
Net sales	201,103,613	165,001,771

Required

1. For each year, compute the percentage (rounded to one decimal) that cash represents of current assets, total assets, current liabilities, and shareholders' equity. Comment on any trends in these percentages.
2. Determine the percentage change (rounded to one decimal) between the current and prior year cash balances.
3. Compute the days' sales uncollected (rounded to one decimal) at the end of both the current year and the prior year. Has the collection of receivables improved? Explain.

ANSWERS TO MULTIPLE CHOICE QUIZ

1. e; The entry follows.

Debits to expenses (or assets)	420
Cash Over and Short	5
Cash.	425

2. a; recognizes cash collection of note by bank.
3. a; the bank reconciliation follows.

4. d; ($6,720/$84,000) × 365 = 29.2 days
5. b; The entry follows.

Merchandise Inventory*	5,880	
Accounts Payable		5,880

*$6,000 × 98%

Bank Reconciliation
November 30

Balance per bank statement	$1,895	Balance per books.	$1,742
Add: Deposit in transit	795	Add: Note collected less fee.	320
Deduct: Outstanding checks	(638)	Deduct: Service charge	(10)
Reconciled balance	$2,052	Reconciled balance	$2,052

7 Reporting and Analyzing Receivables

ACCOUNTS RECEIVABLE	NOTES RECEIVABLE	DISPOSAL AND ANALYSIS OF RECEIVABLES
C1 Recognizing accounts receivable	C2 Computing maturity and interest	C3 Selling and pledging receivables
P1 Valuing accounts receivable	Recognizing notes receivable	A1 Assessing accounts receivable turnover
P2 Estimating and recording bad debts	P3 Valuing and settling notes receivable	

Learning Objectives

C1 Describe accounts receivable and how they occur and are recorded. (p. 310)

P1 Apply the direct write-off method to account for accounts receivable. (p. 314)

P2 Apply the allowance method and estimate uncollectibles based on sales and accounts receivable. (p. 318)

C2 Describe a note receivable, the computation of its maturity date, and the recording of its existence. (p. 322)

P3 Record the honoring and dishonoring of a note and adjustments for interest. (p. 323)

C3 Explain how receivables can be converted to cash before maturity. (p. 325)

A1 Compute accounts receivable turnover and use it to help assess financial condition. (p. 327)

Building Sweat Equity

"Create what the industry is missing"
—KEVIN PLANK

BALTIMORE, MD—"There was a void in apparel and I decided to fill it," explains Kevin Plank, the founder of Under Armour (UnderArmour.com), which is a manufacturer of athletic apparel. Kevin invested his life savings of $20,000 and began by working out of his grandma's basement.

As sales grew, Kevin partnered with a factory in Ohio and hit it off with the factory manager, Sal Fasciana. Sal spent many evenings and weekends teaching Kevin about accounting and cost controls. "I said, 'OK, kid. This is the way it's going to be done,'" recalls Sal. That attention to details carried over to where Kevin learned to monitor receivables.

As shown here, Kevin keeps receivables under 10 percent of net sales.

($ millions)	2010	2011	2012
Accounts receivable	$ 102	$ 134	$ 176
Net sales.............	$1,064	$1,473	$1,835
Accts. rec./Net sales....	9.6%	9.1%	9.6%

Decisions on credit sales and policies for extending credit can make or break a start-up.

Kevin applied well what Sal taught him. He ensured that credit sales were extended to customers in good credit standing. Kevin

Under Armour
NYSE: UA

$1.8 bil. annual sales
6,000 employees

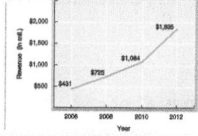

knows his clients, including who pays and when. Says Kevin, we understand our customers—inside and out—including cash payment patterns that allow us to estimate uncollectibles and minimize bad debts. His financial report says, "We make ongoing estimates relating to the collectibility of our accounts receivable and maintain a reserve for estimated losses resulting from the inability of our customers to make required payments."

A commitment to quality customers is propelling Under Armour's sales and shattering Kevin's most optimistic goals. "It's about educating consumers . . . investing in the product." Kevin has also issued notes receivable to select employees. Both accounts and notes receivables receive his attention. His financial report states that they "review the allowance for doubtful accounts monthly."

"When I first started . . . I was a young punk who thought he knew everything,"

explains Kevin. While he admits that insight and ingenuity are vital, he knows accounting reports must show profits for long-term success.

The company's stock price over the past few years reflects the market's support for his efforts and his accounting results.

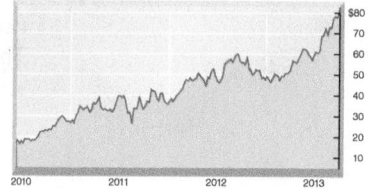

"Most people out there are saying we're going to trip up at some point," says Kevin. "Our job is to prove them wrong." Indeed, his evolving fabrics continue to lead the industry in removing perspiration. He gives us a new perspective on Thomas Edison's assertion that: genius is 99 percent perspiration and 1 percent inspiration.

Sources: *Under Armour Website,* January 2014; *Under Armour 10-K Report,* Filed February 2013; *FastCompany,* 2005; *USA Today,* December 2004; *Inc.com,* 2003 and 2004; *Entrepreneur's Journey,* November 2007

ACCOUNTS RECEIVABLE

A *receivable* is an amount due from another party. The two most common receivables are accounts receivable and notes receivable. Other receivables include interest receivable, rent receivable, tax refund receivable, and receivables from employees. **Accounts receivable** are amounts due from customers for credit sales. This section begins by describing how accounts receivable occur. It includes receivables that occur when customers use credit cards issued by third parties and when a company gives credit directly to customers. When a company does extend credit directly to customers, it (1) maintains a separate account receivable for each customer and (2) accounts for bad debts from credit sales.

Recognizing Accounts Receivable

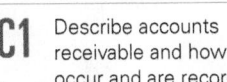

C1 Describe accounts receivable and how they occur and are recorded.

Accounts receivable occur from credit sales to customers. The amount of credit sales has increased in recent years, reflecting several factors including an efficient financial system. Retailers such as Costco and Best Buy hold millions of dollars in accounts receivable. Similar amounts are held by wholesalers such as SUPERVALU and SYSCO. Exhibit 7.1 shows recent dollar amounts of receivables and their percent of total assets for four well-known companies.

EXHIBIT 7.1

Accounts Receivable for Selected Companies

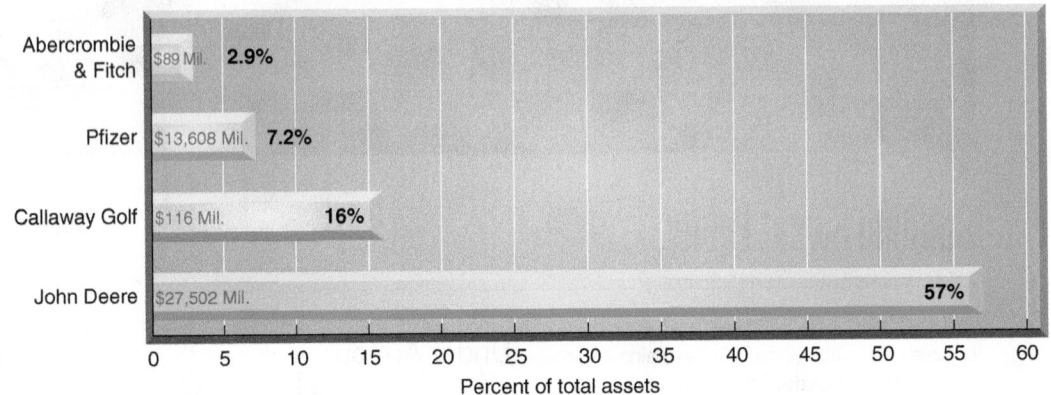

Sales on Credit   Credit sales are recorded by increasing (debiting) Accounts Receivable. A company must also maintain a separate account for each customer that tracks how much that customer purchases, has already paid, and still owes. This information provides the basis for sending bills to customers and for other business analyses. To maintain this information, companies that extend credit directly to their customers keep a separate account receivable for each one of them. The general ledger continues to have a single Accounts Receivable account (called a *control* account) along with the other financial statement accounts, but a supplementary record is created to maintain a separate account for each customer. This supplementary record is called the *accounts receivable ledger* (or *accounts receivable subsidiary ledger*).

Exhibit 7.2 shows the relation between the Accounts Receivable account in the general ledger and its individual customer accounts in the accounts receivable ledger for TechCom, a small electronics wholesaler. This exhibit reports a $3,000 ending balance of TechCom's accounts receivable for June 30. TechCom's transactions are mainly in cash, but it has two

EXHIBIT 7.2

General Ledger and the Accounts Receivable Ledger (before July 1 transactions)

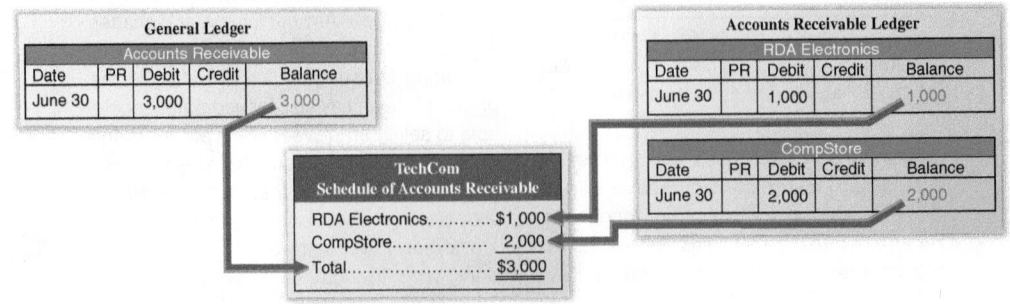

major credit customers: CompStore and RDA Electronics. Its *schedule of accounts receivable* shows that the $3,000 balance of the Accounts Receivable account in the general ledger equals the total of its two customers' balances in the accounts receivable ledger.

To see how accounts receivable from credit sales are recognized in the accounting records, we look at two transactions on July 1 between TechCom and its credit customers—see Exhibit 7.3. The first is a credit sale of $950 to CompStore. A credit sale is posted with both a debit to the Accounts Receivable account in the general ledger and a debit to the customer account in the accounts receivable ledger. The second transaction is a collection of $720 from RDA Electronics from a prior credit sale. Cash receipts from a credit customer are posted with a credit to the Accounts Receivable account in the general ledger and flow through to credit the customer account in the accounts receivable ledger. (Posting debits or credits to Accounts Receivable in two separate ledgers does not violate the requirement that debits equal credits. The equality of debits and credits is maintained in the general ledger. The accounts receivable ledger is a *supplementary* record providing information on each customer.)

EXHIBIT 7.3

Accounts Receivable Transactions

July 1	Accounts Receivable—CompStore	950	
	Sales		950
	*To record credit sales**		
July 1	Cash	720	
	Accounts Receivable—RDA Electronics		720
	To record collection of credit sales.		

Assets = Liabilities + Equity
+ 950   +950

Assets = Liabilities + Equity
+720
−720

* We omit the entry to Dr. Cost of Sales and Cr. Merchandise Inventory to focus on sales and receivables.

Exhibit 7.4 shows the general ledger and the accounts receivable ledger after recording the two July 1 transactions. The general ledger shows the effects of the sale, the collection, and the resulting balance of $3,230. These events are also reflected in the individual customer accounts:

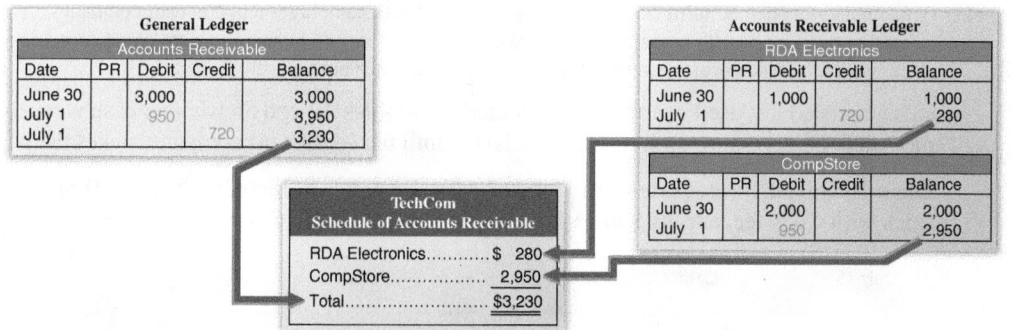

EXHIBIT 7.4

General Ledger and the Accounts Receivable Ledger (after July 1 transactions)

RDA Electronics has an ending balance of $280, and CompStore's ending balance is $2,950. The $3,230 sum of the individual accounts equals the debit balance of the Accounts Receivable account in the general ledger.

Like TechCom, many large retailers such as Target and JCPenney sell on credit. Many also maintain their own credit cards to grant credit to approved customers and to earn interest on any balance not paid within a specified period of time. This allows them to avoid the fee charged by credit card companies. The entries in this case are the same as those for TechCom except for the possibility of added interest revenue. If a customer owes interest on a bill, we debit Interest Receivable and credit Interest Revenue for that amount. (Many retailers require clerks to ask customers during checkout if they wish to apply for a store credit card—sweeteners are often used such as: *save 10% off today's purchases if you apply now.*)

Credit Card Sales   Many companies allow their customers to pay for products and services using third-party credit cards such as Visa, MasterCard, or American Express, and debit cards (also called ATM or bank cards). This practice gives customers the ability to make purchases without cash or checks. Once credit is established with a credit card company or bank, the customer does not have to open an account with each store. Customers using these cards can make single monthly payments instead of several payments to different creditors and can defer their payments.

Point: Visa USA now transacts more than $1 trillion from its credit, debit, and prepaid cards.

Many sellers allow customers to use third-party credit cards and debit cards instead of granting credit directly for several reasons. First, the seller does not have to evaluate each customer's credit standing or make decisions about who gets credit and how much. Second, the seller avoids the risk of extending credit to customers who cannot or do not pay. This risk is transferred to the card company. Third, the seller typically receives cash from the card company sooner than had it granted credit directly to customers. Fourth, a variety of credit options for customers offers a potential increase in sales volume. Sears historically offered credit only to customers using a Sears card but later changed its policy to permit customers to charge purchases to third-party credit card companies in a desire to increase sales. It reported: "SearsCharge increased its share of Sears retail sales even as the company expanded the payment options available to its customers with the acceptance ... of Visa, MasterCard, and American Express in addition to the [Sears] Card."

There are guidelines in how companies account for credit card and debit card sales. Some credit cards, but nearly all debit cards, credit a seller's Cash account immediately upon deposit. In this case the seller deposits a copy of each card sales receipt in its bank account just as it deposits a customer's check. The majority of credit cards, however, require the seller to remit a copy (often electronically) of each receipt to the card company. Until payment is received, the seller has an account receivable from the card company. In both cases, the seller pays a fee for services provided by the card company, often ranging from 1% to 5% of card sales. This charge is deducted from the credit to the seller's account or the cash payment to the seller. (Many retailers accept MasterCard and Visa, but not American Express. The reason is that American Express usually charges retailers a higher percentage fee than other credit card companies.)

Decision Insight

Debit Card vs. Credit Card A buyer's debit card purchase reduces the buyer's cash account balance at the card company, which is often a bank. Since the buyer's cash account balance is a liability (with a credit balance) for the card company to the buyer, the card company would debit that account for a buyer's purchase—hence, the term *debit card*. A credit card reflects authorization by the card company of a line of credit for the buyer with preset interest rates and payment terms—hence, the term *credit card*. Most card companies waive interest charges if the buyer pays its balance each month. ■

Point: Web merchants pay twice as much in credit card association fees as other retailers because they suffer 10 times as much fraud.

The procedures used in accounting for credit card sales depend on whether cash is received immediately on deposit or cash receipt is delayed until the credit card company makes the payment.

Cash Received Immediately on Deposit   To illustrate, if TechCom has $100 of credit card sales with a 4% fee, and its $96 cash is received immediately on deposit, the entry is

Assets = Liabilities + Equity
+96   +100
                        −4

July 15	Cash	96	
	Credit Card Expense	4	
	Sales		100
	*To record credit card sales less a 4% credit card expense.**		

* We omit the entry to Dr. Cost of Sales and Cr. Merchandise Inventory to focus on credit card expense.

Cash Received Some Time after Deposit   However, if instead TechCom must remit electronically the credit card sales receipts to the credit card company and wait for the $96 cash payment, the entry on the date of sale is

Assets = Liabilities + Equity
+96   +100
                        −4

July 15	Accounts Receivable—Credit Card Co.	96	
	Credit Card Expense	4	
	Sales		100
	*To record credit card sales less 4% credit card expense.**		

* We omit the entry to Dr. Cost of Sales and Cr. Merchandise Inventory to focus on credit card expense.

When cash is later received from the credit card company, usually through electronic funds transfer, the entry is

Assets = Liabilities + Equity
+96
−96

July 20	Cash	96	
	Accounts Receivable—Credit Card Co.		96
	To record cash receipt.		

Some firms report credit card expense in the income statement as a type of discount deducted from sales to get net sales. Other companies classify it as a selling expense or even as an administrative expense. Arguments can be made for each approach.

Point: Third-party credit card costs can be large. JCPenney reported third-party credit card costs exceeding $10 million.

Decision Insight

Cabbie Credit Card Sales Thirty New York cabs rolled out the first phase of a new mobile payment system for taxis. These 30 cabs are equipped with an iPad encased in a metal housing that includes a credit card reader. The iPad allows fares to swipe their card, sign their name on the screen with their finger, and then receive a receipt on their phone either by text or email. Taxi drivers are also able to interact with the system, dubbed "Checker," using their own iPhone app. ■

Installment Sales and Receivables Many companies allow their credit customers to make periodic payments over several months. For example, Ford Motor Company reports more than $70 billion in installment receivables. The seller refers to such assets as *installment accounts* (or *finance*) *receivable,* which are amounts owed by customers from credit sales for which payment is required in periodic amounts over an extended time period. Source documents for installment accounts receivable include sales slips or invoices describing the sales transactions. The customer is usually charged interest. Although installment accounts receivable can have credit periods of more than one year, they are classified as current assets if the seller regularly offers customers such terms.

Decision Maker

Entrepreneur As a small retailer, you are considering allowing customers to buy merchandise using credit cards. Until now, your store accepted only cash and checks. What analysis do you use to make this decision? ■ [Answer—p. 330]

A small retailer allows customers to use two different credit cards in charging purchases. With the AA Bank Card, the retailer receives an immediate credit to its account when it deposits sales receipts. AA Bank assesses a 5% service charge for credit card sales. The second credit card that the retailer accepts is the VIZA Card. The retailer sends its accumulated receipts to VIZA on a weekly basis and is paid by VIZA about a week later. VIZA assesses a 3% charge on sales for using its card. Prepare journal entries to record the following selected credit card transactions for the retailer. (The retailer uses the perpetual inventory system for recording sales.)

NEED-TO-KNOW 7.1

C1

Jan. 2 Sold merchandise for $1,000 (that had cost $600) and accepted the customer's AA Bank Card. The AA receipts are immediately deposited in the retailer's bank account.
Jan. 6 Sold merchandise for $400 (that had cost $300) and accepted the customer's VIZA Card. Transferred $400 of credit card receipts to VIZA, requesting payment.
Jan. 16 Received VIZA's check for the January 6 billing, less the service charge.

Solution

Jan. 2	Cash	950	
	Credit Card Expense*	50	
	Sales		1,000
	*To record credit card sales less 5% fee. *($1,000 × .05)*		
Jan. 2	Cost of Goods Sold	600	
	Merchandise Inventory		600
	To record cost of sales.		
Jan. 6	Accounts Receivable—VIZA	388	
	Credit Card Expense*	12	
	Sales		400
	*To record credit card sales less 3% fee. *($400 × .03)*		
Jan. 6	Cost of Goods Sold	300	
	Merchandise Inventory		300
	To record cost of sales.		
Jan. 16	Cash	388	
	Accounts Receivable—VIZA		388
	To record cash received on credit sales less fees.		

Do More: QS 7-1, E 7-1, E 7-2

QC1

| P1 | Apply the direct write-off method to account for accounts receivable. |

Valuing Accounts Receivable—Direct Write-Off Method

When a company directly grants credit to its customers, it expects that some customers will not pay what they promised. The accounts of these customers are *uncollectible accounts,* commonly called **bad debts.** The total amount of uncollectible accounts is an expense of selling on credit. Why do companies sell on credit if they expect some accounts to be uncollectible? The answer is that companies believe that granting credit will increase total sales and net income enough to offset bad debts. Companies use two methods to account for uncollectible accounts: (1) direct write-off method and (2) allowance method. We describe both.

Point: Managers realize that some portion of credit sales will be uncollectible, but which credit sales are uncollectible is unknown.

Recording and Writing Off Bad Debts   The **direct write-off method** of accounting for bad debts records the loss from an uncollectible account receivable when it is determined to be uncollectible. No attempt is made to predict bad debts expense. To illustrate, if TechCom determines on January 23 that it cannot collect $520 owed to it by its customer J. Kent, it recognizes the loss using the direct write-off method as follows:

Assets = Liabilities + Equity
−520   −520

Jan. 23	Bad Debts Expense	520	
	Accounts Receivable—J. Kent		520
	To write off an uncollectible account.		

The debit in this entry charges the uncollectible amount directly to the current period's Bad Debts Expense account. The credit removes its balance from the Accounts Receivable account in the general ledger (and its subsidiary ledger).

Point: If a customer fails to pay within the credit period, most companies send out repeated billings and make other efforts to collect.

Recovering a Bad Debt   Although uncommon, sometimes an account written off is later collected. This can be due to factors such as continual collection efforts or a customer's good fortune. If the account of J. Kent that was written off directly to Bad Debts Expense is later collected in full, the following two entries record this recovery:

Assets = Liabilities + Equity
+520   +520

Assets = Liabilities + Equity
+520
−520

Mar. 11	Accounts Receivable—J. Kent	520	
	Bad Debts Expense		520
	To reinstate account previously written off.		
Mar. 11	Cash	520	
	Accounts Receivable—J. Kent		520
	To record full payment of account.		

Assessing the Direct Write-Off Method   Examples of companies that use the direct write-off method include **Rand Medical Billing, Gateway Distributors, Microwave Satellite Technologies, First Industrial Realty, New Frontier Energy,** and **Sub Surface Waste Management.** The following disclosure by **Pharma-Bio Serv** is typical of the justification for this method: Bad debts are accounted for using the direct write-off method whereby an expense is recognized only when a specific account is determined to be uncollectible. The effect of using this method approximates that of the allowance method. Companies must weigh at least two accounting concepts when considering the use of the direct write-off method: the (1) matching principle and (2) materiality constraint.

Point: Harley-Davidson reports $150 million of credit losses matched against $4,962 million of finance receivables.

Matching principle applied to bad debts.   The **matching (expense recognition) principle** requires expenses to be reported in the same accounting period as the sales they helped produce. This means that if extending credit to customers helped produce sales, the bad debts expense linked to those sales is matched and reported in the same period. The direct write-off method usually does *not* best match sales and expenses because bad debts expense is not recorded until an account becomes uncollectible, which often occurs in a period after that of the credit sale. To match bad debts expense with the sales it produces therefore requires a company to estimate future uncollectibles.

Materiality constraint applied to bad debts.   The **materiality constraint** states that an amount can be ignored if its effect on the financial statements is unimportant to users' business decisions. The materiality constraint permits the use of the direct write-off method when bad debts expenses are very small in relation to a company's other financial statement items such as sales and net income.

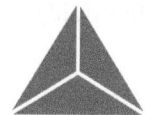

Fraud

Receivables Protection. One accounts receivable fraud involves accepting cash payments from customers and not depositing that money in the company's bank account. Instead, a credit memo is issued to the customer's account, so that there are no collection calls to the customer. This fraud can be exposed by reviewing credit memos issued to customers and confirming the reason they were issued.

A retailer applies the direct write-off method in accounting for uncollectible accounts. Prepare journal entries to record its following selected transactions.

NEED-TO-KNOW 7.2

P1

Feb. 14 The retailer determines that it cannot collect $400 of its accounts receivable from a customer named ZZZ Companay.

April 1 ZZZ Company unexpectedly pays its account in full to the retailer, which then records its recovery of this bad debt.

Solution

Feb. 14	Bad Debts Expense....................................	400	
	Accounts Receivable—ZZZ Co.		400
	To write off an account.		
April 1	Accounts Receivable—ZZZ Co.	400	
	Bad Debts Expense		400
	To reinstate an account previously written off.		
April 1	Cash	400	
	Accounts Receivable—ZZZ Co.		400
	To record cash received on account.		

Do More: QS 7-2, QS 7-9, QS 7-10, E 7-3

Valuing Accounts Receivable—Allowance Method

The **allowance method** of accounting for bad debts matches the *estimated* loss from uncollectible accounts receivable against the sales they helped produce. We must use estimated losses because when sales occur, management does not know which customers will not pay their bills. This means that at the end of each period, the allowance method requires an estimate of the total bad debts expected to result from that period's sales. This method has two advantages over the direct write-off method: (1) it records estimated bad debts expense in the period when the related sales are recorded and (2) it reports accounts receivable on the balance sheet at the estimated amount of cash to be collected.

Point: Under direct write-off, expense is recorded each time an account is written off. Under the allowance method, expense is recorded with an adjusting entry equal to the total estimated uncollectibles for that period's sales.

Recording Bad Debts Expense The allowance method estimates bad debts expense at the end of each accounting period and records it with an adjusting entry. TechCom, for instance, had credit sales of $300,000 during its first year of operations. At the end of the first year, $20,000 of credit sales remained uncollected. Based on the experience of similar businesses, TechCom estimated that $1,500 of its accounts receivable would be uncollectible. This estimated expense is recorded with the following adjusting entry:

	Bad Debts Expense Recognized in
Direct write-off method	The future when account is deemed uncollectible
Allowance method	Current period to yield realizable Accts. Rec. bal.

Dec. 31	Bad Debts Expense	1,500	
	Allowance for Doubtful Accounts		1,500
	To record estimated bad debts.		

Assets = Liabilities + Equity
−1,500   −1,500

Point: Credit approval is usually not assigned to the selling dept. because its goal is to increase sales, and it may approve customers at the cost of increased bad debts. Instead, approval is assigned to a separate credit-granting or administrative dept.

The estimated Bad Debts Expense of $1,500 is reported on the income statement (as either a selling expense or an administrative expense) and offsets the $300,000 credit sales it helped produce. The **Allowance for Doubtful Accounts** is a contra asset account. A contra account is used instead of reducing accounts receivable directly because at the time of the adjusting entry, the company does not know which customers will not pay. After the bad debts adjusting entry is posted, TechCom's account balances (in T-account form) for Accounts Receivable and its Allowance for Doubtful Accounts are as shown in Exhibit 7.5.

EXHIBIT 7.5

General Ledger Entries after Bad Debts Adjusting Entry

Accounts Receivable		Allowance for Doubtful Accounts	
Dec. 31	20,000	Dec. 31	1,500

The Allowance for Doubtful Accounts credit balance of $1,500 has the effect of reducing accounts receivable to its estimated realizable value. **Realizable value** refers to the expected proceeds from converting an asset into cash. Although credit customers owe $20,000 to TechCom, only $18,500 is expected to be realized in cash collections from these customers. In the balance sheet, the Allowance for Doubtful Accounts is subtracted from Accounts Receivable and is often reported as shown in Exhibit 7.6.

Point: Bad Debts Expense is also called *Uncollectible Accounts Expense.* The Allowance for Doubtful Accounts is also called *Allowance for Uncollectible Accounts.*

EXHIBIT 7.6

Balance Sheet Presentation of the Allowance for Doubtful Accounts

Current assets
Accounts receivable............................ $20,000
Less allowance for doubtful accounts 1,500 $18,500

Sometimes the Allowance for Doubtful Accounts is not reported separately. This alternative presentation is shown in Exhibit 7.7 (also see Appendix A).

EXHIBIT 7.7

Alternative Presentation of the Allowance for Doubtful Accounts

Current assets
Accounts receivable (net of $1,500 doubtful accounts) $18,500

Writing Off a Bad Debt   When specific accounts are identified as uncollectible, they are written off against the Allowance for Doubtful Accounts. To illustrate, TechCom decides that J. Kent's $520 account is uncollectible and makes the following entry to write it off.

Assets = Liabilities + Equity
+520
−520

Jan. 23	Allowance for Doubtful Accounts	520	
	Accounts Receivable—J. Kent		520
	To write off an uncollectible account.		

Point: The Bad Debts Expense account is not debited in the write-off entry because it was recorded in the period when sales occurred.

Posting this write-off entry to the Accounts Receivable account removes the amount of the bad debt from the general ledger (it is also posted to the accounts receivable subsidiary ledger). The general ledger accounts now appear as in Exhibit 7.8 (assuming no other transactions affecting these accounts).

EXHIBIT 7.8

General Ledger Entries after Write-Off

Accounts Receivable				Allowance for Doubtful Accounts			
Dec. 31	20,000			Jan. 23	520	Dec. 31	1,500
		Jan. 23	520				

Point: In posting a write-off, the ledger's Explanation column indicates the reason for this credit so it is not misinterpreted as payment in full.

The write-off does *not* affect the realizable value of accounts receivable as shown in Exhibit 7.9. Neither total assets nor net income is affected by the write-off of a specific account. Instead, both assets and net income are affected in the period when bad debts expense is predicted and recorded with an adjusting entry.

EXHIBIT 7.9

Realizable Value before and after Write-Off of a Bad Debt

	Before Write-Off	After Write-Off
Accounts receivable	$ 20,000	$ 19,480
Less allowance for doubtful accounts	1,500	980
Estimated realizable accounts receivable	$18,500	$18,500

Recovering a Bad Debt

Recovering a Bad Debt   When a customer fails to pay and the account is written off as uncollectible, his or her credit standing is jeopardized. To help restore credit standing, a customer sometimes volunteers to pay all or part of the amount owed. A company makes two entries when collecting an account previously written off by the allowance method. The first is to reverse the write-off and reinstate the customer's account. The second entry records the collection of the reinstated account. To illustrate, if on March 11 Kent pays in full his account previously written off, the entries are

Mar. 11	Accounts Receivable—J. Kent.....................	520	
	Allowance for Doubtful Accounts		520
	To reinstate account previously written off.		
Mar. 11	Cash	520	
	Accounts Receivable—J. Kent		520
	To record full payment of account.		

Assets = Liabilities + Equity
+520
−520

Assets = Liabilities + Equity
+520
−520

In this illustration, Kent paid the entire amount previously written off, but sometimes a customer pays only a portion of the amount owed. A question then arises as to whether the entire balance of the account or just the amount paid is returned to accounts receivable. This is a matter of judgment. If we believe this customer will later pay in full, we return the entire amount owed to accounts receivable, but if we expect no further collection, we return only the amount paid.

Example: If TechCom used a collection agency and paid a 35% commission on $520 collected from Kent, how is this recorded? *Answer:*
Cash 338
Collection Expense 182
  Accts. Recble.—J. Kent 520

Decision Insight

PayPal   PayPal is legally just a money transfer agent, but it is increasingly challenging big credit card brands—see chart. PayPal is successful because: (1) online credit card processing fees often exceed $0.15 per dollar, but PayPal's fees are under $0.10 per dollar. (2) PayPal's merchant fraud losses are under 0.2% of revenues, which compares to nearly 2% for online merchants using credit cards. ■

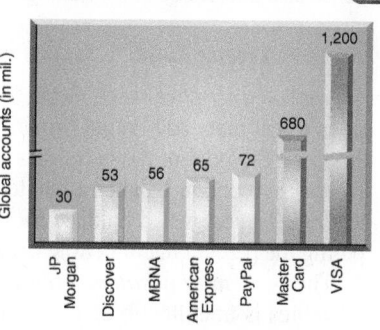

A retailer applies the allowance method in accounting for uncollectible accounts. Prepare journal entries to record its following selected transactions.

NEED-TO-KNOW 7.3

P2

2013
Dec. 31   The retailer estimates $3,000 of its accounts receivable are uncollectible.

2014
Feb. 14   The retailer determines that it cannot collect $400 of its accounts receivable from a customer named ZZZ Companay.

April 1   ZZZ Company unexpectedly pays its account in full to the retailer, which then records its recovery of this bad debt.

Solution

2013			
Dec. 31	Bad Debts Expense.................................	3,000	
	Allowance for Doubtful Accounts		3,000
	To record estimated bad debts.		
2014			
Feb. 14	Allowance for Doubtful Accounts	400	
	Accounts Receivable—ZZZ Co.		400
	To write off an account.		
April 1	Accounts Receivable—ZZZ Co.	400	
	Allowance for Doubtful Accounts		400
	To reinstate an account previously written off.		
April 1	Cash	400	
	Accounts Receivable—ZZZ Co.		400
	To record cash received on account.		

Do More: QS 7-3, E 7-4, E 7-5, E 7-8

Estimating Bad Debts—Percent of Sales Method

The allowance method requires an estimate of bad debts expense to prepare an adjusting entry at the end of each accounting period. There are two common methods. One is based on the income statement relation between bad debts expense and sales. The second is based on the balance sheet relation between accounts receivable and the allowance for doubtful accounts.

The *percent of sales method,* also referred to as the *income statement method,* is based on the idea that a given percent of a company's credit sales for the period is uncollectible. To illustrate, assume that Musicland has credit sales of $400,000 in year 2013. Based on past experience, Musicland estimates 0.6% of credit sales to be uncollectible. This implies that Musicland expects $2,400 of bad debts expense from its sales (computed as $400,000 × 0.006). The adjusting entry to record this estimated expense is

Dec. 31	Bad Debts Expense	2,400	
	Allowance for Doubtful Accounts		2,400
	To record estimated bad debts.		

The allowance account ending balance on the balance sheet for this method would rarely equal the bad debts expense on the income statement. This is so because unless a company is in its first period of operations, its allowance account has a zero balance only if the prior amounts written off as uncollectible *exactly* equal the prior estimated bad debts expenses. (When computing bad debts expense as a percent of sales, managers monitor and adjust the percent so it is not too high or too low.)

Estimating Bad Debts—Percent of Receivables Method

The *accounts receivable methods,* also referred to as *balance sheet methods,* use balance sheet relations to estimate bad debts—mainly the relation between accounts receivable and the allowance amount. The goal of the bad debts adjusting entry for these methods is to make the Allowance for Doubtful Accounts balance equal to the portion of accounts receivable that is estimated to be uncollectible. The estimated balance for the allowance account is obtained in one of two ways: (1) computing the percent uncollectible from the total accounts receivable or (2) aging accounts receivable.

The *percent of accounts receivable method* assumes that a given percent of a company's receivables is uncollectible. This percent is based on past experience and is impacted by current conditions such as economic trends and customer difficulties. The total dollar amount of all receivables is multiplied by this percent to get the estimated dollar amount of uncollectible accounts—reported in the balance sheet as the Allowance for Doubtful Accounts.

To illustrate, assume that Musicland has $50,000 of accounts receivable on December 31, 2013. Experience suggests 5% of its receivables is uncollectible. This means that *after* the adjusting entry is posted, we want the Allowance for Doubtful Accounts to show a $2,500 credit balance (5% of $50,000). We are also told that its beginning balance is $2,200, which is 5% of the $44,000 accounts receivable on December 31, 2012—see Exhibit 7.10.

EXHIBIT 7.10

Allowance for Doubtful Accounts after Bad Debts Adjusting Entry

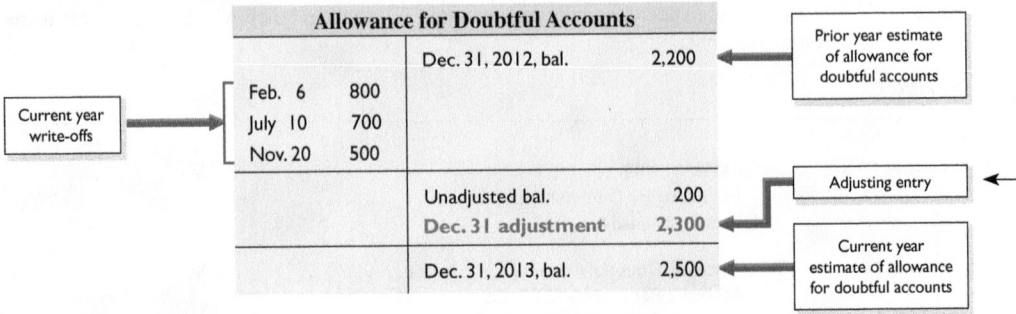

During 2013, accounts of customers are written off on February 6, July 10, and November 20. Thus, the account has a $200 credit balance *before* the December 31, 2013, adjustment. The adjusting entry to give the allowance account the estimated $2,500 balance is

Dec. 31	Bad Debts Expense	2,300	
	Allowance for Doubtful Accounts		2,300
	To record estimated bad debts.		

Decision Insight

Aging Pains   Unlike wine, accounts receivable do not improve with age. Experience shows that .the longer a receivable is past due, the lower is the likelihood of its collection. An *aging schedule* uses this knowledge to estimate bad debts. The chart here is from a survey that reported estimates of bad debts for receivables grouped by how long they were past their due dates. Each company sets its own estimates based on its customers and its experiences with those customers' payment patterns. ■

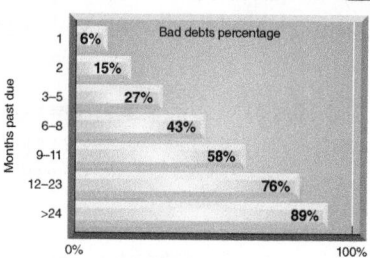

Estimating Bad Debts—Aging of Receivables Method

The **aging of accounts receivable** method uses both past and current receivables information to estimate the allowance amount. Specifically, each receivable is classified by how long it is past its due date. Then estimates of uncollectible amounts are made assuming that the longer an amount is past due, the more likely it is to be uncollectible. Classifications are often based on 30-day periods. After the amounts are classified (or aged), experience is used to estimate the percent of each uncollectible class. These percents are applied to the amounts in each class and then totaled to get the estimated balance of the Allowance for Doubtful Accounts. This computation is performed by setting up a schedule such as Exhibit 7.11.

EXHIBIT 7.11

Aging of Accounts Receivable

Customer	Totals	Not Yet Due	1 to 30 Days Past Due	31 to 60 Days Past Due	61 to 90 Days Past Due	Over 90 Days Past Due
MUSICLAND Schedule of Accounts Receivable by Age December 31, 2013						
Carlie Abbott..............	$ 5,890	$ 5,890				
Jamie Allen.................	710			$ 710		
Chavez Andres............	10,500	10,300	$ 200			
Balicia Company..........	2,800				$1,900	$ 900
Texas Rawhide.............	9,100		6,110	2,990		
Zamora Services..........	21,000	20,810	190			
Total receivables*......	$50,000	$37,000	$6,500	$3,700	$1,900	$ 900
Percent uncollectible.....		×2%	×5%	×10%	×25%	×40%
Estimated uncollectible..	$ 2,270	$ 740	$ 325	$ 370	$ 475	$ 360

Each receivable is grouped by how long it is past its due date

Each age group is multiplied by its estimated bad debts percent

Estimated bad debts for each group are totaled

Exhibit 7.11 lists each customer's individual balances assigned to one of five classes based on its days past due. The amounts in each class are totaled and multiplied by the estimated percent of uncollectible accounts for each class. The percents used are regularly reviewed to reflect changes in the company and economy.

To explain, Musicland has $3,700 in accounts receivable that are 31 to 60 days past due. Its management estimates 10% of the amounts in this age class are uncollectible, or a total of $370 (computed as $3,700 × 10%). Similar analysis is done for each of the other four classes. The final total of $2,270 ($740 + $325 + 370 + $475 + $360) shown in the first column is the estimated balance for the Allowance for Doubtful Accounts. Exhibit 7.12 shows that since the allowance

Unadjusted balance	$ 200 credit
Estimated balance	2,270 credit
Required adjustment	**$2,070 credit**

EXHIBIT 7.12

Computation of the Required Adjustment for the Accounts Receivable Method

Allowance for Doubtful Accounts

	Unadj. bal.	200
	Req. adj.	**2,070**
	Estim. bal.	2,270

Assets = Liabilities + Equity
−2,070   −2,070

account has an unadjusted credit balance of $200, the required adjustment to the Allowance for Doubtful Accounts is $2,070. (We could also use a T-account for this analysis as shown in the margin.) This yields the following end-of-period adjusting entry:

Dec. 31	Bad Debts Expense	2,070	
	Allowance for Doubtful Accounts		2,070
	To record estimated bad debts.		

Point: A debit balance implies that write-offs for that period exceed the total allowance.

Alternatively, if the allowance account had an unadjusted *debit* balance of $500 (instead of the $200 credit balance), its required adjustment would be computed as follows. (Again, a T-account can be used for this analysis as shown in the margin.)

Allowance for Doubtful Accounts

Unadj. bal.	500		
		Req. adj.	**2,770**
		Estim. bal.	2,270

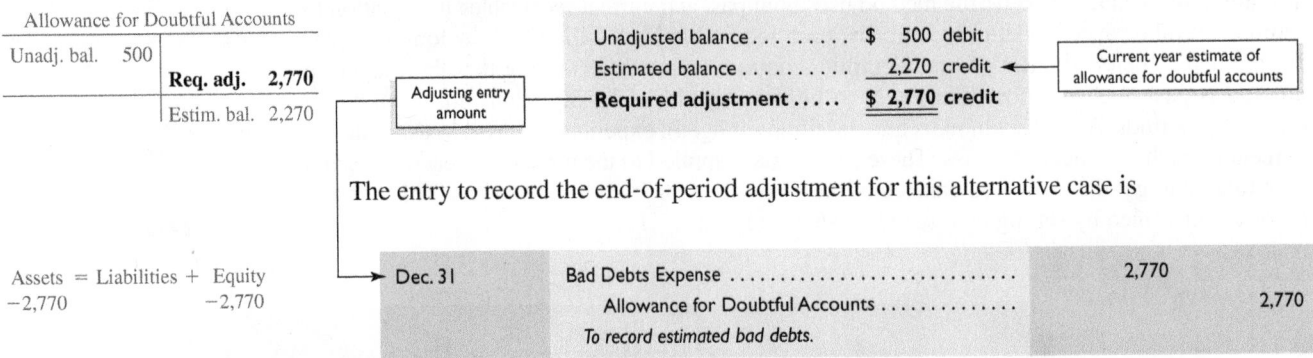

Adjusting entry amount

Unadjusted balance .... $ 500 debit
Estimated balance .... 2,270 credit
Required adjustment ..... **$ 2,770 credit**

Current year estimate of allowance for doubtful accounts

The entry to record the end-of-period adjustment for this alternative case is

Assets = Liabilities + Equity
−2,770   −2,770

Dec. 31	Bad Debts Expense	2,770	
	Allowance for Doubtful Accounts		2,770
	To record estimated bad debts.		

The aging of accounts receivable method is an examination of specific accounts and is usually the most reliable of the estimation methods.

Estimating Bad Debts—Summary of Methods   Exhibit 7.13 summarizes the principles guiding all three estimation methods and their focus of analysis. Percent of sales, with its income statement focus, does a good job at matching bad debts expense with sales. The accounts receivable methods, with their balance sheet focus, do a better job at reporting accounts receivable at realizable value.

EXHIBIT 7.13

Methods to Estimate Bad Debts

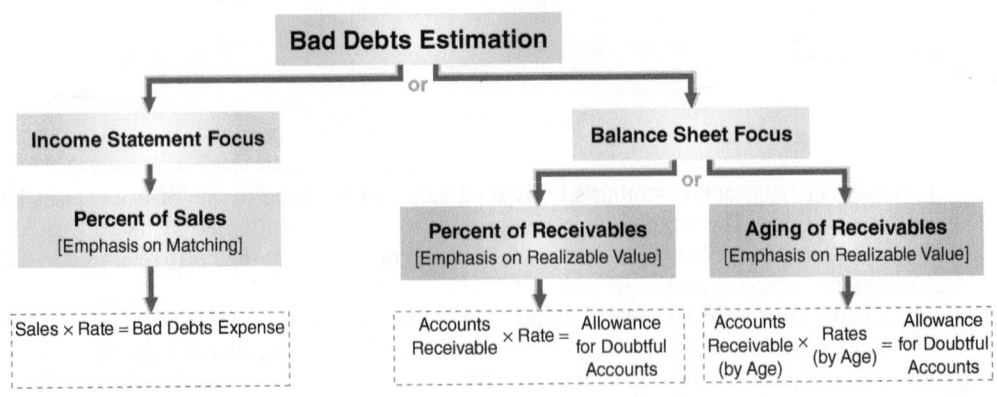

Decision Maker

Labor Union Chief   One week prior to labor contract negotiations, financial statements are released showing no income growth. A 10% growth was predicted. Your analysis finds that the company increased its allowance for uncollectibles from 1.5% to 4.5% of receivables. Without this change, income would show a 9% growth. Does this analysis impact negotiations? ■   [Answer—p. 331]

At its December 31 year-end, a company estimates uncollectible accounts using the allowance method.

1. It prepared the following aging of receivables analysis. (a) Estimate the balance of the Allowance for Doubtful Accounts using the aging of accounts receivable method. (b) Prepare the adjusting entry to record Bad Debts Expense using the estimate from part *a*. Assume the unadjusted balance in the Allowance for Doubtful Accounts is a $10 debit.

				Days Past Due		
	Total	0	I to 30	31 to 60	61 to 90	Over 90
Accounts receivable	$2,600	$2,000	$300	$80	$100	$120
Percent uncollectible		1%	2%	5%	7%	10%

2. (a) Estimate the balance of the Allowance for Doubtful Accounts assuming the company uses 2% of total accounts receivable to estimate uncollectibles, instead of the aging of receivables method in number 1. (b) Prepare the adjusting entry to record Bad Debts Expense using the estimate from part *a*. Assume the unadjusted balance in the Allowance for Doubtful Accounts is a $4 credit.

3. (a) Estimate the balance of the uncollectibles assuming the company uses 0.5% of annual credit sales (annual credit sales were $10,000). (b) Prepare the adjusting entry to record Bad Debts Expense using the estimate from part *a*. Assume the unadjusted balance in the Allowance for Doubtful Accounts is a $4 credit.

Solutions

1a. Computation of the estimated balance of the allowance for uncollectibles:

Not due:	$2,000 × 0.01 =	$20
I to 30:	300 × 0.02 =	6
31 to 60:	80 × 0.05 =	4
61 to 90:	100 × 0.07 =	7
Over 90:	120 × 0.10 =	12
		$49 credit

1b.

Dec. 31	Bad Debts Expense.	59	
	Allowance for Doubtful Accounts		59
	*To record estimated bad debts.**		

*Unadjusted balance	$10 debit
Estimated balance	49 credit
Required adjustment	$59 credit

2a. Computation of the estimated balance of the allowance for uncollectibles:

$$\$2,600 \times 0.02 = \underline{\$52} \text{ credit}$$

2b.

Dec. 31	Bad Debts Expense.	48	
	Allowance for Doubtful Accounts		48
	*To record estimated bad debts.**		

*Unadjusted balance	$ 4 credit
Estimated balance	52 credit
Required adjustment	$48 credit

3a. Computation of the estimated balance of the bad debts expense:

$$\$10,000 \times 0.005 = \underline{\$50} \text{ credit}$$

3b.

Dec. 31	Bad Debts Expense.	50	
	Allowance for Doubtful Accounts		50
	To record estimated bad debts.		

Do More: QS 7-4, E 7-6, E 7-7, E 7-9

QC2

NOTES RECEIVABLE

 C2 Describe a note receivable, the computation of its maturity date, and the recording of its existence.

A **promissory note** is a written promise to pay a specified amount of money, usually with interest, either on demand or at a definite future date. Promissory notes are used in many transactions, including paying for products and services, and lending and borrowing money. Sellers sometimes ask for a note to replace an account receivable when a customer requests additional time to pay a past-due account. For legal reasons, sellers generally prefer to receive notes when the credit period is long and when the receivable is for a large amount. If a lawsuit is needed to collect from a customer, a note is the buyer's written acknowledgment of the debt, its amount, and its terms.

Exhibit 7.14 shows a simple promissory note dated July 10, 2013. For this note, Julia Browne promises to pay TechCom or to its order (according to TechCom's instructions) a specified amount of money ($1,000), called the **principal of a note,** at a definite future date (October 8, 2013). As the one who signed the note and promised to pay it at maturity, Browne is the **maker of the note.** As the person to whom the note is payable, TechCom is the **payee of the note.** To Browne, the note is a liability called a *note payable.* To TechCom, the same note is an asset called a *note receivable.* This note bears interest at 12%, as written on the note. **Interest** is the charge for using the money until its due date. To a borrower, interest is an expense. To a lender, it is revenue.

EXHIBIT 7.14

Promissory Note

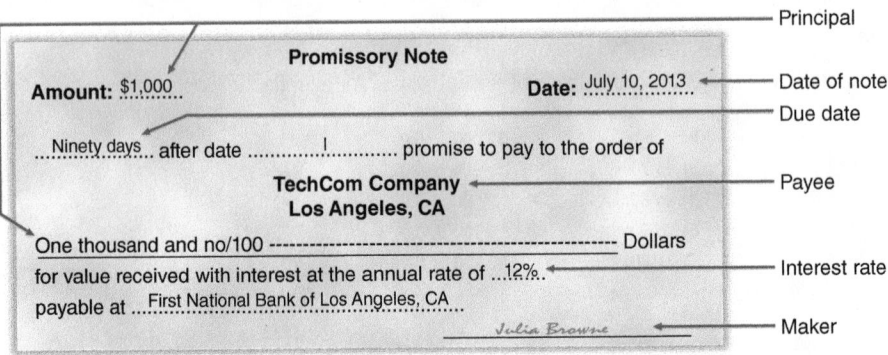

Computing Maturity and Interest

This section describes key computations for notes including the determination of maturity date, period covered, and interest computation.

Maturity Date and Period   The **maturity date of a note** is the day the note (principal and interest) must be repaid. The *period* of a note is the time from the note's (contract) date to its maturity date. Many notes mature in less than a full year, and the period they cover is often expressed in days. When the time of a note is expressed in days, its maturity date is the specified number of days after the note's date. As an example, a five-day note dated June 15 matures and is due on June 20. A 90-day note dated July 10 matures on October 8. This October 8 due date is computed as shown in Exhibit 7.15. The period of a note is sometimes expressed in months or years. When months are used, the note matures and is payable in the month of its maturity on the *same day of the month* as its original date. A nine-month note dated July 10, for instance, is payable on April 10. The same analysis applies when years are used.

EXHIBIT 7.15

Maturity Date Computation

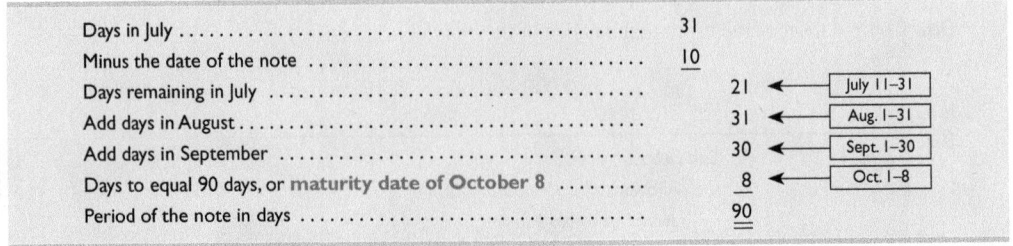

Interest Computation   *Interest* is the cost of borrowing money for the borrower or, alternatively, the profit from lending money for the lender. Unless otherwise stated, the rate of interest on a note is the rate charged for the use of the principal for one year. The formula for computing interest on a note is shown in Exhibit 7.16.

$$\boxed{\begin{array}{c} \text{Principal} \\ \text{of the note} \end{array}} \times \boxed{\begin{array}{c} \text{Annual} \\ \text{interest rate} \end{array}} \times \boxed{\begin{array}{c} \text{Time expressed} \\ \text{in fraction of year} \end{array}} = \boxed{\textbf{Interest}}$$

EXHIBIT 7.16

Computation of Interest Formula

To simplify interest computations, a year is commonly treated as having 360 days (called the *banker's rule* in the business world and widely used in commercial transactions). **We treat a year as having 360 days for interest computations in the examples and assignments.** Using the promissory note in Exhibit 7.14 where we have a 90-day, 12%, $1,000 note, the total interest is computed as follows:

$$\$1,000 \times 12\% \times \frac{90}{360} = \$1,000 \times 0.12 \times 0.25 = \$30$$

Point: If the *banker's rule* is not followed, interest is computed as:

$\$1,000 \times 12\% \times 90/365 = \$29.589041$

The *banker's rule* would yield $30, which is easier to account for than $29.589041.

Recognizing Notes Receivable

Notes receivable are usually recorded in a single Notes Receivable account to simplify record-keeping. The original notes are kept on file, including information on the maker, rate of interest, and due date. (When a company holds a large number of notes, it sometimes sets up a controlling account and a subsidiary ledger for notes. This is similar to the handling of accounts receivable.) To illustrate the recording for the receipt of a note, we use the $1,000, 90-day, 12% promissory note in Exhibit 7.14. TechCom received this note at the time of a product sale to Julia Browne. This transaction is recorded as follows:

July 10*	Notes Receivable	1,000	
	Sales		1,000
	Sold goods in exchange for a 90-day, 12% note.		

Assets = Liabilities + Equity
+1,000   +1,000

* We omit the entry to Dr. Cost of Sales and Cr. Merchandise Inventory to focus on sales and receivables.

When a seller accepts a note from an overdue customer as a way to grant a time extension on a past-due account receivable, it will often collect part of the past-due balance in cash. This partial payment forces a concession from the customer, reduces the customer's debt (and the seller's risk), and produces a note for a smaller amount. To illustrate, assume that TechCom agreed to accept $232 in cash along with a $600, 60-day, 15% note from Jo Cook to settle her $832 past-due account. TechCom made the following entry to record receipt of this cash and note:

Point: Notes receivable often are a major part of a company's assets. Likewise, notes payable often are a large part of a company's liabilities.

Oct. 5	Cash	232	
	Notes Receivable	600	
	Accounts Receivable—J. Cook		832
	Received cash and note to settle account.		

Assets = Liabilities + Equity
+232
+600
−832

Valuing and Settling Notes

Recording an Honored Note   The principal and interest of a note are due on its maturity date. The maker of the note usually *honors* the note and pays it in full. To illustrate, when J. Cook pays the note above on its due date, TechCom records it as follows:

P3 Record the honoring and dishonoring of a note and adjustments for interest.

Dec. 4	Cash	615	
	Notes Receivable		600
	Interest Revenue		15
	Collect note with interest of $600 × 15% × 60/360.		

Assets = Liabilities + Equity
+615   +15
−600

Interest Revenue, also called *Interest Earned,* is reported on the income statement.

Recording a Dishonored Note   When a note's maker is unable or refuses to pay at maturity, the note is *dishonored*. The act of dishonoring a note does not relieve the maker of the obligation to pay. The payee should use every legitimate means to collect. How do companies report this event? The balance of the Notes Receivable account should include only those notes that have not matured. Thus, when a note is dishonored, we remove the amount of this note from the Notes Receivable account and charge it back to an account receivable from its maker. To illustrate, TechCom holds an $800, 12%, 60-day note of Greg Hart. At maturity, Hart dishonors the note. TechCom records this dishonoring of the note as follows:

<table>
<tr><td>**Point:** When posting a dishonored note to a customer's account, an explanation is included so as not to misinterpret the debit as a sale on account.</td></tr>
</table>

Assets = Liabilities + Equity
+816   +16
−800

Oct. 14	Accounts Receivable—G. Hart	816	
	Interest Revenue		16
	Notes Receivable		800
	To charge account of G. Hart for a dishonored note and interest of $800 × 12% × 60/360.		

Point: Reporting the details of notes is consistent with the **full disclosure principle,** which requires financial statements (including footnotes) to report all relevant information.

Charging a dishonored note back to the account of its maker serves two purposes. First, it removes the amount of the note from the Notes Receivable account and records the dishonored note in the maker's account. Second, and more important, if the maker of the dishonored note applies for credit in the future, his or her account will reveal all past dealings, including the dishonored note. Restoring the account also reminds the company to continue collection efforts from Hart for both principal and interest. The entry records the full amount, including interest, to ensure that it is included in collection efforts.

Recording End-of-Period Interest Adjustment   When notes receivable are outstanding at the end of a period, any accrued interest earned is computed and recorded. To illustrate, on December 16, TechCom accepts a $3,000, 60-day, 12% note from a customer in granting an extension on a past-due account. When TechCom's accounting period ends on December 31, $15 of interest has accrued on this note ($3,000 × 12% × 15/360). The following adjusting entry records this revenue:

Assets = Liabilities + Equity
+15   +15

Dec. 31	Interest Receivable	15	
	Interest Revenue		15
	To record accrued interest earned.		

Interest Revenue appears on the income statement, and Interest Receivable appears on the balance sheet as a current asset. When the December 16 note is collected on February 14, TechCom's entry to record the cash receipt is

Assets = Liabilities + Equity
+3,060   +45
−15
−3,000

Feb. 14	Cash	3,060	
	Interest Revenue		45
	Interest Receivable		15
	Notes Receivable		3,000
	Received payment of note and its interest.		

Total interest earned on the 60-day note is $60. The $15 credit to Interest Receivable on February 14 reflects the collection of the interest accrued from the December 31 adjusting entry. The $45 interest earned reflects TechCom's revenue from holding the note from January 1 to February 14 of the current period.

Fraud

Skimming. *Skimming* refers to stealing money from a cash register, a customer's payment, or refunds received. A point-of-sale employee who operates a cash register is especially at risk for skimming. For example, a cash register employee might receive $900 cash but only ring up $600 on the register (or nothing), which enables the employee to steal $300 cash (or the entire amount). A crucial control is to require that each sale is entered into the register. Skimming is then revealed when the record on the register differs from the cash in the register. To ensure that *all* sales are recorded on the register, we use customer help by hanging a sign: "Sales without a receipt are free!"

a. AA Company purchases $1,400 of merchandise from ZZ on December 16, 2014. ZZ accepts AA's $1,400, 90-day, 12% note as payment. ZZ's accounting period ends on December 31, and it does not make reversing entries. Prepare entries for ZZ on December 16, 2014, and December 31, 2014.

b. Using the information in part a, prepare ZZ's March 16, 2015, entry if AA dishonors the note.

c. Instead of the facts in part b, prepare ZZ's March 16, 2015, entry if AA honors the note.

> **NEED-TO-KNOW 7.5**
>
> C2, P3

Solution

a.

Dec. 16	Note Receivable — AA	1,400	
	Sales		1,400
Dec. 31	Interest Receivable...........................	7	
	Interest Revenue		7
	($1,400 × 12% × 15/360)		

b.

Mar. 16	Accounts Receivable — AA....................	1,442	
	Interest Revenue		35
	Interest Receivable......................		7
	Notes Receivable—AA		1,400

c.

Mar. 16	Cash	1,442	
	Interest Revenue		35
	Interest Receivable......................		7
	Notes Receivable—AA		1,400

> Do More: QS 7-5, QS 7-6, QS 7-7, E 7-11, E 7-12, E 7-13, E 7-14
>
> **QC3**

DISPOSAL OF RECEIVABLES

Companies can convert receivables to cash before they are due. Reasons for this include the need for cash or the desire not to be involved in collection activities. Converting receivables is usually done either by (1) selling them or (2) using them as security for a loan. A recent survey shows that about 20% of companies obtain cash from either selling receivables or pledging them as security. In some industries such as textiles, apparel and furniture, this is common practice.

> **C3** Explain how receivables can be converted to cash before maturity.

Selling Receivables

A company can sell all or a portion of its receivables to a finance company or bank. The buyer, called a *factor,* charges the seller a *factoring fee* and then the buyer takes ownership of the receivables and receives cash when they come due. By incurring a factoring fee, the seller receives cash earlier and can pass the risk of bad debts to the factor. The seller can also choose to avoid costs of billing and accounting for the receivables. To illustrate, if TechCom sells $20,000 of its accounts receivable and is charged a 4% factoring fee, it records this sale as follows:

Global: Firms in export sales increasingly sell their receivables to factors.

Aug. 15	Cash	19,200	
	Factoring Fee Expense	800	
	Accounts Receivable		20,000
	Sold accounts receivable for cash, less 4% fee.		

Assets = Liabilities + Equity
+19,200   −800
−20,000

The accounting for sales of notes receivable is similar to that for accounts receivable. The detailed entries are covered in advanced courses. Remember: When factoring receivables, the company selling receivables always receives less cash than the amount of receivables sold due to factoring fees.

Pledging Receivables

A company can raise cash by borrowing money and *pledging* its receivables as security for the loan. Pledging receivables does not transfer the risk of bad debts to the lender because the borrower retains ownership of the receivables. If the borrower defaults on the loan, the lender has a right to be paid from the cash receipts of the receivable when collected. To illustrate, when TechCom borrows $35,000 and pledges its receivables as security, it records this transaction as follows:

Assets = Liabilities + Equity
+35,000   +35,000

Aug. 20	Cash	35,000	
	Notes Payable		35,000
	Borrowed money with a note secured by pledging receivables.		

Since pledged receivables are committed as security for a specific loan, the borrower's financial statements disclose the pledging of them. TechCom, for instance, includes the following note with its statements: Accounts receivable of $40,000 are pledged as security for a $35,000 note payable. Inventory and accounts receivable are two assets commonly demanded by bankers as collateral when making business loans.

■ **Decision** Maker

Analyst/Auditor You are reviewing accounts receivable. Over the past five years, the allowance account as a percentage of gross accounts receivable shows a steady downward trend. What does this finding suggest? ■ [Answer—p. 331]

GLOBAL VIEW

This section discusses similarities and differences between U.S. GAAP and IFRS regarding the recognition, measurement, and disposition of receivables.

Recognition of Receivables Both U.S. GAAP and IFRS have similar asset criteria that apply to recognition of receivables. Further, receivables that arise from revenue-generating activities are subject to broadly similar criteria for U.S. GAAP and IFRS. Specifically, both refer to the realization principle and an earnings process. The realization principle under U.S. GAAP implies an *arm's-length transaction* occurs, whereas under IFRS this notion is applied in terms of reliable measurement and likelihood of economic benefits. Regarding U.S. GAAP's reference to an earnings process, IFRS instead refers to risk transfer and ownership reward. While these criteria are broadly similar, differences do exist, and they arise mainly from industry-specific guidance under U.S. GAAP, which is very limited under IFRS.

Valuation of Receivables Both U.S. GAAP and IFRS require that receivables be reported net of estimated uncollectibles. Further, both systems require that the expense for estimated uncollectibles be recorded in the same period when any revenues from those receivables are recorded. This means that for accounts receivable, both U.S. GAAP and IFRS require the allowance method for uncollectibles (unless uncollectibles are immaterial). The allowance method using percent of sales, percent of receivables, and aging was explained in this chapter. Nokia reports the following for its allowance for uncollectibles:

NOKIA

> Management specifically analyzes accounts receivables and historical bad debt, customer concentrations, customer creditworthiness, current economic trends and changes in our customer payment terms when evaluating the adequacy of the allowance.

Disposition of Receivables Both U.S. GAAP and IFRS apply broadly similar rules in recording dispositions of receivables. Those rules are discussed in this chapter. We should be aware of an important difference in terminology. Companies reporting under U.S. GAAP disclose Bad Debts Expense, which is also referred to as Provision for Bad Debts or the Provision for Uncollectible Accounts. For U.S. GAAP, *provision* here refers to expense. Under IFRS, the term *provision* usually refers to a liability whose amount or timing (or both) is uncertain.

 Accounts Receivable Turnover  **Decision Analysis**

For a company selling on credit, we want to assess both the quality and liquidity of its accounts receivable. *Quality* of receivables refers to the likelihood of collection without loss. Experience shows that the longer receivables are outstanding beyond their due date, the lower the likelihood of collection. *Liquidity* of receivables refers to the speed of collection. **Accounts receivable turnover** is a measure of both the quality and liquidity of accounts receivable. It indicates how often, on average, receivables are received and collected during the period. The formula for this ratio is shown in Exhibit 7.17.

> **A1** Compute accounts receivable turnover and use it to help assess financial condition.

$$\text{Accounts receivable turnover} = \frac{\text{Net sales}}{\text{Average accounts receivable, net}}$$

EXHIBIT 7.17

Accounts Receivable Turnover

We prefer to use net *credit* sales in the numerator because cash sales do not create receivables. However, since financial statements rarely report net credit sales, our analysis uses net sales. The denominator is the *average* accounts receivable balance, computed as (Beginning balance + Ending balance) ÷ 2. TechCom has an accounts receivable turnover of 5.1. This indicates its average accounts receivable balance is converted into cash 5.1 times during the period. Exhibit 7.18 shows graphically this turnover activity for TechCom.

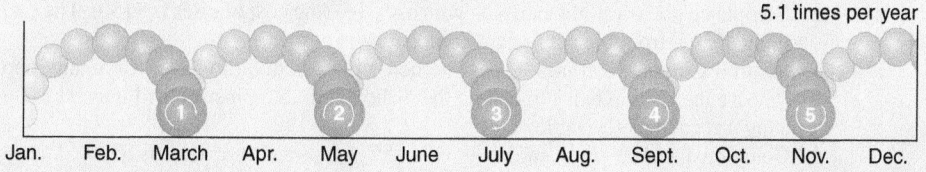

Jan. Feb. March Apr. May June July Aug. Sept. Oct. Nov. Dec.

5.1 times per year

EXHIBIT 7.18

Rate of Accounts Receivable Turnover for TechCom

Accounts receivable turnover also reflects how well management is doing in granting credit to customers in a desire to increase sales. A high turnover in comparison with competitors suggests that management should consider using more liberal credit terms to increase sales. A low turnover suggests management should consider stricter credit terms and more aggressive collection efforts to avoid having its resources tied up in accounts receivable.

To illustrate, we take fiscal year data from two competitors: Dell and Apple. Exhibit 7.19 shows accounts receivable turnover for both companies.

> **Point:** Credit risk ratio is computed by dividing the Allowance for Doubtful Accounts by Accounts Receivable. The higher this ratio, the higher is credit risk.

Company	Figure ($ millions)	2011	2010	2009	2008
Dell	Net sales	$ 61,494	$52,902	$61,101	$61,133
	Average accounts receivable, net	$ 6,165	$ 5,284	$ 5,346	$ 5,292
	Accounts receivable turnover	10.0	10.0	11.4	11.6
Apple	Net sales	$108,249	$65,225	$42,905	$37,491
	Average accounts receivable, net	$ 5,440	$ 4,436	$ 2,892	$ 2,030
	Accounts receivable turnover	19.9	14.7	14.8	18.5

EXHIBIT 7.19

Analysis Using Accounts Receivable Turnover

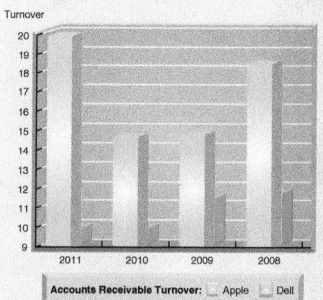

Dell's 2011 turnover is 10.0, computed as $61,494/$6,165 ($ millions). This means that Dell's average accounts receivable balance was converted into cash 10.0 times in 2011. Its turnover was flat in 2011, but it had been slightly declining in recent years. Apple's turnover exceeds that for Dell in each of the past 4 years. Is either company's turnover too high? Since sales are stable or markedly growing over this time period, each company's turnover rate does not appear to be too high. Instead, both Dell and Apple seem to be doing well in managing receivables. This is especially true given the recent recessionary period. Turnover for competitors is generally in the range of 7 to 12 for this same period.[1]

 Decision Maker

Family Physician Your medical practice is barely profitable, so you hire a health care analyst. The analyst highlights several points including the following: *"Accounts receivable turnover is too low. Tighter credit policies are recommended along with discontinuing service to those most delayed in payments."* How do you interpret these recommendations? What actions do you take? ■ [Answer—p. 331]

COMPREHENSIVE...

NEED-TO-KNOW

Clayco Company completes the following selected transactions during year 2013.

July 14 Writes off a $750 account receivable arising from a sale to Briggs Company that dates to 10 months ago. (Clayco Company uses the allowance method.)

30 Clayco Company receives a $1,000, 90-day, 10% note in exchange for merchandise sold to Sumrell Company (the merchandise cost $600).

Aug. 15 Receives $2,000 cash plus a $10,000 note from JT Co. in exchange for merchandise that sells for $12,000 (its cost is $8,000). The note is dated August 15, bears 12% interest, and matures in 120 days.

Nov. 1 Completed a $200 credit card sale with a 4% fee (the cost of sales is $150). The cash is received immediately from the credit card company.

3 Sumrell Company refuses to pay the note that was due to Clayco Company on October 28. Prepare the journal entry to charge the dishonored note plus accrued interest to Sumrell Company's accounts receivable.

5 Completed a $500 credit card sale with a 5% fee (the cost of sales is $300). The payment from the credit card company is received on Nov. 9.

15 Received the full amount of $750 from Briggs Company that was previously written off on July 14. Record the bad debts recovery.

Dec. 13 Received payment of principal plus interest from JT for the August 15 note.

Required

1. Prepare journal entries to record these transactions on Clayco Company's books.

2. Prepare an adjusting journal entry as of December 31, 2013, assuming the following:

  a. Bad debts are estimated to be $20,400 by aging accounts receivable. The unadjusted balance of the Allowance for Doubtful Accounts is $1,000 debit.

  b. Alternatively, assume that bad debts are estimated using the percent of sales method. The Allowance for Doubtful Accounts had a $1,000 debit balance before adjustment, and the company estimates bad debts to be 1% of its credit sales of $2,000,000.

PLANNING THE SOLUTION

● Examine each transaction to determine the accounts affected, and then record the entries.

● For the year-end adjustment, record the bad debts expense for the two approaches.

---

[1] As an estimate of *average days' sales uncollected,* we compute how many days (*on average*) it takes to collect receivables as follows: 365 days ÷ accounts receivable turnover. An increase in this *average collection period* can signal a decline in customers' financial condition.

SOLUTION TO COMPREHENSIVE   NEED-TO-KNOW

1.

July 14	Allowance for Doubtful Accounts	750	
	Accounts Receivable—Briggs Co.		750
	Wrote off an uncollectible account.		
July 30	Notes Receivable—Sumrell Co.	1,000	
	Sales		1,000
	Sold merchandise for a 90-day, 10% note.		
July 30	Cost of Goods Sold	600	
	Merchandise Inventory		600
	To record the cost of July 30 sale.		
Aug. 15	Cash	2,000	
	Notes Receivable—JT Co.	10,000	
	Sales		12,000
	Sold merchandise to customer for $2,000		
	cash and $10,000 note.		
Aug. 15	Cost of Goods Sold	8,000	
	Merchandise Inventory		8,000
	To record the cost of Aug. 15 sale.		
Nov. 1	Cash	192	
	Credit Card Expense	8	
	Sales		200
	To record credit card sale less a 4% credit		
	card expense.		
Nov. 1	Cost of Goods Sold	150	
	Merchandise Inventory		150
	To record the cost of Nov. 1 sale.		
Nov. 3	Accounts Receivable—Sumrell Co.	1,025	
	Interest Revenue		25
	Notes Receivable—Sumrell Co.		1,000
	To charge account of Sumrell Company for		
	a $1,000 dishonored note and interest of		
	$1,000 × 10% × 90/360.		
Nov. 5	Accounts Receivable—Credit Card Co.	475	
	Credit Card Expense	25	
	Sales		500
	To record credit card sale less a 5% credit card expense.		
Nov. 5	Cost of Goods Sold	300	
	Merchandise Inventory		300
	To record the cost of Nov. 5 sale.		
Nov. 9	Cash	475	
	Accounts Receivable—Credit Card Co.		475
	To record cash receipt from Nov. 5 sale.		
Nov. 15	Accounts Receivable—Briggs Co.	750	
	Allowance for Doubtful Accounts		750
	To reinstate the account of Briggs Company		
	previously written off.		
Nov. 15	Cash	750	
	Accounts Receivable—Briggs Co.		750
	Cash received in full payment of account.		
Dec. 13	Cash	10,400	
	Interest Revenue		400
	Note Receivable—JT Co.		10,000
	Collect note with interest of		
	$10,000 × 12% × 120/360.		

2a. Aging of accounts receivable method.

Dec. 31	Bad Debts Expense	21,400	
	Allowance for Doubtful Accounts		21,400
	To adjust allowance account from a $1,000		
	debit balance to a $20,400 credit balance.		

2b. Percent of sales method.*

Dec. 31	Bad Debts Expense	20,000	
	Allowance for Doubtful Accounts		20,000
	To provide for bad debts as 1% × $2,000,000		
	in credit sales.		

* For the income statement approach, which requires estimating bad debts as a percent of sales or credit sales, the Allowance account balance is *not* considered when making the adjusting entry.

Summary

C1 **Describe accounts receivable and how they occur and are recorded.** Accounts receivable are amounts due from customers for credit sales. A subsidiary ledger lists amounts owed by each customer. Credit sales arise from at least two sources: (1) sales on credit and (2) credit card sales. *Sales on credit* refers to a company's granting credit directly to customers. Credit card sales involve customers' use of third-party credit cards.

C2 **Describe a note receivable, the computation of its maturity date, and the recording of its existence.** A note receivable is a written promise to pay a specified amount of money at a definite future date. The maturity date is the day the note (principal and interest) must be repaid. Interest rates are normally stated in annual terms. The amount of interest on the note is computed by expressing time as a fraction of one year and multiplying the note's principal by this fraction and the annual interest rate. A note received is recorded at its principal amount by debiting the Notes Receivable account. The credit amount is to the asset, product, or service provided in return for the note.

C3 **Explain how receivables can be converted to cash before maturity.** Receivables can be converted to cash before maturity in three ways. First, a company can sell accounts receivable to a factor, who charges a factoring fee. Second, a company can borrow money by signing a note payable that is secured by pledging the accounts receivable. Third, notes receivable can be discounted at (sold to) a financial institution.

A1 **Compute accounts receivable turnover and use it to help assess financial condition.** Accounts receivable turnover is a measure of both the quality and liquidity of accounts receivable.

The accounts receivable turnover measure indicates how often, on average, receivables are received and collected during the period. Accounts receivable turnover is computed as net sales divided by average accounts receivable.

P1 **Apply the direct write-off method to account for accounts receivable.** The direct write-off method charges Bad Debts Expense when accounts are written off as uncollectible. This method is acceptable only when the amount of bad debts expense is immaterial.

P2 **Apply the allowance method and estimate uncollectibles based on sales and accounts receivable.** Under the allowance method, bad debts expense is recorded with an adjustment at the end of each accounting period that debits the Bad Debts Expense account and credits the Allowance for Doubtful Accounts. The uncollectible accounts are later written off with a debit to the Allowance for Doubtful Accounts. Uncollectibles are estimated by focusing on either (1) the income statement relation between bad debts expense and credit sales or (2) the balance sheet relation between accounts receivable and the allowance for doubtful accounts. The first approach emphasizes the matching principle using the income statement. The second approach emphasizes realizable value of accounts receivable using the balance sheet.

P3 **Record the honoring and dishonoring of a note and adjustments for interest.** When a note is honored, the payee debits the money received and credits both Notes Receivable and Interest Revenue. Dishonored notes are credited to Notes Receivable and debited to Accounts Receivable (to the account of the maker in an attempt to collect), and Interest Revenue is recorded for interest earned for the time the note is held.

Guidance Answers to Decision Maker **and** Decision Ethics

Entrepreneur Analysis of credit card sales should weigh the benefits against the costs. The primary benefit is the potential to increase sales by attracting customers who prefer the convenience of credit cards. The primary cost is the fee charged by the credit card company for providing this service. Analysis should therefore esti-mate the expected increase in dollar sales from allowing credit card sales and then subtract (1) the normal costs and expenses and (2) the credit card fees associated with this expected increase in dollar sales. If your analysis shows an increase in profit from allowing credit card sales, your store should probably accept them.

Labor Union Chief   Yes, this information is likely to impact your negotiations. The obvious question is why the company markedly increased this allowance. The large increase in this allowance means a substantial increase in bad debts expense *and* a decrease in earnings. This change (coming immediately prior to labor contract discussions) also raises concerns since it reduces the union's bargaining power for increased compensation. You want to ask management for supporting documentation justifying this increase. You also want data for two or three prior years and similar data from competitors. These data should give you some sense of whether the change in the allowance for uncollectibles is justified.

Analyst/Auditor   The downward trend suggests the company is reducing the relative amount charged to bad debts expense each year. This may reflect the company's desire to increase net income. On the other hand, it might be that collections have improved and the lower provision for bad debts is justified. If this is not the case, the lower allowances might be insufficient for bad debts.

Family Physician   The recommendations are twofold. First, the analyst suggests more stringent screening of patients' credit standing. Second, the analyst suggests dropping patients who are most overdue in payments. You are likely bothered by both suggestions. They are probably financially wise recommendations, but you are troubled by eliminating services to those less able to pay. One alternative is to follow the recommendations while implementing a care program directed at patients less able to pay for services. This allows you to continue services to patients less able to pay and lets you discontinue services to patients able but unwilling to pay.

Key Terms

Accounts receivable (p. 310)
Accounts receivable turnover (p. 327)
Aging of accounts receivable (p. 319)
Allowance for Doubtful Accounts (p. 316)
Allowance method (p. 315)
Bad debts (p. 314)

Direct write-off method (p. 314)
Interest (p. 322)
Maker of the note (p. 322)
Matching (expense recognition) principle (p. 314)
Materiality constraint (p. 314)

Maturity date of a note (p. 322)
Payee of the note (p. 322)
Principal of a note (p. 322)
Promissory note (or note) (p. 322)
Realizable value (p. 316)

Multiple Choice Quiz   Answers on p. 343   mhhe.com/wildFA7e

Additional Quiz Questions are available at the book's Website.

1. A company's Accounts Receivable balance at its December 31 year-end is $125,650, and its Allowance for Doubtful Accounts has a credit balance of $328 before year-end adjustment. Its net sales are $572,300. It estimates that 4% of outstanding accounts receivable are uncollectible. What amount of Bad Debts Expense is recorded at December 31?
   a. $5,354
   b. $328
   c. $5,026
   d. $4,698
   e. $34,338

2. A company's Accounts Receivable balance at its December 31 year-end is $489,300, and its Allowance for Doubtful Accounts has a debit balance of $554 before year-end adjustment. Its net sales are $1,300,000. It estimates that 6% of outstanding accounts receivable are uncollectible. What amount of Bad Debts Expense is recorded at December 31?
   a. $29,912
   b. $28,804
   c. $78,000
   d. $29,358
   e. $554

3. Total interest to be earned on a $7,500, 5%, 90-day note is
   a. $93.75
   b. $375.00
   c. $1,125.00
   d. $31.25
   e. $125.00

4. A company receives a $9,000, 8%, 60-day note. The maturity value of the note is
   a. $120
   b. $9,000
   c. $9,120
   d. $720
   e. $9,720

5. A company has net sales of $489,600 and average accounts receivable of $40,800. What is its accounts receivable turnover?
   a. 0.08
   b. 30.41
   c. 1,341.00
   d. 12.00
   e. 111.78

🔘 Icon denotes assignments that involve decision making.

Discussion Questions

1. 🔘 How do sellers benefit from allowing their customers to use credit cards?

2. 🔘 Why does the direct write-off method of accounting for bad debts usually fail to match revenues and expenses?

3. Explain the accounting constraint of materiality.

4. Why might a business prefer a note receivable to an account receivable?

5. Explain why writing off a bad debt against the Allowance for Doubtful Accounts does not reduce the estimated realizable value of a company's accounts receivable.

6. 🔘 Why does the Bad Debts Expense account usually not have the same adjusted balance as the Allowance for Doubtful Accounts?

7. 🔘 Refer to the financial statements and notes of Apple in Appendix A. In its presentation of accounts receivable on the balance sheet, how does it title **APPLE**

accounts receivable? What does it report for its allowance as of September 29, 2012?

8. 🔘 Refer to the balance sheet of Google in **GOOGLE** Appendix A. Does it use the direct write-off method or allowance method in accounting for its accounts receivable? What is the realizable value of its receivable's balance as of December 31, 2012?

9. Refer to the financial statements of Samsung in Appendix A. What does Samsung title its **Samsung** accounts receivable on its consolidated balance sheet? What are Samsung's accounts receivable at December 31, 2012?

10. Refer to the December 31, 2012, financial statements of Samsung in Appendix A. **Samsung** Does Samsung report its accounts receivable as current or non-current asset? Does Samsung report its accounts receivable net of an allowance?

≣ connect

QUICK STUDY

QS 7-1

Credit card sales

C1

Prepare journal entries for the following credit card sales transactions (the company uses the perpetual inventory system).

1. Sold $20,000 of merchandise, that cost $15,000, on MasterCard credit cards. The net cash receipts from sales are immediately deposited in the seller's bank account. MasterCard charges a 5% fee.

2. Sold $5,000 of merchandise, that cost $3,000, on an assortment of credit cards. Net cash receipts are received 5 days later, and a 4% fee is charged.

QS 7-2

Distinguish between the allowance method and direct write-off methods

P1 P2

The following list describes aspects of either the allowance method or the direct write-off method to account for bad debts. For each item listed, indicate if the statement best describes either the allowance method or the direct write-off method.

_____ 1. No attempt is made to predict bad debts expense.

_____ 2. Accounts receivable on the balance sheet is reported at net realizable value.

_____ 3. The write-off of a specific account does not affect net income.

_____ 4. When an account is written off, the debit is to bad debts expense.

_____ 5. Sales and any bad debt expense are usually not recorded in the same period, thus proper matching (of revenue and expense recognition) does not consistently occur.

_____ 6. Requires a company to estimate bad debt expense related to the sales recorded in that period.

QS 7-3

Allowance method for bad debts

P2

Gomez Corp. uses the allowance method to account for uncollectibles. On January 31, it wrote off a $800 account of a customer, C. Green. On March 9, it receives a $300 payment from Green.

1. Prepare the journal entry or entries for January 31.

2. Prepare the journal entry or entries for March 9; assume no additional money is expected from Green.

QS 7-4

Percent of accounts receivable and the percent of sales methods

P2

Warner Company's year-end unadjusted trial balance shows accounts receivable of $99,000, allowance for doubtful accounts of $600 (credit), and sales of $280,000. Uncollectibles are estimated to be 1.5% of accounts receivable.

1. Prepare the December 31 year-end adjusting entry for uncollectibles.

2. What amount would have been used in the year-end adjusting entry if the allowance account had a year-end unadjusted debit balance of $300?

3. Assume the same background facts as above except that Warner estimates uncollectibles as 0.5% of sales. Prepare the December 31 year-end adjusting entry for uncollectibles.

QS 7-5

Note receivable C2

On August 2, 2013, Jun Co. receives a $6,000, 90-day, 12% note from customer Ryan Albany as payment on his $6,000 account. (1) Compute the maturity date for this note. (2) Prepare Jun's journal entry for August 2.

Refer to the information in QS 7-5 and prepare the journal entry assuming the note is honored by the customer on October 31, 2013.

QS 7-6
Note receivable   P3

Dominika Company's December 31 year-end unadjusted trial balance shows a $10,000 balance in Notes Receivable. This balance is from one 6% note dated December 1, with a period of 45 days. Prepare any necessary journal entries for December 31 and for the note's maturity date assuming it is honored.

QS 7-7
Note receivable   P3

Record the sale by Balus Company of $125,000 in accounts receivable on May 1. Balus is charged a 2.5% factoring fee.

QS 7-8
Disposing receivables   C3

Solstice Company determines on October 1 that it cannot collect $50,000 of its accounts receivable from its customer P. Moore. Apply the direct write-off method to record this loss as of October 1.

QS 7-9
Direct write-off method   P1

Refer to the information in QS 7-9. On October 30, P. Moore unexpectedly paid his account in full to Solstice Company. Record Solstice's entry(ies) to reflect this recovery of this bad debt.

QS 7-10
Recovering a bad debt   P1

The following data are taken from the comparative balance sheets of Ruggers Company. Compute and interpret its accounts receivable turnover for year 2013 (competitors average a turnover of 7.5).

QS 7-11
Accounts receivable turnover

A1

	2013	2012
Accounts receivable, net	$153,400	$138,500
Net sales	861,105	910,600

Answer each of the following related to international accounting standards.

a. Explain (in general terms) how the accounting for recognition of receivables is different between IFRS and U.S. GAAP.

b. Explain (in general terms) how the accounting for valuation of receivables is different between IFRS and U.S. GAAP.

QS 7-12
International accounting standards

C1

connect

Morales Company recorded the following selected transactions during November 2013.

EXERCISES

Nov. 5	Accounts Receivable—Ski Shop	4,615	
	Sales		4,615
10	Accounts Receivable—Welcome Enterprises	1,350	
	Sales		1,350
13	Accounts Receivable—Zia Natara	832	
	Sales		832
21	Sales Returns and Allowances	209	
	Accounts Receivable—Zia Natara		209
30	Accounts Receivable—Ski Shop	2,713	
	Sales		2,713

Exercise 7-1
Accounts receivable subsidiary ledger; schedule of accounts receivable

C1

1. Open a general ledger having T-accounts for Accounts Receivable, Sales, and Sales Returns and Allowances. Also open an accounts receivable subsidiary ledger having a T-account for each customer. Post these entries to both the general ledger and the accounts receivable ledger.

2. Prepare a schedule of accounts receivable (see Exhibit 7.4) and compare its total with the balance of the Accounts Receivable controlling account as of November 30.

Check   Accounts Receivable ending balance, $9,301

Levine Company uses the perpetual inventory system and allows customers to use two credit cards in charging purchases. With the Suntrust Bank Card, Levine receives an immediate credit to its account when it deposits sales receipts. Suntrust assesses a 4% service charge for credit card sales. The second credit card that Levine accepts is the Continental Card. Levine sends its accumulated receipts to Continental on a weekly

Exercise 7-2
Accounting for credit card sales

C1

basis and is paid by Continental about a week later. Continental assesses a 2.5% charge on sales for using its card. Prepare journal entries to record the following selected credit card transactions of Levine Company.

Apr. 8   Sold merchandise for $8,400 (that had cost $6,000) and accepted the customer's Suntrust Bank Card. The Suntrust receipts are immediately deposited in Levine's bank account.
      12   Sold merchandise for $5,600 (that had cost $3,500) and accepted the customer's Continental Card. Transferred $5,600 of credit card receipts to Continental, requesting payment.
      20   Received Continental's check for the April 12 billing, less the service charge.

Exercise 7-3
Direct write-off method
P1

Dexter Company applies the direct write-off method in accounting for uncollectible accounts. Prepare journal entries to record the following selected transactions of Dexter.

March 11   Dexter determines that it cannot collect $45,000 of its accounts receivable from its customer Lester Company.
      29   Lester Company unexpectedly pays its account in full to Dexter Company. Dexter records its recovery of this bad debt.

Exercise 7-4
Percent of sales method;
write-off
P2

At year-end (December 31), Chan Company estimates its bad debts as 0.5% of its annual credit sales of $975,000. Chan records its Bad Debts Expense for that estimate. On the following February 1, Chan decides that the $580 account of P. Park is uncollectible and writes it off as a bad debt. On June 5, Park unexpectedly pays the amount previously written off. Prepare the journal entries of Chan to record these transactions and events of December 31, February 1, and June 5.

Exercise 7-5
Percent of accounts receivable
method
P2

At each calendar year-end, Mazie Supply Co. uses the percent of accounts receivable method to estimate bad debts. On December 31, 2013, it has outstanding accounts receivable of $55,000, and it estimates that 2% will be uncollectible. Prepare the adjusting entry to record bad debts expense for year 2013 under the assumption that the Allowance for Doubtful Accounts has (a) a $415 credit balance before the adjustment and (b) a $291 debit balance before the adjustment.

Exercise 7-6
Aging of receivables method
P2

Daley Company estimates uncollectible accounts using the allowance method at December 31. It prepared the following aging of receivables analysis.

				Days Past Due		
	Total	0	1 to 30	31 to 60	61 to 90	Over 90
Accounts receivable	$570,000	$396,000	$90,000	$36,000	$18,000	$30,000
Percent uncollectible		1%	2%	5%	7%	10%

a. Estimate the balance of the Allowance for Doubtful Accounts using the aging of accounts receivable method.
b. Prepare the adjusting entry to record Bad Debts Expense using the estimate from part a. Assume the unadjusted balance in the Allowance for Doubtful Accounts is a $3,600 credit.
c. Prepare the adjusting entry to record Bad Debts Expense using the estimate from part a. Assume the unadjusted balance in the Allowance for Doubtful Accounts is a $100 debit.

Exercise 7-7
Percent of receivables method
P2

Refer to the information in Exercise 7-6 to complete the following requirements.
a. Estimate the balance of the Allowance for Doubtful Accounts assuming the company uses 4.5% of total accounts receivable to estimate uncollectibles, instead of the aging of receivables method.
b. Prepare the adjusting entry to record Bad Debts Expense using the estimate from part a. Assume the unadjusted balance in the Allowance for Doubtful Accounts is a $12,000 credit.
c. Prepare the adjusting entry to record Bad Debts Expense using the estimate from part a. Assume the unadjusted balance in the Allowance for Doubtful Accounts is a $1,000 debit.

Exercise 7-8
Writing off receivables
P2

Refer to the information in Exercise 7-6 to complete the following requirements.
a. On February 1 of the next period, the company determined that $6,800 in customer accounts is uncollectible; specifically, $900 for Oakley Co. and $5,900 for Brookes Co. Prepare the journal entry to write off those accounts.
b. On June 5 of that next period, the company unexpectedly received a $900 payment on a customer account, Oakley Company, that had previously been written off in part a. Prepare the entries necessary to reinstate the account and to record the cash received.

At December 31, Folgeys Coffee Company reports the following results for its calendar year.

Cash sales	$900,000
Credit sales	300,000

Its year-end unadjusted trial balance includes the following items.

Accounts receivable	$125,000 debit
Allowance for doubtful accounts	5,000 debit

a. Prepare the adjusting entry to record Bad Debts Expense assuming uncollectibles are estimated to be 3% of credit sales.

b. Prepare the adjusting entry to record Bad Debts Expense assuming uncollectibles are estimated to be 1% of total sales.

c. Prepare the adjusting entry to record Bad Debts Expense assuming uncollectibles are estimated to be 6% of year-end accounts receivable.

On June 30, Petrov Co. has $128,700 of accounts receivable. Prepare journal entries to record the following selected July transactions. Also prepare any footnotes to the July 31 financial statements that result from these transactions. (The company uses the perpetual inventory system.)

July 4 Sold $7,245 of merchandise (that had cost $5,000) to customers on credit.
      9 Sold $20,000 of accounts receivable to Main Bank. Main charges a 4% factoring fee.
     17 Received $5,859 cash from customers in payment on their accounts.
     27 Borrowed $10,000 cash from Main Bank, pledging $12,500 of accounts receivable as security for the loan.

Prepare journal entries to record these selected transactions for Vitalo Company (no reversing entries are recorded).

Nov. 1 Accepted a $6,000, 180-day, 8% note dated November 1 from Kelly White in granting a time extension on her past-due account receivable.
Dec. 31 Adjusted the year-end accounts for the accrued interest earned on the White note.
Apr. 30 White honors her note when presented for payment; February has 28 days for the current year.

Prepare journal entries to record the following selected transactions of Ridge Company.

Mar. 21 Accepted a $9,500, 180-day, 8% note dated March 21 from Tamara Jackson in granting a time extension on her past-due account receivable.
Sept. 17 Jackson dishonors her note when it is presented for payment.
Dec. 31 After exhausting all legal means of collection, Ridge Company writes off Jackson's account against the Allowance for Doubtful Accounts.

Prepare journal entries for the following selected transactions of Dulcinea Company for 2012.

2012

Dec. 13 Accepted a $9,500, 45-day, 8% note dated December 13 in granting Miranda Lee a time extension on her past-due account receivable.
     31 Prepared an adjusting entry to record the accrued interest on the Lee note.

Refer to the information in Exercise 7-13 and prepare the journal entries for the following selected transactions of Dulcinea Company for 2013.

2013

Jan. 27 Received Lee's payment for principal and interest on the note dated December 13.
Mar. 3 Accepted a $5,000, 10%, 90-day note dated March 3 in granting a time extension on the past-due account receivable of Tomas Company.
     17 Accepted a $2,000, 30-day, 9% note dated March 17 in granting Hiroshi Cheng a time extension on his past-due account receivable.
Apr. 16 Cheng dishonors his note when presented for payment.
May   1 Wrote off the Cheng account against the Allowance for Doubtful Accounts.
June 1 Received the Tomas payment for principal and interest on the note dated March 3.

Exercise 7-15

Accounts receivable turnover

A1

The following information is from the annual financial statements of Raheem Company. Compute its accounts receivable turnover for 2012 and 2013. Compare the two years results and give a possible explanation for any change (competitors average a turnover of 11).

	2013	2012	2011
Net sales	$405,140	$335,280	$388,000
Accounts receivable, net (year-end)	44,800	41,400	34,800

Exercise 7-16

Accounting for bad debts following IFRS

P2

Hitachi, Ltd., reports total revenues of ¥9,315,807 million for its fiscal year ending March 31, 2011, and its March 31, 2011, unadjusted trial balance reports a debit balance for trade receivables (gross) of ¥2,127,682 million.

a. Prepare the adjusting entry to record its Bad Debts Expense assuming uncollectibles are estimated to be 0.4% of total revenues and its unadjusted trial balance reports a credit balance of ¥10,000 million.

b. Prepare the adjusting entry to record Bad Debts Expense assuming uncollectibles are estimated to be 2.1% of year-end trade receivables (gross) and its unadjusted trial balance reports a credit balance of ¥10,000 million.

≣ connect

PROBLEM SET A

Problem 7-1A

Sales on account and credit card sales

C1

Mayfair Co. allows select customers to make purchases on credit. Its other customers can use either of two credit cards: Zisa or Access. Zisa deducts a 3% service charge for sales on its credit card and credits the bank account of Mayfair immediately when credit card receipts are deposited. Mayfair deposits the Zisa credit card receipts each business day. When customers use Access credit cards, Mayfair accumulates the receipts for several days before submitting them to Access for payment. Access deducts a 2% service charge and usually pays within one week of being billed. Mayfair completes the following transactions in June. (The terms of all credit sales are 2/15, n/30, and all sales are recorded at the gross price.)

June 4   Sold $650 of merchandise (that had cost $400) on credit to Natara Morris.
       5   Sold $6,900 of merchandise (that had cost $4,200) to customers who used their Zisa cards.
       6   Sold $5,850 of merchandise (that had cost $3,800) to customers who used their Access cards.
       8   Sold $4,350 of merchandise (that had cost $2,900) to customers who used their Access cards.
      10   Submitted Access card receipts accumulated since June 6 to the credit card company for payment.
      13   Wrote off the account of Abigail McKee against the Allowance for Doubtful Accounts. The $429 balance in McKee's account stemmed from a credit sale in October of last year.
      17   Received the amount due from Access.
      18   Received Morris's check in full payment for the purchase of June 4.

Check   June 17, Dr. Cash $9,996

Required

Prepare journal entries to record the preceding transactions and events. (The company uses the perpetual inventory system. Round amounts to the nearest dollar.)

Problem 7-2A

Accounts receivable transactions and bad debts adjustments

C1 P2

Liang Company began operations on January 1, 2012. During its first two years, the company completed a number of transactions involving sales on credit, accounts receivable collections, and bad debts. These transactions are summarized as follows:

2012

a. Sold $1,345,434 of merchandise (that had cost $975,000) on credit, terms n/30.

b. Wrote off $18,300 of uncollectible accounts receivable.

c. Received $669,200 cash in payment of accounts receivable.

Check   (d) Dr. Bad Debts Expense
            $28,169

d. In adjusting the accounts on December 31, the company estimated that 1.5% of accounts receivable will be uncollectible.

2013

e. Sold $1,525,634 of merchandise (that had cost $1,250,000) on credit, terms n/30.

f. Wrote off $27,800 of uncollectible accounts receivable.

g. Received $1,204,600 cash in payment of accounts receivable.

(h) Dr. Bad Debts Expense
    $32,199

h. In adjusting the accounts on December 31, the company estimated that 1.5% of accounts receivable will be uncollectible.

Required

Prepare journal entries to record Liang's 2012 and 2013 summarized transactions and its year-end adjustments to record bad debts expense. (The company uses the perpetual inventory system and it applies the allowance method for its accounts receivable. Round amounts to the nearest dollar.)

At December 31, 2013, Hawke Company reports the following results for its calendar year.

Cash sales	$1,905,000
Credit sales	5,682,000

In addition, its unadjusted trial balance includes the following items.

Accounts receivable	$1,270,100 debit
Allowance for doubtful accounts	16,580 debit

Required

1. Prepare the adjusting entry for this company to recognize bad debts under each of the following independent assumptions.
   a. Bad debts are estimated to be 1.5% of credit sales.
   b. Bad debts are estimated to be 1% of total sales.
   c. An aging analysis estimates that 5% of year-end accounts receivable are uncollectible.
2. Show how Accounts Receivable and the Allowance for Doubtful Accounts appear on its December 31, 2013, balance sheet given the facts in part 1*a*.
3. Show how Accounts Receivable and the Allowance for Doubtful Accounts appear on its December 31, 2013, balance sheet given the facts in part 1*c*.

Problem 7-3A
Estimating and reporting bad debts

P2

Check Bad Debts Expense:
(1*a*) $85,230, (1*c*) $80,085

Jarden Company has credit sales of $3.6 million for year 2013. On December 31, 2013, the company's Allowance for Doubtful Accounts has an unadjusted credit balance of $14,500. Jarden prepares a schedule of its December 31, 2013, accounts receivable by age. On the basis of past experience, it estimates the percent of receivables in each age category that will become uncollectible. This information is summarized here.

Problem 7-4A
Aging accounts receivable and accounting for bad debts

P2

File Edit View Insert Format Tools Data Accounting Window Help

December 31, 2013 Accounts Receivable	Age of Accounts Receivable	Expected Percent Uncollectible
$830,000	Not yet due	1.25%
254,000	1 to 30 days past due	2.00
86,000	31 to 60 days past due	6.50
38,000	61 to 90 days past due	32.75
12,000	Over 90 days past due	68.00

Sheet1 Sheet2 Sheet3

Required

1. Estimate the required balance of the Allowance for Doubtful Accounts at December 31, 2013, using the aging of accounts receivable method.
2. Prepare the adjusting entry to record bad debts expense at December 31, 2013.

Check (2) Dr. Bad Debts Expense $27,150

Analysis Component

3. On June 30, 2014, Jarden Company concludes that a customer's $4,750 receivable (created in 2013) is uncollectible and that the account should be written off. What effect will this action have on Jarden's 2014 net income? Explain.

Problem 7-5A

Analyzing and journalizing notes
receivable transactions

C2 C3 P3

The following selected transactions are from Ohlmeyer Company.

2012

Dec. 16 Accepted a $10,800, 60-day, 8% note dated this day in granting Danny Todd a time extension
on his past-due account receivable.

31 Made an adjusting entry to record the accrued interest on the Todd note.

2013

Feb. 14 Received Todd's payment of principal and interest on the note dated December 16.

Mar. 2 Accepted an $6,100, 8%, 90-day note dated this day in granting a time extension on the past-
due account receivable from Midnight Co.

17 Accepted a $2,400, 30-day, 7% note dated this day in granting Ava Privet a time extension on
her past-due account receivable.

Apr. 16 Privet dishonored her note when presented for payment.

June 2 Midnight Co. refuses to pay the note that was due to Ohlmeyer Co. on May 31. Prepare the journal
entry to charge the dishonored note plus accrued interest to Midnight Co.'s accounts receivable.

July 17 Received payment from Midnight Co. for the maturity value of its dishonored note plus interest
for 46 days beyond maturity at 8%.

Aug. 7 Accepted an $7,450, 90-day, 10% note dated this day in granting a time extension on the past-
due account receivable of Mulan Co.

Sept. 3 Accepted a $2,100, 60-day, 10% note dated this day in granting Noah Carson a time extension
on his past-due account receivable.

Nov. 2 Received payment of principal plus interest from Carson for the September 3 note.

Nov. 5 Received payment of principal plus interest from Mulan for the August 7 note.

Dec. 1 Wrote off the Privet account against Allowance for Doubtful Accounts.

Required

1. Prepare journal entries to record these transactions and events. (Round amounts to the nearest dollar.)

Analysis Component

2. What reporting is necessary when a business pledges receivables as security for a loan and the loan is
still outstanding at the end of the period? Explain the reason for this requirement and the accounting
principle being satisfied.

PROBLEM SET B

Problem 7-1B

Sales on account and credit
card sales

C1

Archer Co. allows select customers to make purchases on credit. Its other customers can use either of two
credit cards: Commerce Bank or Aztec. Commerce Bank deducts a 3% service charge for sales on its
credit card and immediately credits the bank account of Archer when credit card receipts are deposited.
Archer deposits the Commerce Bank credit card receipts each business day. When customers use the
Aztec card, Archer accumulates the receipts for several days and then submits them to Aztec for payment.
Aztec deducts a 2% service charge and usually pays within one week of being billed. Archer completed
the following transactions in August (terms of all credit sales are 2/10, n/30; and all sales are recorded at
the gross price).

Aug. 4 Sold $3,700 of merchandise (that had cost $2,000) on credit to McKenzie Carpenter.

10 Sold $5,200 of merchandise (that had cost $2,800) to customers who used their Commerce
Bank credit cards.

11 Sold $1,250 of merchandise (that had cost $900) to customers who used their Aztec cards.

14 Received Carpenter's check in full payment for the purchase of August 4.

15 Sold $3,240 of merchandise (that had cost $1,758) to customers who used their Aztec cards.

18 Submitted Aztec card receipts accumulated since August 11 to the credit card company for
payment.

22 Wrote off the account of Craw Co. against the Allowance for Doubtful Accounts. The $498
balance in Craw Co.'s account stemmed from a credit sale in November of last year.

25 Received the amount due from Aztec.

Required

Prepare journal entries to record the preceding transactions and events. (The company uses the perpetual
inventory system. Round amounts to the nearest dollar.)

Sherman Co. began operations on January 1, 2012, and completed several transactions during 2012 and 2013 that involved sales on credit, accounts receivable collections, and bad debts. These transactions are summarized as follows.

2012

a. Sold $685,350 of merchandise (that had cost $500,000) on credit, terms n/30.

b. Received $482,300 cash in payment of accounts receivable.

c. Wrote off $9,350 of uncollectible accounts receivable.

d. In adjusting the accounts on December 31, the company estimated that 1% of accounts receivable will be uncollectible.

2013

e. Sold $870,220 of merchandise (that had cost $650,000) on credit, terms n/30.

f. Received $990,800 cash in payment of accounts receivable.

g. Wrote off $11,090 of uncollectible accounts receivable.

h. In adjusting the accounts on December 31, the company estimated that 1% of accounts receivable will be uncollectible.

Required

Prepare journal entries to record Sherman's 2012 and 2013 summarized transactions and its year-end adjusting entry to record bad debts expense. (The company uses the perpetual inventory system and it applies the allowance method for its accounts receivable. Round amounts to the nearest dollar.)

Problem 7-2B
Accounts receivable transactions and bad debts adjustments
C1 P2

Check *(d)* Dr. Bad Debts Expense
$11,287

(h) Dr. Bad Debts Expense
$9,773

At December 31, 2013, Ingleton Company reports the following results for the year:

Cash sales	$1,025,000
Credit sales	1,342,000

In addition, its unadjusted trial balance includes the following items:

Accounts receivable	$575,000 debit
Allowance for doubtful accounts	7,500 credit

Required

1. Prepare the adjusting entry for Ingleton Co. to recognize bad debts under each of the following independent assumptions.

   a. Bad debts are estimated to be 2.5% of credit sales.

   b. Bad debts are estimated to be 1.5% of total sales.

   c. An aging analysis estimates that 6% of year-end accounts receivable are uncollectible.

2. Show how Accounts Receivable and the Allowance for Doubtful Accounts appear on its December 31, 2013, balance sheet given the facts in part 1*a*.

3. Show how Accounts Receivable and the Allowance for Doubtful Accounts appear on its December 31, 2013, balance sheet given the facts in part 1*c*.

Problem 7-3B
Estimating and reporting bad debts

P2

Check Bad debts expense:
(1*b*) $35,505, (1*c*) $27,000

Hovak Company has credit sales of $4.5 million for year 2013. At December 31, 2013, the company's Allowance for Doubtful Accounts has an unadjusted debit balance of $3,400. Hovak prepares a schedule of its December 31, 2013, accounts receivable by age. On the basis of past experience, it estimates the percent of receivables in each age category that will become uncollectible. This information is summarized here.

Problem 7-4B
Aging accounts receivable and accounting for bad debts

P2

December 31, 2013 Accounts Receivable	Age of Accounts Receivable	Expected Percent Uncollectible
$396,400	Not yet due	2.0%
277,800	1 to 30 days past due	4.0
48,000	31 to 60 days past due	8.5
6,600	61 to 90 days past due	39.0
2,800	Over 90 days past due	82.0

Required

1. Compute the required balance of the Allowance for Doubtful Accounts at December 31, 2013, using the aging of accounts receivable method.

2. Prepare the adjusting entry to record bad debts expense at December 31, 2013.

Analysis Component

3. On July 31, 2014, Hovak concludes that a customer's $3,455 receivable (created in 2013) is uncollectible and that the account should be written off. What effect will this action have on Hovak's 2014 net income? Explain.

Problem 7-5B

Analyzing and journalizing notes receivable transactions

C2 C3 P3

The following selected transactions are from Springer Company.

2012

Nov. 1   Accepted a $4,800, 90-day, 8% note dated this day in granting Steve Julian a time extension on his past-due account receivable.

Dec. 31   Made an adjusting entry to record the accrued interest on the Julian note.

2013

Jan. 30   Received Julian's payment for principal and interest on the note dated November 1.

Feb. 28   Accepted a $12,600, 8%, 30-day note dated this day in granting a time extension on the past-due account receivable from King Co.

Mar. 1   Accepted a $6,200, 60-day, 12% note dated this day in granting Myron Shelley a time extension on his past-due account receivable.

      30   The King Co. dishonored its note when presented for payment.

April 30   Received payment of principal plus interest from M. Shelley for the March 1 note.

June 15   Accepted a $2,000, 72-day, 8% note dated this day in granting a time extension on the past-due account receivable of Ryder Solon.

      21   Accepted a $9,500, 90-day, 8% note dated this day in granting J. Felton a time extension on his past-due account receivable.

Aug. 26   Received payment of principal plus interest from R. Solon for the note of June 15.

Sep. 19   Received payment of principal plus interest from J. Felton for the June 21 note.

Nov. 30   Wrote off King's account against Allowance for Doubtful Accounts.

Required

1. Prepare journal entries to record these transactions and events. (Round amounts to the nearest dollar.)

Analysis Component

2. What reporting is necessary when a business pledges receivables as security for a loan and the loan is still outstanding at the end of the period? Explain the reason for this requirement and the accounting principle being satisfied.

SERIAL PROBLEM

Success Systems

P1 P2

(This serial problem began in Chapter 1 and continues through most of the book. If previous chapter segments were not completed, the serial problem can begin at this point. It is helpful, but not necessary, to use the Working Papers that accompany the book.)

SP 7   Adria Lopez, owner of Success Systems, realizes that she needs to begin accounting for bad debts expense. Assume that Success Systems has total revenues of $43,853 during the first three months of 2014, and that the Accounts Receivable balance on March 31, 2014, is $22,720.

Required

1. Prepare the adjusting entry needed for Success Systems to recognize bad debts expense on March 31, 2014, under each of the following independent assumptions (assume a zero unadjusted balance in the Allowance for Doubtful Accounts at March 31).

   a. Bad debts are estimated to be 1% of total revenues. (Round amounts to the dollar.)

   b. Bad debts are estimated to be 2% of accounts receivable. (Round amounts to the dollar.)

2. Assume that Success Systems' Accounts Receivable balance at June 30, 2014, is $20,250 and that one account of $100 has been written off against the Allowance for Doubtful Accounts since March 31,

2014. If Adria Lopez uses the method prescribed in Part 1*b*, what adjusting journal entry must be made to recognize bad debts expense on June 30, 2014?

3. Should Adria Lopez consider adopting the direct write-off method of accounting for bad debts expense rather than one of the allowance methods considered in part 1? Explain.

The following General Ledger assignment focuses on transactions related to accounts and notes receivable and highlights the impact each transaction has on interest revenue, if any.

GL 7-1 (This assignment is adapted from Problem 7-5.) Prepare the journal entries related to the accounts and notes receivable; the schedule of accounts receivable and the schedule of notes receivable are automatically completed from the journal entries using the **General Ledger** tool. Next, compute both the amount and timing of interest revenue for each note receivable.

GENERAL LEDGER PROBLEM

Available in Connect Only

connect
|ACCOUNTING

Beyond the Numbers

BTN 7-1   Refer to Apple's financial statements in Appendix A to answer the following.

1. What is the amount of Apple's accounts receivable as of September 29, 2012?

2. Compute Apple's accounts receivable turnover as of September 29, 2012.

3. How long does it take, *on average,* for the company to collect receivables?

4. Apple's most liquid assets include (*a*) cash and cash equivalents, (*b*) short-term marketable securities, (*c*) receivables, and (*d*) inventory. Compute the percentage that these liquid assets make up of current liabilities as of September 29, 2012. Do the same computations for September 24, 2011. Comment on the company's ability to satisfy its current liabilities as of its fiscal 2012 year-end compared to its fiscal 2011 year-end.

5. What criteria did Apple use to classify items as cash equivalents? (*Hint:* Refer to Apple's footnotes describing cash equivalent in Appendix A.)

REPORTING IN ACTION

A1

APPLE

Fast Forward

6. Access Apple's financial statements for fiscal years after September 29, 2012, at its Website (www.Apple.com) or the SEC's EDGAR database (www.sec.gov). Recompute parts 2 and 4 and comment on any changes since September 29, 2012.

BTN 7-2   Comparative figures for Apple and Google follow.

COMPARATIVE ANALYSIS

A1 P2

APPLE

GOOGLE

($ millions)	Apple			Google		
	Current Year	One Year Prior	Two Years Prior	Current Year	One Year Prior	Two Years Prior
Accounts receivable, net	$ 10,930	$ 5,369	$ 5,510	$ 7,885	$ 5,427	$ 4,252
Net sales	156,508	108,249	65,225	50,175	37,905	29,321

Required

1. Compute the accounts receivable turnover for Apple and Google for each of the two most recent years using the data shown.

2. Using results from part 1, compute how many days it takes each company, *on average,* to collect receivables. Compare the collection periods for Apple and Google, and suggest at least one explanation for the difference.

3. Which company is more efficient in collecting its accounts receivable? Explain.

Hint: Average collection period equals 365 divided by the accounts receivable turnover.

ETHICS CHALLENGE

P2

BTN 7-3 Anton Blair is the manager of a medium-size company. A few years ago, Blair persuaded the owner to base a part of his compensation on the net income the company earns each year. Each December he estimates year-end financial figures in anticipation of the bonus he will receive. If the bonus is not as high as he would like, he offers several recommendations to the accountant for year-end adjustments. One of his favorite recommendations is for the controller to reduce the estimate of doubtful accounts.

Required

1. What effect does lowering the estimate for doubtful accounts have on the income statement and balance sheet?
2. Do you believe Blair's recommendation to adjust the allowance for doubtful accounts is within his right as manager, or do you believe this action is an ethics violation? Justify your response.
3. What type of internal control(s) might be useful for this company in overseeing the manager's recommendations for accounting changes?

COMMUNICATING IN PRACTICE

P2

BTN 7-4 As the accountant for Pure-Air Distributing, you attend a sales managers' meeting devoted to a discussion of credit policies. At the meeting, you report that bad debts expense is estimated to be $59,000 and accounts receivable at year-end amount to $1,750,000 less a $43,000 allowance for doubtful accounts. Sid Omar, a sales manager, expresses confusion over why bad debts expense and the allowance for doubtful accounts are different amounts. Write a one-page memorandum to him explaining why a difference in bad debts expense and the allowance for doubtful accounts is not unusual. The company estimates bad debts expense as 2% of sales.

TAKING IT TO THE NET

C1

BTN 7-5 Access eBay's, January 31, 2012, filing of its 10-K report for the year ended December 31, 2011, at www.SEC.gov.

Required

1. What is the amount of eBay's net accounts receivable at December 31, 2011, and at December 31, 2010?
2. "Financial Statement Schedule II" to its financial statements lists eBay's allowance for doubtful accounts (including authorized credits). For the two years ended December 31, 2011 and 2010, compute its allowance for doubtful accounts (including authorized credits) as a percent of gross accounts receivable.
3. Do you believe that these percentages are reasonable based on what you know about eBay? Explain.

TEAMWORK IN ACTION

P2

BTN 7-6 Each member of a team is to participate in estimating uncollectibles using the aging schedule and percents shown in Problem 7-4A. The division of labor is up to the team. Your goal is to accurately complete this task as soon as possible. After estimating uncollectibles, check your estimate with the instructor. If the estimate is correct, the team then should prepare the adjusting entry and the presentation of accounts receivable (net) for the December 31, 2013, balance sheet.

ENTREPRENEURIAL DECISION

C1

BTN 7-7 Kevin Plank of Under Armour is introduced in the chapter's opening feature. Kevin currently sells his products through multiple outlets. Assume that he is considering two new selling options.

Plan A. Under Armour would begin selling additional products online directly to customers, which are only currently sold directly to stores. These new online customers would use their credit cards. It currently has the capability of selling through its Website with no additional investment in hardware or software. Credit sales are expected to increase by $250,000 per year. Costs associated with this plan are: cost of these sales will be $135,500, credit card fees will be 4.75% of sales, and additional recordkeeping and shipping costs will be 6% of sales. These online sales will reduce the sales to stores by $35,000 because some customers will now purchase items online. Sales to stores have a 25% gross margin percentage.

Plan B. Under Armour would expand its market to more stores. It would make additional credit sales of $500,000 to those stores. Costs associated with those sales are: cost of sales will be $375,000, additional recordkeeping and shipping will be 4% of sales, and uncollectible accounts will be 6.2% of sales.

Required

1. Compute the additional annual net income or loss expected under (a) Plan A and (b) Plan B.
2. Should Under Armour pursue either plan? Discuss both the financial and nonfinancial factors relevant to this decision.

Check (1*b*) Additional net income, $74,000

BTN 7-8 Many commercials include comments similar to the following: "We accept **VISA**" or "We do not accept **American Express**." Conduct your own research by contacting at least five companies via interviews, phone calls, or the Internet to determine the reason(s) companies discriminate in their use of credit cards. Collect information on the fees charged by the different cards for the companies contacted. (The instructor can assign this as a team activity.)

HITTING THE ROAD

C1

BTN 7-9 Key information from Samsung (www.Samsung.com), which is a leading manufacturer of consumer electronic products, follows.

GLOBAL DECISION

C1 P2

Samsung
APPLE
GOOGLE

₩ in millions	Current Year	Prior Year
Accounts receivable, net*	₩ 26,674,596	₩ 24,153,028
Sales	201,103,613	165,001,771

*Samsung refers to it as "Trade and other receivables."

1. Compute the accounts receivable turnover for the current year.
2. How long does it take on average for Samsung to collect receivables?
3. Refer to BTN 7-2. How does Samsung compare to Apple and Google in terms of its accounts receivable turnover and its collection period?

ANSWERS TO MULTIPLE CHOICE QUIZ

1. d; Desired balance in Allowance for Doubtful Accounts = $ 5,026 cr.
   ($125,650 × 0.04)
   Current balance in Allowance for Doubtful Accounts = _____(328)_ cr.
   Bad Debts Expense to be recorded = $ 4,698

2. a; Desired balance in Allowance for Doubtful Accounts = $29,358 cr.
   ($489,300 × 0.06)
   Current balance in Allowance for Doubtful Accounts = _____554_ dr.
   Bad Debts Expense to be recorded = $29,912

3. a; $7,500 × 0.05 × 90/360 = $93.75

4. c; Principal amount $9,000
   Interest accrued . . . . ___120_ ($9,000 × 0.08 × 60/360)
   Maturity value $9,120

5. d; $489,600/$40,800 = 12

8

Reporting and Analyzing Long-Term Assets

PLANT ASSETS	NATURAL RESOURCES	INTANGIBLE ASSETS
C1 Cost determination	P3 Cost determination	P4 Cost determination
P1 Depreciation	Depletion	Amortization
C2 Partial-years and changes in estimates	Presentation	Types of intangibles
C3 Additional expenditures	Plant assets tied into extracting resources	A1 Analyze asset usage
P2 Disposal		

Learning Objectives

C1 Explain the cost principle for computing the cost of plant assets. (p. 347)

P1 Compute and record depreciation using the straight-line, units-of-production, and declining-balance methods. (p. 349)

C2 Explain depreciation for partial years and changes in estimates. (p. 354)

C3 Distinguish between revenue and capital expenditures, and account for them. (p. 356)

P2 Account for asset disposal through discarding or selling an asset. (p. 358)

P3 Account for natural resource assets and their depletion. (p. 361)

P4 Account for intangible assets. (p. 362)

A1 Compute total asset turnover and apply it to analyze a company's use of assets. (p. 367)

P5 *Appendix 8A*—Account for asset exchanges. (p. 370)

Hot Diggety Dog!

"World's best hot dog"

—**RUDY GIULIANI,** FORMER NEW YORK CITY MAYOR

NEW YORK—Legend has it that on July 4, 1916, four European immigrants held an impromptu hot dog eating contest to settle an argument about who was the most patriotic American. The winner, Irish immigrant James Mullen, ate 13 Nathan's hot dogs with buns in 12 minutes. That contest launched an annual tradition that survives yet today. By 1939, the hot dogs had achieved such success that President Franklin Delano Roosevelt had Nathan's Famous hot dogs sent to Yalta when he met with Winston Churchill and Joseph Stalin. Jump ahead to fiscal 2013, **Nathan's Famous, Inc. (NathansFamous. com)** sells more than 435 million of its world-renowned beef hot dogs around the globe!

From modest beginnings, Nathan's has prospered. Its long-term asset purchases for items such as machinery, equipment, buildings, leasehold improvements, furniture, and fixtures are expensive. Yet, employing an old recipe for success, its total sales from those long-term assets has increased nearly 25% over the past two years. This growth has been achieved with a relatively steady level of investment in a strategic mix of long-term assets as shown below.

Nathan's Famous, Inc.
(NASDAQ: NATH)

Joey Chestnut ate 69 in 10 min. 600,000 hot dogs donated

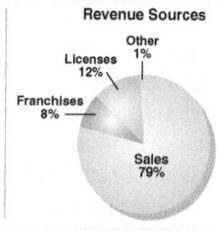

Revenue Sources
- Other 1%
- Licenses 12%
- Franchises 8%
- Sales 79%

($ millions)	2011	2012	2013
Total sales	$57.3	$66.2	$71.5
Long-term assets	8.5	9.0	8.7
Mach, equip, furn & fixtures . .	5.1	5.6	5.5
Leasehold improvements . . .	3.9	4.0	3.9
Buildings & improvements . .	2.2	2.2	2.0
Intangibles & goodwill.	1.4	1.4	1.4

Nathan's efficiency in using its assets, referred to as asset turnover, has been rewarded in the stock market as its stock price has experienced a fairly steady upward climb over the past three years.

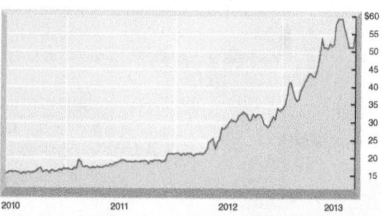

Nathan's Famous is currently on a roll—its products are distributed in 50 states and 6 foreign countries, its restaurant system consists of 263 franchises and 5 company-owned units, and its hot dogs are sold in over 40,000 locations worldwide and in over 500 cinemas nationwide. The challenge for Nathan's will be to maintain the right kind and amount of assets to meet business demands *and* be profitable and growing.

Specifically, management at Nathan's "believes that available cash, marketable securities and cash generated from operations should provide sufficient capital to finance operations." Management also understands that its success depends on continued monitoring and control of the types and costs of its long-term assets. Each of its tangible and intangible assets commands management attention, and the focus is on recovering their costs and returning a profit.

The founder, Nathan Handwerker, who's secret recipe for making hot dogs was developed by his wife Ida, would be proud of his company's continued commitment to excellence. People called him "Mr. Coney Island," and the title still applies today.

Sources: *Nathan's Famous Website,* January 2014; *Nathan's Famous 10-K,* 2013

Section 1—Plant Assets

Plant assets are tangible assets used in a company's operations that have a useful life of more than one accounting period. Plant assets are also called *plant and equipment; property, plant, and equipment;* or *fixed assets.* For many companies, plant assets make up the single largest class of assets they own. Exhibit 8.1 shows plant assets as a percent of total assets for several companies. Not only do they make up a large percent of many companies' assets, but their dollar values are large. **McDonald's** plant assets, for instance, are reported at more than $22 billion, and **Walmart** reports plant assets of more than $107 billion.

EXHIBIT 8.1

Plant Assets of Selected Companies

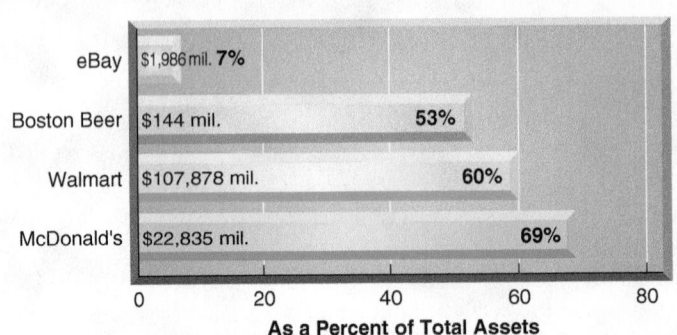

Plant assets are set apart from other assets by two important features. First, *plant assets are used in operations.* This makes them different from, for instance, inventory that is held for sale and not used in operations. The distinctive feature here is use, not type of asset. A company that purchases a computer to resell it reports it on the balance sheet as inventory. If the same company purchases this computer to use in operations, however, it is a plant asset. Another example is land held for future expansion, which is reported as a long-term investment. However, if this land holds a factory used in operations, the land is part of plant assets. Another example is equipment held for use in the event of a breakdown or for peak periods of production, which is reported in plant assets. If this same equipment is removed from use and held for sale, however, it is not reported in plant assets.

The second important feature is that *plant assets have useful lives extending over more than one accounting period.* This makes plant assets different from current assets such as supplies that are normally consumed in a short time period after they are placed in use.

The accounting for plant assets reflects these two features. Since plant assets are used in operations, we try to match their costs against the revenues they generate. Also, since their useful lives extend over more than one period, our matching of costs and revenues must extend over several periods. Specifically, we value plant assets (balance sheet effect) and then, for many of them, we allocate their costs to periods benefiting from their use (income statement effect). An important exception is land; land cost is not allocated to expense when we expect it to have an indefinite life.

Exhibit 8.2 shows four main issues in accounting for plant assets: (1) computing the costs of plant assets, (2) allocating the costs of most plant assets (less any salvage amounts) against

Point: The phrase *capital-intensive* refers to companies with large amounts invested in plant assets. Exhibit 8.1 reveals that McDonalds is more capital-intensive than eBay.

Point: It can help to view plant assets as prepaid expenses that benefit several future accounting periods.

EXHIBIT 8.2

Issues in Accounting for Plant Assets

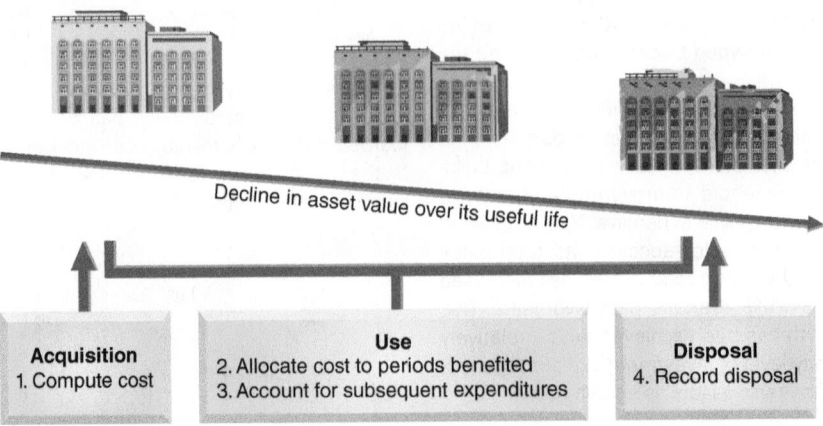

revenues for the periods they benefit, (3) accounting for expenditures such as repairs and improvements to plant assets, and (4) recording the disposal of plant assets. The following sections discuss these issues.

COST DETERMINATION

Plant assets are recorded at cost when acquired. This is consistent with the *cost principle*. **Cost** includes all normal and reasonable expenditures necessary to get the asset in place and ready for its intended use. The cost of a factory machine, for instance, includes its invoice cost less any cash discount for early payment, plus any necessary freight, unpacking, assembling, installing, and testing costs. Examples are the costs of building a base or foundation for a machine, providing electrical hookups, and testing the asset before using it in operations.

> **C1** Explain the cost principle for computing the cost of plant assets.

   To be recorded as part of the cost of a plant asset, an expenditure must be normal, reasonable, and necessary in preparing it for its intended use. If an asset is damaged during unpacking, the repairs are not added to its cost. Instead, they are charged to an expense account. Nor is a paid traffic fine for moving heavy machinery on city streets without a proper permit part of the machinery's cost; but payment for a proper permit is included in the cost of machinery. Charges are sometimes incurred to modify or customize a new plant asset. These charges are added to the asset's cost. We explain in this section how to determine the cost of plant assets for each of its four major classes.

Machinery and Equipment

The costs of machinery and equipment consist of all costs normal and necessary to purchase them and prepare them for their intended use. These include the purchase price, taxes, transportation charges, insurance while in transit, and the installing, assembling, and testing of the machinery and equipment.

Buildings

A Building account is charged for the costs of purchasing or constructing a building that is used in operations. When purchased, a building's costs usually include its purchase price, brokerage

fees, taxes, title fees, and attorney fees. Its costs also include all expenditures to ready it for its intended use, including any necessary repairs or renovations such as wiring, lighting, flooring, and wall coverings. When a company constructs a building or any plant asset for its own use, its costs include materials and labor plus a reasonable amount of indirect overhead cost. Overhead includes the costs of items such as heat, lighting, power, and depreciation on machinery used to construct the asset. Costs of construction also include design fees, building permits, and insurance during construction. However, costs such as insurance to cover the asset *after* it is placed in use are operating expenses.

Land Improvements

Land improvements are additions to land and have limited useful lives. Examples are parking lot surfaces, driveways, walkways, fences, landscaping, and sprinkling and lighting systems. Costs of land improvements include expenditures necessary to make those improvements ready for their intended use. While the costs of these improvements increase the usefulness of the land, they are charged to a separate Land Improvement account so that their costs can be allocated to the periods they benefit.

Land

Land is the earth's surface and has an indefinite (unlimited) life. Costs of land include expenditures necessary to make that property ready for its intended use. When land is purchased for a building site, its cost includes the total amount paid for the land, including any real estate commissions, title insurance fees, legal fees, and any accrued property taxes paid by the purchaser. Payments for surveying, clearing, grading, and draining also are included in the cost of land. Other costs include government assessments, whether incurred at the time of purchase or later, for items such as public roadways, sewers, and sidewalks. These assessments are included because they permanently add to the land's value. Land purchased as a building site sometimes includes structures that must be removed. In such cases, the total purchase price is charged to the Land account as is the cost of removing the structures, less any amounts recovered through sale of salvaged materials. To illustrate, assume that Starbucks paid $167,000 cash to acquire land for a retail store. This land had an old service garage that was removed at a net cost of $13,000 ($15,000 in costs less $2,000 proceeds from salvaged materials). Additional closing costs total $10,000, consisting of brokerage fees ($8,000), legal fees ($1,500), and title costs ($500). The cost of this land to Starbucks is $190,000 and is computed as shown in Exhibit 8.3.

EXHIBIT 8.3

Computing Cost of Land

Cash price of land	$ 167,000
Net cost of garage removal	13,000
Closing costs	10,000
Cost of land	$190,000

Lump-Sum Purchase

Example: If appraised values in Exhibit 8.4 are building, $84,000; land improvements, $12,000; and land, $24,000, what cost is assigned to the building? *Answer:*
(1) $84,000 + $12,000 + $24,000 = $120,000 (total appraisal)
(2) $84,000/$120,000 = 70% (building's percent of total)
(3) 70% × $90,000 = $63,000 (building's apportioned cost)

Plant assets sometimes are purchased as a group in a single transaction for a lump-sum price. This transaction is called a *lump-sum purchase,* or *group, bulk,* or *basket purchase.* When this occurs, we allocate the cost of the purchase among the different types of assets acquired based on their *relative market values,* which can be estimated by appraisal or by using the tax-assessed valuations of the assets. To illustrate, assume CarMax paid $90,000 cash to acquire a group of items consisting of a building appraised at $60,000, land improvements appraised at $10,000, and land appraised at $30,000. The $90,000 cost is allocated on the basis of these appraised values as shown in Exhibit 8.4.

EXHIBIT 8.4

Computing Costs in a Lump-Sum Purchase

	Appraised Value	Percent of Total	Apportioned Cost
Building	$ 60,000	60% ($60,000/$100,000)	$54,000 ($90,000 × 60%)
Land improvements	10,000	10 ($10,000/$100,000)	9,000 ($90,000 × 10%)
Land	30,000	30 ($30,000/$100,000)	27,000 ($90,000 × 30%)
Totals	$100,000	100%	$ 90,000

NEED-TO-KNOW 8.1

C1

Do More: QS 8-1, QS 8-2, E 8-1, E 8-2, E 8-3

QC1

Compute the amount recorded as the cost of a new machine given the following payments related to its purchase: gross purchase price, $700,000; sales tax, $49,000; purchase discount taken, $21,000; freight cost—terms FOB shipping point, $3,500; normal assembly costs, $3,000; cost of necessary machine platform, $2,500; cost of parts used in maintaining machine, $4,200.

Solution

$737,000 = $700,000 + $49,000 − $21,000 + $3,500 + $3,000 + $2,500

DEPRECIATION

Point: Depreciation is cost allocation, not asset valuation.

Depreciation is the process of allocating the cost of a plant asset to expense in the accounting periods benefiting from its use. Depreciation does not measure the decline in the asset's market value each period, nor does it measure the asset's physical deterioration. Since depreciation reflects the cost of using a plant asset, depreciation charges are only recorded when the asset is actually in service. This section describes the factors we must consider in computing depreciation, the depreciation methods used, revisions in depreciation, and depreciation for partial periods.

Factors in Computing Depreciation

Factors that determine depreciation are (1) cost, (2) salvage value, and (3) useful life.

Cost   The **cost** of a plant asset consists of all necessary and reasonable expenditures to acquire it and to prepare it for its intended use.

Salvage Value   The total amount of depreciation to be charged off over an asset's benefit period equals the asset's cost minus its salvage value. **Salvage value,** also called *residual value* or *scrap value,* is an estimate of the asset's value at the end of its benefit period. This is the amount the owner expects to receive from disposing of the asset at the end of its benefit period. If the asset is expected to be traded in on a new asset, its salvage value is the expected trade-in value.

Point: If we expect additional costs in preparing a plant asset for disposal, the salvage value equals the expected amount from disposal less any disposal costs.

Useful Life   The **useful life** of a plant asset is the length of time it is productively used in a company's operations. Useful life, also called *service life,* might not be as long as the asset's total productive life. For example, the productive life of a computer can be eight years or more. Some companies, however, trade in old computers for new ones every two years. In this case, these computers have a two-year useful life, meaning the cost of these computers (less their expected trade-in values) is charged to depreciation expense over a two-year period.

Point: Useful life and salvage value are estimates. Estimates require judgment based on all available information.

Several variables often make the useful life of a plant asset difficult to predict. A major variable is the wear and tear from use in operations. Two other variables, inadequacy and obsolescence, also require consideration. **Inadequacy** refers to the insufficient capacity of a company's plant assets to meet its growing productive demands. **Obsolescence** refers to the condition of a plant asset that is no longer useful in producing goods or services with a competitive advantage because of new inventions and improvements. Both inadequacy and obsolescence are difficult to predict because of demand changes, new inventions, and improvements. A company usually disposes of an inadequate or obsolete asset before it wears out.

A company is often able to better predict a new asset's useful life when it has past experience with a similar asset. When it has no such experience, a company relies on the experience of others or on engineering studies and judgment. In note 1 of its annual report, Tootsie Roll, a snack food manufacturer, reports the following useful lives:

Point: Land is recorded at cost but not depreciated because it normally retains its value over time.

Buildings	20–35 years
Machinery and Equipment	5–20 years

Decision Insight

Life Line   Life expectancy of plant assets is often in the eye of the beholder. For instance, Hershey Foods and Tootsie Roll are competitors and apply similar manufacturing processes, yet their equipment's life expectancies are different. Hershey depreciates equipment over 3 to 15 years, but Tootsie Roll depreciates them over 5 to 20 years. Such differences markedly impact financial statements. ■

Depreciation Methods

Depreciation methods are used to allocate a plant asset's cost over the accounting periods in its useful life. The most frequently used method of depreciation is the straight-line method. Another common depreciation method is the units-of-production method. We explain both of these methods in this section. This section also describes accelerated depreciation methods, with a focus on the declining-balance method.

P1   Compute and record depreciation using the straight-line, units-of-production, and declining-balance methods.

The computations in this section use information about a machine that inspects athletic shoes before packaging. Manufacturers such as Converse, Reebok, adidas, and Fila use this machine. Data for this machine are in Exhibit 8.5.

EXHIBIT 8.5

Data for Athletic Shoe-Inspecting Machine

Cost	$10,000
Salvage value	1,000
Depreciable cost	$ 9,000
Useful life	
Accounting periods	5 years
Units inspected	36,000 shoes

Straight-Line Method **Straight-line depreciation** charges the same amount of expense to each period of the asset's useful life. A two-step process is used. We first compute the *depreciable cost* of the asset, also called the *cost to be depreciated.* It is computed by subtracting the asset's salvage value from its total cost. Second, depreciable cost is divided by the number of accounting periods in the asset's useful life. The formula for straight-line depreciation, along with its computation for the inspection machine just described, is shown in Exhibit 8.6.

EXHIBIT 8.6

Straight-Line Depreciation Formula and Example

$$\frac{\textbf{Cost} - \textbf{Salvage value}}{\textbf{Useful life in periods}} = \frac{\$10,000 - \$1,000}{5 \text{ years}} = \$1,800 \text{ per year}$$

If this machine is purchased on December 31, 2012, and used throughout its predicted useful life of five years, the straight-line method allocates an equal amount of depreciation to each of the years 2013 through 2017. We make the following adjusting entry at the end of each of the five years to record straight-line depreciation of this machine.

Assets = Liabilities + Equity
−1,800   −1,800

Dec. 31	Depreciation Expense	1,800	
	Accumulated Depreciation—Machinery		1,800
	To record annual depreciation.		

Example: If the salvage value of the machine is $2,500, what is the annual depreciation? *Answer:* ($10,000 − $2,500)/5 years = $1,500

The $1,800 Depreciation Expense is reported on the income statement among operating expenses. The $1,800 Accumulated Depreciation is a contra asset account to the Machinery account in the balance sheet. The graph on the left in Exhibit 8.7 shows the $1,800 per year expenses reported in each of the five years. The graph on the right shows the amounts reported on each of the six December 31 balance sheets.

EXHIBIT 8.7

Financial Statement Effects of Straight-Line Depreciation

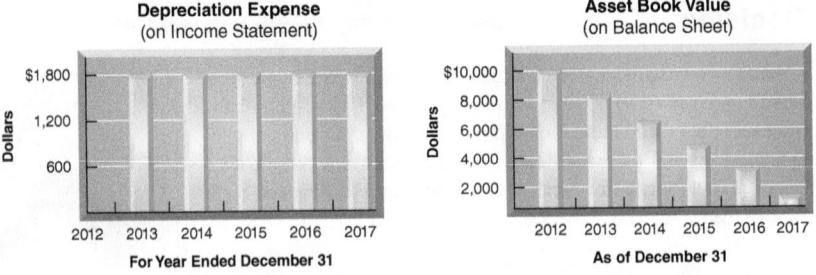

The net balance sheet amount is the **asset book value,** or simply *book value,* and is computed

Book value = Cost − Accumulated depreciation

as the asset's total cost less its accumulated depreciation. For example, at the end of year 2 (December 31, 2014), its book value is $6,400 and is reported in the balance sheet as follows:

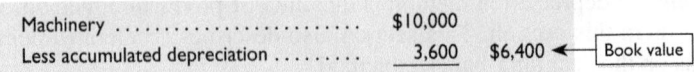

Machinery	$10,000	
Less accumulated depreciation	3,600	$6,400 ◀— Book value

The book value of this machine declines by $1,800 each year due to depreciation. The left-side graphic in Exhibit 8.7 reveals why this method is called straight-line.

We also can compute the *straight-line depreciation rate,* defined as 100% divided by the number of periods in the asset's useful life. For the inspection machine, this rate is 20% (100% ÷ 5 years, or 1/5 per period). We use this rate, along with other information, to compute the machine's *straight-line depreciation schedule* shown in Exhibit 8.8. Note three points in this exhibit. First, depreciation expense is the same each period. Second, accumulated depreciation is the sum of current and prior periods' depreciation expense. Third, book value declines each period until it equals salvage value at the end of the machine's useful life.

Point: Depreciation requires estimates for salvage value and useful life. Ethics are relevant when managers might be tempted to choose estimates to achieve desired results on financial statements.

| Annual Period | | Depreciation for the Period | | | End of Period | |
	Depreciable Cost*	Depreciation Rate	Depreciation Expense	Accumulated Depreciation	Book Value†
2012	—	—	—	—	$10,000
2013	$9,000	20%	$1,800	$1,800	8,200
2014	9,000	20	1,800	3,600	6,400
2015	9,000	20	1,800	5,400	4,600
2016	9,000	20	1,800	7,200	2,800
2017	9,000	20	1,800	9,000	1,000

Salvage value (not depreciated)

* $10,000 − $1,000.   † Book value is total cost minus accumulated depreciation.

EXHIBIT 8.8

Straight-Line Depreciation Schedule

Units-of-Production Method   The straight-line method charges an equal share of an asset's cost to each period. If plant assets are used up in about equal amounts each accounting period, this method produces a reasonable matching of expenses with revenues. However, the use of some plant assets varies greatly from one period to the next. A builder, for instance, might use a piece of construction equipment for a month and then not use it again for several months. When equipment use varies from period to period, the units-of-production depreciation method can better match expenses with revenues. **Units-of-production depreciation** charges a varying amount to expense for each period of an asset's useful life depending on its *usage.*

A two-step process is used to compute units-of-production depreciation. We first compute *depreciation per unit* by subtracting the asset's salvage value from its total cost and then dividing by the total number of units expected to be produced during its useful life. Units of production can be expressed in product or other units such as hours used or miles driven. The second step is to compute depreciation expense for the period by multiplying the units produced in the period by the depreciation per unit. The formula for units-of-production depreciation, along with its computation for the machine described in Exhibit 8.5, is shown in Exhibit 8.9. (7,000 shoes are inspected and sold in its first year.)

EXHIBIT 8.9

Units-of-Production Depreciation Formula and Example

Step 1

$$\text{Depreciation per unit} = \frac{\text{Cost} - \text{Salvage value}}{\text{Total units of production}} = \frac{\$10,000 - \$1,000}{36,000 \text{ shoes}} = \$0.25 \text{ per shoe}$$

Step 2

$$\text{Depreciation expense} = \text{Depreciation per unit} \times \text{Units produced in period}$$
$$\$0.25 \text{ per shoe} \times 7,000 \text{ shoes} = \$1,750$$

Using data on the number of shoes inspected by the machine, we can compute the *units-of-production depreciation schedule* shown in Exhibit 8.10. For example, depreciation for the first year is $1,750 (7,000 shoes at $0.25 per shoe). Depreciation for the second year is $2,000 (8,000 shoes at $0.25 per shoe). Other years are similarly computed. Exhibit 8.10 shows that (1) depreciation expense depends on unit output, (2) accumulated depreciation is the sum of current and prior periods' depreciation expense, and (3) book value declines each period until it

Example: Refer to Exhibit 8.10. If the number of shoes inspected in 2017 is 5,500, what is depreciation for 2017? *Answer:* $1,250 (never depreciate below salvage value)

equals salvage value at the end of the asset's useful life. Deltic Timber is one of many companies using the units-of-production depreciation method. It reports that depreciation "is calculated over the estimated useful lives of the assets by using the units of production method for machinery and equipment."

EXHIBIT 8.10

Units-of-Production
Depreciation Schedule

	Depreciation for the Period			End of Period	
Annual Period	Number of Units	Depreciation per Unit	Depreciation Expense	Accumulated Depreciation	Book Value
2012	—	—	—	—	$10,000
2013	7,000	$0.25	$1,750	$1,750	8,250
2014	8,000	0.25	2,000	3,750	6,250
2015	9,000	0.25	2,250	6,000	4,000
2016	7,000	0.25	1,750	7,750	2,250
2017	5,000	0.25	1,250	9,000	1,000

Salvage value
(not depreciated)

Declining-Balance Method   An **accelerated depreciation method** yields larger depreciation expenses in the early years of an asset's life and less depreciation in later years. The most common accelerated method is the **declining-balance method** of depreciation, which uses a depreciation rate that is a multiple of the straight-line rate and applies it to the asset's beginning-of-period book value. The amount of depreciation declines each period because book value declines each period.

A common depreciation rate for the declining-balance method is double the straight-line rate. This is called the *double-declining-balance (DDB)* method. This method is applied in three steps: (1) compute the asset's straight-line depreciation rate, (2) double the straight-line rate, and (3) compute depreciation expense by multiplying this rate by the asset's beginning-of-period book value. To illustrate, let's return to the machine in Exhibit 8.5 and apply the double-declining-balance method to compute depreciation expense. Exhibit 8.11 shows the first-year depreciation computation for the machine. The three-step process is to (1) divide 100% by five years to determine the straight-line rate of 20%, or 1/5, per year, (2) double this 20% rate to get the declining-balance rate of 40%, or 2/5, per year, and (3) compute depreciation expense as 40%, or 2/5, multiplied by the beginning-of-period book value.

Point: In the DDB method, *double* refers to the rate and *declining balance* refers to book value. The rate is applied to beginning book value each period.

EXHIBIT 8.11

Double-Declining-Balance
Depreciation Formula*

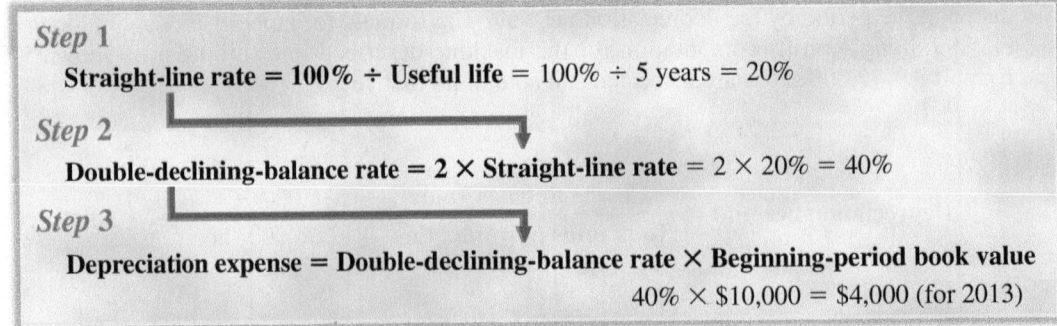

Step 1

Straight-line rate = 100% ÷ Useful life = 100% ÷ 5 years = 20%

Step 2

Double-declining-balance rate = 2 × Straight-line rate = 2 × 20% = 40%

Step 3

Depreciation expense = Double-declining-balance rate × Beginning-period book value
40% × $10,000 = $4,000 (for 2013)

* To simplify: DDB depreciation = (2 × Beginning-period book value)/Useful life.

The *double-declining-balance depreciation schedule* is shown in Exhibit 8.12. The schedule follows the formula except for year 2017, when depreciation expense is $296. This $296 is not equal to 40% × $1,296, or $518.40. If we had used the $518.40 for depreciation expense in 2017, the ending book value would equal $777.60, which is less than the $1,000 salvage value. Instead, the $296 is computed by subtracting the $1,000 salvage value from the $1,296 book value at the beginning of the fifth year (the year when DDB depreciation cuts into salvage value).

Example: What is the DDB depreciation expense in year 2016 if the salvage value is $2,000? *Answer:* $2,160 − $2,000 = $160

| Annual Period | Depreciation for the Period | | | End of Period | |
	Beginning of Period Book Value	Depreciation Rate	Depreciation Expense	Accumulated Depreciation	Book Value
2012	—	—	—	—	$10,000
2013	$10,000	40%	$4,000	$4,000	6,000
2014	6,000	40	2,400	6,400	3,600
2015	3,600	40	1,440	7,840	2,160
2016	2,160	40	864	8,704	1,296
2017	1,296	40	296*	9,000	1,000 ← Salvage value (not depreciated)

EXHIBIT 8.12

Double-Declining-Balance Depreciation Schedule

* Year 2017 depreciation is $1,296 − $1,000 = $296 (never depreciate book value below salvage value).

Comparing Depreciation Methods   Exhibit 8.13 shows depreciation expense for each year of the machine's useful life under each of the three depreciation methods. While depreciation expense per period differs for different methods, total depreciation expense of $9,000 is the same over the machine's useful life.

Period	Straight-Line	Units-of-Production	Double-Declining-Balance
2013	$1,800	$1,750	$4,000
2014	1,800	2,000	2,400
2015	1,800	2,250	1,440
2016	1,800	1,750	864
2017	1,800	1,250	296
Totals	$9,000	$9,000	$9,000

EXHIBIT 8.13

Depreciation Expense for the Different Methods

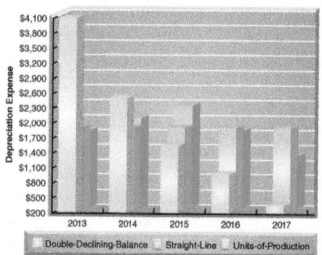

Each method starts with a total cost of $10,000 and ends with a salvage value of $1,000. The difference is the pattern in depreciation expense over the useful life. The book value of the asset when using straight-line is always greater than the book value from using double-declining-balance, except at the beginning and end of the asset's useful life, when it is the same. Also, the straight-line method yields a steady pattern of depreciation expense while the units-of-production depreciation depends on the number of units produced. Each of these methods is acceptable because it allocates cost in a systematic and rational manner.

Decision Insight

In Vogue   About 87% of companies use straight-line depreciation for plant assets, 4% use units-of-production, and 4% use declining-balance. Another 5% use an un-specified accelerated method—most likely declining-balance. ■

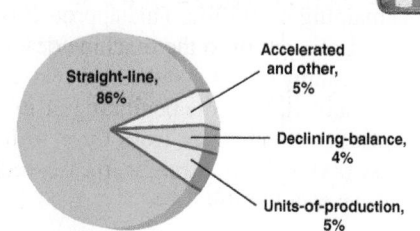

Depreciation for Tax Reporting   The records a company keeps for financial accounting purposes are usually separate from the records it keeps for tax accounting purposes. This is so because financial accounting aims to report useful information on financial performance and position, whereas tax accounting reflects government objectives in raising revenues. Differences between these two accounting systems are normal and expected. Depreciation is a common example of how the records differ. For example, many companies use accelerated depreciation in computing taxable income. Reporting higher depreciation expense in the early years of an asset's life reduces the company's taxable income in those years and increases it in later years, when the depreciation expense is lower. The company's goal here is to *postpone* its tax payments.

Point: Understanding depreciation for financial accounting will help in learning MACRS for tax accounting. Rules for MACRS are available from www.IRS.gov.

The U.S. federal income tax law has rules for depreciating assets. These rules include the **Modified Accelerated Cost Recovery System (MACRS),** which allows straight-line depreciation for some assets but requires accelerated depreciation for most kinds of assets. MACRS separates depreciable assets into different classes and defines the depreciable life and rate for each class. MACRS is *not* acceptable for financial reporting because it often allocates costs over an arbitrary period that is less than the asset's useful life and it fails to estimate salvage value. Details of MACRS are covered in tax accounting courses.

Partial-Year Depreciation

C2 Explain depreciation for partial years and changes in estimates.

Plant assets are purchased and disposed of at various times. When an asset is purchased (or disposed of) at a time other than the beginning or end of an accounting period, depreciation is recorded for part of a year. This is done so that the year of purchase or the year of disposal is charged with its share of the asset's depreciation.

Point: Assets purchased on days 1 through 15 of a month are usually recorded as purchased on the 1st of that month. Assets purchased on days 16 to the month-end are recorded as if purchased on the 1st of the next month.

To illustrate, assume that the machine in Exhibit 8.5 is purchased and placed in service on October 8, 2012, and the annual accounting period ends on December 31. Since this machine is purchased and used for nearly three months in 2012, the calendar-year income statement should report depreciation expense on the machine for that part of the year. Normally, depreciation assumes that the asset is purchased on the first day of the month nearest the actual date of purchase. In this case, since the purchase occurred on October 8, we assume an October 1 purchase date. This means that three months' depreciation is recorded in 2012. Using straight-line depreciation, we compute three months' depreciation of $450 as follows.

$$\frac{\$10,000 - \$1,000}{5 \text{ years}} \times \frac{3}{12} = \$450$$

Example: If the machine's salvage value is zero and purchase occurs on Oct. 8, 2012, how much depreciation is recorded at Dec. 31, 2012?
Answer: $10,000/5 × 3/12 = $500

A similar computation is necessary when an asset disposal occurs during a period. To illustrate, assume that the machine is sold on June 24, 2017. Depreciation is recorded for the period January 1 through June 24 when it is disposed of. This partial year's depreciation, computed to the nearest whole month, is

$$\frac{\$10,000 - \$1,000}{5 \text{ years}} \times \frac{6}{12} = \$900$$

Change in Estimates for Depreciation

Point: Remaining depreciable cost equals book value less revised salvage value at the point of revision.

Depreciation is based on estimates of salvage value and useful life. During the useful life of an asset, new information may indicate that these estimates are inaccurate. If our estimate of an asset's useful life and/or salvage value changes, what should we do? The answer is to use the new estimate to compute depreciation for current and future periods. This means that we revise the depreciation expense computation by spreading the cost yet to be depreciated over the remaining useful life. This approach is used for all depreciation methods.

Point: Income is overstated (and depreciation understated) when useful life is too high; when useful life is too low, the opposite results.

Let's return to the machine described in Exhibit 8.8 using straight-line depreciation. At the beginning of this asset's third year, its book value is $6,400, computed as $10,000 minus $3,600. Assume that at the beginning of its third year, the estimated number of years remaining in its useful life changes from three to four years *and* its estimate of salvage value changes from $1,000 to $400. Straight-line depreciation for each of the four remaining years is computed as shown in Exhibit 8.14.

EXHIBIT 8.14

Computing Revised Straight-Line Depreciation

$$\frac{\text{Book value} - \text{Revised salvage value}}{\text{Revised remaining useful life}} = \frac{\$6,400 - \$400}{4 \text{ years}} = \$1,500 \text{ per year}$$

Example: If at the beginning of its second year the machine's remaining useful life changes from four to three years and salvage value from $1,000 to $400, how much straight-line depreciation is recorded in remaining years?
Answer: Revised depreciation = ($8,200 − $400)/3 = $2,600.

Thus, $1,500 of depreciation expense is recorded for the machine at the end of the third through sixth years—each year of its remaining useful life. Since this asset was depreciated at $1,800 per year for the first two years, it is tempting to conclude that depreciation expense was overstated in the first two years. However, these expenses reflected the best information available at that time. We do not go back and restate prior years' financial statements for this type of new information. Instead, we adjust the current and future periods' statements to reflect this new information. Revising an estimate of the useful life or salvage value of a plant asset is referred to as a **change in an accounting estimate** and is reflected in current and future financial statements, not in prior statements.

Reporting Depreciation

Both the cost and accumulated depreciation of plant assets are reported on the balance sheet or in its notes. Dale Jarrett Racing Adventure, for instance, reports the following.

Office furniture and equipment	$ 54,593
Shop and track equipment	202,973
Race vehicles and other	975,084
Property and equipment, gross	1,232,650
Less accumulated depreciation	628,355
Property and equipment, net	$ 604,295

Many companies also show plant assets on one line with the net amount of cost less accumulated depreciation. When this is done, the amount of accumulated depreciation is disclosed in a note. Apple reports only the net amount of its property, plant and equipment in its balance sheet. To satisfy the full-disclosure principle, Apple describes its depreciation methods in its Note 1 and the amounts comprising plant assets in its Note 5—see its 10-K at www.SEC.gov.

Point: A company usually keeps records for each asset showing its cost and depreciation to date. The combined records for individual assets are a type of *plant asset subsidiary ledger.*

Reporting both the cost and accumulated depreciation of plant assets helps users compare the assets of different companies. For example, a company holding assets costing $50,000 and accumulated depreciation of $40,000 is likely in a situation different from a company with new assets costing $10,000. While the net undepreciated cost of $10,000 is the same in both cases, the first company may have more productive capacity available but likely is facing the need to replace older assets. These insights are not provided if the two balance sheets report only the $10,000 book values.

Users must remember that plant assets are reported on a balance sheet at their undepreciated costs (book value), not at fair (market) values. This emphasis on costs rather than fair values is based on the *going-concern assumption* described in Chapter 1. This assumption states that, unless there is evidence to the contrary, we assume that a company continues in business. This implies that plant assets are held and used long enough to recover their cost through the sale of products and services. Because plant assets are not for sale, their fair values are not reported. An exception is when there is a *permanent decline* in the fair value of an asset relative to its book value, called an asset **impairment.** In this case the company writes the asset down to this fair value (details for the two-step process for assessing and computing the impairment loss are in advanced courses).

Accumulated Depreciation is a contra asset account with a normal credit balance. It does *not* reflect funds accumulated to buy new assets when the assets currently owned are replaced. If a company has funds available to buy assets, the funds are shown on the balance sheet among liquid assets such as Cash or Investments.

Example: Assume equipment carries a book value of $800 ($900 cost less $100 accumulated depreciation) and a fair (market) value of $750, *and* this $50 decline in value meets the 2-step impairment test. The entry to record this impairment is:

Impairment Loss $50
   Accum Depr-Equip. $50

■ Decision Ethics

Controller   You are the controller for a struggling company. Its operations require regular investments in equipment, and depreciation is its largest expense. Its competitors frequently replace equipment—often depreciated over three years. The company president instructs you to revise useful lives of equipment from three to six years and to use a six-year life on all new equipment. What actions do you take? ■ [Answer—p. 372]

NEED-TO-KNOW 8.2

P1, C2

Part 1. A machine costing $22,000 with a five-year life and an estimated $2,000 salvage value is installed on January 1. The factory manager estimates the machine will produce 1,000 units of product during its life. It actually produces the following units: Year 1, 200; Year 2, 400; Year 3, 300; Year 4, 80; and Year 5, 30. The total number of units produced by the end of Year 5 exceeds the original estimate—this difference was not predicted. (The machine must not be depreciated below its estimated salvage value.) Prepare a table with the following four-column headings: Year; Straight-Line; Units-of-Production; Double-Declining-Balance; and then compute depreciation for each year (and total depreciation for all years combined) under each depreciation method.

Part 2. In early January 2013, a company acquires equipment for $3,800. The company estimates this equipment to have a useful life of three years and a salvage value of $200. Early in 2015, the company changes its estimates to a total four-year useful life and zero salvage value. Using the straight-line method, what is depreciation for the year ended 2015?

Solution—Part 1

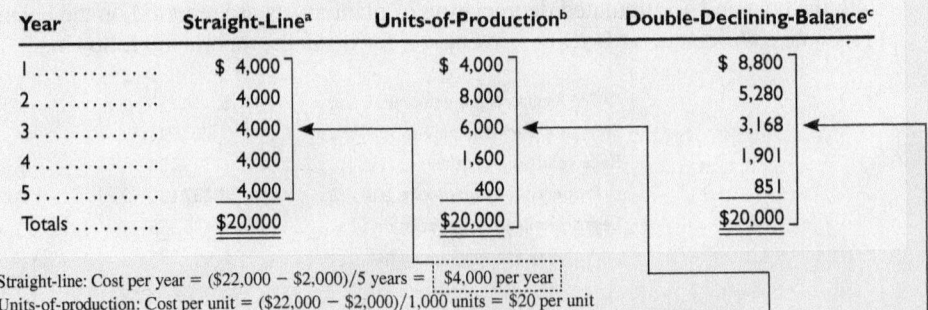

Year	Straight-Line[a]	Units-of-Production[b]	Double-Declining-Balance[c]
1	$ 4,000	$ 4,000	$ 8,800
2	4,000	8,000	5,280
3	4,000	6,000	3,168
4	4,000	1,600	1,901
5	4,000	400	851
Totals	$20,000	$20,000	$20,000

[a]Straight-line: Cost per year = ($22,000 − $2,000)/5 years = $4,000 per year
[b]Units-of-production: Cost per unit = ($22,000 − $2,000)/1,000 units = $20 per unit

Year	Units	Unit Cost	Depreciation
1	200	$20	$ 4,000
2	400	20	8,000
3	300	20	6,000
4	80	20	1,600
5	30	20	400*
Total			$20,000

*Set depreciation in Year 5 to reduce book value to the $20,000 salvage value; namely,
    instead of $600 (30 × $20), we use the maximum of $400 ($20,000 − $19,600 accum depr).
[c]Double-declining-balance: (100%/5) × 2 = 40% depreciation rate

Year	Beginning Book Value	Annual Depreciation (40% of Book Value)	Accumulated Depreciation at the End of the Year	Ending Book Value ($22,000 Cost less Accumulated Depreciation)
1	$22,000	$ 8,800	$ 8,800	$13,200
2	13,200	5,280	14,080	7,920
3	7,920	3,168	17,248	4,752
4	4,752	1,901*	19,149	2,851
5	2,851	851**	20,000	2,000
Total		$20,000		

*Rounded to the nearest dollar.
**Set depreciation in Year 5 to reduce book value to the $20,000 salvage value; namely, instead of $1,140 (2,851 × 40%), we
    use the maximum of $851 ($2,851 − $2,000).

Solution—Part 2

Do More: QS 8-3 through QS 8-7,
E 8-4 through E 8-13

QC2

($3,800 − $200)/3 years = $1,200 (original depreciation per year)

$1,200 × 2 years = $2,400 (accumulated depreciation)

($3,800 − $2,400)/2 years = **$700** (revised depreciation)

ADDITIONAL EXPENDITURES

C3 Distinguish between revenue and capital expenditures, and account for them.

After a company acquires a plant asset and puts it into service, it often makes additional expenditures for that asset's operation, maintenance, repair, and improvement. In recording these expenditures, it must decide whether to capitalize or expense them (to capitalize an expenditure is to debit the asset account). The issue is whether these expenditures are reported as current period expenses or added to the plant asset's cost and depreciated over its remaining useful life.

Revenue expenditures, also called *income statement expenditures,* are additional costs of plant assets that do not materially increase the asset's life or productive capabilities. They are recorded as expenses and deducted from revenues in the current period's income statement. Examples of revenue expenditures are cleaning, repainting, adjustments, and lubricants. **Capital expenditures,** also called *balance sheet expenditures,* are additional costs of plant assets that provide benefits extending beyond the current period. They are debited to asset accounts and reported on the balance sheet. Capital expenditures increase or improve the type or amount of service an asset provides. Examples are roofing replacement, plant expansion, and major overhauls of machinery and equipment.

Financial statements are affected for several years by the accounting choice of recording costs as either revenue expenditures or capital expenditures. This decision is based on whether the expenditures are identified as ordinary repairs or as betterments and extraordinary repairs.

	Financial Statement Effect	
	Accounting	Expense Timing
Revenue expenditure	Income stmt. account debited	Expensed currently
Capital expenditure	Balance sheet account debited	Expensed in future

Decision Maker

Entrepreneur Your start-up Internet services company needs cash, and you are preparing financial statements to apply for a short-term loan. A friend suggests that you treat as many expenses as possible as capital expenditures. What are the impacts on financial statements of this suggestion? What do you think is the aim of this suggestion? ■ [Answer—p. 372]

Ordinary Repairs

Ordinary repairs are expenditures to keep an asset in normal, good operating condition. They are necessary if an asset is to perform to expectations over its useful life. Ordinary repairs do not extend an asset's useful life beyond its original estimate or increase its productivity beyond original expectations. Examples are normal costs of cleaning, lubricating, adjusting, oil changing, and replacing small parts of a machine. Ordinary repairs are treated as *revenue expenditures.* This means their costs are reported as expenses on the current period income statement. Following this rule, Brunswick reports that "maintenance and repair costs are expensed as incurred." If Brunswick's current year repair costs are $9,500, it makes the following entry.

Point: Many companies apply the *materiality constraint* to treat *low-cost plant assets* (say, less than $500) as revenue expenditures. This practice is referred to as a "capitalization policy."

Dec. 31	Repairs Expense	9,500	
	Cash		9,500
	To record ordinary repairs of equipment.		

Assets = Liabilities + Equity
−9,500   −9,500

Betterments and Extraordinary Repairs

Accounting for betterments and extraordinary repairs is similar—both are treated as *capital expenditures.*

Betterments (Improvements) **Betterments,** also called *improvements,* are expenditures that make a plant asset more efficient or productive. A betterment often involves adding a component to an asset or replacing one of its old components with a better one and does not always increase an asset's useful life. An example is replacing manual controls on a machine with automatic controls. One special type of betterment is an *addition,* such as adding a new wing or dock to a warehouse. Since a betterment benefits future periods, it is debited to the asset account as a capital expenditure. The new book value (less salvage value) is then depreciated over the asset's remaining useful life. To illustrate, suppose a company pays $8,000 for a machine with an eight-year useful life and no salvage value. After three years and $3,000 of depreciation, it adds an automated control system to the machine at a cost of $1,800. This results in reduced labor costs in future periods. The cost of the betterment is added to the Machinery account with this entry.

Example: Assume a firm owns a Web server. Identify each cost as a revenue or capital expenditure: (1) purchase price, (2) necessary wiring, (3) platform for operation, (4) circuits to increase capacity, (5) cleaning after each month of use, (6) repair of a faulty switch, and (7) replaced a worn fan. *Answer:* Capital expenditures: 1, 2, 3, 4; revenue expenditures: 5, 6, 7.

Jan. 2	Machinery	1,800	
	Cash		1,800
	To record installation of automated system.		

Assets = Liabilities + Equity
+1,800
−1,800

After the betterment is recorded, the remaining cost to be depreciated is $6,800, computed as $8,000 − $3,000 + $1,800. Depreciation expense for the remaining five years is $1,360 per year, computed as $6,800/5 years.

Point: Both extraordinary repairs and betterments require revising future depreciation.

Extraordinary Repairs (Replacements)   **Extraordinary repairs** are expenditures extending the asset's useful life beyond its original estimate. Extraordinary repairs are *capital expenditures* because they benefit future periods. Their costs are debited to the asset account (or to accumulated depreciation). For example, Delta Air Lines reports, "modifications that . . . extend the useful lives of airframes or engines are capitalized and amortized [depreciated] over the remaining estimated useful life of the asset."

■ **Decision** Insight ━━━━━━━━━━━━━━━━━━━━━━━━━━━━━━━━━━━━━━

Extraordinary Bombers If we owned a 20-year-old truck and planned to use it in our work for another 40 years, we would expect some extraordinary repairs in future years. A similar situation confronts Whiteman Air Force Base, home to the B-2 stealth bomber, which rolled out of a Northrop Grumman hangar in the 1980s. The plan is to keep those bat-winged bombers flying until 2058. The Pentagon is moving forward with a $2 billion, 10-year effort to modernize the bombers' defensive capabilities. ■

DISPOSALS OF PLANT ASSETS

Plant assets are disposed of for several reasons. Some are discarded because they wear out or become obsolete. Others are sold because of changing business plans. Regardless of the reason, disposals of plant assets occur in one of three basic ways: discarding, sale, or exchange. The general steps in accounting for a disposal of plant assets are described in Exhibit 8.15.

EXHIBIT 8.15

Accounting for Disposals of Plant Assets

> 1. Record depreciation up to the date of disposal—this also updates Accumulated Depreciation.
> 2. Record the removal of the disposed asset's account balances—including its Accumulated Depreciation.
> 3. Record any cash (and/or other assets) received or paid in the disposal.
> 4. Record any gain or loss—computed by comparing the disposed asset's book value with the market value of any assets received.*

* An exception to step 4 is the case of an exchange that lacks *commercial substance*—see Appendix 8A.

Discarding Plant Assets

P2 Account for asset disposal through discarding or selling an asset.

A plant asset is *discarded* when it is no longer useful to the company and it has no market value. To illustrate, assume that a machine costing $9,000 with accumulated depreciation of $9,000 is discarded. When accumulated depreciation equals the asset's cost, it is said to be *fully depreciated* (zero book value). The entry to record the discarding of this asset is

Assets = Liabilities + Equity
+9,000
−9,000

June 5	Accumulated Depreciation—Machinery	9,000	
	Machinery		9,000
	To discard fully depreciated machinery.		

This entry reflects all four steps of Exhibit 8.15. Step 1 is unnecessary since the machine is fully depreciated. Step 2 is reflected in the debit to Accumulated Depreciation and credit to Machinery. Since no other asset is involved, step 3 is irrelevant. Finally, since book value is zero and no other asset is involved, no gain or loss is recorded in step 4.

How do we account for discarding an asset that is not fully depreciated or one whose depreciation is not up-to-date? To answer this, consider equipment costing $8,000 with accumulated depreciation of $6,000 on December 31 of the prior fiscal year-end. This equipment is being depreciated using the straight-line method over eight years with zero salvage. On July 1 of the current year it is discarded. Step 1 is to bring depreciation up-to-date.

Point: Recording depreciation expense up-to-date gives an up-to-date book value for determining gain or loss.

Assets = Liabilities + Equity
−500   −500

July 1	Depreciation Expense	500	
	Accumulated Depreciation—Equipment		500
	To record 6 months' depreciation ($1,000 × 6/12).		

Steps 2 through 4 of Exhibit 8.15 are reflected in the second (and final) entry.

July 1	Accumulated Depreciation—Equipment	6,500	
	Loss on Disposal of Equipment	1,500	
	Equipment		8,000
	To discard equipment with a $1,500 book value.		

Assets = Liabilities + Equity
+6,500   −1,500
−8,000

This loss is computed by comparing the equipment's $1,500 book value ($8,000 − $6,000 − $500) with the zero net cash proceeds. The loss is reported in the Other Expenses and Losses section of the income statement. Discarding an asset can sometimes require a cash payment that would increase the loss.

Point: Gain or loss is determined by comparing "value given" (book value) to "value received."

Selling Plant Assets

Companies often sell plant assets when they restructure or downsize operations. To illustrate the accounting for selling plant assets, we consider BTO's March 31 sale of equipment that cost $16,000 and has accumulated depreciation of $12,000 at December 31 of the prior calendar year-end. Annual depreciation on this equipment is $4,000 computed using straight-line depreciation. Step 1 of this sale is to record depreciation expense and update accumulated depreciation to March 31 of the current year.

March 31	Depreciation Expense	1,000	
	Accumulated Depreciation—Equipment		1,000
	To record 3 months' depreciation ($4,000 × 3/12).		

Assets = Liabilities + Equity
−1,000   −1,000

Steps 2 through 4 of Exhibit 8.15 can be reflected in one final entry that depends on the amount received from the asset's sale. We consider three different possibilities.

Sale at Book Value   If BTO receives $3,000 cash, an amount equal to the equipment's book value as of March 31 (book value = $16,000 − $12,000 − $1,000), no gain or loss occurs on disposal. The entry is

Sale price = Book value → No gain or loss

March 31	Cash	3,000	
	Accumulated Depreciation—Equipment	13,000	
	Equipment		16,000
	To record sale of equipment for no gain or loss.		

Assets = Liabilities + Equity
+3,000
+13,000
−16,000

Sale above Book Value   If BTO receives $7,000, an amount that is $4,000 above the equipment's $3,000 book value as of March 31, a gain on disposal occurs. The entry is

Sale price > Book value → Gain

March 31	Cash	7,000	
	Accumulated Depreciation—Equipment	13,000	
	Gain on Disposal of Equipment		4,000
	Equipment		16,000
	To record sale of equipment for a $4,000 gain.		

Assets = Liabilities + Equity
+7,000   +4,000
+13,000
−16,000

Sale below Book Value   If BTO receives $2,500, an amount that is $500 below the equipment's $3,000 book value as of March 31, a loss on disposal occurs. The entry is

Sale price < Book value → Loss

March 31	Cash	2,500	
	Loss on Disposal of Equipment	500	
	Accumulated Depreciation—Equipment	13,000	
	Equipment		16,000
	To record sale of equipment for a $500 loss.		

Assets = Liabilities + Equity
+2,500   −500
+13,000
−16,000

 **IFRS** _____

Unlike U.S. GAAP, IFRS requires an annual review of useful life and salvage value estimates. IFRS also permits revaluation of plant assets to market value if market value is reliably determined. ∎

NEED-TO-KNOW 8.3

C3, P2

Part 1. A company pays $1,000 for equipment expected to last four years and have a $200 salvage value. Prepare journal entries to record the following costs related to the equipment.

a. During the second year of the equipment's life, $400 cash is paid for a new component expected to increase the equipment's productivity by 20% a year.

b. During the third year, $250 cash is paid for normal repairs necessary to keep the equipment in good working order.

c. During the fourth year, $500 is paid for repairs expected to increase the useful life of the equipment from four to five years.

Part 2. A company owns a machine that cost $500 and has accumulated depreciation of $400. Prepare the entry to record the disposal of the machine on January 2 under each of the following independent situations.

a. The machine needed extensive repairs, and it was not worth repairing. The company disposed of the machine, receiving nothing in return.

b. The company sold the machine for $80 cash.

c. The company sold the machine for $100 cash.

d. The company sold the machine for $110 cash.

Solutions—Part 1

a.

Equipment...	400	
Cash		400
To record betterment.		

b.

Repairs Expense	250	
Cash		250
To record ordinary repairs.		

c.

Equipment...	500	
Cash		500
To record extraordinary repairs.		

Solutions—Part 2   [Note: Book value of machine = $500 − $400 = $100]

a. Disposed of at no value

Jan. 2	Loss on Disposal of Machine	100	
	Accumulated Depreciation—Machine	400	
	Machine		500
	To record disposal of machine.		

b. Sold for $80 cash

Jan. 2	Cash	80	
	Loss on Sale of Machine	20	
	Accumulated Depreciation—Machine	400	
	Machine		500
	To record cash sale of machine.		

c. Sold for $100 cash

Jan. 2	Cash	100	
	Accumulated Depreciation—Machine	400	
	Machine		500
	To record cash sale of machine.		

d. Sold for $110 cash

Jan. 2	Cash	110	
	Accumulated Depreciation—Machine	400	
	Gain on Sale of Machine		10
	Machine		500
	To record cash sale of machine.		

Do More: QS 8-8, QS 8-9, E 8-14, E 8-15, E 8-16, E 8-17

QC3

Section 2—Natural Resources

Natural resources are assets that are physically consumed when used. Examples are standing timber, mineral deposits, and oil and gas fields. Since they are consumed when used, they are often called *wasting assets*. These assets represent soon-to-be inventories of raw materials that will be converted into one or more products by cutting, mining, or pumping. Until that conversion takes place, they are noncurrent assets and are shown in a balance sheet using titles such as timberlands, mineral deposits, or oil reserves. Natural resources are reported under either plant assets or their own separate category. Alcoa, for instance, reports its natural resources under the balance sheet title *Properties, plants and equipment.* In a note to its financial statements, Alcoa reports a separate amount for *Land and land rights, including mines.* Weyerhaeuser, on the other hand, reports its timber holdings in a separate balance sheet category titled *Timber and timberlands.*

> **P3** Account for natural resource assets and their depletion.

Cost Determination and Depletion

Natural resources are recorded at cost, which includes all expenditures necessary to acquire the resource and prepare it for its intended use. **Depletion** is the process of allocating the cost of a natural resource to the period when it is consumed. Natural resources are reported on the balance sheet at cost less *accumulated depletion.* The depletion expense per period is usually based on units extracted from cutting, mining, or pumping. This is similar to units-of-production depreciation. Exxon Mobil uses this approach to amortize the costs of discovering and operating its oil wells.

To illustrate depletion of natural resources, let's consider a mineral deposit with an estimated 250,000 tons of available ore. It is purchased for $500,000, and we expect zero salvage value. The depletion charge per ton of ore mined is $2, computed as $500,000 ÷ 250,000 tons. If 85,000 tons are mined and sold in the first year, the depletion charge for that year is $170,000. These computations are detailed in Exhibit 8.16.

Step 1

$$\text{Depletion per unit} = \frac{\text{Cost} - \text{Salvage value}}{\text{Total units of capacity}} = \frac{\$500,000 - \$0}{250,000 \text{ tons}} = \$2 \text{ per ton}$$

Step 2

$$\text{Depletion expense} = \text{Depletion per unit} \times \text{Units extracted and sold in period}$$
$$= \$2 \times 85,000 = \$170,000$$

EXHIBIT 8.16

Depletion Formula and Example

Depletion expense for the first year is recorded as follows.

Dec. 31	Depletion Expense—Mineral Deposit	170,000	
	Accumulated Depletion—Mineral Deposit		170,000
	To record depletion of the mineral deposit.		

Assets = Liabilities + Equity
−170,000   −170,000

The period-end balance sheet reports the mineral deposit as shown in Exhibit 8.17.

| Mineral deposit .... | $500,000 | |
| Less accumulated depletion .... | 170,000 | $330,000 |

EXHIBIT 8.17

Balance Sheet Presentation of Natural Resources

Since all 85,000 tons of the mined ore are sold during the year, the entire $170,000 of depletion is reported on the income statement. If some of the ore remains unsold at year-end, however, the depletion related to the unsold ore is carried forward on the balance sheet and reported as Ore Inventory, a current asset. To illustrate, and continuing with our example, assume that

40,000 tons are mined in the second year, but only 34,000 tons are sold. We record depletion of $68,000 (34,000 tons × $2 depletion per unit) and the remaining Ore Inventory of $12,000 (6,000 tons × $2 depletion per unit) as follows.

Assets = Liabilities + Equity
−80,000   −68,000
+12,000

Dec. 31	Depletion Expense—Mineral Deposit	68,000	
	Ore Inventory	12,000	
	Accumulated Depletion—Mineral Deposit		80,000
	To record depletion and inventory of mineral deposit.		

Plant Assets Tied into Extracting

The conversion of natural resources by mining, cutting, or pumping usually requires machinery, equipment, and buildings. When the usefulness of these plant assets is directly related to the depletion of a natural resource, their costs are depreciated using the units-of-production method in proportion to the depletion of the natural resource. For example, if a machine is permanently installed in a mine and 10% of the ore is mined and sold in the period, then 10% of the machine's cost (less any salvage value) is allocated to depreciation expense. The same procedure is used when a machine is abandoned once resources have been extracted. If, however, a machine will be moved to and used at another site when extraction is complete, the machine is depreciated over its own useful life.

Fraud

Asset Control Long-term assets must be safeguarded against theft, misuse, and other damages. Controls take many forms depending on the asset, including use of security tags, the legal monitoring of rights infringements, and approvals of all asset disposals. A study reports that 43% of employees in operations and service areas witnessed the wasting, mismanaging, or abusing of assets in the past year (KPMG 2011).

NEED-TO-KNOW 8.4

P3

A company acquires a zinc mine at a cost of $750,000. It incurs additional costs of $100,000 to access the mine, which is estimated to hold 200,000 tons of zinc. The estimated value of the land after the zinc is removed is $50,000.

1. Prepare the entry(ies) to record the cost of the zinc mine.
2. Prepare the year-end adjusting entry if 50,000 tons of zinc are mined, but only 40,000 tons are sold the first year.

Solution

1.

Zinc Mine	850,000	
Cash		850,000
To record cost of zinc mine.		

2. Depletion per unit = ($750,000 + $100,000 − $50,000)/200,000 tons = $4.00 per ton

Depletion Expense—Zinc Mine..................................	160,000	
Zinc Inventory..	40,000	
Accumulated Depletion—Zinc Mine		200,000
To record depletion of zinc mine (50,000 × $4.00).		

Do More: QS 8-10, E 8-18

Section 3—Intangible Assets

P4 Account for intangible assets.

Intangible assets are nonphysical assets (used in operations) that confer on their owners long-term rights, privileges, or competitive advantages. Examples are patents, copyrights, licenses, leaseholds, franchises, goodwill, and trademarks. Lack of physical substance does not necessarily imply an intangible asset. Notes and accounts receivable, for instance, lack physical substance, but they are not intangibles. This section identifies the more common types of intangible assets and explains the accounting for them.

Cost Determination and Amortization

An intangible asset is recorded at cost when purchased. Intangibles are then separated into those with limited lives or indefinite lives. If an intangible has a **limited life,** its cost is systematically allocated to expense over its estimated useful life through the process of **amortization.** If an intangible asset has an **indefinite life**—meaning that no legal, regulatory, contractual, competitive, economic, or other factors limit its useful life—it should not be amortized. (If an intangible with an indefinite life is later judged to have a limited life, it is amortized over that limited life.) Amortization of intangible assets is similar to depreciation of plant assets and the depletion of natural resources in that it is a process of cost allocation. However, only the straight-line method is used for amortizing intangibles *unless* the company can show that another method is preferred. The effects of amortization are recorded in a contra account (Accumulated Amortization). The gross acquisition cost of intangible assets is disclosed in the balance sheet along with their accumulated amortization (these disclosures are new). The eventual disposal of an intangible asset involves removing its book value, recording any other asset(s) received or given up, and recognizing any gain or loss for the difference.

Many intangibles have limited lives due to laws, contracts, or other asset characteristics. Examples are patents, copyrights, and leaseholds. Other intangibles such as goodwill, trademarks, and trade names have lives that cannot be easily determined. The cost of intangible assets is amortized over the periods expected to benefit by their use, but in no case can this period be longer than the asset's legal existence. The values of some intangible assets such as goodwill continue indefinitely into the future and are not amortized. (An intangible asset that is not amortized is tested annually for **impairment**—if necessary, an impairment loss is recorded. Details for this test are in advanced courses.)

Intangible assets are often shown in a separate section of the balance sheet immediately after plant assets. Callaway Golf, for instance, follows this approach in reporting over $120 million of intangible assets in its balance sheet. Companies usually disclose their amortization periods for intangibles. The remainder of our discussion focuses on accounting for specific types of intangible assets.

Point: Depreciation, depletion, and amortization are related in that each describes cost allocation.

Point: The cost to acquire a Website address is an intangible asset.

Point: Goodwill is not amortized; instead, it is annually tested for impairment.

Types of Intangibles

Patents   The federal government grants patents to encourage the invention of new technology, mechanical devices, and production processes. A **patent** is an exclusive right granted to its owner to manufacture and sell a patented item or to use a process for 20 years. When patent rights are purchased, the cost to acquire the rights is debited to an account called Patents. If the owner engages in lawsuits to successfully defend a patent, the cost of lawsuits is debited to the Patents account. However, the costs of research and development leading to a new patent are expensed when incurred.

A patent's cost is amortized over its estimated useful life (not to exceed 20 years). If we purchase a patent costing $25,000 with a useful life of 10 years, we make the following adjusting entry at the end of each of the 10 years to amortize one-tenth of its cost.

Dec. 31	Amortization Expense—Patents	2,500	
	Accumulated Amortization—Patents		2,500
	To amortize patent costs over its useful life.		

Assets = Liabilities + Equity
−2,500   −2,500

The $2,500 debit to Amortization Expense appears on the income statement as a cost of the product or service provided under protection of the patent. The Accumulated Amortization—Patents account is a contra asset account to Patents.

 **Decision** Insight

Mention "drug war" and most people think of illegal drug trade. But another drug war is under way: Brand-name drugmakers are fighting to stop generic copies of their products from hitting the market once patents expire. Delaying a generic rival can yield millions in extra sales. One way drugmakers fight patent expirations is to alter *drug delivery.* The first patent might require a patient to take a pill 4×/day. When that patent expires, the drugmaker can "improve" the drug's delivery release system to 2×/day, and then 1×/day, and so forth. ■

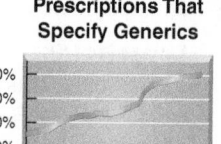

Prescriptions That Specify Generics

Copyrights A **copyright** gives its owner the exclusive right to publish and sell a musical, literary, or artistic work during the life of the creator plus 70 years, although the useful life of most copyrights is much shorter. The costs of a copyright are amortized over its useful life. The only identifiable cost of many copyrights is the fee paid to the Copyright Office of the federal government or international agency granting the copyright. If this fee is immaterial, it is charged directly to an expense account; but if the identifiable costs of a copyright are material, they are capitalized (recorded in an asset account) and periodically amortized by debiting an account called Amortization Expense—Copyrights.

Decision Insight

Mickey Mouse Protection Act The Walt Disney Company successfully lobbied Congress to extend copyright protection from the life of the creator plus 50 years to life of the creator plus 70 years. This extension allows the company to protect its characters for 20 additional years before the right to use them enters the public domain. Mickey Mouse is now protected by copyright law until 2023. The law is officially termed the Copyright Term Extension Act (CTEA) but it is also known as the Mickey Mouse Protection Act. ■

Franchises and Licenses **Franchises** and **licenses** are rights that a company or government grants an entity to deliver a product or service under specified conditions. Many organizations grant franchise and license rights—**McDonald's**, **Pizza Hut**, and **Major League Baseball** are just a few examples. The costs of franchises and licenses are debited to a Franchises and Licenses asset account and are amortized over the lives of the agreements. If an agreement is for an indefinite or perpetual period, those costs are not amortized.

Trademarks and Trade Names Companies often adopt unique symbols or select unique names and brands in marketing their products. A **trademark** or **trade (brand) name** is a symbol, name, phrase, or jingle identified with a company, product, or service. Examples are Nike swoosh, Marlboro Man, Big Mac, Coca-Cola, and Corvette. Ownership and exclusive right to use a trademark or trade name is often established by showing that one company used it before another. Ownership is best established by registering a trademark or trade name with the government's Patent Office. The cost of developing, maintaining, or enhancing the value of a trademark or trade name (such as advertising) is charged to expense when incurred. If a trademark or trade name is purchased, however, its cost is debited to an asset account and then amortized over its expected life. If the company plans to renew indefinitely its right to the trademark or trade name, the cost is not amortized.

Point: McDonald's "golden arches" are one of the world's most valuable trademarks, yet this asset is not shown on McDonald's balance sheet.

Goodwill **Goodwill** has a specific meaning in accounting. Goodwill is the amount by which a company's value exceeds the value of its individual assets and liabilities. This usually implies that the company as a whole has certain valuable attributes not measured among its individual assets and liabilities. These can include superior management, skilled workforce, good supplier or customer relations, quality products or services, good location, or other competitive advantages.

To keep accounting information from being too subjective, goodwill is not recorded unless an entire company or business segment is purchased. Purchased goodwill is measured by taking the purchase price of the company and subtracting the market value of its individual net assets (excluding goodwill). For instance, **Google** paid $1.19 billion to acquire **YouTube**; about $1.13 of the $1.19 billion was for goodwill.

Point: Amortization of goodwill is different for financial accounting and tax accounting. The IRS requires the amortization of goodwill over 15 years.

Example: Assume goodwill carries a book value of $500 and has an implied fair value of $475, *and* this $25 decline in value meets the 2-step impairment test. The entry to record this impairment is:
Impairment Loss $25
  Goodwill $25

Goodwill is measured as the excess of the cost of an acquired entity over the value of the acquired net assets. Goodwill is recorded as an asset, and it is *not* amortized. Instead, goodwill is annually tested for impairment. If the book value of goodwill does not exceed its fair (market) value, goodwill is not impaired. However, if the book value of goodwill does exceed its fair value, an impairment loss is recorded equal to that excess. (Details of this test are in advanced courses.)

Leaseholds Property is rented under a contract called a **lease.** The property's owner, called the **lessor,** grants the lease. The one who secures the right to possess and use the property is called the **lessee.** A **leasehold** refers to the rights the lessor grants to the lessee under the terms of the lease. A leasehold is an intangible asset for the lessee.

Certain leases require no advance payment from the lessee but require monthly rent payments. In this case, we do not set up a Leasehold account. Instead, the monthly payments are debited to a Rent Expense account. If a long-term lease requires the lessee to pay the final period's rent in advance when the lease is signed, the lessee records this advance payment with a debit to the Leasehold account. Since the advance payment is not used until the final period, the Leasehold account balance remains intact until that final period when its balance is transferred to Rent Expense. (Some long-term leases give the lessee essentially the same rights as a purchaser. This results in a tangible asset and a liability reported by the lessee. Chapter 10 describes these so-called *capital leases*.)

A long-term lease can increase in value when current rental rates for similar property rise while the required payments under the lease remain constant. This increase in value of a lease is not reported on the lessee's balance sheet. However, if the property is subleased and the new tenant makes a cash payment to the original lessee for the rights under the old lease, the new tenant debits this payment to a Leasehold account, which is amortized to Rent Expense over the remaining life of the lease.

Point: A leasehold account implies existence of future benefits that the lessee controls because of a prepayment. It also meets the definition of an asset.

Leasehold Improvements   A lessee sometimes pays for alterations or improvements to the leased property such as partitions, painting, and storefronts. These alterations and improvements are called **leasehold improvements,** and the lessee debits these costs to a Leasehold Improvements account. Since leasehold improvements become part of the property and revert to the lessor at the end of the lease, the lessee amortizes these costs over the life of the lease or the life of the improvements, whichever is shorter. The amortization entry debits Amortization Expense—Leasehold Improvements and credits Accumulated Amortization—Leasehold Improvements.

Other Intangibles   There are other types of intangible assets such as *software, noncompete covenants, customer lists,* and so forth. Our accounting for them is the same. First, we record the intangible asset's costs. Second, we determine whether the asset has a limited or indefinite life. If limited, we allocate its costs over that period. If indefinite, its costs are not amortized.

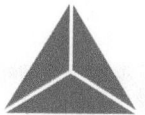

Fraud

Hidden Assets. Most view fraud involving long-term assets as low risk. Yet, the opportunity for fraud in a one-time transaction is reasonably high and requires scrutiny. Concealment of an asset theft can include recording it as scrap, obsolescence, donated, or destroyed. More generally, the following business activities can be used to conceal asset theft:

- Recording an asset disposal as customer adjustment, no charge, or promotional.
- Recording false receiving reports as to asset quantity.
- False counts or record alteration after a physical count.
- Nonbilling of an asset sale.
- Write-off of an asset.

Part 1. A publisher purchases the copyright on a book for $1,000 on January 1 of this year. The copyright legally protects its owner for 5 more years. The company plans to market and sell prints of the original for 7 years. Prepare entries to record the purchase of the copyright on January 1 of this year, and its annual amortization on December 31 of this year.

NEED-TO-KNOW 8.5

P4

Part 2. On January 3 of this year, a retailer incurs a $9,000 cost to modernize its store. Improvements include lighting, partitions, and sound system. These improvements are estimated to yield benefits for 5 years. The retailer leases its store and has 3 years remaining on its lease. Prepare the entry to record (a) the cost of modernization and (b) amortization at the end of this current year.

Part 3. On January 6 of this year, a company pays $6,000 for a patent with a remaining 12-year legal life to produce a supplement expected to be marketable for three years. Prepare entries to record its acquisition and the December 31 amortization entry for this current year.

Solution—Part 1

Jan. 1	Copyright	1,000	
	Cash		1,000
	To record purchase of copyright.		
Dec. 31	Amortization Expense—Copyright	200	
	Accumulated Amortization—Copyright		200
	To record amortization of copyright		
	[$1,000/5 years].		

Solution—Part 2

a.

Jan. 3	Leasehold Improvements	9,000	
	Cash		9,000
	To record leasehold improvements.		

b.

Dec. 31	Amortization Expense–Leasehold Improvements. . .	3,000	
	Accumulated Amortization—Leasehold		
	Improvements		3,000
	To record amortization of leasehold over		
	*remaining lease life.**		

*Amortization = $9,000/3-year-lease-term = $3,000 per year.

Solution—Part 3

Jan. 6	Patents	6,000	
	Cash		6,000
Dec. 31	Amortization Expense*	2,000	
	Accumulated Amortization—Patents.		2,000

*$6,000/3 years = $2,000.

Do More: QS 8-12, E 8-19, E 8-20

QC4

GLOBAL VIEW

This section discusses similarities and differences between U.S. GAAP and IFRS in accounting and reporting for plant assets and intangible assets.

Accounting for Plant Assets   Issues involving cost determination, depreciation, additional expenditures, and disposals of plant assets are subject to broadly similar guidance for both U.S. GAAP and IFRS. Although differences exist, the similarities vastly outweigh the differences. Nokia describes its accounting for plant assets as follows:

NOKIA

> Property, plant and equipment are stated at cost less accumulated depreciation. Depreciation is recorded on a straight-line basis over the expected useful lives of the assets. Maintenance, repairs and renewals are generally charged to expense during the financial period in which they are incurred. However, major renovations are capitalized and included in the carrying amount of the asset . . . Major renovations are depreciated over the remaining useful life of the related asset.

One area where notable differences exist is in accounting for changes in the value of plant assets (between the time they are acquired and when disposed of). Namely, how does IFRS and U.S. GAAP treat decreases and increases in the value of plant assets subsequent to acquisition?

Decreases in the Value of Plant Assets   When the value of plant assets declines after acquisition, but before disposition, both U.S. GAAP and IFRS require companies to record those decreases as *impairment losses*. While the *test for impairment* uses a different base between U.S. GAAP and IFRS, a more fundamental difference is that U.S. GAAP revalues impaired plant assets to *fair value* whereas IFRS revalues them to a *recoverable amount* (defined as fair value less costs to sell).

Increases in the Value of Plant Assets   U.S. GAAP prohibits companies from recording increases in the value of plant assets. However, IFRS permits upward *asset revaluations*. Namely, under IFRS, if an impairment was previously recorded, a company would reverse that impairment to the extent necessary and record that increase in income. If the increase is beyond the original cost, that increase is recorded in comprehensive income.

Accounting for Intangible Assets   For intangible assets, the accounting for cost determination, amortization, additional expenditures, and disposals is subject to broadly similar guidance for U.S. GAAP and IFRS. Although differences exist, the similarities vastly outweigh differences. Again, and consistent with the accounting for plant assets, U.S. GAAP and IFRS handle decreases and increases in the value of intangible assets differently. However, IFRS requirements for recording increases in the value of intangible assets are so restrictive that such increases are rare. Nokia describes its accounting for intangible assets as follows:

> [Intangible assets] are capitalized and amortized using the straight-line method over their useful lives. Where an indication of impairment exists, the carrying amount of any intangible asset is assessed and written down to its recoverable amount.

NOKIA

Total Asset Turnover   **Decision Analysis**

A company's assets are important in determining its ability to generate sales and earn income. Managers devote much attention to deciding what assets a company acquires, how much it invests in assets, and how to use assets most efficiently and effectively. One important measure of a company's ability to use its assets is **total asset turnover,** defined in Exhibit 8.18.

A1 Compute total asset turnover and apply it to analyze a company's use of assets.

EXHIBIT 8.18

Total Asset Turnover

$$\text{Total asset turnover} = \frac{\text{Net sales}}{\text{Average total assets}}$$

The numerator reflects the net amounts earned from the sale of products and services. The denominator reflects the average total resources devoted to operating the company and generating sales.

To illustrate, let's look at total asset turnover in Exhibit 8.19 for two competing companies: Molson Coors and Boston Beer.

EXHIBIT 8.19

Analysis Using Total Asset Turnover

Company	Figure ($ millions)	2011	2010	2009	2008	2007
Molson Coors	Net sales	$ 3,515.7	$ 3,254.4	$ 3,032.4	$ 4,774.3	$ 6,190.6
	Average total assets	$12,560.7	$12,359.4	$11,203.9	$11,934.1	$12,527.5
	Total asset turnover	0.28	0.26	0.27	0.40	0.49
Boston Beer	Net sales	$ 513.000	$ 463.798	$ 415.053	$ 398.400	$ 341.647
	Average total assets	$ 265.509	$ 260.733	$ 241.347	$ 208.856	$ 176.215
	Total asset turnover	1.93	1.78	1.72	1.91	1.94

To show how we use total asset turnover, let's look at Molson Coors. We express Molson Coors's use of assets in generating net sales by saying "it turned its assets over 0.28 times during 2011." This means that each $1.00 of assets produced $0.28 of net sales. Is a total asset turnover of 0.28 good or bad? It is safe to say that all companies desire a high total asset turnover. Like many ratio analyses, however, a company's total asset turnover must be interpreted in comparison with those of prior years and of its competitors. Interpreting the total asset turnover also requires an understanding of the company's operations. Some operations are capital intensive, meaning that a relatively large amount is invested in assets to generate sales. This suggests a relatively lower total asset turnover. Other companies' operations are labor intensive, meaning that they generate sales more by the efforts of people than the use of assets. In that case, we expect a higher total asset turnover. Companies with low total asset turnover require higher profit margins (examples are hotels and real estate); companies with high total asset turnover can succeed with lower profit margins (examples are food stores and toy merchandisers). Molson Coors's turnover recently declined and is now much lower than that for Boston Beer and many other competitors. Total asset turnover for Molson Coors's competitors, available in industry publications such as Dun & Bradstreet, is generally in the range of 0.5 to 1.0 over this same period. Overall, Molson Coors must improve relative to its competitors on total asset turnover.

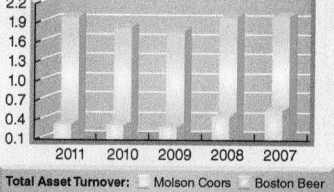

Point: An estimate of **plant asset useful life** equals the plant asset cost divided by depreciation expense.

Point: The **plant asset age** is estimated by dividing accumulated depreciation by depreciation expense. Older plant assets can signal needed asset replacements; they may also signal less efficient assets.

 **Decision** Maker

Environmentalist A paper manufacturer claims it cannot afford more environmental controls. It points to its low total asset turnover of 1.9 and argues that it cannot compete with companies whose total asset turnover is much higher. Examples cited are food stores (5.5) and auto dealers (3.8). How do you respond? ■ [Answer—p. 372]

COMPREHENSIVE...

NEED-TO-KNOW

On July 14, 2013, Tulsa Company pays $600,000 to acquire a fully equipped factory. The purchase involves the following assets and information.

Asset	Appraised Value	Salvage Value	Useful Life	Depreciation Method
Land	$160,000			Not depreciated
Land improvements	80,000	$ 0	10 years	Straight-line
Building	320,000	100,000	10 years	Double-declining-balance
Machinery	240,000	20,000	10,000 units	Units-of-production*
Total	$800,000			

* The machinery is used to produce 700 units in 2013 and 1,800 units in 2014.

Required

1. Allocate the total $600,000 purchase cost among the separate assets.

2. Compute the 2013 (six months) and 2014 depreciation expense for each asset, and compute the company's total depreciation expense for both years.

3. On the last day of calendar year 2015, Tulsa discarded machinery that had been on its books for five years. The machinery's original cost was $12,000 (estimated life of five years) and its salvage value was $2,000. No depreciation had been recorded for the fifth year when the disposal occurred. Journalize the fifth year of depreciation (straight-line method) and the asset's disposal.

4. At the beginning of year 2015, Tulsa purchased a patent for $100,000 cash. The company estimated the patent's useful life to be 10 years. Journalize the patent acquisition and its amortization for the year 2015.

5. Late in the year 2015, Tulsa acquired an ore deposit for $600,000 cash. It added roads and built mine shafts for an additional cost of $80,000. Salvage value of the mine is estimated to be $20,000. The company estimated 330,000 tons of available ore. In year 2015, Tulsa mined and sold 10,000 tons of ore. Journalize the mine's acquisition and its first year's depletion.

6.ᴬ (This requirement involves Appendix 8A.) On the first day of 2015, Tulsa exchanged the machinery that was acquired on July 14, 2013, along with $5,000 cash for machinery with a $210,000 market value. Journalize the exchange of these assets assuming the exchange lacked commercial substance. (Refer to background information in parts 1 and 2.)

PLANNING THE SOLUTION

- Complete a three-column table showing the following amounts for each asset: appraised value, percent of total value, and apportioned cost.

- Using allocated costs, compute depreciation for 2013 (only one-half year) and 2014 (full year) for each asset. Summarize those computations in a table showing total depreciation for each year.

- Depreciation must be recorded up-to-date before discarding an asset. Calculate and record depreciation expense for the fifth year using the straight-line method. Since salvage value is not received at the end of a discarded asset's life, the salvage value becomes a loss on disposal. Record the loss on the disposal as well as the removal of the discarded asset and its related accumulated depreciation.

- Record the patent (an intangible asset) at its purchase price. Use straight-line amortization over its useful life to calculate amortization expense.

- Record the ore deposit (a natural resource asset) at its cost, including any added costs to ready the mine for use. Calculate depletion per ton using the depletion formula. Multiply the depletion per ton by the amount of tons mined and sold to calculate depletion expense for the year.

- Remember that gains and losses on asset exchanges that lack commercial substance are not recognized. Make a journal entry to add the acquired machinery to the books and to remove the old machinery, along with its accumulated depreciation, and to record the cash given in the exchange.

SOLUTION TO COMPREHENSIVE NEED-TO-KNOW

1. Allocation of the total cost of $600,000 among the separate assets.

Asset	Appraised Value	Percent of Total Value	Apportioned Cost
Land	$160,000	20%	$120,000 ($600,000 × 20%)
Land improvements	80,000	10	60,000 ($600,000 × 10%)
Building	320,000	40	240,000 ($600,000 × 40%)
Machinery	240,000	30	180,000 ($600,000 × 30%)
Total	$800,000	100%	$ 600,000

2. Depreciation for each asset. (Land is not depreciated.)

Land Improvements

Cost...	$ 60,000
Salvage value	0
Depreciable cost	$ 60,000
Useful life....................................	10 years
Annual depreciation expense ($60,000/10 years)	$ 6,000
2013 depreciation ($6,000 × 6/12)	$ 3,000
2014 depreciation	$ 6,000

Building

Straight-line rate = 100%/10 years = 10%
Double-declining-balance rate = 10% × 2 = 20%

2013 depreciation ($240,000 × 20% × 6/12)	$ 24,000
2014 depreciation [($240,000 − $24,000) × 20%].........	$ 43,200

Machinery

Cost...	$180,000
Salvage value	20,000
Depreciable cost	$160,000
Total expected units of production	10,000 units
Depreciation per unit ($160,000/10,000 units)	$ 16
2013 depreciation ($16 × 700 units)...................	$ 11,200
2014 depreciation ($16 × 1,800 units)	$ 28,800

Total depreciation expense for each year:

	2013	2014
Land improvements	$ 3,000	$ 6,000
Building	24,000	43,200
Machinery	11,200	28,800
Total	$38,200	$78,000

3. Record the depreciation up-to-date on the discarded asset.

Depreciation Expense—Machinery	2,000	
Accumulated Depreciation—Machinery		2,000
To record depreciation on date of disposal: ($12,000 − $2,000)/5		

Record the removal of the discarded asset and its loss on disposal.

Accumulated Depreciation—Machinery	10,000	
Loss on Disposal of Machinery	2,000	
Machinery		12,000
To record the discarding of machinery with a $2,000 book value.		

4.

Patent	100,000	
Cash		100,000
To record patent acquisition.		

Amortization Expense—Patent	10,000	
Accumulated Amortization—Patent		10,000
To record amortization expense: $100,000/10 years = $10,000.		

5.

Ore Deposit	680,000	
Cash		680,000
To record ore deposit acquisition and its related costs.		

Depletion Expense—Ore Deposit	20,000	
Accumulated Depletion—Ore Deposit		20,000
To record depletion expense: ($680,000 − $20,000)/330,000 tons =		
$2 per ton. 10,000 tons mined and sold × $2 = $20,000 depletion.		

6. Record the asset exchange: The book value on the exchange date is $180,000 (cost) − $40,000 (accumulated depreciation). The book value of the machinery given up in the exchange ($140,000) plus the $5,000 cash paid is less than the $210,000 value of the machine acquired. The entry to record this exchange of assets that lacks commercial substance does not recognize the $65,000 "gain."

Machinery (new)	145,000*	
Accumulated Depreciation—Machinery (old)	40,000	
Machinery (old)		180,000
Cash		5,000
To record asset exchange that lacks commercial substance.		

* Market value of the acquired asset of $210,000 minus $65,000 "gain."

APPENDIX

8A

Exchanging Plant Assets

P5 A Account for asset exchanges.

Many plant assets such as machinery, automobiles, and office equipment are disposed of by exchanging them for newer assets. In a typical exchange of plant assets, a *trade-in allowance* is received on the old asset and the balance is paid in cash. Accounting for the exchange of assets depends on whether the transaction has *commercial substance* (per *SFAS 153,* commercial substance implies that it alters the company's future cash flows). If an asset exchange has commercial substance, a gain or loss is recorded based on the difference between the book value of the asset(s) given up and the market value of the asset(s) received. If an asset exchange lacks commercial substance, no gain or loss is recorded, and the asset(s) received is recorded based on the book value of the asset(s) given up. An exchange has commercial substance if the company's future cash flows change as a result of the transaction. This section describes the accounting for the exchange of assets.

Exchange with Commercial Substance: A Loss　A company acquires $42,000 in new equipment. In exchange, the company pays $33,000 cash and trades in old equipment. The old equipment originally cost $36,000 and has accumulated depreciation of $20,000, which implies a $16,000 book value at the time of exchange. We are told this exchange has commercial substance and that the old equipment has a trade-in allowance of $9,000. This exchange yields a loss as computed in the middle (Loss) columns of Exhibit 8A.1; the loss is computed as Asset received − Assets given = $42,000 − $49,000 = $(7,000). We can also compute the loss as Trade-in allowance − Book value of asset given = $9,000 − $16,000 = $(7,000).

Asset Exchange Has Commercial Substance		Loss		Gain	
Market value of asset received			$ 42,000		$ 52,000
Book value of assets given:					
Equipment ($36,000 − $20,000)		$16,000		$16,000	
Cash		33,000	49,000	33,000	49,000
Gain (loss) on exchange			$(7,000)		$ 3,000

The entry to record this asset exchange is

Jan. 3	Equipment (new)...............................	42,000	
	Loss on Exchange of Assets	7,000	
	Accumulated Depreciation—Equipment (old)	20,000	
	Equipment (old)		36,000
	Cash		33,000
	To record exchange (with commercial substance) of old equipment and cash for new equipment.		

Assets = Liabilities + Equity
+42,000   −7,000
+20,000
−36,000
−33,000

Point: Parenthetical notes to "new" and "old" equipment are for illustration only. Both the debit and credit are to the same Equipment account.

Exchange with Commercial Substance: A Gain   Let's assume the same facts as in the preceding asset exchange *except* that the new equipment received has a market value of $52,000 instead of $42,000. We are told that this exchange has commercial substance and that the old equipment has a trade-in allowance of $19,000. This exchange yields a gain as computed in the right-most (Gain) columns of Exhibit 8A.1; the gain is computed as Asset received − Assets given = $52,000 − $49,000 = $3,000. We can also compute the gain as Trade-in allowance − Book value of asset given = $19,000 − $16,000 = $3,000. The entry to record this asset exchange is

Jan. 3	Equipment (new)	52,000	
	Accumulated Depreciation—Equipment (old)	20,000	
	Equipment (old)		36,000
	Cash		33,000
	Gain on Exchange of Assets		3,000
	To record exchange (with commercial substance) of old equipment and cash for new equipment.		

Assets = Liabilities + Equity
+52,000   +3,000
+20,000
−36,000
−33,000

Exchanges without Commercial Substance   Let's assume the same facts as in the preceding asset exchange involving new equipment received with a market value of $52,000, but let's instead assume the transaction *lacks commercial substance.* The entry to record this asset exchange is

Jan. 3	Equipment (new)	49,000	
	Accumulated Depreciation—Equipment (old)	20,000	
	Equipment (old)		36,000
	Cash		33,000
	To record exchange (without commercial substance) of old equipment and cash for new equipment.		

Assets = Liabilities + Equity
+49,000
+20,000
−36,000
−33,000

The $3,000 gain recorded when the transaction has commercial substance is *not* recognized in this entry because of the rule prohibiting recording a gain or loss on asset exchanges without commercial substance. The $49,000 recorded for the new equipment equals its cash price ($52,000) less the unrecognized gain ($3,000) on the exchange. The $49,000 cost recorded is called the *cost basis* of the new machine. This cost basis is the amount we use to compute depreciation and its book value. The cost basis of the new asset also can be computed by summing the book values of the assets given up as shown in Exhibit 8A.2. The same analysis and approach are taken for a loss on an asset exchange without commercial substance.

Point: No gain or loss is recorded for exchanges *without* commercial substance.

Cost of old equipment	$ 36,000
Less accumulated depreciation	20,000
Book value of old equipment	16,000
Cash paid in the exchange	33,000
Cost recorded for new	
equipment	$49,000

Summary

C1 Explain the cost principle for computing the cost of plant assets. Plant assets are set apart from other tangible assets by two important features: use in operations and useful lives longer than one period. Plant assets are recorded at cost when purchased. Cost includes all normal and reasonable expenditures necessary to get the asset in place and ready for its intended use. The cost of a lump-sum purchase is allocated among its individual assets.

C2 Explain depreciation for partial years and changes in estimates. Partial-year depreciation is often required because assets are bought and sold throughout the year. Depreciation is revised when changes in estimates such as salvage value and useful life occur. If the useful life of a plant asset changes, for instance, the remaining cost to be depreciated is spread over the remaining (revised) useful life of the asset.

C3 Distinguish between revenue and capital expenditures, and account for them. Revenue expenditures expire in the current period and are debited to expense accounts and matched with current revenues. Ordinary repairs are an example of revenue expenditures. Capital expenditures benefit future periods and are debited to asset accounts. Examples of capital expenditures are extraordinary repairs and betterments.

A1 Compute total asset turnover and apply it to analyze a company's use of assets. Total asset turnover measures a company's ability to use its assets to generate sales. It is defined as net sales divided by average total assets. While all companies desire a high total asset turnover, it must be interpreted in comparison with those for prior years and its competitors.

P1 Compute and record depreciation using the straight-line, units-of-production, and declining-balance methods. *Depreciation* is the process of allocating to expense the cost of a plant asset over the accounting periods that benefit from its use. Depreciation does not measure the decline in a plant asset's market value or its physical deterioration. Three factors determine depreciation: cost, salvage value, and useful life. Salvage value is an estimate of the asset's value at the end of its benefit period. Useful (service) life is the length of time an asset is productively used. The straight-line method divides cost less salvage value by the asset's useful life to determine depreciation expense per period. The units-of-production method divides cost less salvage value by the estimated number of units the asset will produce over its life to determine depreciation per unit. The declining-balance method multiplies the asset's beginning-of-period book value by a factor that is often double the straight-line rate.

P2 Account for asset disposal through discarding or selling an asset. When a plant asset is discarded or sold, its cost and accumulated depreciation are removed from the accounts. Any cash proceeds from discarding or selling an asset are recorded and compared to the asset's book value to determine gain or loss.

P3 Account for natural resource assets and their depletion. The cost of a natural resource is recorded in a noncurrent asset account. Depletion of a natural resource is recorded by allocating its cost to depletion expense using the units-of-production method. Depletion is credited to an Accumulated Depletion account.

P4 Account for intangible assets. An intangible asset is recorded at the cost incurred to purchase it. The cost of an intangible asset with a definite useful life is allocated to expense using the straight-line method, and is called *amortization*. Goodwill and intangible assets with an indefinite useful life are not amortized—they are annually tested for impairment. Intangible assets include patents, copyrights, leaseholds, goodwill, and trademarks.

P5A Account for asset exchanges. For an asset exchange with commercial substance, a gain or loss is recorded based on the difference between the book value of the asset given up and the market value of the asset received. For an asset exchange without commercial substance, no gain or loss is recorded, and the asset received is recorded based on the book value of the asset given up.

Guidance Answers to Decision Maker and Decision Ethics

Controller The president's instructions may reflect an honest and reasonable prediction of the future. Since the company is struggling financially, the president may have concluded that the normal pattern of replacing assets every three years cannot continue. Perhaps the strategy is to avoid costs of frequent replacements and stretch use of equipment a few years longer until financial conditions improve. However, if you believe the president's decision is unprincipled, you might confront the president with your opinion that it is unethical to change the estimate to increase income. Another possibility is to wait and see whether the auditor will prohibit this change in estimate. In either case, you should insist that the statements be based on reasonable estimates.

Entrepreneur Treating an expense as a capital expenditure means that reported expenses will be lower and income higher in the short run. This is so because a capital expenditure is not expensed immediately but is spread over the asset's useful life. Treating an expense as a capital expenditure also means that asset and equity totals are reported at larger amounts in the short run. This continues until the asset is fully depreciated. Your friend is probably trying to help, but the suggestion is misguided. Only an expenditure benefiting future periods is a capital expenditure.

Environmentalist The paper manufacturer's comparison of its total asset turnover with food stores and auto dealers is misdirected. These other industries' turnovers are higher because their profit margins are lower (about 2%). Profit margins for the paper industry are usually 3% to 3.5%. You need to collect data from competitors in the paper industry to show that a 1.9 total asset turnover is about the norm for this industry. You might also want to collect data on this company's revenues and expenses, along with compensation data for its high-ranking officers and employees.

Key Terms

Accelerated depreciation method (p. 352)	Impairment (pp. 355, 363)	Natural resources (p. 361)
Amortization (p. 363)	Inadequacy (p. 349)	Obsolescence (p. 349)
Asset book value (p. 350)	Indefinite life (p. 363)	Ordinary repairs (p. 357)
Betterments (p. 357)	Intangible assets (p. 362)	Patent (p. 363)
Capital expenditures (p. 357)	Land improvements (p. 347)	Plant asset age (p. 367)
Change in an accounting estimate (p. 355)	Lease (p. 364)	Plant assets (p. 346)
Copyright (p. 364)	Leasehold (p. 364)	Revenue expenditures (p. 357)
Cost (p. 347)	Leasehold improvements (p. 365)	Salvage value (p. 349)
Declining-balance method (p. 352)	Lessee (p. 364)	Straight-line depreciation (p. 350)
Depletion (p. 361)	Lessor (p. 364)	Total asset turnover (p. 367)
Depreciation (p. 348)	Licenses (p. 364)	Trademark or trade (brand) name (p. 364)
Extraordinary repairs (p. 358)	Limited life (p. 363)	Units-of-production depreciation (p. 351)
Franchises (p. 364)	Modified Accelerated Cost Recovery System (MACRS) (p. 354)	Useful life (p. 349)
Goodwill (p. 364)		

Multiple Choice Quiz

Answers on p. 387   mhhe.com/wildFA7e

Additional Quiz Questions are available at the book's Website.

1. A company paid $326,000 for property that included land, land improvements, and a building. The land was appraised at $175,000, the land improvements were appraised at $70,000, and the building was appraised at $105,000. What is the allocation of property costs to the three assets purchased?
   a. Land, $150,000; Land Improvements, $60,000; Building, $90,000
   b. Land, $163,000; Land Improvements, $65,200; Building, $97,800
   c. Land, $150,000; Land Improvements, $61,600; Building, $92,400
   d. Land, $159,000; Land Improvements, $65,200; Building, $95,400
   e. Land, $175,000; Land Improvements, $70,000; Building, $105,000

2. A company purchased a truck for $35,000 on January 1, 2013. The truck is estimated to have a useful life of four years and an estimated salvage value of $1,000. Assuming that the company uses straight-line depreciation, what is the depreciation expense on the truck for the year ended December 31, 2014?
   a. $8,750
   b. $17,500
   c. $8,500
   d. $17,000
   e. $25,500

3. A company purchased machinery for $10,800,000 on January 1, 2013. The machinery has a useful life of 10 years

and an estimated salvage value of $800,000. What is the depreciation expense on the machinery for the year ended December 31, 2014, assuming that the double-declining-balance method is used?
   a. $2,160,000
   b. $3,888,000
   c. $1,728,000
   d. $2,000,000
   e. $1,600,000

4. A company sold a machine that originally cost $250,000 for $120,000 when accumulated depreciation on the machine was $100,000. The gain or loss recorded on the sale of this machine is
   a. $0 gain or loss.
   b. $120,000 gain.
   c. $30,000 loss.
   d. $30,000 gain.
   e. $150,000 loss.

5. A company had average total assets of $500,000, gross sales of $575,000, and net sales of $550,000. The company's total asset turnover is
   a. 1.15
   b. 1.10
   c. 0.91
   d. 0.87
   e. 1.05

A   *Superscript letter A denotes assignments based on Appendix 8A.*

Ⅰ Icon denotes assignments that involve decision making.

Discussion Questions

1. **Ⅰ** What characteristics of a plant asset make it different from other assets?

2. What is the general rule for cost inclusion for plant assets?

3. What is different between land and land improvements?

4. Why is the cost of a lump-sum purchase allocated to the individual assets acquired?

5. **Ⅰ** Does the balance in the Accumulated Depreciation—Machinery account represent funds to replace the machinery when it wears out? If not, what does it represent?

6. Why is the Modified Accelerated Cost Recovery System not generally accepted for financial accounting purposes?

7. **Ⅰ** What accounting concept justifies charging low-cost plant asset purchases immediately to an expense account?

8. What is the difference between ordinary repairs and extraordinary repairs? How should each be recorded?

9. **Ⅰ** Identify events that might lead to disposal of a plant asset.

10. What is the process of allocating the cost of natural resources to expense as they are used?

11. Is the declining-balance method an acceptable way to compute depletion of natural resources? Explain.

12. What are the characteristics of an intangible asset?

13. What general procedures are applied in accounting for the acquisition and potential cost allocation of intangible assets?

14. **Ⅰ** When do we know that a company has goodwill? When can goodwill appear in a company's balance sheet?

15. **Ⅰ** Assume that a company buys another business and pays for its goodwill. If the company plans to incur costs each year to maintain the value of the goodwill, must it also amortize this goodwill?

16. **Ⅰ** How is total asset turnover computed? Why would a financial statement user be interested in total asset turnover?

17. On its recent balance sheet in Appendix A, **APPLE** Apple lists its plant assets as "Property, plant and equipment, net." What does "net" mean in this title?

18. Refer to Google's recent balance sheet in **GOOGLE** Appendix A. What property, plant and equipment assets does Google list on its balance sheet? What is the book value of its total net property, plant and equipment assets at December 31, 2012?

19. **Ⅰ** Refer to Samsung's balance sheet in **Samsung** Appendix A. What does it title its plant assets? What is the book value of its plant assets at December 31, 2012?

20. Refer to the December 31, 2012, balance **Samsung** sheet of Samsung in Appendix A. What long-term assets discussed in this chapter are reported by the company?

21. Identify the main difference between (a) plant assets and current assets, (b) plant assets and inventory, and (c) plant assets and long-term investments.

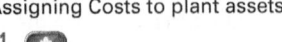 connect

QUICK STUDY

QS 8-1

Assigning Costs to plant assets

C1 **Ⅰ**

Listed below are certain costs (or discounts) incurred in the purchase or construction of new plant assets. Indicate whether the costs should be expensed or included in the cost of the plant assets on the balance sheet. For costs that should be included in plant assets, indicate in which category of plant assets (Equipment, Building, or Land) the related costs should be recorded on the balance sheet.

1. Charges incurred to train employees to use new equipment

2. Invoice cost to purchase new equipment

3. Deduction for an early payment discount taken on the purchase of new equipment

4. Real estate commissions incurred on land purchased for a new plant

5. Property taxes on land incurred after it was purchased

6. Costs to obtain a tune-up for the delivery truck used to deliver new equipment to the warehouse

7. Costs to lay foundation for a new building

8. Insurance on a new building during the construction phase

QS 8-2

Cost of plant assets C1 **Ⅰ**

Kegler Bowling installs automatic scorekeeping equipment with an invoice cost of $190,000. The electrical work required for the installation costs $20,000. Additional costs are $4,000 for delivery and $13,700 for sales tax. During the installation, a component of the equipment is carelessly left on a lane and hit by the automatic lane-cleaning machine. The cost of repairing the component is $1,850. What is the total recorded cost of the automatic scorekeeping equipment?

QS 8-3

Straight-line depreciation

P1

On January 2, 2013, the Cerritos Band acquires sound equipment for concert performances at a cost of $65,800. The band estimates it will use this equipment for four years, during which time it anticipates performing about 200 concerts. It estimates that after four years it can sell the equipment for $2,000. During year 2013, the band performs 45 concerts. Compute the year 2013 depreciation using the straight-line method.

Refer to the information in QS 8-3. Compute the year 2013 depreciation using the units-of-production method.

QS 8-4
Units-of-production depreciation
P1

Refer to the facts in QS 8-3. Assume that the Cerritos Band uses straight-line depreciation but realizes at the start of the second year that due to concert bookings beyond expectations, this equipment will last only a total of three years. The salvage value remains unchanged. Compute the revised depreciation for both the second and third years.

QS 8-5
Computing revised depreciation
C2

A fleet of refrigerated delivery trucks is acquired on January 5, 2013, at a cost of $830,000 with an estimated useful life of eight years and an estimated salvage value of $75,000. Compute the depreciation expense for the first three years using the double-declining-balance method.

QS 8-6
Double-declining-balance
method P1

Assume a company's equipment carries a book value of $16,000 ($16,500 cost less $500 accumulated depreciation) and a fair value of $14,750, *and* that the $1,250 decline in fair value in comparison to the book value meets the 2-step impairment test. Prepare the entry to record this $1,250 impairment.

QS 8-7
Recording plant asset
impairment C2

1. Classify the following as either revenue or capital expenditures.
   a. Paid $40,000 cash to replace a compressor on a refrigeration system that extends its useful life by four years.
   b. Paid $200 cash per truck for the cost of their annual tune-ups.
   c. Paid $175 for the monthly cost of replacement filters on an air-conditioning system.
   d. Completed an addition to an office building for $225,000 cash.
2. Prepare the journal entries to record transactions *a* and *d* of part 1.

QS 8-8
Revenue and capital
expenditures
C3

Hortez Co. owns equipment that cost $76,800, with accumulated depreciation of $40,800. Hortez sells the equipment for cash. Record the sale of the equipment assuming Hortez sells the equipment for (1) $47,000 cash, (2) $36,000 cash, and (3) $31,000 cash.

QS 8-9
Disposal of assets P2

Corentine Company acquires an ore mine at a cost of $1,400,000. It incurs additional costs of $400,000 to access the mine, which is estimated to hold 1,000,000 tons of ore. The estimated value of the land after the ore is removed is $200,000.
1. Prepare the entry(ies) to record the cost of the ore mine.
2. Prepare the year-end adjusting entry if 180,000 tons of ore are mined and sold the first year.

QS 8-10
Natural resources and depletion
P3

Which of the following assets are reported on the balance sheet as intangible assets? Which are reported as natural resources? (*a*) Oil well, (*b*) trademark, (*c*) leasehold, (*d*) gold mine, (*e*) building, (*f*) copyright, (*g*) franchise, (*h*) timberland.

QS 8-11
Classify assets P3 P4

On January 4 of this year, Freckles Boutique incurs a $105,000 cost to modernize its store. Improvements include new floors, ceilings, wiring, and wall coverings. These improvements are estimated to yield benefits for 10 years. Freckles leases its store and has eight years remaining on the lease. Prepare the entry to record (1) the cost of modernization and (2) amortization at the end of this current year.

QS 8-12
Intangible assets and
amortization P4

Aneko Company reports the following ($ 000s): net sales of $14,800 for 2013 and $13,990 for 2012; end-of-year total assets of $19,100 for 2013 and $17,900 for 2012. Compute its total asset turnover for 2013, and assess its level if competitors average a total asset turnover of 2.0 times.

QS 8-13
Computing total asset turnover
A1

Caleb Co. owns a machine that costs $42,400 with accumulated depreciation of $18,400. Caleb exchanges the machine for a newer model that has a market value of $52,000. (1) Record the exchange assuming Caleb paid $30,000 cash and the exchange has commercial substance. (2) Record the exchange assuming Caleb pays $22,000 cash and the exchange lacks commercial substance.

QS 8-14ᴬ
Asset exchange
P5

Answer each of the following related to international accounting standards.
a. Accounting for plant assets involves cost determination, depreciation, additional expenditures, and disposals. Is plant asset accounting broadly similar or dissimilar between IFRS and U.S. GAAP? Identify one notable difference between IFRS and U.S. GAAP in accounting for plant assets.
b. Describe how IFRS and U.S. GAAP treat increases in the value of plant assets subsequent to their acquisition (but before their disposition).

QS 8-15
International accounting
standards
C1 C3

EXERCISES

Exercise 8-1

Cost of plant assets

C1

Rizio Co. purchases a machine for $12,500, terms 2/10, n/60, FOB shipping point. The seller prepaid the $360 freight charges, adding the amount to the invoice and bringing its total to $12,860. The machine requires special steel mounting and power connections costing $895. Another $475 is paid to assemble the machine and get it into operation. In moving the machine to its steel mounting, $180 in damages occurred. Materials costing $40 are used in adjusting the machine to produce a satisfactory product. The adjustments are normal for this machine and are not the result of the damages. Compute the cost recorded for this machine. (Rizio pays for this machine within the cash discount period.)

Exercise 8-2

Recording costs of assets

C1

Cala Manufacturing purchases a large lot on which an old building is located as part of its plans to build a new plant. The negotiated purchase price is $280,000 for the lot plus $110,000 for the old building. The company pays $33,500 to tear down the old building and $47,000 to fill and level the lot. It also pays a total of $1,540,000 in construction costs—this amount consists of $1,452,200 for the new building and $87,800 for lighting and paving a parking area next to the building. Prepare a single journal entry to record these costs incurred by Cala, all of which are paid in cash.

Exercise 8-3

Lump-sum purchase of plant assets   C1

Liltua Company pays $375,280 for real estate plus $20,100 in closing costs. The real estate consists of land appraised at $157,040; land improvements appraised at $58,890; and a building appraised at $176,670. Allocate the total cost among the three purchased assets and prepare the journal entry to record the purchase.

Exercise 8-4

Straight-line depreciation   P1

In early January 2013, NewTech purchases computer equipment for $154,000 to use in operating activities for the next four years. It estimates the equipment's salvage value at $25,000. Prepare a table showing depreciation and book value for each of the four years assuming straight-line depreciation.

Exercise 8-5

Double-declining-balance depreciation   P1

Refer to the information in Exercise 8-4. Prepare a table showing depreciation and book value for each of the four years assuming double-declining-balance depreciation.

Exercise 8-6

Straight-line depreciation

P1

Ramirez Company installs a computerized manufacturing machine in its factory at the beginning of the year at a cost of $43,500. The machine's useful life is estimated at 10 years, or 385,000 units of product, with a $5,000 salvage value. During its second year, the machine produces 32,500 units of product. Determine the machine's second-year depreciation under the straight-line method.

Exercise 8-7

Units-of-production depreciation

P1

Refer to the information in Exercise 8-6. Determine the machine's second-year depreciation using the units-of-production method.

Exercise 8-8

Double-declining-balance depreciation   P1

Refer to the information in Exercise 8-6. Determine the machine's second-year depreciation using the double-declining-balance method.

Exercise 8-9

Straight-line, partial-year depreciation   C2

On April 1, 2012, Cyclone's Backhoe Co. purchases a trencher for $280,000. The machine is expected to last five years and have a salvage value of $40,000. Compute depreciation expense for both 2012 and 2013 assuming the company uses the straight-line method.

Exercise 8-10

Double-declining-balance, partial-year depreciation   C2

Refer to the information in Exercise 8-9. Compute depreciation expense for both 2012 and 2013 assuming the company uses the double-declining-balance method.

Exercise 8-11

Revising depreciation

C2

Apex Fitness Club uses straight-line depreciation for a machine costing $23,860, with an estimated four-year life and a $2,400 salvage value. At the beginning of the third year, Apex determines that the machine has three more years of remaining useful life, after which it will have an estimated $2,000 salvage value. Compute (1) the machine's book value at the end of its second year and (2) the amount of depreciation for each of the final three years given the revised estimates.

Check   (2) $3,710

Tory Enterprises pays $238,400 for equipment that will last five years and have a $43,600 salvage value. By using the equipment in its operations for five years, the company expects to earn $88,500 annually, after deducting all expenses except depreciation. Prepare a table showing income before depreciation, depreciation expense, and net (pretax) income for each year and for the total five-year period, assuming straight-line depreciation.

Exercise 8-12
Straight-line depreciation and income effects P1

Refer to the information in Exercise 8-12. Prepare a table showing income before depreciation, depreciation expense, and net (pretax) income for each year and for the total five-year period, assuming double-declining-balance depreciation is used.

Exercise 8-13
Double-declining-balance depreciation P1

Check   Year 3 NI, $54,170

Veradis Company owns a building that appears on its prior year-end balance sheet at its original $572,000 cost less $429,000 accumulated depreciation. The building is depreciated on a straight-line basis assuming a 20-year life and no salvage value. During the first week in January of the current calendar year, major structural repairs are completed on the building at a $68,350 cost. The repairs extend its useful life for 5 years beyond the 20 years originally estimated.
1. Determine the building's age (plant asset age) as of the prior year-end balance sheet date.
2. Prepare the entry to record the cost of the structural repairs that are paid in cash.
3. Determine the book value of the building immediately after the repairs are recorded.
4. Prepare the entry to record the current calendar year's depreciation.

Exercise 8-14
Extraordinary repairs;
plant asset age
C3

Check   (3) $211,350

Oki Company pays $264,000 for equipment expected to last four years and have a $29,000 salvage value. Prepare journal entries to record the following costs related to the equipment.
1. During the second year of the equipment's life, $22,000 cash is paid for a new component expected to increase the equipment's productivity by 10% a year.
2. During the third year, $6,250 cash is paid for normal repairs necessary to keep the equipment in good working order.
3. During the fourth year, $14,870 is paid for repairs expected to increase the useful life of the equipment from four to five years.

Exercise 8-15
Ordinary repairs, extraordinary repairs and betterments
C3

Diaz Company owns a milling machine that cost $250,000 and has accumulated depreciation of $182,000. Prepare the entry to record the disposal of the milling machine on January 3 under each of the following independent situations.
1. The machine needed extensive repairs, and it was not worth repairing. Diaz disposed of the machine, receiving nothing in return.
2. Diaz sold the machine for $35,000 cash.
3. Diaz sold the machine for $68,000 cash.
4. Diaz sold the machine for $80,000 cash.

Exercise 8-16
Disposal of assets
P2

Rayya Co. purchases and installs a machine on January 1, 2013, at a total cost of $105,000. Straight-line depreciation is taken each year for four years assuming a seven-year life and no salvage value. The machine is disposed of on July 1, 2017, during its fifth year of service. Prepare entries to record the partial year's depreciation on July 1, 2017, and to record the disposal under the following separate assumptions: (1) the machine is sold for $45,500 cash and (2) Rayya receives an insurance settlement of $25,000 resulting from the total destruction of the machine in a fire.

Exercise 8-17
Partial-year depreciation; disposal of plant asset
P2

On April 2, 2013, Montana Mining Co. pays $3,721,000 for an ore deposit containing 1,525,000 tons. The company installs machinery in the mine costing $213,500, with an estimated seven-year life and no salvage value. The machinery will be abandoned when the ore is completely mined. Montana begins mining on May 1, 2013, and mines and sells 166,200 tons of ore during the remaining eight months of 2013. Prepare the December 31, 2013, entries to record both the ore deposit depletion and the mining machinery depreciation. Mining machinery depreciation should be in proportion to the mine's depletion.

Exercise 8-18
Depletion of natural resources
P1   P3

Milano Gallery purchases the copyright on an oil painting for $418,000 on January 1, 2013. The copyright legally protects its owner for 10 more years. The company plans to market and sell prints of the original for 11 years. Prepare entries to record the purchase of the copyright on January 1, 2013, and its annual amortization on December 31, 2013.

Exercise 8-19
Amortization of intangible assets
P4

Exercise 8-20

Goodwill

P4

On January 1, 2013, Robinson Company purchased Franklin Company at a price of $2,500,000. The fair market value of the net assets purchased equals $1,800,000.

1. What is the amount of goodwill that Robinson records at the purchase date?

2. Explain how Robinson would determine the amount of goodwill amortization for the year ended December 31, 2013.

3. Robinson Company believes that its employees provide superior customer service, and through their efforts, Robinson Company believes it has created $900,000 of goodwill. How would Robinson Company record this goodwill?

Exercise 8-21

Cash flows related to assets

C1

GOOGLE

Refer to the statement of cash flows for Google in Appendix A for the fiscal year ended December 31, 2012, to answer the following.

1. What amount of cash is used to purchase property and equipment?

2. How much depreciation and amortization of property and equipment are recorded?

3. What total amount of net cash is used in investing activities?

Exercise 8-22

Evaluating efficient use of assets

A1

Lok Co. reports net sales of $5,856,480 for 2012 and $8,679,690 for 2013. End-of-year balances for total assets are 2011, $1,686,000; 2012, $1,800,000; and 2013, $1,982,000. (*a*) Compute Lok's total asset turnover for 2012 and 2013. (*b*) Comment on Lok's efficiency in using its assets if its competitors average a total asset turnover of 3.0.

Exercise 8-23[A]

Exchanging assets

P5

Check   (2) $14,500

Gilly Construction trades in an old tractor for a new tractor, receiving a $29,000 trade-in allowance and paying the remaining $83,000 in cash. The old tractor had cost $96,000, and straight-line accumulated depreciation of $52,500 had been recorded to date under the assumption that it would last eight years and have a $12,000 salvage value. Answer the following questions assuming the exchange has commercial substance.

1. What is the book value of the old tractor at the time of exchange?

2. What is the loss on this asset exchange?

3. What amount should be recorded (debited) in the asset account for the new tractor?

Exercise 8-24[A]

Recording plant asset disposals

P2 P5

Check   (2) Dr. Machinery (new), $54,575

On January 2, 2013, Bering Co. disposes of a machine costing $44,000 with accumulated depreciation of $24,625. Prepare the entries to record the disposal under each of the following separate assumptions.

1. The machine is sold for $18,250 cash.

2. The machine is traded in for a newer machine having a $60,200 cash price. A $25,000 trade-in allowance is received, and the balance is paid in cash. Assume the asset exchange lacks commercial substance.

3. The machine is traded in for a newer machine having a $60,200 cash price. A $15,000 trade-in allowance is received, and the balance is paid in cash. Assume the asset exchange has commercial substance.

Exercise 8-25

Accounting for plant assets under IFRS

C2 P1 P2

Volkswagen Group reports the following information for property, plant and equipment as of December 31, 2010, along with additions, disposals, depreciation, and impairments for the year ended December 31, 2010 (euros in millions):

Property, plant and equipment, net	€25,847
Additions to property, plant and equipment	5,634
Disposals of property, plant and equipment	2,522
Depreciation on property, plant and equipment	4,731
Impairments to property, plant and equipment	451

1. Prepare Volkswagen's journal entry to record its depreciation for 2010.

2. Prepare Volkswagen's journal entry to record its additions for 2010 assuming they are paid in cash and are treated as "betterments (improvements)" to the assets.

3. Prepare Volkswagen's journal entry to record its €2,522 in disposals for 2010 assuming it receives €700 cash in return and the accumulated depreciation on the disposed assets totals €1,322.

4. Volkswagen reports €451 of impairments. Do these impairments increase or decrease the property, plant and equipment account? And, by what amount?

≡connect

Timberly Construction negotiates a lump-sum purchase of several assets from a company that is going out of business. The purchase is completed on January 1, 2013, at a total cash price of $900,000 for a building, land, land improvements, and four vehicles. The estimated market values of the assets are building, $508,800; land, $297,600; land improvements, $28,800; and four vehicles, $124,800. The company's fiscal year ends on December 31.

PROBLEM SET A

Problem 8-1A
Plant asset costs; depreciation methods C1 P1 [image]

Required

1. Prepare a table to allocate the lump-sum purchase price to the separate assets purchased (round percents to the nearest 1%). Prepare the journal entry to record the purchase.

2. Compute the depreciation expense for year 2013 on the building using the straight-line method, assuming a 15-year life and a $27,000 salvage value.

3. Compute the depreciation expense for year 2013 on the land improvements assuming a five-year life and double-declining-balance depreciation.

Analysis Component

4. Defend or refute this statement: Accelerated depreciation results in payment of less taxes over the asset's life.

Check (2) $30,000

(3) $10,800

In January 2013, Mitzu Co. pays $2,600,000 for a tract of land with two buildings on it. It plans to demolish Building 1 and build a new store in its place. Building 2 will be a company office; it is appraised at $644,000, with a useful life of 20 years and an $60,000 salvage value. A lighted parking lot near Building 1 has improvements (Land Improvements 1) valued at $420,000 that are expected to last another 12 years with no salvage value. Without the buildings and improvements, the tract of land is valued at $1,736,000. The company also incurs the following additional costs:

Problem 8-2A
Asset cost allocation; straight-line depreciation
C1 P1

Cost to demolish Building I	$ 328,400
Cost of additional land grading	175,400
Cost to construct new building (Building 3), having a useful life of 25 years and a $392,000 salvage value	2,202,000
Cost of new land improvements (Land Improvements 2) near Building 2 having a 20-year useful life and no salvage value	164,000

Required

1. Prepare a table with the following column headings: Land, Building 2, Building 3, Land Improvements 1, and Land Improvements 2. Allocate the costs incurred by Mitzu to the appropriate columns and total each column (round percents to the nearest 1%).

2. Prepare a single journal entry to record all the incurred costs assuming they are paid in cash on January 1, 2013.

3. Using the straight-line method, prepare the December 31 adjusting entries to record depreciation for the 12 months of 2013 when these assets were in use.

Check (1) Land costs, $2,115,800; Building 2 costs, $598,000

(3) Depr.—Land Improv. 1 and 2, $32,500 and $8,200

Champion Contractors completed the following transactions and events involving the purchase and operation of equipment in its business.

Problem 8-3A
Computing and revising depreciation; revenue and capital expenditures
C1 C2 C3

2012

Jan. 1   Paid $287,600 cash plus $11,500 in sales tax and $1,500 in transportation (FOB shipping point) for a new loader. The loader is estimated to have a four-year life and a $20,600 salvage value. Loader costs are recorded in the Equipment account.

Jan. 3   Paid $4,800 to enclose the cab and install air conditioning in the loader to enable operations under harsher conditions. This increased the estimated salvage value of the loader by another $1,400.

Dec. 31   Recorded annual straight-line depreciation on the loader.

Check Dec. 31, 2012, Dr. Depr. Expense—Equip., $70,850

2013

Jan. 1   Paid $5,400 to overhaul the loader's engine, which increased the loader's estimated useful life by two years.

Feb. 17   Paid $820 to repair the loader after the operator backed it into a tree.

Dec. 31   Recorded annual straight-line depreciation on the loader.

Check Dec. 31, 2013, Dr. Depr. Expense—Equip., $43,590

Required

Prepare journal entries to record these transactions and events.

Problem 8-4A
Computing and revising depreciation; selling plant assets
C2 P1 P2

Yoshi Company completed the following transactions and events involving its delivery trucks.

2012

Jan. 1   Paid $20,515 cash plus $1,485 in sales tax for a new delivery truck estimated to have a five-year life and a $2,000 salvage value. Delivery truck costs are recorded in the Trucks account.
Dec. 31   Recorded annual straight-line depreciation on the truck.

2013

Check Dec. 31, 2013, Dr. Depr. Expense—Trucks, $5,200

Dec. 31   Due to new information obtained earlier in the year, the truck's estimated useful life was changed from five to four years, and the estimated salvage value was increased to $2,400. Recorded annual straight-line depreciation on the truck.

2014

Dec. 31, 2014, Dr. Loss on Disposal of Trucks, $2,300

Dec. 31   Recorded annual straight-line depreciation on the truck.
Dec. 31   Sold the truck for $5,300 cash.

Required

Prepare journal entries to record these transactions and events.

Problem 8-5A
Depreciation methods
P1

A machine costing $257,500 with a four-year life and an estimated $20,000 salvage value is installed in Luther Company's factory on January 1. The factory manager estimates the machine will produce 475,000 units of product during its life. It actually produces the following units: year 1, 220,000; year 2, 124,600; year 3, 121,800; and year 4, 15,200. The total number of units produced by the end of year 4 exceeds the original estimate—this difference was not predicted. (The machine must not be depreciated below its estimated salvage value.)

Required

Prepare a table with the following column headings and compute depreciation for each year (and total depreciation of all years combined) for the machine under each depreciation method.

Check Year 4: units-of-production depreciation, $4,300; DDB depreciation, $12,187

Year	Straight-Line	Units-of-Production	Double-Declining-Balance

---

Problem 8-6A
Disposal of plant assets
C1 P1 P2

Onslow Co. purchases a used machine for $178,000 cash on January 2 and readies it for use the next day at an $2,840 cost. On January 3, it is installed on a required operating platform costing $1,160, and it is further readied for operations. The company predicts the machine will be used for six years and have a $14,000 salvage value. Depreciation is to be charged on a straight-line basis. On December 31, at the end of its fifth year in operations, it is disposed of.

Required

1. Prepare journal entries to record the machine's purchase and the costs to ready and install it. Cash is paid for all costs incurred.

Check (2b) Depr. Exp., $28,000

2. Prepare journal entries to record depreciation of the machine at December 31 of (a) its first year in operations and (b) the year of its disposal.

(3c) Dr. Loss from Fire, $12,000

3. Prepare journal entries to record the machine's disposal under each of the following separate assumptions: (a) it is sold for $15,000 cash; (b) it is sold for $50,000 cash; and (c) it is destroyed in a fire and the insurance company pays $30,000 cash to settle the loss claim.

Problem 8-7A
Natural resources
P3

On July 23 of the current year, Dakota Mining Co. pays $4,715,000 for land estimated to contain 5,125,000 tons of recoverable ore. It installs machinery costing $410,000 that has a 10-year life and no salvage value and is capable of mining the ore deposit in eight years. The machinery is paid for on July 25, seven days before mining operations begin. The company removes and sells 480,000 tons of ore during its first five months of operations ending on December 31. Depreciation of the machinery is in proportion to the mine's depletion as the machinery will be abandoned after the ore is mined.

Required

Prepare entries to record (*a*) the purchase of the land, (*b*) the cost and installation of machinery, (*c*) the first five months' depletion assuming the land has a net salvage value of zero after the ore is mined, and (*d*) the first five months' depreciation on the machinery.

Check (*c*) Depletion, $441,600
(*d*) Depreciation, $38,400

Analysis Component

Describe both the similarities and differences in amortization, depletion, and depreciation.

On July 1, 2008, Falk Company signed a contract to lease space in a building for 15 years. The lease contract calls for annual (prepaid) rental payments of $80,000 on each July 1 throughout the life of the lease and for the lessee to pay for all additions and improvements to the leased property. On June 25, 2013, Falk decides to sublease the space to Ryan & Associates for the remaining 10 years of the lease—Ryan pays $200,000 to Falk for the right to sublease and it agrees to assume the obligation to pay the $80,000 annual rent to the building owner beginning July 1, 2013. After taking possession of the leased space, Ryan pays for improving the office portion of the leased space at a $130,000 cost. The improvements are paid for by Ryan on July 5, 2013, and are estimated to have a useful life equal to the 16 years remaining in the life of the building.

Problem 8-8A
Intangible assets

P4

Required

1. Prepare entries for Ryan to record (*a*) its payment to Falk for the right to sublease the building space, (*b*) its payment of the 2013 annual rent to the building owner, and (*c*) its payment for the office improvements.

2. Prepare Ryan's year-end adjusting entries required at December 31, 2013, to (*a*) amortize the $200,000 cost of the sublease, (*b*) amortize the office improvements, and (*c*) record rent expense.

Check Dr. Rent Expense for
(2*a*) $10,000, (2*c*) $40,000

Nagy Company negotiates a lump-sum purchase of several assets from a contractor who is relocating. The purchase is completed on January 1, 2013, at a total cash price of $1,800,000 for a building, land, land improvements, and five trucks. The estimated market values of the assets are building, $890,000; land, $427,200; land improvements, $249,200; and five trucks, $213,600. The company's fiscal year ends on December 31.

PROBLEM SET B

Problem 8-1B
Plant asset costs; depreciation methods

C1 P1

Required

1. Prepare a table to allocate the lump-sum purchase price to the separate assets purchased (round percents to the nearest 1%). Prepare the journal entry to record the purchase.

2. Compute the depreciation expense for year 2013 on the building using the straight-line method, assuming a 12-year life and a $120,000 salvage value.

Check (2) $65,000

3. Compute the depreciation expense for year 2013 on the land improvements assuming a 10-year life and double-declining-balance depreciation.

(3) $50,400

Analysis Component

4. Defend or refute this statement: Accelerated depreciation results in payment of more taxes over the asset's life.

In January 2013, ProTech Co. pays $1,550,000 for a tract of land with two buildings. It plans to demolish Building A and build a new shop in its place. Building B will be a company office; it is appraised at $482,800, with a useful life of 15 years and a $99,500 salvage value. A lighted parking lot near Building B has improvements (Land Improvements B) valued at $142,000 that are expected to last another five years with no salvage value. Without the buildings and improvements, the tract of land is valued at $795,200. The company also incurs the following additional costs.

Problem 8-2B
Asset cost allocation; straight-line depreciation

C1 P1

Cost to demolish Building A	$ 122,000
Cost of additional land grading	174,500
Cost to construct new building (Building C), having a useful life of 20 years and a $258,000 salvage value	1,458,000
Cost of new land improvements (Land Improvements C) near Building C, having a 10-year useful life and no salvage value	103,500

Required

1. Prepare a table with the following column headings: Land, Building B, Building C, Land Improvements B, and Land Improvements C. Allocate the costs incurred by ProTech to the appropriate columns and total each column (round percents to the nearest 1%).

2. Prepare a single journal entry to record all incurred costs assuming they are paid in cash on January 1, 2013.

3. Using the straight-line method, prepare the December 31 adjusting entries to record depreciation for the 12 months of 2013 when these assets were in use.

Problem 8-3B
Computing and revising depreciation; revenue and capital expenditures
C1 C2 C3

Mercury Delivery Service completed the following transactions and events involving the purchase and operation of equipment for its business.

2012

Jan. 1 Paid $25,860 cash plus $1,810 in sales tax for a new delivery van that was estimated to have a five-year life and a $3,670 salvage value. Van costs are recorded in the Equipment account.

Jan. 3 Paid $1,850 to install sorting racks in the van for more accurate and quicker delivery of packages. This increases the estimated salvage value of the van by another $230.

Dec. 31 Recorded annual straight-line depreciation on the van.

2013

Jan. 1 Paid $2,064 to overhaul the van's engine, which increased the van's estimated useful life by two years.

May 10 Paid $800 to repair the van after the driver backed it into a loading dock.

Dec. 31 Record annual straight-line depreciation on the van. (Round to the nearest dollar.)

Required

Prepare journal entries to record these transactions and events.

Problem 8-4B
Computing and revising depreciation; selling plant assets
C2 P1 P2

York Instruments completed the following transactions and events involving its machinery.

2012

Jan. 1 Paid $107,800 cash plus $6,470 in sales tax for a new machine. The machine is estimated to have a six-year life and a $9,720 salvage value.

Dec. 31 Recorded annual straight-line depreciation on the machinery.

2013

Dec. 31 Due to new information obtained earlier in the year, the machine's estimated useful life was changed from six to four years, and the estimated salvage value was increased to $14,345. Recorded annual straight-line depreciation on the machinery.

2014

Dec. 31 Recorded annual straight-line depreciation on the machinery.

Dec. 31 Sold the machine for $25,240 cash.

Required

Prepare journal entries to record these transactions and events.

Problem 8-5B
Depreciation methods
P1

On January 2, Manning Co. purchases and installs a new machine costing $324,000 with a five-year life and an estimated $30,000 salvage value. Management estimates the machine will produce 1,470,000 units of product during its life. Actual production of units is as follows: year 1, 355,600; year 2, 320,400; year 3, 317,000; year 4, 343,600; and year 5, 138,500. The total number of units produced by the end of year 5 exceeds the original estimate—this difference was not predicted. (The machine must not be depreciated below its estimated salvage value.)

Required

Prepare a table with the following column headings and compute depreciation for each year (and total depreciation of all years combined) for the machine under each depreciation method.

Year	Straight-Line	Units-of-Production	Double-Declining-Balance

---

On January 1, Walker purchases a used machine for $150,000 and readies it for use the next day at a cost of $3,510. On January 4, it is mounted on a required operating platform costing $4,600, and it is further readied for operations. Management estimates the machine will be used for seven years and have an $18,110 salvage value. Depreciation is to be charged on a straight-line basis. On December 31, at the end of its sixth year of use, the machine is disposed of.

Problem 8-6B
Disposal of plant assets
C1 P1 P2

Required

1. Prepare journal entries to record the machine's purchase and the costs to ready and install it. Cash is paid for all costs incurred.
2. Prepare journal entries to record depreciation of the machine at December 31 of (*a*) its first year in operations and (*b*) the year of its disposal.
3. Prepare journal entries to record the machine's disposal under each of the following separate assumptions: (*a*) it is sold for $28,000 cash; (*b*) it is sold for $52,000 cash; and (*c*) it is destroyed in a fire and the insurance company pays $25,000 cash to settle the loss claim.

On February 19 of the current year, Quartzite Co. pays $5,400,000 for land estimated to contain 4 million tons of recoverable ore. It installs machinery costing $400,000 that has a 16-year life and no salvage value and is capable of mining the ore deposit in 12 years. The machinery is paid for on March 21, eleven days before mining operations begin. The company removes and sells 254,000 tons of ore during its first nine months of operations ending on December 31. Depreciation of the machinery is in proportion to the mine's depletion as the machinery will be abandoned after the ore is mined.

Problem 8-7B
Natural resources
P3

Required

Prepare entries to record (*a*) the purchase of the land, (*b*) the cost and installation of the machinery, (*c*) the first nine months' depletion assuming the land has a net salvage value of zero after the ore is mined, and (*d*) the first nine months' depreciation on the machinery.

Analysis Component

Describe both the similarities and differences in amortization, depletion, and depreciation.

On January 1, 2006, Mason Co. entered into a 12-year lease on a building. The lease contract requires (1) annual (prepaid) rental payments of $36,000 each January 1 throughout the life of the lease and (2) for the lessee to pay for all additions and improvements to the leased property. On January 1, 2013, Mason decides to sublease the space to Stewart Co. for the remaining five years of the lease—Stewart pays $40,000 to Mason for the right to sublease and agrees to assume the obligation to pay the $36,000 annual rent to the building owner beginning January 1, 2013. After taking possession of the leased space, Stewart pays for improving the office portion of the leased space at a $20,000 cost. The improvements are paid for by Stewart on January 3, 2013, and are estimated to have a useful life equal to the 13 years remaining in the life of the building.

Problem 8-8B
Intangible assets
P4

Required

1. Prepare entries for Stewart to record (*a*) its payment to Mason for the right to sublease the building space, (*b*) its payment of the 2013 annual rent to the building owner, and (*c*) its payment for the office improvements.
2. Prepare Stewart's year-end adjusting entries required on December 31, 2013, to (*a*) amortize the $40,000 cost of the sublease, (*b*) amortize the office improvements, and (*c*) record rent expense.

SERIAL PROBLEM
Success Systems
P1 A1

(This serial problem began in Chapter 1 and continues through most of the book. If previous chapter segments were not completed, the serial problem can begin at this point. It is helpful, but not necessary, to use the Working Papers that accompany the book.)

SP 8 Selected ledger account balances for Success Systems follow.

	For Three Months Ended December 31, 2013	For Three Months Ended March 31, 2014
Office equipment	$ 8,000	$ 8,000
Accumulated depreciation—Office equipment	400	800
Computer equipment	20,000	20,000
Accumulated depreciation—Computer equipment	1,250	2,500
Total revenue	31,284	43,853
Total assets	93,248	129,909

Required

1. Assume that Success Systems does not acquire additional office equipment or computer equipment in 2014. Compute amounts for *the year ended* December 31, 2014, for Depreciation Expense—Office Equipment and for Depreciation Expense—Computer Equipment (assume use of the straight-line method).

2. Given the assumptions in part 1, what is the book value of both the office equipment and the computer equipment as of December 31, 2014?

3. Compute the three-month total asset turnover for Success Systems as of March 31, 2014. Use total revenue for the numerator and average the December 31, 2013, total assets and the March 31, 2014, total assets for the denominator. Interpret its total asset turnover if competitors average 2.5 for annual periods. (Round turnover to two decimals.)

Check (3) Three-month (annual) turnover = 0.393 (1.572 annual)

Beyond the Numbers

REPORTING IN ACTION

A1

APPLE

BTN 8-1 Refer to the financial statements of Apple in Appendix A to answer the following.

1. What percent of the original cost of Apple's property and equipment remains to be depreciated as of September 29, 2012 and September 24, 2011? Assume these assets have no salvage value.

2. Over what length(s) of time is Apple depreciating its major categories of property and equipment?

3. What is the change in total property, plant, and equipment (before accumulated depreciation) for the year ended September 29, 2012? What is the amount of cash provided (used) by investing activities for property and equipment for the year ended September 29, 2012? What is one possible explanation for the difference between these two amounts?

4. Compute its total asset turnover for the year ended September 29, 2012, and the year ended September 24, 2011. Assume total assets at September 25, 2010, are $75,183 ($ millions).

Fast Forward

5. Access Apple's financial statements for fiscal years ending after September 29, 2012, at its Website (Apple.com) or the SEC's EDGAR database (www.SEC.gov). Recompute Apple's total asset turnover for the additional years' data you collect. Comment on any differences relative to the turnover computed in part 4.

BTN 8-2   Comparative figures for Apple and Google follow.

($ millions)	Apple			Google		
	Current Year	One Year Prior	Two Years Prior	Current Year	One Year Prior	Two Years Prior
Total assets	$176,064	$116,371	$75,183	$93,798	$72,574	$57,851
Net sales	156,508	108,249	65,225	50,175	37,905	29,321

Required

1. Compute total asset turnover for the most recent two years for Apple and Google using the data shown.
2. Which company is more efficient in generating net sales given the total assets it employs? Assume an industry average of 1.0 for asset turnover.

BTN 8-3   Flo Choi owns a small business and manages its accounting. Her company just finished a year in which a large amount of borrowed funds was invested in a new building addition as well as in equipment and fixture additions. Choi's banker requires her to submit semiannual financial statements so he can monitor the financial health of her business. He has warned her that if profit margins erode, he might raise the interest rate on the borrowed funds to reflect the increased loan risk from the bank's point of view. Choi knows profit margin is likely to decline this year. As she prepares year-end adjusting entries, she decides to apply the following depreciation rule: All asset additions are considered to be in use on the first day of the following month. (The previous rule assumed assets are in use on the first day of the month nearest to the purchase date.)

Required

1. Identify decisions that managers like Choi must make in applying depreciation methods.
2. Is Choi's rule an ethical violation, or is it a legitimate decision in computing depreciation?
3. How will Choi's new depreciation rule affect the profit margin of her business?

BTN 8-4   Teams are to select an industry, and each team member is to select a different company in that industry. Each team member is to acquire the financial statements (Form 10-K) of the company selected— see the company's Website or the SEC's EDGAR database (www.sec.gov). Use the financial statements to compute total asset turnover. Communicate with teammates via a meeting, e-mail, or telephone to discuss the meaning of this ratio, how different companies compare to each other, and the industry norm. The team must prepare a one-page report that describes the ratios for each company and identifies the conclusions reached during the team's discussion.

BTN 8-5   Access the Yahoo! (ticker: YHOO) 10-K report for the year ended December 31, 2011, filed on February 29, 2012, at www.sec.gov.

Required

1. What amount of goodwill is reported on Yahoo!'s balance sheet? What percentage of total assets does its goodwill represent? Is goodwill a major asset for Yahoo!? Explain.
2. Locate Note 5 to its financial statements. Identify the change in goodwill from December 31, 2010, to December 31, 2011. Comment on the change in goodwill over this period.
3. Locate Note 6 to its financial statements. What are the three categories of intangible assets that Yahoo! reports at December 31, 2011? What proportion of total assets do the intangibles represent?
4. What does Yahoo! indicate is the life of "Trade names, trademarks, and domain names" according to its Note 6? Comment on the difference between the estimated useful life and the legal life of Yahoo!'s trademark.

TEAMWORK IN ACTION

P1

Point: This activity can follow an overview of each method. Step 1 allows for three areas of expertise. Larger teams will have some duplication of areas, but the straight-line choice should not be duplicated. Expert teams can use the book and consult with the instructor.

BTN 8-6 Each team member is to become an expert on one depreciation method to facilitate teammates' understanding of that method. Follow these procedures:

a. Each team member is to select an area for expertise from one of the following depreciation methods: straight-line, units-of-production, or double-declining-balance.

b. Expert teams are to be formed from those who have selected the same area of expertise. The instructor will identify the location where each expert team meets.

c. Using the following data, expert teams are to collaborate and develop a presentation answering the requirements. Expert team members must write the presentation in a format they can show to their learning teams.

Data and Requirements On January 8, 2011, Whitewater Riders purchases a van to transport rafters back to the point of departure at the conclusion of the rafting adventures they operate. The cost of the van is $44,000. It has an estimated salvage value of $2,000 and is expected to be used for four years and driven 60,000 miles. The van is driven 12,000 miles in 2011, 18,000 miles in 2012, 21,000 in 2013, and 10,000 in 2014.

1. Compute the annual depreciation expense for each year of the van's estimated useful life.
2. Explain when and how annual depreciation is recorded.
3. Explain the impact on income of this depreciation method versus others over the van's life.
4. Identify the van's book value for each year of its life and illustrate the reporting of this amount for any one year.

d. Re-form original learning teams. In rotation, experts are to present to their teams the results from part c. Experts are to encourage and respond to questions.

ENTREPRENEURIAL DECISION

A1

BTN 8-7 Review the chapter's opening feature involving Nathan's Famous, Inc. Assume that the company currently has net sales of $80,000,000, and that it is planning an expansion that will increase net sales by $28,000,000. To accomplish this expansion, Nathan's Famous, Inc. must increase its average total assets from $50,000,000 to $60,000,000.

Required

1. Compute the company's total asset turnover under (a) current conditions and (b) proposed conditions.
2. Evaluate and comment on the merits of the proposal given your analysis in part 1. Identify any concerns you would express about the proposal.

HITTING THE ROAD

P3 P4

BTN 8-8 Team up with one or more classmates for this activity. Identify companies in your community or area that must account for at least one of the following assets: natural resource; patent; lease; leasehold improvement; copyright; trademark; or goodwill. You might find a company having more than one type of asset. Once you identify a company with a specific asset, describe the accounting this company uses to allocate the cost of that asset to the periods benefited from its use.

GLOBAL DECISION

A1

Samsung
APPLE
GOOGLE

BTN 8-9 Samsung (www.Samsung.com), Apple, and Google are all competitors in the global marketplace. Comparative figures for these companies' recent annual accounting periods follow.

(in millions, except turnover)	Samsung (KRW millions)			Apple		Google	
	Current Year	Prior Year	Two Years Prior	Current Year	Prior Year	Current Year	Prior Year
Total assets	₩181,071,570	₩155,800,263	₩134,308,803	$176,064	$116,371	$93,798	$72,574
Net sales	201,103,613	165,001,771	187,754,283	156,508	108,249	50,175	37,905
Total asset turnover ...	?	?	—	1.07	1.13	0.60	0.58

Required

1. Compute total asset turnover for the most recent two years for Samsung using the data shown.
2. Which company is most efficient in generating net sales given the total assets it employs?

ANSWERS TO MULTIPLE CHOICE QUIZ

1. b;

	Appraisal Value	%	Total Cost	Allocated
Land	$175,000	50%	$326,000	$163,000
Land improvements	70,000	20	326,000	65,200
Building	105,000	30	326,000	97,800
Totals..................	$350,000			$326,000

2. c; ($35,000 − $1,000)/4 years = $8,500 per year.

3. c; 2013: $10,800,000 × (2 × 10%) = $2,160,000
   2014: ($10,800,000 − $2,160,000) × (2 × 10%) = $1,728,000

4. c;

Cost of machine................	$250,000
Accumulated depreciation........	100,000
Book value	150,000
Cash received	120,000
Loss on sale	$ 30,000

5. b; $550,000/$500,000 = 1.10

9 Reporting and Analyzing Current Liabilities

CHARACTERISTICS OF LIABILITIES	KNOWN LIABILITIES	ESTIMATED LIABILITIES	CONTINGENCIES AND ANALYSIS
C1 Reporting liabilities based on: Definition Classification Uncertainty	**C2** Accounts payable, sales taxes payable, and unearned revenues **P1** Short-term notes **P2** Employee deductions **P3** Employer payroll	**P4** Reporting for: Health and pension benefits Vacation benefits Bonus plans Warranty liabilities	**C3** Accounting for contingencies based on notions of probable, possible, remote **A1** Times interest earned ratio

Learning Objectives

C1 Describe current and long-term liabilities and their characteristics. (p. 390)

C2 Identify and describe known current liabilities. (p. 392)

P1 Prepare entries to account for short-term notes payable. (p. 393)

P2 Compute and record *employee* payroll deductions and liabilities. (p. 396)

P3 Compute and record *employer* payroll expenses and liabilities. (p. 398)

P4 Account for estimated liabilities, including warranties and bonuses. (p. 400)

C3 Explain how to account for contingent liabilities. (p. 402)

A1 Compute the times interest earned ratio and use it to analyze liabilities. (p. 405)

P5 *Appendix 9A*—Identify and describe the details of payroll reports, records, and procedures. (p. 408)

Mother Earth

"It's all about word of mouth"
—**ANNIE WITHEY**

BERKELEY, CA—You believe in your product when you put your home phone number on its packaging! Such is the case with Annie Withey. "I am an organic farmer," explains Annie. "We are affecting a lot of people and it's a great thing." She is the proud founder of Annie's, Inc. (**Annies.com**). "We make our products with real ingredients, all found in nature—no artificial anything," insists Annie. The product line began with her original Mac & Cheese, but now extends to pastas, snacks, dressings, pizza, and condiments.

Although Annie insists that her company "remains a purpose-driven company," she explains the importance of focusing on the accounting side. She insists that down-to-earth processes offer their own cost savings and corresponding benefits, including the best ingredients Mother Earth has to offer. Annie describes how good practices include limiting the level of liabilities and other obligations so her business is free to experiment with new offerings. Her balance sheet currently reveals a debt ratio under 27%, meaning that 73% of her business is equity financed.

The result is that Annie's work is paying off as revenues for the past three years

Annie's Inc.
(NYSE: BNNY)

110 employees
135 products

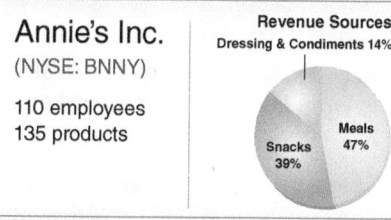

Revenue Sources
Dressing & Condiments 14%
Meals 47%
Snacks 39%

have substantially risen while liabilities remain in check:

($ millions)	2010	2011	2012
Revenues..........	$118	$141	$170
Liabilities	16	25	24

The financial markets, however, are not as convinced. Her company's stock price, while rising, has been somewhat volatile, as shown here:

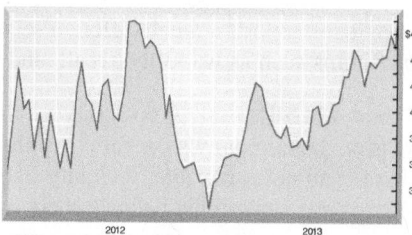

Annie is committed to staying the course, including dealing with the important tasks involving managing liabilities for payroll, supplies, employee benefits, vacations, training, and taxes. She insists that effective management of those liabilities, especially payroll and employee benefits, is crucial to success as she views her employees as part of a larger family. This past year, Annie's payroll went from $2.8 million to $3.8 million, consistent with her view that Annie's keeps a "family feel" while expanding its corporate operations. The company also carefully manages its purchase commitments, which reflect its obligations with many of its key suppliers for organic ingredients.

Ultimately, Annie's must generate sufficient cash to pay off liabilities and to fund its revenue growth and expansion plans. "We are optimistic," insists Annie, "spreading goodness through nourishing foods, honest words, and conduct."

Sources: *Annie's Website,* January 2014; *Annie's 10-K,* 2013; *The Hartford Courant,* July 2012

CHARACTERISTICS OF LIABILITIES

This section discusses important characteristics of liabilities and how liabilities are classified and reported.

Defining Liabilities

Describe current and long-term liabilities and their characteristics.

A *liability* is a probable future payment of assets or services that a company is presently obligated to make as a result of past transactions or events. This definition includes three crucial factors:

1. A past transaction or event.
2. A present obligation.
3. A future payment of assets or services.

These three important elements are portrayed visually in Exhibit 9.1. Liabilities reported in financial statements exhibit those characteristics. No liability is reported when one or more of those characteristics is absent. For example, most companies expect to pay wages to their employees in upcoming months and years, but these future payments are *not* liabilities because no past event such as employee work resulted in a present obligation. Instead, such liabilities arise when employees perform their work and earn the wages.

EXHIBIT 9.1

Characteristics of a Liability

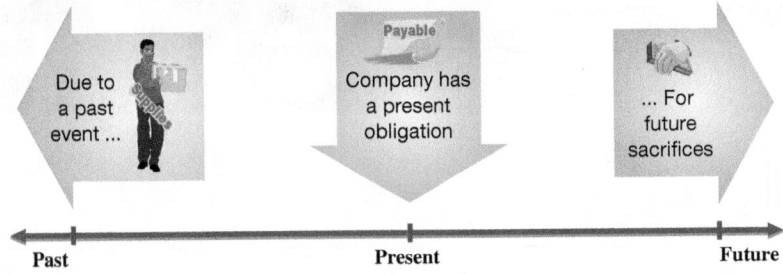

Past	Present	Future
Due to a past event ...	Company has a present obligation	... For future sacrifices

Classifying Liabilities

Point: Account titles using "payable" refer to liabilities.

Information about liabilities is more useful when the balance sheet identifies them as either current or long term. Decision makers need to know when obligations are due so they can plan for them and take appropriate action.

Point: Improper classification of liabilities can distort ratios used in financial statement analysis and business decisions.

Current Liabilities   **Current liabilities,** also called *short-term liabilities,* are obligations due within one year or the company's operating cycle, whichever is longer. They are expected to be paid using current assets or by creating other current liabilities. Common examples of current liabilities are accounts payable, short-term notes payable, wages payable, warranty liabilities, lease liabilities, taxes payable, and unearned revenues.

Current liabilities differ across companies because they depend on the type of company operations. **MGM Mirage**, for instance, included the following current liabilities related to its gaming, hospitality and entertainment operations ($000s):

Advance deposits and ticket sales	$ 97,753
Casino outstanding chip liability	290,238
Casino front money deposits	111,763

Harley-Davidson reports a much different set of current liabilities. It discloses current liabilities made up of items such as warranty, recall, and dealer incentive liabilities.

Long-Term Liabilities   A company's obligations not expected to be paid within the longer of one year or the company's operating cycle are reported as **long-term liabilities.** They can include long-term notes payable, warranty liabilities, lease liabilities, and bonds payable. They are sometimes reported on the balance sheet in a single long-term liabilities total or in multiple categories. **Domino's Pizza**, for instance, reports long-term liabilities of $1,485 million. They are reported after current liabilities. A single liability also can be divided between the current

Point: The current ratio is overstated if a company fails to classify any portion of long-term debt due next period as a current liability.

and noncurrent sections if a company expects to make payments toward it in both the short and long term. Domino's reports long-term debt, $1,451,000,000; and current portion of long-term debt, $835,000, which is less than 1%. The second item is reported in current liabilities. We sometimes see liabilities that do not have a fixed due date but instead are payable on the creditor's demand. These are reported as current liabilities because of the possibility of payment in the near term. Exhibit 9.2 shows amounts of current liabilities and as a percent of total liabilities for selected companies.

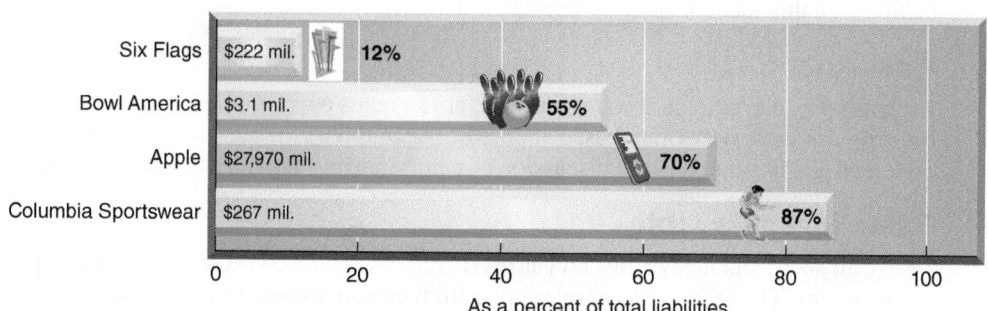

EXHIBIT 9.2

Current Liabilities of Selected Companies

Uncertainty in Liabilities

Accounting for liabilities involves addressing three important questions: Whom to pay? When to pay? How much to pay? Answers to these questions are often decided when a liability is incurred. For example, if a company has a $100 account payable to a specific individual, payable on March 15, the answers are clear. The company knows whom to pay, when to pay, and how much to pay. However, the answers to one or more of these questions are uncertain for some liabilities.

Uncertainty in Whom to Pay Liabilities can involve uncertainty in whom to pay. For instance, a company can create a liability with a known amount when issuing a note that is payable to its holder. In this case, a specific amount is payable to the note's holder at a specified date, but the company does not know who the holder is until that date. Despite this uncertainty, the company reports this liability on its balance sheet.

Point: An *accrued expense* is an unpaid expense, and is also called an *accrued liability*.

Uncertainty in When to Pay A company can have an obligation of a known amount to a known creditor but not know when it must be paid. For example, a legal services firm can accept fees in advance from a client who plans to use the firm's services in the future. This means that the firm has a liability that it settles by providing services at an unknown future date. Although this uncertainty exists, the legal firm's balance sheet must report this liability. These types of obligations are reported as current liabilities because they are likely to be settled in the short term.

Uncertainty in How Much to Pay A company can be aware of an obligation but not know how much will be required to settle it. For example, a company using electrical power is billed only after the meter has been read. This cost is incurred and the liability created before a bill is received. A liability to the power company is reported as an estimated amount if the balance sheet is prepared before a bill arrives.

IFRS

IFRS records a contingent liability when an obligation exists from a past event if there is a "probable" outflow of resources and the amount can be estimated reliably. However, IFRS defines probable as "more likely than not" while U.S. GAAP defines it as "likely to occur." ■

QC1

KNOWN LIABILITIES

C2 Identify and describe known current liabilities.

Most liabilities arise from situations with little uncertainty. They are set by agreements, contracts, or laws and are measurable. These liabilities are **known liabilities,** also called *definitely determinable liabilities.* Known liabilities include accounts payable, notes payable, payroll, sales taxes, unearned revenues, and leases. We describe how to account for these known liabilities in this section.

Accounts Payable

Accounts payable, or trade accounts payable, are amounts owed to suppliers, also called *vendors,* for products or services purchased on credit. Accounting for accounts payable is primarily explained and illustrated in our discussion of merchandising activities in Chapters 4 and 5.

Sales Taxes Payable

Nearly all states and many cities levy taxes on retail sales. Sales taxes are stated as a percent of selling prices. The seller collects sales taxes from customers when sales occur and remits these collections (often monthly) to the proper government agency. Since sellers currently owe these collections to the government, this amount is a current liability. Home Depot, for instance, reports sales taxes payable of $391 million in its recent annual report. To illustrate, if Home Depot sells materials on August 31 for $6,000 cash that are subject to a 5% sales tax, the revenue portion of this transaction is recorded as follows:

Assets = Liabilities + Equity
+6,300   +300   +6,000

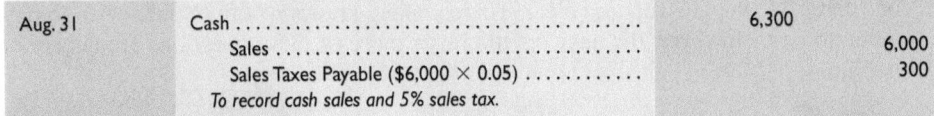

Aug. 31	Cash	6,300	
	Sales		6,000
	Sales Taxes Payable ($6,000 × 0.05)		300
	To record cash sales and 5% sales tax.		

Sales Taxes Payable is debited and Cash credited when it remits these collections to the government. Sales Taxes Payable is not an expense. It arises because laws require sellers to collect this cash from customers for the government.[1]

Unearned Revenues

Unearned revenues (also called *deferred revenues, collections in advance,* and *prepayments*) are amounts received in advance from customers for future products or services. Advance ticket sales for sporting events or music concerts are examples. Rihanna, for instance, has "deferred revenues" from advance ticket sales. To illustrate, assume that Rihanna sells $5 million in tickets for eight concerts; the entry is

Point: To *defer* a revenue means to postpone recognition of a revenue collected in advance until it is earned. Sport teams must defer recognition of ticket sales until games are played.

Assets   = Liabilities + Equity
+5,000,000   +5,000,000

June 30	Cash	5,000,000	
	Unearned Ticket Revenue		5,000,000
	To record sale of concert tickets.		

When a concert is played, Rihanna would record revenue for the portion earned.

Assets = Liabilities + Equity
         −625,000   +625,000

Oct. 31	Unearned Ticket Revenue	625,000	
	Ticket Revenue		625,000
	To record concert ticket revenues earned.		

---

[1] Sales taxes can be computed from total sales receipts when sales taxes are not separately identified on the register. To illustrate, assume a 5% sales tax and $420 in total sales receipts (which includes sales taxes). Sales are computed as follows:

$$\text{Sales} = \text{Total sales receipts}/(1 + \text{Sales tax percentage}) = \$420/1.05 = \$400$$

Thus, the sales tax amount equals total sales receipts minus sales, or $420 − $400 = $20. Sellers are required to act as "agents" for the government and collect sales tax. This extra work can be offset by the sellers' ability to use or invest that cash until it must be paid to the government.

Unearned Ticket Revenue is an unearned revenue account and is reported as a current liability. Unearned revenues also arise with airline ticket sales, magazine subscriptions, construction projects, hotel reservations, and custom orders.

Decision *Insight*

Reward Programs   Gift card sales now exceed $100 billion annually, and reward (also called loyalty) programs are growing. There are no exact rules for how retailers account for rewards. When **Best Buy** launched its "Reward Zone," shoppers earned $5 on each $125 spent and had 90 days to spend it. Retailers make assumptions about how many reward program dollars will be spent and how to report it. Best Buy sets up a liability and reduces revenue by the same amount. **Talbots** does not reduce revenue but instead increases selling expense. **Men's Wearhouse** records rewards in cost of goods sold, whereas **Neiman Marcus** subtracts them from revenue. The FASB continues to review reward programs. ■

Short-Term Notes Payable

A **short-term note payable** is a written promise to pay a specified amount on a definite future date within one year or the company's operating cycle, whichever is longer. These promissory notes are negotiable (as are checks), meaning they can be transferred from party to party by endorsement. The written documentation provided by notes is helpful in resolving disputes and for pursuing legal actions involving these liabilities. Most notes payable bear interest to compensate for use of the money until payment is made. Short-term notes payable can arise from many transactions. A company that purchases merchandise on credit can sometimes extend the credit period by signing a note to replace an account payable. Such notes also can arise when money is borrowed from a bank. We describe both of these cases.

> **P1** Prepare entries to account for short-term notes payable.

> **Point:** Required characteristics for negotiability of a note: (1) unconditional promise, (2) in writing, (3) specific amount, and (4) definite due date.

Note Given to Extend Credit Period   A company can replace an account payable with a note payable. A common example is a creditor that requires the substitution of an interest-bearing note for an overdue account payable that does not bear interest. A less common situation occurs when a debtor's weak financial condition motivates the creditor to accept a note, sometimes for a lesser amount, and to close the account to ensure that this customer makes no additional credit purchases.

To illustrate, let's assume that on August 23, Brady Company asks to extend its past-due $600 account payable to McGraw. After some negotiations, McGraw agrees to accept $100 cash and a 60-day, 12%, $500 note payable to replace the account payable. Brady records the transaction with this entry:

Aug. 23	Accounts Payable—McGraw	600	
	Cash		100
	Notes Payable—McGraw		500
	Gave $100 cash and a 60-day, 12% note for		
	payment on account.		

Assets = Liabilities + Equity
−100   −600
              +500

Signing the note does not resolve Brady's debt. Instead, the form of debt is changed from an account payable to a note payable. McGraw prefers the note payable over the account payable because it earns interest and it is written documentation of the debt's existence, term, and amount. When the note comes due, Brady pays the note and interest by giving McGraw a check for $510. Brady records that payment with this entry:

> **Point:** Accounts payable are detailed in a subsidiary ledger, but notes payable are sometimes not. A file with copies of notes can serve as a subsidiary ledger.

Oct. 22	Notes Payable—McGraw	500	
	Interest Expense	10	
	Cash		510
	Paid note with interest ($500 × 12% × 60/360).		

Assets = Liabilities + Equity
−510   −500   −10

Interest expense is computed by multiplying the principal of the note ($500) by the annual interest rate (12%) for the fraction of the year the note is outstanding (60 days/360 days).

> **Point:** Commercial companies commonly compute interest using a 360-day year. This is known as the *banker's rule.*

Note Given to Borrow from Bank   A bank nearly always requires a borrower to sign a promissory note when making a loan. When the note matures, the borrower repays the note with an amount larger than the amount borrowed. The difference between the amount borrowed and the amount repaid is *interest*. This section considers a type of note whose signer promises to pay *principal* (the amount borrowed) plus interest. In this case, the *face value* of the note equals principal. Face value is the value shown on the face (front) of the note. To illustrate, assume that a company needs $2,000 for a project and borrows this money from a bank at 12% annual interest. The loan is made on September 30, 2013, and is due in 60 days. Specifically, the borrowing company signs a note with a face value equal to the amount borrowed. The note includes a statement similar to this: *"I promise to pay $2,000 plus interest at 12% within 60 days after September 30."* This simple note is shown in Exhibit 9.3.

Point: When money is borrowed from a bank, the loan is reported as an asset (receivable) on the bank's balance sheet.

EXHIBIT 9.3

Note with Face Value Equal to Amount Borrowed

Promissory Note		
$2,000		Sept. 30, 2013
Face Value		Date
Sixty days after date, _____ I _____ promise to pay to the order of		
National Bank		
Boston, MA		
Two thousand and no/100 ----------------------------- Dollars		
plus interest at the annual rate of _12%_ .		
		Janet Lee

The borrower records its receipt of cash and the new liability with this entry:

Assets = Liabilities + Equity
+2,000   +2,000

Sept. 30	Cash	2,000	
	Notes Payable		2,000
	Borrowed $2,000 cash with a 60-day, 12%, $2,000 note.		

When principal and interest are paid, the borrower records payment with this entry:

Assets = Liabilities + Equity
−2,040   −2,000   −40

Nov. 29	Notes Payable	2,000	
	Interest Expense	40	
	Cash		2,040
	Paid note with interest ($2,000 × 12% × 60/360).		

End-of-period interest adjustment.   When the end of an accounting period occurs between the signing of a note payable and its maturity date, the *expense recognition (matching) principle* requires us to record the accrued but unpaid interest on the note. To illustrate, let's return to the note in Exhibit 9.3, but assume that the company borrows $2,000 cash on December 16, 2013, instead of September 30. This 60-day note matures on February 14, 2014, and the company's fiscal year ends on December 31. Thus, we need to record interest expense for the final 15 days in December. This means that one-fourth (15 days/60 days) of the $40 total interest is an expense of year 2013. The borrower records this expense with the following adjusting entry:

Assets = Liabilities + Equity
        +10   −10

2013			
Dec. 31	Interest Expense	10	
	Interest Payable		10
	To record accrued interest on note ($2,000 × 12% × 15/360).		

Example: If this note is dated Dec. 1 instead of Dec. 16, how much expense is recorded on Dec. 31? *Answer:* $2,000 × 12% × 30/360 = $20

When this note matures on February 14, the borrower must recognize 45 days of interest expense for year 2014 and remove the balances of the two liability accounts:

Assets = Liabilities + Equity
−2,040   −10   −30
       −2,000

2014			
Feb. 14	Interest Expense*	30	
	Interest Payable	10	
	Notes Payable	2,000	
	Cash		2,040
	*Paid note with interest. *($2,000 × 12% × 45/360)*		

■ **Decision** Insight

Many franchisors such as **Baskin-Robbins**, **Dunkin' Donuts**, and **Cold Stone Creamery**, use notes to help entrepreneurs acquire their own franchises, including using notes to pay for the franchise fee and any equipment. Payments on these notes are usually collected monthly and often are secured by the franchisees' assets. For example, a **McDonald's** franchise can cost from under $200,000 to over $2 million, depending on the type selected, see **FranchiseFoundations.com**. ■

Part 1. A retailer sells merchandise for $500 cash on June 30 (cost of merchandise is $300). The sales tax law requires the retailer to collect 7% sales tax on every dollar of merchandise sold. Record the entry for the $500 sale and its applicable sales tax. Also record the entry that shows the remittance of the 7% tax on this sale to the state government on July 15.

Part 2. A ticket agency receives $40,000 cash in advance ticket sales for a four-date tour of Haim. Record the advance ticket sales on April 30. Record the revenue earned for the first concert date of May 15, assuming it represents one-fourth of the advance ticket sales.

Part 3. On November 25 of the current year, a company borrows $8,000 cash by signing a 90-day, 5% note payable with a face value of $8,000. (a) Compute the accrued interest payable on December 31 of the current year, (b) prepare the journal entry to record the accrued interest expense at December 31 of the current year, and (c) prepare the journal entry to record payment of the note at maturity.

NEED-TO-KNOW 9.1

P1, C2

Solution—Part 1.

June 30	Cash	535	
	Sales		500
	Sales Taxes Payable		35
	To record cash sales and 5% sales tax.		
June 30	Cost of Goods Sold	300	
	Merchandise Inventory		300
	To record cost of June 30 sales.		
July 15	Sales Taxes Payable	35	
	Cash		35
	To record remittance of sales taxes to govt.		

Solution—Part 2.

April 30	Cash	40,000	
	Unearned Ticket Revenue		40,000
	To record sales in advance of concerts.		
May 15	Unearned Ticket Revenue	10,000	
	Earned Ticket Revenue		10,000
	To record concert revenues earned.		

Solution—Part 3.

a.

Computation of interest payable at December 31:
Days from November 25 to December 31 .... 36 days
Accrued interest (5% × $8,000 × 36/360) $40

b.

Dec. 31	Interest Expense	40	
	Interest Payable		40
	To record accrued interest (5% × $8,000 × 36/360).		

c.

Feb. 23	Interest Expense	60	
	Interest Payable	40	
	Notes Payable	8,000	
	Cash		8,100
	To record payment of note plus interest (5% × $8,000 × 90/360 = 100).		

Do More: QS 9-2, QS 9-3, QS 9-5, E 9-2, E 9-4, E 9-5

Payroll Liabilities

An employer incurs several expenses and liabilities from having employees. These expenses and liabilities are often large and arise from salaries and wages earned, from employee benefits, and from payroll taxes levied on the employer. Boston Beer, for instance, reports payroll-related current liabilities of more than $9.6 million from accrued "employee wages, benefits and reimbursements." We discuss payroll liabilities and related accounts in this section. Appendix 9A describes details about payroll reports, records, and procedures.

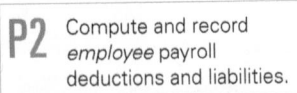

P2 Compute and record *employee* payroll deductions and liabilities.

Point: Deductions at some companies, such as those for insurance coverage, are "required" under its own labor contracts.

Employee Payroll Deductions **Gross pay** is the total compensation an employee earns including wages, salaries, commissions, bonuses, and any compensation earned before deductions such as taxes. (*Wages* usually refer to payments to employees at an hourly rate. *Salaries* usually refer to payments to employees at a monthly or yearly rate.) **Net pay,** also called *take-home pay,* is gross pay less all deductions. **Payroll deductions,** commonly called *withholdings,* are amounts withheld from an employee's gross pay, either required or voluntary. Required deductions result from laws and include income taxes and Social Security taxes. Voluntary deductions, at an employee's option, include pension and health contributions, health and life insurance premiums, union dues, and charitable giving. Exhibit 9.4 shows the typical payroll deductions of an employee. The employer withholds payroll deductions from employees' pay and is obligated to transmit this money to the designated organization. The employer records payroll deductions as current liabilities until these amounts are transmitted. This section discusses the major payroll deductions.

EXHIBIT 9.4

Payroll Deductions

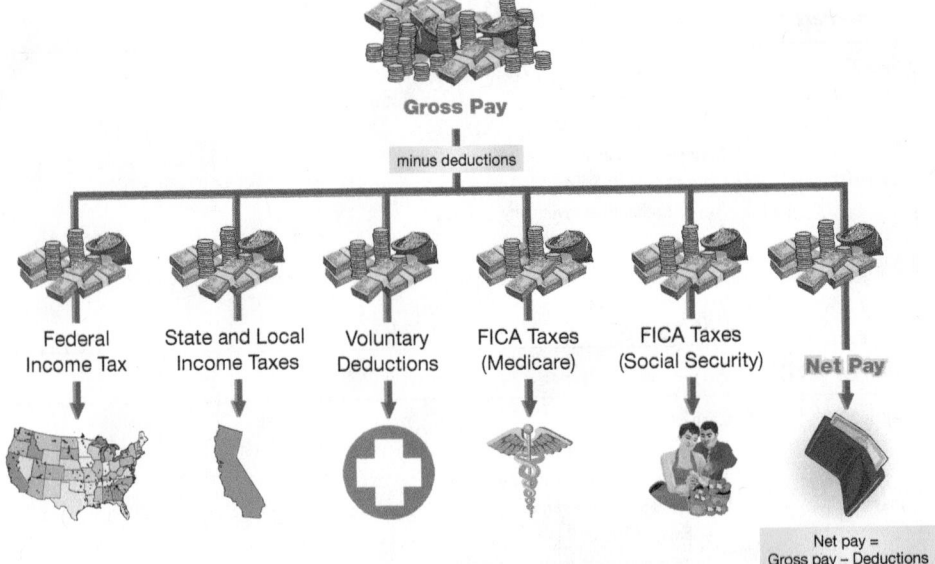

Employee FICA taxes. The federal Social Security system provides retirement, disability, survivorship, and medical benefits to qualified workers. Laws *require* employers to withhold **Federal Insurance Contributions Act (FICA) taxes** from employees' pay to cover costs of the system. Employers usually separate FICA taxes into two groups: (1) retirement, disability, and survivorship and (2) medical. For the first group, the Social Security system provides monthly cash payments to qualified retired workers for the rest of their lives. These payments are often called *Social Security benefits.* Taxes related to this group are often called *Social Security taxes.* For the second group, the system provides monthly payments to deceased workers' surviving families and to disabled workers who qualify for assistance. These payments are commonly called *Medicare benefits;* like those in the first group, they are paid with *Medicare taxes* (part of FICA taxes).

Law requires employers to withhold FICA taxes from each employee's salary or wages on each payday. The taxes for Social Security and Medicare are computed separately. For example, for 2013, the amount scheduled to be withheld from each employee's pay for Social Security tax is 6.2% of the first $113,700 the employee earns in the calendar year. The Medicare tax is 1.45% of *all* amounts the employee earns; there is no maximum limit to Medicare tax. Beginning in 2013, a 0.9% Additional Medicare Tax is imposed on the employee only for pay in excess of $200,000 (this additional tax is *not* imposed on the employer).

Employers must pay withheld taxes to the Internal Revenue Service (IRS) on specific filing dates during the year. Employers who fail to send the withheld taxes to the IRS on time can be assessed substantial penalties. Until all the taxes are sent to the IRS, they are included in employers' current liabilities. For any changes in rates or with the maximum earnings level, check the IRS Website at www.IRS.gov or the SSA Website at www.SSA.gov.

Employee income tax.   Most employers are required to withhold federal income tax from each employee's paycheck. The amount withheld is computed using tables published by the IRS. The amount depends on the employee's annual earnings rate and the number of *withholding allowances* the employee claims. Allowances reduce the amount of taxes one owes the government. The more allowances one claims, the less tax the employer will withhold. Employees can claim allowances for themselves and their dependents. They also can claim additional allowances if they expect major declines in their taxable income for medical expenses. (An employee who claims more allowances than appropriate is subject to a fine.) Most states and many local governments require employers to withhold income taxes from employees' pay and to remit them promptly to the proper government agency. Until they are paid, withholdings are reported as a current liability on the employer's balance sheet.

Employee voluntary deductions.   Beyond Social Security, Medicare, and income taxes, employers often withhold other amounts from employees' earnings. These withholdings arise from employee requests, contracts, unions, or other agreements. They can include amounts for charitable giving, medical and life insurance premiums, pension contributions, and union dues. Until they are paid, such withholdings are reported as part of employers' current liabilities.

Recording employee payroll deductions.   Employers must accrue payroll expenses and liabilities at the end of each pay period. To illustrate, assume that an employee earns a salary of $2,000 per month. At the end of January, the employer's entry to accrue payroll expenses and liabilities for this employee is

Jan. 31	Salaries Expense	2,000	
	FICA—Social Security Taxes Payable (6.2%)		124
	FICA—Medicare Taxes Payable (1.45%)		29
	Employee Federal Income Taxes Payable*		213
	Employee Medical Insurance Payable*		85
	Employee Union Dues Payable*		25
	Salaries Payable		1,524
	To record accrued payroll for January.		

Assets = Liabilities + Equity
+124 −2,000
+29
+213
+85
+25
+1,524

*Amounts taken from employer's accounting records.

Salaries Expense (debit) shows that the employee earns a gross salary of $2,000. The first five payables (credits) show the liabilities the employer owes on behalf of this employee to cover FICA taxes, income taxes, medical insurance, and union dues. The Salaries Payable account (credit) records the $1,524 net pay the employee receives from the $2,000 gross pay earned. When the employee is paid, another entry (or a series of entries) is required to record the check written and distributed (or funds transferred). The entry to record cash payment to this employee is to debit Salaries Payable and credit Cash for $1,524.

Salaries Payable 1,524
  Cash 1,524

Decision Insight

Pay or Else   "Failure to pay employment taxes is stealing from the employees of the business," said IRS Commissioner Mark W. Everson. "The IRS pursues business owners who don't follow the law, and those who embrace these schemes face civil or criminal sanctions." There are many reasons employers do not withhold or pay employment taxes. For some, they attempt to use the government as a "bank to borrow money for a short time," some others collect the taxes and keep it, and still others object to U.S. tax laws. Regardless, federal law requires employment tax withholding and payment by employers. (IRS.gov/newsroom).

Point margins: The sources of U.S. tax receipts are roughly as follows: 50% Personal income tax; 35 FICA and FUTA taxes; 10 Corporate income tax; 5 Other taxes.

Employer Payroll Taxes Employers must pay payroll taxes in addition to those required of employees. Employer taxes include FICA and unemployment taxes.

Employer FICA tax. Employers must pay FICA taxes on their payroll to employees. For 2012, the employer must pay Social Security tax of 6.2% on the first $113,700 earned by each employee, and 1.45% Medicare tax on all earnings of each employee. An employer's tax is credited to the same FICA Taxes Payable accounts used to record the Social Security and Medicare taxes withheld from employees. (A self-employed person must pay both the employee and employer FICA taxes.)

Federal and state unemployment taxes. The federal government participates with states in a joint federal and state unemployment insurance program. Each state administers its program. These programs provide unemployment benefits to qualified workers. The federal government approves state programs and pays a portion of their administrative expenses.

  Federal Unemployment Taxes (FUTA). Employers are subject to a federal unemployment tax on wages and salaries paid to their employees. For the recent year, employers were required to pay FUTA taxes of as much as 6.0% of the first $7,000 earned by each employee. This federal tax can be reduced by a credit of up to 5.4% for taxes paid to a state program. As a result, the net federal unemployment tax is often only 0.6%.

  State Unemployment Taxes (SUTA). All states support their unemployment insurance programs by placing a payroll tax on employers. (A few states require employees to make a contribution. In the book's assignments, we assume that this tax is only on the employer.) In most states, the base rate for SUTA taxes is 5.4% of the first $7,000 paid each employee. This base rate is adjusted according to an employer's merit rating. The state assigns a **merit rating** that reflects a company's stability or instability in employing workers. A good rating reflects stability in employment and means an employer can pay less than the 5.4% base rate. A low rating reflects high turnover or seasonal hirings and layoffs. To illustrate, an employer with 50 employees each of whom earns $7,000 or more per year saves $15,400 annually if it has a merit rating of 1.0% versus 5.4%. This is computed by comparing taxes of $18,900 at the 5.4% rate to only $3,500 at the 1.0% rate.

Recording employer payroll taxes. Employer payroll taxes are an added expense beyond the wages and salaries earned by employees. These taxes are often recorded in an entry separate from the one recording payroll expenses and deductions. To illustrate, assume that the $2,000 recorded salaries expense from the previous example is earned by an employee whose earnings have not yet reached $5,000 for the year. This means the entire salaries expense for this period is subject to tax because year-to-date pay is under $7,000. Also assume that the federal unemployment tax rate is 0.6% and the state unemployment tax rate is 5.4%. Consequently, the FICA portion of the employer's tax is $153, computed by multiplying both the 6.2% and 1.45% by the $2,000 gross pay. Moreover, state unemployment (SUTA) taxes are $108 (5.4% of the $2,000 gross pay), and federal unemployment (FUTA) taxes are $12 (0.6% of $2,000). The entry to record the employer's payroll tax expense and related liabilities is

Assets = Liabilities + Equity
        +124   −273
        +29
        +108
        +12

Jan. 31	Payroll Taxes Expense	273	
	FICA—Social Security Taxes Payable (6.2%)		124
	FICA—Medicare Taxes Payable (1.45%)		29
	State Unemployment Taxes Payable		108
	Federal Unemployment Taxes Payable		12
	To record employer payroll taxes.		

▮ Decision Ethics ━━━━━━━━━━━━━━━━━━━━━━

Web Designer You take a summer job working for a family friend who runs a small IT service. On your first payday, the owner slaps you on the back, gives you full payment in cash, winks, and adds: "No need to pay those high taxes, eh." What action, if any, do you take? ▮ [Answer—p. 416]

Multi-Period Known Liabilities

Many known liabilities extend over multiple periods. These often include unearned revenues and notes payable. For example, if Sports Illustrated sells a four-year magazine subscription, it records amounts received for this subscription in an Unearned Subscription Revenues account. Amounts in this account are liabilities, but are they current or long term? They are *both*. The portion of the Unearned Subscription Revenues account that will be fulfilled in the next year is reported as a current liability. The remaining portion is reported as a long-term liability.

The same analysis applies to notes payable. For example, a borrower reports a three-year note payable as a long-term liability in the first two years it is outstanding. In the third year, the borrower reclassifies this note as a current liability since it is due within one year or the operating cycle, whichever is longer. The **current portion of long-term debt** refers to that part of long-term debt due within one year or the operating cycle, whichever is longer. Long-term debt is reported under long-term liabilities, but the *current portion due* is reported under current liabilities. To illustrate, assume that a $7,500 debt is paid in installments of $1,500 per year for five years. The $1,500 due within the year is reported as a current liability. No journal entry is necessary for this reclassification. Instead, we simply classify the amounts for debt as either current or long term when the balance sheet is prepared.

Some known liabilities are rarely reported in long-term liabilities. These include accounts payable, sales taxes, and wages and salaries.

Point: If *Sports Illustrated* offers you a sweatshirt of your favorite team if you subscribe, it must account for the sweatshirts using a *promotions liability account.*

Point: Some accounting systems do make an entry to transfer the current amount due out of Long-Term Debt and into the Current Portion of Long-Term Debt as follows:

Long-Term Debt 1,500
    Current Portion of L-T Debt . . . 1,500

Fraud

Liability Limits Probably the greatest number of frauds involve payroll. Companies must safeguard payroll activities. Controls include proper approvals and processes for employee additions, deletions, and pay rate changes. A common fraud is a manager adding a fictitious employee to the payroll and then cashing the fictitious employee's check. A study reports that 28% of employees in operations and service areas witnessed violations of employee wage, overtime, or benefit rules in the past year (KPMG 2009). Another 21% observed falsifying of time and expense reports.

Ceridian Connection (Oct. 2010) reports: 8.5% of workplace fraud is tied to payroll. $72,000 is median loss per payroll fraud. 24 months is median time to uncover payroll fraud.

A company's first weekly pay period of the year ends on January 8. On that date, the column totals in its payroll register show that sales employees earned $30,000, and office employees earned $20,000 in salaries. The employees are to have withheld from their salaries FICA Social Security taxes at the rate of 6.2%, FICA Medicare taxes at the rate of 1.45%, $9,000 of federal income taxes, $2,000 of medical insurance deductions, and $1,000 of pension contributions. No employee earned more than $7,000 in the first pay period.

NEED-TO-KNOW 9.2

P2, P3

Part 1. Compute FICA Social Security taxes payable and FICA Medicare taxes payable. Prepare the journal entry to record the company's January 8 (employee) payroll expenses and liabilities. (Round amounts to cents.)

Part 2. Prepare the journal entry to record the company's (employer) payroll taxes resulting from the January 8 payroll. Its merit rating reduces its state unemployment tax rate to 3.4% of the first $7,000 paid to each employee. The federal unemployment tax rate is 0.6%. (Round amounts to cents.)

Solution—Part 1

Jan. 8	Sales Salaries Expense	30,000.00	
	Office Salaries Expense	20,000.00	
	FICA—Social Security Taxes Payable*		3,100.00
	FICA—Medicare Taxes Payable**		725.00
	Employee Fed. Income Taxes Payable		9,000.00
	Employee Med. Insurance Payable		2,000.00
	Employee Pensions Payable		1,000.00
	Salaries Payable		34,175.00
	To record payroll for period.		

*$50,000 × 6.2% = $3,100.00
**$50,000 × 1.45% = $725.00

Solution—Part 2

Jan. 8	Payroll Taxes Expense	5,825.00	
	FICA—Social Security Taxes Payable		3,100.00
	FICA—Medicare Taxes Payable		725.00
	State Unemployment Taxes Payable*		1,700.00
	Federal Unemployment Taxes Payable**		300.00
	To record employer payroll taxes.		

Do More: QS 9-6, QS 9-7, E 9-6, E 9-7, E 9-8, E 9-15, E 9-16

QC2

*$50,000 × 0.034 = $1,700.00
**$50,000 × 0.006 = $300.00

ESTIMATED LIABILITIES

P4 Account for estimated liabilities, including warranties and bonuses.

An **estimated liability** is a known obligation that is of an uncertain amount but that can be reasonably estimated. Common examples are employee benefits such as pensions, health care and vacation pay, and warranties offered by a seller. We discuss each of these in this section. Other examples of estimated liabilities include property taxes and certain contracts to provide future services.

Health and Pension Benefits

Many companies provide **employee benefits** beyond salaries and wages. An employer often pays all or part of medical, dental, life, and disability insurance. Many employers also contribute to *pension plans,* which are agreements by employers to provide benefits (payments) to employees after retirement. Many companies also provide medical care and insurance benefits to their retirees. When payroll taxes and charges for employee benefits are totaled, payroll cost often exceeds employees' gross earnings by 25% or more.

To illustrate, assume that an employer agrees to (1) pay an amount for medical insurance equal to $8,000 and (2) contribute an additional 10% of the employees' $120,000 gross salary to a retirement program. The entry to record these accrued benefits is

Assets = Liabilities + Equity
　　　　　+8,000　　−20,000
　　　　　+12,000

Dec. 31	Employee Benefits Expense	20,000	
	Employee Medical Insurance Payable		8,000
	Employee Retirement Program Payable		12,000
	To record costs of employee benefits.		

● **Decision** Insight

Postgame Spoils Baseball was the first pro sport to set up a pension, originally up to $100 per month depending on years played. Many former players now take home six-figure pensions. Cal Ripken Jr.'s pension when he reaches 62 is estimated at $160,000 per year (he played 21 seasons). The requirement is only 43 games for a full pension and just one game for full medical benefits. ■

Vacation Benefits

Many employers offer paid vacation benefits, also called *paid absences* or *compensated absences.* To illustrate, assume that salaried employees earn 2 weeks' vacation per year. This benefit increases employers' payroll expenses because employees are paid for 52 weeks but work for only 50 weeks. Total annual salary is the same, but the cost per week worked is greater than the amount paid per week. For example, if an employee is paid $20,800 for 52 weeks but works only 50 weeks, the total weekly expense to the employer is $416 ($20,800/50 weeks) instead of the $400 cash paid weekly to the employee ($20,800/52 weeks). The $16 difference between these two amounts is recorded weekly as follows:

Assets = Liabilities + Equity
　　　　　+16　　　−16

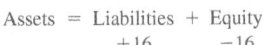

	Vacation Benefits Expense	16	
	Vacation Benefits Payable		16
	To record vacation benefits accrued.		

Vacation Benefits Expense is an operating expense, and Vacation Benefits Payable is a current liability. When the employee takes a vacation, the employer reduces (debits) the Vacation Benefits Payable and credits Cash (no additional expense is recorded).

| Vacation Benefits Payable .... | # |
| Cash .... | # |

Bonus Plans

Many companies offer bonuses to employees, and many of the bonuses depend on net income. To illustrate, assume that an employer offers a bonus to its employees equal to 5% of the company's annual net income (to be equally shared by all). The company's expected annual *pre-bonus* net income is $210,000. The year-end adjusting entry to record this benefit is

Dec. 31	Employee Bonus Expense*	10,000	
	Bonus Payable		10,000
	To record expected bonus costs.		

Assets = Liabilities + Equity
+10,000   −10,000

* Bonus Expense (B) equals 5% of net income, where net income equals $210,000 minus the bonus; the bonus is computed as:

$$B = 0.05 (\$210,000 - B)$$
$$B = \$10,500 - 0.05B$$
$$1.05B = \$10,500$$
$$\mathbf{B = \$10,500/1.05 = \$10,000}$$

When the bonus is paid, Bonus Payable is debited and Cash is credited for $10,000.

Warranty Liabilities

A **warranty** is a seller's obligation to replace or correct a product (or service) that fails to perform as expected within a specified period. Most new cars, for instance, are sold with a warranty covering parts for a specified period of time. Ford Motor Company reported almost $7 billion in "dealer and customer allowances and claims" in its annual report. To comply with the *full disclosure* and *matching principles,* the seller reports the expected warranty expense in the period when revenue from the sale of the product or service is reported. The seller reports this warranty obligation as a liability, although the existence, amount, payee, and date of future sacrifices are uncertain. This is because such warranty costs are probable and the amount can be estimated using, for instance, past experience with warranties.

Point: Kodak recently reported $46 million in warranty obligations.

To illustrate, a dealer sells a used car for $16,000 on December 1, 2013, with a maximum one-year or 12,000-mile warranty covering parts. This dealer's experience shows that warranty expense averages about 4% of a car's selling price, or $640 in this case ($16,000 × 4%). The dealer records the estimated expense and liability related to this sale with this entry:

2013			
Dec. 1	Warranty Expense	640	
	Estimated Warranty Liability		640
	To record estimated warranty expense.		

Assets = Liabilities + Equity
+640   −640

This entry alternatively could be made as part of end-of-period adjustments. Either way, the estimated warranty expense is reported on the 2013 income statement and the warranty liability on the 2013 balance sheet. To further extend this example, suppose the customer returns the car for warranty repairs on January 9, 2014. The dealer performs this work by replacing parts costing $200. The entry to record partial settlement of the estimated warranty liability is

Point: Recognition of warranty liabilities is necessary to comply with the matching and full disclosure principles.

2014			
Jan. 9	Estimated Warranty Liability	200	
	Auto Parts Inventory		200
	To record costs of warranty repairs.		

Assets = Liabilities + Equity
−200   −200

This entry reduces the balance of the estimated warranty liability. Warranty expense was previously recorded in 2013, the year the car was sold with the warranty. Finally, what happens if total warranty expenses are more or less than the estimated 4%, or $640? The answer is that management should monitor actual warranty expenses to see whether the 4% rate is accurate. If experience reveals a large difference from the estimate, the rate for current and future sales should be changed. Differences are expected, but they should be small.

Point: Both U.S. GAAP and IFRS account for restructuring costs in a manner similar to accounting for warranties.

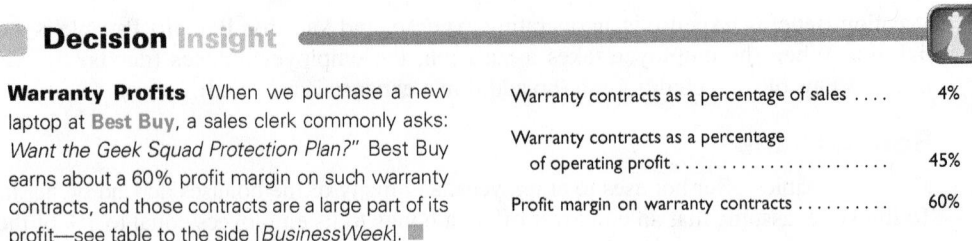

Decision Insight

Warranty Profits When we purchase a new laptop at **Best Buy**, a sales clerk commonly asks: *Want the Geek Squad Protection Plan?"* Best Buy earns about a 60% profit margin on such warranty contracts, and those contracts are a large part of its profit—see table to the side [*BusinessWeek*]. ■

Warranty contracts as a percentage of sales	4%
Warranty contracts as a percentage of operating profit	45%
Profit margin on warranty contracts	60%

Multi-Period Estimated Liabilities

QC3

Estimated liabilities can be both current and long term. For example, pension liabilities to employees are long term to workers who will not retire within the next period. For employees who are retired or will retire within the next period, a portion of pension liabilities is current. Other examples include employee health benefits and warranties. Specifically, many warranties are for 30 or 60 days in length. Estimated costs under these warranties are properly reported in current liabilities. Many other automobile warranties are for three years or 36,000 miles. A portion of these warranties is reported as long term.

CONTINGENT LIABILITIES

C3 Explain how to account for contingent liabilities.

A **contingent liability** is a potential obligation that depends on a future event arising from a past transaction or event. An example is a pending lawsuit. Here, a past transaction or event leads to a lawsuit whose result depends on the outcome of the suit. Future payment of a contingent liability depends on whether an uncertain future event occurs.

Accounting for Contingent Liabilities

Accounting for contingent liabilities depends on the likelihood that a future event will occur and the ability to estimate the future amount owed if this event occurs. Three different possibilities are identified in the following chart: record liability, disclose in notes, or no disclosure.

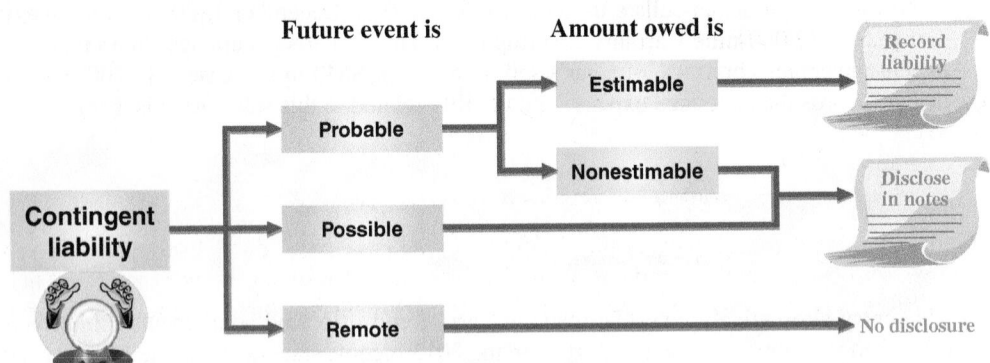

The conditions that determine each of these three possibilities follow:

1. The future event is *probable* (likely) and the amount owed can be *reasonably estimated*. We then record this amount as a liability. Examples are the estimated liabilities described earlier such as warranties, vacation pay, and income taxes.
2. The future event is *reasonably possible* (could occur). We disclose information about this type of contingent liability in notes to the financial statements.
3. The future event is *remote* (unlikely). We do not record or disclose information on remote contingent liabilities.

Point: A contingency is an *if*. Namely, if a future event occurs, then financial consequences are likely for the entity.

Reasonably Possible Contingent Liabilities

This section identifies and discusses contingent liabilities that commonly fall in the second category—when the future event is reasonably possible. Disclosing information about contingencies in this category is motivated by the *full-disclosure principle,* which requires information relevant to decision makers be reported and not ignored.

Potential Legal Claims   Many companies are sued or at risk of being sued. The accounting issue is whether the defendant should recognize a liability on its balance sheet or disclose a contingent liability in its notes while a lawsuit is outstanding and not yet settled. The answer is that a potential claim is recorded in the accounts *only* if payment for damages is probable and the amount can be reasonably estimated. If the potential claim cannot be reasonably estimated or is less than probable but reasonably possible, it is disclosed. Ford Motor Company, for example, includes the following note in its annual report: "Various legal actions, governmental investigations and proceedings and claims are pending . . . arising out of alleged defects in our products."

Point: A sale of a note receivable is often a contingent liability. It becomes a liability if the original signer of the note fails to pay it at maturity.

Debt Guarantees   Sometimes a company guarantees the payment of debt owed by a supplier, customer, or another company. The guarantor usually discloses the guarantee in its financial statement notes as a contingent liability. If it is probable that the debtor will default, the guarantor needs to record and report the guarantee in its financial statements as a liability. The Boston Celtics report a unique guarantee when it comes to coaches and players: "Certain of the contracts provide for guaranteed payments which must be paid even if the employee [player] is injured or terminated."

Other Contingencies   Other examples of contingencies include environmental damages, possible tax assessments, insurance losses, and government investigations. Sunoco, for instance, reports that "federal, state and local laws . . . result in liabilities and loss contingencies. Sunoco accrues . . . cleanup costs [that] are probable and reasonably estimable. Management believes it is reasonably possible (i.e., less than probable but greater than remote) that additional . . . losses will be incurred." Many of Sunoco's contingencies are revealed only in notes.

Point: Auditors and managers often have different views about whether a contingency is recorded, disclosed, or omitted.

Decision Insight

Pricing Priceless   What's it worth to see from one side of the Grand Canyon to the other? What's the cost when gulf coast beaches are closed due to an oil well disaster? A method to measure environmental liabilities is *contingent valuation,* by which people answer such questions. Regulators use their answers to levy fines and assess punitive damages. ▪

Uncertainties that Are Not Contingencies

All organizations face uncertainties from future events such as natural disasters and the development of new competing products or services. These uncertainties are not contingent liabilities because they are future events *not* arising from past transactions. Accordingly, they are not disclosed.

Fraud

Risky Payables. Following are some warning signs of potential fraud involving payables:

- **Duplicate** payments in the same or similar amount to the same vendor (or invoices to the same vendor with the same or similar date).
- **Invoices** at amounts just below the limit requiring managerial approval.
- **Irregular vendor information** such as the absence of a business/home phone number or phone numbers that always go to an answering system; multiple vendors with the same phone number; vendors with PO box billing addresses; vendors with similar-sounding or similar-spelled names.
- **Unusual invoice activity** such as increases or decreases in invoice activity, or above-average invoice amounts, or activity at abnormal dates.

NEED-TO-KNOW 9.3

P4, C3

Part 1. A company's salaried employees earn two weeks vacation per year. It pays $208,000.00 in total employee salaries for 52 weeks but its employees work only 50 weeks. This means its total weekly expense is $4,160 ($208,000/50 weeks) instead of the $4,000 cash paid weekly to the employees ($208,000/52 weeks). Record the company's regular weekly vacation benefits expense.

Part 2. For the current year ended December 31, a company has implemented an employee bonus program equal to 5% of its net income, which employees share equally. Its net income (pre-bonus) is expected to be $840,000, and bonus expense is deducted in computing net income. (a) Compute the bonus payable to the employees at year-end using the method described in the chapter and round to the nearest dollar; then prepare the journal entry at December 31 of the current year to record the bonus due. (b) Prepare the journal entry at January 20 of the following year to record payment of that bonus to employees.

Part 3. On June 11 of the current year, a retailer sells a trimmer for $400 with a one-year warranty that covers parts. Warranty expense is estimated at 5% of sales. On March 24 of the next year, the trimmer is brought in for repairs covered under the warranty requiring $15 in materials taken from the Repair Parts Inventory. Prepare the (a) June 11 entry to record the trimmer sale, and (b) March 24 entry to record warranty repairs.

Part 4. The following legal claims exist for a company. Identify the accounting treatment for each claim as either (i) a liability that is recorded or (ii) an item described in notes to its financial statements. If an item is to be recorded, prepare the entry.

a. The company (defendant) estimates that a pending lawsuit could result in damages of $500,000; it is reasonably possible that the plaintiff will win the case.

b. The company faces a probable loss on a pending lawsuit; the amount is not reasonably estimable.

c. The company estimates environmental damages in a pending case at $900,000 with a high probability of losing the case.

Solution—Part 1

Vacation Benefits Expense*	160	
Vacation Benefits Payable		160
To record vacation benefits accrued.		

*($4,160 − 4,000)

Solution—Part 2

a. $B \quad = 0.05\ (\$840,000 - B)$
$\ B \quad = \$42,000 - 0.05B$
$\ 1.05B = \$42,000$
$\ B \quad = \underline{\$40,000}$

Dec. 31	Employee Bonus Expense	40,000	
	Bonus Payable		40,000
	To record expected bonus costs.		

b.

Jan. 20	Bonus Payable	40,000	
	Cash		40,000
	To record payment of bonus.		

Solution—Part 3

June 11	Cash	400	
	Sales		400
	To record trimmer sales.		
June 11	Warranty Expense	20	
	Estimated Warranty Liability		20
	To record estimated warranty expense. ($400 × 5%)		
March 24	Estimated Warranty Liability	15	
	Repair Parts Inventory		15
	To record cost of warranty repairs.		

Solution—Part 4

a. (ii); reason—is reasonably estimated but not a probable loss.

b. (ii); reason—probable loss but cannot be reasonably estimated.

c. (i); reason—can be reasonably estimated and loss is probable.

Do More: QS 9-4, QS 9-8, QS 9-9, QS 9-10, E 9-3, E 9-9, E 9-10, E 9-11

Environmental Contingent Expense	900,000	
Environmental Contingent Liability		900,000
To record environmental contingent liability.		

QC4

GLOBAL VIEW

This section discusses similarities and differences between U.S. GAAP and IFRS in accounting and reporting for current liabilities.

Characteristics of Liabilities   The definitions and characteristics of current liabilities are broadly similar for both U.S. GAAP and IFRS. Although differences exist, the similarities vastly outweigh any differences. Remembering that "provision" is typically used under IFRS to refer to what is titled "liability" under U.S. GAAP, Nokia describes its recognition of liabilities as follows:

> Provisions are recognized when the Group has a present legal or constructive obligation as a result of past events, it is probable that an outflow of resources will be required to settle the obligation and a reliable estimate of the amount can be made.

NOKIA

Known (Determinable) Liabilities   When there is little uncertainty surrounding current liabilities, both U.S. GAAP and IFRS require companies to record them in a similar manner. This correspondence in accounting applies to accounts payable, sales taxes payable, unearned revenues, short-term notes, and payroll liabilities. Of course, tax regulatory systems of countries are different, which implies use of different rates and levels. Still, the basic approach is the same.

Estimated Liabilities   When there is a known current obligation that involves an uncertain amount, but one that can be reasonably estimated, both U.S. GAAP and IFRS require similar treatment. This treatment extends to many obligations such as those arising from vacations, warranties, restructurings, pensions, and health care. Both accounting systems require that companies record estimated expenses related to these obligations when they can reasonably estimate the amounts. Nokia reports wages, salaries and bonuses of €6,284 million. It also reports pension expenses of €445 million.

Times Interest Earned Ratio ▢▢▢ **Decision Analysis**

A company incurs interest expense on many of its current and long-term liabilities. Examples extend from its short-term notes and the current portion of long-term liabilities to its long-term notes and bonds. Interest expense is often viewed as a *fixed expense* because the amount of these liabilities is likely to remain in one form or another for a substantial period of time. This means that the amount of interest is unlikely to vary due to changes in sales or other operating activities. While fixed expenses can be advantageous when a company is growing, they create risk. This risk stems from the possibility that a company might be unable to pay fixed expenses if sales decline. To illustrate, consider Diego Co.'s results for 2013 and two possible outcomes for year 2014 in Exhibit 9.5.

A1 Compute the times interest earned ratio and use it to analyze liabilities.

		2014 Projections	
($ thousands)	**2013**	**Sales Increase**	**Sales Decrease**
Sales	$600	$900	$300
Expenses (75% of sales)	450	675	225
Income before interest	150	225	75
Interest expense (fixed)	60	60	60
Net income	$ 90	$165	$ 15

EXHIBIT 9.5

Actual and Projected Results

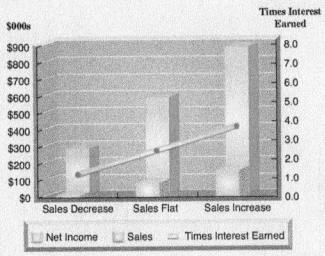

EXHIBIT 9.6

Times Interest Earned

Expenses excluding interest are at, and expected to remain at, 75% of sales. Expenses such as these that change with sales volume are called *variable expenses*. However, interest expense is at, and expected to remain at, $60,000 per year due to its fixed nature.

The middle numerical column of Exhibit 9.5 shows that Diego's income increases by 83% to $165,000 if sales increase by 50% to $900,000. In contrast, the far right column shows that income decreases by 83% if sales decline by 50%. These results reveal that the amount of fixed interest expense affects a company's risk of its ability to pay interest, which is numerically reflected in the **times interest earned** ratio in Exhibit 9.6.

$$\text{Times interest earned} = \frac{\text{Income before interest expense and income taxes}}{\text{Interest expense}}$$

For 2013, Diego's times interest earned is computed as $150,000/$60,000, or 2.5 times. This ratio suggests that Diego faces low to moderate risk because its sales must decline sharply before it would be unable to cover its interest expenses. (Diego is an LLC and does not pay income taxes.)

Experience shows that when times interest earned falls below 1.5 to 2.0 and remains at that level or lower for several periods, the default rate on liabilities increases sharply. This reflects increased risk for companies and their creditors. We also must interpret the times interest earned ratio in light of information about the variability of a company's income before interest. If income is stable from year to year or if it is growing, the company can afford to take on added risk by borrowing. If its income greatly varies from year to year, fixed interest expense can increase the risk that it will not earn enough income to pay interest.

■ **Decision Maker**

Entrepreneur   You wish to invest in a franchise for either one of two national chains. Each franchise has an expected annual net income *after* interest and taxes of $100,000. Net income for the first franchise includes a regular fixed interest charge of $200,000. The fixed interest charge for the second franchise is $40,000. Which franchise is riskier to you if sales forecasts are not met? Does your decision change if the first franchise has more variability in its income stream? ■   [Answer—p. 416]

COMPREHENSIVE...

NEED-TO-KNOW

The following transactions and events took place at Kern Company during its recent calendar-year reporting period (Kern does not use reversing entries).

a. In September 2013, Kern sold $140,000 of merchandise covered by a 180-day warranty. Prior experience shows that costs of the warranty equal 5% of sales. Compute September's warranty expense and prepare the adjusting journal entry for the warranty liability as recorded at September 30. Also prepare the journal entry on October 8 to record a $300 cash expenditure to provide warranty service on an item sold in September.

b. On October 12, 2013, Kern arranged with a supplier to replace Kern's overdue $10,000 account payable by paying $2,500 cash and signing a note for the remainder. The note matures in 90 days and has a 12% interest rate. Prepare the entries recorded on October 12, December 31, and January 10, 2014, related to this transaction.

c. In late December, Kern learns it is facing a product liability suit filed by an unhappy customer. Kern's lawyer advises that although it will probably suffer a loss from the lawsuit, it is not possible to estimate the amount of damages at this time.

d. Sally Bline works for Kern. For the pay period ended November 30, her gross earnings are $3,000. Bline has $800 deducted for federal income taxes and $200 for state income taxes from each paycheck. Additionally, a $35 premium for her health care insurance and a $10 donation for the United Way are deducted. Bline pays FICA Social Security taxes at a rate of 6.2% and FICA Medicare taxes at a rate of 1.45%. She has not earned enough this year to be exempt from any FICA taxes. Journalize the accrual of salaries expense of Bline's wages by Kern.

e. On November 1, Kern borrows $5,000 cash from a bank in return for a 60-day, 12%, $5,000 note. Record the note's issuance on November 1 and its repayment with interest on December 31.

f.ᴮ Kern has estimated and recorded its quarterly income tax payments. In reviewing its year-end tax adjustments, it identifies an additional $5,000 of income tax expense that should be recorded. A portion of this additional expense, $1,000, is deferrable to future years. Record this year-end income taxes expense adjusting entry.

g. For this calendar year, Kern's net income is $1,000,000, its interest expense is $275,000, and its income taxes expense is $225,000. Calculate Kern's times interest earned ratio.

PLANNING THE SOLUTION

- For *a*, compute the warranty expense for September and record it with an estimated liability. Record the October expenditure as a decrease in the liability.
- For *b*, eliminate the liability for the account payable and create the liability for the note payable. Compute interest expense for the 80 days that the note is outstanding in 2013 and record it as an additional liability. Record the payment of the note, being sure to include the interest for the 10 days in 2014.
- For *c*, decide whether the company's contingent liability needs to be disclosed or accrued (recorded) according to the two necessary criteria: probable loss and reasonably estimable.
- For *d*, set up payable accounts for all items in Bline's paycheck that require deductions. After deducting all necessary items, credit the remaining amount to Salaries Payable.
- For *e*, record the issuance of the note. Calculate 60 days' interest due using the 360-day convention in the interest formula.
- For *f*, determine how much of the income taxes expense is payable in the current year and how much needs to be deferred.
- For *g*, apply and compute times interest earned.

SOLUTION TO COMPREHENSIVE NEED-TO-KNOW

a. Warranty expense = 5% × $140,000 = $7,000

Sept. 30	Warranty Expense	7,000	
	Estimated Warranty Liability		7,000
	To record warranty expense for the month.		
Oct. 8	Estimated Warranty Liability	300	
	Cash		300
	To record the cost of the warranty service.		

b. Interest expense for 2013 = 12% × $7,500 × 80/360 = $200
Interest expense for 2014 = 12% × $7,500 × 10/360 = $25

Oct. 12	Accounts Payable	10,000	
	Notes Payable		7,500
	Cash		2,500
	Paid $2,500 cash and gave a 90-day, 12% note to extend the due date on the account.		
Dec. 31	Interest Expense	200	
	Interest Payable		200
	To accrue interest on note payable.		
Jan. 10	Interest Expense	25	
	Interest Payable	200	
	Notes Payable	7,500	
	Cash		7,725
	Paid note with interest, including the accrued interest payable.		

c. Disclose the pending lawsuit in the financial statement notes. Although the loss is probable, no liability can be accrued since the loss cannot be reasonably estimated.

d.

Nov. 30	Salaries Expense	3,000.00	
	FICA—Social Security Taxes Payable (6.2%)		186.00
	FICA—Medicare Taxes Payable (1.45%)		43.50
	Employee Federal Income Taxes Payable		800.00
	Employee State Income Taxes Payable		200.00
	Employee Medical Insurance Payable		35.00
	Employee United Way Payable		10.00
	Salaries Payable		1,725.50
	To record Bline's accrued payroll.		

e.

Nov. 1	Cash	5,000	
	Notes Payable		5,000
	Borrowed cash with a 60-day, 12% note.		

When the note and interest are paid 60 days later, Kern Company records this entry:

Dec. 31	Notes Payable	5,000	
	Interest Expense	100	
	Cash		5,100
	Paid note with interest ($5,000 × 12% × 60/360).		

f.

Dec. 31	Income Taxes Expense	5,000	
	Income Taxes Payable		4,000
	Deferred Income Tax Liability		1,000
	To record added income taxes expense and the deferred tax liability.		

g. Times interest earned $= \dfrac{\$1,000,000 + \$275,000 + \$225,000}{\$275,000} = \underline{\underline{5.45 \text{ times}}}$

9A   Payroll Reports, Records, and Procedures

Understanding payroll procedures and keeping adequate payroll reports and records are essential to a company's success. This appendix focuses on payroll accounting and its reports, records, and procedures.

> **P5** Identify and describe the details of payroll reports, records, and procedures.

Payroll Reports   Most employees and employers are required to pay local, state, and federal payroll taxes. Payroll expenses involve liabilities to individual employees, to federal and state governments, and to other organizations such as insurance companies. Beyond paying these liabilities, employers are required to prepare and submit reports explaining how they computed these payments.

Reporting FICA Taxes and Income Taxes   The Federal Insurance Contributions Act (FICA) requires each employer to file an Internal Revenue Service (IRS) **Form 941,** the *Employer's Quarterly Federal Tax Return,* within one month after the end of each calendar quarter. A sample Form 941 is shown in Exhibit 9A.1 for Phoenix Sales & Service, a landscape design company. Accounting information and software are helpful in tracking payroll transactions and reporting the accumulated information on Form 941. Specifically, the employer reports total wages subject to income tax withholding on line 2 of Form 941. (For simplicity, this appendix uses *wages* to refer to both wages and salaries.) The income tax withheld is reported on line 3. The combined amount of employee and employer FICA (Social Security) taxes

Form 941

Employer's QUARTERLY Federal Tax Return
Department of the Treasury — Internal Revenue Service

(EIN)
Employer identification number: 8 6 – 3 2 1 4 5 8 7

Name (not your trade name): *Phoenix Sales & Service*

Trade name (if any):

Address: 1214 *Mill Road*
Number / Street / Suite or room number

Phoenix / AZ / 85621
City / State / ZIP code

Report for this Quarter ...
(Check one.)

1: January, February, March
2: April, May, June
3: July, August, September
[X] 4: October, November, December

Part 1: Answer these questions for this quarter.

1 Number of employees who received wages, tips, or other compensation for the pay period including: *Mar. 12* (Quarter 1), *June 12* (Quarter 2), *Sept. 12* (Quarter 3), *Dec. 12* (Quarter 4) · **1** | 1

2 Wages, tips, and other compensation · **2** | 36,599.00

3 Total income tax withheld from wages, tips, and other compensation · **3** | 3,056.47

4 If no wages, tips, and other compensation are subject to social security or Medicare tax · ☐ Check and go to line 6.

5 Taxable social security and Medicare wages and tips:

	Column 1		Column 2
5a Taxable social security wages	36,599.00	× .124 =	4,538.28
5b Taxable social security tips		× .124 =	
5c Taxable Medicare wages & tips	36,599.00	× .029 =	1,061.37

5d Total social security and Medicare taxes (*Column 2*, lines 5a + 5b + 5c = line 5d) · **5d** | 5,599.65

6 Total taxes before adjustments (lines 3 + 5d = line 6) · **6** | 8,656.12

7 TAX ADJUSTMENTS (Read the instructions for line 7 before completing lines 7a through 7h.):

7a Current quarter's fractions of cents · | .

7b Current quarter's sick pay · | .

7c Current quarter's adjustments for tips and group-term life insurance | .

7d Current year's income tax withholding (attach Form 941c) · | .

7e Prior quarters' social security and Medicare taxes (attach Form 941c) · | .

7f Special additions to federal income tax (attach Form 941c) · | .

7g Special additions to social security and Medicare (attach Form 941c) · | .

7h TOTAL ADJUSTMENTS (Combine all amounts: lines 7a through 7g.) · **7h** | 0.00

8 Total taxes after adjustments (Combine lines 6 and 7h.) · **8** | 8,656.12

9 Advance earned income credit (EIC) payments made to employees · **9** | .

10 Total taxes after adjustment for advance EIC (lines 8 – line 9 = line 10) · **10** | 8,656.12

11 Total deposits for this quarter, including overpayment applied from a prior quarter · **11** | 8,656.12

12 Balance due (If line 10 is more than line 11, write the difference here.) · **12** | 0.00
Make checks payable to *United States Treasury.*

13 Overpayment (If line 11 is more than line 10, write the difference here.) | 0.00 | Check one ☐ Apply to next return. ☐ Send a refund.

Part 2: Tell us about your deposit schedule and tax liability for this quarter.

If you are unsure about whether you are a monthly schedule depositor or a semiweekly schedule depositor, see *Pub. 15 (Circular E)*, section 11.

14 [A][Z] Write the state abbreviation for the state where you made your deposits OR write "MU" if you made your deposits in *multiple* states.

15 Check one: ☐ Line 10 is less than $2,500. Go to Part 3.

[X] You were a monthly schedule depositor for the entire quarter. Fill out your tax liability for each month. Then go to Part 3.

Tax liability: Month 1 | 3,079.11
Month 2 | 2,049.77
Month 3 | 3,527.24

Total liability for quarter | 8,656.12 | Total must equal line 10.

☐ You were a semiweekly schedule depositor for any part of this quarter. Fill out *Schedule B (Form 941): Report of Tax Liability for Semiweekly Schedule Depositors*, and attach it to this form.

Part 3: Tell us about your business. If a question does NOT apply to your business, leave it blank.

16 If your business has closed or you stopped paying wages · ☐ Check here, and
enter the final date you paid wages / /

17 If you are a seasonal employer and you do not have to file a return for every quarter of the year · ☐ Check here.

Part 4: May we speak with your third-party designee?

Do you want to allow an employee, a paid tax preparer, or another person to discuss this return with the IRS? See the instructions for details.
☐ Yes. Designee's name
Phone ( ) – Personal Identification Number (PIN) ☐☐☐☐☐
[X] No.

Part 5: Sign here. You MUST fill out both sides of this form and SIGN it.

Under penalties of perjury, I declare that I have examined this return, including accompanying schedules and statements, and to the best of my knowledge and belief, it is true, correct, and complete.

✗ Sign your name here
Print name and title
Date / / Phone ( ) –

Point: Line 5a shows the matching nature of the FICA tax as 6.2% × 2, or 12.4%; which is shown as 0.124.

Point: Auditors rely on the four 941 forms filed during a year when auditing a company's annual wage and salaries expense account.

for Phoenix Sales & Service is reported on line 5a (taxable Social Security wages, \$36,599 × 12.4% = \$4,538.28). The 12.4% is the sum of the Social Security tax withheld, computed as 6.2% tax withheld from the employee wages for the quarter plus the 6.2% tax levied on the employer. The combined amount of employee Medicare wages is reported on line 5c. The 2.9% is the sum of 1.45% withheld from employee wages for the quarter plus 1.45% tax levied on the employer. Total FICA taxes are reported on line 5d and are added to the total income taxes withheld of \$3,056.47 to yield a total of \$8,656.12. For this year, assume that income up to \$113,700 is subject to Social Security tax. There is no income limit on amounts subject to Medicare tax. Congress sets rates owed for Social Security tax (and it typically changes each year).

Federal depository banks are authorized to accept deposits of amounts payable to the federal government. Deposit requirements depend on the amount of tax owed. For example, when the sum of FICA taxes plus the employee income taxes is less than \$2,500 for a quarter, the taxes can be paid when Form 941 is filed. Companies with large payrolls are often required to pay monthly or even semiweekly.

Reporting FUTA Taxes and SUTA Taxes An employer's federal unemployment taxes (FUTA) are reported on an annual basis by filing an *Annual Federal Unemployment Tax Return,* IRS **Form 940.** It must be mailed on or before January 31 following the end of each tax year. Ten more days are allowed if all required tax deposits are filed on a timely basis and the full amount of tax is paid on or before January 31. FUTA payments are made quarterly to a federal depository bank if the total amount due exceeds \$500. If \$500 or less is due, the taxes are remitted annually. Requirements for paying and reporting state unemployment taxes (SUTA) vary depending on the laws of each state. Most states require quarterly payments and reports.

Reporting Wages and Salaries Employers are required to give each employee an annual report of his or her wages subject to FICA and federal income taxes along with the amounts of these taxes withheld. This report is called a *Wage and Tax Statement,* or **Form W-2.** It must be given to employees before January 31 following the year covered by the report. Exhibit 9A.2 shows Form W-2 for one of the employees at Phoenix Sales & Service. Copies of the W-2 Form must be sent to the Social Security Administration, where the amount of the employee's wages subject to FICA taxes and FICA taxes withheld are posted to each employee's Social Security account. These posted amounts become the basis for determining an employee's retirement and survivors' benefits. The Social Security Administration also transmits to the IRS the amount of each employee's wages subject to federal income taxes and the amount of taxes withheld.

EXHIBIT 9A.2

Form W-2

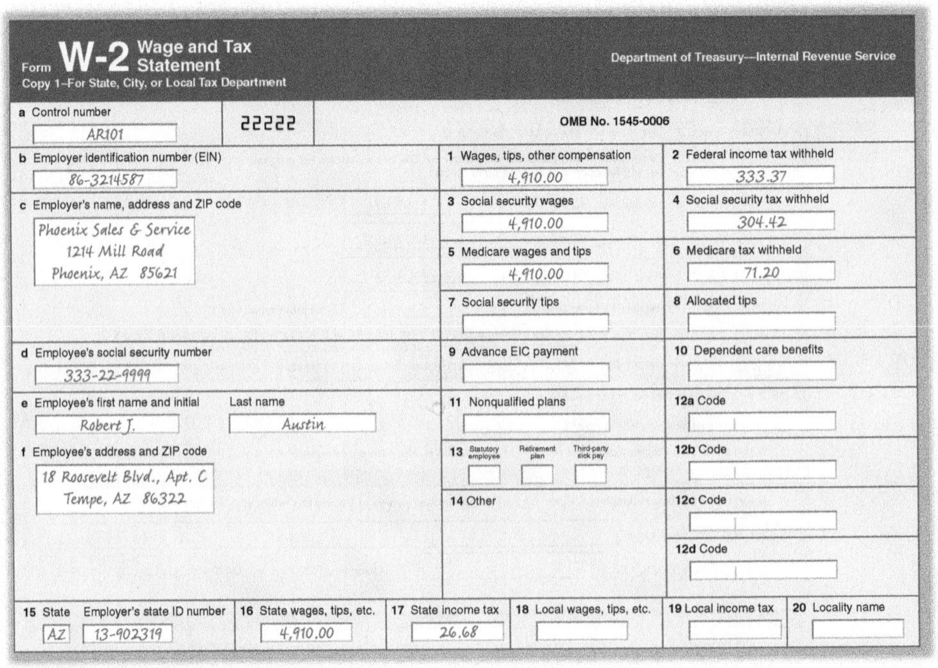
Form W-2 Wage and Tax Statement
Copy 1–For State, City, or Local Tax Department
Department of Treasury—Internal Revenue Service

a Control number: AR101 — 22222 — OMB No. 1545-0006
b Employer identification number (EIN): 86-3214587
c Employer's name, address and ZIP code: Phoenix Sales & Service, 1214 Mill Road, Phoenix, AZ 85621
d Employee's social security number: 333-22-9999
e Employee's first name and initial: Robert J. — Last name: Austin
f Employee's address and ZIP code: 18 Roosevelt Blvd., Apt. C, Tempe, AZ 86322
1 Wages, tips, other compensation: 4,910.00
2 Federal income tax withheld: 333.37
3 Social security wages: 4,910.00
4 Social security tax withheld: 304.42
5 Medicare wages and tips: 4,910.00
6 Medicare tax withheld: 71.20
7 Social security tips
8 Allocated tips
9 Advance EIC payment
10 Dependent care benefits
11 Nonqualified plans
12a Code
13 Statutory employee / Retirement plan / Third-party sick pay
12b Code
14 Other
12c Code
12d Code
15 State: AZ — Employer's state ID number: 13-902319
16 State wages, tips, etc.: 4,910.00
17 State income tax: 26.68
18 Local wages, tips, etc.
19 Local income tax
20 Locality name

Payroll Records Employers must keep payroll records in addition to reporting and paying taxes. These records usually include a payroll register and an individual earnings report for each employee.

Accounting System: Exhibit A.3   _ □ ×

File   Edit   Maintain   Tasks   Analysis   Options   Reports   Window   Help

Phoenix Sales & Service
Payroll Register
For Week Ended Oct. 8, 2013

Employee ID / Employee SS No. Refer., Date	Gross Pay			FIT [blank] FUTA	SIT [blank] SUTA	FICA-SS_EE [blank] FICA-SS_ER	FICA-Med_EE [blank] FICA-Med_ER	Net Pay
	Pay Type	Pay Hours	Gross Pay					
AR101	Regular	40.00	400.00	−28.99	−2.32	−24.80	−5.80	338.09
Robert Austin	Overtime	0.00	0.00					
333-22-9999			400.00	−2.40	−10.80	−24.80	−5.80	
9001, 10/8/13								
CJ102	Regular	40.00	560.00	−52.97	−4.24	−36.02	−8.42	479.35
Judy Cross	Overtime	1.00	21.00					
299-11-9201			581.00	−3.49	−15.69	−36.02	−8.42	
9002, 10/8/13								
DJ103	Regular	40.00	560.00	−48.33	−3.87	−37.32	−8.73	503.75
John Diaz	Overtime	2.00	42.00					
444-11-9090			602.00	−3.61	−16.25	−37.32	−8.73	
9003, 10/8/13								
KK104	Regular	40.00	560.00	−68.57	−5.49	−34.72	−8.12	443.10
Kay Keife	Overtime	0.00	0.00					
909-11-3344			560.00	−3.36	−15.12	−34.72	−8.12	
9004, 10/8/13								
ML105	Regular	40.00	560.00	−34.24	−2.74	−34.72	−8.12	480.18
Lee Miller	Overtime	0.00	0.00					
444-56-3211			560.00	−3.36	−15.12	−34.72	−8.12	
9005, 10/8/13								
SD106	Regular	40.00	560.00	−68.57	−5.49	−34.72	−8.12	443.10
Dale Sears	Overtime	0.00	0.00					
909-33-1234			560.00	−3.36	−15.12	−34.72	−8.12	
9006, 10/8/13								
Totals	Regular	240.00	3,200.00	−301.67	−24.15	−202.30	−47.31	2,687.57
	Overtime	3.00	63.00					
			3,263.00	−19.58	−88.10	−202.30	−47.31	

Sales   Purchases   General Ledger   Payroll   Inventory   Company   Analysis

Payroll Register   A **payroll register** usually shows the pay period dates, hours worked, gross pay, deductions, and net pay of each employee for each pay period. Exhibit 9A.3 shows a payroll register for Phoenix Sales & Service. It is organized into nine columns:

Col. 1   Employee identification (ID); Employee name; Social Security number (SS No.); Reference (check number); and Date (date check issued)
Col. 2   Pay Type (regular and overtime)
Col. 3   Pay Hours (number of hours worked as regular and overtime)
Col. 4   Gross Pay (amount of gross pay)[2]
Col. 5   FIT (federal income taxes withheld); FUTA (federal unemployment taxes)
Col. 6   SIT (state income taxes withheld); SUTA (state unemployment taxes)
Col. 7   FICA-SS_EE (social security taxes withheld, employee); FICA-SS_ER (social security taxes, employer)
Col. 8   FICA-Med_EE (medicare tax withheld, employee); FICA-Med_ER (medicare tax, employer)
Col. 9   Net pay (Gross pay less amounts withheld from employees)

Net pay for each employee is computed as gross pay minus the items on the first line of columns 5–8. The employer's payroll tax for each employee is computed as the sum of items on the third line of columns 5–8.

---

[2] The Gross Pay column shows regular hours worked on the first line multiplied by the regular pay rate—this equals regular pay. Overtime hours multiplied by the overtime premium rate equals overtime premium pay reported on the second line. If employers are engaged in interstate commerce, federal law sets a minimum overtime rate of pay to employees. For this company, workers earn 150% of their regular rate for hours in excess of 40 per week.

A payroll register includes all data necessary to record payroll. In some software programs the entries to record payroll are made in a special *payroll journal*.

Payroll Check   Payment of payroll is usually done by check or electronic funds transfer. Exhibit 9A.4 shows a *payroll check* for a Phoenix employee. This check is accompanied with a detachable *statement of earnings* (at top) showing gross pay, deductions, and net pay.

EXHIBIT 9A.4

Check and Statement of Earnings

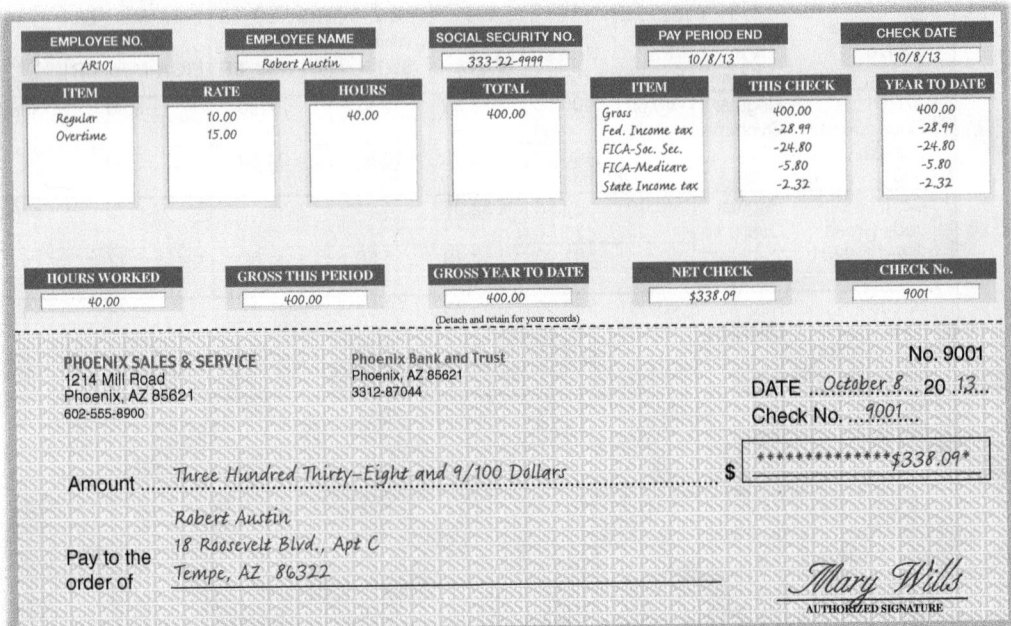

Employee Earnings Report   An **employee earnings report** is a cumulative record of an employee's hours worked, gross earnings, deductions, and net pay. Payroll information on this report is taken from the payroll register. The employee earnings report for R. Austin at Phoenix Sales & Service is shown in Exhibit 9A.5. An employee earnings report accumulates information that can show when an employee's earnings reach the tax-exempt points for FICA, FUTA, and SUTA taxes. It also gives data an employer needs to prepare Form W-2.

Payroll Procedures   Employers must be able to compute federal income tax for payroll purposes. This section explains how we compute this tax and how to use a payroll bank account.

Computing Federal Income Taxes   To compute the amount of taxes withheld from each employee's wages, we need to determine both the employee's wages earned and the employee's number of *withholding allowances*. Each employee records the number of withholding allowances claimed on a withholding allowance certificate, **Form W-4,** filed with the employer. When the number of withholding allowances increases, the amount of income taxes withheld decreases.

Employers often use a **wage bracket withholding table** similar to the one shown in Exhibit 9A.6 to compute the federal income taxes withheld from each employee's gross pay. The table in Exhibit 9A.6 is for a single employee paid weekly. Tables are also provided for married employees and for biweekly, semimonthly, and monthly pay periods (most payroll software includes these tables). When using a wage bracket withholding table to compute federal income tax withheld from an employee's gross wages, we need to locate an employee's wage bracket within the first two columns. We then find the amount withheld by looking in the withholding allowance column for that employee.

Payroll Bank Account   Companies with few employees often pay them with checks drawn on the company's regular bank account. Companies with many employees often use a special **payroll bank account** to pay employees. When this account is used, a company either (1) draws one check for total payroll on the regular bank account and deposits it in the payroll bank account or (2) executes an *electronic funds transfer* to the payroll bank account. Individual payroll checks are then drawn on this payroll bank account. Since only one check for the total payroll is drawn on the regular bank account each payday, use of a special payroll bank account helps with internal control. It also helps in reconciling the regular bank

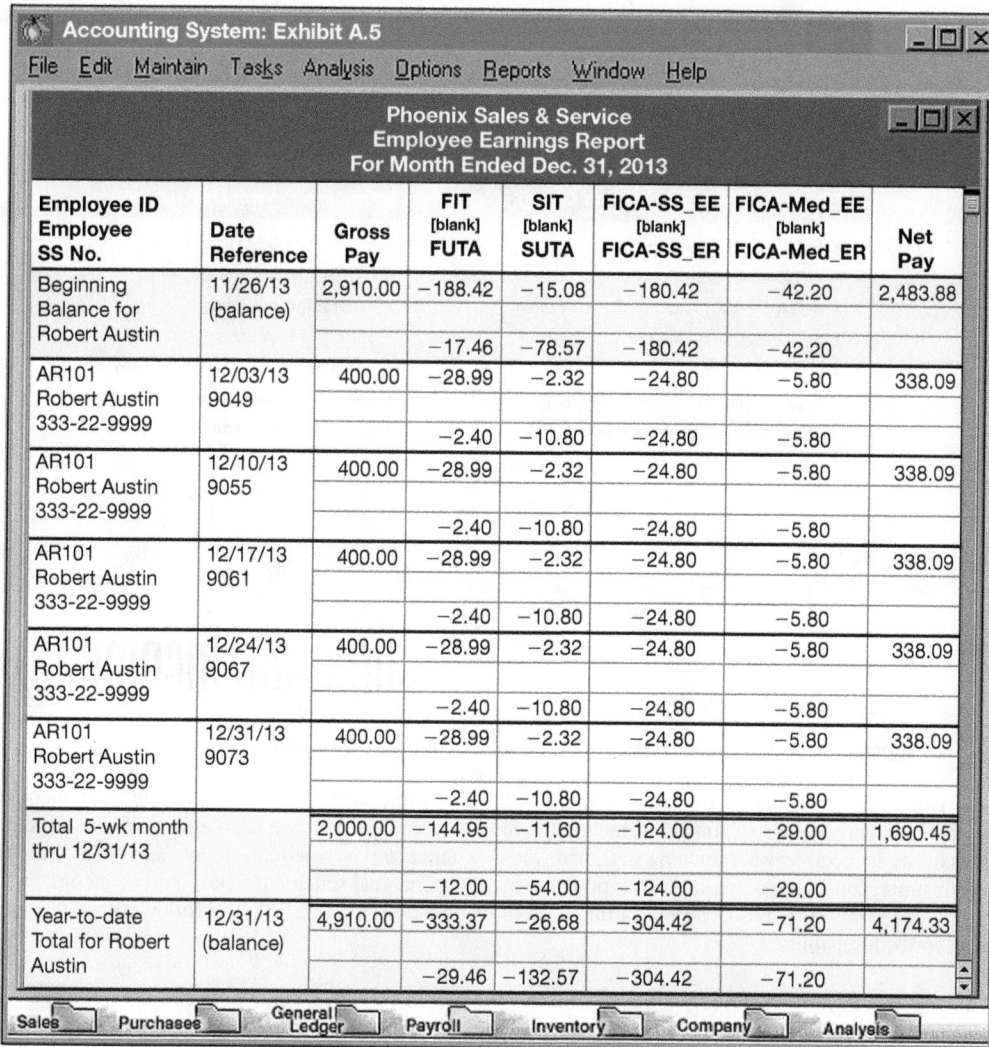

EXHIBIT 9A.5

Employee Earnings Report

EXHIBIT 9A.6

Wage Bracket Withholding Table

account. When companies use a payroll bank account, they usually include check numbers in the payroll register. The payroll register in Exhibit 9A.3 shows check numbers in column 1. For instance, Check No. 9001 is issued to Robert Austin. With this information, the payroll register serves as a supplementary record of wages earned by and paid to employees.

Who Pays What Payroll Taxes and Benefits   We conclude this appendix with the following table identifying who pays which payroll taxes and which common employee benefits such as medical, disability, pension, charitable, and union costs. Who pays which employee benefits, and what portion, is subject to agreements between companies and their workers. Also, self-employed workers must pay both the employer and employee FICA taxes for Social Security and Medicare.

Point: IRS Statistics of Income Bulletin (Winter 2012) reports the following average (effective) income tax rate for different categories of U.S. income earners:

Top 1%	24%
Top 5%	20%
Top 10%	18%
Bottom 50%	1.85%

Employer Payroll Taxes and Costs	Employee Payroll Deductions
• FICA—Social Security Taxes	• FICA—Social Security taxes
• FICA—Medicare Taxes	• FICA—Medicare taxes
• FUTA (Federal Unemployment Taxes)	• Federal Income taxes
• SUTA (State Unemployment Taxes)	• State and local income taxes
• Share of medical coverage, if any	• Share of medical coverage, if any
• Share of pension coverage, if any	• Share of pension coverage, if any
• Share of other benefits, if any	• Share of other benefits, if any

---

APPENDIX

9B

Corporate Income Taxes

This appendix explains current liabilities involving income taxes for corporations.

Income Tax Liabilities   Corporations are subject to income taxes and must estimate their income tax liability when preparing financial statements. Since income tax expense is created by earning income, a liability is incurred when income is earned. This tax must be paid quarterly under federal regulations. To illustrate, consider a corporation that prepares monthly financial statements. Based on its income in January 2013, this corporation estimates that it owes income taxes of $12,100. The following adjusting entry records this estimate:

Assets = Liabilities + Equity
+12,100   −12,100

Jan. 31	Income Taxes Expense	12,100	
	Income Taxes Payable		12,100
	To accrue January income taxes.		

The tax liability is recorded each month until the first quarterly payment is made. If the company's estimated taxes for this first quarter total $30,000, the entry to record its payment is

Assets = Liabilities + Equity
−30,000   −30,000

Apr. 10	Income Taxes Payable	30,000	
	Cash		30,000
	Paid estimated quarterly income taxes based on first quarter income.		

This process of accruing and then paying estimated income taxes continues through the year. When annual financial statements are prepared at year-end, the corporation knows its actual total income and the actual amount of income taxes it must pay. This information allows it to properly record income taxes expense for the fourth quarter so that the total of the four quarters' expense amounts equals the actual taxes paid to the government.

Deferred Income Tax Liabilities   An income tax liability for corporations can arise when the amount of income before taxes that the corporation reports on its income statement is not the same as the amount of income reported on its income tax return. This difference occurs because income tax laws and GAAP measure income differently. (Differences between tax laws and GAAP arise because Congress uses tax laws to generate receipts, stimulate the economy, and influence behavior, whereas GAAP are intended to provide financial information useful for business decisions. Also, tax accounting often follows the cash basis, whereas GAAP follows the accrual basis.)

Some differences between tax laws and GAAP are temporary. *Temporary differences* arise when the tax return and the income statement report a revenue or expense in different years. As an example, companies are often able to deduct higher amounts of depreciation in the early years of an asset's life and smaller amounts in later years for tax reporting in comparison to GAAP. This means that in the early years, depreciation for tax reporting is often more than depreciation on the income statement. In later years, depreciation for tax reporting is often less than depreciation on the income statement. When temporary differences exist between taxable income on the tax return and the income before taxes on the income statement, corporations compute income taxes expense based on the income reported on the income statement. The result is that income taxes expense reported in the income statement is often different from the amount of income taxes payable to the government. This difference is the **deferred income tax liability.**

To illustrate, assume that in recording its usual quarterly income tax payments, a corporation computes $25,000 of income taxes expense. It also determines that only $21,000 is currently due and $4,000 is deferred to future years (a timing difference). The entry to record this end-of-period adjustment is

Dec. 31	Income Taxes Expense	25,000	
	Income Taxes Payable		21,000
	Deferred Income Tax Liability		4,000
	To record tax expense and deferred tax liability.		

Assets = Liabilities + Equity
+21,000   −25,000
+4,000

The credit to Income Taxes Payable reflects the amount currently due to be paid. The credit to Deferred Income Tax Liability reflects tax payments deferred until future years when the temporary difference reverses.

Temporary differences also can cause a company to pay income taxes *before* they are reported on the income statement as expense. If so, the company reports a *Deferred Income Tax Asset* on its balance sheet.

Summary

C1 Describe current and long-term liabilities and their characteristics. Liabilities are probable future payments of assets or services that past transactions or events obligate an entity to make. Current liabilities are due within one year or the operating cycle, whichever is longer. All other liabilities are long term.

C2 Identify and describe known current liabilities. Known (determinable) current liabilities are set by agreements or laws and are measurable with little uncertainty. They include accounts payable, sales taxes payable, unearned revenues, notes payable, payroll liabilities, and the current portion of long-term debt.

C3 Explain how to account for contingent liabilities. If an uncertain future payment depends on a probable future event and the amount can be reasonably estimated, the payment is recorded as a liability. The uncertain future payment is reported as a contingent liability (in the notes) if (*a*) the future event is reasonably possible but not probable or (*b*) the event is probable but the payment amount cannot be reasonably estimated.

A1 Compute the times interest earned ratio and use it to analyze liabilities. Times interest earned is computed by dividing a company's net income before interest expense and income taxes by the amount of interest expense. The times interest earned ratio reflects a company's ability to pay interest obligations.

P1 Prepare entries to account for short-term notes payable. Short-term notes payable are current liabilities; most bear

interest. When a short-term note's face value equals the amount borrowed, it identifies a rate of interest to be paid at maturity.

P2 Compute and record *employee* payroll deductions and liabilities. Employee payroll deductions include FICA taxes, income taxes, and voluntary deductions such as for pensions and charities. They make up the difference between gross and net pay.

P3 Compute and record *employer* payroll expenses and liabilities. An employer's payroll expenses include employees' gross earnings, any employee benefits, and the payroll taxes levied on the employer. Payroll liabilities include employees' net pay amounts, withholdings from employee wages, any employer-promised benefits, and the employer's payroll taxes.

P4 Account for estimated liabilities, including warranties and bonuses. Liabilities for health and pension benefits, warranties, and bonuses are recorded with estimated amounts. These items are recognized as expenses when incurred and matched with revenues generated.

P5ᴬ Identify and describe the details of payroll reports, records, and procedures. Employers report FICA taxes and federal income tax withholdings using Form 941. FUTA taxes are reported on Form 940. Earnings and deductions are reported to each employee and the federal government on Form W-2. An employer's payroll records often include a payroll register for each pay period, payroll checks and statements of earnings, and individual employee earnings reports.

Guidance Answers to Decision Maker and Decision Ethics

Web Designer   You need to be concerned about being an accomplice to unlawful payroll activities. Not paying federal and state taxes on wages earned is illegal and unethical. Such payments also will not provide the employee with Social Security and some Medicare credits. The best course of action is to request payment by check. If this fails to change the owner's payment practices, you must consider quitting this job.

Entrepreneur   Risk is partly reflected by the times interest earned ratio. This ratio for the first franchise is 1.5 [($100,000 +

$200,000)/$200,000], whereas the ratio for the second franchise is 3.5 [($100,000 + $40,000)/$40,000]. This analysis shows that the first franchise is more at risk of incurring a loss if its sales decline. The second question asks about variability of income. If income greatly varies, this increases the risk an owner will not earn sufficient income to cover interest. Since the first franchise has the greater variability, it is a riskier investment.

Key Terms

Contingent liability (p. 402)
Current liabilities (p. 390)
Current portion of long-term debt (p. 399)
Deferred income tax liability (p. 415)
Employee benefits (p. 400)
Employee earnings report (p. 412)
Estimated liability (p. 400)
Federal depository bank (p. 410)
Federal Insurance Contributions Act
  (FICA) Taxes (p. 396)

Federal Unemployment Taxes
  (FUTA) (p. 398)
Form 940 (p. 410)
Form 941 (p. 408)
Form W-2 (p. 410)
Form W-4 (p. 412)
Gross pay (p. 396)
Known liabilities (p. 392)
Long-term liabilities (p. 390)
Merit rating (p. 398)

Net pay (p. 396)
Payroll bank account (p. 412)
Payroll deductions (p. 396)
Payroll register (p. 411)
Short-term note payable (p. 393)
State Unemployment Taxes
  (SUTA) (p. 398)
Times interest earned (p. 406)
Wage bracket withholding table (p. 412)
Warranty (p. 401)

Multiple Choice Quiz   Answers on p. 433   mhhe.com/wildFA7e

Additional Quiz Questions are available at the book's Website.

1. On December 1, a company signed a $6,000, 90-day, 5% note payable, with principal plus interest due on March 1 of the following year. What amount of interest expense should be accrued at December 31 on the note?
   a. $300
   b. $25
   c. $100
   d. $75
   e. $0

2. An employee earned $50,000 during the year. FICA tax for social security is 6.2% and FICA tax for Medicare is 1.45%. The employer's share of FICA taxes is
   a. Zero, since the employee's pay exceeds the FICA limit.
   b. Zero, since FICA is not an employer tax.
   c. $3,100
   d. $725
   e. $3,825

3. Assume the FUTA tax rate is 0.6% and the SUTA tax rate is 5.4%. Both taxes are applied to the first $7,000 of an employee's pay. What is the total unemployment tax an employer must pay on an employee's annual wages of $40,000?
   a. $2,400
   b. $420
   c. $42
   d. $378
   e. Zero; the employee's wages exceed the $7,000 maximum.

4. A company sells big screen televisions for $3,000 each. Each television has a two-year warranty that covers the replacement of defective parts. It is estimated that 1% of all televisions sold will be returned under warranty at an average cost of $250 each. During July, the company sold 10,000 big screen televisions, and 80 were serviced under the warranty during July at a total cost of $18,000. The credit balance in the Estimated Warranty Liability account at July 1 was $26,000. What is the company's warranty expense for the month of July?
   a. $51,000
   b. $1,000
   c. $25,000
   d. $33,000
   e. $18,000

5. Employees earn vacation pay at the rate of 1 day per month. During October, 150 employees qualify for one vacation day each. Their average daily wage is $175 per day. What is the amount of vacation benefit expense for October?
   a. $26,250
   b. $175
   c. $2,100
   d. $63,875
   e. $150

A(B) Superscript letter A (B) denotes assignments based on Appendix 9A (9B).

⚊ Icon denotes assignments that involve decision making.

Discussion Questions

1. ⚊ What is the difference between a current and a long-term liability?

2. What is an estimated liability?

3. ⚊ What are the three important questions concerning the uncertainty of liabilities?

4. If $988 is the total of a sale that includes its sales tax of 4%, what is the selling price of the item only?

5. What is the combined amount (in percent) of the employee and employer Social Security tax rate? (Assume wages do not exceed $200,000 per year.)

6. What is the current Medicare tax rate? This rate is applied to what maximum level of salary and wages?

7. Which payroll taxes are the employee's responsibility and which are the employer's responsibility?

8. What determines the amount deducted from an employee's wages for federal income taxes?

9. What is an employer's unemployment merit rating? How are these ratings assigned to employers?

10. ⚊ Why are warranty liabilities usually recognized on the balance sheet as liabilities even when they are uncertain?

11. ⚊ Suppose that a company has a facility located where disastrous weather conditions often occur. Should it report a probable loss from a future disaster as a liability on its balance sheet? Explain.

12.^A What is a wage bracket withholding table?

13.^A What amount of income tax is withheld from the salary of an employee who is single with two withholding allowances and earning $725 per week? What if the employee earned $625 and has no withholding allowances? (Use Exhibit 9A.6.)

14. Refer to Apple's balance sheet in Appendix A. What is the amount of Apple's accounts payable as of September 29, 2012? **APPLE**

15. ⚊ Refer to Google's balance sheet in Appendix A. What accrued expenses (liabilities) does Google report at December 31, 2012? **GOOGLE**

16. ⚊ Refer to Samsung's balance sheet in Appendix A. List Samsung's current liabilities as of December 31, 2012. **Samsung**

17. ⚊ Refer to Samsung's recent balance sheet in Appendix A. What current liabilities related to income taxes are on its balance sheet? Explain the meaning of each income tax account identified. **Samsung**

⊟ connect

Which of the following items are normally classified as a current liability for a company that has a 15-month operating cycle?

1. Note payable due in 18 months.
2. Note payable maturing in 2 years.
3. Portion of long-term note due in 15 months.
4. Salaries payable.
5. FICA taxes payable.
6. Note payable due in 11 months.

QUICK STUDY

QS 9-1
Classifying liabilities C1 ⚊

Ticketsales, Inc., receives $5,000,000 cash in advance ticket sales for a four-date tour of Bon Jovi. Record the advance ticket sales on October 31. Record the revenue earned for the first concert date of November 5, assuming it represents one-fourth of the advance ticket sales.

QS 9-2
Unearned revenue C2

Dextra Computing sells merchandise for $6,000 cash on September 30 (cost of merchandise is $3,900). The sales tax law requires Dextra to collect 5% sales tax on every dollar of merchandise sold. Record the entry for the $6,000 sale and its applicable sales tax. Also record the entry that shows the remittance of the 5% tax on this sale to the state government on October 15.

QS 9-3
Accounting for sales taxes
C2

The following legal claims exist for Huprey Co. Identify the accounting treatment for each claim as either (a) a liability that is recorded or (b) an item described in notes to its financial statements.

1. Huprey (defendant) estimates that a pending lawsuit could result in damages of $1,250,000; it is reasonably possible that the plaintiff will win the case.
2. Huprey faces a probable loss on a pending lawsuit; the amount is not reasonably estimable.
3. Huprey estimates damages in a case at $3,500,000 with a high probability of losing the case.

QS 9-4
Accounting for contingent liabilities

C3 ⚊

On November 7, 2013, Mura Company borrows $160,000 cash by signing a 90-day, 8% note payable with a face value of $160,000. (1) Compute the accrued interest payable on December 31, 2013, (2) prepare the journal entry to record the accrued interest expense at December 31, 2013, and (3) prepare the journal entry to record payment of the note at maturity.

QS 9-5
Interest-bearing note transactions P1

QS 9-6 Record employee payroll taxes **P2**	On January 15, the end of the first biweekly pay period of the year, North Company's payroll register showed that its employees earned $35,000 of sales salaries. Withholdings from the employees' salaries include FICA Social Security taxes at the rate of 6.2%, FICA Medicare taxes at the rate of 1.45%, $6,500 of federal income taxes, $772.50 of medical insurance deductions, and $120 of union dues. No employee earned more than $7,000 in this first period. Prepare the journal entry to record North Company's January 15 (employee) payroll expenses and liabilities. (Round amounts to cents.)
QS 9-7 Record employer payroll taxes **P3**	Merger Co. has ten employees, each of whom earns $2,000 per month and has been employed since January 1. FICA Social Security taxes are 6.2% of the first $113,700 paid to each employee, and FICA Medicare taxes are 1.45% of gross pay. FUTA taxes are 0.6% and SUTA taxes are 5.4% of the first $7,000 paid to each employee. Prepare the March 31 journal entry to record the March payroll taxes expenses. (Round amounts to cents.)
QS 9-8 Accounting for bonuses **P4**	Noura Company offers an annual bonus to employees if the company meets certain net income goals. Prepare the journal entry to record a $15,000 bonus owed to its workers (to be shared equally) at calendar year-end.
QS 9-9 Accounting for vacations **P4**	Chavez Co.'s salaried employees earn four weeks vacation per year. It pays $312,000.00 in total employee salaries for 52 weeks but its employees work only 48 weeks. This means Chavez's total weekly expense is $6,500 ($312,000/48 weeks) instead of the $6,000 cash paid weekly to the employees ($312,000/52 weeks). Record Chavez's weekly vacation benefits expense.
QS 9-10 Recording warranty repairs **P4**	On September 11, 2012, Home Store sells a mower for $500 with a one-year warranty that covers parts. Warranty expense is estimated at 8% of sales. On July 24, 2013, the mower is brought in for repairs covered under the warranty requiring $35 in materials taken from the Repair Parts Inventory. Prepare the September 11, 2012, entry to record the mower sale, and the July 24, 2013, entry to record the warranty repairs.
QS 9-11 Times interest earned **A1** 🔲	Compute the times interest earned for Park Company, which reports income before interest expense and income taxes of $1,885,000, and interest expense of $145,000. Interpret its times interest earned (assume that its competitors average a times interest earned of 4.0).
QS 9-12ᴬ Net pay and tax computations **P5** **Check** Net pay, $579.99	The payroll records of Speedy Software show the following information about Marsha Gottschalk, an employee, for the weekly pay period ending September 30, 2013. Gottschalk is single and claims one allowance. Compute her Social Security tax (6.2%), Medicare tax (1.45%), federal income tax withholding, state income tax (1.0%), and net pay for the current pay period. (Use the withholding table in Exhibit 9A.6 and round tax amounts to the nearest cent.) Total (gross) earnings for current pay period . . . . $ 740 Cumulative earnings of previous pay periods $9,700
QS 9-13ᴮ Record deferred income tax liability **P4**	Sera Corporation has made and recorded its quarterly income tax payments. After a final review of taxes for the year, the company identifies an additional $40,000 of income tax expense that should be recorded. A portion of this additional expense, $6,000, is deferred for payment in future years. Record Sera's year-end adjusting entry for income tax expense.
QS 9-14 International accounting standards **C1 C2** 🌐	Answer each of the following related to international accounting standards. **a.** In general, how similar or different are the definitions and characteristics of current liabilities between IFRS and U.S. GAAP? **b.** Companies reporting under IFRS often reference a set of current liabilities with the title *financial liabilities*. Identify two current liabilities that would be classified under financial liabilities per IFRS. (*Hint:* Nokia provides examples in this chapter.)

≣ connect

EXERCISES

Exercise 9-1
Classifying liabilities
C1 🔲

The following items appear on the balance sheet of a company with a two-month operating cycle. Identify the proper classification of each item as follows: *C* if it is a current liability, *L* if it is a long-term liability, or *N* if it is not a liability.

_____	**1.** Notes payable (due in 120 days).	_____	**6.** Sales taxes payable.
_____	**2.** Notes payable (mature in five years).	_____	**7.** Accounts receivable.
_____	**3.** Notes payable (due in 6 to 12 months).	_____	**8.** Wages payable.
_____	**4.** Current portion of long-term debt.	_____	**9.** FUTA taxes payable.
_____	**5.** Notes payable (due in 13 to 24 months).	_____	**10.** Salaries payable.

Prepare any necessary adjusting entries at December 31, 2013, for Piper Company's year-end financial statements for each of the following separate transactions and events.

1. Piper Company records an adjusting entry for $10,000,000 of previously unrecorded cash sales (costing $5,000,000) and its sales taxes at a rate of 4%.

2. The company earned $50,000 of $125,000 previously received in advance for services.

Exercise 9-2
Recording known current liabilities
C2

Prepare any necessary adjusting entries at December 31, 2013, for Melbourn Company's year-end financial statements for each of the following separate transactions and events.

1. Melbourn Company guarantees the $100,000 debt of a supplier. The supplier will probably not default on the debt.

2. A disgruntled employee is suing Melbourn Company. Legal advisers believe that the company will probably need to pay damages, but the amount cannot be reasonably estimated.

Exercise 9-3
Accounting for contingent liabilities
C3

Sylvestor Systems borrows $110,000 cash on May 15, 2013, by signing a 60-day, 12% note.

1. On what date does this note mature?

2. Suppose the face value of the note equals $110,000, the principal of the loan. Prepare the journal entries to record (*a*) issuance of the note and (*b*) payment of the note at maturity.

Exercise 9-4
Accounting for note payable
P1

Check   (2b) Interest expense, $2,200

Keesha Co. borrows $200,000 cash on November 1, 2013, by signing a 90-day, 9% note with a face value of $200,000.

1. On what date does this note mature? (Assume that February of 2013 has 28 days.)

2. How much interest expense results from this note in 2013? (Assume a 360-day year.)

3. How much interest expense results from this note in 2014? (Assume a 360-day year.)

4. Prepare journal entries to record (*a*) issuance of the note, (*b*) accrual of interest at the end of 2013, and (*c*) payment of the note at maturity.

Exercise 9-5
Interest-bearing notes payable with year-end adjustments
P1

Check   (2) $3,000
            (3) $1,500

BMX Company has one employee. FICA Social Security taxes are 6.2% of the first $113,700 paid to its employee, and FICA Medicare taxes are 1.45% of gross pay. For BMX, its FUTA taxes are 0.6% and SUTA taxes are 2.9% of the first $7,000 paid to its employee. Compute BMX's amounts for each of these four taxes as applied to the employee's gross earnings for September under each of three separate situations (*a*), (*b*), and (*c*). (Round amounts to cents.)

Exercise 9-6
Computing payroll taxes
P2   P3

	Gross Pay through August	Gross Pay for September
a.	$ 6,400	$ 800
b.	18,200	2,100
c.	107,400	8,000

Check   (*a*) FUTA, $3.60; SUTA, $17.40

Using the data in situation *a* of Exercise 9-6, prepare the employer's September 30 journal entries to record salary expense and its related payroll liabilities for this employee. The employee's federal income taxes withheld by the employer are $80 for this pay period. (Round amounts to cents.)

Exercise 9-7
Payroll-related journal entries   P2

Using the data in situation *a* of Exercise 9-6, prepare the employer's September 30 journal entries to record the *employer's* payroll taxes expense and its related liabilities. (Round amounts to cents.)

Exercise 9-8
Payroll-related journal entries   P3

Hitzu Co. sold a copier costing $4,800 with a two-year parts warranty to a customer on August 16, 2013, for $6,000 cash. Hitzu uses the perpetual inventory system. On November 22, 2014, the copier requires on-site repairs that are completed the same day. The repairs cost $209 for materials taken from the Repair Parts Inventory. These are the only repairs required in 2014 for this copier. Based on experience, Hitzu expects to incur warranty costs equal to 4% of dollar sales. It records warranty expense with an adjusting entry at the end of each year.

1. How much warranty expense does the company report in 2013 for this copier?

2. How much is the estimated warranty liability for this copier as of December 31, 2013?

3. How much warranty expense does the company report in 2014 for this copier?

4. How much is the estimated warranty liability for this copier as of December 31, 2014?

5. Prepare journal entries to record (*a*) the copier's sale; (*b*) the adjustment on December 31, 2013, to recognize the warranty expense; and (*c*) the repairs that occur in November 2014.

Exercise 9-9
Warranty expense and liability computations and entries   P4

Check   (1) $240

            (4) $31

Exercise 9-10

Computing and recording bonuses   P4

Check   (1) $14,563

For the year ended December 31, 2013, Lopez Company has implemented an employee bonus program equal to 3% of Lopez's net income, which employees will share equally. Lopez's net income (prebonus) is expected to be $500,000, and bonus expense is deducted in computing net income.

1. Compute the amount of the bonus payable to the employees at year-end (use the method described in the chapter and round to the nearest dollar).

2. Prepare the journal entry at December 31, 2013, to record the bonus due the employees.

3. Prepare the journal entry at January 19, 2014, to record payment of the bonus to employees.

Exercise 9-11

Accounting for estimated liabilities

P4

Prepare any necessary adjusting entries at December 31, 2013, for Maxum Company's year-end financial statements for each of the following separate transactions and events.

1. Employees earn vacation pay at a rate of one day per month. During December, 20 employees qualify for one vacation day each. Their average daily wage is $160 per employee.

2. During December, Maxum Company sold 12,000 units of a product that carries a 60-day warranty. December sales for this product total $460,000. The company expects 10% of the units to need warranty repairs, and it estimates the average repair cost per unit will be $15.

Exercise 9-12

Computing and interpreting times interest earned

A1

Check   (b) 11.00

Use the following information from separate companies *a* through *f* to compute times interest earned. Which company indicates the strongest ability to pay interest expense as it comes due? (Round ratios to two decimals.)

	Net Income (Loss)	Interest Expense	Income Taxes
a.	$115,000	$44,000	$ 35,000
b.	110,000	16,000	50,000
c.	100,000	12,000	70,000
d.	235,000	14,000	130,000
e.	59,000	14,000	30,000
f.	(5,000)	10,000	0

Exercise 9-13[B]

Accounting for income taxes

P4

Check   (1) $3,610

Nishi Corporation prepares financial statements for each month-end. As part of its accounting process, estimated income taxes are accrued each month for 30% of the current month's net income. The income taxes are paid in the first month of each quarter for the amount accrued for the prior quarter. The following information is available for the fourth quarter of year 2013. When tax computations are completed on January 20, 2014, Nishi determines that the quarter's Income Taxes Payable account balance should be $28,300 on December 31, 2013 (its unadjusted balance is $24,690).

October 2013 net income	$28,600
November 2013 net income	19,100
December 2013 net income	34,600

1. Determine the amount of the accounting adjustment (dated as of December 31, 2013) to produce the proper ending balance in the Income Taxes Payable account.

2. Prepare journal entries to record (*a*) the December 31, 2013, adjustment to the Income Taxes Payable account and (*b*) the January 20, 2014, payment of the fourth-quarter taxes.

Exercise 9-14[A]

Gross and net pay computation

P5

Check   Net pay, $596.30

Lenny Florita, an unmarried employee, works 48 hours in the week ended January 12. His pay rate is $14 per hour, and his wages are subject to no deductions other than FICA—Social Security, FICA—Medicare, and federal income taxes. He claims two withholding allowances. Compute his regular pay, overtime pay (for this company, workers earn 150% of their regular rate for hours in excess of 40 per week), and gross pay. Then compute his FICA tax deduction (use 6.2% for the Social Security portion and 1.45% for the Medicare portion), income tax deduction (use the wage bracket withholding table of Exhibit 9A.6), total deductions, and net pay. (Round tax amounts to the nearest cent.)

Exercise 9-15

Recording payroll

P2   P3

The following monthly data are taken from Ramirez Company at July 31: Sales salaries, $200,000; Office salaries, $160,000; Federal income taxes withheld, $90,000; State income taxes withheld, $20,000; Social security taxes withheld, $22,320; Medicare taxes withheld, $5,220; Medical insurance premiums, $7,000; Life insurance premiums, $4,000; Union dues deducted, $1,000; and Salaries subject to unemployment taxes, $50,000. The employee pays forty percent of medical and life insurance premiums.

Prepare journal entries to record: (1) accrued payroll, including employee deductions, for July; (2) cash payment of the net payroll (salaries payable) for July; (3) accrued employer payroll taxes, and other related employment expenses, for July—assume that FICA taxes are identical to those on employees and that SUTA taxes are 5.4% and FUTA taxes are 0.6%; and (4) cash payment of all liabilities related to the July payroll.

Mester Company has 10 employees. FICA Social Security taxes are 6.2% of the first $113,700 paid to each employee, and FICA Medicare taxes are 1.45% of gross pay. FUTA taxes are 0.6% and SUTA taxes are 5.4% of the first $7,000 paid to each employee. Cumulative pay for the current year for each of its employees follows.

Exercise 9-16
Computing payroll taxes
P2 P3

Employee	Cumulative Pay	Employee	Cumulative Pay	Employee	Cumulative Pay
Ken S.........	$ 6,000	Christina S.	$152,800	Lori K.	$116,600
Tim V.........	60,200	Kathleen K.	106,900	Matt B.........	36,800
Steve S.	87,000	Michelle H.	113,700	John W.	4,000

a. Prepare a table with the following column headings: Employee; Cumulative Pay; Pay Subject to FICA Social Security Taxes; Pay Subject to FICA Medicare Taxes; Pay Subject to FUTA Taxes; Pay Subject to SUTA Taxes. Compute the amounts in this table for each employee and total the columns.

b. For the company, compute each total for: FICA Social Security taxes, FICA Medicare taxes, FUTA taxes, and SUTA taxes. (*Hint:* Remember to include in those totals any employee share of taxes that the company must collect.) (Round amounts to cents.)

Stark Company has five employees. Employees paid by the hour receive a $10 per hour pay rate for the regular 40-hour work week plus one and one-half times the hourly rate for each overtime hour beyond the 40-hours per week. Hourly employees are paid every two weeks, but salaried employees are paid monthly on the last biweekly payday of each month. FICA Social Security taxes are 6.2% of the first $113,700 paid to each employee, and FICA Medicare taxes are 1.45% of gross pay. FUTA taxes are 0.6% and SUTA taxes are 5.4% of the first $7,000 paid to each employee. The company has a benefits plan that includes medical insurance, life insurance, and retirement funding for employees. Under this plan, employees must contribute 5 percent of their gross income as a payroll withholding, which the company matches with double the amount. Following is the partially completed payroll register for the biweekly period ending August 31, which is the last payday of August.

Exercise 9-17
Preparing payroll register and
related entries P5

Employee	Cumulative Pay (Excludes Current Period)	Pay Type	Pay Hours	Gross Pay	FIT / SIT	FUTA / SUTA	FICA-SS_EE / FICA-SS_ER	FICA-Med_EE / FICA-Med_ER	EE-Ben_Plan Withholding / ER-Ben_Plan Withholding	Employee Net Pay
Kathleen	$111,900.00	Salary	---	$7,000.00	$2,000.00					
					300.00					
Anthony	6,800.00	Salary	---	500.00	80.00					
					20.00					
Nichole	15,000.00	Regular	80		110.00					
		Overtime	8		25.00					
Zoey	6,500.00	Regular	80		100.00					
		Overtime	4		22.00					
Gracie	5,000.00	Regular	74	740.00	90.00					
		Overtime	0	0.00	21.00					
Totals	145,200.00				2,380.00					
					388.00					

Note: Table abbreviations follow those in Exhibit 9A.3 (see page 411); and, "Ben_Plan" refers to employee (EE) or employer (ER) withholding for the benefits plan.

a. Complete this payroll register by filling in all cells for the pay period ended August 31. *Hint:* See Exhibit 9A.5 for guidance. (Round amounts to cents.)

b. Prepare the August 31 journal entry to record the accrued biweekly payroll and related liabilities for deductions.

c. Prepare the August 31 journal entry to record the employer's cash payment of the net payroll of part *b.*

d. Prepare the August 31 journal entry to record the employer's payroll taxes including the contribution to the benefits plan.

e. Prepare the August 31 journal entry to pay all liabilities (expect net payroll in part *c*) for this biweekly period.

Volvo Group reports the following information for its product warranty costs as of December 31, 2011, along with provisions and utilizations of warranty liabilities for the year ended December 31, 2011 (SEK in millions).

Exercise 9-18
Accounting for current liabilities
under IFRS
P4

Provision for product warranty Warranty provisions are estimated with consideration of historical claims statistics, the warranty period, the average time-lag between faults occurring and claims to the company and anticipated changes in quality indexes. Estimated costs for product warranties are charged to cost of sales when the products are sold. Differences between actual warranty claims and the estimated claims generally affect the recognized expense and provisions in future periods. Refunds from suppliers, that decrease Volvo's warranty costs, are recognized to the extent these are considered to be certain. At December 31, 2011 (2010) warranty cost provisions amounted to 8,652 (7,841).

Product warranty liabilities, December 31, 2010	SEK 7,841
Additional provisions to product warranty liabilities	7,749
Utilizations and reductions of product warranty liabilities	(6,938)
Product warranty liabilities, December 31, 2011	8,652

1. Prepare Volvo's journal entry to record its estimated warranty liabilities (provisions) for 2011.
2. Prepare Volvo's journal entry to record its costs (utilizations) related to its warranty program for 2011. Assume those costs involve replacements taken out of Inventory, with no cash involved.
3. How much warranty expense does Volvo report for 2011?

connect

PROBLEM SET A

Problem 9-1A
Short-term notes payable transactions and entries
P1

Tyrell Co. entered into the following transactions involving short-term liabilities in 2012 and 2013.

2012

Apr. 20   Purchased $40,250 of merchandise on credit from Locust, terms are 1/10, n/30. Tyrell uses the perpetual inventory system.

May 19   Replaced the April 20 account payable to Locust with a 90-day, $35,000 note bearing 10% annual interest along with paying $5,250 in cash.

July 8   Borrowed $80,000 cash from National Bank by signing a 120-day, 9% interest-bearing note with a face value of $80,000.

___?___   Paid the amount due on the note to Locust at the maturity date.

___?___   Paid the amount due on the note to National Bank at the maturity date.

Nov. 28   Borrowed $42,000 cash from Fargo Bank by signing a 60-day, 8% interest-bearing note with a face value of $42,000.

Dec. 31   Recorded an adjusting entry for accrued interest on the note to Fargo Bank.

2013

___?___   Paid the amount due on the note to Fargo Bank at the maturity date.

Required

1. Determine the maturity date for each of the three notes described.
2. Determine the interest due at maturity for each of the three notes. (Assume a 360-day year.)
3. Determine the interest expense to be recorded in the adjusting entry at the end of 2012.
4. Determine the interest expense to be recorded in 2013.
5. Prepare journal entries for all the preceding transactions and events for years 2012 and 2013.

Check (2) Locust, $875
(3) $308
(4) $252

Problem 9-2A
Payroll expenses, withholdings, and taxes **P2 P3**

Paloma Co. Stars has four employees. FICA Social Security taxes are 6.2% of the first $113,700 paid to each employee, and FICA Medicare taxes are 1.45% of gross pay. Also, for the first $7,000 paid to each employee, the company's FUTA taxes are 0.6% and SUTA taxes are 2.15%. The company is preparing its payroll calculations for the week ended August 25. Payroll records show the following information for the company's four employees.

Name	**Gross Pay through 8/18**	**Gross Pay**	**Income Tax Withholding**
		Current Week	
Dahlia	$112,600	$2,000	$284
Trey	112,800	900	145
Kiesha	7,100	450	39
Chee	1,050	400	30

In addition to gross pay, the company must pay one-half of the $60 per employee weekly health insurance; each employee pays the remaining one-half. The company also contributes an extra 8% of each employee's gross pay (at no cost to employees) to a pension fund.

Required

Compute the following for the week ended August 25 (round amounts to the nearest cent):

1. Each employee's FICA withholdings for Social Security.
2. Each employee's FICA withholdings for Medicare.
3. Employer's FICA taxes for Social Security.
4. Employer's FICA taxes for Medicare.
5. Employer's FUTA taxes.
6. Employer's SUTA taxes.
7. Each employee's net (take-home) pay.
8. Employer's total payroll-related expense for each employee.

Check   (3) $176.70
(4) $54.38
(5) $2.40

(7) Total net pay, $2,900.92

On January 8, the end of the first weekly pay period of the year, Regis Company's payroll register showed that its employees earned $22,760 of office salaries and $65,840 of sales salaries. Withholdings from the employees' salaries include FICA Social Security taxes at the rate of 6.2%, FICA Medicare taxes at the rate of 1.45%, $12,860 of federal income taxes, $1,340 of medical insurance deductions, and $840 of union dues. No employee earned more than $7,000 in this first period.

Problem 9-3A
Entries for payroll transactions
P2 P3

Required

1. Calculate FICA Social Security taxes payable and FICA Medicare taxes payable. Prepare the journal entry to record Regis Company's January 8 (employee) payroll expenses and liabilities. (Round amounts to cents.)

2. Prepare the journal entry to record Regis's (employer) payroll taxes resulting from the January 8 payroll. Regis's merit rating reduces its state unemployment tax rate to 4% of the first $7,000 paid each employee. The federal unemployment tax rate is 0.6%. (Round amounts to cents.)

Check   (1) Cr. Salaries Payable, $66,782.10

(2) Dr. Payroll Taxes Expense, $10,853.50

On October 29, 2012, Lobo Co. began operations by purchasing razors for resale. Lobo uses the perpetual inventory method. The razors have a 90-day warranty that requires the company to replace any nonworking razor. When a razor is returned, the company discards it and mails a new one from Merchandise Inventory to the customer. The company's cost per new razor is $20 and its retail selling price is $75 in both 2012 and 2013. The manufacturer has advised the company to expect warranty costs to equal 8% of dollar sales. The following transactions and events occurred.

Problem 9-4A
Warranty expense and liability estimation
P4

2012

Nov. 11 Sold 105 razors for $7,875 cash.
    30 Recognized warranty expense related to November sales with an adjusting entry.
Dec. 9 Replaced 15 razors that were returned under the warranty.
    16 Sold 220 razors for $16,500 cash.
    29 Replaced 30 razors that were returned under the warranty.
    31 Recognized warranty expense related to December sales with an adjusting entry.

2013

Jan. 5 Sold 150 razors for $11,250 cash.
    17 Replaced 50 razors that were returned under the warranty.
    31 Recognized warranty expense related to January sales with an adjusting entry.

Required

1. Prepare journal entries to record these transactions and adjustments for 2012 and 2013.
2. How much warranty expense is reported for November 2012 and for December 2012?
3. How much warranty expense is reported for January 2013?
4. What is the balance of the Estimated Warranty Liability account as of December 31, 2012?
5. What is the balance of the Estimated Warranty Liability account as of January 31, 2013?

Check   (3) $900
(4) $1,050 Cr.
(5) $950 Cr.

Problem 9-5A
Computing and analyzing times interest earned

A1

Shown here are condensed income statements for two different companies (both are organized as LLCs and pay no income taxes).

Miller Company	
Sales	$1,000,000
Variable expenses (80%)	800,000
Income before interest	200,000
Interest expense (fixed)	60,000
Net income	$ 140,000

Weaver Company	
Sales	$1,000,000
Variable expenses (60%)	600,000
Income before interest	400,000
Interest expense (fixed)	260,000
Net income	$ 140,000

Required

1. Compute times interest earned for Miller Company.
2. Compute times interest earned for Weaver Company.
3. What happens to each company's net income if sales increase by 30%?
4. What happens to each company's net income if sales increase by 50%?
5. What happens to each company's net income if sales increase by 80%?
6. What happens to each company's net income if sales decrease by 10%?
7. What happens to each company's net income if sales decrease by 20%?
8. What happens to each company's net income if sales decrease by 40%?

Check (3) Miller net income, $200,000 (43% increase)

(6) Weaver net income, $100,000 (29% decrease)

Analysis Component

9. Comment on the results from parts 3 through 8 in relation to the fixed-cost strategies of the two companies and the ratio values you computed in parts 1 and 2.

Problem 9-6A[A]
Entries for payroll transactions

P2 P3 P5

Francisco Company has 10 employees, each of whom earns $2,800 per month and is paid on the last day of each month. All 10 have been employed continuously at this amount since January 1. On March 1, the following accounts and balances exist in its general ledger:

a. FICA—Social Security Taxes Payable, $3,472; FICA—Medicare Taxes Payable, $812. (The balances of these accounts represent total liabilities for *both* the employer's and employees' FICA taxes for the February payroll only.)
b. Employees' Federal Income Taxes Payable, $4,000 (liability for February only).
c. Federal Unemployment Taxes Payable, $448 (liability for January and February together).
d. State Unemployment Taxes Payable, $2,240 (liability for January and February together).

During March and April, the company had the following payroll transactions.

Mar. 15   Issued check payable to Swift Bank, a federal depository bank authorized to accept employers' payments of FICA taxes and employee income tax withholdings. The $8,284 check is in payment of the February FICA and employee income taxes.

31   Record the journal entry for the March salaries payable. Then record the cash payment of the March payroll (the company issued checks payable to each employee in payment of the March payroll). The payroll register shows the following summary totals for the March pay period.

Check March 31: Salaries Payable, $21,858

	Salaries				Federal	
Office Salaries	Shop Salaries	Gross Pay	FICA Taxes*	Income Taxes	Net Pay
$11,200	$16,800	$28,000	$1,736	$4,000	$21,858
			$ 406		

* FICA taxes are Social Security and Medicare, respectively.

March 31: Dr. Payroll Taxes Expenses, $2,786

31   Recorded the employer's payroll taxes resulting from the March payroll. The company has a merit rating that reduces its state unemployment tax rate to 4.0% of the first $7,000 paid each employee. The federal rate is 0.6%.

Apr. 15   Issued check to Swift Bank in payment of the March FICA and employee income taxes.

15   Issued check to the State Tax Commission for the January, February, and March state unemployment taxes. Mailed the check and the first quarter tax return to the Commission.

30   Issued check payable to Swift Bank in payment of the employer's FUTA taxes for the first quarter of the year.

30   Mailed Form 941 to the IRS, reporting the FICA taxes and the employees' federal income tax withholdings for the first quarter.

April 15: Cr. Cash, $8,284 (Swift Bank)

Required

Prepare journal entries to record the transactions and events for both March and April.

Warner Co. entered into the following transactions involving short-term liabilities in 2012 and 2013.

PROBLEM SET B

Problem 9-1B
Short-term notes payable transactions and entries
P1

2012

Apr. 22   Purchased $5,000 of merchandise on credit from Fox Products, terms are 1/10, n/30. Warner uses the perpetual inventory system.

May 23   Replaced the April 22 account payable to Fox Products with a 60-day, $4,600 note bearing 15% annual interest along with paying $400 in cash.

July 15   Borrowed $12,000 cash from Spring Bank by signing a 120-day, 10% interest-bearing note with a face value of $12,000.

_?_   Paid the amount due on the note to Fox Products at maturity.

_?_   Paid the amount due on the note to Spring Bank at maturity.

Dec. 6   Borrowed $8,000 cash from City Bank by signing a 45-day, 9% interest-bearing note with a face value of $8,000.

31   Recorded an adjusting entry for accrued interest on the note to City Bank.

2013

_?_   Paid the amount due on the note to City Bank at maturity.

Required

1. Determine the maturity date for each of the three notes described.
2. Determine the interest due at maturity for each of the three notes. (Assume a 360-day year.)
3. Determine the interest expense to be recorded in the adjusting entry at the end of 2012.
4. Determine the interest expense to be recorded in 2013.
5. Prepare journal entries for all the preceding transactions and events for years 2012 and 2013.

Check   (2) Fox, $115
(3) $50
(4) $40

Fishing Guides Co. has four employees. FICA Social Security taxes are 6.2% of the first $113,700 paid to each employee, and FICA Medicare taxes are 1.45% of gross pay. Also, for the first $7,000 paid to each employee, the company's FUTA taxes are 0.6% and SUTA taxes are 1.75%. The company is preparing its payroll calculations for the week ended September 30. Payroll records show the following information for the company's four employees.

Problem 9-2B
Payroll expenses, withholdings, and taxes
P2 P3

| | Gross Pay through 9/23 | Current Week | |
Name		Gross Pay	Income Tax Withholding
Ahmed	$112,100	$2,500	$198
Carlos	112,185	1,515	182
June	6,650	475	32
Marie	22,200	1,000	68

In addition to gross pay, the company must pay one-half of the $50 per employee weekly health insurance; each employee pays the remaining one-half. The company also contributes an extra 5% of each employee's gross pay (at no cost to employees) to a pension fund.

Required

Compute the following for the week ended September 30 (round amounts to the nearest cent):

1. Each employee's FICA withholdings for Social Security.
2. Each employee's FICA withholdings for Medicare.
3. Employer's FICA taxes for Social Security.
4. Employer's FICA taxes for Medicare.

5. Employer's FUTA taxes.
6. Employer's SUTA taxes.
7. Each employee's net (take-home) pay.
8. Employer's total payroll-related expense for each employee.

Check (3) $284.58
          (4) $79.61
          (5) $2.10
          (7) Total net pay, $4,545.81

Problem 9-3B

Entries for payroll transactions

P2 P3

Tavella Company's first weekly pay period of the year ends on January 8. On that date, the column totals in Tavella's payroll register indicate its sales employees earned $34,745, its office employees earned $21,225, and its delivery employees earned $1,030 in salaries. The employees are to have withheld from their salaries FICA Social Security taxes at the rate of 6.2%, FICA Medicare taxes at the rate of 1.45%, $8,625 of federal income taxes, $1,160 of medical insurance deductions, and $138 of union dues. No employee earned more than $7,000 in the first pay period.

Required

Check (1) Cr. Salaries Payable,
              $42,716.50

          (2) Dr. Payroll Taxes
              Expense, $6,640.50

1. Calculate FICA Social Security taxes payable and FICA Medicare taxes payable. Prepare the journal entry to record Tavella Company's January 8 (employee) payroll expenses and liabilities. (Round amounts to cents.)

2. Prepare the journal entry to record Tavella's (employer) payroll taxes resulting from the January 8 payroll. Tavella's merit rating reduces its state unemployment tax rate to 3.4% of the first $7,000 paid each employee. The federal unemployment tax rate is 0.6%. (Round amounts to cents.)

Problem 9-4B

Warranty expense and liability estimation

P4

On November 10, 2013, Lee Co. began operations by purchasing coffee grinders for resale. Lee uses the perpetual inventory method. The grinders have a 60-day warranty that requires the company to replace any nonworking grinder. When a grinder is returned, the company discards it and mails a new one from Merchandise Inventory to the customer. The company's cost per new grinder is $24 and its retail selling price is $50 in both 2013 and 2014. The manufacturer has advised the company to expect warranty costs to equal 10% of dollar sales. The following transactions and events occurred.

2013

Nov. 16 Sold 50 grinders for $2,500 cash.
     30 Recognized warranty expense related to November sales with an adjusting entry.
Dec. 12 Replaced six grinders that were returned under the warranty.
     18 Sold 200 grinders for $10,000 cash.
     28 Replaced 17 grinders that were returned under the warranty.
     31 Recognized warranty expense related to December sales with an adjusting entry.

2014

Jan. 7 Sold 40 grinders for $2,000 cash.
     21 Replaced 36 grinders that were returned under the warranty.
     31 Recognized warranty expense related to January sales with an adjusting entry.

Required

1. Prepare journal entries to record these transactions and adjustments for 2013 and 2014.
2. How much warranty expense is reported for November 2013 and for December 2013?
3. How much warranty expense is reported for January 2014?
4. What is the balance of the Estimated Warranty Liability account as of December 31, 2013?
5. What is the balance of the Estimated Warranty Liability account as of January 31, 2014?

Check (3) $200
          (4) $698 Cr.
          (5) $34 Cr.

Problem 9-5B

Computing and analyzing times interest earned

A1

Shown here are condensed income statements for two different companies (both are organized as LLCs and pay no income taxes).

Ellis Company	
Sales	$240,000
Variable expenses (50%)	120,000
Income before interest	120,000
Interest expense (fixed)	90,000
Net income	$ 30,000

Seidel Company	
Sales	$240,000
Variable expenses (75%)	180,000
Income before interest	60,000
Interest expense (fixed)	30,000
Net income	$ 30,000

Required

1. Compute times interest earned for Ellis Company.

2. Compute times interest earned for Seidel Company.

3. What happens to each company's net income if sales increase by 10%?

4. What happens to each company's net income if sales increase by 40%?

5. What happens to each company's net income if sales increase by 90%?

6. What happens to each company's net income if sales decrease by 20%?

7. What happens to each company's net income if sales decrease by 50%?

8. What happens to each company's net income if sales decrease by 80%?

Check (4) Ellis net income, $78,000 (160% increase)

(6) Seidel net income, $18,000 (40% decrease)

Analysis Component

9. Comment on the results from parts 3 through 8 in relation to the fixed-cost strategies of the two companies and the ratio values you computed in parts 1 and 2.

MLS Company has five employees, each of whom earns $1,600 per month and is paid on the last day of each month. All five have been employed continuously at this amount since January 1. On June 1, the following accounts and balances exist in its general ledger:

a. FICA—Social Security Taxes Payable, $992; FICA—Medicare Taxes Payable, $232. (The balances of these accounts represent total liabilities for *both* the employer's and employees' FICA taxes for the May payroll only.)

b. Employees' Federal Income Taxes Payable, $1,050 (liability for May only).

c. Federal Unemployment Taxes Payable, $88 (liability for April and May together).

d. State Unemployment Taxes Payable, $440 (liability for April and May together).

During June and July, the company had the following payroll transactions.

Problem 9-6B[A]
Entries for payroll transactions
P2 P3 P5

June 15 Issued check payable to Security Bank, a federal depository bank authorized to accept employers' payments of FICA taxes and employee income tax withholdings. The $2,274 check is in payment of the May FICA and employee income taxes.

30 Record the journal entry for the June salaries payable. Then record the cash payment of the June payroll (the company issued checks payable to each employee in payment of the June payroll).The payroll register shows the following summary totals for the June pay period.

Check June 30: Cr. Salaries Payable, $6,338

	Salaries				Federal	
Office Salaries	Shop Salaries	Gross Pay	FICA Taxes*	Income Taxes	Net Pay
$3,800	$4,200	$8,000	$496 $116	$1,050	$6,338

* FICA taxes are Social Security and Medicare, respectively.

30 Recorded the employer's payroll taxes resulting from the June payroll. The company has a merit rating that reduces its state unemployment tax rate to 4.0% of the first $7,000 paid each employee. The federal rate is 0.6%.

July 15 Issued check payable to Security Bank in payment of the June FICA and employee income taxes.

15 Issued check to the State Tax Commission for the April, May and June state unemployment taxes. Mailed the check and the second quarter tax return to the State Tax Commission.

31 Issued check payable to Security Bank in payment of the employer's FUTA taxes for the first quarter of the year.

31 Mailed Form 941 to the IRS, reporting the FICA taxes and the employees' federal income tax withholdings for the second quarter.

Check June 30: Dr. Payroll Taxes Expenses, $612

July 15: Cr. Cash $2,274 (Security Bank)

Required

Prepare journal entries to record the transactions and events for both June and July.

SERIAL PROBLEM

Success Systems

P2 P3 C2

(This serial problem began in Chapter 1 and continues through most of the book. If previous chapter segments were not completed, the serial problem can begin at this point. It is helpful, but not necessary, to use the Working Papers that accompany the book.)

SP 9 Review the February 26 and March 25 transactions for Success Systems (SP 4) from Chapter 4.

Required

1. Assume that Lyn Addie is an unmarried employee. Her $1,000 of wages are subject to no deductions other than FICA Social Security taxes, FICA Medicare taxes, and federal income taxes. Her federal income taxes for this pay period total $159. Compute her net pay for the eight days' work paid on February 26. (Round amounts to the nearest cent.)
2. Record the journal entry to reflect the payroll payment to Lyn Addie as computed in part 1.
3. Record the journal entry to reflect the (employer) payroll tax expenses for the February 26 payroll payment. Assume Lyn Addie has not met earnings limits for FUTA and SUTA—the FUTA rate is 0.6% and the SUTA rate is 4% for Success Systems. (Round amounts to the nearest cent.)
4. Record the entry(ies) for the merchandise sold on March 25 if a 4% sales tax rate applies.

COMPREHENSIVE PROBLEM

Bug-Off Exterminators

(Review of Chapters 1–9)

CP 9 Bug-Off Exterminators provides pest control services and sells extermination products manufactured by other companies. The following six-column table contains the company's unadjusted trial balance as of December 31, 2013.

BUG-OFF EXTERMINATORS December 31, 2013					
	Unadjusted Trial Balance		Adjustments	Adjusted Trial Balance	
Cash	$ 17,000				
Accounts receivable	4,000				
Allowance for doubtful accounts		$ 828			
Merchandise inventory	11,700				
Trucks	32,000				
Accum. depreciation—Trucks		0			
Equipment	45,000				
Accum. depreciation—Equipment		12,200			
Accounts payable....................		5,000			
Estimated warranty liability		1,400			
Unearned services revenue		0			
Interest payable		0			
Long-term notes payable		15,000			
Common stock		10,000			
Retained earnings		49,700			
Dividends.........................	10,000				
Extermination services revenue		60,000			
Interest revenue		872			
Sales (of merchandise)		71,026			
Cost of goods sold	46,300				
Depreciation expense—Trucks	0				
Depreciation expense—Equipment	0				
Wages expense	35,000				
Interest expense	0				
Rent expense	9,000				
Bad debts expense	0				
Miscellaneous expense	1,226				
Repairs expense	8,000				
Utilities expense	6,800				
Warranty expense	0				
Totals	$226,026	$226,026			

The following information in *a* through *h* applies to the company at the end of the current year.

a. The bank reconciliation as of December 31, 2013, includes the following facts.

Cash balance per bank	$15,100
Cash balance per books	17,000
Outstanding checks	1,800
Deposit in transit	2,450
Interest earned (on bank account)	52
Bank service charges (miscellaneous expense)	15

Reported on the bank statement is a canceled check that the company failed to record. (Information from the bank reconciliation allows you to determine the amount of this check, which is a payment on an account payable.)

b. An examination of customers' accounts shows that accounts totaling $679 should be written off as uncollectible. Using an aging of receivables, the company determines that the ending balance of the Allowance for Doubtful Accounts should be $700.

c. A truck is purchased and placed in service on January 1, 2013. Its cost is being depreciated with the straight-line method using the following facts and estimates.

Original cost	$32,000
Expected salvage value	8,000
Useful life (years)	4

d. Two items of equipment (a sprayer and an injector) were purchased and put into service in early January 2011. They are being depreciated with the straight-line method using these facts and estimates.

	Sprayer	Injector
Original cost	$27,000	$18,000
Expected salvage value	3,000	2,500
Useful life (years)	8	5

e. On August 1, 2013, the company is paid $3,840 cash in advance to provide monthly service for an apartment complex for one year. The company began providing the services in August. When the cash was received, the full amount was credited to the Extermination Services Revenue account.

f. The company offers a warranty for the services it sells. The expected cost of providing warranty service is 2.5% of the extermination services revenue of $57,760 for 2013. No warranty expense has been recorded for 2013. All costs of servicing warranties in 2013 were properly debited to the Estimated Warranty Liability account.

g. The $15,000 long-term note is an 8%, five-year, interest-bearing note with interest payable annually on December 31. The note was signed with First National Bank on December 31, 2013.

h. The ending inventory of merchandise is counted and determined to have a cost of $11,700. Bug-Off uses a perpetual inventory system.

Required

1. Use the preceding information to determine amounts for the following items.

a. Correct (reconciled) ending balance of Cash, and the amount of the omitted check.

b. Adjustment needed to obtain the correct ending balance of the Allowance for Doubtful Accounts.

c. Depreciation expense for the truck used during year 2013.

d. Depreciation expense for the two items of equipment used during year 2013.

e. The adjusted 2013 ending balances of the Extermination Services Revenue and Unearned Services Revenue accounts.

f. The adjusted 2013 ending balances of the accounts for Warranty Expense and Estimated Warranty Liability.

g. The adjusted 2013 ending balances of the accounts for Interest Expense and Interest Payable. (Round amounts to nearest whole dollar.)

Check   (1*a*) Cash bal. $15,750
(1*b*) $551 credit

(1*f*) Estim. warranty liability, $2,844 Cr.

(2) Adjusted trial balance totals, $238,207

2. Use the results of part 1 to complete the six-column table by first entering the appropriate adjustments for items *a* through *g* and then completing the adjusted trial balance columns. (*Hint:* Item *b* requires two adjustments.)

3. Prepare journal entries to record the adjustments entered on the six-column table. Assume Bug-Off's adjusted balance for Merchandise Inventory matches the year-end physical count.

(4) Net income, $9,274; Total assets, $82,771

4. Prepare a single-step income statement, a statement of retained earnings (cash dividends during 2013 were $10,000), and a classified balance sheet.

GL GENERAL LEDGER PROBLEM

Available in Connect Only

connect
|ACCOUNTING

The following General Ledger assignment highlights the impact, or lack thereof, for transactions related to short-term liabilities involving accounts and notes payable.

GL 9-1 (This assignment is adapted from Problem 9-1.) Prepare the journal entries related to the accounts and notes payable; the schedule of accounts payable and the schedule of notes payable are automatically completed from the journal entries using the **General Ledger** tool. Next, compute both the amount and timing of interest expense for each note. Finally, prepare the subsequent period journal entry(ies) related to the accrual of interest.

Beyond the Numbers

REPORTING IN ACTION

A1 P4

APPLE

BTN 9-1   Refer to the financial statements of Apple in Appendix A to answer the following.

1. Compute times interest earned for the fiscal years ended 2012, 2011, and 2010. Apple reports that it "had no debt outstanding and accordingly did not incur any related interest expense;" however, for purposes of learning from this assignment, assume that Apple had interest expense of $1,000 million for each year. Comment on Apple's ability to cover its interest expense for this period. Assume an industry average of 10 for times interest earned.

2. Apple's current liabilities include "Deferred revenue"; assume that this account reflects "Loyalty reward liabilities." Is this a known or an estimated liability? Explain how this liability is created.

3. Identify its total of accrued expenses and search its footnotes to list the six accounts that make up accrued expenses.

Fast Forward

4. Access Apple's financial statements for fiscal years ending after September 29, 2012, at its Website (Apple.com) or the SEC's EDGAR database (www.sec.gov). Compute its times interest earned for years ending after September 29, 2012, and compare your results to those in part 1. If no interest expense is reported, assume $1,000 million of interest expense in each year.

COMPARATIVE ANALYSIS

A1

APPLE GOOGLE

BTN 9-2   Key figures for Apple and Google follow.

($ millions)	Apple			Google		
	Current Year	One Year Prior	Two Years Prior	Current Year	One Year Prior	Two Years Prior
Net income	$41,733	$25,922	$14,013	$10,737	$9,737	$8,505
Income taxes	14,030	8,283	4,527	2,598	2,589	2,291
Interest expense*	1,000	1,000	1,000	84	58	5

*Apple did not report interest expense for these periods. Amounts included in this table are assumed for purposes of this analysis.

Required

1. Compute times interest earned for the three years' data shown for each company.

2. Comment on which company appears stronger in its ability to pay interest obligations if income should decline. Assume an industry average of 10.

BTN 9-3 Cameron Bly is a sales manager for an automobile dealership. He earns a bonus each year based on revenue from the number of autos sold in the year less related warranty expenses. Actual warranty expenses have varied over the prior 10 years from a low of 3% of an automobile's selling price to a high of 10%. In the past, Bly has tended to estimate warranty expenses on the high end to be conservative. He must work with the dealership's accountant at year-end to arrive at the warranty expense accrual for cars sold each year.

1. Does the warranty accrual decision create any ethical dilemma for Bly?

2. Since warranty expenses vary, what percent do you think Bly should choose for the current year? Justify your response.

ETHICS CHALLENGE

P4

BTN 9-4 Dusty Johnson is the accounting and finance manager for a manufacturer. At year-end, he must determine how to account for the company's contingencies. His manager, Tom Pretti, objects to Johnson's proposal to recognize an expense and a liability for warranty service on units of a new product introduced in the fourth quarter. Pretti comments, "There's no way we can estimate this warranty cost. We don't owe anyone anything until a product fails and it is returned. Let's report an expense if and when we do any warranty work."

COMMUNICATING IN PRACTICE

C3

Required

Prepare a one-page memorandum for Johnson to send to Pretti defending his proposal.

BTN 9-5 Access the February 24, 2012, filing of the December 31, 2011, annual 10-K report of McDonald's Corporation (Ticker: MCD), which is available from www.sec.gov.

TAKING IT TO THE NET

C1   A1

Required

1. Identify the current liabilities on McDonald's balance sheet as of December 31, 2011.

2. What portion (in percent) of McDonald's long-term debt matures within the next 12 months?

3. Use the consolidated statement of income for the year ended December 31, 2011, to compute McDonald's times interest earned ratio. Comment on the result. Assume an industry average of 15.0.

BTN 9-6 Assume that your team is in business and you must borrow $6,000 cash for short-term needs. You have been shopping banks for a loan, and you have the following two options.

A. Sign a $6,000, 90-day, 10% interest-bearing note dated June 1.

B. Sign a $6,000, 120-day, 8% interest-bearing note dated June 1.

TEAMWORK IN ACTION

C2 P1

Required

1. Discuss these two options and determine the best choice. Ensure that all teammates concur with the decision and understand the rationale.

2. Each member of the team is to prepare *one* of the following journal entries.

   a. Option A—at date of issuance.

   b. Option B—at date of issuance.

   c. Option A—at maturity date.

   d. Option B—at maturity date.

3. In rotation, each member is to explain the entry he or she prepared in part 2 to the team. Ensure that all team members concur with and understand the entries.

4. Assume that the funds are borrowed on December 1 (instead of June 1) and your business operates on a calendar-year reporting period. Each member of the team is to prepare *one* of the following entries.

   a. Option A—the year-end adjustment.

   b. Option B—the year-end adjustment.

   c. Option A—at maturity date.

   d. Option B—at maturity date.

5. In rotation, each member is to explain the entry he or she prepared in part 4 to the team. Ensure that all team members concur with and understand the entries.

ENTREPRENEURIAL DECISION

A1

BTN 9-7   Review the chapter's opening feature about Annie Withey and her start-up company, Annie's, Inc. Assume that she is considering expanding her business to open a headquarters in Europe. Assume her current income statement is as follows.

ANNIE'S, INC. Income Statement For Year Ended December 31, 2013	
Sales	$10,000,000
Operating expenses (55% of sales) .	5,500,000
Net income	$ 4,500,000

Also assume that Annie's, Inc. currently has no interest-bearing debt. If it expands to open a European location, it will require a $3,000,000 loan. Annie's, Inc. has found a bank that will loan it the money by taking on a 7% note payable. The company believes that, at least for the first few years, sales at its European location will be $2,500,000, and that all expenses will follow the same patterns as its current locations.

Required

1. Prepare an income statement (showing three separate columns for current operations, European, and total) for the company assuming that it borrows the funds and expands to Europe. Annual revenues for current operations are expected to remain at $10,000,000.
2. Compute the company's times interest earned under the expansion assumptions in part 1.
3. Assume sales at its European location are $4,000,000. Prepare an income statement (with columns for current operations, European, and total) for the company and compute times interest earned.
4. Assume sales at its European location are $1,000,000. Prepare an income statement (with columns for current operations, European, and total) for the company and compute times interest earned.
5. Comment on your results from parts 1 through 4.

HITTING THE ROAD

P2

BTN 9-8   Check your phone book or the Social Security Administration Website (www.ssa.gov) to locate the Social Security office near you. Visit the office to request a personal earnings and estimate form. Fill out the form and mail according to the instructions. You will receive a statement from the Social Security Administration regarding your earnings history and future Social Security benefits you can receive. (Formerly the request could be made online. The online service has been discontinued and is now under review by the Social Security Administration due to security concerns.) It is good to request an earnings and benefit statement every 5 to 10 years to make sure you have received credit for all wages earned and for which you and your employer have paid taxes into the system.

GLOBAL DECISION

A1

Samsung
APPLE
GOOGLE

BTN 9-9   Samsung, Apple, and Google are all competitors in the global marketplace. Comparative figures for Samsung (www.Samsung.com), along with selected figures from Apple and Google, follow.

Key Figures	Samsung (₩ millions)		Apple		Google	
	Current Year	Prior Year	Current Year	Prior Year	Current Year	Prior Year
Net income	₩23,845,285	₩13,759,043	—	—	—	—
Income taxes	6,069,732	3,432,875	—	—	—	—
Interest expense	7,934,450	7,893,421	—	—	—	—
Times interest earned	?	?	56.76	35.21	159.75	213.52

Required

1. Compute the times interest earned ratio for the most recent two years for Samsung using the data shown.
2. Which company of the three presented provides the best coverage of interest expense? Explain.

ANSWERS TO MULTIPLE CHOICE QUIZ

1. b; $6,000 × 0.05 × 30/360 = $25

2. e; $50,000 × (.062 + .0145) = $3,825

3. b; $7,000 × (.006 + .054) = $420

4. c; 10,000 television sets × .01 × $250 = $25,000

5. a; 150 employees × $175 per day × 1 vacation day earned = $26,250

10 Reporting and Analyzing Long-Term Liabilities

BOND BASICS	BOND ISSUANCES	BOND RETIREMENT	LONG-TERM NOTES
A1 Fundamentals of: Bond financing Bond trading Bond issuance procedures	**P1** Issuance at par **P2** Issuance at a discount **P3** Issuance at a premium Bond pricing	**P4** Accounting for bond retirement: At maturity Before maturity By conversion	**C1** Types of notes **P5** Recording notes **ANALYSIS OF DEBT** **A2** Debt features **A3** Debt-to-equity

Learning Objectives

A1 Compare bond financing with stock financing. (p. 436)

P1 Prepare entries to record bond issuance and interest expense. (p. 438)

P2 Compute and record amortization of bond discount using straight-line method. (p. 439)

P3 Compute and record amortization of bond premium using straight-line method. (p. 442)

P4 Record the retirement of bonds. (p. 446)

C1 Explain the types and payment patterns of notes. (p. 447)

P5 Prepare entries to account for notes. (p. 447)

A2 Assess debt features and their implications. (p. 451)

A3 Compute the debt-to-equity ratio and explain its use. (p. 451)

C2 *Appendix 10A*—Explain and compute the present value of an amount(s) to be paid at a future date(s). (p. 455)

P6 *Appendix 10B*—Compute and record amortization of bond discount using effective interest method. (p. 457)

P7 *Appendix 10B*—Compute and record amortization of bond premium using effective interest method. (p. 458)

C3 *Appendix 10C*—Describe interest accrual when bond payment periods differ from accounting periods. (p. 458)

C4 *Appendix 10D*—Describe accounting for leases and pensions. (p. 460)

Accounting With Friends

"The biggest opportunities are ahead of us"

——MARK PINCUS

SEATTLE—"It's important to know what your goal is," asserts Mark Pincus, "because if you don't know what your goal is, you will definitely never achieve it." His goal was to create **Zynga (Zynga.com),** a social gaming company with hit titles such as *FarmVille, CityVille, Words with Friends, Draw Something,* and *Café World.* "I knew I wanted to be an entrepreneur," says Mark. "I knew I wanted to create these breakthrough products."

But financing his business proved challenging. "I'm very focused on delivering a positive return on investment for the user," explains Mark. "I'm hoping that we don't just give you entertainment, but we actually enhance the relationships in your life." To achieve this, Mark set out to finance Zynga. According to **Capital IQ,** Zynga received $10 million in financing in 2008 from three venture capital firms. Zynga then sold stock in three more financing rounds, resulting in Mark owning less than 25% of Zynga (although he did maintain voting control).

Zynga
(NASDAQ: ZNGA)

3,000 employees
$1.3 bil. revenues

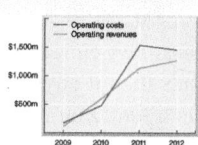

Alternatively, Mark could have pursued debt financing through the use of bonds and notes. This would have had the benefit of greater owner investment in a growing company and, potentially, a greater owner commitment in working toward its future success. In its recent annual report, Zynga reports $1.8 billion in stock financing compared to $0.8 billion in debt financing. Explains Mark, "A lot of companies get to a point where they no longer have a really interested party" if ownership is spread out.

Zynga's financing preferences, however, might be changing. In the past year, Zynga took out a $100 million loan, which is collateralized by its buildings. In addition, the

year before, it entered into a revolving credit agreement with lenders to borrow up to $1 billion in revolving loans. Mark knows that effective management of these liabilities, especially long-term financing from sources such as bonds and notes, is crucial. Namely, Zynga must produce sufficient income to pay for interest and principal. Its recent two income statements reveal operating losses and, to meet these obligations, operating results must turn positive for long-run success.

Still, the larger message of Zynga according to Mark is: "We want to change the world, make history." To help, former head of Microsoft's Xbox and gaming division, Dan Mattrick, agreed to be Zynga's new CEO. "It's still a work in progress," explains Mark. "We are still inventing Zynga."

Sources: *Zynga Website,* January 2014; *Forbes,* July 2013; *The Motley Fool,* June 2013; *GeekWire,* April 2011; *USA Today,* April 2012

BASICS OF BONDS

This section explains the basics of bonds and a company's motivation for issuing them.

Bond Financing

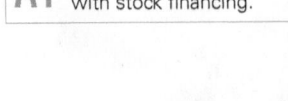

A1   Compare bond financing with stock financing.

Projects that demand large amounts of money often are funded from bond issuances. (Both for-profit and nonprofit companies, as well as governmental units, such as nations, states, cities, and school districts, issue bonds.) A **bond** is its issuer's written promise to pay an amount identified as the par value of the bond with interest. The **par value of a bond,** also called the *face amount* or *face value*, is paid at a specified future date known as the bond's *maturity date*. Most bonds also require the issuer to make semiannual interest payments. The amount of interest paid each period is determined by multiplying the par value of the bond by the bond's contract rate of interest for that same period. This section explains both advantages and disadvantages of bond financing.

Advantages of Bonds   There are three main advantages of bond financing:

1. *Bonds do not affect owner control.* Equity financing reflects ownership in a company, whereas bond financing does not. A person who contributes $1,000 of a company's $10,000 equity financing typically controls one-tenth of all owner decisions. A person who owns a $1,000, 11%, 20-year bond has no ownership right. This person, or bond-holder, is to receive from the bond issuer 11% interest, or $110, each year the bond is outstanding and $1,000 when it matures in 20 years.

2. *Interest on bonds is tax deductible.* Bond interest payments are tax deductible for the issuer, but equity payments (distributions) to owners are not. To illustrate, assume that a corporation with no bond financing earns $15,000 in income *before* paying taxes at a 40% tax rate, which amounts to $6,000 ($15,000 × 40%) in taxes. If a portion of its financing is in bonds, however, the resulting bond interest is deducted in computing taxable income. That is, if bond interest expense is $10,000, the taxes owed would be $2,000 ([$15,000 − $10,000] × 40%), which is less than the $6,000 owed with no bond financing.

3. *Bonds can increase return on equity.* A company that earns a higher return with borrowed funds than it pays in interest on those funds increases its return on equity. This process is called *financial leverage* or *trading on the equity*.

Point: Financial leverage reflects issuance of bonds, notes, or preferred stock.

To illustrate the third point, consider Magnum Co., which has $1 million in equity and is planning a $500,000 expansion to meet increasing demand for its product. Magnum predicts the $500,000 expansion will yield $125,000 in additional income before paying any interest. It currently earns $100,000 per year and has no interest expense. Magnum is considering three plans. Plan A is to not expand. Plan B is to expand and raise $500,000 from equity financing. Plan C is to expand and issue $500,000 of bonds that pay 10% annual interest ($50,000). Exhibit 10.1 shows how these three plans affect Magnum's net income, equity, and return on equity (net income/equity). The owner(s) will earn a higher return on equity if expansion occurs. Moreover, the preferred expansion plan is to issue bonds. Projected net income under Plan C ($175,000) is smaller than under Plan B ($225,000), but the return on equity is larger because of less equity investment. Plan C has another advantage if income is taxable. This illustration reflects a general rule: *Return on equity increases when the expected rate of return from the new assets is higher than the rate of interest expense on the debt financing.*

Example: Compute return on equity for all three plans if Magnum currently earns $150,000 instead of $100,000. *Answer ($ 000s):*
Plan A = 15%   ($150/$1,000)
Plan B = 18.3%   ($275/$1,500)
Plan C = 22.5%   ($225/$1,000)

EXHIBIT 10.1

Financing with Bonds versus Equity

	Plan A: Do Not Expand	Plan B: Equity Financing	Plan C: Bond Financing
Income before interest expense	$ 100,000	$ 225,000	$ 225,000
Interest expense	—	—	(50,000)
Net income	**$ 100,000**	**$ 225,000**	**$ 175,000**
Equity	$1,000,000	$1,500,000	$1,000,000
Return on equity	10.0%	15.0%	17.5%

Disadvantages of Bonds   The two main disadvantages of bond financing are these:

1. *Bonds can decrease return on equity.* When a company earns a lower return with the borrowed funds than it pays in interest, it decreases its return on equity. This downside risk of financial leverage is more likely to arise when a company has periods of low income or net losses.

2. *Bonds require payment of both periodic interest and the par value at maturity.* Bond payments can be especially burdensome when income and cash flow are low. Equity financing, in contrast, does not require any payments because cash withdrawals (dividends) are paid at the discretion of the owner (or board).

A company must weigh the risks and returns of the disadvantages and advantages of bond financing when deciding whether to issue bonds to finance operations.

Point: Debt financing is desirable when interest is tax deductible, when owner control is preferred, and when return on equity exceeds the debt's interest rate.

Bond Trading

Bonds are securities that can be readily bought and sold. A large number of bonds trade on both the New York Exchange and the American Exchange. A bond *issue* consists of a number of bonds, usually in denominations of $1,000 or $5,000, and is sold to many different lenders. After bonds are issued, they often are bought and sold by investors, meaning that any particular bond probably has a number of owners before it matures. Since bonds are exchanged (bought and sold) in the market, they have a market value (price). For convenience, bond market values are expressed as a percent of their par (face) value. For example, a company's bonds might be trading at 103½, meaning they can be bought or sold for 103.5% of their par value. Bonds can also trade below par value. For instance, if a company's bonds are trading at 95, they can be bought or sold at 95% of their par value.

Point: The phrase: *debt is cheaper than equity,* refers in part to interest expense on bonds being tax deductible whereas dividends on stock are not.

Decision Insight

Quotes   The IBM bond quote here is interpreted (left to right) as **Bonds,** issuer name; **Rate,** contract interest rate (5.7%); **Mat,** matures in year 2017 when principal is paid; **Yld,** yield rate (4.7%) of bond at current price; **Vol,** daily dollar worth ($130,000) of trades (in 1,000s); **Close,** closing price (121.18) for the day as percentage of par value; **Chg,** change (+0.24%) in closing price from prior day's close. ■

Bonds	Rate	Mat	Yld	Vol	Close	Chg
IBM	5.7	17	4.7	130	121.18	+0.24%

Bond-Issuing Procedures

State and federal laws govern bond issuances. Bond issuers also want to ensure that they do not violate any of their existing contractual agreements when issuing bonds. Authorization of bond issuances includes the number of bonds authorized, their par value, and the contract interest rate. The legal document identifying the rights and obligations of both the bondholders and the issuer is called the **bond indenture,** which is the legal contract between the issuer and the bondholders (and specifies how often interest is paid). A bondholder may also receive a bond certificate as evidence of the company's debt. A **bond certificate,** such as that shown in Exhibit 10.2, includes specifics such as the issuer's name, the par value, the contract interest rate, and the maturity date. Many companies reduce costs by not issuing paper certificates to bondholders.[1]

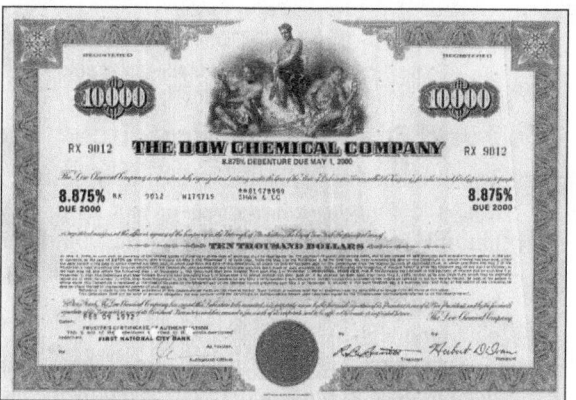

EXHIBIT 10.2

Bond Certificate

Point: *Indenture* refers to a bond's legal contract; *debenture* refers to an unsecured bond.

---

[1] The issuing company normally sells its bonds to an investment firm called an *underwriter,* which resells them to the public. An issuing company can also sell bonds directly to investors. When an underwriter sells bonds to a large number of investors, a *trustee* represents and protects the bondholders' interests. The trustee monitors the issuer to ensure that it complies with the obligations in the bond indenture. Most trustees are large banks or trust companies. The trustee writes and accepts the terms of a bond indenture before it is issued. When bonds are offered to the public, called *floating an issue,* they must be registered with the Securities and Exchange Commission (SEC). SEC registration requires the issuer to file certain financial information. Most company bonds are issued in par value units of $1,000 or $5,000. *A baby bond* has a par value of less than $1,000, such as $100.

Point: The *spread* between the dealer's cost and what buyers pay can be huge. Dealers earn more than $25 billion in annual spread revenue.

Global: In the United Kingdom, government bonds are called *gilts—* short for gilt-edged investments.

BOND ISSUANCES

This section explains accounting for bond issuances at par, below par (discount), and above par (premium). It also describes how to amortize a discount or premium and record bonds issued between interest payment dates.

Issuing Bonds at Par

P1 Prepare entries to record bond issuance and interest expense.

To illustrate an issuance of bonds at par value, suppose a company receives authorization to issue $800,000 of 9%, 20-year bonds dated January 1, 2013, that mature on December 31, 2032, and pay interest semiannually on each June 30 and December 31. After accepting the bond indenture on behalf of the bondholders, the trustee can sell all or a portion of the bonds to an underwriter. If all bonds are sold at par value, the issuer records the sale as follows.

Assets = Liabilities + Equity
+800,000   +800,000

2013			
Jan. 1	Cash	800,000	
	Bonds Payable		800,000
	Sold bonds at par.		

This entry reflects increases in the issuer's cash *and* long-term liabilities.
The issuer records the first semiannual interest payment as follows.

Assets = Liabilities + Equity
−36,000   −36,000

2013			
June 30	Bond Interest Expense	36,000	
	Cash		36,000
	Paid semiannual interest (9% × $800,000 × ½ year).		

The issuer pays and records its semiannual interest obligation every six months until the bonds mature. When they mature, the issuer records its payment of principal as follows.

Assets = Liabilities + Equity
−800,000   −800,000

2032			
Dec. 31	Bonds Payable	800,000	
	Cash		800,000
	Paid bond principal at maturity.		

Bond Discount or Premium

The bond issuer pays the interest rate specified in the indenture, the **contract rate,** also referred to as the *coupon rate, stated rate,* or *nominal rate.* The annual interest paid is determined by multiplying the bond par value by the contract rate. The contract rate is usually stated on an annual basis, even if interest is paid semiannually. For example, if a company issues a $1,000, 8% bond paying interest semiannually, it pays annual interest of $80 (8% × $1,000) in two semiannual payments of $40 each.

The contract rate sets the amount of interest the issuer pays in *cash,* which is not necessarily the *bond interest expense* actually incurred by the issuer. Bond interest expense depends on the bond's market value at issuance, which is determined by market expectations of the risk of lending to the issuer. The bond's **market rate** of interest is the rate that borrowers are willing to pay and lenders are willing to accept for a particular bond and its risk level. As the risk level increases, the rate increases to compensate purchasers for the bonds' increased risk. Also, the market rate is generally higher when the time period until the bond matures is longer due to the risk of adverse events occurring over a longer time period.

Many bond issuers try to set a contract rate of interest equal to the market rate they expect as of the bond issuance date. When the contract rate and market rate are equal, a bond sells at par value, but when they are not equal, a bond does not sell at par value. Instead, it is sold at a *premium* above par value or at a *discount* below par value. Exhibit 10.3 shows the relation between the contract rate, market rate, and a bond's issue price.

QC1

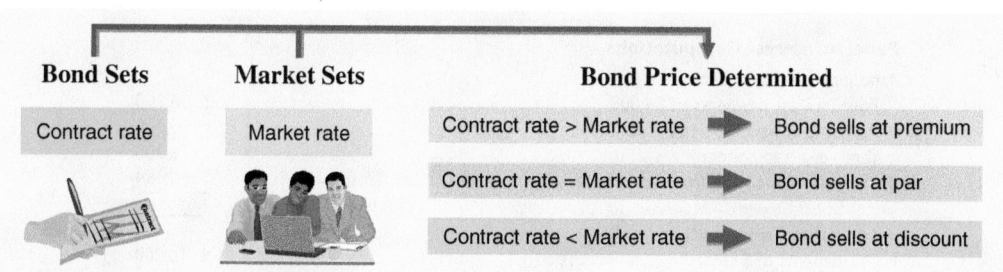

EXHIBIT 10.3

Relation between Bond Issue Price, Contract Rate, and Market Rate

Issuing Bonds at a Discount

A **discount on bonds payable** occurs when a company issues bonds with a contract rate less than the market rate. This means that the issue price is less than par value. To illustrate, assume that Fila announces an offer to issue bonds with a $100,000 par value, an 8% annual contract rate (paid semiannually), and a two-year life. Also assume that the market rate for Fila bonds is 10%. These bonds then will sell at a discount since the contract rate is less than the market rate. The exact issue price for these bonds is stated as 96.454 (implying 96.454% of par value, or $96,454); we show how to compute this issue price later in the chapter. These bonds obligate the issuer to pay two separate types of future cash flows:

1. Par value of $100,000 cash at the end of the bonds' two-year life.
2. Cash interest payments of $4,000 (4% × $100,000) at the end of each semiannual period during the bonds' two-year life.

P2 Compute and record amortization of bond discount using straight-line method.

Point: The difference between the contract rate and the market rate of interest on a new bond issue is usually a fraction of a percent. We use a difference of 2% to emphasize the effects.

The exact pattern of cash flows for the Fila bonds is shown in Exhibit 10.4.

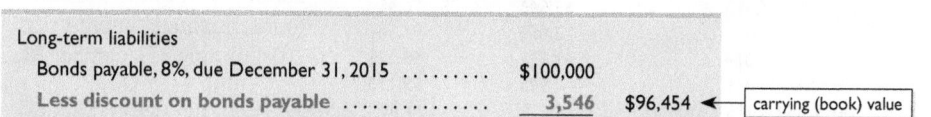

EXHIBIT 10.4

Cash Flows for Fila Bonds

When Fila accepts $96,454 cash for its bonds on the issue date of December 31, 2013, it records the sale as follows.

Dec. 31	Cash	96,454	
	Discount on Bonds Payable	3,546	
	Bonds Payable		100,000
	Sold bonds at a discount on their issue date.		

Assets = Liabilities + Equity
+96,454   +100,000
            −3,546

These bonds are reported in the long-term liability section of the issuer's December 31, 2013, balance sheet as shown in Exhibit 10.5. A discount is deducted from the par value of bonds to yield the **carrying (book) value of bonds.** Discount on Bonds Payable is a contra liability account.

Point: Book value at issuance always equals the issuer's cash borrowed.

Long-term liabilities		
Bonds payable, 8%, due December 31, 2015	$100,000	
Less discount on bonds payable	3,546	$96,454 ◄ carrying (book) value

EXHIBIT 10.5

Balance Sheet Presentation of Bond Discount

Amortizing a Bond Discount   Fila receives $96,454 for its bonds; in return it must pay bondholders $100,000 after two years (plus semiannual interest payments). The $3,546 discount is paid to bondholders at maturity and is part of the cost of using the $96,454 for two years. The upper portion of panel A in Exhibit 10.6 shows that total bond interest expense of $19,546 is the difference between the total amount repaid to bondholders ($116,000) and the amount borrowed from bondholders ($96,454). Alternatively, we can compute total bond interest expense as the sum of the four interest payments and the bond discount. This alternative computation is shown in the lower portion of panel A.

The total $19,546 bond interest expense must be allocated across the four semiannual periods in the bonds' life, and the bonds' carrying value must be updated at each balance sheet date.

Point: *Zero-coupon bonds* do not pay periodic interest (contract rate is zero). These bonds always sell at a discount because their 0% contract rate is always below the market rate.

EXHIBIT 10.6

Interest Computation and Entry for
Bonds Issued at a Discount

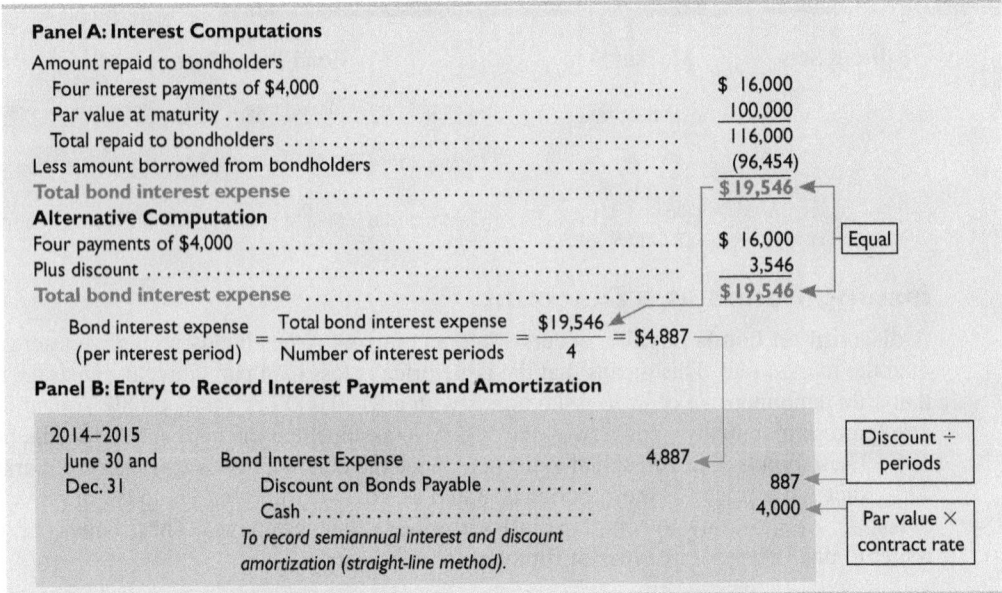

Panel A: Interest Computations

Amount repaid to bondholders
  Four interest payments of $4,000 .... $ 16,000
  Par value at maturity 100,000
  Total repaid to bondholders 116,000
Less amount borrowed from bondholders .... (96,454)
Total bond interest expense $19,546

Alternative Computation

Four payments of $4,000 .... $ 16,000
Plus discount 3,546
Total bond interest expense $19,546

Equal

$$\frac{\text{Bond interest expense}}{\text{(per interest period)}} = \frac{\text{Total bond interest expense}}{\text{Number of interest periods}} = \frac{\$19,546}{4} = \$4,887$$

Panel B: Entry to Record Interest Payment and Amortization

2014–2015		
June 30 and	Bond Interest Expense	4,887
Dec. 31	Discount on Bonds Payable	887
	Cash	4,000
	To record semiannual interest and discount amortization (straight-line method).	

Discount ÷ periods

Par value × contract rate

This is accomplished using the straight-line method (or the effective interest method in Appendix 10B). Both methods systematically reduce the bond discount to zero over the two-year life. This process is called *amortizing a bond discount*.

The following section on discount amortization uses the straight-line method. Appendix 10B uses the effective interest method. An instructor can choose to cover either one or both methods. If the straight-line method is skipped, then read Appendix 10B and return to the section (on page 442) titled "Issuing Bonds at a Premium."

Straight-Line Method   The **straight-line bond amortization** method allocates an equal portion of the total bond interest expense to each interest period. To apply the straight-line method to Fila's bonds, we divide the total bond interest expense of $19,546 by 4 (the number of semiannual periods in the bonds' life). This gives a bond interest expense of $4,887 per period, which is $4,886.5 rounded to the nearest dollar per period (all computations, including those for assignments, are rounded to the nearest whole dollar). Alternatively, we can find this number by first dividing the $3,546 discount by 4, which yields the $887 amount of discount to be amortized each interest period. When the $887 is added to the $4,000 cash payment, the bond interest expense for each period

EXHIBIT 10.7

Straight-Line Amortization
of Bond Discount

Semiannual Period-End	Unamortized Discount*	Carrying Value†
(0) 12/31/2013	$3,546	$ 96,454
(1) 6/30/2014	2,659	97,341
(2) 12/31/2014	1,772	98,228
(3) 6/30/2015	885	99,115
(4) 12/31/2015	0‡	100,000

The two columns always sum to
par value for a discount bond.

* Total bond discount (of $3,546) less accumulated periodic amortization
($887 per semiannual interest period).

† Bond par value (of $100,000) less unamortized discount.

‡ Adjusted for rounding.

is $4,887. Panel B of Exhibit 10.6 shows how the issuer records bond interest expense and updates the balance of the bond liability account at the end of *each* of the four semiannual interest periods (June 30, 2014, through December 31, 2015).

Exhibit 10.7 shows the pattern of decreases in the Discount on Bonds Payable account and the pattern of increases in the bonds' carrying value. The following points summarize the discount bonds' straight-line amortization:

1. At issuance, the $100,000 par value consists of the $96,454 cash received by the issuer plus the $3,546 discount.

2. During the bonds' life, the (unamortized) discount decreases each period by the $887 amortization ($3,546/4), and the carrying value (par value less unamortized discount) increases each period by $887.

3. At maturity, the unamortized discount equals zero, and the carrying value equals the $100,000 par value that the issuer pays the holder.

[Graph: Carrying value, with y-axis labeled $104,000, $100,000, $96,000 and x-axis labeled 12/31/2013, 6/30/2014, 12/31/2014, 6/30/2015, 12/31/2015]

We see that the issuer incurs a $4,887 bond interest expense each period but pays only $4,000 cash. The $887 unpaid portion of this expense is added to the bonds' carrying value. (The total $3,546 unamortized discount is "paid" when the bonds mature; $100,000 is paid at maturity but only $96,454 was received at issuance.)

■ **Decision** Insight ━━━━━━━━━━━━━━━━━━━━

Ratings Game   Many bond buyers rely on rating services to assess bond risk. The best known are Standard & Poor's, Moody's, and Fitch. These services focus on the issuer's financial statements and other factors in setting ratings. Standard & Poor's ratings, from best quality to default, are AAA, AA, A, BBB, BB, B, CCC, CC, C, and D. Ratings can include a plus (+) or minus (−) to show relative standing within a category. Bonds rated in the A and B range are referred to as *investment grade;* lower-rated bonds are considered much riskier. ■

A company issues 8%, two-year bonds on December 31, 2013, with a par value of $7,000 and semiannual interest payments. On the issue date, the annual market rate for these bonds is 10%, which implies a selling price of 96.46 or $6,752. (*a*) Prepare an amortization table such as Exhibit 10.7 for these bonds; use the straight-line method to amortize the discount. Then, prepare journal entries to record (*b*) the issuance of bonds on December 31, 2013; (*c*) the first through fourth interest payments on each June 30 and December 31; and (*d*) the maturity of the bond on December 31, 2015.

> **NEED-TO-KNOW 10.1**
>
> P1, P2

Solution

a.

Semiannual Period-End	Unamortized Discount	Carrying Value
(0) 12/31/2013	$248	$6,752
(1) 6/30/2014	186	6,814
(2) 12/31/2014	124	6,876
(3) 6/30/2015	62	6,938
(4) 12/31/2015	0	7,000

b.

2013			
Dec. 31	Cash	6,752	
	Discount on Bonds Payable	248	
	Bonds Payable		7,000
	Sold bonds at discount.		

c.

2014			
June 30	Bond Interest Expense	342	
	Discount on Bonds Payable*		62
	Cash**		280
	Paid semiannual interest and record amortization.		
2014			
Dec. 31	Bond Interest Expense	342	
	Discount on Bonds Payable*		62
	Cash**		280
	Paid semiannual interest and record amortization.		
2015			
June 30	Bond Interest Expense	342	
	Discount on Bonds Payable*		62
	Cash**		280
	Paid semiannual interest and record amortization.		
2015			
Dec. 31	Bond Interest Expense	342	
	Discount on Bonds Payable*		62
	Cash**		280
	Paid semiannual interest and record amortization.		

*$248/4   **$7,000 × 8% × ½

d.

2015			
Dec. 31	Bonds Payable	7,000	
	Cash		7,000
	Record maturity and payment of bonds.		

> Do More: QS 10-1, QS 10-3, QS 10-5, E 10-1, E 10-2, E 10-6, E 10-7

QC2

Issuing Bonds at a Premium

> **P3** Compute and record amortization of bond premium using straight-line method.

When the contract rate of bonds is higher than the market rate, the bonds sell at a price higher than par value. The amount by which the bond price exceeds par value is the **premium on bonds.** To illustrate, assume that Adidas issues bonds with a $100,000 par value, a 12% annual contract rate, semiannual interest payments, and a two-year life. Also assume that the market rate for Adidas bonds is 10% on the issue date. The Adidas bonds will sell at a premium because the contract rate is higher than the market rate. The issue price for these bonds is stated as 103.546 (implying 103.546% of par value, or $103,546); we show how to compute this issue price later in the chapter. These bonds obligate the issuer to pay out two separate future cash flows:

1. Par value of $100,000 cash at the end of the bonds' two-year life.
2. Cash interest payments of $6,000 (6% × $100,000) at the end of each semiannual period during the bonds' two-year life.

The exact pattern of cash flows for the Adidas bonds is shown in Exhibit 10.8.

EXHIBIT 10.8

Cash Flows for Adidas Bonds

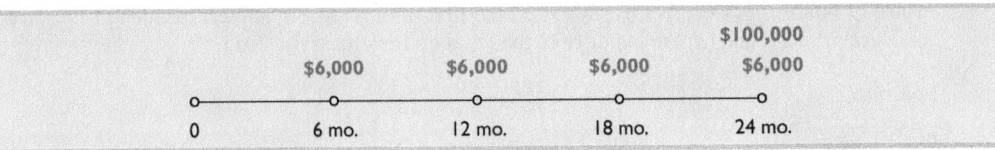

When Adidas accepts $103,546 cash for its bonds on the issue date of December 31, 2013, it records this transaction as follows.

Assets	= Liabilities + Equity
+103,546	+100,000
	+3,546

Dec. 31	Cash	103,546	
	Premium on Bonds Payable		3,546
	Bonds Payable		100,000
	Sold bonds at a premium on their issue date.		

These bonds are reported in the long-term liability section of the issuer's December 31, 2013, balance sheet as shown in Exhibit 10.9. A premium is added to par value to yield the carrying (book) value of bonds. Premium on Bonds Payable is an adjunct (also called *accretion*) liability account.

EXHIBIT 10.9

Balance Sheet Presentation of Bond Premium

Long-term liabilities		
Bonds payable, 12%, due December 31, 2015	$100,000	
Plus premium on bonds payable	3,546	$103,546

Amortizing a Bond Premium   Adidas receives $103,546 for its bonds; in return, it pays bondholders $100,000 after two years (plus semiannual interest payments). The $3,546 premium not repaid to issuer's bondholders at maturity goes to reduce the issuer's expense of using the $103,546 for two years. The upper portion of panel A of Exhibit 10.10 shows that total bond interest expense of $20,454 is the difference between the total amount repaid to bondholders ($124,000) and the amount borrowed from bondholders ($103,546). Alternatively, we can compute total bond interest expense as the sum of the four interest payments less the bond premium. The premium is subtracted because it will not be paid to bondholders when the bonds mature; see the lower portion of panel A. Total bond interest expense must be allocated over the four semiannual periods using the straight-line method (or the effective interest method in Appendix 10B).

Point: The phrase: *ability to service debt,* refers to making interest and principal payments on time.

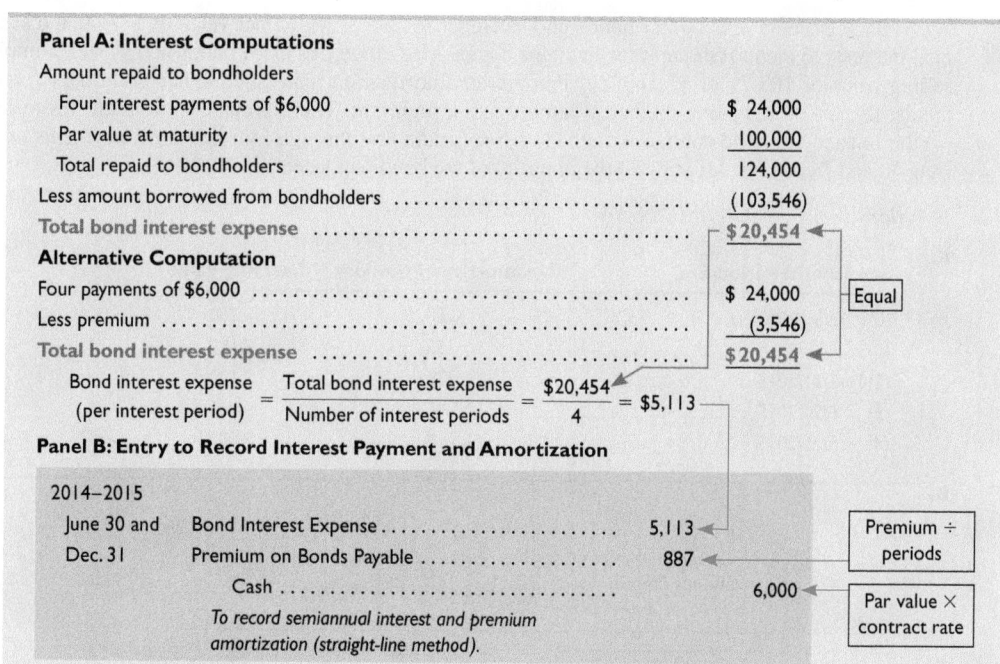

Panel A: Interest Computations

Amount repaid to bondholders

Four interest payments of $6,000	$ 24,000
Par value at maturity	100,000
Total repaid to bondholders	124,000
Less amount borrowed from bondholders	(103,546)
Total bond interest expense	$ 20,454

Alternative Computation

Four payments of $6,000	$ 24,000
Less premium	(3,546)
Total bond interest expense	$ 20,454

$$\frac{\text{Bond interest expense}}{\text{(per interest period)}} = \frac{\text{Total bond interest expense}}{\text{Number of interest periods}} = \frac{\$20,454}{4} = \$5,113$$

Panel B: Entry to Record Interest Payment and Amortization

2014–2015			
June 30 and	Bond Interest Expense	5,113	
Dec. 31	Premium on Bonds Payable	887	
	Cash		6,000
	To record semiannual interest and premium amortization (straight-line method).		

Premium ÷ periods

Par value × contract rate

EXHIBIT 10.10

Interest Computation and Entry for Bonds Issued at a Premium

The following section on premium amortization uses the straight-line method. Appendix 10B uses the effective interest method. An instructor can choose to cover either one or both methods. If the straight-line method is skipped, then read Appendix 10B and return to the section (next page) titled "Bond Pricing."

Straight-Line Method   The straight-line method allocates an equal portion of total bond interest expense to each of the bonds' semiannual interest periods. To apply this method to Adidas bonds, we divide the two years' total bond interest expense of $20,454 by 4 (the number of semiannual periods in the bonds' life). This gives a total bond interest expense of $5,113 per period, which is $5,113.5 rounded down so that the journal entry balances and for simplicity in presentation (alternatively, one could carry cents). Panel B of Exhibit 10.10 shows how the issuer records bond interest expense and updates the balance of the bond liability account for *each* semiannual period (June 30, 2014, through December 31, 2015).

Point: A premium decreases Bond Interest Expense; a discount increases it.

EXHIBIT 10.11

Straight-Line Amortization of Bond Premium

Semiannual Period-End	Unamortized Premium*	Carrying Value†
(0) 12/31/2013	$3,546	$103,546
(1) 6/30/2014	2,659	102,659
(2) 12/31/2014	1,772	101,772
(3) 6/30/2015	885	100,885
(4) 12/31/2015	0‡	100,000

* Total bond premium (of $3,546) less accumulated periodic amortization ($887 per semiannual interest period).

† Bond par value (of $100,000) plus unamortized premium.

‡ Adjusted for rounding.

Exhibit 10.11 shows the pattern of decreases in the unamortized Premium on Bonds Payable account and in the bonds' carrying value. The following points summarize straight-line amortization of the premium bonds:

1. At issuance, the $100,000 par value plus the $3,546 premium equals the $103,546 cash received by the issuer.

2. During the bonds' life, the (unamortized) premium decreases each period by the $887 amortization ($3,546/4), and the carrying value decreases each period by the same $887.

3. At maturity, the unamortized premium equals zero, and the carrying value equals the $100,000 par value that the issuer pays the holder.

During the bond life, carrying value is adjusted to par and the amortized premium to zero.

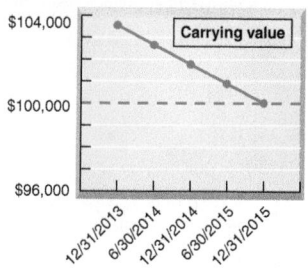

Point: There are nearly 5 million individual U.S. bond issues, ranging from huge treasuries to tiny municipalities. This compares to about 12,000 individual U.S. stocks that are traded.

NEED-TO-KNOW 10.2

P3

A company issues 8%, two-year bonds on December 31, 2013, with a par value of $7,000 and semiannual interest payments. On the issue date, the annual market rate for these bonds is 6%, which implies a selling price of 103.71 or $7,260. (*a*) Prepare an amortization table such as Exhibit 10.11 for these bonds; use the straight-line method to amortize the premium. Then, prepare journal entries to record (*b*) the issuance of bonds on December 31, 2013; (*c*) the first through fourth interest payments on each June 30 and December 31; and (*d*) the maturity of the bond on December 31, 2015.

Solution

a.

Semiannual Period-End	Unamortized Premium	Carrying Value
(0) 12/31/2013	$260	$7,260
(1) 6/30/2014	195	7,195
(2) 12/31/2014	130	7,130
(3) 6/30/2015	65	7,065
(4) 12/31/2015	0	7,000

b.

2013			
Dec. 31	Cash	7,260	
	Premium on Bonds Payable		260
	Bonds Payable		7,000
	Sold bonds at premium.		

c.

2014			
June 30	Bond Interest Expense............................	215	
	Premium on Bonds Payable*	65	
	Cash**		280
	Paid semiannual interest and record amortization.		
2014			
Dec. 31	Bond Interest Expense	215	
	Premium on Bonds Payable*	65	
	Cash**		280
	Paid semiannual interest and record amortization.		
2015			
June 30	Bond Interest Expense	215	
	Premium on Bonds Payable*.......................	65	
	Cash**		280
	Paid semiannual interest and record amortization.		
2015			
Dec. 31	Bond Interest Expense	215	
	Premium on Bonds Payable*	65	
	Cash**		280
	Paid semiannual interest and record amortization.		

*$260/4   **$7,000 × 8% × ½

d.

2015			
Dec. 31	Bonds Payable	7,000	
	Cash		7,000
	Record maturity and payment of bonds.		

Do More: E 10-4, E 10-8, P 10-3, P 10-4

The next section describes bond pricing. An instructor can choose to cover bond pricing or not. Assignments requiring the next section are Quick Study 10-4 and Exercises 10-9 and 10-10.

Bond Pricing

Prices for bonds traded on an organized exchange are often published in newspapers and through online services. This information normally includes the bond price (called *quote*), its contract rate, and its current market (called *yield*) rate. However, only a fraction of bonds are traded on organized exchanges. To compute the price of a bond, we apply present value concepts. This section explains how to use *present value concepts* to price the Fila discount bond and the Adidas premium bond described earlier.

Point: InvestingInBonds.com is a bond research and learning source.

Present Value of a Discount Bond The issue price of bonds is found by computing the present value of the bonds' cash payments, discounted at the bonds' market rate. When computing the present value of the Fila bonds, we work with *semiannual* compounding periods because this is the time between interest payments; the annual market rate of 10% is considered a semiannual rate of 5%. Also, the two-year bond life is viewed as four semiannual periods. The price computation is twofold: (1) Find the present value of the $100,000 par value paid at maturity and (2) find the present value of the series of four semiannual payments of $4,000 each; see Exhibit 10.4. These present values can be found by using *present value tables.* Appendix B at the end of this book shows present value tables and describes their use. Table B.1 at the end of Appendix B is used for the single $100,000 maturity payment, and Table B.3 in Appendix B is used for the $4,000 series of interest payments. Specifically, we go to Table B.1, row 4, and across to the 5% column to identify the present value factor of 0.8227 for the maturity payment. Next, we go to Table B.3, row 4, and across to the 5% column, where the present value factor is 3.5460 for the series of interest payments. We compute bond price by multiplying the cash flow payments by their corresponding present value factors and adding them together; see Exhibit 10.12.

Cash Flow	Table	Present Value Factor	Amount	Present Value
$100,000 par (maturity) value	B.1	0.8227	× $100,000 =	$ 82,270
$4,000 interest payments	B.3	3.5460	× 4,000 =	14,184
Price of bond				$96,454

EXHIBIT 10.12

Computing Issue Price for the Fila Discount Bonds

Calculator	
N = 4	PMT = 4,000
I/Yr = 5	FV = 100,000
	PV = 96,454

Present Value of a Premium Bond We find the issue price of the Adidas bonds by using the market rate to compute the present value of the bonds' future cash flows. When computing the present value of these bonds, we again work with *semiannual* compounding periods because this is the time between interest payments. The annual 10% market rate is applied as a semiannual rate of 5%, and the two-year bond life is viewed as four semiannual periods. The computation is twofold: (1) Find the present value of the $100,000 par value paid at maturity and (2) find the present value of the series of four payments of $6,000 each; see Exhibit 10.8. These present values can be found by using present value tables. First, go to Table B.1, row 4, and across to the 5% column where the present value factor is 0.8227 for the maturity payment. Second, go to Table B.3, row 4, and across to the 5% column, where the present value factor is 3.5460 for the series of interest payments. The bonds' price is computed by multiplying the cash flow payments by their corresponding present value factors and adding them together; see Exhibit 10.13.

Cash Flow	Table	Present Value Factor	Amount	Present Value
$100,000 par (maturity) value	B.1	0.8227	× $100,000 =	$ 82,270
$6,000 interest payments	B.3	3.5460	× 6,000 =	21,276
Price of bond				$103,546

EXHIBIT 10.13

Computing Issue Price for the Adidas Premium Bonds

Calculator	
N = 4	PMT = 6,000
I/Yr = 5	FV = 100,000
	PV = 103,546

Fraud

Unreported Liabilities Drove U.S. Financial Crisis? Many argue that unreported liabilities were a major cause of the financial crisis. They assert that "off-balance-sheet accounting" encouraged bad loans, securitizations, and derivatives that drove much of the crisis. It is argued that balance sheets failed to report many of these liabilities. For example, because bank liabilities used to finance assets were not transparent, the markets failed to penalize banks that used derivatives and variable interest entities (VIEs) to take excessive risks. Arguably, such accounting is fraudulent.

QC3

BOND RETIREMENT

P4 Record the retirement of bonds.

This section describes the retirement of bonds (1) at maturity, (2) before maturity, and (3) by conversion to stock.

Bond Retirement at Maturity

The carrying value of bonds at maturity always equals par value. For example, both Exhibits 10.7 (a discount) and 10.11 (a premium) show that the carrying value of bonds at the end of their lives equals par value ($100,000). The retirement of these bonds at maturity, assuming interest is already paid and entered, is recorded as follows:

Assets = Liabilities + Equity
−100,000   −100,000

2015 Dec. 31	Bonds Payable	100,000	
	Cash		100,000
	To record retirement of bonds at maturity.		

Bond Retirement before Maturity

Point: Bond retirement is also referred to as *bond redemption.*

Point: Gains and losses from retiring bonds were *previously* reported as extraordinary items. New standards require that they now be judged by the "unusual and infrequent" criteria for reporting purposes.

Issuers sometimes wish to retire some or all of their bonds prior to maturity. For instance, if interest rates decline greatly, an issuer may wish to replace high-interest-paying bonds with new low-interest bonds. Two common ways to retire bonds before maturity are to (1) exercise a call option or (2) purchase them on the open market. In the first instance, an issuer can reserve the right to retire bonds early by issuing callable bonds. The bond indenture can give the issuer an option to *call* the bonds before they mature by paying the par value plus a *call premium* to bondholders. In the second case, the issuer retires bonds by repurchasing them on the open market at their current price. Whether bonds are called or repurchased, the issuer is unlikely to pay a price that exactly equals their carrying value. When a difference exists between the bonds' carrying value and the amount paid, the issuer records a gain or loss equal to the difference.

To illustrate the accounting for retiring callable bonds, assume that a company issued callable bonds with a par value of $100,000. The call option requires the issuer to pay a call premium of $3,000 to bondholders in addition to the par value. Next, assume that after the June 30, 2013, interest payment, the bonds have a carrying value of $104,500. Then on July 1, 2013, the issuer calls these bonds and pays $103,000 to bondholders. The issuer recognizes a $1,500 gain from the difference between the bonds' carrying value of $104,500 and the retirement price of $103,000. The issuer records this bond retirement as follows.

Assets = Liabilities + Equity
−103,000   −100,000   +1,500
                −4,500

July 1	Bonds Payable	100,000	
	Premium on Bonds Payable	4,500	
	Gain on Bond Retirement		1,500
	Cash		103,000
	To record retirement of bonds before maturity.		

An issuer usually must call all bonds when it exercises a call option. However, to retire as many or as few bonds as it desires, an issuer can purchase them on the open market. If it retires less than the entire class of bonds, it recognizes a gain or loss for the difference between the carrying value of those bonds retired and the amount paid to acquire them.

Bond Retirement by Conversion

Holders of convertible bonds have the right to convert their bonds to stock. When conversion occurs, the bonds' carrying value is transferred to equity accounts and no gain or loss is recorded. (We further describe convertible bonds in the Decision Analysis section of this chapter.)

To illustrate, assume that on January 1 the $100,000 par value bonds of Converse, with a carrying value of $100,000, are converted to 15,000 shares of $2 par value common stock. The

Convertible Bond

entry to record this conversion follows (the market prices of the bonds and stock are *not* relevant to this entry; the material in Chapter 11 is helpful in understanding this transaction):

Jan. 1	Bonds Payable	100,000	
	Common Stock		30,000
	Paid-In Capital in Excess of Par Value		70,000
	To record retirement of bonds by conversion.		

Assets = Liabilities + Equity
−100,000   +30,000
+70,000

QC4

LONG-TERM NOTES PAYABLE

Like bonds, notes are issued to obtain assets such as cash. Unlike bonds, notes are typically transacted with a *single* lender such as a bank. An issuer initially records a note at its selling price—that is, the note's face value minus any discount or plus any premium. Over the note's life, the amount of interest expense allocated to each period is computed by multiplying the market rate (at issuance of the note) by the beginning-of-period note balance. The note's carrying (book) value at any time equals its face value minus any unamortized discount or plus any unamortized premium; carrying value is also computed as the present value of all remaining payments, discounted using the market rate at issuance.

C1 Explain the types and payment patterns of notes.

Installment Notes

An **installment note** is an obligation requiring a series of payments to the lender. Installment notes are common for franchises and other businesses when lenders and borrowers agree to spread payments over several periods. To illustrate, assume that Foghog borrows $60,000 from a bank to purchase equipment. It signs an 8% installment note requiring six annual payments of principal plus interest and it records the note's issuance at January 1, 2013, as follows.

Point: Banks sometimes reject loans when risk of default by borrowers is high. Then, bonds can serve as another way borrowers can finance operations or expansion.

Jan. 1	Cash	60,000	
	Notes Payable		60,000
	Borrowed $60,000 by signing an 8%, six-year installment note.		

Assets = Liabilities + Equity
+60,000   +60,000

Payments on an installment note normally include the accrued interest expense plus a portion of the amount borrowed (the *principal*). This section describes an installment note with equal payments.

The equal total payments pattern consists of changing amounts of both interest and principal. To illustrate, assume that Foghog borrows $60,000 by signing a $60,000 note that requires six *equal payments* of $12,979 at the end of each year. (The present value of an annuity of six annual payments of $12,979, discounted at 8%, equals $60,000; we show this computation in footnote 2 on the next page.) The $12,979 includes both interest and principal, the amounts of which change with each payment. Exhibit 10.14 shows the pattern of equal total payments and its two parts, interest and principal. Column A shows the note's beginning balance. Column B shows accrued interest for each year at 8% of the beginning note balance. Column C shows the impact on the note's principal, which equals the difference between the total payment in column D and the interest expense in column B. Column E shows the note's year-end balance.

Years
2013 2014 2015 2016 2017 2018
$12,979 ×6

Point: Most consumer notes are installment notes that require equal total payments.

Fraud

Missing Debt A study reports that 13% of employees in finance and accounting witnessed the falsifying or manipulating of accounting information in the past year (KPMG 2009). This includes nondisclosure of special concern with long-term liabilities. Another study reports that most people committing fraud (36%) work in the finance function of their firm (KPMG 2011). For example, Enron violated GAAP to keep debt off its balance sheet.

Although the six cash payments are equal, accrued interest decreases each year because the principal balance of the note declines. As the amount of interest decreases each year, the portion of each payment applied to principal increases. This pattern is graphed in the lower part of

P5 Prepare entries to account for notes.

EXHIBIT 10.14

Installment Note: Equal
Total Payments

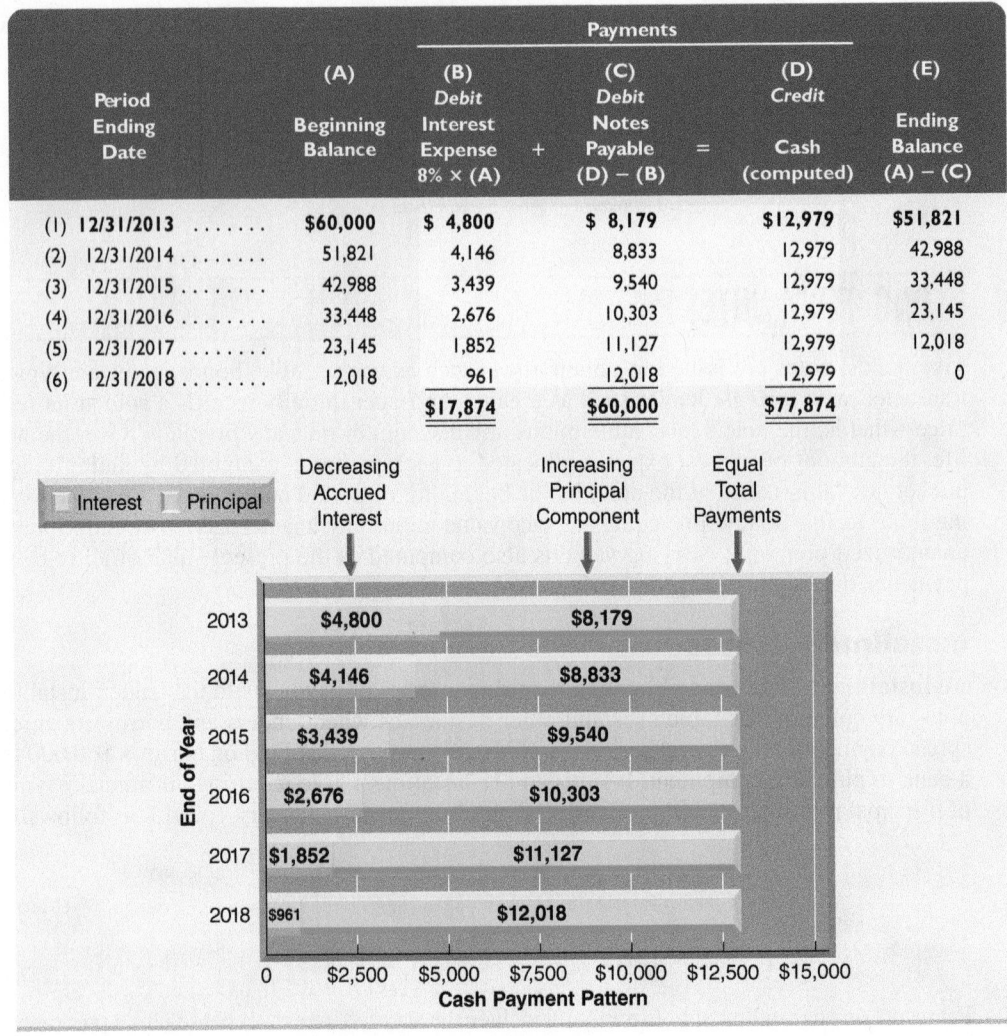

	Period Ending Date	(A) Beginning Balance	(B) Debit Interest Expense 8% × (A)	+	(C) Debit Notes Payable (D) − (B)	=	(D) Credit Cash (computed)	(E) Ending Balance (A) − (C)
(1)	12/31/2013	$60,000	$ 4,800		$ 8,179		$12,979	$51,821
(2)	12/31/2014	51,821	4,146		8,833		12,979	42,988
(3)	12/31/2015	42,988	3,439		9,540		12,979	33,448
(4)	12/31/2016	33,448	2,676		10,303		12,979	23,145
(5)	12/31/2017	23,145	1,852		11,127		12,979	12,018
(6)	12/31/2018	12,018	961		12,018		12,979	0
			$17,874		$60,000		$77,874	

Exhibit 10.14. Foghog uses the amounts in Exhibit 10.14 to record its first two payments (for years 2013 and 2014) as follows:

Assets = Liabilities + Equity
−12,979   −8,179   −4,800

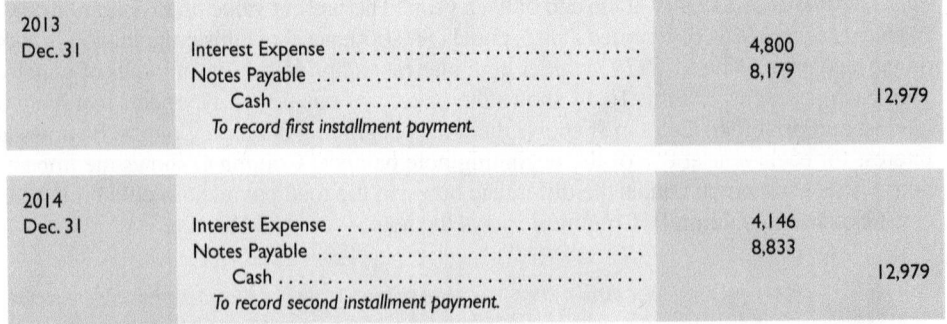

2013 Dec. 31	Interest Expense	4,800	
	Notes Payable	8,179	
	Cash		12,979
	To record first installment payment.		

Assets = Liabilities + Equity
−12,979   −8,833   −4,146

2014 Dec. 31	Interest Expense	4,146	
	Notes Payable	8,833	
	Cash		12,979
	To record second installment payment.		

Foghog records similar entries but with different amounts for each of the remaining four payments. After six years, the Notes Payable account balance is zero.[2]

---

[2] Table B.3 in Appendix B is used to compute the dollar amount of the six payments that equal the initial note balance of $60,000 at 8% interest. We go to Table B.3, row 6, and across to the 8% column, where the present value factor is 4.6229. The dollar amount is then computed by solving this relation:

Example: Suppose the $60,000 installment loan has an 8% interest rate with eight equal annual payments. What is the annual payment? *Answer* (using Table B.3): $60,000/5.7466 = $10,441

Table	Present Value Factor	Dollar Amount	Present Value
B.3	4.6229	× ?	= $60,000

The dollar amount is computed by dividing $60,000 by 4.6229, yielding $12,979.

■ **Decision Maker**

Entrepreneur   You are a furniture retailer planning a Super Bowl sale on a home theater seating that requires no payments for two years. At the end of two years, buyers must pay the full amount. The system's suggested retail price is $4,100, but you are willing to sell it today for $3,000 cash. What is your sale price if payment will not occur for two years and the market interest rate is 10%? ■   [Answer—p. 463]

Mortgage Notes and Bonds

A **mortgage** is a legal agreement that helps protect a lender if a borrower fails to make required payments on notes or bonds. A mortgage gives the lender a right to be paid from the cash proceeds of the sale of a borrower's assets identified in the mortgage. A legal document, called a *mortgage contract,* describes the mortgage terms.

Mortgage notes carry a mortgage contract pledging title to specific assets as security for the note. Mortgage notes are especially popular in the purchase of homes and the acquisition of plant assets. Less common *mortgage bonds* are backed by the issuer's assets. Accounting for mortgage notes and bonds is similar to that for unsecured notes and bonds, except that the mortgage agreement must be disclosed. For example, **TIBCO Software** reports that its "**mortgage note payable ... is collateralized by the commercial real property acquired [corporate headquarters]**."

Point: The Truth-in-Lending Act requires lenders to provide information about loan costs including finance charges and interest rate.

Global: Countries vary in the preference given to debtholders vs. stockholders when a company is in financial distress. Some countries such as Germany, France, and Japan give preference to stockholders over debtholders.

Fraud

Hidden Liabilities. Some companies arguably "hide" debt from their balance sheets by pursuing joint ventures, R&D partnerships, operating leases, and the like. While there are many sound economic reasons to pursue these activities, they also present the "less-principled" company with an opportunity to deceive readers of its balance sheet. Specifically, under certain conditions, companies can hide liabilities from such transactions when the economics suggest they should not. Notes to financial statements can often reveal this risk, but not always.

On January 1, 2013, a company borrows $1,000 cash by signing a four-year, 5% installment note. The note requires four equal total payments of accrued interest and principal on December 31 of each year from 2013 through 2016.

NEED-TO-KNOW 10.3

1. Compute the amount of each of the four equal total payments.

C1, P5

2. Prepare an amortization table for this installment note like the one in Exhibit 10.14.

3. Prepare journal entries to record the loan on January 1, 2013, and the four payments from December 31, 2013, through December 31, 2016.

Solution

1. Amount of each payment = Initial note balance/PV of Annuity (from Table B.3)

= $1,000/3.5460 = $282 (rounded)

2. Amortization table for loan

		Payments			
	(A)	**(B)** **Debit**	**(C)** **Debit**	**(D)**	**(E)**
Period Ending Date	**Beginning Balance [Prior (E)]**	**Interest Expense [5% × (A)] +**	**Notes Payable [(D) − (B)] =**	**Credit Cash [computed]**	**Ending Balance [(A) − (C)]**
2013................	$1,000	$ 50	$ 232	$ 282	$768
2014................	768	38	244	282	524
2015................	524	26	256	282	268
2016................	268	14*	268	282	0
		$128	$1,000	$1,128	

*Adjusted for rounding.

3.

2013 Jan. 1	Cash	1,000	
	Notes Payable		1,000
	Borrowed $1,000 by signing a 5% installment note.		
2013 Dec. 31	Interest Expense	50	
	Notes Payable	232	
	Cash		282
	To record first installment payment.		
2014 Dec. 31	Interest Expense	38	
	Notes Payable	244	
	Cash		282
	To record second installment payment.		
2015 Dec. 31	Interest Expense	26	
	Notes Payable	256	
	Cash		282
	To record third installment payment.		
2016 Dec. 31	Interest Expense	14	
	Notes Payable	268	
	Cash		282
	To record fourth installment payment.		

Do More: QS 10-9, E 10-14, E 10-15

QC5

GLOBAL VIEW

This section discusses similarities and differences between U.S. GAAP and IFRS in accounting and reporting for long-term liabilities such as bonds and notes.

Accounting for Bonds and Notes   The definitions and characteristics of bonds and notes are broadly similar for both U.S. GAAP and IFRS. Although slight differences exist, accounting for bonds and notes under U.S. GAAP and IFRS is similar. Specifically, the accounting for issuances (including recording discounts and premiums), market pricing, and retirement of both bonds and notes follows the procedures in this chapter. Nokia describes its accounting for bonds, which follows the amortized cost approach explained in this chapter (and in Appendix 10B), as follows: **Loans payable [bonds] are recognized initially at fair value, net of transaction costs incurred. In the subsequent periods, they are stated at amortized cost.**

NOKIA

Both U.S. GAAP and IFRS allow companies to account for bonds and notes using fair value (different from the amortized value described in this chapter). This method is referred to as the **fair value option.** This method is similar to that applied in measuring and accounting for debt and equity securities. *Fair value* is the amount a company would receive if it settled a liability (or sold an asset) in an orderly transaction as of the balance sheet date. Companies can use several sources of inputs to determine fair value, and those inputs fall into three classes (ranked in order of preference):

Level 1: Observable quoted market prices in active markets for identical items.
Level 2: Observable inputs other than those in Level 1 such as prices from inactive markets or from similar, but not identical, items.
Level 3: Unobservable inputs reflecting a company's assumptions about value.

The procedures for marking liabilities to fair value at each balance sheet date are in advanced courses.

Accounting for Leases and Pensions   Both U.S. GAAP and IFRS require companies to distinguish between operating leases and capital leases; the latter is referred to as *finance leases* under IFRS. The accounting and reporting for leases are broadly similar for both U.S. GAAP and IFRS. The main difference is the criteria for identifying a lease as a capital lease are more general under IFRS. However, the basic approach applies.

Point: Lease accounting is expected to change over the next year or so.

For pensions, both U.S. GAAP and IFRS require companies to record costs of retirement benefits as employees work and earn them. The basic methods are similar in accounting and reporting for pensions.

Debt Features and the Debt-to-Equity Ratio **Decision Analysis**

Collateral agreements can reduce the risk of loss for both bonds and notes. Unsecured bonds and notes are riskier because the issuer's obligation to pay interest and principal has the same priority as all other unsecured liabilities in the event of bankruptcy. If a company is unable to pay its debts in full, the unsecured creditors (including the holders of debentures) lose all or a portion of their balances. These types of legal agreements and other characteristics of long-term liabilities are crucial for effective business decisions. The first part of this section describes the different types of features sometimes included with bonds and notes. The second part explains and applies the debt-to-equity ratio.

Features of Bonds and Notes

This section describes common features of debt securities.

A2 Assess debt features and their implications.

Secured or Unsecured Secured bonds (and notes) have specific assets of the issuer pledged (or *mortgaged*) as collateral. This arrangement gives holders added protection against the issuer's default. If the issuer fails to pay interest or par value, the secured holders can demand that the collateral be sold and the proceeds used to pay the obligation. **Unsecured bonds** (and notes), also called *debentures,* are backed by the issuer's general credit standing. Unsecured debt is riskier than secured debt. *Subordinated debentures* are liabilities that are not repaid until the claims of the more senior, unsecured (and secured) liabilities are settled.

Secured Debt   **Unsecured Debt**

Term or Serial Term bonds (and notes) are scheduled for maturity on one specified date. **Serial bonds** (and notes) mature at more than one date (often in series) and thus are usually repaid over a number of periods. For instance, $100,000 of serial bonds might mature at the rate of $10,000 each year from 6 to 15 years after they are issued. Many bonds are **sinking fund bonds,** which to reduce the holder's risk require the issuer to create a *sinking fund* of assets set aside at specified amounts and dates to repay the bonds.

Point: More than a million municipal bonds, or "munis," exist, and many are tax exempt. Munis are issued by state, city, town, and county governments to pay for public projects including schools, libraries, roads, bridges, and stadiums.

Registered or Bearer Bonds issued in the names and addresses of their holders are **registered bonds.** The issuer makes bond payments by sending checks (or cash transfers) to registered holders. A registered holder must notify the issuer of any ownership change. Registered bonds offer the issuer the practical advantage of not having to actually issue bond certificates. Bonds payable to whoever holds them (the *bearer*) are called **bearer bonds** or *unregistered bonds*. Sales or exchanges might not be recorded, so the holder of a bearer bond is presumed to be its rightful owner. As a result, lost bearer bonds are difficult to replace. Many bearer bonds are also **coupon bonds.** This term reflects interest coupons that are attached to the bonds. When each coupon matures, the holder presents it to a bank or broker for collection. At maturity, the holder follows the same process and presents the bond certificate for collection. Issuers of coupon bonds cannot deduct the related interest expense for taxable income. This is to prevent abuse by taxpayers who own coupon bonds but fail to report interest income on their tax returns.

Convertible and/or Callable Convertible bonds (and notes) can be exchanged for a fixed number of shares of the issuing corporation's common stock. Convertible debt offers holders the potential to participate in future increases in stock price. Holders still receive periodic interest while the debt is held and the par value if they hold the debt to maturity. In most cases, the holders decide whether and when to convert debt to stock. **Callable bonds** (and notes) have an option exercisable by the issuer to retire them at a stated dollar amount before maturity.

Convertible Debt   **Callable Debt**

> ## Decision Insight
>
> **Collateral** Lenders prefer that more liquid assets serve as collateral for loans. These usually are current assets such as accounts receivable or inventory. The reason is if borrowers default and collateral must be seized, then lenders desire assets that are easily sold to recover losses. ◼

Debt-to-Equity Ratio

Beyond assessing different characteristics of debt as just described, we want to know the level of debt, especially in relation to total equity. Such knowledge helps us assess the risk of a company's financing structure. A company financed mainly with debt is more risky because liabilities must be repaid—usually

A3 Compute the debt-to-equity ratio and explain its use.

with periodic interest—whereas equity financing does not. A measure to assess the risk of a company's financing structure is the **debt-to-equity ratio** (see Exhibit 10.15).

EXHIBIT 10.15

Debt-to-Equity Ratio

$$\text{Debt-to-equity} = \frac{\text{Total liabilities}}{\text{Total equity}}$$

The debt-to-equity ratio varies across companies and industries. To apply the debt-to-equity ratio, let's look at this measure for Cedar Fair in Exhibit 10.16.

EXHIBIT 10.16

Cedar Fair's Debt-to-Equity Ratio

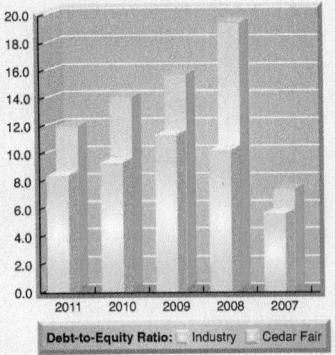

($ millions)	2011	2010	2009	2008	2007
Total liabilities	$1,915.837	$1,945.308	$2,017.577	$2,079.297	$2,133.576
Total equity	$ 158.720	$ 137.136	$ 127.862	$ 106.786	$ 285.092
Debt-to-equity.	12.1	14.2	15.8	19.5	7.5
Industry debt-to-equity	8.5	9.3	11.4	10.3	5.7

Cedar Fair's 2011 debt-to-equity ratio is 12.1, meaning that debtholders contributed $12.10 for each $1 contributed by equityholders. This implies a fairly risky financing structure for Cedar Fair. A similar concern is drawn from a comparison of Cedar Fair with its competitors, where the 2011 industry ratio is 8.5. Analysis across the years shows that Cedar Fair's financing structure has grown to a risky level in recent years. Given its sluggish revenues and increasing operating expenses in recent years (see its annual report), Cedar Fair is increasingly at risk of financial distress.

■ **Decision** Maker ━━━━━━━━━━━━━━━━━━━━━━━━━━━━━━━━

Bond Investor   You plan to purchase debenture bonds from one of two companies in the same industry that are similar in size and performance. The first company has $350,000 in total liabilities, and $1,750,000 in equity. The second company has $1,200,000 in total liabilities, and $1,000,000 in equity. Which company's debenture bonds are less risky based on the debt-to-equity ratio? ■ [Answer—p. 463]

COMPREHENSIVE...

NEED-TO-KNOW

Water Sports Company (WSC) patented and successfully test-marketed a new product. To expand its ability to produce and market the new product, WSC needs to raise $800,000 of financing. On January 1, 2013, the company obtained the money in two ways:

a. WSC signed a $400,000, 10% installment note to be repaid with five equal annual installments to be made on December 31 of 2013 through 2017.

b. WSC issued five-year bonds with a par value of $400,000. The bonds have a 12% annual contract rate and pay interest on June 30 and December 31. The bonds' annual market rate is 10% as of January 1, 2013.

Required

1. For the installment note, (*a*) compute the size of each annual payment, (*b*) prepare an amortization table such as Exhibit 10.14, and (*c*) prepare the journal entry for the first payment.

2. For the bonds, (*a*) compute their issue price; (*b*) prepare the January 1, 2013, journal entry to record their issuance; (*c*) prepare an amortization table using the straight-line method; (*d*) prepare the June 30, 2013, journal entry to record the first interest payment; and (*e*) prepare a journal entry to record retiring the bonds at a $416,000 call price on January 1, 2015.

3.[B] Redo parts 2(*c*), 2(*d*), and 2(*e*) assuming the bonds are amortized using the effective interest method.

PLANNING THE SOLUTION

● For the installment note, divide the borrowed amount by the annuity factor (from Table B.3) using the 10% rate and five payments to compute the amount of each payment. Prepare a table similar to Exhibit 10.14 and use the numbers in the table's first line for the journal entry.

● Compute the bonds' issue price by using the market rate to find the present value of their cash flows (use tables found in Appendix B). Then use this result to record the bonds' issuance. Next, prepare an amortization table like Exhibit 10.11 (and Exhibit 10B.2) and use it to get the numbers needed for the journal entry. Also use the table to find the carrying value as of the date of the bonds' retirement that you need for the journal entry.

SOLUTION TO COMPREHENSIVE NEED-TO-KNOW

Part 1: Installment Note

a. Annual payment = Note balance/Annuity factor = $400,000/3.7908 = $105,519 (The annuity factor is for five payments and a rate of 10%.)

b. An amortization table follows.

Annual Period Ending	(a) Beginning Balance	(b) Debit Interest Expense +	(c) Debit Notes Payable =	(d) Credit Cash	(e) Ending Balance
(1) 12/31/2013	$400,000	$ 40,000	$ 65,519	$105,519	$334,481
(2) 12/31/2014	334,481	33,448	72,071	105,519	262,410
(3) 12/31/2015	262,410	26,241	79,278	105,519	183,132
(4) 12/31/2016	183,132	18,313	87,206	105,519	95,926
(5) 12/31/2017	95,926	9,593	95,926	105,519	0
		$127,595	$400,000	$527,595	

c. Journal entry for December 31, 2013, payment.

Dec. 31	Interest Expense	40,000	
	Notes Payable	65,519	
	Cash		105,519
	To record first installment payment.		

Part 2: Bonds (Straight-Line Amortization)

a. Compute the bonds' issue price.

Cash Flow	Table	Present Value Factor*	Amount	Present Value
Par (maturity) value	B.1 in App. B (PV of 1)	0.6139	× 400,000	= $245,560
Interest payments	B.3 in App. B (PV of annuity)	7.7217	× 24,000	= 185,321
Price of bond				$430,881

* Present value factors are for 10 payments using a semiannual market rate of 5%.

b. Journal entry for January 1, 2013, issuance.

Jan. 1	Cash	430,881	
	Premium on Bonds Payable		30,881
	Bonds Payable		400,000
	Sold bonds at a premium.		

c. Straight-line amortization table for premium bonds.

Semiannual Period-End	Unamortized Premium	Carrying Value
(0) 1/1/2013	$30,881	$430,881
(1) 6/30/2013	27,793	427,793
(2) 12/31/2013	24,705	424,705
(3) 6/30/2014	21,617	421,617
(4) 12/31/2014	18,529	418,529
(5) 6/30/2015	15,441	415,441
(6) 12/31/2015	12,353	412,353
(7) 6/30/2016	9,265	409,265
(8) 12/31/2016	6,177	406,177
(9) 6/30/2017	3,089	403,089
(10) 12/31/2017	0*	400,000

* Adjusted for rounding.

d. Journal entry for June 30, 2013, bond payment.

June 30	Bond Interest Expense	20,912	
	Premium on Bonds Payable	3,088	
	Cash		24,000
	Paid semiannual interest on bonds.		

e. Journal entry for January 1, 2015, bond retirement.

Jan. 1	Bonds Payable	400,000	
	Premium on Bonds Payable	18,529	
	Cash		416,000
	Gain on Retirement of Bonds		2,529
	To record bond retirement (carrying value as of Dec. 31, 2014).		

Part 3: Bonds (Effective Interest Amortization)[B]

c. The effective interest amortization table for premium bonds.

Semiannual Interest Period	(A) Cash Interest Paid 6% × $400,000	(B) Interest Expense 5% × Prior (E)	(C) Premium Amortization (A) − (B)	(D) Unamortized Premium Prior (D) − (C)	(E) Carrying Value $400,000 + (D)
(0) 1/1/2013				$30,881	$430,881
(1) 6/30/2013	$ 24,000	$ 21,544	$ 2,456	28,425	428,425
(2) 12/31/2013	24,000	21,421	2,579	25,846	425,846
(3) 6/30/2014	24,000	21,292	2,708	23,138	423,138
(4) 12/31/2014	24,000	21,157	2,843	20,295	420,295
(5) 6/30/2015	24,000	21,015	2,985	17,310	417,310
(6) 12/31/2015	24,000	20,866	3,134	14,176	414,176
(7) 6/30/2016	24,000	20,709	3,291	10,885	410,885
(8) 12/31/2016	24,000	20,544	3,456	7,429	407,429
(9) 6/30/2017	24,000	20,371	3,629	3,800	403,800
(10) 12/31/2017	24,000	20,200*	3,800	0	400,000
	$240,000	$209,119	$30,881		

* Adjusted for rounding

d. Journal entry for June 30, 2013, bond payment.

June 30	Bond Interest Expense	21,544	
	Premium on Bonds Payable	2,456	
	Cash		24,000
	Paid semiannual interest on bonds.		

e. Journal entry for January 1, 2015, bond retirement.

Jan. 1	Bonds Payable	400,000	
	Premium on Bonds Payable	20,295	
	Cash		416,000
	Gain on Retirement of Bonds		4,295
	To record bond retirement (carrying value as of December 31, 2014).		

Present Values of Bonds and Notes

This appendix explains how to apply present value techniques to measure a long-term liability when it is created and to assign interest expense to the periods until it is settled. Appendix B at the end of the book provides additional discussion of present value concepts.

Present Value Concepts The basic present value concept is that cash paid (or received) in the future has less value now than the same amount of cash paid (or received) today. To illustrate, if we must pay $1 one year from now, its present value is less than $1. To see this, assume that we borrow $0.9259 today that must be paid back in one year with 8% interest. Our interest expense for this loan is computed as $0.9259 × 8%, or $0.0741. When the $0.0741 interest is added to the $0.9259 borrowed, we get the $1 payment necessary to repay our loan with interest. This is formally computed in Exhibit 10A.1. The $0.9259 borrowed is the present value of the $1 future payment. More generally, an amount borrowed equals the present value of the future payment. (This same interpretation applies to an investment. If $0.9259 is invested at 8%, it yields $0.0741 in revenue after one year. This amounts to $1, made up of principal and interest.)

> **C2** Explain and compute the present value of an amount(s) to be paid at a future date(s).

Amount borrowed	**$0.9259**
Interest for one year at 8%	0.0741
Amount owed after 1 year	$ 1.0000

EXHIBIT 10A.1

Components of a One-Year Loan

To extend this example, assume that we owe $1 two years from now instead of one year, and the 8% interest is compounded annually. *Compounded* means that interest during the second period is based on the total of the amount borrowed plus the interest accrued from the first period. The second period's interest is then computed as 8% multiplied by the sum of the amount borrowed plus interest earned in the first period. Exhibit 10A.2 shows how we compute the present value of $1 to be paid in two years. This amount is $0.8573. The first year's interest of $0.0686 is added to the principal so that the second year's interest is based on $0.9259. Total interest for this two-year period is $0.1427, computed as $0.0686 plus $0.0741.

Point: Benjamin Franklin is said to have described compounding as "the money, money makes, makes more money."

Amount borrowed	**$0.8573**
Interest for first year ($0.8573 × 8%)	0.0686
Amount owed after 1 year	0.9259
Interest for second year ($0.9259 × 8%)	0.0741
Amount owed after 2 years	$ 1.0000

EXHIBIT 10A.2

Components of a Two-Year Loan

Present Value Tables The present value of $1 that we must repay at some future date can be computed by using this formula: $1/(1 + i)^n$. The symbol i is the interest rate per period and n is the number of periods until the future payment must be made. Applying this formula to our two-year loan, we get $1/(1.08)^2$, or $0.8573. This is the same value shown in Exhibit 10A.2. We can use this formula to find any present value. However, a simpler method is to use a *present value table,* which lists present values computed with this formula for various interest rates and time periods. Many people find it helpful in learning present value concepts to first work with the table and then move to using a calculator.

Exhibit 10A.3 shows a present value table for a future payment of 1 for up to 10 periods at three different interest rates. Present values in this table are rounded to four decimal places. This table is drawn from the larger and more complete Table B.1 in Appendix B at the end of the book. Notice that the first value in the 8% column is 0.9259, the value we computed earlier for the present value of a $1 loan for one year at 8% (see Exhibit 10A.1). Go to the second row in the same 8% column and find the present value of 1 discounted at 8% for two years, or 0.8573. This $0.8573 is the present value of our obligation to repay $1 after two periods at 8% interest (see Exhibit 10A.2).

EXHIBIT 10A.3

Present Value of 1

	Rate		
Periods	**6%**	**8%**	**10%**
1	0.9434	**0.9259**	0.9091
2	0.8900	**0.8573**	0.8264
3	0.8396	0.7938	0.7513
4	0.7921	0.7350	0.6830
5	0.7473	0.6806	0.6209
6	0.7050	0.6302	0.5645
7	0.6651	0.5835	0.5132
8	0.6274	0.5403	0.4665
9	0.5919	0.5002	0.4241
10	0.5584	0.4632	0.3855

Example: Use Exhibit 10A.3 to find the present value of $1 discounted for 2 years at 6%. *Answer:* $0.8900

EXHIBIT 10A.4

Present Value of a Series of Unequal Payments

Periods	Payments	Present Value of 1 at 10%	Present Value of Payments
1	$2,000	0.9091	$ 1,818
2	3,000	0.8264	2,479
3	5,000	0.7513	3,757
Present value of all payments			**$8,054**

Applying a Present Value Table   To illustrate how to measure a liability using a present value table, assume that a company plans to borrow cash and repay it as follows: $2,000 after one year, $3,000 after two years, and $5,000 after three years. How much does this company receive today if the interest rate on this loan is 10%? To answer, we need to compute the present value of the three future payments, discounted at 10%. This computation is shown in Exhibit 10A.4 using present values from Exhibit 10A.3. The company can borrow $8,054 today at 10% interest in exchange for its promise to make these three payments at the scheduled dates.

Present Value of an Annuity   The $8,054 present value for the loan in Exhibit 10A.4 equals the sum of the present values of the three payments. When payments are not equal, their combined present value is best computed by adding the individual present values as shown in Exhibit 10A.4. Sometimes payments follow an **annuity,** which is a series of *equal* payments at equal time intervals. The present value of an annuity is readily computed.

EXHIBIT 10A.5

Present Value of a Series of Equal Payments (Annuity) by Discounting Each Payment

Periods	Payments	Present Value of 1 at 6%	Present Value of Payments
1	$5,000	0.9434	$ 4,717
2	5,000	0.8900	4,450
3	5,000	0.8396	4,198
4	5,000	0.7921	3,961
Present value of all payments		**3.4651**	**$17,326**

To illustrate, assume that a company must repay a 6% loan with a $5,000 payment at each year-end for the next four years. This loan amount equals the present value of the four payments discounted at 6%. Exhibit 10A.5 shows how to compute this loan's present value of $17,326 by multiplying each payment by its matching present value factor taken from Exhibit 10A.3.

However, the series of $5,000 payments is an annuity, so we can compute its present value with either of two shortcuts. First, the third column of Exhibit 10A.5 shows that the sum of the present values of 1 at 6% for periods 1 through 4 equals 3.4651. One shortcut is to multiply this total of 3.4651 by the $5,000 annual payment to get the combined present value of $17,326. It requires one multiplication instead of four.

The second shortcut uses an *annuity table* such as the one shown in Exhibit 10A.6, which is drawn from the more complete Table B.3 in Appendix B. We go directly to the annuity table to get the present value factor for a specific number of payments and interest rate. We then multiply this factor by the amount of the payment to find the present value of the annuity. Specifically, find the row for four periods and go across to the 6% column, where the factor is 3.4651. This factor equals the present value of an annuity with four payments of 1, discounted at 6%. We then multiply 3.4651 by $5,000 to get the $17,326 present value of the annuity.

EXHIBIT 10A.6

Present Value of an Annuity of 1

Periods	Rate		
	6%	8%	10%
1	0.9434	0.9259	0.9091
2	1.8334	1.7833	1.7355
3	2.6730	2.5771	2.4869
4	3.4651	3.3121	3.1699
5	4.2124	3.9927	3.7908
6	4.9173	4.6229	4.3553
7	5.5824	5.2064	4.8684
8	6.2098	5.7466	5.3349
9	6.8017	6.2469	5.7590
10	7.3601	6.7101	6.1446

Example: Use Exhibit 10A.6 to find the present value of an annuity of eight $15,000 payments with an 8% interest rate. *Answer:* $15,000 × 5.7466 = $86,199

Example: If this borrower makes five semiannual payments of $8,000, what is the present value of this annuity at a 12% rate? *Answer:* 4.2124 × $8,000 = $33,699

Compounding Periods Shorter Than a Year   The present value examples all involved periods of one year. In many situations, however, interest is compounded over shorter periods. For example, the interest rate on bonds is usually stated as an annual rate but interest is often paid every six months (semiannually). This means that the present value of interest payments from such bonds must be computed using interest periods of six months.

Assume that a borrower wants to know the present value of a series of 10 *semiannual payments* of $4,000 made over five years at an *annual interest rate* of 12%. The interest rate is stated as an annual rate of 12%, but it is actually a rate of 6% per semiannual interest period. To compute the present value of this series of $4,000 payments, go to row 10 of Exhibit 10A.6 and across to the 6% column to find the factor 7.3601. The present value of this annuity is $29,440 (7.3601 × $4,000).

Appendix B further describes present value concepts and includes more complete present value tables and assignments.

Effective Interest Amortization

10B

Effective Interest Amortization of a Discount Bond   The straight-line method yields changes in the bonds' carrying value while the amount for bond interest expense remains constant. This gives the impression of a changing interest rate when users divide a constant bond interest expense over a changing carrying value. As a result, accounting standards allow use of the straight-line method only when its results do not differ materially from those obtained using the effective interest method. The **effective interest method,** or simply *interest method,* allocates total bond interest expense over the bonds' life in a way that yields a constant rate of interest. This constant rate of interest is the market rate at the issue date. Thus, bond interest expense for a period equals the carrying value of the bond at the beginning of that period multiplied by the market rate when issued.

Exhibit 10B.1 shows an effective interest amortization table for the Fila bonds (as described in Exhibit 10.4). The key difference between the effective interest and straight-line methods lies in computing bond interest expense. Instead of assigning an equal amount of bond interest expense to each period, the effective interest method assigns a bond interest expense amount that increases over the life of a discount bond. **Both methods allocate the *same* $19,546 of total bond interest expense to the bonds' life, but in different patterns.** Specifically, the amortization table in Exhibit 10B.1 shows that the balance of the discount (column D) is amortized until it reaches zero. Also, the bonds' carrying value (column E) changes each period until it equals par value at maturity. Compare columns D and E to the corresponding columns in Exhibit 10.7 to see the amortization patterns. Total bond interest expense is $19,546, consisting of $16,000 of semiannual cash payments and $3,546 of the original bond discount, the same for both methods.

P6   *Appendix 10B*—Compute and record amortization of bond discount using effective interest method.

Point: The effective interest method computes bond interest expense using the market rate at issuance. This rate is applied to a changing carrying value.

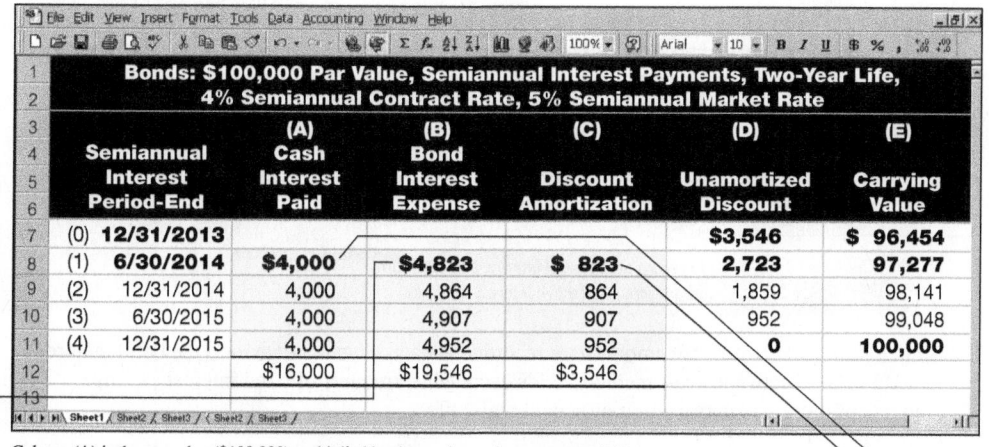

EXHIBIT 10B.1

Effective Interest Amortization of Bond Discount

Bonds: $100,000 Par Value, Semiannual Interest Payments, Two-Year Life, 4% Semiannual Contract Rate, 5% Semiannual Market Rate

Semiannual Interest Period-End	(A) Cash Interest Paid	(B) Bond Interest Expense	(C) Discount Amortization	(D) Unamortized Discount	(E) Carrying Value
(0) 12/31/2013				$3,546	$ 96,454
(1) 6/30/2014	$4,000	$4,823	$ 823	2,723	97,277
(2) 12/31/2014	4,000	4,864	864	1,859	98,141
(3) 6/30/2015	4,000	4,907	907	952	99,048
(4) 12/31/2015	4,000	4,952	952	0	100,000
	$16,000	$19,546	$3,546		

Column (**A**) is the par value ($100,000) multiplied by the semiannual contract rate (4%).
Column (**B**) is the prior period's carrying value multiplied by the semiannual market rate (5%).
Column (**C**) is the difference between interest paid and bond interest expense, or [(B) − (A)].
Column (**D**) is the prior period's unamortized discount less the current period's discount amortization.
Column (**E**) is the par value less unamortized discount, or [$100,000 − (D)].

Except for differences in amounts, journal entries recording the expense and updating the liability balance are the same under the effective interest method and the straight-line method. We can use the numbers in Exhibit 10B.1 to record each semiannual entry during the bonds' two-year life (June 30, 2014, through December 31, 2015). For instance, we record the interest payment at the end of the first semiannual period as follows:

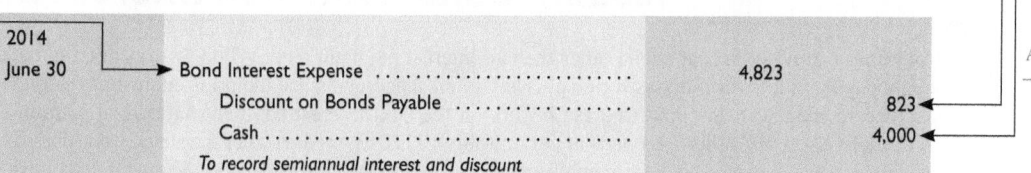

2014			
June 30	Bond Interest Expense	4,823	
	Discount on Bonds Payable		823
	Cash		4,000
	To record semiannual interest and discount amortization (effective interest method).		

Assets = Liabilities + Equity
−4,000   +823   −4,823

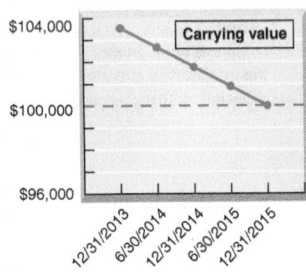

P7   *Appendix 10B—Compute and record amortization of bond premium using effective interest method.*

Effective Interest Amortization of a Premium Bond   Exhibit 10B.2 shows the amortization table using the effective interest method for the Adidas bonds (as described in Exhibit 10.8). Column A lists the semiannual cash payments. Column B shows the amount of bond interest expense, computed as the 5% semiannual market rate at issuance multiplied by the beginning-of-period carrying value. The amount of cash paid in column A is larger than the bond interest expense because the cash payment is based on the higher 6% semiannual contract rate. The excess cash payment over the interest expense reduces the principal. These amounts are shown in column C. Column E shows the carrying value after deducting the

EXHIBIT 10B.2

Effective Interest Amortization of Bond Premium

Bonds: $100,000 Par Value, Semiannual Interest Payments, Two-Year Life, 6% Semiannual Contract Rate, 5% Semiannual Market Rate

	Semiannual Interest Period-End	(A) Cash Interest Paid	(B) Bond Interest Expense	(C) Premium Amortization	(D) Unamortized Premium	(E) Carrying Value
(0)	12/31/2013				$3,546	$103,546
(1)	6/30/2014	$6,000	$5,177	$ 823	2,723	102,723
(2)	12/31/2014	6,000	5,136	864	1,859	101,859
(3)	6/30/2015	6,000	5,093	907	952	100,952
(4)	12/31/2015	6,000	5,048	952	0	100,000
		$24,000	$20,454	$3,546		

Column (**A**) is the par value ($100,000) multiplied by the semiannual contract rate (6%).
Column (**B**) is the prior period's carrying value multiplied by the semiannual market rate (5%).
Column (**C**) is the difference between interest paid and bond interest expense, or [(A) − (B)].
Column (**D**) is the prior period's unamortized premium less the current period's premium amortization.
Column (**E**) is the par value plus unamortized premium, or [$100,000 + (D)].

amortized premium in column C from the prior period's carrying value. Column D shows the premium's reduction by periodic amortization. When the issuer makes the first semiannual interest payment, the effect of premium amortization on bond interest expense and bond liability is recorded as follows:

Assets = Liabilities + Equity
−6,000   − 823   − 5,177

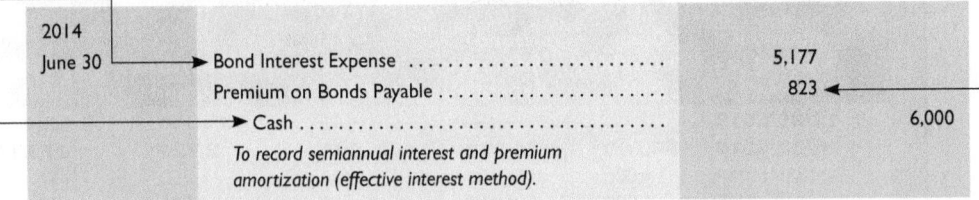

2014
June 30   Bond Interest Expense   5,177
         Premium on Bonds Payable   823
         Cash   6,000
         To record semiannual interest and premium amortization (effective interest method).

Similar entries with different amounts are recorded at each payment date until the bond matures at the end of 2015. The effective interest method yields decreasing amounts of bond interest expense and increasing amounts of premium amortization over the bonds' life.

IFRS

Unlike U.S. GAAP, IFRS requires that interest expense be computed using the effective interest method with *no exemptions*. ■

APPENDIX

10C   Issuing Bonds between Interest Dates

C3   Describe interest accrual when bond payment periods differ from accounting periods.

An issuer can sell bonds at a date other than an interest payment date. When this occurs, the buyers normally pay the issuer the purchase price plus any interest accrued since the prior interest payment date. This accrued interest is then repaid to these buyers on the next interest payment date. To illustrate, suppose **Avia** sells $100,000 of its 9% bonds at par on March 1, 2013, 60 days after the stated issue date. The interest on Avia bonds is payable semiannually on each June 30 and December 31. Since 60 days have passed, the issuer collects accrued interest from the buyers at the time of issuance. This amount is $1,500 ($100,000 × 9% × 60/360 year). This case is reflected in Exhibit 10C.1.

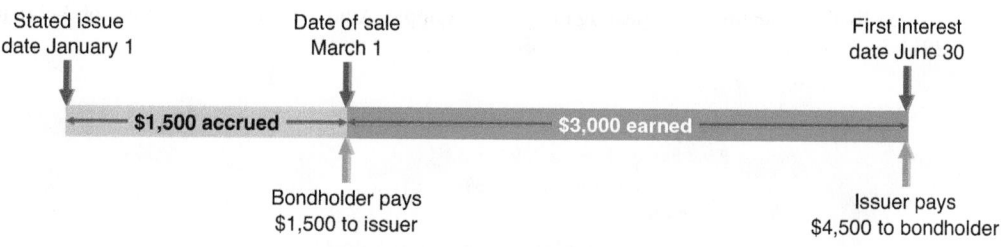

EXHIBIT 10C.1

Accruing Interest between Interest Payment Dates

Avia records the issuance of these bonds on March 1, 2013, as follows:

Mar. 1	Cash	101,500	
	Interest Payable		1,500
	Bonds Payable.............................		100,000
	Sold bonds at par with accrued interest.		

Assets   = Liabilities + Equity
+101,500   +100,000
+1,500

Liabilities for interest payable and bonds payable are recorded in separate accounts. When the June 30, 2013, semiannual interest date arrives, Avia pays the full semiannual interest of $4,500 ($100,000 × 9% × ½ year) to the bondholders. This payment includes the four months' interest of $3,000 earned by the bondholders from March 1 to June 30 *plus* the repayment of the 60 days' accrued interest collected by Avia when the bonds were sold. Avia records this first semiannual interest payment as follows:

Example: How much interest is collected from a buyer of $50,000 of Avia bonds sold at par 150 days after the contract issue date? *Answer:* $1,875 (computed as $50,000 × 9% × $^{150}\!/_{360}$ year)

June 30	Interest Payable	1,500	
	Bond Interest Expense.......................	3,000	
	Cash		4,500
	Paid semiannual interest on the bonds.		

Assets = Liabilities + Equity
−4,500   −1,500   −3,000

The practice of collecting and then repaying accrued interest with the next interest payment is to simplify the issuer's administrative efforts. To explain, suppose an issuer sells bonds on 15 or 20 different dates between the stated issue date and the first interest payment date. If the issuer does not collect accrued interest from buyers, it needs to pay different amounts of cash to each of them according to the time that passed after purchasing the bonds. The issuer needs to keep detailed records of buyers and the dates they bought bonds. Issuers avoid this recordkeeping by having each buyer pay accrued interest at purchase. Issuers then pay the full semiannual interest to all buyers, regardless of when they bought bonds.

Accruing Bond Interest Expense   If a bond's interest period does not coincide with the issuer's accounting period, an adjusting entry is needed to recognize bond interest expense accrued since the most recent interest payment. To illustrate, assume that the stated issue date for Adidas bonds described in Exhibit 10.10 is September 1, 2013, instead of December 31, 2013, and that the bonds are sold on September 1, 2013. As a result, four months' interest (and premium amortization) accrue before the end of the 2013 calendar year. Interest for this period equals $3,409, or ⅔ of the first six months' interest of $5,113. Also, the premium amortization is $591, or ⅔ of the first six months' amortization of $887. The sum of the bond interest expense and the amortization is $4,000 ($3,409 + $591), which equals ⅔ of the $6,000 cash payment due on February 28, 2014. Adidas records these effects with an adjusting entry at December 31, 2013.

Point: Computation of accrued bond interest may use months instead of days for simplicity purposes. For example, the accrued interest computation for the Adidas bonds is based on months.

Dec. 31	Bond Interest Expense	3,409	
	Premium on Bonds Payable	591	
	Interest Payable		4,000
	To record four months' accrued interest and premium amortization.		

Assets = Liabilities + Equity
            −591   −3,409
            +4,000

Similar entries are made on each December 31 throughout the bonds' two-year life. When the $6,000 cash payment occurs on each February 28 interest payment date, Adidas must recognize bond interest expense and amortization for January and February. It must also eliminate the interest payable liability created by the December 31 adjusting entry. For example, Adidas records its payment on February 28, 2014, as follows:

Assets = Liabilities + Equity
−6,000   −4,000   −1,704
         −296

Feb. 28	Interest Payable	4,000	
	Bond Interest Expense ($5,113 × ⅔)	1,704	
	Premium on Bonds Payable ($887 × ⅔)	296	
	Cash		6,000
	To record 2 months' interest and amortization, and		
	eliminate accrued interest liability.		

The interest payments made each August 31 are recorded as usual because the entire six-month interest period is included within this company's calendar-year reporting period.

QC7

Decision Maker

Bond Rater   You work for **Moody's** rating service and it's your job to assist in assigning a rating to a bond that reflects its risk to bondholders. Identify factors you consider in assessing bond risk. Indicate the likely levels (relative to the norm) for the factors you identify for a bond that sells at a discount. ■   [Answer—p. 463]

APPENDIX

10D

Leases and Pensions

This appendix briefly explains the accounting and analysis for both leases and pensions.

C4   Describe accounting for leases and pensions.

Lease Liabilities   A **lease** is a contractual agreement between a *lessor* (asset owner) and a *lessee* (asset renter or tenant) that grants the lessee the right to use the asset for a period of time in return for cash (rent) payments. Nearly one-fourth of all equipment purchases are financed with leases. The advantages of lease financing include the lack of an immediate large cash payment and the potential to deduct rental payments in computing taxable income. From an accounting perspective, leases can be classified as either operating or capital leases. (Lease accounting will change over the next few years, whereby operating leases are likely to be accounted for similar to capital leases . . . stay tuned!)

Point: Home Depot reports that its rental expenses from operating leases total more than $900 million.

Operating Leases   **Operating leases** are short-term (or cancelable) leases in which the lessor retains the risks and rewards of ownership. Examples include most car and apartment rental agreements. The lessee records such lease payments as expenses; the lessor records them as revenue. The lessee does not report the leased item as an asset or a liability (it is the lessor's asset). To illustrate, if an employee of Amazon leases a car for $300 at an airport while on company business, Amazon (lessee) records this cost as follows:

Assets = Liabilities + Equity
−300   −300

July 4	Rental Expense	300	
	Cash		300
	To record lease rental payment.		

Capital Leases   **Capital leases** are long-term (or noncancelable) leases by which the lessor transfers substantially all risks and rewards of ownership to the lessee.[3] Examples include most leases of airplanes and department store buildings. The lessee records the leased item as its own asset along with a lease liability at the start of the lease term; the amount recorded equals the present value of all lease payments. To illustrate, assume that K2 Co. enters into a six-year lease of a building in which it will sell sporting

---

[3] A *capital lease* meets any one or more of four criteria: (1) transfers title of leased asset to lessee, (2) contains a bargain purchase option, (3) has a lease term that is 75% or more of the leased asset's useful life, or (4) has a present value of lease payments that is 90% or more of the leased asset's market value.

equipment. The lease transfers all building ownership risks and rewards to K2 (the present value of its $12,979 annual lease payments is $60,000). K2 records this transaction as follows:

2013 Jan. 1	Leased Asset—Building	60,000	
	Lease Liability		60,000
	To record leased asset and lease liability.		

Assets = Liabilities + Equity
+60,000   +60,000

K2 reports the leased asset as a plant asset and the lease liability as a long-term liability. The portion of the lease liability expected to be paid in the next year is reported as a current liability.[4] At each year-end, K2 records depreciation on the leased asset (assume straight-line depreciation, six-year lease term, and no salvage value) as follows:

Point: Home Depot reports *"certain locations ... are leased under capital leases."* The net present value of this Lease Liability is about $400 million.

Dec. 31	Depreciation Expense—Building	10,000	
	Accumulated Depreciation—Building		10,000
	To record depreciation on leased asset.		

Assets = Liabilities + Equity
−10,000   −10,000

K2 also accrues interest on the lease liability at each year-end. Interest expense is computed by multiplying the remaining lease liability by the interest rate on the lease. Specifically, K2 records its annual interest expense as part of its annual lease payment ($12,979) as follows (for its first year):

2013 Dec. 31	Interest Expense	4,800	
	Lease Liability	8,179	
	Cash		12,979
	*To record first annual lease payment.**		

Assets = Liabilities + Equity
−12,979   −8,179   −4,800

* These numbers are computed from a *lease payment schedule*. For simplicity, we use the same numbers from Exhibit 10.14 for this lease payment schedule—with different headings as follows:

			Payments		
	(A)	(B)	(C)	(D)	(E)
		·Debit	Debit	Credit	
Period Ending Date	Beginning Balance of Lease Liability	Interest on Lease Liability 8% × (A)	+ Lease Liability (D) − (B)	= Cash Lease Payment	Ending Balance of Lease Liability (A) − (C)
12/31/2013	$60,000	$ 4,800	$ 8,179	$12,979	$51,821
12/31/2014	51,821	4,146	8,833	12,979	42,988
12/31/2015	42,988	3,439	9,540	12,979	33,448
12/31/2016	33,448	2,676	10,303	12,979	23,145
12/31/2017	23,145	1,852	11,127	12,979	12,018
12/31/2018	12,018	961	12,018	12,979	0
		$17,874	$60,000	$77,874	

Pension Liabilities   A **pension plan** is a contractual agreement between an employer and its employees for the employer to provide benefits (payments) to employees after they retire. Most employers pay the full cost of the pension, but sometimes employees pay part of the cost. An employer records its payment into a pension plan with a debit to Pension Expense and a credit to Cash. A *plan administrator* receives payments from the employer, invests them in pension assets, and makes benefit payments to *pension recipients* (retired employees). Insurance and trust companies often serve as pension plan administrators.

Point: Fringe benefits are often 40% or more of salaries and wages, and pension benefits make up nearly 15% of fringe benefits.

Many pensions are known as *defined benefit plans* that define future benefits; the employer's contributions vary, depending on assumptions about future pension assets and liabilities. Several disclosures are necessary in this case. Specifically, a pension liability is reported when the accumulated benefit obligation

---

[4] Most lessees try to keep leased assets and lease liabilities off their balance sheets by failing to meet any one of the four criteria of a capital lease. This is because a lease liability increases a company's total liabilities, making it more difficult to obtain additional financing. The acquisition of assets without reporting any related liabilities (or other asset outflows) on the balance sheet is called **off-balance-sheet financing.**

Point: Two types of pension plans are (1) *defined benefit plan*—the retirement benefit is defined and the employer estimates the contribution necessary to pay these benefits—and (2) *defined contribution plan*—the pension contribution is defined and the employer and/or employee contributes amounts specified in the pension agreement.

is *more than* the plan assets, a so-called *underfunded plan*. The accumulated benefit obligation is the present value of promised future pension payments to retirees. *Plan assets* refer to the market value of assets the plan administrator holds. A pension asset is reported when the accumulated benefit obligation is *less than* the plan assets, a so-called *overfunded plan*. An employer reports pension expense when it receives the benefits from the employees' services, which is sometimes decades before it pays pension benefits to employees. (*Other Postretirement Benefits* refer to nonpension benefits such as health care and life insurance benefits. Similar to a pension, costs of these benefits are estimated and liabilities accrued when the employees earn them.)

Summary

C1 **Explain the types and payment patterns of notes.** Notes repaid over a period of time are called *installment notes* and usually follow one of two payment patterns: (1) decreasing payments of interest plus equal amounts of principal or (2) equal total payments. Mortgage notes also are common.

C2^A **Explain and compute the present value of an amount(s) to be paid at a future date(s).** The basic concept of present value is that an amount of cash to be paid or received in the future is worth less than the same amount of cash to be paid or received today. Another important present value concept is that interest is compounded, meaning interest is added to the balance and used to determine interest for succeeding periods. An annuity is a series of equal payments occurring at equal time intervals. An annuity's present value can be computed using the present value table for an annuity (or a calculator).

C3^C **Describe interest accrual when bond payment periods differ from accounting periods.** Issuers and buyers of debt record the interest accrued when issue dates or accounting periods do not coincide with debt payment dates.

C4^D **Describe accounting for leases and pensions.** A lease is a rental agreement between the lessor and the lessee. When the lessor retains the risks and rewards of asset ownership (an *operating lease*), the lessee debits Rent Expense and credits Cash for its lease payments. When the lessor substantially transfers the risks and rewards of asset ownership to the lessee (a *capital lease*), the lessee capitalizes the leased asset and records a lease liability. Pension agreements can result in either pension assets or pension liabilities.

A1 **Compare bond financing with stock financing.** Bond financing is used to fund business activities. Advantages of bond financing versus stock include (1) no effect on owner control, (2) tax savings, and (3) increased earnings due to financial leverage. Disadvantages include (1) interest and principal payments and (2) amplification of poor performance.

A2 **Assess debt features and their implications.** Certain bonds are secured by the issuer's assets; other bonds, called *debentures*, are unsecured. Serial bonds mature at different points in time; term bonds mature at one time. Registered bonds have each bondholder's name recorded by the issuer; bearer bonds are payable to the holder. Convertible bonds are exchangeable for shares of the issuer's stock. Callable bonds can be retired by the issuer at a set price. Debt features alter the risk of loss for creditors.

A3 **Compute the debt-to-equity ratio and explain its use.** Both creditors and equity holders are concerned about the relation between the amount of liabilities and the amount of equity. A company's financing structure is at less risk when the debt-to-equity ratio is lower, as liabilities must be paid and usually with periodic interest.

P1 **Prepare entries to record bond issuance and interest expense.** When bonds are issued at par, Cash is debited and Bonds Payable is credited for the bonds' par value. At bond interest payment dates (usually semiannual), Bond Interest Expense is debited and Cash credited—the latter for an amount equal to the bond par value multiplied by the bond contract rate.

P2 **Compute and record amortization of bond discount using straight-line method.** Bonds are issued at a discount when the contract rate is less than the market rate, making the issue (selling) price less than par. When this occurs, the issuer records a credit to Bonds Payable (at par) and debits both Discount on Bonds Payable and Cash. The amount of bond interest expense assigned to each period is computed using the straight-line method.

P3 **Compute and record amortization of bond premium using straight-line method.** Bonds are issued at a premium when the contract rate is higher than the market rate, making the issue (selling) price greater than par. When this occurs, the issuer records a debit to Cash and credits both Premium on Bonds Payable and Bonds Payable (at par). The amount of bond interest expense assigned to each period is computed using the straight-line method. The Premium on Bonds Payable is allocated to reduce bond interest expense over the life of the bonds.

P4 **Record the retirement of bonds.** Bonds are retired at maturity with a debit to Bonds Payable and a credit to Cash at par value. The issuer can retire the bonds early by exercising a call option or purchasing them in the market. Bondholders can also retire bonds early by exercising a conversion feature on convertible bonds. The issuer recognizes a gain or loss for the difference between the amount paid and the bond carrying value.

P5 **Prepare entries to account for notes.** Interest is allocated to each period in a note's life by multiplying its beginning-period carrying value by its market rate at issuance. If a note is repaid with equal payments, the payment amount is computed by dividing the borrowed amount by the present value of an annuity factor (taken from a present value table) using the market rate and the number of payments.

P6^B **Compute and record amortization of bond discount using effective interest method.** Bonds are issued at a discount when the contract rate is less than the market rate, making the issue (selling) price less than par. The amount of bond interest expense assigned to each period, including amortization of the discount, is computed using the effective interest method.

P7^B **Compute and record amortization of bond premium using effective interest method.** Bonds are issued at a premium when the contract rate is higher than the market rate, making the issue (selling) price greater than par. The amount of bond interest expense assigned to each period, including amortization of the premium, is computed using the effective interest method.

Guidance Answers to Decision Maker

Entrepreneur   This is a "present value" question. The market interest rate (10%) and present value ($3,000) are known, but the payment required two years later is unknown. This amount ($3,630) can be computed as $3,000 × 1.10 × 1.10. Thus, the sale price is $3,630 when no payments are received for two years. The $3,630 received two years from today is equivalent to $3,000 cash today.

Bond Investor   The debt-to-equity ratio for the first company is 0.2 ($350,000/$1,750,000) and for the second company is 1.2 ($1,200,000/$1,000,000), suggesting that the financing structure of the second company is more risky than that of the first company. Consequently, as a buyer of unsecured debenture bonds, you prefer the first company (all else equal).

Bond Rater   Bonds with longer repayment periods (life) have higher risk. Also, bonds issued by companies in financial difficulties or facing higher than normal uncertainties have higher risk. Moreover, companies with higher than normal debt and large fluctuations in earnings are considered of higher risk. Discount bonds are more risky on one or more of these factors.

Key Terms

Annuity (p. 456)

Bearer bonds (p. 451)

Bond (p. 436)

Bond certificate (p. 437)

Bond indenture (p. 437)

Callable bonds (p. 451)

Capital leases (p. 460)

Carrying (book) value of bonds (p. 439)

Contract rate (p. 438)

Convertible bonds (p. 451)

Coupon bonds (p. 451)

Debt-to-equity ratio (p. 452)

Discount on bonds payable (p. 439)

Effective interest method (p. 457)

Fair value option (p. 450)

Installment note (p. 447)

Lease (p. 460)

Market rate (p. 438)

Mortgage (p. 449)

Off-balance-sheet financing (p. 461)

Operating leases (p. 460)

Par value of a bond (p. 436)

Pension plan (p. 461)

Premium on bonds (p. 442)

Registered bonds (p. 451)

Secured bonds (p. 451)

Serial bonds (p. 451)

Sinking fund bonds (p. 451)

Straight-line bond amortization (p. 440)

Term bonds (p. 451)

Unsecured bonds (p. 451)

Multiple Choice Quiz   Answers on p. 477   mhhe.com/wildFA7e

Additional Quiz Questions are available at the book's Website.

1. A bond traded at 97½ means that
   a. The bond pays 97½% interest.
   b. The bond trades at $975 per $1,000 bond.
   c. The market rate of interest is below the contract rate of interest for the bond.
   d. The bonds can be retired at $975 each.
   e. The bond's interest rate is 2½%.

2. A bondholder that owns a $1,000, 6%, 15-year bond has
   a. The right to receive $1,000 at maturity.
   b. Ownership rights in the bond-issuing entity.
   c. The right to receive $60 per month until maturity.
   d. The right to receive $1,900 at maturity.
   e. The right to receive $600 per year until maturity.

3. A company issues 8%, 20-year bonds with a par value of $500,000. The current market rate for the bonds is 8%. The amount of interest owed to the bondholders for each semiannual interest payment is
   a. $40,000.
   b. $0.
   c. $20,000.
   d. $800,000.
   e. $400,000.

4. A company issued 5-year, 5% bonds with a par value of $100,000. The company received $95,735 for the bonds. Using the straight-line method, the company's interest expense for the first semiannual interest period is
   a. $2,926.50.
   b. $5,853.00.
   c. $2,500.00.
   d. $5,000.00.
   e. $9,573.50.

5. A company issued 8-year, 5% bonds with a par value of $350,000. The company received proceeds of $373,745. Interest is payable semiannually. The amount of premium amortized for the first semiannual interest period, assuming straight-line bond amortization, is
   a. $2,698.
   b. $23,745.
   c. $8,750.
   d. $9,344.
   e. $1,484.

B(C,D) *Superscript letter B(C, D) denotes assignments based on Appendix 10B (10C, 10D).*

🎲 Icon denotes assignments that involve decision making.

Discussion Questions

1. What is the main difference between notes payable and bonds payable?

2. What is the main difference between a bond and a share of stock?

3. 🎲 What is the advantage of issuing bonds instead of obtaining financing from the company's owners?

4. What is a bond indenture? What provisions are usually included in it?

5. What are the duties of a trustee for bondholders?

6. What are the *contract* rate and the *market* rate for bonds?

7. 🎲 What factors affect the market rates for bonds?

8.^B 🎲 Does the straight-line or effective interest method produce an interest expense allocation that yields a constant rate of interest over a bond's life? Explain.

9.^C Why does a company that issues bonds between interest dates collect accrued interest from the bonds' purchasers?

10. 🎲 If you know the par value of bonds, the contract rate, and the market rate, how do you compute the bonds' price?

11. What is the issue price of a $2,000 bond sold at 98¼? What is the issue price of a $6,000 bond sold at 101½?

12. Describe the debt-to-equity ratio and explain how creditors and owners would use this ratio to evaluate a company's risk.

13. 🎲 What obligation does an entrepreneur (owner) have to investors that purchase bonds to finance the business?

14. Refer to Apple's annual report in Appendix A. Is there any indication that Apple has issued long-term debt?   **APPLE**

15. By what amount did Samsung's long-term borrowings increase or decrease in 2012?   **Samsung**

16. Refer to the statement of cash flows for Samsung in Appendix A. For the year ended December 31, 2012, what was the amount for repayment of long-term borrowings and debentures?   **Samsung**

17. Refer to the statements for Google in Appendix A. For the year ended December 31, 2012, what is its debt-to-equity ratio? What does this ratio tell us?   **GOOGLE**

18.^D When can a lease create both an asset and a liability for the lessee?

19.^D Compare and contrast an operating lease with a capital lease.

20.^D Describe the two basic types of pension plans.

≣ **connect**

QUICK STUDY

Round dollar amounts to the nearest whole dollar.

QS 10-1

Straight-Line: Bond computations

P1 P2

Enviro Company issues 8%, 10-year bonds with a par value of $250,000 and semiannual interest payments. On the issue date, the annual market rate for these bonds is 10%, which implies a selling price of 87½. The straight-line method is used to allocate interest expense.

1. What are the issuer's cash proceeds from issuance of these bonds?

2. What total amount of bond interest expense will be recognized over the life of these bonds?

3. What is the amount of bond interest expense recorded on the first interest payment date?

QS 10-2^B

Effective Interest: Bond computations

P1 P7

Garcia Company issues 10%, 15-year bonds with a par value of $240,000 and semiannual interest payments. On the issue date, the annual market rate for these bonds is 8%, which implies a selling price of 117¼. The effective interest method is used to allocate interest expense.

1. What are the issuer's cash proceeds from issuance of these bonds?

2. What total amount of bond interest expense will be recognized over the life of these bonds?

3. What amount of bond interest expense is recorded on the first interest payment date?

QS 10-3

Journalize bond issuance P1

Prepare the journal entries for the issuance of the bonds in both QS 10-1 and QS 10-2. Assume that both bonds are issued for cash on January 1, 2013.

QS 10-4

Computing bond price P1

Using the bond details in both QS 10-1 and QS 10-2, confirm that the bonds' selling prices given in each problem are approximately correct (within $100 of each other). Use the present value tables B.1 and B.3 in Appendix B.

QS 10-5

Recording bond issuance and discount amortization P1 P2

Sylvestor Company issues 10%, five-year bonds, on December 31, 2012, with a par value of $100,000 and semiannual interest payments. Use the following bond amortization table and prepare journal entries to record (a) the issuance of bonds on December 31, 2012; (b) the first interest payment on June 30, 2013; and (c) the second interest payment on December 31, 2013.

Semiannual Period-End	Unamortized Discount	Carrying Value
(0) 12/31/2012	$7,360	$92,640
(1) 6/30/2013	6,624	93,376
(2) 12/31/2013	5,888	94,112

On July 1, 2013, Advocate Company exercises a $8,000 call option (plus par value) on its outstanding bonds that have a carrying value of $416,000 and par value of $400,000. The company exercises the call option after the semiannual interest is paid on June 30, 2013. Record the entry to retire the bonds.

QS 10-6
Bond retirement by call option
P4

On January 1, 2013, the $2,000,000 par value bonds of Spitz Company with a carrying value of $2,000,000 are converted to 1,000,000 shares of $1.00 par value common stock. Record the entry for the conversion of the bonds.

QS 10-7
Bond retirement by stock conversion   P4

Enter the letter of the description A through H that best fits each term or phrase 1 through 8.
A. Records and tracks the bondholders' names.
B. Is unsecured; backed only by the issuer's credit standing.
C. Has varying maturity dates for amounts owed.
D. Identifies rights and responsibilities of the issuer and the bondholders.
E. Can be exchanged for shares of the issuer's stock.
F. Is unregistered; interest is paid to whoever possesses them.
G. Maintains a separate asset account from which bondholders are paid at maturity.
H. Pledges specific assets of the issuer as collateral.

QS 10-8
Bond features and terminology
A2

1. _____ Registered bond   **5.** _____ Convertible bond
2. _____ Serial bond   **6.** _____ Bond indenture
3. _____ Secured bond   **7.** _____ Sinking fund bond
4. _____ Bearer bond   **8.** _____ Debenture

Murray Company borrows $340,000 cash from a bank and in return signs an installment note for five annual payments of equal amount, with the first payment due one year after the note is signed. Use Table B.3 in Appendix B to compute the amount of the annual payment for each of the following annual market rates: (a) 4%, (b) 8%, and (c) 12%.

QS 10-9
Computing payments for an installment note   C1

Compute the debt-to-equity ratio for each of the following companies. Which company appears to have a riskier financing structure? Explain.

QS 10-10
Debt-to-equity ratio
A2

	Atlanta Company	Spokane Company
Total liabilities	$429,000	$ 548,000
Total equity	572,000	1,827,000

Madrid Company plans to issue 8% bonds on January 1, 2013, with a par value of $4,000,000. The company sells $3,600,000 of the bonds on January 1, 2013. The remaining $400,000 sells at par on March 1, 2013. The bonds pay interest semiannually as of June 30 and December 31. Record the entry for the March 1 cash sale of bonds.

QS 10-11ᶜ
Issuing bonds between interest dates   P1

Jin Li, an employee of ETrain.com, leases a car at O'Hare airport for a three-day business trip. The rental cost is $250. Prepare the entry by ETrain.com to record Jin Li's short-term car lease cost.

QS 10-12ᴰ
Recording operating leases   C4

Algoma, Inc., signs a five-year lease for office equipment with Office Solutions. The present value of the lease payments is $15,499. Prepare the journal entry that Algoma records at the inception of this capital lease.

QS 10-13ᴰ
Recording capital leases   C4

QS 10-14
International liabilities
disclosures

P1

Vodafone Group Plc reports the following information among its bonds payable as of March 31, 2011 (pounds in millions).

Financial Long-Term Liabilities Measured at Amortised Cost			
(£ millions)	Nominal (par) Value	Carrying Value	Fair Value
4.625% (US dollar 500 million) bond due July 2018	£311	£338	£327

a. What is the par value of the 4.625% bond issuance? What is its book (carrying) value?

b. Was the 4.625% bond sold at a discount or a premium? Explain.

QS 10-15
International liabilities
disclosures and interpretations

P1

Refer to the information in QS 10-14 for Vodafone Group Plc. The following price quotes (from Yahoo! Finance Bond Center) relate to its bonds payable. For example, the price quote indicates that the 4.625% bonds have a market price of 98.0 (98.0% of par value), resulting in a yield to maturity of 4.899%.

Price	Contract Rate (coupon)	Maturity Date	Market Rate (YTM)
98.0	4.625%	15-Jul-2018	4.899%

a. Assuming that the 4.625% bonds were originally issued at par value, what does the market price reveal about interest rate changes since bond issuance? (Assume that Vodafone's credit rating has remained the same.)

b. Does the change in market rates since the issuance of these bonds affect the amount of interest expense reported on Vodafone's income statement? Explain.

c. How much cash would Vodafone need to pay to repurchase the 4.625% bonds at the quoted market price of 98.0? (Assume no interest is owed when the bonds are repurchased.)

d. Assuming that the 4.625% bonds remain outstanding until maturity, at what market price will the bonds sell on the due date in 2018?

≡ connect

EXERCISES

> Round dollar amounts to the nearest whole dollar. Assume no reversing entries are used.

Exercise 10-1
Recording bond issuance and
interest

P1

On January 1, 2013, Boston Enterprises issues bonds that have a $3,400,000 par value, mature in 20 years, and pay 9% interest semiannually on June 30 and December 31. The bonds are sold at par.

1. How much interest will Boston pay (in cash) to the bondholders every six months?

2. Prepare journal entries to record (*a*) the issuance of bonds on January 1, 2013; (*b*) the first interest payment on June 30, 2013; and (*c*) the second interest payment on December 31, 2013.

3. Prepare the journal entry for issuance assuming the bonds are issued at (*a*) 98 and (*b*) 102.

Exercise 10-2
Straight-Line: Amortization of
bond discount

P2

Tano issues bonds with a par value of $180,000 on January 1, 2013. The bonds' annual contract rate is 8%, and interest is paid semiannually on June 30 and December 31. The bonds mature in three years. The annual market rate at the date of issuance is 10%, and the bonds are sold for $170,862.

1. What is the amount of the discount on these bonds at issuance?

2. How much total bond interest expense will be recognized over the life of these bonds?

3. Prepare an amortization table like the one in Exhibit 10.7 for these bonds; use the straight-line method to amortize the discount.

Exercise 10-3[B]
Effective Interest: Amortization
of bond discount

P6

Stanford issues bonds dated January 1, 2013, with a par value of $500,000. The bonds' annual contract rate is 9%, and interest is paid semiannually on June 30 and December 31. The bonds mature in three years. The annual market rate at the date of issuance is 12%, and the bonds are sold for $463,140.

1. What is the amount of the discount on these bonds at issuance?

2. How much total bond interest expense will be recognized over the life of these bonds?

3. Prepare an amortization table like the one in Exhibit 10B.1 for these bonds; use the effective interest method to amortize the discount.

Quatro Co. issues bonds dated January 1, 2013, with a par value of $400,000. The bonds' annual contract rate is 13%, and interest is paid semiannually on June 30 and December 31. The bonds mature in three years. The annual market rate at the date of issuance is 12%, and the bonds are sold for $409,850.

1. What is the amount of the premium on these bonds at issuance?

2. How much total bond interest expense will be recognized over the life of these bonds?

3. Prepare an amortization table like the one in Exhibit 10.11 for these bonds; use the straight-line method to amortize the premium.

Exercise 10-4
Straight-Line: Amortization of bond premium
P3

Refer to the bond details in Exercise 10-4 and prepare an amortization table like the one in Exhibit 10B.2 for these bonds using the effective interest method to amortize the premium.

Exercise 10-5^B
Effective Interest: Amortization of bond premium   P7

Paulson Company issues 6%, four-year bonds, on December 31, 2013, with a par value of $200,000 and semiannual interest payments. Use the following bond amortization table and prepare journal entries to record (a) the issuance of bonds on December 31, 2013; (b) the first interest payment on June 30, 2014; and (c) the second interest payment on December 31, 2014.

Exercise 10-6
Straight-Line: Recording bond issuance and discount amortization

P1 P2

Semiannual Period-End	Unamortized Discount	Carrying Value
(0) 12/31/2013	$13,466	$186,534
(1) 6/30/2014	11,782	188,218
(2) 12/31/2014	10,098	189,902

Dobbs Company issues 5%, two-year bonds, on December 31, 2013, with a par value of $200,000 and semiannual interest payments. Use the following bond amortization table and prepare journal entries to record (a) the issuance of bonds on December 31, 2013; (b) the first through fourth interest payments on each June 30 and December 31; and (c) the maturity of the bond on December 31, 2015.

Exercise 10-7
Straight-Line: Recording bond issuance and discount amortization

P1 P2

Semiannual Period-End	Unamortized Discount	Carrying Value
(0) 12/31/2013	$12,000	$188,000
(1) 6/30/2014	9,000	191,000
(2) 12/31/2014	6,000	194,000
(3) 6/30/2015	3,000	197,000
(4) 12/31/2015	0	200,000

Woodwick Company issues 10%, five-year bonds, on December 31, 2012, with a par value of $200,000 and semiannual interest payments. Use the following bond amortization table and prepare journal entries to record (a) the issuance of bonds on December 31, 2012; (b) the first interest payment on June 30, 2013; and (c) the second interest payment on December 31, 2013.

Exercise 10-8
Straight-Line: Recording bond issuance and premium amortization

P1 P3

Semiannual Period-End	Unamortized Premium	Carrying Value
(0) 12/31/2012	$16,222	$216,222
(1) 6/30/2013	14,600	214,600
(2) 12/31/2013	12,978	212,978

Bringham Company issues bonds with a par value of $800,000 on their stated issue date. The bonds mature in 10 years and pay 6% annual interest in semiannual payments. On the issue date, the annual market rate for the bonds is 8%.

1. What is the amount of each semiannual interest payment for these bonds?

2. How many semiannual interest payments will be made on these bonds over their life?

3. Use the interest rates given to determine whether the bonds are issued at par, at a discount, or at a premium.

4. Compute the price of the bonds as of their issue date.

5. Prepare the journal entry to record the bonds' issuance.

Exercise 10-9
Computing bond interest and price; recording bond issuance

P2

Check (4) $691,287

Exercise 10-10

Computing bond interest and price; recording bond issuance

P3

Check   (4) $162,172

Citywide Company issues bonds with a par value of $150,000 on their stated issue date. The bonds mature in five years and pay 10% annual interest in semiannual payments. On the issue date, the annual market rate for the bonds is 8%.

1. What is the amount of each semiannual interest payment for these bonds?
2. How many semiannual interest payments will be made on these bonds over their life?
3. Use the interest rates given to determine whether the bonds are issued at par, at a discount, or at a premium.
4. Compute the price of the bonds as of their issue date.
5. Prepare the journal entry to record the bonds' issuance.

Exercise 10-11

Straight-Line: Bond computations, amortization, and bond retirement

P2   P4

Check   (6) $8,190 loss

On January 1, 2013, Shay issues $700,000 of 10%, 15-year bonds at a price of 97¾. Six years later, on January 1, 2019, Shay retires 20% of these bonds by buying them on the open market at 104½. All interest is accounted for and paid through December 31, 2018, the day before the purchase. The straight-line method is used to amortize any bond discount.

1. How much does the company receive when it issues the bonds on January 1, 2013?
2. What is the amount of the discount on the bonds at January 1, 2013?
3. How much amortization of the discount is recorded on the bonds for the entire period from January 1, 2013, through December 31, 2018?
4. What is the carrying (book) value of the bonds as of the close of business on December 31, 2018? What is the carrying value of the 20% soon-to-be-retired bonds on this same date?
5. How much did the company pay on January 1, 2019, to purchase the bonds that it retired?
6. What is the amount of the recorded gain or loss from retiring the bonds?
7. Prepare the journal entry to record the bond retirement at January 1, 2019.

Exercise 10-12^C

Recording bond issuance with accrued interest

C4   P1

Check   (1) $102,000

On May 1, 2013, Brussels Enterprises issues bonds dated January 1, 2013, that have a $3,400,000 par value, mature in 20 years, and pay 9% interest semiannually on June 30 and December 31. The bonds are sold at par plus four months' accrued interest.

1. How much accrued interest do the bond purchasers pay Brussels on May 1, 2013?
2. Prepare Brussels' journal entries to record (a) the issuance of bonds on May 1, 2013; (b) the first interest payment on June 30, 2013; and (c) the second interest payment on December 31, 2013.

Exercise 10-13

Straight-Line: Amortization and accrued bond interest expense

P1   P2

Duval Co. issues four-year bonds with a $100,000 par value on June 1, 2013, at a price of $95,948. The annual contract rate is 7%, and interest is paid semiannually on November 30 and May 31.

1. Prepare an amortization table like the one in Exhibit 10.7 for these bonds. Use the straight-line method of interest amortization.
2. Prepare journal entries to record the first two interest payments and to accrue interest as of December 31, 2013.

Exercise 10-14

Installment note with equal total payments   **C1   P5**

Check   (1) $29,523

On January 1, 2013, Eagle borrows $100,000 cash by signing a four-year, 7% installment note. The note requires four equal total payments of accrued interest and principal on December 31 of each year from 2013 through 2016.

1. Compute the amount of each of the four equal total payments.
2. Prepare an amortization table for this installment note like the one in Exhibit 10.14.

Exercise 10-15

Installment note entries   **P5**

Use the information in Exercise 10-14 to prepare the journal entries for Eagle to record the loan on January 1, 2013, and the four payments from December 31, 2013, through December 31, 2016.

Exercise 10-16

Applying debt-to-equity ratio

A3

Montclair Company is considering a project that will require a $500,000 loan. It presently has total liabilities of $220,000, and total assets of $610,000.

1. Compute Montclair's (a) present debt-to-equity ratio and (b) the debt-to-equity ratio assuming it borrows $500,000 to fund the project.
2. Evaluate and discuss the level of risk involved if Montclair borrows the funds to pursue the project.

Exercise 10-17^D

Identifying capital and operating leases   **C4**

Indicate whether the company in each separate case 1 through 3 has entered into an operating lease or a capital lease.

1. The lessor retains title to the asset, and the lease term is three years on an asset that has a five-year useful life.

2. The title is transferred to the lessee, the lessee can purchase the asset for $1 at the end of the lease, and the lease term is five years. The leased asset has an expected useful life of six years.

3. The present value of the lease payments is 95% of the leased asset's market value, and the lease term is 70% of the leased asset's useful life.

Harbor (lessee) signs a five-year capital lease for office equipment with a $10,000 annual lease payment. The present value of the five annual lease payments is $41,000, based on a 7% interest rate.

1. Prepare the journal entry Harbor will record at inception of the lease.

2. If the leased asset has a five-year useful life with no salvage value, prepare the journal entry Harbor will record each year to recognize depreciation expense related to the leased asset.

Exercise 10-18[D]
Accounting for capital lease
C4

General Motors advertised three alternatives for a 25-month lease on a new Blazer: (1) zero dollars down and a lease payment of $1,750 per month for 25 months, (2) $5,000 down and $1,500 per month for 25 months, or (3) $38,500 down and no payments for 25 months. Use the present value Table B.3 in Appendix B to determine which is the best alternative (assume you have enough cash to accept any alternative and the annual interest rate is 12% compounded monthly).

Exercise 10-19[D]
Analyzing lease options
C2 C3 C4

Heineken N.V. reports the following information for its Loans and Borrowings as of December 31, 2010, including proceeds and repayments for the year ended December 31, 2010 (euros in millions).

Exercise 10-20
Accounting for long-term liabilities under IFRS

P1

Loans and borrowings (noncurrent liabilities)	
Loans and borrowings, December 31, 2010	€ 8,078
Proceeds (cash) from issuances of loans and borrowings	1,920
Repayments (in cash) of loans and borrowings	(3,127)

1. Prepare Heineken's journal entry to record its cash proceeds from issuances of its loans and borrowings for 2010. Assume that the par value of these issuances is €2,000.

2. Prepare Heineken's journal entry to record its cash repayments of its loans and borrowings for 2010. Assume that the par value of these issuances is €3,000, and the premium on them is €32.

3. Compute the discount or premium on its loans and borrowings as of December 31, 2010, assuming that the par value of these liabilities is €8,000.

4. Given the facts in part 3 and viewing the entirety of loans and borrowings as one issuance, was the contract rate on these loans and borrowings higher or lower than the market rate at the time of issuance? Explain. (Assume that Heineken's credit rating has remained the same.)

connect

Round dollar amounts to the nearest whole dollar. Assume no reversing entries are used.

PROBLEM SET A

Hartford Research issues bonds dated January 1, 2013, that pay interest semiannually on June 30 and December 31. The bonds have a $40,000 par value and an annual contract rate of 10%, and they mature in 10 years.

Problem 10-1A
Computing bond price and recording issuance

P1

Required

For each of the following three separate situations, (a) determine the bonds' issue price on January 1, 2013, and (b) prepare the journal entry to record their issuance.

1. The market rate at the date of issuance is 8%.

2. The market rate at the date of issuance is 10%.

3. The market rate at the date of issuance is 12%.

Check (1) Premium, $5,437

(3) Discount, $4,588

Hillside issues $4,000,000 of 6%, 15-year bonds dated January 1, 2013, that pay interest semiannually on June 30 and December 31. The bonds are issued at a price of $3,456,448.

Problem 10-2A
Straight-Line: Amortization of bond discount P1 P2

Required

1. Prepare the January 1, 2013, journal entry to record the bonds' issuance.

2. For each semiannual period, compute (a) the cash payment, (b) the straight-line discount amortization, and (c) the bond interest expense.

3. Determine the total bond interest expense to be recognized over the bonds' life.

4. Prepare the first two years of an amortization table like Exhibit 10.7 using the straight-line method.

5. Prepare the journal entries to record the first two interest payments.

Check (3) $4,143,552
(4) 12/31/2014 carrying value, $3,528,920

Problem 10-3A

Straight Line: Amortization of bond premium

P1 P3

Check   (3) $2,704,020
            (4) 12/31/2014 carrying
                value, $4,776,516

Refer to the bond details in Problem 10-2A, *except* assume that the bonds are issued at a price of $4,895,980.

Required

1. Prepare the January 1, 2013, journal entry to record the bonds' issuance.
2. For each semiannual period, compute (*a*) the cash payment, (*b*) the straight-line premium amortization, and (*c*) the bond interest expense.
3. Determine the total bond interest expense to be recognized over the bonds' life.
4. Prepare the first two years of an amortization table like Exhibit 10.11 using the straight-line method.
5. Prepare the journal entries to record the first two interest payments.

Problem 10-4A

Straight-Line: Amortization of bond premium

P1 P3

Check   (2) 6/30/2015 carrying
                value, $252,668

Ellis issues 6.5%, five-year bonds dated January 1, 2013, with a $250,000 par value. The bonds pay interest on June 30 and December 31 and are issued at a price of $255,333. The annual market rate is 6% on the issue date.

Required

1. Calculate the total bond interest expense over the bonds' life.
2. Prepare a straight-line amortization table like Exhibit 10.11 for the bonds' life.
3. Prepare the journal entries to record the first two interest payments.

Problem 10-5A[B]

Effective Interest: Amortization of bond premium; computing bond price P1 P7

Check   (2) 6/30/2015 carrying
                value, $252,865
            (4) $252,326

Refer to the bond details in Problem 10-4A.

Required

1. Compute the total bond interest expense over the bonds' life.
2. Prepare an effective interest amortization table like the one in Exhibit 10B.2 for the bonds' life.
3. Prepare the journal entries to record the first two interest payments.
4. Use the market rate at issuance to compute the present value of the remaining cash flows for these bonds as of December 31, 2015. Compare your answer with the amount shown on the amortization table as the balance for that date (from part 2) and explain your findings.

Problem 10-6A

Straight-Line: Amortization of bond

P1 P2 P3

Check   (2) $97,819
            (3) 12/31/2014 carrying
                value, $308,589

Legacy issues $325,000 of 5%, four-year bonds dated January 1, 2013, that pay interest semiannually on June 30 and December 31. They are issued at $292,181 and their market rate is 8% at the issue date.

Required

1. Prepare the January 1, 2013, journal entry to record the bonds' issuance.
2. Determine the total bond interest expense to be recognized over the bonds' life.
3. Prepare a straight-line amortization table like the one in Exhibit 10.7 for the bonds' first two years.
4. Prepare the journal entries to record the first two interest payments.

Analysis Component

5. Assume the market rate on January 1, 2013, is 4% instead of 8%. Without providing numbers, describe how this change affects the amounts reported on Legacy's financial statements.

Problem 10-7A[B]

Effective Interest: Amortization of bond discount P1 P6

Check   (2) $97,819
            (3) 12/31/2014 carrying
                value, $307,308

Refer to the bond details in Problem 10-6A.

Required

1. Prepare the January 1, 2013, journal entry to record the bonds' issuance.
2. Determine the total bond interest expense to be recognized over the bonds' life.
3. Prepare an effective interest amortization table like the one in Exhibit 10B.1 for the bonds' first two years.
4. Prepare the journal entries to record the first two interest payments.

Ike issues $180,000 of 11%, three-year bonds dated January 1, 2013, that pay interest semiannually on June 30 and December 31. They are issued at $184,566. Their market rate is 10% at the issue date.

Required

1. Prepare the January 1, 2013, journal entry to record the bonds' issuance.
2. Determine the total bond interest expense to be recognized over the bonds' life.
3. Prepare an effective interest amortization table like Exhibit 10B.2 for the bonds' first two years.
4. Prepare the journal entries to record the first two interest payments.
5. Prepare the journal entry to record the bonds' retirement on January 1, 2015, at 98.

Analysis Component

6. Assume that the market rate on January 1, 2013, is 12% instead of 10%. Without presenting numbers, describe how this change affects the amounts reported on Ike's financial statements.

Problem 10-8A[B]

Effective Interest: Amortization of bond; retiring bonds

P1 P4 P6 P7

Check   (3) 6/30/2014 carrying value, $182,448

(5) $5,270 gain

On November 1, 2013, Norwood borrows $200,000 cash from a bank by signing a five-year installment note bearing 8% interest. The note requires equal total payments each year on October 31.

Required

1. Compute the total amount of each installment payment.
2. Complete an amortization table for this installment note similar to the one in Exhibit 10.14.
3. Prepare the journal entries in which Norwood records (*a*) accrued interest as of December 31, 2013 (the end of its annual reporting period), and (*b*) the first annual payment on the note.

Problem 10-9A

Installment notes

C1 P5

Check   (2) 10/31/2017 ending balance, $46,382

At the end of the current year, the following information is available for both Pulaski Company and Scott Company.

	Pulaski Company	Scott Company
Total assets	$900,000	$450,000
Total liabilities	360,000	240,000
Total equity	540,000	210,000

Required

1. Compute the debt-to-equity ratios for both companies.
2. Comment on your results and discuss the riskiness of each company's financing structure.

Problem 10-10A

Applying the debt-to-equity ratio

A3

Rogers Company signs a five-year capital lease with Packer Company for office equipment. The annual year-end lease payment is $10,000 (due at the end of each year), and the interest rate is 8%.

Required

1. Compute the present value of Rogers' five-year lease payments.
2. Prepare the journal entry to record Rogers' capital lease at its inception.
3. Complete a lease payment schedule for the five years of the lease with the following headings. Assume that the beginning balance of the lease liability (present value of lease payments) is $39,927. (*Hint:* To find the amount allocated to interest in year 1, multiply the interest rate by the beginning-of-year lease liability. The amount of the annual lease payment not allocated to interest is allocated to principal. Reduce the lease liability by the amount allocated to principal to update the lease liability at each year-end.)

Problem 10-11A[D]

Capital lease accounting

C4

Check   (1) $39,927

(3) Year 3 ending balance, $17,833

Period Ending Date	Beginning Balance of Lease Liability	Interest on Lease Liability	Reduction of Lease Liability	Cash Lease Payment	Ending Balance of Lease Liability

4. Use straight-line depreciation and prepare the journal entry to depreciate the leased asset at the end of year 1. Assume zero salvage value and a five-year life for the office equipment.

PROBLEM SET B

| Round dollar amounts to the nearest whole dollar. Assume no reversing entries are used. |

Problem 10-1B
Computing bond price and recording issuance
P1

Flagstaff Systems issues bonds dated January 1, 2013, that pay interest semiannually on June 30 and December 31. The bonds have a $90,000 par value and an annual contract rate of 12%, and they mature in five years.

Required

For each of the following three separate situations, (*a*) determine the bonds' issue price on January 1, 2013, and (*b*) prepare the journal entry to record their issuance.

Check (1) Premium, $6,948

       (3) Discount, $6,326

1. The market rate at the date of issuance is 10%.
2. The market rate at the date of issuance is 12%.
3. The market rate at the date of issuance is 14%.

Problem 10-2B
Straight-Line: Amortization of bond discount
P1 P2

Romero issues $3,400,000 of 10%, 10-year bonds dated January 1, 2013, that pay interest semiannually on June 30 and December 31. The bonds are issued at a price of $3,010,000.

Required

1. Prepare the January 1, 2013, journal entry to record the bonds' issuance.
2. For each semiannual period, compute (*a*) the cash payment, (*b*) the straight-line discount amortization, and (*c*) the bond interest expense.

Check (3) $3,790,000

      (4) 6/30/2014 carrying
         value, $3,068,500

3. Determine the total bond interest expense to be recognized over the bonds' life.
4. Prepare the first two years of an amortization table like Exhibit 10.7 using the straight-line method.
5. Prepare the journal entries to record the first two interest payments.

Problem 10-3B
Straight-line: Amortization of bond premium
P1 P3

Refer to the bond details in Problem 10-2B, *except* assume that the bonds are issued at a price of $4,192,932.

Required

1. Prepare the January 1, 2013, journal entry to record the bonds' issuance.
2. For each semiannual period, compute (*a*) the cash payment, (*b*) the straight-line premium amortization, and (*c*) the bond interest expense.

Check (3) $2,607,068
      (4) 6/30/2014 carrying value,
         4,073,991

3. Determine the total bond interest expense to be recognized over the bonds' life.
4. Prepare the first two years of an amortization table like Exhibit 10.11 using the straight-line method.
5. Prepare the journal entries to record the first two interest payments.

Problem 10-4B
Straight-Line: Amortization of bond premium
P1 P3

Ripkin Company issues 9%, five-year bonds dated January 1, 2013, with a $320,000 par value. The bonds pay interest on June 30 and December 31 and are issued at a price of $332,988. Their annual market rate is 8% on the issue date.

Required

1. Calculate the total bond interest expense over the bonds' life.

Check (2) 6/30/2015 carrying
        value, $326,493

2. Prepare a straight-line amortization table like Exhibit 10.11 for the bonds' life.
3. Prepare the journal entries to record the first two interest payments.

Problem 10-5B[B]
Effective Interest: Amortization of bond premium; computing bond price P1 P7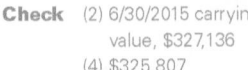

Refer to the bond details in Problem 10-4B.

Required

1. Compute the total bond interest expense over the bonds' life.
2. Prepare an effective interest amortization table like the one in Exhibit 10B.2 for the bonds' life.

Check (2) 6/30/2015 carrying
        value, $327,136
      (4) $325,807

3. Prepare the journal entries to record the first two interest payments.
4. Use the market rate at issuance to compute the present value of the remaining cash flows for these bonds as of December 31, 2015. Compare your answer with the amount shown on the amortization table as the balance for that date (from part 2) and explain your findings.

Gomez issues $240,000 of 6%, 15-year bonds dated January 1, 2013, that pay interest semiannually on June 30 and December 31. They are issued at $198,494, and their market rate is 8% at the issue date.

Required

1. Prepare the January 1, 2013, journal entry to record the bonds' issuance.
2. Determine the total bond interest expense to be recognized over the life of the bonds.
3. Prepare a straight-line amortization table like the one in Exhibit 10.7 for the bonds' first two years.
4. Prepare the journal entries to record the first two interest payments.

Problem 10-6B
Straight-Line: Amortization of bond discount
P1 P2

Check (2) $257,506
(3) 6/30/2014 carrying value, $202,646

Refer to the bond details in Problem 10-6B.

Required

1. Prepare the January 1, 2013, journal entry to record the bonds' issuance.
2. Determine the total bond interest expense to be recognized over the bonds' life.
3. Prepare an effective interest amortization table like the one in Exhibit 10B.1 for the bonds' first two years.
4. Prepare the journal entries to record the first two interest payments.

Problem 10-7B[B]
Effective Interest: Amortization of bond discount
P1 P6

Check (2) $257,506;
(3) 6/30/2014 carrying value, $200,803

Valdez issues $450,000 of 13%, four-year bonds dated January 1, 2013, that pay interest semiannually on June 30 and December 31. They are issued at $493,608, and their market rate is 10% at the issue date.

Required

1. Prepare the January 1, 2013, journal entry to record the bonds' issuance.
2. Determine the total bond interest expense to be recognized over the bonds' life.
3. Prepare an effective interest amortization table like the one in Exhibit 10B.2 for the bonds' first two years.
4. Prepare the journal entries to record the first two interest payments.
5. Prepare the journal entry to record the bonds' retirement on January 1, 2015, at 106.

Problem 10-8B[B]
Effective Interest: Amortization of bond; retiring bonds
P1 P4 P6 P7

Check (3) 6/30/2014 carrying value, $479,202

(5) $3,088 loss

Analysis Component

6. Assume that the market rate on January 1, 2013, is 14% instead of 10%. Without presenting numbers, describe how this change affects the amounts reported on Valdez's financial statements.

On October 1, 2013, Gordon Enterprises borrows $150,000 cash from a bank by signing a three-year install-ment note bearing 10% interest. The note requires equal total payments each year on September 30.

Required

1. Compute the total amount of each installment payment.
2. Complete an amortization table for this installment note similar to the one in Exhibit 10.14.
3. Prepare the journal entries to record (*a*) accrued interest as of December 31, 2013 (the end of its annual reporting period) and (*b*) the first annual payment on the note.

Problem 10-9B
Installment notes
C1 P5

Check (2) 9/30/2015 ending balance, $54,836

At the end of the current year, the following information is available for both Atlas Company and Bryan Company.

Problem 10-10B
Applying the debt-to-equity ratio
A3

	Atlas Company	Bryan Company
Total assets	$180,000	$750,000
Total liabilities	81,000	562,500
Total equity	99,000	187,500

Required

1. Compute the debt-to-equity ratios for both companies.
2. Comment on your results and discuss what they imply about the relative riskiness of these companies.

Problem 10-11B^D

Capital lease accounting

C4

Check   (1) $75,816

(3) Year 3 ending balance,
$34,712

Braun Company signs a five-year capital lease with Verdi Company for office equipment. The annual year-end lease payment is $20,000 (due at the end of each year), and the interest rate is 10%.

Required

1. Compute the present value of Braun's lease payments.
2. Prepare the journal entry to record Braun's capital lease at its inception.
3. Complete a lease payment schedule for the five years of the lease with the following headings. Assume that the beginning balance of the lease liability (present value of lease payments) is $75,816. (*Hint:* To find the amount allocated to interest in year 1, multiply the interest rate by the beginning-of-year lease liability. The amount of the annual lease payment not allocated to interest is allocated to principal. Reduce the lease liability by the amount allocated to principal to update the lease liability at each year-end.)

Period Ending Date	Beginning Balance of Lease Liability	Interest on Lease Liability	Reduction of Lease Liability	Cash Lease Payment	Ending Balance of Lease Liability

4. Use straight-line depreciation and prepare the journal entry to depreciate the leased asset at the end of year 1. Assume zero salvage value and a five-year life for the office equipment.

SERIAL PROBLEM

Success Systems

A1   A3

(This serial problem began in Chapter 1 and continues through most of the book. If previous chapter segments were not completed, the serial problem can begin at this point. It is helpful, but not necessary, to use the Working Papers that accompany the book.)

SP 10   Adria Lopez has consulted with her local banker and is considering financing an expansion of her business by obtaining a long-term bank loan. Selected account balances at March 31, 2014, for Success Systems follow.

Total assets	$129,909	Total liabilities	$875	Total equity	$129,034

Check   (1) $102,352

Required

1. The bank has offered a long-term secured note to Success Systems. The bank's loan procedures require that a client's debt-to-equity ratio not exceed 0.8. As of March 31, 2014, what is the maximum amount that Success Systems could borrow from this bank (rounded to nearest dollar)?
2. If Success Systems borrows the maximum amount allowed from the bank, what percentage of assets would be financed (*a*) by debt and (*b*) by equity?
3. What are some factors Adria Lopez should consider before borrowing the funds?

REPORTING IN ACTION

A1   A2

APPLE

BTN 10-1   Refer to Apple's financial statements in Appendix A to answer the following.

1. Identify the items, if any, that make up Apple's long-term debt as reported on its balance sheet at September 29, 2012.
2. Assume that Apple has $100 million in convertible debentures that carry a 4.25% contract rate of interest. How much annual cash interest must be paid on those convertible debentures?
3. Assume that the convertible bonds discussed in part 2 are convertible into 20,000 shares of Apple's stock. If the carrying value of these bonds is $100 million, what is the entry recorded by Apple upon conversion?

Fast Forward

4. Access Apple's financial statements for the years ending after September 29, 2012, from its Website (Apple.com) or the SEC's EDGAR database (www.sec.gov). Has it issued additional long-term debt since the year-end September 29, 2012? If yes, identify the amount(s).

BTN 10-2   Key figures for Apple and Google follow.

($ millions)	Apple		Google	
	Current Year	Prior Year	Current Year	Prior Year
Total assets	$176,064	$116,371	$93,798	$72,574
Total liabilities	57,854	39,756	22,083	14,429
Total equity	118,210	76,615	71,715	58,145

COMPARATIVE ANALYSIS

A3

APPLE
GOOGLE

Required

1. Compute the debt-to-equity ratios for Apple and Google for both the current year and the prior year.

2. Use the ratios you computed in part 1 to determine which company's financing structure is least risky. Assume an industry average of 0.44 for debt-to-equity.

BTN 10-3   Traverse County needs a new county government building that would cost $10 million. The politicians feel that voters will not approve a municipal bond issue to fund the building since it would increase taxes. They opt to have a state bank issue $10 million of tax-exempt securities to pay for the building construction. The county then will make yearly lease payments (of principal and interest) to repay the obligation. Unlike conventional municipal bonds, the lease payments are not binding obligations on the county and, therefore, require no voter approval.

ETHICS CHALLENGE

C4 A1

Required

1. Do you think the actions of the politicians and the bankers in this situation are ethical?

2. How do the tax-exempt securities used to pay for the building compare in risk to a conventional municipal bond issued by Traverse County?

BTN 10-4   Your business associate mentions that she is considering investing in corporate bonds currently selling at a premium. She says that since the bonds are selling at a premium, they are highly valued and her investment will yield more than the going rate of return for the risk involved. Reply with a memorandum to confirm or correct your associate's interpretation of premium bonds.

COMMUNICATING IN PRACTICE

P3

BTN 10-5   Access the March 22, 2012, filing of the 10-K report of Home Depot for the year ended January 31, 2012, from www.sec.gov (Ticker: HD). Refer to Home Depot's balance sheet, including its note 4 (on debt).

TAKING IT TO THE NET

A2

Required

1. Identify Home Depot's long-term liabilities and the amounts for those liabilities from Home Depot's balance sheet at January 31, 2012.

2. Review Home Depot's note 4. The note reports that as of January 31, 2012, it had $2.961 billion of "5.875% Senior Notes; due December 16, 2036; interest payable semiannually on June 16 and December 16." These notes have a face value of $3.0 billion and were originally issued at $2.958 billion.

  a. Why would Home Depot issue $3.0 billion of its notes for only $2.958 billion?

  b. How much cash interest must Home Depot pay each June 16 and December 16 on these notes?

TEAMWORK IN ACTION

P2 P3

BTN 10-6[B]   Break into teams and complete the following requirements related to *effective interest* amortization for a premium bond.

1. Each team member is to independently prepare a blank table with proper headings for amortization of a bond premium. When all have finished, compare tables and ensure that all are in agreement.

Parts 2 and 3 require use of these facts: On January 1, 2013, McElroy issues $100,000, 9%, five-year bonds at 104.1. The market rate at issuance is 8%. McElroy pays interest semiannually on June 30 and December 31.

2. In rotation, *each* team member must explain how to complete *one* line of the bond amortization table, including all computations for his or her line. (Round amounts to the nearest dollar.) All members are to fill in their tables during this process. You need not finish the table; stop after all members have explained a line.

3. In rotation, *each* team member is to identify a separate column of the table and indicate what the final number in that column will be and explain the reasoning.

4. Reach a team consensus as to what the total bond interest expense on this bond issue will be if the bond is not retired before maturity.

5. As a team, prepare a list of similarities and differences between the amortization table just prepared and the amortization table if the bond had been issued at a discount.

Hint: Rotate teams to report on parts 4 and 5. Consider requiring entries for issuance and interest payments.

ENTREPRENEURIAL DECISION

A1

BTN 10-7   Mark Pincus is the founder of Zynga. Assume that his company currently has $250,000 in equity, and he is considering a $100,000 expansion to meet increased demand. The $100,000 expansion would yield $16,000 in additional annual income before interest expense. Assume that the business currently earns $40,000 annual income before interest expense of $10,000, yielding a return on equity of 12% ($30,000/$250,000). To fund the expansion, he is considering the issuance of a 10-year, $100,000 note with annual interest payments (the principal due at the end of 10 years).

Required

1. Using return on equity as the decision criterion, show computations to support or reject the expansion if interest on the $100,000 note is (*a*) 10%, (*b*) 15%, (*c*) 16%, (*d*) 17%, and (*e*) 20%.

2. What general rule do the results in part 1 illustrate?

HITTING THE ROAD

A1

BTN 10-8   Visit your city or county library. Ask the librarian to help you locate the recent financial records of your city or county government. Examine those records.

Required

1. Determine the amount of long-term bonds and notes currently outstanding.

2. Read the supporting information to your municipality's financial statements and record
   a. The market interest rate(s) when the bonds and/or notes were issued.
   b. The date(s) when the bonds and/or notes will mature.
   c. Any rating(s) on the bonds and/or notes received from Moody's, Standard & Poor's, or another rating agency.

GLOBAL DECISION

A3

Samsung
APPLE
GOOGLE

BTN 10-9   Samsung (www.Samsung.com), Apple, and Google are competitors in the global marketplace. Selected results from these companies follow.

Key Figures	Samsung (₩ millions) Current Year	Samsung (₩ millions) Prior Year	Apple ($ millions) Current Year	Apple ($ millions) Prior Year	Google ($ millions) Current Year	Google ($ millions) Prior Year
Total assets	₩181,071,570	₩155,800,263	$176,064	$116,371	$93,798	$72,574
Total liabilities	59,591,364	54,486,633	57,854	39,756	22,083	14,429
Total equity	121,480,206	101,313,630	118,210	76,615	71,715	58,145
Debt-to-equity ratio	?	?	0.49	0.52	0.31	0.25

Required

1. Compute Samsung's debt-to-equity ratio for the current year and the prior year.

2. Use the data provided and the ratios computed in part 1 to determine which company's financing structure is least risky.

ANSWERS TO MULTIPLE CHOICE QUIZ

1. b

2. a

3. c; $500,000 × 0.08 × ½ year = $20,000

4. a; Cash interest paid = $100,000 × 5% × ½ year = $2,500
Discount amortization = ($100,000 − $95,735)/10 periods = $426.50
Interest expense = $2,500.00 + $426.50 = $2,926.50

5. e; ($373,745 − $350,000)/16 periods = $1,484

11

Reporting and Analyzing Equity

COMMON STOCK	DIVIDENDS	PREFERRED STOCK	TREASURY STOCK	REPORTING AND ANALYSIS
C1 Stock basics	P2 Cash dividends	C2 Issuance	P3 Purchasing treasury stock	C3 Statements of retained earnings and equity
P1 Issuance at:	Stock dividends	Dividend preferences	Reissuing treasury stock	
Par value	Stock splits	Convertible and callable	Retiring stock	A1 EPS
No-par value		Rationale		A2 PE ratio
Stated value				A3 Dividend yield
Noncash assets				A4 Book value

Learning Objectives

C1 Identify characteristics of corporations and their organization. (p. 480)

P1 Record the issuance of corporate stock. (p. 484)

P2 Record transactions involving cash dividends, stock dividends, and stock splits. (p. 487)

C2 Explain characteristics of, and distribute dividends between, common and preferred stock. (p. 491)

P3 Record purchases and sales of treasury stock and the retirement of stock. (p. 495)

C3 Explain the items reported in retained earnings. (p. 498)

A1 Compute earnings per share and describe its use. (p. 500)

A2 Compute price-earnings ratio and describe its use in analysis. (p. 501)

A3 Compute dividend yield and explain its use in analysis. (p. 501)

A4 Compute book value and explain its use in analysis. (p. 501)

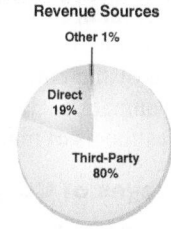

Groupon Clipper

"Make the product awesome for consumers"
—ANDREW MASON

CHICAGO—"I've never been driven to create a huge company and make a lot of money or run my own business," insists Andrew Mason. "I've always just been motivated to be working on interesting things." What interested Andrew was the launch of a Website called **Groupon** (**Groupon.com**). "A Groupon is, essentially, a voucher that's worth money that you can take into a business and use like cash," explains Andrew. "It's a great way to explore your city and find out about really cool, local things to do."

Andrew explains that his success would not have been possible without equity financing and knowledge of business operations. To make it happen, says Andrew, he studied corporate formation, equity issuance, stock types, retaining earnings, and dividend policies. After that analysis, Andrew set up Groupon as a corporation, which had several benefits given his business goals and strategies.

With his corporate structure in place, Andrew was ready to attack the market. Revenues skyrocketed as shown here:

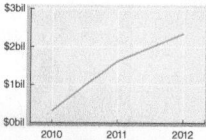

Groupon
(NASDAQ:GRPN)

11,000 employees
41 mil. customers
$2.3 bil. revenue

Revenue Sources

- Other 1%
- Direct 19%
- Third-Party 80%

"We found a way to make e-commerce work for local businesses online," asserts Andrew. "We found a way to deliver effective marketing results for brick and mortar businesses."

The success of Andrew's corporate structure and his equity financing brings both opportunities and challenges. The positive is being part of empowering consumers. "We get crazy emails that feel like they're written by a PR company . . . from our customers about how their marriage was at its end and then Groupon came along and they started going out more," says Andrew. "Now they're happier than ever. We're affecting people's lives in real ways."

The challenge for Andrew is effectively using accounting as a tool to achieve his objectives. That includes his goal to learn more about reporting and analyzing equity transactions. This is important as the SEC has raised questions about Groupon's accounting, including its revenue and expense recognition. Admits Andrew, "There are things we would've done differently and we would've loved to avoid."

While Andrew must improve his accounting, he presently owns over 45 million shares, or 6.9 percent, of Class A common stock, and nearly 1 million shares, or 41.7 percent, of Class B common stock. This equates to a net worth in the hundreds of millions of dollars.

Interestingly, Google is reported to have made a $6 billion offer to acquire Groupon, which was rejected. As it turns out, Groupon had one of the largest initial public stock offerings of any Internet company since Google. Groupon's value skyrocketed to $18 billion on the first day of trading. "It caught me by surprise," says Andrew. "It was just this rocket ship ride that you couldn't let go. And, you didn't want to let go!"

Sources: *Groupon Website and 10-K,* January 2014; *Mixergy.com,* July 2010; *The Wall Street Journal,* December 2010; *Time,* February 2011; *CBS News, 60 Minutes,* January 2012; *Forbes,* March 2013

CORPORATE FORM OF ORGANIZATION

 C1 Identify characteristics of corporations and their organization.

A **corporation** is an entity created by law that is separate from its owners. It has most of the rights and privileges granted to individuals. Owners of corporations are called *stockholders* or *shareholders*. Corporations can be separated into two types. A *privately held* (or *closely held*) corporation does not offer its stock for public sale and usually has few stockholders. A *publicly held* corporation offers its stock for public sale and can have thousands of stockholders. *Public sale* usually refers to issuance and trading on an organized stock market.

Characteristics of Corporations

Corporations represent an important type of organization. Their unique characteristics offer advantages and disadvantages.

Advantages of Corporate Form

- **Separate legal entity:** A corporation conducts its affairs with the same rights, duties, and responsibilities of a person. It takes actions through its agents, who are its officers and managers.
- **Limited liability of stockholders:** Stockholders are liable for neither corporate acts nor corporate debt.
- **Transferable ownership rights:** The transfer of shares from one stockholder to another usually has no effect on the corporation or its operations except when this causes a change in the directors who control or manage the corporation.
- **Continuous life:** A corporation's life continues indefinitely because it is not tied to the physical lives of its owners.
- **Lack of mutual agency for stockholders:** A corporation acts through its agents, who are its officers and managers. Stockholders, who are not its officers and managers, do not have the power to bind the corporation to contracts—referred to as *lack of mutual agency*.
- **Ease of capital accumulation:** Buying stock is attractive to investors because (1) stockholders are not liable for the corporation's acts and debts, (2) stocks usually are transferred easily, (3) the life of the corporation is unlimited, and (4) stockholders are not corporate agents. These advantages enable corporations to accumulate large amounts of capital from the combined investments of many stockholders.

Disadvantages of Corporate Form

- **Government regulation:** A corporation must meet requirements of a state's incorporation laws, which subject the corporation to state regulation and control. Proprietorships and partnerships avoid many of these regulations and governmental reports.
- **Corporate taxation:** Corporations are subject to the same property and payroll taxes as proprietorships and partnerships plus *additional* taxes. The most burdensome of these are federal and state income taxes that together can take 40% or more of corporate pretax income. Moreover, corporate income is usually taxed a second time as part of stockholders' personal income when they receive cash distributed as dividends. This is called *double taxation*. (Dividends are normally taxed at the individual's income tax rate; for "qualified" dividends, the tax rate is 0%, 15%, or 20%, depending on the individual's tax bracket.)

Point: The *business entity assumption* requires a corporation to be accounted for separately from its owners (shareholders).

Global: U.S., U.K., and Canadian corporations finance much of their operations with stock issuances, but companies in countries such as France, Germany, and Japan finance mainly with note and bond issuances.

Point: Proprietorships and partnerships are not subject to income taxes. Their income is taxed as the personal income of their owners.

Point: Double taxation is less severe when a corporation's owner-manager collects a salary that is taxed only once as part of his or her personal income.

Decision Insight

Stock Financing   Mark Zuckerberg took his company, Facebook, public by issuing its first shares on the Nasdaq exchange in 2012. This initial public offering (IPO) of Facebook shares raised billions in equity financing. It also raised the importance of accounting reports versus market hype. The IPO of Facebook shares comes 8 years after the company was founded by Zuckerberg in his college dorm room. ■

Corporate Organization and Management

This section describes the incorporation, costs, and management of corporate organizations.

Incorporation A corporation is created by obtaining a charter from a state government. A charter application usually must be signed by the prospective stockholders called *incorporators* or *promoters* and then filed with the proper state official. When the application process is complete and fees paid, the charter is issued and the corporation is formed. Investors then purchase the corporation's stock, meet as stockholders, and elect a board of directors. Directors oversee a corporation's affairs.

Point: A corporation is not required to have an office in its state of incorporation. Delaware is viewed as having favorable corporate laws and about half of all corporations listed on the NYSE are incorporated there.

Organization Expenses Organization expenses (also called *organization costs*) are the costs to organize a corporation; they include legal fees, promoters' fees, and amounts paid to obtain a charter. The corporation records (debits) these costs to an expense account called *Organization Expenses*. Organization costs are expensed as incurred because it is difficult to determine the amount and timing of their future benefits.

Management of a Corporation The ultimate control of a corporation rests with stockholders who control a corporation by electing its *board of directors,* or simply, *directors.* Each stockholder usually has one vote for each share of stock owned. This control relation is shown in Exhibit 11.1. Directors are responsible for and have final authority for managing corporate activities. A board can act only as a collective body and usually limits its actions to setting general policy.

A corporation usually holds a stockholder meeting at least once a year to elect directors and transact business as its bylaws require. A group of stockholders owning or controlling votes of more than a 50% share of a corporation's stock can elect the board and control the corporation. Stockholders who do not attend stockholders' meetings must have an opportunity to delegate their voting rights to an agent by signing a **proxy,** a document that gives a designated agent the right to vote the stock.

Day-to-day direction of corporate business is delegated to executive officers appointed by the board. A corporation's chief executive officer (CEO) is often its president. Several vice presidents, who report to the president, are commonly assigned specific areas of management responsibility such as finance, production, and marketing. One person often has the dual role of chairperson of the board of directors and CEO. In this case, the president is usually designated the chief operating officer (COO).

EXHIBIT 11.1

Corporate Structure

Stockholders

Board of Directors

President, Vice President, and Other Officers

Employees of the Corporation

Corporate governance is the system by which companies are directed and controlled.

Point: *Bylaws* are guidelines that govern the behavior of individuals employed by and managing the corporation.

▣ **Decision** Insight

Seed Money Sources for start-up money include (1) "angel" investors such as family, friends, or anyone who believes in a company, (2) employees, investors, and even suppliers who can be paid with stock, and (3) venture capitalists (investors) who have a record of entrepreneurial success. See the National Venture Capital Association (**NVCA.org**) for information. ■

Global: Some corporate labels are:

Country	Label
United States	Inc.
France	SA
United Kingdom	
Public	PLC
Private	Ltd
Germany & Austria	
Public	AG
Private	GmbH
Sweden & Finland	AB
Italy	SpA
Netherlands	NV
Australia	AG
Mexico	SA
Bahamas	IBC

Stockholders of Corporations

This section explains stockholder rights, stock purchases and sales, and the role of registrar and transfer agents.

Rights of Stockholders When investors buy stock, they acquire all *specific* rights the corporation's charter grants to stockholders. They also acquire *general* rights granted stockholders by the laws of the state in which the company is incorporated. When a corporation has only one class of stock, it is identified as **common stock.** State laws vary, but common stockholders usually have the general right to

1. Vote at stockholders' meetings (or register proxy votes electronically).
2. Sell or otherwise dispose of their stock.
3. Purchase their proportional share of any common stock later issued by the corporation. This **preemptive right** protects stockholders' proportionate interest in the corporation. For example, a stockholder who owns 25% of a corporation's common stock has the first opportunity to buy 25% of any new common stock issued.
4. Receive the same dividend, if any, on each common share of the corporation.
5. Share in any assets remaining after creditors and preferred stockholders are paid when, and if, the corporation is liquidated. Each common share receives the same amount.

Stockholders also have the right to receive timely financial reports.

Stock Certificates and Transfer   Investors who buy a corporation's stock, sometimes receive a *stock certificate* as proof of share ownership. Many corporations issue only one

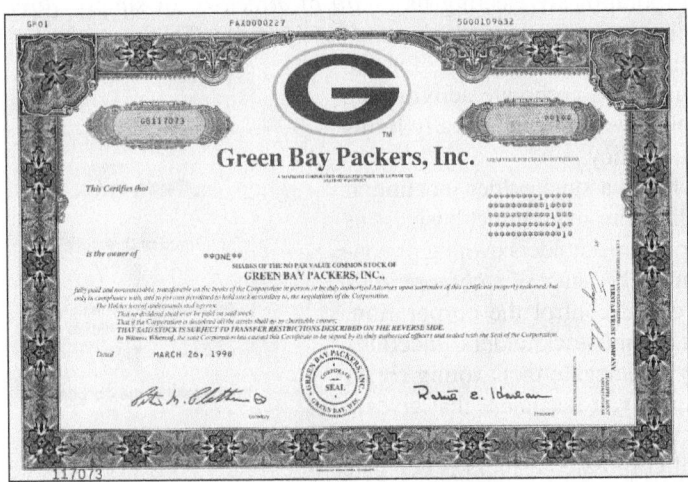

EXHIBIT 11.2

Stock Certificate

Point: The Green Bay Packers is the only nonprofit, community-owned major league professional sports team. The NFL now prohibits any other teams from becoming community-owned.

certificate for each block of stock purchased. A certificate can be for any number of shares. Exhibit 11.2 shows a stock certificate of the Green Bay Packers. A certificate shows the company name, stockholder name, number of shares, and other crucial information. Issuance of certificates is becoming less common. Instead, many stockholders maintain accounts with the corporation or their stockbrokers and never receive actual certificates.

Registrar and Transfer Agents   If a corporation's stock is traded on a major stock exchange, the corporation must have a registrar and a transfer agent. A *registrar* keeps stockholder records and prepares official lists of stockholders for stockholder meetings and dividend payments. A *transfer agent* assists with purchases and sales of shares by receiving and issuing certificates as necessary. Registrars and transfer agents are usually large banks or trust companies with computer facilities and staff to do this work.

Decision Insight

Pricing Stock   A prospectus accompanies a stock's initial public offering (IPO), giving financial information about the company issuing the stock. A prospectus should help answer these questions to price an IPO: (1) Is the underwriter reliable? (2) Is there growth in revenues, profits, and cash flows? (3) What is management's view of operations? (4) Are current owners selling? (5) What are the risks? ■

Basics of Capital Stock

Capital stock is a general term that refers to any shares issued to obtain capital (owner financing). This section introduces terminology and accounting for capital stock.

Authorized Stock   Authorized stock is the number of shares that a corporation's charter allows it to sell. The number of authorized shares usually exceeds the number of shares issued (and outstanding), often by a large amount. (*Outstanding stock* refers to issued stock held by stockholders.) No formal journal entry is required for stock authorization. A corporation must apply to the state for a change in its charter if it wishes to issue more shares than previously authorized. A corporation discloses the number of shares authorized in the equity section of its balance sheet or notes. Apple's balance sheet reports 1.8 billion common shares authorized as of the start of its 2012 fiscal year.

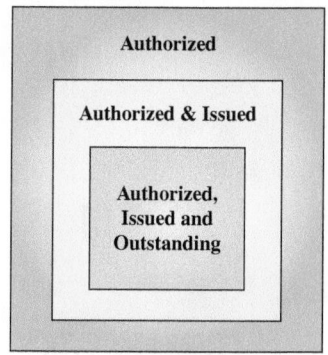

The inner-most box shows that shares issued decline if a company buys back its stock previously issued.

Selling (Issuing) Stock   A corporation can sell stock directly or indirectly. To *sell directly,* it advertises its stock issuance to potential buyers. This type of issuance is most common with privately held corporations. To *sell indirectly,* a corporation pays a brokerage house (investment banker) to issue its stock. Some brokerage houses *underwrite* an indirect issuance of stock; that is, they buy the stock from the corporation and take all gains or losses from its resale.

Market Value of Stock   **Market value per share** is the price at which a stock is bought and sold. Expected future earnings, dividends, growth, and other company and economic factors influence market value. Traded stocks' market values are available daily in newspapers such as *The Wall Street Journal* and online. The current market value of previously issued shares (for example, the price of stock in trades between investors) does not impact the issuing corporation's stockholders' equity.

Classes of Stock   When all authorized shares have the same rights and characteristics, the stock is called *common stock*. A corporation is sometimes authorized to issue more than one class of stock, including preferred stock and different classes of common stock. American Greetings, for instance, has two types of common stock: Class A stock has 1 vote per share and Class B stock has 10 votes per share.

Par Value Stock   **Par value stock** is stock that is assigned a **par value,** which is an amount assigned per share by the corporation in its charter. For example, Monster Worldwide, Inc.'s common stock has a par value of $0.001. Other commonly assigned par values are $10, $5, $1 and $0.01. There is no restriction on the assigned par value. In many states, the par value of a stock establishes **minimum legal capital,** which refers to the least amount that the buyers of stock must contribute to the corporation or be subject to paying at a future date. For example, if a corporation issues 1,000 shares of $10 par value stock, the corporation's minimum legal capital in these states would be $10,000. Minimum legal capital is intended to protect a corporation's creditors. Since creditors cannot demand payment from stockholders' personal assets, their claims are limited to the corporation's assets and any minimum legal capital. At liquidation, creditor claims are paid before any amounts are distributed to stockholders.

Point: Managers are motivated to set a low par value when minimum legal capital or state issuance taxes are based on par value.

Point: Minimum legal capital was intended to protect creditors by requiring a minimum level of net assets.

No-Par Value Stock   **No-par value stock,** or simply *no-par stock,* is stock *not* assigned a value per share by the corporate charter. Its advantage is that it can be issued at any price without the possibility of a minimum legal capital deficiency.

Point: Par, no-par, and stated value do *not* set the stock's market value.

Stated Value Stock   **Stated value stock** is no-par stock to which the directors assign a "stated" value per share. Stated value per share becomes the minimum legal capital per share in this case.

Stockholders' Equity   A corporation's equity is known as **stockholders' equity,** also called *shareholders' equity* or *corporate capital*. Stockholders' equity consists of (1) paid-in (or contributed) capital and (2) retained earnings; see Exhibit 11.3. **Paid-in capital** is the total amount of cash and other assets the corporation receives from its stockholders in exchange for its stock. **Retained earnings** is the cumulative net income (and loss) not distributed as dividends to its stockholders.

Corporation

Common Stock
Normal bal.

Paid-In Capital in Excess of Par
Normal bal.

Total Paid-In Capital

Retained Earnings
Normal bal.

EXHIBIT 11.3

Equity Composition

Point: Paid-in capital comes from stock-related transactions, whereas retained earnings comes from operations; if retained earnings has a debit balance, it is often titled Accumulated Deficit.

Decision Insight

Stock Quote The **Target** stock quote is interpreted as (left to right): **Hi**, highest price in past 52 weeks; **Lo**, lowest price in past 52 weeks;

52 Weeks				Yld		Vol				Net
Hi	Lo	Sym	Div	%	PE	mil.	Hi	Lo	Close	Chg
58.95	45.28	TGT	1.20	2.07	13.5	668	58.06	57.40	57.63	−0.30

Sym, company exchange symbol; **Div**, dividends paid per share in past year; **Yld %**, dividend divided by closing price; **PE**, stock price per share divided by earnings per share; **Vol mil.**, number (in millions) of shares traded; **Hi**, highest price for the day; **Lo**, lowest price for the day; **Close**, closing price for the day; **Net Chg**, change in closing price from prior day. ■

QC1

COMMON STOCK

P1 Record the issuance of corporate stock.

Accounting for the issuance of common stock affects only paid-in (contributed) capital accounts; no retained earnings accounts are affected.

Issuing Par Value Stock

Par value stock can be issued at par, at a premium (above par), or at a discount (below par). In each case, stock can be exchanged for either cash or noncash assets.

Issuing Par Value Stock at Par When common stock is issued at par value, we record amounts for both the asset(s) received and the par value stock issued. To illustrate, the entry to record Dillon Snowboards' issuance of 30,000 shares of $10 par value stock for $300,000 cash on June 5, 2013, follows:

Assets = Liabilities + Equity
+300,000   +300,000

$10 par value × 30,000 shares

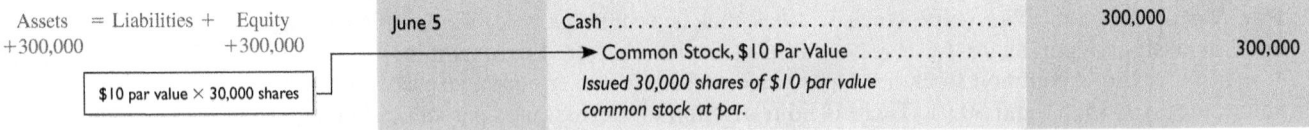

June 5	Cash	300,000	
	Common Stock, $10 Par Value		300,000
	Issued 30,000 shares of $10 par value		
	common stock at par.		

Exhibit 11.4 shows the stockholders' equity of Dillon Snowboards at year-end 2013 (its first year of operations) after income of $65,000 and no dividend payments.

EXHIBIT 11.4

Stockholders' Equity for Stock Issued at Par

Stockholders' Equity	
Common Stock—$10 par value; 50,000 shares authorized; 30,000 shares issued and outstanding	$300,000
Retained earnings	65,000
Total stockholders' equity	$365,000

Issuing Par Value Stock at a Premium A **premium on stock** occurs when a corporation sells its stock for more than par (or stated) value. To illustrate, if Dillon Snowboards issues its $10 par value common stock at $12 per share, its stock is sold at a $2 per share premium. The premium, known as **paid-in capital in excess of par value,** is reported as part of equity; it is not revenue and is not listed on the income statement. The entry to record Dillon Snowboards' issuance of 30,000 shares of $10 par value stock for $12 per share on June 5, 2013, follows:

Point: A *premium* is the amount by which issue price exceeds par (or stated) value. It is recorded in the "Paid-In Capital in Excess of Par Value, Common Stock" account; also called "Additional Paid-In Capital, Common Stock."

Assets = Liabilities + Equity
+360,000   +300,000
                             +60,000

$10 par value × 30,000 shares

[$12 issue price − $10 par value] × 30,000 shares

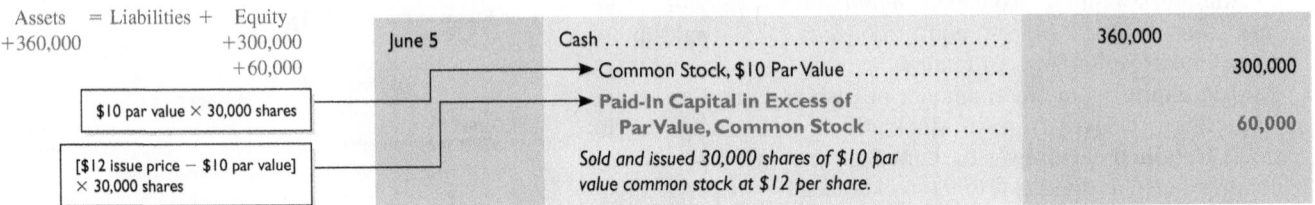

June 5	Cash	360,000	
	Common Stock, $10 Par Value		300,000
	Paid-In Capital in Excess of Par Value, Common Stock		60,000
	Sold and issued 30,000 shares of $10 par		
	value common stock at $12 per share.		

The Paid-In Capital in Excess of Par Value account is added to the par value of the stock in the equity section of the balance sheet as shown in Exhibit 11.5.

Point: The *Paid-In Capital* terminology is interchangeable with *Contributed Capital.*

Stockholders' Equity	
Common Stock—$10 par value; 50,000 shares authorized;	
30,000 shares issued and outstanding	$300,000
Paid-in capital in excess of par value, common stock	60,000
Retained earnings	65,000
Total stockholders' equity	$425,000

EXHIBIT 11.5

Stockholders' Equity for Stock Issued at a Premium

Issuing Par Value Stock at a Discount

Issuing Par Value Stock at a Discount   A **discount on stock** occurs when a corporation sells its stock for less than par (or stated) value. Most states prohibit the issuance of stock at a discount. In states that allow stock to be issued at a discount, its buyers usually become contingently liable to creditors for the discount. If stock is issued at a discount, the amount by which issue price is less than par is debited to a *Discount on Common Stock* account, a contra to the common stock account, and its balance is subtracted from the par value of stock in the equity section of the balance sheet. This discount is not an expense and does not appear on the income statement.

Point: Retained earnings can be negative, reflecting accumulated losses. **Pandora Media** had an accumulated deficit of $101 million at the start of 2012.

Issuing No-Par Value Stock

When no-par stock is issued and is not assigned a stated value, the amount the corporation receives becomes legal capital and is recorded as Common Stock. This means that the entire proceeds are credited to a no-par stock account. To illustrate, a corporation records its October 20 issuance of 1,000 shares of no-par stock for $40 cash per share as follows:

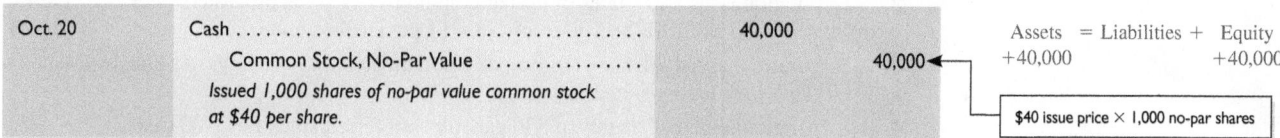

Oct. 20	Cash	40,000	
	Common Stock, No-Par Value		40,000
	Issued 1,000 shares of no-par value common stock at $40 per share.		

Assets = Liabilities + Equity
+40,000   +40,000

$40 issue price × 1,000 no-par shares

Issuing Stated Value Stock

When no-par stock is issued and assigned a stated value, its stated value becomes legal capital and is credited to a stated value stock account. Assuming that stated value stock is issued at an amount in excess of stated value (the usual case), the excess is credited to Paid-In Capital in Excess of Stated Value, Common Stock, which is reported in the stockholders' equity section. To illustrate, a corporation that issues 1,000 shares of no-par common stock having a stated value of $40 per share in return for $50 cash per share records this as follows:

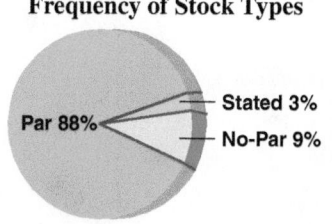

Frequency of Stock Types

Par 88%   Stated 3%   No-Par 9%

Oct. 20	Cash	50,000	
	Common Stock, $40 Stated Value		40,000
	Paid-In Capital in Excess of Stated Value, Common Stock		10,000
	Issued 1,000 shares of $40 per share stated value stock at $50 per share.		

Assets = Liabilities + Equity
+50,000   +40,000
                           +10,000

$40 stated value × 1,000 shares

[$50 issue price − $40 stated value] × 1,000 shares

Issuing Stock for Noncash Assets

A corporation can receive assets other than cash in exchange for its stock. (It can also assume liabilities on the assets received such as a mortgage on property received.) The corporation records the assets received at their market values as of the date of the transaction. The stock given in exchange is recorded at its par (or stated) value with any excess recorded in the Paid-In Capital in Excess of Par (or Stated) Value account. (If no-par stock is issued, the stock is recorded at the assets' market value.) To illustrate, the entry to record receipt of land

Point: Stock issued for noncash assets should be recorded at the market value of either the stock or the noncash asset, whichever is more clearly determinable.

valued at $105,000 in return for issuance of 4,000 shares of $20 par value common stock on June 10 is

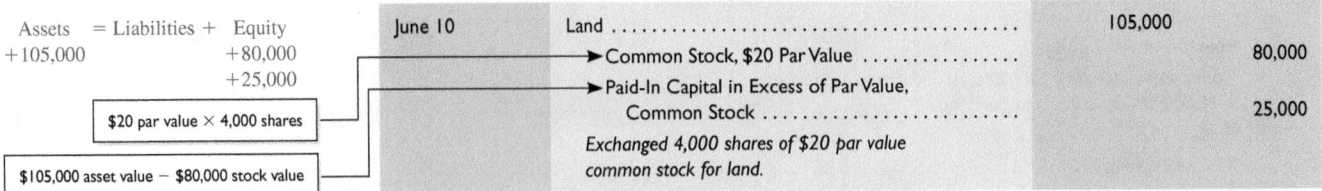

Assets	= Liabilities +	Equity
+105,000		+80,000
		+25,000

$20 par value × 4,000 shares

$105,000 asset value − $80,000 stock value

June 10	Land	105,000	
	➤Common Stock, $20 Par Value		80,000
	➤Paid-In Capital in Excess of Par Value, Common Stock		25,000
	Exchanged 4,000 shares of $20 par value common stock for land.		

Point: Any type of stock can be issued for noncash assets.

A corporation sometimes gives shares of its stock to promoters in exchange for their services in organizing the corporation, which the corporation records as Organization Expenses. The entry to record receipt of services valued at $12,000 in organizing the corporation in return for 600 shares of $15 par value common stock on June 5 is

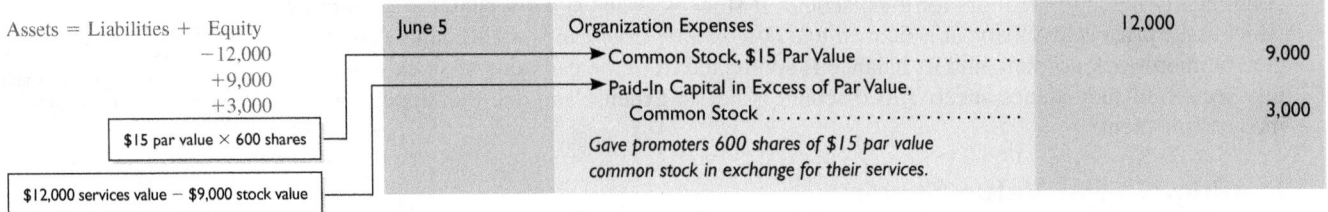

Assets	= Liabilities +	Equity
		−12,000
		+9,000
		+3,000

$15 par value × 600 shares

$12,000 services value − $9,000 stock value

June 5	Organization Expenses	12,000	
	➤Common Stock, $15 Par Value		9,000
	➤Paid-In Capital in Excess of Par Value, Common Stock		3,000
	Gave promoters 600 shares of $15 par value common stock in exchange for their services.		

NEED-TO-KNOW 11.1

P1

Prepare journal entries to record the following four separate (independent) issuances of stock.
1. A corporation issued 80 shares of $5 par value common stock for $700 cash.
2. A corporation issued 40 shares of no-par common stock to its promoters in exchange for their efforts, estimated to be worth $800. The stock has a $1 per share stated value.
3. A corporation issued 40 shares of no-par common stock in exchange for land, estimated to be worth $800. The stock has no stated value.
4. A corporation issued 20 shares of $30 par value preferred stock for $900 cash.

Solution

1.

Cash	700	
Common Stock, $5 Par Value*		400
Paid-In Capital in Excess of Par Value, Common Stock**		300
Issued common stock for cash.		

*80 shares × $5 per share = $400   **$700 − $400 = $300

2.

Organization Expenses.........................	800	
Common Stock, $1 Stated Value		40
Paid-In Capital in Excess of Stated Value, Common Stock		760
Issued stock to promoters.		

3.

Land	800	
Common Stock, No-Par Value		800
Issued stock in exchange for land.		

Do More: QS 11-2, QS 11-3, QS 11-4, QS 11-5, E 11-2, E 11-3, E 11-4

QC2

4.

Cash	900	
Preferred Stock, $30 Par Value*		600
Paid-In Capital in Excess of Par Value, Preferred Stock**		300
Issued preferred stock for cash.		

*20 shares × $30 per share = $600   **$900 − $600 = $300

DIVIDENDS

This section describes both cash and stock dividend transactions.

Cash Dividends

The decision to pay cash dividends rests with the board of directors and involves more than evaluating the amounts of retained earnings and cash. The directors, for instance, may decide to keep the cash to invest in the corporation's growth, to meet emergencies, to take advantage of unexpected opportunities, or to pay off debt. Alternatively, many corporations pay cash dividends to their stockholders at regular dates. These cash flows provide a return to investors and almost always affect the stock's market value.

> **P2** Record transactions involving cash dividends, stock dividends, and stock splits.

Accounting for Cash Dividends   Dividend payment involves three important dates: declaration, record, and payment. **Date of declaration** is the date the directors vote to declare and pay a dividend. This creates a legal liability of the corporation to its stockholders. **Date of record** is the future date specified by the directors for identifying those stockholders listed in the corporation's records to receive dividends. The date of record usually follows the date of declaration by at least two weeks. Persons who own stock on the date of record receive dividends. **Date of payment** is the date when the corporation makes payment; it follows the date of record by enough time to allow the corporation to arrange checks, money transfers, or other means to pay dividends.

Percent of Corporations Paying Dividends

Cash Dividend to Common	75%
Cash Dividend to Preferred	22%

0%   20%   40%   60%   80%   100%

To illustrate, the entry to record a January 9 declaration of a $1 per share cash dividend by the directors of Z-Tech, Inc., with 5,000 outstanding shares is

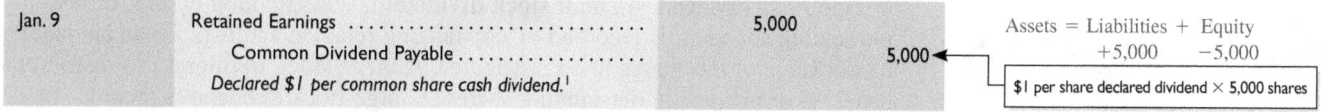

Date of Declaration

Jan. 9	Retained Earnings	5,000	
	Common Dividend Payable..................		5,000
	Declared $1 per common share cash dividend.[1]		

Assets = Liabilities + Equity
          +5,000   −5,000

$1 per share declared dividend × 5,000 shares

Common Dividend Payable is a current liability. The date of record for the Z-Tech dividend is January 22. *No formal journal entry is needed on the date of record.* The February 1 date of payment requires an entry to record both the settlement of the liability and the reduction of the cash balance, as follows:

Date of Payment

Feb. 1	Common Dividend Payable......................	5,000	
	Cash		5,000
	Paid $1 per common share cash dividend.		

Assets = Liabilities + Equity
−5,000   −5,000

Deficits and Cash Dividends   A corporation with a debit (abnormal) balance for retained earnings is said to have a **retained earnings deficit,** which arises when a company incurs cumulative losses and/or pays more dividends than total earnings from current and prior years. A deficit is reported as a deduction on the balance sheet, as shown in Exhibit 11.6. Most states prohibit a corporation with a deficit from paying a cash dividend to its stockholders. This legal restriction is designed to protect creditors by preventing distribution of assets to stockholders when the company may be in financial difficulty.

Point: It is often said a dividend is a distribution of retained earnings, but it is more precise to describe a dividend as a distribution of assets to satisfy stockholder claims.

Point: The Retained Earnings Deficit account is also called *Accumulated Deficit.*

---

[1] An alternative entry is to debit Dividends instead of Retained Earnings. The balance in Dividends is then closed to Retained Earnings at the end of the reporting period. The effect is the same: Retained Earnings is decreased and a Dividend Payable is increased. For simplicity, all assignments in this chapter use the Retained Earnings account to record dividend declarations.

EXHIBIT 11.6

Stockholders' Equity
with a Deficit

Common stock—$10 par value, 5,000 shares authorized, issued, and outstanding	$50,000
Retained earnings deficit	(6,000)
Total stockholders' equity	$44,000

Some state laws allow cash dividends to be paid by returning a portion of the capital contributed by stockholders. This type of dividend is called a **liquidating cash dividend,** or simply *liquidating dividend,* because it returns a part of the original investment back to the stockholders. This requires a debit entry to one of the contributed capital accounts instead of Retained Earnings at the declaration date.

Stock Dividends

Point: Amazon.com has never declared a cash dividend.

A **stock dividend,** declared by a corporation's directors, is a distribution of additional shares of the corporation's own stock to its stockholders without the receipt of any payment in return. Stock dividends and cash dividends are different. A stock dividend does not reduce assets and equity but instead transfers a portion of equity from retained earnings to contributed capital.

Reasons for Stock Dividends   Stock dividends exist for at least two reasons. First, directors are said to use stock dividends to keep the market price of the stock affordable. For example, if a corporation continues to earn income but does not issue cash dividends, the price of its common stock likely increases. The price of such a stock may become so high that it discourages some investors from buying the stock (especially in lots of 100 and 1,000). When a corporation has a stock dividend, it increases the number of outstanding shares and lowers the per share stock price. Another reason for a stock dividend is to provide evidence of management's confidence that the company is doing well and will continue to do well.

Accounting for Stock Dividends   A stock dividend affects the components of equity by transferring part of retained earnings to contributed capital accounts, sometimes described as *capitalizing* retained earnings. Accounting for a stock dividend depends on whether it is a small or large stock dividend. A **small stock dividend** is a distribution of 25% or less of previously outstanding shares. It is recorded by capitalizing retained earnings for an amount equal to the market value of the shares to be distributed. A **large stock dividend** is a distribution of more than 25% of previously outstanding shares. A large stock dividend is recorded by capitalizing retained earnings for the minimum amount required by state law governing the corporation. Most states require capitalizing retained earnings equal to the par or stated value of the stock.

To illustrate stock dividends, we use the equity section of Quest's balance sheet shown in Exhibit 11.7 just *before* its declaration of a stock dividend on December 31.

EXHIBIT 11.7

Stockholders' Equity *before*
Declaring a Stock Dividend

Stockholders' Equity (before dividend)	
Common stock—$10 par value, 15,000 shares authorized, 10,000 shares issued and outstanding	$100,000
Paid-in capital in excess of par value, common stock	8,000
Retained earnings	35,000
Total stockholders' equity	$143,000

Recording a small stock dividend.   Assume that Quest's directors declare a 10% stock dividend on December 31. This stock dividend of 1,000 shares, computed as 10% of its 10,000 issued and outstanding shares, is to be distributed on January 20 to the stockholders of record on January 15. Since the market price of Quest's stock on December 31 is $15 per share, this small stock dividend declaration is recorded as follows:

Point: Small stock dividends are recorded at market value.

Assets = Liabilities + Equity
−15,000
+10,000
+5,000

10% dividend × 10,000 issued shares × $10 par value

10% dividend × 10,000 issued shares × [$15 market price − $10 par value]

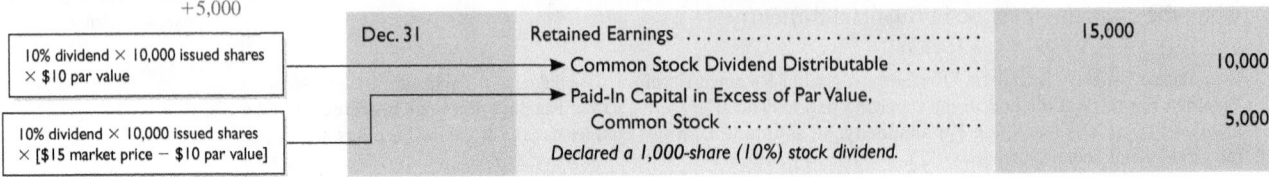

Date of Declaration—Small Stock Dividend

Dec. 31	Retained Earnings	15,000	
	Common Stock Dividend Distributable		10,000
	Paid-In Capital in Excess of Par Value, Common Stock		5,000
	Declared a 1,000-share (10%) stock dividend.		

The $10,000 credit in the declaration entry equals the par value of the shares and is recorded in *Common Stock Dividend Distributable,* an equity account. Its balance exists only until the shares are issued. The $5,000 credit equals the amount by which market value exceeds par value. This amount increases the Paid-In Capital in Excess of Par Value account in anticipation of the issuance of shares. In general, the balance sheet changes in three ways when a stock dividend is declared. First, the amount of equity attributed to common stock increases; for Quest, from $100,000 to $110,000 for 1,000 additional declared shares. Second, paid-in capital in excess of par increases by the excess of market value over par value for the declared shares. Third, retained earnings decreases, reflecting the transfer of amounts to both common stock and paid-in capital in excess of par. The stockholders' equity of Quest is shown in Exhibit 11.8 *after* its 10% stock dividend is declared on December 31—the items impacted are in bold.

Point: The term *Distributable* (not *Payable*) is used for stock dividends. A stock dividend is never a liability because it never reduces assets.

Point: The credit to Paid-In Capital in Excess of Par Value is recorded when the stock dividend is declared. This account is not affected when stock is later distributed.

EXHIBIT 11.8

Stockholders' Equity *after* Declaring a Stock Dividend

Stockholders' Equity (after dividend)

Common stock—$10 par value, 15,000 shares authorized, 10,000 shares issued and outstanding	$100,000
Common stock dividend distributable—1,000 shares	10,000
Paid-in capital in excess of par value, common stock	13,000
Retained earnings	20,000
Total stockholders' equity	$143,000

No entry is made on the date of record for a stock dividend. On January 20, the date of payment, Quest distributes the new shares to stockholders and records this entry:

Date of Payment—Small Stock Dividend

Jan. 20	Common Stock Dividend Distributable	10,000	
	Common Stock, $10 Par Value		10,000
	To record issuance of common stock dividend.		

Assets = Liabilities + Equity
−10,000
+10,000

The combined effect of these stock dividend entries is to transfer (or capitalize) $15,000 of retained earnings to paid-in capital accounts. The amount of capitalized retained earnings equals the market value of the 1,000 issued shares ($15 × 1,000 shares). A stock dividend has no effect on the ownership percent of individual stockholders.

Point: A stock dividend does not affect assets.

Recording a large stock dividend.   A corporation capitalizes retained earnings equal to the minimum amount required by state law for a large stock dividend. For most states, this amount is the par or stated value of the newly issued shares. To illustrate, suppose Quest's board declares a stock dividend of 30% instead of 10% on December 31. Since this dividend is more than 25%, it is treated as a large stock dividend. Thus, the par value of the 3,000 dividend shares is capitalized at the date of declaration with this entry:

Point: Large stock dividends are recorded at par or stated value.

Date of Declaration—Large Stock Dividend

Dec. 31	Retained Earnings	30,000	
	Common Stock Dividend Distributable		30,000
	Declared a 3,000-share (30%) stock dividend.		

Assets = Liabilities + Equity
−30,000
+30,000

30% dividend × 10,000 issued shares × $10 par value

This transaction decreases retained earnings and increases contributed capital by $30,000. On the date of payment the company debits Common Stock Dividend Distributable and credits Common Stock for $30,000. The effects from a large stock dividend on balance sheet accounts are similar to those for a small stock dividend except for the absence of any effect on paid-in capital in excess of par.

Stock Splits

A **stock split** is the distribution of additional shares to stockholders according to their percent ownership. When a stock split occurs, the corporation "calls in" its outstanding shares and issues more than one new share in exchange for each old share. Splits can be done in any ratio, including 2-for-1,

Before 5:1 Split: 1 share, $50 par

After 5:1 Split: 5 shares, $10 par

Point: Berkshire Hathaway has resisted a stock split. Its recent stock price was $170,000 per share.

Point: A reverse stock split is the opposite of a stock split. It increases both the market value per share and the par or stated value per share with a split ratio less than 1-for-1, such as 1-for-2. A reverse split results in fewer shares. Markets often read bad news into reverse splits.

3-for-1, or higher. In 2012, Google directors approved a 2-for-1 stock split. Stock splits reduce the par or stated value per share. The reasons for stock splits are similar to those for stock dividends.

To illustrate, CompTec has 100,000 outstanding shares of $20 par value common stock with a current market value of $88 per share. A 2-for-1 stock split cuts par value in half as it replaces 100,000 shares of $20 par value stock with 200,000 shares of $10 par value stock. Market value is reduced from $88 per share to about $44 per share. The split does not affect any equity amounts reported on the balance sheet or any individual stockholder's percent ownership. Both the Paid-In Capital and Retained Earnings accounts are unchanged by a split, and *no journal entry is made.* The only effect on the accounts is a change in the stock account description. CompTec's 2-for-1 split on its $20 par value stock means that after the split, it changes its stock account title to Common Stock, $10 Par Value. This stock's description on the balance sheet also changes to reflect the additional authorized, issued, and outstanding shares and the new par value.

The difference between stock splits and large stock dividends is often blurred. Many companies report stock splits in their financial statements without calling in the original shares by simply changing their par value. This type of "split" is really a large stock dividend and results in additional shares issued to stockholders by capitalizing retained earnings or transferring other paid-in capital to Common Stock. This approach avoids administrative costs of splitting the stock. Harley-Davidson recently declared a 2-for-1 stock split executed in the form of a 100% stock dividend.

◼ **Decision Maker** ━━━━━━━━━━━━━━━━━━━━━━━━

Entrepreneur A company you cofounded and own stock in announces a 50% stock dividend. Has the value of your stock investment increased, decreased, or remained the same? Would it make a difference if it was a 3-for-2 stock split executed in the form of a dividend? ◼ [Answer—p. 505]

NEED-TO-KNOW 11.2

P2

A company began the current year with the following balances in its stockholders' equity accounts.

Common stock—$10 par, 500 shares authorized, 200 shares issued and outstanding	$2,000
Paid-in capital in excess of par, common stock	1,000
Retained earnings	5,000
Total	$8,000

All outstanding common stock was issued for $15 per share when the company was created. Prepare journal entries to account for the following transactions during the current year.

Jan. 10   The board declared a $0.10 cash dividend per share to shareholders of record Jan. 28.
Feb. 15   Paid the cash dividend declared on January 10.
Mar. 31   Declared a 20% stock dividend. The market value of the stock is $18 per share.
May   1   Distributed the stock dividend declared on March 31.
Dec. 1   Declared a 40% stock dividend. The market value of the stock is $25 per share.
Dec. 31   Distributed the stock dividend declared on December 1.

Jan. 10	Retained Earnings	20	
	Common Dividend Payable		20
	Declared a $0.10 per share cash dividend.		
Feb. 15	Common Dividend Payable	20	
	Cash		20
	Paid $0.10 per share cash dividend.		
Mar. 31	Retained Earnings	720	
	Common Stock Dividend Distributable		400
	Paid-In Capital in Excess of Par Value, Common Stock		320
	Declared a small stock dividend of 20% or 40 shares; market value is $18 per share.		

[continued on next page]

Do More: QS 11-7, QS 11-8, QS 11-9, E 11-6, E 11-7

QC4

[continued from previous page]

May 1	Common Stock Dividend Distributable	400	
	Common Stock		400
	Distributed 40 shares of common stock.		
Dec. 1	Retained Earnings	960	
	Common Stock Dividend Distributable		960
	Declared a large stock dividend of 40% or 96 shares		
	(40% × [200 + 40]); market is $25 per share.		
Dec. 31	Common Stock Dividend Distributable	960	
	Common Stock		960
	Distributed 96 shares of common stock.		

PREFERRED STOCK

A corporation can issue two basic kinds of stock, common and preferred. **Preferred stock** has special rights that give it priority (or senior status) over common stock in one or more areas. Special rights typically include a preference for receiving dividends and for the distribution of assets if the corporation is liquidated. Preferred stock carries all rights of common stock unless the corporate charter nullifies them. Most preferred stock, for instance, does not confer the right to vote. Exhibit 11.9 shows that preferred stock is issued by about one-fourth of corporations. All corporations issue common stock. (While rare, not all common stock carries voting rights; Google's C class common shares are non-voting.)

C2 Explain characteristics of, and distribute dividends between, common and preferred stock.

EXHIBIT 11.9

Corporations and Preferred Stock

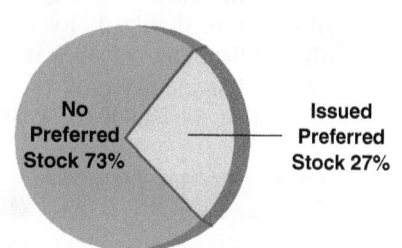

Issuance of Preferred Stock

Preferred stock usually has a par value. Like common stock, it can be sold at a price different from par. Preferred stock is recorded in its own separate capital accounts. To illustrate, if Dillon Snowboards issues 50 shares of $100 par value preferred stock for $6,000 cash on July 1, 2013, the entry is

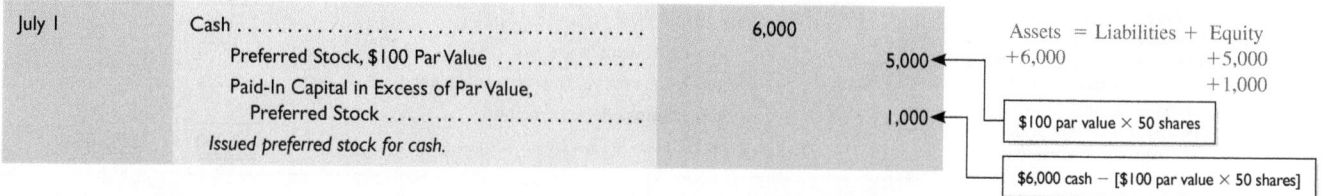

The equity section of the year-end balance sheet for Dillon Snowboards, including preferred stock, is shown in Exhibit 11.10. (This exhibit assumes that common stock was issued at par.) Issuing no-par preferred stock is similar to issuing no-par common stock. Also, the entries for issuing preferred stock for noncash assets are similar to those for common stock.

EXHIBIT 11.10

Stockholders' Equity with Common and Preferred Stock

Stockholders' Equity	
Common stock—$10 par value; 50,000 shares authorized;	
30,000 shares issued and outstanding	$300,000
Preferred stock—$100 par value; 1,000 shares authorized;	
50 shares issued and outstanding.............................	5,000
Paid-in capital in excess of par value, preferred stock	1,000
Retained earnings	65,000
Total stockholders' equity	$371,000

Dividend Preference of Preferred Stock

Preferred stock usually carries a preference for dividends, meaning that preferred stockholders are allocated their dividends before any dividends are allocated to common stockholders. The dividends allocated to preferred stockholders are usually expressed as a dollar amount per share or a percent applied to par value. A preference for dividends does *not* ensure dividends. If the directors do not declare a dividend, neither the preferred nor the common stockholders receive one.

Point: Dividend preference does not imply that preferred stockholders receive more dividends than common stockholders, nor does it guarantee a dividend.

Cumulative or Noncumulative Dividend   Most preferred stocks carry a cumulative dividend right. **Cumulative preferred stock** has a right to be paid both the current and all prior periods' unpaid dividends before any dividend is paid to common stockholders. When preferred stock is cumulative and the directors either do not declare a dividend to preferred stockholders or declare one that does not cover the total amount of cumulative dividend, the unpaid dividend amount is called **dividend in arrears.** Accumulation of dividends in arrears on cumulative preferred stock does not guarantee they will be paid. **Noncumulative preferred stock** confers no right to prior periods' unpaid dividends if they were not declared in those prior periods.

To illustrate the difference between cumulative and noncumulative preferred stock, assume that a corporation's outstanding stock includes (1) 1,000 shares of $100 par, 9% preferred stock—yielding $9,000 per year in potential dividends, and (2) 4,000 shares of $50 par value common stock. During 2012, the first year of operations, the directors declare cash dividends of $5,000. In year 2013, they declare cash dividends of $42,000. See Exhibit 11.11 for the allocation of dividends for these two years. Allocation of year 2013 dividends depends on whether the preferred stock is noncumulative or cumulative. With noncumulative preferred, the preferred stockholders never receive the $4,000 skipped in 2012. If the preferred stock is cumulative, the $4,000 in arrears is paid in 2013 before any other dividends are paid.

EXHIBIT 11.11

Allocation of Dividends (noncumulative vs. cumulative preferred stock)

Example: What dividends do cumulative preferred stockholders receive in 2013 if the corporation paid only $2,000 of dividends in 2012? How does this affect dividends to common stockholders in 2013? *Answers:* $16,000 ($7,000 dividends in arrears, plus $9,000 current preferred dividends). Dividends to common stockholders decrease to $26,000.

	Preferred	Common
Preferred Stock Is Noncumulative		
Year 2012	$ 5,000	$ 0
Year 2013		
Step 1: Current year's preferred dividend	$ 9,000	
Step 2: Remainder to common		$33,000
Preferred Stock Is Cumulative		
Year 2012	$ 5,000	$ 0
Year 2013		
Step 1: Dividend in arrears	$ 4,000	
Step 2: Current year's preferred dividend	9,000	
Step 3: Remainder to common		$29,000
Totals for year 2013	$13,000	$29,000

A liability for a dividend does not exist until the directors declare a dividend. If a preferred dividend date passes and the corporation's board fails to declare the dividend on its cumulative preferred stock, the dividend in arrears is not a liability. The *full-disclosure principle* requires a corporation to report (usually in a note) the amount of preferred dividends in arrears as of the balance sheet date.

Participating or Nonparticipating Dividend   **Nonparticipating preferred stock** has a feature that limits dividends to a maximum amount each year. This maximum is often stated as a percent of the stock's par value or as a specific dollar amount per share. Once preferred stockholders receive this amount, the common stockholders receive any and all additional dividends. **Participating preferred stock** has a feature allowing preferred stockholders to share with common stockholders in any dividends paid in excess of the percent or dollar amount stated on the preferred stock. This participation feature does not apply until common stockholders receive dividends equal to the preferred stock's dividend percent. Many corporations are authorized to issue participating preferred stock but rarely do, and most managers never expect to issue it.[2]

Convertible Preferred Stock

Preferred stock is more attractive to investors if it carries a right to exchange preferred shares for a fixed number of common shares. **Convertible preferred stock** gives holders the option to exchange their preferred shares for common shares at a specified rate. When a company prospers and its common stock increases in value, convertible preferred stockholders can share in this success by converting their preferred stock into more valuable common stock.

Callable Preferred Stock

Callable preferred stock gives the issuing corporation the right to purchase (retire) this stock from its holders at specified future prices and dates. The amount paid to call and retire a preferred share is its **call price,** or *redemption value,* and is set when the stock is issued. The call price normally includes the stock's par value plus a premium giving holders additional return on their investment. When the issuing corporation calls and retires a preferred stock, the terms of the agreement often require it to pay the call price *and* any dividends in arrears.

Point: The issuing corporation has the right, or option, to retire its callable preferred stock.

 **IFRS**

Like U.S. GAAP, IFRS requires that preferred stocks be classified as debt or equity based on analysis of the stock's contractual terms. However, IFRS uses different criteria for such classification. ■

Reasons for Issuing Preferred Stock

Corporations issue preferred stock for several reasons. One is to raise capital without sacrificing control. For example, suppose a company's organizers have $100,000 cash to invest and organize a corporation that needs $200,000 of capital to start. If they sell $200,000 worth of common stock (with $100,000 to the organizers), they would have only 50% control and would need to negotiate extensively with other stockholders in making policy. However, if they issue $100,000 worth of common stock to themselves and sell outsiders $100,000 of 8%, cumulative preferred stock with no voting rights, they retain control.

A second reason to issue preferred stock is to boost the return earned by common stockholders. To illustrate, suppose a corporation's organizers expect to earn an annual after-tax income of $24,000 on an investment of $200,000. If they sell and issue $200,000 worth of common stock, the $24,000 income produces a 12% return on the $200,000 of common stockholders' equity. However, if they issue $100,000 of 8% preferred stock to outsiders and $100,000 of common stock to themselves, their own return increases to 16% per year, as shown in Exhibit 11.12.

Net (after-tax) income	$24,000
Less preferred dividends at 8%	(8,000)
Balance to common stockholders	$16,000
Return to common stockholders ($16,000/$100,000)	16%

EXHIBIT 11.12

Return to Common Stockholders When Preferred Stock Is Issued

---

[2] Participating preferred stock is usually authorized as a defense against a possible corporate *takeover* by an "unfriendly" investor (or a group of investors) who intends to buy enough voting common stock to gain control. Taking a term from spy novels, the financial world refers to this type of plan as a *poison pill* that a company swallows if enemy investors threaten its capture. A poison pill usually works as follows: A corporation's common stockholders on a given date are granted the right to purchase a large amount of participating preferred stock at a very low price. This right to purchase preferred shares is *not* transferable. If an unfriendly investor buys a large block of common shares (whose right to purchase participating preferred shares does *not* transfer to this buyer), the board can issue preferred shares at a low price to the remaining common shareholders who retained the right to purchase. Future dividends are then divided between the newly issued participating preferred shares and the common shares. This usually transfers value from common shares to preferred shares, causing the unfriendly investor's common stock to lose much of its value and reduces the potential benefit of a hostile takeover.

Point: Financial leverage also occurs when debt is issued and the interest rate paid on it is less than the rate earned from using the assets the creditors lend the company.

Common stockholders earn 16% instead of 12% because assets contributed by preferred stockholders are invested to earn $12,000 while the preferred dividend is only $8,000. Use of preferred stock to increase return to common stockholders is an example of **financial leverage** (also called *trading on the equity*). As a general rule, when the dividend rate on preferred stock is less than the rate the corporation earns on its assets, the effect of issuing preferred stock is to increase (or *lever*) the rate earned by common stockholders.

Other reasons for issuing preferred stock include its appeal to some investors who believe that the corporation's common stock is too risky or that the expected return on common stock is too low.

■ Decision Maker

Concert Organizer   Assume that you alter your business strategy from organizing concerts targeted at under 1,000 people to those targeted at between 5,000 to 20,000 people. You also incorporate because of increased risk of lawsuits and a desire to issue stock for financing. It is important that you control the company for decisions on whom to schedule. What types of stock do you offer? ■   [Answer—p. 505]

NEED-TO-KNOW 11.3

C2

A company's outstanding stock consists of 80 shares of *noncumulative* 5% preferred stock with a $5 par value and also 200 shares of common stock with a $1 par value. During its first three years of operation, the corporation declared and paid the following total cash dividends:

2013	$ 15
2014	5
2015	200

Part 1. Determine the amount of dividends paid each year to each of the two classes of stockholders: preferred and common. Also compute the total dividends paid to each class for the three years combined.

Part 2. Determine the amount of dividends paid each year to each of the two classes of stockholders assuming that the preferred stock is *cumulative*. Also determine the total dividends paid to each class for the three years combined.

Solution—Part 1

	Non-Cumulative Preferred	Common
2013 ($15 paid)		
Preferred*	$15	
Common—remainder	___	$ 0
Total for the year	$15	$ 0
2014 ($5 paid)		
Preferred*	$ 5	
Common—remainder	___	$ 0
Total for the year	$ 5	$ 0
2015 ($200 paid)		
Preferred*	$20	
Common—remainder	___	$180
Total for the year	$20	$180
2013–2015 (combined $220 paid)	___	___
Total for three years	$40	$180

* Holders of noncumulative preferred stock are entitled to no more than $20 of dividends in any one year (5% × $5 × 80 shares).

Solution—Part 2

	Cumulative Preferred	Common
2013 ($15 paid)		
Preferred*	$15	
Common—remainder		$ 0
Total for the year	$15	$ 0
(Note: $5 in preferred stock dividends in arrears.)		
2014 ($5 paid)		
Preferred—arrears from 2013	$ 5	
Preferred*	0	
Common—remainder		$ 0
Total for the year	$ 5	$ 0
(Note: $20 in preferred stock dividends in arrears.)		
2015 ($200 paid)		
Preferred—arrears from 2014 ($0 arrears from 2013)	$20	
Preferred*	20	
Common—remainder		$160
Total for the year	$40	$160
(Note: $0 in preferred stock dividends in arrears.)		
2013–2015 (combined $220 paid)		
Total for three years	$60	$160

> Do More: QS 11-6, QS 11-10, E 11-5, E 11-8, E 11-9

QC5

* Holders of cumulative preferred stock are entitled to no more than $20 of dividends declared in any year (5% × $5 × 80 shares) plus any dividends in arrears.

TREASURY STOCK

Corporations acquire shares of their own stock for several reasons: (1) to use their shares to acquire another corporation, (2) to purchase shares to avoid a hostile takeover of the company, (3) to reissue them to employees as compensation, and (4) to maintain a strong market for their stock or to show management confidence in the current price.

A corporation's reacquired shares are called **treasury stock,** which is similar to unissued stock in several ways: (1) neither treasury stock nor unissued stock is an asset, (2) neither receives cash dividends or stock dividends, and (3) neither allows the exercise of voting rights. However, treasury stock does differ from unissued stock in one major way: The corporation can resell treasury stock at less than par without having the buyers incur a liability, provided it was originally issued at par value or higher. Treasury stock purchases also require management to exercise ethical sensitivity because funds are being paid to specific stockholders instead of all stockholders. Managers must be sure the purchase is in the best interest of all stockholders. These concerns cause companies to fully disclose treasury stock transactions.

P3 Record purchases and sales of treasury stock and the retirement of stock.

Corporations and Treasury Stock

With Treasury Stock 62% / No Treasury Stock 38%

Purchasing Treasury Stock

Purchasing treasury stock reduces the corporation's assets and equity by equal amounts. (We describe the *cost method* of accounting for treasury stock, which is the most widely used method. The *par value* method is another method explained in advanced courses.) To illustrate, Exhibit 11.13 shows Cyber Corporation's account balances *before* any treasury stock purchase (Cyber has no liabilities).

Assets		Stockholders' Equity	
Cash	$ 30,000	Common stock—$10 par; 10,000 shares authorized, issued, and outstanding	$100,000
Other assets	95,000	Retained earnings	25,000
Total assets	$125,000	Total stockholders' equity	$125,000

EXHIBIT 11.13

Account Balances *before* Purchasing Treasury Stock

Cyber then purchases 1,000 of its own shares for $11,500 on May 1, which is recorded as follows:

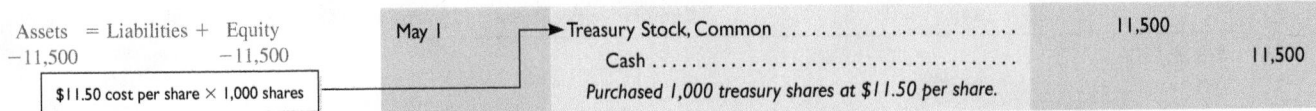

Assets = Liabilities + Equity
−11,500   −11,500

$11.50 cost per share × 1,000 shares

May 1	Treasury Stock, Common	11,500	
	Cash		11,500
	Purchased 1,000 treasury shares at $11.50 per share.		

This entry reduces equity through the debit to the Treasury Stock account, which is a contra equity account. Exhibit 11.14 shows account balances *after* this transaction.

EXHIBIT 11.14

Account Balances *after* Purchasing Treasury Stock

Assets		Stockholders' Equity	
Cash	$ 18,500	Common stock—$10 par; 10,000 shares authorized and issued; 1,000 shares in treasury	$100,000
Other assets	95,000	Retained earnings, $11,500 restricted by treasury stock purchase	25,000
		Less cost of treasury stock	(11,500)
Total assets	$113,500	Total stockholders' equity	$113,500

Point: The Treasury Stock account is *not* an asset. Treasury stock does not carry voting or dividend rights.

Point: A treasury stock purchase is also called a *stock buyback*.

The treasury stock purchase reduces Cyber's cash, total assets, and total equity by $11,500 but does not reduce the balance of either the Common Stock or the Retained Earnings account. The equity reduction is reported by deducting the cost of treasury stock in the equity section. Also, two disclosures are evident. First, the stock description reveals that 1,000 issued shares are in treasury, leaving only 9,000 shares still outstanding. Second, the description for retained earnings reveals that it is partly restricted.

Reissuing Treasury Stock

Treasury stock can be reissued by selling it at cost, above cost, or below cost.

Selling Treasury Stock at Cost   If treasury stock is reissued at cost, the entry is the reverse of the one made to record the purchase. For instance, if on May 21 Cyber reissues 100 of the treasury shares purchased on May 1 at the same $11.50 per share cost, the entry is

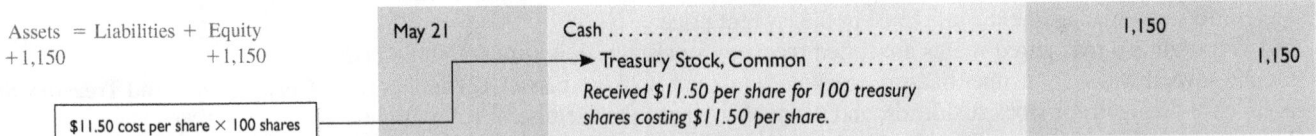

Assets = Liabilities + Equity
+1,150   +1,150

$11.50 cost per share × 100 shares

May 21	Cash	1,150	
	Treasury Stock, Common		1,150
	Received $11.50 per share for 100 treasury shares costing $11.50 per share.		

Point: Treasury stock does not represent ownership. A company cannot own a part of itself.

Selling Treasury Stock *above* Cost   If treasury stock is sold for more than cost, the amount received in excess of cost is credited to the Paid-In Capital, Treasury Stock account. This account is reported as a separate item in the stockholders' equity section. No gain is ever reported from the sale of treasury stock. To illustrate, if Cyber receives $12 cash per share for 400 treasury shares costing $11.50 per share on June 3, the entry is

Assets = Liabilities + Equity
+4,800   +4,600
                         +200

$11.50 cost per share × 400 shares

[$12 issue price − $11.50 cost per share] × 400 shares

June 3	Cash	4,800	
	Treasury Stock, Common		4,600
	Paid-In Capital, Treasury Stock		**200**
	Received $12 per share for 400 treasury shares costing $11.50 per share.		

Point: The phrase *treasury stock* is believed to arise from the fact that reacquired stock is held in a corporation's treasury.

Point: The Paid-In Capital, Treasury Stock account can have a zero or credit balance but never a debit balance.

Selling Treasury Stock *below* Cost   When treasury stock is sold below cost, the entry to record the sale depends on whether the Paid-In Capital, Treasury Stock account has a credit balance. If it has a zero balance, the excess of cost over the sales price is debited to Retained Earnings. If the Paid-In Capital, Treasury Stock account has a credit balance, it is debited for the excess of the cost over the selling price but not to exceed the balance in this account. When the credit balance in this paid-in capital account is eliminated, any remaining difference between the cost and selling price is debited to Retained Earnings. To illustrate, if Cyber sells its remaining 500 shares of treasury stock at $10 per share on July 10, equity is reduced by $750 (500 shares × $1.50 per share excess of cost over selling price), as shown in this entry:

July 10	Cash	5,000	
	Paid-In Capital, Treasury Stock	200 ◄	
	Retained Earnings	550 ◄	
	Treasury Stock, Common		5,750◄
	Received $10 per share for 500 treasury		
	shares costing $11.50 per share.		

Assets = Liabilities + Equity
+5,000   −200
                          −550
                          +5,750

[$10 issue price − $11.50 cost per share] × 500 shares; not to exceed $200

For any amount exceeding $200 PIC from TS

$11.50 cost per share × 500 shares

This entry eliminates the $200 credit balance in the paid-in capital account created on June 3 and then reduces the Retained Earnings balance by the remaining $550 excess of cost over selling price. A company never reports a loss (or gain) from the sale of treasury stock.

Retiring Stock

A corporation can purchase its own stock and retire it. Retiring stock reduces the number of issued shares. Retired stock is the same as authorized and unissued shares. Purchases and retirements of stock are permissible under state law only if they do not jeopardize the interests of creditors and stockholders. When stock is purchased for retirement, we remove all capital amounts related to the retired shares. If the purchase price exceeds the net amount removed, this excess is debited to Retained Earnings. If the net amount removed from all capital accounts exceeds the purchase price, this excess is credited to the Paid-In Capital from Retirement of Stock account. A company's assets and equity are always reduced by the amount paid for the retiring stock.

Point: Recording stock retirement results in canceling the equity from the original issuance of the shares.

A company began the current year with the following balances in its stockholders' equity accounts.

NEED-TO-KNOW 11.4

P3

Common stock—$10 par, 500 shares authorized, 200 shares		
issued and outstanding	$2,000	
Paid-in capital in excess of par, common stock	1,000	
Retained earnings	5,000	
Total	$8,000	

All outstanding common stock was issued for $15 per share when the company was created. Prepare journal entries to account for the following transactions during the current year.

July   1   Purchased 30 shares of treasury stock at $20 per share.
Sept. 1   Sold 20 treasury shares at $26 cash per share.
Dec.   1   Sold the remaining 10 shares of treasury stock at $7 cash per share.

July 1	Treasury Stock, Common	600	
	Cash		600
	Purchased 30 common shares at $20 per share.		
Sept. 1	Cash	520	
	Treasury Stock, Common		400
	Paid-In Capital, Treasury Stock		120
	Sold 20 treasury shares at $26 per share.		
Dec. 1	Cash	70	
	Paid-In Capital, Treasury Stock	120	
	Retained Earnings	10	
	Treasury Stock, Common		200
	Sold 10 treasury shares at $7 per share.		

Do More: QS 11-11, E 11-10

QC6

REPORTING OF EQUITY

C3 Explain the items reported in retained earnings.

Statement of Retained Earnings

Retained earnings generally consist of a company's cumulative net income less any net losses and dividends declared since its inception. Retained earnings are part of stockholders' claims on the company's net assets, but this does *not* imply that a certain amount of cash or other assets is available to pay stockholders. For example, Abercrombie & Fitch has $2,320,571 thousand in retained earnings, but only $583,495 thousand in cash. This section describes events and transactions affecting retained earnings and how retained earnings are reported.

Restrictions and Appropriations   The term **restricted retained earnings** refers to both statutory and contractual restrictions. A common *statutory* (or *legal*) *restriction* is to limit treasury stock purchases to the amount of retained earnings. The balance sheet in Exhibit 11.14 provides an example. A common *contractual restriction* involves loan agreements that restrict paying dividends beyond a specified amount or percent of retained earnings. Restrictions are usually described in the notes. The term **appropriated retained earnings** refers to a voluntary transfer of amounts from the Retained Earnings account to the Appropriated Retained Earnings account to inform users of special activities that require funds.

Prior Period Adjustments   **Prior period adjustments** are corrections of material errors in prior period financial statements. These errors include arithmetic mistakes, unacceptable accounting, and missed facts. Prior period adjustments are reported in the *statement of retained earnings* (or the statement of stockholders' equity), net of any income tax effects. Prior period adjustments result in changing the beginning balance of retained earnings for events occurring prior to the earliest period reported in the current set of financial statements. To illustrate, assume that ComUS makes an error in a 2011 journal entry for the purchase of land by incorrectly debiting an expense account. When this is discovered in 2013, the statement of retained earnings includes a prior period adjustment, as shown in Exhibit 11.15. This exhibit also shows the usual format of the statement of retained earnings.

Point: If a year 2011 error is discovered in 2012, the company records the adjustment in 2012. But if the financial statements include 2011 and 2012 figures, the statements report the correct amounts for 2011, and a note describes the correction.

EXHIBIT 11.15

Statement of Retained Earnings with a Prior Period Adjustment

ComUS Statement of Retained Earnings For Year Ended December 31, 2013	
Retained earnings, Dec. 31, 2012, as previously reported	$4,745,000
Prior period adjustment	
Cost of land incorrectly expensed (net of $63,000 income taxes)	147,000
Retained earnings, Dec. 31, 2012, as adjusted	4,892,000
Plus net income	1,224,300
Less cash dividends declared	(301,800)
Retained earnings, Dec. 31, 2013	$5,814,500

Many items reported in financial statements are based on estimates. Future events are certain to reveal that some of these estimates were inaccurate even when based on the best data available at the time. These inaccuracies are *not* considered errors and are *not* reported as prior period adjustments. Instead, they are identified as **changes in accounting estimates** and are accounted for in current and future periods. To illustrate, we know that depreciation is based on estimated useful lives and salvage values. As time passes and new information becomes available, managers may need to change these estimates and the resulting depreciation expense for current and future periods.

Point: Accounting for changes in estimates is sometimes criticized as two wrongs to make a right. Consider a change in an asset's life. Depreciation neither before nor after the change is the amount computed if the revised estimate were originally selected. Regulators chose this approach to avoid restating prior period numbers.

Closing Process   The closing process was explained earlier in the book as: (1) Close credit balances in revenue accounts to Income Summary, (2) Close debit balances in expense accounts to Income Summary, and (3) Close Income Summary to Retained Earnings. If dividends are recorded in a Dividends account, and not as an immediate reduction to Retained Earnings (as shown in this chapter), a fourth step is necessary to close the Dividends account to Retained Earnings.

Statement of Stockholders' Equity

Instead of a separate statement of retained earnings, companies commonly report a statement of stockholders' equity that includes changes in retained earnings. A **statement of stockholders' equity** lists the beginning and ending balances of key equity accounts and describes the changes that occur during the period. The companies in Appendix A report such a statement. The usual format is to provide a column for each component of equity and use the rows to describe events occurring in the period. Exhibit 11.16 shows a condensed statement for Apple.

APPLE Statement of Stockholders' Equity					
($ millions, shares in thousands)	Common Stock Shares	Common Stock Amount	Retained Earnings	Other	Total Equity
Balance, Sept. 25, 2010	915,970	$10,668	$37,169	$ (46)	$47,791
Net income	—	—	25,922	—	25,922
Issuance of Common Stock	13,307	1,729	(250)	—	1,479
Other	—	934	—	489	1,423
Cash Dividends ($0.00 per share)	—	—	—	—	—
Balance, Sept. 24, 2011	929,277	$13,331	$62,841	$443	$76,615

EXHIBIT 11.16

Statement of Stockholders' Equity

APPLE

Reporting Stock Options

The majority of corporations whose shares are publicly traded issue **stock options,** which are rights to purchase common stock at a fixed price over a specified period. As the stock's price rises, the option's value increases. Starbucks and Home Depot offer stock options to both full- and part-time employees. Stock options are said to motivate managers and employees to (1) focus on company performance, (2) take a long-run perspective, and (3) remain with the company. A stock option is like having an investment with no risk ("a carrot with no stick").

To illustrate, Quantum grants each of its employees the option to purchase 100 shares of its $1 par value common stock at its current market price of $50 per share anytime within the next 10 years. If the stock price rises to $70 per share, an employee can exercise the option at a gain of $20 per share (acquire a $70 stock at the $50 option price). With 100 shares, a single employee would have a total gain of $2,000, computed as $20 × 100 shares. Companies report the cost of stock options in the income statement. Measurement of this cost is explained in advanced courses.

Fraud

Pump 'n Dump Fraudulent information can be used by the owners of a company's stock to pump it up and claim it is undervalued, which causes naïve investors to seek to acquire the stock and drive up its price. After that, those behind the release of fraudulent information dump the stock at an inflated price. When later information reveals that the stock is overvalued, its price declines and investors still holding the stock lose value. This scheme is called *pump 'n dump.* Jonathan Lebed, at 15 years old, is one of the most infamous cases of pump 'n dump, in which he allegedly made about $1 million.

GLOBAL VIEW

This section discusses similarities and differences between U.S. GAAP and IFRS in accounting and reporting for equity.

Accounting for Common Stock The accounting for and reporting of common stock under U.S. GAAP and IFRS are similar. Specifically, procedures for issuing common stock at par, at a premium, at a discount, and for noncash assets are similar across the two systems. However, we must be aware of legal

Samsung

and cultural differences across the world that can impact the rights and responsibilities of common share-holders. Samsung's terminology is a bit different as it uses the phrase "share premium" in reference to what U.S. GAAP would title "paid-in capital in excess of par value" (see Appendix A).

Accounting for Dividends Accounting for and reporting of dividends under U.S. GAAP and IFRS are consistent. This applies to cash dividends, stock dividends, and stock splits. For Samsung, it "declared cash dividends to shareholders of common stock and preferred stock as interim dividends for the six-month periods . . . and as year-end dividends." Samsung, like many other companies, follows a dividend policy set by management and its board.

Accounting for Preferred Stock Accounting and reporting for preferred stock are similar for U.S. GAAP and IFRS, but there are some important differences. First, preferred stock that is redeemable at the option of the preferred stockholders is reported *between* liabilities and equity in U.S. GAAP balance sheets. However, that same stock is reported as a liability in IFRS balance sheets. Second, the issue price of convertible preferred stock (and bonds) is recorded entirely under preferred stock (or bonds) *and none is assigned to the conversion feature* under U.S. GAAP. However, IFRS requires that a portion of the issue price be allocated to the conversion feature when it exists. Samsung has preferred stock, which is non-cumulative and non-voting.

Accounting for Treasury Stock Both U.S. GAAP and IFRS apply the principle that companies do not record gains or losses on transactions involving their own stock. This applies to purchases, reissuances, and retirements of treasury stock. Consequently, the accounting for treasury stock explained in this chapter is consistent with that under IFRS. However, IFRS in this area is less detailed than that of U.S. GAAP.

Decision Analysis  Earnings per Share, Price-Earnings Ratio, Dividend Yield, and Book Value per Share

---

Earnings per Share

 A1 Compute earnings per share and describe its use.

The income statement reports **earnings per share,** also called *EPS* or *net income per share,* which is the amount of income earned per each share of a company's outstanding common stock. The **basic earnings per share** formula is shown in Exhibit 11.17. When a company has no preferred stock, then preferred dividends are zero. The weighted-average common shares outstanding is measured over the income reporting period; its computation is explained in advanced courses.

EXHIBIT 11.17

Basic Earnings per Share

$$\text{Basic earnings per share} = \frac{\text{Net income} - \text{Preferred dividends}}{\text{Weighted-average common shares outstanding}}$$

To illustrate, assume that Quantum Co. earns $40,000 net income in 2013 and declares dividends of $7,500 on its noncumulative preferred stock. (If preferred stock is *non*cumulative, the income available [numerator] is the current period net income less any preferred dividends *declared* in that same period. If preferred stock is cumulative, the income available [numerator] is the current period net income less the preferred dividends whether declared or not.) Quantum has 5,000 weighted-average common shares outstanding during 2013. Its basic EPS[3] is

$$\text{Basic earnings per share} = \frac{\$40,000 - \$7,500}{5,000 \text{ shares}} = \$6.50$$

---

[3] A corporation can be classified as having either a simple or complex capital structure. The term **simple capital structure** refers to a company with only common stock and nonconvertible preferred stock outstanding. The term **complex capital structure** refers to companies with dilutive securities. **Dilutive securities** include options, rights to purchase common stock, and any bonds or preferred stock that are convertible into common stock. A company with a complex capital structure must often report two EPS figures: basic and diluted. **Diluted earnings per share** is computed by adding all dilutive securities to the denominator of the basic EPS computation. It reflects the decrease in basic EPS *assuming* that all dilutive securities are converted into common shares.

Price-Earnings Ratio

A stock's market value is determined by its *expected* future cash flows. A comparison of a company's EPS and its market value per share reveals information about market expectations. This comparison is traditionally made using a **price-earnings (or PE) ratio,** expressed also as *price earnings, price to earnings,* or *PE.* Some analysts interpret this ratio as what price the market is willing to pay for a company's current earnings stream. Price-earnings ratios can differ across companies that have similar earnings because of either higher or lower expectations of future earnings. The price-earnings ratio is defined in Exhibit 11.18.

A2 Compute price-earnings ratio and describe its use in analysis.

Point: The average PE ratio of stocks in the 1950–2012 period is about 14.

EXHIBIT 11.18

Price-Earnings Ratio

$$\text{Price-earnings ratio} = \frac{\text{Market value (price) per share}}{\text{Earnings per share}}$$

This ratio is often computed using EPS from the most recent period (for Amazon, its PE is 138; for Altria, its PE is 19). However, many users compute this ratio using *expected* EPS for the next period.

Some analysts view stocks with high PE ratios (higher than 20 to 25) as more likely to be overpriced and stocks with low PE ratios (less than 5 to 8) as more likely to be underpriced. These investors prefer to sell or avoid buying stocks with high PE ratios and to buy or hold stocks with low PE ratios. However, investment decision making is rarely so simple as to rely on a single ratio. For instance, a stock with a high PE ratio can prove to be a good investment if its earnings continue to increase beyond current expectations. Similarly, a stock with a low PE ratio can prove to be a poor investment if its earnings decline below expectations.

Point: Average PE ratios for U.S. stocks increased over the past two decades. Some analysts interpret this as a signal the market is overpriced. But higher ratios can at least partly reflect accounting changes that have reduced reported earnings.

■ Decision Maker

Money Manager You plan to invest in one of two companies identified as having identical future prospects. One has a PE of 19 and the other a PE of 25. Which do you invest in? Does it matter if your *estimate* of PE for these two companies is 29 as opposed to 22? ■ [Answer—p. 505]

Dividend Yield

Investors buy shares of a company's stock in anticipation of receiving a return from either or both cash dividends and stock price increases. Stocks that pay large dividends on a regular basis, called *income stocks,* are attractive to investors who want recurring cash flows from their investments. In contrast, some stocks pay little or no dividends but are still attractive to investors because of their expected stock price increases. The stocks of companies that distribute little or no cash but use their cash to finance expansion are called *growth stocks.* One way to help identify whether a stock is an income stock or a growth stock is to analyze its dividend yield. **Dividend yield,** defined in Exhibit 11.19, shows the annual amount of cash dividends distributed to common shares relative to their market value.

A3 Compute dividend yield and explain its use in analysis.

$$\text{Dividend yield} = \frac{\text{Annual cash dividends per share}}{\text{Market value per share}}$$

EXHIBIT 11.19

Dividend Yield

Dividend yield can be computed for current and prior periods using actual dividends and stock prices and for future periods using expected values. Exhibit 11.20 shows recent dividend and stock price data for Amazon and Altria Group to compute dividend yield.

Company	Cash Dividends per Share	Market Value per Share	Dividend Yield
Amazon	$0.00	$310	0.0%
Altria Group.	$1.70	$ 32	5.3%

EXHIBIT 11.20

Dividend and Stock Price Information

Dividend yield is zero for Amazon, implying it is a growth stock. An investor in Amazon would look for increases in stock prices (and eventual cash from the sale of stock). Altria has a dividend yield of 5.3%, implying it is an income stock for which dividends are important in assessing its value.

Point: The *payout ratio* equals cash dividends declared on common stock divided by net income. A low payout ratio suggests that a company is retaining earnings for future growth.

Book Value per Share

Case 1: Common Stock (Only) Outstanding. **Book value per common share,** defined in Exhibit 11.21, reflects the amount of equity applicable to *common* shares on a per share basis. To illustrate, we use Dillon Snowboards' data from Exhibit 11.4. Dillon has 30,000 outstanding common shares, and the stockholders'

A4 Compute book value and explain its use in analysis.

equity applicable to common shares is $365,000. Dillon's book value per common share is $12.17, computed as $365,000 divided by 30,000 shares.

EXHIBIT 11.21

Book Value per Common Share

$$\text{Book value per common share} = \frac{\text{Stockholders' equity applicable to common shares}}{\text{Number of common shares outstanding}}$$

Point: Book value per share is also referred to as *stockholders' claim to assets on a per share basis.*

Case 2: Common and Preferred Stock Outstanding. To compute book value when both common and preferred shares are outstanding, we allocate total equity between the two types of shares. The **book value per preferred share** is computed first; its computation is shown in Exhibit 11.22.

EXHIBIT 11.22

Book Value per Preferred Share

$$\text{Book value per preferred share} = \frac{\text{Stockholders' equity applicable to preferred shares}}{\text{Number of preferred shares outstanding}}$$

The equity applicable to preferred shares equals the preferred share's call price (or par value if the preferred is not callable) plus any cumulative dividends in arrears. The remaining equity is the portion applicable to common shares. To illustrate, consider LTD's equity in Exhibit 11.23. Its preferred stock is callable at $108 per share, and two years of cumulative preferred dividends are in arrears.

EXHIBIT 11.23

Stockholders' Equity with Preferred and Common Stock

Stockholders' Equity	
Preferred stock—$100 par value, 7% cumulative, 2,000 shares authorized, 1,000 shares issued and outstanding	$100,000
Common stock—$25 par value, 12,000 shares authorized, 10,000 shares issued and outstanding	250,000
Paid-in capital in excess of par value, common stock	15,000
Retained earnings	82,000
Total stockholders' equity	$447,000

The book value computations are in Exhibit 11.24. Equity is first allocated to preferred shares before the book value of common shares is computed.

EXHIBIT 11.24

Computing Book Value per Preferred and Common Share

Total stockholders' equity		$447,000
Less equity applicable to preferred shares		
Call price (1,000 shares × $108)	$108,000	
Dividends in arrears ($100,000 × 7% × 2 years)	14,000	(122,000)
Equity applicable to common shares		$325,000
Book value per preferred share ($122,000/1,000 shares)		$ 122.00
Book value per common share ($325,000/10,000 shares)		$ 32.50

Book value per share reflects the value per share if a company is liquidated at balance sheet amounts. Book value is also the starting point in many stock valuation models, merger negotiations, price setting for public utilities, and loan contracts. The main limitation in using book value is the potential difference between recorded value and market value for assets and liabilities. Investors often adjust their analysis for estimates of these differences.

◼ Decision Maker

Investor   You are considering investing in BMX, whose book value per common share is $4 and price per common share on the stock exchange is $7. From this information, are BMX's net assets priced higher or lower than its recorded values? ◼   [Answer—p. 505]

Barton Corporation began operations on January 1, 2012. The following transactions relating to stock-holders' equity occurred in the first two years of the company's operations.

2012

Jan. 1   Authorized the issuance of 2 million shares of $5 par value common stock and 100,000 shares of $100 par value, 10% cumulative, preferred stock.
Jan. 2   Issued 200,000 shares of common stock for $12 cash per share.
Jan. 3   Issued 100,000 shares of common stock in exchange for a building valued at $820,000 and mer-chandise inventory valued at $380,000.
Jan. 4   Paid $10,000 cash to the company's founders for organization activities.
Jan. 5   Issued 12,000 shares of preferred stock for $110 cash per share.

2013

June 4   Issued 100,000 shares of common stock for $15 cash per share.

Required

1. Prepare journal entries to record these transactions.
2. Prepare the stockholders' equity section of the balance sheet as of December 31, 2012, and December 31, 2013, based on these transactions.
3. Prepare a table showing dividend allocations and dividends per share for 2012 and 2013 assuming Barton declares the following cash dividends: 2012, $50,000, and 2013, $300,000.
4. Prepare the January 2, 2012, journal entry for Barton's issuance of 200,000 shares of common stock for $12 cash per share assuming.
   a. Common stock is no-par stock without a stated value.
   b. Common stock is no-par stock with a stated value of $10 per share.

PLANNING THE SOLUTION

● Record journal entries for the transactions for 2012 and 2013.
● Determine the balances for the 2012 and 2013 equity accounts for the balance sheet.
● Prepare the contributed capital portion of the 2012 and 2013 balance sheets.
● Prepare a table similar to Exhibit 11.11 showing dividend allocations for 2012 and 2013.
● Record the issuance of common stock under both specifications of no-par stock.

SOLUTION TO COMPREHENSIVE NEED-TO-KNOW

1. Journal entries.

2012			
Jan. 2	Cash	2,400,000	
	Common Stock, $5 Par Value		1,000,000
	Paid-In Capital in Excess of Par Value,		
	Common Stock		1,400,000
	Issued 200,000 shares of common stock.		
Jan. 3	Building	820,000	
	Merchandise Inventory	380,000	
	Common Stock, $5 Par Value		500,000
	Paid-In Capital in Excess of Par Value,		
	Common Stock		700,000
	Issued 100,000 shares of common stock.		
Jan. 4	Organization Expenses	10,000	
	Cash		10,000
	Paid founders for organization costs.		
Jan. 5	Cash	1,320,000	
	Preferred Stock, $100 Par Value		1,200,000
	Paid-In Capital in Excess of Par Value,		
	Preferred Stock		120,000
	Issued 12,000 shares of preferred stock.		
2013			
June 4	Cash	1,500,000	
	Common Stock, $5 Par Value		500,000
	Paid-In Capital in Excess of Par Value,		
	Common Stock		1,000,000
	Issued 100,000 shares of common stock.		

2. Balance sheet presentations (at December 31 year-end).

Stockholders' Equity	2013	2012
Preferred stock—$100 par value, 10% cumulative, 100,000 shares authorized, 12,000 shares issued and outstanding	$1,200,000	$1,200,000
Paid-in capital in excess of par value, preferred stock....................	120,000	120,000
Total paid-in capital by preferred stockholders	1,320,000	1,320,000
Common stock—$5 par value, 2,000,000 shares authorized, 300,000 shares issued and outstanding in 2012, and 400,000 shares issued and outstanding in 2013.......................	2,000,000	1,500,000
Paid-in capital in excess of par value, common stock	3,100,000	2,100,000
Total paid-in capital by common stockholders	5,100,000	3,600,000
Total paid-in capital	$6,420,000	$4,920,000

3. Dividend allocation table.

	Common	Preferred
2012 ($50,000)		
Preferred—current year (12,000 shares × $10 = $120,000)	$ 0	$ 50,000
Common—remainder (300,000 shares outstanding)	0	0
Total for the year	$ 0	$ 50,000
2013 ($300,000)		
Preferred—dividend in arrears from 2012 ($120,000 − $50,000)	$ 0	$ 70,000
Preferred—current year	0	120,000
Common—remainder (400,000 shares outstanding)	110,000	0
Total for the year	$110,000	$190,000
Dividends per share		
2012	$ 0.00	$ 4.17
2013	$ 0.28	$ 15.83

4. Journal entries.

   a. For 2012 (no-par stock without a stated value):

Jan. 2	Cash	2,400,000	
	Common Stock, No-Par Value		2,400,000
	Issued 200,000 shares of no-par common stock at $12 per share.		

   b. For 2012 (no-par stock with a stated value):

Jan. 2	Cash	2,400,000	
	Common Stock, $10 Stated Value		2,000,000
	Paid-In Capital in Excess of Stated Value, Common Stock		400,000
	Issued 200,000 shares of $10 stated value common stock at $12 per share.		

Summary

C1 **Identify characteristics of corporations and their organization.** Corporations are legal entities whose stockholders are not liable for its debts. Stock is easily transferred, and the life of a corporation does not end with the incapacity of a stockholder. A cor-poration acts through its agents, who are its officers and managers. Corporations are regulated and subject to income taxes. Authorized stock is the stock that a corporation's charter authorizes it to sell. Issued stock is the portion of authorized shares sold. Par value stock is a value per share assigned by the charter. No-par value stock is stock *not* assigned a value per share by the charter. Stated value stock is no-par stock to which the directors assign a value per share.

C2 **Explain characteristics of, and distribute dividends between, common and preferred stock.** Preferred stock has a priority (or senior status) relative to common stock in one or more areas, usually (1) dividends and (2) assets in case of liquidation. Preferred stock usually does not carry voting rights and can be convertible or callable. Convertibility permits the holder to convert preferred to common. Callability permits the issuer to buy back preferred stock under specified conditions. Preferred stockholders usually hold the right to dividend distributions before common stockholders. When preferred stock is cumulative and in arrears, the amount in arrears must be distributed to preferred before any dividends are distributed to common.

C3 **Explain the items reported in retained earnings.** Stockholders' equity is made up of (1) paid-in capital and (2) retained earnings. Paid-in capital consists of funds raised by stock issuances. Retained earnings consists of cumulative net income (losses) not distributed. Many companies face statutory and contractual restrictions on retained earnings. Corporations can voluntarily appropriate retained earnings to inform others about their disposition. Prior period adjustments are corrections of errors in prior financial statements.

A1 **Compute earnings per share and describe its use.** A company with a simple capital structure computes basic EPS by dividing net income less any preferred dividends by the weighted-average number of outstanding common shares. A company with a complex capital structure must usually report both basic and diluted EPS.

A2 **Compute price-earnings ratio and describe its use in analysis.** A common stock's price-earnings (PE) ratio is computed by dividing the stock's market value (price) per share by its EPS. A stock's PE is based on expectations that can prove to be better or worse than eventual performance.

A3 **Compute dividend yield and explain its use in analysis.** Dividend yield is the ratio of a stock's annual cash dividends per share to its market value (price) per share. Dividend yield can be compared with the yield of other companies to determine whether the stock is expected to be an income or growth stock.

A4 **Compute book value and explain its use in analysis.** Book value per common share is equity applicable to common shares divided by the number of outstanding common shares. Book value per preferred share is equity applicable to preferred shares divided by the number of outstanding preferred shares.

P1 **Record the issuance of corporate stock.** When stock is issued, its par or stated value is credited to the stock account and any excess is credited to a separate contributed capital account. If a stock has neither par nor stated value, the entire proceeds are credited to the stock account. Stockholders must contribute assets equal to minimum legal capital or be potentially liable for the deficiency.

P2 **Record transactions involving cash dividends, stock dividends, and stock splits.** Cash dividends involve three events. On the date of declaration, the directors bind the company to pay the dividend. A dividend declaration reduces retained earnings and creates a current liability. On the date of record, recipients of the dividend are identified. On the date of payment, cash is paid to stockholders and the current liability is removed. Neither a stock dividend nor a stock split alters the value of the company. However, the value of each share is less due to the distribution of additional shares. The distribution of additional shares is according to individual stockholders' ownership percent. Small stock dividends ($\leq$25%) are recorded by capitalizing retained earnings equal to the market value of distributed shares. Large stock dividends (>25%) are recorded by capitalizing retained earnings equal to the par or stated value of distributed shares. Stock splits do not necessitate journal entries but do necessitate changes in the description of stock.

P3 **Record purchases and sales of treasury stock and the retirement of stock.** When a corporation purchases its own previously issued stock, it debits the cost of these shares to Treasury Stock. Treasury stock is subtracted from equity in the balance sheet. If treasury stock is reissued, any proceeds in excess of cost are credited to Paid-In Capital, Treasury Stock. If the proceeds are less than cost, they are debited to Paid-In Capital, Treasury Stock to the extent a credit balance exists. Any remaining amount is debited to Retained Earnings. When stock is retired, all accounts related to the stock are removed.

Guidance Answers to Decision Maker and Decision Ethics

Entrepreneur The 50% stock dividend provides you no direct income. A stock dividend often reveals management's optimistic expectations about the future and can improve a stock's marketability by making it affordable to more investors. Accordingly, a stock dividend usually reveals "good news" and because of this, it likely increases (slightly) the market value for your stock. The same conclusions apply to the 3-for-2 stock split.

Concert Organizer You have two basic options: (1) different classes of common stock or (2) common and preferred stock. Your objective is to issue to yourself stock that has all or a majority of the voting power. The other class of stock would carry limited or no voting rights. In this way, you maintain control and are able to raise the necessary funds.

Money Manager Since one company requires a payment of $19 for each $1 of earnings, and the other requires $25, you would prefer the stock with the PE of 19; it is a better deal given identical prospects. You should make sure these companies' earnings computations are roughly the same, for example, no extraordinary items, unusual events, and so forth. Also, your PE estimates for these companies do matter. If you are willing to pay $29 for each $1 of earnings for these companies, you obviously expect both to exceed current market expectations.

Investor Book value reflects recorded values. BMX's book value is $4 per common share. Stock price reflects the market's expectation of net asset value (both tangible and intangible items). BMX's market value is $7 per common share. Comparing these figures suggests BMX's market value of net assets is higher than its recorded values (by an amount of $7 versus $4 per share).

Key Terms

Appropriated retained earnings (p. 498)
Authorized stock (p. 482)
Basic earnings per share (p. 500)
Book value per common share (p. 501)
Book value per preferred share (p. 502)
Call price (p. 493)
Callable preferred stock (p. 493)
Capital stock (p. 482)
Changes in accounting estimates (p. 498)
Common stock (p. 482)
Complex capital structure (p. 500)
Convertible preferred stock (p. 493)
Corporation (p. 480)
Cumulative preferred stock (p. 492)
Date of declaration (p. 487)
Date of payment (p. 487)
Date of record (p. 487)
Diluted earnings per share (p. 500)
Dilutive securities (p. 500)

Discount on stock (p. 485)
Dividend in arrears (p. 492)
Dividend yield (p. 501)
Earnings per share (EPS) (p. 500)
Financial leverage (p. 494)
Large stock dividend (p. 488)
Liquidating cash dividend (p. 488)
Market value per share (p. 483)
Minimum legal capital (p. 483)
Noncumulative preferred stock (p. 492)
Nonparticipating preferred stock (p. 492)
No-par value stock (p. 483)
Organization expenses (p. 481)
Paid-in capital (p. 483)
Paid-in capital in excess of par value (p. 484)
Participating preferred stock (p. 492)
Par value (p. 483)
Par value stock (p. 483)

Preemptive right (p. 482)
Preferred stock (p. 491)
Premium on stock (p. 484)
Price-earnings (PE) ratio (p. 501)
Prior period adjustments (p. 498)
Proxy (p. 481)
Restricted retained earnings (p. 498)
Retained earnings (p. 483)
Retained earnings deficit (p. 487)
Reverse stock split (p. 490)
Simple capital structure (p. 500)
Small stock dividend (p. 488)
Stated value stock (p. 483)
Statement of stockholders' equity (p. 499)
Stock dividend (p. 488)
Stock options (p. 499)
Stock split (p. 489)
Stockholders' equity (p. 483)
Treasury stock (p. 495)

Multiple Choice Quiz   Answers on p. 521   mhhe.com/wildFA7e

Additional Quiz Questions are available at the book's Website.

1. A corporation issues 6,000 shares of $5 par value common stock for $8 cash per share. The entry to record this transaction includes:
   a. A debit to Paid-In Capital in Excess of Par Value for $18,000.
   b. A credit to Common Stock for $48,000.
   c. A credit to Paid-In Capital in Excess of Par Value for $30,000.
   d. A credit to Cash for $48,000.
   e. A credit to Common Stock for $30,000.

2. A company reports net income of $75,000. Its weighted-average common shares outstanding is 19,000. It has no other stock outstanding. Its earnings per share is:
   a. $4.69
   b. $3.95
   c. $3.75
   d. $2.08
   e. $4.41

3. A company has 5,000 shares of $100 par preferred stock and 50,000 shares of $10 par common stock outstanding. Its total stockholders' equity is $2,000,000. Its book value per common share is:
   a. $100.00
   b. $ 10.00
   c. $ 40.00
   d. $ 30.00
   e. $ 36.36

4. A company paid cash dividends of $0.81 per share. Its earnings per share is $6.95 and its market price per share is $45.00. Its dividend yield is:
   a. 1.8%
   b. 11.7%
   c. 15.4%
   d. 55.6%
   e. 8.6%

5. A company's shares have a market value of $85 per share. Its net income is $3,500,000, and its weighted-average common shares outstanding is 700,000. Its price-earnings ratio is:
   a. 5.9
   b. 425.0
   c. 17.0
   d. 10.4
   e. 41.2

Ⅰ Icon denotes assignments that involve decision making.

Discussion Questions

1. What are organization expenses? Provide examples.
2. How are organization expenses reported?
3. **Ⅰ** Who is responsible for directing a corporation's affairs?
4. What is the difference between authorized shares and outstanding shares?
5. What is the preemptive right of common stockholders?
6. List the general rights of common stockholders.
7. What is the difference between the market value per share and the par value per share?
8. What is the difference between the par value and the call price of a share of preferred stock?
9. **Ⅰ** Why would an investor find convertible preferred stock attractive?
10. Identify and explain the importance of the three dates relevant to corporate dividends.
11. Why is the term *liquidating dividend* used to describe cash dividends debited against paid-in capital accounts?
12. **Ⅰ** How does declaring a stock dividend affect the corporation's assets, liabilities, and total equity? What are the effects of the eventual distribution of that stock?
13. **Ⅰ** What is the difference between a stock dividend and a stock split?

14. **Ⅰ** Courts have ruled that a stock dividend is not taxable income to stockholders. What justifies this decision?
15. How does the purchase of treasury stock affect the purchaser's assets and total equity?
16. **Ⅰ** Why do laws place limits on treasury stock purchases?
17. How are EPS results computed for a corporation with a simple capital structure?
18. What is a stock option?
19. How is book value per share computed for a corporation with no preferred stock? What is the main limitation of using book value per share to value a corporation?
20. Refer to Apple's fiscal 2012 balance sheet in Appendix A. How many shares of common stock are authorized? How many shares of voting common stock are issued?   **APPLE**
21. **Ⅰ** Refer to the 2012 balance sheet for Google in Appendix A. What is the par value per share of its preferred stock? Suggest a rationale for the amount of par value it assigned.   **GOOGLE**
22. **Ⅰ** Refer to the financial statements for Samsung in Appendix A. How much were its cash payments for treasury stock purchases for the year ended December 31, 2012?   **Samsung**

▤ connect

Of the following statements, which are true for the corporate form of organization?
1. Ownership rights cannot be easily transferred.
2. Owners have unlimited liability for corporate debts.
3. Capital is more easily accumulated than with most other forms of organization.
4. Corporate income that is distributed to shareholders is usually taxed twice.
5. It is a separate legal entity.
6. It has a limited life.
7. Owners are not agents of the corporation.

QUICK STUDY

QS 11-1
Characteristics of corporations
C1

Prepare the journal entry to record Autumn Company's issuance of 63,000 shares of no-par value common stock assuming the shares:
a. Sell for $29 cash per share.
b. Are exchanged for land valued at $1,827,000.

QS 11-2
Issuance of no-par common stock
P1

Prepare the journal entry to record Zende Company's issuance of 75,000 shares of $5 par value common stock assuming the shares sell for:
a. $5 cash per share.
b. $6 cash per share.

QS 11-3
Issuance of common stock
P1

Prepare the journal entry to record Jevonte Company's issuance of 36,000 shares of its common stock assuming the shares have a:
a. $2 par value and sell for $18 cash per share.
b. $2 stated value and sell for $18 cash per share.

QS 11-4
Issuance of par and stated value common stock
P1

QS 11-5

Issuance of common stock

P1

Prepare the issuer's journal entry for each separate transaction. (*a*) On March 1, Atlantic Co. issues 42,500 shares of $4 par value common stock for $297,500 cash. (*b*) On April 1, OP Co. issues no-par value common stock for $70,000 cash. (*c*) On April 6, MPG issues 2,000 shares of $25 par value common stock for $45,000 of inventory, $145,000 of machinery, and acceptance of an $94,000 note payable.

QS 11-6

Preferred stock issuance and dividends

C2

a. Prepare the journal entry to record Tamasine Company's issuance of 5,000 shares of $100 par value 7% cumulative preferred stock for $102 cash per share.

b. Assuming the facts in part 1, if Tamasine declares a year-end cash dividend, what is the amount of dividend paid to preferred shareholders? (Assume no dividends in arrears.)

QS 11-7

Accounting for dividends

P2

Which of the following statements are true regarding dividends?

1. Cash and stock dividends reduce retained earnings.

2. Dividends payable is recorded at the time a cash dividend is declared.

3. The date of record refers to the date a cash dividend is paid to stockholders.

4. Stock dividends are a mechanism to keep the market price of stock affordable.

QS 11-8

Accounting for cash dividends

P2

Prepare journal entries to record the following transactions for Emerson Corporation.

July 15   Declared a cash dividend payable to common stockholders of $165,000.

August 15 Date of record is August 15 for the cash dividend declared on July 15.

August 31 Paid the dividend declared on July 15.

QS 11-9

Accounting for small stock dividend

P2

The stockholders' equity section of Jun Company's balance sheet as of April 1 follows. On April 2, Jun declares and distributes a 10% stock dividend. The stock's per share market value on April 2 is $20 (prior to the dividend). Prepare the stockholders' equity section immediately after the stock dividend.

Common stock—$5 par value, 375,000 shares authorized, 200,000 shares issued and outstanding	$1,000,000
Paid-in capital in excess of par value, common stock	600,000
Retained earnings	833,000
Total stockholders' equity	$2,433,000

QS 11-10

Dividend allocation between classes of shareholders

C2

Stockholders' equity of Ernst Company consists of 80,000 shares of $5 par value, 8% cumulative preferred stock and 250,000 shares of $1 par value common stock. Both classes of stock have been outstanding since the company's inception. Ernst did not declare any dividends in the prior year, but it now declares and pays a $110,000 cash dividend at the current year-end. Determine the amount distributed to each class of stockholders for this two-year-old company.

QS 11-11

Purchase and sale of treasury stock P3

On May 3, Zirbal Corporation purchased 4,000 shares of its own stock for $36,000 cash. On November 4, Zirbal reissued 850 shares of this treasury stock for $8,500. Prepare the May 3 and November 4 journal entries to record Zirbal's purchase and reissuance of treasury stock.

QS 11-12

Impacts of stock issuances, dividends, splits and treasury transactions

P1 P2 P3

Listed below are various transactions that a company incurred during the current year. Indicate the impact on total stockholders' equity for each scenario. Specifically state whether stockholders' equity would 'Increase', 'Decrease', or have 'No Effect' as a result of each transaction listed below. Consider each transaction independently.

1. A stock dividend equal to 30% of the previously outstanding shares is declared.

2. New shares of common stock are issued for cash.

3. Treasury shares of common stock are purchased (assume the cost method).

4. Cash dividends are paid to shareholders.

QS 11-13

Accounting for changes in estimates; error adjustments

C3

Answer the following questions related to a company's activities for the current year:

1. A review of the notes payable files discovers that three years ago the company reported the entire amount of a payment (principal and interest) on an installment note payable as interest expense. This mistake had a material effect on the amount of income in that year. How should the correction be reported in the current year financial statements?

2. After using an expected useful life of seven years and no salvage value to depreciate its office equipment over the preceding three years, the company decided early this year that the equipment will last only two more years. How should the effects of this decision be reported in the current year financial statements?

Murray Company reports net income of $770,000 for the year. It has no preferred stock, and its weighted-average common shares outstanding is 280,000 shares. Compute its basic earnings per share.

QS 11-14
Basic earnings per share A1

Epic Company earned net income of $900,000 this year. The number of common shares outstanding during the entire year was 400,000, and preferred shareholders received a $20,000 cash dividend. Compute Epic Company's basic earnings per share.

QS 11-15
Basic earnings per share A1

Compute Topp Company's price-earnings ratio if its common stock has a market value of $20.54 per share and its EPS is $3.95. Would an analyst likely consider this stock potentially overpriced- or underpriced or neither? Explain.

QS 11-16
Price-earnings ratio A2

Foxburo Company expects to pay a $2.34 per share cash dividend this year on its common stock. The current market value of Foxburo stock is $32.50 per share. Compute the expected dividend yield on the Foxburo stock. Would you classify the Foxburo stock as a growth or an income stock? Explain.

QS 11-17
Dividend yield A3

The stockholders' equity section of Montel Company's balance sheet follows. The preferred stock's call price is $40. Determine the book value per share of the common stock.

QS 11-18
Book value per common share

A4

Preferred stock—5% cumulative, $10 par value, 20,000 shares authorized, issued and outstanding	$ 200,000
Common stock—$5 par value, 200,000 shares authorized, 150,000 shares issued and outstanding	750,000
Retained earnings	900,000
Total stockholders' equity	$1,850,000

Air France-KLM reports the following equity information for its fiscal year ended March 31, 2012 (euros in millions). Prepare its journal entry, using its account titles, to record the issuance of capital stock assuming that its entire par value stock was issued on March 31, 2012, for cash.

QS 11-19
International equity disclosures

P1

March 31	2012
Issued capital	€ 300
Additional paid-in capital	2,971

---

connect

Describe how each of the following characteristics of organizations applies to corporations.

1. Owner authority and control	5. Duration of life
2. Ease of formation	6. Owner liability
3. Transferability of ownership	7. Legal status
4. Ability to raise large capital amounts	8. Tax status of income

EXERCISES

Exercise 11-1
Characteristics of corporations
C1

Rodriguez Corporation issues 19,000 shares of its common stock for $152,000 cash on February 20. Prepare journal entries to record this event under each of the following separate situations.
1. The stock has a $2 par value.
2. The stock has neither par nor stated value.
3. The stock has an $5 stated value.

Exercise 11-2
Accounting for par, stated, and no-par stock issuances
P1

Prepare journal entries to record the following four separate issuances of stock.
1. A corporation issued 4,000 shares of $5 par value common stock for $35,000 cash.
2. A corporation issued 2,000 shares of no-par common stock to its promoters in exchange for their efforts, estimated to be worth $40,000. The stock has a $1 per share stated value.
3. A corporation issued 2,000 shares of no-par common stock to its promoters in exchange for their efforts, estimated to be worth $40,000. The stock has no stated value.
4. A corporation issued 1,000 shares of $50 par value preferred stock for $60,000 cash.

Exercise 11-3
Recording stock issuances
P1

Exercise 11-4

Stock issuance for noncash assets

P1

Sudoku Company issues 7,000 shares of $7 par value common stock in exchange for land and a building. The land is valued at $45,000 and the building at $85,000. Prepare the journal entry to record issuance of the stock in exchange for the land and building.

Exercise 11-5

Identifying characteristics of preferred stock

C2

Match each description 1 through 6 with the characteristic of preferred stock that it best describes by writing the letter of that characteristic in the blank next to each description.

A. Callable   **B.** Convertible   **C.** Cumulative
D. Noncumulative   **E.** Nonparticipating   **F.** Participating

_____ **1.** Holders of the stock are entitled to receive current and all past dividends before common stockholders receive any dividends.

_____ **2.** The issuing corporation can retire the stock by paying a prespecified price.

_____ **3.** Holders of the stock can receive dividends exceeding the stated rate under certain conditions.

_____ **4.** Holders of the stock are not entitled to receive dividends in excess of the stated rate.

_____ **5.** Holders of this stock can exchange it for shares of common stock.

_____ **6.** Holders of the stock lose any dividends that are not declared in the current year.

Exercise 11-6

Stock dividends and splits

P2

On June 30, 2013, Sharper Corporation's common stock is priced at $62 per share before any stock dividend or split, and the stockholders' equity section of its balance sheet appears as follows.

Common stock—$10 par value, 120,000 shares authorized, 50,000 shares issued and outstanding	$ 500,000
Paid-in capital in excess of par value, common stock	200,000
Retained earnings	660,000
Total stockholders' equity	$1,360,000

1. Assume that the company declares and immediately distributes a 50% stock dividend. This event is recorded by capitalizing retained earnings equal to the stock's par value. Answer these questions about stockholders' equity as it exists *after* issuing the new shares.

  a. What is the retained earnings balance?

Check (1*b*) $1,360,000

  b. What is the amount of total stockholders' equity?

  c. How many shares are outstanding?

2. Assume that the company implements a 3-for-2 stock split instead of the stock dividend in part 1. Answer these questions about stockholders' equity as it exists *after* issuing the new shares.

(2*a*) $660,000

  a. What is the retained earnings balance?

  b. What is the amount of total stockholders' equity?

  c. How many shares are outstanding?

3. Explain the difference, if any, to a stockholder from receiving new shares distributed under a large stock dividend versus a stock split.

Exercise 11-7

Stock dividends and per share book values

P2

The stockholders' equity of TVX Company at the beginning of the day on February 5 follows:

Common stock—$10 par value, 150,000 shares authorized, 60,000 shares issued and outstanding	$ 600,000
Paid-in capital in excess of par value, common stock	425,000
Retained earnings	550,000
Total stockholders' equity	$1,575,000

On February 5, the directors declare a 20% stock dividend distributable on February 28 to the February 15 stockholders of record. The stock's market value is $40 per share on February 5 before the stock dividend. The stock's market value is $33.40 per share on February 28.

1. Prepare entries to record both the dividend declaration and its distribution.

Check (2) Book value per share: before, $26.250; after, $21.875

2. One stockholder owned 800 shares on February 5 before the dividend. Compute the book value per share and total book value of this stockholder's shares immediately before *and* after the stock dividend of February 5.

3. Compute the total market value of the investor's shares in part 2 as of February 5 and February 28.

York's outstanding stock consists of 80,000 shares of *noncumulative* 7.5% preferred stock with a $5 par value and also 200,000 shares of common stock with a $1 par value. During its first four years of operation, the corporation declared and paid the following total cash dividends:

2013	$ 20,000
2014	28,000
2015	200,000
2016	350,000

Determine the amount of dividends paid each year to each of the two classes of stockholders: preferred and common. Also compute the total dividends paid to each class for the four years combined.

Exercise 11-8
Dividends on common and noncumulative preferred stock
C2

Check 4-year total paid to preferred, $108,000

Use the data in Exercise 11-8 to determine the amount of dividends paid each year to each of the two classes of stockholders assuming that the preferred stock is *cumulative*. Also determine the total dividends paid to each class for the four years combined.

Exercise 11-9
Dividends on common and cumulative preferred stock C2

On October 10, the stockholders' equity of Sherman Systems appears as follows:

Common stock—$10 par value, 72,000 shares authorized, issued, and outstanding	$ 720,000
Paid-in capital in excess of par value, common stock	216,000
Retained earnings	864,000
Total stockholders' equity	$1,800,000

Exercise 11-10
Recording and reporting treasury stock transactions
P3

1. Prepare journal entries to record the following transactions for Sherman Systems.
   a. Purchased 5,000 shares of its own common stock at $25 per share on October 11.
   b. Sold 1,000 treasury shares on November 1 for $31 cash per share.
   c. Sold all remaining treasury shares on November 25 for $20 cash per share.
2. Explain how the company's equity section changes after the October 11 treasury stock purchase, and prepare the revised equity section of its balance sheet at that date.

Check (1c) Dr. Retained Earnings, $14,000

The following information is available for Amos Company for the year ended December 31, 2013.
a. Balance of retained earnings, December 31, 2012, prior to discovery of error, $1,375,000.
b. Cash dividends declared and paid during 2013, $43,000.
c. It neglected to record 2011 depreciation expense of $55,500, which is net of $4,500 in income taxes.
d. The company earned $126,000 in 2013 net income.
Prepare a 2013 statement of retained earnings for Amos Company.

Exercise 11-11
Preparing a statement of retained earnings
C3

Ecker Company reports $2,700,000 of net income for 2013 and declares $388,020 of cash dividends on its preferred stock for 2013. At the end of 2013, the company had 678,000 weighted-average shares of common stock.
1. What amount of net income is available to common stockholders for 2013?
2. What is the company's basic EPS for 2013?

Exercise 11-12
Earnings per share
A1

Check (2) $3.41

Kelley Company reports $960,000 of net income for 2013 and declares $120,000 of cash dividends on its preferred stock for 2013. At the end of 2013, the company had 400,000 weighted-average shares of common stock.
1. What amount of net income is available to common stockholders for 2013?
2. What is the company's basic EPS for 2013? Round your answer to the nearest whole cent.

Exercise 11-13
Earnings per share
A1

Check (2) $2.10

Exercise 11-14
Price-earnings ratio computation and interpretation

A2

Compute the price-earnings ratio for each of these four separate companies. Which stock might an analyst likely investigate as being potentially undervalued by the market? Explain.

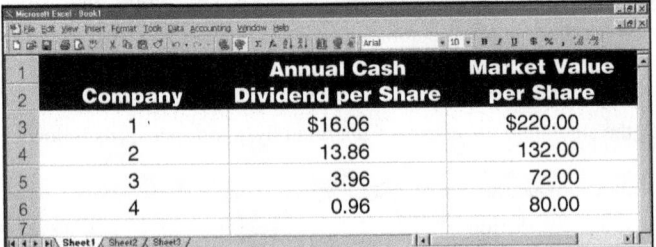

Company	Earnings per Share	Market Value per Share
1	$12.00	$176.40
2	10.00	96.00
3	7.50	93.75
4	50.00	250.00

Exercise 11-15
Dividend yield computation and interpretation

A3

Compute the dividend yield for each of these four separate companies. Which company's stock would probably *not* be classified as an income stock? Explain.

Company	Annual Cash Dividend per Share	Market Value per Share
1	$16.06	$220.00
2	13.86	132.00
3	3.96	72.00
4	0.96	80.00

Exercise 11-16
Book value per share

A4

The equity section of Cyril Corporation's balance sheet shows the following:

Preferred stock—6% cumulative, $25 par value, $30 call price, 10,000 shares issued and outstanding	$ 250,000
Common stock—$10 par value, 80,000 shares issued and outstanding	800,000
Retained earnings	535,000
Total stockholders' equity	$1,585,000

Determine the book value per share of the preferred and common stock under two separate situations.

Check   (1) Book value of common, $16.06

1. No preferred dividends are in arrears.
2. Three years of preferred dividends are in arrears.

Exercise 11-17
Accounting for equity under IFRS

C3 P1

Unilever Group reports the following equity information for the years ended December 31, 2009 and 2010 (euros in millions).

December 31	2010	2009
Share capital	€ 484	€ 484
Share premium	134	131
Other reserves	(5,406)	(5,900)
Retained profit	19,273	17,350
Shareholders' equity	€14,485	€12,065

1. For each of the three account titles *share capital, share premium,* and *retained profit,* match it with the usual account title applied under U.S. GAAP from the following options:
   a. Paid-in capital in excess of par value, common stock
   b. Retained earnings
   c. Common stock, par value

2. Prepare Unilever's journal entry, using its account titles, to record the issuance of capital stock assuming that its entire par value stock was issued on December 31, 2009, for cash.

3. What were Unilever's 2010 dividends assuming that only dividends and income impacted retained profit for 2010 and that its 2010 income totaled €4,232?

Alexander Corporation reports the following components of stockholders' equity on December 31, 2013:

Exercise 11-18
Cash dividends, treasury stock, and statement of retained earnings
C3 P2 P3

Common stock—$25 par value, 50,000 shares authorized, 30,000 shares issued and outstanding	$ 750,000
Paid-in capital in excess of par value, common stock	50,000
Retained earnings	340,000
Total stockholders' equity	$1,140,000

In year 2014, the following transactions affected its stockholders' equity accounts.

Jan.   2   Purchased 3,000 shares of its own stock at $25 cash per share.
Jan.   7   Directors declared a $1.50 per share cash dividend payable on Feb. 28 to the Feb. 9 stockholders of record.
Feb. 28   Paid the dividend declared on January 7.
July   9   Sold 1,200 of its treasury shares at $30 cash per share.
Aug. 27   Sold 1,500 of its treasury shares at $20 cash per share.
Sept. 9   Directors declared a $2 per share cash dividend payable on October 22 to the September 23 stockholders of record.
Oct. 22   Paid the dividend declared on September 9.
Dec. 31   Closed the $52,000 credit balance (from net income) in the Income Summary account to Retained Earnings.

Required

1. Prepare journal entries to record each of these transactions for 2014.
2. Prepare a statement of retained earnings for the year ended December 31, 2014.
3. Prepare the stockholders' equity section of the company's balance sheet as of December 31, 2014.

connect

Kinkaid Co. is incorporated at the beginning of this year and engages in a number of transactions. The following journal entries impacted its stockholders' equity during its first year of operations.

PROBLEM SET A

Problem 11-1A
Stockholders' equity transactions and analysis
C2 P1

a.	Cash	300,000
	Common Stock, $25 Par Value	250,000
	Paid-In Capital in Excess of Par Value, Common Stock	50,000
b.	Organization Expenses	150,000
	Common Stock, $25 Par Value	125,000
	Paid-In Capital in Excess of Par Value, Common Stock	25,000
c.	Cash	43,000
	Accounts Receivable	15,000
	Building	81,500
	Notes Payable	59,500
	Common Stock, $25 Par Value	50,000
	Paid-In Capital in Excess of Par Value, Common Stock	30,000
d.	Cash	120,000
	Common Stock, $25 Par Value	75,000
	Paid-In Capital in Excess of Par Value, Common Stock	45,000

Required

1. Explain the transaction(s) underlying each journal entry (*a*) through (*d*).
2. How many shares of common stock are outstanding at year-end?
3. What is the amount of minimum legal capital (based on par value) at year-end?
4. What is the total paid-in capital at year-end?
5. What is the book value per share of the common stock at year-end if total paid-in capital plus retained earnings equals $695,000?

Check (2) 20,000 shares
(3) $500,000
(4) $650,000

Problem 11-2A
Cash dividends, treasury stock, and statement of retained earnings

C3 P2 P3

Kohler Corporation reports the following components of stockholders' equity on December 31, 2013:

Common stock—$10 par value, 100,000 shares authorized, 40,000 shares issued and outstanding	$400,000
Paid-in capital in excess of par value, common stock	60,000
Retained earnings	270,000
Total stockholders' equity	$730,000

In year 2014, the following transactions affected its stockholders' equity accounts.

Jan.   1   Purchased 4,000 shares of its own stock at $20 cash per share.
Jan.   5   Directors declared a $2 per share cash dividend payable on Feb. 28 to the Feb. 5 stockholders of record.
Feb. 28   Paid the dividend declared on January 5.
July   6   Sold 1,500 of its treasury shares at $24 cash per share.
Aug. 22   Sold 2,500 of its treasury shares at $17 cash per share.
Sept. 5   Directors declared a $2 per share cash dividend payable on October 28 to the September 25 stockholders of record.
Oct. 28   Paid the dividend declared on September 5.
Dec. 31   Closed the $388,000 credit balance (from net income) in the Income Summary account to Retained Earnings.

Required

1. Prepare journal entries to record each of these transactions for 2014.

Check   (2) Retained earnings, Dec. 31, 2014, $504,500.

2. Prepare a statement of retained earnings for the year ended December 31, 2014.
3. Prepare the stockholders' equity section of the company's balance sheet as of December 31, 2014.

Problem 11-3A
Equity analysis—journal entries and account balances

P2

At September 30, the end of Beijing Company's third quarter, the following stockholders' equity accounts are reported.

Common stock, $12 par value	$360,000
Paid-in capital in excess of par value, common stock	90,000
Retained earnings	320,000

In the fourth quarter, the following entries related to its equity are recorded:

Oct. 2	Retained Earnings	60,000	
	Common Dividend Payable		60,000
Oct. 25	Common Dividend Payable	60,000	
	Cash		60,000
Oct. 31	Retained Earnings	75,000	
	Common Stock Dividend Distributable		36,000
	Paid-In Capital in Excess of Par Value, Common Stock		39,000
Nov. 5	Common Stock Dividend Distributable	36,000	
	Common Stock, $12 Par Value		36,000
Dec. 1	Memo—Change the title of the common stock account to reflect the new par value of $4.		
Dec. 31	Income Summary	210,000	
	Retained Earnings		210,000

Required

1. Explain the transaction(s) underlying each journal entry.
2. Complete the following table showing the equity account balances at each indicated date (include the balances from September 30).

	Oct. 2	Oct. 25	Oct. 31	Nov. 5	Dec. 1	Dec. 31
Common stock	$____	$____	$____	$____	$____	$____
Common stock dividend distributable	____	____	____	____	____	____
Paid-in capital in excess of par, common stock	____	____	____	____	____	____
Retained earnings	____	____	____	____	____	____
Total equity........................	$____	$____	$____	$____	$____	$____

Check   Total equity: Oct. 2, $710,000; Dec. 31, $920,000

The equity sections from Atticus Group's 2013 and 2014 year-end balance sheets follow.

Problem 11-4A
Analysis of changes in stockholders' equity accounts

C3 P2 P3

Stockholders' Equity (December 31, 2013)

Common stock—$4 par value, 100,000 shares authorized, 40,000 shares issued and outstanding	$160,000
Paid-in capital in excess of par value, common stock	120,000
Retained earnings	320,000
Total stockholders' equity	$600,000

Stockholders' Equity (December 31, 2014)

Common stock—$4 par value, 100,000 shares authorized, 47,400 shares issued, 3,000 shares in treasury	$189,600
Paid-in capital in excess of par value, common stock	179,200
Retained earnings ($30,000 restricted by treasury stock)	400,000
	768,800
Less cost of treasury stock	(30,000)
Total stockholders' equity	$738,800

The following transactions and events affected its equity during year 2014.

Jan.   5   Declared a $0.50 per share cash dividend, date of record January 10.
Mar. 20   Purchased treasury stock for cash.
Apr.   5   Declared a $0.50 per share cash dividend, date of record April 10.
July   5   Declared a $0.50 per share cash dividend, date of record July 10.
July 31   Declared a 20% stock dividend when the stock's market value is $12 per share.
Aug. 14   Issued the stock dividend that was declared on July 31.
Oct.   5   Declared a $0.50 per share cash dividend, date of record October 10.

Required

1. How many common shares are outstanding on each cash dividend date?
2. What is the total dollar amount for each of the four cash dividends?
3. What is the amount of the capitalization of retained earnings for the stock dividend?
4. What is the per share cost of the treasury stock purchased?
5. How much net income did the company earn during year 2014?

Check   (3) $88,800
(4) $10
(5) $248,000

Raphael Corporation's common stock is currently selling on a stock exchange at $85 per share, and its current balance sheet shows the following stockholders' equity section:

Problem 11-5A
Computation of book values and dividend allocations

C2 A4

Preferred stock—5% cumulative, $___ par value, 1,000 shares authorized, issued, and outstanding	$ 50,000
Common stock—$___ par value, 4,000 shares authorized, issued, and outstanding	80,000
Retained earnings	150,000
Total stockholders' equity	$280,000

Required (Round per share amounts to cents.)

1. What is the current market value (price) of this corporation's common stock?

2. What are the par values of the corporation's preferred stock and its common stock?

3. If no dividends are in arrears, what are the book values per share of the preferred stock and the common stock?

Check   (4) Book value of common, $56.25

4. If two years' preferred dividends are in arrears, what are the book values per share of the preferred stock and the common stock?

(5) Book value of common, $55

5. If two years' preferred dividends are in arrears and the preferred stock is callable at $55 per share, what are the book values per share of the preferred stock and the common stock?

(6) Dividends per common share, $1.00

6. If two years' preferred dividends are in arrears and the board of directors declares cash dividends of $11,500, what total amount will be paid to the preferred and to the common shareholders? What is the amount of dividends per share for the common stock?

Analysis Component

7. What are some factors that can contribute to a difference between the book value of common stock and its market value (price)?

PROBLEM SET B

Problem 11-1B
Stockholders' equity
transactions and analysis

C2 P1

Weiss Company is incorporated at the beginning of this year and engages in a number of transactions. The following journal entries impacted its stockholders' equity during its first year of operations.

a.	Cash	120,000	
	Common Stock, $1 Par Value		3,000
	Paid-In Capital in Excess of Par Value, Common Stock		117,000
b.	Organization Expenses	40,000	
	Common Stock, $1 Par Value		1,000
	Paid-In Capital in Excess of Par Value, Common Stock		39,000
c.	Cash	13,300	
	Accounts Receivable	8,000	
	Building	37,000	
	Notes Payable		18,300
	Common Stock, $1 Par Value		800
	Paid-In Capital in Excess of Par Value, Common Stock		39,200
d.	Cash	60,000	
	Common Stock, $1 Par Value		1,200
	Paid-In Capital in Excess of Par Value, Common Stock		58,800

Required

1. Explain the transaction(s) underlying each journal entry (*a*) through (*d*).

Check   (2) 6,000 shares

2. How many shares of common stock are outstanding at year-end?

(3) $6,000

3. What is the amount of minimum legal capital (based on par value) at year-end?

(4) $260,000

4. What is the total paid-in capital at year-end?

5. What is the book value per share of the common stock at year-end if total paid-in capital plus retained earnings equals $283,000?

Problem 11-2B
Cash dividends, treasury stock,
and statement of retained
earnings

C3 P2 P3

Balthus Corp. reports the following components of stockholders' equity on December 31, 2013:

Common stock—$1 par value, 320,000 shares authorized, 200,000 shares issued and outstanding	$ 200,000
Paid-in capital in excess of par value, common stock	1,400,000
Retained earnings	2,160,000
Total stockholders' equity	$3,760,000

It completed the following transactions related to stockholders' equity in year 2014:

Jan. 10   Purchased 40,000 shares of its own stock at $12 cash per share.
Mar. 2   Directors declared a $1.50 per share cash dividend payable on March 31 to the March 15 stock-
          holders of record.
Mar. 31   Paid the dividend declared on March 2.
Nov. 11   Sold 24,000 of its treasury shares at $13 cash per share.
Nov. 25   Sold 16,000 of its treasury shares at $9.50 cash per share.
Dec. 1   Directors declared a $2.50 per share cash dividend payable on January 2 to the December 10
          stockholders of record.
Dec. 31   Closed the $1,072,000 credit balance (from net income) in the Income Summary account to
          Retained Earnings.

Required

1. Prepare journal entries to record each of these transactions for 2014.
2. Prepare a statement of retained earnings for the year ended December 31, 2014.
3. Prepare the stockholders' equity section of the company's balance sheet as of December 31, 2014.

Check   (2) Retained earnings, Dec. 31, 2014, $2,476,000

At December 31, the end of Chilton Communication's third quarter, the following stockholders' equity accounts are reported:

Problem 11-3B
Equity analysis—journal entries and account balances
P2

Common stock, $10 par value	$ 960,000
Paid-in capital in excess of par value, common stock	384,000
Retained earnings	1,600,000

In the fourth quarter, the following entries related to its equity are recorded:

Jan. 17	Retained Earnings	96,000	
	Common Dividend Payable		96,000
Feb. 5	Common Dividend Payable	96,000	
	Cash		96,000
Feb. 28	Retained Earnings	252,000	
	Common Stock Dividend Distributable		120,000
	Paid-In Capital in Excess of Par Value, Common Stock		132,000
Mar. 14	Common Stock Dividend Distributable	120,000	
	Common Stock, $10 Par Value		120,000
Mar. 25	Memo—Change the title of the common stock account to reflect the new par value of $5.		
Mar. 31	Income Summary	720,000	
	Retained Earnings		720,000

Required

1. Explain the transaction(s) underlying each journal entry.
2. Complete the following table showing the equity account balances at each indicated date (include the
balances from December 31).

	Jan. 17	Feb. 5	Feb. 28	Mar. 14	Mar. 25	Mar. 31
Common stock	$_____	$_____	$_____	$_____	$_____	$_____
Common stock dividend distributable	_____	_____	_____	_____	_____	_____
Paid-in capital in excess of par, common stock	_____	_____	_____	_____	_____	_____
Retained earnings	_____	_____	_____	_____	_____	_____
Total equity	$_____	$_____	$_____	$_____	$_____	$_____

Check   Total equity: Jan. 17, $2,848,000; Mar. 31, $3,568,000

Problem 11-4B

Analysis of changes in stockholders' equity accounts

C3 P2 P3

The equity sections from Hovo Corporation's 2013 and 2014 balance sheets follow.

Stockholders' Equity (December 31, 2013)	
Common stock—$20 par value, 30,000 shares authorized,	
17,000 shares issued and outstanding	$340,000
Paid-in capital in excess of par value, common stock	60,000
Retained earnings	270,000
Total stockholders' equity	$670,000

Stockholders' Equity (December 31, 2014)	
Common stock—$20 par value, 30,000 shares authorized,	
19,000 shares issued, 1,000 shares in treasury	$380,000
Paid-in capital in excess of par value, common stock	104,000
Retained earnings ($40,000 restricted by treasury stock)	295,200
	779,200
Less cost of treasury stock	(40,000)
Total stockholders' equity	$739,200

The following transactions and events affected its equity during year 2014.

Feb. 15   Declared a $0.40 per share cash dividend, date of record five days later.
Mar. 2   Purchased treasury stock for cash.
May 15   Declared a $0.40 per share cash dividend, date of record five days later.
Aug. 15   Declared a $0.40 per share cash dividend, date of record five days later.
Oct.   4   Declared a 12.5% stock dividend when the stock's market value is $42 per share.
Oct. 20   Issued the stock dividend that was declared on October 4.
Nov. 15   Declared a $0.40 per share cash dividend, date of record five days later.

Required

1. How many common shares are outstanding on each cash dividend date?
2. What is the total dollar amount for each of the four cash dividends?
3. What is the amount of the capitalization of retained earnings for the stock dividend?
4. What is the per share cost of the treasury stock purchased?
5. How much net income did the company earn during year 2014?

Check (3) $84,000
            (4) $40
            (5) $136,000

Problem 11-5B

Computation of book values and dividend allocations

C2 A4

Soltech Company's common stock is currently selling on a stock exchange at $90 per share, and its current balance sheet shows the following stockholders' equity section.

Preferred stock—8% cumulative, $___ par value, 1,500 shares	
authorized, issued, and outstanding	$ 375,000
Common stock—$___ par value, 18,000 shares	
authorized, issued, and outstanding	900,000
Retained earnings	1,125,000
Total stockholders' equity	$2,400,000

Required (Round per share amounts to cents.)

1. What is the current market value (price) of this corporation's common stock?
2. What are the par values of the corporation's preferred stock and its common stock?
3. If no dividends are in arrears, what are the book values per share of the preferred stock and the common stock? (Round per share values to the nearest cent.)
4. If two years' preferred dividends are in arrears, what are the book values per share of the preferred stock and the common stock? (Round per share values to the nearest cent.)
5. If two years' preferred dividends are in arrears and the preferred stock is callable at $280 per share, what are the book values per share of the preferred stock and the common stock? (Round per share values to the nearest cent.)
6. If two years' preferred dividends are in arrears and the board of directors declares cash dividends of $100,000, what total amount will be paid to the preferred and to the common shareholders? What is the amount of dividends per share for the common stock? (Round per share values to the nearest cent.)

Check (4) Book value of common, $109.17

           (5) Book value of common, $106.67

           (6) Dividends per common share, $0.56

Analysis Component

7. Discuss why the book value of common stock is not always a good estimate of its market value.

SERIAL PROBLEM
Success Systems
P1 C1 C2

(This serial problem began in Chapter 1 and continues through most of the book. If previous chapter segments were not completed, the serial problem can begin at this point. It is helpful, but not necessary, to use the Working Papers that accompany the book.)

SP 11 Adria Lopez created Success Systems on October 1, 2013. The company has been successful, and Adria plans to expand her business. She believes that an additional $86,000 is needed and is investigating three funding sources.

a. Adria's sister Cicely is willing to invest $86,000 in the business as a common shareholder. Since Adria currently has about $129,000 invested in the business, Cicely's investment will mean that Adria will maintain about 60% ownership, and Cicely will have 40% ownership of Success Systems.

b. Adria's uncle Marcello is willing to invest $86,000 in the business as a preferred shareholder. Marcello would purchase 860 shares of $100 par value, 7% preferred stock.

c. Adria's banker is willing to lend her $86,000 on a 7%, 10-year note payable. She would make monthly payments of $1,000 per month for 10 years.

Required

1. Prepare the journal entry to reflect the initial $86,000 investment under each of the options (a), (b), and (c).

2. Evaluate the three proposals for expansion, providing the pros and cons of each option.

3. Which option do you recommend Adria adopt? Explain.

The following General Ledger assignments highlight the impact, or lack thereof, on financial statements from equity-based transactions.

GENERAL LEDGER PROBLEM

Available in Connect Only

connect
|ACCOUNTING

GL 11-1 (This assignment is adapted from Problem 11-1, including beginning equity balances.) Prepare journal entries for key equity transactions; each transaction is automatically posted to the ledger using the **General Ledger** tool. Then, prepare period-end closing entries, the statement of retained earnings, and the stockholders' equity section of the balance sheet.

GL 11-2 (This assignment is adapted from Problem 11-4, including beginning and ending equity balances.) Prepare journal entries that reflect changes in equity balances for the period; each transaction is automatically posted to the ledger using the **General Ledger** tool. Required computations include the number of shares outstanding, the amount of net income, and the impact on retained earnings resulting from a stock dividend.

Beyond the Numbers

BTN 11-1 Refer to Apple's financial statements in Appendix A to answer the following.

REPORTING IN ACTION
C2 A1 A4

APPLE

1. How many shares of common stock are issued and outstanding at September 29, 2012, and September 24, 2011? How do these numbers compare with the basic weighted-average common shares outstanding at September 29, 2012, and September 24, 2011?

2. What is the book value of its entire common stock at September 29, 2012?

3. What is the total amount of cash dividends paid to common stockholders for the years ended September 29, 2012, and September 24, 2011?

4. Identify and compare basic EPS amounts across fiscal years 2012, 2011, and 2010. Identify and comment on any notable changes.

5. How many shares does Apple hold in treasury stock, if any, as of September 29, 2012, and September 24, 2011?

Fast Forward

6. Access Apple's financial statements for fiscal years ending after September 29, 2012, from its Website (Apple.com) or the SEC's EDGAR database (www.SEC.gov). Has the number of common shares outstanding increased since that date? Has the company increased the total amount of cash dividends paid compared to the total amount for fiscal year 2012?

COMPARATIVE ANALYSIS

A1 A2 A3 A4

APPLE
GOOGLE

BTN 11-2 Key comparative figures for Apple and Google follow.

Key Figures	Apple	Google
Net income (in millions)	$ 41,733	$ 10,737
Cash dividends declared per common share	$ 2.65	$ —
Common shares outstanding (in millions)	939,208	329,979
Weighted-average common shares outstanding (in millions)	934,818	327,213
Market value (price) per share	$ 655.88	$ 707.38
Equity applicable to common shares (in millions)	$118,210	$ 71,715

Required

1. Compute the book value per common share for each company using these data.
2. Compute the basic EPS for each company using these data.
3. Compute the dividend yield for each company using these data. Does the dividend yield of either of the companies characterize it as an income or growth stock? Explain.
4. Compute, compare, and interpret the price-earnings ratio for each company using these data.

ETHICS CHALLENGE

C3

BTN 11-3 Harriet Moore is an accountant for New World Pharmaceuticals. Her duties include tracking research and development spending in the new product development division. Over the course of the past six months, Harriet notices that a great deal of funds have been spent on a particular project for a new drug. She hears "through the grapevine" that the company is about to patent the drug and expects it to be a major advance in antibiotics. Harriet believes that this new drug will greatly improve company performance and will cause the company's stock to increase in value. Harriet decides to purchase shares of New World in order to benefit from this expected increase.

Required

What are Harriet's ethical responsibilities, if any, with respect to the information she has learned through her duties as an accountant for New World Pharmaceuticals? What are the implications to her planned purchase of New World shares?

COMMUNICATING IN PRACTICE

A1 A2

Hint: Make a transparency of each team's memo for a class discussion.

BTN 11-4 Teams are to select an industry, and each team member is to select a different company in that industry. Each team member then is to acquire the selected company's financial statements (or Form 10-K) from the SEC site (www.SEC.gov). Use these data to identify basic EPS. Use the financial press (or finance.yahoo.com) to determine the market price of this stock, and then compute the price-earnings ratio. Communicate with teammates via a meeting, e-mail, or telephone to discuss the meaning of this ratio, how companies compare, and the industry norm. The team must prepare a single memorandum reporting the ratio for each company and identifying the team conclusions or consensus of opinion. The memorandum is to be duplicated and distributed to the instructor and teammates.

TAKING IT TO THE NET

C1 C3

BTN 11-5 Access the February 24, 2012, filing of the 2011 calendar-year 10-K report of McDonald's, (ticker MCD) from www.SEC.gov.

Required

1. Review McDonald's balance sheet and identify how many classes of stock it has issued.
2. What are the par values, number of authorized shares, and issued shares of the classes of stock you identified in part 1?
3. Review its statement of cash flows and identify what total amount of cash it paid in 2011 to purchase treasury stock.
4. What amount did McDonald's pay out in common stock cash dividends for 2011?

TEAMWORK IN ACTION

P3

Hint: Instructor should be sure each team accurately completes part 1 before proceeding.

BTN 11-6 This activity requires teamwork to reinforce understanding of accounting for treasury stock.

1. Write a brief team statement (a) generalizing what happens to a corporation's financial position when it engages in a stock "buyback" and (b) identifying reasons why a corporation would engage in this activity.
2. Assume that an entity acquires 100 shares of its $100 par value common stock at a cost of $134 cash per share. Discuss the entry to record this acquisition. Next, assign *each* team member to prepare *one* of the following entries (assume each entry applies to all shares):
   a. Reissue treasury shares at cost.
   b. Reissue treasury shares at $150 per share.

c. Reissue treasury shares at $120 per share; assume the paid-in capital account from treasury shares has a $1,500 balance.

d. Reissue treasury shares at $120 per share; assume the paid-in capital account from treasury shares has a $1,000 balance.

e. Reissue treasury shares at $120 per share; assume the paid-in capital account from treasury shares has a zero balance.

3. In sequence, each member is to present his/her entry to the team and explain the *similarities* and *differences* between that entry and the previous entry.

BTN 11-7 Assume that Groupon decides to launch a new Website to market discount bookkeeping services to consumers. This chain, named Servon, requires $500,000 of start-up capital. The founder contributes $375,000 of personal assets in return for 15,000 shares of common stock, but he must raise another $125,000 in cash. There are two alternative plans for raising the additional cash. *Plan A* is to sell 3,750 shares of common stock to one or more investors for $125,000 cash. *Plan B* is to sell 1,250 shares of cumulative preferred stock to one or more investors for $125,000 cash (this preferred stock would have a $100 par value, an annual 8% dividend rate, and be issued at par).

1. If the new business is expected to earn $72,000 of after-tax net income in the first year, what rate of return on beginning equity will the founder earn under each alternative plan? Which plan will provide the higher expected return?

2. If the new business is expected to earn $16,800 of after-tax net income in the first year, what rate of return on beginning equity will the founder earn under each alternative plan? Which plan will provide the higher expected return?

3. Analyze and interpret the differences between the results for parts 1 and 2.

ENTREPRENEURIAL DECISION

C2 P2

BTN 11-8 Review 30 to 60 minutes of financial news programming on television. Take notes on companies that are catching analysts' attention. You might hear reference to over- and undervaluation of firms and to reports about PE ratios, dividend yields, and earnings per share. Be prepared to give a brief description to the class of your observations.

HITTING THE ROAD

A1 A2 A3

BTN 11-9 Financial information for Samsung (www.Samsung.com) follows (drawn from its financial statements and footnotes):

GLOBAL DECISION

A1 C3

Samsung

Net income less dividends available to preferred shares (in millions)	₩ 20,130,020
Cash dividends declared for common stock (in millions).	₩ 981,359
Cash dividends declared per common share	₩ 7,500
Number of common shares outstanding (in millions)*	130.848
Weighted average common shares outstanding (in millions)	130.698
Equity applicable to common shares (in millions)†	₩121,360,739

*Computed as 147.299 mil. issued shares less 16.451 mil. treasury shares.
†Computed as ₩121,480,206 total equity less ₩119,467 preferred stock.

Required

1. Compute book value per share for Samsung.
2. Compute earnings per share (EPS) for Samsung.
3. Compare Samsung's dividends per share with its EPS. Is Samsung paying out a large or small amount of its income as dividends? Explain.

ANSWERS TO MULTIPLE CHOICE QUIZ

1. e; Entry to record this stock issuance is:

Cash (6,000 × $8)	48,000	
Common Stock (6,000 × $5)		30,000
Paid-In Capital in Excess of Par Value, Common Stock		18,000

2. b; $75,000/19,000 shares = $3.95 per share

3. d; Preferred stock = 5,000 × $100 = $500,000

Book value per share = ($2,000,000 − $500,000)/50,000 shares = $30 per common share

4. a; $0.81/$45.00 = 1.8%

5. c; Earnings per share = $3,500,000/700,000 shares = $5 per share
PE ratio = $85/$5 = 17.0

12

Reporting and Analyzing Cash Flows

BASICS OF CASH FLOW REPORTING	CASH FLOWS FROM OPERATING	CASH FLOWS FROM INVESTING	CASH FLOWS FROM FINANCING
C1 Purpose, measurement and classification	**P2** Indirect and direct methods of reporting	**P3** Three-stage process of analysis	**P3** Three-stage process of analysis
Noncash activities	Illustration of indirect method	Analysis of noncurrent assets	Analysis of non-current liabilities
P1 Format and preparation	Summary of indirect method adjustments	Analysis of other assets	Analysis of equity
			A1 Analysis of cash

Learning Objectives

C1 Distinguish between operating, investing, and financing activities, and describe how noncash investing and financing activities are disclosed. (p. 525)

P1 Prepare a statement of cash flows. (p. 527)

P2 Compute cash flows from operating activities using the indirect method. (p. 532)

P3 Determine cash flows from both investing and financing activities. (p. 537)

A1 Analyze the statement of cash flows and apply the cash flow on total assets ratio. (p. 542)

P4 *Appendix 12A*—Illustrate use of a spreadsheet to prepare a statement of cash flows. (p. 546)

P5 *Appendix 12B*—Compute cash flows from operating activities using the direct method. (p. 549)

Cash in the Cloud

"We want to create the future"
—MARC BENIOFF

SAN FRANCISCO—We all know to be wary of companies with declining income, declining working capital, and rising debt. One of those companies is **salesforce.com (salesforce.com)**, a service provider of social and mobile cloud technology solutions. Its goal is to "help customers transform themselves into 'customer companies'," meaning they provide "customer relationship management, or CRM, via the Internet, or 'cloud'." Marc Benioff, co-founder, explains, "We want to be the company that you turn to connect your customers with you, and that means you have to do it in sales, you have to do it in service, and you have to do it in marketing."

The company's net income, working capital, and total liabilities for the past four years follow:

($ billions)	2010	2011	2012	2013
Net income......	$ 85	$ 70	$ (12)	$ (270)
Working capital. . .	798	(202)	(628)	(902)
Liabilities........	1,404	1,815	2,498	3,158

While its accounting results reveal declining income and working capital at the same time its debt is rising, the markets see the company in a positive light. Moreover, the following graph shows its stock price exhibiting a substantial increase over the past four years.

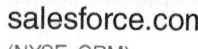

salesforce.com
(NYSE: CRM)

10,000 employees
$3.1 bil. revenue

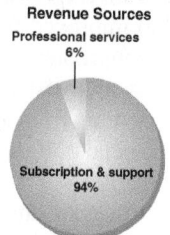

Revenue Sources

Professional services 6%

Subscription & support 94%

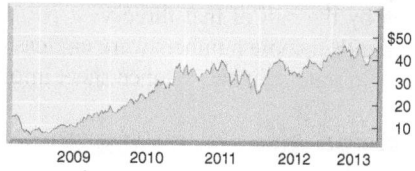

Are the markets wrong? Further, publications such as *Forbes* named salesforce.com the "Most Innovative Company in the World" for the second consecutive year in 2012. What's going on here?

Let's dig a bit deeper. Its financial statements reveal increasing deferred revenues arising from advance customer payments to perform future services (a good thing!). We also see rising sales, nearly doubling over the past two years. Although costs did outstrip sales, the growth in deferred revenues foretells a positive future. This is the source

of the market enthusiasm, along with even greater growth potential.

This picture is readily apparent when looking at salesforce.com's cash flows:

($ billions)	2010	2011	2012	2013
Operating CF	$271	$ 459	$592	$737
Investing CF	(379)	(1,063)	(490)	(939)
Financing CF	637	14	76	335

The key line here is its operating cash flows, which have increased 270% over the past three years! The large investing cash outflows are what we would expect from a growth company. Further, its financing cash inflows are relatively small for a growth company, suggesting that much of its expansion is self-funded.

Our analysis of salesforce.com, a potential game-changer, was greatly aided by examining the statement of cash flows. Although there is risk with deferred revenues, the market is seeing those numbers as a precursor to future revenues and potentially greater growth in sales and net income. While only the future can reveal the success or failure of those expectations, it is clear that the market is relying on cash flow numbers in foretelling a rosy future.

Sources: *salesforce.com Website,* January 2014; *salesforce.com 10-K,* 2013; *Forbes,* September 2013

BASICS OF CASH FLOW REPORTING

This section describes the basics of cash flow reporting, including its purpose, measurement, classification, format, and preparation.

Purpose of the Statement of Cash Flows

The purpose of the **statement of cash flows** is to report cash receipts (inflows) and cash payments (outflows) during a period. This includes separately identifying the cash flows related to operating, investing, and financing activities. The statement of cash flows does more than simply report changes in cash. It is the detailed disclosure of individual cash flows that makes this statement useful to users. Information in this statement helps users answer questions such as these:

Point: Internal users rely on the statement of cash flows to make investing and financing decisions. External users rely on this statement to assess the amount and timing of a company's cash flows.

- How does a company obtain its cash?
- Where does a company spend its cash?
- What explains the change in the cash balance?

The statement of cash flows addresses important questions such as these by summarizing, classifying, and reporting a company's cash inflows and cash outflows for each period.

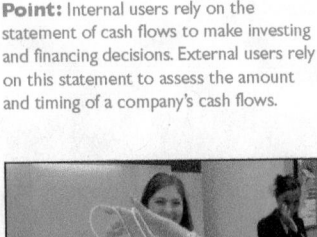

Importance of Cash Flows

Information about cash flows can influence decision makers in important ways. For instance, we look more favorably at a company that is financing its expenditures with cash from operations than one that does it by selling its assets. Information about cash flows helps users decide whether a company has enough cash to pay its existing debts as they mature. It is also relied upon to evaluate a company's ability to meet unexpected obligations and pursue unexpected opportunities. External information users especially want to assess a company's ability to take advantage of new business opportunities. Internal users such as managers use cash flow information to plan day-to-day operating activities and make long-term investment decisions.

Macy's striking turnaround is an example of how analysis and management of cash flows can lead to improved financial stability. Several years ago Macy's obtained temporary protection from bankruptcy, at which time it desperately needed to improve its cash flows. It did so by engaging in aggressive cost-cutting measures. As a result, Macy's annual cash flow rose to $210 million, up from a negative cash flow of $38.9 million in the prior year. Macy's eventually met its financial obligations and then successfully merged with Federated Department Stores.

The case of W. T. Grant Co. is a classic example of the importance of cash flow information in predicting a company's future performance and financial strength. Grant reported net income of more than $40 million per year for three consecutive years. At that same time, it was experiencing an alarming decrease in cash provided by operations. For instance, net cash outflow was more than $90 million by the end of that three-year period. Grant soon went bankrupt. Users who relied solely on Grant's income numbers were unpleasantly surprised. This reminds us that cash flows as well as income statement and balance sheet information are crucial in making business decisions.

▮ Decision Insight

Cash Savvy "A lender must have a complete understanding of a borrower's cash flows to assess both the borrowing needs and repayment sources. This requires information about the major types of cash inflows and outflows. I have seen many companies, whose financial statements indicate good profitability, experience severe financial problems because the owners or managers lacked a good understanding of cash flows."—Mary E. Garza, **Bank of America** ▮

Measurement of Cash Flows

Cash Equivalents

Cash flows are defined to include both *cash* and *cash equivalents*. The statement of cash flows explains the difference between the beginning and ending balances of cash and cash equivalents. We continue to use the phrases *cash flows* and the *statement of cash flows,* but we must remember that both phrases refer to cash and cash equivalents. Recall that a cash equivalent must satisfy two criteria: (1) be readily convertible to a known amount of cash and (2) be sufficiently close to its maturity so its market value is unaffected by interest rate changes. In most cases, a debt security must be within three months of its maturity to satisfy these criteria. Companies must disclose and follow a clear policy for determining cash and cash equivalents and apply it consistently from period to period. American Express, for example, defines its cash equivalents as "time deposits and other highly liquid investments with original maturities of 90 days or less."

Classification of Cash Flows

Since cash and cash equivalents are combined, the statement of cash flows does not report transactions between cash and cash equivalents such as cash paid to purchase cash equivalents and cash received from selling cash equivalents. However, all other cash receipts and cash payments are classified and reported on the statement as operating, investing, or financing activities. Individual cash receipts and payments for each of these three categories are labeled to identify their originating transactions or events. A net cash inflow (source) occurs when the receipts in a category exceed the payments. A net cash outflow (use) occurs when the payments in a category exceed the receipts.

> **C1** Distinguish between operating, investing, and financing activities, and describe how noncash investing and financing activities are disclosed.

Operating Activities   Operating activities include those transactions and events that determine net income. Examples are the production and purchase of merchandise, the sale of goods and services to customers, and the expenditures to administer the business. Not all items in income, such as unusual gains and losses, are operating activities (we discuss these exceptions later in the chapter). Exhibit 12.1 lists the more common cash inflows and outflows from operating activities. (Although cash receipts and cash payments from buying and selling trading securities are often reported under operating activities, new standards require that these receipts and payments be classified based on the nature and purpose of those securities.)

OPERATING

EXHIBIT 12.1

Cash Flows from Operating Activities

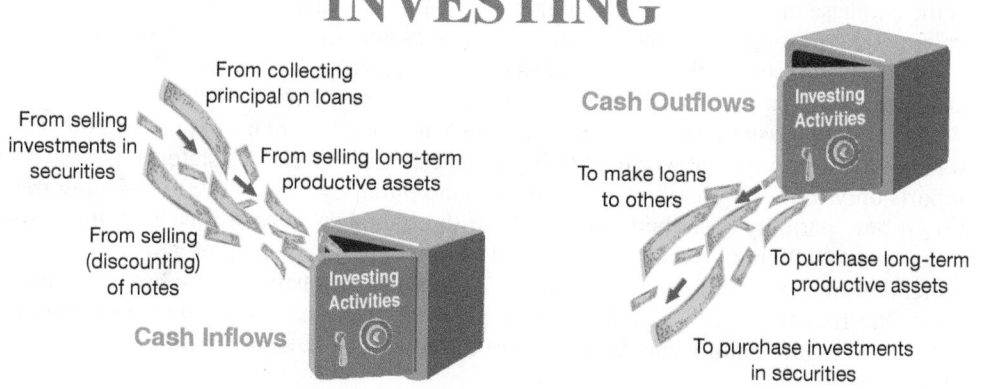

Investing Activities   Investing activities generally include those transactions and events that affect long-term assets—namely, the purchase and sale of long-term assets. They also include (1) the purchase and sale of short-term investments in the securities of other entities, other than cash equivalents and trading securities and (2) lending and collecting money for notes receivable. Exhibit 12.2 lists examples of cash flows from investing activities. Proceeds

Point: The FASB requires that *cash dividends received* and *cash interest received* be reported as operating activities.

EXHIBIT 12.2

Cash Flows from Investing Activities

INVESTING

From collecting
principal on loans

From selling
investments in
securities

From selling long-term
productive assets

From selling
(discounting)
of notes

Investing
Activities

Cash Inflows

Cash Outflows   Investing
Activities

To make loans
to others

To purchase long-term
productive assets

To purchase investments
in securities

from collecting the principal amounts of notes deserve special mention. If the note results from sales to customers, its cash receipts are classified as operating activities whether short-term or long-term. If the note results from a loan to another party apart from sales, however, the cash receipts from collecting the note principal are classified as an investing activity. The FASB requires that the collection of interest on loans be reported as an operating activity.

Financing Activities   **Financing activities** include those transactions and events that affect long-term liabilities and equity. Examples are (1) obtaining cash from issuing debt and repaying the amounts borrowed and (2) receiving cash from or distributing cash to owners. These activities involve transactions with a company's owners and creditors. They also often involve borrowing and repaying principal amounts relating to both short- and long-term debt. GAAP requires that payments of interest expense be classified as operating activities. Also, cash payments to settle credit purchases of merchandise, whether on account or by note, are operating activities. Exhibit 12.3 lists examples of cash flows from financing activities.

EXHIBIT 12.3

Cash Flows from
Financing Activities

Point: Interest payments on a loan are classified as operating activities, but payments of loan principal are financing activities.

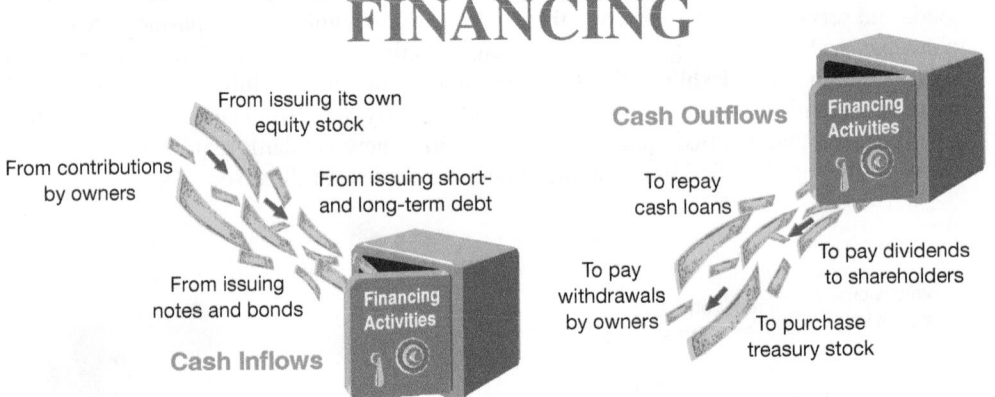

FINANCING

From issuing its own
equity stock

From contributions
by owners

From issuing short-
and long-term debt

Cash Outflows

Financing
Activities

To repay
cash loans

To pay dividends
to shareholders

From issuing
notes and bonds

Financing
Activities

To pay
withdrawals
by owners

To purchase
treasury stock

Cash Inflows

▲ **Fraud**

Cash Monitoring Cash flows can be delayed or accelerated at the end of a period to improve or reduce current period cash flows. Also, cash flows can be misclassified. Cash outflows reported under operations are interpreted as expense payments. However, cash outflows reported under investing activities are interpreted as a positive sign of growth potential. Thus, managers face incentives to misclassify cash flows. For these reasons, cash flow reporting warrants our scrutiny.

Noncash Investing and Financing

When important investing and financing activities do not affect cash receipts or payments, they are still disclosed at the bottom of the statement of cash flows or in a note to the statement because of their importance and the *full-disclosure principle*. One example of such a transaction is the purchase of long-term assets using a long-term note payable (loan). This transaction involves both investing and financing activities but does not affect any cash inflow or outflow and is not reported in any of the three sections of the statement of cash flows. This disclosure rule also extends to transactions with partial cash receipts or payments.

Point: A stock dividend transaction involving a transfer from retained earnings to common stock or a credit to contributed capital is *not* considered a noncash investing and financing activity because the company receives no consideration for shares issued.

To illustrate, assume that Goorin purchases land for $12,000 by paying $5,000 cash and trading in used equipment worth $7,000. The investing section of the statement of cash flows reports only the $5,000 cash outflow for the land purchase. The $12,000 investing transaction is only partially described in the body of the statement of cash flows, yet this information is potentially important to users because it changes the makeup of assets. Goorin could either describe the transaction in a footnote or include information at the bottom of its statement that lists the $12,000 land purchase along with the cash financing of $5,000 and a $7,000 trade-in of equipment. As another example, Borg Co. acquired $900,000 of assets in exchange for $200,000 cash and a $700,000 long-term note, which should be reported as follows:

Fair value of assets acquired	$900,000
Less cash paid	200,000
Liabilities incurred or assumed	$700,000

Exhibit 12.4 lists transactions commonly disclosed as noncash investing and financing activities.

- Retirement of debt by issuing equity stock.
- Conversion of preferred stock to common stock.
- Lease of assets in a capital lease transaction.
- Purchase of long-term assets by issuing a note or bond.
- Exchange of noncash assets for other noncash assets.
- Purchase of noncash assets by issuing equity or debt.

EXHIBIT 12.4

Examples of Noncash Investing and Financing Activities

Format of the Statement of Cash Flows

Accounting standards require companies to include a statement of cash flows in a complete set of financial statements. This statement must report information about a company's cash receipts and cash payments during the period. Exhibit 12.5 shows the usual format. A company must report cash flows from three activities: operating, investing, and financing. The statement explains how transactions and events impact the prior period-end cash (and cash equivalents) balance to produce its current period-end balance.

COMPANY NAME
Statement of Cash Flows
For period Ended date

Cash flows from operating activities	
[List of individual inflows and outflows]	
Net cash provided (used) by operating activities	$ #
Cash flows from investing activities	
[List of individual inflows and outflows]	
Net cash provided (used) by investing activities	#
Cash flows from financing activities	
[List of individual inflows and outflows]	
Net cash provided (used) by financing activities	#
Net increase (decrease) in cash	$ #
Cash (and equivalents) balance at prior period-end	#
Cash (and equivalents) balance at current period-end	$ #

Separate schedule or note disclosure of any "noncash investing and financing transactions" is required.

EXHIBIT 12.5

Format of the Statement of Cash Flows

Point: Positive cash flows for a section are titled net cash "provided by" or "from." Negative cash flows are labeled as net cash "used by."

Decision Maker

Entrepreneur   You are considering purchasing a start-up business that recently reported a $110,000 annual net loss and a $225,000 annual net cash inflow. How are these results possible? ■   [Answer—p. 554]

Preparing the Statement of Cash Flows

Preparing a statement of cash flows involves five steps: ①compute the net increase or decrease in cash; ②compute and report the net cash provided or used by operating activities (using either the direct or indirect method; both are explained); ③compute and report the net cash provided or used by investing activities; ④compute and report the net cash provided or used by financing activities; and ⑤compute the net cash flow by combining net cash provided or used by

P1 Prepare a statement of cash flows.

operating, investing, and financing activities and then *prove it* by adding it to the beginning cash balance to show that it equals the ending cash balance.

Step 1 Compute net increase or decrease in cash

Step 2 Compute net cash from operating activities

Step 3 Compute net cash from investing activities

Step 4 Compute net cash from financing activities

Step 5 Prove and report beginning and ending cash balances

Point: View the change in cash as a *target* number (or check figure) that we will fully explain and prove in the statement of cash flows.

Computing the net increase or net decrease in cash is a simple but crucial computation. It equals the current period's cash balance minus the prior period's cash balance. This is the *bottom-line* figure for the statement of cash flows and is a check on accuracy. The information we need to prepare a statement of cash flows comes from various sources including comparative balance sheets at the beginning and end of the period, and an income statement for the period. There are two alternative approaches to preparing the statement: (1) analyzing the Cash account and (2) analyzing noncash accounts.

Analyzing the Cash Account   A company's cash receipts and cash payments are recorded in the Cash account in its general ledger. The Cash account is therefore a natural place to look for information about cash flows from operating, investing, and financing activities. To illustrate, review the summarized Cash T-account of Genesis, Inc., in Exhibit 12.6. Individual cash transactions are summarized in this Cash account according to the major types of cash receipts and cash payments. For instance, only the total of cash receipts from all customers is listed. Individual cash transactions underlying these totals can number in the thousands. Accounting software is available to provide summarized cash accounts.

EXHIBIT 12.6

Summarized Cash Account

Cash change

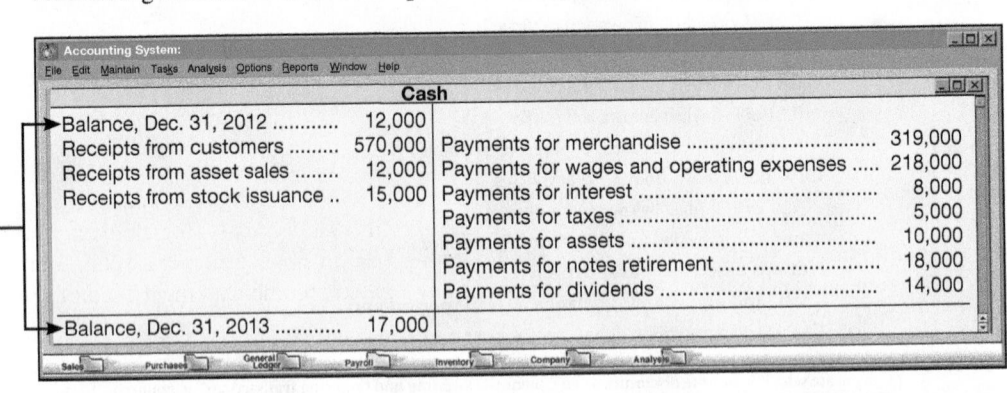

Cash			
Balance, Dec. 31, 2012	12,000		
Receipts from customers	570,000	Payments for merchandise	319,000
Receipts from asset sales	12,000	Payments for wages and operating expenses	218,000
Receipts from stock issuance	15,000	Payments for interest	8,000
		Payments for taxes	5,000
		Payments for assets	10,000
		Payments for notes retirement	18,000
		Payments for dividends	14,000
Balance, Dec. 31, 2013	17,000		

Preparing a statement of cash flows from Exhibit 12.6 requires determining whether an individual cash inflow or outflow is an operating, investing, or financing activity, and then listing each by activity. This yields the statement shown in Exhibit 12.7. However, preparing the statement of cash flows from an analysis of the summarized Cash account has two limitations. First, most companies have many individual cash receipts and payments, making it difficult to review them all. Accounting software minimizes this burden, but it is still a task requiring professional judgment for many transactions. Second, the Cash account does not usually carry an adequate description of each cash transaction, making assignment of all cash transactions according to activity difficult.

Analyzing Noncash Accounts   A second approach to preparing the statement of cash flows is analyzing noncash accounts. This approach uses the fact that when a company records cash inflows and outflows with debits and credits to the Cash account (see Exhibit 12.6), it also

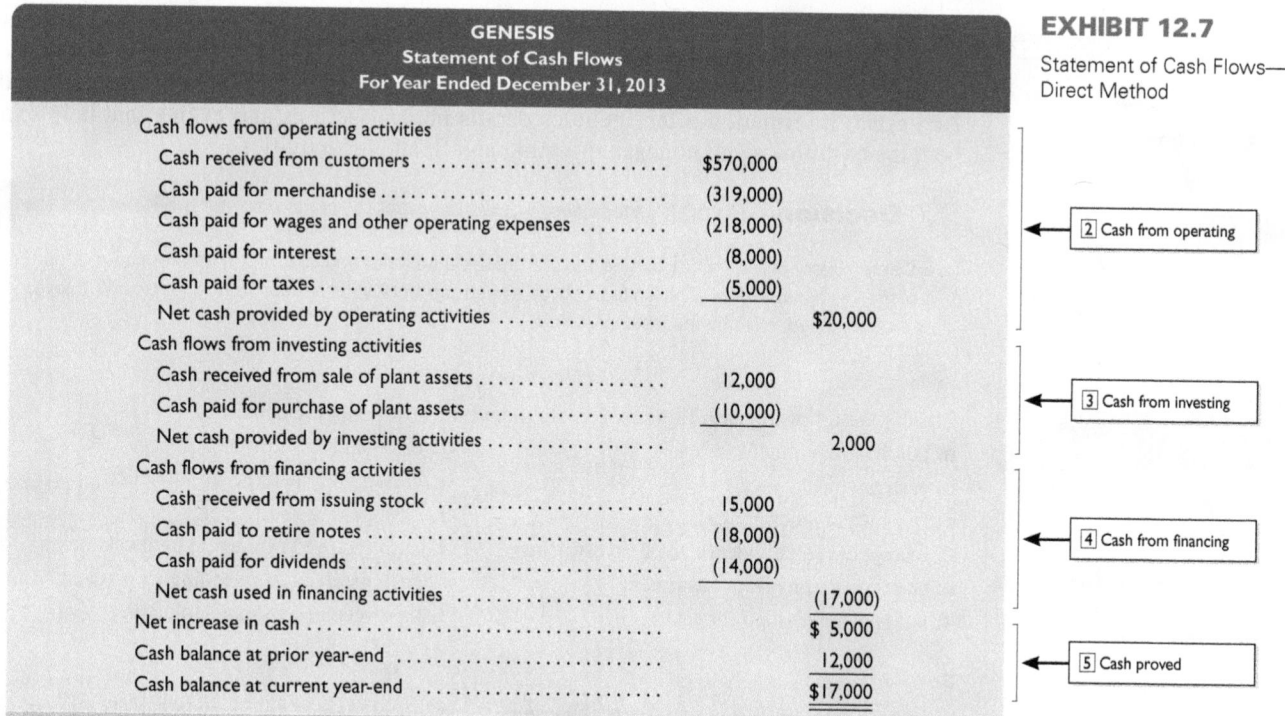

EXHIBIT 12.7

Statement of Cash Flows—
Direct Method

GENESIS Statement of Cash Flows For Year Ended December 31, 2013		
Cash flows from operating activities		
Cash received from customers	$570,000	
Cash paid for merchandise	(319,000)	
Cash paid for wages and other operating expenses	(218,000)	
Cash paid for interest	(8,000)	
Cash paid for taxes	(5,000)	
Net cash provided by operating activities		$20,000
Cash flows from investing activities		
Cash received from sale of plant assets	12,000	
Cash paid for purchase of plant assets	(10,000)	
Net cash provided by investing activities		2,000
Cash flows from financing activities		
Cash received from issuing stock	15,000	
Cash paid to retire notes	(18,000)	
Cash paid for dividends	(14,000)	
Net cash used in financing activities		(17,000)
Net increase in cash		$ 5,000
Cash balance at prior year-end		12,000
Cash balance at current year-end		$17,000

[2] Cash from operating

[3] Cash from investing

[4] Cash from financing

[5] Cash proved

records credits and debits in noncash accounts (reflecting double-entry accounting). Many of these noncash accounts are balance sheet accounts—for instance, from the sale of land for cash. Others are revenue and expense accounts that are closed to equity. For instance, the sale of services for cash yields a credit to Services Revenue that is closed to Retained Earnings for a corporation. In sum, *all cash transactions eventually affect noncash balance sheet accounts*. Thus, we can determine cash inflows and outflows by analyzing changes in noncash balance sheet accounts.

Exhibit 12.8 uses the accounting equation to show the relation between the Cash account and the noncash balance sheet accounts. This exhibit starts with the accounting equation at the top. It is then expanded in line (2) to separate cash from noncash asset accounts. Line (3) moves noncash asset accounts to the right-hand side of the equality where they are subtracted. This shows that cash equals the sum of the liability and equity accounts *minus* the noncash asset accounts. Line (4) points out that *changes* on one side of the accounting equation equal *changes* on the other side. It shows that we can explain changes in cash by analyzing changes in the noncash accounts consisting of liability accounts, equity accounts, and noncash asset accounts. By analyzing noncash balance sheet accounts and any related income statement accounts, we can prepare a statement of cash flows.

Information to Prepare the Statement   Information to prepare the statement of cash flows usually comes from three sources: (1) comparative balance sheets, (2) the

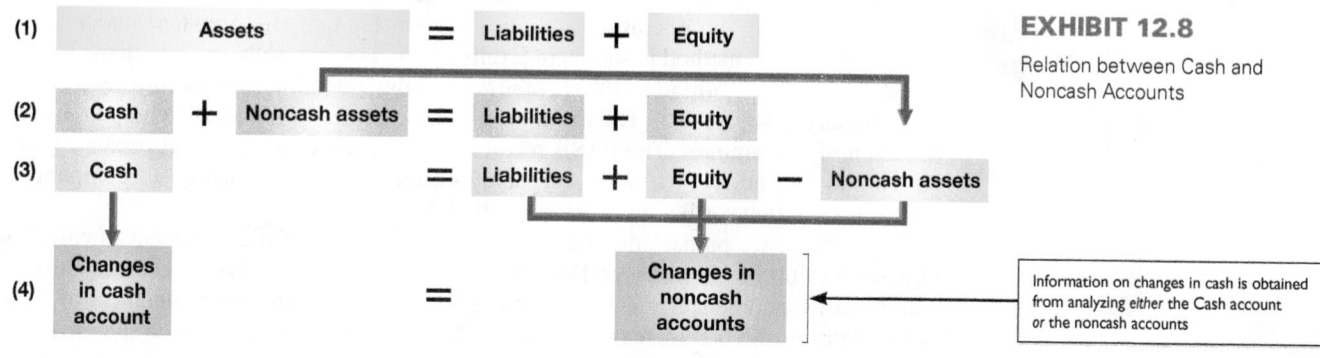

EXHIBIT 12.8

Relation between Cash and Noncash Accounts

(1) Assets = Liabilities + Equity

(2) Cash + Noncash assets = Liabilities + Equity

(3) Cash = Liabilities + Equity − Noncash assets

(4) Changes in cash account = Changes in noncash accounts

Information on changes in cash is obtained from analyzing *either* the Cash account *or* the noncash accounts

current income statement, and (3) additional information. Comparative balance sheets are used to compute changes in noncash accounts from the beginning to the end of the period. The current income statement is used to help compute cash flows from operating activities. Additional information often includes details on transactions and events that help explain both the cash flows and noncash investing and financing activities.

Decision Insight

e-Cash   Every credit transaction on the Net leaves a trail that a hacker or a marketer can pick up. Enter e-cash—or digital money. The encryption of e-cash protects your money from snoops and thieves and cannot be traced, even by the issuing bank. ■

NEED-TO-KNOW 12.1

C1

Classify the following cash flows as operating, investing, or financing activities.

a. purchase equipment for cash
b. cash payment of wages
c. issuance of stock for cash
d. receipt of cash dividends from investments
e. cash collections from customers
f. note payable issued for cash

g. cash paid for utilities
h. cash paid to acquire investments
i. cash paid to retire debt
j. cash received as interest on investments
k. cash received from selling investments
l. cash received from a bank loan

Solution

a. Investing	**c.** Financing	**e.** Operating	**g.** Operating	**i.** Financing	**k.** Investing
b. Operating	**d.** Operating	**f.** Financing	**h.** Investing	**j.** Operating	**l.** Financing

Do More: QS 12-1, QS 12-2, E 12-1

CASH FLOWS FROM OPERATING

Indirect and Direct Methods of Reporting

Cash flows provided (used) by operating activities are reported in one of two ways: the *direct method* or the *indirect method.* These two different methods apply only to the operating activities section.

The **direct method** separately lists each major item of operating cash receipts (such as cash received from customers) and each major item of operating cash payments (such as cash paid for merchandise). The cash payments are subtracted from cash receipts to determine the net cash provided (used) by operating activities. The operating activities section of Exhibit 12.7 reflects the direct method of reporting operating cash flows.

The **indirect method** reports net income and then adjusts it for items necessary to obtain net cash provided or used by operating activities. It does *not* report individual items of cash inflows and cash outflows from operating activities. Instead, the indirect method reports the necessary adjustments to reconcile net income to net cash provided or used by operating activities. The operating activities section for Genesis prepared under the indirect method is shown in Exhibit 12.9. The net cash amount provided by operating activities is *identical* under both the direct and indirect methods.

Point: To better understand the direct and indirect methods of reporting operating cash flows, identify similarities and differences between Exhibits 12.7 and 12.11.

This equality always exists. The difference in these methods is with the computation and presentation of this amount. The FASB recommends the direct method, but because it is not required and the indirect method is arguably easier to compute, nearly all companies report operating cash flows using the indirect method.

To illustrate, we prepare the operating activities section of the statement of cash flows for Genesis. Exhibit 12.10 shows the December 31, 2012 and 2013, balance sheets of Genesis along with its 2013 income statement. We use this information to prepare a statement of cash flows that explains the $5,000 increase in cash for 2013 as reflected in its balance sheets. This $5,000

EXHIBIT 12.9

Operating Activities Section—Indirect Method

Cash flows from operating activities		
Net income		$ 38,000
Adjustments to reconcile net income to net cash provided by operating activities		
Increase in accounts receivable	(20,000)	
Increase in merchandise inventory	(14,000)	
Increase in prepaid expenses.......................	(2,000)	
Decrease in accounts payable	(5,000)	
Decrease in interest payable	(1,000)	
Increase in income taxes payable	10,000	
Depreciation expense	24,000	
Loss on sale of plant assets	6,000	
Gain on retirement of notes	(16,000)	
Net cash provided by operating activities		**$20,000**

is computed as Cash of $17,000 at the end of 2013 minus Cash of $12,000 at the end of 2012. Genesis discloses additional information on its 2013 transactions:

a. The accounts payable balances result from merchandise inventory purchases.

b. Purchased $70,000 in plant assets by paying $10,000 cash and issuing $60,000 of notes payable.

c. Sold plant assets with an original cost of $30,000 and accumulated depreciation of $12,000 for $12,000 cash, yielding a $6,000 loss.

d. Received $15,000 cash from issuing 3,000 shares of common stock.

e. Paid $18,000 cash to retire notes with a $34,000 book value, yielding a $16,000 gain.

f. Declared and paid cash dividends of $14,000.

EXHIBIT 12.10

Financial Statements

GENESIS Balance Sheets December 31, 2013 and 2012	2013	2012
Assets		
Current assets		
Cash	$ 17,000	$ 12,000
Accounts receivable	60,000	40,000
Merchandise inventory	84,000	70,000
Prepaid expenses	6,000	4,000
Total current assets	167,000	126,000
Long-term assets		
Plant assets	250,000	210,000
Accumulated depreciation	(60,000)	(48,000)
Total assets	$357,000	$288,000
Liabilities		
Current liabilities		
Accounts payable	$ 35,000	$ 40,000
Interest payable	3,000	4,000
Income taxes payable	22,000	12,000
Total current liabilities	60,000	56,000
Long-term notes payable	90,000	64,000
Total liabilities	150,000	120,000
Equity		
Common stock, $5 par	95,000	80,000
Retained earnings	112,000	88,000
Total equity	207,000	168,000
Total liabilities and equity	$357,000	$288,000

GENESIS Income Statement For Year Ended December 31, 2013		
Sales		$590,000
Cost of goods sold	$300,000	
Wages and other operating expenses ..	216,000	
Interest expense	7,000	
Depreciation expense	24,000	(547,000)
		43,000
Other gains (losses)		
Gain on retirement of notes	16,000	
Loss on sale of plant assets	(6,000)	10,000
Income before taxes		53,000
Income taxes expense		(15,000)
Net income		$ 38,000

> *The next section describes the indirect method. Appendix 12B describes the direct method. An instructor can choose to cover either one or both methods. Neither section depends on the other. If the indirect method is skipped, then read Appendix 12B and return to the section (seven pages ahead) titled "Cash Flows from Investing."*

Application of the Indirect Method of Reporting

P2 Compute cash flows from operating activities using the indirect method.

Net income is computed using accrual accounting, which recognizes revenues when earned and expenses when incurred. Revenues and expenses do not necessarily reflect the receipt and payment of cash. The indirect method of computing and reporting net cash flows from operating activities involves adjusting the net income figure to obtain the net cash provided or used by operating activities. This includes subtracting noncash increases (credits) from net income and adding noncash charges (debits) back to net income.

To illustrate, the indirect method begins with Genesis's net income of $38,000 and adjusts it to obtain net cash provided by operating activities of $20,000. Exhibit 12.11 shows the results of the indirect method of reporting operating cash flows, which adjusts net income for three types of adjustments. There are adjustments ① to reflect changes in noncash current assets and current liabilities related to operating activities, ② to income statement items involving operating activities that do not affect cash inflows or outflows, and ③ to eliminate gains and losses resulting from investing and financing activities (not part of operating activities). This section describes each of these adjustments.

Point: *Noncash credits* refer to *revenue* amounts reported on the income statement that are *not collected in cash* this period. *Noncash charges* refer to *expense* amounts reported on the income statement that are *not paid* this period.

① Adjustments for Changes in Current Assets and Current Liabilities This section describes adjustments for changes in noncash current assets and current liabilities.

Point: Operating activities are typically those that determine income, which are often reflected in changes in current assets and current liabilities.

Adjustments for changes in noncash current assets. Changes in noncash current assets normally result from operating activities. Examples are sales affecting accounts receivable and building usage affecting prepaid rent. Decreases in noncash current assets yield the following adjustment:

Decreases in noncash current assets are added to net income.

To see the logic for this adjustment, consider that a decrease in a noncash current asset such as accounts receivable suggests more available cash at the end of the period compared to the beginning. This is so because a decrease in accounts receivable implies higher cash receipts than reflected in sales. We add these higher cash receipts (from decreases in noncash current assets) to net income when computing cash flow from operations.

In contrast, an increase in noncash current assets such as accounts receivable implies less cash receipts than reflected in sales. As another example, an increase in prepaid rent indicates that more cash is paid for rent than is deducted as rent expense. Increases in noncash current assets yield the following adjustment:

Increases in noncash current assets are subtracted from net income.

To illustrate, these adjustments are applied to the noncash current assets in Exhibit 12.10.

Accounts receivable. Accounts receivable *increase* $20,000, from a beginning balance of $40,000 to an ending balance of $60,000. This increase implies that Genesis collects less cash than is reported in sales. That is, some of these sales were in the form of accounts receivable and that amount increased during the period. To see this it is helpful to use *account analysis.* This usually involves setting up a T-account and reconstructing its major entries to compute cash receipts or payments. The following reconstructed Accounts Receivable T-account reveals that cash receipts are less than sales:

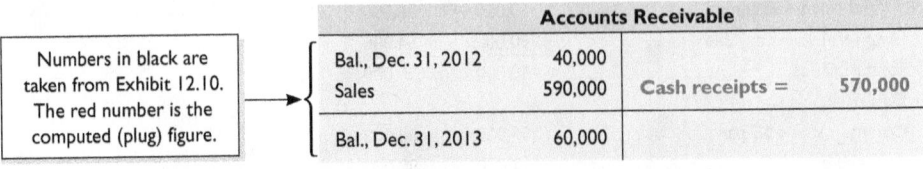

	Accounts Receivable			
Bal., Dec. 31, 2012	40,000			
Sales	590,000	Cash receipts =	570,000	
Bal., Dec. 31, 2013	60,000			

Numbers in black are taken from Exhibit 12.10. The red number is the computed (plug) figure.

We see that sales are $20,000 greater than cash receipts. This $20,000—as reflected in the $20,000 increase in Accounts Receivable—is subtracted from net income when computing cash provided by operating activities (see Exhibit 12.11).

GENESIS		
Statement of Cash Flows		
For Year Ended December 31, 2013		

Cash flows from operating activities

Net income	$ 38,000	
Adjustments to reconcile net income to net cash provided by operating activities		
① ⎧ Increase in accounts receivable.................	(20,000)	
Increase in merchandise inventory	(14,000)	
Increase in prepaid expenses	(2,000)	
Decrease in accounts payable..................	(5,000)	
Decrease in interest payable...................	(1,000)	
⎩ Increase in income taxes payable	10,000	
② { Depreciation expense.......................	24,000	
③ ⎧ Loss on sale of plant assets...................	6,000	
⎩ Gain on retirement of notes..................	(16,000)	
Net cash provided by operating activities		$20,000
Cash flows from investing activities		
Cash received from sale of plant assets	12,000	
Cash paid for purchase of plant assets	(10,000)	
Net cash provided by investing activities		2,000
Cash flows from financing activities		
Cash received from issuing stock	15,000	
Cash paid to retire notes	(18,000)	
Cash paid for dividends.........................	(14,000)	
Net cash used in financing activities		(17,000)
Net increase in cash		$ 5,000
Cash balance at prior year-end......................		12,000
Cash balance at current year-end...................		$17,000

EXHIBIT 12.11

Statement of Cash Flows—
Indirect Method

Point: Refer to Exhibit 12.10 and
identify the $5,000 change in cash.
This change is what the statement of
cash flows explains; it serves as a check.

Point: The statement of cash flows
is usually the last prepared of the four
required financial statements.

Merchandise inventory. Merchandise inventory *increases* by $14,000, from a $70,000 beginning balance to an $84,000 ending balance. This increase implies that Genesis had greater cash purchases than cost of goods sold. This larger amount of cash purchases is in the form of inventory, as reflected in the following account analysis:

Merchandise Inventory			
Bal., Dec. 31, 2012	70,000		
Purchases =	314,000	Cost of goods sold	300,000
Bal., Dec. 31, 2013	84,000		

The amount by which purchases exceed cost of goods sold—as reflected in the $14,000 increase in inventory—is subtracted from net income when computing cash provided by operating activities (see Exhibit 12.11).

Prepaid expenses. Prepaid Expenses *increase* $2,000, from a $4,000 beginning balance to a $6,000 ending balance, implying that Genesis's cash payments exceed its recorded prepaid expenses. These higher cash payments increase the amount of Prepaid Expenses, as reflected in its reconstructed T-account:

Prepaid Expenses			
Bal., Dec. 31, 2012	4,000		
Cash payments =	218,000	Wages and other operating exp.	216,000
Bal., Dec. 31, 2013	6,000		

The amount by which cash payments exceed the recorded operating expenses—as reflected in the $2,000 increase in Prepaid Expenses—is subtracted from net income when computing cash provided by operating activities (see Exhibit 12.11).

Adjustments for changes in current liabilities.   Changes in current liabilities normally result from operating activities. An example is a purchase that affects accounts payable. Increases in current liabilities yield the following adjustment to net income when computing operating cash flows:

Increases in current liabilities are added to net income.

To see the logic for this adjustment, consider that an increase in the Accounts Payable account suggests that cash payments are less than the related (cost of goods sold) expense. As another example, an increase in wages payable implies that cash paid for wages is less than the recorded wages expense. Since the recorded expense is greater than the cash paid, we add the increase in wages payable to net income to compute net cash flow from operations.

Conversely, when current liabilities decrease, the following adjustment is required:

Decreases in current liabilities are subtracted from net income.

To illustrate, these adjustments are applied to the current liabilities in Exhibit 12.10.

Accounts payable. Accounts payable *decrease* $5,000, from a beginning balance of $40,000 to an ending balance of $35,000. This decrease implies that cash payments to suppliers exceed purchases by $5,000 for the period, which is reflected in the reconstructed Accounts Payable T-account:

Accounts Payable			
		Bal., Dec. 31, 2012	40,000
Cash payments =	319,000	Purchases	314,000
		Bal., Dec. 31, 2013	35,000

The amount by which cash payments exceed purchases—as reflected in the $5,000 decrease in Accounts Payable—is subtracted from net income when computing cash provided by operating activities (see Exhibit 12.11).

Interest payable. Interest payable *decreases* $1,000, from a $4,000 beginning balance to a $3,000 ending balance. This decrease indicates that cash paid for interest exceeds interest expense by $1,000, which is reflected in the Interest Payable T-account:

Interest Payable			
		Bal., Dec. 31, 2012	4,000
Cash paid for interest =	8,000	Interest expense	7,000
		Bal., Dec. 31, 2013	3,000

The amount by which cash paid exceeds recorded expense—as reflected in the $1,000 decrease in Interest Payable—is subtracted from net income (see Exhibit 12.11).

Income taxes payable. Income taxes payable *increase* $10,000, from a $12,000 beginning balance to a $22,000 ending balance. This increase implies that reported income taxes exceed the cash paid for taxes, which is reflected in the Income Taxes Payable T-account:

Income Taxes Payable			
		Bal., Dec. 31, 2012	12,000
Cash paid for taxes =	5,000	Income taxes expense	15,000
		Bal., Dec. 31, 2013	22,000

Summary Adjustments for Changes in Current Assets and Current Liabilities

Account	Increases	Decreases
Noncash current assets	Deduct from NI	Add to NI
Current liabilities	Add to NI	Deduct from NI

The amount by which cash paid falls short of the reported taxes expense—as reflected in the $10,000 increase in Income Taxes Payable—is added to net income when computing cash provided by operating activities (see Exhibit 12.11).

② **Adjustments for Operating Items Not Providing or Using Cash**   The income statement usually includes some expenses that do not reflect cash outflows in the period. Examples are depreciation, amortization, depletion, and bad debts expense. The indirect method for reporting operating cash flows requires that

> *Expenses with no cash outflows are added back to net income.*

To see the logic of this adjustment, recall that items such as depreciation, amortization, depletion, and bad debts originate from debits to expense accounts and credits to noncash accounts. These entries have *no* cash effect, and we add them back to net income when computing net cash flows from operations. Adding them back cancels their deductions.

Similarly, when net income includes revenues that do not reflect cash inflows in the period, the indirect method for reporting operating cash flows requires that

> *Revenues with no cash inflows are subtracted from net income.*

We apply these adjustments to the Genesis operating items that do not provide or use cash.

Depreciation.   Depreciation expense is the only Genesis operating item that has no effect on cash flows in the period. We must add back the $24,000 depreciation expense to net income when computing cash provided by operating activities. (We later explain that any cash outflow to acquire a plant asset is reported as an investing activity.)

③ **Adjustments for Nonoperating Items**   Net income often includes losses that are not part of operating activities but are part of either investing or financing activities. Examples are a loss from the sale of a plant asset and a loss from retirement of notes payable. The indirect method for reporting operating cash flows requires that

> *Nonoperating losses are added back to net income.*

To see the logic, consider that items such as a plant asset sale and a notes retirement are normally recorded by recognizing the cash, removing all plant asset or notes accounts, and recognizing any loss or gain. The cash received or paid is not part of operating activities but is part of either investing or financing activities. *No* operating cash flow effect occurs. However, because the nonoperating loss is a deduction in computing net income, we need to add it back to net income when computing cash flow from operations. Adding it back cancels the deduction.

Similarly, when net income includes gains not part of operating activities, the indirect method for reporting operating cash flows requires that

> *Nonoperating gains are subtracted from net income.*

To illustrate these adjustments, we consider the nonoperating items of Genesis.

Loss on sale of plant assets.   Genesis reports a $6,000 loss on sale of plant assets as part of net income. This loss is a proper deduction in computing income, but it is *not part of operating activities*. Instead, a sale of plant assets is part of investing activities. Thus, the $6,000 nonoperating loss is added back to net income (see Exhibit 12.11). Adding it back cancels the loss. We later explain how to report the cash inflow from the asset sale in investing activities.

Gain on retirement of debt.   A $16,000 gain on retirement of debt is properly included in net income, but it is *not part of operating activities*. This means the $16,000 nonoperating gain must be subtracted from net income to obtain net cash provided by operating activities (see Exhibit 12.11). Subtracting it cancels the recorded gain. We later describe how to report the cash outflow to retire debt.

Summary of Adjustments for Indirect Method

Exhibit 12.12 summarizes the most common adjustments to net income when computing net cash provided or used by operating activities under the indirect method.

Point: An income statement reports revenues, gains, expenses, and losses on an accrual basis. The statement of cash flows reports cash received and cash paid for operating, financing, and investing activities.

Point: By adding back nonoperating items such as 'Loss on sale of plant assets' to net income, we get operating income, which is the starting point for the operating section of the statement of cash flows.

EXHIBIT 12.12

Summary of Selected Adjustments for Indirect Method

Net Income
+ Decrease in noncash current asset
− Increase in noncash current asset   ① Adjustments for changes in current
+ Increase in current liability*   assets and current liabilities
− Decrease in current liability*

+ Depreciation, depletion, and amortization   ② Adjustments for operating items
                                                 not providing or using cash

+ Losses from disposal of long-term assets   ③ Adjustments for nonoperating items
   and retirement of debt
− Gains from disposal of long-term assets
   and retirement of debt

Net cash provided (used) by operating activities

* Excludes current portion of long-term debt and any (nonsales-related) short-term notes payable—both are financing activities.

The computations in determining cash provided or used by operating activities are different for the indirect and direct methods, but the result is identical. Both methods yield the same $20,000 figure for cash from operating activities for Genesis; see Exhibits 12.7 and 12.11.

Decision Insight

Cash or Income   The difference between net income and operating cash flows can be large and sometimes reflects on the quality of earnings. This bar chart shows the net income and operating cash flows of three companies. Operating cash flows can be either higher or lower than net income. ■

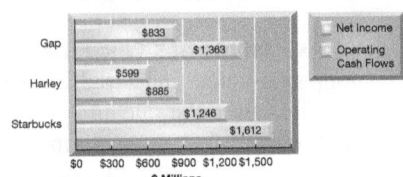

	Net Income	Operating Cash Flows
Gap	$833	$1,363
Harley	$599	$885
Starbucks	$1,246	$1,612

$0 $300 $600 $900 $1,200 $1,500
$ Millions

NEED-TO-KNOW 12.2

P2

A company's current year income statement and selected balance sheet data at December 31 of the current and prior years follow. Prepare the cash flows from operating activities section only of its statement of cash flows using the indirect method for the current year.

Income Statement For Current Year Ended December 31	
Sales revenue	$120
Expenses	
Cost of goods sold	50
Depreciation expense	30
Salaries expense	17
Interest expense	3
Net income	$ 20

Selected Balance Sheet Accounts		
At December 31	Current Yr	Prior Yr
Accounts receivable	$12	$10
Inventory	6	9
Accounts payable	7	11
Salaries payable	8	3
Interest payable	1	0

Solution

Cash Flows from Operating Activities—Indirect Method For Current Year Ended December 31		
Cash flows from operating activities		
Net income		$20
Adjustments to reconcile net income to net cash provided by operating activities		
Depreciation expense	$30	
Increase in accounts receivable	(2)	
Decrease in merchandise inventory	3	
Decrease in accounts payable	(4)	
Increase in salaries payable	5	
Increase in interest payable	1	33
Net cash provided by operating activities		$53

Do More: QS 12-3, QS 12-6, QS 12-14, E 12-3, E 12-4, E 12-6

QC2

CASH FLOWS FROM INVESTING

The third major step in preparing the statement of cash flows is to compute and report cash flows from investing activities. We normally do this by identifying changes in (1) all noncurrent asset accounts and (2) the current accounts for both notes receivable and investments in securities (excluding trading securities). We then analyze changes in these accounts to determine their effect, if any, on cash and report the cash flow effects in the investing activities section of the statement of cash flows. Reporting of investing activities is identical under the direct method and indirect method.

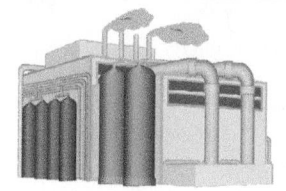

Three-Stage Process of Analysis

Information to compute cash flows from investing activities is usually taken from beginning and ending balance sheets and the income statement. We use a three-stage process to determine cash provided or used by investing activities: (1) identify changes in investing-related accounts, (2) explain these changes using reconstruction analysis, and (3) report their cash flow effects.

P3 Determine cash flows from both investing and financing activities.

Analysis of Noncurrent Assets

Information about the Genesis transactions provided earlier reveals that the company both purchased and sold plant assets during the period. Both transactions are investing activities and are analyzed for their cash flow effects in this section.

Plant Asset Transactions   The first stage in analyzing the Plant Assets account and its related Accumulated Depreciation is to identify any changes in these accounts from comparative balance sheets in Exhibit 12.10. This analysis reveals a $40,000 increase in plant assets from $210,000 to $250,000 and a $12,000 increase in accumulated depreciation from $48,000 to $60,000.

The second stage is to explain these changes. Items *b* and *c* of the additional information for Genesis (page 531) are relevant in this case. Recall that the Plant Assets account is affected by both asset purchases and sales, while its Accumulated Depreciation account is normally increased from depreciation and decreased from the removal of accumulated depreciation in asset sales. To explain changes in these accounts and to identify their cash flow effects, we prepare *reconstructed entries* from prior transactions; *they are not the actual entries by the preparer.*

To illustrate, item *b* reports that Genesis purchased plant assets of $70,000 by issuing $60,000 in notes payable to the seller and paying $10,000 in cash. The reconstructed entry for analysis of item *b* follows:

Point: Investing activities include (1) purchasing and selling long-term assets, (2) lending and collecting on notes receivable, and (3) purchasing and selling short-term investments other than cash equivalents and trading securities.

Point: Financing and investing info is available in ledger accounts to help explain changes in comparative balance sheets. Post references lead to relevant entries and explanations.

Reconstruction	Plant Assets	70,000	
	Notes Payable		60,000
	Cash		**10,000**

This entry reveals a $10,000 cash outflow for plant assets and a $60,000 noncash investing and financing transaction involving notes exchanged for plant assets.

Next, item *c* reports that Genesis sold plant assets costing $30,000 (with $12,000 of accumulated depreciation) for $12,000 cash, resulting in a $6,000 loss. The reconstructed entry for analysis of item *c* follows:

Reconstruction	**Cash**	**12,000**	
	Accumulated Depreciation	12,000	
	Loss on Sale of Plant Assets	6,000	
	Plant Assets		30,000

This entry reveals a $12,000 cash inflow from assets sold. The $6,000 loss is computed by comparing the asset book value to the cash received and does not reflect any cash inflow or outflow.

Point: When determining cash flows from investing, T-account analysis is key to reconstructing accounts and amounts.

We also reconstruct the entry for Depreciation Expense using information from the income statement.

| Reconstruction | Depreciation Expense .... | 24,000 | |
| | Accumulated Depreciation .... | | 24,000 |

This entry shows that Depreciation Expense results in no cash flow effect. These three reconstructed entries are reflected in the following plant asset and related T-accounts.

Plant Assets					Accumulated Depreciation—Plant Assets			
Bal., Dec. 31, 2012	210,000						Bal., Dec. 31, 2012	48,000
Purchase	**70,000**	**Sale**	**30,000**	**Sale**	**12,000**	**Depr. expense**	**24,000**
Bal., Dec. 31, 2013	250,000						Bal., Dec. 31, 2013	60,000

Example: If a plant asset costing $40,000 with $37,000 of accumulated depreciation is sold at a $1,000 loss, what is the cash flow? What is the cash flow if this asset is sold at a gain of $3,000? *Answers:* +$2,000; +$6,000.

This reconstruction analysis is complete in that the change in plant assets from $210,000 to $250,000 is fully explained by the $70,000 purchase and the $30,000 sale. Also, the change in accumulated depreciation from $48,000 to $60,000 is fully explained by depreciation expense of $24,000 and the removal of $12,000 in accumulated depreciation from an asset sale. (Preparers of the statement of cash flows have the entire ledger and additional information at their disposal, but for brevity reasons only the information needed for reconstructing accounts is given.)

The third stage looks at the reconstructed entries for identification of cash flows. The two identified cash flow effects are reported in the investing section of the statement as follows (also see Exhibit 12.7 or 12.11):

Cash flows from investing activities

| Cash received from sale of plant assets .... | $12,000 |
| Cash paid for purchase of plant assets .... | (10,000) |

The $60,000 portion of the purchase described in item *b* and financed by issuing notes is a noncash investing and financing activity. It is reported in a note or in a separate schedule to the statement as follows:

Noncash investing and financing activity

| Purchased plant assets with issuance of notes .... | $60,000 |

Analysis of Other Assets

Many other asset transactions (including those involving current notes receivable and investments in certain securities) are considered investing activities and can affect a company's cash flows. Since Genesis did not enter into other investing activities impacting assets, we do not need to extend our analysis to these other assets. If such transactions did exist, we would analyze them using the same three-stage process illustrated for plant assets.

Fraud

Cash Control. For frauds involving misappropriation of assets, cash is the target over 90% of the time. Further, frauds involving cash theft are not restricted to employees stealing currency but include bank deposits, checks, bank drafts, and money orders. Following are common types of cash schemes.

- *Fraudulent disbursements* of cash include falsification of invoices to nonexistent parties and recording extra hours not really worked.
- *Skimming* of cash is most frequent in the retail industry at the point of sale when an employee receives cash from a customer but does not record it.
- *Lapping/hiking* of cash occurs when customer payments are stolen and then concealed by recording later customer payments to those accounts, and so forth; to avoid lapping, one must separate cash recordkeeping from cash custody.

Use the following information to determine this company's cash flows from investing activities.

a. A factory with a book value of $100 and an original cost of $800 was sold at a loss of $10.

b. Paid $70 cash for new equipment.

c. Long-term stock investments were sold for $20 cash, yielding a loss of $4.

d. Sold land costing $175 for $160 cash, yielding a loss of $15.

NEED-TO-KNOW 12.3

P3

Solution

Cash flows from investing activities	
Cash received from sale of factory*	$ 90
Cash paid for new equipment	(70)
Cash received from sale of long-term investments	20
Cash received from sale of land	160
Net cash provided by investing activities	$200

*Cash received from sale of factory = Book value − Loss = $100 − $10 = $90

Do More: QS 12-4, QS 12-7, QS 12-15, E 12-8

QC3

CASH FLOWS FROM FINANCING

The fourth major step in preparing the statement of cash flows is to compute and report cash flows from financing activities. We normally do this by identifying changes in all noncurrent liability accounts (including the current portion of any notes and bonds) and the equity accounts. These accounts include long-term debt, notes payable, bonds payable, common stock, and retained earnings. Changes in these accounts are then analyzed using available information to determine their effect, if any, on cash. Results are reported in the financing activities section of the statement. Reporting of financing activities is identical under the direct method and indirect method.

Three-Stage Process of Analysis

We again use a three-stage process to determine cash provided or used by financing activities: (1) identify changes in financing-related accounts, (2) explain these changes using reconstruction analysis, and (3) report their cash flow effects.

Analysis of Noncurrent Liabilities

Information about Genesis provided earlier reveals two transactions involving noncurrent liabilities. We analyzed one of those, the $60,000 issuance of notes payable to purchase plant assets. This transaction is reported as a significant noncash investing and financing activity in a footnote or a separate schedule to the statement of cash flows. The other remaining transaction involving noncurrent liabilities is the cash retirement of notes payable.

Point: Financing activities generally refer to changes in the noncurrent liability and the equity accounts. Examples are (1) receiving cash from issuing debt or repaying amounts borrowed and (2) receiving cash from or distributing cash to owners.

Notes Payable Transactions   The first stage in analysis of notes is to review the comparative balance sheets from Exhibit 12.10. This analysis reveals an increase in notes payable from $64,000 to $90,000.

The second stage explains this change. Item *e* of the additional information for Genesis (page 531) reports that notes with a carrying value of $34,000 are retired for $18,000 cash, resulting in a $16,000 gain. The reconstructed entry for analysis of item *e* follows:

Reconstruction	Notes Payable	34,000	
	Gain on retirement of debt		16,000
	Cash		**18,000**

This entry reveals an $18,000 cash outflow for retirement of notes and a $16,000 gain from comparing the notes payable carrying value to the cash received. This gain does not reflect any cash inflow or outflow. Also, item *b* of the additional information reports that Genesis purchased plant assets costing $70,000 by issuing $60,000 in notes payable to the seller and paying $10,000 in cash. We reconstructed this entry when analyzing investing activities: It showed a $60,000 increase to notes payable that is reported as a noncash investing and financing transaction. The Notes Payable account reflects (and is fully explained by) these reconstructed entries as follows:

Notes Payable			
		Bal., Dec. 31, 2012	64,000
Retired notes	**34,000**	**Issued notes**	**60,000**
		Bal., Dec. 31, 2013	90,000

The third stage is to report the cash flow effect of the notes retirement in the financing section of the statement as follows (also see Exhibit 12.7 or 12.11):

Cash flows from financing activities	
Cash paid to retire notes	$(18,000)

Analysis of Equity

The Genesis information reveals two transactions involving equity accounts. The first is the issuance of common stock for cash. The second is the declaration and payment of cash dividends. We analyze both.

Common Stock Transactions   The first stage in analyzing common stock is to review the comparative balance sheets from Exhibit 12.10, which reveal an increase in common stock from $80,000 to $95,000.

The second stage explains this change. Item *d* of the additional information (page 531) reports that 3,000 shares of common stock are issued at par for $5 per share. The reconstructed entry for analysis of item *d* follows:

Reconstruction	**Cash**	**15,000**	
	Common Stock		15,000

This entry reveals a $15,000 cash inflow from stock issuance and is reflected in (and explains) the Common Stock account as follows:

Common Stock		
	Bal., Dec. 31, 2012	80,000
	Issued stock	**15,000**
	Bal., Dec. 31, 2013	95,000

The third stage discloses the cash flow effect from stock issuance in the financing section of the statement as follows (also see Exhibit 12.7 or 12.11):

Cash flows from financing activities	
Cash received from issuing stock	$15,000

Retained Earnings Transactions   The first stage in analyzing the Retained Earnings account is to review the comparative balance sheets from Exhibit 12.10. This reveals an increase in retained earnings from $88,000 to $112,000.

The second stage explains this change. Item *f* of the additional information (page 531) reports that cash dividends of $14,000 are paid. The reconstructed entry follows:

Reconstruction	Retained Earnings	14,000	
	Cash		14,000

This entry reveals a $14,000 cash outflow for cash dividends. Also see that the Retained Earnings account is impacted by net income of $38,000. (Net income was analyzed under the operating section of the statement of cash flows.) The reconstructed Retained Earnings account follows:

Retained Earnings			
		Bal., Dec. 31, 2012	88,000
Cash dividend	14,000	Net income	38,000
		Bal., Dec. 31, 2013	112,000

The third stage reports the cash flow effect from the cash dividend in the financing section of the statement as follows (also see Exhibit 12.7 or 12.11):

Cash flows from financing activities	
Cash paid for dividends	$(14,000)

Point: Financing activities not affecting cash flow include *declaration* of a cash dividend, *declaration* of a stock dividend, payment of a stock dividend, and a stock split.

We now have identified and explained all of the Genesis cash inflows and cash outflows and one noncash investing and financing transaction. Specifically, our analysis has reconciled changes in all noncash balance sheet accounts.

Global: There are no requirements to separate domestic and international cash flows, leading some users to ask, "Where in the world is cash flow?"

Proving Cash Balances

The fifth and final step in preparing the statement is to report the beginning and ending cash balances and prove that the *net change in cash* is explained by operating, investing, and financing cash flows. This step is shown here for Genesis.

Net cash provided by operating activities	$20,000
Net cash provided by investing activities	2,000
Net cash used in financing activities	(17,000)
Net increase in cash	**$ 5,000**
Cash balance at 2012 year-end	12,000
Cash balance at 2013 year-end	$17,000

The preceding table shows that the $5,000 net increase in cash, from $12,000 at the beginning of the period to $17,000 at the end, is reconciled by net cash flows from operating ($20,000 inflow), investing ($2,000 inflow), and financing ($17,000 outflow) activities. This is formally reported at the bottom of the statement of cash flows as shown in both Exhibits 12.7 and 12.11.

■ Decision Maker

Reporter   Management is in labor contract negotiations and grants you an interview. It highlights a recent $600,000 net loss that involves a $930,000 extraordinary loss and a total net cash outflow of $550,000 (which includes net cash outflows of $850,000 for investing activities and $350,000 for financing activities). What is your assessment of this company? ■   [Answer—p. 554]

Use the following information to determine this company's cash flows from financing activities.
a. Issued common stock for $40 cash.
b. Paid $70 cash to retire a note payable at its $70 maturity value.
c. Paid cash dividend of $15.
d. Paid $5 cash to acquire its treasury stock.

NEED-TO-KNOW 12.4

P3

Solution

Cash flows from financing activities	
Cash received from issuance of common stock	$ 40
Cash paid to settle note payable	(70)
Cash paid for dividend	(15)
Cash paid to acquire treasury stock	(5)
Net cash used by financing activities	$(50)

Do More: QS 12-5, QS 12-8, QS 12-16, E 12-9

GLOBAL VIEW

The statement of cash flows, which explains changes in cash (including cash equivalents) from period to period, is required under both U.S. GAAP and IFRS. This section discusses similarities and differences between U.S. GAAP and IFRS in reporting that statement.

Reporting Cash Flows from Operating   Both U.S. GAAP and IFRS permit the reporting of cash flows from operating activities using either the direct or indirect method. Further, the basic requirements underlying the application of both methods are fairly consistent across these two accounting systems. Appendix A shows that Samsung reports its cash flows from operating activities using the indirect method, and in a manner similar to that explained in this chapter. Further, the definition of cash and cash equivalents is roughly similar for U.S. GAAP and IFRS.

Samsung

There are, however, some differences between U.S. GAAP and IFRS in reporting operating cash flows. We mention two of the more notable. First, U.S. GAAP requires cash inflows from interest revenue and dividend revenue be classified as operating, whereas IFRS permits classification under operating or investing provided that this classification is consistently applied across periods. Samsung reports its cash from interest received under operating, consistent with U.S. GAAP (no mention is made of any dividends received). Second, U.S. GAAP requires cash outflows for interest expense be classified as operating, whereas IFRS again permits classification under operating or financing provided that it is consistently applied across periods. (Some believe that interest payments, like dividends payments, are better classified as financing because they represent payments to financiers.) Samsung reports cash outflows for interest under operating, which is consistent with U.S. GAAP and acceptable under IFRS.

Reporting Cash Flows from Investing and Financing   U.S. GAAP and IFRS are broadly similar in computing and classifying cash flows from investing and financing activities. A quick review of these two sections for Samsung's statement of cash flows shows a structure similar to that explained in this chapter. One notable exception is that U.S. GAAP requires cash outflows for income tax be classified as operating, whereas IFRS permits the splitting of those cash flows among operating, investing, and financing depending on the sources of that tax. Samsung reports its cash outflows for income tax under operating, which is similar to U.S. GAAP.

Decision Analysis    Cash Flow Analysis

Analyzing Cash Sources and Uses

A1   Analyze the statement of cash flows and apply the cash flow on total assets ratio.

Most managers stress the importance of understanding and predicting cash flows for business decisions. Creditors evaluate a company's ability to generate cash before deciding whether to lend money. Investors also assess cash inflows and outflows before buying and selling stock. Information in the statement of cash flows helps address these and other questions such as (1) How much cash is generated from or used in operations? (2) What expenditures are made with cash from operations? (3) What is the source of cash for debt payments? (4) What is the source of cash for distributions to owners? (5) How is the increase in investing activities financed? (6) What is the source of cash for new plant assets? (7) Why is cash flow from operations different from income? (8) How is cash from financing used?

To effectively answer these questions, it is important to separately analyze investing, financing, and operating activities. To illustrate, consider data from three different companies in Exhibit 12.13. These companies operate in the same industry and have been in business for several years.

EXHIBIT 12.13

Cash Flows of Competing Companies

($ thousands)	BMX	ATV	Trex
Cash provided (used) by operating activities	$90,000	$40,000	$(24,000)
Cash provided (used) by investing activities			
Proceeds from sale of plant assets			26,000
Purchase of plant assets	(48,000)	(25,000)	
Cash provided (used) by financing activities			
Proceeds from issuance of debt			13,000
Repayment of debt	(27,000)		
Net increase (decrease) in cash	$15,000	$15,000	$ 15,000

Each company generates an identical $15,000 net increase in cash, but its sources and uses of cash flows are very different. BMX's operating activities provide net cash flows of $90,000, allowing it to purchase plant assets of $48,000 and repay $27,000 of its debt. ATV's operating activities provide $40,000 of cash flows, limiting its purchase of plant assets to $25,000. Trex's $15,000 net cash increase is due to selling plant assets and incurring additional debt. Its operating activities yield a net cash outflow of $24,000. Overall, analysis of these cash flows reveals that BMX is more capable of generating future cash flows than is ATV or Trex.

 Decision Insight ●━━━━━━━━━━━━━━━━━━━━━━━━━ ♟

Free Cash Flows   Many investors use cash flows to value company stock. However, cash-based valuation models often yield different stock values due to differences in measurement of cash flows. Most models require cash flows that are "free" for distribution to shareholders. These *free cash flows* are defined as cash flows available to shareholders after operating asset reinvestments and debt payments. Knowledge of the statement of cash flows is key to proper computation of free cash flows. A company's growth and financial flexibility depend on adequate free cash flows. ■

Point: CFO (Cash flow from operations)
Less: Capital Expenditures
Less: Debt Repayments
= FCF (free cash flows)

Cash Flow on Total Assets

Cash flow information has limitations, but it can help measure a company's ability to meet its obligations, pay dividends, expand operations, and obtain financing. Users often compute and analyze a cash-based ratio similar to return on total assets except that its numerator is net cash flows from operating activities. The **cash flow on total assets** ratio is in Exhibit 12.14.

$$\text{Cash flow on total assets} = \frac{\text{Cash flow from operations}}{\text{Average total assets}}$$

EXHIBIT 12.14

Cash Flow on Total Assets

This ratio reflects actual cash flows and is not affected by accounting income recognition and measurement. It can help business decision makers estimate the amount and timing of cash flows when planning and analyzing operating activities.

To illustrate, the 2011 cash flow on total assets ratio for Nike is 12.3%—see Exhibit 12.15. Is a 12.3% ratio good or bad? To answer this question, we compare this ratio with the ratios of prior years (we could also compare its ratio with those of its competitors and the market). Nike's cash flow on total assets ratio for several prior years is in the second column of Exhibit 12.15. Results show that its 12.3% return is the lowest return over the past several years. This is probably reflective of the recent recessionary period.

EXHIBIT 12.15

Nike's Cash Flow on Total Assets

Year	Cash Flow on Total Assets	Return on Total Assets
2011.........	12.3%	14.5%
2010.........	22.9	13.8
2009.........	13.5	11.6
2008.........	16.7	16.3
2007.........	18.3	14.5

As an indicator of *earnings quality,* some analysts compare the cash flow on total assets ratio to the return on total assets ratio. Nike's return on total assets is provided in the third column of Exhibit 12.15. Nike's cash flow on total assets ratio exceeds its return on total assets in four of the five years, leading some analysts to infer that Nike's earnings quality is high for that period because more earnings are realized in the form of cash.

Point: Cash flow ratios are often used by financial analysts.

 Decision Insight ●━━━━━━━━━━━━━━━━━━━━━━━━━ ♟

Cash Flow Ratios   Analysts use various other cash-based ratios, including the following two:

(1) $$\text{Cash coverage of growth} = \frac{\text{Operating cash flow}}{\text{Cash outflow for plant assets}}$$

where a low ratio (less than 1) implies cash inadequacy to meet asset growth, whereas a high ratio implies cash adequacy for asset growth.

(2) $$\text{Operating cash flow to sales} = \frac{\text{Operating cash flow}}{\text{Net sales}}$$

When this ratio substantially and consistently differs from the operating income to net sales ratio, the risk of accounting improprieties increases. ■

Point: The following ratio helps assess whether operating cash flow is adequate to meet long-term obligations:
Cash coverage of debt = Cash flow from operations ÷ Noncurrent liabilities. A low ratio suggests a higher risk of insolvency; a high ratio suggests a greater ability to meet long-term obligations.

COMPREHENSIVE...

NEED-TO-KNOW

Umlauf's comparative balance sheets, income statement, and additional information follow.

UMLAUF COMPANY
Income Statement
For Year Ended December 31, 2013

Sales		$446,100
Cost of goods sold	$222,300	
Other operating expenses	120,300	
Depreciation expense	25,500	(368,100)
		78,000
Other gains (losses)		
Loss on sale of equipment	3,300	
Loss on retirement of bonds ..	825	(4,125)
Income before taxes		73,875
Income taxes expense		(13,725)
Net income		$ 60,150

UMLAUF COMPANY
Balance Sheets
December 31, 2013 and 2012

	2013	2012
Assets		
Cash	$ 43,050	$ 23,925
Accounts receivable	34,125	39,825
Merchandise inventory	156,000	146,475
Prepaid expenses	3,600	1,650
Equipment	135,825	146,700
Accum. depreciation—Equipment	(61,950)	(47,550)
Total assets	$310,650	$311,025
Liabilities and Equity		
Accounts payable	$ 28,800	$ 33,750
Income taxes payable	5,100	4,425
Dividends payable	0	4,500
Bonds payable	0	37,500
Common stock, $10 par	168,750	168,750
Retained earnings	108,000	62,100
Total liabilities and equity	$310,650	$311,025

Additional Information

a. Equipment costing $21,375 with accumulated depreciation of $11,100 is sold for cash.

b. Equipment purchases are for cash.

c. Accumulated Depreciation is affected by depreciation expense and the sale of equipment.

d. The balance of Retained Earnings is affected by dividend declarations and net income.

e. All sales are made on credit.

f. All merchandise inventory purchases are on credit.

g. Accounts Payable balances result from merchandise inventory purchases.

h. Prepaid expenses relate to "other operating expenses."

Required

1. Prepare a statement of cash flows using the indirect method for year 2013.

2.ᴮPrepare a statement of cash flows using the direct method for year 2013.

PLANNING THE SOLUTION

- Prepare two blank statements of cash flows with sections for operating, investing, and financing activities using the (1) indirect method format and (2) direct method format.

- Compute the cash paid for equipment and the cash received from the sale of equipment using the additional information provided along with the amount for depreciation expense and the change in the balances of equipment and accumulated depreciation. Use T-accounts to help chart the effects of the sale and purchase of equipment on the balances of the Equipment account and the Accumulated Depreciation account.

- Compute the effect of net income on the change in the Retained Earnings account balance. Assign the difference between the change in retained earnings and the amount of net income to dividends declared. Adjust the dividends declared amount for the change in the Dividends Payable balance.

- Compute cash received from customers, cash paid for merchandise, cash paid for other operating expenses, and cash paid for taxes as illustrated in the chapter.

- Enter the cash effects of reconstruction entries to the appropriate section(s) of the statement.

- Total each section of the statement, determine the total net change in cash, and add it to the beginning balance to get the ending balance of cash.

SOLUTION TO COMPREHENSIVE NEED-TO-KNOW

Supporting computations for cash receipts and cash payments.

(1)	*Cost of equipment sold	$ 21,375
	Accumulated depreciation of equipment sold	(11,100)
	Book value of equipment sold	10,275
	Loss on sale of equipment	(3,300)
	Cash received from sale of equipment	$ 6,975
	Cost of equipment sold	$ 21,375
	Less decrease in the equipment account balance	(10,875)
	Cash paid for new equipment	$ 10,500
(2)	Loss on retirement of bonds	$ 825
	Carrying value of bonds retired	37,500
	Cash paid to retire bonds	$ 38,325
(3)	Net income	$ 60,150
	Less increase in retained earnings	45,900
	Dividends declared	14,250
	Plus decrease in dividends payable	4,500
	Cash paid for dividends	$ 18,750
(4)B	Sales	$ 446,100
	Add decrease in accounts receivable	5,700
	Cash received from customers	$451,800
(5)B	Cost of goods sold	$ 222,300
	Plus increase in merchandise inventory	9,525
	Purchases	231,825
	Plus decrease in accounts payable	4,950
	Cash paid for merchandise	$236,775
(6)B	Other operating expenses	$ 120,300
	Plus increase in prepaid expenses	1,950
	Cash paid for other operating expenses	$122,250
(7)B	Income taxes expense	$ 13,725
	Less increase in income taxes payable	(675)
	Cash paid for income taxes	$ 13,050

*Supporting T-account analysis for part 1 follows:

Equipment				
Bal., Dec. 31, 2012	146,700			
Cash purchase	10,500	Sale		21,375
Bal., Dec. 31, 2013	135,825			

Accumulated Depreciation—Equipment				
			Bal., Dec. 31, 2012	47,550
Sale	11,100		Depr. expense	25,500
			Bal., Dec. 31, 2013	61,950

UMLAUF COMPANY
Statement of Cash Flows (Indirect Method)
For Year Ended December 31, 2013

Cash flows from operating activities		
Net income	$60,150	
Adjustments to reconcile net income to net cash provided by operating activities		
Decrease in accounts receivable	5,700	
Increase in merchandise inventory	(9,525)	
Increase in prepaid expenses	(1,950)	
Decrease in accounts payable	(4,950)	
Increase in income taxes payable	675	
Depreciation expense	25,500	
Loss on sale of plant assets	3,300	
Loss on retirement of bonds	825	
Net cash provided by operating activities		$79,725

[continued on next page]

[continued from previous page]

Cash flows from investing activities		
Cash received from sale of equipment	6,975	
Cash paid for equipment	(10,500)	
Net cash used in investing activities		(3,525)
Cash flows from financing activities		
Cash paid to retire bonds payable	(38,325)	
Cash paid for dividends	(18,750)	
Net cash used in financing activities		(57,075)
Net increase in cash		$19,125
Cash balance at prior year-end		23,925
Cash balance at current year-end		$43,050

UMLAUF COMPANY
Statement of Cash Flows (Direct Method)
For Year Ended December 31, 2013

Cash flows from operating activities		
Cash received from customers	$451,800	
Cash paid for merchandise	(236,775)	
Cash paid for other operating expenses	(122,250)	
Cash paid for income taxes	(13,050)	
Net cash provided by operating activities		$79,725
Cash flows from investing activities		
Cash received from sale of equipment	6,975	
Cash paid for equipment	(10,500)	
Net cash used in investing activities		(3,525)
Cash flows from financing activities		
Cash paid to retire bonds payable	(38,325)	
Cash paid for dividends	(18,750)	
Net cash used in financing activities		(57,075)
Net increase in cash		$19,125
Cash balance at prior year-end		23,925
Cash balance at current year-end		$43,050

APPENDIX

12A

Spreadsheet Preparation of the Statement of Cash Flows

This appendix explains how to use a spreadsheet to prepare the statement of cash flows under the indirect method.

Preparing the Indirect Method Spreadsheet   Analyzing noncash accounts can be challenging when a company has a large number of accounts and many operating, investing, and financing transactions. A *spreadsheet,* also called *work sheet* or *working paper,* can help us organize the information needed to prepare a statement of cash flows. A spreadsheet also makes it easier to check the accuracy of our work. To illustrate, we return to the comparative balance sheets and income statement shown in Exhibit 12.10. We use the following identifying letters *a* through *g* to code changes in accounts, and letters *h* through *m* for additional information, to prepare the statement of cash flows:

   a. Net income is $38,000.

   b. Accounts receivable increase by $20,000.

   c. Merchandise inventory increases by $14,000.

   d. Prepaid expenses increase by $2,000.

   e. Accounts payable decrease by $5,000.

f. Interest payable decreases by $1,000.

g. Income taxes payable increase by $10,000.

h. Depreciation expense is $24,000.

i. Plant assets costing $30,000 with accumulated depreciation of $12,000 are sold for $12,000 cash. This yields a loss on sale of assets of $6,000.

j. Notes with a book value of $34,000 are retired with a cash payment of $18,000, yielding a $16,000 gain on retirement.

k. Plant assets costing $70,000 are purchased with a cash payment of $10,000 and an issuance of notes payable for $60,000.

l. Issued 3,000 shares of common stock for $15,000 cash.

m. Paid cash dividends of $14,000.

Exhibit 12A.1 shows the indirect method spreadsheet for Genesis. We enter both beginning and ending balance sheet amounts on the spreadsheet. We also enter information in the Analysis of Changes columns

EXHIBIT 12A.1

Spreadsheet for Preparing Statement of Cash Flows—Indirect Method

File Edit View Insert Format Tools Data Accounting Window Help				
GENESIS				
Spreadsheet for Statement of Cash Flows—Indirect Method				
For Year Ended December 31, 2013				
		Analysis of Changes		
	Dec. 31, 2012	**Debit**	**Credit**	**Dec. 31, 2013**
Balance Sheet—Debit Bal. Accounts				
Cash	$ 12,000			$ 17,000
Accounts receivable	40,000	(b) $ 20,000		60,000
Merchandise inventory	70,000	(c) 14,000		84,000
Prepaid expenses	4,000	(d) 2,000		6,000
Plant assets	210,000	(k1) 70,000	(i) $ 30,000	250,000
	$336,000			$417,000
Balance Sheet—Credit Bal. Accounts				
Accumulated depreciation	$ 48,000	(i) 12,000	(h) 24,000	$ 60,000
Accounts payable	40,000	(e) 5,000		35,000
Interest payable	4,000	(f) 1,000		3,000
Income taxes payable	12,000		(g) 10,000	22,000
Notes payable	64,000	(j) 34,000	(k2) 60,000	90,000
Common stock, $5 par value	80,000		(l) 15,000	95,000
Retained earnings	88,000	(m) 14,000	(a) 38,000	112,000
	$336,000			$417,000
Statement of Cash Flows				
Operating activities				
Net income		(a) 38,000		
Increase in accounts receivable			(b) 20,000	
Increase in merchandise inventory			(c) 14,000	
Increase in prepaid expenses			(d) 2,000	
Decrease in accounts payable			(e) 5,000	
Decrease in interest payable			(f) 1,000	
Increase in income taxes payable		(g) 10,000		
Depreciation expense		(h) 24,000		
Loss on sale of plant assets		(i) 6,000		
Gain on retirement of notes			(j) 16,000	
Investing activities				
Receipts from sale of plant assets		(i) 12,000		
Payment for purchase of plant assets			(k1) 10,000	
Financing activities				
Payment to retire notes			(j) 18,000	
Receipts from issuing stock		(l) 15,000		
Payment of cash dividends			(m) 14,000	
Noncash Investing and Financing Activities				
Purchase of plant assets with notes		(k2) 60,000	(k1) 60,000	
		$337,000	$337,000	

(keyed to the additional information items *a* through *m*) to explain changes in the accounts and determine the cash flows for operating, investing, and financing activities. Information about noncash investing and financing activities is reported near the bottom.

Entering the Analysis of Changes on the Spreadsheet   The following sequence of procedures is used to complete the spreadsheet after the beginning and ending balances of the balance sheet accounts are entered:

① Enter net income as the first item in the Statement of Cash Flows section for computing operating cash inflow (debit) and as a credit to Retained Earnings.

② In the Statement of Cash Flows section, adjustments to net income are entered as debits if they increase cash flows and as credits if they decrease cash flows. Applying this same rule, adjust net income for the change in each noncash current asset and current liability account related to operating activities. For each adjustment to net income, the offsetting debit or credit must help reconcile the beginning and ending balances of a current asset or current liability account.

③ Enter adjustments to net income for income statement items not providing or using cash in the period. For each adjustment, the offsetting debit or credit must help reconcile a noncash balance sheet account.

④ Adjust net income to eliminate any gains or losses from investing and financing activities. Because the cash from a gain must be excluded from operating activities, the gain is entered as a credit in the operating activities section. Losses are entered as debits. For each adjustment, the related debit and/or credit must help reconcile balance sheet accounts and involve reconstructed entries to show the cash flow from investing or financing activities.

⑤ After reviewing any unreconciled balance sheet accounts and related information, enter the remaining reconciling entries for investing and financing activities. Examples are purchases of plant assets, issuances of long-term debt, stock issuances, and dividend payments. Some of these may require entries in the noncash investing and financing section of the spreadsheet (reconciled).

⑥ Check accuracy by totaling the Analysis of Changes columns and by determining that the change in each balance sheet account has been explained (reconciled).

We illustrate these steps in Exhibit 12A.1 for Genesis:

Point: Analysis of the changes on the spreadsheet are summarized here:

1. Cash flows from operating activities generally affect net income, current assets, and current liabilities.

2. Cash flows from investing activities generally affect noncurrent asset accounts.

3. Cash flows from financing activities generally affect noncurrent liability and equity accounts.

Step	Entries
①.........	(*a*)
②.........	(*b*) through (*g*)
③.........	(*h*)
④.........	(*i*) through (*j*)
⑤.........	(*k*) through (*m*)

Since adjustments *i, j,* and *k* are more challenging, we show them in the following debit and credit format. These entries are for purposes of our understanding; they are *not* the entries actually made in the journals. Changes in the Cash account are identified as sources or uses of cash.

i.	Loss from sale of plant assets	6,000	
	Accumulated depreciation	12,000	
	Receipt from sale of plant assets **(source of cash)**	12,000	
	Plant assets		30,000
	To describe sale of plant assets.		
j.	Notes payable	34,000	
	Payments to retire notes **(use of cash)**		18,000
	Gain on retirement of notes................................		16,000
	To describe retirement of notes.		
k1.	Plant assets	70,000	
	Payment to purchase plant assets **(use of cash)**		10,000
	Purchase of plant assets financed by notes		60,000
	To describe purchase of plant assets.		
k2.	Purchase of plant assets financed by notes	60,000	
	Notes payable		60,000
	To issue notes for purchase of assets.		

Direct Method of Reporting Operating Cash Flows 12B

We compute cash flows from operating activities under the direct method by adjusting accrual-based income statement items to the cash basis. The usual approach is to adjust income statement accounts related to operating activities for changes in their related balance sheet accounts as follows:

P5 Compute cash flows from operating activities using the direct method.

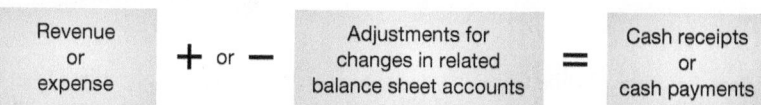

The framework for reporting cash receipts and cash payments for the operating section of the cash flow statement under the direct method follows. We consider cash receipts first and then cash payments.

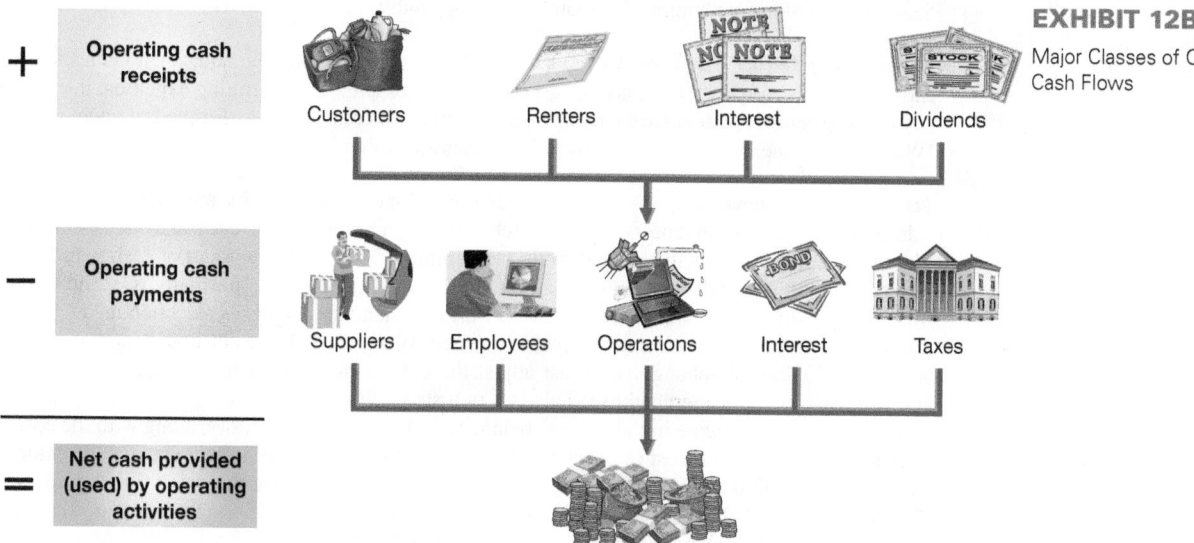

EXHIBIT 12B.1

Major Classes of Operating Cash Flows

Operating Cash Receipts A review of Exhibit 12.10 and the additional information reported by Genesis suggests only one potential cash receipt: sales to customers. This section, therefore, starts with sales to customers as reported on the income statement and then adjusts it as necessary to obtain cash received from customers to report on the statement of cash flows.

Cash Received from Customers If all sales are for cash, the amount received from customers equals the sales reported on the income statement. When some or all sales are on account, however, we must adjust the amount of sales for the change in Accounts Receivable. It is often helpful to use *account analysis* to do this. This usually involves setting up a T-account and reconstructing its major entries, with emphasis on cash receipts and payments. To illustrate, we use a T-account that includes accounts receivable balances for Genesis on December 31, 2012 and 2013. The beginning balance is $40,000 and the ending balance is $60,000. Next, the income statement shows sales of $590,000, which we enter on the debit side of this account. We now can reconstruct the Accounts Receivable account to determine the amount of cash received from customers as follows:

Point: An accounts receivable increase implies that cash received from customers is less than sales (the converse is also true).

Accounts Receivable			
Bal., Dec. 31, 2012	40,000		
Sales	590,000	Cash receipts =	570,000
Bal., Dec. 31, 2013	60,000		

Example: If the ending balance of accounts receivable is $20,000 (instead of $60,000), what is cash received from customers? *Answer:* $610,000

EXHIBIT 12B.2

Formula to Compute Cash Received from Customers— Direct Method

Point: Net income is measured using accrual accounting. Cash flows from operations are measured using cash basis accounting.

This T-account shows that the Accounts Receivable balance begins at $40,000 and increases to $630,000 from sales of $590,000, yet its ending balance is only $60,000. This implies that cash receipts from customers are $570,000, computed as $40,000 + $590,000 − [?] = $60,000. This computation can be rearranged to express cash received as equal to sales of $590,000 minus a $20,000 increase in accounts receivable. This computation is summarized as a general rule in Exhibit 12B.2. The statement of cash flows in Exhibit 12.7 reports the $570,000 cash received from customers as a cash inflow from operating activities.

$$\text{Cash received from customers} = \text{Sales} \begin{bmatrix} + \text{ Decrease in accounts receivable} \\ \text{or} \\ - \text{ Increase in accounts receivable} \end{bmatrix}$$

Other Cash Receipts   While Genesis's cash receipts are limited to collections from customers, we often see other types of cash receipts, most commonly cash receipts involving rent, interest, and dividends. We compute cash received from these items by subtracting an increase in their respective receivable or adding a decrease. For instance, if rent receivable increases in the period, cash received from renters is less than rent revenue reported on the income statement. If rent receivable decreases, cash received is more than reported rent revenue. The same logic applies to interest and dividends. The formulas for these computations are summarized later in this appendix.

Operating Cash Payments   A review of Exhibit 12.10 and the additional Genesis information shows four operating expenses: cost of goods sold; wages and other operating expenses; interest expense; and taxes expense. We analyze each expense to compute its cash amounts for the statement of cash flows. (We then examine depreciation and the other losses and gains.)

Cash Paid for Merchandise   We compute cash paid for merchandise by analyzing both cost of goods sold and merchandise inventory. If all merchandise purchases are for cash and the ending balance of Merchandise Inventory is unchanged from the beginning balance, the amount of cash paid for merchandise equals cost of goods sold—an uncommon situation. Instead, there normally is some change in the Merchandise Inventory balance. Also, some or all merchandise purchases are often made on credit, and this yields changes in the Accounts Payable balance. When the balances of both Merchandise Inventory and Accounts Payable change, we must adjust the cost of goods sold for changes in both accounts to compute cash paid for merchandise. This is a two-step adjustment.

First, we use the change in the account balance of Merchandise Inventory, along with the cost of goods sold amount, to compute cost of purchases for the period. An increase in merchandise inventory implies that we bought more than we sold, and we add this inventory increase to cost of goods sold to compute cost of purchases. A decrease in merchandise inventory implies that we bought less than we sold, and we subtract the inventory decrease from cost of goods sold to compute purchases. We illustrate the *first step* by reconstructing the Merchandise Inventory account of Genesis:

Merchandise Inventory			
Bal., Dec. 31, 2012	70,000		
Purchases =	314,000	Cost of goods sold	300,000
Bal., Dec. 31, 2013	84,000		

The beginning balance is $70,000, and the ending balance is $84,000. The income statement shows that cost of goods sold is $300,000, which we enter on the credit side of this account. With this information, we determine the amount for cost of purchases to be $314,000. This computation can be rearranged to express cost of purchases as equal to cost of goods sold of $300,000 plus the $14,000 increase in inventory.

The second step uses the change in the balance of Accounts Payable, and the amount of cost of purchases, to compute cash paid for merchandise. A decrease in accounts payable implies that we paid for more goods than we acquired this period, and we would then add the accounts payable decrease to cost of purchases to compute cash paid for merchandise. An increase in accounts payable implies that we paid for less than the amount of goods acquired, and we would subtract the accounts payable increase from purchases to compute cash paid for merchandise. The *second step* is applied to Genesis by reconstructing its Accounts Payable account:

Accounts Payable			
		Bal., Dec. 31, 2012	40,000
Cash payments =	319,000	Purchases	314,000
		Bal., Dec. 31, 2013	35,000

Its beginning balance of $40,000 plus purchases of $314,000 minus an ending balance of $35,000 yields cash paid of $319,000 (or $40,000 + $314,000 − [?] = $35,000). Alternatively, we can express cash paid for merchandise as equal to purchases of $314,000 plus the $5,000 decrease in accounts payable. The $319,000 cash paid for merchandise is reported on the statement of cash flows in Exhibit 12.7 as a cash outflow under operating activities.

We summarize this two-step adjustment to cost of goods sold to compute cash paid for merchandise inventory in Exhibit 12B.3.

Example: If the ending balances of Inventory and Accounts Payable are $60,000 and $50,000, respectively (instead of $84,000 and $35,000), what is cash paid for merchandise? *Answer:* $280,000

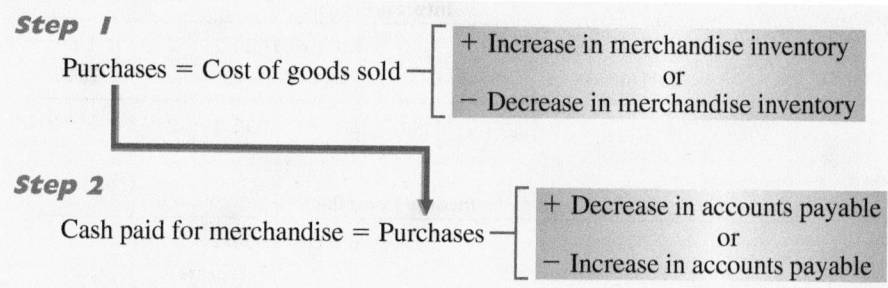

EXHIBIT 12B.3

Two Steps to Compute Cash Paid for Merchandise—Direct Method

Cash Paid for Wages and Operating Expenses (Excluding Depreciation)   The income statement of Genesis shows wages and other operating expenses of $216,000 (see Exhibit 12.10). To compute cash paid for wages and other operating expenses, we adjust this amount for any changes in their related balance sheet accounts. We begin by looking for any prepaid expenses and accrued liabilities related to wages and other operating expenses in the balance sheets of Genesis in Exhibit 12.10. The balance sheets show prepaid expenses but no accrued liabilities. Thus, the adjustment is limited to the change in prepaid expenses. The amount of adjustment is computed by assuming that all cash paid for wages and other operating expenses is initially debited to Prepaid Expenses. This assumption allows us to reconstruct the Prepaid Expenses account:

Prepaid Expenses			
Bal., Dec. 31, 2012	4,000		
Cash payments =	218,000	Wages and other operating exp.	216,000
Bal., Dec. 31, 2013	6,000		

Prepaid Expenses increase by $2,000 in the period, meaning that cash paid for wages and other operating expenses exceeds the reported expense by $2,000. Alternatively, we can express cash paid for wages and other operating expenses as equal to its reported expenses of $216,000 plus the $2,000 increase in prepaid expenses.[1]

Exhibit 12B.4 summarizes the adjustments to wages (including salaries) and other operating expenses. The Genesis balance sheet did not report accrued liabilities, but we include them in the formula to explain the adjustment to cash when they do exist. A decrease in accrued liabilities implies that we paid cash for more goods or services than received this period, so we add the decrease in accrued liabilities to the expense amount to obtain cash paid for these goods or services. An increase in accrued liabilities implies that we paid cash for less than what was acquired, so we subtract this increase in accrued liabilities from the expense amount to get cash paid.

Point: A decrease in prepaid expenses implies that reported expenses include an amount(s) that did not require a cash outflow in the period.

---

[1] The assumption that all cash payments for wages and operating expenses are initially debited to Prepaid Expenses is not necessary for our analysis to hold. If cash payments are debited directly to the expense account, the total amount of cash paid for wages and other operating expenses still equals the $216,000 expense plus the $2,000 increase in Prepaid Expenses (which arise from end-of-period adjusting entries).

EXHIBIT 12B.4

Formula to Compute Cash Paid for Wages and Operating Expenses—Direct Method

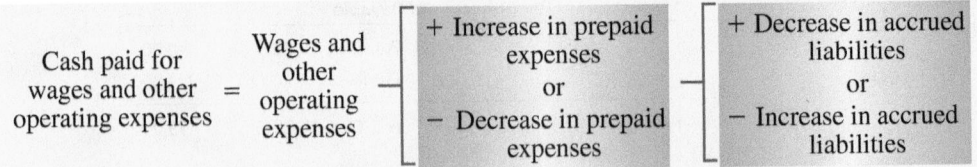

Cash paid for interest and income taxes   Computing operating cash flows for interest and taxes is similar to that for operating expenses. Both require adjustments to their amounts reported on the income statement for changes in their related balance sheet accounts. We begin with the Genesis income statement showing interest expense of $7,000 and income taxes expense of $15,000. To compute the cash paid, we adjust interest expense for the change in interest payable and then the income taxes expense for the change in income taxes payable. These computations involve reconstructing both liability accounts:

Interest Payable			
		Bal., Dec. 31, 2012	4,000
Cash paid for interest =	8,000	Interest expense	7,000
		Bal., Dec. 31, 2013	3,000

Income Taxes Payable			
		Bal., Dec. 31, 2012	12,000
Cash paid for taxes =	5,000	Income taxes expense	15,000
		Bal., Dec. 31, 2013	22,000

These accounts reveal cash paid for interest of $8,000 and cash paid for income taxes of $5,000. The formulas to compute these amounts are in Exhibit 12B.5. Both of these cash payments are reported as operating cash outflows on the statement of cash flows in Exhibit 12.7.

EXHIBIT 12B.5

Formulas to Compute Cash Paid for Both Interest and Taxes—Direct Method

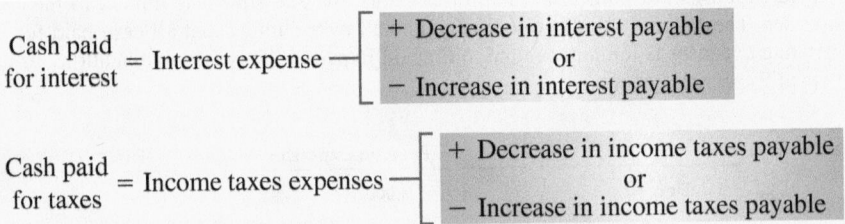

Analysis of Additional Expenses, Gains, and Losses   Genesis has three additional items reported on its income statement: depreciation, loss on sale of assets, and gain on retirement of debt. We must consider each for its potential cash effects.

Depreciation Expense   Depreciation expense is $24,000. It is often called a *noncash expense* because depreciation has no cash flows. Depreciation expense is an allocation of an asset's depreciable cost. The cash outflow with a plant asset is reported as part of investing activities when it is paid for. Thus, depreciation expense is *never* reported on a statement of cash flows using the direct method; nor is depletion or amortization expense.

Loss on Sale of Assets   Sales of assets frequently result in gains and losses reported as part of net income, but the amount of recorded gain or loss does *not* reflect any cash flows in these transactions. Asset sales result in cash inflow equal to the cash amount received, regardless of whether the asset was sold at a gain or a loss. This cash inflow is reported under investing activities. Thus, the loss or gain on a sale of assets is *never* reported on a statement of cash flows using the direct method.

Gain on Retirement of Debt   Retirement of debt usually yields a gain or loss reported as part of net income, but that gain or loss does *not* reflect cash flow in this transaction. Debt retirement results in cash outflow equal to the cash paid to settle the debt, regardless of whether the debt is retired at a gain or loss.

This cash outflow is reported under financing activities; the loss or gain from retirement of debt is *never* reported on a statement of cash flows using the direct method.

Summary of Adjustments for Direct Method Exhibit 12B.6 summarizes common adjustments for net income to yield net cash provided (used) by operating activities under the direct method.

Item	From Income Statement	Adjustments to Obtain Cash Flow Numbers	
Receipts			
From sales	Sales Revenue	┌ +Decrease in Accounts Receivable └ −Increase in Accounts Receivable	
From rent	Rent Revenue	┌ +Decrease in Rent Receivable └ −Increase in Rent Receivable	
From interest	Interest Revenue	┌ +Decrease in Interest Receivable └ −Increase in Interest Receivable	
From dividends	Dividend Revenue	┌ +Decrease in Dividends Receivable └ −Increase in Dividends Receivable	
Payments			
To suppliers	Cost of Goods Sold	┌ +Increase in Inventory └ −Decrease in Inventory	┌ +Decrease in Accounts Payable └ −Increase in Accounts Payable
For operations	Operating Expense	┌ +Increase in Prepaids └ −Decrease in Prepaids	┌ +Decrease in Accrued Liabilities └ −Increase in Accrued Liabilities
To employees	Wages (Salaries) Expense	┌ +Decrease in Wages (Salaries) Payable └ −Increase in Wages (Salaries) Payable	
For interest	Interest Expense	┌ +Decrease in Interest Payable └ −Increase in Interest Payable	
For taxes	Income Tax Expense	┌ +Decrease in Income Tax Payable └ −Increase in Income Tax Payable	

EXHIBIT 12B.6

Summary of Selected Adjustments for Direct Method

Direct Method Format of Operating Activities Section Exhibit 12.7 shows the Genesis statement of cash flows using the direct method. Major items of cash inflows and cash outflows are listed separately in the operating activities section. The format requires that operating cash outflows be subtracted from operating cash inflows to get net cash provided (used) by operating activities. The FASB recommends that the operating activities section of the statement of cash flows be reported using the direct method, which is considered more useful to financial statement users. *However, the FASB requires a reconciliation of net income to net cash provided (used) by operating activities when the direct method is used* (which can be reported in the notes). This reconciliation is similar to preparation of the operating activities section of the statement of cash flows using the indirect method.

Point: Some preparers argue that it is easier to prepare a statement of cash flows using the indirect method. This likely explains its greater frequency in financial statements.

 **IFRS**

Currently, U.S. GAAP and IFRS allow cash flows from operating activities to be reported using either the indirect method or the direct method. The IASB and FASB are working on joint guidance that would require the direct method for the operating section with the indirect method's operating section disclosed in the footnotes. Stay tuned . . . ∎

QC4

Summary

C1 **Distinguish between operating, investing, and financing activities, and describe how noncash investing and financing activities are disclosed.** The purpose of the statement of cash flows is to report major cash receipts and cash payments relating to operating, investing, or financing activities. Operating activities include transactions and events that determine net income. Investing activities include transactions and events that mainly affect long-term assets. Financing activities include transactions and events that mainly affect long-term liabilities and equity. Noncash investing and financing activities must be disclosed in either a note or a separate schedule to

the statement of cash flows. Examples are the retirement of debt by issuing equity and the exchange of a note payable for plant assets.

A1 **Analyze the statement of cash flows and apply the cash flow on total assets ratio.** To understand and predict cash flows, users stress identification of the sources and uses of cash flows by operating, investing, and financing activities. Emphasis is on operating cash flows since they derive from continuing operations. The cash flow on total assets ratio is defined as operating cash flows divided by average total assets. Analysis of current and past values for this ratio can reflect a company's ability to yield regular and positive cash flows. It is also viewed as a measure of earnings quality.

P1 **Prepare a statement of cash flows.** Preparation of a statement of cash flows involves five steps: (1) Compute the net increase or decrease in cash; (2) compute net cash provided or used by operating activities (*using either the direct or indirect method*); (3) compute net cash provided or used by investing activities; (4) compute net cash provided or used by financing activities; and (5) report the beginning and ending cash balance and prove that it is explained by net cash flows. Noncash investing and financing activities are also disclosed.

P2 **Compute cash flows from operating activities using the indirect method.** The indirect method for reporting net cash provided or used by operating activities starts with net income and then adjusts it for three items: (1) changes in noncash current assets and current liabilities related to operating activities, (2) revenues and expenses not providing or using cash, and (3) gains and losses from investing and financing activities.

P3 **Determine cash flows from both investing and financing activities.** Cash flows from both investing and financing activities are determined by identifying the cash flow effects of transactions and events affecting each balance sheet account related to these activities. All cash flows from these activities are identified when we can explain changes in these accounts from the beginning to the end of the period.

P4A **Illustrate use of a spreadsheet to prepare a statement of cash flows.** A spreadsheet is a useful tool in preparing a statement of cash flows. Six key steps (see Appendix 12A) are applied when using the spreadsheet to prepare the statement.

P5B **Compute cash flows from operating activities using the direct method.** The direct method for reporting net cash provided or used by operating activities lists major operating cash inflows less cash outflows to yield net cash inflow or outflow from operations.

Guidance Answers to Decision Maker

Entrepreneur Several factors might explain an increase in net cash flows when a net loss is reported, including (1) early recognition of expenses relative to revenues generated (such as research and development), (2) cash advances on long-term sales contracts not yet recognized in income, (3) issuances of debt or equity for cash to finance expansion, (4) cash sale of assets, (5) delay of cash payments, and (6) cash prepayment on sales. Analysis needs to focus on the components of both the net loss and the net cash flows and their implications for future performance.

Reporter Your initial reaction based on the company's $600,000 loss with a $550,000 decrease in net cash flows is not positive. However, closer scrutiny reveals a more positive picture of this company's performance. Cash flow from operating activities is $650,000, computed as [?] − $850,000 − $350,000 = $(550,000). You also note that net income *before* the extraordinary loss is $330,000, computed as [?] − $930,000 = $(600,000).

Key Terms

Multiple Choice Quiz   Answers on p. 575   mhhe.com/wildFA7e

Additional Quiz Questions are available at the book's Website.

1. A company uses the indirect method to determine its cash flows from operating activities. Use the following information to determine its net cash provided or used by operating activities.

Net income	$15,200
Depreciation expense	10,000
Cash payment on note payable	8,000
Gain on sale of land	3,000
Increase in inventory	1,500
Increase in accounts payable	2,850

   a. $23,550 used by operating activities
   b. $23,550 provided by operating activities
   c. $15,550 provided by operating activities
   d. $42,400 provided by operating activities
   e. $20,850 provided by operating activities

2. A machine with a cost of $175,000 and accumulated depreciation of $94,000 is sold for $87,000 cash. The amount reported as a source of cash under cash flows from investing activities is
   a. $81,000.
   b. $6,000.

c. $87,000.

d. Zero; this is a financing activity.

e. Zero; this is an operating activity.

3. A company settles a long-term note payable plus interest by paying $68,000 cash toward the principal amount and $5,440 cash for interest. The amount reported as a use of cash under cash flows from financing activities is

a. Zero; this is an investing activity.

b. Zero; this is an operating activity.

c. $73,440.

d. $68,000.

e. $5,440.

4. The following information is available regarding a company's annual salaries and wages. What amount of cash is paid for salaries and wages?

Salaries and wages expense	$255,000
Salaries and wages payable, prior year-end	8,200
Salaries and wages payable, current year-end	10,900

a. $252,300

b. $257,700

c. $255,000

d. $274,100

e. $235,900

5. The following information is available for a company. What amount of cash is paid for merchandise for the current year?

Cost of goods sold	$545,000
Merchandise inventory, prior year-end	105,000
Merchandise inventory, current year-end	112,000
Accounts payable, prior year-end	98,500
Accounts payable, current year-end	101,300

a. $545,000

b. $554,800

c. $540,800

d. $535,200

e. $549,200

$^{A(B)}$ Superscript letter A (B) denotes assignments based on Appendix 12A (12B).

Icon denotes assignments that involve decision making.

Discussion Questions

1. What is the reporting purpose of the statement of cash flows? Identify at least two questions that this statement can answer.

2. What are some investing activities reported on the statement of cash flows?

3. What are some financing activities reported on the statement of cash flows?

4. Describe the direct method of reporting cash flows from operating activities.

5. When a statement of cash flows is prepared using the direct method, what are some of the operating cash flows?

6. Describe the indirect method of reporting cash flows from operating activities.

7. Where on the statement of cash flows is the payment of cash dividends reported?

8. Assume that a company purchases land for $1,000,000, paying $400,000 cash and borrowing the remainder with a long-term note payable. How should this transaction be reported on a statement of cash flows?

9. On June 3, a company borrows $200,000 cash by giving its bank a 90-day, interest-bearing note. On the statement of cash flows, where should this be reported?

10. If a company reports positive net income for the year, can it also show a net cash outflow from operating activities? Explain.

11. Is depreciation a source of cash flow?

12. Refer to Apple's statement of cash flows in Appendix A. (*a*) Which method is used to compute its net cash provided by operating activities? (*b*) Its balance sheet shows an increase in accounts (trade) receivables from September 24, 2011, to September 29, 2012; why is this increase in accounts (trade) receivables subtracted when computing net cash provided by operating activities for the fiscal year ended September 29, 2012? **APPLE**

13. Refer to Google's statement of cash flows in Appendix A. What are its cash flows from financing activities for the year ended December 31, 2012? List the items and amounts. **GOOGLE**

14. Refer to Samsung's 2012 statement of cash flows in Appendix A. List its cash flows from operating activities, investing activities, and financing activities. **Samsung**

15. Refer to Samsung's statement of cash flows in Appendix A. What investing activities result in cash outflows for the year ended December 31, 2012? List items and amounts. **Samsung**

QUICK STUDY

QS 12-1

Statement of cash flows

C1

Complete the following explanations 1 through 4 regarding the statement of cash flows by filling in the blank(s) with the best phrase from *a* through *f*.

a. Statement of cash flows

b. Cash operating activity

c. Cash investing activity

d. Cash financing activity

e. Noncash activity

f. Net change in cash balance

1. Conversion of bonds into stock is an example of a/an _____.

2. An example of a/an _____ is cash paid for dividends.

3. The _____ reports the cash (and cash equivalent) activities of a business for a specific accounting period.

4. The beginning cash balance plus the _____ equals the ending cash balance reported on a statement of cash flows.

QS 12-2

Transaction classification by activity

C1

Classify the following cash flows as either operating, investing, or financing activities.

1. Sold long-term investments for cash.

2. Received cash payments from customers.

3. Paid cash for wages and salaries.

4. Purchased inventories for cash.

5. Paid cash dividends.

6. Issued common stock for cash.

7. Received cash interest on a note.

8. Paid cash interest on outstanding notes.

9. Received cash from sale of land at a loss.

10. Paid cash for property taxes on building.

QS 12-3

Indirect: Computing cash from operations

P2

Use the following information to determine this company's cash flows from operating activities using the indirect method.

MOSS COMPANY
Selected Balance Sheet Information
December 31, 2013 and 2012

	2013	2012
Current assets		
Cash	$84,650	$26,800
Accounts receivable	25,000	32,000
Inventory	60,000	54,100
Current liabilities		
Accounts payable	30,400	25,700
Income taxes payable	2,050	2,200

MOSS COMPANY
Income Statement
For Year Ended December 31, 2013

Sales		$515,000
Cost of goods sold		331,600
Gross profit		183,400
Operating expenses		
Depreciation expense	$ 36,000	
Other expenses	121,500	157,500
Income before taxes		25,900
Income taxes expense		7,700
Net income		$ 18,200

QS 12-4

Computing cash from asset sales

P3

The following selected information is from Ellerby Company's comparative balance sheets.

At December 31	2013	2012
Furniture	$132,000	$ 184,500
Accumulated depreciation—Furniture	(88,700)	(110,700)

The income statement reports depreciation expense for the year of $18,000. Also, furniture costing $52,500 was sold for its book value. Compute the cash received from the sale of furniture.

The following selected information is from the Princeton Company's comparative balance sheets.

QS 12-5
Computing financing cash flows
P3

At December 31	2013	2012
Common stock, $10 par value	$105,000	$100,000
Paid-in capital in excess of par	567,000	342,000
Retained earnings	313,500	287,500

The company's net income for the year ended December 31, 2013, was $48,000.

1. Compute the cash received from the sale of its common stock during 2013.
2. Compute the cash paid for dividends during 2013.

Use the following balance sheets and income statement to answer QS 12-6 through QS 12-11.

QS 12-6
Indirect: Computing cash from operations P2

CRUZ, INC. Comparative Balance Sheets December 31, 2013		
	2013	2012
Assets		
Cash	$ 94,800	$ 24,000
Accounts receivable, net	41,000	51,000
Inventory	85,800	95,800
Prepaid expenses	5,400	4,200
Furniture	109,000	119,000
Accum. depreciation—Furniture	(17,000)	(9,000)
Total assets	$319,000	$285,000
Liabilities and Equity		
Accounts payable	$ 15,000	$ 21,000
Wages payable	9,000	5,000
Income taxes payable	1,400	2,600
Notes payable (long-term)	29,000	69,000
Common stock, $5 par value	229,000	179,000
Retained earnings	35,600	8,400
Total liabilities and equity	$319,000	$285,000

CRUZ, INC. Income Statement For Year Ended December 31, 2013		
Sales		$488,000
Cost of goods sold		314,000
Gross profit		174,000
Operating expenses		
Depreciation expense	$37,600	
Other expenses	89,100	126,700
Income before taxes		47,300
Income taxes expense		17,300
Net income		$ 30,000

Required

Use the indirect method to prepare the cash provided or used from operating activities section only of the statement of cash flows for this company.

Refer to the data in QS 12-6.
Furniture costing $55,000 is sold at its book value in 2013. Acquisitions of furniture total $45,000 cash, on which no depreciation is necessary because it is acquired at year-end. What is the cash inflow related to the sale of furniture?

QS 12-7
Computing cash from asset sales
P3

Refer to the data in QS 12-6.

1. Assume that all common stock is issued for cash. What amount of cash dividends is paid during 2013?
2. Assume that no additional notes payable are issued in 2013. What cash amount is paid to reduce the notes payable balance in 2013?

QS 12-8
Computing financing cash outflows P3

Refer to the data in QS 12-6.

1. How much cash is received from sales to customers for year 2013?
2. What is the net increase or decrease in cash for year 2013?

QS 12-9ᴮ
Direct: Computing cash received from customers P5

QS 12-10^B

Direct: Computing operating cash outflows **P5**

Refer to the data in QS 12-6.

1. How much cash is paid to acquire merchandise inventory during year 2013?
2. How much cash is paid for operating expenses during year 2013?

QS 12-11^B

Direct: Computing cash from operations **P5**

Refer to the data in QS 12-6.
Use the direct method to prepare the cash provided or used from operating activities section only of the statement of cash flows for this company.

QS 12-12

Analyses of sources and uses of cash **A1**

Financial data from three competitors in the same industry follow.

1. Which of the three competitors is in the strongest position as shown by its statement of cash flows?
2. Analyze and compare the strength of Moore's cash flow on total assets ratio to that of Sykes.

($ thousands)	Moore	Sykes	Kritch
Cash provided (used) by operating activities	$ 70,000	$ 60,000	$ (24,000)
Cash provided (used) by investing activities			
Proceeds from sale of operating assets			26,000
Purchase of operating assets	(28,000)	(34,000)	
Cash provided (used) by financing activities			
Proceeds from issuance of debt			23,000
Repayment of debt	(6,000)		
Net increase (decrease) in cash	$ 36,000	$ 26,000	$ 25,000
Average total assets	$ 790,000	$ 625,000	$ 300,000

QS 12-13^A

Noncash accounts on a spreadsheet **P4**

When a spreadsheet for a statement of cash flows is prepared, all changes in noncash balance sheet accounts are fully explained on the spreadsheet. Explain how these noncash balance sheet accounts are used to fully account for cash flows on a spreadsheet.

QS 12-14

Indirect: Computing cash flows from operations

P2

For each of the following three separate cases, compute cash flows from operations. The list includes all balance sheet accounts related to cash from operating activities.

	Case X	Case Y	Case Z
Net income	$ 4,000	$100,000	$72,000
Depreciation expense	30,000	8,000	24,000
Accounts receivable increase (decrease)	40,000	20,000	(4,000)
Inventory increase (decrease)	(20,000)	(10,000)	10,000
Accounts payable increase (decrease)	24,000	(22,000)	14,000
Accrued liabilities increase (decrease)	(44,000)	12,000	(8,000)

QS 12-15

Computing cash flows from investing

P3

Compute cash flows from investing activities using the following company information.

Sale of short-term investments	$ 6,000
Cash collections from customers	16,000
Purchase of used equipment	5,000
Depreciation expense	2,000

Compute cash flows from financing activities using the following company information.

QS 12-16
Computing cash flows from financing
P3

Additional short-term borrowings	$20,000
Purchase of short-term investments	5,000
Cash dividends paid	16,000
Interest paid	8,000

Use the following financial statements and additional information to (1) prepare a statement of cash flows for the year ended December 31, 2014, using the *indirect method,* and (2) analyze and briefly discuss the statement prepared in part 1 with special attention to operating activities and to the company's cash level.

QS 12-17
Indirect: Preparation of statement of cash flows
P1

MONTGOMERY INC.
Comparative Balance Sheets
December 31, 2014 and 2013

	2014	2013
Assets		
Cash	$ 30,400	$ 30,550
Accounts receivable, net	10,050	12,150
Inventory	90,100	70,150
Equipment	49,900	41,500
Accum. depreciation—Equipment	(22,500)	(15,300)
Total assets	$157,950	$139,050
Liabilities and Equity		
Accounts payable	$ 23,900	$ 25,400
Salaries payable	500	600
Common stock, no par value	110,000	100,000
Retained earnings	23,550	13,050
Total liabilities and equity	$157,950	$139,050

MONTGOMERY INC.
Income Statement
For Year Ended December 31, 2014

Sales		$45,575
Cost of goods sold		(18,950)
Gross profit		26,625
Operating expenses		
Depreciation expense	$7,200	
Other expenses	5,550	
Total operating expense		12,750
Income before taxes		13,875
Income tax expense		3,375
Net income		$10,500

Additional Information

a. No dividends are declared or paid in 2014.

b. Issued additional stock for $10,000 cash in 2014.

c. Purchased equipment for cash in 2014; no equipment was sold in 2014.

Answer each of the following related to international accounting standards.

1. Which method, indirect or direct, is acceptable for reporting operating cash flows under IFRS?

2. For each of the following four cash flows, identify whether it is reported under the operating, investing, or financing section (or some combination) within the indirect format of the statement of cash flows reported under IFRS and under U.S. GAAP.

QS 12-18
International cash flow disclosures
C1

Cash Flow Source	US GAAP Reporting	IFRS Reporting
a. Interest paid		
b. Dividends paid		
c. Interest received		
d. Dividends received		

EXERCISES

Exercise 12-1
Indirect: Cash flow classification

C1

The following transactions and events occurred during the year. Assuming that this company uses the *indirect method* to report cash provided by operating activities, indicate where each item would appear on its statement of cash flows by placing an *x* in the appropriate column.

	Statement of Cash Flows			Noncash Investing and Financing Activities	Not Reported on Statement or in Notes
	Operating Activities	Investing Activities	Financing Activities		
a. Declared and paid a cash dividend	——	——	——	——	——
b. Recorded depreciation expense	——	——	——	——	——
c. Paid cash to settle long-term note payable	——	——	——	——	——
d. Prepaid expenses increased in the year	——	——	——	——	——
e. Accounts receivable decreased in the year	——	——	——	——	——
f. Purchased land by issuing common stock	——	——	——	——	——
g. Paid cash to purchase inventory	——	——	——	——	——
h. Sold equipment for cash, yielding a loss	——	——	——	——	——
i. Accounts payable decreased in the year	——	——	——	——	——
j. Income taxes payable increased in the year	——	——	——	——	——

Exercise 12-2ᴮ
Direct: Cash flow classification

C1 P5

The following transactions and events occurred during the year. Assuming that this company uses the *direct method* to report cash provided by operating activities, indicate where each item would appear on the statement of cash flows by placing an *x* in the appropriate column.

	Statement of Cash Flows			Noncash Investing and Financing Activities	Not Reported on Statement or in Notes
	Operating Activities	Investing Activities	Financing Activities		
a. Retired long-term notes payable by issuing common stock	——	——	——	——	——
b. Paid cash toward accounts payable	——	——	——	——	——
c. Sold inventory for cash	——	——	——	——	——
d. Paid cash dividend that was declared in a prior period	——	——	——	——	——
e. Accepted six-month note receivable in exchange for plant assets	——	——	——	——	——
f. Recorded depreciation expense	——	——	——	——	——
g. Paid cash to acquire treasury stock	——	——	——	——	——
h. Collected cash from sales	——	——	——	——	——
i. Borrowed cash from bank by signing a nine-month note payable	——	——	——	——	——
j. Paid cash to purchase a patent	——	——	——	——	——

Exercise 12-3
Indirect: Cash flows from operating activities

P2

Fitzpatrick Company's calendar-year 2013 income statement shows the following: Net Income, $374,000; Depreciation Expense, $44,000; Amortization Expense, $7,200; Gain on Sale of Plant Assets, $6,000. An examination of the company's current assets and current liabilities reveals the following changes (all from operating activities): Accounts Receivable decrease, $17,100; Merchandise Inventory decrease, $42,000; Prepaid Expenses increase, $4,700; Accounts Payable decrease, $8,200; Other Payables increase, $1,200. Use the *indirect method* to compute cash flow from operating activities.

Salud Company reports net income of $400,000 for the year ended December 31, 2013. It also reports $80,000 depreciation expense and a $20,000 gain on the sale of machinery. Its comparative balance sheets reveal a $40,000 increase in accounts receivable, $6,000 increase in accounts payable, $12,000 decrease in prepaid expenses, and $2,000 decrease in wages payable.

Exercise 12-4

Indirect: Cash flow from operations

P2

Required

Prepare only the operating activities section of the statement of cash flows for 2013 using the *indirect method.*

For each of the following three separate cases, use the information provided about the calendar-year 2014 operations of Sahim Company to compute the required cash flow information.

Exercise 12-5ᴮ

Direct: Computation of cash flows

P5

Case X: Compute cash received from customers:

Sales	$515,000
Accounts receivable, December 31, 2013	27,200
Accounts receivable, December 31, 2014	33,600

Case Y: Compute cash paid for rent:

Rent expense	$139,800
Rent payable, December 31, 2013	7,800
Rent payable, December 31, 2014	6,200

Case Z: Compute cash paid for merchandise:

Cost of goods sold	$525,000
Merchandise inventory, December 31, 2013	158,600
Accounts payable, December 31, 2013	66,700
Merchandise inventory, December 31, 2014	130,400
Accounts payable, December 31, 2014	82,000

Information: The following income statement and information about changes in noncash current assets and current liabilities are reported.

Exercise 12-6

Indirect: Cash flows from operating activities

P2

SONAD COMPANY
Income Statement
For Year Ended December 31, 2013

Sales		$1,828,000
Cost of goods sold		991,000
Gross profit		837,000
Operating expenses		
Salaries expense	$245,535	
Depreciation expense	44,200	
Rent expense	49,600	
Amortization expenses—Patents	4,200	
Utilities expense	18,125	361,660
		475,340
Gain on sale of equipment		6,200
Net income		$ 481,540

Changes in current asset and current liability accounts for the year that relate to operations follow.

Accounts receivable	$30,500 increase	Accounts payable	$12,500 decrease
Merchandise inventory	25,000 increase	Salaries payable	3,500 decrease

Required

Prepare only the cash flows from operating activities section of the statement of cash flows using the *indirect* method.

Exercise 12-7ᴮ
Direct: Cash flows from operating activities P5

Refer to the information about Sonad Company in Exercise 12-6.
Use the *direct method* to prepare only the cash provided or used by operating activities section of the statement of cash flows for this company.

Exercise 12-8
Cash flows from investing activities
P3

Use the following information to determine this company's cash flows from investing activities.
a. Equipment with a book value of $65,300 and an original cost of $133,000 was sold at a loss of $14,000.
b. Paid $89,000 cash for a new truck.
c. Sold land costing $154,000 for $198,000 cash, yielding a gain of $44,000.
d. Long-term investments in stock were sold for $60,800 cash, yielding a gain of $4,150.

Exercise 12-9
Cash flows from financing activities
P3

Use the following information to determine this company's cash flows from financing activities.
a. Net income was $35,000.
b. Issued common stock for $64,000 cash.
c. Paid cash dividend of $14,600.
d. Paid $50,000 cash to settle a note payable at its $50,000 maturity value.
e. Paid $12,000 cash to acquire its treasury stock.
f. Purchased equipment for $39,000 cash.

Exercise 12-10
Indirect: Preparation of statement of cash flows P1

Information: The following financial statements and additional information are reported.

IKIBAN INC. Income Statement For Year Ended June 30, 2013		
Sales		$678,000
Cost of goods sold		411,000
Gross profit		267,000
Operating expenses		
Depreciation expense	$58,600	
Other expenses	67,000	
Total operating expenses		125,600
		141,400
Other gains (losses)		
Gain on sale of equipment		2,000
Income before taxes		143,400
Income taxes expense		43,890
Net income		$ 99,510

IKIBAN INC. Comparative Balance Sheets June 30, 2013 and 2012		
	2013	**2012**
Assets		
Cash	$ 87,500	$ 44,000
Accounts receivable, net	65,000	51,000
Inventory	63,800	86,500
Prepaid expenses	4,400	5,400
Equipment	124,000	115,000
Accum. depreciation—Equipment	(27,000)	(9,000)
Total assets	$317,700	$292,900
Liabilities and Equity		
Accounts payable	$ 25,000	$ 30,000
Wages payable	6,000	15,000
Income taxes payable	3,400	3,800
Notes payable (long term)	30,000	60,000
Common stock, $5 par value	220,000	160,000
Retained earnings	33,300	24,100
Total liabilities and equity	$317,700	$292,900

Additional Information
a. A $30,000 note payable is retired at its $30,000 carrying (book) value in exchange for cash.
b. The only changes affecting retained earnings are net income and cash dividends paid.
c. New equipment is acquired for $57,600 cash.
d. Received cash for the sale of equipment that had cost $48,600, yielding a $2,000 gain.
e. Prepaid Expenses and Wages Payable relate to Other Expenses on the income statement.
f. All purchases and sales of merchandise inventory are on credit.

Check (b) Cash dividends, $90,310

(d) Cash from equip. sale, $10,000

Required
(1) prepare a statement of cash flows for the year ended June 30, 2013, using the *indirect method,* and
(2) compute the company's cash flow on total assets ratio for its fiscal year 2013.

Refer to the information in Exercise 12-10.
Using the *direct method,* prepare the statement of cash flows for the year ended June 30, 2013.

Exercise 12-11[B]
Direct: Preparation of statement
of cash flows   P1

Hampton Company reports the following information for its recent calendar year.

Exercise 12-12
Indirect: Reporting cash flows
from operations
P2

Sales	$160,000
Expenses	
Cost of goods sold	100,000
Salaries expense	24,000
Depreciation expense	12,000
Net income	$ 24,000
Accounts receivable increase	$ 10,000
Inventory decrease	16,000
Salaries payable increase	1,000

Required

Prepare the operating activities section of the statement of cash flows for Hampton Company using the indirect method.

Arundel Company disclosed the following information for its recent calendar year.

Exercise 12-13
Indirect: Reporting and
interpreting cash flows from
operations
P2

Revenues	$100,000
Expenses	
Salaries expense	84,000
Utilities expense	14,000
Depreciation expense	14,600
Other expenses	3,400
Net loss	$ (16,000)
Accounts receivable decrease	$ 24,000
Purchased a machine	10,000
Salaries payable increase	18,000
Other accrued liabilities decrease	8,000

Required

1. Prepare the operating activities section of the statement of cash flows using the indirect method.
2. What were the major reasons that this company was able to report a net loss but positive cash flow from operations?
3. Of the potential causes of differences between cash flow from operations and net income, which are the most important to investors?

Complete the following spreadsheet in preparation of the statement of cash flows. (The statement of cash flows is not required.) Prepare the spreadsheet as in Exhibit 12A.1; report operating activities under the indirect method. Identify the debits and credits in the Analysis of Changes columns with letters that correspond to the following transactions and events *a* through *h*.

Exercise 12-14
Indirect: Cash flows
spreadsheet
P4

a. Net income for the year was $100,000.
b. Dividends of $80,000 cash were declared and paid.
c. Scoreteck's only noncash expense was $70,000 of depreciation.
d. The company purchased plant assets for $70,000 cash.
e. Notes payable of $20,000 were issued for $20,000 cash.
f. Change in accounts receivable.
g. Change in merchandise inventory.
h. Change in accounts payable.

	File Edit View Insert Format Tools Data Accounting Window Help				
	SCORETECK CORPORATION				
	Spreadsheet for Statement of Cash Flows—Indirect Method				
	For Year Ended December 31, 2013				
		Dec. 31,	Analysis of Changes		Dec. 31,
		2012	Debit	Credit	2013
8	**Balance Sheet—Debit Bal. Accounts**				
9	Cash	$ 80,000			$ 60,000
10	Accounts receivable	120,000			190,000
11	Merchandise inventory	250,000			230,000
12	Plant assets	600,000			670,000
13		$1,050,000			$1,150,000
15	**Balance Sheet—Credit Bal. Accounts**				
16	Accumulated depreciation	$100,000			$ 170,000
17	Accounts payable	150,000			140,000
18	Notes payable	370,000			390,000
19	Common stock	200,000			200,000
20	Retained earnings	230,000			250,000
21		$1,050,000			$1,150,000
23	**Statement of Cash Flows**				
24	Operating activities				
25	Net income				
26	Increase in accounts receivable				
27	Decrease in merchandise inventory				
28	Decrease in accounts payable				
29	Depreciation expense				
30	Investing activities				
31	Cash paid to purchase plant assets				
32	Financing activities				
33	Cash paid for dividends				
34	Cash from issuance of notes				

Exercise 12-15[B]

Direct: Preparation of statement of cash flows and supporting note

P1

Use the following information about the cash flows of Ferron Company to prepare a complete statement of cash flows (*direct method*) for the year ended December 31, 2013. Use a note disclosure for any noncash investing and financing activities.

Cash and cash equivalents balance, December 31, 2012	$ 40,000
Cash and cash equivalents balance, December 31, 2013	148,000
Cash received as interest	3,500
Cash paid for salaries	76,500
Bonds payable retired by issuing common stock (no gain or loss on retirement)	185,500
Cash paid to retire long-term notes payable	100,000
Cash received from sale of equipment	60,250
Cash received in exchange for six-month note payable	35,000
Land purchased by issuing long-term note payable	105,250
Cash paid for store equipment	24,750
Cash dividends paid	10,000
Cash paid for other expenses	20,000
Cash received from customers	495,000
Cash paid for merchandise	254,500

The following summarized Cash T-account reflects the total debits and total credits to the Cash account of Thomas Corporation for calendar year 2013.

(1) Use this information to prepare a complete statement of cash flows for year 2013. The cash provided or used by operating activities should be reported using the *direct method*.

(2) Refer to the statement of cash flows prepared for part 1 to answer the following questions *a* through *d*: (*a*) Which section—operating, investing, or financing—shows the largest cash (i) inflow and (ii) outflow? (*b*) What is the largest individual item among the investing cash outflows? (*c*) Are the cash proceeds larger from issuing notes or issuing stock? (*d*) Does the company have a net cash inflow or outflow from borrowing activities?

Exercise 12-16ᴮ
Direct: Preparation of statement of cash flows from Cash T-account

P1

Accounting System:				
File Edit Maintain Tasks Analysis Options Reports Window Help				

Cash			
Balance, Dec. 31, 2012	333,000		
Receipts from customers	5,000,000	Payments for merchandise	2,590,000
Receipts from dividends	208,400	Payments for wages	550,000
Receipts from land sale	220,000	Payments for rent	320,000
Receipts from machinery sale	710,000	Payments for interest	218,000
Receipts from issuing stock	1,540,000	Payments for taxes	450,000
Receipts from borrowing	3,600,000	Payments for machinery	2,236,000
		Payments for long-term investments	1,260,000
		Payments for note payable	386,000
		Payments for dividends	500,000
		Payments for treasury stock	218,000
Balance, Dec. 31, 2013	$?		

| Sales | Purchases | General Ledger | Payroll | Inventory | Company | Analysis |

A company reported average total assets of $1,240,000 in 2012 and $1,510,000 in 2013. Its net operating cash flow in 2012 was $102,920 and $138,920 in 2013. Calculate its cash flow on total assets ratio for both years. Comment on the results and any change in performance.

Exercise 12-17
Analyses of cash flow on total assets A1

Peugeot S.A. reports the following financial information for the year ended December 31, 2011 (euros in millions). Prepare its statement of cash flows under the indirect method. (*Hint:* Each line item below is titled, and any necessary parentheses added, as it is reported in the statement of cash flows.)

Exercise 12-18
Indirect: Statement of cash flows under IFRS

P1

Net income	€ 784	Cash paid for purchases of treasury stock	€ (199)
Depreciation and amortization	3,037	Cash paid for other financing activities...........	(2,282)
Gains on disposals and other	(883)	Cash from disposal of plant assets and intangibles ...	189
Net increase in current operating assets....	(1,183)	Cash paid for plant assets and intangibles	(3,921)
Cash paid for dividends	(290)	Cash and cash equivalents, December 31, 2010	10,442

connect

Forten Company, a merchandiser, recently completed its calendar-year 2013 operations. For the year, (1) all sales are credit sales, (2) all credits to Accounts Receivable reflect cash receipts from customers, (3) all purchases of inventory are on credit, (4) all debits to Accounts Payable reflect cash payments for inventory, and (5) Other Expenses are paid in advance and are initially debited to Prepaid Expenses. The company's balance sheets and income statement follow.

PROBLEM SET A

Problem 12-1A
Indirect: Statement of cash flows

A1 P1 P2 P3

FORTEN COMPANY
Income Statement
For Year Ended December 31, 2013

Sales		$582,500
Cost of goods sold		285,000
Gross profit		297,500
Operating expenses		
Depreciation expense	$ 20,750	
Other expenses.................	132,400	153,150
Other gains (losses)		
Loss on sale of equipment		(5,125)
Income before taxes		139,225
Income taxes expense		24,250
Net income		$114,975

FORTEN COMPANY
Comparative Balance Sheets
December 31, 2013 and 2012

	2013	2012
Assets		
Cash	$ 49,800	$ 73,500
Accounts receivable	65,810	50,625
Merchandise inventory	275,656	251,800
Prepaid expenses	1,250	1,875
Equipment	157,500	108,000
Accum. depreciation—Equipment	(36,625)	(46,000)
Total assets	$513,391	$439,800
Liabilities and Equity		
Accounts payable	$ 53,141	$114,675
Short-term notes payable	10,000	6,000
Long-term notes payable	65,000	48,750
Common stock, $5 par value	162,750	150,250
Paid-in capital in excess		
of par, common stock	37,500	0
Retained earnings	185,000	120,125
Total liabilities and equity	$513,391	$439,800

Additional Information on Year 2013 Transactions

a. The loss on the cash sale of equipment was $5,125 (details in *b*).

b. Sold equipment costing $46,875, with accumulated depreciation of $30,125, for $11,625 cash.

c. Purchased equipment costing $96,375 by paying $30,000 cash and signing a long-term note payable for the balance.

d. Borrowed $4,000 cash by signing a short-term note payable.

e. Paid $50,125 cash to reduce the long-term notes payable.

f. Issued 2,500 shares of common stock for $20 cash per share.

g. Declared and paid cash dividends of $50,100.

Required

Check Cash from operating activities, $40,900

1. Prepare a complete statement of cash flows; report its operating activities using the *indirect method*. Disclose any noncash investing and financing activities in a note.

Analysis Component

2. Analyze and discuss the statement of cash flows prepared in part 1, giving special attention to the wisdom of the cash dividend payment.

Problem 12-2A[A]

Indirect: Cash flows spreadsheet

P1 P2 P3 P4

Refer to the information reported about Forten Company in Problem 12-1A.

Required

Prepare a complete statement of cash flows using a spreadsheet as in Exhibit 12A.1; report its operating activities using the indirect method. Identify the debits and credits in the Analysis of Changes columns with letters that correspond to the following list of transactions and events.

a. Net income was $114,975.

b. Accounts receivable increased.

c. Merchandise inventory increased.

d. Prepaid expenses decreased.

e. Accounts payable decreased.

f. Depreciation expense was $20,750.

g. Sold equipment costing $46,875, with accumulated depreciation of $30,125, for $11,625 cash. This yielded a loss of $5,125.

h. Purchased equipment costing $96,375 by paying $30,000 cash and **(i.)** by signing a long-term note payable for the balance.

j. Borrowed $4,000 cash by signing a short-term note payable.

k. Paid $50,125 cash to reduce the long-term notes payable.

l. Issued 2,500 shares of common stock for $20 cash per share.

m. Declared and paid cash dividends of $50,100.

Check Analysis of Changes column totals, $600,775

Refer to Forten Company's financial statements and related information in Problem 12-1A.

Problem 12-3A[B]
Direct: Statement of cash flows P1 P3 P5

Required

Prepare a complete statement of cash flows; report its operating activities according to the *direct method.* Disclose any noncash investing and financing activities in a note.

Check Cash used in financing activities, $(46,225)

Golden Corp., a merchandiser, recently completed its 2013 operations. For the year, (1) all sales are credit sales, (2) all credits to Accounts Receivable reflect cash receipts from customers, (3) all purchases of inventory are on credit, (4) all debits to Accounts Payable reflect cash payments for inventory, (5) Other Expenses are all cash expenses, and (6) any change in Income Taxes Payable reflects the accrual and cash payment of taxes. The company's balance sheets and income statement follow.

Problem 12-4A
Indirect: Statement of cash flows
P1 P2 P3

GOLDEN CORPORATION
Comparative Balance Sheets
December 31, 2013 and 2012

	2013	2012
Assets		
Cash	$ 164,000	$107,000
Accounts receivable	83,000	71,000
Merchandise inventory	601,000	526,000
Equipment	335,000	299,000
Accum. depreciation—Equipment	(158,000)	(104,000)
Total assets	$1,025,000	$899,000
Liabilities and Equity		
Accounts payable	$ 87,000	$ 71,000
Income taxes payable	28,000	25,000
Common stock, $2 par value	592,000	568,000
Paid-in capital in excess of par value, common stock	196,000	160,000
Retained earnings	122,000	75,000
Total liabilities and equity	$1,025,000	$899,000

GOLDEN CORPORATION
Income Statement
For Year Ended December 31, 2013

Sales		$1,792,000
Cost of goods sold		1,086,000
Gross profit		706,000
Operating expenses		
Depreciation expense	$ 54,000	
Other expenses	494,000	548,000
Income before taxes		158,000
Income taxes expense		22,000
Net income		$ 136,000

Additional Information on Year 2013 Transactions

a. Purchased equipment for $36,000 cash.

b. Issued 12,000 shares of common stock for $5 cash per share.

c. Declared and paid $89,000 in cash dividends.

Required

Prepare a complete statement of cash flows; report its cash inflows and cash outflows from operating activities according to the *indirect method.*

Check Cash from operating activities, $122,000

Problem 12-5A^A

Indirect: Cash flows spreadsheet

P1 P2 P3 P4

Refer to the information reported about Golden Corporation in Problem 12-4A.

Required

Prepare a complete statement of cash flows using a spreadsheet as in Exhibit 12A.1; report operating activities under the indirect method. Identify the debits and credits in the Analysis of Changes columns with letters that correspond to the following list of transactions and events.

   a. Net income was $136,000.

   b. Accounts receivable increased.

   c. Merchandise inventory increased.

   d. Accounts payable increased.

   e. Income taxes payable increased.

   f. Depreciation expense was $54,000.

   g. Purchased equipment for $36,000 cash.

Check Analysis of Changes column totals, $481,000

   h. Issued 12,000 shares at $5 cash per share.

   i. Declared and paid $89,000 of cash dividends.

Problem 12-6A^B

Direct: Statement of cash flows P1 P3 P5

Check Cash used in financing activities, $(29,000)

Refer to Golden Corporation's financial statements and related information in Problem 12-4A.

Required

Prepare a complete statement of cash flows; report its cash flows from operating activities according to the *direct method*.

Problem 12-7A

Indirect: Computing cash flows from operations

P2

Lansing Company's 2013 income statement and selected balance sheet data at December 31, 2012 and 2013, follow.

LANSING COMPANY Income Statement For Year Ended December 31, 2013	
Sales revenue	$97,200
Expenses	
Cost of goods sold	42,000
Depreciation expense	12,000
Salaries expense	18,000
Rent expense	9,000
Insurance expense	3,800
Interest expense	3,600
Utilities expense	2,800
Net income	$ 6,000

LANSING COMPANY Selected Balance Sheet Accounts		
At December 31	2013	2012
Accounts receivable	$5,600	$5,800
Inventory	1,980	1,540
Accounts payable.......	4,400	4,600
Salaries payable	880	700
Utilities payable	220	160
Prepaid insurance	260	280
Prepaid rent	220	180

Required

Check Cash from operating activities, $17,780

Prepare the cash flows from operating activities section only of the company's 2013 statement of cash flows using the indirect method.

Problem 12-8A^B

Direct: Computing cash flows from operations

P5

Refer to the information in Problem 12-7A.

Required

Prepare the cash flows from operating activities section only of the company's 2013 statement of cash flows using the direct method.

PROBLEM SET B

Problem 12-1B

Indirect: Statement of cash flows A1 P1 P2 P3

Gazelle Corporation, a merchandiser, recently completed its calendar-year 2013 operations. For the year, (1) all sales are credit sales, (2) all credits to Accounts Receivable reflect cash receipts from customers, (3) all purchases of inventory are on credit, (4) all debits to Accounts Payable reflect cash payments for inventory, and (5) Other Expenses are paid in advance and are initially debited to Prepaid Expenses. The company's balance sheets and income statement follow.

GAZELLE CORPORATION
Comparative Balance Sheets
December 31, 2013 and 2012

	2013	2012
Assets		
Cash	$123,450	$ 61,550
Accounts receivable	77,100	80,750
Merchandise inventory	240,600	250,700
Prepaid expenses	15,100	17,000
Equipment	262,250	200,000
Accum. depreciation—Equipment	(110,750)	(95,000)
Total assets	$607,750	$515,000
Liabilities and Equity		
Accounts payable	$ 17,750	$102,000
Short-term notes payable	15,000	10,000
Long-term notes payable	100,000	77,500
Common stock, $5 par	215,000	200,000
Paid-in capital in excess of par, common stock	30,000	0
Retained earnings	230,000	125,500
Total liabilities and equity	$607,750	$515,000

GAZELLE CORPORATION
Income Statement
For Year Ended December 31, 2013

Sales		$1,185,000
Cost of goods sold		595,000
Gross profit		590,000
Operating expenses		
Depreciation expense	$ 38,600	
Other expenses	362,850	
Total operating expenses		401,450
		188,550
Other gains (losses)		
Loss on sale of equipment		(2,100)
Income before taxes		186,450
Income taxes expense		28,350
Net income		$ 158,100

Additional Information on Year 2013 Transactions

a. The loss on the cash sale of equipment was $2,100 (details in *b*).
b. Sold equipment costing $51,000, with accumulated depreciation of $22,850, for $26,050 cash.
c. Purchased equipment costing $113,250 by paying $43,250 cash and signing a long-term note payable for the balance.
d. Borrowed $5,000 cash by signing a short-term note payable.
e. Paid $47,500 cash to reduce the long-term notes payable.
f. Issued 3,000 shares of common stock for $15 cash per share.
g. Declared and paid cash dividends of $53,600.

Required

1. Prepare a complete statement of cash flows; report its operating activities using the *indirect method*. Disclose any noncash investing and financing activities in a note.

Check Cash from operating activities, $130,200

Analysis Component

2. Analyze and discuss the statement of cash flows prepared in part 1, giving special attention to the wisdom of the cash dividend payment.

Refer to the information reported about Gazelle Corporation in Problem 12-1B.

Problem 12-2B[A]
Indirect: Cash flows spreadsheet

P1 P2 P3 P4

Required

Prepare a complete statement of cash flows using a spreadsheet as in Exhibit 12A.1; report its operating activities using the *indirect method*. Identify the debits and credits in the Analysis of Changes columns with letters that correspond to the following list of transactions and events.

a. Net income was $158,100.
b. Accounts receivable decreased.
c. Merchandise inventory decreased.
d. Prepaid expenses decreased.
e. Accounts payable decreased.
f. Depreciation expense was $38,600.

[continued on next page]

g. Sold equipment costing $51,000, with accumulated depreciation of $22,850, for $26,050 cash. This yielded a loss of $2,100.

h. Purchased equipment costing $113,250 by paying $43,250 cash and **(i.)** by signing a long-term note payable for the balance.

j. Borrowed $5,000 cash by signing a short-term note payable.

k. Paid $47,500 cash to reduce the long-term notes payable.

l. Issued 3,000 shares of common stock for $15 cash per share.

m. Declared and paid cash dividends of $53,600.

Check Analysis of Changes column totals, $681,950

Problem 12-3B[B]
Direct: Statement of
cash flows   P1 P3 P5

Check Cash used in financing activities, $(51,100)

Refer to Gazelle Corporation's financial statements and related information in Problem 12-1B.

Required

Prepare a complete statement of cash flows; report its operating activities according to the *direct method*. Disclose any noncash investing and financing activities in a note.

Problem 12-4B
Indirect: Statement of
cash flows

P1 P2 P3

Satu Company, a merchandiser, recently completed its 2013 operations. For the year, (1) all sales are credit sales, (2) all credits to Accounts Receivable reflect cash receipts from customers, (3) all purchases of inventory are on credit, (4) all debits to Accounts Payable reflect cash payments for inventory, (5) Other Expenses are cash expenses, and (6) any change in Income Taxes Payable reflects the accrual and cash payment of taxes. The company's balance sheets and income statement follow.

SATU COMPANY Comparative Balance Sheets December 31, 2013 and 2012		
	2013	**2012**
Assets		
Cash	$ 58,750	$ 28,400
Accounts receivable	20,222	25,860
Merchandise inventory	165,667	140,320
Equipment	107,750	77,500
Accum. depreciation—Equipment	(46,700)	(31,000)
Total assets	$305,689	$241,080
Liabilities and Equity		
Accounts payable	$ 20,372	$157,530
Income taxes payable	2,100	6,100
Common stock, $5 par value	40,000	25,000
Paid-in capital in excess of par, common stock	68,000	20,000
Retained earnings	175,217	32,450
Total liabilities and equity	$305,689	$241,080

SATU COMPANY Income Statement For Year Ended December 31, 2013		
Sales		$750,800
Cost of goods sold		269,200
Gross profit		481,600
Operating expenses		
Depreciation expense	$ 15,700	
Other expenses..............	173,933	189,633
Income before taxes		291,967
Income taxes expense		89,200
Net income		$202,767

Additional Information on Year 2013 Transactions

a. Purchased equipment for $30,250 cash.

b. Issued 3,000 shares of common stock for $21 cash per share.

c. Declared and paid $60,000 of cash dividends.

Required

Prepare a complete statement of cash flows; report its cash inflows and cash outflows from operating activities according to the *indirect method*.

Check Cash from operating activities, $57,600

Refer to the information reported about Satu Company in Problem 12-4B.

Required

Prepare a complete statement of cash flows using a spreadsheet as in Exhibit 12A.1; report operating activities under the *indirect method.* Identify the debits and credits in the Analysis of Changes columns with letters that correspond to the following list of transactions and events.

a. Net income was $202,767.

b. Accounts receivable decreased.

c. Merchandise inventory increased.

d. Accounts payable decreased.

e. Income taxes payable decreased.

f. Depreciation expense was $15,700.

g. Purchased equipment for $30,250 cash.

h. Issued 3,000 shares at $21 cash per share.

i. Declared and paid $60,000 of cash dividends.

Problem 12-5B[A]

Indirect: Cash flows spreadsheet

P1 P2 P3 P4

Check   Analysis of Changes column totals, $543,860

Refer to Satu Company's financial statements and related information in Problem 12-4B.

Required

Prepare a complete statement of cash flows; report its cash flows from operating activities according to the *direct method.*

Problem 12-6B[B]

Direct: Statement of cash flows

P1 P3 P5

Check   Cash provided by financing activities, $3,000

Salt Lake Company's 2013 income statement and selected balance sheet data at December 31, 2012 and 2013, follow.

Problem 12-7B

Indirect: Computing cash flows from operations

P2

SALT LAKE COMPANY
Income Statement
For Year Ended December 31, 2013

Sales revenue	$156,000
Expenses	
Cost of goods sold	72,000
Depreciation expense	32,000
Salaries expense	20,000
Rent expense	5,000
Insurance expense	2,600
Interest expense	2,400
Utilities expense	2,000
Net income	$ 20,000

SALT LAKE COMPANY
Selected Balance Sheet Accounts

At December 31	2013	2012
Accounts receivable	$3,600	$3,000
Inventory	860	980
Accounts payable	2,400	2,600
Salaries payable	900	600
Utilities payable	200	0
Prepaid insurance	140	180
Prepaid rent	100	200

Required

Prepare the cash flows from operating activities section only of the company's 2013 statement of cash flows using the indirect method.

Check   Cash from operating activities, $51,960

Refer to the information in Problem 12-7B.

Required

Prepare the cash flows from operating activities section only of the company's 2013 statement of cash flows using the direct method.

Problem 12-8B[B]

Direct: Computing cash flows from operations

P5

SERIAL PROBLEM
Success Systems (Indirect)

P1 P2 P3

(This serial problem began in Chapter 1 and continues through most of the book. If previous chapter segments were not completed, the serial problem can begin at this point. It is helpful, but not necessary, to use the Working Papers that accompany the book.)

SP 12   Adria Lopez, owner of Success Systems, decides to prepare a statement of cash flows for her business. (Although the serial problem allowed for various ownership changes in earlier chapters, we will prepare the statement of cash flows using the following financial data.)

SUCCESS SYSTEMS Income Statement For Three Months Ended March 31, 2014		
Computer services revenue		$25,160
Net sales		18,693
Total revenue...................		43,853
Cost of goods sold	$14,052	
Depreciation expense— Office equipment	400	
Depreciation expense— Computer equipment	1,250	
Wages expense	3,250	
Insurance expense	555	
Rent expense	2,475	
Computer supplies expense	1,305	
Advertising expense	600	
Mileage expense	320	
Repairs expense—Computer	960	
Total expenses		25,167
Net income		$18,686

SUCCESS SYSTEMS Comparative Balance Sheets December 31, 2013, and March 31, 2014		
	2014	**2013**
Assets		
Cash	$ 77,845	$58,160
Accounts receivable	22,720	5,668
Merchandise inventory	704	0
Computer supplies	2,005	580
Prepaid insurance	1,110	1,665
Prepaid rent	825	825
Office equipment	8,000	8,000
Accumulated depreciation—Office equipment	(800)	(400)
Computer equipment	20,000	20,000
Accumulated depreciation— Computer equipment	(2,500)	(1,250)
Total assets	$129,909	$93,248
Liabilities and Equity		
Accounts payable	$ 0	$ 1,100
Wages payable................	875	500
Unearned computer service revenue	0	1,500
Common stock	108,000	83,000
Retained earnings	21,034	7,148
Total liabilities and equity	$129,909	$93,248

Required

Check   Cash flows used by operations: $(515)

Prepare a statement of cash flows for Success Systems using the *indirect method* for the three months ended March 31, 2014. Recall that the owner Adria Lopez contributed $25,000 to the business in exchange for additional stock in the first quarter of 2014 and has received $4,800 in cash dividends.

GL GENERAL LEDGER PROBLEM

Available in Connect Only

connect
|ACCOUNTING

The following General Ledger assignments highlight the impact, or lack thereof, on the statement of cash flows from summary journal entries derived from consecutive trial balances.

GL 12-1 (This assignment is adapted from Exercise 12-11.) Prepare summary journal entries reflecting changes in consecutive trial balances. Then prepare the statement of cash flows (direct method) from those entries.

GL 12-2 (This assignment is adapted from Problem 12-3.) Prepare summary journal entries reflecting changes in consecutive trial balances. Then prepare the statement of cash flows (direct method) from those entries.

GL 12-3 (This assignment is adapted from Problem 12-6.) Prepare summary journal entries reflecting changes in consecutive trial balances. Then prepare the statement of cash flows (direct method) from those entries.

Beyond the Numbers

BTN 12-1   Refer to Apple's financial statements in Appendix A to answer the following.

1. Is Apple's statement of cash flows prepared under the direct method or the indirect method? How do you know?

2. For each fiscal year 2012, 2011, and 2010, is the amount of cash provided by operating activities more or less than the cash paid for dividends?

3. What is the largest amount in reconciling the difference between net income and cash flow from operating activities in fiscal 2012? In fiscal 2011? In fiscal 2010?

4. Identify the largest cash inflow and cash outflow for investing *and* for financing activities, in fiscal 2012 and in fiscal 2011.

Fast Forward

5. Obtain Apple's financial statements for a fiscal year ending after September 29, 2012, from either its Website (Apple.com) or the SEC's database (www.sec.gov). Since September 29, 2012, what are Apple's largest cash outflows and cash inflows in the investing and in the financing sections of its statement of cash flows?

REPORTING IN ACTION

A1

APPLE

BTN 12-2   Key figures for Apple and Google follow.

($ millions)	Apple			Google		
	Current Year	1 Year Prior	2 Years Prior	Current Year	1 Year Prior	2 Years Prior
Operating cash flows	$ 50,856	$ 37,529	$18,595	$16,619	$14,565	$11,081
Total assets	176,064	116,371	75,183	93,798	72,574	57,851

COMPARATIVE ANALYSIS

A1

APPLE

GOOGLE

Required

1. Compute the recent two years' cash flow on total assets ratios for Apple and Google.

2. What does the cash flow on total assets ratio measure?

3. Which company has the highest cash flow on total assets ratio for the periods shown?

4. Does the cash flow on total assets ratio reflect on the quality of earnings? Explain.

BTN 12-3   Katie Murphy is preparing for a meeting with her banker. Her business is finishing its fourth year of operations. In the first year, it had negative cash flows from operations. In the second and third years, cash flows from operations were positive. However, inventory costs rose significantly in year 4, and cash flows from operations will probably be down 25%. Murphy wants to secure a line of credit from her banker as a financing buffer. From experience, she knows the banker will scrutinize operating cash flows for years 1 through 4 and will want a projected number for year 5. Murphy knows that a steady progression upward in operating cash flows for years 1 through 4 will help her case. She decides to use her discretion as owner and considers several business actions that will turn her operating cash flow in year 4 from a decrease to an increase.

ETHICS CHALLENGE

C1 A1

Required

1. Identify two business actions Murphy might take to improve cash flows from operations.

2. Comment on the ethics and possible consequences of Murphy's decision to pursue these actions.

BTN 12-4   Your friend, Diana Wood, recently completed the second year of her business and just received annual financial statements from her accountant. Wood finds the income statement and balance sheet informative but does not understand the statement of cash flows. She says the first section is especially confusing because it contains a lot of additions and subtractions that do not make sense to her. Wood adds, "The income statement tells me the business is more profitable than last year and that's most important. If I want to know how cash changes, I can look at comparative balance sheets."

COMMUNICATING IN PRACTICE

C1

Required

Write a half-page memorandum to your friend explaining the purpose of the statement of cash flows. Speculate as to why the first section is so confusing and how it might be rectified.

TAKING IT TO THE NET

A1

BTN 12-5   Access the March 30, 2012, filing of the 10-K report (for year ending December 31, 2011) of Mendocino Brewing Company, Inc., at www.sec.gov.

Required

1. Does Mendocino Brewing use the direct or indirect method to construct its consolidated statement of cash flows?
2. For the year ended December 31, 2011, what is the largest item in reconciling the net income to net cash provided by operating activities?
3. In the recent two years, has the company been more successful in generating operating cash flows or in generating net income? Identify the figures to support the answer.
4. In the year ended December 31, 2011, what was the largest cash outflow for investing activities *and* for financing activities?
5. What item(s) does Mendocino Brewing report as supplementary cash flow information?
6. Does Mendocino Brewing report any noncash financing activities for 2011? Identify them, if any.

TEAMWORK IN ACTION

C1   A1   P2   P5

BTN 12-6   Team members are to coordinate and independently answer one question within each of the following three sections. Team members should then report to the team and confirm or correct teammates' answers.

1. Answer *one* of the following questions about the statement of cash flows.
   a. What are this statement's reporting objectives?
   b. What two methods are used to prepare it? Identify similarities and differences between them.
   c. What steps are followed to prepare the statement?
   d. What types of analyses are often made from this statement's information?
2. Identify and explain the adjustment from net income to obtain cash flows from operating activities using the indirect method for *one* of the following items.
   a. Noncash operating revenues and expenses.
   b. Nonoperating gains and losses.
   c. Increases and decreases in noncash current assets.
   d. Increases and decreases in current liabilities.
3.^BIdentify and explain the formula for computing cash flows from operating activities using the direct method for *one* of the following items.
   a. Cash receipts from sales to customers.
   b. Cash paid for merchandise inventory.
   c. Cash paid for wages and operating expenses.
   d. Cash paid for interest and taxes.

Note: For teams of more than four, some pairing within teams is necessary. Use as an in-class activity or as an assignment. If used in class, specify a time limit on each part. Conclude with reports to the entire class, using team rotation. Each team can prepare responses on a transparency.

ENTREPRENEURIAL DECISION

C1   A1

BTN 12-7   Review the chapter's opener involving salesforce.com and its co-founder, Marc Benioff.

Required

1. In a business such as salesforce.com, monitoring cash flow is always a priority. Even though salesforce.com now has billions in annual sales and sometimes earns a positive net income, explain how cash flow can lag behind net income.
2. Salesforce.com is a publicly traded corporation. What are potential sources of financing for its future expansion?

BTN 12-8   Jenna and Matt Wilder are completing their second year operating Mountain High, a downhill ski area and resort. Mountain High reports a net loss of $(10,000) for its second year, which includes an $85,000 extraordinary loss from fire. This past year also involved major purchases of plant assets for renovation and expansion, yielding a year-end total asset amount of $800,000. Mountain High's net cash outflow for its second year is $(5,000); a summarized version of its statement of cash flows follows:

Net cash flow provided by operating activities	$295,000
Net cash flow used by investing activities	(310,000)
Net cash flow provided by financing activities	10,000

Required

Write a one-page memorandum to the Wilders evaluating Mountain High's current performance and assessing its future. Give special emphasis to cash flow data and their interpretation.

BTN 12-9   Visit The Motley Fool's Website (Fool.com). Enter the *Fool's School* (at *Fool.com/School*). Identify and select the link *How to Value Stocks*. (Please note the site may ask you to register with your email address. Registration is free and grants access to full articles on the site.)

HITTING THE ROAD
C1

Required

1. Click on *Introduction to Valuation Methods,* and then *Cash-Flow-Based Valuations.* How does the Fool's school define cash flow? What is the school's reasoning for this definition?
2. Per the school's instruction, why do analysts focus on earnings before interest and taxes (EBIT)?
3. Visit other links at this Website that interest you such as "How to Read a Balance Sheet," or find out what the "Fool's Ratio" is. Write a half-page report on what you find.

BTN 12-10   Key comparative information for Samsung (www.Samsung.com), which is a leading manufacturer of electronic consumer products, follows.

GLOBAL DECISION
C1

**Samsung
APPLE
GOOGLE**

(₩ in millions)	Current Year	I Year Prior	2 Years Prior
Operating cash flows	₩ 37,972,809	₩ 22,917,901	₩ 35,452,160
Total assets	181,071,570	155,800,263	134,308,803

Required

1. Compute the recent two years' cash flow on total assets ratio for Samsung.
2. How does Samsung's ratio compare to Apple's and Google's ratios from BTN 12-2?

ANSWERS TO MULTIPLE CHOICE QUIZ

1. b;

Net income	$15,200
Depreciation expense	10,000
Gain on sale of land	(3,000)
Increase in inventory	(1,500)
Increase in accounts payable	2,850
Net cash provided by operations	$23,550

2. c; cash received from sale of machine is reported as an investing activity.

3. d; FASB requires cash interest paid to be reported under operating.
4. a; Cash paid for salaries and wages = $255,000 + $8,200 − $10,900 = $252,300
5. e; Increase in inventory = $112,000 − $105,000 = $7,000
Increase in accounts payable = $101,300 − $98,500 = $2,800
Cash paid for merchandise = $545,000 + $7,000 − $2,800 = $549,200

13

Analyzing and Interpreting Financial Statements

BASICS OF ANALYSIS	HORIZONTAL ANALYSIS	VERTICAL ANALYSIS	RATIO ANALYSIS AND REPORTING
C1 Analysis: Its purpose, building blocks, and information needs C2 Standards for comparisons, and analysis tools	P1 Application of: Comparative balance sheets Comparative income statements Trend analysis	P2 Application of: Common-size balance sheet Common-size income statement Common-size graphics	P3 Liquidity and efficiency Solvency Profitability Market prospects A1 Analysis reports

Learning Objectives

C1 Explain the purpose and identify the building blocks of analysis. (p. 578)

C2 Describe standards for comparisons in analysis. (p. 579)

P1 Explain and apply methods of horizontal analysis. (p. 580)

P2 Describe and apply methods of vertical analysis. (p. 585)

P3 Define and apply ratio analysis. (p. 589)

A1 Summarize and report results of analysis. (p. 599)

A2 *Appendix 13A*—Explain the form and assess the content of a complete income statement. (p. 602)

A Winning Analysis

"We are in the business of helping people"

—JAMES GORMAN, CEO

NEW YORK—In preschool, most of the children get trophies. At **Morgan Stanley (MorganStanley.com),** the young financiers can earn trophies, or "deal toys," when they complete a deal, according to Nina Godiwalla, who put together a collection of such stories. Fortunately, work is not always about trophies at Morgan Stanley, which is one of the most respected financial services companies in the world. Morgan Stanley analyzes financial statements for profit. Moreover, based on its stock price over the past year (see below), the company's analysis techniques are paying off.

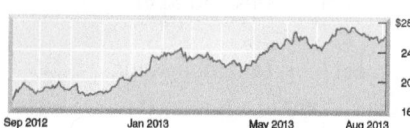

One of Morgan Stanley's key tools for company analysis is **ModelWare.** ModelWare is a framework to analyze the nuts and bolts of companies' financial statements, and then to compare those companies on the basis of head-to-head performance metrics. One of its key aims is to provide comparable informa-

Morgan Stanley

(NYSE: MS)

57,000 employees
$26 bil. revenues

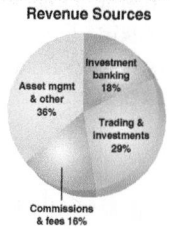

Revenue Sources

Asset mgmt & other 36%

Investment banking 18%

Trading & investments 29%

Commissions & fees 16%

tion that focuses on sustainable performance. To do this, it works with the underlying accounting numbers and footnotes.

Specifically, Morgan Stanley draws on the accounting numbers in financial statements to produce comparable metrics using techniques such as horizontal and vertical analysis. It also computes financial ratios for analysis and interpretation. Those ratios include return on equity, return on assets, asset turnover, profit margin, price-to-earnings, and numerous others. The focus is to uncover the drivers of profitability and to predict the future levels of those drivers.

The company has experienced decades of success through analyzing financial statements. Despite its best efforts, however, people still do not fully use the information available in financial statements. Accordingly, Morgan Stanley will continue to reap profits from financial statement analysis and interpretation.

Morgan Stanley is also proud to play by the rules. *Fortune* writes, "Five years after the collapse of Lehman Brothers, Morgan Stanley has earned some bragging rights. It's the only major bank that hasn't paid a federal fine related to the financial crisis. [It] hasn't even been accused of breaking the law." James Gorman, its CEO, asserts that the "firm's reputation is our most precious asset." James also offers some personal advice for budding analysts: "If you [let] your compensation . . . define your overall level of happiness, you have a problem . . . I mean, life's too short."

Sources: *Morgan Stanley Website*, January 2014; *Bloomberg*, January 2012; *Business Insider*, January 2011; *Fortune*, August 2013; *MorganStanleyIQ*, 8 November 2007; *The Wall Street Journal*, March 2006

BASICS OF ANALYSIS

C1 Explain the purpose and identify the building blocks of analysis.

Financial statement analysis applies analytical tools to general-purpose financial statements and related data for making business decisions. It involves transforming accounting data into more useful information. Financial statement analysis reduces our reliance on hunches, guesses, and intuition as well as our uncertainty in decision making. It does not lessen the need for expert judgment; instead, it provides us an effective and systematic basis for making business decisions. This section describes the purpose of financial statement analysis, its information sources, the use of comparisons, and some issues in computations.

Purpose of Analysis

Internal users of accounting information are those involved in strategically managing and operating the company. They include managers, officers, internal auditors, consultants, budget directors, and market researchers. The purpose of financial statement analysis for these users is to provide strategic information to improve company efficiency and effectiveness in providing products and services.

Point: Financial statement analysis tools are also used for personal financial investment decisions.

External users of accounting information are *not* directly involved in running the company. They include shareholders, lenders, directors, customers, suppliers, regulators, lawyers, brokers, and the press. External users rely on financial statement analysis to make better and more informed decisions in pursuing their own goals.

We can identify other uses of financial statement analysis. Shareholders and creditors assess company prospects to make investing and lending decisions. A board of directors analyzes financial statements in monitoring management's decisions. Employees and unions use financial statements in labor negotiations. Suppliers use financial statement information in establishing credit terms. Customers analyze financial statements in deciding whether to establish supply relationships. Public utilities set customer rates by analyzing financial statements. Auditors use financial statements in assessing the "fair presentation" of their clients' financial results. Analyst services such as **Dun & Bradstreet**, **Moody's**, and **Standard & Poor's** use financial statements in making buy-sell recommendations and in setting credit ratings. The common goal of these users is to evaluate company performance and financial condition. This includes evaluating (1) past and current performance, (2) current financial position, and (3) future performance and risk.

Point: Financial statement analysis is a topic on the CPA, CMA, CIA, and CFA exams.

Building Blocks of Analysis

Financial statement analysis focuses on one or more elements of a company's financial condition or performance. Our analysis emphasizes four areas of inquiry—with varying degrees of importance. These four areas are described and illustrated in this chapter and are considered the *building blocks* of financial statement analysis:

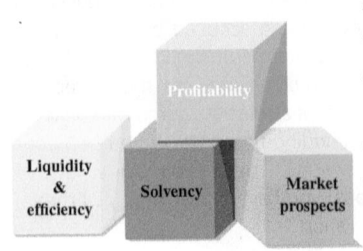

- **Liquidity** and **efficiency**—ability to meet short-term obligations and to efficiently generate revenues.
- **Solvency**—ability to generate future revenues and meet long-term obligations.
- **Profitability**—ability to provide financial rewards sufficient to attract and retain financing.
- **Market prospects**—ability to generate positive market expectations.

Applying the building blocks of financial statement analysis involves determining (1) the objectives of analysis and (2) the relative emphasis among the building blocks. We distinguish among these four building blocks to emphasize the different aspects of a company's financial condition or performance, yet we must remember that these areas of analysis are interrelated. For instance, a company's operating performance is affected by the availability of financing and short-term liquidity conditions. Similarly, a company's credit standing is not limited to satisfactory short-term liquidity but depends also on its profitability and efficiency in using assets. Early in our analysis, we need to determine the relative emphasis of each building block. Emphasis and analysis can later change as a result of evidence collected.

Decision Insight

Chips and Brokers The phrase *blue chips* refers to stock of big, profitable companies. The phrase comes from poker; where the most valuable chips are blue. The term *brokers* refers to those who execute orders to buy or sell stock. The term comes from wine retailers—individuals who broach (break) wine casks. ■

Information for Analysis

Some users, such as managers and regulatory authorities, are able to receive special financial reports prepared to meet their analysis needs. However, most users must rely on **general-purpose financial statements** that include the (1) income statement, (2) balance sheet, (3) statement of stockholders' equity (or statement of retained earnings), (4) statement of cash flows, and (5) notes to these statements.

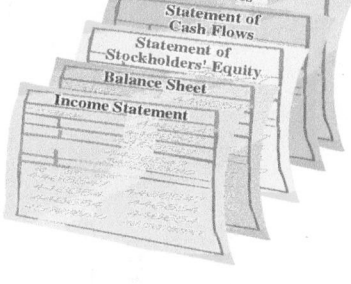

Financial reporting refers to the communication of financial information useful for making investment, credit, and other business decisions. Financial reporting includes not only general-purpose financial statements but also information from SEC 10-K or other filings, press releases, shareholders' meetings, forecasts, management letters, auditors' reports, and Webcasts.

Management's Discussion and Analysis (MD&A) is one example of useful information outside traditional financial statements. **Apple**'s MD&A (available at <u>Investor.Apple.com</u> and is 'Item 7' in the annual report), for example, begins with an overview, followed by critical accounting policies and estimates. It then discusses operating results followed by financial condition (liquidity, capital resources, and cash flows). The final few parts discuss legal proceedings, market risk of financial instruments, and risks from interest rate and foreign currency fluctuations. The MD&A is an excellent starting point in understanding a company's business activities.

Decision Insight

Analysis Online Many Websites offer free access and screening of companies by key numbers such as earnings, sales, and book value. For instance, **Investor's Business Daily** has information for more than 10,000 stocks (<u>www.investors.com</u>). ■

Standards for Comparisons

When interpreting measures from financial statement analysis, we need to decide whether the measures indicate good, bad, or average performance. To make such judgments, we need standards (benchmarks) for comparisons that include the following:

C2 Describe standards for comparisons in analysis.

- *Intracompany*—The company under analysis can provide standards for comparisons based on its own prior performance and relations between its financial items. **Apple**'s current net income, for instance, can be compared with its prior years' net income and in relation to its revenues or total assets.
- *Competitor*—One or more direct competitors of the company being analyzed can provide standards for comparisons. **Coca-Cola**'s profit margin, for instance, can be compared with **PepsiCo**'s profit margin.
- *Industry*—Industry statistics can provide standards of comparisons. Such statistics are available from services such as **Dun & Bradstreet**, **Standard & Poor's**, and **Moody's**.
- *Guidelines (rules of thumb)*—General standards of comparisons can develop from experience. Examples are the 2:1 level for the current ratio or 1:1 level for the acid-test ratio. Guidelines, or rules of thumb, must be carefully applied because context is crucial.

Point: Each chapter's *Reporting in Action* problems engage students in *intracompany* analysis, whereas *Comparative Analysis* problems require competitor analysis (Apple vs. Google vs. Samsung).

All of these comparison standards are useful when properly applied, yet measures taken from a selected competitor or group of competitors are often best. Intracompany and industry measures are also important. Guidelines or rules of thumb should be applied with care, and then only if they seem reasonable given past experience and industry norms.

Tools of Analysis

Three of the most common tools of financial statement analysis are

1. **Horizontal analysis**—Comparison of a company's financial condition and performance across time.
2. **Vertical analysis**—Comparison of a company's financial condition and performance to a base amount.
3. **Ratio analysis**—Measurement of key relations between financial statement items.

The remainder of this chapter describes these analysis tools and how to apply them.

QC1

Fraud

Fraud Fighters. Horizontal, vertical, and ratio analysis tools can uncover fraud by identifying amounts out of line with expectations. One can then follow up and ask questions that can either identify a logical reason for such results or confirm/raise suspicions of fraud. Many past fraud schemes could have been identified much earlier had people applied these tools and pressured management for explanations.

HORIZONTAL ANALYSIS

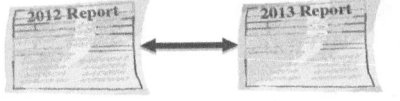

Analysis of any single financial number is of limited value. Instead, much of financial statement analysis involves identifying and describing relations between numbers, groups of numbers, and changes in those numbers. Horizontal analysis refers to examination of financial statement data *across time*. [The term *horizontal analysis* arises from the left-to-right (or right-to-left) movement of our eyes as we review comparative financial statements across time.]

Comparative Statements

P1 Explain and apply methods of horizontal analysis.

Comparing amounts for two or more successive periods often helps in analyzing financial statements. **Comparative financial statements** facilitate this comparison by showing financial amounts in side-by-side columns on a single statement, called a *comparative format*. Using figures from **Apple**'s financial statements, this section explains how to compute dollar changes and percent changes for comparative statements.

Computation of Dollar Changes and Percent Changes Comparing financial statements over relatively short time periods—two to three years—is often done by analyzing changes in line items. A change analysis usually includes analyzing absolute dollar amount changes and percent changes. Both analyses are relevant because dollar changes can yield large percent changes inconsistent with their importance. For instance, a 50% change from a base figure of $100 is less important than the same percent change from a base amount of $100,000 in the same statement. Reference to dollar amounts is necessary to retain a proper perspective and to assess the importance of changes. We compute the *dollar change* for a financial statement item as follows:

Example: What is a more significant change, a 70% increase on a $1,000 expense or a 30% increase on a $400,000 expense? *Answer:* The 30% increase.

$$\text{Dollar change} = \text{Analysis period amount} - \text{Base period amount}$$

Analysis period is the point or period of time for the financial statements under analysis, and *base period* is the point or period of time for the financial statements used for comparison purposes. The prior year is commonly used as a base period. We compute the *percent change* by dividing the dollar change by the base period amount and then multiplying this quantity by 100 as follows:

$$\text{Percent change (\%)} = \frac{\text{Analysis period amount} - \text{Base period amount}}{\text{Base period amount}} \times 100$$

We can always compute a dollar change, but we must be aware of a few rules in working with percent changes. To illustrate, look at four separate cases in this chart:

Case	Analysis Period	Base Period	Change Analysis	
			Dollar	Percent
A	$ 1,500	$(4,500)	$ 6,000	—
B	(1,000)	2,000	(3,000)	—
C	8,000	—	8,000	—
D	0	10,000	(10,000)	(100%)

When a negative amount appears in the base period and a positive amount in the analysis period (or vice versa), we cannot compute a meaningful percent change; see cases A and B. Also, when no value is in the base period, no percent change is computable; see case C. Finally, when an item has a value in the base period and zero in the analysis period, the decrease is 100 percent; see case D.

It is common when using horizontal analysis to compare amounts to either average or median values from prior periods (average and median values smooth out erratic or unusual fluctuations).[1] We also commonly round percents and ratios to one or two decimal places, but practice on this matter is not uniform. Computations are as detailed as necessary, which is judged by whether rounding potentially affects users' decisions. Computations should not be excessively detailed so that important relations are lost among a mountain of decimal points and digits.

Comparative Balance Sheets Comparative balance sheets consist of balance sheet amounts from two or more balance sheet dates arranged side by side. Its usefulness is often improved by showing each item's dollar change and percent change to highlight large changes.

Analysis of comparative financial statements begins by focusing on items that show large dollar or percent changes. We then try to identify the reasons for these changes and, if possible, determine whether they are favorable or unfavorable. We also follow up on items with small changes when we expected the changes to be large.

Exhibit 13.1 shows comparative balance sheets for Apple, Inc. (NASDAQ: AAPL). A few items stand out on the asset side. Apple's accounts receivable show a substantial 103.6% increase. Although much of this increase stems from Apple's 45% increase in sales, the additional growth appears to stem from an increase in receivables from its cellular network customers (however, there is no evidence of any increased risk from nonpayment). Other notable increases occur with (1) long-term (and short-term) securities, reflecting Apple's success but with an absence of vision for reinvestment, and (2) property, plant and equipment, reflecting Apple's growth. Its sizable total asset growth of 51.3% must be accompanied by future income to validate Apple's asset reinvestments. Many of its shareholders question its recent growth, which is one factor in its declining stock price from late 2012 through much of 2013.

We see most increases on Apple's financing side mimic its 45% sales growth, which is to be expected. Due to its success, Apple has little long-term debt. We also see a 61.2% growth in retained earnings, which reflects its success in generating net income. This has also created more calls from its shareholders to increase cash dividends (as its liquid assets balloon).

Comparative Income Statements Comparative income statements are prepared similarly to comparative balance sheets. Amounts for two or more periods are placed side by side, with additional columns for dollar and percent changes. Exhibit 13.2 shows Apple's comparative income statements.

Apple has substantial sales growth of 44.6% in 2012. This finding helps support management's growth strategy as reflected in the comparative balance sheets. Apple evidences an ability to control cost of goods sold (36.3% increase) and its operating expenses (33.8% increase), which all grew but at a rate less than its 44.6% sales growth (very good news). In addition, Apple's net income growth of 61.0% on revenue growth of 44.6% is very good.

Example: When there is a value in the base period and zero in the analysis period, the decrease is 100%. Why isn't the reverse situation an increase of 100%? *Answer:* A 100% increase of zero is still zero.

Point: Spreadsheet programs can help with horizontal, vertical, and ratio analyses, including graphical depictions of financial relations.

Point: Business consultants use comparative statement analysis to provide management advice.

Point: Percent change can also be computed by dividing the current period by the prior period and subtracting 1.0. For example, the 44.6% sales increase of Exhibit 13.2 is computed as: ($156,508/$108,249) − 1.

---

[1] *Median* is the middle value in a group of numbers. For instance, if five prior years' incomes are (in 000s) $15, $19, $18, $20, and $22, the median value is $19. When there are two middle numbers, we can take their average. For instance, if four prior years' sales are (in 000s) $84, $91, $96, and $93, the median is $92 (computed as the average of $91 and $93).

EXHIBIT 13.1

Comparative Balance Sheets

APPLE

APPLE, INC. Comparative Balance Sheets September 29, 2012 and September 24, 2011				
(in millions)	2012	2011	Dollar Change	Percent Change
Assets				
Cash and cash equivalents........................	$ 10,746	$ 9,815	$ 931	9.5%
Short-term marketable securities.................	18,383	16,137	2,246	13.9
Accounts receivable, net	10,930	5,369	5,561	103.6
Inventories......................................	791	776	15	1.9
Deferred tax assets	2,583	2,014	569	28.3
Vendor non-trade receivables	7,762	6,348	1,414	22.3
Other current assets	6,458	4,529	1,929	42.6
Total current assets	57,653	44,988	12,665	28.2
Long-term marketable securities..................	92,122	55,618	36,504	65.6
Property, plant and equipment, net	15,452	7,777	7,675	98.7
Goodwill..	1,135	896	239	26.7
Acquired intangible assets, net...................	4,224	3,536	688	19.5
Other assets....................................	5,478	3,556	1,922	54.0
Total assets..................................	$176,064	$116,371	$59,693	51.3
Liabilities				
Accounts payable...............................	$ 21,175	$ 14,632	$ 6,543	44.7%
Accrued expenses	11,414	9,247	2,167	23.4
Deferred revenue...............................	5,953	4,091	1,862	45.5
Total current liabilities	38,542	27,970	10,572	37.8
Deferred revenue—noncurrent	2,648	1,686	962	57.1
Other noncurrent liabilities......................	16,664	10,100	6,564	65.0
Total liabilities	57,854	39,756	18,098	45.5
Stockholders' Equity				
Common stock	16,422	13,331	3,091	23.2
Retained earnings...............................	101,289	62,841	38,448	61.2
Accumulated other comprehensive income	499	443	56	12.6
Total stockholders' equity	118,210	76,615	41,595	54.3
Total liabilities and stockholders' equity	$176,064	$116,371	$59,693	51.3

EXHIBIT 13.2

Comparative Income Statements

APPLE

APPLE, INC. Comparative Income Statements For Years Ended September 29, 2012, and September 24, 2011				
(in millions, except per share)	2012	2011	Dollar Change	Percent Change
Net sales	$156,508	$108,249	$48,259	44.6%
Cost of sales...................................	87,846	64,431	23,415	36.3
Gross margin	68,662	43,818	24,844	56.7
Research and development	3,381	2,429	952	39.2
Selling, general and administrative................	10,040	7,599	2,441	32.1
Total operating expenses........................	13,421	10,028	3,393	33.8
Operating income	55,241	33,790	21,451	63.5
Other income, net	522	415	107	25.8
Income before provision for income taxes	55,763	34,205	21,558	63.0
Provision for income taxes	14,030	8,283	5,747	69.4
Net income	$ 41,733	$ 25,922	15,811	61.0
Basic earnings per share	$ 44.64	$ 28.05	$ 16.59	59.1
Diluted earnings per share	$ 44.15	$ 27.68	$ 16.47	59.5

Trend Analysis

Trend analysis, also called *trend percent analysis* or *index number trend analysis,* is a form of horizontal analysis that can reveal patterns in data across successive periods. It involves computing trend percents for a series of financial numbers and is a variation on the use of percent changes. The difference is that trend analysis does not subtract the base period amount in the numerator. To compute trend percents, we do the following:

1. Select a *base period* and assign each item in the base period a weight of 100%.
2. Express financial numbers as a percent of their base period number.

Specifically, a *trend percent,* also called an *index number,* is computed as follows:

$$\text{Trend percent (\%)} = \frac{\text{Analysis period amount}}{\text{Base period amount}} \times 100$$

Point: *Index* refers to the comparison of the analysis period to the base period. Percents determined for each period are called *index numbers.*

To illustrate trend analysis, we use the Apple data shown in Exhibit 13.3.

(in millions)	2012	2011	2010	2009	2008
Net sales.................	$156,508	$108,249	$65,225	$36,537	$32,479
Cost of sales	87,846	64,431	39,541	23,397	21,334
Operating expenses	13,421	10,028	7,299	5,482	4,870

EXHIBIT 13.3

Sales and Expenses

These data are from Apple's current and prior financial statements. The base period is 2008 and the trend percent is computed in each subsequent year by dividing that year's amount by its 2008 amount. For instance, the revenue trend percent for 2012 is 481.9%, computed as $156,508/$32,479. The trend percents—using the data from Exhibit 13.3—are shown in Exhibit 13.4.

	2012	2011	2010	2009	2008
Net sales.................	481.9%	333.3%	200.8%	112.5%	100.0%
Cost of sales	411.8	302.0	185.3	109.7	100.0
Operating expenses	275.6	205.9	149.9	112.6	100.0

EXHIBIT 13.4

Trend Percents for Sales and Expenses

Graphical depictions often aid analysis of trend percents. Exhibit 13.5 shows the trend percents from Exhibit 13.4 in a *line graph,* which can help us identify trends and detect changes in direction or magnitude. It reveals that the trend line for revenue consistently exceeds that for both cost of sales and for operating expenses. Moreover, the magnitude of that difference has grown. This result bodes well for Apple because profitability of the company will suffer if costs and operating expenses cannot be controlled. Management must continue to control these costs in future years. In summary, the trend lines for both costs and expenses are encouraging because revenue growth outpaces their growth for each year from 2010–2012.

Point: Trend analysis expresses a percent of base, not a percent of change.

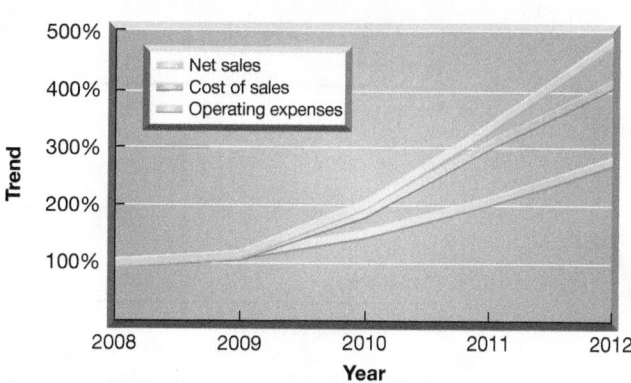

EXHIBIT 13.5

Trend Percent Lines for Sales and Expenses of Apple

Exhibit 13.6 compares Apple's revenue trend line to that of Google and Samsung for this same period. Apple is able to grow its revenue in each year relative to its base year. In this respect Apple soundly outperforms its competitors, although both Google and Samsung performed very well over

EXHIBIT 13.6

Trend Percent Lines—Apple, Google and Samsung

APPLE

GOOGLE

Samsung

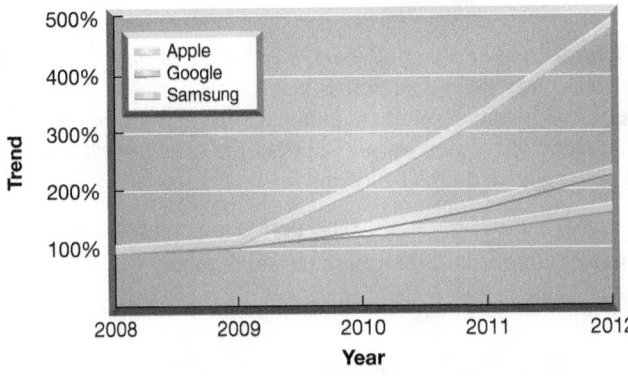

this same period of time. These data indicate that Apple's products and services have met with great consumer acceptance.

Trend analysis of financial statement items can include comparisons of relations between items on different financial statements. For instance, Exhibit 13.7 compares Apple's revenue and total assets. The rate of increase in total assets (444.9%) is less than the increase in revenues (481.9%) since 2008. Is this result favorable or not? The answer is that Apple was *more* efficient in using its assets in 2012. Management has generated revenues sufficient to more than compensate for this asset growth.

EXHIBIT 13.7

Sales and Asset Data for Apple

(in millions)	2012	2008	Trend Percent (2012 vs. 2008)
Net sales	$156,508	$32,479	481.9%
Total assets	176,064	39,572	444.9

Overall we must remember that an important role of financial statement analysis is identifying questions and areas of interest, which often direct us to important factors bearing on a company's future. Accordingly, financial statement analysis should be seen as a continuous process of refining our understanding and expectations of company performance and financial condition.

■ **Decision Maker**

Auditor   Your tests reveal a 3% increase in sales from $200,000 to $206,000 and a 4% decrease in expenses from $190,000 to $182,400. Both changes are within your "reasonableness" criterion of ±5%, and thus you don't pursue additional tests. The audit partner in charge questions your lack of follow-up and mentions the *joint relation* between sales and expenses. To what is the partner referring? ■   [Answer—p. 604]

NEED-TO-KNOW 13.1

P1

Compute trend percents for the following accounts, using 2012 as the base year (round percents to whole numbers). State whether the situation as revealed by the trends appears to be favorable or unfavorable for each account.

($ millions)	2015	2014	2013	2012
Sales	$500	$350	$250	$200
Cost of goods sold.........	400	175	100	50

Solution

($ millions)	2015	2014	2013	2012
Sales	250% ($500/$200)	175% ($350/$200)	125% ($250/$200)	100% ($200/$200)
Cost of goods sold.........	800% ($400/$50)	350% ($175/$50)	200% ($100/$50)	100% ($50/$50)

Analysis: The trend in sales is favorable; however, we need more information about economic conditions such as inflation rates and competitors' performances to better assess it. Cost of sales is also rising (as expected with increasing sales); however, cost of sales is rising faster than the increase in sales, which is unfavorable and bad news. A quick analysis of the gross margin percentage would highlight this concern.

Do More: QS 13-2, QS 13-4, E 13-3

VERTICAL ANALYSIS

Vertical analysis is a tool to evaluate individual financial statement items or a group of items in terms of a specific base amount. We usually define a key aggregate figure as the base, which for an income statement is usually revenue and for a balance sheet is usually total assets. This section explains vertical analysis and applies it to Apple. [The term *vertical analysis* arises from the up-down (or down-up) movement of our eyes as we review common-size financial statements. Vertical analysis is also called *common-size analysis*.]

Income Statement	
Sales	10,000
Expenses	6,000
Income	4,000

Common-Size Statements

The comparative statements in Exhibits 13.1 and 13.2 show the change in each item over time, but they do not emphasize the relative importance of each item. We use **common-size financial statements** to reveal changes in the relative importance of each financial statement item. All individual amounts in common-size statements are redefined in terms of common-size percents. A *common-size percent* is measured by dividing each individual financial statement amount under analysis by its base amount:

P2 Describe and apply methods of vertical analysis.

$$\text{Common-size percent (\%)} = \frac{\text{Analysis amount}}{\text{Base amount}} \times 100$$

Common-Size Balance Sheets   Common-size statements express each item as a percent of a *base amount*, which for a common-size balance sheet is usually total assets. The base amount is assigned a value of 100%. (This implies that the total amount of liabilities plus equity equals 100% since this amount equals total assets.) We then compute a common-size percent for each asset, liability, and equity item using total assets as the base amount. When we present a company's successive balance sheets in this way, changes in the mixture of assets, liabilities, and equity are apparent.

Point: The *base* amount in common-size analysis is an *aggregate* amount from that period's financial statement.

Exhibit 13.8 shows common-size comparative balance sheets for Apple. Some relations that stand out on both a magnitude and percentage basis include (1) a 4.5% point increase in long-term securities, which equates to a $36,504 million increase, (2) a 2.1% point increase in property, plant and equipment, and (3) a 3.5% increase in retained earnings, which equates to a $38,448 million increase. Some of these changes reflect a company with huge successes, but some with lack of focus as evidenced by the increasing size of long-term securities. This buildup in securities is a concern as the return on securities is historically smaller than the return on operating assets from successful reinvestment. Time well tell whether Apple can continue to generate sufficient revenue and income from its growing asset base.

Point: Common-size statements often are used to compare two or more companies in the same industry.

Point: Common-size statements are also useful in comparing firms that report in different currencies.

Common-Size Income Statements   Analysis also benefits from use of a common-size income statement. Revenue is usually the base amount, which is assigned a value of 100%. Each common-size income statement item appears as a percent of revenue. If we think of the 100% revenue amount as representing one sales dollar, the remaining items show how each revenue dollar is distributed among costs, expenses, and income.

Exhibit 13.9 shows common-size comparative income statements for each dollar of Apple's revenue. The past two years' common-size numbers are similar with a few exceptions. What is very good news is that Apple has gained 2.8 cents in net income per net sales dollar—evidenced by the 23.9% to 26.7% increase in income as a percent of net sales. This implies that management is effectively controlling costs. Much of this is attributed to the decline in cost of sales from 59.5% to 56.1% as a percent of net sales. However, we also see a nice decline in total operating expenses from 9.3% to 8.6% as a percent of net sales. In sum, analysis here shows that common-size percents for successive income statements can uncover potentially important changes in a company's cost management. (Evidence of no changes, especially when changes are expected, is also informative.)

Global: International companies sometimes disclose "convenience" financial statements, which are statements translated in other languages and currencies. However, these statements rarely adjust for differences in accounting principles across countries.

Common-Size Graphics

Two of the most common tools of common-size analysis are trend analysis of common-size statements and graphical analysis. The trend analysis of common-size statements is similar to that of comparative statements discussed under vertical analysis. It is not illustrated here because the only difference is the substitution of common-size percents for trend percents. Instead, this section discusses graphical analysis of common-size statements.

EXHIBIT 13.8

Common-Size Comparative
Balance Sheets

APPLE

APPLE, INC. Common-Size Comparative Balance Sheets September 29, 2012, and September 24, 2011			Common-Size Percents*	
(in millions)	2012	2011	2012	2011
Assets				
Cash and cash equivalents	$ 10,746	$ 9,815	6.1%	8.4%
Short-term marketable securities	18,383	16,137	10.4	13.9
Accounts receivable, net	10,930	5,369	6.2	4.6
Inventories	791	776	0.4	0.7
Deferred tax assets	2,583	2,014	1.5	1.7
Vendor non-trade receivables	7,762	6,348	4.4	5.5
Other current assets	6,458	4,529	3.7	3.9
Total current assets.	57,653	44,988	32.7	38.7
Long-term marketable securities	92,122	55,618	52.3	47.8
Property, plant and equipment, net	15,452	7,777	8.8	6.7
Goodwill.	1,135	896	0.6	0.8
Acquired intangible assets, net.	4,224	3,536	2.4	3.0
Other assets.	5,478	3,556	3.1	3.1
Total assets	$176,064	$116,371	100.0%	100.0%
Liabilities				
Accounts payable	$ 21,175	$ 14,632	12.0%	12.6%
Accrued expenses	11,414	9,247	6.5	7.9
Deferred revenue.	5,953	4,091	3.4	3.5
Total current liabilities	38,542	27,970	21.9	24.0
Deferred revenue—noncurrent.	2,648	1,686	1.5	1.4
Other noncurrent liabilities	16,664	10,100	9.5	8.7
Total liabilities	57,854	39,756	32.9	34.2
Stockholders' Equity				
Common stock.	16,422	13,331	9.3	11.5
Retained earnings	101,289	62,841	57.5	54.0
Accumulated other comprehensive income	499	443	0.3	0.4
Total stockholders' equity	118,210	76,615	67.1	65.8
Total liabilities and stockholders' equity	$176,064	$116,371	100.0%	100.0%

* Percents are rounded to tenths and thus may not exactly sum to totals and subtotals.

EXHIBIT 13.9

Common-Size Comparative
Income Statements

APPLE

APPLE, INC. Common-Size Comparative Income Statements For Years Ended September 29, 2012, and September 24, 2011			Common-Size Percents*	
(in millions)	2012	2011	2012	2011
Net sales	$156,508	$108,249	100.0%	100.0%
Cost of sales.	87,846	64,431	56.1	59.5
Gross margin	68,662	43,818	43.9	40.5
Research and development	3,381	2,429	2.2	2.2
Selling, general and administrative	10,040	7,599	6.4	7.0
Total operating expenses.	13,421	10,028	8.6	9.3
Operating income	55,241	33,790	35.3	31.2
Other income, net	522	415	0.3	0.4
Income before provision for income taxes	55,763	34,205	35.6	31.6
Provision for income taxes	14,030	8,283	9.0	7.7
Net income	$ 41,733	$ 25,922	26.7%	23.9%

* Percents are rounded to tenths and thus may not exactly sum to totals and subtotals.

An income statement readily lends itself to common-size graphical analysis. This is so because revenues affect nearly every item in an income statement. Exhibit 13.10 shows Apple's 2012 common-size income statement in graphical form. This pie chart highlights the contribution of each cost component of net sales for net income (for this graph, 'other income, net' is included in selling, general and administrative costs).

Exhibit 13.11 previews more complex graphical analyses available and the insights they provide. The data for this exhibit are taken from Apple's *Segments* footnote. Apple reports five operating segments for 2012: (1) Americas, (2) Europe, (3) Japan, (4) Asia-Pacific, and (5) Retail.

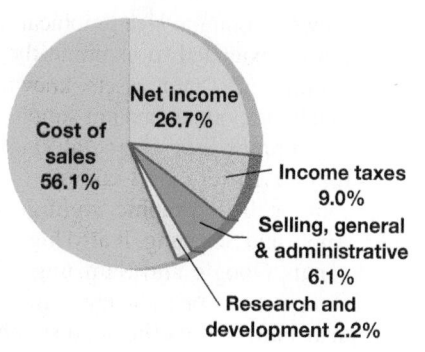

EXHIBIT 13.10

Common-Size Graphic of Income Statement

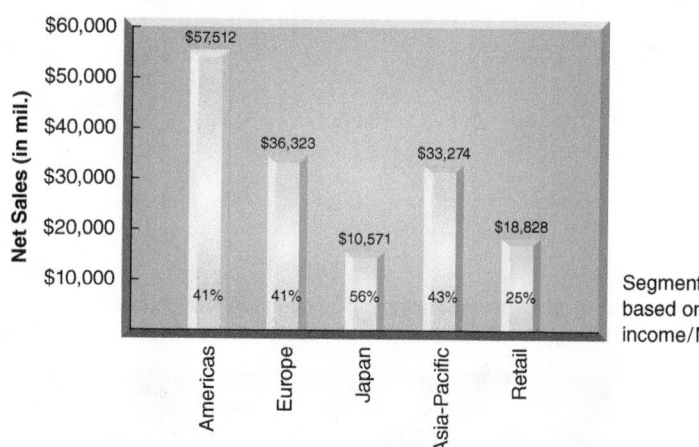

EXHIBIT 13.11

Sales and Operating Income Margin Breakdown by Segment

The bars in Exhibit 13.11 show the level of net sales for each of the five reportable segments of Apple. Its Americas segment generates $57,512 million of its total net sales, which is roughly 37% of its total. The four other bars show the level of sales generated from each of the other four international segments, including its retail segment. At the bottom of each bar is that segment's operating income margin, defined as segment operating income divided by segment net sales. The Americas segment is seen to yield a 41% operating income margin; margins for the other four segments are shown at the bottom of each of the other four segment bars. This type of graphic presentation can lead to questions about the profitability of each segment and discussion of potential expansions into the more lucrative segments. For example, the Japan segment yields an operating margin of 56%. A natural question for management is what potential is there to further expand sales into the segment and maintain the similar operating margin? This type of analysis can help users in determining strategic plans and actions.

Graphical analysis is also useful in identifying (1) sources of financing including the distribution among current liabilities, noncurrent liabilities, and equity capital and (2) focuses of investing activities, including the distribution among current and noncurrent assets. To illustrate, Exhibit 13.12

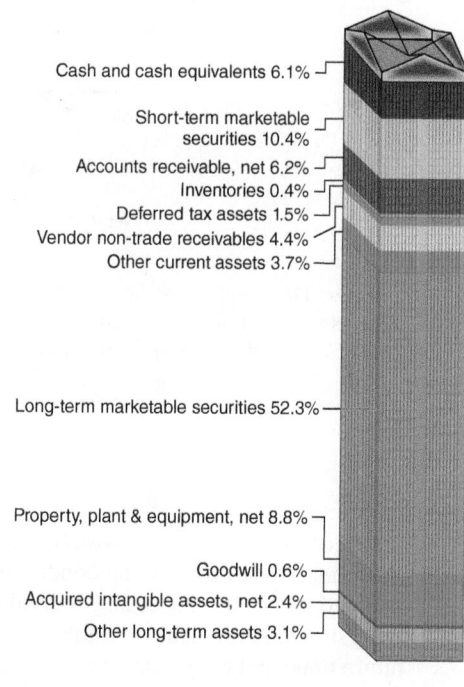

EXHIBIT 13.12

Common-Size Graphic of Asset Components

shows a common-size graphical display of Apple's assets. Common-size balance sheet analysis can be extended to examine the composition of these subgroups. For instance, in assessing liquidity of current assets, knowing what proportion of *current* assets consists of inventories is usually important, and not simply what proportion inventories are of *total* assets.

Common-size financial statements are also useful in comparing different companies. Exhibit 13.13 shows common-size graphics of Apple, Google, and Samsung on financing sources. This graphic highlights the larger percent of equity financing for Google versus Apple and Samsung. It also highlights the somewhat larger noncurrent (debt) financing of Apple versus Google and Samsung. Comparison of a company's common-size statements with competitors' or industry common-size statistics alerts us to differences in the structure or distribution of its financial statements but not to their dollar magnitude.

EXHIBIT 13.13

Common-Size Graphic of Financing Sources—Competitor Analysis

APPLE

GOOGLE

Samsung

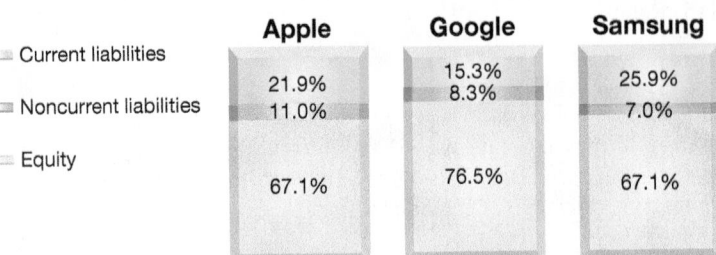

	Apple	Google	Samsung
Current liabilities	21.9%	15.3%	25.9%
Noncurrent liabilities	11.0%	8.3%	7.0%
Equity	67.1%	76.5%	67.1%

NEED-TO-KNOW 13.2

P2

Express the following comparative income statements in common-size percents and assess whether or not this company's situation has improved in the most recent year (round percents to whole numbers).

Comparative Income Statements For Years Ended December 31, 2014 and 2013		
	2014	**2013**
Sales	$800	$500
Total expenses	560	400
Net income	$240	$100

Solution

	2014	**2013**
Sales	100% ($800/$800)	100% ($500/$500)
Total expenses	70% ($560/$800)	80% ($400/$500)
Net income	30%	20%

Do More: QS 13-3, E 13-5, E 13-7

QC2

Analysis: This company's situation has improved. This is evident from its substantial increase in net income as a percent of sales for 2014 (30%) relative to 2013 (20%). Further, the company's sales increased from $500 in 2013 to $800 in 2014 (while expenses declined as a percent of sales from 80% to 70%).

RATIO ANALYSIS

P3   Define and apply ratio analysis.

Ratios are among the more widely used tools of financial analysis because they provide clues to and symptoms of underlying conditions. A ratio can help us uncover conditions and trends difficult to detect by inspecting individual components making up the ratio. Ratios, like other analysis tools, are usually future oriented; that is, they are often adjusted for their probable future trend and magnitude, and their usefulness depends on skillful interpretation.

A ratio expresses a mathematical relation between two quantities. It can be expressed as a percent, rate, or proportion. For instance, a change in an account balance from $100 to $250 can be expressed as (1) 150% increase, (2) 2.5 times, or (3) 2.5 to 1 (or 2.5:1). Computation of a ratio is a simple arithmetic operation, but its interpretation is not. To be meaningful, a ratio must refer to an economically important relation. For example, a direct and crucial relation exists between an item's sales price and its cost. Accordingly, the ratio of cost of goods sold to sales is meaningful. In contrast, no obvious relation exists between freight costs and the balance of long-term investments.

This section describes an important set of financial ratios and its application. The selected ratios are organized into the four building blocks of financial statement analysis: (1) liquidity and efficiency, (2) solvency, (3) profitability, and (4) market prospects. All of these ratios were explained at relevant points in prior chapters. The purpose here is to organize and apply them under a summary framework. We use four common standards, in varying degrees, for comparisons: intracompany, competitor, industry, and guidelines.

Point: Some sources for industry norms are *Annual Statement Studies* by Robert Morris Associates, *Industry Norms & Key Business Ratios* by Dun & Bradstreet, *Standard & Poor's Industry Surveys,* and Reuters.com/finance.

Liquidity and Efficiency

Liquidity refers to the availability of resources to meet short-term cash requirements. It is affected by the timing of cash inflows and outflows along with prospects for future performance. Analysis of liquidity is aimed at a company's funding requirements. *Efficiency* refers to how productive a company is in using its assets. Efficiency is usually measured relative to how much revenue is generated from a certain level of assets.

Both liquidity and efficiency are important and complementary. If a company fails to meet its current obligations, its continued existence is doubtful. Viewed in this light, all other measures of analysis are of secondary importance. Although accounting measurements assume the company's continued existence, our analysis must always assess the validity of this assumption using liquidity measures. Moreover, inefficient use of assets can cause liquidity problems. A lack of liquidity often precedes lower profitability and fewer opportunities. It can foretell a loss of owner control. To a company's creditors, lack of liquidity can yield delays in collecting interest and principal payments or the loss of amounts due them. A company's customers and suppliers of goods and services also are affected by short-term liquidity problems. Implications include a company's inability to execute contracts and potential damage to important customer and supplier relationships. This section describes and illustrates key ratios relevant to assessing liquidity and efficiency.

Working Capital and Current Ratio   The amount of current assets less current liabilities is called **working capital,** or *net working capital.* A company needs adequate working capital to meet current debts, to carry sufficient inventories, and to take advantage of cash discounts. A company that runs low on working capital is less likely to meet current obligations or to continue operating. When evaluating a company's working capital, we must not only look at the dollar amount of current assets less current liabilities, but also at their ratio. The *current ratio* is defined as follows (see Chapter 3 for additional explanation):

$$\text{Current ratio} = \frac{\text{Current assets}}{\text{Current liabilities}}$$

Drawing on information in Exhibit 13.1, Apple's working capital and current ratio for both 2012 and 2011 are shown in Exhibit 13.14. Also, Google (4.22), Samsung (1.86), and the industry's current ratio (2.5) are shown in the margin. Apple's 2012 ratio (1.50) is lower than competitors' ratios, but it is not in danger of defaulting on loan payments. A high current ratio suggests a strong liquidity position and an ability to meet current obligations. A company can, however, have a current ratio that is too high. An excessively high current ratio means that the company has invested too much in current assets compared to its current

(in millions)	2012	2011
Current assets	$ 57,653	$ 44,988
Current liabilities	38,542	27,970
Working capital	$19,111	$17,018
Current ratio		
$57,623/$38,542 =	1.50 to 1	
$44,988/$27,970 =		1.61 to 1

EXHIBIT 13.14

Apple's Working Capital and Current Ratio

Current ratio
Google = 4.22
Samsung = 1.86
Industry = 2.5

obligations. An excessive investment in current assets is not an efficient use of funds because current assets normally generate a low return on investment (compared with long-term assets).

Many users apply a guideline of 2:1 (or 1.5:1) for the current ratio in helping evaluate a company's debt-paying ability. A company with a 2:1 or higher current ratio is generally thought to be a good credit risk in the short run. Such a guideline or any analysis of the current ratio must recognize at least three additional factors: (1) type of business, (2) composition of current assets, and (3) turnover rate of current asset components.

Type of business.   A service company that grants little or no credit and carries few inventories can probably operate on a current ratio of less than 1:1 if its revenues generate enough cash to pay its current liabilities. On the other hand, a company selling high-priced clothing or furniture requires a higher ratio because of difficulties in judging customer demand and cash receipts. For instance, if demand falls, inventory may not generate as much cash as expected. Accordingly, analysis of the current ratio should include a comparison with ratios from successful companies in the same industry and from prior periods. We must also recognize that a company's accounting methods, especially choice of inventory method, affect the current ratio. For instance, when costs are rising, a company using LIFO tends to report a smaller amount of current assets than when using FIFO.

Point: When a firm uses LIFO in a period of rising costs, the standard for an adequate current ratio usually is lower than if it used FIFO.

Composition of current assets.   The composition of a company's current assets is important to an evaluation of short-term liquidity. For instance, cash, cash equivalents, and short-term investments are more liquid than accounts and notes receivable. Also, short-term receivables normally are more liquid than inventory. Cash, of course, can be used to immediately pay current debts. Items such as accounts receivable and inventory, however, normally must be converted into cash before payment is made. An excessive amount of receivables and inventory weakens a company's ability to pay current liabilities. The acid-test ratio (see below) can help with this assessment.

Turnover rate of assets.   Asset turnover measures a company's efficiency in using its assets. One relevant measure of asset efficiency is the revenue generated. A measure of total asset turnover is revenues divided by total assets, but evaluation of turnover for individual assets is also useful. We discuss both receivables turnover and inventory turnover on the next page.

■ Decision Maker

Banker   A company requests a one-year, $200,000 loan for expansion. This company's current ratio is 4:1, with current assets of $160,000. Key competitors carry a current ratio of about 1.9:1. Using this information, do you approve the loan application? Does your decision change if the application is for a 10-year loan? ■   [Answer—p. 604]

Acid-Test Ratio   Quick assets are cash, short-term investments, and current receivables. These are the most liquid types of current assets. The *acid-test ratio,* also called *quick ratio,* and introduced in Chapter 4, reflects on a company's short-term liquidity.

$$\text{Acid-test ratio} = \frac{\text{Cash} + \text{Short-term investments} + \text{Current receivables}}{\text{Current liabilities}}$$

Apple's acid-test ratio is computed in Exhibit 13.15. Apple's 2012 acid-test ratio (0.56) is lower than that for Google (3.90) and Samsung (1.37), and is less than the 1:1 common guideline for

EXHIBIT 13.15

Acid-Test Ratio

(in millions)	2012	2011
Cash and equivalents	$10,746	$ 9,815
Current receivables	10,930	5,369
Total quick assets	$21,676	$ 15,184
Current liabilities	$38,542	$ 27,970
Acid-test ratio		
$21,676/$38,542	0.56 to 1	
$15,184/$27,970		0.54 to 1

Acid-test ratio
Google = 3.90
Samsung = 1.37
Industry = 0.9

an acceptable acid-test ratio. The ratio for Apple is also less than the 0.9 industry norm; however, we are not concerned. As with analysis of the current ratio, we need to consider other factors. For instance, the frequency with which a company converts its current assets into cash affects its working capital requirements. This implies that analysis of short-term liquidity should also include an analysis of receivables and inventories, which we consider next.

Global: Ratio analysis helps overcome currency translation problems, but it does *not* overcome differences in accounting principles.

Accounts Receivable Turnover   We can measure how frequently a company converts its receivables into cash by computing the *accounts receivable turnover*. This ratio is defined as follows (see Chapter 7 for additional explanation):

$$\text{Accounts receivable turnover} = \frac{\text{Net sales}}{\text{Average accounts receivable, net}}$$

Short-term receivables from customers are often included in the denominator along with accounts receivable. Also, accounts receivable turnover is more precise if credit sales are used for the numerator, but external users generally use net sales (or net revenues) because information about credit sales is typically not reported. Apple's 2012 accounts receivable turnover is computed as follows ($ millions).

Point: Some users prefer using gross accounts receivable (before subtracting the allowance for doubtful accounts) to avoid the influence of a manager's bad debts estimate.

$$\frac{\$156,508}{(\$5,369 + \$10,930)/2} = 19.2 \text{ times}$$

Apple's value of 19.2 exceeds that of both Google's 7.5 and Samsung's 7.9. Accounts receivable turnover is high when accounts receivable are quickly collected. A high turnover is favorable because it means the company need not commit large amounts of funds to accounts receivable. However, an accounts receivable turnover can be too high; this can occur when credit terms are so restrictive that they negatively affect sales volume.

Accounts receivable turnover
Google = 7.5
Samsung = 7.9
Industry = 5.0

Point: Ending accounts receivable can be substituted for the average balance in computing accounts receivable turnover if the difference between ending and average receivables is small.

Inventory Turnover   How long a company holds inventory before selling it will affect working capital requirements. One measure of this effect is *inventory turnover,* also called *merchandise turnover* or *merchandise inventory turnover,* which is defined as follows (see Chapter 5 for additional explanation):

$$\text{Inventory turnover} = \frac{\text{Cost of goods sold}}{\text{Average inventory}}$$

Using Apple's cost of goods sold and inventories information, we compute its inventory turnover for 2012 as follows (if the beginning and ending inventories for the year do not represent the usual inventory amount, an average of quarterly or monthly inventories can be used).

Inventory turnover
Google = 76.42
Samsung = 7.57
Industry = 7.0

$$\frac{\$87,846}{(\$776 + \$791)/2} = 112.12 \text{ times}$$

Apple's inventory turnover of 112.12 is more than Google's 76.42 and Samsung's 7.57, and the industry's 7.0. A company with a high turnover requires a smaller investment in inventory than one producing the same sales with a lower turnover. Inventory turnover can be too high, however, if the inventory a company keeps is so small that it restricts sales volume.

Days' Sales Uncollected   Accounts receivable turnover provides insight into how frequently a company collects its accounts. Days' sales uncollected is one measure of this activity, which is defined as follows (Chapter 6 provides additional explanation):

$$\text{Days' sales uncollected} = \frac{\text{Accounts receivable, net}}{\text{Net sales}} \times 365$$

Any short-term notes receivable from customers are normally included in the numerator.

Apple's 2012 days' sales uncollected follows.

Day's sales uncollected
Google = 57.4
Samsung = 48.4

$$\frac{\$10,930}{\$156,508} \times 365 = 25.5 \text{ days}$$

Both Google's days' sales uncollected of 57.4 days and Samsung's 48.4 days are more than the 25.5 days for Apple. Days' sales uncollected is more meaningful if we know company credit terms. A rough guideline states that days' sales uncollected should not exceed $1\frac{1}{3}$ times the days in its (1) credit period, *if* discounts are not offered or (2) discount period, *if* favorable discounts are offered.

Days' Sales in Inventory   *Days' sales in inventory* is a useful measure in evaluating inventory liquidity. Days' sales in inventory is linked to inventory in a way that days' sales uncollected is linked to receivables. We compute days' sales in inventory as follows (Chapter 5 provides additional explanation).

$$\text{Days' sales in inventory} = \frac{\text{Ending inventory}}{\text{Cost of goods sold}} \times 365$$

Apple's days' sales in inventory for 2012 follows.

$$\frac{\$791}{\$87,846} \times 365 = 3.3 \text{ days}$$

Days' sales in inventory
Google = 8.9
Samsung = 51.1
Industry = 35

Point: *Average collection period* is estimated by dividing 365 by the accounts receivable turnover ratio. For example, 365 divided by an accounts receivable turnover of 6.1 indicates a 60-day average collection period.

If the products in Apple's inventory are in demand by customers, this formula estimates that its inventory will be converted into receivables (or cash) in 3.3 days. If all of Apple's sales were credit sales, the conversion of inventory to receivables in 3.3 days *plus* the conversion of receivables to cash in 25.5 days implies that inventory will be converted to cash in about 28.8 days (3.3 + 25.5).

Total Asset Turnover   *Total asset turnover* reflects a company's ability to use its assets to generate sales and is an important indication of operating efficiency. The definition of this ratio follows (Chapter 8 offers additional explanation).

$$\text{Total asset turnover} = \frac{\text{Net sales}}{\text{Average total assets}}$$

QC3

Apple's total asset turnover of 1.07 for 2012 follows, which is greater than that for Google (0.60) but less than that for Samsung (1.19).

Total asset turnover
Google = 0.60
Samsung = 1.19
Industry = 1.2

$$\frac{\$156,508}{(\$116,371 + \$176,064)/2} = 1.07 \text{ times}$$

Solvency

Solvency refers to a company's long-run financial viability and its ability to cover long-term obligations. All of a company's business activities—financing, investing, and operating—affect its solvency. Analysis of solvency is long term and uses less precise but more encompassing measures than liquidity. One of the most important components of solvency analysis is the composition of a company's capital structure. *Capital structure* refers to a company's financing sources. It ranges from relatively permanent equity financing to riskier or more temporary short-term financing. Assets represent security for financiers, ranging from loans secured by specific assets to the assets available as general security to unsecured creditors. This section describes the tools of solvency analysis. Our analysis focuses on a company's ability to both meet its obligations and provide security to its creditors *over the long run*. Indicators of this ability include

debt and *equity* ratios, the relation between *pledged assets and secured liabilities,* and the company's capacity to earn sufficient income to *pay fixed interest charges.*

Debt and Equity Ratios   One element of solvency analysis is to assess the portion of a company's assets contributed by its owners and the portion contributed by creditors. This relation is reflected in the debt ratio (also described in Chapter 2). The *debt ratio* expresses total liabilities as a percent of total assets. The **equity ratio** provides complementary information by expressing total equity as a percent of total assets. Apple's debt and equity ratios follow.

Point: For analysis purposes, Noncontrolling Interest is usually included in equity.

(in millions)	2012	Ratios	
Total liabilities	$ 57,854	32.9%	[Debt ratio]
Total equity	118,210	67.1	[Equity ratio]
Total liabilities and equity	$176,064	100.0%	

Debt ratio :: Equity ratio
Google = 23.5% :: 76.5%
Samsung = 32.9% :: 67.1%
Industry = 35% :: 65%

Apple's financial statements reveal more equity than debt. A company is considered less risky if its capital structure (equity and long-term debt) contains more equity. One risk factor is the required payment for interest and principal when debt is outstanding. Another factor is the greater the stockholder financing, the more losses a company can absorb through equity before the assets become inadequate to satisfy creditors' claims. From the stockholders' point of view, if a company earns a return on borrowed capital that is higher than the cost of borrowing, the difference represents increased income to stockholders. The inclusion of debt is described as *financial leverage* because debt can have the effect of increasing the return to stockholders. Companies are said to be highly leveraged if a large portion of their assets is financed by debt.

Point: Bank examiners from the FDIC and other regulatory agencies use debt and equity ratios to monitor compliance with regulatory capital requirements imposed on banks and S&Ls.

Debt-to-Equity Ratio   The ratio of total liabilities to equity is another measure of solvency. We compute the ratio as follows (Chapter 10 offers additional explanation).

$$\text{Debt-to-equity ratio} = \frac{\text{Total liabilities}}{\text{Total equity}}$$

Apple's debt-to-equity ratio for 2012 is

$$\$57,854/\$118,210 = 0.49$$

Debt-to-equity
Google = 0.31
Samsung = 0.49
Industry = 0.6

Apple's 0.49 debt-to-equity ratio is equal to that of Samsung (0.49), higher than the 0.31 ratio for Google, but lower than the industry ratio of 0.6. Consistent with our inferences from the debt ratio, Apple's capital structure has less debt than equity, which helps limit risk. Recall that debt must be repaid with interest, while equity does not. These debt requirements can be burdensome when the industry and/or the economy experience a downturn. A larger debt-to-equity ratio also implies less opportunity to expand through use of debt financing.

Times Interest Earned   The amount of income before deductions for interest expense and income taxes is the amount available to pay interest expense. The following *times interest earned* ratio reflects the creditors' risk of loan repayments with interest (see Chapter 9 for additional explanation).

Point: The times interest earned ratio and the debt and equity ratios are of special interest to bank lending officers.

$$\text{Times interest earned} = \frac{\text{Income before interest expense and income taxes}}{\text{Interest expense}}$$

The larger this ratio, the less risky is the company for creditors. One guideline says that creditors are reasonably safe if the company earns its fixed interest expense two or more times each year. Apple's times interest earned ratio follows (its annual report says "the company had no debt outstanding and accordingly did not incur any related interest expense"). The absence of interest expense means this ratio is not meaningful to Apple because of zero interest expense; the same is true for Google. This means their creditors have little risk of nonrepayment.

$$\frac{\$41,733 + \$0 + \$14,030}{\$0} = \underset{\text{[not interpretable]}}{—} \text{ times}$$

Decision Insight

Bears and Bulls   A *bear market* is a declining market. The phrase comes from bear-skin jobbers who often sold the skins before the bears were caught. The term *bear* was then used to describe investors who sold shares they did not own in anticipation of a price decline. A *bull market* is a rising market. This phrase comes from the once popular sport of bear and bull baiting. The term *bull* came to mean the opposite of *bear*. ■

Profitability

We are especially interested in a company's ability to use its assets efficiently to produce profits (and positive cash flows). *Profitability* refers to a company's ability to generate an adequate return on invested capital. Return is judged by assessing earnings relative to the level and sources of financing. Profitability is also relevant to solvency. This section describes key profitability measures and their importance to financial statement analysis.

Profit Margin   A company's operating efficiency and profitability can be expressed by two components. The first is *profit margin,* which reflects a company's ability to earn net income from sales (Chapter 3 offers additional explanation). It is measured by expressing net income as a percent of sales (*sales* and *revenues* are similar terms). **Apple**'s profit margin follows.

$$\textbf{Profit margin} = \frac{\textbf{Net income}}{\textbf{Net sales}} = \frac{\$41,733}{\$156,508} = 26.7\%$$

To evaluate profit margin, we must consider the industry. For instance, an appliance company might require a profit margin between 10% and 15%; whereas a retail supermarket might require a profit margin of 1% or 2%. Both profit margin and *total asset turnover* make up the two basic components of operating efficiency. These ratios reflect on management because managers are ultimately responsible for operating efficiency. The next section explains how we use both measures to analyze return on total assets.

Return on Total Assets   *Return on total assets* is defined as follows.

$$\textbf{Return on total assets} = \frac{\textbf{Net income}}{\textbf{Average total assets}}$$

Apple's 2012 return on total assets is

$$\frac{\$41,733}{(\$116,371 + \$176,064)/2} = 28.5\%$$

Apple's 28.5% return on total assets is higher than that for many businesses and is higher than Google's 12.9%, Samsung's 14.2%, and the industry's 9% return. We also should evaluate any trend in the rate of return.

The following equation shows the important relation between profit margin, total asset turnover, and return on total assets.

$$\textbf{Profit margin} \times \textbf{Total asset turnover} = \textbf{Return on total assets}$$

or

$$\frac{\textbf{Net income}}{\textbf{Net sales}} \times \frac{\textbf{Net sales}}{\textbf{Average total assets}} = \frac{\textbf{Net income}}{\textbf{Average total assets}}$$

Both profit margin and total asset turnover contribute to overall operating efficiency, as measured by return on total assets. If we apply this formula to Apple, we get

$$26.7\% \times 1.07 = 28.5\% \text{ (with rounding)}$$

Google: 21.4% × 0.60 = 12.9%
Samsung: 11.9% × 1.19 = 14.2%
(with rounding)

This analysis shows that Apple's superior return on assets versus that of both Google and Samsung is driven by its higher profit and, in the case of Google, also by its better asset turnover.

Return on Common Stockholders' Equity   Perhaps the most important goal in operating a company is to earn net income for its owner(s). *Return on common stockholders' equity* measures a company's success in reaching this goal and is defined as follows.

$$\textbf{Return on common stockholders' equity} = \frac{\textbf{Net income} - \textbf{Preferred dividends}}{\textbf{Average common stockholders' equity}}$$

Apple's 2012 return on common stockholders' equity is computed as follows:

$$\frac{\$41,733 - \$0}{(\$76,615 + \$118,210)/2} = 42.8\%$$

Return on common equity
Google = 16.5%
Samsung = 21.4%
Industry = 15%

The denominator in this computation is the book value of common equity (noncontrolling interest is often included in common equity for this ratio). In the numerator, the dividends on cumulative preferred stock are subtracted whether they are declared or are in arrears. If preferred stock is noncumulative, its dividends are subtracted only if declared. Apple's return on common stockholders' equity (42.8%) is superior to Google's 16.5% and Samsung's 21.4%.

 Decision Insight

Wall Street   *Wall Street* is synonymous with financial markets, but its name comes from the street location of the original New York Stock Exchange. The street's name derives from stockades built by early settlers to protect New York from pirate attacks. ■

Market Prospects

Market measures are useful for analyzing corporations with publicly traded stock. These market measures use stock price, which reflects the market's (public's) expectations for the company. This includes expectations of both company return and risk—as the market perceives it.

Price-Earnings Ratio   Computation of the *price-earnings ratio* follows (Chapter 11 provides additional explanation).

$$\textbf{Price-earnings ratio} = \frac{\textbf{Market price per common share}}{\textbf{Earnings per share}}$$

Point: PE ratio can be viewed as an indicator of the market's expected growth and risk for a stock. High expected risk suggests a low PE ratio. High expected growth suggests a high PE ratio.

Predicted earnings per share for the next period is often used in the denominator of this computation. Reported earnings per share for the most recent period is also commonly used. In both cases, the ratio is used as an indicator of the future growth and risk of a company's earnings as perceived by the stock's buyers and sellers.

The market price of Apple's common stock at the start of fiscal year 2013 was $659.39. Using Apple's $44.64 basic earnings per share, we compute its price-earnings ratio as follows (some analysts compute this ratio using the median of the low and high stock price).

PE (year-end)
Google = 21.6
Samsung = 9.9

$$\frac{\$659.39}{\$44.64} = 14.8$$

Point: Some investors avoid stocks with high PE ratios under the belief they are "overpriced." Alternatively, some investors *sell these stocks short*—hoping for price declines.

Apple's price-earnings ratio is less than that for Google, but is higher than that for Samsung and the norm for this period.

Dividend Yield   *Dividend yield* is used to compare the dividend-paying performance of different investment alternatives. We compute dividend yield as follows (Chapter 11 offers additional explanation).

$$\text{Dividend yield} = \frac{\textbf{Annual cash dividends per share}}{\textbf{Market price per share}}$$

Apple's dividend yield, based on its fiscal year-end market price per share of $659.39 and its policy of $2.65 cash dividends per share, is computed as follows.

Dividend yield
Google = 0.0%
Samsung = 0.5%

$$\frac{\$2.65}{\$659.39} = 0.4\%$$

Some companies, such as Google, do not declare and pay dividends because they wish to reinvest the cash.

Summary of Ratios

Point: Corporate PE ratios and dividend yields are found in daily stock market quotations listed in *The Wall Street Journal, Investor's Business Daily,* or other publications and Web services.

Exhibit 13.16 summarizes the major financial statement analysis ratios illustrated in this chapter and throughout the book. This summary includes each ratio's title, its formula, and the purpose for which it is commonly used.

▌ **Decision** Insight

Ticker Prices   *Ticker prices* refer to a band of moving data on a monitor carrying up-to-the-minute stock prices. The phrase comes from *ticker tape,* a 1-inch-wide strip of paper spewing stock prices from a printer that ticked as it ran. Most of today's investors have never seen actual ticker tape, but the phrase survives. ▪

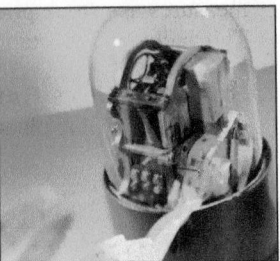

EXHIBIT 13.16

Financial Statement Analysis Ratios*

Ratio	Formula	Measure of
Liquidity and Efficiency		
Current ratio	$= \dfrac{\text{Current assets}}{\text{Current liabilities}}$	Short-term debt-paying ability
Acid-test ratio	$= \dfrac{\text{Cash + Short-term investments + Current receivables}}{\text{Current liabilities}}$	Immediate short-term debt-paying ability
Accounts receivable turnover	$= \dfrac{\text{Net sales}}{\text{Average accounts receivable, net}}$	Efficiency of collection
Inventory turnover	$= \dfrac{\text{Cost of goods sold}}{\text{Average inventory}}$	Efficiency of inventory management
Days' sales uncollected	$= \dfrac{\text{Accounts receivable, net}}{\text{Net sales}} \times 365$	Liquidity of receivables
Days' sales in inventory	$= \dfrac{\text{Ending inventory}}{\text{Cost of goods sold}} \times 365$	Liquidity of inventory
Total asset turnover	$= \dfrac{\text{Net sales}}{\text{Average total assets}}$	Efficiency of assets in producing sales
Solvency		
Debt ratio	$= \dfrac{\text{Total liabilities}}{\text{Total assets}}$	Creditor financing and leverage
Equity ratio	$= \dfrac{\text{Total equity}}{\text{Total assets}}$	Owner financing
Debt-to-equity ratio	$= \dfrac{\text{Total liabilities}}{\text{Total equity}}$	Debt versus equity financing
Times interest earned	$= \dfrac{\text{Income before interest expense and income taxes}}{\text{Interest expense}}$	Protection in meeting interest payments
Profitability		
Profit margin ratio	$= \dfrac{\text{Net income}}{\text{Net sales}}$	Net income in each sales dollar
Gross margin ratio	$= \dfrac{\text{Net sales} - \text{Cost of goods sold}}{\text{Net sales}}$	Gross margin in each sales dollar
Return on total assets	$= \dfrac{\text{Net income}}{\text{Average total assets}}$	Overall profitability of assets
Return on common stockholders' equity	$= \dfrac{\text{Net income} - \text{Preferred dividends}}{\text{Average common stockholders' equity}}$	Profitability of owner investment
Book value per common share	$= \dfrac{\text{Shareholders' equity applicable to common shares}}{\text{Number of common shares outstanding}}$	Liquidation at reported amounts
Basic earnings per share	$= \dfrac{\text{Net income} - \text{Preferred dividends}}{\text{Weighted-average common shares outstanding}}$	Net income per common share
Market Prospects		
Price-earnings ratio	$= \dfrac{\text{Market price per common share}}{\text{Earnings per share}}$	Market value relative to earnings
Dividend yield	$= \dfrac{\text{Annual cash dividends per share}}{\text{Market price per share}}$	Cash return per common share

* Additional ratios also examined in previous chapters included credit risk ratio; plant asset useful life; plant asset age; days' cash expense coverage; cash coverage of growth; cash coverage of debt; free cash flow; cash flow on total assets; and payout ratio.

NEED-TO-KNOW 13.3

P3

For each ratio listed, identify whether the change in ratio value from 2013 to 2014 is regarded as favorable or unfavorable.

Ratio	2014	2013	Ratio	2014	2013
1. Profit margin	6%	8%	4. Accounts receivable turnover	8.8	9.4
2. Debt ratio	50%	70%	5. Basic earnings per share	$2.10	$2.00
3. Gross margin	40%	36%	6. Inventory turnover	3.6	4.0

Solution

Ratio	2014	2013	Change
1. Profit margin ratio..................	6%	8%	Unfavorable
2. Debt ratio	50%	70%	Favorable
3. Gross margin ratio	40%	36%	Favorable
4. Accounts receivable turnover..........	8.8	9.4	Unfavorable
5. Basic earnings per share	$2.10	$2.00	Favorable
6. Inventory turnover	3.6	4.0	Unfavorable

Do More: QS 13-6, E 13-8, E 13-9, E 13-10, E 13-11, E 13-12, P 13-4

QC4

GLOBAL VIEW

The analysis and interpretation of financial statements is, of course, impacted by the accounting system in effect. This section discusses similarities and differences for analysis of financial statements when prepared under U.S. GAAP vis-à-vis IFRS.

Horizontal and Vertical Analyses   Horizontal and vertical analyses help eliminate many differences between U.S. GAAP and IFRS when analyzing and interpreting financial statements. Financial numbers are converted to percentages that are, in the best case scenario, consistently applied across and within periods. This enables users to effectively compare companies across reporting regimes. However, when fundamental differences in reporting regimes impact financial statements, such as with certain recognition rule differences, the user must exercise caution when drawing conclusions. Some users will reformulate one set of numbers to be more consistent with the other system to enable comparative analysis. This reformulation process is covered in advanced courses. The important point is that horizontal and vertical analyses help strip away differences between the reporting regimes, but several key differences sometimes remain and require adjustment of the numbers.

Ratio Analysis   Ratio analysis of financial statement numbers has many of the advantages and disadvantages of horizontal and vertical analyses discussed above. Importantly, ratio analysis is useful for business decisions, with some possible changes in interpretation depending on what is and what is not included in accounting measures across U.S. GAAP and IFRS. Still, we must take care in drawing inferences from a comparison of ratios across reporting regimes because what a number measures can differ across regimes. Piaggio offers the following example of its own ratio analysis applied to its financing objectives: "The object of capital management . . . , [and] consistent with others in the industry, the Company monitors capital on the basis of a total liabilities to equity ratio. This ratio is calculated as total liabilities divided by equity."

Fraud

Not Created Equal Financial regulation has several goals. Two of them are to ensure adequate accounting disclosure and to strengthen corporate governance. For disclosure purposes, companies must now provide details of related-party transactions and material off-balance-sheet agreements. This is motivated by several major frauds. For corporate governance, the CEO and CFO must now certify the fairness of financial statements and the effectiveness of internal controls. Yet, concerns remain. A study reports that 23% of management and administrative employees observed activities that posed a conflict of interest in the past year (KPMG 2009). Another 12% witnessed the falsifying or manipulating of accounting information. The bottom line: All financial statements are not of equal quality.

Understanding the purpose of financial statement analysis is crucial to the usefulness of any analysis. This understanding leads to efficiency of effort, effectiveness in application, and relevance in focus. The purpose of most financial statement analyses is to reduce uncertainty in business decisions through a rigorous and sound evaluation. A *financial statement analysis report* helps by directly addressing the building blocks of analysis and by identifying weaknesses in inference by requiring explanation: It forces us to organize our reasoning and to verify its flow and logic. A report also serves as a communication link with readers, and the writing process reinforces our judgments and vice versa. Finally, the report helps us (re)evaluate evidence and refine conclusions on key building blocks. A good analysis report usually consists of six sections:

> **A1** Summarize and report results of analysis.

1. **Executive summary**—brief focus on important analysis results and conclusions.
2. **Analysis overview**—background on the company, its industry, and its economic setting.
3. **Evidential matter**—financial statements and information used in the analysis, including ratios, trends, comparisons, statistics, and all analytical measures assembled; often organized under the building blocks of analysis.
4. **Assumptions**—identification of important assumptions regarding a company's industry and economic environment, and other important assumptions for estimates.
5. **Key factors**—list of important favorable and unfavorable factors, both quantitative and qualitative, for company performance; usually organized by areas of analysis.
6. **Inferences**—forecasts, estimates, interpretations, and conclusions drawing on all sections of the report.

We must remember that the user dictates relevance, meaning that the analysis report should include a brief table of contents to help readers focus on those areas most relevant to their decisions. All irrelevant matter must be eliminated. For example, decades-old details of obscure transactions and detailed miscues of the analysis are irrelevant. Ambiguities and qualifications to avoid responsibility or hedging inferences must be eliminated. Finally, writing is important. Mistakes in grammar and errors of fact compromise the report's credibility.

Decision Insight

Short Selling *Short selling* refers to selling stock before you buy it. Here's an example: You borrow 100 shares of Nike stock, sell them at $40 each, and receive money from their sale. You then wait. You hope that Nike's stock price falls to, say, $35 each and you can replace the borrowed stock for less than you sold it for, reaping a profit of $5 each less any transaction costs. ■

Use the following financial statements of Precision Co. to complete these requirements.

> **COMPREHENSIVE...**
>
> **NEED-TO-KNOW**

1. Prepare comparative income statements showing the percent increase or decrease for year 2013 in comparison to year 2012.
2. Prepare common-size comparative balance sheets for years 2013 and 2012.
3. Compute the following ratios as of December 31, 2013, or for the year ended December 31, 2013, and identify its building block category for financial statement analysis.
   a. Current ratio
   b. Acid-test ratio
   c. Accounts receivable turnover
   d. Days' sales uncollected
   e. Inventory turnover
   f. Debt ratio
   g. Debt-to-equity ratio
   h. Times interest earned
   i. Profit margin ratio
   j. Total asset turnover
   k. Return on total assets
   l. Return on common stockholders' equity

PRECISION COMPANY
Comparative Income Statements
For Years Ended December 31, 2013 and 2012

	2013	2012
Sales	$2,486,000	$2,075,000
Cost of goods sold	1,523,000	1,222,000
Gross profit	963,000	853,000
Operating expenses		
Advertising expense	145,000	100,000
Sales salaries expense	240,000	280,000
Office salaries expense	165,000	200,000
Insurance expense	100,000	45,000
Supplies expense	26,000	35,000
Depreciation expense	85,000	75,000
Miscellaneous expenses	17,000	15,000
Total operating expenses	778,000	750,000
Operating income	185,000	103,000
Interest expense	44,000	46,000
Income before taxes	141,000	57,000
Income taxes	47,000	19,000
Net income	$ 94,000	$ 38,000
Earnings per share	$ 0.99	$ 0.40

PRECISION COMPANY
Comparative Balance Sheets
December 31, 2013 and 2012

	2013	2012
Assets		
Current assets		
Cash	$ 79,000	$ 42,000
Short-term investments	65,000	96,000
Accounts receivable, net	120,000	100,000
Merchandise inventory	250,000	265,000
Total current assets	514,000	503,000
Plant assets		
Store equipment, net	400,000	350,000
Office equipment, net	45,000	50,000
Buildings, net	625,000	675,000
Land	100,000	100,000
Total plant assets	1,170,000	1,175,000
Total assets	$1,684,000	$1,678,000
Liabilities		
Current liabilities		
Accounts payable	$ 164,000	$ 190,000
Short-term notes payable	75,000	90,000
Taxes payable	26,000	12,000
Total current liabilities	265,000	292,000
Long-term liabilities		
Notes payable (secured by mortgage on buildings)	400,000	420,000
Total liabilities	665,000	712,000
Stockholders' Equity		
Common stock, $5 par value	475,000	475,000
Retained earnings	544,000	491,000
Total stockholders' equity	1,019,000	966,000
Total liabilities and equity	$1,684,000	$1,678,000

PLANNING THE SOLUTION

- Set up a four-column income statement; enter the 2013 and 2012 amounts in the first two columns and then enter the dollar change in the third column and the percent change from 2012 in the fourth column.
- Set up a four-column balance sheet; enter the 2013 and 2012 year-end amounts in the first two columns and then compute and enter the amount of each item as a percent of total assets.
- Compute the required ratios using the data provided. Use the average of beginning and ending amounts when appropriate (see Exhibit 13.16 for definitions).

SOLUTION TO COMPREHENSIVE NEED-TO-KNOW

1.

PRECISION COMPANY
Comparative Income Statements
For Years Ended December 31, 2013 and 2012

	2013	2012	Increase (Decrease) in 2013 Amount	Percent
Sales	$2,486,000	$2,075,000	$411,000	19.8%
Cost of goods sold	1,523,000	1,222,000	301,000	24.6
Gross profit	963,000	853,000	110,000	12.9

[continued on next page]

[continued from previous page]

Operating expenses				
Advertising expense	145,000	100,000	45,000	45.0
Sales salaries expense	240,000	280,000	(40,000)	(14.3)
Office salaries expense	165,000	200,000	(35,000)	(17.5)
Insurance expense	100,000	45,000	55,000	122.2
Supplies expense	26,000	35,000	(9,000)	(25.7)
Depreciation expense	85,000	75,000	10,000	13.3
Miscellaneous expenses	17,000	15,000	2,000	13.3
Total operating expenses	778,000	750,000	28,000	3.7
Operating income	185,000	103,000	82,000	79.6
Interest expense	44,000	46,000	(2,000)	(4.3)
Income before taxes	141,000	57,000	84,000	147.4
Income taxes	47,000	19,000	28,000	147.4
Net income	$ 94,000	$ 38,000	$ 56,000	147.4
Earnings per share	$ 0.99	$ 0.40	$ 0.59	147.5

2.

PRECISION COMPANY Common-Size Comparative Balance Sheets December 31, 2013 and 2012				
	December 31		Common-Size Percents	
	2013	2012	2013*	2012*
Assets				
Current assets				
Cash	$ 79,000	$ 42,000	4.7%	2.5%
Short-term investments	65,000	96,000	3.9	5.7
Accounts receivable, net	120,000	100,000	7.1	6.0
Merchandise inventory	250,000	265,000	14.8	15.8
Total current assets	514,000	503,000	30.5	30.0
Plant assets				
Store equipment, net	400,000	350,000	23.8	20.9
Office equipment, net	45,000	50,000	2.7	3.0
Buildings, net	625,000	675,000	37.1	40.2
Land	100,000	100,000	5.9	6.0
Total plant assets	1,170,000	1,175,000	69.5	70.0
Total assets	$1,684,000	$1,678,000	100.0	100.0
Liabilities				
Current liabilities				
Accounts payable	$ 164,000	$ 190,000	9.7%	11.3%
Short-term notes payable	75,000	90,000	4.5	5.4
Taxes payable	26,000	12,000	1.5	0.7
Total current liabilities	265,000	292,000	15.7	17.4
Long-term liabilities				
Notes payable (secured by mortgage on buildings)	400,000	420,000	23.8	25.0
Total liabilities	665,000	712,000	39.5	42.4
Stockholders' equity				
Common stock, $5 par value	475,000	475,000	28.2	28.3
Retained earnings	544,000	491,000	32.3	29.3
Total stockholders' equity	1,019,000	966,000	60.5	57.6
Total liabilities and equity	$1,684,000	$1,678,000	100.0	100.0

* Columns do not always exactly add to 100 due to rounding.

3. Ratios for 2013:

a. Current ratio: $514,000/$265,000 = 1.9:1 (liquidity and efficiency)

b. Acid-test ratio: ($79,000 + $65,000 + $120,000)/$265,000 = 1.0:1 (liquidity and efficiency)

c. Average receivables: ($120,000 + $100,000)/2 = $110,000
Accounts receivable turnover: $2,486,000/$110,000 = 22.6 times (liquidity and efficiency)

d. Days' sales uncollected: ($120,000/$2,486,000) × 365 = 17.6 days (liquidity and efficiency)

e. Average inventory: ($250,000 + $265,000)/2 = $257,500
Inventory turnover: $1,523,000/$257,500 = 5.9 times (liquidity and efficiency)

f. Debt ratio: $665,000/$1,684,000 = 39.5% (solvency)

g. Debt-to-equity ratio: $665,000/$1,019,000 = 0.65 (solvency)

h. Times interest earned: $185,000/$44,000 = 4.2 times (solvency)

i. Profit margin ratio: $94,000/$2,486,000 = 3.8% (profitability)

j. Average total assets: ($1,684,000 + $1,678,000)/2 = $1,681,000
Total asset turnover: $2,486,000/$1,681,000 = 1.48 times (liquidity and efficiency)

k. Return on total assets: $94,000/$1,681,000 = 5.6% or 3.8% × 1.48 = 5.6% (profitability)

l. Average total common equity: ($1,019,000 + $966,000)/2 = $992,500
Return on common stockholders' equity: $94,000/$992,500 = 9.5% (profitability)

APPENDIX

13A

Sustainable Income

> **A2** Explain the form and assess the content of a complete income statement.

When a company's revenue and expense transactions are from normal, continuing operations, a simple income statement is usually adequate. When a company's activities include income-related events not part of its normal, continuing operations, it must disclose information to help users understand these events and predict future performance. To meet these objectives, companies separate the income statement into continuing operations, discontinued segments, extraordinary items, comprehensive income, and earnings per share. For illustration, Exhibit 13A.1 shows such an income statement for ComUS. These separate distinctions help us measure *sustainable income,* which is the income level most likely to continue into the future. Sustainable income is commonly used in PE ratios and other market-based measures of performance.

Continuing Operations   The first major section (①) shows the revenues, expenses, and income from continuing operations. Users especially rely on this information to predict future operations. Many users view this section as the most important. Earlier chapters explained the items comprising income from continuing operations.

Discontinued Segments   A **business segment** is a part of a company's operations that serves a particular line of business or class of customers. A segment has assets, liabilities, and financial results of operations that can be distinguished from those of other parts of the company. A company's gain or loss from selling or closing down a segment is separately reported. Section ② of Exhibit 13A.1 reports both (1) income from operating the discontinued segment for the current period prior to its disposal and (2) the loss from disposing of the segment's net assets. The income tax effects of each are reported separately from the income taxes expense in section ①.

Extraordinary Items   Section ③ reports **extraordinary gains and losses,** which are those that are *both unusual* and *infrequent.* An **unusual gain or loss** is abnormal or otherwise unrelated to the company's regular activities and environment. An **infrequent gain or loss** is not expected to recur given the company's operating environment. Reporting extraordinary items in a separate category helps users predict future performance, absent the effects of extraordinary items. Items usually considered extraordinary include (1) expropriation (taking away) of property by a foreign government, (2) condemning of property by a domestic government body, (3) prohibition against using an asset by a newly enacted law, and (4) losses and gains from an unusual and infrequent calamity ("act of God"). Items *not* considered

ComUS
Income Statement
For Year Ended December 31, 2013

Net sales		$8,478,000
Operating expenses		
① { Cost of goods sold	$5,950,000	
Depreciation expense	35,000	
Other selling, general, and administrative expenses	515,000	
Interest expense	20,000	
Total operating expenses		(6,520,000)
Other gains (losses)		
Loss on plant relocation		(45,000)
Gain on sale of surplus land		72,000
Income from continuing operations before taxes		1,985,000
Income taxes expense		(595,500)
Income from continuing operations		1,389,500
Discontinued segment		
② { Income from operating Division A (net of $180,000 taxes)	420,000	
Loss on disposal of Division A (net of $66,000 tax benefit)	(154,000)	266,000
Income before extraordinary items		1,655,500
Extraordinary items		
③ { Gain on land expropriated by state (net of $85,200 taxes)	198,800	
Loss from earthquake damage (net of $270,000 tax benefit)	(630,000)	(431,200)
Net income		$1,224,300
Earnings per common share (200,000 outstanding shares)		
Income from continuing operations		$ 6.95
④ { Discontinued operations		1.33
Income before extraordinary items		8.28
Extraordinary items		(2.16)
Net income (basic earnings per share)		$ 6.12

extraordinary include (1) write-downs of inventories and write-offs of receivables, (2) gains and losses from disposing of segments, and (3) financial effects of labor strikes.

Gains and losses that are neither unusual nor infrequent are reported as part of continuing operations. Gains and losses that are *either* unusual *or* infrequent, but *not* both, are reported as part of continuing operations *but* after the normal revenues and expenses.

■ Decision Maker

Small Business Owner You own an orange grove near Jacksonville, Florida. A bad frost destroys about one-half of your oranges. You are currently preparing an income statement for a bank loan. Can you claim the loss of oranges as extraordinary? ■ [Answer—p. 605]

Earnings per Share The final section ④ of the income statement in Exhibit 13A.1 reports earnings per share for each of the three subcategories of income (continuing operations, discontinued segments, and extraordinary items) when they exist. Earnings per share is discussed in Chapter 11.

Changes in Accounting Principles The *consistency concept* directs a company to apply the same accounting principles across periods. Yet a company can change from one acceptable accounting principle (such as FIFO, LIFO, or weighted-average) to another as long as the change improves the usefulness of information in its financial statements. A footnote would describe the accounting change and why it is an improvement.

Changes in accounting principles require retrospective application to prior periods' financial statements. *Retrospective application* involves applying a different accounting principle to prior periods as if

Point: Changes in principles are sometimes required when new accounting standards are issued.

QC5

that principle had always been used. Retrospective application enhances the consistency of financial information between periods, which improves the usefulness of information, especially with comparative analyses. (Prior to 2005, the cumulative effect of changes in accounting principles was recognized in net income in the period of the change.) Accounting standards also require that *a change in depreciation, amortization, or depletion method for long-term operating assets is accounted for as a change in accounting estimate*—that is, prospectively over current and future periods. This reflects the notion that an entity should change its depreciation, amortization, or depletion method only with changes in estimated asset benefits, the pattern of benefit usage, or information about those benefits.

Summary

C1 Explain the purpose and identify the building blocks of analysis. The purpose of financial statement analysis is to help users make better business decisions. Internal users want information to improve company efficiency and effectiveness in providing products and services. External users want information to make better and more informed decisions in pursuing their goals. The common goals of all users are to evaluate a company's (1) past and current performance, (2) current financial position, and (3) future performance and risk. Financial statement analysis focuses on four "building blocks" of analysis: (1) liquidity and efficiency—ability to meet short-term obligations and efficiently generate revenues; (2) solvency—ability to generate future revenues and meet long-term obligations; (3) profitability—ability to provide financial rewards sufficient to attract and retain financing; and (4) market prospects—ability to generate positive market expectations.

C2 Describe standards for comparisons in analysis. Standards for comparisons include (1) intracompany—prior performance and relations between financial items for the company under analysis; (2) competitor—one or more direct competitors of the company; (3) industry—industry statistics; and (4) guidelines (rules of thumb)—general standards developed from past experiences and personal judgments.

A1 Summarize and report results of analysis. A financial statement analysis report is often organized around the building blocks of analysis. A good report separates interpretations and conclusions of analysis from the information underlying them. An analysis report often consists of six sections: (1) executive summary, (2) analysis overview, (3) evidential matter, (4) assumptions, (5) key factors, and (6) inferences.

A2A Explain the form and assess the content of a complete income statement. An income statement has four *potential* sections: (1) continuing operations, (2) discontinued segments, (3) extraordinary items, and (4) earnings per share.

P1 Explain and apply methods of horizontal analysis. Horizontal analysis is a tool to evaluate changes in data across time. Two important tools of horizontal analysis are comparative statements and trend analysis. Comparative statements show amounts for two or more successive periods, often with changes disclosed in both absolute and percent terms. Trend analysis is used to reveal important changes occurring from one period to the next.

P2 Describe and apply methods of vertical analysis. Vertical analysis is a tool to evaluate each financial statement item or group of items in terms of a base amount. Two tools of vertical analysis are common-size statements and graphical analyses. Each item in common-size statements is expressed as a percent of a base amount. For the balance sheet, the base amount is usually total assets, and for the income statement, it is usually sales.

P3 Define and apply ratio analysis. Ratio analysis provides clues to and symptoms of underlying conditions. Ratios, properly interpreted, identify areas requiring further investigation. A ratio expresses a mathematical relation between two quantities such as a percent, rate, or proportion. Ratios can be organized into the building blocks of analysis: (1) liquidity and efficiency, (2) solvency, (3) profitability, and (4) market prospects.

Guidance Answers to Decision Maker

Auditor The *joint relation* referred to is the combined increase in sales and the decrease in expenses yielding more than a 5% increase in income. Both *individual* accounts (sales and expenses) yield percent changes within the ±5% acceptable range. However, a joint analysis suggests a different picture. For example, consider a joint analysis using the profit margin ratio. The client's profit margin is 11.46% ($206,000 − $182,400/$206,000) for the current year compared with 5.0% ($200,000 − $190,000/$200,000) for the prior year—yielding a 129% increase in profit margin! This is what concerns the partner, and it suggests expanding audit tests to verify or refute the client's figures.

Banker Your decision on the loan application is positive for at least two reasons. First, the current ratio suggests a strong ability to meet short-term obligations. Second, current assets of $160,000 and a current ratio of 4:1 imply current liabilities of $40,000 (one-fourth of current assets) and a working capital excess of $120,000. This working capital excess is 60% of the loan amount. However, if the application is for a 10-year loan, our decision is less optimistic. The current ratio and working capital suggest a good safety margin, but indications of inefficiency in operations exist. In particular, a 4:1 current ratio is more than double its key competitors' ratio. This is characteristic of inefficient asset use.

Small Business Owner The frost loss is probably not extraordinary. Jacksonville experiences enough recurring frost damage to make it difficult to argue this event is both unusual and infrequent. Still, you want to highlight the frost loss and hope the bank views this uncommon event separately from continuing operations.

Key Terms

Business segment (p. 602)
Common-size financial statement (p. 585)
Comparative financial statements (p. 580)
Efficiency (p. 578)
Equity ratio (p. 593)
Extraordinary gains and losses (p. 602)
Financial reporting (p. 579)

Financial statement analysis (p. 578)
General-purpose financial statements (p. 579)
Horizontal analysis (p. 580)
Infrequent gain or loss (p. 602)
Liquidity (p. 578)
Market prospects (p. 578)

Profitability (p. 578)
Ratio analysis (p. 580)
Solvency (p. 578)
Unusual gain or loss (p. 602)
Vertical analysis (p. 580)
Working capital (p. 589)

Multiple Choice Quiz

Answers on p. 622

mhhe.com/wildFA7e

Additional Quiz Questions are available at the book's Website.

1. A company's sales in 2012 were $300,000 and in 2013 were $351,000. Using 2012 as the base year, the sales trend percent for 2013 is:
   a. 17%
   b. 85%
   c. 100%
   d. 117%
   e. 48%

Use the following information for questions 2 through 5.

GALLOWAY COMPANY
Balance Sheet
December 31, 2013

Assets

Cash	$ 86,000
Accounts receivable	76,000
Merchandise inventory	122,000
Prepaid insurance	12,000
Long-term investments	98,000
Plant assets, net	436,000
Total assets	$830,000

Liabilities and Equity

Current liabilities	$124,000
Long-term liabilities	90,000
Common stock	300,000
Retained earnings	316,000
Total liabilities and equity	$830,000

2. What is Galloway Company's current ratio?
   a. 0.69
   b. 1.31
   c. 3.88
   d. 6.69
   e. 2.39

3. What is Galloway Company's acid-test ratio?
   a. 2.39
   b. 0.69
   c. 1.31
   d. 6.69
   e. 3.88

4. What is Galloway Company's debt ratio?
   a. 25.78%
   b. 100.00%
   c. 74.22%
   d. 137.78%
   e. 34.74%

5. What is Galloway Company's equity ratio?
   a. 25.78%
   b. 100.00%
   c. 34.74%
   d. 74.22%
   e. 137.78%

A
Superscript letter A denotes assignments based on Appendix 13A.

🔲 Icon denotes assignments that involve decision making.

Discussion Questions

1. Explain the difference between financial reporting and financial statements.

2. What is the difference between comparative financial statements and common-size comparative statements?

3. Which items are usually assigned a 100% value on (a) a common-size balance sheet and (b) a common-size income statement?

4. 🔲 What three factors would influence your evaluation as to whether a company's current ratio is good or bad?

5. 🔲 Suggest several reasons why a 2:1 current ratio might not be adequate for a particular company.

6. 🔲 Why is working capital given special attention in the process of analyzing balance sheets?

7. 🔲 What does the number of days' sales uncollected indicate?

8. 🔲 What does a relatively high accounts receivable turnover indicate about a company's short-term liquidity?

9. 🔲 Why is a company's capital structure, as measured by debt and equity ratios, important to financial statement analysts?

10. 🔲 How does inventory turnover provide information about a company's short-term liquidity?

11. 🔲 What ratios would you compute to evaluate management performance?

12. 🔲 Why would a company's return on total assets be different from its return on common stockholders' equity?

13. Where on the income statement does a company report an unusual gain not expected to occur more often than once every two years or so?

14. Refer to Apple's financial statements in Appendix A. Compute its profit margin for the years ended September 29, 2012, and September 24, 2011.   **APPLE**

15. Refer to Google's financial statements in Appendix A to compute its equity ratio as of December 31, 2012, and December 31, 2011.   **GOOGLE**

16. Refer to Samsung's financial statements in Appendix A. Compute its debt ratio as of December 31, 2012, and December 31, 2011.   **Samsung**

17. Use Samsung's financial statements in Appendix A to compute its return on total assets for fiscal year ended December 31, 2012.   **Samsung**

≡ **connect**

QUICK STUDY

QS 13-1
Financial reporting   C1

Which of the following items (a) through (i) are part of financial reporting but are *not* included as part of general-purpose financial statements? (a) balance sheet, (b) financial statement notes, (c) statement of shareholders' equity, (d) prospectus, (e) stock price information and analysis, (f) statement of cash flows, (g) management discussion and analysis of financial performance, (h) income statement, (i) company news releases.

QS 13-2
Trend percents

P1

Use the following information for Tide Corporation to determine the 2012 and 2013 trend percents for net sales using 2012 as the base year.

($ thousands)	2013	2012
Net sales	$801,810	$453,000
Cost of goods sold	392,887	134,088

QS 13-3
Common-size analysis   P2

Refer to the information in QS 13-2. Use that information for Tide Corporation to determine the 2012 and 2013 common-size percents for cost of goods sold using net sales as the base.

QS 13-4
Horizontal analysis

P1

Compute the annual dollar changes and percent changes for each of the following accounts.

	2013	2012
Short-term investments	$374,634	$234,000
Accounts receivable	97,364	101,000
Notes payable	0	88,000

Identify which standard of comparison, (*a*) intracompany, (*b*) competitor, (*c*) industry, or (*d*) guidelines, is best described by each of the following.

1. _____ Is often viewed as the best standard of comparison.

2. _____ Rules of thumb developed from past experiences.

3. _____ Provides analysis based on a company's prior performance.

4. _____ Compares a company against industry statistics.

QS 13-5
Standard of comparison C2

For each ratio listed, identify whether the change in ratio value from 2012 to 2013 is usually regarded as favorable or unfavorable.

QS 13-6
Ratio interpretation
P3

Ratio	2013	2012	Ratio	2013	2012
1. Profit margin	9%	8%	5. Accounts receivable turnover	5.5	6.7
2. Debt ratio	47%	42%	6. Basic earnings per share	$1.25	$1.10
3. Gross margin	34%	46%	7. Inventory turnover	3.6	3.4
4. Acid-test ratio	1.00	1.15	8. Dividend yield	2.0%	1.2%

The following information is available for Morgan Company and Parker Company, similar firms operating in the same industry. Write a half-page report comparing Morgan and Parker using the available information. Your discussion should include their ability to meet current obligations and to use current assets efficiently.

QS 13-7
Analysis of short-term
financial condition

A1

	Morgan			Parker		
	2014	2013	2012	2014	2013	2012
Current ratio	1.7	1.6	2.1	3.2	2.7	1.9
Acid-test ratio	1.0	1.1	1.2	2.8	2.5	1.6
Accounts receivable turnover	30.5	25.2	29.2	16.4	15.2	16.0
Merchandise inventory turnover	24.2	21.9	17.1	14.5	13.0	12.6
Working capital	$70,000	$58,000	$52,000	$131,000	$103,000	$78,000

Team Project: Assume that the two companies apply for a one-year loan from the team. Identify additional information the companies must provide before the team can make a loan decision.

A review of the notes payable files discovers that three years ago the company reported the entire $1,000 cash payment (consisting of $800 principal and $200 interest) toward an installment note payable as interest expense. This mistake had a material effect on the amount of income in that year. How should the correction be reported in the current year financial statements?

QS 13-8ᴬ
Error adjustments
A2

Answer each of the following related to international accounting and analysis.

a. Identify a limitation to using ratio analysis when examining companies reporting under different accounting systems such as IFRS versus U.S. GAAP.

b. Identify an advantage to using horizontal and vertical analyses when examining companies reporting under different currencies.

QS 13-9
International ratio analysis
C2

---

connect

Match the ratio to the building block of financial statement analysis to which it best relates.

A. Liquidity and efficiency **C.** Profitability

B. Solvency **D.** Market prospects

1. _____ Equity ratio

2. _____ Return on total assets

3. _____ Dividend yield

4. _____ Book value per common share

5. _____ Days' sales in inventory

6. _____ Accounts receivable turnover

7. _____ Debt-to-equity

8. _____ Times interest earned

9. _____ Gross margin ratio

10. _____ Acid-test ratio

EXERCISES

Exercise 13-1
Building blocks of analysis
C1

Exercise 13-2

Identifying financial ratios

C2

1. Which two ratios are key components in measuring a company's operating efficiency? Which ratio summarizes these two components?
2. What measure reflects the difference between current assets and current liabilities?
3. Which two short-term liquidity ratios measure how frequently a company collects its accounts?

Exercise 13-3

Computation and analysis of trend percents

P1

Compute trend percents for the following accounts, using 2011 as the base year (round the percents to whole numbers). State whether the situation as revealed by the trends appears to be favorable or unfavorable for each account.

	2015	2014	2013	2012	2011
Sales	$282,880	$270,800	$252,600	$234,560	$150,000
Cost of goods sold	128,200	122,080	115,280	106,440	67,000
Accounts receivable	18,100	17,300	16,400	15,200	9,000

Exercise 13-4

Determination of income effects from common-size and trend percents

P1 P2

Common-size and trend percents for Rustynail Company's sales, cost of goods sold, and expenses follow. Determine whether net income increased, decreased, or remained unchanged in this three-year period.

	Common-Size Percents			Trend Percents		
	2014	2013	2012	2014	2013	2012
Sales	100.0%	100.0%	100.0%	105.4%	104.2%	100.0%
Cost of goods sold	63.4	61.9	59.1	113.1	109.1	100.0
Total expenses	15.3	14.8	15.1	106.8	102.1	100.0

Exercise 13-5

Common-size percent computation and interpretation

P2

Express the following comparative income statements in common-size percents and assess whether or not this company's situation has improved in the most recent year (round the percents to one decimal).

GOMEZ CORPORATION Comparative Income Statements For Years Ended December 31, 2013 and 2012		
	2013	2012
Sales	$740,000	$625,000
Cost of goods sold	560,300	290,800
Gross profit	179,700	334,200
Operating expenses	128,200	218,500
Net income	$ 51,500	$115,700

Exercise 13-6

Analysis of efficiency and financial leverage

A1

Roak Company and Clay Company are similar firms that operate in the same industry. Clay began operations in 2013 and Roak in 2010. In 2015, both companies pay 7% interest on their debt to creditors. The following additional information is available.

	Roak Company			Clay Company		
	2015	2014	2013	2015	2014	2013
Total asset turnover	3.1	2.8	3.0	1.7	1.5	1.1
Return on total assets	9.0%	9.6%	8.8%	5.9%	5.6%	5.3%
Profit margin ratio	2.4%	2.5%	2.3%	2.8%	3.0%	2.9%
Sales	$410,000	$380,000	$396,000	$210,000	$170,000	$110,000

Write a half-page report comparing Roak and Clay using the available information. Your analysis should include their ability to use assets efficiently to produce profits. Also comment on their success in employing financial leverage in 2015.

Simon Company's year-end balance sheets follow. Express the balance sheets in common-size percents. Round amounts to the nearest one-tenth of a percent. Analyze and comment on the results.

Exercise 13-7

Common-size percents

P2

At December 31	2014	2013	2012
Assets			
Cash	$ 31,800	$ 35,625	$ 37,800
Accounts receivable, net	89,500	62,500	50,200
Merchandise inventory	112,500	82,500	54,000
Prepaid expenses	10,700	9,375	5,000
Plant assets, net	278,500	255,000	230,500
Total assets	$523,000	$445,000	$377,500
Liabilities and Equity			
Accounts payable	$129,900	$ 75,250	$ 51,250
Long-term notes payable secured by			
mortgages on plant assets	98,500	101,500	83,500
Common stock, $10 par value	163,500	163,500	163,500
Retained earnings	131,100	104,750	79,250
Total liabilities and equity	$523,000	$445,000	$377,500

Refer to Simon Company's balance sheets in Exercise 13-7. Analyze its year-end short-term liquidity position at the end of 2014, 2013, and 2012 by computing (1) the current ratio and (2) the acid-test ratio. Comment on the ratio results. (Round ratio amounts to two decimals.)

Exercise 13-8

Liquidity analysis

P3

Refer to the Simon Company information in Exercise 13-7. The company's income statements for the years ended December 31, 2014 and 2013, follow. Assume that all sales are on credit and then compute: (1) days' sales uncollected, (2) accounts receivable turnover, (3) inventory turnover, and (4) days' sales in inventory. Comment on the changes in the ratios from 2013 to 2014. (Round amounts to one decimal.)

Exercise 13-9

Liquidity analysis and interpretation

P3

For Year Ended December 31		2014		2013
Sales		$673,500		$532,000
Cost of goods sold	$411,225		$345,500	
Other operating expenses	209,550		134,980	
Interest expense	12,100		13,300	
Income taxes	9,525		8,845	
Total costs and expenses		642,400		502,625
Net income		$ 31,100		$ 29,375
Earnings per share..............		$ 1.90		$ 1.80

Refer to the Simon Company information in Exercises 13-7 and 13-9. Compare the company's long-term risk and capital structure positions at the end of 2014 and 2013 by computing these ratios: (1) debt and equity ratios—percent rounded to one decimal, (2) debt-to-equity ratio—rounded to two decimals, and (3) times interest earned—rounded to one decimal. Comment on these ratio results.

Exercise 13-10

Risk and capital structure analysis

P3

Exercise 13-11
Efficiency and
profitability analysis

P3

Refer to Simon Company's financial information in Exercises 13-7 and 13-9. Evaluate the company's efficiency and profitability by computing the following for 2014 and 2013: (1) profit margin ratio—percent rounded to one decimal, (2) total asset turnover—rounded to one decimal, and (3) return on total assets—percent rounded to one decimal. Comment on these ratio results.

Exercise 13-12
Profitability analysis

P3

Refer to Simon Company's financial information in Exercises 13-7 and 13-9. Additional information about the company follows. To help evaluate the company's profitability, compute and interpret the following ratios for 2014 and 2013: (1) return on common stockholders' equity—percent rounded to one decimal, (2) price-earnings ratio on December 31—rounded to one decimal, and (3) dividend yield—percent rounded to one decimal.

Common stock market price, December 31, 2014.........	$30.00
Common stock market price, December 31, 2013.........	28.00
Annual cash dividends per share in 2014	0.29
Annual cash dividends per share in 2013	0.24

Exercise 13-13ᴬ
Income statement categories

A2

In 2013, Randa Merchandising, Inc., sold its interest in a chain of wholesale outlets, taking the company completely out of the wholesaling business. The company still operates its retail outlets. A listing of the major sections of an income statement follows:

A. Income (loss) from continuing operations

B. Income (loss) from operating, or gain (loss) from disposing, a discontinued segment

C. Extraordinary gain (loss)

Indicate where each of the following income-related items for this company appears on its 2013 income statement by writing the letter of the appropriate section in the blank beside each item.

Section	Item	Debit	Credit
_____	1. Net sales		$2,900,000
_____	2. Gain on state's condemnation of company property (net of tax)		230,000
_____	3. Cost of goods sold	$1,480,000	
_____	4. Income taxes expense	217,000	
_____	5. Depreciation expense	232,500	
_____	6. Gain on sale of wholesale business segment (net of tax)		775,000
_____	7. Loss from operating wholesale business segment (net of tax)	444,000	
_____	8. Salaries expense	640,000	

Exercise 13-14ᴬ
Income statement presentation

A2

Use the financial data for Randa Merchandising, Inc., in Exercise 13-13 to prepare its income statement for calendar year 2013. (Ignore the earnings per share section.)

Exercise 13-15
Ratio analysis under different currencies

P3

Nintendo Company, Ltd., reports the following financial information as of, or for the year ended, March 31, 2011. Nintendo reports its financial statements in both Japanese yen and U.S. dollars as shown (amounts in millions).

Current assets	¥1,468,706	$17,695,254
Total assets	1,634,297	19,690,330
Current liabilities	333,301	4,015,683
Net sales	1,014,345	12,221,031
Net income	77,621	935,200

1. Compute Nintendo's current ratio, net profit margin, and sales-to-total-assets using the financial information reported in (a) yen and (b) dollars. Round amounts to two decimals.

2. What can we conclude from a review of the results for part 1?

connect

Selected comparative financial statements of Korbin Company follow.

PROBLEM SET A

Problem 13-1A
Ratios, common-size statements, and trend percents

P1 P2 P3

KORBIN COMPANY Comparative Income Statements For Years Ended December 31, 2014, 2013, and 2012			
	2014	2013	2012
Sales	$555,000	$340,000	$278,000
Cost of goods sold	283,500	212,500	153,900
Gross profit	271,500	127,500	124,100
Selling expenses	102,900	46,920	50,800
Administrative expenses	50,668	29,920	22,800
Total expenses	153,568	76,840	73,600
Income before taxes	117,932	50,660	50,500
Income taxes	40,800	10,370	15,670
Net income	$ 77,132	$ 40,290	$ 34,830

KORBIN COMPANY Comparative Balance Sheets December 31, 2014, 2013, and 2012			
	2014	2013	2012
Assets			
Current assets	$ 52,390	$ 37,924	$ 51,748
Long-term investments	0	500	3,950
Plant assets, net	100,000	96,000	60,000
Total assets	$152,390	$134,424	$115,698
Liabilities and Equity			
Current liabilities	$ 22,800	$ 19,960	$ 20,300
Common stock	72,000	72,000	60,000
Other paid-in capital	9,000	9,000	6,000
Retained earnings	48,590	33,464	29,398
Total liabilities and equity	$152,390	$134,424	$115,698

Required

1. Compute each year's current ratio. (Round ratio amounts to one decimal.)

2. Express the income statement data in common-size percents. (Round percents to two decimals.)

Check   (3) 2014, Total assets trend, 131.71%

3. Express the balance sheet data in trend percents with 2012 as the base year. (Round percents to two decimals.)

Analysis Component

4. Comment on any significant relations revealed by the ratios and percents computed.

Problem 13-2A
Calculation and analysis of trend percents

A1 P1

Selected comparative financial statements of Haroun Company follow.

HAROUN COMPANY Comparative Income Statements For Years Ended December 31, 2014–2008							
($ thousands)	2014	2013	2012	2011	2010	2009	2008
Sales	$1,694	$1,496	$1,370	$1,264	$1,186	$1,110	$928
Cost of goods sold	1,246	1,032	902	802	752	710	586
Gross profit	448	464	468	462	434	400	342
Operating expenses	330	256	234	170	146	144	118
Net income	$ 118	$ 208	$ 234	$ 292	$ 288	$ 256	$224

HAROUN COMPANY Comparative Balance Sheets December 31, 2014–2008							
($ thousands)	2014	2013	2012	2011	2010	2009	2008
Assets							
Cash	$ 58	$ 78	$ 82	$ 84	$ 88	$ 86	$ 89
Accounts receivable, net	490	514	466	360	318	302	216
Merchandise inventory	1,838	1,364	1,204	1,032	936	810	615
Other current assets	36	32	14	34	28	28	9
Long-term investments	0	0	0	146	146	146	146
Plant assets, net	2,020	2,014	1,752	944	978	860	725
Total assets	$4,442	$4,002	$3,518	$2,600	$2,494	$2,232	$1,800
Liabilities and Equity							
Current liabilities	$1,220	$1,042	$ 718	$ 614	$ 546	$ 522	$ 282
Long-term liabilities	1,294	1,140	1,112	570	580	620	400
Common stock	1,000	1,000	1,000	850	850	650	650
Other paid-in capital	250	250	250	170	170	150	150
Retained earnings	678	570	438	396	348	290	318
Total liabilities and equity	$4,442	$4,002	$3,518	$2,600	$2,494	$2,232	$1,800

Required

Check   (1) 2014, Total assets trend, 246.8%

1. Compute trend percents for all components of both statements using 2008 as the base year. (Round percents to one decimal.)

Analysis Component

2. Analyze and comment on the financial statements and trend percents from part 1.

Problem 13-3A
Transactions, working capital, and liquidity ratios

P3

Plum Corporation began the month of May with $700,000 of current assets, a current ratio of 2.50:1, and an acid-test ratio of 1.10:1. During the month, it completed the following transactions (the company uses a perpetual inventory system).

May 2 Purchased $50,000 of merchandise inventory on credit.
    8 Sold merchandise inventory that cost $55,000 for $110,000 cash.
    10 Collected $20,000 cash on an account receivable.
    15 Paid $22,000 cash to settle an account payable.

17 Wrote off a $5,000 bad debt against the Allowance for Doubtful Accounts account.

22 Declared a $1 per share cash dividend on its 50,000 shares of outstanding common stock.

26 Paid the dividend declared on May 22.

27 Borrowed $100,000 cash by giving the bank a 30-day, 10% note.

28 Borrowed $80,000 cash by signing a long-term secured note.

29 Used the $180,000 cash proceeds from the notes to buy new machinery.

Check May 22: Current ratio, 2.19; Acid-test ratio, 1.11

May 29: Current ratio, 1.80; Working capital, $325,000

Required

Prepare a table showing Plum's (1) current ratio, (2) acid-test ratio, and (3) working capital, after each transaction. Round ratios to two decimals.

Selected year-end financial statements of Cabot Corporation follow. (All sales were on credit; selected balance sheet amounts at December 31, 2012, were inventory, $48,900; total assets, $189,400; common stock, $90,000; and retained earnings, $22,748.)

Problem 13-4A
Calculation of financial statement ratios

P3

CABOT CORPORATION Income Statement For Year Ended December 31, 2013	
Sales	$448,600
Cost of goods sold	297,250
Gross profit	151,350
Operating expenses	98,600
Interest expense	4,100
Income before taxes	48,650
Income taxes	19,598
Net income	$ 29,052

CABOT CORPORATION
Balance Sheet
December 31, 2013

Assets		Liabilities and Equity	
Cash	$ 10,000	Accounts payable	$ 17,500
Short-term investments	8,400	Accrued wages payable	3,200
Accounts receivable, net	29,200	Income taxes payable	3,300
Notes receivable (trade)*	4,500	Long-term note payable, secured	
Merchandise inventory	32,150	by mortgage on plant assets	63,400
Prepaid expenses	2,650	Common stock	90,000
Plant assets, net	153,300	Retained earnings	62,800
Total assets	$240,200	Total liabilities and equity	$240,200

* These are short-term notes receivable arising from customer (trade) sales.

Required

Compute the following: (1) current ratio, (2) acid-test ratio, (3) days' sales uncollected, (4) inventory turnover, (5) days' sales in inventory, (6) debt-to-equity ratio, (7) times interest earned, (8) profit margin ratio, (9) total asset turnover, (10) return on total assets, and (11) return on common stockholders' equity. Round to one decimal place, except for part 6 round to two decimals.

Check Acid-test ratio, 2.2 to 1; Inventory turnover, 7.3

Summary information from the financial statements of two companies competing in the same industry follows.

Problem 13-5A
Comparative ratio analysis

A1 P3

	Barco Company	Kyan Company		Barco Company	Kyan Company
Data from the current year-end balance sheets			**Data from the current year's income statement**		
Assets			Sales	$770,000	$880,200
Cash	$ 19,500	$ 34,000	Cost of goods sold	585,100	632,500
Accounts receivable, net	37,400	57,400	Interest expense	7,900	13,000
Current notes receivable (trade)	9,100	7,200	Income tax expense	14,800	24,300
Merchandise inventory	84,440	132,500	Net income	162,200	210,400
Prepaid expenses	5,000	6,950	Basic earnings per share	4.51	5.11
Plant assets, net	290,000	304,400			
Total assets	$445,440	$542,450			
			Beginning-of-year balance sheet data		
			Accounts receivable, net	$ 29,800	$ 54,200
Liabilities and Equity			Current notes receivable (trade)	0	0
Current liabilities	$ 61,340	$ 93,300	Merchandise inventory	55,600	107,400
Long-term notes payable	80,800	101,000	Total assets	398,000	382,500
Common stock, $5 par value	180,000	206,000	Common stock, $5 par value	180,000	206,000
Retained earnings	123,300	142,150	Retained earnings	98,300	93,600
Total liabilities and equity	$445,440	$542,450			

Required

Check (1) Kyan: Accounts receivable turnover, 14.8; Inventory turnover, 5.3

(2) Barco: Profit margin, 21.1%; PE, 16.6

1. For both companies compute the (*a*) current ratio, (*b*) acid-test ratio, (*c*) accounts (including notes) receivable turnover, (*d*) inventory turnover, (*e*) days' sales in inventory, and (*f*) days' sales uncollected. Identify the company you consider to be the better short-term credit risk and explain why. Round to one decimal place.

2. For both companies compute the (*a*) profit margin ratio, (*b*) total asset turnover, (*c*) return on total assets, and (*d*) return on common stockholders' equity. Assuming that each company paid cash dividends of $3.80 per share and each company's stock can be purchased at $75 per share, compute their (*e*) price-earnings ratios and (*f*) dividend yields. Round to one decimal place. Identify which company's stock you would recommend as the better investment and explain why.

Problem 13-6A^A

Income statement computations and format

A2

Selected account balances from the adjusted trial balance for Olinda Corporation as of its calendar year-end December 31, 2013, follow.

	Debit	Credit
a. Interest revenue..		$ 14,000
b. Depreciation expense—Equipment..............................	$ 34,000	
c. Loss on sale of equipment...	25,850	
d. Accounts payable		44,000
e. Other operating expenses...	106,400	
f. Accumulated depreciation—Equipment		71,600
g. Gain from settlement of lawsuit		44,000
h. Accumulated depreciation—Buildings.........................		174,500
i. Loss from operating a discontinued segment (pretax).....	18,250	
j. Gain on insurance recovery of tornado damage (pretax and extraordinary)........		29,120
k. Net sales..		998,500
l. Depreciation expense—Buildings	52,000	
m. Correction of overstatement of prior year's sales (pretax)........	16,000	
n. Gain on sale of discontinued segment's assets (pretax)............		34,000
o. Loss from settlement of lawsuit	23,750	
p. Income taxes expense	?	
q. Cost of goods sold	482,500	

Required

Answer each of the following questions by providing supporting computations.

1. Assume that the company's income tax rate is 30% for all items. Identify the tax effects and after-tax amounts of the four items labeled pretax.

2. What is the amount of income from continuing operations before income taxes? What is the amount of the income taxes expense? What is the amount of income from continuing operations?

3. What is the total amount of after-tax income (loss) associated with the discontinued segment?

4. What is the amount of income (loss) before the extraordinary items?

5. What is the amount of net income for the year?

Check (3) $11,025

(4) $243,425

(5) $263,809

Selected comparative financial statement information of Bluegrass Corporation follows.

PROBLEM SET B

Problem 13-1B
Ratios, common-size statements, and trend percents

P1   P2   P3

BLUEGRASS CORPORATION Comparative Income Statements For Years Ended December 31, 2014, 2013, and 2012			
	2014	**2013**	**2012**
Sales	$198,800	$166,000	$143,800
Cost of goods sold	108,890	86,175	66,200
Gross profit	89,910	79,825	77,600
Selling expenses	22,680	19,790	18,000
Administrative expenses	16,760	14,610	15,700
Total expenses	39,440	34,400	33,700
Income before taxes	50,470	45,425	43,900
Income taxes	6,050	5,910	5,300
Net income	$ 44,420	$ 39,515	$ 38,600

BLUEGRASS CORPORATION Comparative Balance Sheets December 31, 2014, 2013, and 2012			
	2014	**2013**	**2012**
Assets			
Current assets	$ 54,860	$ 32,660	$ 36,300
Long-term investments	0	1,700	10,600
Plant assets, net	112,810	113,660	79,000
Total assets	$167,670	$148,020	$125,900
Liabilities and Equity			
Current liabilities	$ 22,370	$ 19,180	$ 16,500
Common stock	46,500	46,500	37,000
Other paid-in capital	13,850	13,850	11,300
Retained earnings	84,950	68,490	61,100
Total liabilities and equity	$167,670	$148,020	$125,900

Required

1. Compute each year's current ratio. (Round ratio amounts to one decimal.)

2. Express the income statement data in common-size percents. (Round percents to two decimals.)

3. Express the balance sheet data in trend percents with 2012 as the base year. (Round percents to two decimals.)

Check (3) 2014, Total assets trend, 133.18%

Analysis Component

4. Comment on any significant relations revealed by the ratios and percents computed.

Problem 13-2B
Calculation and analysis of
trend percents

A1 P1

Selected comparative financial statements of Tripoly Company follow.

TRIPOLY COMPANY Comparative Income Statements For Years Ended December 31, 2014–2008							
($ thousands)	2014	2013	2012	2011	2010	2009	2008
Sales	$560	$610	$630	$680	$740	$770	$860
Cost of goods sold	276	290	294	314	340	350	380
Gross profit	284	320	336	366	400	420	480
Operating expenses	84	104	112	126	140	144	150
Net income	$200	$216	$224	$240	$260	$276	$330

TRIPOLY COMPANY Comparative Balance Sheets December 31, 2014–2008							
($ thousands)	2014	2013	2012	2011	2010	2009	2008
Assets							
Cash	$ 44	$ 46	$ 52	$ 54	$ 60	$ 62	$ 68
Accounts receivable, net	130	136	140	144	150	154	160
Merchandise inventory	166	172	178	180	186	190	208
Other current assets	34	34	36	38	38	40	40
Long-term investments	36	30	26	110	110	110	110
Plant assets, net	510	514	520	412	420	428	454
Total assets	$920	$932	$952	$938	$964	$984	$1,040
Liabilities and Equity							
Current liabilities	$148	$156	$186	$190	$210	$260	$280
Long-term liabilities	92	120	142	148	194	214	260
Common stock	160	160	160	160	160	160	160
Other paid-in capital	70	70	70	70	70	70	70
Retained earnings	450	426	394	370	330	280	270
Total liabilities and equity	$920	$932	$952	$938	$964	$984	$1,040

Required

Check (1) 2014, Total assets trend, 88.5%

1. Compute trend percents for all components of both statements using 2008 as the base year. (Round percents to one decimal.)

Analysis Component

2. Analyze and comment on the financial statements and trend percents from part 1.

Problem 13-3B
Transactions, working capital, and liquidity ratios P3

Koto Corporation began the month of June with $300,000 of current assets, a current ratio of 2.5:1, and an acid-test ratio of 1.4:1. During the month, it completed the following transactions (the company uses a perpetual inventory system).

Check June 1: Current ratio, 2.88; Acid-test ratio, 2.40

June	1	Sold merchandise inventory that cost $75,000 for $120,000 cash.
	3	Collected $88,000 cash on an account receivable.
	5	Purchased $150,000 of merchandise inventory on credit.
	7	Borrowed $100,000 cash by giving the bank a 60-day, 10% note.
	10	Borrowed $120,000 cash by signing a long-term secured note.
	12	Purchased machinery for $275,000 cash.
	15	Declared a $1 per share cash dividend on its 80,000 shares of outstanding common stock.
	19	Wrote off a $5,000 bad debt against the Allowance for Doubtful Accounts account.
	22	Paid $12,000 cash to settle an account payable.
	30	Paid the dividend declared on June 15.

June 30: Working capital, $(10,000); Current ratio, 0.97

Required

Prepare a table showing the company's (1) current ratio, (2) acid-test ratio, and (3) working capital after each transaction. Round ratios to two decimals.

Selected year-end financial statements of Overton Corporation follow. (All sales were on credit; selected balance sheet amounts at December 31, 2012, were inventory, $17,400; total assets, $94,900; common stock, $35,500; and retained earnings, $18,800.)

Problem 13-4B

Calculation of financial statement ratios

P3

OVERTON CORPORATION
Income Statement
For Year Ended December 31, 2013

Sales	$315,500
Cost of goods sold	236,100
Gross profit	79,400
Operating expenses	49,200
Interest expense	2,200
Income before taxes	28,000
Income taxes	4,200
Net income	$ 23,800

OVERTON CORPORATION
Balance Sheet
December 31, 2013

Assets		Liabilities and Equity	
Cash	$ 6,100	Accounts payable	$ 11,500
Short-term investments	6,900	Accrued wages payable	3,300
Accounts receivable, net	12,100	Income taxes payable	2,600
Notes receivable (trade)*	3,000	Long-term note payable, secured	
Merchandise inventory	13,500	by mortgage on plant assets	30,000
Prepaid expenses	2,000	Common stock, $5 par value	35,000
Plant assets, net	73,900	Retained earnings	35,100
Total assets	$117,500	Total liabilities and equity	$117,500

* These are short-term notes receivable arising from customer (trade) sales.

Required

Compute the following: (1) current ratio, (2) acid-test ratio, (3) days' sales uncollected, (4) inventory turnover, (5) days' sales in inventory, (6) debt-to-equity ratio, (7) times interest earned, (8) profit margin ratio, (9) total asset turnover, (10) return on total assets, and (11) return on common stockholders' equity. Round to one decimal place, except for part 6 round to two decimals.

Check Acid-test ratio, 1.6 to 1; Inventory turnover, 15.3

Summary information from the financial statements of two companies competing in the same industry follows.

Problem 13-5B

Comparative ratio analysis

A1 P3

	Fargo Company	Ball Company		Fargo Company	Ball Company
Data from the current year-end balance sheets			**Data from the current year's income statement**		
Assets			Sales	$393,600	$667,500
Cash	$ 20,000	$ 36,500	Cost of goods sold	290,600	480,000
Accounts receivable, net	77,100	70,500	Interest expense	5,900	12,300
Current notes receivable (trade)	11,600	9,000	Income tax expense	5,700	12,300
Merchandise inventory	86,800	82,000	Net income	33,850	61,700
Prepaid expenses	9,700	10,100	Basic earnings per share	1.27	2.19
Plant assets, net	176,900	252,300			
Total assets	$382,100	$460,400			
			Beginning-of-year balance sheet data		
Liabilities and Equity			Accounts receivable, net	$ 72,200	$ 73,300
Current liabilities	$ 90,500	$ 97,000	Current notes receivable (trade)	0	0
Long-term notes payable	93,000	93,300	Merchandise inventory	105,100	80,500
Common stock, $5 par value	133,000	141,000	Total assets	383,400	443,000
Retained earnings	65,600	129,100	Common stock, $5 par value	133,000	141,000
Total liabilities and equity	$382,100	$460,400	Retained earnings	49,100	109,700

Required

1. For both companies compute the (*a*) current ratio, (*b*) acid-test ratio, (*c*) accounts (including notes) receivable turnover, (*d*) inventory turnover, (*e*) days' sales in inventory, and (*f*) days' sales uncollected. Identify the company you consider to be the better short-term credit risk and explain why. Round to one decimal place.

2. For both companies compute the (*a*) profit margin ratio, (*b*) total asset turnover, (*c*) return on total assets, and (*d*) return on common stockholders' equity. Assuming that each company paid cash dividends of $1.50 per share and each company's stock can be purchased at $25 per share, compute their (*e*) price-earnings ratios and (*f*) dividend yields. Round to one decimal place, except for part *b* round to two decimals. Identify which company's stock you would recommend as the better investment and explain why.

Problem 13-6B[A]

Income statement computations and format

A2

Selected account balances from the adjusted trial balance for Harbor Corp. as of its calendar year-end December 31, 2013, follow.

	Debit	Credit
a. Accumulated depreciation—Buildings		$ 400,000
b. Interest revenue		20,000
c. Net sales		2,640,000
d. Income taxes expense	$?	
e. Loss on hurricane damage (pretax and extraordinary)	64,000	
f. Accumulated depreciation—Equipment		220,000
g. Other operating expenses	328,000	
h. Depreciation expense—Equipment	100,000	
i. Loss from settlement of lawsuit	36,000	
j. Gain from settlement of lawsuit		68,000
k. Loss on sale of equipment	24,000	
l. Loss from operating a discontinued segment (pretax)	120,000	
m. Depreciation expense—Buildings	156,000	
n. Correction of overstatement of prior year's expense (pretax)		48,000
o. Cost of goods sold	1,040,000	
p. Loss on sale of discontinued segment's assets (pretax)	180,000	
q. Accounts payable		132,000

Required

Answer each of the following questions by providing supporting computations.

1. Assume that the company's income tax rate is 25% for all items. Identify the tax effects and after-tax amounts of the four items labeled pretax.

2. What is the amount of income from continuing operations before income taxes? What is the amount of income taxes expense? What is the amount of income from continuing operations?

3. What is the total amount of after-tax income (loss) associated with the discontinued segment?

4. What is the amount of income (loss) before the extraordinary items?

5. What is the amount of net income for the year?

SERIAL PROBLEM

Success Systems

P3

(This serial problem began in Chapter 1 and continues through most of the book. If previous chapter segments were not completed, the serial problem can begin at this point. It is helpful, but not necessary, to use the Working Papers that accompany the book.)

SP 13 Use the following selected data from Success Systems' income statement for the three months ended March 31, 2014, and from its March 31, 2014, balance sheet to complete the requirements below: computer services revenue, $25,160; net sales (of goods), $18,693; total sales and revenue, $43,853; cost of goods sold, $14,052; net income, $18,686; quick assets, $100,205; current assets, $105,209; total assets, $129,909; current liabilities, $875; total liabilities, $875; and total equity, $129,034.

Required

1. Compute the gross margin ratio (both with and without services revenue) and net profit margin ratio (round the percent to one decimal).

2. Compute the current ratio and acid-test ratio (round to one decimal).

3. Compute the debt ratio and equity ratio (round the percent to one decimal).

4. What percent of its assets are current? What percent are long term (round the percent to one decimal)?

Beyond the Numbers

BTN 13-1 Refer to Apple's financial statements in Appendix A to answer the following.

1. Using fiscal 2010 as the base year, compute trend percents for fiscal years 2010, 2011, and 2012 for net sales, cost of sales, operating income, other income (expense) net, provision for income taxes, and net income. (Round percents to one decimal.)

2. Compute common-size percents for fiscal years 2011 and 2012 for the following categories of assets: (a) total current assets, (b) property, plant and equipment, net, and (c) goodwill plus acquired intangible assets net. (Round percents to one decimal.)

3. Comment on any notable changes across the years for the income statement trends computed in part 1 and the balance sheet percents computed in part 2.

Fast Forward

4. Access Apple's financial statements for fiscal years ending after September 29, 2012, from its Website (Apple.com) or the SEC database (www.SEC.gov). Update your work for parts 1, 2, and 3 using the new information accessed.

REPORTING IN ACTION

A1 P1 P2

APPLE

BTN 13-2 Key figures for Apple and Google follow.

($ millions)	Apple	Google
Cash and equivalents	$ 10,746	$14,778
Accounts receivable, net	10,930	7,885
Inventories	791	505
Retained earnings	101,289	48,342
Cost of sales	87,846	20,634
Revenues	156,508	50,175
Total assets	176,064	93,798

COMPARATIVE ANALYSIS

C2 P2

APPLE

GOOGLE

Required

1. Compute common-size percents for each of the companies using the data provided. (Round percents to one decimal.)

2. Which company retains a higher portion of cumulative net income in the company?

3. Which company has a higher gross margin ratio on sales?

4. Which company holds a higher percent of its total assets as inventory?

BTN 13-3 As Beacon Company controller, you are responsible for informing the board of directors about its financial activities. At the board meeting, you present the following information.

ETHICS CHALLENGE

A1

	2013	2012	2011
Sales trend percent	147.0%	135.0%	100.0%
Selling expenses to sales	10.1%	14.0%	15.6%
Sales to plant assets ratio	3.8 to 1	3.6 to 1	3.3 to 1
Current ratio	2.9 to 1	2.7 to 1	2.4 to 1
Acid-test ratio	1.1 to 1	1.4 to 1	1.5 to 1
Inventory turnover	7.8 times	9.0 times	10.2 times
Accounts receivable turnover	7.0 times	7.7 times	8.5 times
Total asset turnover	2.9 times	2.9 times	3.3 times
Return on total assets	10.4%	11.0%	13.2%
Return on stockholders' equity.........	10.7%	11.5%	14.1%
Profit margin ratio	3.6%	3.8%	4.0%

After the meeting, the company's CEO holds a press conference with analysts in which she mentions the following ratios.

	2013	2012	2011
Sales trend percent	147.0%	135.0%	100.0%
Selling expenses to sales	10.1%	14.0%	15.6%
Sales to plant assets ratio	3.8 to 1	3.6 to 1	3.3 to 1
Current ratio	2.9 to 1	2.7 to 1	2.4 to 1

Required

1. Why do you think the CEO decided to report 4 ratios instead of the 11 prepared?
2. Comment on the possible consequences of the CEO's reporting of the ratios selected.

**COMMUNICATING
IN PRACTICE**

A1   P3

BTN 13-4   Each team is to select a different industry, and each team member is to select a different company in that industry and acquire its financial statements. Use those statements to analyze the company, including at least one ratio from each of the four building blocks of analysis. When necessary, use the financial press to determine the market price of its stock. Communicate with teammates via a meeting, e-mail, or telephone to discuss how different companies compare to each other and to industry norms. The team is to prepare a single one-page memorandum reporting on its analysis and the conclusions reached.

**TAKING IT TO
THE NET**

P3

BTN 13-5   Access the February 17, 2012, filing of the December 31, 2011, 10-K report of The Hershey Company (ticker HSY) at www.SEC.gov and complete the following requirements.

Required

Compute or identify the following profitability ratios of Hershey for its years ending December 31, 2011, *and* December 31, 2010. Interpret its profitability using the results obtained for these two years.

1. Profit margin ratio (round the percent to one decimal).
2. Gross profit ratio (round the percent to one decimal).
3. Return on total assets (round the percent to one decimal). (Total assets at year-end 2009 were $3,675,031,000.)
4. Return on common stockholders' equity (round the percent to one decimal). (Total shareholders' equity at year-end 2009 was $760,339,000.)
5. Basic net income per common share (round to the nearest cent).

**TEAMWORK IN
ACTION**

P1   P2   P3

BTN 13-6   A team approach to learning financial statement analysis is often useful.

Required

1. Each team should write a description of horizontal and vertical analysis that all team members agree with and understand. Illustrate each description with an example.
2. *Each* member of the team is to select *one* of the following categories of ratio analysis. Explain what the ratios in that category measure. Choose one ratio from the category selected, present its formula, and explain what it measures.
   - **a.** Liquidity and efficiency
   - **c.** Profitability
   - **b.** Solvency
   - **d.** Market prospects
3. Each team member is to present his or her notes from part 2 to teammates. Team members are to confirm or correct other teammates' presentation.

Hint: Pairing within teams may be necessary for part 2. Use as an in-class activity or as an assignment. Consider presentations to the entire class using team rotation with transparencies.

BTN 13-7 Assume that James Gorman of Morgan Stanley (MorganStanley.com) has impressed you with the company's success and its commitment to ethical behavior. You learn of a staff opening at Morgan Stanley and decide to apply for it. Your resume is successfully screened from the thousands received and you advance to the interview process. You learn that the interview consists of analyzing the following financial facts and answering analysis questions below. (The data are taken from a small merchandiser in outdoor recreational equipment.)

ENTREPRENEURIAL DECISION
A1 P1 P2 P3

	2012	2011	2010
Sales trend percents	137.0%	125.0%	100.0%
Selling expenses to sales	9.8%	13.7%	15.3%
Sales to plant assets ratio	3.5 to 1	3.3 to 1	3.0 to 1
Current ratio	2.6 to 1	2.4 to 1	2.1 to 1
Acid-test ratio	0.8 to 1	1.1 to 1	1.2 to 1
Merchandise inventory turnover	7.5 times	8.7 times	9.9 times
Accounts receivable turnover	6.7 times	7.4 times	8.2 times
Total asset turnover	2.6 times	2.6 times	3.0 times
Return on total assets	8.8%	9.4%	11.1%
Return on equity	9.75%	11.50%	12.25%
Profit margin ratio	3.3%	3.5%	3.7%

Required

Use these data to answer each of the following questions with explanations.

1. Is it becoming easier for the company to meet its current liabilities on time and to take advantage of any available cash discounts? Explain.

2. Is the company collecting its accounts receivable more rapidly? Explain.

3. Is the company's investment in accounts receivable decreasing? Explain.

4. Is the company's investment in plant assets increasing? Explain.

5. Is the owner's investment becoming more profitable? Explain.

6. Did the dollar amount of selling expenses decrease during the three-year period? Explain.

BTN 13-8 You are to devise an investment strategy to enable you to accumulate $1,000,000 by age 65. Start by making some assumptions about your salary. Next compute the percent of your salary that you will be able to save each year. If you will receive any lump-sum monies, include those amounts in your calculations. Historically, stocks have delivered average annual returns of 10–11%. Given this history, you should probably not assume that you will earn above 10% on the money you invest. It is not necessary to specify exactly what types of assets you will buy for your investments; just assume a rate you expect to earn. Use the future value tables in Appendix B to calculate how your savings will grow. Experiment a bit with your figures to see how much less you have to save if you start at, for example, age 25 versus age 35 or 40. (For this assignment, do not include inflation in your calculations.)

HITTING THE ROAD
C1 P3

BTN 13-9 Samsung (www.Samsung.com), which is a leading manufacturer of consumer electronic products, along with Apple and Google, are competitors in the global marketplace. Key figures for Samsung follow (in KRW millions).

GLOBAL DECISION
A1

Samsung
APPLE
GOOGLE

Cash and equivalents	₩ 18,791,460
Accounts receivable, net	26,674,596
Inventories	17,747,413
Retained earnings	119,985,689
Cost of sales	126,651,931
Revenues	201,103,613
Total assets	181,071,570

Required

1. Compute common-size percents for Samsung using the data provided. (Round percents to one decimal.)
2. Compare the results with Apple and Google from BTN 13-2.

ANSWERS TO MULTIPLE CHOICE QUIZ

1. d; ($351,000/$300,000) × 100 = 117%

2. e; ($86,000 + $76,000 + $122,000 + $12,000)/$124,000 = 2.39

3. c; ($86,000 + $76,000)/$124,000 = 1.31

4. a; ($124,000 + $90,000)/$830,000 = 25.78%

5. d; ($300,000 + $316,000)/$830,000 = 74.22%

Appendix

A

Financial Statement Information

This appendix includes financial information for (1) Apple, (2) Google, and (3) Samsung. Apple says it designs, manufactures, and markets mobile communication and media devices, personal computers, and portable digital music players, and sells a variety of related software, services, peripherals, networking solutions, and third-party digital content and applications; it competes with both Google and Samsung in the United States and globally. The information in this Appendix is taken from their annual 10-K reports (or annual report for Samsung) filed with the SEC or other regulatory agency. An **annual report** is a summary of a company's financial results for the year along with its current financial condition and future plans. This report is directed to external users of financial information, but it also affects the actions and decisions of internal users.

A company often uses an annual report to showcase itself and its products. Many annual reports include photos, diagrams, and illustrations related to the company. The primary objective of annual reports, however, is the *financial section*, which communicates much information about a company, with most data drawn from the accounting information system. The layout of an annual report's financial section is fairly established and typically includes the following:

- Letter to Shareholders
- Financial History and Highlights
- Management Discussion and Analysis
- Management's Report on Financial Statements and on Internal Controls
- Report of Independent Accountants (Auditor's Report) and on Internal Controls
- Financial Statements
- Notes to Financial Statements
- List of Directors and Officers

This appendix provides the financial statements for Apple (plus selected notes), Google, and Samsung. The appendix is organized as follows:

- Apple **A-2** through **A-9**
- Google **A-10** through **A-13**
- Samsung **A-14** through **A-17**

APPLE
GOOGLE
Samsung

Many assignments at the end of each chapter refer to information in this appendix. We encourage readers to spend time with these assignments; they are especially useful in showing the relevance and diversity of financial accounting and reporting.

Special note: The SEC maintains the EDGAR (**E**lectronic **D**ata **G**athering, **A**nalysis, and **R**etrieval) database at www.sec.gov for U.S. filers. The **Form 10-K** is the annual report form for most companies. It provides electronically accessible information. The **Form 10-KSB** is the annual report form filed by small businesses. It requires slightly less information than the Form 10-K. One of these forms must be filed within 90 days after the company's fiscal year-end. (Forms 10-K405, 10-KT, 10-KT405, and 10-KSB405 are slight variations of the usual form due to certain regulations or rules.)

APPLE

CONSOLIDATED BALANCE SHEETS

(In millions, except number of shares which are reflected in thousands)

	September 29, 2012	September 24, 2011
ASSETS		
Current assets		
Cash and cash equivalents	$ 10,746	$ 9,815
Short-term marketable securities	18,383	16,137
Accounts receivable, less allowances of $98 and $53, respectively	10,930	5,369
Inventories	791	776
Deferred tax assets	2,583	2,014
Vendor non-trade receivables	7,762	6,348
Other current assets	6,458	4,529
Total current assets	57,653	44,988
Long-term marketable securities	92,122	55,618
Property, plant and equipment, net	15,452	7,777
Goodwill	1,135	896
Acquired intangible assets, net	4,224	3,536
Other assets	5,478	3,556
Total assets	$176,064	$116,371
LIABILITIES AND SHAREHOLDERS' EQUITY		
Current liabilities		
Accounts payable	$ 21,175	$ 14,632
Accrued expenses	11,414	9,247
Deferred revenue	5,953	4,091
Total current liabilities	38,542	27,970
Deferred revenue - non-current	2,648	1,686
Other non-current liabilities	16,664	10,100
Total liabilities	57,854	39,756
Commitments and contingencies		
Shareholders' equity		
Common stock, no par value; 1,800,000 shares authorized; 939,208 and 929,277 shares issued and outstanding, respectively	16,422	13,331
Retained earnings	101,289	62,841
Accumulated other comprehensive income	499	443
Total shareholders' equity	118,210	76,615
Total liabilities and shareholders' equity	$176,064	$116,371

See accompanying Notes to Consolidated Financial Statements.

CONSOLIDATED STATEMENTS OF OPERATIONS

(In millions, except number of shares which are reflected in thousands and per share amounts)

	Years ended		
	September 29, 2012	September 24, 2011	September 25, 2010
Net sales	$156,508	$108,249	$ 65,225
Cost of sales	87,846	64,431	39,541
Gross margin	68,662	43,818	25,684
Operating expenses			
Research and development	3,381	2,429	1,782
Selling, general and administrative	10,040	7,599	5,517
Total operating expenses	13,421	10,028	7,299
Operating income	55,241	33,790	18,385
Other income (expense), net	522	415	155
Income before provision for income taxes	55,763	34,205	18,540
Provision for income taxes	14,030	8,283	4,527
Net income	$ 41,733	$ 25,922	$ 14,013
Earnings per share:			
Basic	$ 44.64	$ 28.05	$ 15.41
Diluted	$ 44.15	$ 27.68	$ 15.15
Shares used in computing earnings per share:			
Basic	934,818	924,258	909,461
Diluted	945,355	936,645	924,712
Cash dividends declared per common share	$ 2.65	$ 0.00	$ 0.00

See accompanying Notes to Consolidated Financial Statements.

CONSOLIDATED STATEMENTS OF SHAREHOLDERS' EQUITY
(In millions, except number of shares which are reflected in thousands)

	Common Stock		Retained Earnings	Accumulated Other Comprehensive Income/ (Loss)	Total Share-holders' Equity
	Shares	Amount			
Balances as of September 26, 2009	899,806	$ 8,210	$ 23,353	$ 77	$ 31,640
Components of comprehensive income:					
Net income	0	0	14,013	0	14,013
Change in foreign currency translation	0	0	0	7	7
Change in unrealized gains/losses on marketable securities, net of tax	0	0	0	123	123
Change in unrecognized gains/losses on derivative instruments, net of tax	0	0	0	(253)	(253)
Total comprehensive income					13,890
Share-based compensation	0	876	0	0	876
Common stock issued under stock plans, net of shares withheld for employee taxes	16,164	703	(197)	0	506
Tax benefit from equity awards, including transfer pricing adjustments	0	879	0	0	879
Balances as of September 25, 2010	915,970	10,668	37,169	(46)	47,791
Components of comprehensive income:					
Net income	0	0	25,922	0	25,922
Change in foreign currency translation	0	0	0	(12)	(12)
Change in unrealized gains/losses on marketable securities, net of tax	0	0	0	(41)	(41)
Change in unrecognized gains/losses on derivative instruments, net of tax	0	0	0	542	542
Total comprehensive income					26,411
Share-based compensation	0	1,168	0	0	1,168
Common stock issued under stock plans, net of shares withheld for employee taxes	13,307	561	(250)	0	311
Tax benefit from equity awards, including transfer pricing adjustments	0	934	0	0	934
Balances as of September 24, 2011	929,277	13,331	62,841	443	76,615
Components of comprehensive income:					
Net income	0	0	41,733	0	41,733
Change in foreign currency translation	0	0	0	(15)	(15)
Change in unrealized gains/losses on marketable securities, net of tax	0	0	0	601	601
Change in unrecognized gains/losses on derivative instruments, net of tax	0	0	0	(530)	(530)
Total comprehensive income					41,789
Dividends and dividend equivalent rights declared	0	0	(2,523)	0	(2,523)
Share-based compensation	0	1,740	0	0	1,740
Common stock issued under stock plans, net of shares withheld for employee taxes	9,931	200	(762)	0	(562)
Tax benefit from equity awards, including transfer pricing adjustments	0	1,151	0	0	1,151
Balances as of September 29, 2012	939,208	$ 16,422	$101,289	$ 499	$118,210

See accompanying Notes to Consolidated Financial Statements.

CONSOLIDATED STATEMENTS OF CASH FLOWS
(In millions)

	Years ended		
	September 29, 2012	September 24, 2011	September 25, 2010
Cash and cash equivalents, beginning of the year	$ 9,815	$ 11,261	$ 5,263
Operating activities			
Net income	41,733	25,922	14,013
Adjustments to reconcile net income to cash generated by operating activities:			
Depreciation and amortization	3,277	1,814	1,027
Share-based compensation expense	1,740	1,168	879
Deferred income tax expense	4,405	2,868	1,440
Changes in operating assets and liabilities:			
Accounts receivable, net	(5,551)	143	(2,142)
Inventories	(15)	275	(596)
Vendor non-trade receivables	(1,414)	(1,934)	(2,718)
Other current and non-current assets	(3,162)	(1,391)	(1,610)
Accounts payable	4,467	2,515	6,307
Deferred revenue	2,824	1,654	1,217
Other current and non-current liabilities	2,552	4,495	778
Cash generated by operating activities	50,856	37,529	18,595
Investing activities			
Purchases of marketable securities	(151,232)	(102,317)	(57,793)
Proceeds from maturities of marketable securities	13,035	20,437	24,930
Proceeds from sales of marketable securities	99,770	49,416	21,788
Payments made in connection with business acquisitions, net of cash acquired	(350)	(244)	(638)
Payments for acquisition of property, plant and equipment	(8,295)	(4,260)	(2,005)
Payments for acquisition of intangible assets	(1,107)	(3,192)	(116)
Other	(48)	(259)	(20)
Cash used in investing activities	(48,227)	(40,419)	(13,854)
Financing activities			
Proceeds from issuance of common stock	665	831	912
Excess tax benefits from equity awards	1,351	1,133	751
Dividends and dividend equivalent rights paid	(2,488)	0	0
Taxes paid related to net share settlement of equity awards	(1,226)	(520)	(406)
Cash (used in)/generated by financing activities	(1,698)	1,444	1,257
Increase/(decrease) in cash and cash equivalents	931	(1,446)	5,998
Cash and cash equivalents, end of the year	$ 10,746	$ 9,815	$ 11,261
Supplemental cash flow disclosure:			
Cash paid for income taxes, net	$ 7,682	$ 3,338	$ 2,697

See accompanying Notes to Consolidated Financial Statements.

APPLE INC.
SELECTED NOTES TO CONSOLIDATED FINANCIAL STATEMENTS

Basis of Presentation and Preparation

The Company's fiscal year is the 52 or 53-week period that ends on the last Saturday of September. The Company's fiscal years 2012, 2011 and 2010 ended on September 29, 2012, September 24, 2011, and September 25, 2010, respectively. An additional week is included in the first fiscal quarter approximately every six years to realign fiscal quarters with calendar quarters. Fiscal year 2012 spanned 53 weeks, with a 14th week included in the first quarter of 2012. Fiscal years 2011 and 2010 spanned 52 weeks each. Unless otherwise stated, references to particular years or quarters refer to the Company's fiscal years ended in September and the associated quarters of those fiscal years.

Revenue Recognition

Net sales consist primarily of revenue from the sale of hardware, software, digital content and applications, peripherals, and service and support contracts. The Company recognizes revenue when persuasive evidence of an arrangement exists, delivery has occurred, the sales price is fixed or determinable, and collection is probable. Product is considered delivered to the customer once it has been shipped and title and risk of loss have been transferred. For most of the Company's product sales, these criteria are met at the time the product is shipped. For online sales to individuals, for some sales to education customers in the U.S., and for certain other sales, the Company defers revenue until the customer receives the product because the Company retains a portion of the risk of loss on these sales during transit. The Company recognizes revenue from the sale of hardware products, software bundled with hardware that is essential to the functionality of the hardware, and third-party digital content sold on the iTunes Store in accordance with general revenue recognition accounting guidance. The Company recognizes revenue in accordance with industry specific software accounting guidance for the following types of sales transactions: (i) standalone sales of software products, (ii) sales of software upgrades and (iii) sales of software bundled with hardware not essential to the functionality of the hardware.

For the sale of most third-party products, the Company recognizes revenue based on the gross amount billed to customers because the Company establishes its own pricing for such products, retains related inventory risk for physical products, is the primary obligor to the customer and assumes the credit risk for amounts billed to its customers. For third-party applications sold through the App Store and Mac App Store and certain digital content sold through the iTunes Store, the Company does not determine the selling price of the products and is not the primary obligor to the customer. Therefore, the Company accounts for such sales on a net basis by recognizing in net sales only the commission it retains from each sale. The portion of the gross amount billed to customers that is remitted by the Company to third-party app developers and certain digital content owners is not reflected in the Company's Consolidated Statements of Operations.

The Company records deferred revenue when it receives payments in advance of the delivery of products or the performance of services. This includes amounts that have been deferred for unspecified and specified software upgrade rights and non-software services that are attached to hardware and software products. The Company sells gift cards redeemable at its retail and online stores, and also sells gift cards redeemable on the iTunes Store for the purchase of digital content and software. The Company records deferred revenue upon the sale of the card, which is relieved upon redemption of the card by the customer. Revenue from AppleCare service and support contracts is deferred and recognized over the service coverage periods. AppleCare service and support contracts typically include extended phone support, repair services, web-based support resources and diagnostic tools offered under the Company's standard limited warranty.

The Company records reductions to revenue for estimated commitments related to price protection and other customer incentive programs. For transactions involving price protection, the Company recognizes revenue net of the estimated amount to be refunded. For the Company's other customer incentive programs, the estimated cost of these programs is recognized at the later of the date at which the Company has sold the product or the date at which the program is offered. The Company also records reductions to revenue for expected future product returns based on the Company's historical experience. Revenue is recorded net of taxes collected from customers that are remitted to governmental authorities, with the collected taxes recorded as current liabilities until remitted to the relevant government authority.

Revenue Recognition for Arrangements with Multiple Deliverables   For multi-element arrangements that include hardware products containing software essential to the hardware product's functionality, undelivered software elements that relate to the hardware product's essential software, and undelivered non-software services, the Company allocates revenue to all deliverables based on their relative selling prices. In such circumstances, the Company uses a hierarchy to determine the selling price to be used for allocating revenue to deliverables: (i) vendor-specific objective evidence of fair value ("VSOE"), (ii) third-party evidence of selling price ("TPE"), and (iii) best estimate of selling price ("ESP"). VSOE generally exists only when the Company sells the deliverable separately and is the price actually charged by the Company for that deliverable. ESPs reflect the Company's best estimates of what the selling prices of elements would be if they were sold regularly on a stand-alone basis. For multi-element arrangements accounted for in accordance with industry specific software accounting guidance, the Company allocates revenue to all deliverables based on the VSOE of each element, and if VSOE does not exist revenue is recognized when elements lacking VSOE are delivered.

For sales of qualifying versions of iPhone, iPad and iPod touch ("iOS devices"), Mac and Apple TV, the Company has indicated it may from time to time provide future unspecified software upgrades and features to the essential software bundled with each of these hardware products free of charge to customers. Essential software for iOS devices includes iOS and related applications and for Mac includes OS X, related applications and iLife. The Company also provides various non-software services to owners of qualifying versions of iOS devices and Mac. The Company has identified up to three deliverables regularly included in arrangements involving the sale of these devices. The first deliverable is the hardware and software essential to the functionality of the hardware device delivered at the time of sale. The second deliverable is the embedded right included with the purchase of iOS devices, Mac and Apple TV to receive on a when-and-if-available basis, future unspecified software upgrades and features relating to the product's essential software. The third deliverable is the non-software services to be provided to qualifying versions of iOS devices and Mac. The Company allocates revenue between these deliverables using the relative selling price method. Because the Company has neither VSOE nor TPE for these deliverables, the allocation of revenue is based on the Company's ESPs. Revenue allocated to the delivered hardware and the related essential software is recognized at the time of sale provided the other conditions for revenue recognition have been met. Revenue allocated to the embedded unspecified software upgrade rights and the non-software services is deferred and recognized on a straight-line basis over the estimated period the software upgrades and non-software services are expected to be provided for each of these devices, which ranges from two to four years. Cost of sales related to delivered hardware and related essential software, including estimated warranty costs, are recognized at the time of sale. Costs incurred to provide non-software services are recognized as cost of sales as incurred, and engineering and sales and marketing costs are recognized as operating expenses as incurred.

The Company's process for determining its ESP for deliverables without VSOE or TPE considers multiple factors that may vary depending upon the unique facts and circumstances related to each deliverable. The Company believes its customers would be reluctant to buy unspecified software upgrade rights for the essential software included with its qualifying hardware products. This view is primarily based on the fact that unspecified software upgrade rights do not obligate the Company to provide upgrades at a particular time or at all, and do not specify to customers which upgrades or features will be delivered. The Company also believes its customers would be unwilling to pay a significant amount for access to the non-software services because other companies offer similar services at little or no cost to users. Therefore, the Company has concluded that if it were to sell upgrade rights or access to the non-software services on a standalone basis, including those rights and services attached to iOS devices, Mac and Apple TV, the selling prices would be relatively low. Key factors considered by the Company in developing the ESPs for software upgrade rights include prices charged by the Company for similar offerings, market trends in the pricing of Apple-branded and third-party Mac and iOS compatible software, the nature of the upgrade rights (e.g., unspecified versus specified), and the relative ESP of the upgrade rights as compared to the total selling price of the product. The Company may also consider additional factors as appropriate, including the impact of other products and services provided to customers, the pricing of competitive alternatives if they exist, product-specific business objectives, and the length of time a particular version of a device has been available. When relevant, the same factors are considered by the Company in developing ESPs for offerings such as the non-software services; however, the primary consideration in developing ESPs for the non-software services is the estimated cost to provide such services, including consideration for a reasonable profit margin.

For the three years ended September 29, 2012, the Company's combined ESPs for the unspecified software upgrade rights and the rights to receive the non-software services included with its qualifying hardware devices have ranged from $5 to $25. Revenue allocated to such rights included with iOS devices and Apple TV is recognized on a straight-line basis over two years, and revenue allocated to such rights included with Mac is recognized on a straight-line basis over four years.

Shipping Costs

For all periods presented, amounts billed to customers related to shipping and handling are classified as revenue, and the Company's shipping and handling costs are included in cost of sales.

Warranty Expense

The Company generally provides for the estimated cost of hardware and software warranties at the time the related revenue is recognized. The Company assesses the adequacy of its pre-existing warranty liabilities and adjusts the amounts as necessary based on actual experience and changes in future estimates.

APPLE

Software Development Costs

Research and development costs are expensed as incurred. Development costs of computer software to be sold, leased, or otherwise marketed are subject to capitalization beginning when a product's technological feasibility has been established and ending when a product is available for general release to customers. In most instances, the Company's products are released soon after technological feasibility has been established. Costs incurred subsequent to achievement of technological feasibility were not significant, and generally software development costs were expensed as incurred during 2012, 2011 and 2010.

Advertising Costs

Advertising costs are expensed as incurred. Advertising expense was $1.0 billion, $933 million and $691 million for 2012, 2011 and 2010, respectively.

Earnings Per Share

Basic earnings per share is computed by dividing income available to common shareholders by the weighted-average number of shares of common stock outstanding during the period. Diluted earnings per share is computed by dividing income available to common shareholders by the weighted-average number of shares of common stock outstanding during the period increased to include the number of additional shares of common stock that would have been outstanding if the potentially dilutive securities had been issued.

Cash Equivalents and Marketable Securities

All highly liquid investments with maturities of three months or less at the date of purchase are classified as cash equivalents. The Company's marketable debt and equity securities have been classified and accounted for as available-for-sale. Management determines the appropriate classification of its investments at the time of purchase and reevaluates the designations at each balance sheet date. The Company classifies its marketable debt securities as either short-term or long-term based on each instrument's underlying contractual maturity date. Marketable debt securities with maturities of 12 months or less are classified as short-term and marketable debt securities with maturities greater than 12 months are classified as long-term. The Company classifies its marketable equity securities, including mutual funds, as either short-term or long-term based on the nature of each security and its availability for use in current operations. The Company's marketable debt and equity securities are carried at fair value, with the unrealized gains and losses, net of taxes, reported as a component of shareholders' equity. The cost of securities sold is based upon the specific identification method.

Allowance for Doubtful Accounts

The Company records its allowance for doubtful accounts based upon its assessment of various factors. The Company considers historical experience, the age of the accounts receivable balances, credit quality of the Company's customers, current economic conditions, and other factors that may affect customers' ability to pay.

Inventories

Inventories are stated at the lower of cost, computed using the first-in, first-out method, or market. If the cost of the inventories exceeds their market value, provisions are made currently for the difference between the cost and the market value. The Company's inventories consist primarily of components and finished goods for all periods presented.

Property, Plant and Equipment

Property, plant and equipment are stated at cost. Depreciation is computed by use of the straight-line method over the estimated useful lives of the assets, which for buildings is the lesser of 30 years or the remaining life of the underlying building; between two to five years for machinery and equipment, including product tooling and manufacturing process equipment; and the shorter of lease terms or ten years for leasehold improvements. The Company capitalizes eligible costs to acquire or develop internal-use software that are incurred subsequent to the preliminary project stage. Capitalized costs related to internal-use software are amortized using the straight-line method over the estimated useful lives of the assets, which range from three to five years. Depreciation and amortization expense on property and equipment was $2.6 billion, $1.6 billion and $815 million during 2012, 2011 and 2010, respectively.

	2012	2011
Land and buildings......................	$ 2,439	$ 2,059
Machinery, equipment and internal-use software	15,743	6,926
Office furniture and equipment	241	184
Leasehold improvements.................	3,464	2,599
Gross property, plant and equipment.......	21,887	11,768
Accumulated depreciation and amortization ..	(6,435)	(3,991)
Net property, plant and equipment	$15,452	$ 7,777

Long-Lived Assets Including Goodwill and Other Acquired Intangible Assets

The Company reviews property, plant and equipment, inventory component prepayments, and certain identifiable intangibles, excluding goodwill, for impairment. Long-lived assets are reviewed for impairment whenever events or changes in circumstances indicate the carrying amount of an asset may not be recoverable. Recoverability of these assets is measured by comparison of their carrying amounts to future undiscounted cash flows the assets are expected to generate. If property, plant and equipment, inventory component prepayments, and certain identifiable intangibles are considered to be impaired, the impairment to be recognized equals the amount by which the carrying value of the assets exceeds its fair market value. The Company did not record any significant impairments during 2012, 2011 and 2010.

The Company does not amortize goodwill and intangible assets with indefinite useful lives, rather such assets are required to be tested for impairment at least annually or sooner whenever events or changes in circumstances indicate that the assets may be impaired. The Company performs its goodwill and intangible asset impairment tests in the fourth quarter of each fiscal year. The Company did not recognize any impairment charges related to goodwill or indefinite lived intangible assets during 2012, 2011 and 2010. The Company established reporting units based on its current reporting structure. For purposes of testing goodwill for impairment, goodwill has been allocated to these reporting units to the extent it relates to each reporting unit. In 2012 and 2011, the Company's goodwill was allocated to the Americas and Europe reportable operating segments.

The Company amortizes its intangible assets with definite lives over their estimated useful lives and reviews these assets for impairment. The Company is currently amortizing its acquired intangible assets with definite lives over periods typically from three to seven years.

Fair Value Measurements

The Company applies fair value accounting for all financial assets and liabilities and non-financial assets and liabilities that are recognized or disclosed at fair value in the financial statements on a recurring basis. The Company defines fair value as the price that would be received from selling an asset or paid to transfer a liability in an orderly transaction between market participants at the measurement date. When determining the fair value measurements for assets and liabilities, which are required to be recorded at fair value, the Company considers the principal or most advantageous market in which the Company would transact and the market-based risk measurements or assumptions that market participants would use in pricing the asset or liability, such as risks inherent in valuation techniques, transfer restrictions and credit risk. Fair value is estimated

by applying the following hierarchy, which prioritizes the inputs used to measure fair value into three levels and bases the categorization within the hierarchy upon the lowest level of input that is available and significant to the fair value measurement:

Level 1—Quoted prices in active markets for identical assets or liabilities.

Level 2—Observable inputs other than quoted prices in active markets for identical assets and liabilities, quoted prices for identical or similar assets or liabilities in inactive markets, or other inputs that are observable or can be corroborated by observable market data for substantially the full term of the assets or liabilities.

Level 3—Inputs that are generally unobservable and typically reflect management's estimate of assumptions that market participants would use in pricing the asset or liability.

The Company's valuation techniques used to measure the fair value of money market funds and certain marketable equity securities were derived from quoted prices in active markets for identical assets or liabilities. The valuation techniques used to measure the fair value of all other financial instruments, all of which have counterparties with high credit ratings, were valued based on quoted market prices or model driven valuations using significant inputs derived from or corroborated by observable market data. In accordance with the fair value accounting requirements, companies may choose to measure eligible financial instruments and certain other items at fair value. The Company has not elected the fair value option for any eligible financial instruments.

Accrued Expenses

	2012	2011
Accrued warranty and related costs............	$ 1,638	$1,240
Accrued taxes..............................	1,535	1,140
Deferred margin on component sales...........	1,492	2,038
Accrued marketing and selling expenses........	910	598
Accrued compensation and employee benefits	735	590
Other current liabilities	5,104	3,641
Total accrued expenses....................	$11,414	$9,247

Non-Current Liabilities

	2012	2011
Deferred tax liabilities	$13,847	$ 8,159
Other non-current liabilities..................	2,817	1,941
Total other non-current liabilities............	$16,664	$10,100

Google Inc.
Consolidated Balance Sheets

(In millions, except share and par value amounts which are reflected in thousands, and par value per share amounts)	As of December 31, 2011	As of December 31, 2012
ASSETS		
Current assets		
Cash and cash equivalents	$ 9,983	$14,778
Marketable securities	34,643	33,310
Total cash, cash equivalents, and marketable securities (including securities loaned of $2,778 and $3,160)	44,626	48,088
Accounts receivable, net of allowance of $133 and $581	5,427	7,885
Inventories	35	505
Receivable under reverse repurchase agreements	745	700
Deferred income taxes, net	215	1,144
Prepaid revenue share, expenses and other assets	1,710	2,132
Total current assets	52,758	60,454
Prepaid revenue share, expenses and other assets, non-current	499	2,011
Non-marketable equity securities	790	1,469
Property and equipment, net	9,603	11,854
Intangible assets, net	1,578	7,473
Goodwill	7,346	10,537
Total assets	$72,574	$93,798
LIABILITIES AND STOCKHOLDERS' EQUITY		
Current liabilities		
Accounts payable	$ 588	$ 2,012
Short-term debt	1,218	2,549
Accrued compensation and benefits	1,818	2,239
Accrued expenses and other current liabilities	1,370	3,258
Accrued revenue share	1,168	1,471
Securities lending payable	2,007	1,673
Deferred revenue	547	895
Income taxes payable, net	197	240
Total current liabilities	8,913	14,337
Long-term debt	2,986	2,988
Deferred revenue, non-current	44	100
Income taxes payable, non-current	1,693	2,046
Deferred income taxes, net, non-current	287	1,872
Other long-term liabilities	506	740
Commitments and contingencies		
Stockholders' equity		
Convertible preferred stock, $0.001 par value per share, 100,000 shares authorized; no shares issued and outstanding	0	0
Class A and Class B common stock and additional paid-in capital, $0.001 par value per share: 9,000,000 shares authorized (Class A 6,000,000, Class B 3,000,000) and 12,000,000 shares authorized (Class A 9,000,000, Class B 3,000,000); 324,895 (Class A 257,553, Class B 67,342) and par value of $325 (Class A $258, Class B $67) and 329,979 (Class A 267,448, Class B 62,531) and par value of $330 (Class A $267, Class B $63) shares issued and outstanding	20,264	22,835
Class C capital stock, $0.001 par value per share, 3,000,000 shares authorized; no shares issued and outstanding	0	0
Accumulated other comprehensive income	276	538
Retained earnings	37,605	48,342
Total stockholders' equity	58,145	71,715
Total liabilities and stockholders' equity	$72,574	$93,798

See accompanying notes.

Google Inc.
Consolidated Statements of Income

(In millions, except per share amounts)	Year Ended December 31,		
	2010	2011	2012
Revenues			
Google (advertising and other)	$29,321	$37,905	$46,039
Motorola Mobile (hardware and other)	0	0	4,136
Total revenues	$29,321	$37,905	$50,175
Costs and expenses			
Cost of revenues—Google (advertising and other)[1]	$10,417	$13,188	$17,176
Cost of revenues—Motorola Mobile (hardware and other)[1]	0	0	3,458
Research and development[1]	3,762	5,162	6,793
Sales and marketing[1]	2,799	4,589	6,143
General and administrative[1]	1,962	2,724	3,845
Charge related to the resolution of Department of Justice investigation	0	500	0
Total costs and expenses	18,940	26,163	37,415
Income from operations	10,381	11,742	12,760
Interest and other income, net	415	584	626
Income from continuing operations before income taxes	10,796	12,326	13,386
Provision for income taxes	2,291	2,589	2,598
Net income from continuing operations	$ 8,505	$ 9,737	$10,788
Net loss from discontinued operations	0	0	(51)
Net income	$ 8,505	$ 9,737	$10,737
Net income (loss) per share of Class A and Class B common stock—basic:			
Continuing operations	$ 26.69	$ 30.17	$ 32.97
Discontinued operations	0.00	0.00	(0.16)
Net income per share of Class A and Class B common stock—basic	$ 26.69	$ 30.17	$ 32.81
Net income (loss) per share of Class A and Class B common stock—diluted:			
Continuing operations	$ 26.31	$ 29.76	$ 32.46
Discontinued operations	0.00	0.00	(0.15)
Net income per share of Class A and Class B common stock—diluted	$ 26.31	$ 29.76	$ 32.31

(1) Includes stock-based compensation expense as follows:

Cost of revenues—Google (advertising and other)	$ 67	$ 249	$ 359
Cost of revenues—Motorola Mobile (hardware and other)	0	0	14
Research and development	861	1,061	1,325
Sales and marketing	261	361	498
General and administrative	187	303	453
	$ 1,376	$ 1,974	$ 2,649

See accompanying notes.

Google Inc.
Consolidated Statements of Stockholders' Equity

(In millions, except for share amounts which are reflected in thousands)	Class A and Class B Common Stock and Additional Paid-In Capital		Accumulated Other Comprehensive Income	Retained Earnings	Total Stockholders' Equity
	Shares	Amount			
Balance at January 1, 2010	317,772	$15,817	$105	$20,082	$36,004
Common stock issued	5,126	1,412	0	0	1,412
Common stock repurchased	(1,597)	(82)	0	(719)	(801)
Stock-based compensation expense		1,376	0	0	1,376
Stock-based compensation tax benefits		72	0	0	72
Tax withholding related to vesting of restricted stock units		(360)	0	0	(360)
Net income		0	0	8,505	8,505
Other comprehensive income		0	33	0	33
Balance at December 31, 2010	321,301	18,235	138	27,868	46,241
Common stock issued	3,594	621	0	0	621
Stock-based compensation expense		1,974	0	0	1,974
Stock-based compensation tax benefits		60	0	0	60
Tax withholding related to vesting of restricted stock units		(626)	0	0	(626)
Net income		0	0	9,737	9,737
Other comprehensive income		0	138	0	138
Balance at December 31, 2011	324,895	20,264	276	37,605	58,145
Common stock issued	5,084	736	0	0	736
Stock-based compensation expense		2,692	0	0	2,692
Stock-based compensation tax benefits		166	0	0	166
Tax withholding related to vesting of restricted stock units		(1,023)	0	0	(1,023)
Net income		0	0	10,737	10,737
Other comprehensive income		0	262	0	262
Balance at December 31, 2012	329,979	$22,835	$538	$48,342	$71,715

See accompanying notes.

Google Inc.
Consolidated Statements of Comprehensive Income

(In millions)	Year Ended December 31,		
	2010	2011	2012
Net income	$8,505	$9,737	$10,737
Other comprehensive income:			
Change in foreign currency translation adjustment	(124)	(107)	75
Available-for-sale investments:			
Change in net unrealized gains	232	348	493
Less: reclassification adjustment for net gains included in net income	(151)	(115)	(216)
Net change (net of tax effect of $52, $54, $68)	81	233	277
Cash flow hedges:			
Change in unrealized gains	196	39	47
Less: reclassification adjustment for gains included in net income	(120)	(27)	(137)
Net change (net of tax effect of $52, $2, $53)	76	12	(90)
Other comprehensive income	33	138	262
Comprehensive income	$8,538	$9,875	$10,999

See accompanying notes.

Google Inc.
Consolidated Statements of Cash Flows

(In millions)	Year Ended December 31,		
	2010	2011	2012
Operating activities			
Net income	$ 8,505	$ 9,737	$ 10,737
Adjustments:			
Depreciation and amortization of property and equipment	1,067	1,396	1,988
Amortization of intangible and other assets	329	455	974
Stock-based compensation expense	1,376	1,974	2,692
Excess tax benefits from stock-based award activities	(94)	(86)	(188)
Deferred income taxes	9	343	(266)
Impairment of equity investments	0	110	0
Gain on divestiture of business	0	0	(188)
Other	(12)	6	(28)
Changes in assets and liabilities, net of effects of acquisitions:			
Accounts receivable	(1,129)	(1,156)	(787)
Income taxes, net	102	731	1,492
Inventories	0	(30)	301
Prepaid revenue share, expenses and other assets	(414)	(232)	(833)
Accounts payable	272	101	(499)
Accrued expenses and other liabilities	745	795	762
Accrued revenue share	214	259	299
Deferred revenue	111	162	163
Net cash provided by operating activities	11,081	14,565	16,619
Investing activities			
Purchases of property and equipment	(4,018)	(3,438)	(3,273)
Purchases of marketable securities	(43,985)	(61,672)	(33,410)
Maturities and sales of marketable securities	37,099	48,746	35,180
Investments in non-marketable equity securities	(320)	(428)	(696)
Cash collateral related to securities lending	2,361	(354)	(334)
Investments in reverse repurchase agreements	(750)	5	45
Acquisitions, net of cash acquired and proceeds received from divestiture, and purchases of intangible and other assets	(1,067)	(1,900)	(10,568)
Net cash used in investing activities	(10,680)	(19,041)	(13,056)
Financing activities			
Net proceeds (payments) from stock-based award activities	294	(5)	(287)
Excess tax benefits from stock-based award activities	94	86	188
Repurchase of common stock in connection with acquisitions	(801)	0	0
Proceeds from issuance of debt, net of costs	5,246	10,905	16,109
Repayment of debt	(1,783)	(10,179)	(14,781)
Net cash provided by financing activities	3,050	807	1,229
Effect of exchange rate changes on cash and cash equivalents	(19)	22	3
Net increase (decrease) in cash and cash equivalents	3,432	(3,647)	4,795
Cash and cash equivalents at beginning of year	10,198	13,630	9,983
Cash and cash equivalents at end of year	$ 13,630	$ 9,983	$ 14,778
Supplemental disclosures of cash flow information			
Cash paid for interest	$ 0	$ 40	$ 74
Cash paid for taxes	$ 2,175	$ 1,471	$ 2,034
Non-cash financing activity:			
Fair value of stock-based awards assumed in connection with acquisitions	$ 750	$ 0	$ 41

See accompanying notes.

CONSOLIDATED STATEMENTS OF FINANCIAL POSITION

Samsung Electronics Co., Ltd. and its subsidiaries

(In millions of Korean won, in thousands of U.S dollars)

	December 31 2012 KRW	December 31 2011 KRW	January 1 2011 KRW
Assets			
Current Assets			
Cash and cash equivalents	18,791,460	14,691,761	9,791,419
Short-term financial instruments	17,397,937	11,529,905	11,529,392
Available-for-sale financial assets	1,258,874	655,969	1,159,152
Trade and other receivables	26,674,596	24,153,028	21,308,834
Advances	1,674,428	1,436,288	1,302,428
Prepaid expenses	2,262,234	2,329,463	2,200,739
Inventories	17,747,413	15,716,715	13,364,524
Other current assets	1,462,075	988,934	746,101
Total current assets	87,269,017	71,502,063	61,402,589
Non-current assets			
Available-for-sale financial assets	5,229,175	3,223,598	3,040,206
Associates and joint ventures	8,785,489	9,204,169	8,335,290
Property, plant and equipment	68,484,743	62,043,951	52,964,594
Intangible assets	3,729,705	3,355,236	2,779,439
Deposits	814,693	791,863	655,662
Long-term prepaid expenses	3,515,479	3,454,205	3,544,572
Deferred income tax assets	2,516,080	1,783,086	1,144,068
Other non-current assets	727,189	442,092	442,383
Total assets	181,071,570	155,800,263	134,308,803
Liabilities and Equity			
Current liabilities			
Trade and other payables	16,889,350	18,509,490	16,049,800
Short-term borrowings	8,443,752	9,653,722	8,429,721
Advance received	1,517,672	1,450,733	883,585
Withholdings	966,374	1,715,070	1,052,555
Accrued expenses	9,495,156	7,823,728	7,102,427
Income tax payable	3,222,934	1,262,798	2,051,452
Current portion of long-term borrowings and debentures	999,010	30,292	1,123,934
Provisions	5,054,853	3,514,536	2,917,919
Other current liabilities	343,951	358,645	333,328
Total current liabilities	46,933,052	44,319,014	39,944,721
Non-current liabilities			
Non-current liabilities			
Long-term trade and other payables	1,165,881	1,024,804	1,072,661
Debentures	1,829,374	1,280,124	587,338
Long-term borrowings	3,623,028	3,682,472	634,381
Retirement benefit liabilities	1,729,939	1,119,188	823,486
Deferred income tax liabilities	3,429,467	2,333,442	1,618,523
Provisions	408,529	363,223	295,357
Other non-current liabilities	472,094	364,366	154,700
Total liabilities	59,591,364	54,486,633	45,131,167
Equity attributable to owners of the parent			
Preferred stock	119,467	119,467	119,467
Common stock	778,047	778,047	778,047
Share premium	4,403,893	4,403,893	4,403,893
Retained earnings	119,985,689	97,622,872	85,071,444
Other components of equity	(8,193,044)	(5,833,896)	(4,931,290)
Non-controlling interests	4,386,154	4,223,247	3,736,075
Total equity	121,480,206	101,313,630	89,177,636
Total liabilities and equity	181,071,570	155,800,263	134,308,803

The accompanying notes are an integral part of these financial statements.

CONSOLIDATED STATEMENTS OF INCOME

Samsung Electronics Co., Ltd. and its subsidiaries

(In millions of Korean won, in thousands of U.S dollars)

| | For the year ended December 31, | |
| | 2012 | 2011 |
	KRW	KRW
Revenue	201,103,613	165,001,771
Cost of sales	126,651,931	112,145,120
Gross profit	74,451,682	52,856,651
Selling, general and administrative expenses	45,402,344	37,212,360
Operating profit	29,049,338	15,644,291
Other non-operating income	1,552,989	2,251,019
Other non-operating expense	1,576,025	1,612,690
Share of profit or loss of associates and joint ventures	986,611	1,399,194
Finance income	7,836,554	7,403,525
Finance expense	7,934,450	7,893,421
Profit before income tax	29,915,017	17,191,918
Income tax expense	6,069,732	3,432,875
Profit for the year	23,845,285	13,759,043
Profit attributable to owners of the parent	23,185,375	13,382,645
Profit attributable to non-controlling interests	659,910	376,398
Earnings per share for profit attributable to the owners of the parent		
- Basic (in Korean won and US dollars)	154,020	89,229
- Diluted (in Korean won and US dollars)	153,950	89,146

The accompanying notes are an integral part of these financial statements.

CONSOLIDATED STATEMENTS OF COMPREHENSIVE INCOME

Samsung Electronics Co., Ltd. and its subsidiaries

(In millions of Korean won, in thousands of U.S dollars)

| | For the year ended December 31, | |
| | 2012 | 2011 |
	KRW	KRW
Profit for the year	23,845,285	13,759,043
Items not to be reclassified subsequently to profit or loss:		
Remeasurement effect of employee benefit, net of tax	(504,120)	(385,214)
Items to be reclassified subsequently to profit or loss :		
Changes in value of available-for-sale financial assets, net of tax	962,184	(572,028)
Share of associates and joint ventures, net of tax	(350,491)	(113,898)
Foreign currency translation, net of tax	(1,824,653)	183,655
Consolidated comprehensive income	22,128,205	12,871,558
Consolidated comprehensive income attributable to:		
Owners of the parent	21,499,343	12,439,116
Non-controlling interests	628,862	432,442

The accompanying notes are an integral part of these financial statements.

CONSOLIDATED STATEMENTS OF CHANGES IN EQUITY

Samsung Electronics Co., Ltd. and its subsidiaries

(In millions of Korean won)

2011 KRW	Preferred stock	Common stock	Share premium	Retained earnings	Other reserves	Equity attributable to owners of the parent	Non-controlling interests	Total
Balance at January 1, 2011	119,467	778,047	4,403,893	85,014,550	(4,726,398)	85,589,559	3,759,532	89,349,091
Cumulative effect of change in accounting policy	-	-	-	56,894	(204,892)	(147,998)	(23,457)	(171,455)
Revised balance at January 1, 2011	119,467	778,047	4,403,893	85,071,444	(4,931,290)	85,441,561	3,736,075	89,177,636
Profit for the year	-	-	-	13,382,645		13,382,645	376,398	13,759,043
Available-for-sale financial assets, net of tax,	-	-	-	-	(567,186)	(567,186)	(4,842)	(572,028)
Share of associates and joint ventures, net of tax	-	-	-	-	(113,898)	(113,898)	-	(113,898)
Foreign currency translation, net of tax	-	-	-	-	123,434	123,434	60,221	183,655
Remeasurement effect of employee benefit, net of tax	-	-	-	-	(385,879)	(385,879)	665	(385,214)
Total comprehensive income	-	-	-	13,382,645	(943,529)	12,439,116	432,442	12,871,558
Dividends	-	-	-	(824,478)	-	(824,478)	(156,388)	(980,866)
Capital transaction under common control	-	-	-	-	(108,840)	(108,840)	78,155	(30,685)
Effect of business combination	-	-	-	-		-	131,564	131,564
Disposal of treasury stock	-	-	-	-	288,773	288,773	-	288,773
Stock option activities	-	-	-	-	(73,008)	(73,008)	-	(73,008)
Others	-	-	-	(6,739)	(66,002)	(72,741)	1,399	(71,342)
Total transactions with owners	-	-	-	(831,217)	40,923	(790,294)	54,730	(735,564)
Balance at December 31, 2011	119,467	778,047	4,403,893	97,622,872	(5,833,896)	97,090,383	4,223,247	101,313,630

The accompanying notes are an integral part of these consolidated financial statements.

2012 KRW	Preferred stock	Common stock	Share premium	Retained earnings	Other reserves	Equity attributable to owners of the parent	Non-controlling interests	Total
Balance at January 1, 2012	119,467	778,047	4,403,893	97,622,872	(5,833,896)	97,090,383	4,223,247	101,313,630
Profit for the year	-	-	-	23,185,375	-	23,185,375	659,910	23,845,285
Available-for-sale financial assets, net of tax	-	-	-	-	960,688	960,688	1,496	962,184
Share of associates and joint ventures, net of tax	-	-	-	-	(350,491)	(350,491)	-	(350,491)
Foreign currency translation, net of tax	-	-	-	-	(1,789,877)	(1,789,877)	(34,776)	(1,824,653)
Remeasurement effect of employee benefit, net of tax	-	-	-	-	(506,351)	(506,351)	2,231	(504,120)
Total comprehensive income	-	-	-	23,185,375	(1,686,031)	21,499,344	628,861	22,128,205
Dividends	-	-	-	(827,501)	-	(827,501)	(373,632)	(1,201,133)
Capital transaction under common control	-	-	-	-	(1,089,835)	(1,089,835)	(104,395)	(1,194,230)
Effect of business combination	-	-	-	-		-	12,844	12,844
Disposal of treasury stock	-	-	-	-	455,377	455,377	-	455,377
Stock option activities	-	-	-	-	(33,071)	(33,071)	-	(33,071)
Others	-	-	-	4,943	(5,588)	(645)	(771)	(1,416)
Total transactions with owners	-	-	-	(822,558)	(673,117)	(1,495,675)	(465,954)	(1,961,629)
Balance at December 31, 2012	119,467	778,047	4,403,893	119,985,689	(8,193,044)	117,094,052	4,386,154	121,480,206

The accompanying notes are an integral part of these consolidated financial statements.

SAMSUNG

CONSOLIDATE STATEMENTS OF CASH FLOWS

Samsung Electronics Co., Ltd. and its subsidiaries

(In millions of Korean won, in thousands of U.S dollars)

		For the year ended December 31,	
		2012	2011
		KRW	KRW
Cash flows from operating activities			
Profit for the year		23,845,285	13,759,043
Adjustments		22,759,559	16,450,629
Changes in operating assets and liabilities		(5,777,949)	(4,057,345)
Cash flows from operating activities		40,826,895	26,152,327
Interest received		789,397	755,859
Interest paid		(576,379)	(641,462)
Dividend received		1,112,940	628,585
Income tax paid		(4,180,044)	(3,977,408)
Net cash generated from operating activities		37,972,809	22,917,901
Cash flows from investing activities			
Net decrease (increase) in short-term financial instruments		(5,965,611)	75,666
Net decrease (increase) in short-term available-for-sale financial assets		(589,072)	518,479
Proceeds from disposal of long-term available-for-sale financial assets		106,208	415,096
Acquisition of long-term available-for-sale financial assets		(870,249)	(419,678)
Proceeds from disposal of associates and joint ventures		41,091	306,804
Acquisition of associates and joint ventures		(279,022)	(403,538)
Disposal of property and equipment		644,062	379,878
Purchases of property and equipment		(22,965,271)	(21,965,678)
Disposal of intangible assets		61,497	9,703
Purchases of intangible assets		(650,884)	(663,678)
Proceeds from deposits		313,043	461,454
Payment for deposits		(347,746)	(594,067)
Cash outflows from business combination		(464,279)	(522,740)
Cash inflows from disposal of business		-	925,454
Others		(355,321)	364,281
Net cash used in investing activities		(31,321,554)	(21,112,564)
Cash flows from financing activities			
Net (repayment) proceeds from shortterm borrowings		(800,579)	977,315
Disposal of treasury stock		88,473	160,827
Proceeds from long-term borrowings and debentures		1,862,256	3,925,406
Repayment of long-term borrowings and debentures		(522,899)	(1,145,167)
Payment of dividends		(1,265,137)	(874,608)
Net increase (decrease) in Non-controlling interests		(1,200,134)	363,417
Others		(26,488)	(297,461)
Net cash provided by (used in) financing activities		(1,864,508)	3,109,729
Effect of exchange rate changes on cash and cash equivalents		(687,048)	(14,724)
Net increase (decrease) in cash and cash equivalents		4,099,699	4,900,342
Cash and cash equivalents			
Beginning of the year		14,691,761	9,791,419
End of the year		18,791,460	14,691,761

The accompanying notes are an integral part of these consolidated financial statements.

Appendix

B

Applying Present and Future Values

PRESENT AND FUTURE VALUE CONCEPTS	VALUE OF A SINGLE AMOUNT	VALUE OF AN ANNUITY
C1 Time is money and the concept of interest	P1 Present value of a single amount P2 Future value of a single amount	P3 Present value of an annuity P4 Future value of an annuity

Learning Objectives

C1 Describe the earning of interest and the concepts of present and future values. (p. B-1)

P1 Apply present value concepts to a single amount by using interest tables. (p. B-2)

P2 Apply future value concepts to a single amount by using interest tables. (p. B-3)

P3 Apply present value concepts to an annuity by using interest tables. (p. B-5)

P4 Apply future value concepts to an annuity by using interest tables. (p. B-6)

PRESENT AND FUTURE VALUE CONCEPTS

The old saying "Time is money" reflects the notion that as time passes, the values of our assets and liabilities change. This change is due to *interest,* which is a borrower's payment to the owner of an asset for its use. The most common example of interest is a savings account asset. As we keep a balance of cash in the account, it earns interest that the financial institution pays us. An example of a liability is a car loan. As we carry the balance of the loan, we accumulate interest costs on it. We must ultimately repay this loan with interest.

Present and future value computations enable us to measure or estimate the interest component of holding assets or liabilities over time. The present value computation is important when we want to know the value of future-day assets *today*. The future value computation is important when we want to know the value of present-day assets *at a future date*. The first section focuses on the present value of a single amount. The second section focuses on the future value of a single amount. Then both the present and future values of a series of amounts (called an *annuity*) are defined and explained.

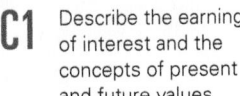

C1   Describe the earning of interest and the concepts of present and future values.

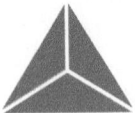

Fraud

Happy Ending A New York maintenance worker duped out of a $5 million scratch-off ticket got his winnings seven years later. Robert Miles bought the ticket in 2006 at a convenience store where the owner and his two sons convinced Miles the ticket was worth $5,000 and paid him $4,000 for it. The brothers waited until 2012 to claim the jackpot, prompting an investigation, which uncovered the fraud. The $5 million will be paid to Miles as a $250,000 annuity over 20 years or as a lump-sum payment of $3,210,000, which would yield $2,124,378 after taxes.

PRESENT VALUE OF A SINGLE AMOUNT

We graphically express the present value, called p, of a single future amount, called f, that is received or paid at a future date in Exhibit B.1.

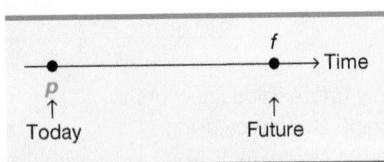

EXHIBIT B.1

Present Value of a Single Amount Diagram

The formula to compute the present value of a single amount is shown in Exhibit B.2, where p = present value; f = future value; i = rate of interest per period; and n = number of periods. (Interest is also called the *discount,* and an interest rate is also called the *discount rate.*)

$$p = \frac{f}{(1 + i)^n}$$

EXHIBIT B.2

Present Value of a Single Amount Formula

To illustrate present value concepts, assume that we need $220 one period from today. We want to know how much we must invest now, for one period, at an interest rate of 10% to provide for this $220. For this illustration, the p, or present value, is the unknown amount—the specifics are shown graphically as follows:

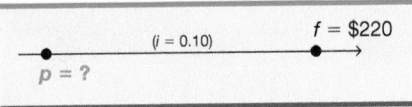

Conceptually, we know p must be less than $220. This is obvious from the answer to this question: Would we rather have $220 today or $220 at some future date? If we had $220 today, we could invest it and see it grow to something more than $220 in the future. Therefore, we would prefer the $220 today. This means that if we were promised $220 in the future, we would take less than $220 today. But how much less? To answer that question, we compute an estimate of the present value of the $220 to be received one period from now using the formula in Exhibit B.2 as follows:

$$p = \frac{f}{(1 + i)^n} = \frac{\$220}{(1 + 0.10)^1} = \$200$$

We interpret this result to say that given an interest rate of 10%, we are indifferent between $200 today or $220 at the end of one period.

We can also use this formula to compute the present value for *any number of periods.* To illustrate, consider a payment of $242 at the end of two periods at 10% interest. The present value of this $242 to be received two periods from now is computed as follows:

$$p = \frac{f}{(1 + i)^n} = \frac{\$242}{(1 + 0.10)^2} = \$200$$

I will pay your allowance at the end of the month. Do you want to wait or receive its present value today?

Together, these results tell us we are indifferent between $200 today, or $220 one period from today, or $242 two periods from today given a 10% interest rate per period.

The number of periods (n) in the present value formula does not have to be expressed in years. Any period of time such as a day, a month, a quarter, or a year can be used. Whatever period is used, the interest rate (i) must be compounded for the same period. This means that if a situation expresses n in months and i equals 12% per year, then i is transformed into interest earned per month (or 1%). In this case, interest is said to be *compounded monthly.*

A present value table helps us with present value computations. It gives us present values (factors) for a variety of both interest rates (i) and periods (n). Each present value in a present value table assumes that the future value (f) equals 1. When the future value (f) is different from 1, we simply multiply the present value (p) from the table by that future value to give us the estimate. The formula used to construct a table of present values for a single future amount of 1 is shown in Exhibit B.3.

EXHIBIT B.3

Present Value of 1 Formula

$$p = \frac{1}{(1 + i)^n}$$

P1 Apply present value concepts to a single amount by using interest tables.

This formula is identical to that in Exhibit B.2 except that f equals 1. Table B.1 at the end of this appendix is such a present value table. It is often called a **present value of 1 table**. A present value table involves three factors: p, i, and n. Knowing two of these three factors allows us to compute the third. (A fourth is f, but as already explained, we need only multiply the 1 used in the formula by f.) To illustrate the use of a present value table, consider three cases.

Case 1   (solve for p when knowing i and n). To show how we use a present value table, let's look again at how we estimate the present value of $220 (the f value) at the end of one period ($n = 1$) where the interest rate (i) is 10%. To solve this case, we go to the present value table (Table B.1) and look in the row for 1 period and in the column for 10% interest. Here we find a present value (p) of 0.9091 based on a future value of 1. This means, for instance, that $1 to be received one period from today at 10% interest is worth $0.9091 today. Since the future value in this case is not $1 but $220, we multiply the 0.9091 by $220 to get an answer of $200.

Case 2   (solve for n when knowing p and i). To illustrate, assume a $100,000 future value ($f$) that is worth $13,000 today ($p$) using an interest rate of 12% (i) but where n is unknown. In particular, we want to know how many periods (n) there are between the present value and the future value. To put this in context, it would fit a situation in which we want to retire with $100,000 but currently have only $13,000 that is earning a 12% return and we will be unable to save any additional money. How long will it be before we can retire? To answer this, we go to Table B.1 and look in the 12% interest column. Here we find a column of present values (*p*) based on a future value of 1. To use the present value table for this solution, we must divide $13,000 (*p*) by $100,000 (*f*), which equals 0.1300. This is necessary because *a present value table defines* f *equal to 1, and* p *as a fraction of 1.* We look for a value nearest to 0.1300 (*p*), which we find in the row for 18 periods (*n*). This means that the present value of $100,000 at the end of 18 periods at 12% interest is $13,000; alternatively stated, we must work 18 more years.

Case 3   (solve for *i* when knowing *p* and *n*). In this case, we have, say, a $120,000 future value (*f*) worth $60,000 today (*p*) when there are nine periods (*n*) between the present and future values, but the interest rate is unknown. As an example, suppose we want to retire with $120,000, but we have only $60,000 and we will be unable to save any additional money, yet we hope to retire in nine years. What interest rate must we earn to retire with $120,000 in nine years? To answer this, we go to the present value table (Table B.1) and look in the row for nine periods. To use the present value table, we must divide $60,000 (*p*) by $120,000 (*f*), which equals 0.5000. Recall that this step is necessary because a present value table defines *f* equal to 1 and *p* as a fraction of 1. We look for a value in the row for nine periods that is nearest to 0.5000 (*p*), which we find in the column for 8% interest (*i*). This means that the present value of $120,000 at the end of nine periods at 8% interest is $60,000 or, in our example, we must earn 8% annual interest to retire in nine years.

A company is considering an investment expected to yield $70,000 after six years. If this company demands an 8% return, how much is it willing to pay for this investment today?

NEED-TO-KNOW B.1

Solution

$70,000 × 0.6302 = $44,114 (use Table B.1, *i* = 8%, *n* = 6).

FUTURE VALUE OF A SINGLE AMOUNT

We must modify the formula for the present value of a single amount to obtain the formula for the future value of a single amount. In particular, we multiply both sides of the equation in Exhibit B.2 by $(1 + i)^n$ to get the result shown in Exhibit B.4.

$$f = p \times (1 + i)^n$$

EXHIBIT B.4

Future Value of a Single Amount Formula

The future value (*f*) is defined in terms of *p*, *i*, and *n*. We can use this formula to determine that $200 (*p*) invested for 1 (*n*) period at an interest rate of 10% (*i*) yields a future value of $220 as follows:

$$f = p \times (1 + i)^n$$
$$= \$200 \times (1 + 0.10)^1$$
$$= \$220$$

This formula can also be used to compute the future value of an amount for *any number of periods* into the future. To illustrate, assume that $200 is invested for three periods at 10%. The future value of this $200 is $266.20, computed as follows:

P2   Apply future value concep to a single amount by usi interest tables.

$$f = p \times (1 + i)^n$$
$$= \$200 \times (1 + 0.10)^3$$
$$= \$266.20$$

A future value table makes it easier for us to compute future values (f) for many different combinations of interest rates (i) and time periods (n). Each future value in a future value table assumes the present value (p) is 1. As with a present value table, if the future amount is something other than 1, we simply multiply our answer by that amount. The formula used to construct a table of future values (factors) for a single amount of 1 is in Exhibit B.5.

EXHIBIT B.5

Future Value of 1 Formula

$$f = (1 + i)^n$$

Table B.2 at the end of this appendix shows a table of future values for a current amount of 1. This type of table is called a **future value of 1 table**.

There are some important relations between Tables B.1 and B.2. In Table B.2, for the row where $n = 0$, the future value is 1 for each interest rate. This is so because no interest is earned when time does not pass. We also see that Tables B.1 and B.2 report the same information but in a different manner. In particular, one table is simply the *inverse* of the other. To illustrate this inverse relation, let's say we invest $100 for a period of five years at 12% per year. How much do we expect to have after five years? We can answer this question using Table B.2 by finding the future value (f) of 1, for five periods from now, compounded at 12%. From that table we find $f = 1.7623$. If we start with $100, the amount it accumulates to after five years is $176.23 ($100 × 1.7623). We can alternatively use Table B.1. Here we find that the present value (p) of 1, discounted five periods at 12%, is 0.5674. Recall the inverse relation between present value and future value. This means that $p = 1/f$ (or equivalently, $f = 1/p$). We can compute the future value of $100 invested for five periods at 12% as follows: $f = \$100 \times (1/0.5674) = \$176.24$ (which equals the $176.23 just computed, except for a 1 cent rounding difference).

A future value table involves three factors: f, i, and n. Knowing two of these three factors allows us to compute the third. To illustrate, consider these three possible cases.

Case 1 (solve for f when knowing i and n). Our preceding example fits this case. We found that $100 invested for five periods at 12% interest accumulates to $176.24.

Case 2 (solve for n when knowing f and i). In this case, we have, say, $2,000 ($p$) and we want to know how many periods (n) it will take to accumulate to $3,000 ($f$) at 7% ($i$) interest. To answer this, we go to the future value table (Table B.2) and look in the 7% interest column. Here we find a column of future values (f) based on a present value of 1. To use a future value table, we must divide $3,000 ($f$) by $2,000 ($p$), which equals 1.500. This is necessary because *a future value table defines* p *equal to 1, and* f *as a multiple of 1*. We look for a value nearest to 1.50 (f), which we find in the row for six periods (n). This means that $2,000 invested for six periods at 7% interest accumulates to $3,000.

Case 3 (solve for i when knowing f and n). In this case, we have, say, $2,001 ($p$), and in nine years ($n$) we want to have $4,000 ($f$). What rate of interest must we earn to accomplish this? To answer that, we go to Table B.2 and search in the row for nine periods. To use a future value table, we must divide $4,000 ($f$) by $2,001 ($p$), which equals 1.9990. Recall that this is necessary because a future value table defines p equal to 1 and f as a multiple of 1. We look for a value nearest to 1.9990 (f), which we find in the column for 8% interest (i). This means that $2,001 invested for nine periods at 8% interest accumulates to $4,000.

NEED-TO-KNOW B.2

Assume that you win a $150,000 cash sweepstakes today. You decide to deposit this cash in an account earning 8% annual interest, and you plan to quit your job when the account equals $555,000. How many years will it be before you can quit working?

Solution

$555,000/$150,000 = 3.7000; Table B.2 shows this value is not achieved until after 17 years at 8% interest.

PRESENT VALUE OF AN ANNUITY

An *annuity* is a series of equal payments occurring at equal intervals. One example is a series of three annual payments of $100 each. An *ordinary annuity* is defined as equal end-of-period payments at equal intervals. An ordinary annuity of $100 for three periods and its present value (*p*) are illustrated in Exhibit B.6.

EXHIBIT B.6

Present Value of an Ordinary Annuity Diagram

One way to compute the present value of an ordinary annuity is to find the present value of each payment using our present value formula from Exhibit B.3. We then add each of the three present values. To illustrate, let's look at three $100 payments at the end of each of the next three periods with an interest rate of 15%. Our present value computations are

P3 Apply present value concepts to an annuity by using interest tables.

$$p = \frac{\$100}{(1 + 0.15)^1} + \frac{\$100}{(1 + 0.15)^2} + \frac{\$100}{(1 + 0.15)^3} = \$228.32$$

This computation is identical to computing the present value of each payment (from Table B.1) and taking their sum or, alternatively, adding the values from Table B.1 for each of the three payments and multiplying their sum by the $100 annuity payment.

A more direct way is to use a present value of annuity table. Table B.3 at the end of this appendix is one such table. This table is called a **present value of an annuity of 1 table**. If we look at Table B.3 where $n = 3$ and $i = 15\%$, we see the present value is 2.2832. This means that the present value of an annuity of 1 for three periods, with a 15% interest rate, equals 2.2832.

A present value of an annuity formula is used to construct Table B.3. It can also be constructed by adding the amounts in a present value of 1 table. To illustrate, we use Tables B.1 and B.3 to confirm this relation for the prior example:

From Table B.1		From Table B.3	
$i = 15\%, n = 1$	0.8696		
$i = 15\%, n = 2$	0.7561		
$i = 15\%, n = 3$	0.6575		
Total	2.2832	$i = 15\%, n = 3$	2.2832

We can also use business calculators or spreadsheet programs to find the present value of an annuity.

Decision Insight

Blessed Winnings   "I don't have good luck—I'm blessed," proclaimed Andrew "Jack" Whittaker, 55, a sewage treatment contractor, after winning the largest ever undivided jackpot in a U.S. lottery. Whittaker had to choose between $315 million in 30 annual installments or $170 million in one lump sum ($112 million after-tax). ■

A company is considering an investment that would produce payments of $10,000 every six months for three years. The first payment would be received in six months. If this company requires an 8% annual return, what is the maximum amount it is willing to pay for this investment today?

NEED-TO-KNOW B.3

Solution

$10,000 × 5.2421 = $52,421 (use Table B.3, $i = 4\%, n = 6$).

FUTURE VALUE OF AN ANNUITY

The future value of an *ordinary annuity* is the accumulated value of each annuity payment with interest as of the date of the final payment. To illustrate, let's consider the earlier annuity of three annual payments of $100. Exhibit B.7 shows the point in time for the future value (f). The first payment is made two periods prior to the point when future value is determined, and the final payment occurs on the future value date.

EXHIBIT B.7

Future Value of an Ordinary Annuity Diagram

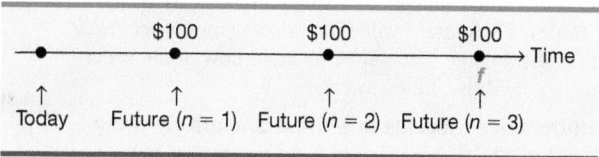

One way to compute the future value of an annuity is to use the formula to find the future value of *each* payment and add them. If we assume an interest rate of 15%, our calculation is

$$f = \$100 \times (1 + 0.15)^2 + \$100 \times (1 + 0.15)^1 + \$100 \times (1 + 0.15)^0 = \$347.25$$

This is identical to using Table B.2 and summing the future values of each payment, or adding the future values of the three payments of 1 and multiplying the sum by $100.

P4 Apply future value concepts to an annuity by using interest tables.

A more direct way is to use a table showing future values of annuities. Such a table is called a **future value of an annuity of 1 table**. Table B.4 at the end of this appendix is one such table. Note that in Table B.4 when $n = 1$, the future values equal 1 ($f = 1$) for all rates of interest. This is so because such an annuity consists of only one payment and the future value is determined on the date of that payment—no time passes between the payment and its future value. The future value of an annuity formula is used to construct Table B.4. We can also construct it by adding the amounts from a future value of 1 table. To illustrate, we use Tables B.2 and B.4 to confirm this relation for the prior example:

	From Table B.2		From Table B.4	
$i = 15\%, n = 0$	1.0000			
$i = 15\%, n = 1$	1.1500			
$i = 15\%, n = 2$	1.3225			
Total	3.4725	$i = 15\%, n = 3$	3.4725	

Note that the future value in Table B.2 is 1.0000 when $n = 0$, but the future value in Table B.4 is 1.0000 when $n = 1$. Is this a contradiction? No. When $n = 0$ in Table B.2, the future value is determined on the date when a single payment occurs. This means that no interest is earned because no time has passed, and the future value equals the payment. Table B.4 describes annuities with equal payments occurring at the end of each period. When $n = 1$, the annuity has one payment, and its future value equals 1 on the date of its final and only payment. Again, no time passes between the payment and its future value date.

NEED-TO-KNOW B.4

A company invests $45,000 per year for five years at 12% annual interest. Compute the value of this annuity investment at the end of five years.

Solution

$45,000 × 6.3528 = $285,876 (use Table B.4, $i = 12\%, n = 5$).

Summary

C1 **Describe the earning of interest and the concepts of present and future values.** Interest is payment by a borrower to the owner of an asset for its use. Present and future value computations are a way for us to estimate the interest component of holding assets or liabilities over a period of time.

P1 **Apply present value concepts to a single amount by using interest tables.** The present value of a single amount received at a future date is the amount that can be invested now at the specified interest rate to yield that future value.

P2 **Apply future value concepts to a single amount by using interest tables.** The future value of a single amount invested

at a specified rate of interest is the amount that would accumulate by the future date.

P3 **Apply present value concepts to an annuity by using interest tables.** The present value of an annuity is the amount that can be invested now at the specified interest rate to yield that series of equal periodic payments.

P4 **Apply future value concepts to an annuity by using interest tables.** The future value of an annuity invested at a specific rate of interest is the amount that would accumulate by the date of the final payment.

connect

Assume that you must make future value estimates using the *future value of 1 table* (Table B.2). Which interest rate column do you use when working with the following rates?

1. 8% annual rate, compounded quarterly

2. 12% annual rate, compounded annually

3. 6% annual rate, compounded semiannually

4. 12% annual rate, compounded monthly

QUICK STUDY

QS B-1
Identifying interest rates in tab
C1

Ken Francis is offered the possibility of investing $2,745 today and in return to receive $10,000 after 15 years. What is the annual rate of interest for this investment? (Use Table B.1.)

QS B-2
Interest rate on an investment
P1

Megan Brink is offered the possibility of investing $6,651 today at 6% interest per year in a desire to accumulate $10,000. How many years must Brink wait to accumulate $10,000? (Use Table B.1.)

QS B-3
Number of periods
of an investment
P1

Flaherty is considering an investment that, if paid for immediately, is expected to return $140,000 five years from now. If Flaherty demands a 9% return, how much is she willing to pay for this investment?

QS B-4
Present value of an amount
P1

CII, Inc., invests $630,000 in a project expected to earn a 12% annual rate of return. The earnings will be reinvested in the project each year until the entire investment is liquidated 10 years later. What will the cash proceeds be when the project is liquidated?

QS B-5
Future value of an amount
P2

Beene Distributing is considering a project that will return $150,000 annually at the end of each year for the next six years. If Beene demands an annual return of 7% and pays for the project immediately, how much is it willing to pay for the project?

QS B-6
Present value
of an annuity
P3

Claire Fitch is planning to begin an individual retirement program in which she will invest $1,500 at the end of each year. Fitch plans to retire after making 30 annual investments in the program earning a return of 10%. What is the value of the program on the date of the last payment (30 years from the present)?

QS B-7
Future value
of an annuity
P4

EXERCISES

Exercise B-1
Number of periods
of an investment   P2

Bill Thompson expects to invest $10,000 at 12% and, at the end of a certain period, receive $96,463. How many years will it be before Thompson receives the payment? (Use Table B.2.)

Exercise B-2
Interest rate on
an investment   P2

Ed Summers expects to invest $10,000 for 25 years, after which he wants to receive $108,347. What rate of interest must Summers earn? (Use Table B.2.)

Exercise B-3
Interest rate on
an investment   P3

Jones expects an immediate investment of $57,466 to return $10,000 annually for eight years, with the first payment to be received one year from now. What rate of interest must Jones earn? (Use Table B.3.)

Exercise B-4
Number of periods
of an investment   P3

Keith Riggins expects an investment of $82,014 to return $10,000 annually for several years. If Riggins earns a return of 10%, how many annual payments will he receive? (Use Table B.3.)

Exercise B-5
Interest rate on
an investment   P4

Algoe expects to invest $1,000 annually for 40 years to yield an accumulated value of $154,762 on the date of the last investment. For this to occur, what rate of interest must Algoe earn? (Use Table B.4.)

Exercise B-6
Number of periods
of an investment   P4

Kate Beckwith expects to invest $10,000 annually that will earn 8%. How many annual investments must Beckwith make to accumulate $303,243 on the date of the last investment? (Use Table B.4.)

Exercise B-7
Present value
of an annuity   P3

Sam Weber finances a new automobile by paying $6,500 cash and agreeing to make 40 monthly payments of $500 each, the first payment to be made one month after the purchase. The loan bears interest at an annual rate of 12%. What is the cost of the automobile?

Exercise B-8
Present value of bonds

P1   P3

Spiller Corp. plans to issue 10%, 15-year, $500,000 par value bonds payable that pay interest semiannually on June 30 and December 31. The bonds are dated December 31, 2013, and are issued on that date. If the market rate of interest for the bonds is 8% on the date of issue, what will be the total cash proceeds from the bond issue?

Exercise B-9
Present value of an amount   P1

McAdams Company expects to earn 10% per year on an investment that will pay $606,773 six years from now. Use Table B.1 to compute the present value of this investment. (Round the amount to the nearest dollar.)

Exercise B-10
Present value of
an amount and
of an annuity   P1   P3

Compute the amount that can be borrowed under each of the following circumstances:
1. A promise to repay $90,000 seven years from now at an interest rate of 6%.
2. An agreement made on February 1, 2013, to make three separate payments of $20,000 on February 1 of 2014, 2015, and 2016. The annual interest rate is 10%.

Exercise B-11
Present value of an amount   P1

On January 1, 2013, a company agrees to pay $20,000 in three years. If the annual interest rate is 10%, determine how much cash the company can borrow with this agreement.

Exercise B-12
Practical applications of the time
value of money

P1   P2   P3   P4

a. How much would you have to deposit today if you wanted to have $60,000 in 4 years? Annual interest rate is 9%.

b. Assume that you are saving up for a trip around the world when you graduate in 2 years. If you can earn 8% on your investments, how much would you have to deposit today to have $15,000 when you graduate?

c. Would you rather have $463 now or $1,000 ten years from now? Assume that you can earn 9% on your investments.

d. Assume that a college parking sticker today costs $90. If the cost of parking is increasing at the rate of 5% per year, how much will the college parking sticker cost in 8 years?

e. Assume that the average price of a new home is $158,500. If new homes are increasing at a rate of 10% per year, how much will a new home cost in 8 years?

f. An investment will pay you $10,000 in 10 years, and it will also pay you $400 at the end of *each* of the next 10 years (years 1 thru 10). If the annual interest rate is 6%, how much would you be willing to pay today for this type of investment?

g. A college student is reported in the newspaper as having won $10,000,000 in the Kansas State Lottery. However, as is often the custom with lotteries, she does *not* actually receive the entire $10 million now. Instead she will receive $500,000 at the end of the year for *each* of the next 20 years. If the annual interest rate is 6%, what is the present value (today's amount) that she won? (Ignore taxes.)

C&H Ski Club recently borrowed money and agrees to pay it back with a series of six annual payments of $5,000 each. C&H subsequently borrows more money and agrees to pay it back with a series of four annual payments of $7,500 each. The annual interest rate for both loans is 6%.

1. Use Table B.1 to find the present value of these two separate annuities. (Round amounts to the nearest dollar.)

2. Use Table B.3 to find the present value of these two separate annuities. (Round amounts to the nearest dollar.)

Exercise B-13
Present values of annuities
P3

Otto Co. borrows money on April 30, 2013, by promising to make four payments of $13,000 each on November 1, 2013; May 1, 2014; November 1, 2014; and May 1, 2015.

1. How much money is Otto able to borrow if the interest rate is 8%, compounded semiannually?

2. How much money is Otto able to borrow if the interest rate is 12%, compounded semiannually?

3. How much money is Otto able to borrow if the interest rate is 16%, compounded semiannually?

Exercise B-14
Present value with semiannual compounding
C1 P3

Mark Welsch deposits $7,200 in an account that earns interest at an annual rate of 8%, compounded quarterly. The $7,200 plus earned interest must remain in the account 10 years before it can be withdrawn. How much money will be in the account at the end of 10 years?

Exercise B-15
Future value of an amount   P2

Kelly Malone plans to have $50 withheld from her monthly paycheck and deposited in a savings account that earns 12% annually, compounded monthly. If Malone continues with her plan for two and one-half years, how much will be accumulated in the account on the date of the last deposit?

Exercise B-16
Future value of an annuity   P4

Starr Company decides to establish a fund that it will use 10 years from now to replace an aging production facility. The company will make a $100,000 initial contribution to the fund and plans to make quarterly contributions of $50,000 beginning in three months. The fund earns 12%, compounded quarterly. What will be the value of the fund 10 years from now?

Exercise B-17
Future value of an amount plus an annuity   P2 P4

Catten, Inc., invests $163,170 today earning 7% per year for nine years. Use Table B.2 to compute the future value of the investment nine years from now. (Round the amount to the nearest dollar.)

Exercise B-18
Future value of an amount   P2

For each of the following situations, identify (1) the case as either (*a*) a present or a future value and (*b*) a single amount or an annuity, (2) the table you would use in your computations (but do not solve the problem), and (3) the interest rate and time periods you would use.

a. You need to accumulate $10,000 for a trip you wish to take in four years. You are able to earn 8% compounded semiannually on your savings. You plan to make only one deposit and let the money accumulate for four years. How would you determine the amount of the one-time deposit?

b. Assume the same facts as in part (*a*) except that you will make semiannual deposits to your savings account.

c. You want to retire after working 40 years with savings in excess of $1,000,000. You expect to save $4,000 a year for 40 years and earn an annual rate of interest of 8%. Will you be able to retire with more than $1,000,000 in 40 years? Explain.

d. A sweepstakes agency names you a grand prize winner. You can take $225,000 immediately or elect to receive annual installments of $30,000 for 20 years. You can earn 10% annually on any investments you make. Which prize do you choose to receive?

Exercise B-19
Using present and future value tables
C1 P1 P2 P3 P4

TABLE B.1

Present Value of 1

$$p = 1/(1 + i)^n$$

Periods	1%	2%	3%	4%	5%	6%	7%	8%	9%	10%	12%	15%
1	0.9901	0.9804	0.9709	0.9615	0.9524	0.9434	0.9346	0.9259	0.9174	0.9091	0.8929	0.8696
2	0.9803	0.9612	0.9426	0.9246	0.9070	0.8900	0.8734	0.8573	0.8417	0.8264	0.7972	0.7561
3	0.9706	0.9423	0.9151	0.8890	0.8638	0.8396	0.8163	0.7938	0.7722	0.7513	0.7118	0.6575
4	0.9610	0.9238	0.8885	0.8548	0.8227	0.7921	0.7629	0.7350	0.7084	0.6830	0.6355	0.5718
5	0.9515	0.9057	0.8626	0.8219	0.7835	0.7473	0.7130	0.6806	0.6499	0.6209	0.5674	0.4972
6	0.9420	0.8880	0.8375	0.7903	0.7462	0.7050	0.6663	0.6302	0.5963	0.5645	0.5066	0.4323
7	0.9327	0.8706	0.8131	0.7599	0.7107	0.6651	0.6227	0.5835	0.5470	0.5132	0.4523	0.3759
8	0.9235	0.8535	0.7894	0.7307	0.6768	0.6274	0.5820	0.5403	0.5019	0.4665	0.4039	0.3269
9	0.9143	0.8368	0.7664	0.7026	0.6446	0.5919	0.5439	0.5002	0.4604	0.4241	0.3606	0.2843
10	0.9053	0.8203	0.7441	0.6756	0.6139	0.5584	0.5083	0.4632	0.4224	0.3855	0.3220	0.2472
11	0.8963	0.8043	0.7224	0.6496	0.5847	0.5268	0.4751	0.4289	0.3875	0.3505	0.2875	0.2149
12	0.8874	0.7885	0.7014	0.6246	0.5568	0.4970	0.4440	0.3971	0.3555	0.3186	0.2567	0.1869
13	0.8787	0.7730	0.6810	0.6006	0.5303	0.4688	0.4150	0.3677	0.3262	0.2897	0.2292	0.1625
14	0.8700	0.7579	0.6611	0.5775	0.5051	0.4423	0.3878	0.3405	0.2992	0.2633	0.2046	0.1413
15	0.8613	0.7430	0.6419	0.5553	0.4810	0.4173	0.3624	0.3152	0.2745	0.2394	0.1827	0.1229
16	0.8528	0.7284	0.6232	0.5339	0.4581	0.3936	0.3387	0.2919	0.2519	0.2176	0.1631	0.1069
17	0.8444	0.7142	0.6050	0.5134	0.4363	0.3714	0.3166	0.2703	0.2311	0.1978	0.1456	0.0929
18	0.8360	0.7002	0.5874	0.4936	0.4155	0.3503	0.2959	0.2502	0.2120	0.1799	0.1300	0.0808
19	0.8277	0.6864	0.5703	0.4746	0.3957	0.3305	0.2765	0.2317	0.1945	0.1635	0.1161	0.0703
20	0.8195	0.6730	0.5537	0.4564	0.3769	0.3118	0.2584	0.2145	0.1784	0.1486	0.1037	0.0611
25	0.7798	0.6095	0.4776	0.3751	0.2953	0.2330	0.1842	0.1460	0.1160	0.0923	0.0588	0.0304
30	0.7419	0.5521	0.4120	0.3083	0.2314	0.1741	0.1314	0.0994	0.0754	0.0573	0.0334	0.0151
35	0.7059	0.5000	0.3554	0.2534	0.1813	0.1301	0.0937	0.0676	0.0490	0.0356	0.0189	0.0075
40	0.6717	0.4529	0.3066	0.2083	0.1420	0.0972	0.0668	0.0460	0.0318	0.0221	0.0107	0.0037

TABLE B.2

Future Value of 1

$$f = (1 + i)^n$$

Periods	1%	2%	3%	4%	5%	6%	7%	8%	9%	10%	12%	15%
0	1.0000	1.0000	1.0000	1.0000	1.0000	1.0000	1.0000	1.0000	1.0000	1.0000	1.0000	1.0000
1	1.0100	1.0200	1.0300	1.0400	1.0500	1.0600	1.0700	1.0800	1.0900	1.1000	1.1200	1.1500
2	1.0201	1.0404	1.0609	1.0816	1.1025	1.1236	1.1449	1.1664	1.1881	1.2100	1.2544	1.3225
3	1.0303	1.0612	1.0927	1.1249	1.1576	1.1910	1.2250	1.2597	1.2950	1.3310	1.4049	1.5209
4	1.0406	1.0824	1.1255	1.1699	1.2155	1.2625	1.3108	1.3605	1.4116	1.4641	1.5735	1.7490
5	1.0510	1.1041	1.1593	1.2167	1.2763	1.3382	1.4026	1.4693	1.5386	1.6105	1.7623	2.0114
6	1.0615	1.1262	1.1941	1.2653	1.3401	1.4185	1.5007	1.5869	1.6771	1.7716	1.9738	2.3131
7	1.0721	1.1487	1.2299	1.3159	1.4071	1.5036	1.6058	1.7138	1.8280	1.9487	2.2107	2.6600
8	1.0829	1.1717	1.2668	1.3686	1.4775	1.5938	1.7182	1.8509	1.9926	2.1436	2.4760	3.0590
9	1.0937	1.1951	1.3048	1.4233	1.5513	1.6895	1.8385	1.9990	2.1719	2.3579	2.7731	3.5179
10	1.1046	1.2190	1.3439	1.4802	1.6289	1.7908	1.9672	2.1589	2.3674	2.5937	3.1058	4.0456
11	1.1157	1.2434	1.3842	1.5395	1.7103	1.8983	2.1049	2.3316	2.5804	2.8531	3.4785	4.6524
12	1.1268	1.2682	1.4258	1.6010	1.7959	2.0122	2.2522	2.5182	2.8127	3.1384	3.8960	5.3503
13	1.1381	1.2936	1.4685	1.6651	1.8856	2.1329	2.4098	2.7196	3.0658	3.4523	4.3635	6.1528
14	1.1495	1.3195	1.5126	1.7317	1.9799	2.2609	2.5785	2.9372	3.3417	3.7975	4.8871	7.0757
15	1.1610	1.3459	1.5580	1.8009	2.0789	2.3966	2.7590	3.1722	3.6425	4.1772	5.4736	8.1371
16	1.1726	1.3728	1.6047	1.8730	2.1829	2.5404	2.9522	3.4259	3.9703	4.5950	6.1304	9.3576
17	1.1843	1.4002	1.6528	1.9479	2.2920	2.6928	3.1588	3.7000	4.3276	5.0545	6.8660	10.7613
18	1.1961	1.4282	1.7024	2.0258	2.4066	2.8543	3.3799	3.9960	4.7171	5.5599	7.6900	12.3755
19	1.2081	1.4568	1.7535	2.1068	2.5270	3.0256	3.6165	4.3157	5.1417	6.1159	8.6128	14.2318
20	1.2202	1.4859	1.8061	2.1911	2.6533	3.2071	3.8697	4.6610	5.6044	6.7275	9.6463	16.3665
25	1.2824	1.6406	2.0938	2.6658	3.3864	4.2919	5.4274	6.8485	8.6231	10.8347	17.0001	32.9190
30	1.3478	1.8114	2.4273	3.2434	4.3219	5.7435	7.6123	10.0627	13.2677	17.4494	29.9599	66.2118
35	1.4166	1.9999	2.8139	3.9461	5.5160	7.6861	10.6766	14.7853	20.4140	28.1024	52.7996	133.1755
40	1.4889	2.2080	3.2620	4.8010	7.0400	10.2857	14.9745	21.7245	31.4094	45.2593	93.0510	267.8635

$$p = \left[1 - \frac{1}{(1 + i)^n}\right]/i$$

	Rate											
Periods	**1%**	**2%**	**3%**	**4%**	**5%**	**6%**	**7%**	**8%**	**9%**	**10%**	**12%**	**15%**
1	0.9901	0.9804	0.9709	0.9615	0.9524	0.9434	0.9346	0.9259	0.9174	0.9091	0.8929	0.8696
2	1.9704	1.9416	1.9135	1.8861	1.8594	1.8334	1.8080	1.7833	1.7591	1.7355	1.6901	1.6257
3	2.9410	2.8839	2.8286	2.7751	2.7232	2.6730	2.6243	2.5771	2.5313	2.4869	2.4018	2.2832
4	3.9020	3.8077	3.7171	3.6299	3.5460	3.4651	3.3872	3.3121	3.2397	3.1699	3.0373	2.8550
5	4.8534	4.7135	4.5797	4.4518	4.3295	4.2124	4.1002	3.9927	3.8897	3.7908	3.6048	3.3522
6	5.7955	5.6014	5.4172	5.2421	5.0757	4.9173	4.7665	4.6229	4.4859	4.3553	4.1114	3.7845
7	6.7282	6.4720	6.2303	6.0021	5.7864	5.5824	5.3893	5.2064	5.0330	4.8684	4.5638	4.1604
8	7.6517	7.3255	7.0197	6.7327	6.4632	6.2098	5.9713	5.7466	5.5348	5.3349	4.9676	4.4873
9	8.5660	8.1622	7.7861	7.4353	7.1078	6.8017	6.5152	6.2469	5.9952	5.7590	5.3282	4.7716
10	9.4713	8.9826	8.5302	8.1109	7.7217	7.3601	7.0236	6.7101	6.4177	6.1446	5.6502	5.0188
11	10.3676	9.7868	9.2526	8.7605	8.3064	7.8869	7.4987	7.1390	6.8052	6.4951	5.9377	5.2337
12	11.2551	10.5753	9.9540	9.3851	8.8633	8.3838	7.9427	7.5361	7.1607	6.8137	6.1944	5.4206
13	12.1337	11.3484	10.6350	9.9856	9.3936	8.8527	8.3577	7.9038	7.4869	7.1034	6.4235	5.5831
14	13.0037	12.1062	11.2961	10.5631	9.8986	9.2950	8.7455	8.2442	7.7862	7.3667	6.6282	5.7245
15	13.8651	12.8493	11.9379	11.1184	10.3797	9.7122	9.1079	8.5595	8.0607	7.6061	6.8109	5.8474
16	14.7179	13.5777	12.5611	11.6523	10.8378	10.1059	9.4466	8.8514	8.3126	7.8237	6.9740	5.9542
17	15.5623	14.2919	13.1661	12.1657	11.2741	10.4773	9.7632	9.1216	8.5436	8.0216	7.1196	6.0472
18	16.3983	14.9920	13.7535	12.6593	11.6896	10.8276	10.0591	9.3719	8.7556	8.2014	7.2497	6.1280
19	17.2260	15.6785	14.3238	13.1339	12.0853	11.1581	10.3356	9.6036	8.9501	8.3649	7.3658	6.1982
20	18.0456	16.3514	14.8775	13.5903	12.4622	11.4699	10.5940	9.8181	9.1285	8.5136	7.4694	6.2593
25	22.0232	19.5235	17.4131	15.6221	14.0939	12.7834	11.6536	10.6748	9.8226	9.0770	7.8431	6.4641
30	25.8077	22.3965	19.6004	17.2920	15.3725	13.7648	12.4090	11.2578	10.2737	9.4269	8.0552	6.5660
35	29.4086	24.9986	21.4872	18.6646	16.3742	14.4982	12.9477	11.6546	10.5668	9.6442	8.1755	6.6166
40	32.8347	27.3555	23.1148	19.7928	17.1591	15.0463	13.3317	11.9246	10.7574	9.7791	8.2438	6.6418

$$f = [(1 + i)^n - 1]/i$$

	Rate											
Periods	**1%**	**2%**	**3%**	**4%**	**5%**	**6%**	**7%**	**8%**	**9%**	**10%**	**12%**	**15%**
1	1.0000	1.0000	1.0000	1.0000	1.0000	1.0000	1.0000	1.0000	1.0000	1.0000	1.0000	1.0000
2	2.0100	2.0200	2.0300	2.0400	2.0500	2.0600	2.0700	2.0800	2.0900	2.1000	2.1200	2.1500
3	3.0301	3.0604	3.0909	3.1216	3.1525	3.1836	3.2149	3.2464	3.2781	3.3100	3.3744	3.4725
4	4.0604	4.1216	4.1836	4.2465	4.3101	4.3746	4.4399	4.5061	4.5731	4.6410	4.7793	4.9934
5	5.1010	5.2040	5.3091	5.4163	5.5256	5.6371	5.7507	5.8666	5.9847	6.1051	6.3528	6.7424
6	6.1520	6.3081	6.4684	6.6330	6.8019	6.9753	7.1533	7.3359	7.5233	7.7156	8.1152	8.7537
7	7.2135	7.4343	7.6625	7.8983	8.1420	8.3938	8.6540	8.9228	9.2004	9.4872	10.0890	11.0668
8	8.2857	8.5830	8.8923	9.2142	9.5491	9.8975	10.2598	10.6366	11.0285	11.4359	12.2997	13.7268
9	9.3685	9.7546	10.1591	10.5828	11.0266	11.4913	11.9780	12.4876	13.0210	13.5795	14.7757	16.7858
10	10.4622	10.9497	11.4639	12.0061	12.5779	13.1808	13.8164	14.4866	15.1929	15.9374	17.5487	20.3037
11	11.5668	12.1687	12.8078	13.4864	14.2068	14.9716	15.7836	16.6455	17.5603	18.5312	20.6546	24.3493
12	12.6825	13.4121	14.1920	15.0258	15.9171	16.8699	17.8885	18.9771	20.1407	21.3843	24.1331	29.0017
13	13.8093	14.6803	15.6178	16.6268	17.7130	18.8821	20.1406	21.4953	22.9534	24.5227	28.0291	34.3519
14	14.9474	15.9739	17.0863	18.2919	19.5986	21.0151	22.5505	24.2149	26.0192	27.9750	32.3926	40.5047
15	16.0969	17.2934	18.5989	20.0236	21.5786	23.2760	25.1290	27.1521	29.3609	31.7725	37.2797	47.5804
16	17.2579	18.6393	20.1569	21.8245	23.6575	25.6725	27.8881	30.3243	33.0034	35.9497	42.7533	55.7175
17	18.4304	20.0121	21.7616	23.6975	25.8404	28.2129	30.8402	33.7502	36.9737	40.5447	48.8837	65.0751
18	19.6147	21.4123	23.4144	25.6454	28.1324	30.9057	33.9990	37.4502	41.3013	45.5992	55.7497	75.8364
19	20.8109	22.8406	25.1169	27.6712	30.5390	33.7600	37.3790	41.4463	46.0185	51.1591	63.4397	88.2118
20	22.0190	24.2974	26.8704	29.7781	33.0660	36.7856	40.9955	45.7620	51.1601	57.2750	72.0524	102.4436
25	28.2432	32.0303	36.4593	41.6459	47.7271	54.8645	63.2490	73.1059	84.7009	98.3471	133.3339	212.7930
30	34.7849	40.5681	47.5754	56.0849	66.4388	79.0582	94.4608	113.2832	136.3075	164.4940	241.3327	434.7451
35	41.6603	49.9945	60.4621	73.6522	90.3203	111.4348	138.2369	172.3168	215.7108	271.0244	431.6635	881.1702
40	48.8864	60.4020	75.4013	95.0255	120.7998	154.7620	199.6351	259.0565	337.8824	442.5926	767.0914	1,779.0903

Appendix

C Investments and International Operations

BASICS OF INVESTMENTS	NONINFLUENTIAL INVESTMENTS	INFLUENTIAL INVESTMENTS
C1 Motivation for investments	**P1** Trading securities	**P4** Securities with significant influence
Short-term versus long-term	**P2** Held-to-maturity securities	**C2** Securities with controlling influence
Classification and reporting	**P3** Available-for-sale securities	
Accounting basics		**A1** Analyze components of return on assets

---

Learning Objectives

C1 Distinguish between debt and equity securities and between short-term and long-term investments. (p. C-1)

P1 Account for trading securities. (p. C-3)

P2 Account for held-to-maturity securities. (p. C-5)

P3 Account for available-for-sale securities. (p. C-5)

P4 Account for equity securities with significant influence. (p. C-7)

C2 Describe how to report equity securities with controlling influence. (p. C-9)

A1 Compute and analyze the components of return on total assets. (p. C-11)

C3 *Appendix C-A*—Explain foreign exchange rates and record transactions listed in a foreign currency. (p. C-15)

BASICS OF INVESTMENTS

This section describes the motivation for investments, the distinction between short- and long-term investments, and the different classes of investments.

C1   Distinguish between debt and equity securities and between short-term and long-term investments.

Motivation for Investments

Companies make investments for at least three reasons. First, companies transfer *excess cash* into investments to produce higher income. Second, some entities, such as mutual funds and pension funds, are set up to produce income from investments. Third, companies make investments for strategic reasons. Examples are investments in competitors, suppliers, and even customers. Exhibit C.1 shows short-term (S-T) and long-term (L-T) investments as a percent of total assets for several companies.

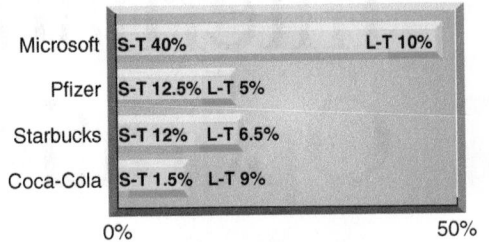

EXHIBIT C.1

Investments of Selected Companies

Short-Term Investments   Cash equivalents are investments that are both readily converted to known amounts of cash and mature within three months. Many investments, however, mature between 3 and 12 months. These investments are **short-term investments,** also called *temporary investments* and *marketable securities.* Specifically, short-term investments are securities that (1) management intends to convert to cash within one year or the operating cycle, whichever is longer, and (2) are readily convertible to cash. Short-term investments are reported under current assets and serve a purpose similar to cash equivalents.

Long-Term Investments   **Long-term investments** in securities are defined as those securities that are not readily convertible to cash or are not intended to be converted into cash in the short term. Long-term investments can also include funds earmarked for a special purpose, such as bond sinking funds and investments in land or other assets not used in the company's operations. Long-term investments are reported in the noncurrent section of the balance sheet, often in its own separate line titled *Long-Term Investments.*

Debt Securities versus Equity Securities   Investments in securities can include both debt and equity securities. *Debt securities* reflect a creditor relationship such as investments in notes, bonds, and certificates of deposit; they are issued by governments, companies, and individuals. *Equity securities* reflect an owner relationship such as shares of stock issued by companies.

Classification and Reporting

Accounting for investments in securities depends on three factors: (1) security type, either debt or equity, (2) the company's intent to hold the security either short term or long term, and (3) the company's (investor's) percent ownership in the other company's (investee's) equity securities. Exhibit C.2 identifies five classes of securities using these three factors. It describes each of these five classes of securities and the standard reporting required under each class.

Debt Securities: Accounting Basics

This section explains the accounting basics for *debt securities,* including that for acquisition, disposition, and any interest.

Acquisition.   Debt securities are recorded at cost when purchased. To illustrate, assume that Music City paid $29,500 plus a $500 brokerage fee on September 1, 2012, to buy Dell's 7%, two-year bonds payable with a $30,000 par value. The bonds pay interest semiannually on August 31 and February 28.

EXHIBIT C.2

Investments in Securities

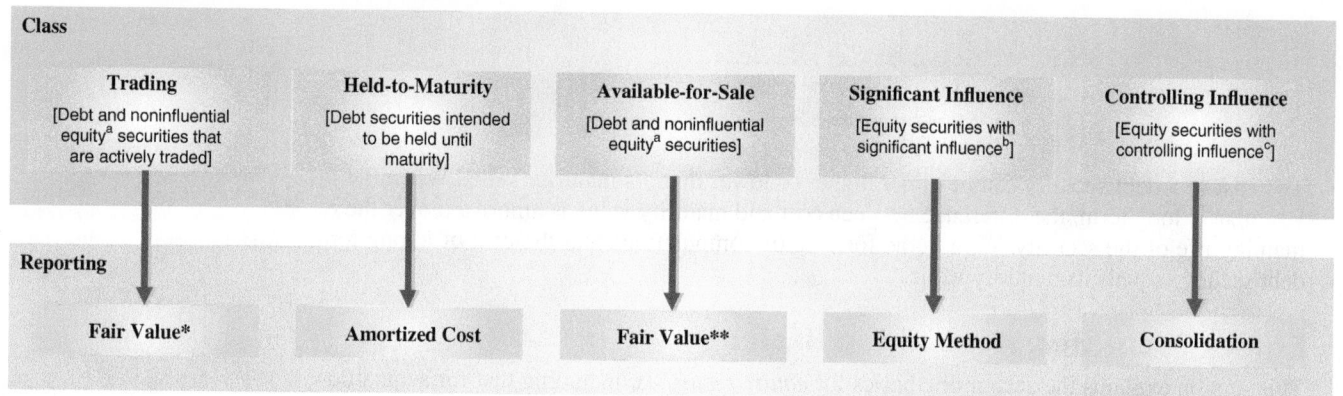

[a] Holding less than 20% of voting stock (equity securities only).   [b] Holding 20% or more, but not more than 50%, of voting stock.   [c] Holding more than 50% of voting stock.
* Unrealized gains and losses reported on the income statement.
** Unrealized gains and losses reported in the equity section of the balance sheet and in comprehensive income.

Music City intends to hold the bonds until they mature on August 31, 2014; consequently, they are classified as held-to-maturity (HTM) securities. The entry to record this purchase follows. (If the maturity of the securities was short term, and management's intent was to hold them until they mature, then they would be classified as Short-Term Investments—HTM.)

Assets = Liabilities + Equity
+30,000
−30,000

2012 Sept. 1	Long-Term Investments—HTM (Dell)	30,000	
	Cash		30,000
	Purchased bonds to be held to maturity.		

Interest earned.   Interest revenue for investments in debt securities is recorded when earned. To illustrate, on December 31, 2012, at the end of its accounting period, Music City accrues interest receivable as follows.

Assets = Liabilities + Equity
+700   +700

Dec. 31	Interest Receivable	700	
	Interest Revenue		700
	Accrued interest earned ($30,000 × 7% × 4/12).		

The $700 reflects 4/6 of the semiannual cash receipt of interest—the portion Music City earned as of December 31. Relevant sections of Music City's financial statements at December 31, 2012, are shown in Exhibit C.3.

EXHIBIT C.3

Financial Statement Presentation of Debt Securities

On the income statement for year 2012:	
Interest revenue	**$ 700**
On the December 31, 2012, balance sheet:	
Long-term investments—Held-to-maturity securities (at amortized cost)	**$30,000**

On February 28, 2013, Music City records receipt of semiannual interest.

Assets = Liabilities + Equity
+1,050   +350
−700

Feb. 28	Cash	1,050	
	Interest Receivable		700
	Interest Revenue		350
	Received six months' interest on Dell bonds.		

Disposition.   When the bonds mature, the proceeds (not including the interest entry) are recorded as:

2014 Aug. 31	Cash	30,000	
	Long-Term Investments—HTM (Dell)...........		30,000
	Received cash from matured bonds.		

Assets   = Liabilities + Equity
+30,000
−30,000

The cost of a debt security can be either higher or lower than its maturity value. When the investment is long term, the difference between cost and maturity value is amortized over the remaining life of the security. We assume for ease of computations that the cost of a long-term debt security equals its maturity value.

Example: What is cost per share?
Answer: Cost per share is the total cost of acquisition, including broker fees, divided by number of shares acquired.

Equity Securities: Accounting Basics

This section explains the accounting basics for *equity securities,* including that for acquisition, dividends, and disposition.

Acquisition.   Equity securities are recorded at cost when acquired, including commissions or brokerage fees paid. To illustrate, assume that Music City purchases 1,000 shares of Intex common stock at par value for $86,000 on October 10, 2012. It records this purchase of available-for-sale (AFS) securities as follows.

Oct. 10	Long-Term Investments—AFS (Intex)	86,000	
	Cash		86,000
	Purchased 1,000 shares of Intex.		

Assets   = Liabilities + Equity
+86,000
−86,000

Dividend earned.   Any cash dividends received are credited to Dividend Revenue and reported in the income statement. To illustrate, on November 2, Music City receives a $1,720 quarterly cash dividend on the Intex shares, which it records as:

Nov. 2	Cash	1,720	
	Dividend Revenue		1,720
	Received dividend of $1.72 per share.		

Assets   = Liabilities + Equity
+1,720   +1,720

Disposition.   When the securities are sold, sale proceeds are compared with the cost, and any gain or loss is recorded. To illustrate, on December 20, Music City sells 500 of the Intex shares for $45,000 cash and records this sale as:

Dec. 20	Cash	45,000	
	Long-Term Investments—AFS (Intex)		43,000
	Gain on Sale of Long-Term Investments		2,000
	Sold 500 Intex shares ($86,000 × 500/1,000).		

Assets   = Liabilities + Equity
+45,000   +2,000
−43,000

REPORTING OF NONINFLUENTIAL INVESTMENTS

Companies must value and report most noninfluential investments at *fair value.* The exact reporting requirements depend on whether the investments are classified as (1) trading, (2) held-to-maturity, or (3) available-for-sale.

Trading Securities

Trading securities are *debt and equity securities* that the company intends to actively manage and trade for profit. Frequent purchases and sales are expected and are made to earn profits on short-term price changes. Trading securities are *always* reported as current assets.

P1 Account for trading securities.

Valuing and reporting trading securities.   The entire portfolio of trading securities is reported at its fair value; this requires a "fair value adjustment" from the cost of the portfolio. The term *portfolio* refers to a group of securities. Any unrealized gain (or loss) from a change in the fair value of the portfolio of trading securities is reported on the income statement. Most users believe accounting reports are more useful when changes in fair value for trading securities are reported in income.

To illustrate, TechCom's portfolio of trading securities had a total cost of $11,500 and a fair value of $13,000 on December 31, 2012, the first year it held trading securities. The difference between the $11,500 cost and the $13,000 fair value reflects a $1,500 gain. It is an unrealized gain because it is not yet confirmed by actual sales. The fair value adjustment for trading securities is recorded with an adjusting entry at the end of each period to equal the difference between the portfolio's cost and its fair value. TechCom records this gain as follows.

Point: *'Unrealized gain (or loss)'* refers to a change in fair value that is not yet realized through actual sale.

Point: 'Fair Value Adjustment—Trading' is a *permanent account*, shown as a deduction or addition to 'Short-Term Investments—Trading.'

Assets = Liabilities + Equity
+1,500   +1,500

Dec. 31	Fair Value Adjustment—Trading	1,500	
	Unrealized Gain—Income		1,500
	To reflect an unrealized gain in fair values of trading securities.		

Example: If TechCom's trading securities have a cost of $14,800 and a fair value of $16,100 at Dec. 31, 2013, its adjusting entry is
Unrealized Loss—Income 200
   Fair Value Adj.—Trading 200
This is computed as: $1,500 Beg. Dr. bal. + $200 Cr. = $1,300 End. Dr. bal.

The **Unrealized Gain (or Loss)** is reported in the Other Revenues and Gains (or Expenses and Losses) section on the income statement. Unrealized Gain (or Loss)—Income is a *temporary* account that is closed to Income Summary at the end of each period. Fair Value Adjustment—Trading is a *permanent* account, which adjusts the reported value of the trading securities portfolio from its prior period fair value to the current period fair value. The total cost of the trading securities portfolio is maintained in one account, and the fair value adjustment is recorded in a separate account. For example, TechCom's investment in trading securities is reported in the current assets section of its balance sheet as follows.

Current Assets		
Short-term investments—Trading (at cost)	$11,500	
Fair Value adjustment—Trading	1,500	
Short-term investments—Trading (at fair value)		$13,000
or simply		
Short-term investments—Trading (at fair value; cost is $11,500)		$13,000

Selling trading securities.   When individual trading securities are sold, the difference between the net proceeds (sale price less fees) and the cost of the individual trading securities that are sold is recognized as a gain or a loss. Any prior period fair value adjustment to the portfolio is *not* used to compute the gain or loss from sale of individual trading securities. For example, if TechCom sold some of its trading securities that had cost $1,000 for $1,200 cash on January 9, 2013, it would record the following.

Point: Reporting securities at fair value is referred to as *mark-to-market* accounting.

Assets = Liabilities + Equity
+1,200   +200
−1,000

Jan. 9	Cash	1,200	
	Short-Term Investments—Trading		1,000
	Gain on Sale of Short-Term Investments		200
	Sold trading securities costing $1,000 for $1,200 cash.		

A gain is reported in the Other Revenues and Gains section on the income statement, whereas a loss is shown in Other Expenses and Losses. When the period-end fair value adjustment for the portfolio of trading securities is computed, it excludes the cost and fair value of any securities sold.

Held-to-Maturity Securities

Held-to-maturity (HTM) securities are *debt* securities a company intends and is able to hold until maturity. They are reported in current assets if their maturity dates are within one year or the operating cycle, whichever is longer. HTM securities are reported in long-term assets when the maturity dates extend beyond one year or the operating cycle, whichever is longer. All HTM securities are recorded at cost when purchased, and interest revenue is recorded when earned.

The portfolio of HTM securities is usually reported at (amortized) cost, which is explained in advanced courses. There is no fair value adjustment to the portfolio of HTM securities—neither to the short-term nor long-term portfolios. The basics of accounting for HTM securities were described earlier in this appendix.

P2 Account for held-to-maturity securities.

Point: Only debt securities can be classified as *held-to-maturity*; equity securities have no maturity date.

■ Decision Maker

Money Manager   You expect interest rates to sharply fall within a few weeks and remain at this lower rate. What is your strategy for holding investments in fixed-rate bonds and notes? ■ [Answer—p. C-18]

Available-for-Sale Securities

Available-for-sale (AFS) securities are *debt and equity securities* not classified as trading or held-to-maturity securities. AFS securities are purchased to yield interest, dividends, or increases in fair value. They are not actively managed like trading securities. If the intent is to sell AFS securities within the longer of one year or operating cycle, they are classified as short-term investments. Otherwise, they are classified as long-term.

P3 Account for available-for-sale securities.

Valuing and reporting available-for-sale securities.   As with trading securities, companies adjust the cost of the portfolio of AFS securities to reflect changes in fair value. This is done with a fair value adjustment to its total portfolio cost. However, any unrealized gain or loss for the portfolio of AFS securities is *not* reported on the income statement. Instead, it is reported in the equity section of the balance sheet (and is part of *comprehensive income*, explained later). To illustrate, assume that Music City had no prior period investments in available-for-sale securities other than those purchased in the current period. Exhibit C.4 shows both the cost and fair value of those investments on December 31, 2012, the end of its reporting period.

Example: If fair value in Exhibit C.4 $70,000 (instead of $74,550), what entr is made? *Answer:*
Unreal. Loss—Equity   3,000
  Fair Value Adj.—AFS. . .   3,0

	Cost	Fair Value	Unrealized Gain (Loss)
Improv bonds	$30,000	$29,050	$ (950)
Intex common stock, 500 shares	43,000	45,500	2,500
Total	$73,000	$74,550	$1,550

EXHIBIT C.4

Cost and Fair Value of Available-for-Sale Securities

The year-end adjusting entry to record the fair value of these investments follows.

Dec. 31	Fair Value Adjustment—Available-for-Sale (LT)	1,550	
	Unrealized Gain—Equity		1,550
	To record adjustment to fair value of		
	available-for-sale securities.		

Assets = Liabilities + Equity
+1,550   +1,550

Exhibit C.5 shows the December 31, 2012, balance sheet presentation—it assumes these investments are long term, but they can also be short term. It is also common to combine the cost of investments with the balance in the Fair Value Adjustment account and report the net as a single amount.

Point: 'Unrealized Loss—Equity' and 'Unrealized Gain—Equity' are *permanel* (balance sheet) equity *accounts.*

EXHIBIT C.5

Balance Sheet Presentation of
Available-for-Sale Securities

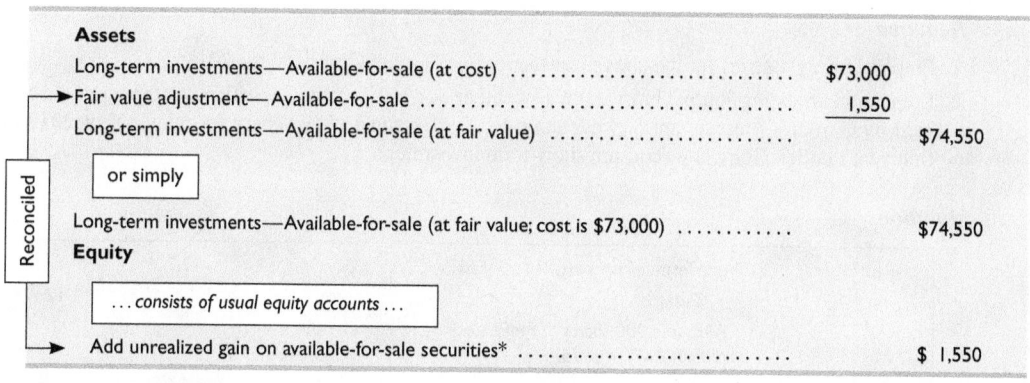

* Often included under the caption Accumulated Other Comprehensive Income.

Point: Income can be window-dressed upward by selling AFS securities with unrealized gains; income is reduced by selling those with unrealized losses.

Assets = Liabilities + Equity
−550   −550

Let's extend this illustration and assume that at the end of its next calendar year (December 31, 2013), Music City's portfolio of long-term AFS securities has an $81,000 cost and an $82,000 fair value. It records the adjustment to fair value as follows.

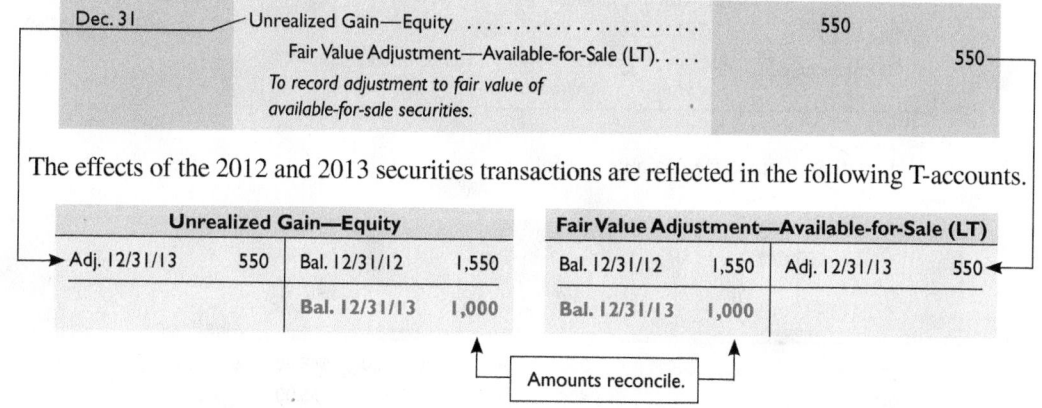

Example: If cost is $83,000 and fair value is $82,000 at Dec. 31, 2013, it records the following adjustment:
Unreal. Gain—Equity 1,550
Unreal. Loss—Equity 1,000
     Fair Value Adj.—AFS . .   2,550

The effects of the 2012 and 2013 securities transactions are reflected in the following T-accounts.

Unrealized Gain—Equity				Fair Value Adjustment—Available-for-Sale (LT)			
Adj. 12/31/13	550	Bal. 12/31/12	1,550	Bal. 12/31/12	1,550	Adj. 12/31/13	550
		Bal. 12/31/13	1,000	Bal. 12/31/13	1,000		

Amounts reconcile.

Point: 'Fair Value Adjustment—Available-for-Sale' is a permanent account, shown as a deduction or addition to the Investment account.

Selling available-for-sale securities.   Accounting for the sale of individual AFS securities is identical to that described for the sale of trading securities. When individual AFS securities are sold, the difference between the cost of the individual securities sold and the net proceeds (sale price less fees) is recognized as a gain or loss.

Alert   Both U.S. GAAP (and IFRS) permit companies to use fair value in reporting financial assets (referred to as the fair value option). This option allows companies to report any financial asset at fair value and recognize value changes in income. This method was previously reserved only for trading securities, but is now an option for available-for-sale and held-to-maturity securities (and other 'financial assets and liabilities' such as accounts and notes receivable, accounts and notes payable, and bonds). U.S. standards also set a 3-level system to determine fair value:
—Level 1: Use quoted market values
—Level 2: Use observable values from related assets or liabilities
—Level 3: Use unobservable values from estimates or assumptions
To date, a fairly small set of companies has chosen to broadly apply the fair value option—but, we continue to monitor its use ...

NEED-TO-KNOW C.1

P3

Garden Company completes the following selected transactions related to its short-term investments during 2013.

May 8   Purchased 300 shares of FedEx stock as a short-term investment in available-for-sale securities at $40 per share plus $975 in broker fees.

Sept. 2   Sold 100 shares of its investment in FedEx stock at $47 per share and held the remaining 200 shares; broker's commission was $225.

Oct. 2   Purchased 400 shares of Ajay stock for $60 per share plus $1,600 in commissions. The stock is held as a short-term investment in available-for-sale securities.

Required

1. Prepare journal entries for the above transactions of Garden Company for 2013.

2. Prepare an adjusting journal entry as of December 31, 2013, if the fair values of the equity securities held by Garden Company are $48 per share for FedEx and $55 per share for Ajay. (Year 2013 is the first year Garden Company acquired short-term investments.)

Solution

1.

May 8	Short-Term Investments—AFS (FedEx)	12,975	
	Cash		12,975
	Purchased 300 shares of FedEx stock (300 × $40) + $975.		
Sept. 2	Cash	4,475	
	Gain on Sale of Short-Term Investment		150
	Short-Term Investments—AFS (FedEx)		4,325
	Sold 100 shares of FedEx for $47 per share less a $225 commission. The original cost is ($12,975 × 100/300).		
Oct. 2	Short-Term Investments—AFS (Ajay)	25,600	
	Cash		25,600
	Purchased 400 shares of Ajay for $60 per share plus $1,600 in commissions.		

2. Computation of unrealized gain or loss follows.

Short-Term Investments in Available-for-Sale Securities	Shares	Cost per Share	Total Cost	Fair Value per Share	Total Fair Value	Unrealized Gain (Loss)
FedEx	200	$43.25	$ 8,650	$48.00	$ 9,600	
Ajay	400	64.00	25,600	55.00	22,000	
Totals			$34,250		$31,600	$(2,650)

The adjusting entry follows:

Dec. 31	Unrealized Loss—Equity	2,650	
	Fair Value Adjustment—Available-for-Sale (ST)		2,650
	To reflect an unrealized loss in fair values of available-for-sale securities.		

QC1

REPORTING OF INFLUENTIAL INVESTMENTS

Investment in Securities with Significant Influence

A long-term investment classified as **equity securities with significant influence** implies that the investor can exert significant influence over the investee. An investor that owns 20% or more (but not more than 50%) of a company's voting stock is usually presumed to have a significant influence over the investee. In some cases, however, the 20% test of significant influence is overruled by other, more persuasive, evidence. This evidence can either lower the 20% requirement or increase it. The **equity method** of accounting and reporting is used for long-term investments in equity securities with significant influence, which is explained in this section.

P4 Account for equity securities with significant influence.

Long-term investments in equity securities with significant influence are recorded at cost when acquired. To illustrate, Micron Co. records the purchase of 3,000 shares (30%) of Star Co. common stock at a total cost of $70,650 on January 1, 2012, as follows.

Assets = Liabilities + Equity
+70,650
−70,650

Jan. I	Long-Term Investments—Star	70,650	
	Cash		70,650
	To record purchase of 3,000 Star shares.		

The investee's (Star) earnings increase both its net assets and the claim of the investor (Micron) on the investee's net assets. Thus, when the investee reports its earnings, the investor records its share of those earnings in its investment account. To illustrate, assume that Star reports net income of $20,000 for 2012. Micron then records its 30% share of those earnings as follows.

Assets = Liabilities + Equity
+6,000   +6,000

Dec. 31	Long-Term Investments—Star	6,000	
	Earnings from Long-Term Investment		6,000
	To record 30% equity in investee earnings.		

The debit reflects the increase in Micron's equity in Star. The credit reflects 30% of Star's net income. Earnings from Long-Term Investment is a *temporary* account (closed to Income Summary at each period-end) and is reported on the investor's (Micron's) income statement. If the investee incurs a net loss instead of a net income, the investor records its share of the loss and reduces (credits) its investment account. The investor closes this earnings or loss account to Income Summary.

The receipt of cash dividends is not revenue under the equity method because the investor has already recorded its share of the investee's earnings. Instead, cash dividends received by an investor from an investee are viewed as a conversion of one asset to another; that is, dividends reduce the balance of the investment account. To illustrate, Star declares and pays $10,000 in cash dividends on its common stock. Micron records its 30% share of these dividends received on January 9, 2013, as:

Assets = Liabilities + Equity
+3,000
−3,000

Jan. 9	Cash	3,000	
	Long-Term Investments—Star		3,000
	To record share of dividend paid by Star.		

The book value of an investment under the equity method equals the cost of the investment plus (minus) the investor's equity in the *undistributed* (*distributed*) earnings of the investee. Once Micron records these transactions, its Long-Term Investments account appears as in Exhibit C.6.

EXHIBIT C.6

Investment in Star Common Stock (Ledger Account)

Long-Term Investment—Star				
I/ 1/2012 Investment acquisition	70,650			
12/31/2012 Share of earnings	6,000			
12/31/2012 Balance	76,650			
		I/ 9/2013 Share of dividend	3,000	
I/ 9/2013 Balance	73,650			

Micron's account balance on January 9, 2013, for its investment in Star is $73,650. This is the investment's cost *plus* Micron's equity in Star's earnings since its purchase *less* Micron's equity in Star's cash dividends since its purchase. When an investment in equity securities is sold, the gain or loss is computed by comparing proceeds from the sale with the book value of the investment on the date of sale. If Micron sells its Star stock for $80,000 on January 10, 2013, it records the sale as:

Jan. 10	Cash	80,000	
	Long-Term Investments—Star		73,650
	Gain on Sale of Investment		6,350
	Sold 3,000 shares of stock for $80,000.		

Assets = Liabilities + Equity
+80,000   +6,350
−73,650

Investment in Securities with Controlling Influence

A long-term investment classified as **equity securities with controlling influence** implies that the investor can exert a controlling influence over the investee. An investor who owns more than 50% of a company's voting stock has control over the investee. This investor can dominate all other shareholders in electing the corporation's board of directors and has control over the investee's management. In some cases, controlling influence can extend to situations of less than 50% ownership. Exhibit C.7 summarizes the accounting for investments in equity securities based on an investor's ownership in the stock.

The *equity method with consolidation* is used to account for long-term investments in equity securities with controlling influence. The investor reports *consolidated financial statements* when owning such securities. The controlling investor is called the **parent,** and the investee is called the **subsidiary.** Many companies are parents with subsidiaries. Examples are (1) Gap, Inc., the parent of Gap, Old Navy, and Banana Republic; and (2) Brunswick, the parent of Mercury Marine, Sea Ray, and U.S. Marine. A company owning all the outstanding stock of a subsidiary can, if it desires, take over the subsidiary's assets, retire the subsidiary's stock, and merge the subsidiary into the parent. However, there often are financial, legal, and tax advantages if a business operates as a parent controlling one or more subsidiaries. When a company operates as a parent with subsidiaries, each entity maintains separate accounting records. From a legal viewpoint, the parent and each subsidiary are separate entities with all rights, duties, and responsibilities of individual companies.

Consolidated financial statements show the financial position, results of operations, and cash flows of all entities under the parent's control, including all subsidiaries. These statements are prepared as if the business were organized as one entity. The parent uses the equity method in its accounts, but the investment account is *not* reported on the parent's financial statements. Instead, the individual assets and liabilities of the parent and its subsidiaries are combined on one balance sheet. Their revenues and expenses also are combined on one income statement, and their cash flows are combined on one statement of cash flows. The procedures for preparing consolidated financial statements are in advanced courses.

C2 Describe how to report equity securities with controlling influence.

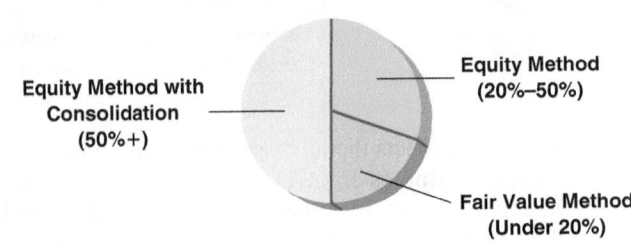

EXHIBIT C.7

Accounting for Equity Investments by Percent of Ownership

🌐 **IFRS**

Unlike U.S. GAAP, IFRS requires uniform accounting policies be used throughout the group of consolidated subsidiaries. Also, unlike U.S. GAAP, IFRS offers no detailed guidance on valuation procedures. ■

Accounting Summary for Investments in Securities

Exhibit C.8 summarizes the standard accounting for investments in securities. Recall that many investment securities are classified as either short term or long term depending on management's intent and ability to convert them in the future. Understanding the accounting for these investments enables us to draw better conclusions from financial statements in making business decisions.

EXHIBIT C.8

Accounting for Investments
in Securities

Classification	Accounting
Short-Term Investment in Securities	
Held-to-maturity (debt) securities	Cost (without any discount or premium amortization)
Trading (debt and equity) securities	Fair value (with fair value adjustment to income)
Available-for-sale (debt and equity) securities	Fair value (with fair value adjustment to equity)
Long-Term Investment in Securities	
Held-to-maturity (debt) securities	Cost (with any discount or premium amortization)
Available-for-sale (debt and equity) securities	Fair value (with fair value adjustment to equity)
Equity securities with significant influence	Equity method
Equity securities with controlling influence	Equity method (with consolidation)

Comprehensive Income   Comprehensive income is defined as all changes in equity during a period except those from owners' investments and dividends. Specifically, comprehensive income is computed by adding or subtracting *other comprehensive income* to net income:

Net income	$ #
Other comprehensive income	#
Comprehensive income	$ #

Point: Some users believe that since AFS securities are not actively traded, reporting fair value changes in income would unnecessarily increase income variability and decrease usefulness.

Other comprehensive income includes unrealized gains and losses on available-for-sale securities, foreign currency translation adjustments, and certain pension adjustments. (*Accumulated other comprehensive income* is defined as the cumulative impact of *other comprehensive income.*)

Comprehensive income is reported in financial statements in one of two ways (which reflects new FASB guidance as of 2012):

1. On a separate *statement of comprehensive income* that immediately follows the income statement.
2. On the lower section of the income statement (as a single continuous *statement of income and comprehensive income*).

Option 1 is the most common. Google, for example, reports a statement of comprehensive income following its income statement. Following is an abbreviated version of the Google statement:

GOOGLE

Net income	**$10,737**
Available-for-sale investments, net of tax.	277
Foreign currency translation	75
Cash flow hedges, net of tax	(90)
Other comprehensive income	262
Total comprehensive income	**$10,999**

Other comprehensive income

Option 2 adds the components of other comprehensive income to net income on the bottom of the income statement to compute a continuous statement of income and comprehensive income. There is no difference in the numbers; it is simply a matter of how those numbers are presented. A third option, which is no longer generally acceptable by itself, was to include the components of other comprehensive income and its total along with the total of comprehensive income in the statement of equity.

QC2

GLOBAL VIEW

This section discusses similarities and differences for the accounting and reporting of investments when financial statements are prepared under U.S. GAAP vis-à-vis IFRS.

Accounting for Noninfluential Securities   The accounting for noninfluential securities is broadly similar between U.S. GAAP and IFRS. *Trading securities* are accounted for using fair values with unrealized gains and losses reported in net income as fair values change. *Available-for-sale securities* are accounted for using fair values with unrealized gains and losses reported in other comprehensive income as fair values change (and later in net income when realized). *Held-to-maturity securities* are accounted for using amortized cost. Similarly, companies have the option under both systems to apply the fair value option for available-for-sale and held-to-maturity securities. Also, both systems review held-to-maturity securities for impairment. There are some differences in terminology under IFRS: (1) trading securities are commonly referred to as *financial assets at fair value through profit and loss,* and (2) available-for-sale securities are commonly referred to as *available-for-sale financial assets.* NOKIA reports the following categories for noninfluential securities: (1) *Financial assets at fair value through profit or loss,* consisting of financial assets held for trading and financial assets designated upon initial recognition as at fair value through profit or loss, (2) *Available-for-sale financial assets,* which are measured at fair value.

NOKIA

Accounting for Influential Securities   The accounting for influential securities is broadly similar across U.S. GAAP and IFRS. Specifically, under the *equity method,* the share of investee's net income is reported in the investor's income in the same period the investee earns that income; also, the investment account equals the acquisition cost plus the share of investee income less the share of investee dividends (minus amortization of excess on purchase price above fair value of identifiable, limited-life assets). Under the *consolidation method,* investee and investor revenues and expenses are combined, absent intercompany transactions, and subtracting noncontrolling interests. Also, nonintercompany assets and liabilities are similarly combined (eliminating the need for an investment account), and noncontrolling interests are subtracted from equity. There are some differences in terminology: (1) U.S. GAAP companies commonly refer to earnings from long-term investments as *equity in earnings of affiliates* whereas IFRS companies commonly use *equity in earnings of associated (or associate) companies,* (2) U.S. GAAP companies commonly refer to noncontrolling interests in consolidated subsidiaries as *minority interests* whereas IFRS companies commonly use *noncontrolling interests.*

Components of Return on Total Assets   ◻◻◻   **Decision Analysis**

A company's **return on total assets** (or simply *return on assets*) is important in assessing financial performance. The return on total assets can be separated into two components, profit margin and total asset turnover, for additional analyses. Exhibit C.9 shows how these two components determine return on total assets.

A1 Compute and analyze th
components of return or
total assets.

$$\text{Return on total assets} = \text{Profit margin} \times \text{Total asset turnover}$$

$$\frac{\text{Net income}}{\text{Average total assets}} = \frac{\text{Net income}}{\text{Net sales}} \times \frac{\text{Net sales}}{\text{Average total assets}}$$

EXHIBIT C.9

Components of Return on Total Assets

Profit margin reflects the percent of net income in each dollar of net sales. Total asset turnover reflects a company's ability to produce net sales from total assets. All companies desire a high return on total assets. By considering these two components, we can often discover strengths and weaknesses not revealed by return on total assets alone. This improves our ability to assess future performance and company strategy.

To illustrate, consider return on total assets and its components for Gap Inc. in Exhibit C.10.

EXHIBIT C.10

Gap's Components of Return on Total Assets

Fiscal Year	Return on Total Assets	=	Profit Margin	×	Total Asset Turnover
2012	11.5%	=	5.7%	×	2.01
2011	16.0	=	8.2	×	1.95
2010	14.1	=	7.7	×	1.83
2009	12.6*	=	6.7	×	1.89
2008	10.2	=	5.3	×	1.92

* Differences due to rounding.

At least three findings emerge. First, Gap's return on total assets improved from 10.2% in 2008 to 11.5% in 2012. Second, total asset turnover has slightly improved over this period, from 1.92 to 2.01. Third, Gap's profit margin steadily increased over this period, from 2008's level of 5.3%. These components reveal the dual role of profit margin and total asset turnover in determining return on total assets. They also reveal that the driver of Gap's recent improvement in return on total assets is not total asset turnover but profit margin.

Generally, if a company is to maintain or improve its return on total assets, it must meet any decline in either profit margin or total asset turnover with an increase in the other. If not, return on assets will decline. Companies consider these components in planning strategies. A component analysis can also reveal where a company is weak and where changes are needed, especially in a competitor analysis. If asset turnover is lower than the industry norm, for instance, a company should focus on raising asset turnover at least to the norm. The same applies to profit margin.

Decision Maker

Retailer You are an entrepreneur and owner of a retail sporting goods store. The store's recent annual performance reveals (industry norms in parentheses): return on total assets = 11% (11.2%); profit margin = 4.4% (3.5%); and total asset turnover = 2.5 (3.2). What does your analysis of these figures reveal? ■
[Answer—p. C-18]

COMPREHENSIVE...

NEED-TO-KNOW

The following transactions relate to Brown Company's long-term investments during 2012 and 2013. Brown did not own any long-term investments prior to 2012. Show (1) the appropriate journal entries and (2) the relevant portions of each year's balance sheet and income statement that reflect these transactions for both 2012 and 2013.

2012

Sept. 9 Purchased 1,000 shares of Packard, Inc., common stock for $80,000 cash. These shares represent 30% of Packard's outstanding shares.

Oct. 2 Purchased 2,000 shares of AT&T common stock for $60,000 cash as a long-term investment. These shares represent less than a 1% ownership in AT&T.

17 Purchased as a long-term investment 1,000 shares of Apple Computer common stock for $40,000 cash. These shares are less than 1% of Apple's outstanding shares.

Nov. 1 Received $5,000 cash dividend from Packard.

30 Received $3,000 cash dividend from AT&T.

Dec. 15 Received $1,400 cash dividend from Apple.

31 Packard's net income for this year is $70,000.

31 Fair values for the investments in equity securities are Packard, $84,000; AT&T, $48,000; and Apple Computer, $45,000.

31 For preparing financial statements, note the following post-closing account balances: Common Stock, $500,000, and Retained Earnings, $350,000.

2013

Jan. 1 Sold Packard, Inc., shares for $108,000 cash.

May 30 Received $3,100 cash dividend from AT&T.

June 15 Received $1,600 cash dividend from Apple.

Aug. 17 Sold the AT&T stock for $52,000 cash.
  19 Purchased 2,000 shares of Coca-Cola common stock for $50,000 cash as a long-term invest-
      ment. The stock represents less than a 5% ownership in Coca-Cola.
Dec. 15 Received $1,800 cash dividend from Apple.
  31 Fair values of the investments in equity securities are Apple, $39,000, and Coca-Cola, $48,000.
  31 For preparing financial statements, note the following post-closing account balances: Common
      Stock, $500,000, and Retained Earnings, $410,000.

PLANNING THE SOLUTION

- Account for the investment in Packard under the equity method.
- Account for the investments in AT&T, Apple, and Coca-Cola as long-term investments in available-for-
  sale securities.
- Prepare the information for the two years' balance sheets by including the relevant asset and equity
  accounts, and the two years' income statements by identifying the relevant revenues, earnings, gains,
  and losses.

SOLUTION TO COMPREHENSIVE NEED-TO-KNOW

1. Journal entries for 2012.

Sept. 9	Long-Term Investments—Packard	80,000	
	Cash		80,000
	Acquired 1,000 shares, representing a 30% equity in Packard.		
Oct. 2	Long-Term Investments—AFS (AT&T)	60,000	
	Cash		60,000
	Acquired 2,000 shares as a long-term investment in available-for-sale securities.		
Oct. 17	Long-Term Investments—AFS (Apple)	40,000	
	Cash		40,000
	Acquired 1,000 shares as a long-term investment in available-for-sale securities.		
Nov. 1	Cash	5,000	
	Long-Term Investments—Packard		5,000
	Received dividend from Packard.		
Nov. 30	Cash	3,000	
	Dividend Revenue		3,000
	Received dividend from AT&T.		
Dec. 15	Cash	1,400	
	Dividend Revenue		1,400
	Received dividend from Apple.		
Dec. 31	Long-Term Investments—Packard	21,000	
	Earnings from Investment (Packard)		21,000
	To record 30% share of Packard's annual earnings of $70,000.		
Dec. 31	Unrealized Loss—Equity	7,000	
	Fair Value Adjustment—Available-for-Sale (LT)* ...		7,000
	To record change in fair value of long-term available-for-sale securities.		

* Fair value adjustment computations:

	Cost	Fair Value	Unrealized Gain (Loss)
AT&T	$ 60,000	$48,000	$(12,000)
Apple	40,000	45,000	5,000
Total	$100,000	$93,000	$ (7,000)

Required balance of the Fair Value
Adjustment—Available-for-Sale
(LT) account (credit) .... $(7,000)
Existing balance 0
Necessary adjustment (credit) ...... $(7,000)

2. The December 31, 2012, selected balance sheet items appear as follows.

Assets	
Long-term investments	
Available-for-sale securities (at fair value; cost is $100,000)	$ 93,000
Investment in equity securities	96,000
Total long-term investments	189,000
Stockholders' Equity	
Common stock	500,000
Retained earnings	350,000
Unrealized loss—Equity	(7,000)

The relevant income statement items for the year ended December 31, 2012, follow.

Dividend revenue	$ 4,400
Earnings from investment	21,000

1. Journal entries for 2013.

Jan. 1	Cash	108,000	
	Long-Term Investments—Packard		96,000
	Gain on Sale of Long-Term Investments		12,000
	Sold 1,000 shares for cash.		
May 30	Cash	3,100	
	Dividend Revenue		3,100
	Received dividend from AT&T.		
June 15	Cash	1,600	
	Dividend Revenue		1,600
	Received dividend from Apple.		
Aug. 17	Cash	52,000	
	Loss on Sale of Long-Term Investments	8,000	
	Long-Term Investments—AFS (AT&T)		60,000
	Sold 2,000 shares for cash.		
Aug. 19	Long-Term Investments—AFS (Coca-Cola)	50,000	
	Cash		50,000
	Acquired 2,000 shares as a long-term investment in available-for-sale securities.		
Dec. 15	Cash	1,800	
	Dividend Revenue		1,800
	Received dividend from Apple.		
Dec. 31	Fair Value Adjustment—Available-for-Sale (LT)*	4,000	
	Unrealized Loss—Equity		4,000
	To record change in fair value of long-term available-for-sale securities.		

* Fair value adjustment computations:

	Cost	Fair Value	Unrealized Gain (Loss)
Apple	$40,000	$39,000	$(1,000)
Coca-Cola	50,000	48,000	(2,000)
Total	$90,000	$87,000	$(3,000)

Required balance of the Fair Value Adjustment—Available-for-Sale (LT) account (credit)	$(3,000)
Existing balance (credit)	(7,000)
Necessary adjustment (debit)	$ 4,000

2. The December 31, 2013, balance sheet items appear as follows.

Assets

Long-term investments

Available-for-sale securities (at fair value; cost is $90,000) . . . . $ 87,000

Stockholders' Equity

Common stock   500,000

Retained earnings   410,000

Unrealized loss—Equity . . . .   (3,000)

The relevant income statement items for the year ended December 31, 2013, follow.

Dividend revenue . . . . $ 6,500

Gain on sale of long-term investments   12,000

Loss on sale of long-term investments . . . .   (8,000)

Investments in International Operations

C-A

Many entities from small entrepreneurs to large corporations conduct business internationally. Some entities' operations occur in so many different countries that the companies are called **multinationals.** Many of us think of Coca-Cola and McDonald's, for example, as primarily U.S. companies, but most of their sales occur outside the United States. Exhibit C-A.1 shows the percent of international sales and income for selected U.S. companies. Managing and accounting for multinationals present challenges. This section describes some of these challenges and how to account for and report these activities.

Two major accounting challenges that arise when companies have international operations relate to transactions that involve more than one currency. The first is to account for sales and purchases listed in a foreign currency. The second is to prepare consolidated financial statements with international subsidiaries. For ease in this discussion, we use companies with a U.S. base of operations and assume the need to prepare financial statements in U.S. dollars. This means the *reporting currency* of these companies is the U.S. dollar.

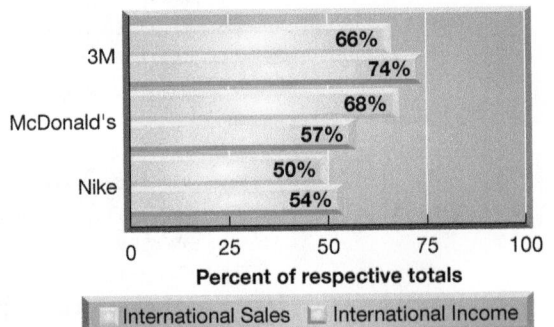

EXHIBIT C-A.1

International Sales and Income as a Percent of Their Totals

Point: Transactions *listed* or *stated* in a foreign currency are said to be *denominated* in that currency.

Exchange Rates between Currencies   Markets for the purchase and sale of foreign currencies exist all over the world. In these markets, U.S. dollars can be exchanged for Canadian dollars, British pounds, Japanese yen, Euros, or any other legal currencies. The price of one currency stated in terms of another currency is called a **foreign exchange rate.** Exhibit C-A.2 lists recent exchange rates for selected currencies. The exchange rate for British pounds and U.S. dollars is $1.8980, meaning 1 British pound could be purchased for $1.8980. On that same day, the exchange rate between Mexican pesos and U.S. dollars is $0.0925, or 1 Mexican peso can be purchased for $0.0925. Exchange rates fluctuate due to changing economic and political conditions, including the supply and demand for currencies and expectations about future events.

C3   Explain foreign exchange rates and record transactions listed in a foreign currency.

Point: To convert currency, see XE.c[

Decision Insight

Greek Haircut   Investors in government debt securities in the Eurozone must be careful of the heightened default risk associated with securities issued by certain Eurozone member nations. For example, in 2012, buyers of certain Greek bonds were repaid only 30% of principal because of the government's inability to honor its full obligation on the bonds. ■

EXHIBIT C-A.2

Foreign Exchange Rates for Selected Currencies*

Source (unit)	Price in $U.S.	Source (unit)	Price in $U.S.
Britain (pound)	$1.8980	Canada (dollar)	$0.9793
Mexico (peso)	0.0925	Japan (yen)	0.0090
Taiwan (dollar)	0.0305	Europe (Euro)	1.2920

* Rates will vary over time based on economic, political, and other changes.

Sales and Purchases Listed in a Foreign Currency   When a U.S. company makes a credit sale to an international customer, accounting for the sale and the account receivable is straightforward if sales terms require the international customer's payment in U.S. dollars. If sale terms require (or allow) payment in a foreign currency, however, the U.S. company must account for the sale and the account receivable in a different manner.

Sales in a Foreign Currency   To illustrate, consider the case of the U.S.-based manufacturer Boston Company, which makes credit sales to London Outfitters, a British retail company. A sale occurs on December 12, 2012, for a price of £10,000 with payment due on February 10, 2013. Boston Company keeps its accounting records in U.S. dollars. To record the sale, Boston Company must translate the sales price from pounds to dollars. This is done using the exchange rate on the date of the sale. Assuming the exchange rate on December 12, 2012, is $1.80, Boston records this sale as follows.

Assets = Liabilities + Equity
+18,000   +18,000

Dec. 12	Accounts Receivable—London Outfitters	18,000	
	Sales*		18,000
	To record a sale at £10,000, when the exchange rate equals $1.80. * (£10,000 × $1.80/£)		

When Boston Company prepares its annual financial statements on December 31, 2012, the current exchange rate is $1.84. Thus, the current dollar value of Boston Company's receivable is $18,400 (£10,000 × $1.84/£). This amount is $400 higher than the amount recorded on December 12. Accounting principles require a receivable to be reported in the balance sheet at its current dollar value. Thus, Boston Company must make the following entry to record the increase in the dollar value of this receivable at year-end.

Assets = Liabilities + Equity
+400   +400

Dec. 31	Accounts Receivable—London Outfitters	400	
	Foreign Exchange Gain		400
	To record the increased value of the British pound for the receivable.		

Point: Foreign exchange gains are credits, and foreign exchange losses are debits.

On February 10, 2013, Boston Company receives London Outfitters' payment of £10,000. It immediately exchanges the pounds for U.S. dollars. On this date, the exchange rate for pounds is $1.78. Thus, Boston Company receives only $17,800 (£10,000 × $1.78/£). It records the cash receipt and the loss associated with the decline in the exchange rate as follows.

Assets = Liabilities + Equity
+17,800   −600
−18,400

Feb. 10	Cash	17,800	
	Foreign Exchange Loss	600	
	Accounts Receivable—London Outfitters		18,400
	Received foreign currency payment of an account and converted it into dollars.		

Gains and losses from foreign exchange transactions are accumulated in the Foreign Exchange Gain (or Loss) account. After year-end adjustments, the balance in the Foreign Exchange Gain (or Loss) account is reported on the income statement and closed to the Income Summary account.

Example: Assume that a U.S. company makes a credit purchase from a British company for £10,000 when the exchange rate is $1.62. At the balance sheet date, this rate is $1.72. Does this imply a gain or loss for the U.S. company? *Answer:* A loss.

Purchases in a Foreign Currency   Accounting for credit purchases from an international seller is similar to the case of a credit sale to an international customer. In particular, if the U.S. company is required to make payment in a foreign currency, the account payable must be translated into dollars before the U.S. company can record it. If the exchange rate is different when preparing financial statements and when paying for the purchase, the U.S. company must recognize a foreign exchange gain or loss at those dates. To illustrate, assume NC Imports, a U.S. company, purchases products costing €20,000 (euros) from

Hamburg Brewing on January 15, when the exchange rate is $1.20 per euro. NC records this transaction as follows.

Jan. 15	Inventory	24,000	
	Accounts Payable—Hamburg Brewing		24,000
	To record a €20,000 purchase when exchange rate is $1.20 (€20,000 × $1.20/€)		

Assets = Liabilities + Equity
+24,000   +24,000

NC Imports makes payment in full on February 14 when the exchange rate is $1.25 per euro, which is recorded as follows.

Feb. 14	Accounts Payable—Hamburg Brewing	24,000	
	Foreign Exchange Loss	1,000	
	Cash		25,000
	To record cash payment towards €20,000 account when exchange rate is $1.25 (€20,000 × $1.25/€).		

Assets = Liabilities + Equity
−25,000   −24,000   −1,000

Decision Insight

Global Greenback   What do changes in foreign exchange rates mean? A decline in the price of the U.S. dollar against other currencies usually yields increased international sales for U.S. companies, without hiking prices or cutting costs, and puts them on a stronger competitive footing abroad. At home, they can raise prices without fear that foreign rivals will undercut them. ∎

Consolidated Statements with International Subsidiaries   A second challenge in accounting for international operations involves preparing consolidated financial statements when the parent company has one or more international subsidiaries. Consider a U.S.-based company that owns a controlling interest in a French subsidiary. The reporting currency of the U.S. parent is the dollar. The French subsidiary maintains its financial records in euros. Before preparing consolidated statements, the parent must translate financial statements of the French company into U.S. dollars. After this translation is complete (including that for accounting differences), it prepares consolidated statements the same as for domestic subsidiaries. Procedures for translating an international subsidiary's account balances depend on the nature of the subsidiary's operations. The process requires the parent company to select appropriate foreign exchange rates and to apply those rates to the foreign subsidiary's account balances. This is described in advanced courses.

Global: A weaker U.S. dollar often increases global sales for U.S. companie[s]

Decision Maker

Entrepreneur   Assume that Ben and Jerry's purchases milk from dairies in both the U.S. and Canada. The price of the Canadian dollar in terms of the U.S. dollar jumps from US$0.70 to US$0.80. Is the ice cream maker now more or less likely to buy milk from Canadian or U.S. suppliers? ∎   [Answer—p. C-18]

Summary

C1   **Distinguish between debt and equity securities and between short-term and long-term investments.** *Debt securities* reflect a creditor relationship and include investments in notes, bonds, and certificates of deposit. *Equity securities* reflect an owner relationship and include shares of stock issued by other companies. Short-term investments in securities are current assets that meet two criteria: (1) They are expected to be converted into cash within one year or the current operating cycle of the business, whichever is longer and (2) they are readily convertible to cash, or *marketable*. All other investments in securities are long-term. Long-term investments also include assets not used in operations and those held for special purposes, such as land for expansion. Investments in securities are classified into one of five groups: (1) trading securities, which are always short-term, (2) debt securi-

ties held-to-maturity, (3) debt and equity securities available-for-sale, (4) equity securities in which an investor has a significant influence over the investee, and (5) equity securities in which an investor has a controlling influence over the investee.

C2   **Describe how to report equity securities with controlling influence.** If an investor owns more than 50% of another company's voting stock and controls the investee, the investor's financial reports are prepared on a consolidated basis. These repo[rts] are prepared as if the company were organized as one entity.

C3A   **Explain foreign exchange rates and record transactions listed in a foreign currency.** A foreign exchange rate is t[he] price of one currency stated in terms of another. An entity with transactions in a foreign currency when the exchange rate chang[es] between the transaction dates and their settlement will experience exchange gains or losses. When a company makes a credit sale to a foreign customer and sales terms call for payment in a foreign currency, the company must translate the foreign currency into dollars to record the receivable. If the exchange rate changes before payment is received, exchange gains or losses are recognized in the year they occur. The same treatment is used when a company makes a credit purchase from a foreign supplier and is required to make payment in a foreign currency.

A1 **Compute and analyze the components of return on total assets.** Return on total assets has two components: profit margin and total asset turnover. A decline in one component must be met with an increase in another if return on assets is to be maintained. Component analysis is helpful in assessing company performance compared to that of competitors and its own past.

P1 **Account for trading securities.** Investments are initially recorded at cost, and any dividend or interest from these investments is recorded in the income statement. Investments classified as trading securities are reported at fair value. Unrealized gains and losses on trading securities are reported in income. When investments are sold, the difference between the net proceeds from the sale and the cost of the securities is recognized as a gain or loss.

P2 **Account for held-to-maturity securities.** Debt securities held-to-maturity are reported at cost when purchased. Interest revenue is recorded as it accrues. The cost of long-term held-to-maturity securities is adjusted for the amortization of any difference between cost and maturity value.

P3 **Account for available-for-sale securities.** Debt and equity securities available-for-sale are recorded at cost when purchased. Available-for-sale securities are reported at their fair values on the balance sheet with unrealized gains or losses shown in the equity section. Gains and losses realized on the sale of these investments are reported in the income statement.

P4 **Account for equity securities with significant influence.** The equity method is used when an investor has a significant influence over an investee. This usually exists when an investor owns 20% or more of the investee's voting stock but not more than 50%. The equity method means an investor records its share of investee earnings with a debit to the investment account and a credit to a revenue account. Dividends received reduce the investment account balance.

Guidance Answers to Decision Maker

Money Manager If you have investments in fixed-rate bonds and notes when interest rates fall, the value of your investments increases. This is so because the bonds and notes you hold continue to pay the same (high) rate while the market is demanding a new lower interest rate. Your strategy is to continue holding your investments in bonds and notes, and, potentially, to increase these holdings through additional purchases.

Retailer Your store's return on assets is 11%, which is similar to the industry norm of 11.2%. However, disaggregation of return on assets reveals that your store's profit margin of 4.4% is much higher than the norm of 3.5%, but your total asset turnover of 2.5 is much lower than the norm of 3.2. These results suggest that, as compared with competitors, you are less efficient in using assets. You need to

focus on increasing sales or reducing assets. You might consider reducing prices to increase sales, provided such a strategy does not reduce your return on assets. For instance, you could reduce your profit margin to 4% to increase sales. If total asset turnover increases to more than 2.75 when profit margin is lowered to 4%, your overall return on assets is improved.

Entrepreneur You are now less likely to buy Canadian milk products because it takes more U.S. money to buy a Canadian dollar (and milk). For instance, the purchase of milk from a Canadian dairy with a $1,000 (Canadian dollars) price would have cost the U.S. company $700 (U.S. dollars, computed as C$1,000 × US$0.70) before the rate change, and $800 (US dollars, computed as C$1,000 × US$0.80) after the rate change.

Key Terms

Available-for-sale (AFS) securities (p. C-5)

Comprehensive income (p. C-10)

Consolidated financial statements (p. C-9)

Equity method (p. C-7)

Equity securities with controlling influence (p. C-9)

Equity securities with significant influence (p. C-7)

Foreign exchange rate (p. C-15)

Held-to-maturity (HTM) securities (p. C-5)

Long-term investments (p. C-1)

Multinational (p. C-15)

Other comprehensive income (p. C-10)

Parent (p. C-9)

Return on total assets (p. C-11)

Short-term investments (p. C-1)

Subsidiary (p. C-9)

Trading securities (p. C-3)

Unrealized gain (loss) (p. C-4)

1. A company purchased $30,000 of 5% bonds for investment purposes on May 1. The bonds pay interest on February 1 and August 1. The amount of interest revenue accrued at December 31 (the company's year-end) is:
   a. $1,500
   b. $1,375
   c. $1,000
   d. $625
   e. $300

2. Earlier this period, Amadeus Co. purchased its only available-for-sale investment in the stock of Bach Co. for $83,000. The period-end fair value of this stock is $84,500. Amadeus records a:
   a. Credit to Unrealized Gain—Equity for $1,500.
   b. Debit to Unrealized Loss—Equity for $1,500.
   c. Debit to Investment Revenue for $1,500.
   d. Credit to Fair Value Adjustment—Available-for-Sale for $3,500.
   e. Credit to Cash for $1,500.

3. Mozart Co. owns 35% of Melody Inc. Melody pays $50,000 in cash dividends to its shareholders for the period. Mozart's entry to record the Melody dividend includes a:
   a. Credit to Investment Revenue for $50,000.
   b. Credit to Long-Term Investments for $17,500.

   c. Credit to Cash for $17,500.
   d. Debit to Long-Term Investments for $17,500.
   e. Debit to Cash for $50,000.

4. A company has net income of $300,000, net sales of $2,500,000, and total assets of $2,000,000. Its return on total assets equals:
   a. 6.7%
   b. 12.0%
   c. 8.3%
   d. 80.0%
   e. 15.0%

5. A company had net income of $80,000, net sales of $600,000, and total assets of $400,000. Its profit margin and total asset turnover are:

	Profit Margin	Total Asset Turnover
a.	1.5%	13.3
b.	13.3%	1.5
c.	13.3%	0.7
d.	7.0%	13.3
e.	10.0%	26.7

^A Superscript A denotes assignments based on Appendix C-A.

Icon denotes assignments that involve decision making.

Discussion Questions

1. Under what two conditions should investments be classified as current assets?

2. On a balance sheet, what valuation must be reported for short-term investments in trading securities?

3. If a short-term investment in available-for-sale securities costs $10,000 and is sold for $12,000, how should the difference between these two amounts be recorded?

4. Identify the three classes of noninfluential and two classes of influential investments in securities.

5. Under what conditions should investments be classified as current assets? As long-term assets?

6. For investments in available-for-sale securities, how are unrealized (holding) gains and losses reported?

7. If a company purchases its only long-term investments in available-for-sale debt securities this period and their fair value is below cost at the balance sheet date, what entry is required to recognize this unrealized loss?

8. On a balance sheet, what valuation must be reported for debt securities classified as available-for-sale?

9. Under what circumstances are long-term investments in debt securities reported at cost and adjusted for amortization of any difference between cost and maturity value?

10. In accounting for investments in equity securities, when should the equity method be used?

11. Under what circumstances does a company prepare consoli dated financial statements?

12.^A What are two major challenges in accounting for interna tional operations?

13.^A Assume a U.S. company makes a credit sale to a foreign customer that is required to make payment in its foreign cur rency. In the current period, the exchange rate is $1.40 on the date of the sale and is $1.30 on the date the customer pays the receivable. Will the U.S. company record an exchange gain or loss?

14.^A If a U.S. company makes a credit sale to a foreign custome required to make payment in U.S. dollars, can the U.S. compan have an exchange gain or loss on this sale?

QUICK STUDY

QS C-1

Short-term equity investments

P1

On April 18, Riley Co. made a short-term investment in 300 common shares of XLT Co. The purchase price is $42 per share and the broker's fee is $250. The intent is to actively manage these shares for profit. On May 30, Riley Co. receives $1 per share from XLT in dividends. Prepare the April 18 and May 30 journal entries to record these transactions.

QS C-2

Available-for-sale securities

P3

Journ Co. purchased short-term investments in available-for-sale securities at a cost of $50,000 on November 25, 2013. At December 31, 2013, these securities had a fair value of $47,000. This is the first and only time the company has purchased such securities.

1. Prepare the December 31, 2013, year-end adjusting entry for the securities' portfolio.

2. For each account in the entry for part 1, explain how it is reported in financial statements.

3. Prepare the April 6, 2014, entry when Journ sells one-half of these securities for $26,000.

QS C-3

Available-for-sale securities

P3

Prepare Hertog Company's journal entries to reflect the following transactions for the current year.

May 7   Purchases 200 shares of Kraft stock as a short-term investment in available-for-sale securities at a cost of $50 per share plus $300 in broker fees.

June 6   Sells 200 shares of its investment in Kraft stock at $56 per share. The broker's commission on this sale is $150.

QS C-4

Available-for-sale securities

P3

Hiker Company completes the following transactions during the current year.

May 9   Purchases 200 shares of Higo stock as a short-term investment in available-for-sale securities at a cost of $25 per share plus $150 in broker fees.

June 2   Sells 100 shares of its investment in Higo stock at $28 per share. The broker's commission on this sale is $90.

Dec. 31   The closing market price (fair value) of the Higo stock is $23 per share.

Prepare the May 9 and June 2 journal entries and the December 31 adjusting entry. This is the first and only time the company purchased such securities.

QS C-5

Identifying long-term investments

C1

Which of the following statements are true of long-term investments?

a. They are held as an investment of cash available for current operations.

b. They can include funds earmarked for a special purpose, such as bond sinking funds.

c. They can include investments in trading securities.

d. They can include debt securities held-to-maturity.

e. They are always easily sold and therefore qualify as being marketable.

f. They can include debt and equity securities available-for-sale.

g. They can include bonds and stocks not intended to serve as a ready source of cash.

QS C-6

Describing investments in securities

C1 C2

Complete the following descriptions by filling in the blanks.

1. Equity securities giving an investor significant influence are accounted for using the _____ _____.

2. Available-for-sale debt securities are reported on the balance sheet at _____ _____.

3. Trading securities are classified as _____ assets.

4. Accrual of interest on bonds held as long-term investments requires a credit to _____ _____.

5. The controlling investor (more than 50% ownership) is called the _____, and the investee company is called the _____.

QS C-7

Debt securities transactions

P2

On February 1, 2013, Garzon purchased 6% bonds issued by PBS Utilities at a cost of $40,000, which is their par value. The bonds pay interest semiannually on July 31 and January 31. For 2013, prepare entries to record Garzon's July 31 receipt of interest and its December 31 year-end interest accrual.

QS C-8

Recording equity securities

P3

On May 20, 2013, Montero Co. paid $1,000,000 to acquire 25,000 common shares (10%) of ORD Corp. as a long-term investment. On August 5, 2014, Montero sold one-half of these shares for $625,000. What valuation method should be used to account for this stock investment? Prepare entries to record both the acquisition and the sale of these shares.

Assume the same facts as in QS C-8 except that the stock acquired represents 40% of ORD Corp.'s outstanding stock. Also assume that ORD Corp. paid a $100,000 dividend on November 1, 2013, and reported a net income of $700,000 for 2013. Prepare the entries to record (a) the receipt of the dividend and (b) the December 31, 2013, year-end adjustment required for the investment account.

QS C-9
Equity method transactions
P4

During the current year, Reed Consulting Group acquired long-term available-for-sale securities at a $70,000 cost. At its December 31 year-end, these securities had a fair value of $58,000. This is the first and only time the company purchased such securities.
1. Prepare the necessary year-end adjusting entry related to these securities.
2. Explain how each account used in part 1 is reported in the financial statements.

QS C-10
Recording fair value adjustment for securities
P3

Complete the following descriptions by filling in the blanks.
1. The controlling investor is called the _____, and the investee is called the _____.
2. A long-term investment classified as equity securities with controlling influence implies that the investor can exert a _____ influence over the investee.

QS C-11
Equity securities with controlling influence
C2

The return on total assets is the focus of analysts, creditors, and other users of financial statements.
1. How is the return on total assets computed?
2. What does this important ratio reflect?

QS C-12
Return on total assets   A1

Return on total assets can be separated into two important components.
1. Write the formula to separate the return on total assets into its two basic components.
2. Explain how these components of the return on total assets are helpful to financial statement users for business decisions.

QS C-13
Component return on total assets   A1

A U.S. company sells a product to a British company with the transaction listed in British pounds. On the date of the sale, the transaction total of $14,500 is billed as £10,000, reflecting an exchange rate of 1.45 (that is, $1.45 per pound). Prepare the entry to record (1) the sale and (2) the receipt of payment in pounds when the exchange rate is 1.35.

QS C-14ᴬ
Foreign currency transactions
C3

On March 1, 2013, a U.S. company made a credit sale requiring payment in 30 days from a Malaysian company, Hamac Sdn. Bhd., in 20,000 Malaysian ringgits. Assuming the exchange rate between Malaysian ringgits and U.S. dollars is $0.4538 on March 1 and $0.4899 on March 31, prepare the entries to record the sale on March 1 and the cash receipt on March 31.

QS C-15ᴬ
Foreign currency transactions
C3

The Carrefour Group reports the following description of its trading securities (titled "financial assets reported at fair value in the income statement").

> These are financial assets held by the Group in order to make a short-term profit on the sale. These assets are valued at their fair value with variations in value recognized in the income statement.

Note 10 to Carrefour's 2010 financial statements reports €7 million in unrealized gains for 2010 and €26 million in unrealized losses for 2010, both included in the fair value of those financial assets held for trading. What amount of these unrealized gains and unrealized losses, if any, are reported in its 2010 income statement? Explain.

QS C-16
International accounting for investments
P1

---

connect

Prepare journal entries to record the following transactions involving the short-term securities investments of Duke Co., all of which occurred during year 2013.
a. On March 22, purchased 1,000 shares of RIP Company stock at $10 per share plus a $80 brokerage fee. These shares are categorized as trading securities.
b. On September 1, received a $1.00 per share cash dividend on the RIP Company stock purchased in transaction a.
c. On October 8, sold 500 shares of RIP Co. stock for $15 per share, less a $50 brokerage fee.

EXERCISES

Exercise C-1
Accounting for short-term trading securities
P1

(c) Dr. Cash $7,450

Exercise C-2

Accounting for short-term held-to-maturity securities   P2

Prepare journal entries to record the following transactions involving the short-term securities investments of Natura Co., all of which occurred during year 2013.

a. On June 15, paid $1,000,000 cash to purchase Remedy's 90-day short-term debt securities ($1,000,000 principal), dated June 15, that pay 10% interest (categorized as held-to-maturity securities).

b. On September 16, received a check from Remedy in payment of the principal and 90 days' interest on the debt securities purchased in transaction *a*.

Exercise C-3

Accounting for short-term available-for-sale securities

P3

Prepare journal entries to record the following transactions involving the short-term securities investments of Krum Co., all of which occurred during year 2013.

a. On August 1, paid $450,000 cash to purchase Houtte's 9% debt securities ($450,000 principal), dated July 30, 2013, and maturing January 30, 2014 (categorized as available-for-sale securities).

b. On October 30, received a check from Houtte for 90 days' interest on the debt securities purchased in transaction *a*.

Exercise C-4

Debt and equity securities and short- and long-term investments

C1

Complete the following descriptions by filling in the blanks.

1. Debt securities reflect a _____ relationship such as investments in notes, bonds, and certificates of deposit.

2. Equity securities reflect an _____ relationship such as shares of stock issued by companies.

3. Short-term investments are securities that (1) management intends to convert to cash within ___ ___ or the ___ ___ whichever is longer, and (2) are readily convertible to _____.

4. Long-term investments in securities are defined as those securities that are ___ ___ convertible to cash or are ___ ___ to be converted into cash in the short term.

Exercise C-5

Equity securities with controlling influence

C2

Complete the following descriptions by filling in the blanks.

1. Consolidated _____ _____ show the financial position, results of operations, and cash flows of all entities under the parent's control, including all subsidiaries.

2. The equity method with _____ is used to account for long-term investments in equity securities with controlling influence.

Exercise C-6

Accounting for trading securities

P1

Check   (3) Gain, $2,000

Brooks Co. purchases various investments in trading securities at a cost of $66,000 on December 27, 2013. (This is its first and only purchase of such securities.) At December 31, 2013, these securities had a fair value of $72,000.

1. Prepare the December 31, 2013, year-end adjusting entry for the trading securities' portfolio.

2. Explain how each account in the entry of part 1 is reported in financial statements.

3. Prepare the January 3, 2014, entry when Brooks sells a portion of its trading securities (that had originally cost $33,000) for $35,000.

Exercise C-7

Adjusting available-for-sale securities to fair value

P3

Check   Unrealized loss, $9,100

On December 31, 2013, Reggit Company held the following short-term investments in its portfolio of available-for-sale securities. Reggit had no short-term investments in its prior accounting periods. Prepare the December 31, 2013, adjusting entry to report these investments at fair value.

	Cost	Fair Value
Verrizano Corporation bonds payable	$89,600	$91,600
Preble Corporation notes payable	70,600	62,900
Lucerne Company common stock	86,500	83,100

Exercise C-8

Transactions in short-term and long-term investments

P1 P2 P3

Prepare journal entries to record the following transactions involving both the short-term and long-term investments of Cancun Corp., all of which occurred during calendar year 2013. Use the account Short-Term Investments for any transactions that you determine are short term.

a. On February 15, paid $160,000 cash to purchase American General's 90-day short-term notes at par, which are dated February 15 and pay 10% interest (classified as held-to-maturity).

b. On March 22, bought 700 shares of Fran Industries common stock at $51 cash per share plus a $150 brokerage fee (classified as long-term available-for-sale securities).

c. On May 15, received a check from American General in payment of the principal and 90 days' interest on the notes purchased in transaction *a*.

d. On July 30, paid $100,000 cash to purchase MP3 Electronics' 8% notes at par, dated July 30, 2013, and maturing on January 30, 2014 (classified as trading securities).

e. On September 1, received a $1.00 per share cash dividend on the Fran Industries common stock purchased in transaction *b*.

f. On October 8, sold 350 shares of Fran Industries common stock for $64 cash per share, less a $125 brokerage fee.

g. On October 30, received a check from MP3 Electronics for three months' interest on the notes purchased in transaction *d*.

On December 31, 2013, Lujack Co. held the following short-term available-for-sale securities.

	Cost	Fair Value
Nintendo Co. common stock	$44,450	$48,900
Atlantic bonds payable	49,000	47,000
Kellogg Co. notes payable	25,000	23,200
McDonald's Corp. common stock	46,300	44,800

Lujack had no short-term investments prior to the current period. Prepare the December 31, 2013, year-end adjusting entry to record the fair value adjustment for these securities.

Exercise C-9
Fair value adjustment to available-for-sale securities

P3

Prescrip Co. began operations in 2012. The cost and fair values for its long-term investments portfolio in available-for-sale securities are shown below. Prepare Prescrip's December 31, 2013, adjusting entry to reflect any necessary fair value adjustment for these investments.

	Cost	Fair Value
December 31, 2012.........	$120,483	$118,556
December 31, 2013.........	60,120	90,271

Exercise C-10
Fair value adjustment to available-for-sale securities

P3

Ticker Services began operations in 2011 and maintains long-term investments in available-for-sale securities. The year-end cost and fair values for its portfolio of these investments follow. Prepare journal entries to record each year-end fair value adjustment for these securities.

	Cost	Fair Value
December 31, 2011	$372,000	$360,860
December 31, 2012	428,500	455,800
December 31, 2013	600,200	700,500
December 31, 2014	876,900	780,200

Exercise C-11
Multiyear fair value adjustment to available-for-sale securities

P3

Information regarding Carperk Company's individual investments in securities during its calendar-year 2013, along with the December 31, 2013, fair values, follows.

a. Investment in Brava Company bonds: $420,500 cost, $457,000 fair value. Carperk intends to hold these bonds until they mature in 2018.

b. Investment in Baybridge common stock: 29,500 shares; $362,450 cost; $391,375 fair value. Carperk owns 32% of Baybridge's voting stock and has a significant influence over Baybridge.

c. Investment in Buffa common stock: 12,000 shares; $165,500 cost; $178,000 fair value. This investment amounts to 3% of Buffa's outstanding shares, and Carperk's goal with this investment is to earn dividends over the next few years.

d. Investment in Newton common stock: 3,500 shares; $90,300 cost; $88,625 fair value. Carperk's goal with this investment is to reap an increase in fair value of the stock over the next three to five years. Newton has 30,000 common shares outstanding.

e. Investment in Farmers common stock: 16,300 shares; $100,860 cost; $111,210 fair value. This stock is marketable and is held as an investment of cash available for operations.

Exercise C-12
Classifying investments in securities; recording fair values

C1 P2 P3 P4

Required

1. Identify whether each investment should be classified as a short-term or long-term investment. For each long-term investment, indicate in which of the long-term investment classifications it should be placed.

2. Prepare a journal entry dated December 31, 2013, to record the fair value adjustment of the long-term investments in available-for-sale securities. Carperk had no long-term investments prior to year 2013.

Exercise C-13
Securities transactions;
equity method
P4

Prepare journal entries to record the following transactions and events of Kodax Company.

2013

Jan.   2   Purchased 30,000 shares of Grecco Co. common stock for $408,000 cash plus a broker's fee of $3,000 cash. Bushtex has 90,000 shares of common stock outstanding and its policies will be significantly influenced by Kodax.
Sept. 1   Grecco declared and paid a cash dividend of $1.50 per share.
Dec. 31   Grecco announced that net income for the year is $486,900.

2014

June   1   Grecco declared and paid a cash dividend of $2.10 per share.
Dec. 31   Grecco announced that net income for the year is $702,750.
Dec. 31   Kodax sold 10,000 shares of Grecco for $320,000 cash.

Exercise C-14
Return on total assets
A1

The following information is available from the financial statements of Regae Industries. Compute Regae's return on total assets for 2013 and 2014. (Round returns to one-tenth of a percent.) Comment on the company's efficiency in using its assets in 2013 and 2014.

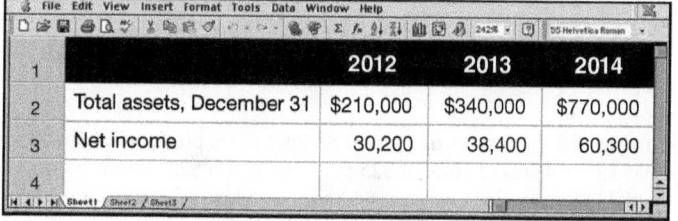

	2012	2013	2014
Total assets, December 31	$210,000	$340,000	$770,000
Net income	30,200	38,400	60,300

Exercise C-15^A

Exercise C-15^A
Foreign currency transactions
C3

Leigh of New York sells its products to customers in the United States and the United Kingdom. On December 16, 2013, Leigh sold merchandise on credit to Bronson Ltd. of London at a price of 17,000 pounds. The exchange rate on that day for £1 was $1.4583. On December 31, 2013, when Leigh prepared its financial statements, the rate was £1 for $1.4382. Bronson paid its bill in full on January 15, 2014, at which time the exchange rate was £1 for $1.4482. Leigh immediately exchanged the 17,000 pounds for U.S. dollars. Prepare Leigh's journal entries on December 16, December 31, and January 15 (round to the nearest dollar).

Exercise C-16^A
Computing foreign exchange
gains and losses on receivables
C3

On May 8, 2013, Jett Company (a U.S. company) made a credit sale to Lopez (a Mexican company). The terms of the sale required Lopez to pay 800,000 pesos on February 10, 2014. Jett prepares quarterly financial statements on March 31, June 30, September 30, and December 31. The exchange rates for pesos during the time the receivable is outstanding follow.

May 8, 2013	$0.1323
June 30, 2013	0.1352
September 30, 2013	0.1368
December 31, 2013	0.1335
February 10, 2014	0.1386

Compute the foreign exchange gain or loss that Jett should report on each of its quarterly income statements for the last three quarters of 2013 and the first quarter of 2014. Also compute the amount reported on Jett's balance sheets at the end of each of its last three quarters of 2013.

The Carrefour Group reports the following description of its financial assets available-for-sale.

Exercise C-17
International accounting
for investments

P3

> Assets available for sale are . . . valued at fair value. Unrealized . . . gains or losses are recorded as shareholders' equity until they are sold.

Note 10 to Carrefour's 2010 financial statements reports €18 million in *net* unrealized losses (net of unrealized gains) for 2010, which is included in the fair value of its available-for-sale securities reported on the balance sheet.

1. What amount of the €18 million net unrealized losses, if any, is reported in its 2010 income statement? Explain.

2. If the €18 million net unrealized losses are not reported in the income statement, in which statement are they reported, if any? Explain.

connect

Carlsville Company, which began operations in 2013, invests its idle cash in trading securities. The following transactions are from its short-term investments in its trading securities.

PROBLEM SET A

Problem C-1A
Recording transactions and
fair value adjustments for
trading securities

P1

2013

Jan. 20   Purchased 800 shares of Ford Motor Co. at $26 per share plus a $125 commission.
Feb. 9   Purchased 2,200 shares of Lucent at $44.25 per share plus a $578 commission.
Oct. 12   Purchased 750 shares of Z-Seven at $7.50 per share plus a $200 commission.

2014

Apr. 15   Sold 800 shares of Ford Motor Co. at $29 per share less a $285 commission.
July 5   Sold 750 shares of Z-Seven at $10.25 per share less a $102.50 commission.
July 22   Purchased 1,600 shares of Hunt Corp. at $30 per share plus a $444 commission.
Aug. 19   Purchased 1,800 shares of Donna Karan at $18.25 per share plus a $290 commission.

2015

Feb. 27   Purchased 3,400 shares of HCA at $34 per share plus a $420 commission.
Mar. 3   Sold 1,600 shares of Hunt at $25 per share less a $250 commission.
June 21   Sold 2,200 shares of Lucent at $42 per share less a $420 commission.
June 30   Purchased 1,200 shares of Black & Decker at $47.50 per share plus a $595 commission.
Nov. 1   Sold 1,800 shares of Donna Karan at $18.25 per share less a $309 commission.

Required

1. Prepare journal entries to record these short-term investment activities for the years shown. (Ignore any year-end adjusting entries.)

2. On December 31, 2015, prepare the adjusting entry to record any necessary fair value adjustment for the portfolio of trading securities when HCA's share price is $36 and Black & Decker's share price is $43.50. (Assume the Fair Value Adjustment—Trading account had an unadjusted balance of zero.)

Check (2) Dr. Fair Value
Adjustment—Trading $985

Rose Company had no short-term investments prior to year 2013. It had the following transactions involving short-term investments in available-for-sale securities during 2013.

Problem C-2A
Recording, adjusting, and
reporting short-term available-
for-sale securities

P3

Apr. 16   Purchased 4,000 shares of Gem Co. stock at $24.25 per share plus a $180 brokerage fee.
May 1   Paid $100,000 to buy 90-day U.S. Treasury bills (debt securities): $100,000 principal amount, 6% interest, securities dated May 1.
July 7   Purchased 2,000 shares of PepsiCo stock at $49.25 per share plus a $175 brokerage fee.
      20   Purchased 1,000 shares of Xerox stock at $16.75 per share plus a $205 brokerage fee.
Aug. 3   Received a check for principal and accrued interest on the U.S. Treasury bills that matured on July 29.
      15   Received an $0.85 per share cash dividend on the Gem Co. stock.
      28   Sold 2,000 shares of Gem Co. stock at $30 per share less a $225 brokerage fee.
Oct. 1   Received a $1.90 per share cash dividend on the PepsiCo shares.
Dec. 15   Received a $1.05 per share cash dividend on the remaining Gem Co. shares.
      31   Received a $1.30 per share cash dividend on the PepsiCo shares.

Required

1. Prepare journal entries to record the preceding transactions and events.

2. Prepare a table to compare the year-end cost and fair values of Rose's short-term investments in available-for-sale securities. The year-end fair values per share are: Gem Co., $26.50; PepsiCo, $46.50; and Xerox, $13.75.

3. Prepare an adjusting entry, if necessary, to record the year-end fair value adjustment for the portfolio of short-term investments in available-for-sale securities.

Analysis Component

4. Explain the balance sheet presentation of the fair value adjustment for Rose's short-term investments.

5. How do these short-term investments affect Rose's (*a*) income statement for year 2013 and (*b*) the equity section of its balance sheet at year-end 2013?

Problem C-3A
Recording, adjusting, and reporting long-term available-for-sale securities

P3

Grass Security, which began operations in 2013, invests in long-term available-for-sale securities. Following is a series of transactions and events determining its long-term investment activity.

2013

Jan. 20 Purchased 1,000 shares of Johnson & Johnson at $20.50 per share plus a $240 commission.
Feb.   9 Purchased 1,200 shares of Sony at $46.20 per share plus a $225 commission.
June 12 Purchased 1,500 shares of Mattel at $27.00 per share plus an $195 commission.
Dec. 31 Per share fair values for stocks in the portfolio are Johnson & Johnson, $21.50; Mattel, $30.90; Sony, $38.

2014

Apr. 15 Sold 1,000 shares of Johnson & Johnson at $23.50 per share less a $525 commission.
July   5 Sold 1,500 shares of Mattel at $23.90 per share less a $235 commission.
July 22 Purchased 600 shares of Sara Lee at $22.50 per share plus a $480 commission.
Aug. 19 Purchased 900 shares of Eastman Kodak at $17 per share plus a $198 commission.
Dec. 31 Per share fair values for stocks in the portfolio are: Kodak, $19.25; Sara Lee, $20.00; Sony, $35.00.

2015

Feb. 27 Purchased 2,400 shares of Microsoft at $67.00 per share plus a $525 commission.
June 21 Sold 1,200 shares of Sony at $48.00 per share less a $880 commission.
June 30 Purchased 1,400 shares of Black & Decker at $36.00 per share plus a $435 commission.
Aug.   3 Sold 600 shares of Sara Lee at $16.25 per share less a $435 commission.
Nov.   1 Sold 900 shares of Eastman Kodak at $22.75 per share less a $625 commission.
Dec. 31 Per share fair values for stocks in the portfolio are: Black & Decker, $39.00; Microsoft, $69.00.

Required

1. Prepare journal entries to record these transactions and events and any year-end fair value adjustments to the portfolio of long-term available-for-sale securities.

2. Prepare a table that summarizes the (*a*) total cost, (*b*) total fair value adjustment, and (*c*) total fair value of the portfolio of long-term available-for-sale securities at each year-end.

3. Prepare a table that summarizes (*a*) the realized gains and losses and (*b*) the unrealized gains or losses for the portfolio of long-term available-for-sale securities at each year-end.

Problem C-4A
Long-term investment transactions; unrealized and realized gains and losses

C2 P3 P4

Stoll Co.'s long-term available-for-sale portfolio at December 31, 2012, consists of the following.

Available-for-Sale Securities	Cost	Fair Value
40,000 shares of Company A common stock	$535,300	$490,000
7,000 shares of Company B common stock	159,380	154,000
17,500 shares of Company C common stock	662,750	640,938

Stoll enters into the following long-term investment transactions during year 2013.

Jan. 29 Sold 3,500 shares of Company B common stock for $79,188 less a brokerage fee of $1,500.
Apr. 17 Purchased 10,000 shares of Company W common stock for $197,500 plus a brokerage fee of $2,400. The shares represent a 30% ownership in Company W.

July   6   Purchased 4,500 shares of Company X common stock for $126,562 plus a brokerage fee of $1,750. The shares represent a 10% ownership in Company X.

Aug. 22   Purchased 50,000 shares of Company Y common stock for $375,000 plus a brokerage fee of $1,200. The shares represent a 51% ownership in Company Y.

Nov. 13   Purchased 8,500 shares of Company Z common stock for $267,900 plus a brokerage fee of $2,450. The shares represent a 5% ownership in Company Z.

Dec. 9   Sold 40,000 shares of Company A common stock for $515,000 less a brokerage fee of $4,100.

The fair values of its investments at December 31, 2013, are: B, $81,375; C, $610,312; W, $191,250; X, $118,125; Y, $531,250; and Z, $278,800.

Required

1. Determine the amount Stoll should report on its December 31, 2013, balance sheet for its long-term investments in available-for-sale securities.

2. Prepare any necessary December 31, 2013, adjusting entry to record the fair value adjustment for the long-term investments in available-for-sale securities.

3. What amount of gains or losses on transactions relating to long-term investments in available-for-sale securities should Stoll report on its December 31, 2013, income statement?

Check (2) Cr. Unrealized Loss— Equity, $20,002

Selk Steel Co., which began operations on January 4, 2013, had the following subsequent transactions and events in its long-term investments.

Problem C-5A
Accounting for long-term investments in securities; with and without significant influer

2013

Jan.   5   Selk purchased 60,000 shares (20% of total) of Kildaire's common stock for $1,560,000.

Oct. 23   Kildaire declared and paid a cash dividend of $3.20 per share.

Dec. 31   Kildaire's net income for 2013 is $1,164,000, and the fair value of its stock at December 31 is $30.00 per share.

P3 P4

2014

Oct. 15   Kildaire declared and paid a cash dividend of $2.60 per share.

Dec. 31   Kildaire's net income for 2014 is $1,476,000, and the fair value of its stock at December 31 is $32.00 per share.

2015

Jan.   2   Selk sold all of its investment in Kildaire for $1,894,000 cash.

Part 1

Assume that Selk has a significant influence over Kildaire with its 20% share of stock.

Required

1. Prepare journal entries to record these transactions and events for Selk.

2. Compute the carrying (book) value per share of Selk's investment in Kildaire common stock as reflected in the investment account on January 1, 2015.

Check (2) Carrying value per sh $29

3. Compute the net increase or decrease in Selk's equity from January 5, 2013, through January 2, 2015, resulting from its investment in Kildaire.

Part 2

Assume that although Selk owns 20% of Kildaire's outstanding stock, circumstances indicate that it does not have a significant influence over the investee and that it is classified as an available-for-sale security investment.

Required

1. Prepare journal entries to record the preceding transactions and events for Selk. Also prepare an entry dated January 2, 2015, to remove any balance related to the fair value adjustment.

(1) 1/2/2015 Dr. Unrealiz Gain—Equity $360,000

2. Compute the cost per share of Selk's investment in Kildaire common stock as reflected in the investment account on January 1, 2015.

3. Compute the net increase or decrease in Selk's equity from January 5, 2013, through January 2, 2015, resulting from its investment in Kildaire.

(3) Net increase, $682,0

Problem C-6Aᴬ
Foreign currency transactions
C3

Doering Company, a U.S. corporation with customers in several foreign countries, had the following selected transactions for 2013 and 2014.

2013

Apr. 8 Sold merchandise to Salinas & Sons of Mexico for $5,938 cash. The exchange rate for pesos is $0.1043 on this day.

July 21 Sold merchandise on credit to Sumito Corp. in Japan. The price of 1.5 million yen is to be paid 120 days from the date of sale. The exchange rate for yen is $0.0094 on this day.

Oct. 14 Sold merchandise for 19,000 pounds to Smithers Ltd. of Great Britain, payment in full to be received in 90 days. The exchange rate for pounds is $1.4566 on this day.

Nov. 18 Received Sumito's payment in yen for its July 21 purchase and immediately exchanged the yen for dollars. The exchange rate for yen is $0.0092 on this day.

Dec. 20 Sold merchandise for 17,000 ringgits to Hamid Albar of Malaysia, payment in full to be received in 30 days. On this day, the exchange rate for ringgits is $0.4501.

Dec. 31 Recorded adjusting entries to recognize exchange gains or losses on Doering's annual financial statements. Rates for exchanging foreign currencies on this day follow.

Pesos (Mexico)	$0.1055
Yen (Japan)	0.0093
Pounds (Britain)	1.4620
Ringgits (Malaysia)	0.4456

2014

Jan. 12 Received full payment in pounds from Smithers for the October 14 sale and immediately exchanged the pounds for dollars. The exchange rate for pounds is $1.4699 on this day.

Jan. 19 Received Hamid Albar's full payment in ringgits for the December 20 sale and immediately exchanged the ringgits for dollars. The exchange rate for ringgits is $0.4420 on this day.

Required

1. Prepare journal entries for the Doering transactions and adjusting entries (round amounts to the nearest dollar).

Check (2) 2013 total foreign exchange loss, $274

2. Compute the foreign exchange gain or loss to be reported on Doering's 2013 income statement.

Analysis Component

3. What actions might Doering consider to reduce its risk of foreign exchange gains or losses?

PROBLEM SET B

Problem C-1B
Recording transactions and fair value adjustments for trading securities P1

Harris Company, which began operations in 2013, invests its idle cash in trading securities. The following transactions relate to its short-term investments in its trading securities.

2013

Mar. 10 Purchased 2,400 shares of AOL at $59.15 per share plus a $1,545 commission.
May 7 Purchased 5,000 shares of MTV at $36.25 per share plus a $2,855 commission.
Sept. 1 Purchased 1,200 shares of UPS at $57.25 per share plus a $1,250 commission.

2014

Apr. 26 Sold 5,000 shares of MTV at $34.50 per share less a $2,050 commission.
Apr. 27 Sold 1,200 shares of UPS at $60.50 per share less an $1,788 commission.
June 2 Purchased 3,600 shares of SPW at $172 per share plus a $3,250 commission.
June 14 Purchased 900 shares of Walmart at $50.25 per share plus a $1,082 commission.

2015

Jan. 28 Purchased 2,000 shares of PepsiCo at $43 per share plus a $2,890 commission.
Jan. 31 Sold 3,600 shares of SPW at $168 per share less a $2,040 commission.
Aug. 22 Sold 2,400 shares of AOL at $56.75 per share less a $2,480 commission.
Sept. 3 Purchased 1,500 shares of Vodaphone at $40.50 per share plus an $1,680 commission.
Oct. 9 Sold 900 shares of Walmart at $53.75 per share less a $1,220 commission.

Required

1. Prepare journal entries to record these short-term investment activities for the years shown. (Ignore any year-end adjusting entries.)

2. On December 31, 2015, prepare the adjusting entry to record any necessary fair value adjustment for the portfolio of trading securities when PepsiCo's share price is $41 and Vodaphone's share price is $37. (Assume the Fair Value Adjustment—Trading account had an unadjusted balance of zero.)

Check   (2) Cr. Fair Value
Adjustment—Trading $13,820

Slip Systems had no short-term investments prior to 2013. It had the following transactions involving short-term investments in available-for-sale securities during 2013.

Problem C-2B
Recording, adjusting, and reporting short-term available-for-sale securities

P3

Feb.	6	Purchased 3,400 shares of Nokia stock at $41.25 per share plus a $3,000 brokerage fee.
	15	Paid $20,000 to buy six-month U.S. Treasury bills (debt securities): $20,000 principal amount, 6% interest, securities dated February 15.
Apr.	7	Purchased 1,200 shares of Dell Co. stock at $39.50 per share plus a $1,255 brokerage fee.
June	2	Purchased 2,500 shares of Merck stock at $72.50 per share plus a $2,890 brokerage fee.
	30	Received a $0.19 per share cash dividend on the Nokia shares.
Aug.	11	Sold 850 shares of Nokia stock at $46 per share less a $1,050 brokerage fee.
	16	Received a check for principal and accrued interest on the U.S. Treasury bills purchased February 15.
	24	Received a $0.10 per share cash dividend on the Dell shares.
Nov.	9	Received a $0.20 per share cash dividend on the remaining Nokia shares.
Dec.	18	Received a $0.15 per share cash dividend on the Dell shares.

Required

1. Prepare journal entries to record the preceding transactions and events.

2. Prepare a table to compare the year-end cost and fair values of the short-term investments in available-for-sale securities. The year-end fair values per share are: Nokia, $40.25; Dell, $40.50; and Merck, $59.

3. Prepare an adjusting entry, if necessary, to record the year-end fair value adjustment for the portfolio of short-term investments in available-for-sale securities.

Check   (2) Cost = $340,232

(3) Dr. Unrealized Loss—
Equity, $41,494

Analysis Component

4. Explain the balance sheet presentation of the fair value adjustment to Slip's short-term investments.

5. How do these short-term investments affect (a) its income statement for year 2013 and (b) the equity section of its balance sheet at the 2013 year-end?

Paris Enterprises, which began operations in 2013, invests in long-term available-for-sale securities. Following is a series of transactions and events involving its long-term investment activity.

Problem C-3B
Recording, adjusting, and reporting long-term available-for-sale securities

P3

2013

Mar.	10	Purchased 1,200 shares of Apple at $25.50 per share plus $800 commission.
Apr.	7	Purchased 2,500 shares of Ford at $22.50 per share plus $1,033 commission.
Sept.	1	Purchased 600 shares of Polaroid at $47.00 per share plus $890 commission.
Dec.	31	Per share fair values for stocks in the portfolio are: Apple, $27.50; Ford, $21.00; Polaroid, $49.00.

2014

Apr.	26	Sold 2,500 shares of Ford at $20.50 per share less a $1,207 commission.
June	2	Purchased 1,800 shares of Duracell at $19.25 per share plus a $1,050 commission.
June	14	Purchased 1,200 shares of Sears at $21 per share plus a $280 commission.
Nov.	27	Sold 600 shares of Polaroid at $51 per share less a $845 commission.
Dec.	31	Per share fair values for stocks in the portfolio are: Apple, $29.00; Duracell, $18.00; Sears, $23.00.

2015

Jan.	28	Purchased 1,000 shares of Coca-Cola Co. at $40 per share plus a $1,480 commission.
Aug.	22	Sold 1,200 shares of Apple at $21.50 per share less a $1,850 commission.
Sept.	3	Purchased 3,000 shares of Motorola at $28 per share plus a $780 commission.
Oct.	9	Sold 1,200 shares of Sears at $24.00 per share less a $599 commission.
Oct.	31	Sold 1,800 shares of Duracell at $15.00 per share less a $898 commission.
Dec.	31	Per share fair values for stocks in the portfolio are: Coca-Cola, $48.00; Motorola, $24.00.

Required

1. Prepare journal entries to record these transactions and events and any year-end fair value adjustments to the portfolio of long-term available-for-sale securities.

2. Prepare a table that summarizes the (a) total cost, (b) total fair value adjustment, and (c) total fair value for the portfolio of long-term available-for-sale securities at each year-end.

3. Prepare a table that summarizes (a) the realized gains and losses and (b) the unrealized gains or losses for the portfolio of long-term available-for-sale securities at each year-end.

Check   (2b) Fair Value Adjustment bal.: 12/31/13, ($2,873); 12/31/14, $2,220

(3b) Unrealized Loss at 12/31/2015, $6,260

Problem C-4B
Long-term investment transactions; unrealized and realized gains and losses

C2 P3 P4

Troyer's long-term available-for-sale portfolio at December 31, 2012, consists of the following.

Available-for-Sale Securities	Cost	Fair Value
27,500 shares of Company R common stock	$559,125	$599,063
8,500 shares of Company S common stock	308,380	293,250
11,000 shares of Company T common stock	147,295	151,800

Troyer enters into the following long-term investment transactions during year 2013.

Jan. 13   Sold 2,125 shares of Company S stock for $72,250 less a brokerage fee of $1,195.
Mar. 24   Purchased 15,500 shares of Company U common stock for $282,875 plus a brokerage fee of $1,980. The shares represent a 62% ownership interest in Company U.
Apr. 5   Purchased 42,500 shares of Company V common stock for $133,875 plus a brokerage fee of $1,125. The shares represent a 10% ownership in Company V.
Sept. 2   Sold 11,000 shares of Company T common stock for $156,750 less a brokerage fee of $2,700.
Sept. 27 Purchased 2,500 shares of Company W common stock for $50,500 plus a brokerage fee of $1,050. The shares represent a 25% ownership interest in Company W.
Oct. 30   Purchased 5,000 shares of Company X common stock for $48,750 plus a brokerage fee of $1,170. The shares represent a 13% ownership interest in Company X.

The fair values of its investments at December 31, 2013, are: R, $568,125; S, $210,375; U, $272,800; V, $134,938; W, $54,689; and X, $45,625.

Required

1. Determine the amount Troyer should report on its December 31, 2013, balance sheet for its long-term investments in available-for-sale securities.

2. Prepare any necessary December 31, 2013, adjusting entry to record the fair value adjustment of the long-term investments in available-for-sale securities.

3. What amount of gains or losses on transactions relating to long-term investments in available-for-sale securities should Troyer report on its December 31, 2013, income statement?

Check   (2) Dr. Unrealized Loss—Equity, $16,267; Cr. Fair Value Adjustment—AFS (LT), $45,580

Problem C-5B
Accounting for long-term investments in securities; with and without significant influence

P3 P4

Brinkley Company, which began operations on January 3, 2013, had the following subsequent transactions and events in its long-term investments.

2013

Jan. 5   Brinkley purchased 20,000 shares (25% of total) of Bloch's common stock for $200,500.
Aug. 1   Bloch declared and paid a cash dividend of $1.05 per share.
Dec. 31   Bloch's net income for 2013 is $82,000, and the fair value of its stock is $11.90 per share.

2014

Aug. 1   Bloch declared and paid a cash dividend of $1.35 per share.
Dec. 31   Bloch's net income for 2014 is $78,000, and the fair value of its stock is $13.65 per share.

2015

Jan. 8   Brinkley sold all of its investment in Bloch for $375,000 cash.

Part 1

Assume that Brinkley has a significant influence over Bloch with its 25% share.

Required

1. Prepare journal entries to record these transactions and events for Brinkley.
2. Compute the carrying (book) value per share of Brinkley's investment in Bloch common stock as reflected in the investment account on January 7, 2015.
3. Compute the net increase or decrease in Brinkley's equity from January 5, 2013, through January 8, 2015, resulting from its investment in Bloch.

Check   (2) Carrying value per share $9.63

Part 2

Assume that although Brinkley owns 25% of Bloch's outstanding stock, circumstances indicate that it does not have a significant influence over the investee and that it is classified as an available-for-sale security investment.

Required

1. Prepare journal entries to record these transactions and events for Brinkley. Also prepare an entry dated January 8, 2015, to remove any balance related to the fair value adjustment.
2. Compute the cost per share of Brinkley's investment in Bloch common stock as reflected in the investment account on January 7, 2015.
3. Compute the net increase or decrease in Brinkley's equity from January 5, 2013, through January 8, 2015, resulting from its investment in Bloch.

(1) 1/8/2015 Dr. Unrealized Gain—Equity $72,500

(3) Net increase, $222,500

Datamix, a U.S. corporation with customers in several foreign countries, had the following selected transactions for 2013 and 2014.

Problem C-6B[A]
Foreign currency transactions
C3

2013

May 26   Sold merchandise for 6.5 million yen to Fuji Company of Japan, payment in full to be received in 60 days. On this day, the exchange rate for yen is $0.0093.

June   1   Sold merchandise to Fordham Ltd. of Great Britain for $64,800 cash. The exchange rate for pounds is $1.4498 on this day.

July 25   Received Fuji's payment in yen for its May 26 purchase and immediately exchanged the yen for dollars. The exchange rate for yen is $0.0092 on this day.

Oct. 15   Sold merchandise on credit to Martinez Brothers of Mexico. The price of 378,000 pesos is to be paid 90 days from the date of sale. On this day, the exchange rate for pesos is $0.1020.

Dec.   6   Sold merchandise for 250,000 yuans to Chi-Ying Company of China, payment in full to be received in 30 days. The exchange rate for yuans is $0.1439 on this day.

Dec. 31   Recorded adjusting entries to recognize exchange gains or losses on Datamix's annual financial statements. Rates of exchanging foreign currencies on this day follow.

Yen (Japan)	$0.0094
Pounds (Britain)	1.4580
Pesos (Mexico)	0.1060
Yuans (China)	0.1450

2014

Jan.   5   Received Chi-Ying's full payment in yuans for the December 6 sale and immediately exchanged the yuans for dollars. The exchange rate for yuans is $0.1580 on this day.

Jan. 13   Received full payment in pesos from Martinez for the October 15 sale and immediately exchanged the pesos for dollars. The exchange rate for pesos is $0.1039 on this day.

Required

1. Prepare journal entries for the Datamix transactions and adjusting entries.
2. Compute the foreign exchange gain or loss to be reported on Datamix's 2013 income statement.

Check   (2) 2013 total foreign exchange gain, $1,137

Analysis Component

3. What actions might Datamix consider to reduce its risk of foreign exchange gains or losses?

SERIAL PROBLEM
Success Systems

P1

(This serial problem began in Chapter 1 and continues through most of the book. If previous chapter segments were not completed, the serial problem can begin at this point. It is helpful, but not necessary, to use the Working Papers that accompany the book.)

SP C While reviewing the March 31, 2014, balance sheet of Success Systems, Adria Lopez notes that the business has built a large cash balance of $77,845. Its most recent bank money market statement shows that the funds are earning an annualized return of 0.75%. Adria Lopez decides to make several investments with the desire to earn a higher return on the idle cash balance. Accordingly, in April 2014, Success Systems makes the following investments in trading securities:

April 16 Purchases 400 shares of Johnson & Johnson stock at $50 per share plus $300 commission.
April 30 Purchases 200 shares of Starbucks Corporation at $22 per share plus $250 commission.

On June 30, 2014, the per share market price (fair value) of the Johnson & Johnson shares is $55 and the Starbucks shares is $19.

Required

1. Prepare journal entries to record the April purchases of trading securities by Success Systems.
2. On June 30, 2014, prepare the adjusting entry to record any necessary fair value adjustment to its portfolio of trading securities.

Beyond the Numbers

ETHICS CHALLENGE
P2 P3

BTN C-1 Kasey Hartman is the controller for Wholemart Company, which has numerous long-term investments in debt securities. Wholemart's investments are mainly in 5-year bonds. Hartman is preparing its year-end financial statements. In accounting for long-term debt securities, she knows that each long-term investment must be designated as a held-to-maturity or an available-for-sale security. Interest rates rose sharply this past year causing the portfolio's fair value to substantially decline. The company does not intend to hold the bonds for the entire 5 years. Hartman also earns a bonus each year, which is computed as a percent of net income.

Required

1. Will Hartman's bonus depend in any way on the classification of the debt securities? Explain.
2. What criteria must Hartman use to classify the securities as held-to-maturity or available-for-sale?
3. Is there likely any company oversight of Hartman's classification of the securities? Explain.

COMMUNICATING IN PRACTICE

P4

BTN C-2 Assume that you are Jolee Company's accountant. Company owner Mary Jolee has reviewed the 2013 financial statements you prepared and questions the $6,000 loss reported on the sale of its investment in Kemper Co. common stock. Jolee acquired 50,000 shares of Kemper's common stock on December 31, 2011, at a cost of $500,000. This stock purchase represented a 40% interest in Kemper. The 2012 income statement reported that earnings from all investments were $126,000. On January 3, 2013, Jolee Company sold the Kemper stock for $575,000. Kemper did not pay any dividends during 2012 but reported a net income of $202,500 for that year. Mary Jolee believes that because the Kemper stock purchase price was $500,000 and was sold for $575,000, the 2013 income statement should report a $75,000 gain on the sale.

Required

Draft a one-half page memorandum to Mary Jolee explaining why the $6,000 loss on sale of Kemper stock is correctly reported.

TAKING IT TO THE NET

C1

BTN C-3 Access the July 28, 2011, 10-K filing (for year-end June 30, 2011) of Microsoft (MSFT) at www.sec.gov. Review its note 4, "Investments."

Required

1. How does the "cost-basis" total amount for its investments as of June 30, 2011, compare to the prior year-end amount?
2. Identify at least eight types of short-term investments held by Microsoft as of June 30, 2011.

3. What were Microsoft's unrealized gains and its unrealized losses from its investments for 2011?

4. Was the cost or fair value ("recorded basis") of the investments higher as of June 30, 2011?

BTN C-4 Each team member is to become an expert on a specific classification of long-term investments. This expertise will be used to facilitate other teammates' understanding of the concepts and procedures relevent to the classification chosen.

TEAMWORK IN ACTION
C1 C2 P1 P2 P3 P4

1. Each team member must select an area for expertise by choosing one of the following classifications of long-term investments.
   a. Held-to-maturity debt securities
   b. Available-for-sale debt and equity securities
   c. Equity securities with significant influence
   d. Equity securities with controlling influence

2. Learning teams are to disburse and expert teams are to be formed. Expert teams are made up of those who select the same area of expertise. The instructor will identify the location where each expert team will meet.

3. Expert teams will collaborate to develop a presentation based on the following requirements. Students must write the presentation in a format they can show to their learning teams in part (4).

Requirements for Expert Presentation

   a. Write a transaction for the acquisition of this type of investment security. The transaction description is to include all necessary data to reflect the chosen classification.

   b. Prepare the journal entry to record the acquisition.

   [*Note:* The expert team on equity securities with controlling influence will substitute requirements (*d*) and (*e*) with a discussion of the reporting of these investments.]

   c. Identify information necessary to complete the end-of-period adjustment for this investment.

   d. Assuming that this is the only investment owned, prepare any necessary year-end entries.

   e. Present the relevant balance sheet section(s).

4. Re-form learning teams. In rotation, experts are to present to their teams the presentations they developed in part 3. Experts are to encourage and respond to questions.

BTN C-5ᴬ Assume that you are planning a spring break trip to Europe. Identify three locations where you can find exchange rates for the dollar relative to the Euro or other currencies.

HITTING THE ROAD
C3

ANSWERS TO MULTIPLE CHOICE QUIZ

1. d; $30,000 \times 5\% \times 5/12 = $625

2. a; Unrealized gain = $84,500 − $83,000 = $1,500

3. b; $50,000 \times 35\% = $17,500

4. e; $300,000/$2,000,000 = 15\%

5. b; Profit margin = $80,000/$600,000 = 13.3\%
   Total asset turnover = $600,000/$400,000 = 1.5

Appendix

D Reporting and Analyzing Partnerships

PARTNERSHIP ORGANIZATION	BASIC PARTNERSHIP ACCOUNTING	PARTNER ADMISSION AND WITHDRAWAL	PARTNERSHIP LIQUIDATION
C1 Characteristics Organizations with partnership characteristics Choice of business form	P1 Organizing a partnership P2 Dividing income or loss Partnership financial statements	P3 Admission of partner Withdrawal of partner Death of partner	P4 No capital deficiency Capital deficiency A1 Analyze partner return on equity

Learning Objectives

C1 Identify characteristics of partnerships and similar organizations. (p. D-2)

P1 Prepare entries for partnership formation. (p. D-4)

P2 Allocate and record income and loss among partners. (p. D-5)

P3 Account for the admission and withdrawal of partners. (p. D-7)

P4 Prepare entries for partnership liquidation. (p. D-11)

A1 Compute partner return on equity and use it to evaluate partnership performance. (p. D-13)

PARTNERSHIP FORM OF ORGANIZATION

C1 Identify characteristics of partnerships and similar organizations.

A **partnership** is an unincorporated association of two or more people to pursue a business for profit as co-owners. Many businesses are organized as partnerships. They are especially common in small retail and service businesses. Many professional practitioners, including physicians, lawyers, investors, and accountants, also organize their practices as partnerships.

Characteristics of Partnerships

Partnerships are an important type of organization because they offer certain advantages with their unique characteristics. We describe these characteristics in this section.

Voluntary Association   A partnership is a voluntary association between partners. Joining a partnership increases the risk to one's personal financial position. Some courts have ruled that partnerships are created by the actions of individuals even when there is no *express agreement* to form one. Omar Soliman and Nick Friedman are partners who voluntarily created the company **College Hunks Hauling Junk.**

Point: When a new partner is admitted, all parties usually must agree to the admission.

Partnership Agreement   Forming a partnership requires that two or more legally competent people (who are of age and of sound mental capacity) agree to be partners. Their agreement becomes a **partnership contract,** also called *articles of copartnership.* Although it should be in writing, the contract is binding even if it is only expressed verbally. Partnership agreements normally include details of the partners' (1) names and contributions, (2) rights and duties, (3) sharing of income and losses, (4) withdrawal arrangement, (5) dispute procedures, (6) admission and withdrawal of partners, and (7) rights and duties in the event a partner dies.

Point: The end of a partnership is referred to as its *dissolution.*

Limited Life   The life of a partnership is limited. Death, bankruptcy, or any event taking away the ability of a partner to enter into or fulfill a contract ends a partnership. Any one of the partners can also terminate a partnership at will.

Point: Partners are taxed on their share of partnership income, not on their withdrawals. Partners receive a "K-1" form each year showing their share of income they must report on their personal tax return.

Taxation   A partnership is not subject to taxes on its income. The income or loss of a partnership is allocated to the partners according to the partnership agreement, and it is included in determining the taxable income for each partner's tax return. Partnership income or loss is allocated each year whether or not cash is distributed to partners.

Mutual Agency   Mutual agency implies that each partner is a fully authorized agent of the partnership. As its agent, a partner can commit or bind the partnership to any contract within the scope of the partnership business. For instance, a partner in a merchandising business can sign contracts binding the partnership to buy merchandise, lease a store building, borrow money, or hire employees. These activities are all within the scope of a merchandising firm. A partner in a law firm, acting alone, however, cannot bind the other partners to a contract to buy snowboards for resale or rent an apartment for parties. These actions are outside the normal scope of a law firm's business. Partners also can agree to limit the power of any one or more of the partners to negotiate contracts for the partnership. This agreement is binding on the partners and on outsiders who know it exists. It is not binding on outsiders who do not know it exists. Outsiders unaware of the agreement have the right to assume each partner has normal agency powers for the partnership. Mutual agency exposes partners to the risk of unwise actions by any one partner.

Point: The majority of states adhere to the Uniform Partnership Act for the basic rules of partnership formation, operation, and dissolution.

Unlimited Liability   Unlimited liability implies that each partner can be called on to pay a partnership's debts. When a partnership cannot pay its debts, creditors usually can apply their claims to partners' *personal* assets. If a partner does not have enough assets to meet his or her share of the partnership debt, the creditors can apply their claims to the assets of the other partners. A partnership in which all partners have *mutual agency* and *unlimited liability* is called a **general partnership.** Mutual agency and unlimited liability are two main reasons that most general partnerships have only a few members.

Point: Limited life, mutual agency, and unlimited liability are disadvantages of a partnership.

Co-Ownership of Property   Partnership assets are owned jointly by all partners. Any investment by a partner becomes the joint property of all partners. Partners have a claim on partnership assets based on their capital account and the partnership contract.

Organizations with Partnership Characteristics

Organizations exist that combine certain characteristics of partnerships with other forms of organizations. We discuss several of these forms in this section.

Limited Partnerships   Some individuals who want to invest in a partnership are unwilling to accept the risk of unlimited liability. Their needs can be met with a **limited partnership.** This type of organization is identified in its name with the words "Limited Partnership" or "Ltd." or "LP." A limited partnership has two classes of partners, general and limited. At least one partner must be a **general partner,** who assumes management duties and unlimited liability for the debts of the partnership. The **limited partners** have no personal liability beyond the amounts they invest in the partnership. Limited partners have no active role except as specified in the partnership agreement. A limited partnership agreement often specifies unique procedures for allocating income and losses between general and limited partners. The accounting procedures are similar for both limited and general partnerships.

Limited Liability Partnerships   Most states allow individuals to form a **limited liability partnership.** This is identified in its name with the words "Limited Liability Partnership" or by "LLP." This type of partnership is designed to protect innocent partners from malpractice or negligence claims resulting from the acts of another partner. When a partner provides service resulting in a malpractice claim, that partner has personal liability for the claim. The remaining partners who were not responsible for the actions resulting in the claim are not personally liable for it. However, most states hold all partners personally liable for other partnership debts. Accounting for a limited liability partnership is the same as for a general partnership.

Point: Many accounting, law, consulting, and architectural firms are set up as LLPs.

 **Decision** Insight

Pencil Pushing Partners   Most states allow any business to form as a limited liability partnership (LLP); however, some states only allow approved professional service companies to form them. Of the four largest CPA firms in the United States (KPMG, Deloitte, PricewaterhouseCoopers, and Ernst & Young), all are set up as LLPs. ∎

S Corporations   Certain corporations with 100 or fewer stockholders can elect to be treated as a partnership for income tax purposes. These corporations are called *Sub-Chapter S* or simply **S corporations.** This distinguishes them from other corporations, called *Sub-Chapter C* or simply **C corporations.** S corporations provide stockholders the same limited liability feature that C corporations do. The advantage of an S corporation is that it does not pay income taxes. If stockholders work for an S corporation, their salaries are treated as expenses of the corporation. The remaining income or loss of the corporation is allocated to stockholders for inclusion on their personal tax returns. Except for C corporations having to account for income tax expenses and liabilities, the accounting procedures are the same for both S and C corporations.

Global: Forms of business organizations allowed vary by country.

Limited Liability Companies   A relatively new form of business organization is the **limited liability company.** The names of these businesses usually include the words "Limited Liability Company" or an abbreviation such as "LLC" or "LC." This form of business has certain features similar to a corporation and others similar to a limited partnership. The owners, who are called *members,* are protected with the same limited liability feature as owners of corporations. While limited partners cannot actively participate in the management of a limited partnership, the members of a limited liability company can assume an active management role. A limited liability company usually has a limited life. For income tax purposes, a limited liability company is typically treated as a partnership. This treatment depends on factors such as whether the members' equity interests are freely transferable and whether the company has continuity of life. A limited liability company's accounting system is designed to help management comply with the dictates of the articles of organization and company regulations adopted by its members. The accounting

Point: The majority of proprietorships and partnerships that are organized today are set up as LLCs.

Point: Accounting for LLCs is similar to that for partnerships (and proprietorships). One difference is that Owner (Partner), Capital is usually called *Members, Capital* for LLCs.

system also must provide information to support the company's compliance with state and federal laws, including taxation. The company **College Hunks Hauling Junk** is an LLC.

Choosing a Business Form

Choosing the proper business form is crucial. Many factors should be considered, including taxes, liability risk, tax and fiscal year-end, ownership structure, estate planning, business risks, and earnings and property distributions. The following table summarizes several important characteristics of business organizations:

	Proprietorship	Partnership	LLP	LLC	S Corp.	Corporation
Business entity	Yes	Yes	Yes	Yes	Yes	Yes
Legal entity	No	No	No	Yes	Yes	Yes
Limited liability	No	No	Limited*	Yes	Yes	Yes
Business taxed	No	No	No	No	No	Yes
One owner allowed	Yes	No	No	Yes	Yes	Yes

* A partner's personal liability for LLP debts is limited. Most LLPs carry insurance to protect against malpractice.

Point: The Small Business Administration provides suggestions and information on setting up the proper form for your organization—see **SBA.gov**.

We must remember that this table is a summary, not a detailed list. Many details underlie each of these business forms, and several details differ across states. Also, state and federal laws change, and a body of law is still developing around LLCs. Business owners should look at these details and consider unique business arrangements such as organizing various parts of their businesses in different forms.

BASIC PARTNERSHIP ACCOUNTING

Since ownership rights in a partnership are divided among partners, partnership accounting

- Uses a capital account for each partner.
- Uses a withdrawals account for each partner.
- Allocates net income or loss to partners according to the partnership agreement.

This section describes partnership accounting for organizing a partnership, distributing income and loss, and preparing financial statements.

Organizing a Partnership

P1 Prepare entries for partnership formation.

When partners invest in a partnership, their capital accounts are credited for the invested amounts. Partners can invest both assets and liabilities. Each partner's investment is recorded at an agreed-on value, normally the market values of the contributed assets and liabilities at the date of contribution. To illustrate, Kayla Zayn and Hector Perez organize a partnership on January 11 called BOARDS that offers year-round facilities for skateboarding and snowboarding. Zayn's initial net investment in BOARDS is $30,000, made up of cash ($7,000), boarding facilities ($33,000), and a note payable reflecting a bank loan for the new business ($10,000). Perez's initial investment is cash of $10,000. These amounts are the values agreed on by both partners. The entries to record these investments follow.

Zayn's Investment

Assets = Liabilities + Equity
+7,000   +10,000   +30,000
+33,000

Jan. 11	Cash	7,000	
	Boarding facilities	33,000	
	Note payable		10,000
	K. Zayn, Capital		30,000
	To record the investment of Zayn.		

Perez's Investment

Assets = Liabilities + Equity
+10,000   +10,000

Jan. 11	Cash	10,000	
	H. Perez, Capital		10,000
	To record the investment of Perez.		

In accounting for a partnership, the following additional relations hold true: (1) Partners' withdrawals are debited to their own separate withdrawals accounts. (2) Partners' capital accounts are credited (or debited) for their shares of net income (or net loss) when closing the accounts at the end of a period. (3) Each partner's withdrawals account is closed to that partner's capital account. Separate capital and withdrawals accounts are kept for each partner.

Point: Both equity and cash are reduced when a partner withdraws cash from a partnership.

Decision Insight

Broadway Partners **Big River Productions** is a partnership that owns the rights to the play *Big River*. The play is performed on tour and periodically on Broadway. For a recent year-end, its Partners' Capital was approximately $300,000, and it was distributed in its entirety to the partners. ■

Dividing Income or Loss

Partners are not employees of the partnership but are its owners. If partners devote their time and services to their partnership, they are understood to do so for profit, not for salary. This means there are no salaries to partners that are reported as expenses on the partnership income statement. However, when net income or loss of a partnership is allocated among partners, the partners can agree to allocate "salary allowances" reflecting the relative value of services provided. Partners also can agree to allocate "interest allowances" based on the amount invested. For instance, since Zayn contributes three times the investment of Perez, it is only fair that this be considered when allocating income between them. Like salary allowances, these interest allowances are not expenses on the income statement.

P2 Allocate and record income and loss among partners.

Partners can agree to any method of dividing income or loss. In the absence of an agreement, the law says that the partners share income or loss of a partnership equally. If partners agree on how to share income but say nothing about losses, they share losses the same way they share income. Three common methods to divide income or loss use (1) a stated ratio basis, (2) the ratio of capital balances, or (3) salary and interest allowances and any remainder according to a fixed ratio. We explain each of these methods in this section.

Point: Partners can agree on a ratio to divide income and another ratio to divide a loss.

Allocation on Stated Ratios The *stated ratio* (also called the *income-and-loss-sharing ratio*, the *profit and loss ratio*, or the *P&L ratio*) method of allocating partnership income or loss gives each partner a fraction of the total. Partners must agree on the fractional share each receives. To illustrate, assume the partnership agreement of K. Zayn and H. Perez says Zayn receives two-thirds and Perez one-third of partnership income and loss. If their partnership's net income is $60,000, it is allocated to the partners when the Income Summary account is closed as follows.

Point: The fractional basis can be stated as a proportion, ratio, or percent. For example, a 3:2 basis is the same as ⅗ and ⅖, or 60% and 40%.

Dec. 31	Income Summary	60,000	
	K. Zayn, Capital		40,000
	H. Perez, Capital		20,000
	To allocate income and close Income Summary.		

Assets = Liabilities + Equity
$-60,000$
$+40,000$
$+20,000$

Allocation on Capital Balances The *capital balances* method of allocating partnership income or loss assigns an amount based on the ratio of each partner's relative capital balance. If Zayn and Perez agree to share income and loss on the ratio of their beginning capital balances—Zayn's $30,000 and Perez's $10,000—Zayn receives three-fourths of any income or loss ($30,000/$40,000) and Perez receives one-fourth ($10,000/$40,000). The journal entry follows the same format as that using stated ratios (see the preceding entries).

Point: To determine the percent of income received by each partner, divide an individual partner's share by total net income.

Allocation on Services, Capital, and Stated Ratios The *services, capital, and stated ratio* method of allocating partnership income or loss recognizes that service and capital contributions of partners often are not equal. Salary allowances can make up for differences in service contributions. Interest allowances can make up for unequal capital contributions. Also, the allocation of income and loss can include *both* salary and interest allowances. To illustrate, assume that the partnership agreement of K. Zayn and H. Perez reflects differences in service and capital contributions as follows: (1) annual salary allowances of $36,000 to Zayn and $24,000 to Perez, (2) annual interest allowances of 10% of a partner's beginning-year capital balance, and (3) equal share of any remaining balance of income or loss. These salaries and interest allowances are *not* reported as expenses on the income statement. They are simply a means of dividing partnership income or loss. The remainder of this section provides two illustrations using this three-point allocation agreement.

Illustration when income exceeds allowance.   If BOARDS has first-year net income of $70,000, and Zayn and Perez apply the three-point partnership agreement described in the prior paragraph, income is allocated as shown in Exhibit D.1. Zayn gets $42,000 and Perez gets $28,000 of the $70,000 total.

EXHIBIT D.1

Dividing Income When Income Exceeds Allowances

	Zayn	Perez	Total
Net income			**$70,000**
Salary allowances			
Zayn	$ 36,000		
Perez		$ 24,000	
Interest allowances			
Zayn (10% × $30,000)	3,000		
Perez (10% × $10,000)		1,000	
Total salaries and interest	39,000	25,000	64,000
Balance of income			6,000
Balance allocated equally			
Zayn	3,000 ←		
Perez		3,000 ←	
Total allocated			6,000
Balance of income			$ 0
Income of each partner	$42,000	$28,000	

Illustration when allowances exceed income.   The sharing agreement between Zayn and Perez must be followed even if net income is less than the total of the allowances. For example, if BOARDS' first-year net income is $50,000 instead of $70,000, it is allocated to the partners as shown in Exhibit D.2. Computations for salaries and interest are identical to those in Exhibit D.1. However, when we apply the total allowances against income, the balance of income is negative.

Point: When allowances exceed income, the amount of this negative balance often is referred to as a *sharing agreement loss* or *deficit.*

EXHIBIT D.2

Dividing Income When Allowances Exceed Income

	Zayn	Perez	Total
Net income			**$50,000**
Salary allowances			
Zayn	$ 36,000		
Perez		$ 24,000	
Interest allowances			
Zayn (10% × $30,000)	3,000		
Perez (10% × $10,000)		1,000	
Total salaries and interest	39,000	25,000	64,000
Balance of income			(14,000)
Balance allocated equally			
Zayn	(7,000) ←		
Perez		(7,000) ←	
Total allocated			(14,000)
Balance of income			$ 0
Income of each partner	$32,000	$18,000	

This $(14,000) negative balance is allocated equally to the partners per their sharing agreement. This means that a negative $(7,000) is allocated to each partner. In this case, Zayn ends up with $32,000 and Perez with $18,000. If BOARDS had experienced a net loss, Zayn and Perez would share it in the same manner as the $50,000 income. The only difference is that they would have begun with a negative amount because of the loss. Specifically, the partners would still have been allocated their salary and interest allowances, further adding to the negative balance of the loss. This *total* negative balance *after* salary and interest allowances would have been allocated equally between the partners. These allocations would have been applied against the positive numbers from any allowances to determine each partner's share of the loss.

Point: Check to make sure the sum of the dollar amounts allocated to each partner equals net income or loss.

Point: When a loss occurs, it is possible for a specific partner's capital to increase (when closing income summary) if that partner's allowance is in excess of his or her share of the negative balance. This implies that decreases to the capital balances of other partners exceed the partnership's loss amount.

Partnership Financial Statements

Partnership financial statements are similar to those of other organizations. The **statement of partners' equity,** also called *statement of partners' capital,* is one exception. It shows *each* partner's beginning capital balance, additional investments, allocated income or loss, withdrawals, and ending capital balance. To illustrate, Exhibit D.3 shows the statement of partners' equity for BOARDS prepared using the sharing agreement of Exhibit D.1. Recall that BOARDS' income was $70,000; also, assume that Zayn withdrew $20,000 and Perez $12,000 at year-end.

BOARDS Statement of Partners' Equity For Year Ended December 31, 2013				
		Zayn	**Perez**	**Total**
Beginning capital balances		$ 0	$ 0	$ 0
Plus				
Investments by owners		30,000	10,000	40,000
Net income				
Salary allowances	$36,000		$24,000	
Interest allowances	3,000		1,000	
Balance allocated	3,000		3,000	
Total net income		42,000	28,000	70,000
		72,000	38,000	110,000
Less partners' withdrawals		(20,000)	(12,000)	(32,000)
Ending capital balances		$52,000	$26,000	$78,000

EXHIBIT D.3

Statement of Partners' Equity

The equity section of the balance sheet of a partnership usually shows the separate capital account balance of each partner. In the case of BOARDS, both K. Zayn, Capital, and H. Perez, Capital, are listed in the equity section along with their balances of $52,000 and $26,000, respectively.

Decision Insight

Double Draw Partnerships sometimes use two accounts to reflect a partner's withdrawal of cash from a partnership. For example, a "Drawing" account might be used for regular withdrawals such as for a monthly salary allowance. A second "Withdrawals" account might be used for infrequent or personal draws such as to help pay for a daughter/son's wedding or a lake home. ■

ADMISSION AND WITHDRAWAL OF PARTNERS

A partnership is based on a contract between individuals. When a partner is admitted or withdraws, the present partnership ends. Still, the business can continue to operate as a new partnership consisting of the remaining partners. This section considers how to account for the admission and withdrawal of partners.

P3 Account for the admission and withdrawal of partners.

Admission of a Partner

A new partner is admitted in one of two ways: by purchasing an interest from one or more current partners or by investing cash or other assets in the partnership.

Purchase of Partnership Interest   The purchase of partnership interest is a *personal transaction between one or more current partners and the new partner.* To become a partner, the current partners must accept the purchaser. Accounting for the purchase of partnership interest involves reallocating current partners' capital to reflect the transaction. To illustrate, at the end of BOARDS' first year, H. Perez sells one-half of his partnership interest to Tyrell Rasheed for $18,000. This means that Perez gives up a $13,000 recorded interest ($26,000 × 1/2) in the partnership (see the ending capital balance in Exhibit D.3). The partnership records this January 4 transaction as follows.

Assets = Liabilities + Equity
       −13,000
       +13,000

Jan. 4	H. Perez, Capital	13,000	
	T. Rasheed, Capital		13,000
	To record admission of Rasheed by purchase.		

After this entry is posted, BOARDS' equity shows K. Zayn, Capital; H. Perez, Capital; and T. Rasheed, Capital, and their respective balances of $52,000, $13,000, and $13,000.

Two aspects of this transaction are important. First, the partnership does *not* record the $18,000 Rasheed paid Perez. The partnership's assets, liabilities, and *total equity* are unaffected by this transaction among partners. Second, Zayn and Perez must agree that Rasheed is to become a partner. If they agree to accept Rasheed, a new partnership is formed and a new contract with a new income-and-loss-sharing agreement is prepared. If Zayn or Perez refuses to accept Rasheed as a partner, then (under the Uniform Partnership Act) Rasheed gets Perez's sold share of partnership income and loss. If the partnership is liquidated, Rasheed gets Perez's sold share of partnership assets. Rasheed gets no voice in managing the company unless Rasheed is admitted as a partner.

Point: Partners' withdrawals are not constrained by the partnership's annual income or loss.

Investing Assets in a Partnership   Admitting a partner by accepting assets is a *transaction between the new partner and the partnership.* The invested assets become partnership property. To illustrate, if Zayn (with a $52,000 interest) and Perez (with a $26,000 interest) agree to accept Rasheed as a partner in BOARDS after an investment of $22,000 cash, this is recorded as follows.

Assets = Liabilities + Equity
+22,000   +22,000

Jan. 4	Cash	22,000	
	T. Rasheed, Capital		22,000
	To record admission of Rasheed by investment.		

After this entry is posted, both assets (cash) and equity (T. Rasheed, Capital) increase by $22,000. Rasheed now has a 22% equity in the assets of the business, computed as $22,000 divided by the entire partnership equity ($52,000 + $26,000 + $22,000). Rasheed does not necessarily have a right to 22% of income. Dividing income and loss is a separate matter on which partners must agree.

Bonus to old partners.   When the current value of a partnership is greater than the recorded amounts of equity, the partners usually require a new partner to pay a bonus for the privilege of joining. To illustrate, assume that Zayn and Perez agree to accept Rasheed as a partner with a 25% interest in BOARDS if Rasheed invests $42,000. Recall that the partnership's accounting records show that Zayn's recorded equity in the business is $52,000 and Perez's recorded equity is $26,000 (see Exhibit D.3). Rasheed's equity is determined as follows.

Equities of existing partners ($52,000 + $26,000)	$ 78,000
Investment of new partner	42,000
Total partnership equity	$120,000
Equity of Rasheed (25% × $120,000)	$ 30,000

Although Rasheed invests $42,000, the equity attributed to Rasheed in the new partnership is only $30,000. The $12,000 difference is called a *bonus* and is allocated to existing partners (Zayn and Perez) according to their income-and-loss-sharing agreement. A bonus is shared in this way because it is viewed as reflecting a higher value of the partnership that is not yet reflected in income. The entry to record this transaction follows.

Jan. 4			
	Cash	42,000	
	T. Rasheed, Capital		30,000
	K. Zayn, Capital ($12,000 × ½)		6,000
	H. Perez, Capital ($12,000 × ½)		6,000
	To record admission of Rasheed and bonus.		

Assets = Liabilities + Equity
+42,000   +30,000
                                 +6,000
                                 +6,000

Bonus to new partner.   Alternatively, existing partners can grant a bonus to a new partner. This usually occurs when they need additional cash or the new partner has exceptional talents. The bonus to the new partner is in the form of a larger share of equity than the amount invested. To illustrate, assume that Zayn and Perez agree to accept Rasheed as a partner with a 25% interest in the partnership, but they require Rasheed to invest only $18,000. Rasheed's equity is determined as follows.

Equities of existing partners ($52,000 + $26,000)	$78,000
Investment of new partner	18,000
Total partnership equity	$96,000
Equity of Rasheed (25% × $96,000)	$24,000

The old partners contribute the $6,000 bonus (computed as $24,000 minus $18,000) to Rasheed according to their income-and-loss-sharing ratio. Moreover, Rasheed's 25% equity does not necessarily entitle Rasheed to 25% of future income or loss. This is a separate matter for agreement by the partners. The entry to record the admission and investment of Rasheed is

Jan. 4			
	Cash	18,000	
	K. Zayn, Capital ($6,000 × ½)	3,000	
	H. Perez, Capital ($6,000 × ½)	3,000	
	T. Rasheed, Capital		24,000
	To record Rasheed's admission and bonus.		

Assets = Liabilities + Equity
+18,000   −3,000
                                −3,000
                              +24,000

Withdrawal of a Partner

A partner generally withdraws from a partnership in one of two ways. (1) First, the withdrawing partner can sell his or her interest to another person who pays for it in cash or other assets. For this, we need only debit the withdrawing partner's capital account and credit the new partner's capital account. (2) The second case is when cash or other assets of the partnership are distributed to the withdrawing partner in settlement of his or her interest. To illustrate these cases, assume that Perez withdraws from the partnership of BOARDS in some future period. The partnership shows the following capital balances at the date of Perez's withdrawal: K. Zayn, $84,000; H. Perez, $38,000; and T. Rasheed, $38,000. The partners (Zayn, Perez, and Rasheed) share income and loss equally. Accounting for Perez's withdrawal depends on whether a bonus is paid. We describe three possibilities.

No Bonus   If Perez withdraws and takes cash equal to Perez's capital balance, the entry is

Oct. 31			
	H. Perez, Capital	38,000	
	Cash		38,000
	To record withdrawal of Perez from partnership		
	with no bonus.		

Assets = Liabilities + Equity
−38,000   −38,000

Perez can take any combination of assets to which the partners agree to settle Perez's equity. Perez's withdrawal creates a new partnership between the remaining partners. A new partnership contract and a new income-and-loss-sharing agreement are required.

Bonus to Remaining Partners   A withdrawing partner is sometimes willing to take less than the recorded value of his or her equity to get out of the partnership or because the recorded value is overstated. Whatever the reason, when this occurs, the withdrawing partner in effect gives the remaining partners a bonus equal to the equity left behind. The remaining partners share this unwithdrawn equity according to their income-and-loss-sharing ratio. To illustrate, if Perez withdraws and agrees to take $34,000 cash in settlement of Perez's capital balance, the entry is

Assets	= Liabilities +	Equity
−34,000		−38,000
		+2,000
		+2,000

Oct. 31	H. Perez, Capital	38,000	
	Cash		34,000
	K. Zayn, Capital		2,000
	T. Rasheed, Capital		2,000
	To record withdrawal of Perez and bonus to remaining partners.		

Perez withdrew $4,000 less than Perez's recorded equity of $38,000. This $4,000 is divided between Zayn and Rasheed according to their income-and-loss-sharing ratio.

Bonus to Withdrawing Partner   A withdrawing partner may be able to receive more than his or her recorded equity for at least two reasons. First, the recorded equity may be understated. Second, the remaining partners may agree to remove this partner by giving assets of greater value than this partner's recorded equity. In either case, the withdrawing partner receives a bonus. The remaining partners reduce their equity by the amount of this bonus according to their income-and-loss-sharing ratio. To illustrate, if Perez withdraws and receives $40,000 cash in settlement of Perez's capital balance, the entry is

Assets	= Liabilities +	Equity
−40,000		−38,000
		−1,000
		−1,000

Oct. 31	H. Perez, Capital	38,000	
	K. Zayn, Capital	1,000	
	T. Rasheed, Capital	1,000	
	Cash		40,000
	To record Perez's withdrawal from partnership with a bonus to Perez.		

Falcon Cable Communications set up a partnership withdrawal agreement. Falcon owns and operates cable television systems and had two managing general partners. The partnership agreement stated that either partner "can offer to sell to the other partner the offering partner's entire partnership interest . . . for a negotiated price. If the partner receiving such an offer rejects it, the offering partner may elect to cause [the partnership] . . . to be liquidated and dissolved."

Death of a Partner

A partner's death dissolves a partnership. A deceased partner's estate is entitled to receive his or her equity. The partnership contract should contain provisions for settlement in this case. These provisions usually require (1) closing the books to determine income or loss since the end of the previous period and (2) determining and recording current market values for both assets and liabilities. The remaining partners and the deceased partner's estate then must agree to a settlement of the deceased partner's equity. This can involve selling the equity to remaining partners or to an outsider, or it can involve withdrawing assets.

▌ Decision Ethics

Financial Planner   You are hired by the two remaining partners of a three-member partnership after the third partner's death. The partnership agreement states that a deceased partner's estate is entitled to a "share of partnership assets equal to the partner's relative equity balance" (partners' equity balances are equal). The estate argues that it is entitled to one-third of the current value of partnership assets. The remaining partners say the distribution should use asset book values, which are 75% of current value. They also point to partnership liabilities, which equal 40% of total asset book value and 30% of current value. How would you resolve this situation? ▌   [Answer—p. D-16]

LIQUIDATION OF A PARTNERSHIP

When a partnership is liquidated, its business ends and three concluding steps are required.

> **P4** Prepare entries for partnership liquidation.

1. Record the sale of noncash assets for cash, and any gain or loss from liquidation is allocated to partners *using their income-and-loss-sharing agreement.*
2. Pay or settle all partner liabilities.
3. Distribute any remaining cash to partners *based on their capital balances.*

Partnership liquidation usually falls into one of two cases, as described in this section.

No Capital Deficiency

No capital deficiency means that all partners have a zero or credit balance in their capital accounts for final distribution of cash. To illustrate, assume that Zayn, Perez, and Rasheed operate their partnership in BOARDS for several years, sharing income and loss equally. The partners then decide to liquidate. On the liquidation date, the current period's income or loss is transferred to the partners' capital accounts according to the sharing agreement. After that transfer, assume the partners' recorded account balances (immediately prior to liquidation) are:

Cash ...	$178,000	Accounts payable ...	$20,000	H. Perez, Capital	$66,000
Land ...	40,000	K. Zayn, Capital	70,000	T. Rasheed, Capital	62,000

We apply three steps for liquidation. ① *The partnership sells its noncash assets, and any losses or gains from liquidation are shared among partners according to their income-and-loss-sharing agreement* (equal for these partners). Assume that BOARDS sells its noncash assets consisting of $40,000 in land for $46,000 cash, yielding a net gain of $6,000. In a liquidation, gains or losses usually result from the sale of noncash assets, which are called *losses and gains from liquidation.* The entry to sell its assets for $46,000 follows.

Jan. 15			
	Cash	46,000	
	Land		40,000
	Gain from Liquidation		6,000
	Sold noncash assets at a gain.		

Assets = Liabilities + Equity
−40,000   +6,000
+46,000

Allocation of the gain from liquidation per the partners' income-and-loss-sharing agreement follows.

Jan. 15			
	Gain from Liquidation	6,000	
	K. Zayn, Capital		2,000
	H. Perez, Capital		2,000
	T. Rasheed, Capital		2,000
	To allocate liquidation gain to partners.		

Assets = Liabilities + Equity
                            −6,000
                            +2,000
                            +2,000
                            +2,000

② *The partnership pays its liabilities, and any losses or gains from liquidation of liabilities are shared among partners according to their income-and-loss-sharing agreement.* BOARDS' only liability is $20,000 in accounts payable, and no gain or loss occurred.

Jan. 15			
	Accounts Payable	20,000	
	Cash		20,000
	To pay claims of creditors.		

Assets = Liabilities + Equity
−20,000   −20,000

After step 2, we have the following capital balances along with the remaining cash balance.

K. Zayn			H. Perez, Capital			T. Rasheed, Capital			Cash			
	Bal.	70,000		Bal.	66,000		Bal.	62,000	Bal.	178,000	(3)	20,000
	(2)	2,000		(2)	2,000		(2)	2,000	(1)	46,000		
	Bal.	72,000		Bal.	68,000		Bal.	64,000	Bal.	204,000		

③ *Any remaining cash is divided among the partners **according to their capital account balances.*** The entry to record the final distribution of cash to partners follows.

Assets	= Liabilities +	Equity
−204,000		−72,000
		−68,000
		−64,000

Jan. 15	K. Zayn, Capital	72,000	
	H. Perez, Capital	68,000	
	T. Rasheed, Capital	64,000	
	Cash		204,000
	To distribute remaining cash to partners.		

It is important to remember that the final cash payment is distributed to partners according to their capital account balances, whereas gains and losses from liquidation are allocated according to the income-and-loss-sharing ratio. The following *statement of liquidation* summarizes the three steps in this section.

Statement of Liquidation	Cash	Noncash Assets	=	Liabilities	K. Zayn, Capital	H. Perez, Capital	T. Rasheed, Capital
Balances prior to liquidation. . . .	$178,000	$ 40,000		$ 20,000	$ 70,000	$66,000	$62,000
① Sale of noncash assets	46,000	(40,000)			2,000	2,000	2,000
② Payment of liabilities	(20,000)			(20,000)	0	0	0
Balances for distribution	204,000	$ 0		$ 0	72,000	68,000	64,000
③ Distribution of cash to partners	(204,000)				(72,000)	(68,000)	(64,000)
	$ 0				$ 0	$ 0	$ 0

Capital Deficiency

Capital deficiency means that at least one partner has a debit balance in his or her capital account at the point of final cash distribution (during step ③ as explained in the prior section). This can arise from liquidation losses, excessive withdrawals before liquidation, or recurring losses in prior periods. A partner with a capital deficiency must, if possible, cover the deficit by paying cash into the partnership.

To illustrate, assume that Zayn, Perez, and Rasheed operate their partnership in BOARDS for several years, sharing income and losses equally. The partners then decide to liquidate. Immediately prior to the final distribution of cash, the partners' recorded capital balances are Zayn, $19,000; Perez, $8,000; and Rasheed, $(3,000). Rasheed's capital deficiency means that Rasheed owes the partnership $3,000. Both Zayn and Perez have a legal claim against Rasheed's personal assets. The final distribution of cash in this case depends on how this capital deficiency is handled. Two possibilities exist: the partner pays the deficiency or the partner cannot pay the deficiency.

Partner Pays Deficiency   Rasheed is obligated to pay $3,000 into the partnership to cover the deficiency. If Rasheed is willing and able to pay, the entry to record receipt of payment from Rasheed follows.

Assets	= Liabilities +	Equity
+3,000		+3,000

Jan. 15	Cash	3,000	
	T. Rasheed, Capital		3,000
	To record payment of deficiency by Rasheed.		

After the $3,000 payment, the partners' capital balances are Zayn, $19,000; Perez, $8,000; and Rasheed, $0. The entry to record the final cash distributions to partners is

Assets	= Liabilities +	Equity
−27,000		−19,000
		−8,000

Jan. 15	K. Zayn, Capital	19,000	
	H. Perez, Capital	8,000	
	Cash		27,000
	To distribute remaining cash to partners.		

Partner Cannot Pay Deficiency   The remaining partners with credit balances absorb any partner's unpaid deficiency according to their income-and-loss-sharing ratio. To illustrate, if Rasheed is unable to pay the $3,000 deficiency, Zayn and Perez absorb it. Since they share income and loss equally, Zayn and Perez each absorb $1,500 of the deficiency. This is recorded as follows.

Jan. 15	K. Zayn, Capital	1,500		Assets = Liabilities + Equity
	H. Perez, Capital	1,500		−1,500
	T. Rasheed, Capital		3,000	−1,500
	To transfer Rasheed deficiency to Zayn and Perez.			+3,000

After Zayn and Perez absorb Rasheed's deficiency, the capital accounts of the partners are Zayn, $17,500; Perez, $6,500; and Rasheed, $0. The entry to record the final cash distribution to the partners is

Jan. 15	K. Zayn, Capital	17,500		Assets = Liabilities + Equity
	H. Perez, Capital	6,500		−24,000 −17,500
	Cash		24,000	−6,500
	To distribute remaining cash to partners.			

Rasheed's inability to cover this deficiency does not relieve Rasheed of the liability. If Rasheed becomes able to pay at a future date, Zayn and Perez can each collect $1,500 from Rasheed.

GLOBAL VIEW

Partnership accounting according to U.S. GAAP is similar, but not identical, to that under IFRS. This section discusses broad differences in partnership accounting, organization, admission, withdrawal, and liquidation.

Both U.S. GAAP and IFRS include broad and similar guidance for partnership accounting. Further, partnership organization is similar worldwide; however, different legal and tax systems dictate different implications and motivations for how a partnership is effectively set up.

The accounting for partnership admission, withdrawal, and liquidation is likewise similar worldwide. Specifically, procedures for admission, withdrawal, and liquidation depend on the partnership agreements constructed by all parties involved. However, different legal and tax systems impact those agreements and their implications to the parties.

Partner Return on Equity    **Decision Analysis**

An important role of partnership financial statements is to aid current and potential partners in evaluating partnership success compared with other opportunities. One measure of this success is the **partner return on equity** ratio:

A1 Compute partner return on equity and use it to evaluate partnership performance.

$$\text{Partner return on equity} = \frac{\text{Partner net income}}{\text{Average partner equity}}$$

This measure is separately computed for each partner. To illustrate, Exhibit D.4 reports selected data from the Boston Celtics LP. The return on equity for the *total* partnership is computed as $216/[($85 + $253)/2] = 127.8\%$. However, return on equity is quite different across the partners. For example, the Boston Celtics LP I partner return on equity is computed as $44/[($122 + $166)/2] = 30.6\%$, whereas the Celtics LP partner return on equity is computed as $111/[($270 + $333)/2] = 36.8\%$. Partner return on equity provides *each* partner an assessment of its return on its equity invested in the partnership. A specific partner often uses this return to decide whether additional investment or withdrawal of resources is best for that partner. Exhibit D.4 reveals that the year shown produced good returns for all

EXHIBIT D.4

Selected Data from
Boston Celtics LP

($ thousands)	Total*	Boston Celtics LP I	Boston Celtics LP II	Celtics LP
Beginning-year balance	$ 85	$122	$(307)	$270
Net income (loss) for year	216	44	61	111
Cash distribution	(48)	—	—	(48)
Ending-year balance	$253	$166	$(246)	$333
Partner return on equity	127.8%	30.6%	n.a.	36.8%

* Totals may not add up due to rounding.

partners (the Boston Celtics LP II return is not computed because its average equity is negative due to an unusual and large distribution in the prior year).

COMPREHENSIVE...

NEED-TO-KNOW

The following transactions and events affect the partners' capital accounts in several successive partnerships. Prepare a table with six columns, one for each of the five partners along with a total column to show the effects of the following events on the five partners' capital accounts.

Part 1

4/13/2011   Ries and Bax create R&B Company. Each invests $10,000, and they agree to share income and losses equally.

12/31/2011   R&B Co. earns $15,000 in income for its first year. Ries withdraws $4,000 from the partnership, and Bax withdraws $7,000.

1/1/2012   Royce is made a partner in RB&R Company after contributing $12,000 cash. The partners agree that a 10% interest allowance will be given on each partner's beginning-year capital balance. In addition, Bax and Royce are to receive $5,000 salary allowances. The remainder of the income or loss is to be divided evenly.

12/31/2012   The partnership's income for the year is $40,000, and withdrawals at year-end are Ries, $5,000; Bax, $12,500; and Royce, $11,000.

1/1/2013   Ries sells her interest for $20,000 to Murdock, whom Bax and Royce accept as a partner in the new BR&M Co. Income or loss is to be shared equally after Bax and Royce receive $25,000 salary allowances.

12/31/2013   The partnership's income for the year is $35,000, and year-end withdrawals are Bax, $2,500, and Royce, $2,000.

1/1/2014   Elway is admitted as a partner after investing $60,000 cash in the new Elway & Associates partnership. He is given a 50% interest in capital after the other partners transfer $3,000 to his account from each of theirs. A 20% interest allowance (on the beginning-year capital balances) will be used in sharing any income or loss, there will be no salary allowances, and Elway will receive 40% of the remaining balance—the other three partners will each get 20%.

12/31/2014   Elway & Associates earns $127,600 in income for the year, and year-end withdrawals are Bax, $25,000; Royce, $27,000; Murdock, $15,000; and Elway, $40,000.

1/1/2015   Elway buys out Bax and Royce for the balances of their capital accounts after a revaluation of the partnership assets. The revaluation gain is $50,000, which is divided in using a 1:1:1:2 ratio (Bax:Royce:Murdock:Elway). Elway pays the others from personal funds. Murdock and Elway will share income on a 1:9 ratio.

2/28/2015   The partnership earns $10,000 of income since the beginning of the year. Murdock retires and receives partnership cash equal to her capital balance. Elway takes possession of the partnership assets in his own name, and the partnership is dissolved.

Part 2

Journalize the events affecting the partnership for the year ended December 31, 2012.

PLANNING THE SOLUTION

- Evaluate each transaction's effects on the capital accounts of the partners.
- Each time a new partner is admitted or a partner withdraws, allocate any bonus based on the income-or-loss-sharing agreement.

- Each time a new partner is admitted or a partner withdraws, allocate subsequent net income or loss in accordance with the new partnership agreement.
- Prepare entries to (1) record Royce's initial investment; (2) record the allocation of interest, salaries, and remainder; (3) show the cash withdrawals from the partnership; and (4) close the withdrawal accounts on December 31, 2012.

SOLUTION TO COMPREHENSIVE NEED-TO-KNOW

Part 1

Event	Ries	Bax	Royce	Murdock	Elway	Total
4/13/2011						
Initial investment	$10,000	$10,000				$ 20,000
12/31/2011						
Income (equal)	7,500	7,500				15,000
Withdrawals	(4,000)	(7,000)				(11,000)
Ending balance	$13,500	$10,500				$ 24,000
1/1/2012						
New investment			$12,000			$ 12,000
12/31/2012						
10% interest	1,350	1,050	1,200			3,600
Salaries		5,000	5,000			10,000
Remainder (equal)	8,800	8,800	8,800			26,400
Withdrawals	(5,000)	(12,500)	(11,000)			(28,500)
Ending balance	$18,650	$12,850	$16,000			$ 47,500
1/1/2013						
Transfer interest	(18,650)			$18,650		$ 0
12/31/2013						
Salaries		25,000	25,000			50,000
Remainder (equal)		(5,000)	(5,000)	(5,000)		(15,000)
Withdrawals		(2,500)	(2,000)			(4,500)
Ending balance	$ 0	$30,350	$34,000	$13,650		$ 78,000
1/1/2014						
New investment					$ 60,000	60,000
Bonuses to Elway		(3,000)	(3,000)	(3,000)	9,000	0
Adjusted balance		$27,350	$31,000	$10,650	$ 69,000	$138,000
12/31/2014						
20% interest..............		5,470	6,200	2,130	13,800	27,600
Remainder (1:1:1:2)........		20,000	20,000	20,000	40,000	100,000
Withdrawals..............		(25,000)	(27,000)	(15,000)	(40,000)	(107,000)
Ending balance		$27,820	$30,200	$17,780	$ 82,800	$158,600
1/1/2015						
Gain (1:1:1:2)		10,000	10,000	10,000	20,000	50,000
Adjusted balance		$37,820	$40,200	$27,780	$102,800	$208,600
Transfer interests		(37,820)	(40,200)		78,020	0
Adjusted balance		$ 0	$ 0	$27,780	$180,820	$208,600
2/28/2015						
Income (1:9)..............				1,000	9,000	10,000
Adjusted balance				$28,780	$189,820	$218,600
Settlements				(28,780)	(189,820)	(218,600)
Final balance..............				$ 0	$ 0	$ 0

Part 2

2012			
Jan. 1	Cash	12,000	
	Royce, Capital		12,000
	To record investment of Royce.		
Dec. 31	Income Summary	40,000	
	Ries, Capital		10,150
	Bax, Capital		14,850
	Royce, Capital		15,000
	To allocate interest, salaries, and remainders.		
Dec. 31	Ries, Withdrawals	5,000	
	Bax, Withdrawals	12,500	
	Royce, Withdrawals	11,000	
	Cash		28,500
	To record cash withdrawals by partners.		
Dec. 31	Ries, Capital	5,000	
	Bax, Capital	12,500	
	Royce, Capital	11,000	
	Ries, Withdrawals		5,000
	Bax, Withdrawals		12,500
	Royce, Withdrawals		11,000
	To close withdrawal accounts.		

Summary

C1 **Identify characteristics of partnerships and similar organizations.** Partnerships are voluntary associations, involve partnership agreements, have limited life, are not subject to income tax, include mutual agency, and have unlimited liability. Organizations that combine selected characteristics of partnerships and corporations include limited partnerships, limited liability partnerships, S corporations, and limited liability companies.

A1 **Compute partner return on equity and use it to evaluate partnership performance.** Partner return on equity provides each partner an assessment of his or her return on equity invested in the partnership.

P1 **Prepare entries for partnership formation.** A partner's initial investment is recorded at the market value of the assets contributed to the partnership.

P2 **Allocate and record income and loss among partners.** A partnership agreement should specify how to allocate partnership income or loss among partners. Allocation can be based on a stated ratio, capital balances, or salary and interest allowances

to compensate partners for differences in their service and capital contributions.

P3 **Account for the admission and withdrawal of partners.** When a new partner buys a partnership interest directly from one or more existing partners, the amount of cash paid from one partner to another does not affect the partnership total recorded equity. When a new partner purchases equity by investing additional assets in the partnership, the new partner's investment can yield a bonus either to existing partners or to the new partner. The entry to record a withdrawal can involve payment from either (1) the existing partners' personal assets or (2) partnership assets. The latter can yield a bonus to either the withdrawing or remaining partners.

P4 **Prepare entries for partnership liquidation.** When a partnership is liquidated, losses and gains from selling partnership assets are allocated to the partners according to their income-and-loss-sharing ratio. If a partner's capital account has a deficiency that the partner cannot pay, the other partners share the deficit according to their relative income-and-loss-sharing ratio.

Guidance Answers to Decision Ethics

Financial Planner The partnership agreement apparently fails to mention liabilities or use the term *net assets*. To give the estate one-third of total assets is not fair to the remaining partners because if the partner had lived and the partners had decided to liquidate, the liabilities would need to be paid out of assets before any liquidation. Also, a

settlement based on the deceased partner's recorded equity would fail to recognize excess of current value over book value. This value increase would be realized if the partnership were liquidated. A fair settlement would seem to be a payment to the estate for the balance of the deceased partner's equity based on the *current value of net assets*.

Key Terms

C corporation (p. D-3)

General partner (p. D-3)

General partnership (p. D-2)

Limited liability company (LLC) (p. D-3)

Limited liability partnership (p. D-3)

Limited partners (p. D-3)

Limited partnership (p. D-3)

Mutual agency (p. D-2)

Partner return on equity (p. D-13)

Partnership (p. D-2)

Partnership contract (p. D-2)

Partnership liquidation (p. D-11)

S corporation (p. D-3)

Statement of partners' equity (p. D-7)

Unlimited liability (p. D-2)

Multiple Choice Quiz   Answers on p. D-26

1. Stokely and Leder are forming a partnership. Stokely invests a building that has a market value of $250,000; and the partnership assumes responsibility for a $50,000 note secured by a mortgage on that building. Leder invests $100,000 cash. For the partnership, the amounts recorded for the building and for Stokely's Capital account are these:
   a. Building, $250,000; Stokely, Capital, $250,000.
   b. Building, $200,000; Stokely, Capital, $200,000.
   c. Building, $200,000; Stokely, Capital, $100,000.
   d. Building, $200,000; Stokely, Capital, $250,000.
   e. Building, $250,000; Stokely, Capital, $200,000.

2. Katherine, Alliah, and Paulina form a partnership. Katherine contributes $150,000, Alliah contributes $150,000, and Paulina contributes $100,000. Their partnership agreement calls for the income or loss division to be based on the ratio of capital invested. If the partnership reports income of $90,000 for its first year of operations, what amount of income is credited to Paulina's capital account?
   a. $22,500
   b. $25,000
   c. $45,000
   d. $30,000
   e. $90,000

3. Jamison and Blue form a partnership with capital contributions of $600,000 and $800,000, respectively. Their partnership agreement calls for Jamison to receive $120,000 per year in salary. Also, each partner is to receive an interest allowance equal to 10% of the partner's beginning capital contributions, with any remaining income or loss divided equally. If net income for its initial year is $270,000, then Jamison's and Blue's respective shares are
   a. $135,000; $135,000.
   b. $154,286; $115,714.
   c. $120,000; $150,000.
   d. $185,000; $85,000.
   e. $85,000; $185,000.

4. Hansen and Fleming are partners and share equally in income or loss. Hansen's current capital balance in the partnership is $125,000 and Fleming's is $124,000. Hansen and Fleming agree to accept Black with a 20% interest. Black invests $75,000 in the partnership. The bonus granted to Hansen and Fleming equals
   a. $13,000 each.
   b. $5,100 each.
   c. $4,000 each.
   d. $5,285 to Hansen; $4,915 to Fleming.
   e. $0; Hansen and Fleming grant a bonus to Black.

5. Mee Su is a partner in Hartford Partners, LLC. Her partnership capital balance at the beginning of the current year was $110,000, and her ending balance was $124,000. Her share of the partnership income is $10,500. What is her partner return on equity?
   a. 8.97%
   b. 1060.00%
   c. 9.54%
   d. 1047.00%
   e. 8.47%

Icon denotes assignments that involve decision making.

Discussion Questions

1. If a partnership contract does not state the period of time the partnership is to exist, when does the partnership end?

2. What does the term *mutual agency* mean when applied to a partnership?

3. How does a general partnership differ from a limited partnership?

4. Can partners limit the right of a partner to commit their partnership to contracts? Would such an agreement be binding (*a*) on the partners and (*b*) on outsiders?

5. Assume that Amey and Lacey are partners. Lacey dies, and her son claims the right to take his mother's place in the partnership. Does he have this right? Why or why not?

6. Assume that the Barnes and Ardmore partnership agreement provides for a two-third/one-third sharing of income but says nothing about losses. The first year of partnership operation resulted in a loss, and Barnes argues that the loss should be shared equally because the partnership agreement said nothing about sharing losses. Is Barnes correct? Explain.

7. Allocation of partnership income among the partners appears on what financial statement?

8. What does the term *unlimited liability* mean when it is applied to partnership members?

9. 🔲 George, Burton, and Dillman have been partners for three years. The partnership is being dissolved. George is leaving the firm, but Burton and Dillman plan to carry on the business. In the final settlement, George places a $75,000 salary claim against the partnership. He contends that he has a claim for a salary of $25,000 for each year because he devoted all of his time for three years to the affairs of the partnership. Is his claim valid? Why or why not?

10. 🔲 Kay, Kat, and Kim are partners. In a liquidation, Kay's share of partnership losses exceeds her capital account balance.

Moreover, she is unable to meet the deficit from her personal assets, and her partners shared the excess losses. Does this relieve Kay of liability?

11. After all partnership assets have been converted to cash and all liabilities paid, the remaining cash should equal the sum of the balances of the partners' capital accounts. Why?

12. Assume a partner withdraws from a partnership and receives assets of greater value than the book value of his equity. Should the remaining partners share the resulting reduction in their equities in the ratio of their relative capital balances or according to their income-and-loss-sharing ratio?

QUICK STUDY

QS D-1
Partnership liability
C1

Amy and Lester are partners in operating a store. Without consulting Amy, Lester enters into a contract to purchase merchandise for the store. Amy contends that she did not authorize the order and refuses to pay for it. The vendor sues the partners for the contract price of the merchandise. (*a*) Must the partnership pay for the merchandise? Why? (*b*) Does your answer differ if Amy and Lester are partners in a public accounting firm? Explain.

QS D-2
Partnership income allocation
P2

Ann Stolton and Susie Bright are partners in a business they started two years ago. The partnership agreement states that Stolton should receive a salary allowance of $15,000 and that Bright should receive a $20,000 salary allowance. Any remaining income or loss is to be shared equally. Determine each partner's share of the current year's net income of $52,000.

QS D-3
Partnership income allocation
P2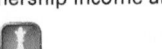

Blake and Matthew are partners who agree that Blake will receive a $100,000 salary allowance and that any remaining income or loss will be shared equally. If Matthew's capital account is credited for $2,000 as his share of the net income in a given period, how much net income did the partnership earn in that period?

QS D-4
Liability in limited partnerships
P1

Fancher organized a limited partnership and is the only general partner. Carley invested $20,000 in the partnership and was admitted as a limited partner with the understanding that she would receive 10% of the profits. After two unprofitable years, the partnership ceased doing business. At that point, partnership liabilities were $85,000 larger than partnership assets. How much money can the partnership's creditors obtain from Carley's personal assets to satisfy the unpaid partnership debts?

QS D-5
Partner admission through purchase of interest
P3

Stein agrees to pay Choi and Amal $10,000 each for a one-third (33⅓%) interest in the Choi and Amal partnership. Immediately prior to Stein's admission, each partner had a $30,000 capital balance. Make the journal entry to record Stein's purchase of the partners' interest.

QS D-6
Admission of a partner
P3

Jules and Johnson are partners, each with $40,000 in their partnership capital accounts. Kwon is admitted to the partnership by investing $40,000 cash. Make the entry to show Kwon's admission to the partnership.

The Field, Brown & Snow partnership was begun with investments by the partners as follows: Field, $131,250; Brown, $165,000; and Snow, $153,750. The operations did not go well, and the partners eventually decided to liquidate the partnership, sharing all losses equally. On May 31, after all assets were converted to cash and all creditors were paid, only $45,000 in partnership cash remained.

1. Compute the capital account balance of each partner after the liquidation of assets and the payment of creditors.

2. Assume that any partner with a deficit agrees to pay cash to the partnership to cover the deficit. Present the journal entries on May 31 to record (*a*) the cash receipt from the deficient partner(s) and (*b*) the final disbursement of cash to the partners.

3. Assume that any partner with a deficit is not able to reimburse the partnership. Present journal entries (*a*) to transfer the deficit of any deficient partners to the other partners and (*b*) to record the final disbursement of cash to the partners.

QS D-7
Liquidation of partnership
P4

Check   (1) Field, $(3,750)

Howe and Duley's company is organized as a partnership. At the prior year-end, partnership equity totaled $150,000 ($100,000 from Howe and $50,000 from Duley). For the current year, partnership net income is $24,990 ($20,040 allocated to Howe and $4,950 allocated to Duley), and year-end total partnership equity is $200,000 ($140,000 from Howe and $60,000 from Duley). Compute the total partnership return on equity *and* the individual partner return on equity ratios.

QS D-8
Partner return on equity
A1

▦connect

Next to the following list of eight characteristics of business organizations, enter a brief description of how each characteristic applies to general partnerships.

EXERCISES

Exercise D-1
Characteristics of partnerships
C1

Characteristic	Application to General Partnerships
1. Life	
2. Owners' liability	
3. Legal status	
4. Tax status of income	
5. Owners' authority	
6. Ease of formation	
7. Transferability of ownership	
8. Ability to raise large amounts of capital	

For each of the following separate cases, recommend a form of business organization. With each recommendation, explain how business income would be taxed if the owners adopt the form of organization recommended. Also list several advantages that the owners will enjoy from the form of business organization that you recommend.

a. Sharif, Henry and Korb are recent college graduates in computer science. They want to start a Website development company. They all have college debts and currently do not own any substantial computer equipment needed to get the company started.

b. Dr. Ward and Dr. Liu are recent graduates from medical residency programs. Both are family practice physicians and would like to open a clinic in an underserved rural area. Although neither has any funds to bring to the new venture, an investor has expressed interest in making a loan to provide start-up funds for their practice.

c. Munson has been out of school for about five years and has become quite knowledgeable about the residential real estate market. He would like to organize a company that buys and sells real estate. Munson believes he has the expertise to manage the company but needs funds to invest in residential property.

Exercise D-2
Forms of organization
C1

On March 1, 2013, Eckert and Kelley formed a partnership. Eckert contributed $82,500 cash and Kelley contributed land valued at $60,000 and a building valued at $100,000. The partnership also assumed responsibility for Kelley's $92,500 long-term note payable associated with the land and building. The partners agreed to share income as follows: Eckert is to receive an annual salary allowance of $25,000, both are to receive an annual interest allowance of 10% of their beginning-year capital investment, and

Exercise D-3
Journalizing partnership transactions
P2

any remaining income or loss is to be shared equally. On October 20, 2013, Eckert withdrew $34,000 cash and Kelley withdrew $20,000 cash. After the adjusting and closing entries are made to the revenue and expense accounts at December 31, 2013, the Income Summary account had a credit balance of $90,000.

1. Prepare journal entries to record (*a*) the partners' initial capital investments, (*b*) their cash withdrawals, and (*c*) the December 31 closing of both the Withdrawals and Income Summary accounts.

Check (2) Kelley, $79,250

2. Determine the balances of the partners' capital accounts as of December 31, 2013.

Exercise D-4
Journalizing partnership formation
P2

Angela Moss and Autumn Barber organize a partnership on January 1. Moss's initial net investment is $75,000, consisting of cash ($17,500), equipment ($82,500), and a note payable reflecting a bank loan for the new business ($25,000). Barber's initial investment is cash of $31,250. These amounts are the values agreed on by both partners. Prepare journal entries to record (1) Moss's investment and (2) Barber's investment.

Exercise D-5
Income allocation in a partnership
P2

Kramer and Knox began a partnership by investing $60,000 and $80,000, respectively. During its first year, the partnership earned $160,000. Prepare calculations showing how the $160,000 income should be allocated to the partners under each of the following three separate plans for sharing income and loss: (1) the partners failed to agree on a method to share income; (2) the partners agreed to share income and loss in proportion to their initial investments (round amounts to the nearest dollar); and (3) the partners agreed to share income by granting a $50,000 per year salary allowance to Kramer, a $40,000 per year salary allowance to Knox, 10% interest on their initial capital investments, and the remaining balance shared equally.

Check Plan 3, Kramer, $84,000

Exercise D-6
Income allocation in a partnership
P2

Assume that the partners of Exercise D-5 agreed to share net income and loss by granting annual salary allowances of $50,000 to Kramer and $40,000 to Knox, 10% interest allowances on their investments, and any remaining balance shared equally.

1. Determine the partners' shares of Kramer and Knox given a first-year net income of $98,800.

Check (2) Kramer, $(4,400)

2. Determine the partners' shares of Kramer and Knox given a first-year net loss of $16,800.

Exercise D-7
Admission of new partner
P3

The Struter Partnership has total partners' equity of $510,000, which is made up of Main, Capital, $400,000, and Frist, Capital, $110,000. The partners share net income and loss in a ratio of 80% to Main and 20% to Frist. On November 1, Madison is admitted to the partnership and given a 15% interest in equity and a 15% share in any income and loss. Prepare the journal entry to record the admission of Madison under each of the following separate assumptions: Madison invests cash of (1) $90,000; (2) $120,000; and (3) $80,000.

Exercise D-8
Retirement of partner
P3

Hunter, Folgers, and Tulip have been partners while sharing net income and loss in a 5:3:2 ratio. On January 31, the date Tulip retires from the partnership, the equities of the partners are Hunter, $150,000; Folgers, $90,000; and Tulip, $60,000. Present journal entries to record Tulip's retirement under each of the following separate assumptions: Tulip is paid for her equity using partnership cash of (1) $60,000; (2) $80,000; and (3) $30,000.

Exercise D-9
Sale of partnership interest
P3

The partners in the Biz Partnership have agreed that partner Mandy may sell her $100,000 equity in the partnership to Brittney, for which Brittney will pay Mandy $85,000. Present the partnership's journal entry to record the sale of Mandy's interest to Brittney on September 30.

Exercise D-10
Liquidation of partnership
P4

Turner, Roth, and Lowe are partners who share income and loss in a 1:4:5 ratio. After lengthy disagreements among the partners and several unprofitable periods, the partners decide to liquidate the partnership. Immediately before liquidation, the partnership balance sheet shows total assets, $126,000; total liabilities, $78,000; Turner, Capital, $2,500; Roth, Capital, $14,000; and Lowe, Capital, $31,500. The cash proceeds from selling the assets were sufficient to repay all but $28,000 to the creditors. (*a*) Calculate the loss from selling the assets. (*b*) Allocate the loss to the partners. (*c*) Determine how much of the remaining liability should be paid by each partner.

Check (b) Lowe, Capital after allocation, $(6,500)

Exercise D-11
Liquidation of limited partnership
P4

Assume that the Turner, Roth, and Lowe partnership of Exercise D-10 is a limited partnership. Turner and Roth are general partners and Lowe is a limited partner. How much of the remaining $28,000 liability should be paid by each partner? (Round amounts to the nearest dollar.)

Rugged Sports Enterprises LP is organized as a limited partnership consisting of two individual partners: Hockey LP and Football LP. Both partners separately operate a minor league hockey team and a semipro football team. Compute partner return on equity for each limited partnership (and the total) for the year ended June 30, 2013, using the following selected data on partner capital balances from Rugged Sports Enterprises LP.

Exercise D-12
Partner return on equity

A1

	Hockey LP	Football LP	Total
Balance at 6/30/2012	$189,000	$ 758,000	$ 947,000
Annual net income	22,208	445,473	468,032
Cash distribution	—	(50,000)	(50,000)
Balance at 6/30/2013	$211,134	$1,153,898	$1,365,032

connect

Kara Ries, Tammy Bax, and Joe Thomas invested $80,000, $112,000, and $128,000, respectively, in a partnership. During its first calendar year, the firm earned $249,000.

PROBLEM SET A

Problem D-1A
Allocating partnership income
P2

Required

Prepare the entry to close the firm's Income Summary account as of its December 31 year-end and to allocate the $249,000 net income to the partners under each of the following separate assumptions: The partners (1) have no agreement on the method of sharing income and loss; (2) agreed to share income and loss in the ratio of their beginning capital investments; and (3) agreed to share income and loss by providing annual salary allowances of $66,000 to Ries, $56,000 to Bax, and $80,000 to Thomas; granting 10% interest on the partners' beginning capital investments; and sharing the remainder equally.

Check   (3) Thomas, Capital, $97,800

Irene Watts and John Lyon are forming a partnership to which Watts will devote one-half time and Lyon will devote full time. They have discussed the following alternative plans for sharing income and loss: (*a*) in the ratio of their initial capital investments, which they have agreed will be $42,000 for Watts and $63,000 for Lyon; (*b*) in proportion to the time devoted to the business; (*c*) a salary allowance of $6,000 per month to Lyon and the balance in accordance with the ratio of their initial capital investments; or (*d*) a salary allowance of $6,000 per month to Lyon, 10% interest on their initial capital investments, and the balance shared equally. The partners expect the business to perform as follows: year 1, $36,000 net loss; year 2, $90,000 net income; and year 3, $150,000 net income.

Problem D-2A
Allocating partnership income and loss; sequential years
P2

Required

Prepare three tables with the following column headings.

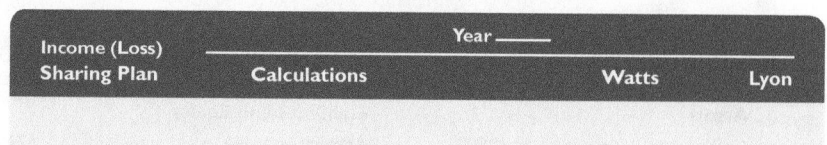

Income (Loss) Sharing Plan	Year ————		
	Calculations	Watts	Lyon

Complete the tables, one for each of the first three years, by showing how to allocate partnership income or loss to the partners under each of the four plans being considered. (Round answers to the nearest whole dollar.)

Check   Plan d, year 1, Lyon's share, $19,050

Bill Beck, Bruce Beck, and Barb Beck formed the BBB Partnership by making capital contributions of $67,500, $262,500, and $420,000, respectively. They predict annual partnership net income of $450,000 and are considering the following alternative plans of sharing income and loss: (*a*) equally; (*b*) in the ratio of their initial capital investments; or (*c*) salary allowances of $80,000 to Bill, $60,000 to Bruce, and $90,000 to Barb; interest allowances of 10% on their initial capital investments; and the balance shared as follows: 20% to Bill, 40% to Bruce, and 40% to Barb.

Problem D-3A
Partnership income allocation, statement of partners' equity, and closing entries
P2

Required

1. Prepare a table with the following column headings.

Income (Loss) Sharing Plan	Calculations	Bill	Bruce	Barb	Total

Use the table to show how to distribute net income of $450,000 for the calendar year under each of the alternative plans being considered. (Round answers to the nearest whole dollar.)

2. Prepare a statement of partners' equity showing the allocation of income to the partners assuming they agree to use plan (c), that income earned is $209,000, and that Bill, Bruce, and Barb withdraw $34,000, $48,000, and $64,000, respectively, at year-end.

3. Prepare the December 31 journal entry to close Income Summary assuming they agree to use plan (c) and that net income is $209,000. Also close the withdrawals accounts.

Problem D-4A
Partner withdrawal and admission

P3

Part 1. Meir, Benson, and Lau are partners and share income and loss in a 3:2:5 ratio. The partnership's capital balances are as follows: Meir, $168,000; Benson, $138,000; and Lau, $294,000. Benson decides to withdraw from the partnership, and the partners agree to not have the assets revalued upon Benson's retirement. Prepare journal entries to record Benson's February 1 withdrawal from the partnership under each of the following separate assumptions: Benson (a) sells her interest to North for $160,000 after Meir and Lau approve the entry of North as a partner; (b) gives her interest to a son-in-law, Schmidt, and thereafter Meir and Lau accept Schmidt as a partner; (c) is paid $138,000 in partnership cash for her equity; (d) is paid $214,000 in partnership cash for her equity; and (e) is paid $30,000 in partnership cash plus equipment recorded on the partnership books at $70,000 less its accumulated depreciation of $23,200.

Part 2. Assume that Benson does not retire from the partnership described in Part 1. Instead, Rhode is admitted to the partnership on February 1 with a 25% equity. Prepare journal entries to record Rhode's entry into the partnership under each of the following separate assumptions: Rhode invests (a) $200,000; (b) $145,000; and (c) $262,000.

Problem D-5A
Liquidation of a partnership

P4

Kendra, Cogley, and Mei share income and loss in a 3:2:1 ratio. The partners have decided to liquidate their partnership. On the day of liquidation their balance sheet appears as follows.

KENDRA, COGLEY, AND MEI Balance Sheet May 31			
Assets		**Liabilities and Equity**	
Cash	$180,800	Accounts payable	$245,500
Inventory	537,200	Kendra, Capital	93,000
		Cogley, Capital	212,500
		Mei, Capital	167,000
Total assets	$718,000	Total liabilities and equity	$718,000

Required

Prepare journal entries for (a) the sale of inventory, (b) the allocation of its gain or loss, (c) the payment of liabilities at book value, and (d) the distribution of cash in each of the following separate cases: Inventory is sold for (1) $600,000; (2) $500,000; (3) $320,000 and any partners with capital deficits pay in the amount of their deficits; and (4) $250,000 and the partners have no assets other than those invested in the partnership. (Round to the nearest dollar.)

Mark Albin, Roland Peters and Sam Ramsey invested $164,000, $98,400 and $65,600, respectively, in a partnership. During its first calendar year, the firm earned $270,000.

Required

Prepare the entry to close the firm's Income Summary account as of its December 31 year-end and to allocate the $270,000 net income to the partners under each of the following separate assumptions. (Round answers to whole dollars.) The partners (1) have no agreement on the method of sharing income and loss; (2) agreed to share income and loss in the ratio of their beginning capital investments; and (3) agreed to share income and loss by providing annual salary allowances of $96,000 to Albin, $72,000 to Peters, and $50,000 to Ramsey; granting 10% interest on the partners' beginning capital investments; and sharing the remainder equally.

PROBLEM SET B

Problem D-1B
Allocating partnership income
P2

Check   (3) Ramsey, Capital, $62,960

Maria Bell and J.R. Green are forming a partnership to which Bell will devote one-third time and Green will devote full time. They have discussed the following alternative plans for sharing income and loss: (*a*) in the ratio of their initial capital investments, which they have agreed will be $104,000 for Bell and $156,000 for Green; (*b*) in proportion to the time devoted to the business; (*c*) a salary allowance of $4,000 per month to Green and the balance in accordance with the ratio of their initial capital investments; or (*d*) a salary allowance of $4,000 per month to Green, 10% interest on their initial capital investments, and the balance shared equally. The partners expect the business to perform as follows: year 1, $36,000 net loss; year 2, $76,000 net income; and year 3, $188,000 net income.

Problem D-2B
Allocating partnership income and loss; sequential years
P2

Required

Prepare three tables with the following column headings.

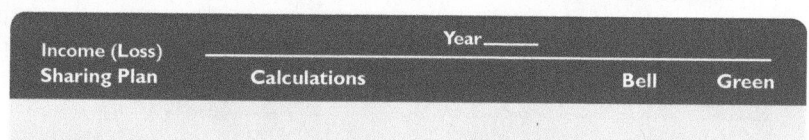

Complete the tables, one for each of the first three years, by showing how to allocate partnership income or loss to the partners under each of the four plans being considered. (Round answers to the nearest whole dollar.)

Check   Plan d, year 1, Green's share, $8,600

Sally Cook, Lin Xi, and Ken Schwartz formed the CXS Partnership by making capital contributions of $144,000, $216,000, and $120,000, respectively. They predict annual partnership net income of $240,000 and are considering the following alternative plans of sharing income and loss: (*a*) equally; (*b*) in the ratio of their initial capital investments; or (*c*) salary allowances of $40,000 to Cook, $30,000 to Xi, and $80,000 to Schwartz; interest allowances of 12% on their initial capital investments; and the balance shared equally.

Problem D-3B
Partnership income allocation, statement of partners' equity, and closing entries
P2

Required

1. Prepare a table with the following column headings.

Use the table to show how to distribute net income of $240,000 for the calendar year under each of the alternative plans being considered. (Round answers to the nearest whole dollar.)

2. Prepare a statement of partners' equity showing the allocation of income to the partners assuming they agree to use plan (*c*), that income earned is $87,600, and that Cook, Xi, and Schwartz withdraw $18,000, $38,000, and $24,000, respectively, at year-end.

3. Prepare the December 31 journal entry to close Income Summary assuming they agree to use plan (*c*) and that net income is $87,600. Also close the withdrawals accounts.

Check   (2) Schwartz, Ending Capital, $150,400

Problem D-4B
Partner withdrawal
and admission
P3

Check (1e) Cr. Chan, Capital,
$163,200

Part 1. Gibbs, Cook, and Chan are partners and share income and loss in a 5:1:4 ratio. The partnership's capital balances are as follows: Gibbs, $606,000; Cook, $148,000; and Chan, $446,000. Gibbs decides to withdraw from the partnership, and the partners agree not to have the assets revalued upon Gibbs's retirement. Prepare journal entries to record Gibbs's April 30 withdrawal from the partnership under each of the following separate assumptions: Gibbs (a) sells her interest to Brady for $250,000 after Cook and Chan approve the entry of Brady as a partner; (b) gives her interest to a daughter-in-law, Cannon, and thereafter Cook and Chan accept Cannon as a partner; (c) is paid $606,000 in partnership cash for her equity; (d) is paid $350,000 in partnership cash for her equity; and (e) is paid $200,000 in partnership cash plus manufacturing equipment recorded on the partnership books at $538,000 less its accumulated depreciation of $336,000.

Check (2c) Cr. Cook, Capital,
$10,080

Part 2. Assume that Gibbs does not retire from the partnership described in Part 1. Instead, Chip is admitted to the partnership on April 30 with a 20% equity. Prepare journal entries to record the entry of Brise under each of the following separate assumptions: Chip invests (a) $300,000; (b) $196,000; and (c) $426,000.

Problem D-5B
Liquidation of a partnership
P4

Lasure, Ramirez, and Toney, who share income and loss in a 2:1:2 ratio, plan to liquidate their partnership. At liquidation, their balance sheet appears as follows.

LASURE, RAMIREZ, AND TONEY
Balance Sheet
January 18

Assets		**Liabilities and Equity**	
Cash	$348,600	Accounts payable	$342,600
Equipment	617,200	Lasure, Capital	300,400
		Ramirez, Capital	195,800
		Toney, Capital	127,000
Total assets	$965,800	Total liabilities and equity	$965,800

Required

Prepare journal entries for (a) the sale of equipment, (b) the allocation of its gain or loss, (c) the payment of liabilities at book value, and (d) the distribution of cash in each of the following separate cases: Equipment is sold for (1) $650,000; (2) $530,000; (3) $200,000 and any partners with capital deficits pay in the amount of their deficits; and (4) $150,000 and the partners have no assets other than those invested in the partnership. (Round amounts to the nearest dollar.)

Check (4) Cash distribution:
Lasure, $73,600

SERIAL PROBLEM
Success Systems
P3

(This serial problem began in Chapter 1 and continues through most of the book. If previous chapter segments were not completed, the serial problem can begin at this point. It is helpful, but not necessary, to use the Working Papers that accompany the book.)

SP D   At the start of 2014, Adria Lopez is considering adding a partner to her business. She envisions the new partner taking the lead in generating sales of both services and merchandise for Success Systems. A. Lopez's equity in Success Systems as of January 1, 2014, is reflected in the following capital balance.

A. Lopez, Capital $90,148

Required

1. A. Lopez is evaluating whether the prospective partner should be an equal partner with respect to capital investment and profit sharing (1:1) or whether the agreement should be 4:1 with Lopez retaining four-fifths interest with rights to four-fifths of the net income or loss. What factors should she consider in deciding which partnership agreement to offer?

2. Prepare the January 1, 2014, journal entry(ies) necessary to admit a new partner to Success Systems through the purchase of a partnership interest for each of the following two separate cases: (a) 1:1 sharing agreement and (b) 4:1 sharing agreement.

3. Prepare the January 1, 2014, journal entry(ies) required to admit a new partner if the new partner invests cash of $22,537.

4. After posting the entry in part 3, what would be the new partner's equity percentage?

Beyond the Numbers

BTN D-1   Doctors Mobey, Oak, and Chesterfield have been in a group practice for several years. Mobey and Oak are family practice physicians, and Chesterfield is a general surgeon. Chesterfield receives many referrals for surgery from his family practice partners. Upon the partnership's original formation, the three doctors agreed to a two-part formula to share income. Every month each doctor receives a salary allowance of $3,000. Additional income is divided according to a percent of patient charges the doctors generate for the month. In the current month, Mobey generated 10% of the billings, Oak 30%, and Chesterfield 60%. The group's income for this month is $50,000. Chesterfield has expressed dissatisfaction with the income-sharing formula and asks that income be split entirely on patient charge percents.

ETHICS CHALLENGE

P2

Required

1. Compute the income allocation for the current month using the original agreement.
2. Compute the income allocation for the current month using Chesterfield's proposed agreement.
3. Identify the ethical components of this partnership decision for the doctors.

BTN D-2   Assume that you are studying for an upcoming accounting exam with a good friend. Your friend says that she has a solid understanding of general partnerships but is less sure that she understands organizations that combine certain characteristics of partnerships with other forms of business organization. You offer to make some study notes for your friend to help her learn about limited partnerships, limited liability partnerships, S corporations, and limited liability companies. Prepare a one-page set of well-organized, complete study notes on these four forms of business organization.

COMMUNICATING IN PRACTICE

C1

BTN D-3   Access the March 14, 2011, filing of the December 31, 2010, 10-K of America First Tax Exempt Investors LP. This company deals with tax-exempt mortgage revenue bonds that, among other things, finance student housing properties.

TAKING IT TO THE NET

P1 P2

1. Locate its December 31, 2010, balance sheet and list the account titles reported in the equity section of the balance sheet.
2. Locate its statement of partners' capital and comprehensive income (loss). How many units of limited partnership (known as "beneficial unit certificate holders") are outstanding at December 31, 2010?
3. What is the partnership's largest asset and its amount at December 31, 2010?

BTN D-4   This activity requires teamwork to reinforce understanding of accounting for partnerships.

TEAMWORK IN ACTION

P2

Required

1. Assume that Baker, Warner, and Rice form the BWR Partnership by making capital contributions of $200,000, $300,000, and $500,000, respectively. BWR predicts annual partnership net income of $450,000. The partners are considering various plans for sharing income and loss. Assign a different team member to compute how the projected $450,000 income would be shared under each of the following separate plans:
   a. Shared equally.
   b. In the ratio of the partners' initial capital investments.
   c. Salary allowances of $50,000 to Baker, $60,000 to Warner, and $70,000 to Rice, with the remaining balance shared equally.
   d. Interest allowances of 10% on the partners' initial capital investments, with the remaining balance shared equally.
2. In sequence, each member is to present his or her income-sharing calculations with the team.
3. As a team, identify and discuss at least one other possible way that income could be shared.

**ENTREPRENEURIAL
DECISION**

C1

BTN D-5 Omar Soliman and Nick Friedman are founding partners of their company, College Hunks Hauling Junk LLC. Assume that Omar and Nick decide to expand their business with the help of general partners.

Required

1. What details should Omar, Nick, and their future partners specify in the general partnership agreements?
2. What advantages should Omar, Nick, and their future partners be aware of with respect to organizing as a general partnership?
3. What disadvantages should Omar, Nick, and their future partners be aware of with respect to organizing as a general partnership?

ANSWERS TO MULTIPLE CHOICE QUIZ

1. e; Capital = $250,000 − $50,000
2. a; $90,000 × [$100,000/($150,000 + $150,000 + $100,000)]
   = $22,500
3. d;

	Jamison	Blue	Total
Net income			$ 270,000
Salary allowance	$120,000		(120,000)
Interest allowance	60,000	$80,000	(140,000)
Balance of income			10,000
Balance divided equally	5,000	5,000	(10,000)
Totals	$185,000	$85,000	$ 0

4. b; Total partnership equity = $125,000 + $124,000 + $75,000
   = $324,000
   Equity of Black = $324,000 × 20% = $64,800
   Bonus to old partners = $75,000 − $64,800 = $10,200, split equally
5. a; $10,500/[($110,000 + $124,000)/2] = 8.97%

Appendix

E Reporting and Preparing Special Journals

SYSTEM PRINCIPLES	SYSTEM COMPONENTS	SPECIAL JOURNALS	SYSTEM TECHNOLOGY
C1 Control Relevance Compatibility Flexibility Cost-Benefit	C1 Source documents Input devices Processors Storage Output devices	C2 Goals and uses C3 Subsidiary ledgers P1 Sales journal Cash receipts journal Purchases journal Cash disbursements journal P2 Proving the ledgers	Computers Data processing Networks Enterprise resource planning (ERP)

Learning Objectives

C1 Identify the principles and components of accounting information systems. (p. E-2)

C2 Explain the goals and uses of special journals. (p. E-5)

C3 Describe the use of controlling accounts and subsidiary ledgers. (p. E-6)

P1 Journalize and post transactions using special journals. (p. E-7)

P2 Prepare and prove the accuracy of subsidiary ledgers. (p. E-8)

A1 Compute segment return on assets and use it to evaluate segment performance. (p. E-18)

P3 *Appendix E-A*—Journalize and post transactions using special journals in a periodic inventory system. (p. E-25)

FUNDAMENTAL SYSTEM PRINCIPLES

C1 Identify the principles and components of accounting information systems.

EXHIBIT E.1

System Principles

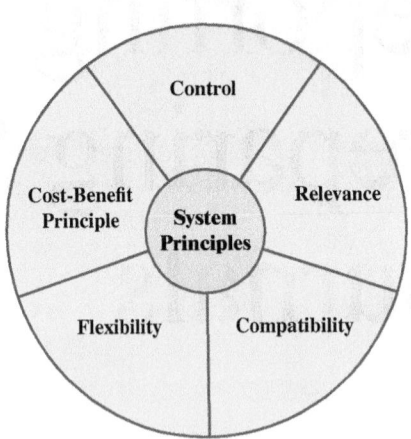

Accounting information systems collect and process data from transactions and events, organize them in useful reports, and communicate results to decision makers. With the increasing complexity of business and the growing need for information, accounting information systems are more important than ever. All decision makers need to have a basic knowledge of how accounting information systems work. This knowledge gives decision makers a competitive edge as they gain a better understanding of information constraints, measurement limitations, and potential applications. It allows them to make more informed decisions and to better balance the risks and returns of different strategies. This section explains five basic principles of accounting information systems, shown in Exhibit E.1.

Control Principle

Managers need to control and monitor business activities. The **control principle** prescribes that an accounting information system have internal controls. **Internal controls** are methods and procedures allowing managers to control and monitor business activities. They include policies to direct operations toward common goals, procedures to ensure reliable financial reports, safeguards to protect company assets, and methods to achieve compliance with laws and regulations.

Point: Hackers stole 45 million debit and credit card numbers from **T.J. Maxx.** The security breach is estimated to have cost the company $100 per card or $4.5 billion.

Relevance Principle

Decision makers need relevant information to make informed decisions. The **relevance principle** prescribes that an accounting information system report useful, understandable, timely, and pertinent information for effective decision making. The system must be designed to capture data that make a difference in decisions. To ensure this, we must consider all decision makers when identifying relevant information for disclosure.

Compatibility Principle

Accounting information systems must be consistent with the aims of a company. The **compatibility principle** prescribes that an accounting information system conform with a company's activities, personnel, and structure. It also must adapt to a company's unique characteristics. The system must not be intrusive but must work in harmony with and be driven by company goals. Most start-up entrepreneurs require only a simple information system. Starbucks, on the other hand, demands both a merchandising and a manufacturing information system able to assemble data from its global operations.

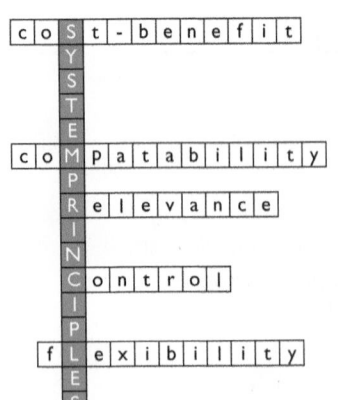

Flexibility Principle

Accounting information systems must be able to adjust to changes. The **flexibility principle** prescribes that an accounting information system be able to adapt to changes in the company, business environment, and needs of decisions makers. Technological advances, competitive pressures, consumer tastes, regulations, and company activities constantly evolve. A system must be designed to adapt to these changes.

Cost-Benefit Principle

Point: Law requires that *all* employers destroy credit-check and other employee records *before* tossing them. A cross-cut shredder is the tool of choice.

The **cost-benefit principle** prescribes that the benefits from an activity in an accounting information system outweigh the costs of that activity. The costs and benefits of an activity such as producing a specific report will impact the decisions of both external and internal users. Decisions regarding other systems principles (control, relevance, compatibility, and flexibility) are also affected by the cost-benefit principle.

Digitals Are Forever   E-communications have helped bring down many employees, including the former CEO of Boeing. To comply with Sarbanes-Oxley, more and more companies now archive and monitor e-mails, instant messages, blog postings, and Net-based phone calls. Using natural-language software, companies sift through digital communications in milliseconds, checking for trade secrets, bad language, porn, and pirated files. Also, employers should draft policies for employee use and access to electronic media to preserve company property interest and access rights to electronic data. ■

COMPONENTS OF ACCOUNTING SYSTEMS

Accounting information systems consist of people, records, methods, and equipment. The systems are designed to capture information about a company's transactions and to provide output including financial, managerial, and tax reports. All accounting information systems have these same goals, and thus share some basic components. These components apply whether or not a system is heavily computerized, yet the components of computerized systems usually provide more accuracy, speed, efficiency, and convenience than those of manual systems.

The five basic **components of accounting systems** are source documents, input devices, information processors, information storage, and output devices. Exhibit E.2 shows these components as a series of steps, yet we know that much two-way communication occurs between many of these components. We briefly describe each of these key components in this section.

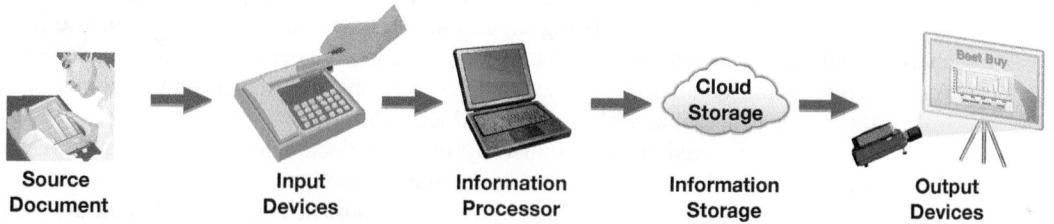

| Source Document | Input Devices | Information Processor | Information Storage | Output Devices |

EXHIBIT E.2

Accounting System Components

Source Documents

We introduced source documents in Chapters 1 and 2 and explained their importance for both business transactions and information collection. Source documents provide the basic information processed by an accounting system. Examples of source documents include bank statements and checks, invoices from suppliers, billings to customers, cash register files, and employee earnings records. Source documents can be paper, although they increasingly are taking the form of electronic files and Web communications. A growing number of companies are sending documents directly from their systems to their customers' and suppliers' systems. The Web is playing a major role in this transformation from paper-based to *paperless* systems.

Accurate source documents are crucial to accounting information systems. Input of faulty or incomplete information seriously impairs the reliability and relevance of the information system. We commonly refer to this as "garbage in, garbage out." Information systems are set up with attention on control procedures to limit the possibility of entering faulty data in the system.

Input Devices

Input devices capture information from source documents and enable its transfer to the system's information processing component. These devices often involve converting data on source documents from written or electronic form to a form usable for the system. Journal entries, both electronic and paper based, are a type of input device. Keyboards, scanners, and modems are some of the most common input devices in practice today. For example, bar code readers capture code numbers and transfer them to the organization's computer for processing. Moreover, a scanner can capture writing samples and other input directly from source documents. Cell phone cameras also can serve as input devices via bar codes.

Controls are used to ensure that only authorized individuals input data to the system. Controls increase the system's reliability and allow information to be traced back to its source.

Point: Understanding a manual accounting system is useful in understanding an electronic system.

Decision Insight

Siri Exposure Siri (Speech Interpretation and Recognition Interface) is an intelligent personal assistant and knowledge navigator that works as an application for Apple's iOS. The latest iPhones include Siri, including its voice recognition capabilities. Companies should ask: *Siri, do we have adequate controls for inputs to our system via voice recognition?* ■

Information Processors

Information processors are systems that interpret, transform, and summarize information for use in analysis and reporting. An important part of an information processor in accounting systems is professional judgment. Accounting principles are never so structured that they limit the need for professional judgment. Other parts of an information processor include journals, ledgers, working papers, and posting procedures. Each assists in transforming raw data to useful information.

Increasingly, computer technology (both computing hardware and software) is assisting manual information processors. This assistance is freeing accounting professionals to take on increased analysis, interpretive, and managerial roles. Web-based application service providers (ASPs) offer another type of information processor.

Information Storage

Information storage is the accounting system component that keeps data in a form accessible to information processors. After being input and processed, data are stored for use in future analyses and reports. The database must be accessible to preparers of periodic financial reports. Auditors rely on this database when they audit both financial statements and a company's controls. Companies also maintain files of source documents.

Older systems consisted almost exclusively of paper documents, but most modern systems depend on electronic storage devices or, increasingly, cloud storage. Advances in information storage enable accounting systems to increasingly store more detailed data. This means managers have more data to access and work with in planning and controlling business activities. Information storage can be online, meaning that data can be accessed whenever, and from wherever, it is needed. Off-line storage means access often requires assistance and authorization. Information storage is increasingly augmented by Web sources such as SEC databases, benchmarking services, and financial and product markets. Also, audit technology allows external auditors 365-day real-time access to client records from remote locations.

Decision Insight

Virtual Output A screenless computer display, called *virtual retinal display* (VRD), scans rows of pixels directly onto the user's retina by means of a laser. VRDs can simulate three-dimensional virtual worlds, including 3D financial graphics. ■

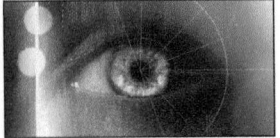

Output Devices

Output devices are the means to take information out of an accounting system and make it available to users. Common output devices are printers, monitors, projectors, and Web communications. Output devices provide users a variety of items including graphics, analysis reports, bills to customers, checks to suppliers, employee paychecks, financial statements, and internal reports. When requests for output occur, an information processor takes the needed data from a database and prepares the necessary report, which is then sent to an output device. A special type of output is an electronic funds transfer (EFT). One example is the transfer of payroll from the company's bank account to its employees' bank accounts. This requires an interface to allow a company's accounting system to send payroll data directly to the bank's accounting system. This interface can involve a company recording its payroll data in an encrypted zip file and forwarding it to the bank. The bank then uses this output to transfer wages earned to employees' accounts.

■ **Decision** Ethics

Accountant   Your client requests advice in purchasing software for its accounting system. You have been offered a 10% commission by a software company for each purchase of its system by one of your clients. Does this commission arrangement affect your evaluation of software? Do you tell your client about the commission arrangement? ■   [Answer—p. E-27]

SPECIAL JOURNALS IN ACCOUNTING

This section describes the underlying records of accounting information systems. Designed correctly, these records support efficiency in processing transactions and events. They are part of all systems in various forms and are increasingly electronic. Even in technologically advanced systems, a basic understanding of the records we describe in this section aids in using, interpreting, and applying accounting information. It also improves our knowledge of computer-based systems. Remember that all accounting systems have common purposes and internal workings whether or not they depend on technology. (Popular accounting software that utilizes special journals includes *Great Plains* and *QuickBooks*.)

   This section focuses on special journals and subsidiary ledgers that are an important part of accounting systems. We describe how special journals are used to capture transactions, and we explain how subsidiary ledgers are set up to capture details of accounts. This section uses a *perpetual* inventory system, and the special journals are set up using this system. We include a note at the bottom of each of the special journals explaining the change required if a company uses a periodic system.

C2   Explain the goals and uses of special journals.

Basics of Special Journals

A **general journal** is an all-purpose journal in which we can record any transaction. Use of a general journal for all transactions is usually more costly for a business *and* is a less effective control procedure. Moreover, for less technologically advanced systems, use of a general journal requires that each debit and each credit entered be individually posted to its respective ledger account. To enhance internal control and reduce costs, transactions are organized into common groups. A **special journal** is used to record and post transactions of similar type. Most transactions of a merchandiser, for instance, can be categorized into the journals shown in Exhibit E.3. This section assumes the use of these four special journals along with the general journal. The general journal continues to be used for transactions not covered by special journals and for adjusting, closing, and correcting entries. We show in the following discussion that special journals are *efficient tools in helping journalize and post transactions*. This is done, for instance, by accumulating debits and credits of similar transactions, which allows posting of amounts as column *totals* rather than as individual amounts. The advantage of this system increases as the number of transactions increases. Special journals allow an *efficient division of labor*, which is also an effective control procedure.

Point: Companies can use as many special journals as necessary given their unique business activities.

Point: A specific transaction is recorded in only *one* journal.

EXHIBIT E.3

Using Special Journals with a General Journal

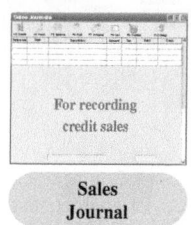

For recording credit sales

Sales Journal

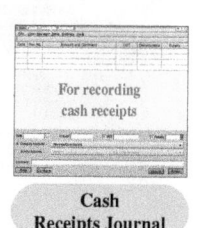

For recording cash receipts

Cash Receipts Journal

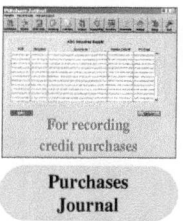

For recording credit purchases

Purchases Journal

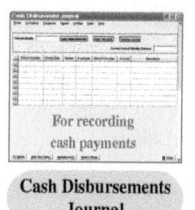

For recording cash payments

Cash Disbursements Journal

For transactions not in special journals

General Journal

   It is important to note that special journals and subsidiary ledgers *are designed in a manner that is best suited for each business*. The most likely candidates for special journal status are recurring transactions—for many businesses those are sales, cash receipts, purchases, and cash disbursements. However, good systems design for a business could involve collapsing sales and cash receipts in one journal, or purchases and cash disbursements in another. It could also involve adding more special journals or additional subsidiary ledgers for other recurring transactions. This design decision extends to journal and ledger format. That is, the selection on number of columns, column headings, and so forth is based on what is best suited for each business. Thus, read the following sections as one example of a common systems design, but not the only design. (Proprietary software is internally developed by companies to meet system needs not met by off-the-shelf accounting software.)

Subsidiary Ledgers

To understand special journals, it is necessary to understand the workings of a **subsidiary ledger,** which is a list of individual accounts with a common characteristic. A subsidiary ledger contains detailed information on specific accounts in the general ledger. Information systems often include several subsidiary ledgers. Two of the most important are:

- *Accounts receivable ledger*—stores transaction data of individual customers.
- *Accounts payable ledger*—stores transaction data of individual suppliers.

Individual accounts in subsidiary ledgers are often arranged alphabetically, which is the approach taken here. We describe accounts receivable and accounts payable ledgers in this section. Our discussion of special journals uses these ledgers.

Accounts Receivable Ledger   When we recorded credit sales in prior chapters, we debited (increased) Accounts Receivable. When a company has more than one credit customer, the accounts receivable records must show how much *each* customer purchased, paid, and has yet to pay. This information is collected by keeping a separate account receivable for each credit customer. A separate account for each customer *could* be kept in the general ledger with the other financial statement accounts, but this is uncommon. Instead, the general ledger usually has a single Accounts Receivable account, and a *subsidiary ledger* is set up to keep a separate account for each customer. This subsidiary ledger is called the **accounts receivable ledger** (also called *accounts receivable subsidiary ledger* or *customers ledger*), and it can exist in electronic or paper form.

Exhibit E.4 shows the relation between the Accounts Receivable account and its individual accounts in the subsidiary ledger. After all items are posted, the balance in the Accounts Receivable account must equal the sum of all balances of its customers' accounts. The Accounts Receivable account is said to control the accounts receivable ledger and is called a **controlling account.** Since the accounts receivable ledger is a supplementary record controlled by an account in the general ledger, it is called a *subsidiary* ledger.

Point: When a general ledger account has a subsidiary ledger, any transaction that impacts one of them also impacts the other—some refer to this as *general and subsidiary ledgers kept in tandem.*

EXHIBIT E.4

Accounts Receivable Controlling Account and Its Subsidiary Ledger

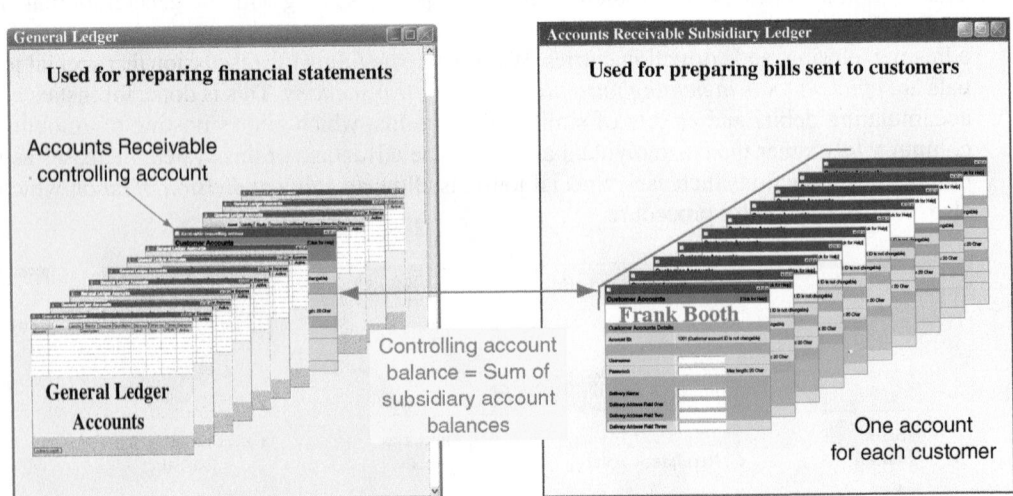

Point: A control account refers to any general ledger account that summarizes subsidiary ledger data.

Accounts Payable Ledger   There are other controlling accounts and subsidiary ledgers. We know, for example, that many companies buy on credit from several suppliers. This means that companies must keep a separate account for each supplier by keeping an Accounts Payable controlling account in the general ledger and a separate account for each supplier (creditor) in an **accounts payable ledger** (also called *accounts payable subsidiary ledger* or *creditors ledger*).

Other Subsidiary Ledgers Subsidiary ledgers are common for several other accounts. A company with many classes of equipment, for example, might keep only one Equipment account in its general ledger, but its Equipment account would control a subsidiary ledger in which each class of equipment is recorded in a separate account. Similar treatment is common for investments, inventory, and any accounts needing separate detailed records. Genmar Holdings, which manufactures boats by Champion, Glastron, Four Winns, and Larson, reports sales information by product line in its report. Yet its accounting system keeps much more detailed sales records. Genmar Holdings, for instance, sells hundreds of different products and must be able to analyze the sales performance of each. This detail can be captured by many different general ledger sales accounts but is instead captured by using supplementary records that function like subsidiary ledgers. Overall, subsidiary ledgers are applied in many different ways to ensure that the accounting system captures sufficient details to support analyses that decision makers need. At least four benefits derive from subsidiary ledgers:

1. Removal of excessive details, and detailed accounts, from the general ledger.
2. Up-to-date information readily available on specific customers and suppliers.
3. Aid in error identification for specific accounts.
4. Potential efficiencies in recordkeeping through division of labor in posting.

Sales Journal

A typical **sales journal** is used to record sales of inventory *on credit*. Sales of inventory for cash are not recorded in a sales journal but in a cash receipts journal. Sales of noninventory assets on credit are recorded in the general journal.

P1 Journalize and post transactions using special journals.

Journalizing Credit sale transactions are recorded with information about each sale entered separately in a sales journal. This information is often taken from a copy of the sales ticket or invoice prepared at the time of sale. The top portion of Exhibit E.5 shows a typical sales journal from a merchandiser. It has columns for recording the date, customer's name, invoice number, posting reference, and the retail and cost amounts of each credit sale. The sales journal in this exhibit is called a **columnar journal,** which is any journal with more than one column.

Each transaction recorded in the sales journal yields an entry in the "Accounts Receivable Dr., Sales Cr." column. We usually need only one column for these two accounts. (An exception is when managers need more information about taxes, returns, and other sales details.) Each transaction in the sales journal also yields an entry in the "Cost of Goods Sold Dr., Inventory Cr." column. This entry reflects the perpetual inventory system of tracking costs with each sale. To illustrate, on February 2, this company sold merchandise on account to Jason Henry for $450. The invoice number is 307, and the cost of this merchandise is $315. This information is captured on one line in the sales journal. No further explanations or entries are necessary, saving time and effort. Moreover, this sales journal is consistent with most inventory systems that use bar codes to record both sales and costs with each sale transaction. Note that the Posting Reference (PR) column is not used when entering transactions but instead is used when posting.

Point: Each transaction in the sales journal includes a debit to accounts receivable and a credit to sales.

Point: Continuously updated customer accounts provide timely information for customer inquiries on those accounts and on current amounts owed.

Posting A sales journal is posted as reflected in the arrow lines of Exhibit E.5. Two types of posting can be identified: (1) posting to the subsidiary ledger(s) and (2) posting to the general ledger.

Posting to subsidiary ledger. Individual transactions in the sales journal are posted regularly (typically concurrently) to customer accounts in the accounts receivable ledger. These postings keep customer accounts up-to-date, which is important for the person granting credit to customers. When sales recorded in the sales journal are individually posted to customer accounts in the accounts receivable ledger, check marks are entered in the sales journal's PR column. Check marks are used rather than account numbers because customer accounts usually are arranged alphabetically in the accounts receivable ledger. Note that posting debits to Accounts Receivable twice—once to Accounts Receivable and once to the customer's subsidiary account—does not violate the accounting equation of debits equal credits. The equality of debits and credits is always maintained in the general ledger.

Point: PR column is only checked *after* the amount(s) is posted.

EXHIBIT E.5

Sales Journal with Posting*

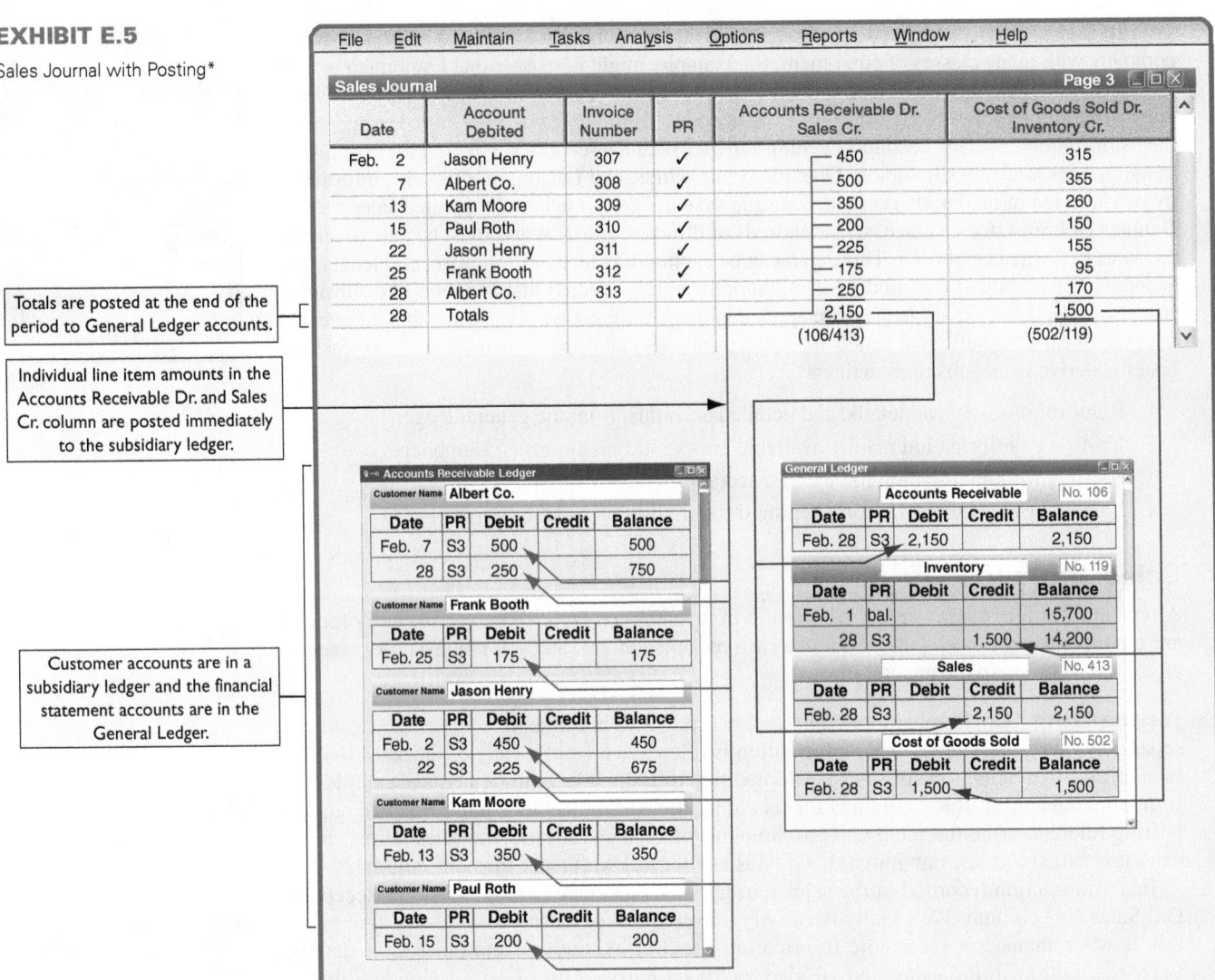

Totals are posted at the end of the period to General Ledger accounts.

Individual line item amounts in the Accounts Receivable Dr. and Sales Cr. column are posted immediately to the subsidiary ledger.

Customer accounts are in a subsidiary ledger and the financial statement accounts are in the General Ledger.

*The Sales Journal in a *periodic* system would exclude the column on the far right titled "Cost of Goods Sold Dr., Inventory Cr."

Posting to general ledger.   The sales journal's account columns are totaled at the end of each period (the month of February in this case). For the "sales" column, the $2,150 total is debited to Accounts Receivable and credited to Sales in the general ledger (see Exhibit E.5). For the "cost" column, the $1,500 total is debited to Cost of Goods Sold and credited to Inventory in the general ledger. When totals are posted to accounts in the general ledger, the account numbers are entered below the column total in the sales journal for tracking. For example, we enter (106/413) below the total in the sales column after this amount is posted to account number 106 (Accounts Receivable) and account number 413 (Sales).

Point: Postings are automatic in a computerized system.

A company identifies in the PR column of its subsidiary ledgers the journal and page number from which an amount is taken. We identify a journal by using an initial. Items posted from the sales journal carry the initial *S* before their journal page numbers in a PR column. Likewise, items from the cash receipts journal carry the initial *R*; items from the cash disbursements journal carry the initial *D*; items from the purchases journal carry the initial *P*; and items from the general journal carry the initial *G*.

Proving the Ledgers   Account balances in the general ledger and subsidiary ledgers are periodically proved (or reviewed) for accuracy after posting. To do this we first prepare a trial balance of the general ledger to confirm that debits equal credits. Second, we test a subsidiary ledger by preparing a *schedule* of individual accounts and amounts. A **schedule of accounts receivable** lists each customer and the balance owed. If this total equals the balance of the

P2   Prepare and prove the accuracy of subsidiary ledgers.

Accounts Receivable controlling account, the accounts in the accounts receivable ledger are assumed correct. Exhibit E.6 shows a schedule of accounts receivable drawn from the accounts receivable ledger of Exhibit E.5. (Accountants may use the expression "tie out" when checking whether the balance of the accounts receivable control account matches the total balance on the subsidiary listing of accounts receivable.)

Schedule of Accounts Receivable February 28	
Albert Co.	$ 750
Frank Booth	175
Jason Henry	675
Kam Moore	350
Paul Roth	200
Total accounts receivable	$2,150

EXHIBIT E.6

Schedule of Accounts Receivable

Additional Issues   We consider three additional issues with the sales journal: (1) recording sales taxes, (2) recording sales returns and allowances, and (3) using actual sales invoices as a journal.

Point: In accounting, the word *schedule* generally means a list.

Sales taxes.   Governmental agencies such as cities and states often require sellers to collect sales taxes from customers and to periodically send these taxes to the appropriate agency. When using a columnar sales journal, we can keep a record of taxes collected by adding a Sales Taxes Payable column as follows.

File	Edit	Maintain	Tasks	Analysis	Options	Reports	Window	Help

| | | | | | | | Sales Journal Page 3 | |

Date	Account Debited	Invoice Number	PR	Accounts Receivable Dr.	Sales Taxes Payable Cr.	Sales Cr.	Cost of Goods Sold Dr. Inventory Cr.
Dec. 1	Favre Co.	7-1698		103	3	100	75

Individual amounts in the Accounts Receivable column would continue to be posted immediately to customer accounts in the accounts receivable ledger. Individual amounts in the Sales Taxes Payable and Sales columns are not posted. Column totals would continue to be posted as usual. (A company that collects sales taxes on its cash sales can also use a Sales Taxes Payable column in its cash receipts journal.)

Sales returns and allowances.   A company with only a few sales returns and allowances can record them in a general journal with an entry such as the following:

May 17	Sales Returns and Allowances	414	175	
	Accounts Receivable—Ray Ball	106/✓		175
	Customer returned merchandise.			

Assets = Liabilities + Equity
−175   −175

The debit in this entry is posted to the Sales Returns and Allowances account (no. 414). The credit is posted to both the Accounts Receivable controlling account (no. 106) and to the customer's account. When we enter the account number and the check mark, 106/✓, in the PR column on the credit line, this means both the Accounts Receivable controlling account in the general ledger and the Ray Ball account in the accounts receivable ledger are credited for $175. [*Note:* If the returned goods can be resold to another customer, the company would debit (increase) the Inventory account and credit (decrease) the Cost of Goods Sold account. If the returned goods are defective (worthless), the company could simply leave their costs in the Cost of Goods Sold account (see Chapter 4).] A company with a large number of sales returns and allowances can save time by recording them in a separate sales returns and allowances journal.

Sales invoices as a sales journal.   To save costs, some small companies avoid using a sales journal for credit sales and instead post each sales invoice amount directly to the customer's account in the accounts receivable ledger. They then put copies of invoices in a file. At the end of the period, they total all invoices for that period and make a general journal entry to debit

Accounts Receivable and credit Sales for the total amount. The file of invoice copies acts as a sales journal. This is called *direct posting of sales invoices*.

Cash Receipts Journal

A **cash receipts journal** is typically used to record all receipts of cash. Exhibit E.7 shows one common form of the cash receipts journal.

EXHIBIT E.7

Cash Receipts Journal with Posting*

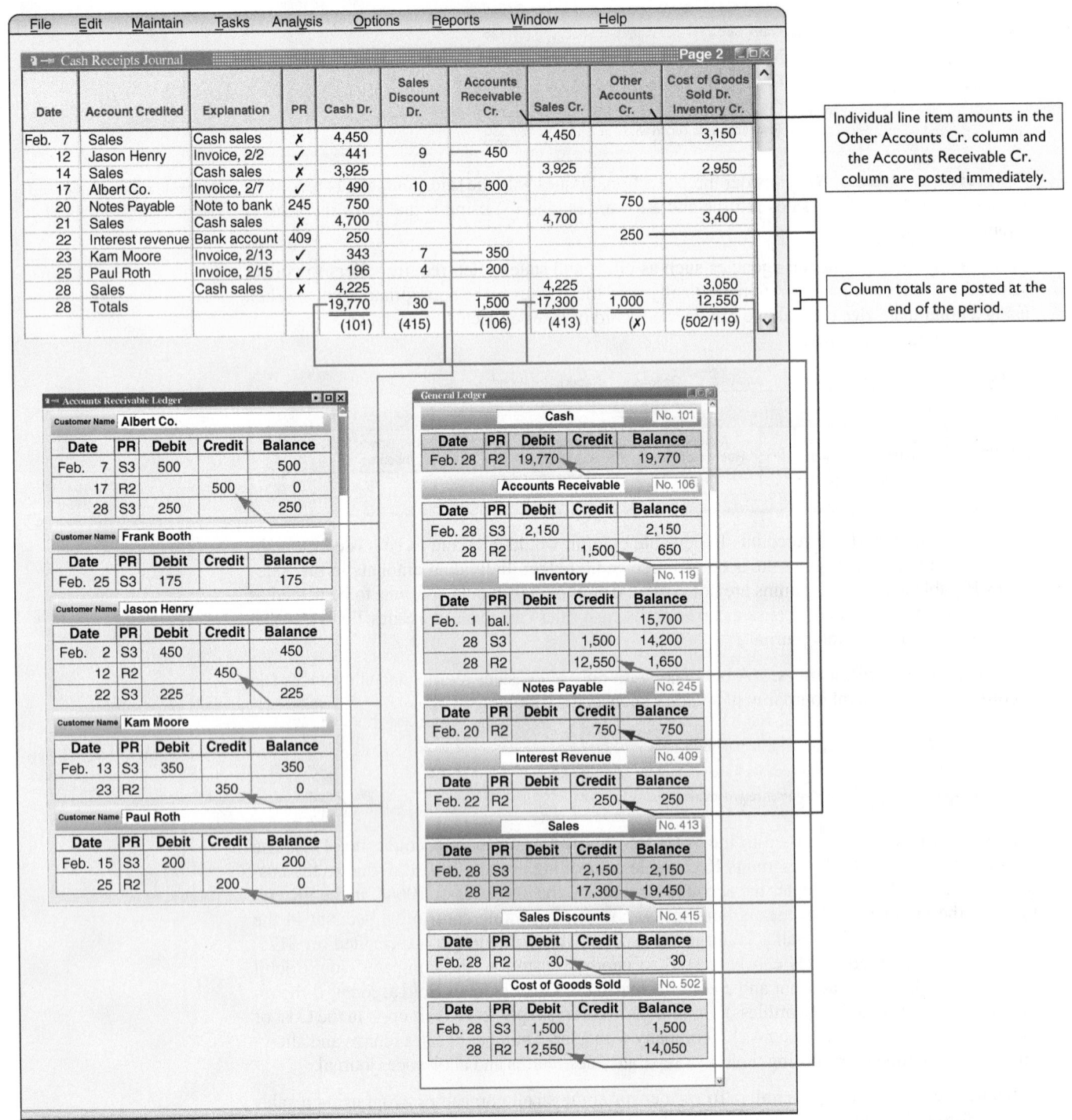

*The Cash Receipts Journal in a *periodic* system would exclude the column on the far right titled "Cost of Goods Dr., Inventory Cr."

Journalizing and Posting   Cash receipts can be separated into one of three types: (1) cash from credit customers in payment of their accounts, (2) cash from cash sales, and (3) cash from other sources. The cash receipts journal in Exhibit E.7 has a separate credit column for each of these three sources. We describe how to journalize transactions from each of these three sources. (An Explanation column is included in the cash receipts journal to identify the source.)

Point: Each transaction in the cash receipts journal involves a debit to Cash. Credit accounts will vary.

Cash from credit customers.   *Journalizing.* To record cash received in payment of a customer's account, the customer's name is first entered in the Account Credited column—see transactions dated February 12, 17, 23, and 25. Then the amounts debited to both Cash and the Sales Discount (if any) are entered in their respective columns, and the amount credited to the customer's account is entered in the Accounts Receivable Cr. column.

Posting. Individual amounts in the Accounts Receivable Cr. column are posted immediately to customer accounts in the subsidiary accounts receivable ledger. The $1,500 column total is posted at the end of the period (month in this case) as a credit to the Accounts Receivable controlling account in the general ledger.

Cash sales.   *Journalizing.* The amount for each cash sale is entered in the Cash Dr. column and the Sales Cr. column. The February 7, 14, 21, and 28 transactions are examples. (Cash sales are usually journalized daily or at point of sale, but are journalized weekly in Exhibit E.7 for brevity.) Each cash sale also yields an entry to Cost of Goods Sold Dr. and Inventory Cr. for the cost of merchandise—see the far right column.

Point: Some software packages put cash sales in the sales journal.

Posting. For cash sales, we place an *x* in the PR column to indicate that its amount is not individually posted. We do post the $17,300 Sales Cr. total and the $12,550 total from the "cost" column.

Cash from other sources.   *Journalizing.* Examples of cash from other sources are money borrowed from a bank, cash interest received on account, and cash sale of noninventory assets. The transactions of February 20 and 22 are illustrative. The Other Accounts Cr. column is used for these transactions.

Example: Record in the cash receipts journal a $700 cash sale of land when the land carries a $700 original cost. *Answer:* Debit the Cash column for $700, and credit the Other Accounts column for $700 (the account credited is Land).

Posting. Amounts from these transactions are immediately posted to their general ledger accounts and the PR column identifies those accounts.

Footing, Crossfooting, and Posting   To be sure that total debits and credits in a columnar journal are equal, we often crossfoot column totals before posting them. To *foot* a column of numbers is to add it. To *crossfoot* in this case is to add the Debit column totals, then add the Credit column totals, and compare the two sums for equality. Footing and crossfooting of the numbers in Exhibit E.7 result in the report in Exhibit E.8.

Point: Subsidiary ledgers and their controlling accounts are in *balance* only after all posting is complete.

Debit Columns		Credit Columns	
Cash Dr.	$19,770	Accounts Receivable Cr.	$ 1,500
Sales Discounts Dr.	30	Sales Cr.	17,300
Cost of Goods Sold Dr.	12,550	Other Accounts Cr.	1,000
		Inventory Cr.	12,550
Total	$32,350	Total	$32,350

EXHIBIT E.8

Footing and Crossfooting Journal Totals

At the end of the period, after crossfooting the journal to confirm that debits equal credits, the total amounts from the columns of the cash receipts journal are posted to their general ledger accounts. The Other Accounts Cr. column total is not posted because the individual amounts are directly posted to their general ledger accounts. We place an *x* below the Other Accounts Cr. column to indicate that this column total is not posted. The account numbers for the column totals that are posted are entered in parentheses below each column. (*Note:* Posting items immediately from the Other Accounts Cr. column with a delayed posting of their offsetting items in the Cash column total causes the general ledger to be out of balance during the period. Posting the Cash Dr. column total at the end of the period corrects this imbalance in the general ledger before the trial balance and financial statements are prepared.)

■ Decision Maker

Entrepreneur You want to know how promptly customers are paying their bills. This information can help you decide whether to extend credit and to plan your cash payments. Where do you find this information? ■ [Answer—p. E-27]

Purchases Journal

A **purchases journal** is typically used to record all credit purchases, including those for inventory. Purchases for cash are recorded in the Cash Disbursements Journal.

Point: The number of special journals and the design of each are based on a company's specific needs.

Journalizing Entries in the purchases journal in Exhibit E.9 reflect purchase invoices or other source documents. We use the invoice date and terms to compute the date when payment for each purchase is due. The Accounts Payable Cr. column is used to record the amounts owed to each creditor. Inventory purchases are recorded in the Inventory Dr. column.

To illustrate, inventory costing $200 is purchased from Ace Manufacturing on February 5. The creditor's name (Ace) is entered in the Account column, the invoice date is entered in the Date of Invoice column, the purchase terms are entered in the Terms column, and the $200 amount is entered in the Accounts Payable Cr. and the Inventory Dr. columns. When a purchase involves an amount recorded in the Other Accounts Dr. column, we use the Account column to identify the general ledger account debited. For example, the February 28 transaction involves purchases of inventory, office supplies, and store supplies from ITT. The journal has no column for store supplies, so the Other Accounts Dr. column is used. In this case, Store Supplies is

Point: Each transaction in the purchases journal has a credit to Accounts Payable. Debit accounts will vary.

EXHIBIT E.9

Purchases Journal with Posting*

File	Edit	Maintain	Tasks	Analysis	Options	Reports	Window	Help

Purchases Journal   Page 1

Date	Account	Date of Invoice	Terms	PR	Accounts Payable Cr.	Inventory Dr.	Office Supplies Dr.	Other Accounts Dr.
Feb. 3	Horning Supply Co.	2/2	n/30	✓	350	275	75	
5	Ace Mfg. Co.	2/5	2/10, n/30	✓	200	200		
13	Wynet & Co.	2/10	2/10, n/30	✓	150	150		
20	Smite Co.	2/18	2/10, n/30	✓	300	300		
25	Ace Mfg. Co.	2/24	2/10, n/30	✓	100	100		
28	Store Supplies/ITT Co.	2/28	n/30	125/✓	225	125	25	75
28	Totals				1,325	1,150	100	75
					(201)	(119)	(124)	(X)

Individual amounts in the Other Accounts Dr. column and the Accounts Payable Cr. column are posted immediately.

Column totals, except for Other Accounts Dr. column, are posted at the end of the period.

Accounts Payable Ledger

Company Name **Ace Mfg. Company**

Date	PR	Debit	Credit	Balance
Feb. 5	P1		200	200
25	P1		100	300

Company Name **Horning Supply Company**

Date	PR	Debit	Credit	Balance
Feb. 3	P1		350	350

Company Name **ITT Company**

Date	PR	Debit	Credit	Balance
Feb. 28	P1		225	225

Company Name **Smite Company**

Date	PR	Debit	Credit	Balance
Feb. 20	P1		300	300

Company Name **Wynet and Company**

Date	PR	Debit	Credit	Balance
Feb. 13	P1		150	150

General Ledger

Inventory   No. 119

Date	PR	Debit	Credit	Balance
Feb. 1	bal.			15,700
28	S3		1,500	14,200
28	R2		12,550	1,650
28	P1	1,150		2,800

Office Supplies   No. 124

Date	PR	Debit	Credit	Balance
Feb. 28	P1	100		100

Store Supplies   No. 125

Date	PR	Debit	Credit	Balance
Feb. 28	P1	75		75

Accounts Payable   No. 201

Date	PR	Debit	Credit	Balance
Feb. 28	P1		1,325	1,325

*The Purchases Journal in a *periodic* system replaces "Inventory Dr." with "Purchases Dr."

entered in the Account column along with the creditor's name (ITT). This purchases journal also includes a separate column for credit purchases of office supplies. A separate column such as this is useful when several transactions involve debits to the same account. Each company uses its own judgment in deciding on the number of separate columns necessary.

Point: The Other Accounts Dr. column allows the purchases journal to be used for any purchase on credit.

Posting   The amounts in the Accounts Payable Cr. column are immediately posted to individual creditor accounts in the accounts payable subsidiary ledger. Individual amounts in the Other Accounts Dr. column are immediately posted to their general ledger accounts. At the end of the period, all column totals except the Other Accounts Dr. column are posted to their general ledger accounts.

Proving the Ledger   Accounts payable balances in the subsidiary ledger can be periodically proved after posting. We prove the subsidiary ledger by preparing a **schedule of accounts payable,** which is a list of accounts from the accounts payable ledger with their balances and the total. If this total of the individual balances equals the balance of the Accounts Payable controlling account, the accounts in the accounts payable ledger are assumed correct. Exhibit E.10 shows a schedule of accounts payable drawn from the accounts payable ledger of Exhibit E.9. (This schedule can be done after any posting; for example, we could prepare another schedule of accounts payable after the postings in Exhibit E.11.)

Point: The balance in the Accounts Payable controlling account must equal the sum of the individual account balances in the accounts payable subsidiary ledger after posting.

EXHIBIT E.10

Schedule of Accounts Payable

Schedule of Accounts Payable February 28	
Ace Mfg. Company	$ 300
Horning Supply Company	350
ITT Company	225
Smite Company	300
Wynet & Company	150
Total accounts payable	$1,325

Cash Disbursements Journal

A **cash disbursements journal,** also called a *cash payments journal,* is typically used to record all cash payments.

Journalizing   The cash disbursements journal shown in Exhibit E.11 illustrates repetitive entries to the Cash Cr. column of this journal (reflecting cash payments). Also note the frequent credits to Inventory (which reflect purchase discounts) and the debits to Accounts Payable. For example, on February 15, the company pays Ace on account (credit terms of 2/10, n/30—see February 5 transaction in Exhibit E.9). Since payment occurs in the discount period, the company pays $196 ($200 invoice less $4 discount). The $4 discount is credited to Inventory. Note that when this company purchases inventory for cash, it is recorded using the Other Accounts Dr. column and the Cash Cr. column as illustrated in the February 3 and 12 transactions. Generally, the Other Accounts column is used to record cash payments on items for which no column exists. For example, on February 15, the company pays salaries expense of $250. The title of the account debited (Salaries Expense) is entered in the Account Debited column.

Point: Each transaction in the cash disbursements journal involves a credit to Cash. The debit accounts will vary.

The cash disbursements journal has a column titled Ck. No. (check number). For control over cash disbursements, all payments except for those of small amounts are made by check. Checks should be prenumbered and each check's number entered in the journal in numerical order in the column headed Ck. No. This makes it possible to scan the numbers in the column for omitted checks. When a cash disbursements journal has a column for check numbers, it is sometimes called a **check register.**

Posting   Individual amounts in the Other Accounts Dr. column of a cash disbursements journal are immediately posted to their general ledger accounts. Individual amounts in the Accounts Payable Dr. column are also immediately posted to creditors' accounts in the subsidiary Accounts Payable ledger. At the end of the period, we crossfoot column totals and post

EXHIBIT E.11

Cash Disbursements Journal with Posting*

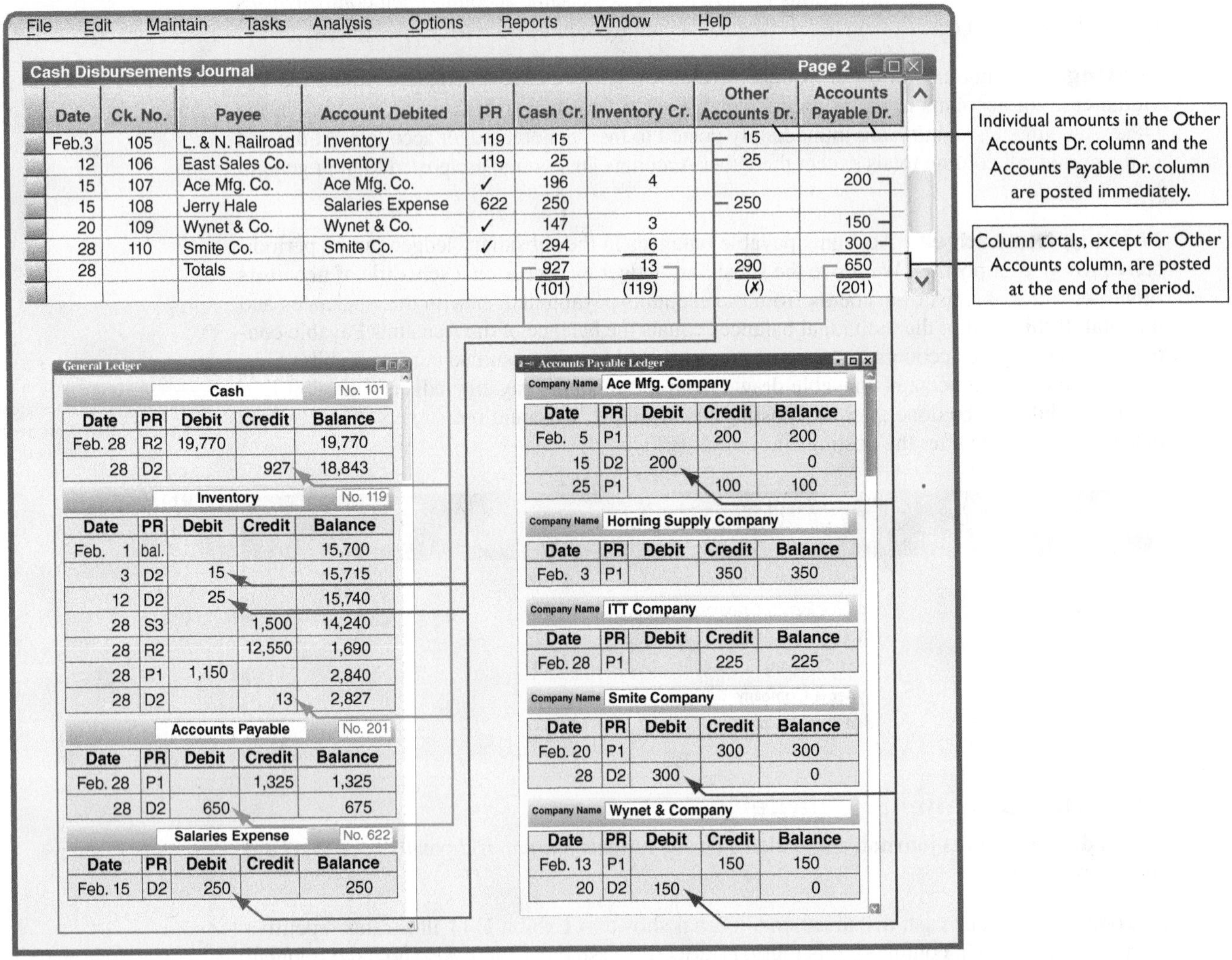

File	Edit	Maintain	Tasks	Analysis	Options	Reports	Window	Help

Cash Disbursements Journal — Page 2

Date	Ck. No.	Payee	Account Debited	PR	Cash Cr.	Inventory Cr.	Other Accounts Dr.	Accounts Payable Dr.
Feb.3	105	L. & N. Railroad	Inventory	119	15		15	
12	106	East Sales Co.	Inventory	119	25		25	
15	107	Ace Mfg. Co.	Ace Mfg. Co.	✓	196	4		200
15	108	Jerry Hale	Salaries Expense	622	250		250	
20	109	Wynet & Co.	Wynet & Co.	✓	147	3		150
28	110	Smite Co.	Smite Co.	✓	294	6		300
28		Totals			927	13	290	650
					(101)	(119)	(X)	(201)

> Individual amounts in the Other Accounts Dr. column and the Accounts Payable Dr. column are posted immediately.

> Column totals, except for Other Accounts column, are posted at the end of the period.

General Ledger

Cash — No. 101

Date	PR	Debit	Credit	Balance
Feb. 28	R2	19,770		19,770
28	D2		927	18,843

Inventory — No. 119

Date	PR	Debit	Credit	Balance
Feb. 1	bal.			15,700
3	D2	15		15,715
12	D2	25		15,740
28	S3		1,500	14,240
28	R2		12,550	1,690
28	P1	1,150		2,840
28	D2		13	2,827

Accounts Payable — No. 201

Date	PR	Debit	Credit	Balance
Feb. 28	P1		1,325	1,325
28	D2	650		675

Salaries Expense — No. 622

Date	PR	Debit	Credit	Balance
Feb. 15	D2	250		250

Accounts Payable Ledger

Company Name **Ace Mfg. Company**

Date	PR	Debit	Credit	Balance
Feb. 5	P1		200	200
15	D2	200		0
25	P1		100	100

Company Name **Horning Supply Company**

Date	PR	Debit	Credit	Balance
Feb. 3	P1		350	350

Company Name **ITT Company**

Date	PR	Debit	Credit	Balance
Feb. 28	P1		225	225

Company Name **Smite Company**

Date	PR	Debit	Credit	Balance
Feb. 20	P1		300	300
28	D2	300		0

Company Name **Wynet & Company**

Date	PR	Debit	Credit	Balance
Feb. 13	P1		150	150
20	D2	150		0

*The Cash Disbursements Journal in a *periodic* system replaces "Inventory Cr." with "Purchases Discounts Cr."

the Accounts Payable Dr. column total to the Accounts Payable controlling account. Also, the Inventory Cr. column total is posted to the Inventory account, and the Cash Cr. column total is posted to the Cash account.

Decision Maker

Controller   You wish to analyze your company's cash payments to suppliers and its purchases discounts. Where do you find this information? ■   [Answer—p. E-27]

General Journal Transactions

When special journals are used, we still need a general journal for adjusting, closing, and any other transactions for which no special journal has been set up. Examples of these other transactions might include purchases returns and allowances, purchases of plant assets by issuing a note payable, sales returns if a sales returns and allowances journal is not used, and receipt of a note receivable from a customer. We described the recording of transactions in a general journal in Chapters 2 and 3.

TECHNOLOGY-BASED ACCOUNTING SYSTEMS

Accounting information systems are supported with technology, which can range from simple calculators to advanced computerized systems. Since technology is increasingly important in accounting information systems, we discuss the impact of computer technology, how data processing works with accounting data, and the role of computer networks.

Computer Technology in Accounting

Computer technology provides accuracy, speed, efficiency, and convenience in performing accounting tasks. A program can be written, for instance, to process customers' merchandise orders. Multipurpose off-the-shelf software applications exist for a variety of business operations. These include familiar accounting programs such as Sage 50 Complete Accounting (formerly known as Peachtree®) and QuickBooks®. Off-the-shelf programs are designed to be user friendly and menu driven, and many operate more efficiently as *integrated* systems. In an integrated system, actions taken in one part of the system automatically affect related parts. When a credit sale is recorded in an integrated system, for instance, several parts of the system are automatically updated, such as posting.

Point: Companies that have reported missing or stolen employee data such as Social Security numbers include Time Warner, Polo Ralph Lauren, Lexis/Nexis, ChoicePoint, and DSW Shoes.

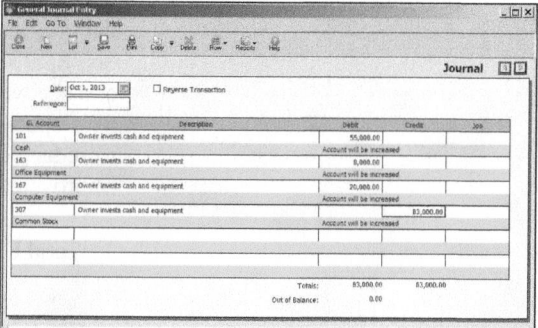

Computer technology can dramatically reduce the time and effort devoted to recordkeeping. Less effort spent on recordkeeping means more time for accounting professionals to concentrate on analysis and managerial decision making. These advances have created a greater demand for accounting professionals who understand financial reports and can draw insights and information from mountains of processed data. Accounting professionals have expertise in determining relevant and reliable information for decision making. They also can assess the effects of transactions and events on a company and its financial statements. (The IRS allows individuals to enter tax info online and receive free processing of such returns.)

Decision Insight

Middleware is software allowing different computer programs in a company or across companies to work together. It allows transfer of purchase orders, invoices, and other electronic documents between accounting systems. For example, suppliers can monitor inventory levels of their buyers for production and shipping purposes. ■

Data Processing in Accounting

Accounting systems differ with regard to how input is entered and processed. **Online processing** enters and processes data as soon as source documents are available. This means that databases are immediately updated. **Batch processing** accumulates source documents for a period of time and then processes them all at once such as daily, weekly, or monthly. The advantage of online processing is timeliness. This often requires additional costs related to both software and hardware requirements. Companies such as Intuit (Intuit.com) are making online processing of accounting data a reality for many businesses. The advantage of batch processing is that it requires only periodic updating of databases. Records used to send bills to customers, for instance, might require updating only once a month. The disadvantage of batch processing is the lack of updated databases for management to use when making business decisions. (Businesses and individuals can now deposit checks into bank accounts using scanners with capabilities of reading amounts, ensuring that each item passes a specified image quality standard, and reducing the risk that the scanned image is a duplicate of a previously scanned check.)

Computer Networks in Accounting

Networking, or linking computers with each other, can create information advantages (and cost efficiencies). **Computer networks** are links among computers giving different users and different computers access to common databases, programs, and hardware. Many college computer labs, for instance, are networked. A small computer network is called a *local area network (LAN)*; it links machines with *hard-wire* hookups. Large computer networks extending over long distances often rely on *modem* or *wireless* communication.

Demand for information sometimes requires advanced networks such as the systems Federal Express and UPS use to track packages and bill customers and the system Walmart uses to monitor inventory levels in its stores. These networks include many computers and satellite communications to gather information and to provide ready access to its databases from all locations.

Enterprise Resource Planning Software

Enterprise resource planning (ERP) software includes the programs that manage a company's vital operations. They extend from order taking to manufacturing to accounting. (Your college likely relies on ERP software to track its budget and student records information.) When working properly, these integrated programs can speed decision making, identify costs for reduction, and give managers control over operations with the click of a mouse. For many managers, ERP software allows them to scrutinize business, identify where inventories are piling up, and see what plants are most efficient. The software is designed to link every part of a company's operations. This software allowed Butterball, one of America's leading poultry brands, to reduce costs, enable rapid acquisitions, realize return on IT investment, and drive business improvements.

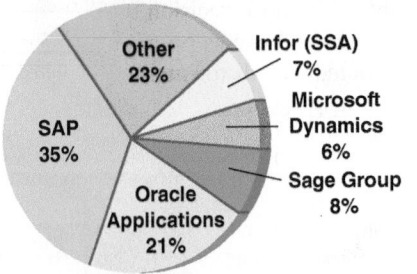

Total ERP Market: About $30 Billion

Other 23%
Infor (SSA) 7%
Microsoft Dynamics 6%
SAP 35%
Sage Group 8%
Oracle Applications 21%

ERP has several suppliers. SAP leads the market, with Oracle, which gobbled up PeopleSoft and J. D. Edwards, a distant second (*AMR Research*). SAP software is used by more than half of the world's 500 largest companies. It links ordering, inventory, production, purchasing, planning, tracking, and human resources. A transaction or event triggers an immediate chain reaction of events throughout the enterprise. It is making companies more efficient and profitable. Tasty Baking Company, a leading U.S. producer of snack cakes and other baked goods, uses SAP solutions to access real-time information, gain greater efficiencies, plan and respond to business needs, and achieve measurable results.

ERP is pushing into cyberspace and customer relationship management (CRM). Now companies can share data with customers and suppliers. Applesauce maker Mott's is using SAP so that distributors can check the status of orders and place them over the Net, and the Coca-Cola Company uses it to ship soda on time. ERP is also increasingly used by small business. One-third of Oracle's sales in North America are to companies with less than $500 million in annual revenue. Worldwide, small and midsize companies are 25% to 30% of Oracle's sales. For example, NetSuite's accounting services to small and medium businesses are powered by Oracle's system. Jeff Johanson, director of channel operations of SAP's practice for small and midsize businesses asserts that: "Small and medium businesses don't have different needs from larger companies, but they generally can't afford customized solutions."

Decision Insight

A new generation of accounting support is available. With the touch of a key, users can create real-time inventory reports showing all payments, charges, and credit limits at any point in the accounting cycle. Many services also include "alert signals" notifying the company when, for example, a large order exceeds a customer's credit limit or when purchases need to be made or when a bank balance is running low. These alerts occur via e-mail, fax, PDA, or phone. ■

Cloud Computing

Cloud computing is the delivery of computing as a service rather than a product. Many argue that its introduction will revolutionize information systems applications. Cloud computing uses applications via the Web instead of installing them on individual computers. This means that companies lease, rather than purchase, those applications, which also means that the user does not need to update applications as that is the job of the computing service provider. Thus, as tax laws change or when rates are revised, the service provider takes on that responsibility (and cost).

When a company transfers computing applications to a provider, there is much less risk if a user's computers crash or are stolen. Further, many users and their clients can access the same applications and share data. Accountants, lawyers, and analysts can similarly access data for quicker and easier processing and analysis. For example, all invoices could be offloaded to a Web-based bill management system, where documentation, disbursement, and record keeping could all be handled in the cloud. However, the user does lose control over the data and is dependent on the provider's control system. Today, many companies are exploring cloud computing and often begin with applications that are independent of other systems so that if problems arise, they are concentrated within that application only. Examples are training programs and workflow systems. Further, many argue that the gains of cloud computing are great for small and medium-sized companies, which do not have large IT departments or require unique information systems.

Cloud computing has enormous potential for greater efficiency and effectiveness with information systems applications. The future will reveal whether or not that potential will be achieved. Cloud computing has the potential to improve controls due to data centralization and the enhanced security from providers who can spread that cost over many customers. Still, some users worry about exposure to sensitive data. Users should consider the following factors when looking at providers of cloud computing:

- Provider's knowledge of the user's business.
- Security of the provider's cloud, including firewalls.
- Provider's history, reputation, and references.
- Service level agreement for hardware and software.
- Provider's cloud compatibility with user's system.

 **GLOBAL VIEW**

This section discusses similarities and differences between U.S. GAAP and IFRS regarding system principles and components, and special journals.

System Principles and Components   Both U.S. GAAP and IFRS aim for high-quality financial reporting. That aim implies that sound information system principles and components are applied worldwide. However, while system principles and components are fundamentally similar across the globe, culture and other realities often mean different emphases are placed on the mix of system controls. BMW provides the following description of its system controls:

> The internal control system ensures that all the information needed to achieve the objectives set for the internal control system is made available to those responsible in an appropriate and timely manner. Controls are carried out with the aid of the IT applications, thus reducing the incidence of process risks.

Special Journals   Accounting systems for recording sales, purchases, cash receipts, and cash disbursements are similar worldwide. Although the exact structure of special journals is unique to each company, the basic structure is identical. Companies desire to apply accounting in an efficient manner. Accordingly, systems that employ special journals are applied worldwide.

A1 Compute segment return on assets and use it to evaluate segment performance.

Good accounting information systems collect financial data for a company's various segments. A *segment* refers to a part of a company that is separately identified by its products or services, or by the geographic market it serves. Callaway Golf Company reports that it operates in two business segments: (1) golf clubs and (2) golf balls. Users of financial statements are especially interested in segment information to better understand a company's activities because segments often vary on profitability, risk, and growth.

Companies must report segment information, including their sales, operating income, identifiable assets, capital expenditures, and depreciation. However, managers are reluctant to release information that can harm competitive position. Exhibit E.12 shows survey results on the number of companies with different (reported) segments.

EXHIBIT E.12

Companies Reporting Operations by Types of Segments*

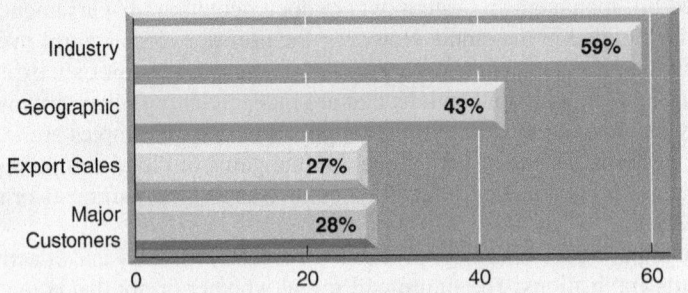

*Total exceeds 100% because companies can report more than one segment.

One measure of success for business segments is the **segment return on assets** ratio defined as follows.

$$\text{Segment return on assets} = \frac{\text{Segment operating income}}{\text{Segment average assets}}$$

EXHIBIT E.13

Callaway Golf's Segment Return on Assets

This ratio reflects on the profitability of a segment. Exhibit E.13 shows the segments' operating income, average assets, and return on assets for Callaway Golf Company.

Golf Segment* ($ thousands)	2011 Clubs	2011 Balls	2010 Clubs	2010 Balls	2009 Clubs	2009 Balls	2008 Clubs	2008 Balls
Operating income	$ (3,899)	$(12,655)	$ 39,176	$ 2,559	$ 34,502	$ (9,427)	$134,018	$ 6,903
Average assets	$423,538	$107,214	$422,419	$125,972	$418,003	$138,326	$421,261	$143,793
Segment return on assets ...	n.a.	n.a.	9%	2%	8%	n.a.	32%	5%

* A segment's operating income is usually measured as pretax income, and assets is usually measured as identifiable assets.

The trend in Callaway's segment return on assets is up-and-down for its golf club segment, and similarly mixed for its golf balls segment. Importantly, its golf clubs segment makes up a much greater portion of its operations; for example, 2010 income of $39,176 from golf clubs make up 94% of its total income of $41,735 from both segments. 2011 was a poor year for Callaway as both segments reported losses, which meant its returns for 2011 were not applicable (n.a.) for analysis. Still, those negative returns must return to positive levels as losses are not sustainable in the long run. Callaway should continue its emphasis on its golf club segment vis-a-vis its golf balls segment given the greater returns and larger total income from that segment. Analysis can also be extended to geographical segments and any other segments that companies report.

Decision Maker

Banker   A soccer equipment merchandiser requests a loan from you to expand operations. Its net income is $220,000, reflecting a 10% increase over the prior year. You ask about segment results. The owner reports that $160,000 of net income is from Cuban operations, reflecting a 60% increase over the prior year. The remaining $60,000 of net income is from U.S. operations, reflecting a 40% decrease. Does this segment information impact your loan decision? ■   [Answer—p. E-27]

Pepper Company completed the following selected transactions and events during March of this year. (Terms of all credit sales for the company are 2/10, n/30.)

Mar. 4   Sold merchandise on credit to Jennifer Nelson, Invoice No. 954, for $16,800 (cost is $12,200).

6   Purchased $1,220 of office supplies on credit from Mack Company. Invoice dated March 3, terms n/30.

6   Sold merchandise on credit to Dennie Hoskins, Invoice No. 955, for $10,200 (cost is $8,100).

11   Purchased $52,600 of merchandise, invoice dated March 6, terms 2/10, n/30, from Defore Industries.

12   Borrowed $26,000 cash by giving Commerce Bank a long-term promissory note payable.

14   Received cash payment from Jennifer Nelson for the March 4 sale less the discount (Invoice No. 954).

16   Received a $200 credit memorandum from Defore Industries for unsatisfactory merchandise Pepper purchased on March 11 and later returned.

16   Received cash payment from Dennie Hoskins for the March 6 sale less the discount (Invoice No. 955).

18   Purchased $22,850 of store equipment on credit from Schmidt Supply, invoice dated March 15, terms n/30.

20   Sold merchandise on credit to Marjorie Allen, Invoice No. 956, for $5,600 (cost is $3,800).

21   Sent Defore Industries Check No. 516 in payment of its March 6 dated invoice less the return and the discount.

22   Purchased $41,625 of merchandise, invoice dated March 18, terms 2/10, n/30, from Welch Company.

26   Issued a $600 credit memorandum to Marjorie Allen for defective merchandise Pepper sold on March 20 and Allen later returned.

31   Issued Check No. 517, payable to Payroll, in payment of $15,900 sales salaries for the month. Cashed the check and paid the employees.

31   Cash sales for the month are $134,680 (cost is $67,340). (Cash sales are recorded daily but are recorded only once here to reduce repetitive entries.)

Required

1. Open the following selected general ledger accounts: Cash (101), Accounts Receivable (106) Inventory (119), Office Supplies (124), Store Equipment (165), Accounts Payable (201), Long-Term Notes Payable (251), Sales (413), Sales Returns and Allowances (414), Sales Discounts (415), Cost of Goods Sold (502), and Sales Salaries Expense (621). Open the following accounts receivable ledger accounts: Marjorie Allen, Dennie Hoskins, and Jennifer Nelson. Open the following accounts payable ledger accounts: Defore Industries, Mack Company, Schmidt Supply, and Welch Company.

2. Enter the transactions using a sales journal, a purchases journal, a cash receipts journal, a cash disbursements journal, and a general journal similar to the ones illustrated in this appendix. Regularly post to the individual customer and creditor accounts. Also, post any amounts that should be posted as individual amounts to general ledger accounts. Foot and crossfoot the journals and make the month-end postings. *Pepper Co. uses the perpetual inventory system.*

3. Prepare a trial balance for the selected general ledger accounts in part 1 and prove the accuracy of subsidiary ledgers by preparing schedules of accounts receivable and accounts payable.

PLANNING THE SOLUTION

- Set up the required general ledger, the subsidiary ledger accounts, and the five required journals as illustrated in this appendix.

- Read and analyze each transaction and decide in which special journal (or general journal) the transaction is recorded.

- Record each transaction in the proper journal (and post the appropriate individual amounts).

- Once you have recorded all transactions, total the journal columns. Post from each journal to the appropriate ledger accounts.

- Prepare a trial balance to prove the equality of the debit and credit balances in your general ledger.

- Prepare schedules of accounts receivable and accounts payable. Compare the totals of these schedules to the Accounts Receivable and Accounts Payable controlling account balances, making sure that they agree.

SOLUTION TO COMPREHENSIVE NEED-TO-KNOW—PERPETUAL SYSTEM

Sales Journal — Page 2

Date	Account Debited	Invoice Number	PR	Accounts Receivable Dr. Sales Cr.	Cost of Goods Sold Dr. Inventory Cr.
Mar. 4	Jennifer Nelson	954	✓	16,800	12,200
6	Dennie Hoskins	955	✓	10,200	8,100
20	Marjorie Allen	956	✓	5,600	3,800
31	Totals			32,600	24,100
				(106/413)	(502/119)

Cash Receipts Journal — Page 3

Date	Account Credited	Explanation	PR	Cash Dr.	Sales Discount Dr.	Accounts Receivable Cr.	Sales Cr.	Other Accounts Cr.	Cost of Goods Sold Dr. Inventory Cr.
Mar. 12	L.T. Notes Payable	Note to bank	251	26,000				26,000	
14	Jennifer Nelson	Invoice 954, 3/4	✓	16,464	336	16,800			
16	Dennie Hoskins	Invoice 955, 3/6	✓	9,996	204	10,200			
31	Sales	Cash sales	x	134,680			134,680		67,340
31	Totals			187,140	540	27,000	134,680	26,000	67,340
				(101)	(415)	(106)	(413)	(x)	(502/119)

Purchases Journal — Page 3

Date	Account	Date of Invoice	Terms	PR	Accounts Payable Cr.	Inventory Dr.	Office Supplies Dr.	Other Accounts Dr.
Mar. 6	Office Supplies/Mack Co	3/3	n/30	✓	1,220		1,220	
11	Defore Industries	3/6	2/10, n/30	✓	52,600	52,600		
18	Store Equipment/Schmidt Supp	3/15	n/30	165/✓	22,850			22,850
22	Welch Company	3/18	2/10, n/30	✓	41,625	41,625		
31	Totals				118,295	94,225	1,220	22,850
					(201)	(119)	(124)	(x)

Cash Disbursements Journal — Page 3

Date	Ck. No.	Payee	Account Debited	PR	Cash Cr.	Inventory Cr.	Other Accounts Dr.	Accounts Payable Dr.
Mar. 21	516	Defore Industries	Defore Industries	✓	51,352	1,048		52,400
31	517	Payroll	Sales Salaries Expense	621	15,900		15,900	
31		Totals			67,252	1,048	15,900	52,400
					(101)	(119)	(x)	(201)

General Journal — Page 2

Mar. 16	Accounts Payable—Defore Industries	201/✓	200	
	Inventory	119		200
	To record credit memorandum received.			
26	Sales Returns and Allowances	414	600	
	Accounts Receivable—Marjorie Allen	106/✓		600
	To record credit memorandum issued.			

Accounts Receivable Ledger

Marjorie Allen

Date	PR	Debit	Credit	Balance
Mar. 20	S2	5,600		5,600
26	G2		600	5,000

Dennie Hoskins

Date	PR	Debit	Credit	Balance
Mar. 6	S2	10,200		10,200
16	R3		10,200	0

Jennifer Nelson

Date	PR	Debit	Credit	Balance
Mar. 4	S2	16,800		16,800
14	R3		16,800	0

Accounts Payable Ledger

Defore Industries

Date	PR	Debit	Credit	Balance
Mar. 11	P3		52,600	52,600
16	G2	200		52,400
21	D3	52,400		0

Mack Company

Date	PR	Debit	Credit	Balance
Mar. 6	P3		1,220	1,220

Schmidt Supply

Date	PR	Debit	Credit	Balance
Mar. 18	P3		22,850	22,850

Welch Company

Date	PR	Debit	Credit	Balance
Mar. 22	P3		41,625	41,625

General Ledger (Partial Listing)

Cash   Acct. No. 101

Date	PR	Debit	Credit	Balance
Mar. 31	R3	187,140		187,140
31	D3		67,252	119,888

Accounts Receivable   Acct. No. 106

Date	PR	Debit	Credit	Balance
Mar. 26	G2		600	(600)
31	S2	32,600		32,000
31	R3		27,000	5,000

Inventory   Acct. No. 119

Date	PR	Debit	Credit	Balance
Mar. 16	G2		200	(200)
21	D3		1,048	(1,248)
31	P3	94,225		92,977
31	S2		24,100	68,877
31	R3		67,340	1,537

Office Supplies   Acct. No. 124

Date	PR	Debit	Credit	Balance
Mar. 31	P3	1,220		1,220

Store Equipment   Acct. No. 165

Date	PR	Debit	Credit	Balance
Mar. 18	P3	22,850		22,850

Accounts Payable   Acct. No. 201

Date	PR	Debit	Credit	Balance
Mar. 16	G2	200		(200)
31	P3		118,295	118,095
31	D3	52,400		65,695

Long-Term Notes Payable   Acct. No. 251

Date	PR	Debit	Credit	Balance
Mar. 12	R3		26,000	26,000

Sales   Acct. No. 413

Date	PR	Debit	Credit	Balance
Mar. 31	S2		32,600	32,600
31	R3		134,680	167,280

Sales Returns and Allowances   Acct. No. 414

Date	PR	Debit	Credit	Balance
Mar. 26	G2	600		600

Sales Discounts   Acct. No. 415

Date	PR	Debit	Credit	Balance
Mar. 31	R3	540		540

Cost of Goods Sold   Acct. No. 502

Date	PR	Debit	Credit	Balance
Mar. 31	R3	67,340		67,340
31	S2	24,100		91,440

Sales Salaries Expense   Acct. No. 621

Date	PR	Debit	Credit	Balance
Mar. 31	D3	15,900		15,900

PEPPER COMPANY
Trial Balance (partial)
March 31

	Debit	Credit
Cash	$119,888	
Accounts receivable	5,000	
Inventory	1,537	
Office supplies	1,220	
Store equipment	22,850	
Accounts payable		$ 65,695
Long-term notes payable		26,000
Sales		167,280
Sales returns and allowances	600	
Sales discounts	540	
Cost of goods sold	91,440	
Sales salaries expense	15,900	
Totals	$258,975	$258,975

reconciled

reconciled

PEPPER COMPANY
Schedule of Accounts Receivable
March 31

Marjorie Allen	$5,000
Total accounts receivable	$5,000

PEPPER COMPANY
Schedule of Accounts Payable
March 31

Mack Company	$ 1,220
Schmidt Supply	22,850
Welch Company	41,625
Total accounts payable	$65,695

COMPREHENSIVE...

NEED-TO-KNOW

—PERIODIC SYSTEM

This example relies on procedures in Appendix E-A. Pepper Company completed the following selected transactions and events during March of this year. (Terms of all credit sales for the company are 2/10, n/30.)

Mar. 4 Sold merchandise on credit to Jennifer Nelson, Invoice No. 954, for $16,800 (cost is $12,200).

6 Purchased $1,220 of office supplies on credit from Mack Company. Invoice dated March 3, terms n/30.

6 Sold merchandise on credit to Dennie Hoskins, Invoice No. 955, for $10,200 (cost is $8,100).

11 Purchased $52,600 of merchandise, invoice dated March 6, terms 2/10, n/30, from Defore Industries.

12 Borrowed $26,000 cash by giving Commerce Bank a long-term promissory note payable.

14 Received cash payment from Jennifer Nelson for the March 4 sale less the discount (Invoice No. 954).

16 Received a $200 credit memorandum from Defore Industries for unsatisfactory merchandise Pepper purchased on March 11 and later returned.

16 Received cash payment from Dennie Hoskins for the March 6 sale less the discount (Invoice No. 955).

18 Purchased $22,850 of store equipment on credit from Schmidt Supply, invoice dated March 15, terms n/30.

20 Sold merchandise on credit to Marjorie Allen, Invoice No. 956, for $5,600 (cost is $3,800).

21 Sent Defore Industries Check No. 516 in payment of its March 6 dated invoice less the return and the discount.

22 Purchased $41,625 of merchandise, invoice dated March 18, terms 2/10, n/30, from Welch Company.

26 Issued a $600 credit memorandum to Marjorie Allen for defective merchandise Pepper sold on March 20 and Allen later returned.

31 Issued Check No. 517, payable to Payroll, in payment of $15,900 sales salaries for the month. Cashed the check and paid the employees.

31 Cash sales for the month are $134,680 (cost is $67,340). (Cash sales are recorded daily but are recorded only once here to reduce repetitive entries.)

Required

1. Open the following selected general ledger accounts: Cash (101), Accounts Receivable (106), Office Supplies (124), Store Equipment (165), Accounts Payable (201), Long-Term Notes Payable (251),

Sales (413), Sales Returns and Allowances (414), Sales Discounts (415), Purchases (505), Purchases Returns and Allowances (506), Purchases Discounts (507), and Sales Salaries Expense (621). Open the following accounts receivable ledger accounts: Marjorie Allen, Dennie Hoskins, and Jennifer Nelson. Open the following accounts payable ledger accounts: Defore Industries, Mack Company, Schmidt Supply, and Welch Company.

2. Enter the transactions using a sales journal, a purchases journal, a cash receipts journal, a cash disbursements journal, and a general journal similar to the ones illustrated in Appendix E-A. Regularly post to the individual customer and creditor accounts. Also, post any amounts that should be posted as individual amounts to general ledger accounts. Foot and crossfoot the journals and make the month-end postings. *Pepper Co. uses the periodic inventory system in this problem.*

3. Prepare a trial balance for the selected general ledger accounts in part 1 and prove the accuracy of subsidiary ledgers by preparing schedules of accounts receivable and accounts payable.

SOLUTION TO COMPREHENSIVE NEED-TO-KNOW—PERIODIC SYSTEM

Sales Journal — Page 2

Date	Account Debited	Invoice Number	PR	Accounts Receivable Dr. Sales Cr.
Mar. 4	Jennifer Nelson	954	✓	16,800
6	Dennie Hoskins	955	✓	10,200
20	Marjorie Allen	956	✓	5,600
31	Totals			32,600
				(106/413)

Cash Receipts Journal — Page 3

Date	Account Credited	Explanation	PR	Cash Dr.	Sales Discount Dr.	Accounts Receivable Cr.	Sales Cr.	Other Accounts Cr.
Mar. 12	L.T. Notes Payable	Note to bank	251	26,000				26,000
14	Jennifer Nelson	Invoice 954, 3/4	✓	16,464	336	16,800		
16	Dennie Hoskins	Invoice 955, 3/6	✓	9,996	204	10,200		
31	Sales	Cash sales	x	134,680			134,680	
31	Totals			187,140	540	27,000	134,680	26,000
				(101)	(415)	(106)	(413)	(x)

Purchases Journal — Page 3

Date	Account	Date of Invoice	Terms	PR	Accounts Payable Cr.	Purchases Dr.	Office Supplies Dr.	Other Accounts Dr.
Mar. 6	Office Supplies/Mack Co	3/3	n/30	✓	1,220		1,220	
11	Defore Industries	3/6	2/10, n/30	✓	52,600	52,600		
18	Store Equipment/Schmidt Supp	3/15	n/30	165/✓	22,850			22,850
22	Welch Company	3/18	2/10, n/30	✓	41,625	41,625		
31	Totals				118,295	94,225	1,220	22,850
					(201)	(505)	(124)	(x)

Cash Disbursements Journal — Page 3

Date	Ck. No.	Payee	Account Debited	PR	Cash Cr.	Purchases Discount Cr.	Other Accounts Dr.	Accounts Payable Dr.
Mar. 21	516	Defore Industries	Defore Industries	✓	51,352	1,048		52,400
31	517	Payroll	Sales Salaries Expense	621	15,900		15,900	
31		Totals			67,252	1,048	15,900	52,400
					(101)	(507)	(x)	(201)

General Journal — Page 2

Mar. 16	Accounts Payable—Defore Industries	201/✓	200	
	Purchases Returns and Allowances	506		200
	To record credit memorandum received.			
26	Sales Returns and Allowances	414	600	
	Accounts Receivable—Marjorie Allen	106/✓		600
	To record credit memorandum issued.			

Accounts Receivable Ledger

Marjorie Allen

Date	PR	Debit	Credit	Balance
Mar. 20	S2	5,600		5,600
26	G2		600	5,000

Dennie Hoskins

Date	PR	Debit	Credit	Balance
Mar. 6	S2	10,200		10,200
16	R3		10,200	0

Jennifer Nelson

Date	PR	Debit	Credit	Balance
Mar. 4	S2	16,800		16,800
14	R3		16,800	0

Accounts Payable Ledger

Defore Industries

Date	PR	Debit	Credit	Balance
Mar. 11	P3		52,600	52,600
16	G2	200		52,400
21	D3	52,400		0

Mack Company

Date	PR	Debit	Credit	Balance
Mar. 6	P3		1,220	1,220

Schmidt Supply

Date	PR	Debit	Credit	Balance
Mar. 18	P3		22,850	22,850

Welch Company

Date	PR	Debit	Credit	Balance
Mar. 22	P3		41,625	41,625

General Ledger (Partial Listing)

Cash   Acct. No. 101

Date	PR	Debit	Credit	Balance
Mar. 31	R3	187,140		187,140
31	D3		67,252	119,888

Accounts Receivable   Acct. No. 106

Date	PR	Debit	Credit	Balance
Mar. 26	G2		600	(600)
31	S2	32,600		32,000
31	R3		27,000	5,000

Office Supplies   Acct. No. 124

Date	PR	Debit	Credit	Balance
Mar. 31	P3	1,220		1,220

Store Equipment   Acct. No. 165

Date	PR	Debit	Credit	Balance
Mar. 18	P3	22,850		22,850

Accounts Payable   Acct. No. 201

Date	PR	Debit	Credit	Balance
Mar. 16	G2	200		(200)
31	P3		118,295	118,095
31	D3	52,400		65,695

Long-Term Notes Payable   Acct. No. 251

Date	PR	Debit	Credit	Balance
Mar. 12	R3		26,000	26,000

Sales   Acct. No. 413

Date	PR	Debit	Credit	Balance
Mar. 31	S2		32,600	32,600
31	R3		134,680	167,280

Sales Returns and Allowances   Acct. No. 414

Date	PR	Debit	Credit	Balance
Mar. 26	G2	600		600

Sales Discounts   Acct. No. 415

Date	PR	Debit	Credit	Balance
Mar. 31	R3	540		540

Purchases   Acct. No. 505

Date	PR	Debit	Credit	Balance
Mar. 31	P3	94,225		94,225

Purchases Returns and Allowances   Acct. No. 506

Date	PR	Debit	Credit	Balance
Mar. 16	G2		200	200

Purchases Discounts   Acct. No. 507

Date	PR	Debit	Credit	Balance
Mar. 31	D3		1,048	1,048

Sales Salaries Expense   Acct. No. 621

Date	PR	Debit	Credit	Balance
Mar. 31	D3	15,900		15,900

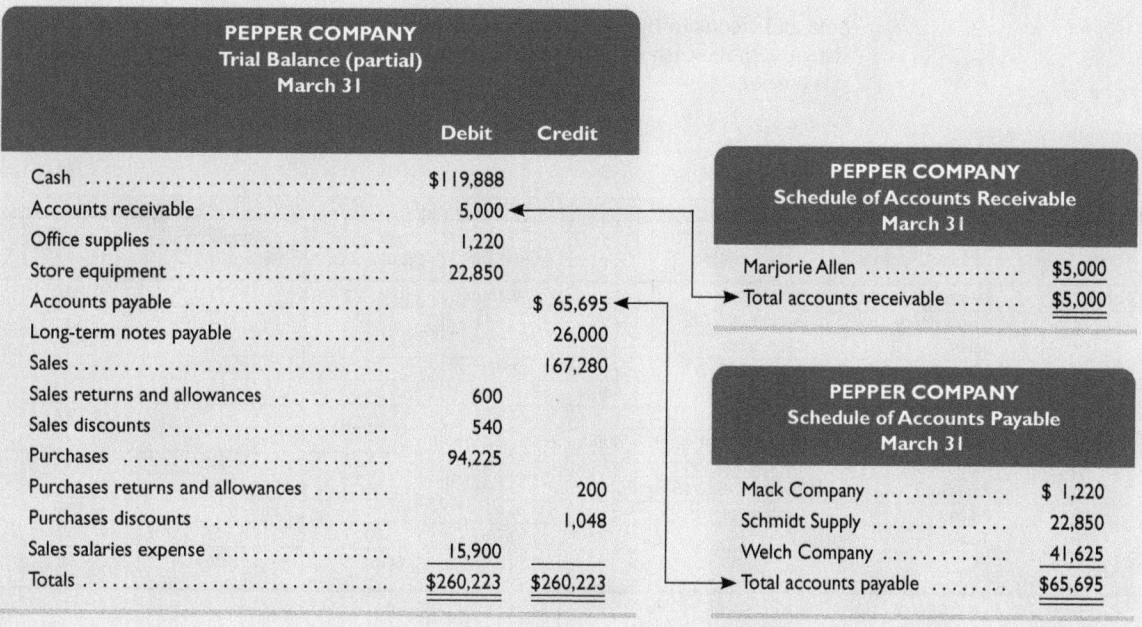

PEPPER COMPANY
Trial Balance (partial)
March 31

	Debit	Credit
Cash	$119,888	
Accounts receivable	5,000	
Office supplies	1,220	
Store equipment	22,850	
Accounts payable		$ 65,695
Long-term notes payable		26,000
Sales		167,280
Sales returns and allowances	600	
Sales discounts	540	
Purchases	94,225	
Purchases returns and allowances		200
Purchases discounts		1,048
Sales salaries expense	15,900	
Totals	$260,223	$260,223

PEPPER COMPANY
Schedule of Accounts Receivable
March 31

Marjorie Allen	$5,000
Total accounts receivable	$5,000

PEPPER COMPANY
Schedule of Accounts Payable
March 31

Mack Company	$ 1,220
Schmidt Supply	22,850
Welch Company	41,625
Total accounts payable	$65,695

Special Journals under a Periodic System

This appendix describes special journals under a periodic inventory system. Each journal is slightly impacted. The sales journal and the cash receipts journal both require one less column (namely that of Cost of Goods Sold Dr., Inventory Cr.). The Purchases Journal replaces the Inventory Dr. column with a Purchases Dr. column in a periodic system. The cash disbursements journal replaces the Inventory Cr. column with a Purchases Discounts Cr. column in a periodic system. These changes are illustrated.

P3 Journalize and post transactions using special journals in a periodic inventory system.

Sales Journal   The sales journal using the periodic inventory system is shown in Exhibit E-A.1. The difference in the sales journal between the perpetual and periodic system is the exclusion of the column to record cost of goods sold and inventory amounts for each sale. The periodic system does *not* record the increase in cost of goods sold and the decrease in inventory at the time of each sale.

Sales Journal   Page 3 ☐◻☒

Date	Account Debited	Invoice Number	PR	Accounts Receivable Dr. Sales Cr.
Feb. 2	Jason Henry	307	✓	450
7	Albert Co.	308	✓	500
13	Kam Moore	309	✓	350
15	Paul Roth	310	✓	200
22	Jason Henry	311	✓	225
25	Frank Booth	312	✓	175
28	Albert Co.	313	✓	250
28	Total			2,150
				(106/413)

EXHIBIT E-A.1

Sales Journal—Periodic System

Cash Receipts Journal   The cash receipts journal using the periodic system is shown in Exhibit E-A.2. Note the absence of the column on the far right side to record debits to Cost of Goods

Sold and credits to Inventory for the cost of merchandise sold (seen under the perpetual system). Consistent with the cash receipts journal shown in Exhibit E.7, we show only the weekly (summary) cash sale entries.

EXHIBIT E-A.2

Cash Receipts Journal—Periodic System

Cash Receipts Journal   Page 2

Date	Account Credited	Explanation	PR	Cash Dr.	Sales Discount Dr.	Accounts Receivable Cr.	Sales Cr.	Other Accounts Cr.
Feb. 7	Sales	Cash sales	x	4,450			4,450	
12	Jason Henry	Invoice 307, 2/2	✓	441	9	450		
14	Sales	Cash sales	x	3,925			3,925	
17	Albert Co.	Invoice 308, 2/7	✓	490	10	500		
20	Notes Payable	Note to bank	245	750				750
21	Sales	Cash sales	x	4,700			4,700	
22	Interest revenue	Bank account	409	250				250
23	Kam Moore	Invoice 309, 2/13	✓	343	7	350		
25	Paul Roth	Invoice 310, 2/15	✓	196	4	200		
28	Sales	Cash sales	x	4,225			4,225	
28	Totals			19,770	30	1,500	17,300	1,000
				(101)	(415)	(106)	(413)	(x)

Purchases Journal   The purchases journal using the periodic system is shown in Exhibit E-A.3. This journal under a perpetual system included an Inventory column where the periodic system now has a Purchases column.

EXHIBIT E-A.3

Purchases Journal—Periodic System

Purchases Journal   Page 1

Date	Account	Date of Invoice	Terms	PR	Accounts Payable Cr.	Purchases Dr.	Office Supplies Dr.	Other Accounts Dr.
Feb. 3	Horning Supply Co.	2/2	n/30	✓	350	275	75	
5	Ace Mfg. Co.	2/5	2/10, n/30	✓	200	200		
13	Wynet and Co.	2/10	2/10, n/30	✓	150	150		
20	Smite Co.	2/18	2/10, n/30	✓	300	300		
25	Ace Mfg. Co.	2/24	2/10, n/30	✓	100	100		
28	Store Supplies/ITT Co.	2/28	n/30	125/✓	225	125	25	75
28	Totals				1,325	1,150	100	75
					(201)	(505)	(124)	(x)

Cash Disbursements Journal   The cash disbursements journal using a periodic system is shown in Exhibit E-A.4. This journal under the perpetual system included an Inventory column where the periodic system now has the Purchases Discounts column.

EXHIBIT E-A.4

Cash Disbursements Journal—Periodic System

Cash Disbursements Journal   Page 2

Date	Ck. No.	Payee	Account Debited	PR	Cash Cr.	Purchases Discounts Cr.	Other Accounts Dr.	Accounts Payable Dr.
Feb. 3	105	L. and N. Railroad	Purchases	505	15		15	
12	106	East Sales Co.	Purchases	505	25		25	
15	107	Ace Mfg. Co.	Ace Mfg. Co.	✓	196	4		200
15	108	Jerry Hale	Salaries Expense	622	250		250	
20	109	Wynet and Co.	Wynet and Co.	✓	147	3		150
28	110	Smite Co.	Smite Co.	✓	294	6		300
28		Totals			927	13	290	650
					(101)	(507)	(x)	(201)

Summary

C1 **Identify the principles and components of accounting information systems.** Accounting information systems are governed by five fundamental principles: control, relevance, compatibility, flexibility, and cost-benefit. The five basic components of an accounting information system are source documents, input devices, information processors, information storage, and output devices.

C2 **Explain the goals and uses of special journals.** Special journals are used for recording transactions of similar type, each meant to cover one kind of transaction. Four of the most common special journals are the sales journal, cash receipts journal, purchases journal, and cash disbursements journal. Special journals are efficient and cost-effective tools in the journalizing and posting processes.

C3 **Describe the use of controlling accounts and subsidiary ledgers.** A general ledger keeps controlling accounts such as Accounts Receivable and Accounts Payable, but details on individual accounts making up the controlling account are kept in subsidiary ledgers (such as an accounts receivable ledger). The balance in a controlling account must equal the sum of its subsidiary account balances after posting is complete.

A1 **Compute segment return on assets and use it to evaluate segment performance.** A business segment is a part of a company that is separately identified by its products or services or by the geographic market it serves. Analysis of a company's segments is aided by the segment return on assets (segment operating income divided by segment average assets).

P1 **Journalize and post transactions using special journals.** Each special journal is devoted to similar kinds of transactions. Transactions are journalized on one line of a special journal, with columns devoted to specific accounts, dates, names, posting references, explanations, and other necessary information. Posting is threefold: (1) individual amounts in the Other Accounts column are posted to their general ledger accounts on a regular (daily) basis, (2) individual amounts in a column whose total is *not* posted to a controlling account at the end of a period (month) are posted regularly (daily) to their general ledger accounts, and (3) total amounts for all columns except the Other Accounts column are posted at the end of a period (month) to their column's account title in the general ledger.

P2 **Prepare and prove the accuracy of subsidiary ledgers.** Account balances in the general ledger and its subsidiary ledgers are tested for accuracy after posting is complete. This procedure is twofold: (1) prepare a trial balance of the general ledger to confirm that debits equal credits and (2) prepare a schedule to confirm that the controlling account's balance equals the subsidiary ledger's balance.

P3A **Journalize and post transactions using special journals in a periodic inventory system.** Transactions are journalized and posted using special journals in a periodic system. The methods are similar to those in a perpetual system; the primary difference is that both cost of goods sold and inventory are not adjusted at the time of each sale. This usually results in the deletion (or renaming) of one or more columns devoted to these accounts in each special journal.

Guidance Answers to Decision Maker and Decision Ethics

Accountant The main issue is whether commissions have an actual or perceived impact on the integrity and objectivity of your advice. You probably should not accept a commission arrangement (the AICPA Code of Ethics prohibits it when you perform the audit or a review). In any event, you should tell the client of your commission arrangement. Also, you need to seriously examine the merits of agreeing to a commission arrangement when you are in a position to exploit it.

Entrepreneur The accounts receivable ledger has much of the information you need. It lists detailed information for each customer's account, including the amounts, dates for transactions, and dates of payments. It can be reorganized into an "aging schedule" to show how long customers wait before paying their bills.

Controller Much of the information you need is in the accounts payable ledger. It contains information for each supplier, the amounts due, and when payments are made. This subsidiary ledger along with information on credit terms should enable you to conduct your analyses.

Banker This merchandiser's segment information is likely to greatly impact your loan decision. The risks associated with the company's two sources of net income are quite different. While net income is up by 10%, U.S. operations are performing poorly and Cuban operations are subject to many uncertainties. These uncertainties depend on political events, legal issues, business relationships, Cuban economic conditions, and a host of other risks. Overall, net income results suggested a low-risk loan opportunity, but the segment information reveals a high-risk situation.

Key Terms

Accounting information systems (p. E-2)
Accounts payable ledger (p. E-6)
Accounts receivable ledger (p. E-6)
Batch processing (p. E-15)

Cash disbursements journal (p. E-13)
Cash receipts journal (p. E-10)
Check register (p. E-13)
Columnar journal (p. E-7)

Compatibility principle (p. E-2)
Components of accounting systems (p. E-3)
Computer network (p. E-5)

Control principle (p. E-2)
Controlling account (p. E-6)
Cost-benefit principle (p. E-2)
Enterprise resource planning (ERP)
software (p. E-16)
Flexibility principle (p. E-2)
General journal (p. E-5)

Information processor (p. E-4)
Information storage (p. E-4)
Input device (p. E-3)
Internal controls (p. E-2)
Online processing (p. E-15)
Output devices (p. E-4)
Purchases journal (p. E-12)

Relevance principle (p. E-2)
Sales journal (p. E-7)
Schedule of accounts payable (p. E-13)
Schedule of accounts receivable (p. E-8)
Segment return on assets (p. E-18)
Special journal (p. E-5)
Subsidiary ledger (p. E-6)

Multiple Choice Quiz   Answers on p. E-42

1. The sales journal is used to record
   a. Credit sales
   b. Cash sales
   c. Cash receipts
   d. Cash purchases
   e. Credit purchases
2. The purchases journal is used to record
   a. Credit sales
   b. Cash sales
   c. Cash receipts
   d. Cash purchases
   e. Credit purchases
3. The ledger that contains the financial statement accounts of a company is the
   a. General journal
   b. Column balance journal

   c. Special ledger
   d. General ledger
   e. Special journal
4. A subsidiary ledger that contains a separate account for each supplier (creditor) to the company is the
   a. Controlling account
   b. Accounts payable ledger
   c. Accounts receivable ledger
   d. General ledger
   e. Special journal
5. Enterprise resource planning software
   a. Refers to programs that help manage company operations.
   b. Is another name for spreadsheet programs.
   c. Uses batch processing of business information.
   d. Is substantially declining in use.
   e. Is another name for database programs.

Icon denotes assignments that involve decision making.

Discussion Questions

1. What are five basic components of an accounting system?
2. What are source documents? Give two examples.
3. What are the five fundamental principles of accounting information systems?
4. What is the purpose of an input device? Give examples of input devices for computer systems.
5. What is the difference between data that are stored off-line and data that are stored online?
6. What purpose is served by the output devices of an accounting system?
7. When special journals are used, they are usually used to record each of four different types of transactions. What are these four types of transactions?

8. What notations are entered into the Posting Reference column of a ledger account?
9. When a general journal entry is used to record sales returns, the credit of the entry must be posted twice. Does this cause the trial balance to be out of balance? Explain.
10. Describe the procedures involving the use of copies of a company's sales invoices as a sales journal.
11. Credits to customer accounts and credits to Other Accounts are individually posted from a cash receipts journal such as the one in Exhibit E.7. Why not put both types of credits in the same column and save journal space?
12. Why should sales to and receipts of cash from credit customers be recorded and posted immediately?

≣connect

For account titles and numbers, use the Chart of Accounts at the end of the book.

Enter the letter of each system principle in the blank next to its best description.

A. Control principle
D. Flexibility principle
B. Relevance principle
E. Cost-benefit principle
C. Compatibility principle

1. _____ The principle prescribes the accounting information system to help monitor activities.
2. _____ The principle prescribes the accounting information system to adapt to the unique characteristics of the company.
3. _____ The principle prescribes the accounting information system to change in response to technological advances and competitive pressures.
4. _____ The principle that affects all other accounting information system principles.
5. _____ The principle prescribes the accounting information system to provide timely information for effective decision making.

QUICK STUDY

QS E-1

Accounting information
system principles

C1

Fill in the blanks to complete the following descriptions.

1. With _____ processing, source documents are accumulated for a period and then processed all at the same time, such as once a day, week, or month.
2. A computer _____ allows different computer users to share access to data and programs.
3. A _____ is an input device that captures writing and other input directly from source documents.
4. _____ _____ _____ software comprises programs that help manage a company's vital operations, from manufacturing to accounting.

QS E-2

Accounting information system

C1

Identify the most likely role in an accounting system played by each of the numbered items 1 through 12 by assigning a letter from the list A through E on the left.

A. Source documents
B. Input devices
C. Information processors
D. Information storage
E. Output devices

_____ **1.** Computer keyboard
_____ **2.** Computer printer
_____ **3.** Computer monitor
_____ **4.** MP3 player
_____ **5.** Bank statement
_____ **6.** Computer software
_____ **7.** Bar code reader
_____ **8.** Digital camera
_____ **9.** Invoice from a supplier
_____ **10.** Zip drive
_____ **11.** Computer scanner
_____ **12.** Filing cabinet

QS E-3

Accounting information
system components

C1

Wilcox Electronics uses a sales journal, a purchases journal, a cash receipts journal, a cash disbursements journal, and a general journal as illustrated in this appendix. Wilcox recently completed the following transactions *a* through *h*. Identify the journal in which each transaction should be recorded.

a. Sold merchandise on credit.
b. Purchased shop supplies on credit.
c. Paid an employee's salary in cash.
d. Borrowed cash from the bank.

e. Sold merchandise for cash.
f. Purchased merchandise on credit.
g. Purchased inventory for cash.
h. Paid cash to a creditor.

QS E-4

Identifying the special journal
of entry

C2

QS E-5

Entries in the general journal

C2

Biloxi Gifts uses a sales journal, a purchases journal, a cash receipts journal, a cash disbursements journal, and a general journal as illustrated in this appendix. Journalize its November transactions that should be recorded in the general journal. For those not recorded in the general journal, identify the special journal where each should be recorded.

Nov. 2 The company purchased $2,600 of merchandise on credit from the Midland Co., terms 2/10, n/30.
     12 The owner, T. Biloxi, contributed an automobile worth $17,000 to the company in exchange for common stock.
     16 The company sold $1,200 of merchandise (cost is $800) on credit to K. Myer, terms n/30.
     19 K. Myer returned $175 of (worthless) merchandise to the company originally purchased on November 16 (assume the cost of this merchandise is left in cost of goods sold).

QS E-6

Controlling accounts and subsidiary ledgers

C3

Following is information from Fredrickson Company for its initial month of business. (1) Identify the balances listed in the accounts receivable subsidiary ledger. (2) Identify the accounts receivable balance listed in the general ledger at month's end.

Credit Sales			Cash Collections		
Jan. 10	Stern Company	$4,000	Jan. 20	Stern Company	$2,000
19	Diaz Brothers	1,600	28	Diaz Brothers	1,600
23	Rex Company	2,500	31	Rex Company	1,300

QS E-7

Purchases journal—perpetual

P1

Peachtree Company uses a sales journal, a purchases journal, a cash receipts journal, a cash disbursements journal, and a general journal. The following transactions occur in the month of May.

May 1 Purchased $10,100 of merchandise on credit from Krause, Inc., terms n/30.
     8 Sold merchandise costing $900 on credit to G. Seles for $1,500 subject to a $30 sales discount if paid by the end of the month.
     14 Purchased $240 of store supplies from Chang Company on credit, terms n/30.
     17 Purchased $260 of office supplies on credit from Monder Company, terms n/30.
     24 Sold merchandise costing $400 to D. Air for $650 cash.
     28 Purchased store supplies from Porter's for $90 cash.
     29 Paid Krause, Inc., $10,100 cash for the merchandise purchased on May 1.

Prepare headings for a purchases journal like the one in Exhibit E.9. Journalize the May transactions that should be recorded in the purchases journal.

QS E-8

Identifying journal of entry   C2

Refer to QS E-7 and for each of the May transactions identify the journal in which it would be recorded. Assume the company uses a sales journal, purchases journal, cash receipts journal, cash disbursements journal, and general journal as illustrated in this appendix.

QS E-9

Accounts receivable ledger; posting from sales journal

P2

Warton Company posts its sales invoices directly and then binds them into a Sales Journal. The company had the following credit sales to these customers during July.

July 2	Mary Mack	$ 8,600
8	Eric Horner	11,100
10	Troy Wilson	13,400
14	Hong Jiang	20,500
20	Troy Wilson	11,200
29	Mary Mack	7,300
	Total credit sales	$72,100

Required

1. Open an accounts receivable subsidiary ledger having a T-account for each customer. Post the invoices to the subsidiary ledger.
2. Open an Accounts Receivable controlling T-account and a Sales T-account to reflect general ledger accounts. Post the end-of-month total from the sales journal to these accounts.
3. Prepare a schedule of accounts receivable and prove that its total equals the Accounts Receivable controlling account balance.

Apple reports the following operating income (and average assets in parentheses) in a recent year for each of its geographic segments—$ millions: Americas, $13,538 ($3,308); Europe, $11,528 ($2,456); and Japan, $2,481 ($898). Apple also reports the following sales (only) by product segments: iPhone, $47,057; iPad, $20,358; iPod, $7,453; Desktops, $6,439; Portables, $15,344; Other, $11,598. Compute Apple's return on assets for each of its geographic segments, and assess the relative performance of these segments. Compute the percentage of total sales for each of its five product segments.

QS E-10

Analyzing segment reports

A1

Apple

Nestlé, a Switzerland-based company, uses a sales journal, a purchases journal, a cash receipts journal, a cash disbursements journal, and a general journal in a manner similar to that explained in this appendix. Journalize the following summary transactions of Nestlé transactions that should be recorded in the general journal. For those not recorded in the general journal, identify only the special journal where each should be recorded. (All amounts in millions of Swiss franc, CHF.)

1. Assume Nestlé purchased CHF 17,000 of merchandise on credit from the suppliers.

2. Assume Nestlé sold CHF 94,000 of merchandise (cost is CHF 42,300) on credit to customers.

3. Assume a key customer returned CHF 2,400 of (worthless) merchandise to Nestlé (assume the cost of this merchandise is left in cost of goods sold).

QS E-11

International accounting and special journals

C2

Prepare headings for a purchases journal like the one in Exhibit E-A.3. Journalize the May transactions from QS E-7 that should be recorded in the purchases journal assuming the periodic inventory system is used.

QS E-12^A

Purchases journal—periodic   P3

connect

For account titles and numbers, use the Chart of Accounts at the end of the book.

EXERCISES

Finer Company uses a sales journal, a purchases journal, a cash receipts journal, a cash disbursements journal, and a general journal. The following transactions occur in the month of May.

Exercise E-1

Sales journal—perpetual

P1

May	2	Sold merchandise costing $300 to B. Facer for $450 cash, invoice no. 5703.
	5	Purchased $2,400 of merchandise on credit from Marchant Corp.
	7	Sold merchandise costing $800 to J. Dryer for $1,250, terms 2/10, n/30, invoice no. 5704.
	8	Borrowed $9,000 cash by signing a note payable to the bank.
	12	Sold merchandise costing $200 to R. Lamb for $340, terms n/30, invoice no. 5705.
	16	Received $1,225 cash from J. Dryer to pay for the purchase of May 7.
	19	Sold used store equipment for $900 cash to Golf, Inc.
	25	Sold merchandise costing $500 to T. Taylor for $750, terms n/30, invoice no. 5706.

Prepare headings for a sales journal like the one in Exhibit E.5. Journalize the May transactions that should be recorded in this sales journal.

Refer to Exercise E-1 and for each of the May transactions identify the journal in which it would be recorded. Assume the company uses a sales journal, purchases journal, cash receipts journal, cash disbursements journal, and general journal as illustrated in this appendix.

Exercise E-2

Identifying journal of entry   C2

Ali Co. uses a sales journal, a purchases journal, a cash receipts journal, a cash disbursements journal, and a general journal. The following transactions occur in the month of November.

Exercise E-3

Cash receipts journal—perpetual

P1

Nov.	3	The company purchased $3,200 of merchandise on credit from Hart Co., terms n/20.
	7	The company sold merchandise costing $840 on credit to J. Than for $1,000, subject to an $20 sales discount if paid by the end of the month.
	9	The company borrowed $3,750 cash by signing a note payable to the bank.
	13	J. Ali, the owner, contributed $5,000 cash to the company in exchange for common stock.
	18	The company sold merchandise costing $250 to B. Cox for $330 cash.
	22	The company paid Hart Co. $3,200 cash for the merchandise purchased on November 3.
	27	The company received $980 cash from J. Than in payment of the November 7 purchase.
	30	The company paid salaries of $1,650 in cash.

Prepare headings for a cash receipts journal like the one in Exhibit E.7. Journalize the November transactions that should be recorded in the cash receipts journal.

Exercise E-4
Identifying journal of entry C2

Refer to Exercise E-3 and for each of the November transactions identify the journal in which it would be recorded. Assume the company uses a sales journal, purchases journal, cash receipts journal, cash disbursements journal, and general journal as illustrated in this appendix.

Exercise E-5
Controlling accounts and subsidiary ledgers
C3

Following is information from Jesper Company for its initial month of business. (1) Identify the balances listed in the accounts payable subsidiary ledger. (2) Identify the accounts payable balance listed in the general ledger at month's end.

Credit Purchases			Cash Paid		
Jan. 9	Bailey Company	$14,000	Jan. 19	Bailey Company	$10,100
18	Johnson Brothers	6,600	27	Johnson Brothers	6,600
22	Preston Company	6,200	31	Preston Company	5,400

Exercise E-6
Cash disbursements journal—perpetual
P1

Marx Supply uses a sales journal, a purchases journal, a cash receipts journal, a cash disbursements journal, and a general journal. The following transactions occur in the month of April.

Apr. 3 Purchased merchandise for $2,950 on credit from Seth, Inc., terms 2/10, n/30.
9 Issued check no. 210 to Kitt Corp. to buy store supplies for $650.
12 Sold merchandise costing $500 on credit to C. Myrs for $770, terms n/30.
17 Issued check no. 211 for $1,400 to pay off a note payable to City Bank.
20 Purchased merchandise for $4,500 on credit from Lite, terms 2/10, n/30.
28 Issued check no. 212 to Lite to pay the amount due for the purchase of April 20, less the discount.
29 Paid salary of $1,800 to B. Dock by issuing check no. 213.
30 Issued check no. 214 to Seth, Inc., to pay the amount due for the purchase of April 3.

Prepare headings for a cash disbursements journal like the one in Exhibit E.11. Journalize the April transactions that should be recorded in the cash disbursements journal.

Exercise E-7
Identifying journal of entry C2

Refer to Exercise E-6 and for each of the April transactions identify the journal in which it would be recorded. Assume the company uses a sales journal, purchases journal, cash receipts journal, cash disbursements journal, and general journal as illustrated in this appendix.

Exercise E-8
Purchases journal and error identification
P1

A company that records credit purchases in a purchases journal and records purchases returns in a general journal made the following errors. Indicate when each error should be discovered.

1. Made an addition error in totaling the Office Supplies column of the purchases journal.
2. Made an addition error in determining the balance of a creditor's subsidiary account.
3. Posted a purchases return to the Accounts Payable account and to the creditor's subsidiary account but did not post the purchases return to the Inventory account.
4. Correctly recorded a $8,000 purchase in the purchases journal but posted it to the creditor's subsidiary account as a $800 purchase.
5. Posted a purchases return to the Inventory account and to the Accounts Payable account but did not post to the creditor's subsidiary account.

Exercise E-9
Special journal transactions and error discovery
P1

Post Pharmacy uses the following journals: sales journal, purchases journal, cash receipts journal, cash disbursements journal, and general journal. On June 5, Post purchased merchandise priced at $14,000, subject to credit terms of 2/10, n/30. On June 14, the pharmacy paid the net amount due for the merchandise. In journalizing the payment, the pharmacy debited Accounts Payable for $14,000 but failed to record the cash discount on the purchases. Cash was properly credited for the actual $13,720 paid. (*a*) In what journals would the June 5 and the June 14 transactions be recorded? (*b*) What procedure is likely to discover the error in journalizing the June 14 transaction?

At the end of May, the sales journal of Mountain View appears as follows.

Sales Journal					Page 2 ☐☒
Date	Account Debited	Invoice Number	PR	Accounts Receivable Dr. Sales Cr.	Cost of Goods Sold Dr. Inventory Cr.
May 6	Aaron Reckers	190		3,880	3,120
10	Sara Reed	191		2,940	2,325
17	Anna Page	192		1,850	1,480
25	Sara Reed	193		1,340	1,075
31	Totals			10,010	8,000

Mountain View also recorded the return of defective merchandise with the following entry.

May 20	Sales Returns and Allowances	350	
	Accounts Receivable—Anna Page		350
	Customer returned (worthless) merchandise.		

Required

1. Open an accounts receivable subsidiary ledger that has a T-account for each customer listed in the sales journal. Post to the customer accounts the entries in the sales journal and any portion of the general journal entry that affects a customer's account.

2. Open a general ledger that has T-accounts for Accounts Receivable, Inventory, Sales, Sales Returns and Allowances, and Cost of Goods Sold. Post the sales journal and any portion of the general journal entry that affects these accounts.

3. Prepare a schedule of accounts receivable and prove that its total equals the balance in the Accounts Receivable controlling account.

Refer to Exhibit E.13 and complete the segment return on assets table for Teton Company (round ratios to three decimals, or one decimal if shown in percent form). Analyze your findings and identify the segment with the highest, and that with the lowest, segment return on assets.

	Segment Operating Income (in $ mil.)		Segment Assets (in $ mil.)		Segment Return on Assets
Segment	2013	2012	2013	2012	2013
Specialty					
Skiing Group	$ 72	$ 68	$ 591	$450	
Skating Group	19	16	63	52	
Specialty Footwear	32	29	165	146	
Other Specialty	21	14	47	34	
Subtotal	144	127	866	682	
General Merchandise					
South America	42	46	315	284	
United States	17	18	62	45	
Europe	15	13	24	22	
Subtotal	74	77	401	351	
Total	$218	$204	$1,267	$1,033	

Prepare headings for a sales journal like the one in Exhibit E-A.1. Journalize the May transactions shown in Exercise E-1 that should be recorded in the sales journal assuming that the periodic inventory system is used.

Prepare headings for a cash receipts journal like the one in Exhibit E-A.2. Journalize the November transactions shown in Exercise E-3 that should be recorded in the cash receipts journal assuming that the periodic inventory system is used.

Exercise E-10
Posting to subsidiary ledger accounts; preparing a schedule of accounts receivable

P2

Check (3) Ending Accounts Receivable, $9,660

Exercise E-11
Computing and analyzing segment return on assets

A1

Check Europe segment return, 65.2%

Exercise E-12ᴬ
Sales journal—periodic   P3

Exercise E-13ᴬ
Cash receipts journal—periodic
P3

Exercise E-14^A

Cash disbursements
journal—periodic   P3

Prepare headings for a cash disbursements journal like the one in Exhibit E-A.4. Journalize the April transactions from Exercise E-6 that should be recorded in the cash disbursements journal assuming that the periodic inventory system is used.

■ connect

PROBLEM SET A

Problem E-1A
Special journals, subsidiary
ledgers, and schedule of
accounts receivable—perpetual

C3   P1   P2

For account titles and numbers, use the Chart of Accounts at the end of the book.

Wiset Company completes these transactions during April of the current year (the terms of all its credit sales are 2/10, n/30).

Apr. 2   Purchased $14,300 of merchandise on credit from Noth Company, invoice dated April 2, terms 2/10, n/60.
 3   Sold merchandise on credit to Page Alistair, Invoice No. 760, for $4,000 (cost is $3,000).
 3   Purchased $1,480 of office supplies on credit from Custer, Inc. Invoice dated April 2, terms n/10 EOM.
 4   Issued Check No. 587 to *World View* for advertising expense, $899.
 5   Sold merchandise on credit to Paula Kohr, Invoice No. 761, for $8,000 (cost is $6,500).
 6   Received an $80 credit memorandum from Custer, Inc., for the return of some of the office supplies received on April 3.
 9   Purchased $12,125 of store equipment on credit from Hal's Supply, invoice dated April 9, terms n/10 EOM.
 11   Sold merchandise on credit to Nic Nelson, Invoice No 762, for $10,500 (cost is $7,000).
 12   Issued Check No. 588 to Noth Company in payment of its April 2 invoice, less the discount.
 13   Received payment from Page Alistair for the April 3 sale, less the discount.
 13   Sold $5,100 of merchandise on credit to Page Alistair (cost is $3,600), Invoice No. 763.
 14   Received payment from Paula Kohr for the April 5 sale, less the discount.
 16   Issued Check No. 589, payable to Payroll, in payment of sales salaries expense for the first half of the month, $10,750. Cashed the check and paid employees.
 16   Cash sales for the first half of the month are $52,840 (cost is $35,880). (Cash sales are recorded daily from cash register data but are recorded only twice in this problem to reduce repetitive entries.)
 17   Purchased $13,750 of merchandise on credit from Grant Company, invoice dated April 17, terms 2/10, n/30.
 18   Borrowed $60,000 cash from First State Bank by signing a long-term note payable.
 20   Received payment from Nic Nelson for the April 11 sale, less the discount.
 20   Purchased $830 of store supplies on credit from Hal's Supply, invoice dated April 19, terms n/10 EOM.
 23   Received a $750 credit memorandum from Grant Company for the return of defective merchandise received on April 17.
 23   Received payment from Page Alistair for the April 13 sale, less the discount.
 25   Purchased $11,375 of merchandise on credit from Noth Company, invoice dated April 24, terms 2/10, n/60.
 26   Issued Check No. 590 to Grant Company in payment of its April 17 invoice, less the return and the discount.
 27   Sold $3,170 of merchandise on credit to Paula Kohr, Invoice No. 764 (cost is $2,520).
 27   Sold $6,700 of merchandise on credit to Nic Nelson, Invoice No. 765 (cost is $4,305).
 30   Issued Check No. 591, payable to Payroll, in payment of the sales salaries expense for the last half of the month, $10,750.
 30   Cash sales for the last half of the month are $73,975 (cost is $58,900).

Required

1. Prepare a sales journal like that in Exhibit E.5 and a cash receipts journal like that in Exhibit E.7. Number both journal pages as page 3. Then review the transactions of Wiset Company and enter those that should be journalized in the sales journal and those that should be journalized in the cash receipts journal. Ignore any transactions that should be journalized in a purchases journal, a cash disbursements journal, or a general journal.

2. Open the following general ledger accounts: Cash, Accounts Receivable, Inventory, Long-Term Notes Payable, Common Stock, Retained Earnings, Sales, Sales Discounts, and Cost of Goods Sold. Enter the March 31 balances for Cash ($85,000), Inventory ($125,000), Long-Term Notes Payable ($110,000), Common Stock ($20,000), and Retained Earnings ($80,000). Also open accounts receivable subsidiary ledger accounts for Paula Kohr, Page Alistair, and Nic Nelson.

3. Verify that amounts that should be posted as individual amounts from the journals have been posted. (Such items are immediately posted.) Foot and crossfoot the journals and make the month-end postings.

4. Prepare a trial balance of the general ledger and prove the accuracy of the subsidiary ledger by preparing a schedule of accounts receivable.

Check   Trial balance totals, $434,285

Analysis Component

5. Assume that the total for the schedule of Accounts Receivable does not equal the balance of the controlling account in the general ledger. Describe steps you would take to discover the error(s).

The April transactions of Wiset Company are described in Problem E-1A.

Problem E-2A
Special journals, subsidiary ledgers, and schedule of accounts payable—perpetual

C3 P1 P2

Required

1. Prepare a general journal, a purchases journal like that in Exhibit E.9, and a cash disbursements journal like that in Exhibit E.11. Number all journal pages as page 3. Review the April transactions of Wiset Company and enter those transactions that should be journalized in the general journal, the purchases journal, or the cash disbursements journal. Ignore any transactions that should be journalized in a sales journal or cash receipts journal.

2. Open the following general ledger accounts: Cash, Inventory, Office Supplies, Store Supplies, Store Equipment, Accounts Payable, Long-Term Notes Payable, Common Stock, Retained Earnings, Sales Salaries Expense, and Advertising Expense. Enter the March 31 balances of Cash ($85,000), Inventory ($125,000), Long-Term Notes Payable ($110,000), Common Stock ($20,000), and Retained Earnings ($80,000). Also open accounts payable subsidiary ledger accounts for Hal's Supply, Noth Company, Grant Company, and Custer, Inc.

3. Verify that amounts that should be posted as individual amounts from the journals have been posted. (Such items are immediately posted.) Foot and crossfoot the journals and make the month-end postings.

4. Prepare a trial balance of the general ledger and a schedule of accounts payable.

Check   Trial balance totals, $235,730

Church Company completes these transactions and events during March of the current year (terms for all its credit sales are 2/10, n/30).

Problem E-3A
Special journals, subsidiary ledgers, trial balance—perpetual

C3 P1 P2

Mar. 1   Purchased $43,600 of merchandise from Van Industries, invoice dated March 1, terms 2/15, n/30.
     2   Sold merchandise on credit to Min Cho, Invoice No. 854, for $16,800 (cost is $8,400).
     3   Purchased $1,230 of office supplies on credit from Gabel Company, invoice dated March 3, terms n/10 EOM.
     3   Sold merchandise on credit to Linda Witt, Invoice No. 855, for $10,200 (cost is $5,800).
     6   Borrowed $82,000 cash from Federal Bank by signing a long-term note payable.
     9   Purchased $21,850 of office equipment on credit from Spell Supply, invoice dated March 9, terms n/10 EOM.
    10   Sold merchandise on credit to Jovita Albany, Invoice No. 856, for $5,600 (cost is $2,900).
    12   Received payment from Min Cho for the March 2 sale less the discount.
    13   Sent Van Industries Check No. 416 in payment of the March 1 invoice less the discount.
    13   Received payment from Linda Witt for the March 3 sale less the discount.
    14   Purchased $32,625 of merchandise from the CD Company, invoice dated March 13, terms 2/10, n/30.
    15   Issued Check No. 417, payable to Payroll, in payment of sales salaries expense for the first half of the month, $18,300. Cashed the check and paid the employees.
    15   Cash sales for the first half of the month are $34,680 (cost is $20,210). (Cash sales are recorded daily, but are recorded only twice here to reduce repetitive entries.)
    16   Purchased $1,770 of store supplies on credit from Gabel Company, invoice dated March 16, terms n/10 EOM.
    17   Received a $2,425 credit memorandum from CD Company for the return of unsatisfactory merchandise purchased on March 14.
    19   Received a $630 credit memorandum from Spell Supply for office equipment received on March 9 and returned for credit.
    20   Received payment from Jovita Albany for the sale of March 10 less the discount.
    23   Issued Check No. 418 to CD Company in payment of the invoice of March 13 less the March 17 return and the discount.
    27   Sold merchandise on credit to Jovita Albany, Invoice No. 857, for $14,910 (cost is $7,220).

28 Sold merchandise on credit to Linda Witt, Invoice No. 858, for $4,315 (cost is $3,280).
31 Issued Check No. 419, payable to Payroll, in payment of sales salaries expense for the last half of the month, $18,300. Cashed the check and paid the employees.
31 Cash sales for the last half of the month are $30,180 (cost is $16,820).
31 Verify that amounts impacting customer and creditor accounts were posted and that any amounts that should have been posted as individual amounts to the general ledger accounts were posted. Foot and crossfoot the journals and make the month-end postings.

Required

1. Open the following general ledger accounts: Cash; Accounts Receivable; Inventory (March 1 beg. bal. is $10,000); Office Supplies; Store Supplies; Office Equipment; Accounts Payable; Long-Term Notes Payable; Common Stock (March 1 beg. bal. is $3,000), and Retained Earnings (March 1 beg. bal. is $7,000); Sales; Sales Discounts; Cost of Goods Sold; and Sales Salaries Expense. Open the following accounts receivable subsidiary ledger accounts: Jovita Albany, Min Cho, and Linda Witt. Open the following accounts payable subsidiary ledger accounts: Gabel Company, Van Industries, Spell Supply, and CD Company.

2. Enter these transactions in a sales journal like Exhibit E.5, a purchases journal like Exhibit E.9, a cash receipts journal like Exhibit E.7, a cash disbursements journal like Exhibit E.11, or a general journal. Number all journal pages as page 2.

Check Trial balance totals, $232,905

3. Prepare a trial balance of the general ledger and prove the accuracy of the subsidiary ledgers by preparing schedules of both accounts receivable and accounts payable.

Problem E-4A[A]
Special journals, subsidiary ledgers, and schedule of accounts receivable—periodic C3 P2 P3

Assume that Wiset Co. in Problem E-1A uses the periodic inventory system.

Required

1. Prepare headings for a sales journal like the one in Exhibit E-A.1. Prepare headings for a cash receipts journal like the one in Exhibit E-A.2. Journalize the April transactions shown in Problem E-1A that should be recorded in the sales journal and the cash receipts journal assuming the *periodic* inventory system is used.

2. Open the general ledger accounts with balances as shown in Problem E-1A (do not open a Cost of Goods Sold ledger account). Also open accounts receivable subsidiary ledger accounts for Page Alistair, Paula Kohr, and Nic Nelson. Under the periodic system, an Inventory account exists but is inactive until its balance is updated to the correct inventory balance at year-end. In this problem, the Inventory account remains inactive but must be included to correctly complete the trial balance.

Check Trial balance totals, $434,285

3. Complete parts 3, 4, and 5 of Problem E-1A using the results of parts 1 and 2 of this problem.

Problem E-5A[A]
Special journals, subsidiary ledgers, and schedule of accounts payable—periodic

C3 P2 P3

Refer to Problem E-1A and assume that Wiset Co. uses the periodic inventory system.

Required

1. Prepare a general journal, a purchases journal like that in Exhibit E-A.3, and a cash disbursements journal like that in Exhibit E-A.4. Number all journal pages as page 3. Review the April transactions of Wiset Company (Problem E-1A) and enter those transactions that should be journalized in the general journal, the purchases journal, or the cash disbursements journal. Ignore any transaction that should be journalized in a sales journal or cash receipts journal.

2. Open the following general ledger accounts: Cash, Inventory, Office Supplies, Store Supplies, Store Equipment, Accounts Payable, Long-Term Notes Payable, Common Stock, Retained Earnings, Purchases, Purchases Returns and Allowances, Purchases Discounts, Sales Salaries Expense, and Advertising Expense. Enter the March 31 balances of Cash ($85,000), Inventory ($125,000), Long-Term Notes Payable ($110,000), Common Stock ($20,000), and Retained Earnings ($80,000). Also open accounts payable subsidiary ledger accounts for Hal's Supply, Noth Company, Grant Company, and Custer, Inc.

Check Trial balance totals, $237,026

3. Complete parts 3 and 4 of Problem E-2A using the results of parts 1 and 2 of this problem.

Assume that Church Company in Problem E-3A uses the periodic inventory system.

Problem E-6A^A

Special journals, subsidiary ledgers, trial balance—periodic

C3 P2 P3

Required

1. Open the following general ledger accounts: Cash; Accounts Receivable; Inventory (March 1 beg. bal. is $10,000); Office Supplies; Store Supplies; Office Equipment; Accounts Payable; Long-Term Notes Payable; Common Stock (March 1 beg. bal. is $3,000), and Retained Earnings (March 1 beg. bal. is $7,000); Sales; Sales Discounts; Purchases; Purchases Returns and Allowances; Purchases Discounts; and Sales Salaries Expense. Open the following accounts receivable subsidiary ledger accounts: Jovita Albany, Min Cho, and Linda Witt. Open the following accounts payable subsidiary ledger accounts: Gabel Company, Van Industries, Spell Supply, and CD Company.

2. Enter the transactions from Problem E-3A in a sales journal like that in Exhibit E-A.1, a purchases journal like that in Exhibit E-A.3, a cash receipts journal like that in Exhibit E-A.2, a cash disbursements journal like that in Exhibit E-A.4, or a general journal. Number journal pages as page 2.

3. Prepare a trial balance of the general ledger and prove the accuracy of the subsidiary ledgers by preparing schedules of both accounts receivable and accounts payable.

Check Trial balance totals, $236,806

For account titles and numbers, use the Chart of Accounts at the end of the book.

PROBLEM SET B

Problem E-1B

Special journals, subsidiary ledgers, schedule of accounts receivable—perpetual

C3 P1 P2

Acorn Industries completes these transactions during July of the current year (the terms of all its credit sales are 2/10, n/30).

July 1   Purchased $6,500 of merchandise on credit from Teton Company, invoice dated June 30, terms 2/10, n/30.

3   Issued Check No. 300 to *The Weekly* for advertising expense, $625.

5   Sold merchandise on credit to Kim Nettle, Invoice No. 918, for $19,200 (cost is $10,500).

6   Sold merchandise on credit to Ruth Blake, Invoice No. 919, for $7,500 (cost is $4,300).

7   Purchased $1,250 of store supplies on credit from Plaine, Inc., invoice dated July 7, terms n/10 EOM.

8   Received a $250 credit memorandum from Plaine, Inc., for the return of store supplies received on July 7.

9   Purchased $38,220 of store equipment on credit from Charm's Supply, invoice dated July 8, terms n/10 EOM.

10   Issued Check No. 301 to Teton Company in payment of its June 30 invoice, less the discount.

13   Sold merchandise on credit to Ashton Moore, Invoice No. 920, for $8,550 (cost is $5,230).

14   Sold merchandise on credit to Kim Nettle, Invoice No. 921, for $5,100 (cost is $3,800).

15   Received payment from Kim Nettle for the July 5 sale, less the discount.

15   Issued Check No. 302, payable to Payroll, in payment of sales salaries expense for the first half of the month, $31,850. Cashed the check and paid employees.

15   Cash sales for the first half of the month are $118,350 (cost is $76,330). (Cash sales are recorded daily using data from the cash registers but are recorded only twice in this problem to reduce repetitive entries.)

16   Received payment from Ruth Blake for the July 6 sale, less the discount.

17   Purchased $7,200 of merchandise on credit from Drake Company, invoice dated July 17, terms 2/10, n/30.

20   Purchased $650 of office supplies on credit from Charm's Supply, invoice dated July 19, terms n/10 EOM.

21   Borrowed $15,000 cash from College Bank by signing a long-term note payable.

23   Received payment from Ashton Moore for the July 13 sale, less the discount.

24   Received payment from Kim Nettle for the July 14 sale, less the discount.

24   Received a $2,400 credit memorandum from Drake Company for the return of defective merchandise received on July 17.

26   Purchased $9,770 of merchandise on credit from Teton Company, invoice dated July 26, terms 2/10, n/30.

27   Issued Check No. 303 to Drake Company in payment of its July 17 invoice, less the return and the discount.

29   Sold merchandise on credit to Ruth Blake, Invoice No. 922, for $17,500 (cost is $10,850).

30   Sold merchandise on credit to Ashton Moore, Invoice No. 923, for $16,820 (cost is $9,840).

31   Issued Check No. 304, payable to Payroll, in payment of the sales salaries expense for the last half of the month, $31,850.

31   Cash sales for the last half of the month are $80,244 (cost is $53,855).

Required

1. Prepare a sales journal like that in Exhibit E.5 and a cash receipts journal like that in Exhibit E.7. Number both journals as page 3. Then review the transactions of Acorn Industries and enter those transactions that should be journalized in the sales journal and those that should be journalized in the cash receipts journal. Ignore any transactions that should be journalized in a purchases journal, a cash disbursements journal, or a general journal.

2. Open the following general ledger accounts: Cash, Accounts Receivable, Inventory, Long-Term Notes Payable, Common Stock, Retained Earnings, Sales, Sales Discounts, and Cost of Goods Sold. Enter the June 30 balances for Cash ($100,000), Inventory ($200,000), Long-Term Notes Payable ($200,000), Common Stock ($10,000), and Retained Earnings ($90,000). Also open accounts receivable subsidiary ledger accounts for Kim Nettle, Ashton Moore, and Ruth Blake.

3. Verify that amounts that should be posted as individual amounts from the journals have been posted. (Such items are immediately posted.) Foot and crossfoot the journals and make the month-end postings.

Check   Trial balance totals, $588,264

4. Prepare a trial balance of the general ledger and prove the accuracy of the subsidiary ledger by preparing a schedule of accounts receivable.

Analysis Component

5. Assume that the total for the schedule of Accounts Receivable does not equal the balance of the controlling account in the general ledger. Describe steps you would take to discover the error(s).

Problem E-2B
Special journals, subsidiary ledgers, and schedule of accounts payable—perpetual

C3 P1 P2

The July transactions of Acorn Industries are described in Problem E-1B.

Required

1. Prepare a general journal, a purchases journal like that in Exhibit E.9, and a cash disbursements journal like that in Exhibit E.11. Number all journal pages as page 3. Review the July transactions of Acorn Industries and enter those transactions that should be journalized in the general journal, the purchases journal, or the cash disbursements journal. Ignore any transactions that should be journalized in a sales journal or cash receipts journal.

2. Open the following general ledger accounts: Cash, Inventory, Office Supplies, Store Supplies, Store Equipment, Accounts Payable, Long-Term Notes Payable, Common Stock, Retained Earnings, Sales Salaries Expense, and Advertising Expense. Enter the June 30 balances of Cash ($100,000), Inventory ($200,000), Long-Term Notes Payable ($200,000), Common Stock ($10,000), and Retained Earnings ($90,000). Also open accounts payable subsidiary ledger accounts for Charm's Supply, Teton Company, Drake Company, and Plaine, Inc.

3. Verify that amounts that should be posted as individual amounts from the journals have been posted. (Such items are immediately posted.) Foot and crossfoot the journals and make the month-end postings.

Check   Trial balance totals, $349,640

4. Prepare a trial balance of the general ledger and a schedule of accounts payable.

Problem E-3B
Special journals, subsidiary ledgers, trial balance—perpetual

C3 P2 P3

Grassley Company completes these transactions during November of the current year (terms for all its credit sales are 2/10, n/30).

Nov. 1 Purchased $5,058 of office equipment on credit from Brun Supply, invoice dated November 1, terms n/10 EOM.

2 Borrowed $88,500 cash from Wisconsin Bank by signing a long-term note payable.

4 Purchased $33,500 of merchandise from BLR Industries, invoice dated November 3, terms 2/10, n/30.

5 Purchased $1,040 of store supplies on credit from Grebe Company, invoice dated November 5, terms n/10 EOM.

8 Sold merchandise on credit to Cyd Rounder, Invoice No. 439, for $6,550 (cost is $3,910).

10 Sold merchandise on credit to Carlos Mantel, Invoice No. 440, for $13,500 (cost is $8,500).

11 Purchased $2,557 of merchandise from Lo Company, invoice dated November 10, terms 2/10, n/30.

12   Sent BLR Industries Check No. 633 in payment of its November 3 invoice less the discount.

15   Issued Check No. 634, payable to Payroll, in payment of sales salaries expense for the first half of the month, $6,585. Cashed the check and paid the employees.

15   Cash sales for the first half of the month are $18,170 (cost is $9,000). (Cash sales are recorded daily but are recorded only twice in this problem to reduce repetitive entries.)

15   Sold merchandise on credit to Tori Tripp, Invoice No. 441, for $5,250 (cost is $2,450).

16   Purchased $459 of office supplies on credit from Grebe Company, invoice dated November 16, terms n/10 EOM.

17   Received a $557 credit memorandum from Lo Company for the return of unsatisfactory merchandise purchased on November 11.

18   Received payment from Cyd Rounder for the November 8 sale less the discount.

19   Received payment from Carlos Mantel for the November 10 sale less the discount.

19   Issued Check No. 635 to Lo Company in payment of its invoice of November 10 less the return and the discount.

22   Sold merchandise on credit to Carlos Mantel, Invoice No. 442, for $3,695 (cost is $2,060).

24   Sold merchandise on credit to Tori Tripp, Invoice No. 443, for $4,280 (cost is $2,130).

25   Received payment from Tori Tripp for the sale of November 15 less the discount.

26   Received a $922 credit memorandum from Brun Supply for the return of office equipment purchased on November 1.

30   Issued Check No. 636, payable to Payroll, in payment of sales salaries expense for the last half of the month, $6,585. Cashed the check and paid the employees.

30   Cash sales for the last half of the month are $16,703 (cost is $10,200).

30   Verify that amounts impacting customer and creditor accounts were posted and that any amounts that should have been posted as individual amounts to the general ledger accounts were posted. Foot and crossfoot the journals and make the month-end postings.

Required

1. Open the following general ledger accounts: Cash; Accounts Receivable; Inventory (November 1 beg. bal. is $40,000); Office Supplies; Store Supplies; Office Equipment; Accounts Payable; Long-Term Notes Payable; Common Stock (Nov. 1 beg. bal. is $10,000), and Retained Earnings (Nov. 1 beg. bal. is $30,000); Sales; Sales Discounts; Cost of Goods Sold; and Sales Salaries Expense. Open the following accounts receivable subsidiary ledger accounts: Carlos Mantel, Tori Tripp, and Cyd Rounder. Open the following accounts payable subsidiary ledger accounts: Grebe Company, BLR Industries, Brun Supply, and Lo Company.

2. Enter these transactions in a sales journal like that in Exhibit E.5, a purchases journal like that in Exhibit E.9, a cash receipts journal like that in Exhibit E.7, a cash disbursements journal like that in Exhibit E.11, or a general journal. Number all journal pages as page 2.

3. Prepare a trial balance of the general ledger and prove the accuracy of the subsidiary ledgers by preparing schedules of both accounts receivable and accounts payable.

Check   Trial balance totals, $202,283

Assume that Acorn Industries in Problem E-1B uses the periodic inventory system.

Problem E-4B[A]
Special journals, subsidiary ledgers, and schedule of accounts receivable—periodic

C3 P2 P3

Required

1. Prepare headings for a sales journal like the one in Exhibit E-A.1. Prepare headings for a cash receipts journal like the one in Exhibit E-A.2. Journalize the July transactions shown in Problem E-1B that should be recorded in the sales journal and the cash receipts journal assuming the periodic inventory system is used.

2. Open the general ledger accounts with balances as shown in Problem E-1B (do not open a Cost of Goods Sold ledger account). Also open accounts receivable subsidiary ledger accounts for Ruth Blake, Ashton Moore, and Kim Nettle. Under the periodic system, an Inventory account exists but is inactive until its balance is updated to the correct inventory balance at year-end. In this problem, the Inventory account remains inactive but must be included to correctly complete the trial balance.

3. Complete parts 3, 4, and 5 of Problem E-1B using the results of parts 1 and 2 of this problem.

Check   Trial balance totals, $588,264

Problem E-5B^A

Special journals, subsidiary
ledgers, and schedule of
accounts payable—periodic

C3 P2 P3

Refer to Problem E-1B and assume that Acorn uses the periodic inventory system.

Required

1. Prepare a general journal, a purchases journal like that in Exhibit E-A.3, and a cash disbursements journal like that in Exhibit E-A.4. Number all journal pages as page 3. Review the July transactions of Acorn Company (Problem E-1B) and enter those transactions that should be journalized in the general journal, the purchases journal, or the cash disbursements journal. Ignore any transaction that should be journalized in a sales journal or cash receipts journal.

2. Open the following general ledger accounts: Cash, Inventory, Office Supplies, Store Supplies, Store Equipment, Accounts Payable, Long-Term Notes Payable, Common Stock, Retained Earnings, Purchases, Purchases Returns and Allowances, Purchases Discounts, Sales Salaries Expense, and Advertising Expense. Enter the June 30 balances of Cash ($100,000), Inventory ($200,000), Long-Term Notes Payable ($200,000), Common Stock ($10,000), and Retained Earnings ($90,000). Also open accounts payable subsidiary ledger accounts for Teton Company, Plaine, Inc., Charm's Supply, and Drake Company.

Check   Trial balance totals, $352,266

3. Complete parts 3 and 4 of Problem E-2B using the results of parts 1 and 2 of this problem.

Problem E-6B^A

Special journals, subsidiary
ledgers, trial balance—periodic

C3 P2 P3

Assume that Grassley Company in Problem E-3B uses the periodic inventory system.

Required

1. Open the following general ledger accounts: Cash; Accounts Receivable; Inventory (November 1 beg. bal. is $40,000); Office Supplies; Store Supplies; Office Equipment; Accounts Payable; Long-Term Notes Payable; Common Stock (Nov. 1 beg. bal. is $10,000), and Retained Earnings (Nov. 1 beg. bal. is $30,000); Sales; Sales Discounts; Purchases; Purchases Returns and Allowances; Purchases Discounts; and Sales Salaries Expense. Open the following accounts receivable subsidiary ledger accounts: Carlos Mantel, Tori Tripp, and Cyd Rounder. Open the following accounts payable subsidiary ledger accounts: Grebe Company, BLR Industries, Brun Supply, and Lo Company.

2. Enter the transactions from Problem E-3B in a sales journal like that in Exhibit E-A.1, a purchases journal like that in Exhibit E-A.3, a cash receipts journal like that in Exhibit E-A.2, a cash disbursements journal like that in Exhibit E-A.4, or a general journal. Number journal pages as page 2.

Check   Trial balance totals, $203,550

3. Prepare a trial balance of the general ledger and prove the accuracy of the subsidiary ledgers by preparing schedules of both accounts receivable and accounts payable.

SERIAL PROBLEM

Success Systems   P1

(This serial problem began in Chapter 1 and continues through most of the book. If previous chapter segments were not completed, the serial problem can begin at this point. It is helpful, but not necessary, to use the Working Papers that accompany the book.)

SP E   Assume that Adria Lopez expands Success Systems' accounting system to include special journals.

Required

1. Locate the transactions related to January through March 2014 for Success Systems in Chapter 4.

2. Enter the Success Systems transactions for January through March in a sales journal like that in Exhibit E.5 (insert "n/a" in the Invoice column), a cash receipts journal like that in Exhibit E.7, a purchases journal like that in Exhibit E.9 (use Computer Supplies heading instead of Office Supplies), and a cash disbursements journal like that in Exhibit E.11 (insert "n/a" in the Check Number column), or a general journal. Number journal pages as page 2. If the transaction does not specify the name of the payee, state "not specified" in the Payee column of the cash disbursements journal.

3. The transactions on the following dates should be journalized in the general journal: January 5, 11, 20, 24, and 29 (no entry required) and March 24. Do not record and post the adjusting entries for the end of March.

Beyond the Numbers

BTN E-1   Erica Gray, CPA, is a sole practitioner. She has been practicing as an auditor for 10 years. Recently a long-standing audit client asked Gray to design and implement an integrated computer-based accounting information system. The fees associated with this additional engagement with the client are very attractive. However, Gray wonders if she can remain objective on subsequent audits in her evaluation of the client's accounting system and its records if she was responsible for its design and implementation. Gray knows that professional auditing standards require her to remain independent in fact and appearance from her auditing clients.

ETHICS CHALLENGE

C1

Required

1. What do you believe auditing standards are mainly concerned with when they require independence in fact? In appearance?

2. Why is it important that auditors remain independent of their clients?

3. Do you think Gray can accept this engagement and remain independent? Justify your response.

BTN E-2   Your friend, Wendy Geiger, owns a small retail store that sells candies and nuts. Geiger acquires her goods from a few select vendors. She generally makes purchase orders by phone and on credit. Sales are primarily for cash. Geiger keeps her own manual accounting system using a general journal and a general ledger. At the end of each business day, she records one summary entry for cash sales. Geiger recently began offering items in creative gift packages. This has increased sales substantially, and she is now receiving orders from corporate and other clients who order large quantities and prefer to buy on credit. As a result of increased credit transactions in both purchases and sales, keeping the accounting records has become extremely time consuming. Geiger wants to continue to maintain her own manual system and calls you for advice. Write a memo to her advising how she might modify her current manual accounting system to accommodate the expanded business activities. Geiger is accustomed to checking her ledger by using a trial balance. Your memo should explain the advantages of what you propose and of any other verification techniques you recommend.

COMMUNICATING IN PRACTICE

C2 C3

BTN E-3   Access the March 13, 2012, filing of the fiscal 2012 10-K report for Dell (ticker DELL) at www.sec.gov. Read its Note 14 that details Dell's segment information and answer the following.

1. Dell's operations are divided among which four global business segments?

2. In fiscal year 2012, which segment had the largest dollar amount of operating income? Which had the largest amount of assets?

3. Compute the return on assets for each segment for fiscal year 2012. Use operating income and average total assets by segment for your calculation. Which segment has the highest return on assets?

4. For what product groups does Dell provide segment data? What percent of Dell's net revenue is earned by each product group?

TAKING IT TO THE NET

A1

BTN E-4   Each member of the team is to assume responsibility for one of the following tasks:

a. Journalizing in the purchases journal.

b. Journalizing in the cash disbursements journal.

c. Maintaining and verifying the Accounts Payable ledger.

d. Journalizing in the sales journal and the general journal.

e. Journalizing in the cash receipts journal.

f. Maintaining and verifying the Accounts Receivable ledger.

The team should abide by the following procedures in carrying out responsibilities.

TEAMWORK IN ACTION

C3 P1 P2

Required

1. After tasks *a–f* are assigned, each team member is to quickly read the list of transactions in Problem E-3A, identifying with initials the journal in which each transaction is to be recorded. Upon completion, the team leader is to read transaction dates, and the appropriate team member is to vocalize responsibility. Any disagreement between teammates must be resolved.

2. Journalize and continually update subsidiary ledgers. Journal recorders should alert teammates assigned to subsidiary ledgers when an entry must be posted to their subsidiary.

3. Team members responsible for tasks *a*, *b*, *d*, and *e* are to summarize and prove journals; members responsible for tasks *c* and *f* are to prepare both payables and receivables schedules.

4. The team leader is to take charge of the general ledger, rotating team members to obtain amounts to be posted. The person responsible for a journal must complete posting references in that journal. Other team members should verify the accuracy of account balance computations. To avoid any abnormal account balances, post in the following order: P, S, G, R, D. (*Note:* Posting any necessary individual general ledger amounts is also done at this time.)

5. The team leader is to read out general ledger account balances while another team member fills in the trial balance form. Concurrently, one member should keep a running balance of debit account balance totals and another credit account balance totals. Verify the final total of the trial balance and the schedules. If necessary, the team must resolve any errors. Turn in the trial balance and schedules to the instructor.

ANSWERS TO MULTIPLE CHOICE QUIZ

1. a
2. e
3. d

4. b
5. a

Glossary

Accelerated depreciation method Method that produces larger depreciation charges in the early years of an asset's life and smaller charges in its later years. *(p. 352)*

Account Record within an accounting system in which increases and decreases are entered and stored in a specific asset, liability, equity, revenue, or expense. *(p. 57)*

Account balance Difference between total debits and total credits (including the beginning balance) for an account. *(p. 61)*

Account form balance sheet Balance sheet that lists assets on the left side and liabilities and equity on the right.

Account payable Liability created by buying goods or services on credit; backed by the buyer's general credit standing.

Accounting Information and measurement system that identifies, records, and communicates relevant information about a company's business activities. *(p. 4)*

Accounting cycle Recurring steps performed each accounting period, starting with analyzing transactions and continuing through the post-closing trial balance (or reversing entries). *(p. 122)*

Accounting equation Equality involving a company's assets, liabilities, and equity; Assets = Liabilities + Equity; also called *balance sheet equation*. *(p. 15)*

Accounting information system People, records, and methods that collect and process data from transactions and events, organize them in useful forms, and communicate results to decision makers. *(App. E)*

Accounting period Length of time covered by financial statements; also called *reporting period*. *(p. 102)*

Accounts payable ledger Subsidiary ledger listing individual creditor (supplier) accounts. *(App. E)*

Accounts receivable Amounts due from customers for credit sales; backed by the customer's general credit standing. *(p. 310)*

Accounts receivable ledger Subsidiary ledger listing individual customer accounts. *(App. E)*

Accounts receivable turnover Measure of both the quality and liquidity of accounts receivable; indicates how often receivables are received and collected during the period; computed by dividing net sales by average accounts receivable. *(p. 327)*

Accrual basis accounting Accounting system that recognizes revenues when earned and expenses when incurred; the basis for GAAP. *(p. 102)*

Accrued expenses Costs incurred in a period that are both unpaid and unrecorded; adjusting entries for recording accrued expenses involve increasing expenses and increasing liabilities. *(p. 111)*

Accrued revenues Revenues earned in a period that are both unrecorded and not yet received in cash (or other assets); adjusting entries for recording accrued revenues involve increasing assets and increasing revenues. *(p. 113)*

Accumulated depreciation Cumulative sum of all depreciation expense recorded for an asset.

Acid-test ratio Ratio used to assess a company's ability to settle its current debts with its most liquid assets; defined as quick assets (cash, short-term investments, and current receivables) divided by current liabilities. *(p. 183)*

Activity-based costing (ABC) Cost allocation method that focuses on activities performed; traces costs to activities and then assigns them to cost objects.

Activity cost driver Variable that causes an activity's cost to go up or down; a causal factor.

Activity cost pool Temporary account that accumulates costs a company incurs to support an activity.

Adjusted trial balance List of accounts and balances prepared after period-end adjustments are recorded and posted. *(p. 116)*

Adjusting entry Journal entry at the end of an accounting period to bring an asset or liability account to its proper amount and update the related expense or revenue account. *(p. 104)*

Aging of accounts receivable Process of classifying accounts receivable by how long they are past due for purposes of estimating uncollectible accounts. *(p. 318)*

Allowance for Doubtful Accounts Contra asset account with a balance approximating uncollectible accounts receivable; also called *Allowance for Uncollectible Accounts*. *(p. 316)*

Allowance method Procedure that (a) estimates and matches bad debts expense with its sales for the period and/or (b) reports accounts receivable at estimated realizable value. *(p. 315)*

Amortization Process of allocating the cost of an intangible asset to expense over its estimated useful life. *(p. 363)*

Annual financial statements Financial statements covering a one-year period; often based on a calendar year, but any consecutive 12-month (or 52-week) period is acceptable. *(p. 102)*

Annual report Summary of a company's financial results for the year with its current financial condition and future plans; directed to external users of financial information. *(p. A-1)*

Annuity Series of equal payments at equal intervals. *(p. 456)*

Appropriated retained earnings Retained earnings separately reported to inform stockholders of funding needs. *(p. 498)*

Asset book value (See *book value*.)

Assets Resources a business owns or controls that are expected to provide current and future benefits to the business. *(p. 15)*

Audit Analysis and report of an organization's accounting system, its records, and its reports using various tests. *(p. 13)*

Auditors Individuals hired to review financial reports and information systems. *Internal auditors* of a company are employed to assess and evaluate its system of internal controls, including the resulting reports. *External auditors* are independent of a company and are hired to assess and evaluate the "fairness" of financial statements (or to perform other contracted financial services). *(p. 13)*

Authorized stock Total amount of stock that a corporation's charter authorizes it to issue. *(p. 482)*

Available-for-sale (AFS) securities Investments in debt and equity securities that are not classified as trading securities or held-to-maturity securities. *(p. C-5)*

Average cost See *weighted average.*

Bad debts Accounts of customers who do not pay what they have promised to pay; an expense of selling on credit; also called *uncollectible accounts.* *(p. 314)*

Balance column account Account with debit and credit columns for recording entries and another column for showing the balance of the account after each entry. *(p. 64)*

Balance sheet Financial statement that lists types and dollar amounts of assets, liabilities, and equity at a specific date. *(p. 21)*

Balance sheet equation (See *accounting equation.*)

Bank reconciliation Report that explains the difference between the book (company) balance of cash and the cash balance reported on the bank statement. *(p. 280)*

Bank statement Bank report on the depositor's beginning and ending cash balances, and a listing of its changes, for a period. *(p. 279)*

Basic earnings per share Net income less any preferred dividends and then divided by weighted-average common shares outstanding. *(p. 500)*

Batch processing Accumulating source documents for a period of time and then processing them all at once such as once a day, week, or month. *(App. E)*

Bearer bonds Bonds made payable to whoever holds them (the *bearer*); also called *unregistered bonds.* *(p. 451)*

Betterments Expenditures to make a plant asset more efficient or productive; also called *improvements.* *(p. 357)*

Bond Written promise to pay the bond's par (or face) value and interest at a stated contract rate; often issued in denominations of $1,000. *(p. 436)*

Bond certificate Document containing bond specifics such as issuer's name, bond par value, contract interest rate, and maturity date. *(p. 437)*

Bond indenture Contract between the bond issuer and the bondholders; identifies the parties' rights and obligations. *(p. 437)*

Book value Asset's acquisition costs less its accumulated depreciation (or depletion, or amortization); also sometimes used synonymously as the *carrying value* of an account. *(pp. 107 & 350)*

Book value per common share Recorded amount of equity applicable to common shares divided by the number of common shares outstanding. *(p. 501)*

Book value per preferred share Equity applicable to preferred shares (equals its call price [or par value if it is not callable] plus any cumulative dividends in arrears) divided by the number of preferred shares outstanding. *(p. 502)*

Bookkeeping (See *recordkeeping.*)

Business An organization of one or more individuals selling product and/or services for profit.

Business entity assumption Principle that requires a business to be accounted for separately from its owner(s) and from any other entity. *(p. 12)*

Business segment Part of a company that can be separately identified by the products or services that it provides or by the geographic market that it serves; also called *segment.* *(p. 602)*

C corporation Corporation that does not qualify for nor elect to be treated as a proprietorship or partnership for income tax purposes and therefore is subject to income taxes; also called *C corp.* *(App. D)*

Call price Amount that must be paid to call and retire a callable preferred stock or a callable bond. *(p. 493)*

Callable bonds Bonds that give the issuer the option to retire them at a stated amount prior to maturity. *(p. 451)*

Callable preferred stock Preferred stock that the issuing corporation, at its option, may retire by paying the call price plus any dividends in arrears. *(p. 493)*

Canceled checks Checks that the bank has paid and deducted from the depositor's account. *(p. 279)*

Capital expenditures Additional costs of plant assets that provide material benefits extending beyond the current period; also called *balance sheet expenditures.* *(p. 357)*

Capital leases Long-term leases in which the lessor transfers substantially all risk and rewards of ownership to the lessee. *(p. 460)*

Capital stock General term referring to a corporation's stock used in obtaining capital (owner financing). *(p. 482)*

Capitalize Record the cost as part of a permanent account and allocate it over later periods.

Carrying (book) value of bonds Net amount at which bonds are reported on the balance sheet; equals the par value of the bonds less any unamortized discount or plus any unamortized premium; also called *carrying amount or book value.* *(p. 439)*

Cash Includes currency, coins, and amounts on deposit in bank checking or savings accounts. *(p. 269)*

Cash basis accounting Accounting system that recognizes revenue when cash is received and records expenses when cash is paid. *(p. 10)*

Cash budget Plan that shows expected cash inflows and outflows during the budget period, including receipts from loans needed to maintain minimum cash balance and repayments of such loans.

Cash disbursements journal Special journal normally used to record all payments of cash; also called *cash payments journal.* *(App. E)*

Cash discount Reduction in the price of merchandise granted by a seller to a buyer when payment is made within the discount period. *(p. 169)*

Cash equivalents Short-term, investment assets that are readily convertible to a known cash amount or sufficiently close to their maturity date (usually within 90 days) so that market value is not sensitive to interest rate changes. *(p. 269)*

Cash flow on total assets Ratio of operating cash flows to average total assets; not sensitive to income recognition and measurement; partly reflects earnings quality. *(p. 543)*

Cash Over and Short Income statement account used to record cash overages and cash shortages arising from errors in cash receipts or payments. *(p. 271)*

Cash receipts journal Special journal normally used to record all receipts of cash. *(App. E)*

Change in an accounting estimate Change in an accounting estimate that results from new information, subsequent developments, or improved judgment that impacts current and future periods. *(pp. 355 & 498)*

Chart of accounts List of accounts used by a company; includes an identification number for each account. *(p. 60)*

Check Document signed by a depositor instructing the bank to pay a specified amount to a designated recipient. *(p. 277)*

Check register Another name for a cash disbursements journal when the journal has a column for check numbers. *(pp. 290 & App. E)*

Classified balance sheet Balance sheet that presents assets and liabilities in relevant subgroups, including current and noncurrent classifications. *(p. 123)*

Closing entries Entries recorded at the end of each accounting period to transfer end-of-period balances in revenue, gain, expense, loss, and withdrawal (dividend for a corporation) accounts to the capital account (to retained earnings for a corporation). *(p. 119)*

Closing process Necessary end-of-period steps to prepare the accounts for recording the transactions of the next period. *(p. 118)*

Columnar journal Journal with more than one column. *(App. E)*

Committee of Sponsoring Organizations (COSO) Committee of Sponsoring Organizations of the Treadway Commission (or COSO) is a joint initiative of five private sector organizations and is dedicated to providing thought leadership through the development of frameworks and guidance on enterprise risk management, internal control, and fraud deterrence. *(p. 265)*

Common stock Corporation's basic ownership share; also generically called *capital stock*. *(pp. 13, 15, 59 & 482)*

Common-size financial statement Statement that expresses each amount as a percent of a base amount. In the balance sheet, total assets is usually the base and is expressed as 100%. In the income statement, net sales is usually the base. *(p. 585)*

Comparative financial statement Statement with data for two or more successive periods placed in side-by-side columns, often with changes shown in dollar amounts and percents. *(p. 580)*

Compatibility principle Information system principle that prescribes an accounting system to conform with a company's activities, personnel, and structure. *(App. E)*

Complex capital structure Capital structure that includes outstanding rights or options to purchase common stock, or securities that are convertible into common stock. *(p. 500)*

Components of accounting systems Five basic components of accounting systems are source documents, input devices, information processors, information storage, and output devices. *(App. E)*

Compound journal entry Journal entry that affects at least three accounts. *(p. 67)*

Comprehensive income Net change in equity for a period, excluding owner investments and distributions. *(p. C-10)*

Computer hardware Physical equipment in a computerized accounting information system.

Computer network Linkage giving different users and different computers access to common databases and programs. *(App. E)*

Computer software Programs that direct operations of computer hardware.

Conceptual framework The basic concepts that underlie the preparation and presentation of financial statements for external users; can serve as a guide in developing future standards and to resolve accounting issues that are not addressed directly in current standards using the definitions, recognition criteria, and measurement concepts for assets, liabilities, revenues, and expenses. *(p. 9)*

Conservatism constraint Principle that prescribes the less optimistic estimate when two estimates are about equally likely. *(p. 224)*

Consignee Receiver of goods owned by another who holds them for purposes of selling them for the owner. *(p. 214)*

Consignor Owner of goods who ships them to another party who will sell them for the owner. *(p. 214)*

Consistency concept Principle that prescribes use of the same accounting method(s) over time so that financial statements are comparable across periods. *(p. 222)*

Consolidated financial statements Financial statements that show all (combined) activities under the parent's control, including those of any subsidiaries. *(p. C-9)*

Contingent liability Obligation to make a future payment if, and only if, an uncertain future event occurs. *(p. 402)*

Contra account Account linked with another account and having an opposite normal balance; reported as a subtraction from the other account's balance. *(p. 107)*

Contract rate Interest rate specified in a bond indenture (or note); multiplied by the par value to determine the interest paid each period; also called *coupon rate, stated rate,* or *nominal rate*. *(p. 438)*

Contributed capital Total amount of cash and other assets received from stockholders in exchange for stock; also called *paid-in capital*. *(pp. 15 & 483)*

Contributed capital in excess of par value Difference between the par value of stock and its issue price when issued at a price above par.

Control principle Information system principle that prescribes an accounting system to aid managers in controlling and monitoring business activities. *(App. E)*

Controlling account General ledger account, the balance of which (after posting) equals the sum of the balances in its related subsidiary ledger. *(App. E)*

Convertible bonds Bonds that bondholders can exchange for a set number of the issuer's shares. *(p. 451)*

Convertible preferred stock Preferred stock with an option to exchange it for common stock at a specified rate. *(p. 493)*

Copyright Right giving the owner the exclusive privilege to publish and sell musical, literary, or artistic work during the creator's life plus 70 years. *(p. 364)*

Corporation Business that is a separate legal entity under state or federal laws with owners called *shareholders* or *stockholders*. *(pp. 12 & 480)*

Cost All normal and reasonable expenditures necessary to get an asset in place and ready for its intended use. *(p. 347)*

Cost accounting system Accounting system for manufacturing activities based on the perpetual inventory system.

Cost-benefit constraint The notion that the benefit of a disclosure exceeds the cost of that disclosure. *(p. 13)*

Cost-benefit principle Information system principle that prescribes the benefits from an activity in an accounting system to outweigh the costs of that activity. *(App. E)*

Cost of goods available for sale Consists of beginning inventory plus net purchases of a period.

Cost of goods sold Cost of inventory sold to customers during a period; also called *cost of sales. (p. 166)*

Cost principle Accounting principle that prescribes financial statement information to be based on actual costs incurred in business transactions. *(p. 10)*

Coupon bonds Bonds with interest coupons attached to their certificates; bondholders detach coupons when they mature and present them to a bank or broker for collection. *(p. 451)*

Credit Recorded on the right side; an entry that decreases asset and expense accounts, and increases liability, revenue, and most equity accounts; abbreviated Cr. *(p. 61)*

Credit memorandum Notification that the sender has credited the recipient's account in the sender's records. *(p. 175)*

Credit period Time period that can pass before a customer's payment is due. *(p. 169)*

Credit terms Description of the amounts and timing of payments that a buyer (debtor) agrees to make in the future. *(p. 169)*

Creditors Individuals or organizations entitled to receive payments. *(p. 58)*

Cumulative preferred stock Preferred stock on which undeclared dividends accumulate until paid; common stockholders cannot receive dividends until cumulative dividends are paid. *(p. 492)*

Current assets Cash and other assets expected to be sold, collected, or used within one year or the company's operating cycle, whichever is longer. *(p. 125)*

Current liabilities Obligations due to be paid or settled within one year or the company's operating cycle, whichever is longer. *(pp. 125 & 390)*

Current portion of long-term debt Portion of long-term debt due within one year or the operating cycle, whichever is longer; reported under current liabilities. *(p. 399)*

Current ratio Ratio used to evaluate a company's ability to pay its short-term obligations, calculated by dividing current assets by current liabilities. *(p. 128)*

Date of declaration Date the directors vote to pay a dividend. *(p. 487)*

Date of payment Date the corporation makes the dividend payment. *(p. 487)*

Date of record Date directors specify for identifying stockholders to receive dividends. *(p. 487)*

Days' sales in inventory Estimate of number of days needed to convert inventory into receivables or cash; equals ending inventory divided by cost of goods sold and then multiplied by 365; also called *days' stock on hand. (p. 228)*

Days' sales uncollected Measure of the liquidity of receivables computed by dividing the current balance of receivables by the annual credit (or net) sales and then multiplying by 365; also called *days' sales in receivables. (p. 285)*

Debit Recorded on the left side; an entry that increases asset and expense accounts, and decreases liability, revenue, and most equity accounts; abbreviated Dr. *(p. 61)*

Debit memorandum Notification that the sender has debited the recipient's account in the sender's records. *(p. 170)*

Debt ratio Ratio of total liabilities to total assets; used to reflect risk associated with a company's debts. *(p. 77)*

Debt-to-equity ratio Defined as total liabilities divided by total equity; shows the proportion of a company financed by non-owners (creditors) in comparison with that financed by owners. *(p. 451)*

Debtors Individuals or organizations that owe money. *(p. 57)*

Declining-balance method Method that determines depreciation charge for the period by multiplying a depreciation rate (often twice the straight-line rate) by the asset's beginning-period book value. *(p. 352)*

Deferred income tax liability Corporation income taxes that are deferred until future years because of temporary differences between GAAP and tax rules. *(p. 415)*

Departmental accounting system Accounting system that provides information useful in evaluating the profitability or cost effectiveness of a department.

Depletion Process of allocating the cost of natural resources to periods when they are consumed and sold. *(p. 361)*

Deposit ticket Lists items such as currency, coins, and checks deposited and their corresponding dollar amounts. *(p. 277)*

Deposits in transit Deposits recorded by the company but not yet recorded by its bank. *(p. 280)*

Depreciable cost Cost of a plant asset less its salvage value.

Depreciation Expense created by allocating the cost of plant and equipment to periods in which they are used; represents the expense of using the asset. *(pp. 106 & 348)*

Diluted earnings per share Earnings per share calculation that requires dilutive securities be added to the denominator of the basic EPS calculation. *(p. 500)*

Dilutive securities Securities having the potential to increase common shares outstanding; examples are options, rights, convertible bonds, and convertible preferred stock. *(p. 500)*

Direct method Presentation of net cash from operating activities for the statement of cash flows that lists major operating cash receipts less major operating cash payments. *(p. 530)*

Direct write-off method Method that records the loss from an uncollectible account receivable at the time it is determined to be uncollectible; no attempt is made to estimate bad debts. *(p. 314)*

Discount on bonds payable Difference between a bond's par value and its lower issue price or carrying value; occurs when the contract rate is less than the market rate. *(p. 439)*

Discount on note payable Difference between the face value of a note payable and the (lesser) amount borrowed; reflects the added interest to be paid on the note over its life.

Discount on stock Difference between the par value of stock and its issue price when issued at a price below par value. *(p. 485)*

Discount period Time period in which a cash discount is available and the buyer can make a reduced payment. *(p. 169)*

Discount rate Expected rate of return on investments; also called *cost of capital, hurdle rate,* or *required rate of return.*

Discounts lost Expenses resulting from not taking advantage of cash discounts on purchases. *(p. 290)*

Dividend in arrears Unpaid dividend on cumulative preferred stock; must be paid before any regular dividends on preferred stock and before any dividends on common stock. *(p. 492)*

Dividend yield Ratio of the annual amount of cash dividends distributed to common shareholders relative to the common stock's market value (price). *(p. 501)*

Dividends Corporation's distributions of assets to its owners. *(pp. 15 & 59)*

Dodd-Frank Wall Street Reform and Consumer Protection Act *(p. 14)*

Double-declining-balance (DDB) depreciation Depreciation equals beginning book value multiplied by 2 times the straight-line rate.

Double-entry accounting Accounting system in which each transaction affects at least two accounts and has at least one debit and one credit. *(p. 61)*

Double taxation Corporate income is taxed and then its later distribution through dividends is normally taxed again for shareholders.

Earnings (See *net income.*)

Earnings per share (EPS) Amount of income earned by each share of a company's outstanding common stock; also called *net income per share. (p. 500)*

Effective interest method Allocates interest expense over the bond life to yield a constant rate of interest; interest expense for a period is found by multiplying the balance of the liability at the beginning of the period by the bond market rate at issuance; also called *interest method. (p. 457)*

Efficiency Company's productivity in using its assets; usually measured relative to how much revenue a certain level of assets generates. *(p. 578)*

Efficiency variance Difference between the actual quantity of an input and the standard quantity of that input.

Electronic funds transfer (EFT) Use of electronic communication to transfer cash from one party to another. *(p. 278)*

Employee benefits Additional compensation paid to or on behalf of employees, such as premiums for medical, dental, life, and disability insurance, and contributions to pension plans. *(p. 400)*

Employee earnings report Record of an employee's net pay, gross pay, deductions, and year-to-date payroll information. *(p. 412)*

Enterprise resource planning (ERP) software Programs that manage a company's vital operations, which range from order taking to production to accounting. *(App. E)*

Entity Organization that, for accounting purposes, is separate from other organizations and individuals.

EOM Abbreviation for *end of month;* used to describe credit terms for credit transactions. *(p. 169)*

Equity Owner's claim on the assets of a business; equals the residual interest in an entity's assets after deducting liabilities; also called *net assets. (p. 15)*

Equity method Accounting method used for long-term investments when the investor has "significant influence" over the investee. *(p. C-7)*

Equity ratio Portion of total assets provided by equity, computed as total equity divided by total assets. *(p. 593)*

Equity securities with controlling influence Long-term investment when the investor is able to exert controlling influence over the investee; investors owning 50% or more of voting stock are presumed to exert controlling influence. *(p. C-9)*

Equity securities with significant influence Long-term investment when the investor is able to exert significant influence over the investee; investors owning 20 percent or more (but less than 50 percent) of voting stock are presumed to exert significant influence. *(p. C-7)*

Estimated liability Obligation of an uncertain amount that can be reasonably estimated. *(p. 400)*

Ethics Codes of conduct by which actions are judged as right or wrong, fair or unfair, honest or dishonest. *(p. 7)*

Events Happenings that both affect an organization's financial position and can be reliably measured. *(p. 16)*

Expanded accounting equation Assets = Liabilities + Equity; Equity equals [Owner capital − Owner withdrawals + Revenues − Expenses] for a noncorporation; Equity equals [Contributed capital + Retained earnings + Revenues − Expenses] for a corporation where dividends are subtracted from retained earnings. *(p. 16)*

Expense recognition (or **matching**) **principle** (See *matching principle.*)

Expenses Outflows or using up of assets as part of operations of a business to generate sales. *(p. 15)*

External transactions Exchanges of economic value between one entity and another entity. *(p. 16)*

External users Persons using accounting information who are not directly involved in running the organization. *(p. 4)*

Extraordinary gains or losses Gains or losses reported separately from continuing operations because they are both unusual and infrequent. *(p. 602)*

Extraordinary repairs Major repairs that extend the useful life of a plant asset beyond prior expectations; treated as a capital expenditure. *(p. 358)*

Fair value option Fair Value Option (FVO) refers to an option to measure eligible items at fair value; eligible items include *financial assets,* such as HTM, AFS, and equity method investments, and *financial liabilities.* FVO is applied "instrument by instrument" and is elected when the eligible item is "first recognized"; once FVO is elected the decision is "irrevocable." When FVO is elected, it is measured at "fair value" and unrealized gains and losses are recognized in earnings. *(p. 450)*

Federal depository bank Bank authorized to accept deposits of amounts payable to the federal government. *(p. 410)*

Federal Insurance Contributions Act (FICA) Taxes Taxes assessed on both employers and employees; for Social Security and Medicare programs. *(p. 396)*

Federal Unemployment Taxes (FUTA) Payroll taxes on employers assessed by the federal government to support its unemployment insurance program. *(p. 398)*

FIFO method (See *first-in, first-out.*)

Financial accounting Area of accounting aimed mainly at serving external users. *(p. 4)*

Financial Accounting Standards Board (FASB) Independent group of full-time members responsible for setting accounting rules. *(p. 9)*

Financial leverage Earning a higher return on equity by paying dividends on preferred stock or interest on debt at a rate lower than the return earned with the assets from issuing preferred stock or debt; also called *trading on the equity*. (p. 494)

Financial reporting Process of communicating information relevant to investors, creditors, and others in making investment, credit, and business decisions. (p. 579)

Financial statement analysis Application of analytical tools to general-purpose financial statements and related data for making business decisions. (p. 578)

Financial statements Includes the balance sheet, income statement, statement of owner's (or stockholders') equity, and statement of cash flows.

Financing activities Transactions with owners and creditors that include obtaining cash from issuing debt, repaying amounts borrowed, and obtaining cash from or distributing cash to owners. (p. 526)

First-in, first-out (FIFO) Method to assign cost to inventory that assumes items are sold in the order acquired; earliest items purchased are the first sold. (pp. 218 & 235)

Fiscal year Consecutive 12-month (or 52-week) period chosen as the organization's annual accounting period. (p. 102)

Flexibility principle Information system principle that prescribes an accounting system be able to adapt to changes in the company, its operations, and needs of decision makers. (App. E)

FOB Abbreviation for *free on board;* the point when ownership of goods passes to the buyer; *FOB shipping point* (or *factory*) means the buyer pays shipping costs and accepts ownership of goods when the seller transfers goods to carrier; *FOB destination* means the seller pays shipping costs and buyer accepts ownership of goods at the buyer's place of business. (p. 171)

Foreign exchange rate Price of one currency stated in terms of another currency. (p. C-15)

Form 940 IRS form used to report an employer's federal unemployment taxes (FUTA) on an annual filing basis. (p. 410)

Form 941 IRS form filed to report FICA taxes owed and remitted. (p. 408)

Form 10-K (or 10-KSB) Annual report form filed with SEC by businesses (small businesses) with publicly traded securities. (p. A-1)

Form W-2 Annual report by an employer to each employee showing the employee's wages subject to FICA and federal income taxes along with amounts withheld. (p. 410)

Form W-4 Withholding allowance certificate, filed with the employer, identifying the number of withholding allowances claimed. (p. 412)

Franchises Privileges granted by a company or government to sell a product or service under specified conditions. (p. 364)

Full disclosure principle Principle that prescribes financial statements (including notes) to report all relevant information about an entity's operations and financial condition. (p. 11)

GAAP (See *generally accepted accounting principles.*)

General and administrative expenses Expenses that support the operating activities of a business. (p. 180)

General journal All-purpose journal for recording the debits and cr its of transactions and events. (pp. 63 & App. E)

General ledger (See *ledger.*) (p. 57)

General partner Partner who assumes unlimited liability for the de of the partnership; responsible for partnership management. (App. D

General partnership Partnership in which all partners have mu agency and unlimited liability for partnership debts. (App. D)

Generally accepted accounting principles (GAAP) Rules that spe acceptable accounting practices. (p. 9)

Generally accepted auditing standards (GAAS) Rules that spe acceptable auditing practices.

General-purpose financial statements Statements published peri cally for use by a variety of interested parties; includes the income st ment, balance sheet, statement of owner's equity (or statement of reta earnings for a corporation), statement of cash flows, and notes to th statements. (p. 579)

Going-concern assumption Principle that prescribes finan statements to reflect the assumption that the business will conti operating. (p. 11)

Goodwill Amount by which a company's (or a segment's) value exce the value of its individual assets less its liabilities. (p. 364)

Gross margin (See *gross profit.*)

Gross margin ratio Gross margin (net sales minus cost of goods s divided by net sales; also called *gross profit ratio.* (p. 183)

Gross method Method of recording purchases at the full invoice p without deducting any cash discounts. (p. 290)

Gross pay Total compensation earned by an employee. (p. 396)

Gross profit Net sales minus cost of goods sold; also called *gross r gin.* (p. 166)

Gross profit method Procedure to estimate inventory by using the gross profit rate to estimate cost of goods sold, which is then subtra from the cost of goods available for sale. (p. 241)

Held-to-maturity (HTM) securities Debt securities that a company the intent and ability to hold until they mature. (p. C-5)

Horizontal analysis Comparison of a company's financial condi and performance across time. (p. 580)

Impairment Diminishment of an asset value. (pp. 355 & 363)

Imprest system Method to account for petty cash; maintains a cons balance in the fund, which equals cash plus petty cash receipts.

Inadequacy Condition in which the capacity of plant assets is too s to meet the company's production demands. (p. 349)

Income (See *net income.*) (p. 16)

Income statement Financial statement that subtracts expenses f revenues to yield a net income or loss over a specified period of t also includes any gains or losses. (p. 21)

Income summary Temporary account used only in the closing pro to which the balances of revenue and expense accounts (including gains or losses) are transferred; its balance is transferred to the ca account (or retained earnings for a corporation). (p. 119)

Indefinite life Asset life that is not limited by legal, regulatory, contractual, competitive, economic, or other factors. *(p. 363)*

Indirect method Presentation that reports net income and then adjusts it by adding and subtracting items to yield net cash from operating activities on the statement of cash flows. *(p. 530)*

Information processor Component of an accounting system that interprets, transforms, and summarizes information for use in analysis and reporting. *(App. E)*

Information storage Component of an accounting system that keeps data in a form accessible to information processors. *(App. E)*

Infrequent gain or loss Gain or loss not expected to recur given the operating environment of the business. *(p. 602)*

Input device Means of capturing information from source documents that enables its transfer to information processors. *(App. E)*

Installment note Liability requiring a series of periodic payments to the lender. *(p. 447)*

Intangible assets Long-term assets (resources) used to produce or sell products or services; usually lack physical form and have uncertain benefits. *(pp. 125 & 362)*

Interest Charge for using money (or other assets) loaned from one entity to another. *(p. 322)*

Interim financial statements Financial statements covering periods of less than one year; usually based on one-, three-, or six-month periods. *(pp. 102 & 240)*

Interim statements (See *interim financial statements.*)

Internal controls or **Internal control system** All policies and procedures used to protect assets, ensure reliable accounting, promote efficient operations, and urge adherence to company policies. *(pp. 264 & App. E)*

Internal transactions Activities within an organization that can affect the accounting equation. *(p. 16)*

Internal users Persons using accounting information who are directly involved in managing the organization. *(p. 5)*

International Accounting Standards Board (IASB) Group that identifies preferred accounting practices and encourages global acceptance; issues International Financial Reporting Standards (IFRS). *(p. 9)*

International Financial Reporting Standards (IFRS) Set of international accounting standards explaining how types of transactions and events are reported in financial statements; IFRS are issued by the International Accounting Standards Board *(p. 9)*

Inventory Goods a company owns and expects to sell in its normal operations. *(p. 167)*

Inventory turnover Number of times a company's average inventory is sold during a period; computed by dividing cost of goods sold by average inventory; also called *merchandise turnover*. *(p. 227)*

Investing activities Transactions that involve purchasing and selling of long-term assets, includes making and collecting notes receivable and investments in other than cash equivalents. *(p. 525)*

Invoice Itemized record of goods prepared by the vendor that lists the customer's name, items sold, sales prices, and terms of sale. *(p. 288)*

Invoice approval Document containing a checklist of steps necessary for approving the recording and payment of an invoice; also called *check authorization*. *(p. 288)*

Journal Record in which transactions are entered before they are posted to ledger accounts; also called *book of original entry*. *(p. 63)*

Journalizing Process of recording transactions in a journal. *(p. 63)*

Known liabilities Obligations of a company with little uncertainty; set by agreements, contracts, or laws; also called *definitely determinable liabilities*. *(p. 392)*

Land improvements Assets that increase the benefits of land, have a limited useful life, and are depreciated. *(p. 347)*

Large stock dividend Stock dividend that is more than 25% of the previously outstanding shares. *(p. 488)*

Last-in, first-out (LIFO) Method for assigning cost to inventory that assumes costs for the most recent items purchased are sold first and charged to cost of goods sold. *(pp. 219 & 236)*

Lease Contract specifying the rental of property. *(pp. 364 & 460)*

Leasehold Rights the lessor grants to the lessee under the terms of a lease. *(p. 364)*

Leasehold improvements Alterations or improvements to leased property such as partitions and storefronts. *(p. 365)*

Ledger Record containing all accounts (with amounts) for a business; also called *general ledger*.

Lessee Party to a lease who secures the right to possess and use the property from another party (the lessor). *(p. 364)*

Lessor Party to a lease who grants another party (the lessee) the right to possess and use its property. *(p. 364)*

Liabilities Creditors' claims on an organization's assets; involves a probable future payment of assets, products, or services that a company is obligated to make due to past transactions or events. *(p. 15)*

Licenses (See *franchises.*)

Limited liability Owner can lose no more than the amount invested.

Limited liability company Organization form that combines select features of a corporation and a limited partnership; provides limited liability to its members (owners), is free of business tax, and allows members to actively participate in management. *(App. D)*

Limited liability partnership Partnership in which a partner is not personally liable for malpractice or negligence unless that partner is responsible for providing the service that resulted in the claim. *(App. D)*

Limited life (See *useful life.*)

Limited partners Partners who have no personal liability for partnership debts beyond the amounts they invested in the partnership. *(App. D)*

Limited partnership Partnership that has two classes of partners, limited partners and general partners. *(App. D)*

Liquid assets Resources such as cash that are easily converted into other assets or used to pay for goods, services, or liabilities. *(p. 269)*

Liquidating cash dividend Distribution of assets that returns part of the original investment to stockholders; deducted from contributed capital accounts. *(p. 488)*

Liquidation Process of going out of business; involves selling assets, paying liabilities, and distributing remainder to owners.

Liquidity Availability of resources to meet short-term cash requirements. *(pp. 269 & 578)*

List price Catalog (full) price of an item before any trade discount is deducted. *(p. 168)*

Long-term investments Long-term assets not used in operating activities such as notes receivable and investments in stocks and bonds. *(pp. 125 & C-2)*

Long-term liabilities Obligations not due to be paid within one year or the operating cycle, whichever is longer. *(pp. 125 & 390)*

Lower of cost or market (LCM) Required method to report inventory at market replacement cost when that market cost is lower than recorded cost. *(p. 223)*

Maker of the note Entity who signs a note and promises to pay it at maturity. *(p. 322)*

Managerial accounting Area of accounting aimed mainly at serving the decision-making needs of internal users; also called *management accounting*. *(p. 5)*

Manufacturer Company that uses labor and operating assets to convert raw materials to finished goods.

Market prospects Expectations (both good and bad) about a company's future performance as assessed by users and other interested parties. *(p. 578)*

Market rate Interest rate that borrowers are willing to pay and lenders are willing to accept for a specific lending agreement given the borrowers' risk level. *(p. 438)*

Market value per share Price at which stock is bought or sold. *(p. 483)*

Matching (or expense recognition) principle Prescribes expenses to be reported in the same period as the revenues that were earned as a result of the expenses. *(pp. 11, 103 & 314)*

Materiality constraint Prescribes that accounting for items that significantly impact financial statement and any inferences from them adhere strictly to GAAP. *(pp. 13 & 314)*

Maturity date of a note Date when a note's principal and interest are due. *(p. 322)*

Measurement principle Principle that prescribes financial statement information, and its underlying transactions and events, be based on relevant measures of valuation; also called the *cost principle*. *(p. 10)*

Merchandise (See *merchandise inventory.*)

Merchandise inventory Goods that a company owns and expects to sell to customers; also called *merchandise* or *inventory*. *(p. 166)*

Merchandiser Entity that earns net income by buying and selling merchandise. *(p. 166)*

Merit rating Rating assigned to an employer by a state based on the employer's record of employment. *(p. 398)*

Minimum legal capital Amount of assets defined by law that stoc[k] holders must (potentially) invest in a corporation; usually defined as p[ar] value of the stock; intended to protect creditors. *(p. 483)*

Modified Accelerated Cost Recovery System (MACRS) Depreciati[on] system required by federal income tax law. *(p. 354)*

Monetary unit assumption Principle that assumes transactions a[nd] events can be expressed in money units. *(p. 11)*

Mortgage Legal loan agreement that protects a lender by giving t[he] lender the right to be paid from the cash proceeds from the sale of a b[or]rower's assets identified in the mortgage. *(p. 449)*

Multinational Company that operates in several countries. *(p. C-15)*

Multiple-step income statement Income statement format that sho[ws] subtotals between sales and net income, categorizes expenses, and oft[en] reports the details of net sales and expenses. *(p. 179)*

Mutual agency Legal relationship among partners whereby each pa[rt]ner is an agent of the partnership and is able to bind the partnership [to] contracts within the scope of the partnership's business. *(App. D)*

Natural business year Twelve-month period that ends when a comp[a]ny's sales activities are at their lowest point. *(p. 102)*

Natural resources Assets physically consumed when used; examp[les] are timber, mineral deposits, and oil and gas fields; also called *wasti[ng] assets*. *(p. 361)*

Net assets (See *equity.*)

Net income Amount earned after subtracting all expenses necessary [for] and matched with sales for a period; also called *income, profit,* or *ear[n]ings.* *(p. 16)*

Net loss Excess of expenses over revenues for a period. *(p. 16)*

Net method Method of recording purchases at the full invoice price le[ss] any cash discounts. *(p. 290)*

Net pay Gross pay less all deductions; also called *take-home pay.* *(p. 39[*)

Net realizable value Expected selling price (value) of an item minus [the] cost of making the sale. *(p. 214)*

Noncumulative preferred stock Preferred stock on which the right [to] receive dividends is lost for any period when dividends are not [de]clared. *(p. 492)*

Noninterest-bearing note Note with no stated (contract) rate of int[er]est; interest is implicitly included in the note's face value.

Nonparticipating preferred stock Preferred stock on which divide[nds] are limited to a maximum amount each year. *(p. 492)*

No-par value stock Stock class that has not been assigned a par [or] stated) value by the corporate charter. *(p. 483)*

Nonsufficient funds (NSF) check Maker's bank account has insu[ffi]cient money to pay the check; also called *hot check.*

Note (See *promissory note.*)

Note payable Liability expressed by a written promise to pay a defin[ite] sum of money on demand or on a specific future date(s).

Note receivable Asset consisting of a written promise to receive a de[fi]nite sum of money on demand or on a specific future date(s).

Objectivity Concept that prescribes independent, unbiased evidence to support financial statement information.

Obsolescence Condition in which, because of new inventions and improvements, a plant asset can no longer be used to produce goods or services with a competitive advantage. *(p. 349)*

Off-balance-sheet financing Acquisition of assets by agreeing to liabilities not reported on the balance sheet. *(p. 461)*

Online processing Approach to inputting data from source documents as soon as the information is available. *(App. E)*

Operating activities Activities that involve the production or purchase of merchandise and the sale of goods or services to customers, including expenditures related to administering the business. *(p. 525)*

Operating cycle Normal time between paying cash for merchandise or employee services and receiving cash from customers. *(p. 123)*

Operating leases Short-term (or cancelable) leases in which the lessor retains risks and rewards of ownership. *(p. 460)*

Ordinary repairs Repairs to keep a plant asset in normal, good operating condition; treated as a revenue expenditure and immediately expensed. *(p. 357)*

Organization expenses (costs) Costs such as legal fees and promoter fees to bring an entity into existence. *(p. 481)*

Other comprehensive income (See *comprehensive income.*)

Output devices Means by which information is taken out of the accounting system and made available for use. *(App. E)*

Outsourcing Manager decision to buy a product or service from another entity; part of a *make-or-buy* decision; also called *make or buy.*

Outstanding checks Checks written and recorded by the depositor but not yet paid by the bank at the bank statement date. *(p. 280)*

Outstanding stock Corporation's stock held by its shareholders.

Owner, Capital Account showing the owner's claim on company assets; equals owner investments plus net income (or less net losses) minus owner withdrawals since the company's inception; also referred to as *equity.*

Owner investment Assets put into the business by the owner.

Owner's equity (See *equity.*)

Owner, Withdrawals Account used to record asset distributions to the owner. *(See also withdrawals.) (p. 15)*

Paid-in capital (See *contributed capital.*)

Paid-in capital in excess of par value Amount received from issuance of stock that is in excess of the stock's par value. *(p. 484)*

Par value Value assigned a share of stock by the corporate charter when the stock is authorized. *(p. 483)*

Par value of a bond Amount the bond issuer agrees to pay at maturity and the amount on which cash interest payments are based; also called *face amount* or *face value* of a bond. *(p. 436)*

Par value stock Class of stock assigned a par value by the corporate charter. *(p. 483)*

Parent Company that owns a controlling interest in a corporation (requires more than 50% of voting stock). *(p. C-9)*

Participating preferred stock Preferred stock that shares with common stockholders any dividends paid in excess of the percent stated on preferred stock. *(p. 492)*

Partner return on equity Partner net income divided by average partner equity for the period. *(App. D)*

Partnership Unincorporated association of two or more persons to pursue a business for profit as co-owners. *(pp. 12 & App. D)*

Partnership contract Agreement among partners that sets terms under which the affairs of the partnership are conducted; also called *articles of partnership.* *(App. D)*

Partnership liquidation Dissolution of a partnership by (1) selling noncash assets and allocating any gain or loss according to partners' income-and-loss ratio, (2) paying liabilities, and (3) distributing any remaining cash according to partners' capital balances. *(App. D)*

Patent Exclusive right granted to its owner to produce and sell an item or to use a process for 17 years. *(p. 363)*

Payee of the note Entity to whom a note is made payable. *(p. 322)*

Payroll bank account Bank account used solely for paying employees; each pay period an amount equal to the total employees' net pay is deposited in it and the payroll checks are drawn on it. *(p. 412)*

Payroll deductions Amounts withheld from an employee's gross pay; also called *withholdings.* *(p. 396)*

Payroll register Record for a pay period that shows the pay period dates, regular and overtime hours worked, gross pay, net pay, and deductions. *(p. 411)*

Pension plan Contractual agreement between an employer and its employees for the employer to provide benefits to employees after they retire; expensed when incurred. *(p. 461)*

Periodic inventory system Method that records the cost of inventory purchased but does not continuously track the quantity available or sold to customers; records are updated at the end of each period to reflect the physical count and costs of goods available. *(p. 167)*

Permanent accounts Accounts that reflect activities related to one or more future periods; balance sheet accounts whose balances are not closed; also called *real accounts.* *(p. 119)*

Perpetual inventory system Method that maintains continuous records of the cost of inventory available and the cost of goods sold. *(p. 167)*

Petty cash Small amount of cash in a fund to pay minor expenses; accounted for using an imprest system. *(p. 274)*

Plant asset age Plant asset age is an approximation of the age of plant assets, which is estimated by dividing accumulated depreciation by depreciation expense. *(p. 367)*

Plant assets Tangible long-lived assets used to produce or sell products and services; also called *property, plant and equipment (PP&E)* or *fixed assets.* *(pp. 106 & 346)*

Post-closing trial balance List of permanent accounts and their balances from the ledger after all closing entries are journalized and posted. *(p. 122)*

Posting Process of transferring journal entry information to the ledger; computerized systems automate this process. *(p. 63)*

Posting reference (PR) column A column in journals in which individual ledger account numbers are entered when entries are posted to those ledger accounts. *(p. 64)*

Preemptive right Stockholders' right to maintain their proportionate interest in a corporation with any additional shares issued. *(p. 482)*

Preferred stock Stock with a priority status over common stockholders in one or more ways, such as paying dividends or distributing assets. *(p. 491)*

Premium on bonds Difference between a bond's par value and its higher carrying value; occurs when the contract rate is higher than the market rate; also called *bond premium*. *(p. 442)*

Premium on stock (See *contributed capital in excess of par value.*) *(p. 484)*

Prepaid expenses Items paid for in advance of receiving their benefits; classified as assets. *(p. 105)*

Price-earnings (PE) ratio Ratio of a company's current market value per share to its earnings per share; also called *price-to-earnings*. *(p. 501)*

Principal of a note Amount that the signer of a note agrees to pay back when it matures, not including interest. *(p. 322)*

Principles of internal control Principles prescribing management to establish responsibility, maintain records, insure assets, separate recordkeeping from custody of assets, divide responsibility for related transactions, apply technological controls, and perform reviews. *(p. 264)*

Prior period adjustment Correction of an error in a prior year that is reported in the statement of retained earnings (or statement of stockholders' equity) net of any income tax effects. *(p. 498)*

Pro forma financial statements Statements that show the effects of proposed transactions and events as if they had occurred. *(p. 134)*

Profit (See *net income.*)

Profit margin Ratio of a company's net income to its net sales; the percent of income in each dollar of revenue; also called *net profit margin*. *(p. 127)*

Profitability Refers to a company's ability to generate an adequate return on invested capital; return is judged by assessing earnings relative to the level and sources of financing. *(p. 578)*

Promissory note (or **note**) Written promise to pay a specified amount either on demand or at a definite future date; is a *note receivable* for the lender but a *note payable* for the lendee. *(p. 322)*

Proprietorship (See *sole proprietorship.*)

Proxy Legal document giving a stockholder's agent the power to exercise the stockholder's voting rights. *(p. 481)*

Purchase discount Term used by a purchaser to describe a cash discount granted to the purchaser for paying within the discount period. *(p. 169)*

Purchase order Document used by the purchasing department to place an order with a seller (vendor). *(p. 287)*

Purchase requisition Document listing merchandise needed by a department and requesting it be purchased. *(p. 287)*

Purchases journal Journal normally used to record all purchases on credit. *(App. E)*

Ratio analysis Determination of key relations between financial statement items as reflected in numerical measures. *(p. 580)*

Realizable value Expected proceeds from converting an asset into cash. *(p. 316)*

Receiving report Form used to report that ordered goods are receive and to describe their quantity and condition. *(p. 288)*

Recordkeeping Part of accounting that involves recording transactions and events, either manually or electronically; also called *boo keeping*. *(p. 4)*

Registered bonds Bonds owned by investors whose names and ad dresses are recorded by the issuer; interest payments are made to th registered owners. *(p. 451)*

Relevance principle Information system principle prescribing that i reports be useful, understandable, timely, and pertinent for decision ma ing. *(App. E)*

Report form balance sheet Balance sheet that lists accounts vertical in the order of assets, liabilities, and equity. *(p. 22)*

Restricted retained earnings Retained earnings not available for div dends because of legal or contractual limitations. *(p. 498)*

Retail inventory method Method for estimating ending inventory bas on the ratio of the amount of goods for sale at cost to the amount goods for sale at retail. *(p. 241)*

Retailer Intermediary that buys products from manufacturers or who salers and sells them to consumers. *(p. 166)*

Retained earnings Cumulative income less cumulative losses and di dends. *(pp. 15 & 483)*

Retained earnings deficit Debit (abnormal) balance in Retained Ear ings; occurs when cumulative losses and dividends exceed cumulati income; also called *accumulated deficit*. *(p. 487)*

Return Monies received from an investment; often in perce form. *(p. 26)*

Return on assets (See *return on total assets.*)

Return on equity Ratio of net income to average equity for the perio

Return on total assets Ratio reflecting operating efficiency; defined net income divided by average total assets for the period; also called *turn on assets* or *return on investment*. *(pp. 26 & C-11)*

Revenue expenditures Expenditures reported on the current inco statement as an expense because they do not provide benefits in fut periods. *(p. 357)*

Revenue recognition principle The principle prescribing that rever is recognized when earned. *(p. 11)*

Revenues Gross increase in equity from a company's business activi that earn income; also called *sales*. *(p. 15)*

Reverse stock split Occurs when a corporation calls in its stock and places each share with less than one new share; increases both mar value per share and any par or stated value per share. *(p. 490)*

Reversing entries Optional entries recorded at the beginning of a per that prepare the accounts for the usual journal entries as if adjusting tries had not occurred in the prior period. *(p. 135)*

Risk Uncertainty about an expected return. *(p. 29)*

S corporation Corporation that meets special tax qualifications so a be treated like a partnership for income tax purposes. *(App. D)*

Sales (See *revenues.*)

Sales discount Term used by a seller to describe a cash discount granted to buyers who pay within the discount period. *(p. 169)*

Sales journal Journal normally used to record sales of goods on credit. *(App. E)*

Salvage value Estimate of amount to be recovered at the end of an asset's useful life; also called *residual value* or *scrap value*. *(p. 349)*

Sarbanes-Oxley Act (SOX) Created the *Public Company Accounting Oversight Board,* regulates analyst conflicts, imposes corporate governance requirements, enhances accounting and control disclosures, impacts insider transactions and executive loans, establishes new types of criminal conduct, and expands penalties for violations of federal securities laws. *(pp. 13 & 264)*

Schedule of accounts payable List of the balances of all accounts in the accounts payable ledger and their totals. *(App. E)*

Schedule of accounts receivable List of the balances of all accounts in the accounts receivable ledger and their totals. *(App. E)*

Section 404 (of SOX) Section 404 of SOX requires management and the external auditor to report on the adequacy of the company's internal control on financial reporting, which is the most costly aspect of SOX for companies to implement as documenting and testing important financial manual and automated controls require enormous efforts. Section 404 also requires management to produce an "internal control report" as part of each annual SEC report that affirms "the responsibility of management for establishing and maintaining an adequate internal control structure and procedures for financial reporting." *(p. 264)*

Secured bonds Bonds that have specific assets of the issuer pledged as collateral. *(p. 451)*

Securities and Exchange Commission (SEC) Federal agency Congress has charged to set reporting rules for organizations that sell ownership shares to the public. *(p. 9)*

Segment return on assets Segment operating income divided by segment average (identifiable) assets for the period. *(App. E)*

Selling expenses Expenses of promoting sales, such as displaying and advertising merchandise, making sales, and delivering goods to customers. *(p. 180)*

Serial bonds Bonds consisting of separate amounts that mature at different dates. *(p. 451)*

Service company Organization that provides services instead of tangible products.

Shareholders Owners of a corporation; also called *stockholders*. *(p. 12)*

Shares Equity of a corporation divided into ownership units; also called *stock*. *(p. 13)*

Short-term investments Debt and equity securities that management expects to convert to cash within the next 3 to 12 months (or the operating cycle if longer); also called *temporary investments* or *marketable securities*. *(p. C-1)*

Short-term note payable Current obligation in the form of a written promissory note. *(p. 393)*

Shrinkage Inventory losses that occur as a result of theft or deterioration. *(p. 176)*

Signature card Includes the signatures of each person authorized to sign checks on the bank account. *(p. 277)*

Simple capital structure Capital structure that consists of only common stock and nonconvertible preferred stock; consists of no dilutive securities. *(p. 500)*

Single-step income statement Income statement format that includes cost of goods sold as an expense and shows only one subtotal for total expenses. *(p. 180)*

Sinking fund bonds Bonds that require the issuer to make deposits to a separate account; bondholders are repaid at maturity from that account. *(p. 451)*

Small stock dividend Stock dividend that is 25% or less of a corporation's previously outstanding shares. *(p. 488)*

Social responsibility Being accountable for the impact that one's actions might have on society.

Sole proprietorship Business owned by one person that is not organized as a corporation; also called *proprietorship*. *(p. 12)*

Solvency Company's long-run financial viability and its ability to cover long-term obligations. *(p. 578)*

Source documents Source of information for accounting entries that can be in either paper or electronic form; also called *business papers*. *(p. 56)*

Special journal Any journal used for recording and posting transactions of a similar type. *(App. E)*

Specific identification Method for assigning cost to inventory when the purchase cost of each item in inventory is identified and used to compute cost of inventory. *(pp. 217 & 234)*

Spreadsheet Computer program that organizes data by means of formulas and format; also called *electronic work sheet*.

State Unemployment Taxes (SUTA) State payroll taxes on employers to support its unemployment programs. *(p. 398)*

Stated value stock No-par stock assigned a stated value per share; this amount is recorded in the stock account when the stock is issued. *(p. 483)*

Statement of cash flows A financial statement that lists cash inflows (receipts) and cash outflows (payments) during a period; arranged by operating, investing, and financing. *(pp. 21 & 524)*

Statement of owner's equity Report of changes in equity over a period; adjusted for increases (owner investment and net income) and for decreases (withdrawals and net loss). *(p. 20)*

Statement of partners' equity Financial statement that shows total capital balances at the beginning of the period, any additional investment by partners, the income or loss of the period, the partners' withdrawals, and the partners' ending capital balances; also called *statement of partners' capital*. *(App. D)*

Statement of retained earnings Report of changes in retained earnings over a period; adjusted for increases (net income), for decreases (dividends and net loss), and for any prior period adjustment. *(p. 21)*

Statement of stockholders' equity Financial statement that lists the beginning and ending balances of each major equity account and describes all changes in those accounts. *(p. 499)*

Statements of Financial Accounting Standards (SFAS) FASB publications that establish U.S. GAAP.

Stock (See also *shares*) *(p. 13)*

Stock dividend Corporation's distribution of its own stock to its stockholders without the receipt of any payment. *(p. 488)*

Stock options Rights to purchase common stock at a fixed price over a specified period of time. *(p. 499)*

Stock split Occurs when a corporation calls in its stock and replaces each share with more than one new share; decreases both the market value per share and any par or stated value per share. *(p. 489)*

Stock subscription Investor's contractual commitment to purchase unissued shares at future dates and prices.

Stockholders (See also *shareholders*.) *(p. 13)*

Stockholders' equity A corporation's equity; also called *shareholders' equity* or *corporate capital*. *(p. 483)*

Straight-line bond amortization Method allocating an equal amount of bond interest expense to each period of the bond life. *(p. 440)*

Straight-line depreciation Method that allocates an equal portion of the depreciable cost of plant asset (cost minus salvage) to each accounting period in its useful life. *(pp. 107 & 350)*

Subsidiary Entity controlled by another entity (parent) in which the parent owns more than 50% of the subsidiary's voting stock. *(p. C-9)*

Subsidiary ledger List of individual subaccounts and amounts with a common characteristic; linked to a controlling account in the general ledger. *(App. E)*

Supplementary records Information outside the usual accounting records; also called *supplemental records*. *(p. 172)*

Supply chain Linkages of services or goods extending from suppliers, to the company itself, and on to customers.

T-account Tool used to show the effects of transactions and events on individual accounts. *(p. 61)*

Temporary accounts Accounts used to record revenues, expenses, and withdrawals (dividends for a corporation); they are closed at the end of each period; also called *nominal accounts*. *(p. 118)*

Term bonds Bonds scheduled for payment (maturity) at a single specified date. *(p. 451)*

Throughput time (See *cycle time*.)

Time period assumption Assumption that an organization's activities can be divided into specific time periods such as months, quarters, or years. *(pp. 11 & 102)*

Times interest earned Ratio of income before interest expense (and any income taxes) divided by interest expense; reflects risk of covering interest commitments when income varies. *(p. 406)*

Total asset turnover Measure of a company's ability to use its assets to generate sales; computed by dividing net sales by average total assets. *(p. 367)*

Trade discount Reduction from a list or catalog price that can var wholesalers, retailers, and consumers. *(p. 168)*

Trademark or **trade (brand) name** Symbol, name, phrase, or j identified with a company, product, or service. *(p. 364)*

Trading on the equity (See *financial leverage*.)

Trading securities Investments in debt and equity securities tha company intends to actively trade for profit. *(p. C-3)*

Transaction Exchange of economic consideration affecting an en financial position that can be reliably measured.

Treasury stock Corporation's own stock that it reacquired and holds. *(p. 495)*

Trial balance List of accounts and their balances at a point in time; debit balances equal total credit balances. *(p. 71)*

Unadjusted trial balance List of accounts and balances prepare fore accounting adjustments are recorded and posted. *(p. 116)*

Unclassified balance sheet Balance sheet that broadly groups as liabilities, and equity accounts. *(p. 123)*

Unearned revenue Liability created when customers pay in advanc products or services; earned when the products or services are later d ered. *(pp. 59 & 109)*

Units-of-production depreciation Method that charges a var amount to depreciation expense for each period of an asset's usefu depending on its usage. *(p. 351)*

Unlimited liability Legal relationship among general partners makes each of them responsible for partnership debts if the other ners are unable to pay their shares. *(App. D)*

Unrealized gain (loss) Gain (loss) not yet realized by an actual tran tion or event such as a sale. *(p. C-4)*

Unsecured bonds Bonds backed only by the issuer's credit st ing; almost always riskier than secured bonds; also ca *debentures*. *(p. 451)*

Unusual gain or loss Gain or loss that is abnormal or unrelated t company's ordinary activities and environment. *(p. 602)*

Useful life Length of time an asset will be productively used in the o tions of a business; also called *service life* or *limited life*. *(pp. 349 & 3*

Vendee Buyer of goods or services. *(p. 288)*

Vendor Seller of goods or services. *(p. 287)*

Vertical analysis Evaluation of each financial statement item or g of items in terms of a specific base amount. *(p. 580)*

Voucher Internal file used to store documents and information to trol cash disbursements and to ensure that a transaction is properly au rized and recorded. *(p. 289)*

Voucher register Journal (referred to as *book of original entry* which all vouchers are recorded after they have been approved. *(p.*

Voucher system Procedures and approvals designed to control cash bursements and acceptance of obligations. *(p. 272)*

Wage bracket withholding table Table of the amounts of income tax withheld from employees' wages. *(p. 412)*

Warranty Agreement that obligates the seller to correct or replace a product or service when it fails to perform properly within a specified period. *(p. 401)*

Weighted average Method for assigning inventory cost to sales; the cost of available-for-sale units is divided by the number of units available to determine per unit cost prior to each sale that is then multiplied by the units sold to yield the cost of that sale. *(pp. 220 & 237)*

Weighted-average method (See *weighted average.*)

Wholesaler Intermediary that buys products from manufacturers or other wholesalers and sells them to retailers or other wholesalers. *(p. 166)*

Work sheet Spreadsheet used to draft an unadjusted trial balance, adjusting entries, adjusted trial balance, and financial statements. (See also *spreadsheet*) *(p. 133)*

Working capital Current assets minus current liabilities at a point in time. *(p. 589)*

Working papers Analyses and other informal reports prepared by accountants and managers when organizing information for formal reports and financial statements. *(p. 133)*

Credits

Index

Chart of Accounts

Following is a typical chart of accounts, which is used in several assignments. Every company has its own unique accounts and numbering system.

Assets

Current Assets

101 Cash
102 Petty cash
103 Cash equivalents
104 Short-term investments
105 Fair value adjustment, _____ securities (S-T)
106 Accounts receivable
107 Allowance for doubtful accounts
108 Legal fees receivable
109 Interest receivable
110 Rent receivable
111 Notes receivable
119 Merchandise inventory
120 _____ inventory
121 _____ inventory
124 Office supplies
125 Store supplies
126 _____ supplies
128 Prepaid insurance
129 Prepaid interest
131 Prepaid rent
132 Raw materials inventory
133 Goods in process inventory, _____
134 Goods in process inventory, _____
135 Finished goods inventory

Long-Term Investments

141 Long-term investments
142 Fair value adjustment, _____ securities (L-T)
144 Investment in _____
145 Bond sinking fund

Plant Assets

151 Automobiles
152 Accumulated depreciation—Automobiles
153 Trucks
154 Accumulated depreciation—Trucks
155 Boats
156 Accumulated depreciation—Boats
157 Professional library
158 Accumulated depreciation—Professional library
159 Law library
160 Accumulated depreciation—Law library
161 Furniture
162 Accumulated depreciation—Furniture
163 Office equipment
164 Accumulated depreciation—Office equipment
165 Store equipment

166 Accumulated depreciation—Store equipment
167 _____ equipment
168 Accumulated depreciation—_____ equipment
169 Machinery
170 Accumulated depreciation—Machinery
173 Building _____
174 Accumulated depreciation—Building _____
175 Building _____
176 Accumulated depreciation—Building _____
179 Land improvements _____
180 Accumulated depreciation—Land improvements _____
181 Land improvements _____
182 Accumulated depreciation—Land improvements _____
183 Land

Natural Resources

185 Mineral deposit
186 Accumulated depletion—Mineral deposit

Intangible Assets

191 Patents
192 Leasehold
193 Franchise
194 Copyrights
195 Leasehold improvements
196 Licenses
197 Accumulated amortization—_____

Liabilities

Current Liabilities

201 Accounts payable
202 Insurance payable
203 Interest payable
204 Legal fees payable
207 Office salaries payable
208 Rent payable
209 Salaries payable
210 Wages payable
211 Accrued payroll payable
214 Estimated warranty liability
215 Income taxes payable
216 Common dividend payable
217 Preferred dividend payable
218 State unemployment taxes payable
219 Employee federal income taxes payable
221 Employee medical insurance payable

222 Employee retirement program payable
223 Employee union dues payable
224 Federal unemployment taxes payable
225 FICA taxes payable
226 Estimated vacation pay liability

Unearned Revenues

230 Unearned consulting fees
231 Unearned legal fees
232 Unearned property management fees
233 Unearned _____ fees
234 Unearned _____ fees
235 Unearned janitorial revenue
236 Unearned _____ revenue
238 Unearned rent

Notes Payable

240 Short-term notes payable
241 Discount on short-term notes payable
245 Notes payable
251 Long-term notes payable
252 Discount on long-term notes payable

Long-Term Liabilities

253 Long-term lease liability
255 Bonds payable
256 Discount on bonds payable
257 Premium on bonds payable
258 Deferred income tax liability

Equity

Owner's Equity

301 _____, Capital
302 _____, Withdrawals
303 _____, Capital
304 _____, Withdrawals
305 _____, Capital
306 _____, Withdrawals

Paid-In Capital

307 Common stock, $_____ par value
308 Common stock, no-par value
309 Common stock, $_____ stated value
310 Common stock dividend distributable
311 Paid-in capital in excess of par value, Common stock

312 Paid-in capital in excess of stated value,
No-par common stock
313 Paid-in capital from retirement of common stock
314 Paid-in capital, Treasury stock
315 Preferred stock
316 Paid-in capital in excess of par value,
Preferred stock

Retained Earnings

318 Retained earnings
319 Cash dividends (or Dividends)
320 Stock dividends

Other Equity Accounts

321 Treasury stock, Common
322 Unrealized gain—Equity
323 Unrealized loss—Equity

Revenues

401 _____ fees earned
402 _____ fees earned
403 _____ services revenue
404 _____ services revenue
405 Commissions earned
406 Rent revenue (or Rent earned)
407 Dividends revenue (or Dividend earned)
408 Earnings from investment in _____
409 Interest revenue (or Interest earned)
410 Sinking fund earnings
413 Sales
414 Sales returns and allowances
415 Sales discounts

Cost of Sales

Cost of Goods Sold

502 Cost of goods sold
505 Purchases
506 Purchases returns and allowances
507 Purchases discounts
508 Transportation-in

Manufacturing

520 Raw materials purchases
521 Freight-in on raw materials
530 Factory payroll
531 Direct labor
540 Factory overhead
541 Indirect materials
542 Indirect labor
543 Factory insurance expired
544 Factory supervision
545 Factory supplies used
546 Factory utilities
547 Miscellaneous production costs
548 Property taxes on factory building
549 Property taxes on factory equipment
550 Rent on factory building
551 Repairs, factory equipment
552 Small tools written off
560 Depreciation of factory equipment
561 Depreciation of factory building

Standard Cost Variance

580 Direct material quantity variance
581 Direct material price variance
582 Direct labor quantity variance
583 Direct labor price variance
584 Factory overhead volume variance
585 Factory overhead controllable variance

Expenses

Amortization, Depletion, and Depreciation

601 Amortization expense—_____
602 Amortization expense—_____
603 Depletion expense—_____
604 Depreciation expense—Boats
605 Depreciation expense—Automobiles
606 Depreciation expense—Building _____
607 Depreciation expense—Building _____
608 Depreciation expense—Land improvements _____
609 Depreciation expense—Land improvements _____
610 Depreciation expense—Law library
611 Depreciation expense—Trucks
612 Depreciation expense—_____ equipment
613 Depreciation expense—_____ equipment
614 Depreciation expense—_____
615 Depreciation expense—_____

Employee-Related Expenses

620 Office salaries expense
621 Sales salaries expense
622 Salaries expense
623 _____ wages expense
624 Employees' benefits expense
625 Payroll taxes expense

Financial Expenses

630 Cash over and short
631 Discounts lost
632 Factoring fee expense
633 Interest expense

Insurance Expenses

635 Insurance expense—Delivery equipment
636 Insurance expense—Office equipment
637 Insurance expense—_____

Rental Expenses

640 Rent expense
641 Rent expense—Office space
642 Rent expense—Selling space
643 Press rental expense
644 Truck rental expense
645 _____ rental expense

Supplies Expenses

650 Office supplies expense
651 Store supplies expense
652 _____ supplies expense
653 _____ supplies expense

Miscellaneous Expenses

655 Advertising expense
656 Bad debts expense
657 Blueprinting expense
658 Boat expense
659 Collection expense
661 Concessions expense
662 Credit card expense
663 Delivery expense
664 Dumping expense
667 Equipment expense
668 Food and drinks expense
671 Gas and oil expense
672 General and administrative expense
673 Janitorial expense
674 Legal fees expense
676 Mileage expense
677 Miscellaneous expenses
678 Mower and tools expense
679 Operating expense
680 Organization expense
681 Permits expense
682 Postage expense
683 Property taxes expense
684 Repairs expense—_____
685 Repairs expense—_____
687 Selling expense
688 Telephone expense
689 Travel and entertainment expense
690 Utilities expense
691 Warranty expense
695 Income taxes expense

Gains and Losses

701 Gain on retirement of bonds
702 Gain on sale of machinery
703 Gain on sale of investments
704 Gain on sale of trucks
705 Gain on _____
706 Foreign exchange gain or loss
801 Loss on disposal of machinery
802 Loss on exchange of equipment
803 Loss on exchange of _____
804 Loss on sale of notes
805 Loss on retirement of bonds
806 Loss on sale of investments
807 Loss on sale of machinery
808 Loss on _____
809 Unrealized gain—Income
810 Unrealized loss—Income
811 Impairment gain
812 Impairment loss

Clearing Accounts

901 Income summary
902 Manufacturing summary

A Rose by Any Other Name

The same financial statement sometimes receives different titles. Following are some of the more common aliases.*

Balance Sheet	Statement of Financial Position Statement of Financial Condition
Income Statement	Statement of Income Operating Statement Statement of Operations Statement of Operating Activity Earnings Statement Statement of Earnings Profit and Loss (P&L) Statement
Statement of Cash Flows	Statement of Cash Flow Cash Flows Statement Statement of Changes in Cash Position Statement of Changes in Financial Position
Statement of Stockholders' Equity	Statement of Shareholders' Equity[†] Statement of Changes in Shareholders' Equity[†] Statement of Stockholders' Equity and Comprehensive Income[†] Statement of Changes in Capital Accounts[†] Statement of Changes in Owner's Equity Statement of Changes in Owner's Capital

*The term **Consolidated** often precedes or follows these statement titles to reflect the combination of different entities, such as a parent company and its subsidiaries.

[†] For corporations only.

We thank Dr. Louella Moore from Arkansas State University for suggesting this listing.

SELECTED TRANSACTIONS AND RELATIONS

① Merchandising Transactions Summary

	Merchandising Transactions	Merchandising Entries	Dr.	Cr.
Purchases	Purchasing merchandise for resale.	• Merchandise Inventory .... Cash or Accounts Payable	#	#
	Paying freight costs on purchases; FOB shipping point.	• Merchandise Inventory .... Cash	#	#
	Paying within discount period.	• Accounts Payable .... Merchandise Inventory .... Cash	#	# #
	Recording purchase returns or allowances.	• Cash or Accounts Payable .... Merchandise Inventory	#	#
Sales	Selling merchandise.	• Cash or Accounts Receivable .... Sales..............................	#	#
		• Cost of Goods Sold................. Merchandise Inventory	#	#
	Receiving payment within discount period.	• Cash .... Sales Discounts .... Accounts Receivable..............	# #	#
	Granting sales returns or allowances.	• Sales Returns and Allowances........... Cash or Accounts Receivable	#	#
		• Merchandise Inventory .... Cost of Goods Sold	#	#
	Paying freight costs on sales; FOB destination.	• Delivery Expense .... Cash	#	#

	Merchandising Events	Adjusting and Closing Entries		
Adjusting	Adjusting due to shrinkage (occurs when recorded amount larger than physical inventory).	Cost of Goods Sold .... Merchandise Inventory	#	#
Closing	Closing temporary accounts with credit balances.	Sales .... Income Summary	#	#
	Closing temporary accounts with debit balances.	Income Summary .... Sales Returns and Allowances .... Sales Discounts .... Cost of Goods Sold .... Delivery Expense .... "Other Expenses"	#	# # # # #

② Merchandising Cost Flows

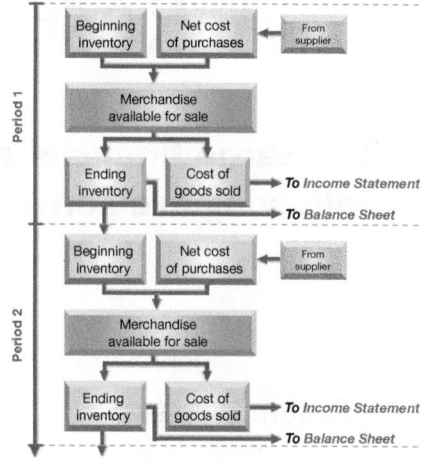

④ Bad Debts Estimation

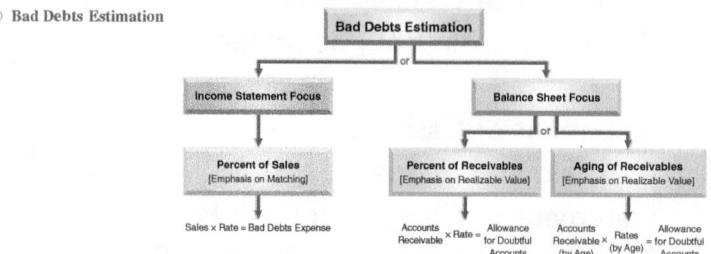

③ Credit Terms and Amounts

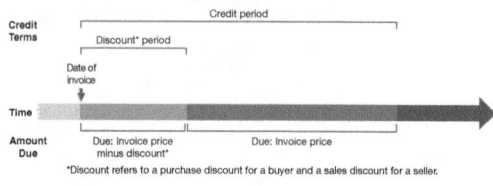

*Discount refers to a purchase discount for a buyer and a sales discount for a seller.

⑤ Bond Valuation

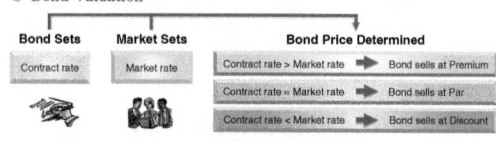

⑦ Dividend Transactions

	Type of Dividend		
Account Affected	**Cash Dividend**	**Stock Dividend**	**Stock Split**
Cash	Decrease	—	—
Common Stock	—	Increase	—
Retained Earnings ..	Decrease	Decrease	—

⑥ Stock Transactions Summary

	Stock Transactions	Stock Entries	Dr.	Cr.
Issue Common Stock	Issue par value common stock at par (par stock recorded at par).	Cash .... Common Stock	#	#
	Issue par value common stock at premium (par stock recorded at par).	Cash .... Common Stock .... Paid-In Capital in Excess of Par Value, Common Stock	#	# #
	Issue no-par value common stock (no-par stock recorded at amount received).	Cash .... Common Stock	#	#
	Issue stated value common stock at stated value (stated stock recorded at stated value).	Cash .... Common stock	#	#
	Issue stated value common stock at premium (stated stock recorded at stated value).	Cash .... Common stock .... Paid-In Capital in Excess of Stated Value, Common Stock	#	# #
Issue Preferred Stock	Issue par value preferred stock at par (par stock recorded at par).	Cash .... Preferred Stock	#	#
	Issue par value preferred stock at premium (par stock recorded at par).	Cash .... Preferred Stock .... Paid-In Capital in Excess of Par Value, Preferred Stock	#	# #
Reacquire Common Stock	Reacquire its own common stock (treasury stock recorded at cost).	Treasury Stock, Common .... Cash	#	#
Reissue Common Stock	Reissue its treasury stock at cost (treasury stock removed at cost).	Cash .... Treasury Stock, Common	#	#
	Reissue its treasury stock above cost (treasury stock removed at cost).	Cash .... Treasury Stock, Common........ Paid-In Capital, Treasury	#	# #
	Reissue its treasury stock below cost (treasury stock removed at cost; if paid-in capital is insufficient to cover amount below cost, retained earnings is debited for remainder).	Cash .... Paid-In Capital, Treasury............ Retained Earnings (if necessary) .... Treasury Stock, Common	# # #	#

⑧ A Rose by Any Other Name

The same financial statement sometimes receives different titles. Following are some of the more common aliases.*

Balance Sheet	Statement of Financial Position Statement of Financial Condition
Income Statement	Statement of Income Operating Statement Statement of Operations Statement of Operating Activity Earnings Statement Statement of Earnings Profit and Loss (P&L) Statement
Statement of Cash Flows	Statement of Cash Flow Cash Flows Statement Statement of Changes in Cash Position Statement of Changes in Financial Position
Statement of Stockholders' Equity	Statement of Shareholders' Equity Statement of Changes in Shareholders' Equity Statement of Stockholders' Equity and Comprehensive Income Statement of Changes in Owner's Equity Statement of Changes in Owner's Capital Statement of Changes in Capital Accounts

*The term **Consolidated** often precedes or follows these statement titles to reflect the combination of different entities, such as a parent company and its subsidiaries.

FUNDAMENTALS

① Accounting Equation

Assets	=	Liabilities	+	Equity
↑ ↓		↓ ↑		↓ ↑
Debit for increases / Credit for decreases		Debit for decreases / Credit for increases		Debit for decreases / Credit for increases

Contributed Capital*	+		Retained Earnings		

Common Stock	−	Dividends	+	Revenues	−	Expenses
Dr. for decreases / Cr. for increases		Dr. for increases / Cr. for decreases		Dr. for decreases / Cr. for increases		Dr. for increases / Cr. for decreases

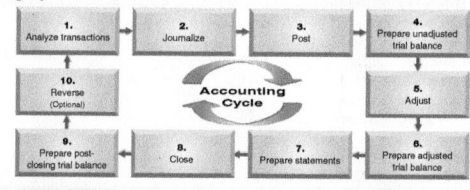 Indicates normal balance.

*Includes common stock and any preferred stock.

② Accounting Cycle

1. Analyze transactions
2. Journalize
3. Post
4. Prepare unadjusted trial balance
5. Adjust
6. Prepare adjusted trial balance
7. Prepare statements
8. Close
9. Prepare post-closing trial balance
10. Reverse (Optional)

(Accounting Cycle)

③ Adjustments and Entries

Type	Adjusting Entry	
Prepaid Expenses	Dr. Expense	Cr. Asset*
Unearned Revenues	Dr. Liability	Cr. Revenue
Accrued Expenses	Dr. Expense	Cr. Liability
Accrued Revenues	Dr. Asset	Cr. Revenue

*For depreciation, credit Accumulated Depreciation (contra asset).

④ 4-Step Closing Process

1. Transfer revenue and gain account balances to Income Summary.
2. Transfer expense and loss account balances to Income Summary.
3. Transfer Income Summary balance to Retained Earnings.
4. Transfer Dividends balance to Retained Earnings.

⑤ Accounting Concepts

Characteristics	Assumptions	Principles	Constraints
Relevance	Business entity	Measurement (historical cost)	Cost-benefit
Reliability	Going concern	Revenue recognition	Materiality
Comparability	Monetary unit	Expense recognition	Industry practice
Consistency	Periodicity	Full disclosure	Conservatism

⑥ Ownership of Inventory

	Ownership Transfers When Goods Passed To	Transportation Costs Paid By
FOB Shipping Point	Carrier	Buyer
FOB Destination	Buyer	Seller

⑦ Inventory Costing Methods

- Specific identification
- First-in, first-out (FIFO)
- Weighted-average
- Last-in, first-out (LIFO)

⑧ Depreciation and Depletion

Straight-line:
$$\frac{\text{Cost} - \text{Salvage value}}{\text{Useful life in periods}} \times \text{Periods expired}$$

Units-of-production:
$$\frac{\text{Cost} - \text{Salvage value}}{\text{Useful life in units}} \times \text{Units produced}$$

Declining-balance: Rate* × Beginning-of-period book value
*Rate is often double the straight-line rate, or 2 × (1/Useful life)

Depletion:
$$\frac{\text{Cost} - \text{Salvage value}}{\text{Total capacity in units}} \times \text{Units extracted}$$

⑨ Interest Computation

Interest = Principal (face) × Rate × Time

⑩ Accounting for Investment Securities

Classification*	Accounting
Short-Term Investment in Securities	
Held-to-maturity (debt) securities	**Cost** (without any discount or premium amortization)
Trading (debt and equity) securities	**Fair value** (with fair value adjustment to income)
Available-for-sale (debt and equity) securities	**Fair value** (with fair value adjustment to equity)
Long-Term Investment in Securities	
Held-to-maturity (debt) securities	**Cost** (with any discount or premium amortization)
Available-for-sale (debt and equity) securities	**Fair value** (with fair value adjustment to equity)
Equity securities with significant influence	Equity method
Equity securities with controlling influence	Equity method (with consolidation)

*A *fair value option* allows companies to report HTM and AFS securities much like trading securities.

ANALYSES

① Liquidity and Efficiency

Current ratio $= \dfrac{\text{Current assets}}{\text{Current liabilities}}$ — pp. 55, 128 & 589

Working capital = Current assets − Current liabilities — p. 589

Acid-test ratio $= \dfrac{\text{Cash} + \text{Short-term investments} + \text{Current receivables}}{\text{Current liabilities}}$ — pp. 183 & 590

Accounts receivable turnover $= \dfrac{\text{Net sales}}{\text{Average accounts receivable, net}}$ — pp. 327 & 591

Credit risk ratio $= \dfrac{\text{Allowance for doubtful accounts}}{\text{Accounts receivable, net}}$ — p. 327

Inventory turnover $= \dfrac{\text{Cost of goods sold}}{\text{Average inventory}}$ — pp. 227 & 591

Days' sales uncollected $= \dfrac{\text{Accounts receivable, net}}{\text{Net sales}} \times 365^*$ — pp. 285 & 591

Days' sales in inventory $= \dfrac{\text{Ending inventory}}{\text{Cost of goods sold}} \times 365^*$ — pp. 228 & 592

Total asset turnover $= \dfrac{\text{Net sales}}{\text{Average total assets}}$ — pp. 367 & 592

Plant asset useful life $= \dfrac{\text{Plant asset cost}}{\text{Depreciation expense}}$ — p. 367

Plant asset age $= \dfrac{\text{Accumulated depreciation}}{\text{Depreciation expense}}$ — p. 367

Days' cash expense coverage $= \dfrac{\text{Cash and cash equivalents}}{\text{Average daily cash expenses}}$ — p. 270

*360 days is also commonly used.

② Solvency

Debt ratio $= \dfrac{\text{Total liabilities}}{\text{Total assets}}$ Equity ratio $= \dfrac{\text{Total equity}}{\text{Total assets}}$ — pp. 55, 77 & 593

Debt-to-equity $= \dfrac{\text{Total liabilities}}{\text{Total equity}}$ — pp. 452 & 593

Times interest earned $= \dfrac{\text{Income before interest expense and income taxes}}{\text{Interest expense}}$ — pp. 406 & 593

Cash coverage of growth $= \dfrac{\text{Cash flow from operations}}{\text{Cash outflow for plant assets}}$ — p. 543

Cash coverage of debt $= \dfrac{\text{Cash flow from operations}}{\text{Total noncurrent liabilities}}$ — p. 543

③ Profitability

Profit margin ratio $= \dfrac{\text{Net income}}{\text{Net sales}}$ — pp. 55, 127 & 594

Gross margin ratio $= \dfrac{\text{Net sales} - \text{Cost of goods sold}}{\text{Net sales}}$ — p. 183

Return on total assets $= \dfrac{\text{Net income}}{\text{Average total assets}}$ — pp. 26 & 594

$\qquad = \text{Profit margin ratio} \times \text{Total asset turnover}$ — p. 595

Return on common stockholders' equity $= \dfrac{\text{Net income} - \text{Preferred dividends}}{\text{Average common stockholders' equity}}$ — p. 595

Book value per common share $= \dfrac{\text{Stockholders' equity applicable to common shares}}{\text{Number of common shares outstanding}}$ — p. 502

Basic earnings per share $= \dfrac{\text{Net income} - \text{Preferred dividends}}{\text{Weighted-average common shares outstanding}}$ — p. 500

Cash flow on total assets $= \dfrac{\text{Cash flow from operations}}{\text{Average total assets}}$ — p. 543

Payout ratio $= \dfrac{\text{Cash dividends declared on common stock}}{\text{Net income}}$ — p. 501

④ Market

Price-earnings ratio $= \dfrac{\text{Market value (price) per share}}{\text{Earnings per share}}$ — pp. 55, 501 & 595

Dividend yield $= \dfrac{\text{Annual cash dividends per share}}{\text{Market price per share}}$ — pp. 501 & 596

Residual income = Net income − Target net income

FINANCIAL REPORTS

Income Statement*
For *period* Ended *date*

Net sales (revenues)	$	#
Cost of goods sold (cost of sales)		#
Gross margin (gross profit)		#
Operating expenses		
Examples: Depreciation, salaries, ...	$ #	
wages, rent, utilities, interest, ...	#	
amortization, advertising, taxes	#	
Total operating expenses		#
Nonoperating gains and losses...................		#
Net income (net profit or earnings)		$ #

* A typical chart of accounts is at the end of the book and classifies all accounts by financial statement categories.

Balance Sheet
Date

ASSETS

Current assets
Examples: Cash, Cash equivalents, Short-term investments,
  Accounts receivable, Current portion of notes .... $ #
  receivable, Inventory, Prepaid expenses .... #
  Total current assets .... $ #

Long-term investments
Examples: Investment in stock, Investment in bonds, ... #
  Land for expansion .... #
  Total long-term investments .... #

Plant assets
Examples: Equipment, Machinery, Buildings, Land .... #
  Total plant assets, net of depreciation .... #

Intangible assets
Examples: Patent, Trademark, Copyright, License, Goodwill .... #
  Total intangible assets, net of amortization .... #
Total assets .... $ #

LIABILITIES AND EQUITY

Current liabilities
Examples: Accounts payable, Wages payable, Salaries............. $ #
  payable, Current notes payable, Taxes payable, ... #
  Interest payable, Unearned revenues................ #
  Total current liabilities .... $ #

Long-term liabilities
Examples: Notes payable, Bonds payable, Lease liability .... #
  Total long-term liabilities......................... #
Total liabilities .... #

Equity
  Common stock .... #
  Paid-in capital in excess of par or stated value .... #
  Retained earnings .... #
Less treasury stock .... (#)
Total liabilities and equity .... $ #

Statement of Cash Flows
For *period* Ended *date*

Cash flows from operating activities
  [Prepared using the indirect (see below)† or direct method]
  Net cash provided (used) by operating activities............................ $ #
Cash flows from investing activities
  [List of individual investing inflows and outflows]
  Net cash provided (used) by investing activities .... #
Cash flows from financing activities
  [List of individual financing inflows and outflows]
  Net cash provided (used) by financing activities .... #
Net increase (decrease) in cash .... $ #
Cash (and equivalents) balance at beginning of period .... #
Cash (and equivalents) balance at end of period.................... $ #

Attach separate schedule or note disclosure of "Noncash investing and financing transactions."

†Indirect Method: Cash Flows from Operating Activities

Cash flows from operating activities
Net income .... $ #
Add: Decreases in noncash current assets .... $ #
  Increases in current liabilities .... #
  Expenses with no cash outflows (examples: depreciation,
    and amortization of both intangibles and bond discounts) ..... #
  Nonoperating losses (examples: losses from asset sales
    and from debt retirements) .... # #
Less: Increases in noncash current assets .... #
  Decreases in current liabilities .... #
  Revenues with no cash inflows (examples:
    amortization of bond premiums) .... #
  Nonoperating gains (examples: gains from asset sales
    and from debt retirements) .... # #
Net cash provided (used) by operating activities .... $ #

Statement of Retained Earnings
For *period* Ended *date*

Retained earnings, beginning	$	#
Add: Net income.....................		#
		#
Less: Dividends declared...............		#
Retained earnings, ending		$ #

Statement of Stockholders' Equity†
For *period* Ended *date*

	Common Stock	Capital in Excess of Par	Retained Earnings	Treasury Stock	Total
Balances, beginning...........	$ #	$ #	$ #	$ #	$ #
Net income					
Cash dividends..............					
Stock issuance					
Treasury stock purchase......					
Treasury stock reissuance.....					
Other.....................					
Balances, ending.............	$ #	$ #	$ #	$ #	$ #

† Additional columns and account titles commonly include number of shares, preferred stock, unrealized gains and losses on available-for-sale securities, foreign currency translation, and comprehensive income.

Premium Bond Amortization (Straight-Line) Table†

Semiannual Period-End	Unamortized Bond Premium*	Bond Carrying Value**
Bond life-start	$ #	$ #
....		
....		
Bond life-end	0	par

† Bond carrying value is adjusted to par and its amortized premium to zero over the bond life (note: carrying value less unamortized bond premium equals par).
* Equals total bond premium less its accumulated amortization.
** Equals bond par value *plus* its unamortized bond premium.

Discount Bond Amortization (Straight-Line) Table†

Semiannual Period-End	Unamortized Bond Discount*	Bond Carrying Value**
Bond life-start	$ #	$ #
....		
....		
Bond life-end	0	par

† Bond carrying value is adjusted to par and its amortized discount to zero over the bond life (note: unamortized bond discount plus carrying value equals par).
* Equals total bond discount less its accumulated amortization.
** Equals bond par value *less* its unamortized bond discount.

Effective Interest Amortization Table for Bonds with Semiannual Interest Payment

Semiannual Interest Period-End	Cash Interest Paid^A	Bond Interest Expense^B	Discount or Premium Amortization^C	Unamortized Discount or Premium^D	Carrying Value^E
#	#	#	#	#	#

^A Par value multiplied by the semiannual contract rate.
^B Prior period's carrying value multiplied by the semiannual market rate.
^C The difference between interest paid and bond interest expense.
^D Prior period's unamortized discount or premium less the current period's discount or premium amortization.
^E Par value less unamortized discount or plus unamortized premium.

Installment Notes Payment Table

Period Ending Date	Beginning Balance	Debit Interest Expense	+	Debit Notes Payable	=	Credit Cash	Ending Balance
#	#	#		#		#	#

Bank Reconciliation
Date

Bank statement balance...........	$#	Book balance			$#
Add: Unrecorded deposits........	#	Add: Unrecorded bank credit memoranda			#
Bank errors understating the balance	#	Book errors understating the balance			#
Less: Outstanding checks	#	Less: Unrecorded bank debit memoranda			#
Bank errors overstating the balance	#	Book errors overstating the balance..............			#
Adjusted bank balance.........	**$#**	**Adjusted book balance..........**			**$#**

↑ Balances are equal (reconciled) ↑

Online Supplements

ConnectPlus Accounting with LearnSmart One-Semester Online Access for Financial Accounting: Information for Decisions, Seventh Edition

McGraw-Hill Connect® is a web-based assignment and assessment platform that gives students the means to better connect with their coursework, with their instructors, and with the important concepts that they will need to know for success now and in the future. With Connect, instructors can deliver assignments, quizzes and tests easily online. Students can practice important skills at their own pace and on their own schedule.

GETTING STARTED:

To get started in Connect, you will need the following:

1. Your instructor's unique Connect URL

    Sample of Connect URL

    http://www.mcgrawhillconnect.com/class/instructorname_section_name

2. Connect Access Code

    Using a Print Book? Your access code will appear at the back of the book. Reference your Table of Contents for an exact page number.

    Using an eBook? Once you have purchased your Create eBook, you will automatically have access to Connect. Simply go to your instructor's unique URL and sign in using the username and password you established when accessing your Create eBook.

REGISTRATION AND SIGN IN:

- Go to the Connect Website address provided by your instructor.
- Click **Register Now**.
- Enter your email address.
    > **TIP:** If you already have a McGraw-Hill account, you will be asked for your password and will not be required to create a new account.
- Enter your access code (This access code appears on the back cover of the Create book and is only redeemable once.)
- Follow the on-screen instructions.
    > **TIP:** Please choose your Security Question carefully. We will ask you for this information if you forget your password.
- When registration is complete, click on **Go to Connect Now**.
- You are now ready to use **Connect.**

Need Help?
Contact us online: www.mcgrawhillconnect.com/support
Give us a call: 1-800-331-5094